THE ENCYCLOPEDIA OF
WESTERNS

THE ENCYCLOPEDIA OF
WESTERNS

HERB FAGEN

Foreword by
TOM SELLECK

Preface by
DALE ROBERTSON

☑®
Facts On File, Inc.

The Encyclopedia of Westerns

Facts On File, Inc.
132 West 31st Street
New York NY 10001

Library of Congress Cataloging-in-Publication Data

Fagen, Herb.
The encyclopedia of westerns / Herb Fagen; foreword by Tom Selleck;
preface by Dale Robertson.
p. cm.
Includes index.
ISBN 0-8160-4456-2
1. Western films—United States—Encyclopedias. 2. Western films—Italy—
Encyclopedias. I. Title
PN1995.9.W4 F27 2002
791.43'63278'03—dc21   2002026355

Facts On File books are available at special discounts when purchased in bulk
quantities for businesses, associations, institutions, or sales promotions.
Please call our Special Sales Department in New York at
(212) 967-8800 or (800) 322-8755.

You can find Facts On File on the World Wide Web at
http://www.factsonfile.com

Text design by Cathy Rincon
Cover design by Nora Wertz

Printed in the United States of America

VB Hermitage 10 9 8 7 6 5 4 3 2 1

This book is printed on acid-free paper.

To the memory of Budd Boetticher
(1916–2001)
The "Last Lion" of Western Films

Contents

Foreword

When I was four years old my parents moved from Detroit to California, and I can honestly say that I grew up on western movies with Roy Rogers, Gene Autry, Hop-Along Cassidy, Hoot Gibson, Ken Maynard, and Bob Steele. However, as a youngster I had never ridden a horse except for those rides at Griffith Park where they strap you on a pony.

Nevertheless, years later when I accidentally fell into acting and made a couple of western-format commercials, at least I wasn't afraid of horses. I was able to get on the horse so they could shoot a half-hour of me looking like an idiot, and maybe three or four seconds of it would look okay for the commercial.

This commercial led to a few parts, including the very first I ever got when I was under contract with Fox. It was in an episode of the western series *Lancer*, which aired on January 14, 1969. I was in what we call a "teaser" to the show—playing a drunken cowboy who unwisely tries to pick a fight with a guy with lots of guns, a hook for a hand, and a big German shepherd. At the end of this "teaser," that big German shepherd had pinned me to the wall.

This was my debut in a TV western.

I then did a bunch of unsold pilots and gained more and more experience. Then came *The Sacketts*. My pal Sam Elliott—we had been under contract together at Fox—was in the movie and put in good word in for me with the higher-ups, including Bob Totten, who was a terrific director. One could see the loyalty he inspired in the marvelous cast he put together. During our interview, Totten asked me if I could ride. I said that while I wasn't afraid of horses and had been on a few of them, my answer had to be 'No!' I assured him, however, that I was a good athlete and I could learn. I think he appreciated my honesty.

The finalists for the last two roles, younger brothers Orrin and Tyrell Sackett, met at the Randall Ranch, where we spent three days auditioning our skills. Jeff Osterhage (who played Tyrell) and I walked over to the grandstands where Bob Totten, Glenn Ford, and Sam Elliott were sitting. Totten said, "OK, I want you to go over and pick out a horse there, put a saddle on it, and ride it back over here." We did what he asked. One actor became indignant and walked out because he obviously had lied about his familiarity with horses.

Totten did not mince words with his actors, nor did he coddle them. We knew that once the filming started, we were going to have to look and act like real cowboys. I spent a lot of time before the movie with wranglers Jay Fishburn and Donna Hall. Donna really taught Jeff and me the ropes, and I

mean she taught us from the ground up—how to get on the horse, get off the horse, and walk the horse.

We were young guys and wanted to gallop, but Donna would have none of it. She said, "You can't do that until you can get on and off a horse, walk him down the street, and make him stop and stand still. That's 90 percent of what you'll do in a movie, and when you learn and look like a cowboy, then I'll let you do the other stuff."

Based on two stories by Louis L'Amour, *The Sacketts* was my indoctrination and my real introduction to the western genre, especially working with such seasoned actors as Jack Elam, Glenn Ford, Slim Pickens, and Ben Johnson. Ben was like a dad to us all, so I can really say that I learned from the best.

A few years later, we did *The Shadow Riders* (also based on a book by Louis L'Amour) for director Andrew V. McLaglen. It was a real honor because I met L'Amour, who gave me a hardbound leather copy of the book and inscribed it with the words, "Tom, you make my people live." I believe it was the only time that Louis L'Amour actually wrote a book from a screenplay he was doing. For legal reasons, he had to write in a new set of brothers, the Cravens. But as in *The Sacketts*, Sam Elliott, Jeff Osterhage, and I played the three brothers.

As an art form, the western film owes a great debt to guys like John Ford. But long before Ford made his mark on the genre, there was Edwin S. Porter's *The Great Train Robbery*, dating back to 1903 and considered by many to be our first real movie. Thanks to Ford and others, the western film has become as much a part of our shared mythology as King Arthur. There has been a yearning in modern culture to go back to simpler times. The frontier spirit is something that never leaves us. The writer Anthony LeJeune once said that the classic western always involves "a moral dilemma and a challenge to the human spirit, the resolution of which, as John Wayne says in the movie *The Alamo*, 'speaks well for men.'"

There have been a lot of directors who have made top-flight western films, but the old guard of the studio days, especially John Ford, was superb. Just look at the top-ten list by anybody who knows Westerns. Invariably, there will be three or four John Ford movies.

Take *My Darling Clementine*. You become riveted by it. Every two or three minutes comes a camera set-up that could be turned into a portrait. It doesn't have that crazy MTV-editing pace we see today. It's an intimate story with an intimate face, and it's one of my very favorite movies. Henry Fonda was spectacular in the film. I've never seen him so tough. He had an easy-going quality and clearly remains one of the quintessential American actors.

Shane also had a huge early influence on me. What was most important was the kind of tension and slow-to-act quality that is a great lesson in any western film. There wasn't a lot of needless gunplay. Yet when a firearm did go off, it had a resounding sound and power, as in that classic scene when Elisha Cook Jr. is knocked off his feet by Jack Palance's bullet. It was appropriately frightening as a kid to see to the power of a firearm and, I might add, the responsible way to see it as well.

Howard Hawks's *Red River* and John Ford's *Rio Grande* are other western favorites. Ford's Cavalry Trilogy (*Fort Apache, She Wore A Yellow Ribbon,* and *Rio Grande*) are all fine movies, yet I particularly like *Rio Grande,* the last entry in this outstanding group. Ben Johnson and Dobe Carey (Harry Carey Jr.) were excellent in that extremely difficult "Roman riding" scene (one person riding two horses, standing, with one foot on each horse's back). Claude Jarman Jr. was also in that scene. He played John Wayne's son and did some "Roman riding" as well. Interestingly, he said that he had never ridden much, but had great big feet and took to that special kind of riding "like crazy."

There are so many actors who I think are indelible in westerns, but none more so than John Wayne. If you put every Academy Award-winning actor, every actor, everybody in the movie business into an ensemble movie with John Wayne, he's going to play the boss or the movie is going to be a lie. That says a lot about him. He was very underrated as an actor, and at the height of his career he played flawed characters. That's something for which I've always had an appetite because flawed characters learn something and consequently can teach us a lot. I met John Wayne twice. We both went to USC and were in the same fraternity, Sigma Chi, and I got to slip him the fraternity grip, which was a big deal because as western stars go, he was "the guy."

I'm really not sure why they aren't making more western movies because when they make good ones they work like crazy. In the last decade alone, two out of the top ten pictures were westerns, Kevin Costner's *Dances with Wolves* and Clint Eastwood's *Unforgiven.* The real problem I think is that the production end of Hollywood doesn't know *how* to make them. They know how to make deals. Some actors can play a period piece like a Western; others are fine actors but have more of a contemporary quality. You just can't put whoever you think is hot into any western and expect it to work.

Somehow, Hollywood started believing that they had to make westerns more contemporary and modernize them. So when the six-guns don't shoot enough bullets, they invent new hardware. I looked into making another western movie a while back. It had a good script, but when I went to talk with the director there were pictures on the wall of trains and other artifacts that never existed. Once he said he designs his own trains and creates his own universe, I knew immediately that he was doomed to fail.

Today the movie crowd is so deal-oriented, so marketing-oriented, that they don't know what to do with a western although they occasionally stumble into one. I feel the major

studios need to rethink how they're doing them and how they're casting them. I don't believe that for a minute that westerns are dated. They don't date if they're made properly and are really very lucrative if they are made by someone with a little vision. Kevin Costner is someone who simply got it right, and so did Simon Wincer (*Quigley Down Under, Lonesome Dove*). Simon is Australian, but he has the right tools.

Today we don't have that stock company of actors we had in the past, so it's very hard to ground yourself. But in every movie I have made with my partner Michael Brandman, I have tried to include a Dobe Carey, a Barry Corbin, or a Wilfred Brimley. These are the people who ground your movie in the specific period and genre. There are not as many around as before, but they are national treasures. We need them, and we need to celebrate them. They are wonderful actors.

The land, too, has to be treated like another character in a western movie. It is usually the central place from which conflict arises and from which romance blooms, even if it is only the romance of the landscape. For example, *Crossfire Trail* evokes a strong sense of the landscape, and I'm not talking about radical environmentalism. Yet I do think that we'd all like to live in a greener, cleaner world, and I believe westerns harken back to that dream.

I am pleased today that *Quigley Down Under* is starting to be recognized and is now even making some top-ten lists. It originally got a terrible distribution because the studio released it the same month as *Dances With Wolves* and two weeks before *Three Men and a Little Lady,* my sequel to *Three Men and a Baby.* It made some money, then they pulled it in, took the cash, and ran. Today, it is hard to obtain in video stores because it usually is rented out. More than any other picture I have done, I get the most response from *Quigley Down Under.* In fact, several rifle companies are now making Quigley rifles. Yet I had to fight to get it made. I had a lot of power at the time and I wanted to make a western. John Hill had written a great story, and quite a few important stars like Steve McQueen had toyed with making a film based on Hill's story.

Another of my westerns, *Crossfire Trail,* is doing extremely well now on DVD. It was a movie made for cable, but we gave it the same type of production value as we would have for the big screen. Moreover, *Last Stand at Saber Ridge* a few years earlier set all records for Turner at the time of its release. Originally designed to be shown on the big screen in the rest of the world, it was shot as such. But Turner Pictures was acquired by Warner Bros., and they let it slip through their fingers. It's a shame because such movies have a very strong after-release value.

But Hollywood seems to be primed for another round. I was recently talking to my good friend Kevin Costner, who is preparing another western, and so am I. Both of us are planning to shoot on location in Calgary, Alberta. I can't wait to get started. And when I get that stupid question as to why people don't want to see westerns any more, I remind them to look at the ratings of my last movies. They were better than good; they were great. *Crossfire Trail* was the highest-rated program in the entire history of cable television. *Monte Walsh* was the most-watched Friday program in basic cable history and a number-four rating for all TV networks. So it's not that westerns don't work; it's that *bad* westerns don't work!

I guess some people have said that I have become the new standard bearer for the western genre. I can't speak to that but I feel very lucky that people not only want to see me in western movies and to see more of them, but also that I am fortunate enough to be able to make them. As I mentioned earlier I did not grow up on a horse, nor was I raised on a ranch—although I probably would have liked to have been.

But just to be a part of that universe, and to be accepted in that universe, makes my whole life as an actor worthwhile.

—Tom Selleck

Preface

Westerns have been very special part of my life as an actor. I made 15 western films between 1950 and 1957, then two successful TV series—*Tales of Wells Fargo* (1957–62) and *The Iron Horse* (1966–68). While my movie career began with uncredited parts in *The Boy with Green Hair* (1948), *Flamingo Road*, and *The Girl from Jones Beach* (1949), I was tapped for movies almost 10 years earlier while still a raw teenager.

It all started in Wichita, Kansas, in 1939. I was 17 years old and boxing in professional prizefights to make money. We fought all matches "winner take all," and we didn't fight for promoters. Harry Cohn, the head of Columbia, had a man out there watching the matches. One night after a fight, he asked me to come to Hollywood to do a test for a picture called *Golden Boy* about a young boxer. I couldn't go because I was still in school, and my mom wasn't about to let me go that far away from home (we listened to our parents in those days). I also had eight horses in training that I was preparing to be polo ponies and couldn't walk away from them. So the part went to another youngster by the name of William Holden.

Then World War II came along and took up the next few years of my life. At one point, I was stationed in California. It looked like we were getting ready to go overseas, so I called my mom and asked her what she wanted for Christmas. She said she had plenty of photographs and newspaper clippings of me but that she didn't have a portrait. She asked me if I could get one for her.

Well, I talked to the guys in the outfit, and soon there were 14 of us who went down to the Amos Carr Studio on Wilcox and Hollywood Boulevard. Each of us got a picture for our parents and gave the lady, Marian Parsons, our addresses.

Later on, I started getting letters from people who had seen my portrait at Amos Carr and wanted me to come to Hollywood for a screen test. What had happened was that she had blown it up and put it in the window. Now, after the war, I didn't have a job to return to. I had been badly injured so I couldn't go back to boxing. I tried to get back into the horse business that I had lost during the war, without success. So when one night, I came across those letters (a serviceman never throws away a letter, I can tell you that), I told my mom that I was going to Hollywood to see if I could get a job. She said, "Well, son, do you think you can do that?" I said, "I know I can't if I don't try."

In February 1946, I arrived in Hollywood. I gave myself 24 months. If I wasn't making a living in two years, it was back to Oklahoma.

After 16 months, I began earning a living.

I got to know every office boy and every secretary in every studio in town. Every time a new screenplay would come in, they would call me. I'd meet them in the parking lot, and they'd give me a script in a plain manila envelope, which I looked at quickly. Then I'd go tell my agent to go to RKO or Warner Bros. or wherever and tell them the name of the part I wanted to read for. I wanted a part that was big enough to be noticed, but not big enough that the audience would get tired of me if I didn't do a good job.

After about 20 or 30 attempts, I finally got a part in *Fighting Man of the Plains* for 20th Century Fox, and that started the whole thing. Directed by Edwin L. Marin, I played Jesse James and helped Randolph Scott clean up the criminal element in a Kansas town. Although I did some nonwestern movies, I basically stayed within the western genre. In 1950, I did *The Caraboo Trail* for 20th Century Fox, also directed by Edwin L. Marin and again with Randolph Scott, and then *Two Flags West* with Joseph Cotten, Linda Darnell, Jeff Chandler, and Cornel Wilde. By the time I did *Return of the Texan* for Fox in 1952, I got top billing.

I like westerns. The story lines are fairly simple, the good guys win and the bad guys lose. I think people today have forgotten what the word *entertainment* means. You don't make movies to show life as it is. You show life as you wish it were or how you would like it to be. Too many films today have lost their imagination. When we made western films, you did not confuse them with today's times and current trends. It was pure entertainment. It took us away from our problems and troubles because we were watching things that happened a long time ago. They also presented a strong leading man who, reluctantly or not, would assume responsibility and set things right. This strong male presence, I feel, is important in a western film.

To me, Gary Cooper epitomized the western hero. Joel McCrea was right up there too, and so, of course, was John Wayne. They were all real men. Yet there was something about Gary Cooper. The toughest men I have known in the world were usually the quietest. You got these guys running around today flexing their muscles and acting tough. Well Coop's the one I would choose if it came to a fight. I got to know him pretty well and would often hunt with him and Clark Gable. Both were pretty much the same off screen. Back then, movies were a business of personalities. That's what motion pictures really are, or should be.

I think Tom Selleck is the standard bearer for Westerns today. He's a leading man in an old-fashioned way. He's handsome, he's strong, and he's big. With the right scripts he could be around for a long time. There are some good actors around like Sam Elliott, but they are more character types. Tom has all the requisites to become a major force in the genre and to continue that great line of western screen heroes.

The guys today try to bring stage techniques to the motion picture industry, but it doesn't work well in westerns. Drama schools are producing the actors, and they have a great influence on casting directors. Consequently, they're using their students, but these guys just don't ring true, and that's what's hurting the western. Most of these kids don't know what a beautiful picture is. Unfortunately, many of the folks making movies recently have tried to destroy the hero image, and that's too bad. Take Custer, for example. Contrary to the contemporary view, he wasn't a dunce, and his life certainly wasn't a failure.

In the mid-1960s, I was offered five spaghetti westerns. Everything was going fine until they told me I'd be away for two years. I said you couldn't stack enough money up in trucks and bring it to me in order for me to spend two years out of the United States. So I didn't go, and I've never been sorry. For one, it helped Clint Eastwood's career. He's a good actor and has been a wonderful box-office attraction.

I think the spaghetti westerns had too much blood and violence. If I had done them, they would have been different, much lighter. Of course, that probably would have made another enemy or two for me. What problems I had with people in the industry were never the result of my being temperamental about a bigger dressing room or things like that. It all had to do with the story. If they were not going to make the best story possible, then we were headed for some real disagreements.

I've worked for lots of directors over the years, but the one who stands out and never got the full credit he deserved was a fellow named R. G. "Buddy" Springsteen. Among other things, he directed the television series *Tales of the Wells Fargo*. He knew and loved his work well and understood the business too.

John Ford made some great pictures, particularly *Stagecoach* and *She Wore a Yellow Ribbon*, although I think there were better directors. I especially liked Ben Johnson's performance in *Yellow Ribbon*. Ben was a real cowboy, a true cowboy. I never was a real cowboy, though some folks think so. I considered myself a horseman, having bred and raised horses all my life— but there's a difference. Sam Peckinpah was good but was his own worst enemy. He brought things to life, but might have brought things too close to life.

Like everyone else I have my favorite western movies, those I enjoy seeing again and again. *High Noon* was a great one. I also liked a film called *Last of the Duanes* with George O'Brien. I knew George and was a big fan of his even as a kid.

He was a real decent man. Most guys never get to be friends with their boyhood heroes. I was lucky. I became friendly with two of my boyhood heroes. George and Hall of Fame baseball player Dizzy Dean. *Wells Fargo* with Joel McCrea remains another favorite. So does *Shane*, an absolutely great movie. Over the years I have really come to appreciate Alan Ladd's work. What a pleasant, pleasant actor he was. He gave a magnificent performance in *Shane*.

As for my own movies, I'd have to say the one I liked best was a 1954 film, *The Gambler from Natchez*. It's an exciting story in which I play a young man who sets out to avenge the murder of his father, falsely accused of cheating at cards and gunned down by three men. Debra Paget was my love interest in the film. She's one of the sweetest people in the world and a very good actress. Another leading lady I really liked was Betty Grable. I played opposite her in the 1951 film, *Call Me Mister* and the 1953 musical, *The Farmer Takes a Wife*. She had a great sense of humor and was a true and sincere person.

I don't believe that westerns are finished, even though most of the new ones aren't very good. What people have to realize is that you must have a good story to make a good western. A strong story must accompany the color and excitement. The movie business follows trends; if someone does a western and it makes lots of money, others will follow suit. But again, the storyline must be there.

Looking back at a film and TV career that goes back more than 50 years and includes more than 40 movies, two television series, and numerous TV guest appearances, you always wish you could have done some of your movies over and made them better. But I have a great deal of pride having worked so much in the western genre. People seem to remember so much of what I did, and it's a nice feeling. One thing I learned early on is even if the stakes are low, never intentionally do a bad job. You work your hardest to do your best work, no matter what. I was lucky enough to work with big-name stars almost from the start. But I never felt intimidated in any way. I was an officer during World War II, so I was used to dealing with men of all stripes.

I am writing stories now and have written seven screenplays in the past three years. Recently, I have been Master of Ceremonies at the annual Golden Boot Awards. It's for a good cause, the Motion Picture and Television Fund. I enjoy seeing everybody, but we are losing so many people now, and that's very sad.

I wish the movies today had the same moral overtones that ours had. The old westerns will always be there. However, I believe the western film can make a comeback. The audience is out there, and so is the interest. All we need are some good stories and the right people to start making them again.

—Dale Robertson

Acknowledgments

A multitude of thanks and appreciation to those who have helped make this project possible.

To Tom Selleck and Dale Robertson, my gratitude for providing the foreword and preface to this project. Your work in the genre has been momentous, and your contributions to our project so much appreciated.

To Gay Hovet, special projects manager for the Golden Boot Awards, and Esme Chandlee, Tom Selleck's publicity associate, a million thanks for your help in arranging interviews with Mr. Selleck and Mr. Robertson.

To Gary Goldstein, who originally brought me into this project, a hearty "Thank you." More of the same to James Chambers, editor-in-chief for arts and humanities at Facts On File; my deep appreciation for your patience and guidance.

To my agent, Jake Elwell at Wieser and Wieser, the usual kudos for continuing to represent my work with skill and integrity. To my research assistant, Nette Ronnow, thanks for your hard work and for meeting some tough deadlines.

To Jeff Schmedinghoff, thanks for your help in preparing the Appendixes.

On a personal level, my continued appreciation to sports agent John Wayslik for taking a chance on a fledgling, mid-dle-aged writer and choosing me from among many prospective scribes to coauthor the autobiography of Windy City baseball legend Minnie Minoso. You jump-started my career, John.

To Sally, for enduring a full plate of western movies for more than two years; thanks for the love and support. To my mom, Gert Fagen, 90 years young, you are a true hero and the unsung "wind beneath my wings."

A special thanks to actress Sue Ane Langdon, writer/producer Andrew J. Fenedy, actors Gregory Walcott and Edward Faulkner, and the late Budd Boetticher (a dear friend) for providing personal photographs especially for this project.

Over the past few years I have had the good fortune of knowing and interviewing many of those who were active participants (actors, directors, stuntmen, etc.) in the world of western filmmaking. So sadly, a growing number are no longer with us. Where possible, I have inserted excerpts from past interviews within the body of the text. To western filmmakers, past and present, forever and always, "Lest We Forget."

—Herb Fagen
Walnut Creek, California

Introduction

The mystique and lure of the American West, so long a part of our national lore and collective dreams, have been elevated to an art form through the medium of film. Images etched out against the big western sky have been part of growing up in America for nearly a century now. Like jazz and jive in the world of music, the western film is a distinct American original.

In 1903 Edwin S. Porter's *The Great Train Robbery* became the first recognizable western film and the blueprint for countless others. Since then moviemakers have attempted to depict the exploits, real or imaginary, of the pioneers and frontiersmen, the lawman and bandits, the heroes and heroines of a sprawling and ever-expanding American West.

The Great Train Robbery was a commercial success as well as a cinematic milestone. Yet in the rash of films to follow, one major ingredient was missing. Western audiences needed a central figure to capture their attention—call him the western star hero.

Three pioneers: Cecil B. DeMille, D. W. Griffith, and Mack Sennett (AUTHOR'S COLLECTION)

He appeared in the stocky person of G. M. Anderson, an actor soon to be known almost exclusively as Broncho Billy. Courageous, rugged, amiable, and basically plain, he was the prototype "good badman," the type of hero who might willingly sacrifice his cherished freedom to help a child in distress. Few of Broncho Billy Anderson's 500 one- or two-reelers survive today. Nevertheless they set the stage for future cowboy heroes like William S. Hart, Tom Mix, and Harry Carey.

The western hero might stray from the righteous path, but he would somehow manage to saddle up on the side of the angels before the final fadeout. Reticent and strong, tender and charming, the western screen hero was more often than not short on commitment and long on independence.

The western as a genre prospered in its formative years because two of the most talented and adept early filmmakers cut their directorial teeth on the genre: David Wark (D. W.) Griffith and Thomas H. Ince. Before their arrival, and before Griffith in particular began to develop a language of film and lay the foundation of cinema as an art form, the western film had developed little in the way of style or shape.

By 1911 the industry had churned out 43 western features, with the number jumping to 99 features in 1915. Popularity held steady, reaching a peak of 205 in 1925. New cowboy heroes like Hoot Gibson, Tim McCoy, Ken Maynard, Buck Jones, Fred Thompson, and the rugged and talented George O'Brien became horse-opera stars in the silent era. Many maintained their appeal into the 1930s, sharing the B-western spotlight with the likes of Johnny Mack Brown, Bob Steele, and an ex-USC football player by the name of John Wayne.

But by the late 1920s westerns were facing a dilemma. Talkies meant big changes. With the advent of sound, for example, the floundering between too much silent action and too much static dialogue became a troubling concern. A major breakthrough came in 1929 with Raoul Walsh's *In Old Arizona*. Because sound-recording equipment was stored in stationary, soundproof booths, the chase scene was dropped, and one-third of the movie was shot indoors. Yet by taking the camera outdoors and by picking up gunshots, hoofbeats, and even the natural noises of frying bacon, it became apparent that the western film could more than cope with sound.

Based on "The Cisco Kid," a story by O. Henry, *In Old Arizona* won a Best Actor Oscar for star Warner Baxter, whose good looks and deep voice brought in lots of dollars and a plethora of mail addressed to him at the Fox studio. Nominated for six Academy Awards, including Best Picture, today it remains mainly a curiosity piece.

The next big western of the formative sound period—and the most commercially successful—was *Cimarron* (1930–31). Directed by Wesley Ruggles and produced by RKO Studio, *Cimarron* won three Academy Awards, including Best Picture of the Year, making for the evening's biggest winner at the awards ceremony. With the addition of music—particularly traditional western folk tunes like those employed by directors such as John Ford—the western's shaky journey into the world of talkies was now complete.

Ford's *Stagecoach* (1939) finally lifted the western from the B genre and into the front rank of American cinema, making a major star out of 32-year-old John Wayne, who had been languishing in the "poverty row" of budget westerns since fizzling in *The Big Trail* nine years earlier in 1930. As the Ringo Kid, Wayne's entrance is simply stunning—a visual treat. The sky, the desert, and the picturesque buttes of Monument Valley create a classic western landscape. The background is brilliant as the camera focuses perfectly against Wayne's sweat-filled face. Instantly, an image is born. Ringo's world, like the film itself, is black and white, his parameters firm, his boundaries clearly defined: "There are some things a man can't run away from."

With *Stagecoach*, the "Golden Age" of the western film had arrived. During the 1940s, the 1950s, even into the 1960s, the movie industry's most popular and appealing stars rode the Western Range. John Wayne, Gary Cooper, Randolph Scott, Joel McCrea, and James Stewart became major players on the western scene. As Michael Parkinson and Clyde Jeavons note in their incisive *Pictorial History of Westerns* (1972), these five, along with predecessors Broncho Billy Anderson, William S. Hart, and Tom Mix rank among the handful of western stars who either worked exclusively in the genre or made their biggest contribution to the cinema in the "Western's broad confines." Add today the name of Clint Eastwood, and that venerated list is now complete.

Since the late 1930s, many big stars who have achieved fame in a variety of roles have also embraced the western with some regularity and a notable degree of success. Henry Fonda, Glenn Ford, Richard Widmark, and Alan Ladd immediately come to mind. So do Errol Flynn, Clark Gable, William Holden, Gregory Peck, Robert Taylor, Charlton Heston, James Garner, John Payne, Kirk Douglas, Burt Lancaster, Robert Ryan, Robert Mitchum, Jack Palance, Ronald Reagan, Ernest Borgnine, Lee Marvin, and many others.

Even James Cagney, Humphrey Bogart, and Marlon Brando have graced the western screen with their inimitable flair. B-western heroes Gene Autry, Roy Rogers, and, to a lesser degree, William Boyd as Hop-Along Cassidy became household names and living legends. Actors George Montgomery, Dale Robertson, Audie Murphy, and Charles Bronson found a home and enduring fame in western movies. In 1971 veteran actor and former World Rodeo champion Ben Johnson became the first authentic cowboy to win an Academy Award for his splendid work in *The Last Picture Show*.

Too often overlooked are the great character actors who supplied a multitude of supporting performances that gave fine films their very foundation: Walter Brennan, Victor McLaglen, Ward Bond, Harry Carey Jr., Charles Bickford, Richard Boone, Andy Devine, Arthur Kennedy, Jack Elam, Pedro Armendáriz, George "Gabby" Hayes, Tim Holt, John Ireland, Brian Keith, Royal Dano, John Mitchum, Edward Faulkner, Gregory Walcott, Warren Oates, Lee Van Cleef, Arthur Hunnicutt, Dan Duryea, and others.

Not lost are contributions to silver screen westerns by a handful of "Golden Age" leading ladies: Barbara Stanwyck, Jean Arthur, Veronica Lake, Claire Trevor, Jennifer Jones, Joan Crawford, Jane Russell, Linda Darnell, Angie Dickinson, Maureen O'Hara, Vera Miles, and Katharine Ross have contributed quality work in a male-dominated genre.

No director could carve a western landscape like John Ford. With the deftness of a Remington, he could capture the snow-topped Sierras, the wailing winds of Monument Valley, nearly every feature of the sprawling western land, expansive and beautiful. Still, as the unmatched poet and romanticist of the cinematic West, Ford's record four Academy Awards do not include a single western film.

But Ford was not alone in helming outstanding westerns during Hollywood's so-called golden years. Howard Hawks, William Wellman, King Vidor, Raoul Walsh, Henry King, Henry Hathaway, Anthony Mann, and Budd Boetticher each contributed brilliantly to the genre. To a lesser degree so did Fritz Lange, Delmer Daves, Michael Curtiz, John Sturges, George Miller, Lesley Selander, and George Sherman. And while George Stevens, Fred Zinnemann, and William Wyler are not recognized as genre masters per se, their masterworks *Shane*, *High Noon*, and even Wyler's *The Westerner* are superb motion pictures and among the best westerns ever filmed.

In the post war era, westerns began taking on controversial themes. William Wellman's *The Ox Bow Incident* (1943), John Ford's *My Darling Clementine* (1944), Raoul Walsh's *Pursued* (1947), André De Toth's *Ramrod* (1947), Howard Hawks's *Red River* (1948), Alfred Greene's *Four Faces West* (1948), Delmer Daves's *Broken Arrow* (1950), Henry King's *The Gunfighter* (1950), Anthony Mann's *The Furies* (1950), Zinnemann's *High Noon* (1952), Stevens's *Shane* (1953), Ford's *The Searchers* (1956), Budd Boetticher's *Seven Men From Now* (1957), Samuel Fuller's *Forty Guns* (1957), and Sam Peckinpah's *Ride the High Country* constitute just a few examples of rich and intelligent filmmaking.

With the changing political and social currents of the 1960s, westerns entered a state of flux. It took 143 films and a career dating back to 1929 for John Wayne to earn a long-awaited Oscar for his work in Henry Hathaway's *True Grit*. The American Indian was given a wide share of dignity and respect in Ford's *Cheyenne Autumn* and in Arthur Penn's *Little Big Man* (1970).

The tough lonely life of the cattle drover was realistically captured in Tom Gries's *Will Penny*, with Charlton Heston reaching his finest film hour in the title role. The bad guys were made into heroes in *The Wild Bunch* (1969), Sam Peckinpah's magnificent, moving, and impeccably violent ode to a dying West. The combination of action and patter reached its peak that same year with George Roy Hill's irresistible *Butch Cassidy and the Sundance Kid*.

On a less positive note, the traditional western had been usurped by a different product. These "revisionist" westerns purported to show the Old West not as we had idealized but as it "really was." Yet many of these new westerns were as highly exaggerated and often more historically flawed than the films they supposedly were replacing. This new realism tended to depict the Old West as dirty, mean-spirited, dangerous, crass, and largely ignoble. The spaghetti westerns (see Appendix I) that enjoyed such enormous popularity from the mid-1960s to the early '70s initiated this viewpoint.

By the 1970s, foul language, graphic violence, and uncovered parts of the human torso began to flash across the western screen as never before, although Howard Hughes's *The Outlaw* [1943] and King Vidor's *Duel in the Sun* [1946] had pushed the steamy envelope to new limits two decades earlier. With the waning of the Western film in this decade and the

demise of the studio system that helped create it, the genre began to be viewed as obsolete. More and more westerns had become the special fodder for revisionist critics and filmmakers and CEOs in business suits.

What was best in the genre had gone from the big screen to the small, with the production of inspired miniseries and movies such as Robert Totten's *The Sacketts* (1979) and Andrew McLaglen's *The Shadow Riders* (1982). Both productions were based on stories by Louis L'Amour and helped to advance the names of two young actors destined to preserve the western ethos: Tom Selleck and Sam Elliott.

In 1989, Larry McMurtry's sprawling novel *Lonesome Dove* was made into superb miniseries starring Tommy Lee Jones and Robert Duvall. Directed by Simon Wincer and with best-of-career performances by Jones and Duvall, it ranks among the best westerns ever produced. The television trend has continued to the present day with two outstanding TNT (Turner Network Television) productions: *Last Stand at Saber Ridge* (1997) and the enormously successful *Crossfire Trail* (2001), both features produced by and starring Tom Selleck.

Could the western film make a comeback? A few people thought so, not least a couple of actors named Kevin Costner and Clint Eastwood.

In 1990, *Dances with Wolves* became the first western to win an Academy Award for Best Picture since *Cimarron* in 1930, with Costner becoming the first director to garner an Oscar for helming a western. Moreover, the film revitalized the western's financial viability. Two years later Clint Eastwood scored big with *Unforgiven*, called by *Time*'s movie critic Richard Corliss "a dark passionate drama with good guys so twisted and bad guys so persuasive that virtue and villainy become two views of the same soul." The *Los Angeles Daily News*' Bob Strauss characterized *Unforgiven* as "a ruthlessly uncompromising western, an unflinching autopsy of Eastwood's screen persona, our frontier legends, and the legacy history bequeathes." Called by some "an old man's movie," three of the four leads in *Unforgiven* were in their 60s, and the other 55, a fact that speaks volumes.

Clint Eastwood may well be the last genre classicist in American film, most certainly the western film. *Unforgiven* won four Oscars: Best Picture; Best Supporting Actor (Gene Hackman); Best Film Editing (Joel Cox); and Best Director (Eastwood). Twenty-three years after handing an Oscar to John Wayne, Barbara Streisand handed a similar gold statuette to another western screen icon. Andrew Sarris remarked of Eastwood in *The New Observer*, "Now at age sixty-two, he joyously joins the gallery of the sunset horsemen previously incarnated in the twilight westerns of John Wayne, Joel McCrea, Randolph Scott, and Gary Cooper, among other grizzled greats."

It was a fitting epitaph to a century of westerns.

Our purpose in producing Facts On File's *Encyclopedia of Westerns* is to present the most comprehensive and annotated volume of westerns available to the public. Entries appear alphabetically, and annotations vary from credits only to one or two lines to three or four pages, depending on available data and the significance of the entry. They may incorporate a synopsis, reviews, sidebars, musical critiques, or statements by filmmakers and performers (many from original interviews with the author). Unlike many film almanacs and directories, there is no overall rating of the entries, but from time to time the author's opinions do surface.

With a project so comprehensive, certain constraints were necessary. The entries are comprised mainly of western films of the sound era. Landmark films from the silent era, such as Edwin S. Porter's *The Great Train Robbery*, James Cruze's *The Covered Wagon*, and John Ford's *The Iron Horse* are fully covered as individual entries. So are such William S. Hart features as *Hell's Hinges* and *Tumbleweeds* as well as such Tom Mix vehicles as *The Great K & A Train Robbery* and *Just Tony*.

We inserted serials selectively because our original plan was to limit our entries to feature films. We employed the same criteria for western movies made explicitly for television. Granted, these are arbitrary decisions.

Because of the sheer numbers, the B westerns present a particular problem. In 1935, for example, more than 150 titles were either produced or released. While such films often overlooked in serious studies of the genre, many have real style and an ability to tackle social issues such as racial discrimination which the A westerns tended to avoid throughout much of the 1930s and 1940s.

To be as inclusive as possible, we employed Master Entries, a few examples of which follow:

- Roy Rogers made more than 90 films for Republic between 1938 and 1952. Some entries are fully annotated with a synopsis and ancillary data. Others include only the credits with a reference to the Master Entry which details all the films in the series with some explanatory comments. Not all films in all series are included.
- Johnny Mack Brown's considerable volume of work includes series features he made for different studios. Consequently, a separate Master Entry will be listed for the appropriate series studio.
- If the entry is part of a series where different actors played the same role, the Master Entry will involve the series—not the actor. Thus any Red Ryder entry not given a full annotation and synopsis will be listed in the master entry.

While purists might disagree, we included films with western themes from the modern era: Hence the likes of *Hud, Junior Bonner, and J.W. Coop* receive full treatment. So were

musicals with a decidedly western bent: *Annie Get Your Gun, Oklahoma!, Rose Marie,* and *Seven Brides for Seven Brothers,* for example.

At the same time, a few films were not included that some might expect: John Huston's brilliant *The Treasure of the Sierra Madre*. The reason is that it crosses genre lines, and a work of such merit deserves greater attention than this volume can allow. Nor have I included George Stevens's highly praised *Giant* (1956). For Stevens, *Shane* was his western film vision, whereas *Giant* was made as the final installment in a trilogy of 1950s films as a testimony to the American experience, the other two being *A Place in the Sun* (1951) and *Shane* (1953).

To further aid the reader, we have included separate appendixes for the spaghetti westerns, Academy Awards nominations and winners in the genre, and literary sources. Also, we have listed all films not cited as entries in the body of the work by year in two separate appendixes, one for sound films and one for silent films.

As a city kid from Chicago, I fell in love with the American West at a very early age. I watched western movies in an assortment of theaters and movies palaces on Chicago's North Side and in downtown Chicago where the Chicago Theater, the Oriental Theater, and the State and Lake ruled supreme. I was awed by an incredibly handsome Alan Ladd in *Shane* and moved by the tears and pathos of an adoring young boy in the film's closing scene, one of the most haunting and memorable in the history of American cinema.

I saw Gary Cooper reach his finest hour as the courageous Will Kane in *High Noon*, and I whistled the haunting theme music for months. My childhood images of John Wayne remain: in *She Wore a Yellow Ribbon*, he reluctantly reaches for a pair of glasses, then wiping an errant tear from his eye, reads the touching inscription inside the silver watch bestowed to Captain Nathan Brittles by his troops—"Lest We Forget."

Nor should we. The western film is an American original, a cultural treasure, a true cinematic art form. It has seen us through changing times and shifting trends. It has comforted us, entertained us, and at times shocked us. But it has never left us. I am proud and honored to have been asked to help keep this marvelous legacy alive.

—Herb Fagen
Walnut Creek, California
June 2002

Entries A to Z

ABILENE TOWN United Artists, 1946, B&W, 89 min, VT. **Producers:** Herbert B. Biberman and Jules Levy; **Director:** Edwin L. Marin; **Screenplay:** Harold Shumate; **Music:** Gerard Carbonara, Albert Glasser, Kermit Goell (songs), Charles Koff, James Mayfield, Fred Speilman (songs), and Max Teer; **Cinematographer:** Archie Stout (as Archie J. Stout); **Editor:** Richard V. Heermance; **Cast:** Randolph Scott, Ann Dvorak, Edgar Buchanan, Rhonda Fleming, Lloyd Bridges, Helen Boyce, Howard Freeman, Richard Hale, Jack Lambert, Dick Curtis.

In this film set in the post-Civil War West, a patient marshal (Randolph Scott) tries to stop homesteader conflicts. Cattlemen and homesteaders are at loggerheads in this fast-paced shoot-em-up western that focuses on the evolution of this Kansas village from an unstable and violent cowboy town into a peaceful frontier community.

Within a historical perspective, Abilene is located where the Chisholm Trail ends and where cattle were put on trains for the packinghouse cities. At the time, businessmen felt that without the cattle business, the town would die. The cattlemen-versus-homesteader conflicts provide a recurring theme in scores of western films.

Randolph Scott is at his stoic best as the taciturn marshal who cleans up the town and manages to tame salty saloon singer Ann Dvorak along the way. Rhonda Fleming and Lloyd Bridges provide appealing second leads, and Jack Lambert makes a believable heavy, but it is veteran character actor Edgar Buchanan who steals the show as Sheriff Bravo Trimble. Based on Ernest Haycox's 1946 novel *Trail Town*, the film features such Kermit Goell/ Fred Speilman songs as "Everytime I Give My Heart," "I Love Out Here in the West" and "All You Gotta Do," spelled with frequent strains of "The Battle Hymn of the Republic." This above-average treatment of a familiar western theme still makes for an entertaining and enjoyable viewing experience.

ABILENE TRAIL Monogram, 1951, B&W, 54 min. **Producer:** Vincent M. Fennelly; **Director:** Lewis D. Collins; **Screenplay:** Harry L. Fraser; **Cinematographer:** Gilbert Warrenton; **Editor:** Richard V. Heermance; **Cast:** Whip Wilson, Andy Clyde, Noel Neill, Steve Clark, Marshall Reed, Dennis Moore, Lee Roberts, Tommy Farrell, Ted Adams, Milburne Morante, Lyle Talbot, Bill Kennedy.

Two suspected horse thieves come to the aid of a young rancher who is having trouble driving his herd to market in this solid Monogram B western series piece with Whip Wilson as Dave "Kansas Kid" Hill and Andy Clyde as "Sagebrush Charlie." Wilson was a feature series player on the Monogram schedules in the 1940s and early 1950s. Although the B western was in decline by the early 1950s, this Whip Wilson vehicle is quite well done. This Monogram feature is the only film where he plays "The Kansas City Kid." Most of his 26 feature films had him playing a character named Whip Wilson or "Whip" because of his skills with that implement.

Wilson's films include *God's Country* (1946); *Silver Trails* (1948); *Crashing Thru, Haunted Trails, Riders of the Dusk, Shadows of the West, Range Land* (1949); *Fence Riders, Gunslingers, Arizona Territory, Cherokee Uprising, Outlaws of Texas, Silver Raiders* (1950); *Canyon Raiders, Nevada Badmen, Lawless Cowboys, Wanted: Dead or Alive, Stagecoach Driver, Stage to Blue River* (1951); *Night Raiders, The Gunman,* aka *Mr. Hobo, Montana Incident* aka *Gunsmoke Range, Wyoming Roundup* (1952).

ACE HIGH (*QUATTRO DEL AVE MARIA*) Paramount, 1969, Color, 132 min. **Producers:** Bino Cicogna and Giuseppe Colizzi; **Director:** Colizzi; **Screenplay:** Colizzi; **Music:** Carlo Rustichelli; **Cinematographer:** Marcello Masciocchi; **Editor:** Marcello Malvestiti; **Cast:** Terence Hill, Bud Spencer, Eli Wallach, Kevin McCarthy, Steffan Zacharias, Livio Lorenzo, Tiffany Hoyveld.

An outlaw who is sentenced to hang is offered a chance to save his life. This better-than-average Giuseppi Colizzi western comedy offers an enjoyable musical score, some beautiful photography, and the usual violent touches. Terence Hill plays Cat Stevens (not to be confused with the former rock star), and Eli Wallach and Kevin McCarthy deliver their usual competent performances. In Great Britain the film was issued as *Revenge of El Paso.* (See also Appendix I, Spaghetti Westerns A–Z.)

ACES AND EIGHTS Puritan Pictures, 1936, B&W, 62 min. **Producers:** Sam Katzman, Sigmond Neufeld, and Leslie Simmons; **Director:** Sam Newfield; **Screenplay:** George Arthur Durlam; **Cinematographer:** Jack Greenhalgh; **Cast:** Tim McCoy, Luanna Walters, Rex Lease, Wheeler Oakman, J. Frank Glendon.

Tim McCoy plays an infamous cardsharp who comes to the aid of a Mexican family unfairly accused of murder. There's not much action here, but the story is well told and pleasant, and McCoy gives a fine performance as a gambler. A colonel in the U.S. Army and an authority on Indian lore, the dignified McCoy achieved a reputation as a more serious actor than did most of his counterparts in the B western arena. (See also *MAN FROM GUNTOWN.*)

ACE'S WILD Commodore, 1936, B&W, 57 min. **Producer:** William Berke; **Director:** Harry L. Fraser; **Screenplay:** Monro Talbot; **Cinematographer:** Robert E. Kline; **Editor:** Arthur A. Brooks; **Cast:** Harry Carey, Gertrude Messinger, Fred "Snowflake" Toones, Ed Cassidy, Phil Dunham, Chuck Morrison.

A newspaper editor is threatened by outlaws when he tries to stop their activities in this low-budget film with an excellent performance by Harry Carey.

ACROSS THE BADLANDS Columbia, 1950, B&W, 55 min. **Producer:** Colbert Carr; **Director:** Fred F. Sears; **Screenplay:** Barry Shipman; **Cinematographer:** Fayte M. Browne; **Editor:** Paul Borofsky; **Cast:** Charles Starrett, Smiley Burnette, Stanley Andrews, Harmonica Bill, Jock (O) Mahoney.

The Durango Kid (Charles Starrett) and sidekick Smiley Burnette are called in by the general manager of a railroad company to expose a gang that is making attacks on a band of surveyors laying a new railway line. Aided by Barry Shipman's fine script and Fred S. Sears's steady direction, this action-packed film is one of Starrett's best series entries. Starrett starred in 60 Durango Kid features beginning with *THE DURANGO KID* in 1940.

ACROSS THE BORDER (aka: LONE RIDER CROSSES THE RIO, THE) Producers Releasing Corporation, 1941, B&W, 63 min. **Producer:** Sigmond Neufeld; **Director:** Sam Newfield; **Screenplay:** William Lively; **Music:** Johnny Lange and Lew Porter; **Cinematographer:** Jack Greenhalgh; **Editor:** Holbrook N. Todd; **Cast:** George Houston, Al St. John, Roquell Verria, Julian Rivero.

While hiding from outlaws in Mexico, Tom Cameron (aka The Lone Rider, played by George Houston) and Fuzzy Jones (Al St. John) help a Mexican official's son fake his kidnapping. The boy's father disapproves of his affair with a cabaret singer. But when the boy is kidnapped for real, Tom and Fuzzy get blamed. They end up solving the "kidnapping" in this somewhat different entry in the Lone Rider series.

Houston played Tom Cameron (The Lone Rider) in 10 films for Producers Releasing Corporation from 1941 until his death in 1944 at age 46, when he was succeeded by Robert Livingston as Rocky Cameron/The Lone Rider. (See also *LONE RIDER AMBUSHED, THE.*)

ACROSS THE GREAT DIVIDE Pacific International, 1977, Color, 101 min. **Producer:** Arthur R. Dubs; **Director:** Stewart Rafill; **Screenplay:** Rafill; **Music:** Gene Kauer and Douglas M. Lackey; **Cinematographer:** Gerard Alcan; **Editors:** R. Hansel Brown and Frank C. Decot; **Cast:** Robert Logan, Heather Rattray, Mark Edward Hall, George "Buck" Flower, Hal Bokar.

In 1876 a vagabond con man and two orphans, intent on traveling west to Oregon, brave the harsh elements so the youngsters can claim inherited land. Praise from viewers is surprisingly high—much higher than critical reviews. Lots of pretty scenery and a plentiful display of animals offer the film's most appealing highlights.

ACROSS THE RIO GRANDE Monogram, 1949, B&W, 56 min. **Producer:** Louis Gray; **Director:** Oliver Drake; **Screenplay:** Ronald Davidson; **Cinematographer:** Harry Neumann; **Editor:** John C. Fuller; **Cast:** Jimmy Wakely, Dub Taylor, Myron Healey, Polly Bergen.

Jimmy Wakely helps straighten out a young lawyer who is involved with border ore smugglers. In the process he captures the killer of the lawyer's father. This excellent Jimmy Wakely film marks the first screen appearance by actress/singer Polly Bergen, who plays a cantina singer. Usually garbed in Gene Autry-like attire, Jimmy Wakely was a Monogram musical mainstay in the 1940s. He appeared in the 1940 film *TEXAS TERROR* (with his group Jimmy Wakely & His Rough Riders) starring Don "Red" Barry, *THE TULSA KID* (1940), and *SAGA OF DEATH VALLEY* (1939) with Roy Rogers and Don "Red" Barry. He went on to work with many of the big B western stars in the early to mid-1940s.

Wakely appeared as an uncredited singer in *Come On Danger* with Tim Holt (1942); with Johnny Mack Brown in *Pony Post* (1940); *Bury Me Not on the Lone Prairie* (1941); *Deep in the Heart of Texas, Little Joe, the Wrangler* (1942); *Cheyenne Roundup, Lone Star Trail, The Old Chisholm Trail, Raiders of San Joaquin, Tenting Tonight on the Old Camp Ground* (1943); *The Marshal's Daughter,* (1953); and with Charles Starrett in *Robin Hood of the Range, Cowboy in the Clouds* (1943); *Sundown Valley, Sagebrush Heroes, Cyclone Prairie Rangers, Saddle Leather Law, Cowboy Canteen, Cowboy from Lonesome River* (1944).

Jimmy Wakely, star of Across the Rio Grande. *Wakely worked with many of the top B western stars in the early to mid-1940s before starring in his own series. His entries were generally low on plot and large in musical content.* (MONOGRAM/AUTHOR'S COLLECTION)

In 1944 he began his own series of films for Monogram which were generally low on plot and heavy on musical content. They include *Song of the Range* (1944); *Lonesome Trail, Springtime in Texas, Saddle Serenade, Riders of the Dawn* (1945); *Moon Over Montana, West of the Alamo, Song of the Sierras, Trail to Mexico* (1946); *Ridin' Down the Trail, Song of the Wasteland, Six Gun Serenade, Rainbow Over the Rockies* (1947); *Partners of the Sunset, Cowboy Cavalier, Silver Trails, Outlaw Brand, Courtin' Trouble, Song of the Drifter, Oklahoma Blues, The Rangers Ride, Range Renegades* (1948); *Across The Rio Grande, Brand of Fear, Gun Runner, Roaring Westward* aka *Boom Town Badmen, Lawless Code, Gun Law Justice* (1949).

ACROSS THE SIERRAS (aka: WELCOME STRANGER) Columbia, 1941, B&W, 59 min. **Producer:** Leon Barsha; **Director:** D. Ross Aldermen; **Screenplay:** Paul Franklin; **Cinematographer:** George Meehan; **Cast:** Bill Elliott, Luana Walters, Dub Taylor, Dick Curtis, Richard Fiske, LeRoy Mason.

Bill Elliott (Wild Bill Hickok) expresses a desire to live peacefully. But events change when he is forced to beat the daylights out of a band of heavies. Mitch Carewe (Dick Curtis) is just released from jail and swears vengeance on Hickok for locking him up years earlier. Although Wild Bill is victorious over the bad guys, he is rejected by his ladylove (Luana Walters) who can't abide a man who carries a six-gun. The unusual plot twist plays quite well.

Elliott was lured to the movies when he first saw his hero William H. Hart on the screen. He was a struggling heavy for 10 years (under the name Gordon Elliott) until Columbia gave him his big break by casting him in its 1938 serial *The Adventures of Wild Bill Hickok*, which is responsible for his name change.

ACROSS THE WIDE MISSOURI MGM, 1951, Color, 78 min, VT. **Producer:** Robert Sisk; **Director:** William Wellman; **Screenplay:** Talbot Jennings, Frank Cavett; **Music:** David Raskin; **Cinematographer:** William C. Mellor; **Editor:** John Dunning; **Cast:** Clark Gable, Ricardo Montalban, John Hodiak, Adolphe Menjou, J. Carrol Naish, Jack Holt, George Chandler, Maria Elena Marqués, Richard Anderson, Alan Napier, Frankie Darro (uncredited), Howard Keel (uncredited as narrator).

Like *BROKEN ARROW* (1950), this film was unique to its day and influenced subsequent films sympathetic to Indians (although Native Americans had on occasion been treated

Clark Gable and Maria Elena Marqués in Across the Wide Missouri (MGM/AUTHOR'S COLLECTION)

sympathetically in earlier films as well). All the Indian dialogue is spoken in native tongue and translated into pidgin English by Adolphe Menjou, cast as a French Canadian. While great care was given to make the spoken word accurate, the long and laborious translations, realistic as they are, slow the pace of the movie and encumber the dialogue.

Clark Gable is his two-fisted best as trapper Flint Mitchell, who falls in love with a beautiful Indian princess played by Mexican film star Maria Elena Marqués. Racial barriers in 1950 did not allow an "important" white star to marry an Indian girl and live "happily ever after." As in *Broken Arrow*, Delmar Daves's compelling film dealing with a similar theme, the Indian maiden is scripted into an untimely and tragic death.

William Wellman's deft direction sets the tone for this adventurous saga about the explorers and trappers who challenged the idyllic majesty of Colorado during the early 1820s. The Rocky Mountain panorama, filmed on location in Colorado, is absolutely stunning, prompting Richard Griffith to write in *The Saturday Review* that Wellman "pitches into his lively material with the zest of a man whose cameras are straining at the leash." Equally impressive is David Raskin's original film score, touched at times by strains of the American folk standard "Shenandoah."

Based on Bernard De Voto's 1947 Pulitzer Prize-winning novel, and a theme first introduced into American literature by James Fenimore Cooper, this impressive yet flawed film captures the destruction of Colorado's seemingly perfect lifestyle and the soiling of its once-pristine fur country. An uncredited Howard Keel narrates the story as the son of Flint Mitchell (Gable) and his Blackhawk Indian mother (Marqués).

ADIOS AMIGO Atlas Productions, 1975, Color, 87 min. **Producer:** Fred Williamson; **Director:** Williamson; **Screenplay:** Williamson; **Music:** Blue Infernal Machine; **Cinematographer:** Tony Palmieri; **Editors:** Eva Ruggiero and Gene Ruggiero; **Cast:** Williamson, Richard Pryor, James Brown, Thalmus Rasulala, Mike Henry.

This was a total venture for Fred Williamson, who wrote, produced, and directed the film. Williamson and his con-man partner (Richard Pryor) bungle their way through a series of misadventures including a stagecoach robbery, a land swindle, and a jailbreak. A departure from the prevailing blaxploitation pictures of the early and mid-1970s, Williamson rejects the violence and the black/white animosity of earlier films, relying on humor instead. The result is a whimsical parody of the Hollywood western cowboy, highlighted mainly by Pryor's irresistible humor.

ADVANCE TO THE REAR (aka: COMPANY OF COWARDS, UK) MGM, 1964, Color, 100 min. **Producer:** Ted Richmond; **Director:** George Marshall; **Screenplay:** Samuel A. Peoples and William Bowers; **Music:** Randy Sparks; **Cinematographer:** Milton Krasner; **Cast:** Glenn Ford, Stella Stevens, Melvin Douglas, Jim Backus, Joan Blondell, Andrew Prine, Alan Hale Jr., Whit Bissell, Michael Pate, Gregg Palmer, Preston Foster.

In this film based on the novel by William Chamberlain III and Jack Schaefer, Glenn Ford and Melvin Douglas play two cavalry officers who lead an inept band of misfits and somehow manage to capture a rebel spy, saving the Union gold shipment in the process. In fact, these guys are so goofy that they'll never be heard from again after being sent so far west.

The only sane man in this brigade of boobs is Glenn Ford. His colleagues include a kleptomaniac, a flagpole sitter, a fellow who loves to play with fire, a trooper with chronic hiccups, a punch-drunk fighter, and a friendly soul named "Smiley Boy" who hugs his pals to death. Stella Stevens and Joan Blondell (Easy Jenny) are the harlots with hearts of gold. Deftly directed by George Marshall, with an intelligent screenplay by William Bowers and Samuel A. Peoples, the film provides good escapist family fun and lots of laughs.

ADVENTURES IN SILVERADO Columbia, 1948, B&W, 75 min. **Producers:** Robert Cohn and Ted Richmond; **Director:** Phil Karlson; **Screenplay:** Kenneth Gamet, Tom Kirkpatrick, and Joe Pagano; **Music:** Misha Bakaleinikoff; **Cinematographer:** Henry Freulich; **Cast:** William Bishop, Gloria Henry, Edgar Buchanan, Forrest Tucker, Irving Bacon, Fred Sears.

Based on Robert Louis Stevenson's novel *Silverado Squatter*, this low-budget western has the famed author as a passenger on a stagecoach headed west to the Napa Valley in search of a story. When the stage is robbed by a hooded highwayman called "The Monk," the driver is accused of being in cahoots with the badman and sets out to capture him. This is an interesting and well-done film by underrated director Phil Karlson, who helmed mainly low-budget actioners until he suddenly gained stature in the 1950s.

ADVENTURES OF BULLWHIP GRIFFIN, THE Disney, 1967, Color, 108 min. **Producer:** Bill Anderson; **Director:** James Neilson; **Screenplay:** Lowell S. Hawley; **Music:** George Bruns; **Cinematographer:** Edward Colman; **Cast:** Roddy McDowall, Karl Malden, Mike Mazurki, Suzanne Pleshette, Harry Guardino, Bryan Russell, Hermione Baddeley, Cecil Kellaway.

Two snooty snobbish types and their butler head to the Wild West and end up taking better care of themselves than anyone thought possible. Roddy McDowall shines as the family butler (Eric "Bullwhip" Griffin), whose unyielding sense of propriety makes him an ideal foil as he heads west during the Gold Rush. Based on Aaron Sidney Fleischman's novel *By the Great Horn Spoon*, this is a bright, well-crafted, and rich spoof.

ADVENTURES OF DON COYOTE United Artists, 1947, B&W, 65 min. **Producers:** Ralph Cohn, Mary Pickford, and Charles "Buddy" Rogers; **Director:** Reginald Le Borg; **Screenplay:** Harold Tarshis; **Music:** David Chudnow; **Cinematographer:** Fred Jackman Jr.; **Editor:** Lynn Harrison; **Cast:** Frances Rafferty, Richard Martin, Marc

Cramer, Benny Bartlett, Frank Fenton, Pierce Lyden, Byron Foulger.

Two pals try to help a girl whose ranch is being attacked by outlaws in this tight little B western produced by Mary Pickford and Buddy Rogers.

ADVENTURES OF FRANK AND JESSE JAMES
Republic, 1948, B&W, 180 min, 13 chapters, VT. **Producer:** Herbert Yates; **Directors:** Frank Bannon and Yakima Canutt; **Screenplay:** Frank Adreon, Basil Dickey, Sol Shor, and Robert G. Walker; **Cinematographer:** John MacBurnie; **Editors:** Cliff Bell Sr. and Sam Starr; **Cast:** Clayton Moore, Steve Darrell, Noel Neill, George J. Lewis, Tom Steele, House Peters Jr., Lane Bradford, Stanley Andrews, George Chesebro, Jack Kirk, Steve Clark, Dub Taylor, George Loftin, Frank Ellis, Bud Osborne.

Jesse and Frank James (Clayton Moore and Steve Darrell) enter the gold-mining business to raise enough money to pay back what they stole in their younger and wilder days. However, a crooked mine foreman tries to stop them from repaying the robbery debts from a gold mine they now operate with a man and his daughter. A top-notch cast and plenty of action, codirected by Yakima Canutt, contributes to an exciting and engrossing western serial that leaves the audience hanging in suspense and waiting for more. Since it is available on video, new genre fans will enjoy the cliff-hanging aspects of the serials their parents and grandparents watched in local theaters decades ago.

ADVENTURES OF FRONTIER FREEMONT
Sunn Classics, 1976, Color, 86 min. **Producers:** David O'Malley and Charles Seller Jr.; **Director:** Richard Friedenberg; **Screenplay:** Friedenberg, O'Malley, and Sellier Jr.; **Cinematographer:** George Stapleford; **Editor:** Sharron Miller; **Cast:** Dan Haggerty, Denver Pyle, Tony Mirrati, Norman Goodman.

A man who decides to live in the wilderness is forced to overcome many hardships and obstacles before finding the peace of mind he is searching for. This low-budget film is a good, clean family adventure.

ADVENTURES OF GALLANT BESS, THE
Eagle Lion Films, 1948, B&W, 71 min. **Producers:** Jerry Briskin and Michael Rapf; **Director:** Lew Landers; **Screenplay:** Rapf; **Music:** Irving Gertz; **Cinematographer:** William Bradford; **Editor:** Harry Komer; **Cast:** Cameron Mitchell, Audrey Long, Fuzzy Knight, John Harmon.

Cameron Mitchell is torn between his girl Penny (Audrey Long) and his love for his horse in this low-key but colorful equestrian story.

ADVENTURES OF RED RYDER, THE
Republic, 1940, B&W, 12 chapters. **Producer:** Herbert Yates; **Directors:** William Witney and John English; **Screenplay:** Ronald Davidson, Franklin Adreon, Norman Hall, and Sol Shore; **Music:** Cy Feuer; **Cinematographer:** William Nobles; **Cast:** Don "Red" Barry, Noah Beery, Tommy Cook, Bob Kortman, William Farnum, Maude Pierce Allen, Vivian Austin (as Vivian Coe), Hal Taliaferro, Harry Worth, Carleton Young, Ray Teal, Gene Alsasce, Gayne Whitman, Hooper Atchley, John Dilson, Lloyd Ingraham, Charles Hutchinson, Gardner James, Wheaton Chambers, Lynton Brent, William "Billy" Benedict.

A crooked banker murders several people in order to seize land to be used by the railroad. After he kills Red Ryder's father, Red and his pal "Little Beaver" vow revenge.

Based on Fred Harmon's newspaper comic strip, this Republic serial was the first portrayal of the Red Ryder character by Donald Barry, who later continued making series westerns for Republic Pictures many times as the Cyclone Kid and the Tulsa Kid. Although he made no other Red Ryder features, Barry became so closely identified with the character that he was frequently billed on the screen as Don "Red" Barry, even though he didn't have red hair. In this serial David Sharpe did most of the acrobatic stunting for Barry.

Starting in 1944, William "Wild Bill" Elliott made the first 16 Red Ryder features for Republic Studios. These were enormously popular with audiences and brought Elliott to the peak of his career with Republic: *Tucson Raiders*, CHEYENNE WILDCAT, MARSHAL OF RENO, THE SAN ANTONIO KID, VIGILANTES OF DODGE CITY, SHERIFF OF LAS VEGAS (1944); THE LONE TEXAS RANGER; *Wagon Wheels Westward*, COLORADO PIONEERS, MARSHAL OF LAREDO, *Great Stagecoach Robbery*, PHANTOM OF THE PLAINS (1945); CONQUEST OF CHEYENNE, CALIFORNIA GOLD RUSH, SHERIFF OF REDWOOD VALLEY, *Sun Valley Cyclone* (1946).

The series continued with Allan "Rocky" Lane in the title role: *Santa Fe Uprising, Stagecoach to Denver* (1946); HOMESTEADERS OF PARADISE VALLEY, *Marshal of Cripple Creek*, OREGON TRAIL SCOUTS, RUSTLERS OF DEVIL'S CANYON, THE, VIGILANTES OF BOOMTOWN (1947). When the series was resumed by Eagle Lion films in 1949, Jim Bannon appeared as Red Ryder in four films: ROLL THUNDER, ROLL; RIDE, RYDER, RIDE, *Cowboy and the Prizefighter* (1949); THE FIGHTING REDHEAD (1949). Film historians generally feel that the best films of the series were those with Bill Elliott in the title role, but both Elliott and Allan Lane contributed some fine features to this popular B western series.

ADVENTURES OF REX AND RINTY, THE
Republic, 1935, B&W, 12 chapters. **Producers:** Nat Levine and Barney A. Serecky (supervising); **Director:** Ford Beebe and Reeves Eason; **Screenplay:** Eason, Maurice Geraghty, John Rathmell, Barney A. Sarecky, and Ray Trampe; **Music:** Lee Zahler; **Cinematographer:** William Nobles; **Cast:** Kane Richmond, Mischa Auer, Norma Taylor, Smiley Burnette, Harry Woods, Wheeler Oakman.

Rex, King of the Wild Horses, is brought from the fictitious island of Sujan, where he is worshiped as a God-Horse, to the United States, where he is to be trained as a polo pony. He escapes his captives and meets Rinty (Rin-Tin-Tin Jr.).

With the help of Frank Bradlley (Kane Richmond), Rex is returned to his native Sujan. But the natives are now persuaded to turn against their God-Horse, and he is rescued just before he is to be burned as a sacrifice.

ADVENTURES OF THE MASKED PHANTOM
Talisman Studios, Inc., 1939, B&W, 60 min. **Producer:** B. F. Zeidman; **Director:** Charles Abbott; **Screenplay:** Joseph O'Donnell and Clifford Sanforth; **Music:** Johnny Lane and Lew Porter; **Cinematographer:** Marcel Le Picard; **Cast:** Monte Rawlins, Larry Mason, Sonny Lamont, Betty Burgess.

A law officer hides his face behind a mask in order to hunt down outlaws who are smuggling stolen gold plates from a mine with an abundance of low-grade ore. The names of the characters are interesting: Alamo, the Stranger, the Minstrel, and Dumpy the Ranch Hand. This campy curio should appeal to certain audiences.

AFTER THE STORM   See *DESERT GOLD* (1914).

AGAINST A CROOKED SKY   Vestron, 1975, Color, 89 min, VT. **Producer:** Lyman Dayton; **Director:** Earl Bellamy; **Screenplay:** Eleanor Lamb and Douglas G. Stewart; **Music:** Lex De Azevedo; **Editor:** Marsh Hendrey; **Cast:** Richard Boone, Stewart Peterson, Henry Wilcoxon, Shannon Farnon, Jewell Branch, Clint Ritchie, Brenda Venus, Vincent St. Cyr.

A teenage girl, the eldest daughter of a pioneer family, is kidnapped by a mysterious Indian tribe. Her brother pursues her, and along the way he recruits a broken-down, drunken prospector (Richard Boone) to help him track the unknown Indians and rescue his sister. Once he finds her, he has to pass a horrifying test called "Crooked Sky," putting his own life in peril by shielding his sister from an executioner's arrow. A fine performance by Boone as "the Russian." Filmed on location in Arches National Park, Utah, this is a good, picturesque, family-oriented movie.

ALAMO, THE   United Artists, 1960, Color, 192 min, VT, DVD. **Producer:** John Wayne; **Director:** John Wayne; **Screenplay:** James Edward Grant; **Music:** Dimitri Tiomkin; **Cinematographer:** William Clothier; **Editor:** Stuart Gilmore; **Cast:** John Wayne, Richard Widmark, Laurence Harvey, Richard Boone, Frankie Avalon, Patrick Wayne, Linda Cristal, Joan O'Brien, Chill Wills, Joseph Calleia, Ken Curtis, Carlos Arruza, Jester Hairston, Veda Ann Borg, John Dierkes, Denver Pyle, Hank Worden, Chuck Roberson, Guinn "Big Boy" Williams, Olive Carey, Aissa Wayne.

In 1836 Texas, the northernmost province of Mexico, rebels against the tyrannical rule of General Santa Anna (Ruben Padilla) and declares itself an independent republic. General Sam Houston (Richard Boone) tries to train and raise an army before Santa Anna's advancing forces. Colonel William Travis

John Wayne (as Davy Crockett) and stuntman/actor Dean Smith in The Alamo, *Wayne's directorial debut. Nominated for six Academy Awards including Best Picture, it won an Oscar only for Best Sound.* (UNITED ARTISTS/COURTESY OF DEAN SMITH)

(Laurence Harvey) arrives with 25 men to establish the first line of defense. Colonel Jim Bowie (Richard Widmark) comes to fight for independence with a small force of volunteers. A strong rivalry immediately develops, which threatens to develop into a private war. But many of their differences are mediated by Colonel Davy Crockett (John Wayne).

In a onetime Spanish mission that is crumbling to the ground, 180 men are now poised to stand against the advancing Mexican army of 7,000. They hope to hold their ground until Sam Houston has enough time to raise his army. But through a series of complications, Houston never arrives.

The story of the Alamo and the courageous men who fought to the last in its defense is well known. For 52-year-old John Wayne, it was the fulfillment of a dream. When he finished the production he told Hedda Hopper, "I wanted to direct from the first time I set foot in a studio. I was sidetracked for something like thirty years—I finally made it."

For more than 14 years, Wayne's dreams centered on creating the epic story. He insisted on directing because he had guided the project through its infancy and had nurtured it through each stage of development. The film was as much a statement of personal conviction as it was the telling of an epic tale.

Wayne first brought the idea to his pal, screenwriter James Grant, in 1947. The two men went to San Antonio and hired a research group to provide every written word about the Alamo and its defenders. Wayne then pitched the idea to Herbert Yates, his boss at Republic Pictures. Yates was leery. He had already done a small-budget picture on the Alamo in 1939 called *Men of Conquest*. Eager to please Wayne, Republic's top star, Yates held out the carrot for years but never formalized the deal. Eventually it was James "Happy" Shahan—who owned a 22,000-acre ranch six miles north of Bracketville,

Texas—who made the film possible. Anxious to lure Hollywood to Bracketville, Shahan contracted for the construction of an elaborate set on his ranch. With the help of art designer Al Ybarra, a completed Alamo compound and a town of 19 buildings were ready for the scheduled arrival of actors and crew in mid-1959.

Casting was a problem. Wayne originally had wanted to play Sam Houston (Boone's role) and devote the rest of his energies toward producing and directing. United Artists, however, said they would only help budget the film on the condition that Wayne himself play Davy Crockett.

Early press releases named William Holden and Rock Hudson to play Jim Bowie and Colonel William Travis, respectively. While Wayne and Holden were good friends, their respective production companies—Batjac and Holden Productions—could not come to terms on shooting schedules and other matters. When Holden bowed out, names like Charlton Heston and James Arness surfaced from time to time. But by summer Wayne had decided on Richard Widmark, whose versatility he admired and whom he felt could provide the proper character balance between the boisterous Davy Crockett and the priggish Colonel Travis. Wayne and Widmark worked well together on camera, but offscreen the relationship was far from amicable and quite strained.

It was John Ford who ultimately sold Wayne on Laurence Harvey for the part of Colonel Travis. A newcomer from England who had scored an Oscar nomination for his work in *Room at the Top*, Harvey's bisexuality proved a bit of a problem for Wayne at first, but he learned to respect and admire Harvey's grit and toughness. The two actors got along fine and developed a mutual respect.

Since *The Alamo* was filled with action and some of the most expansive battle scenes ever put on film, Wayne employed enormous groups of stuntmen. Legendary stuntman Cliff Lyons, Wayne's friend and associate from his early days in film, was named second unit director. Important secondary roles were given to Wayne's son Patrick and a talented stable of buddies like Ken Curtis, Hank Worden, Chuck Roberson, and Jack Pennick.

The end result was an occasionally long-winded and wordy account of a glorious American epoch when heroes prevailed and heroism presided. Despite its obvious flaws, and very lukewarm early reviews, *The Alamo* holds up as a fine film and a testament to Wayne's determination and fortitude.

The final 45 minutes is a study in excellence, and the battle scenes (due largely to Cliff Lyons) are among the best ever put on screen. Dimitri Tiomkin's score is superb, and the song "The Green Leaves of Summer" was worthy of an Oscar (it lost out to "Never on Sunday" from the film of the same name). The thematic use of melody and drama in the final scenes has rarely been duplicated, and "The Green Leaves of Summer" became a big hit for the recording group The Brothers Four, country singer Marty Robbins, and a popular instrumental by the British Dixieland band, Kenny Ball and his Jazzmen.

Nor was *The Alamo* the financial disaster some have assumed. Upon its release, it grossed $8 million, making it one of the year's top-grossing films, and established box-office records in London; Paris; Stockholm; Rome; Denmark; and San Juan, Puerto Rico. In Japan it set a foreign film box-office record, topping the record previously set by *Ben Hur*. While Wayne did not earn personal profits from the film, United Artists and MGM reaped millions from releases, rereleases, and redistribution rights.

It is wrong to dismiss *The Alamo* as the long-winded flop many critics claimed. As a war saga locked into the sentiment and drama of its time, and as an epic slice of Americana, it remains a popular and engaging film. Cut by 26 minutes after its Los Angeles premiere, it was restored to full length for the 1992 tape and laser disc reissues. While the critics were less than friendly, the film earned seven Academy Award nominations.

ALAMO: THIRTEEN DAYS OF GLORY, THE
Finnegan/Pinchuk, 1987, Color, 180 min. **Producers:** Stockton Briggle, Richard Carrothers, Bill Finnegan, Patricia Finnegan, Dennis Hennessy, and Sheldon Pinchuk; **Director:** Burt Kennedy; **Teleplay:** Clyde Ware and Norman McLeod Morill; **Music:** Peter Bernstein; **Cinematographer:** John Elsenbach; **Editor:** Michael N. Knue; **Cast:** James Arness, Brian Keith, Alec Baldwin, Raul Julia, Gene Evans, Ethan Wayne, Lorne Green.

Once again it is the valiant stand made by 180 men against the 7,000-man army of Mexican general Santa Anna in this made-for-television film. Based on the book by Lon Tinkle and directed by Burt Kennedy (who earlier had directed John Wayne in THE WAR WAGON (1967) and THE TRAIN ROBBERS (1973), this production has Brian Keith as Davy Crockett, James Arness as Jim Bowie, and Alec Baldwin as Colonel William Travis. Filmed in Bracketville, Texas (on the same set that John Wayne had built), Kennedy's TV remake features some robust battle scenes and a flamboyant performance by Raul Julia as Santa Anna.

ALBUQUERQUE
Paramount, 1948, Color, 90 min. **Producers:** William H. Pine and William C. Thomas; **Director:** Ray Enright; **Screenplay:** Gene Lewis and Clarence Upson Young; **Music:** Darrell Calker; **Cinematographer:** Fred Jackman Jr.; **Editor:** Howard A. Smith; **Cast:** Randolph Scott, Barbara Britton, George "Gabby" Hayes, Lon Chaney Jr., Russell Hayden.

A young man who finally rebels against an overly strict uncle wins his spurs in life. A solid film, this is an appealing entry for Randolph Scott fans. The Virginia-born Scott, with a college degree in textile engineering, became one of the movies' most dominant stars, appearing in 59 western films. Few stars—even John Wayne—came to be so closely identified with one genre. Based on a story by Luke Short, this picture was filmed in Albuquerque, New Mexico, and Sedona, California.

ALIAS BILLY THE KID
Republic, 1946, B&W, 55 min. **Producer:** Herbert Yates; **Director:** Thomas Carr; **Screenplay:** Betty Burbridge and Earl Snell; **Cinematographer:** Bob Thackery; **Editor:** Charles Craft; **Cast:** Sunset

Carson, Peggy Stewart, Tom London, Roy Barcroft, Pierce Lyden.

A ranger lets a convicted murderer escape from jail so he can trail him to his gang. But the man gets away, and the ranger becomes involved with a female outlaw leader. There is good action in this average Sunset Carson entry. (See also CALL OF THE ROCKIES [1944]).

ALIAS JESSE JAMES United Artists, 1959, Color, 92 min. **Producers:** Bob Hope and Jack Hope; **Director:** Norman Z. McCleod; **Screenplay:** Danile B. Beauchamps and William Bowers/Aubrey; **Music:** Joseph J. Lilley; **Cinematographer:** Lionel Lindon; **Editors:** Jack Bachom and Marvin Coil; **Cast:** Bob Hope, Rhonda Fleming, Wendell Corey, Gloria Talbot, Jim Davis, Bing Crosby, Gary Cooper, James Garner, Mike Mazurki, Jack Lambert, James Arness, Gene Autry, Ward Bond, Gail Davis, Hugh O'Brien, Fess Parker, Roy Rogers, Jay Silverheels, Iron Eyes Cody.

Bob Hope plays Milford Farnsworth, an insurance salesman canvassing the Wild West, where he is mistaken for a gun-slinging sharpshooter. Rhonda Fleming as Cora Lee and Gloria Talbot as the Indian Maiden provide the obligatory female beauty expected from any Hope caper. Moreover, some of the genre's most appealing film and TV westerners appear in a variety of cameo slots. Based on a story by Bert Lawrence, this hilarious western comedy is one of Bob Hope's funniest films. It all makes for a sprightly spoof.

ALIEN THUNDER See DAN CANDY'S LAW.

AL JENNINGS OF OKLAHOMA Columbia, 1951, Color, 79 min. **Producer:** Rudolph Flothow; **Director:** Ray Nazarro; **Screenplay:** George Bricker; **Music:** Misha Bakaleinikoff; **Cinematographer:** W. Howard Greene; **Cast:** Dan Duryea, Gail Storm, Dick Foran, Gloria Henry, Guinn "Big Boy" Williams, Grant Withers.

Oklahoma lawyer-turned-bank robber Al Jennings (Dan Duryea) tries to go straight after being released from prison, but faces a multitude of problems. A real cowboy who gained notoriety in turn-of-the-century Oklahoma by robbing banks and trains, Al Jennings actually journeyed to Hollywood after going straight to work in movies as an actor, writer, and technical advisor, sometimes playing himself. In yet another fictionalized Hollywood attempt to transform true-life figures with less than savory reputations into victimized gunslingers trying to live down their pasts, Duryea—usually the master screen villain—is downright pleasant in the title role.

ALLEGHENY UPRISING (aka: FIRST REBEL, THE, UK) RKO, 1939, B&W/Colorized, 81 min, VT. **Producer:** Pandro S. Berman; **Director:** William H. Seiter; **Screenplay:** P. J. Wolfson; **Music:** Anthony Collins; **Cinematographer:** Nicholas Musuraca; **Editor:** George Crone;

Cast: Claire Trevor, John Wayne, George Sanders, Brian Donlevy, Robert Barrat, John F. Hamilton, Moroni Olson, Eddie Quillan, Chill Wills, Ian Wolfe, Wallis Clark, Monte Montague, Eddy Waller, Olaf Hytten, Clay Clement, Bud Osborne, Charles Middleton.

Set in the American colonies prior to the Revolutionary War, young frontiersman Jim Smith (John Wayne) leads a group of settlers who find themselves in the unenviable position of being threatened by both the British on the one hand and hostile Indians on the other. Based on the novel The First Rebel by Neil H. Swanson and released just six days after DRUMS ALONG THE MOHAWK, which embraces a similar subject, this underrated film deals with the supplying of liquor and firearms to the Pennsylvania Indians by unscrupulous traders.

RKO wanted to capitalize on the success of STAGECOACH (1939) by romantically pairing John Wayne and Claire Trevor for a second time. While their presence illuminates the film, it is also important to note that the film successfully recaptures an almost forgotten chapter in our history, at the same time remaining surprisingly true to historical fact. "There is evidence of careful research in the settings and costumes . . . heretofore neglected, in the screen compilation of historical fiction," Variety noted in its review of the picture. History buffs, especially, should take a look at this film.

ALONG CAME JONES RKO, 1945, B&W, 90 min, VT. **Producer:** Gary Cooper; **Director:** Stuart Heisler; **Screenplay:** Nunnally Johnson; **Music:** Hugo Friendlander, Arthur Lange, and Charles Maxwell; **Cinematographer:** Milton R. Krasner; **Editor:** Thomas Neff and Paul Weatherwax; **Cast:** Gary Cooper, Loretta Young, William Demarest, Dan Duryea, Willard Robertson, Frank Sully, Ray Teal.

Melody Jones (Gary Cooper) rides into town with a saddle, a song, and a sidekick named Fury (William Demarest) in this film based on a novel by Alan LeMay. Sporting the initials M.J. on his saddlebag, Jones is immediately taken for a villainous outlaw named Monte Jarrad (Dan Duryea). He even falls in love with Jarrad's girl Cherry de Longpre (Loretta Young). His adventures and misadventures are fodder for a delightful western spoof with a good share of action and gunplay. Nunnally Johnson's screenplay is punctuated with such patented Cooper idioms as "Nope!" and "Much obliged!" Even the song "Round and Round," written by Al Stewart and Arthur Lange, is sung by Ole Coop himself. The film is great fun from start to finish.

Along Came Jones was Cooper's first effort at producing, and the critics were kind. Variety praised Cooper for playing "his usually languid self impressively." The New York Daily News went even further in its four-star review: "Not since his beloved 'Mr. Deeds' has he [Cooper] been able to expand on all the charm, befuddled naivete and droll humor at his command . . ." Over his long and distinguished film career, the Montana-born, two-time Oscar-winning actor starred in 28 Westerns, garnering his second Oscar for his vintage portrayal of Marshal Will Kane in HIGH NOON (1952).

ALONG THE GREAT DIVIDE Warner Bros., 1951, Color, 88 min, VT. **Producer:** Anthony Vieller; **Director:** Raoul Walsh; **Screenplay:** Walter Doniger, Lewis Meltzer; **Music:** David Buttolph; **Cinematographer:** Sidney Hickox; **Editor:** Thomas Reilly; **Cast:** Kirk Douglas, Virginia Mayo, Walter Brennan, John Agar, Ray Teal, Hugh Sanders, Morris Ankrum, James Anderson.

New federal marshal Ken Merrick (Kirk Douglas) saves an old-timer (Walter Brennan) from being hanged by the Roden family, who are vengefully pursuing the man they believe killed one of their own. The marshal insists on bringing the old fellow to Santa Loma for trial, but the Rodens continue in their personal pursuit. To elude Roden's henchmen, Merrick decides to take the desert route, encountering sleeplessness, sandstorms, and "Pop" Keith's (Brennan's) discordant singing, which prompts Merrick to yell out in frustration, "Mister, they're trying you for the wrong crime."

But Merrick is forced to confront his own demons when a Brennan song conjures a deep, dark secret in the marshal's past. Virginia Mayo as Brennan's daughter provides the female connection. Directed by Raoul Walsh, *Along the Great Divide* was Kirk Douglas's first western. Enhanced by some breathtaking scenery, it is a compelling tale with good performances by all—especially Douglas and Brennan—and a particularly solid portrayal by John Agar as Deputy Billy Shear.

ALONG THE NAVAJO TRAIL Republic, 1945, B&W, 66 min, VT. **Producer:** Edward J. White; **Director:** Frank McDonald; **Screenplay:** Gerald Geraghty; **Music:** Bob Nolan and Morton Scott; **Cinematographer:** William Bradford; **Editor:** Tony Martinelli; **Cast:** Roy Rogers, George "Gabby" Hayes, Dale Evans, Estelita Rodriguez, Douglas Fowley, Nester Paiva, Sam Flint, Roy Barcroft, Bob Nolan.

Deputy Marshal Roy investigates the disappearance of a government agent who came to the Lazy A Ranch owned by Dale's father. Among the fine songs featured in this pleasant and pleasing Roy Rogers entry are the classic "Cool Water," written by Bob Nolan and introduced by the Sons of the Pioneers, of which Nolan and Rogers (then known as Dick Weston) were founding members; and the title song "Along the Navajo Trail" (Charles, DeLange, and Markes), which was turned into a hit record by many artists, including Bing Crosby, the Andrews Sisters, and Gene Krupa.

ALONG THE OREGON TRAIL Republic, 1947, Color, 64 min. **Producer:** Melville Tucker; **Director:** R. G. Springsteen; **Screenplay:** Earle Snell; **Cinematographer:** Alfred S. Keller; **Editor:** Arthur Roberts; **Cast:** Monte Hale, Adrian Booth, Clayton Moore, Roy Barcroft, Max Terhune, Kermit Maynard, Wade Crosby.

A cowboy finds himself at odds with a madman who covets an empire for himself in the West. Average Monte Hale vehicle, enhanced by good color and the comedic aura of Max Terhune. (See also *HOME ON THE RANGE*.)

ALONG THE RIO GRANDE RKO, 1941, B&W, 63 min. **Producer:** Bert Gilroy; **Director:** Edward Killy; **Screenplay:** Stuart Anthony, Morton Grant, and Arthur V. Jones; **Music:** Red Rose and Ray Whitley; **Cinematographer:** Frank Redman; **Editor:** Frederic Knudtson; **Cast:** Tim Holt, Ray Whitley, Betty Jane Rhodes, Emmett Lynn, Robert Fiske, Wally Wales (Hal Taliaferro), Ruth Clifford, Carl Stockdale, Slim Whitaker.

To avenge the murder of their former boss, three men assume the guise of outlaws and join the gang responsible for the killing in this good Tim Holt RKO oater. Ray Whitley makes his first appearance as Smoky.

An RKO staple for many years, Tim Holt was the son of silent and sound action star Jack Holt and the brother of actress Jennifer Holt. Popular and handsome, Holt had a loyal following until the middle 1950s, when the B western all but disappeared. He gave outstanding performances in two highly acclaimed films, *The Magnificent Ambersons* and *The Treasure of the Sierra Madre*, as well as small roles in *STAGECOACH* and *MY DARLING CLEMENTINE*, but most of his career was spent in B westerns.

When George O'Brien, RKO's top cowboy star, quit the studio in 1940, Holt took over his series of low-budget Westerns, beginning with *WAGON TRAIN* and *FARGO* (1940). His career was interrupted in 1943 with a three-year stint in military service. He resumed his post as RKO's resident B western star in 1946, with several adaptations of Zane Grey stories, including *THUNDER MOUNTAIN* (1947), *WILD HORSE MESA* (1947), and *UNDER TONTO RUN* (1947).

He made another two dozen or so westerns which were among the best in the field between 1948 and 1952. At the peak of his B western career in the 1940s, he was "the fastest draw" in the movies and, along with Ben Johnson and Joel McCrea, among the film industry's top horsemen. Of his nearly 50 films for RKO, 13 were with Ray Whitley and another 30 with Richard "Chito" Martin. Holt's joint ventures with Whitley include *THE RENEGADE RANGER* (1938); *WAGON TRAIN, THE FARGO KID* (1940); *Thundering Hoofs, Six-Gun Gold, Robbers of the Range, Riding the Wind, LAND OF THE OPEN RANGE, Dude Cowboy, CYCLONE ON HORSEBACK, The Bandit Trail, ALONG THE RIO GRANDE* (1941); *COME ON DANGER* (1942). Other Holt ventures for RKO made without Whitley are *The Girl and the Gambler* (1939); *Bandit Ranger, Pirates of the Prairie* (1942); *Red River Robin Hood, Sagebrush Law, The Avenging Rider, FIGHTING FRONTIER* (1943).

His features with Richard "Chito" Martin began after Holt's return from war service. These include *Wild Horse Mesa, Under the Tonto Rim, THUNDER MOUNTAIN* (1947); *Gun Smugglers, Guns of Hate, Western Heritage, Indian Agent, THE ARIZONA RANGER* (1948); *Stagecoach Kid, Rustlers, Masked Raiders, BROTHERS IN THE SADDLE, Mysterious Desperado* (1949); *Law of the Badlands, Dynamite Pass, BORDER TREASURE, Rio Grande Patrol, Riders of the Ranger, Rider from Tucson, Storm Over Wyoming* (1950); *Pistol Harvest, Overland Telegraph, Hot Lead, Gunplay, Saddle Legion* (1951); *Road Agent, DESERT PASSAGE* aka *Starlight Canyon, Target, Trail Guide* (1952).

ALONG THE SUNDOWN TRAIL PRC, 1942, B&W, 59 min. **Producer:** Sigmund Neufeld; **Director:** Sam Newfield (as Peter Stewart); **Screenplay:** Arthur St. Claire; **Music:** Johnny Lange and Lew Porter; **Cinematographer:** Jack Greenhalgh; **Editor:** Holbrook N. Todd; **Cast:** Lee Powell, Art Davis, Bill "Cowboy Rambler" Boyd, Julie Duncan, Charles King, Karl Hackett, Howard Masters, Jack Ingram, Kermit Maynard.

Big Ben Salter (Charles King) and Pop Lawrence (Karl Hackett) both mine ore. But Salter has his men planted at Lawrence's mine, where they replace Lawrence's high-grade ore with Salter's lesser product. The marshal (Lee Powell) figures out the scam and with help from deputies Art and Bill go after the bad guys. Actor/composer Bill "Cowboy Rambler" Boyd should not be confused with Bill Boyd of Hopalong Cassidy fame. A typical entry for PRC's *Frontier Marshal* series.

ALVAREZ KELLY Columbia, 1966, Color, 116 min, VT. **Producers:** Ray David and Sol Siegal; **Director:** Edward Dmytryk; **Screenplay:** Elliott Arnold and Franklin Coen (also story); **Music:** Johnny Greene, Johnny Mercer; **Cinematographer:** Joseph McDonald; **Editor:** Harold R. Kress; **Cast:** William Holden, Richard Widmark, Janice Rule, Patrick O'Neal, Victoria Shaw, Robert C. Carmel, Richard Rust, Arthur Rust, Don "Red" Barry, Harry Carey Jr.

Alvarez Kelly (William Holden) is hired to drive a herd of cattle from Texas to the Union Army besieging Richmond. However, his plans are changed when one-eyed Virginia colonel Tom Rossiter (Richard Widmark) takes Kelly's money and forces him to steal the herd for the Confederacy. This is a routine movie based on a true incident. Onetime B western star Don "Red" Barry appears as Lt. Farrow. Good musical score from Johnny Green and four-time Oscar winner Johnny Mercer. The shooting off of Holden's finger in the movie was a portent of the increasing use of violence soon to follow in western films.

AMBUSH MGM, 1949, Color, 89 min. **Producer:** Armand Deutsch; **Director:** Sam Wood; **Screenplay:** Marguerite Roberts; **Music:** Rudolph G. Kopp; **Cinematographer:** Harold Lipstein; **Editor:** Ben Lewis; **Cast:** Robert Taylor, John Hodiak, Arlene Dahl, Don Taylor, Jean Hagen, Bruce Crowling, Leon Ames, John McIntire, Pat Moriarity, Charles Stevens, Chief Thundercloud, Ray Teal, Robin Short, Richard Bailey.

A civilian scout (Robert Taylor) finds himself at odds with a cavalry captain (John Hodiak) when he is forced to bring back a girl captured by some renegade Apache. Although it is a long wait before the real action starts, there is plenty of excitement afterwards, including a knock-down fight between Taylor and Hodiak, a skirmish where the Apache set a trap and massacre most of the whites, and a grand finale that is as bloody and noisy as Sam Wood could make it. Arlene Dahl (adorned in tight frontier costumes and plunging [though anachronistic] décolletage) is the gal Hodiak romances until Taylor manages to alienate her affections. Don Taylor has a subsidiary romance with Jean Hagen, the unhappy wife of villain Bruce Crowley. Both Taylors manage to get their women when their rivals die conveniently at the hands of the Apache. Based on a story by Luke Short, this was director Sam Wood's final picture (he died shortly after the film was finished) and marked the first production assignment for Armand Deutsch.

AMBUSH AT CIMARRON PASS Twentieth Century Fox, 1958, B&W, 73 min. **Producer:** Herbert E. Mendelson; **Director:** Jodie Copeland; **Screenplay:** Richard G. Taylor and John K. Butler; **Music:** Paul Sawtell and Bert Shefter; **Cinematographer:** John M. Nickolaus; **Editor:** Carl L. Peirson; **Cast:** Scott Brady, Margia Dean, Clint Eastwood, Irving Bacon, Frank Gerstle, Dick London, Baynes Barron, William Vaughn, Keith Richards, Ken Mayer, John Frederick (as John Merrick), Dirk London, Desmond Slattery.

A partially decimated army unit teams up with a group of cowboys who have been hit by renegade Indians. The cowboys and cavalrymen try to protect a shipment of guns from reaching the Apache while disagreeing strongly on strategy. A minor western with lots of action and a strong performance by Scott Brady as Sergeant Matt Blake, the film gave a young actor named Clint Eastwood the most important and visible role of his career up to that time. As Keith Williams, a bitter ex-Confederate soldier with a chip on his shoulder, Eastwood received his first favorable critical notices, though he would later jokingly call the film the worst movie ever made.

AMBUSH AT TOMAHAWK GAP Columbia, 1953, Color, 73 min. **Producer:** Wallace McDonald; **Director:** Fred F. Sears; **Screenplay:** David Lange; **Music:** Ross DiMaggio; **Cinematographer:** Henry Freulich; **Editor:** Aaron Snell; **Cast:** John Hodiak, John Derek, David Brian, Maria Elena Marqués, Ray Teal, John Qualen, Otto Hulett, Percy Helton, Trevor Bardette, John Doucette.

Four released convicts (John Hodiak, John Derek, David Brian, and Ray Teal) return to the ghost town of Tomahawk Gap in search of an army payroll they stole years earlier. While hunting for the money, they are attacked by bloodthirsty Indians, and a life-and-death struggle ensues. Lots of gunplay and action in this exciting and suspenseful western, with a superb performance by veteran actor Ray Teal. This was one of last pictures for the underrated and reliable John Hodiak; he died two years later in 1955 at age 41.

AMBUSH VALLEY Reliable Pictures, 1936, B&W, 57 min. **Producer:** Bennett Cohen; **Director:** Bernard A. Ray; **Screenplay:** Cohen; **Cast:** Bob Custer, Victoria Vinton, John Elliott, Vane Calvert, Eddie Phillips, Roger Williams, Victor Adamson, Jack Anderson, Ed Cassidy, Oscar Gahan, Jack Gilman, Wally Wales, Wally West.

Clay Morgan kills Joel Potter, and Marshal Bruce Manning (Bob Custer) must arrest him, even though he is the brother of the girl Manning plans to marry. When the Morgan family help Clay to escape, the Potters retaliate by taking Ann Morgan hostage. Marshal Manning is now caught between the two sides who are about to fight it out.

AMERICAN EMPIRE United Artists, 1942, B&W, 82 min. **Producer:** Harry Sherman; **Director:** William McGann; **Screenplay:** J. Robert Bren, J. Gladys Atwater, and Ben Grauman Kohn; **Music:** Gerard Carbonara; **Cinematographer:** Russell Harlan; **Editors:** Sherman A. Rose and Carroll Lewis; **Cast:** Richard Dix, Leo Carrillo, Preston Foster, Frances Gifford, Robert Barrat, Jack La Rue, Guinn "Big Boy" Williams, Cliff Edwards, Merrill Guy Rodin, Chris-Pin Martin, William Farnum, Etta McDaniel, Hal Taliaferro (as Wally Wales), Richard Webb.

Civil War veterans Don Taylor (Richard Dix) and Paxton Bryce (Preston Foster) head to Texas, settle down, and build a vast empire during the Reconstruction period. *American Empire* is a vivid panorama of the Texas frontier country, which captures the flavor of the Old West if not the precise letter of the times. There is lots of outdoor action that explodes in all directions, from its hearty opening to its breathtaking climax, as sturdy men fight it out with dastardly rustlers.

Both Dix and Foster give top-level performances as one time friends who choose different directions. Leo Carillo is fine as the energetic villain, and comely Frances Gifford supplies a healthy diversion from horses and gunplay. Produced by Harry Sherman, *American Empire* is a worthy addition to the western genre, a well-made film with an interesting array of characters and enough conflict to hold audience interest. This film also shows another side to Richard Dix, an actor whose career has too often been identified and linked with his work in CIMARRON.

AMERICANO, THE RKO, 1955, Color, 85 min. **Producers:** Sam Wiesenthal (executive), Robert Stillman, Benny Dvonisio (Brazil), and Oscar Ferreira (Brazil); **Director:** William Castle; **Screenplay:** Guy Trasper; **Music:** Xavier Cugat, Roy Webb (song, "El Americano"); **Cinematographer:** William E. Snyder; **Editor:** Harry Marker; **Cast:** Glenn Ford, Frank Lovejoy, Cesar Romero, Ursula Thies, Abbe Lane, Rudolfo Hoyos, Salvador Baguez, Tom Powers, Frank Marlow, George Navarro.

American cowboy Sam Dent (Glenn Ford) travels to Brazil with a shipment of prize Brahma bulls for delivery to a wealthy rancher. When he arrives he learns that the rancher has been killed and replaced by a fellow named Bento Hermany (Frank Lovejoy). Dent hires a "bandit chaser" known as El Gato (Cesar Romero) to guide him to the ranch. El Gato disappears mysteriously, and Dent finds romance and intrigue with Marianna (Ursula Thiess), the beautiful owner of the ranch next door. Eventually he learns of Hermany's evil intentions and the true identity of the mysterious bandit chief known as El Gato.

Ford gives his usual stellar performance, and Lovejoy is superb as the demented and dangerous Hermany. Xavier Cugat's melodic score, an evocative dance by the vivacious Abbe Lane, and a dramatic offbeat showdown between Ford and Lovejoy highlight this interesting oater with a South American setting.

AMERICAN TAIL 2: FIEVEL GOES WEST, AN Universal/MCA, 1991, Color, 75 min. **Producer:** Steven Spielberg; **Director:** Phil Nibbelink and Simon Wells; **Screenplay:** Flint Dille and Charles Swenson; **Music:** James Horner; **Special Effects:** Craig Clark; **Voices:** Cathy Cavadini, John Cleese, Dom DeLuise, Amy Irving, Jon Lovitz, Nehemiah Persoff, James Stewart, Erica Yohn, Phillip Glasser.

The Mouskewitz family is settled in America, but Fievel wants to journey west to become a cowboy. His alter ego is Wylie Burp (voice dubbed by Jimmy Stewart), the old lawdog of the west who offers Fievel some sound advice whenever the little mouse finds himself in trouble (not unlike Bogart in Woody Allen's *Play It Again, Sam*).

Some critics call this animated feature about a family of emigre mice who move out west—unaware that they are falling into a trap perpetrated by a smooth-talking cat—a work of art. Others are less enthusiastic, seeing it as being little more than yet another appealing and traditional children's cartoon. Either way it provides an enjoyable sequel to *American Tail*, the 1986 original.

Released roughly around the same time as the ever-popular *Beauty and the Beast*, the film combines some brilliant animation with appealing songs. The James Horner/Will Jennings song "Dreams to Dream" from *Fievel Goes West* won a Golden Globe nomination for Best Original Song in a Motion Picture.

ANCHOR, THE See *PIONEERS OF THE FRONTIER*.

ANGEL AND THE BADMAN Republic, 1947, B&W, 100 min. **Producer:** John Wayne; **Director:** James Edward Grant; **Screenplay:** Grant; **Cinematographer:** Archie Stout; **Music:** Richard Hageman (score), Cy Feuer (director), Kim Gannon and Walter Kent (songs); **Cinematographer:** Archie Stout; **Editor:** Harry Keller; **Cast:** John Wayne, Gail Russell, Harry Carey, Bruce Cabot, Irene Rich, Lee Dixon, Tom Powers, John Halloran, Stephen Grant, Joan Barton, Paul Hurst, Craig Woods, Marshall Reed.

Injured, desperately tired, and pursued by a group of armed horsemen, Quirt Evans (John Wayne) is taken in by Quaker Thomas Worth (John Halloran), his wife (Irene Rich), and their granddaughter Prudence (Gail Russell). They ignore the order of the doctor to get rid of Quirt if they want to keep the peace.

Quirt is attracted to the beautiful Prudence, and she to him. But he feels he must fulfill his vow to kill Laredo

John Wayne and Gail Russell in Angel and the Badman
(REPUBLIC/AUTHOR'S COLLECTION)

Stevens (Bruce Cabot), the murderer of his foster father. When the Worths are at a Quaker meeting, Quirt and two buddies hold up a gambling train owned by Stevens. To the amazement of his friends, when the job is over, Quirt rides back to the Worth ranch.

Quirt has a change of heart. His love for Prudence is so strong that he promises to spare Laredo and give up his gun if she will marry him and settle down on a farm. The pledge is forgotten, though, when the couple is attacked by Stevens and his men, who chase them into a river and leave them to drown. However, Quirt manages to rescue the seriously ill Prudence. He takes his gun and rides into town in search of Stevens.

Sick with fever, Prudence follows and finds Quirt waiting for Stevens in front of the saloon. He silently hands her his gun, unaware that Stevens is standing down the street, his gun directed flush at Quirt. Stevens is about to pull the trigger when he is felled by a shot fired by Marshal Wistful McClintock (Harry Carey). Quirt and Prudence are now able to build a new life together.

Angel and the Badman was Wayne's first endeavor as a producer and was not a big box-office hit. Perhaps the lack of sustained and substantial action so true to most John Wayne westerns proved a detriment. Nevertheless, the picture is an appealing low-budget western that, according to the *New York Times*, was "different and a notch or two superior to the normal sagebrush saga." In the opinion of *Variety*, the offbeat story about a gunslinger who renounces violence after falling in love with a beautiful Quaker girl, while not the typical Wayne shoot-em up adventure yarn, had a compelling warmth and was John Wayne's "best job since *Stagecoach*."

In 1946 Wayne's good friend and favorite writer Jimmy Grant penned a script for Wayne's new production company called *The Angel and the Outlaw*. Always true to his friends, Wayne also honored Grant's request to direct the film, recalling how John Ford had given him his big chance years earlier. A stickler to loyalty, Wayne offered his hero and mentor

Harry Carey the role of Marshal Wistful McClintock and his pal Bruce Cabot the part of Laredo Stevens.

Wayne and leading lady Gail Russell became quite close, and their chemistry on-screen is real and riveting. Whether the two were romantically involved depends mainly on who is telling the story, but there is no doubt that Wayne genuinely cared for the vulnerable and extremely beautiful young actress. When speaking of Wayne shortly before her tragic death due to complications from alcoholism, Russell told a producer friend that "the one word that describes Duke is 'honest.' He's an honest man. He can't be otherwise." John Wayne and Gail Russell would be teamed together once more in *The Wake of the Red Witch* (1948), with the remarkable screen chemistry still intact.

ANGEL IN EXILE (aka: DARK VIOLENCE) Republic, 1948, B&W, 90 min. **Producer:** Herbert Yates; **Directors:** Allen Dwan and Phillip Ford; **Screenplay:** Charles Larson; **Music:** Nathan Scott; **Cinematographer:** Reggie Lansing; **Editor:** Arthur Roberts; **Cast:** John Carroll, Adele Mara, Thomas Gomez, Alfonso Bedova, Grant Withers, Paul Fix.

Ex-con Charlie Dakin (John Carroll) heads for an Arizona gold mine after serving his time in prison. Determined to make his fortune, his trip is interrupted when residents of a small Mexican village believe him to be a sacred religious figure. A top-flight cast and an unusual plot make this long-forgotten Republic film a winner. The film was reissued in 1954 as *Dark Violence*.

ANIMALS, THE (aka: APACHE VENGEANCE, FIVE SAVAGE MEN, UK) XYZ Productions, 1970, Color, 86 min. **Producer:** Richard Bakalvan; **Director:** Ron Joy; **Screenplay:** Bakalvan and Hy Mizrahi; **Music:** Rupert Holmes; **Cinematographer:** Keith C. Smith; **Cast:** Michele Carey, William Bryant, Jake Wade Cox, Steve DeFrance, Pepper Martin, Henry Silva, Peggy Stewart, Neil Summers, Keenan Wynn, John Anderson.

This account of a pretty Apache schoolteacher raped by five brutal men who hold up her stagecoach is overly sadistic. She vows vengeance and tracks down her abusers with a fury.

ANNIE GET YOUR GUN MGM, 1950, Color, 107 min, VT. **Producer:** Arthur Freed; **Director:** George Sidney; **Screenplay:** Sidney Sheldon; **Music:** Adolph Deutsch (director) and Irving Berlin (songs); **Cinematographer:** Charles Rosher; **Editor:** James E. Newcom; **Cast:** Betty Hutton, Howard Keel, Louis Calhern, J. Carrol Naish, Edward Arnold, Keenan Wynn, Benay Venuta, James H. Harrison, Bradley Mora, Susan Odin, Dianne Dick, Chief Yowlachie, Eleanor Brown, Evelyn Beresford, André Charlot, John Mylong, Nini Pipitone.

The hit Broadway musical by Dorothy Fields, Herbert Fields, and Irving Berlin comes to the screen with Betty Hutton as the famed Annie Oakley, a backwoods gal and superb sharpshooter who participates in Buffalo Bill's Wild West Show and soon sets her romantic feelings on the marksman supreme, Frank Butler (Howard Keel).

When Sidney Sheldon adapted this enormously popular Broadway musical for the screen, there were nothing but problems. Producer Arthur Freed had acquired the rights to the hit Broadway play at a cost of $650,000, the highest price to that date for a musical property, with the proviso that Judy Garland would take the part of Annie Oakley, which Ethel Merman had played on stage, because MGM felt the dynamic Merman was too old for the screen. But after recording her songs, Garland's personal problems intervened, leading to numerous delays and the eventual suspension of production. To salvage revenue already expended—and after considering studio players Martha Ray and Betty Garrett for the part—MGM borrowed the acrobatic Betty Hutton from Paramount for the title role.

A search for a suitable Frank Butler persisted. After first considering John Raitt, who had sizzled on Broadway in *Carousel*, the part eventually went to newcomer Howard Keel (making his screen debut), who was then starring in the London production of *Oklahoma!*. On the second day of filming, Keel broke his ankle and was put on the sidelines for nearly three months.

Veteran character actor Frank Morgan, who was to play Buffalo Bill, died in the interim and was replaced by Louis Calhern. Busby Berkeley, originally slated to direct the film, was fired and replaced by Charles Walters. Then when the filming recommenced, Walters was shelved and replaced by George Sidney.

Even Irving Berlin had not been the original choice to write the musical score. When producers Richard Rodgers and Oscar Hammerstein first decided to bring the story to the Broadway stage, they had initially opted for Jerome Kern.

The film project was finally completed in December 1949 at a cost of nearly $4 million. It was a rousing success with audiences and critics alike, as MGM eventually took in over $8 million on the production. Most of the songs from the Broadway score were used in the film, although some lyrics to "Doin' What Comes Naturally" were modified to appease the industry code. In today's musical venue, when a show is lucky to have one memorable song, *Annie Get Your Gun* gave the musical theater more hit songs than any Broadway show with the possible exception of *South Pacific*. Beautifully adapted for the screen, this rip-roaring musical, one of Hollywood's very best, features such songs as "Doin' What Comes Naturally," "The Girl That I Marry," "Anything You can Do," "They Say It's Wonderful," "I've Got the Sun In the Morning," and the signature show tune "There's No Business Like Show Business."

A lively musical tribute to the world of the fabled West which *Variety* called "socko musical entertainment on film," *Annie Get Your Gun* garnered four Oscar nominations and an Academy Award for Best Scoring of a Musical Picture. For her role as the raw western sharpshooter who, after many tries and lots of songs, finally lands her man, Betty Hutton was voted *Photoplay* magazine's Female Star of the Year (1950).

ANNIE OAKLEY RKO, 1935, B&W, 88 min, VT. **Producer:** Cliff Reid; **Director:** George Stevens; **Screenplay:** Joel Sayre and John Twist; **Music:** Alberto Columbo; **Cinematographer:** Roy Hunt; **Editor:** George Hively; **Cast:** Barbara Stanwyck, Preston Foster, Melvyn Douglas, Pert Kelton, Andy Clyde, Moroni Olson, Chief Thunderbird.

Based on a story by Joseph H. Fields and Ewart Adamson, for this film director George Stevens took some liberties with the facts of Annie Oakley's life, investing greatly in her character. Annie (Barbara Stanwyck) is the famed star attraction and crack rifle shot in Buffalo Bill's Wild West Show, whose name was internationally known in the 1890s.

Stanwyck plays the famed sharpshooter with an intelligence and dignity that seems thoroughly modern even today. Perhaps more important, she initiated a line of western heroines she would play throughout her distinguished career. The sexual rivalry so central to the Oakley myth is given an apparent acceptance when her superior talents are recognized and acknowledged by her colleague/lover Toby Walker (Preston Foster). The famed acts of Buffalo Bill's (Moroni Olsen) Wild West Show are faithfully reproduced, and the film's audience appeal is enhanced by several displays of sharpshooting. Never a regular contributor to the western genre, George Stevens would wait 18 years before winning international genre acclaim for *SHANE*, his epic and poetic 1953 western.

ANOTHER MAN, ANOTHER CHANCE (aka: ANOTHER MAN, ANOTHER WOMAN) United Artists, 1977, Color, 131 min. **Producers:** Georges Dancigers and Alexandre Mnouchkine; **Director:** Claude Lelouch; **Screenplay:** Lelouch; **Music:** Francis Lai; **Cinematographer:** Stanley Cortex and Jacques Lefrancois; **Editors:** Georges Klotz and Fabien D. Tordjimann; **Cast:** James Caan, Genevieve Bujold, Frances Hunter, Jennifer Warren.

Set in the late 1800s, this film is a virtual remake of Lelouch's highly acclaimed *A Man and a Woman* (1966)—this time with a western landscape. David Williams (James Caan) and Jeanne Leroy (Genevieve Bujold) are a widower and widow who fall in love. Bujold is a young woman who comes west with a photographer who dies suddenly; she later meets and marries a veterinarian.

Although well-acted and interesting, this film is a bit too long and much too wordy. It fails to engage an audience to the same degree as Lelouch's riveting and romantic *A Man and a Woman* a decade earlier. Made in France as *Un Autre Homme, Une Autre Chance*, an alternate title of the film is *Another Man, Another Woman*.

ANOTHER PAIR OF ACES Pedernales Films, 1991, Color, VT. **Producer:** Cyrus I. Yavneh; **Director:** Bill Bixby; **Teleplay:** Bixby; **Music:** Jay Gruska; **Cinematographer:** Chuck Colwell; **Editor:** Janet Ashiaga; **Cast:** Willie Nelson, Kris Kristofferson, Joan Severance, Rip Torn, Ken Farmer, Daniel Tucker Kamin.

This made-for-television, modern-day western depicts Ranger Kris Kristofferson, con man Willie Nelson, and FBI agent Joan Severance tackling political corruption and murder. After a good start, the film becomes downright silly and predictable, with highly charged FBI agent Susan Davis (Severance) torn between her crime-fighting duties and seducing the not-too-reluctant Kristofferson. The video includes some steamy scenes not included in the original TV movie.

APACHE United Artists, 1954, Color, 91 min, VT. **Producer:** Harold Hecht; **Director:** Robert Aldrich; **Screenplay:** James R. Webb; **Music:** David Raskin; **Cinematographer:** Ernesto Laszlo; **Editor:** Alan Crossland Jr.; **Cast:** Burt Lancaster, Jean Peters, John McIntire, Charles Bronson, John Dehner, Monte Blue.

Based on Paul Wellman's novel *Bronco Apache*, Burt Lancaster plays Massai, the last Apache warrior, who learns from the U.S. cavalry the old adage that "might makes right." Following the surrender of Geronimo (Monte Blue), Massai is captured and scheduled to be transported to a Florida reservation. He manages to escape and heads to his homeland to win back his beautiful squaw (Jean Peters). He wages a one-man war against the cavalry before turning in the gun for the more peaceful life of a farmer. He gives up confronting the white man's world only when he is pacified by the love of his woman and the birth of his child.

Unfortunately, the film falls short of what it might have been. Lancaster's Massai is riddled with overacting. Moreover, director Aldrich's original ending was discarded by the producers. Instead of Massai being shot in the back by federal troops—which might have validated the point of the film—Aldrich was asked to film a new ending where Massai survives and surrenders. Look for a young Charles Bronson—still billed as Charles Buchinsky—in the role of Hondo. The part of Geronimo also marked the last screen appearance for actor Monte Blue, whose film career dated back to a bit part in D. W. Griffith's *Birth of a Nation*. The film's most redeeming factors remain Ernest Laszlo's beautiful photography and David Raskin's excellent musical score.

APACHE AGENT See *WALK THE PROUD LAND*.

APACHE AMBUSH Columbia, 1955, B&W, 68 min. **Producer:** Wallace MacDonald; **Director:** Fred Sears; **Screenplay:** David Lang; **Music:** Mischa Bakaleinikoff; **Cinematographer:** Frank Jackman Jr.; **Editor:** Jerome Thoms; **Cast:** Bill Williams, Richard Jaeckel, Alex Montoya, Adelle August, Tex Ritter, Ray Corrigan, Ray Teal, George Chandler, Harry Lauter, George Keymas.

While leading a cattle drive to Texas after the Civil War, a former Union soldier is faced with trouble from marauding Indians and renegade Confederates. Supporting appearances by genre favorites Tex Ritter, Ray Corrigan, Ray Teal, and Harry Lauter provides an added bonus to this otherwise average oater.

APACHE BLOOD (aka: PURSUIT) Key International Pictures, 1975, Color, 86 min, VT. **Producer:** Vern Piehl; **Director:** Tom Quillen; **Screenplay:** Dewitt Lee and Jack Lee; **Cast:** Ray Danton, Dewitt Lee, Troy Nabors, Diane Taylor, Eva Kovacs, Jason Clark.

An army scout wounded by a bear is tracked through the desert by an Indian brave who plans to kill him.

APACHE CHIEF Lippert Pictures, 1949, B&W, 60 min. **Producer:** Leonard S. Picker; **Director:** Frank McDonald; **Screenplay:** Gerald Green and Leonard Picker; **Cinematographer:** Benjamin H. Kline; **Editor:** Stanley Frazen; **Cast:** Alan Curtis, Tom Neal, Carol Thurston, Russell Hayden, Fuzzy Knight, Trevor Bardette, Francis MacDonald, Ted Hecht, Roy Gordon.

Two Indian brothers, one peaceful and the other warlike, oppose each other as they vie for leadership of their tribe. During the 1930s and 1940s, the B westerns were often more in tune to the plight of Native Americans than the larger studio productions. However, the message is tarnished by budget constraints and the fact that the Indians are adorned with poor costumes, saddled horses, and Brooklyn accents.

APACHE COUNTRY Columbia, 1952, B&W, 62 min. **Producer:** Armand Schaefer; **Director:** George Archainbaud; **Screenplay:** Norman S. Hall; **Music:** Paul Mertz; **Cinematographer:** William Bradford; **Editor:** James Sweeney; **Cast:** Gene Autry, Pat Buttram, Carolina Cotton, Harry Lauter, Francis X. Bushman, Mary Scott, Gregg Barton, Tom London.

A white man sets out to keep the Indians drunk so they will do as he wants. The U.S. government sends Gene Autry to fix things up and make matters right once again.

APACHE DRUMS Universal, 1951, Color, 75 min. **Producer:** Val Lewton; **Director:** Hugo Fregonese; **Screenplay:** David Chandler; **Music:** Hans J. Salter; **Cinematographer:** Charles P. Boyle; **Editor:** Milton Carruth; **Cast:** Stephen McNally, Coleen Gray, Willard Parker, Arthur Shields, James Griffith, James Best, Sherry Jackson.

Based on the Harry Brown novel *Stand at Spanish Boot*, this film features Stephen McNally as gambler Sam "Slick" Leeds who is kicked out of the western town of Spanish Boot and returns on his own to warn its citizens of an impending Apache attack. This taut little western drama is an enjoyable and suspenseful film, highlighted by an excellent acting job from McNally.

APACHE KID, THE Republic, 1941, B&W, 56 min. **Producer:** Herbert Yates; **Director:** George Sherman; **Screenplay:** Eliot Gibbons and Richard Murphy; **Music:** Cy Feuer; **Cinematographer:** Harry Neumann; **Editor:** Lester Orlebech; **Cast:** Don "Red" Barry, Lynn Merrick, LeRoy Mason, Robert Fiske, Al St. John, Fred "Snowflake" Toones.

When the payroll arrives to build a government-contracted road, the crooked sponsors arrange for their gang to rob the stage, enabling them to pay their workers in almost worthless scrip. But Pete Dawson (Don "Red" Barry) becomes the Apache Kid, robs the stage ahead of the gang, and enables the money to get to sheriff in time for the workers to be paid in cash.

APACHE KID'S ESCAPE, THE   Robert S. Horner Productions, 1930, B&W. **Director:** Robert J. Horner; **Screenplay:** Horner; **Cast:** Jack Perrin, Fred Church, Josephine Hill, Virginia Ashcroft, Bud Osborne.

After escaping from the sheriff, the Apache Kid (Jack Perrin) takes a job as a ranch hand under the assumed name of Jim. But another ranch hand named Ted uses the kerchief given to him by Jim and robs a stage. Eventually Jim sets him right, Ted returns the gold, and the Apache Kid's name is cleared.

Others who have played the Apache Kid in films include Max Hoffman in *Rootin' Tootin' Rhythm* (1937), Joe De La Cruz in *The Adventures of Red Ryder* (1940), Keith Larson in *Apache Warrior*, and George Keymas in *The Storm Rider* (1957).

APACHE MASSACRE   See *FACE TO THE WIND*.

APACHE RIFLES   20th Century Fox, 1964, Color, 92 min. **Producer:** Grant Whytock; **Director:** William Witney; **Screenplay:** Charles B. Smith; **Cinematographer:** Archie R. Dalzell; **Editor:** Whytock; **Cast:** Audie Murphy, Michael Dante, Linda Lawson, L. Q. Jones, Ken Lynch, Joseph Vitale.

Jeff Stanton, a young cavalry officer, is assigned to bring in a band of renegade Apache who are terrorizing the countryside. William Witney's skillful direction becomes a big plus in this average Audie Murphy venture.

APACHE ROSE   Republic, 1947, Color, 75 min, VT. **Producer:** Edward J. White; **Director:** William Witney; **Screenplay:** Gerald Geraghty; **Music:** Jack Elliott, Glenn Spencer, and Tim Spencer; **Cinematographer:** Jack A. Marta; **Editor:** Les Orlebeck; **Cast:** Roy Rogers, Dale Evans, Olin Howlin, George Meeker, John Laurenz, Donna Martell (as Donna de Mario), Bob Nolan and the Sons of the Pioneers, Minerva Urecal, LeRoy Mason.

Roy Rogers, an oil prospector, finds his efforts compromised by gamblers from an offshore gambling boat who are determined to control the land and oil for themselves. This is the first feature in Republic's Roy Rogers series to be shot in brilliant Trucolor.

APACHE TERRITORY   Columbia, 1958, B&W, 75 min. **Producers:** Rory Calhoun and V. M. Orsatti; **Director:** Ray Nazarro; **Screenplay:** George W. George and Charles R. Marion; **Music:** Mischa Bakaleinikoff (conductor); **Cine-matographer:** Irving Lippman; **Editor:** Al Clark; **Cast:** Rory Calhoun, Barbara Bates, John Dehner, Leo Gordon, Myron Healey, Caroline Craig.

Logan Cates (Rory Calhoun) sets out to stop an Indian war and singlehandedly routs the rampaging Indians while saving a defenseless girl, the sole survivor of a wagon train attack that claimed her entire family. An old flame and her future husband soon appear at the scene as well as members of the cavalry. Together they hope to hold off a series of Indian attacks while battling the elements and each other. Coproduced by Calhoun and helmed by Ray Nazarro, the film is based on the novel *Last Stand at Papago Wells* by Louis L'Amour.

APACHE TRAIL   MGM, 1942, B&W, 66 min. **Producer:** Samuel Marx; **Director:** Richard Thorpe; **Screenplay:** Maurice Geraghty; **Music:** Sol Kaplan; **Cinematographer:** Sidney Wagner; **Editor:** Frank Sullivan; **Cast:** Lloyd Nolan, Donna Reed, William Lundigan, Anne Ayers, Gloria Holden, Fuzzy Knight, Ray Teal, Chill Wills, Grant Withers, Connie Gilchrist, Tito Renaldo.

When whites desecrate their ceremonial grounds, Indians go on the warpath and innocent settlers must face the consequences. A curio from the World War II era, the film benefits from a strong cast and good direction by Richard Thorpe.

APACHE UPRISING   Paramount, 1966, Color, 90 min, VT. **Producer:** A. C. Lyles; **Director:** R. G. Springsteen; **Screenplay:** Max Lamb and Harry Stanford; **Music:** Jimmy Haskell; **Cinematographer:** W. Wallace Kelley; **Editor:** John F. Schreyer; **Cast:** Rory Calhoun, Corinne Calvet, John Russell, Lon Chaney Jr., Gene Evans, Richard Arlen, Arthur Hunnicutt, DeForest Kelley, George Chandler, Jean Parker, Johnny Mack Brown, Don "Red" Barry, Abel Fernandez.

Based on the book *Way Station* by Lamb and Stanford, this adaptation follows ex-rebel Jim Walker (Rory Calhoun) as he becomes a lawman in a western town and takes on a trio of bad guys (John Russell, Gene Evans, and DeForest Kelley). The trio provides an interesting array of villains, especially Kelley (in his pre-*Star Trek* days), who is positively frightening. But it is veteran character actor Arthur Hunnicutt who steals the show as Bill Gibson, Calhoun's craggy sidekick. As usual, producer A. C. Lyles found time to give work to erstwhile stars such as Johnny Mack Brown and Don "Red" Barry, whose careers were otherwise behind them.

APACHE VENGEANCE   See *ANIMALS, THE*.

APACHE WARRIOR   20th Century Fox, 1957, B&W, 74 min. **Producer:** Plato Skouras; **Director:** Elmo Williams; **Screenplay:** Kurt Neumann, Eric Norden, and Carroll Young; **Music:** Paul Dunlap; **Cinematographer:** John M.

Nicholaus Jr.; **Editor:** Jodie Copelan; **Cast:** Keith Larson, Jim Davis, Rodolfo Acosta, Eugenia Paul, John Miljan, Damian O'Flynn, George Keymas.

The Apache Kid aids in the capture of Geronimo, then becomes a hunted renegade himself when his brother is killed and his former white brother is forced to hunt him down. Lots of action with good performances by Keith Larson as the renegade, Jim Davis as the hunter, and Rodolfo Acosta as the Indian most responsible for the trouble. (See also *APACHE KID'S ESCAPE, THE*.)

APACHE WAR SMOKE   MGM, 1952, B&W, 67 min. **Producer:** Hayes Goetz; **Director:** Harold Kress; **Screenplay:** Jerry Davis; **Cinematographer:** John Alton; **Editor:** Newell P. Kimlin; **Cast:** Gilbert Roland, Glenda Farrell, Robert Horton, Barbara Ruick, Gene Lockhart, Harry Morgan, Patricia Tiernani, Hank Worden, Myron Healey, Robert (Bobby) Blake.

Bandits head for a way station after they rob a stagecoach, only to discover that the station is about to be attacked by Indians. This is a well-done western about a stagecoach robbery and a series of ominous Indian attacks. Based on a story by Ernest Haycox, the film boasts a strong performance by Gilbert Roland as the proverbial good bad man.

APACHE WOMEN   Golden State Productions, 1955, B&W, 69 min, VT. **Producer:** Roger Corman; **Director:** Corman; **Screenplay:** Lou Rusoff; **Music:** Ronald Stein; **Cinematographer:** Floyd Crosby; **Editor:** Ronald Sinclair; **Cast:** Joan Taylor, Lloyd Bridges, Lance Fuller, Morgan Jones, Lou Place, Jonathan Hale.

Government affairs agent Rex Moffett (Lloyd Bridges) is sent to a western town to investigate attacks that the townspeople say are being committed by the rampaging Apache. He is in for a surprise! The tagline reads "Naked Violence . . . with a gun or a knife *she* was a match for any man." That about says it all for Corman's second western.

APPALOOSA, THE   Universal, 1966, Color, 98 min, VT. **Producer:** Alan Miller; **Director:** Sidney J. Furie; **Screenplay:** James Bridges and Roland Kibbee; **Music:** Frank Skinner; **Cinematographer:** Russell Metty; **Editor:** Ted J. Kent; **Cast:** Marlon Brando, Anjanette Comer, John Saxon, Emilio Fernandez, Alex Montova, Miriam Colon, Rafael Campos.

When his cherished Appaloosa horse is stolen by a Mexican bandit, a man takes off across the border to retrieve it. Set at the turn of 20th century, Marlon Brando grimaces and broods his way through this slow-moving western. Brando's method acting proves tedious and pales next to John Saxon's fine performance as a Mexican warlord. Russell Metty's magnificent photography, including a series of stunning facial close-ups and unusual camera angles, highlight this offbeat western, which is not nearly as good as Brando's effort in *ONE EYED JACKS* (1961).

APPLE DUMPLING GANG, THE   Walt Disney Productions/Buena Vista, 1975, Color, 100 min. **Producer:** Bill Anderson; **Director:** Norman Tokar; **Screenplay:** Don Tait; **Music:** Buddy Baker; **Cinematographer:** Frank V. Phillips; **Editor:** Ray de Leuw; **Cast:** Bill Bixby, Susan Clark, Don Knotts, Tim Conway, David Wayne, Slim Pickens, Harry Morgan, Iris Adrian, Bing Russell.

Three orphans are forced on gambler Bill Bixby, a confirmed bachelor who resides in the 19th-century boomtown of Quake City. Following an earthquake that shakes the area, the kids find a large gold nugget worth tens of thousands of dollars. But their new wealth causes a slew of unexpected problems, and they agree to "give" the gold to two bumbling outlaws (Don Knotts and Tim Conway).

Based on a novel by Jack M. Brickham, funnymen Knotts and Conway make a great team in this zany western spoof. Filmed in Bend, Oregon, and directed by Norman Tokar—who helmed many *Leave it to Beaver* episodes for television—the picture provides good, clean family fun.

APPLE DUMPLING GANG RIDES AGAIN, THE   Disney Productions/Buena Vista, 1979, Color, 89 min, VT. **Producers:** Ron Miller and Tom Leetch; **Director:** Vincent McEveety; **Screenplay:** Don Tait; **Music:** Buddy Baker; **Cinematographer:** Frank V. Phillips; **Editor:** Gordon D. Brenner; **Cast:** Tim Conway, Don Knotts, Tim Matheson, Kenneth Mars, Elyssa Davalos, Jack Elam, Harry Morgan, Ruth Buzzi, Audrey Totter, Robert Totten.

Don Knotts and Tim Conway bumble their way through the Old West once more as they are hunted as outlaws. A banal sequel to the original, but an interesting cast helps score a few points.

ARENA   MGM, 1953, Color, 83 min. **Producers:** Arthur M. Loew Jr. and Dore Schary; **Director:** Richard Fleischer; **Screenplay:** Harold Jack Bloon and Arthur M. Loew Jr. (story); **Cinematographer:** Paul Vogel; **Editor:** Cotton Warburton; **Cast:** Gig Young, Jean Hagen, Polly Bergen, Harry Morgan, Barbara Lawrence, Robert Horton, Lee Aaker, Lee Van Cleef.

Rodeo folks Hobb and Ruth Danvers (Gig Young and Polly Bergen) watch their marriage take a nosedive as Hobb becomes more and more successful. Filmed on location in Tucson, Arizona, and shown originally in 3-D, the movie's biggest strength is its realistic rodeo scenes, highlighted by rodeo footage from the annual Fiesta de los Vaqueros in Tucson.

ARIZONA   Columbia, 1940, B&W, 127 min, VT. **Producer:** Wesley Ruggles; **Director:** Ruggles; **Screenplay:** Claude Binyon; **Music:** Victor Young; **Cinematographers:**

Fayte M. Browne, Harry Hallenberger, and Joseph Walker; **Editors:** William A. Lyon and Otto Meyer; **Cast:** Jean Arthur, William Holden, Warren William, Porter Hall, Edgar Buchanan, Paul Harvey, George Chandler, Byron Foulger, Regis Toomey.

Phoebe Titus (Jean Arthur), the independent tough-minded owner of a struggling freight line, is determined to battle corruption and plundering in the Arizona Territory. When forced to deal with a nasty array of crooks and swindlers, she receives unexpected help and a healthy share of romance from a Missouri-bred, California-bound cowboy named Peter Muncie (William Holden).

Director Wesley Ruggles had hoped the film would match the success of *CIMARRON*, his 1931 Oscar-winning epic. But the film fell far short, and Ruggles, who was one of Mack Sennett's original Keystone Cops and began directing in 1917, never helmed another western.

Nevertheless, *Arizona* still packs some solid entertainment punch. Not least is Victor Young's Oscar-nominated musical score and an outstanding villainous performance by Warren William. Jean Arthur is excellent as Phoebe, and her romantic interplay with her wandering cowboy lover is rife with consternation and delight. "Doggone it, Peter!" she laments, "If this is what it's like to be in love, I'm glad I'm only going to be in love once." One of the silver screen's true talents, Arthur retired from films a few years later. She came out of retirement in 1953 to star in *SHANE*, her 92nd and final film role.

ARIZONA BADMAN Kent, 1935, B&W, 58 min. **Producer:** William Kent; **Director:** Roy Luby; **Cinematographer:** James Brown; **Editor:** Roy Claire; **Cast:** Reb Russell, Lois January, Slim Whitaker, Edmund Cobb, Dick Botiller, Tommy Bupp, Ann Howard.

The daughter of a notorious cattle thief falls for a stranger at a dance. The stranger is really a lawman who is after her father. (See also *LIGHTNING TRIGGERS*.)

ARIZONA BOUND Paramount, 1927, B&W. **Producers:** Adolph Zucker and Jesse Lasky; **Director:** John Waters; **Screenplay:** John Stone and Paul Gangelin; **Cinematographer:** C. Edgar Schoenbaum; **Cast:** Gary Cooper, Betty Jewell, Jack Dougherty, Christian J. Frank, El Brendel, Charles Crockett, Joe Butterworth, Guy Oliver, Guinn "Big Boy" Williams.

Gary Cooper plays a rambling cowboy who happens into a small western town the same day a big gold shipment is leaving by stagecoach. However, two different parties are planning to rob the coach. One is the driver who has the confidence of the townsfolk; the other is a stranger who wants to hijack the shipment for himself. The young cowboy becomes embroiled in the action, is accused of being one of the bandits, and narrowly escapes a lynching. In true heroic fashion, he manages to retrieve the gold, establish his innocence, and win the girl he loves.

Gary Cooper's first starring film helped to establish him with movie audiences and assure his future in westerns. "Gary Cooper has the physique, the ability to ride, as well as histrionic ability, for a Western hero," commented the *Exhibitors Daily Review*, while *Variety* decreed that "*Arizona Bound* will give [Cooper] a respectable introduction to his future public." The Montana-born, England-educated Cooper did many of his own stunts in the film, including a jump into a moving stagecoach.

ARIZONA BOUND Monogram, 1941, B&W, 57 min, VT. **Producer:** Scott R. Dunlap; **Director:** Spencer Gordon Bennett; **Screenplay:** Adele S. Buffington (as Jess Bowers); **Music:** Edward J. Kay; **Cinematographer:** Harry Neumann; **Editor:** Carl Pierson; **Cast:** Buck Jones, Tim McCoy, Raymond Hatton, Luana Walters, Tristram Coffin, Slim Whitaker, Dennis Moore, Kathryn Sheldon, Horace Murphy.

The *Rough Riders* are called upon to help save a stagecoach line whose stages are being robbed and whose drivers are being shot. Buck Jones, Tim McCoy, and Raymond Hatton make a top-notch trio, arguably the best cowboy team on the Monogram lot. This feature is the first of the *Rough Rider* series. As *The Rough Riders*, Jones, McCoy, and Hatton made eight fine series entries: *Arizona Bound, Forbidden Trails, Gunman From Bodie* aka *Bad Man from Bodie* (1941); *Below the Border, Down Texas Way, Ghost Town Law, Riders of the West, West of the Law* (1942).

ARIZONA BUSHWACKERS Paramount, 1968, Color, 87 min, VT. **Producer:** A. C. Lyles; **Director:** Lesley Selander; **Screenplay:** Steve Fisher and Andrew Craddock (story); **Music:** Jimmy Haskell; **Cinematographer:** Lester Short; **Editor:** John F. Schrever; **Cast:** Howard Keel, Yvonne De Carlo, John Ireland, Marilyn Maxwell, Scott Brady, Brian Donlevy, James Craig, Roy Rogers Jr., Regis Parton, Monte Montana, Eric Cody, James Cagney.

A confederate spy (Howard Keel) takes a job in a small western town as cover for his espionage activities. He soon finds out that a local businessman (Scott Brady) is selling weapons to a band of rampaging Apache. This good A. C. Lyles western is narrated by James Cagney, a longtime A. C. Lyles friend.

ARIZONA COWBOY Republic, 1950, B&W, 67 min, VT. **Producer:** Franklin Adreon; **Director:** R. C. Springsteen; **Screenplay:** Bradford Ropes; **Music:** Stanley Wilson; **Cinematographer:** William Bradford; **Editor:** Harry Keller; **Cast:** Rex Allen, Teala Loring, Gordon Jones, Minerva Urecal, James Cradwell, Roy Barcroft.

Rex Allen plays an ex-GI who becomes a rodeo star, then is framed for a robbery by a gang of crooks. *Arizona Cowboy* is the first in a series of 19 Rex Allen films for Republic Pictures, giving him the distinction of being the last of the singing cowboys. Usually supported by sidekicks like Buddy Ebsen and Slim Pickens, Allen immediately became a big B western star. From 1952 through 1954—until the B western all but faded out—he was outgrossed at the box office only by Roy Rogers and Gene Autry. Among his better series entries are UNDER MEXICALI STARS (1950), with George Blair directing; and two William Witney features, THE OLD OVERLAND TRAIL (1953) and DOWN LAREDO WAY (1953).

Other series features include *Hills of Oklahoma, Trail of Robin Hood, Redwood Forest Trail* (1950); *Thunder in God's Country, Utah Wagon Train, Silver City Bonanza, Rodeo King and the Senorita* (1951); *Old Oklahoma Plains, The Last Musketeer, I Dream of Jeannie* (as Mr. Tambo and narrator), *Colorado Sundown, Border Saddlemates* (1952); *Iron Mountain Trail, Shadows of Tombstone, Red River Shore* (1953); *Phantom Stallion* (1954).

ARIZONA CYCLONE Imperial, 1934, B&W. **Producer:** William M. Pizor; **Director:** Robert Emmett Tansey; **Screenplay:** Tansey; **Cast:** Wally Wales, Franklyn Farnum, Karla Cowan, Fred Parker, Barney Beasley, Herman Hack.

ARIZONA CYCLONE Universal, 1941, B&W, 59 min. **Producer:** Will Cowan; **Director:** John H. Lewis and Ray Taylor; **Screenplay:** Sherman L. Lowe; **Music:** Hans J. Salter; **Cinematographer:** Charles Van Enger; **Editor:** Paul Landres; **Cast:** Johnny Mack Brown, Fuzzy Knight, Neil O'Day, Kathryn Adams, Herbert Rawlinson, Dick Curtis, Robert Strange, Glenn Strange.

The driver for a freight line tries to find out who murdered his boss over a telegraph hauling contract in this good Johnny Mack Brown entry for Universal. An earlier film by the same name, released in 1934, was directed by Robert Emmett Tansey and featured Wally Wales and Franklyn Farnum in leading roles.

ARIZONA DAYS Grand National Pictures, 1937, B&W, 57 min, VT. **Producer:** Edward Finney; **Director:** John English; **Screenplay:** Sherman Lowe; **Music:** Frank Sanucci; **Cinematographer:** Gus Peterson; **Editor:** John Wilkes; **Cast:** Tex Ritter, Syd Saylor, William Faversham, Eleanor Stewart, Forrest Taylor, "Snub" Pollard, Glenn Strange.

Tex Ritter is a drifter who joins a traveling minstrel show that is burned to the ground by outlaws. He becomes a tax collector in order to replace the show's equipment and expose the villains. Along the way, Tex sings a song or two, knocks out a few bad guys, and woos the girl of his dreams. (See also SONG OF THE GRINGO.)

ARIZONA FRONTIER Monogram, 1940, B&W, 60 min. **Producer:** Edward Finney; **Director:** Albert Herman; **Screenplay:** Robert Emmett Tansey; **Music:** Frank Sanucci; **Cinematographer:** Marcel Le Picard; **Editor:** Frederick Bain; **Cast:** Tex Ritter, Slim Andrews, Evelyn Finley, Tristram Coffin, Jim Thorpe, Gene Alsace, James Pierce.

A government agent is sent to investigate a series of Indian raids and comes to realize that the commander of the local army post is behind the lawlessness. Filmed in Arizona, this better-than-average Tex Ritter venture has Tex singing "Wastin' Time" and the traditional "Red River Valley." Look for Jim Thorpe, voted the World's Greatest Athlete (1900–50), in the role of Gray Cloud. (See also SONG OF THE GRINGO.)

ARIZONA GANGBUSTERS (aka: GANG BUSTERS, GANGBUSTERS) PRC Pictures, 1940, B&W, 60 min. **Producer:** Sigmund Neufeld; **Director:** Sam Newfield (as Peter Stewart); **Screenplay:** William Lively and Joseph O'Donnell; **Music:** Lew Porter; **Cinematographer:** Jack Greenhalgh; **Cast:** Tim McCoy, Pamela Haddon, Forrest Taylor, Lou Fulton, Arno Frey, Julian Rivero, Jack Rutherford, Otto Reichow, Lita Cortez.

An Arizona cowboy (Tim McCoy) uncovers a Nazi fifth-column group and sets out to destroy them.

ARIZONA GUNFIGHTER Republic, 1937, B&W, 58 min. **Producer:** A. W. Hackel; **Director:** Sam Newfield; **Screenplay:** George Plympton and Harry Olmsted (story); **Cinematographer:** Robert E. Cline; **Editor:** Roy Claire; **Cast:** Bob Steele, Jean Carmen, Ted Adams, Ernie Adams, Lew Meehan, Karl Hackett, A. C. Henderson, Frank Ball.

A cowboy sets out to find the man who murdered his father. This interesting and entertaining Bob Steele oater is just one of many series entries Steele made for Republic Pictures, which was formed in 1935 as a result of the merger of four minor studios. Herbert J. Yates, founder and president of Republic, turned the studio into a profitable factory of polished B westerns. Among its leading cowboy stars were Bob Steele, John Wayne, Gene Autry, and Roy Rogers.

ARIZONA KID, THE Fox Film Corporation, 1930, B&W, 88 min. **Director:** Alfred Santell; **Screenplay:** Ralph Block; **Cinematographer:** Glen MacWilliams; **Editor:** Paul Whetherwax; **Cast:** Warner Baxter, Carole Lombard, Theodore von Eltz, Hank Mann, James Gibson, Mona Maris.

A bandit posing as a Mexican miner carries on his illegal activities and romances a series of girls, until he falls for a fashionable girl from the East who is actually married. Based on the O. Henry story, Warner Baxter is the Cisco Kid, the screen's most lovable bandit. The previous year Baxter had won a Best Actor Oscar for the enormously successful IN OLD ARIZONA (1929). (See also CISCO KID, THE.)

ARIZONA KID, THE Republic, 1939, B&W, 61 min, VT. **Producer:** Joseph Kane; **Director:** Kane; **Screenplay:** Gerald Geraghty and Luci Ward; **Music:** Cy Feuer (director); **Cast:** Roy Rogers, George "Gabby" Hayes, Sally March, Stuart Hamblen, Dorothy Sebastian, Robert Middlemass.

Roy Rogers is a Confederate officer stationed in Missouri who rounds up an outlaw gang working under the pretense of service to the Confederacy. Good action sequences aid this well-done Rogers entry. Ohio-born Roy Rogers (Leonard Slye) actually spent a year on a Montana ranch learning to ride and shoot, becoming very adept at basic cowboy skills. He would soon become the undisputed "King of the Cowboys" and biggest money-making western star for a record 12 consecutive years (1943–54).

ARIZONA LEGION   RKO, 1939, B&W, 58 min. **Producer:** Bert Gilroy; **Director:** David Howard; **Screenplay:** Oliver Drake and Bernard McConville (story); **Cinematographer:** Harry J. Wild; **Editor:** Frederick Knudtson; **Cast:** George O'Brien, Laraine Day, Carlyle Moore Jr., Tom Chatterton, Edward Le Saint, Harry Cording, Glenn Strange.

Boone Yeager, an undercover agent with the Arizona Rangers, poses as a hard-drinking, shoot-em-up cowboy so he can infiltrate the Dutton gang, who are running things in lawless Arizona. Laraine Day (billed as Laraine Johnson) plays his love interest Letty Meade in this well-done George O'Brien series entry. (See also *RACKETEERS OF THE RANGE*.)

ARIZONA MAHONEY (aka: ARIZONA THUNDERBOLT, BADMEN OF ARIZONA) Paramount, 1937, B&W, 61 min. **Producer:** A. M. Bottsford; **Director:** J. P. Hogan; **Screenplay:** Stuart Anthony and Robert Yost; **Cast:** Joe Cook, Robert Cummings, Buster Crabbe, Marjorie Gateson, June Martel, Fred Kohler, Irving Bacon.

When Sue Bixby becomes his new boss, stagecoach robber Kirby Talbot (Buster Crabbe) reforms his outlaw ways. But when he and his gang are outnumbered fighting another group of outlaws, Phillip Randell (Robert Cummings) rides to get circus man Arizona Mahoney and his shooting cannon.
  Based on Zane Grey's novel *Stairs of Sand*, this Paramount oater was filmed under the same title in 1929, with Wallace Beery, Jean Arthur, Phillips Holmes, and Fred Kohler in the leading roles.

ARIZONA MANHUNT   Republic, 1951, B&W, 60 min. **Producer:** Rudy Ralston; **Director:** Fred C. Brannon; **Screenplay:** William Lively; **Cinematographer:** John MacBurnie; **Editor:** Irving M. Schoenberg; **Cast:** Michael Chapin, Elaine Janssen, James Bell, Lucile Barkley, Roy Barcroft.

A group of youngsters help an elderly sheriff and his deputy defeat a gang of outlaws in this decent entry in Republic's *Rough Ridin' Kids* series.

ARIZONA MISSION   See *GUN THE MAN DOWN*.

ARIZONA RAIDERS   Columbia, 1965, Color, 88 min, VT. **Producer:** Grant Whytock; **Director:** William Witney; **Screenplay:** Alex Gottlieb, Frank Gruber, Mary Willingham, and Willard Willingham; **Music:** Richard LaSalle; **Cinematographer:** Jacques R. Marquette; **Editor:** Grant Whytock; **Cast:** Audie Murphy, Michael Dante, Ben Cooper, Buster Crabbe, Gloria Talbott, Ray Stricklyn, George Keymas.

Audie Murphy plays an ex-Quantrill raider who is released from jail and deputized as an Arizona Ranger to help hunt down the remnants of Quantrill's band. Ben Cooper plays Murphy's loyal buddy who protects him to the end. This is a good Murphy venture made even better by the directing skills of William Witney.

ARIZONA RAIDERS, THE Paramount, 1936, B&W, 57 min. **Producer:** A. M. Botsford; **Director:** James P. Hogan; **Screenplay:** John W. Kraft and Robert Yost; **Music:** Gerard Carbonara, Hugo Friedlander, John Leipold, and Heinz Rooemheld (all uncredited); **Cinematographer:** Lee Tover; **Editor:** Chandler House; **Cast:** Buster Crabbe, Marsha Hunt, Raymond Hatton, Grant Withers, Johnny Downs, Betty Jean Rhodes, Don Rowen.

After being saved himself from the rope, Laramie Nelson (Buster Crabbe) saves another man (Raymond Hatton) from the same fate. Based on Zane Grey's novel *Raiders of the Spanish Peaks*, this film was reissued in 1951 as *Badmen of Arizona*.

ARIZONA RANGER, THE RKO, 1948, B&W, 63 min. **Producer:** Herman Schlom; **Director:** John Rawlins; **Screenplay:** Norman Houston and Frances Kavanaugh; **Music:** Paul Sawtell; **Cinematographer:** J. Roy Hunt; **Editor:** Desmond Marquette; **Cast:** Tim Holt, Jack Holt, Nan Leslie, Richard Martin, Steve Brodie, Paul Hurst, Robert Bray.

Jack Holt plays a big rancher who believes in handling his own problems without the law's help. His son Tim returns from the Spanish-American War with two buddies intent on forming the Arizona Rangers. The inevitable conflict occurs between father and son before they reunite to fight the bad guys together. This RKO entry is most notable for teaming Tim Holt with dad Jack Holt, the only time these two talents actually play father and son. The picture was part of Tim Holt's post-World War II western series at RKO, and it is a good one. (See also *ALONG THE RIO GRANDE*.)

ARIZONA TERRITORY Monogram, 1950, B&W, 56 min, VT. **Producer:** Vincent M. Fennelly; **Director:** Wallace Fox; **Screenplay:** Adele S. Buffington; **Cinematographer:** Harry Neumann; **Editor:** Richard V. Heermance; **Cast:** Whip Wilson, Andy Clyde, Nancy Saunders, John Merton, Carl Mathews, Carol Henry.

A lawman is on the trail of counterfeiters who are transferring fake currency to Eastern merchants. (See also *ABILENE TRAIL*.)

ARIZONA THUNDERBOLT   See *ARIZONA MAHONEY*.

ARIZONIAN, THE RKO, 1935, B&W, 74 min. **Producer:** Cliff Reid; **Director:** Charles Vidor; **Screenplay:** Dudley Nichols; **Music:** Roy Webb; **Cinematographer:** Harold Wenstrom; **Editor:** Jack Hively; **Cast:** Richard Dix, Preston Foster, Margot Graham, Louis Calhern, James Bush, Ray Meyer, Francis Ford, J. Farrell MacDonald, Joe Sawyer, Jim Thorpe.

Based on Dudley Nichols's novel *The Peacemaker*, Marshal Clay Tallant (Richard Dix) teams with outlaw Tex Randolph (Preston Foster) to clean up the town of Silver City, which is run by corrupt sheriff Jake Mannon (Louis Calhern). Dix is excellent as a Wyatt Earp-type marshal with the ability to disarm villains by merely starring at them and convert outlaws to the side of goodness just by his presence. *The Arizonian* is among the better western films to come out of the 1930s, with Dix and Foster complementing one another on screen in grand style.

ARKANSAS JUDGE Republic, 1941, B&W, 71 min. **Producer:** Armand Schaefer; **Director:** Frank McDonald; **Screenplay:** Ian McLellan Hunter, Ring Lardner Jr., Dorrell McGowan, Stuart McGowan, and Gertrude Purcell; **Music:** Cy Feuer; **Editor:** Ernest J. Nims; **Cast:** Leon Weaver, Frank Weaver, June Weaver, Roy Rogers, Spring Byington, Pauline Moore, Frank M. Thomas, Veda Ann Borg.

A working woman is accused of a crime that was actually committed by the daughter of a judge, the man who wrongly accused the woman. Roy Rogers plays a young lawyer and takes a back seat to the cornball comedy and music of the Weaver Brothers and Elviry (June Weaver).

ARROWHEAD Paramount, 1953, Color, 105 min, VT. **Producer:** Nat Holt; **Director:** Charles Marquis Warren; **Screenplay:** Warren; **Music:** Paul Sawtell; **Cinematographer:** Ray Rennahan; **Editor:** Frank Bracht; **Cast:** Charlton Heston, Jack Palance, Katy Jurado, Brian Keith, Mary Sinclair, Milburn Stone, Richard Shannon, Lewis Martin, Frank De Kova, Robert Wilke, Peter Coe.

Based on W. R. Burnett's novel *Adobe Walls*, Charlton Heston plays Ed Bannon, a white man raised by Apaches who has learned to hate them. Heston's adversary is his former blood brother Torriano (Jack Palance), who has been educated in a white school in the East and has learned the white man's ways. The tension steadily increases, builds in suspense, and culminates with a vicious hand-to-hand battle between Bannon and Torriano. Brian Keith gives a thumbs-up performance as the naïve cavalry commander who grossly underestimates the extent of Torriano's treachery. The character of Ed Bannon was based on the real chief of scouts in the Southwest for the U.S. cavalry, and the picture was shot on location in Bracketville, Texas, where the story actually took place.

ARROW IN THE DUST Allied Artists, 1954, Color, 80 min. **Producer:** Hayes Goetz; **Director:** Leslie Selander;

Screenplay: Don Martin; **Music:** Marlin Skyles; **Cinematographer:** Ellis W. Carter; **Editor:** William Austin; **Cast:** Sterling Hayden, Coleen Gray, Keith Larson, Tom Tully, Jimmy Wakely, Lee Van Cleef, John Pickford, Carlton Young.

Sterling Hayden is a deserting horse soldier who assumes the identity of a dead commanding officer and in the process learns something about duty and honor in this adaptation of L. L. Foreman's novel. Jimmy Wakely sings the song "The Weary Stranger." This well-scripted and well-acted western helmed by the capable Leslie Selander still holds up.

ARYAN, THE Triangle Film Corporation, 1916, B&W, 105 min. **Producer:** Thomas H. Ince; **Directors:** Reginald Barker, William S. Hart, and Clifford Smith; **Cast:** William S. Hart, Gertrude Claire, Charles K. French, Louise Glaum, Ernest Swalloe, Bessie Love.

William S. Hart plays a bitter man who finds peace when he saves a beleaguered farm community from the bad guys in this silent film. Steve Denton (Hart) is rich from years of prospecting when he is fleeced by the "good" citizens of Yellow Ridge. Consumed with anger, he kidnaps the woman most responsible and makes her his slave in a desert hideaway. He refuses to aid a wagon train full of farmers dying in the desert until he meets Mary Jane, an innocent and brave young girl played by Bessie Love. Future screen greats John Gilbert and Jean Hersholt appear in uncredited roles. One of William S. Hart's finest films under the Triangle banner, *The Aryan* was Hart's self-professed favorite.

ASSASSIN, THE See *GUNFIGHTERS, THE*.

AT GUNPOINT Allied Artists, 1955, Color, 81 min. **Producer:** Vincent M. Fennelly; **Director:** Alfred L. Werker; **Screenplay:** Daniel B. Ullman; **Music:** Carmen Dragon and Eric Zeisl; **Cinematographer:** Ellsworth Fredericks; **Editor:** Eda Warren; **Cast:** Fred MacMurray, Dorothy Malone, Walter Brennan, Tommy Rettig, John Qualen, Irving Bacon, Skip Homeier, Whit Bissell, Jack Lambert, Frank Ferguson, Harry Lauter, John Pickard.

A peaceful storekeeper accidentally shoots a bank robber and becomes an instant local hero. However, once the robber's friends swear vengeance, the townsfolk turn against him by boycotting his store and urging him to leave town. He refuses to run away, deciding instead to hold his ground. Eventually the town is shamed into backing him up. This is yet another spin-off of the *High Noon* theme, which became quite popular in the 1950s and early '60s, only this time the good citizens manage to see the light of resistance and help their unlikely hero by the final fadeout.

AVENGING ANGEL, THE Curtis/Lowe Productions/TNT, 1995, Color, 91 min. **Producers:** Tom Berenger and Patrick Curtis; **Director:** Craig Baxley; **Teleplay:** David

Nemec; **Music:** Gary Chang; **Cinematographer:** Mark Irwin; **Editor:** Mark Helfrich; **Cast:** Tom Berenger, James Coburn, Fay Masterson, Charlton Heston, Kevin Tighe, Jeffrey Jones, Patrick Groman.

Based on fact, this little-known episode in U.S. history tells of a Mormon loner who makes it his cause to protect Brigham Young and other Mormon leaders from being assassinated by their enemies. Well produced by Curtis/Lowe Productions with plenty of action, the film boasts riveting performances by Charlton Heston as Brigham Young and Tom Berenger as the bodyguard who is cast in the middle of a dangerous power struggle.

BACK IN THE SADDLE Republic, 1941, B&W, 73 min, VT. **Producer:** Harry Grey; **Director:** Lew Landers; **Screenplay:** Jesse Lasky Jr. and Richard Murphy; **Music:** Raoul Kraushaar; **Cinematographer:** Ernest Miller; **Editor:** Tony Martinelli; **Cast:** Gene Autry, Smiley Burnette, Mary Lee, Edward Norris, Julie Bishop.

Gene Autry foils a nasty mine owner who has been poisoning cattle in an attempt to drive the local ranchers off their land. An exciting shoot-out with flaming hay carts and whizzing bullets set in and around a jail provides an ample supply of action and some great Saturday afternoon entertainment. Of course there is the title song, crooned to perfection by the movie's first frontline singing cowboy. Written by Gene Autry and Ray Whitley and recorded by Autry, it became his theme song. Many years later the song would appear in the soundtrack of the hit movie *Sleepless in Seattle*.

BACKLASH Universal, 1956, Color, 84 min. **Producer:** Aaron Rosenberg; **Director:** John Sturges; **Screenplay:** Borden Chase; **Music:** Herman Stein; **Cinematographer:** Irving Glassberg; **Editor:** Sherman Todd; **Cast:** Richard Widmark, Donna Reed, William Campbell, John McIntire, Barton MacLane, Harry Morgan, Robert J. Wilke, Jack Lambert.

When Jim Slater's (Richard Widmark) father dies in an Apache ambush, he searches for the one survivor who supposedly went for help but instead disappeared with a lot of gold. His mission is complicated by renewed Apache hostilities, an impending range war, and a number of people who think he is in the possession of the gold and seem to be gunning for him too. Donna Reed plays Karyl Orton, a liberated beauty who appears to be on a similar mission. Based on a novel by Frank Gruber, this intelligent film was released one year after Sturges's best-known film, *BAD DAY AT BLACK ROCK*,

and it has that indelible Sturges imprint of people in jeopardy who are trapped in a hostile environment where the only escape is through violent confrontation.

BACK TO THE FUTURE, PART III Universal, 1990, Color, 118 min, VT, CD. **Producers:** Steven Speilberg, Neil Canton, Bob Gale, Kathleen Kennedy, Frank Marshall, and Steve Starkey; **Director:** Robert Zemeckis; **Screenplay:** Zemeckis and Bob Gale; **Music:** Alan Silvestri; **Cinematographer:** Dean Cundey; **Editors:** Harry Keramidas and Arthur Schmidt; **Cast:** Michael J. Fox, Christopher Lloyd, Mary Steenburgen, Elizebeth Shue, Thomas Wilson, Lea Thompson, Harry Carey Jr., Dub Taylor, Pat Buttram.

This time Marty (Michael J. Fox) travels back to 1885 in order to keep Doc (Christopher Lloyd) from being murdered and finds himself in the midst of a band of charging Indians, flush in the middle of John Ford's Monument Valley. Part of the fun is recognizing elements from other genre classics: the dance from *MY DARLING CLEMENTINE*, the sobering-up concoction from *EL DORADO*, and the costume from *A FISTFUL OF DOLLARS*. Doc even has a romance with a spinster schoolmarm (Mary Steenburgen) who shares his passion for Jules Verne.

Fans and patrons of the *Back to the Future* films generally consider this to be a worthy and entertaining conclusion to the time-travel trilogy. The film is enhanced by brilliant imagery, dazzling special effects, and an outstanding musical score. True-blue western fans will delight in seeing venerable stalwarts Harry Carey Jr., Dub Taylor, and Pat Buttram as three saloon old-timers. This fun-filled picture was filmed on location in Sonora, California, and Monument Valley, Utah, as well as Oxnard and Los Angeles, California.

BACK TO THE WOODS Columbia, 1939, B&W, 19 min. **Producer:** Jules White; **Director:** Jack White (as Preston Black); **Screenplay:** Andrew Bennison; **Cinematographer:** George Meehan; **Cast:** Curly Howard, Larry Fine, Moe Howard.

This comedy short with a western tinge and a colonial setting has the Three Stooges as convicted criminals banished by England to the American colonies. When they arrive they find that the colonists are starving because local Indians will not allow them on their hunting grounds. Naturally, the Stooges go hunting, and after a wild chase they are captured by the Indians. They escape, and another wild chase ensues.

BAD BASCOMB MGM, 1946, B&W, 112 min. **Producer:** Orville O. Dull; **Director:** S. Sylvan Simon; **Screenplay:** Grant Garrett and William Lipman; **Music:** David Snell; **Cinematographer:** Charles Edgar Schoenbaum; **Editor:** Ben Lewis; **Cast:** Wallace Beery, Margaret O'Brien, Marjorie Main, J. Carrol Naish, Frances Rafferty, Marshall Thompson.

Bad guy Zeb Bascomb (Wallace Beery) joins a wagon train heading to Utah hoping to keep federal troops from capturing him. Over the long trek he falls under the charms of young Emmy, played by Margaret O'Brien, the consummate child star of the 1940s. Beery, who specialized in softhearted bad-guy roles, stretches his lovable rogue image to the limit as a ruthless outlaw softened and tamed by the gentility of a young girl. When Bascomb's partner (J. Carrol Naish) joins the wagon train and tries to get him to steal Mormon gold to be used for a hospital, Bascomb refuses. He later saves Emmy's life when her wagon overturns and she is forced into the raging river. Emmy in turn helps fend off an Indian attack with a peashooter. Rife with action and sentiment, the film is yet another attempt to use pacifist religious groups to soften the rough-and-tumble lifestyle of the Old West.

BAD COMPANY Paramount, 1972, Color, 93 min, VT. **Producer:** Stanley R. Jaffe; **Director:** Robert Benton; **Screenplay:** Benton and David Newman; **Music:** Harvey Schmidt; **Cinematographer:** Gordon Willis; **Editors:** Ron Kalish and Ralph Rosenbloom; **Cast:** Jeff Bridges, Barry Brown, Jim Davis, David Huddleston, John Savage, Jerry Houser.

Fresh from an Oscar nomination for his work in *The Last Picture Show*, a young Jeff Bridges stars as Jake Rumsey, a well-brought-up boy who finds himself alone in the world. Reluctantly he joins a group of boyish outlaws. His counterpart is Drew Dixon (Barry Brown), who has fled his family home in Ohio to escape conscription in the Union army. With four other teenagers they head west determined to make things better. They soon find out that the West is not a romantic haven, and they are forced to steal to stay alive. Violence abounds, and innocence is lost. At the final fadeout only Jake and Drew survive, assured that they are now ready to pull their first bank robbery. The film marks Robert Benton's directorial debut and boasts a series of good performances, Harvey Schmidt's (*The Fantastics, 110 in the Shade*)

excellent piano score, and Gordon Willis's interesting and subdued camera work.

BAD DAY AT BLACK ROCK MGM, 1955, Color, 1955, 81 min. **Producer:** Dore Schary; **Director:** John Sturges; **Screenplay:** Millard Kauffman and Don McGuire; **Music:** Andre Previn; **Cinematographer:** William C. Mellor; **Editor:** Newell P. Kimlin; **Cast:** Spencer Tracy, Robert Ryan, Anne Francis, Walter Brennan, Dean Jagger, John Ericson, Ernest Borgnine, Lee Marvin, Russell Collins, Walter Sande.

John Macreedy (Spencer Tracy) disembarks a train in the drab and barren Southwest town of Black Rock. The year is 1945, and he is to deliver a posthumous medal to a Japanese-American farmer whose son has died in battle. What he encounters is an antagonistic town and three supreme bullies—Robert Ryan, Ernest Borgnine, and Lee Marvin. This superb picture with a genuine moral tone marked Tracy's last film for MGM, and it was applauded by critics and audiences alike. It also makes a strong statement that Robert Ryan was perhaps the most underappreciated and artistically overlooked movie actor of his day. This is a strong, stand-up, modern-day western with a marvelous cast, a film that writer John O'Hara called "one of the finest motion pictures ever made."

BADGE OF MARSHAL BRENNAN Allied Artists, 1957, B&W, 74 min. **Producer:** Albert C. Gannaway; **Director:** Gannaway; **Screenplay:** Thomas G. Hubbard; **Music:** Ramey Idriss; **Cinematographer:** Charles Straumer; **Editor:** Asa Boyd Clark; **Cast:** Jim Davis, Arleen Whelan, Louis Jean Heydt, Marty Robbins, Harry Lauter, Douglas Fowley, Lawrence Dobkin, Lee Van Cleef.

An outlaw who is on the run is mistaken for a dead marshal and decides to go up against a wicked land baron in this low-budget entry based on the novel *Last of the Badmen*. Jim Davis, excellent in the title role, heads a number of good performances.

BAD GIRLS 20th Century Fox, 1994, Color, 96 min, VT. **Producers:** William Fay, Charles Finch, Bruce Meade, Andre E. Morgan, Lynda Obst, and Albert S. Ruddy; **Director:** Jonathan Kaplan; **Screenplay:** Yolanda Finch and Ken Friedman; **Music:** Jerry Goldsmith; **Cinematographer:** Ralf D. Bode; **Editor:** Jane Kurson; **Cast:** Madeleine Stowe, Mary Stewart Masterson, Andie MacDowell, Drew Barrymore, James Russo, Robert Loggia, Neil Summers, James Le Gros.

Wanted for a bordello shooting, four prostitutes leave the Wild West and head north to make a better life. With guns in tow, they look and talk tough, but the big question becomes how will they fare when Cody Zamora's partner Kid Jarrett takes Cody's money, and the four "Honky Tonk Harlots" set out to recover the loot? The video release of the film contains a few shots with nudity that did not appear in the theatrical release. Interestingly, Kid Jarrett's hideout in *Bad Girls* is actually the interior of the fortress used in the 1960 film *THE ALAMO*.

There were a slew of problems as well as some wholesale production housecleaning. The original filming began with Tamra Davis as director, but Jonathan Kaplan took the helm early on when the production company became disenchanted with the direction the film was taking. When filming began two weeks later, nothing remained of the original project except some of the leading actresses.

BAD JIM 21st Century Film Corporation, 1990, Color, 90 min. **Producers:** Les Greene and Joseph Wouk; **Director:** Clyde Ware; **Screenplay:** Ware; **Music:** Jamie Sheriff; **Cinematographer:** David Golia; **Editor:** Glen Garland; **Cast:** James Brolin, Richard Roundtree, John Clark Gable, Harry Carey Jr., Rory Calhoun, Ty Hardin, Pepe Serna, Bruce Kirby.

Three men purchase Billy the Kid's horse and start passing themselves off as Billy's gang. The movie marks the film debut of Clark Gable's son as the youngest of the bandit trio. Interestingly, John Clark Gable shares the camera's eye with actor James Brolin, who played Clark Gable in the 1976 bio *Gable and Lombard*. Casting of such screen veterans as Richard Roundtree, Rory Calhoun, and Harry Carey Jr. are a big plus and contribute well to the film's leisurely pace.

BADLANDERS, THE MGM, 1958, Color, 83 min, VT. **Producer:** Aaron Rosenberg; **Director:** Delmer Daves; **Screenplay:** Richard Collins; **Cinematographer:** John F. Seitz; **Editors:** James Baiotto and William Webb; **Cast:** Alan Ladd, Ernest Borgnine, Katy Jurado, Claire Kelly, Kent Smith, Nehemiah Persoff, Anthony Caruso, Ann Doran.

Two men (Alan Ladd and Ernest Borgnine) are released from the Arizona Territorial Prison at Yuma in 1898. "The Dutchman" (Ladd) is out for revenge against the people of a small mining town who had him imprisoned unjustly. John McBain (Borgnine) just wants to go straight. However, when "The Dutchman" involves McBain in a gold-theft scheme and they decide to plan a gold robbery, each man tries to outsmart the other in this good reworking of W. R. Burnett's novel *The Asphalt Jungle*.

Alan Ladd gives a solid performance as Peter van Hoek, the man they call "The Dutchman." Ladd's emotional strength lends a casual grace to the character and provides the proper contrast to Borgnine's more bombastic John McBain. In what *Variety* calls "a truly original frontier drama," Delmer Daves is able to throw in a laugh or two to complement the film's escalating suspense. The picture is proof that one can make an effective adult western without it becoming "a psychological" genre piece.

BAD LANDS RKO, 1939, B&W, 70 min. **Producer:** Robert Sisk; **Director:** Lew Landers; **Screenplay:** Clarence Upson Young; **Cinematographer:** Frank Redman; **Editor:** George Hively; **Cast:** Robert Barrat, Noah Beery Jr., Guinn "Big Boy" Williams, Andy Clyde, Francis Ford, Addison Richards.

Sheriff Bill Cummings (Robert Barrat) leads a posse of 10 men into the Arizona Bad Lands, where they are pinned down by a band of Indians. As the men are killed off one by one, the chances for escape become more remote. Eventually only the sheriff is left alive at a water hole when the army finally arrives to "rescue" the group. A thinly disguised remake of RKO's *The Lost Patrol* (1934), *Bad Lands* features no women in the cast. Without any big-name stars, the film still manages to be a cut or two better than most B westerns.

BADLANDS OF DAKOTA Universal, 1941, B&W, 74 min. **Producer:** George Waggner; **Director:** Alfred E. Green; **Screenplay:** Gerald Geraghty and Harold Shumate; **Music:** Hans J. Salter, Ralph Freed (uncredited), Charles Previn (uncredited), Frank Sinner (uncredited); **Cinematographer:** Stanley Cortez; **Cast:** Robert Stack, Ann Rutherford, Richard Dix, Frances Farmer, Broderick Crawford, Hugh Herbert, Andy Devine, Lon Chaney Jr., Fuzzy Knight.

A crooked saloon owner in the town of Deadwood sends his younger brother to bring his fiancé home, but quite predictably the woman and brother fall in love. This well-done Universal western features Frances Farmer as Calamity Jane and Richard Dix as Wild Bill Hickok.

BADLANDS OF MONTANA 20th Century Fox, B&W, 75 min. **Producers:** Daniel B. Ullman and Herbert E. Mendelson; **Director:** Ullman; **Screenplay:** Ullman; **Music:** Irving Gertz; **Cinematographer:** Frederick Gately; **Editor:** Neil Brunnenkant; **Cast:** Rex Reason, Beverly Garland, Emile Meyer, Keith Larson, Jack Kruschen, Margia Dean, Stanley Farrar.

Local citizen Steven Brewster (Rex Reason) is whipped and forced to leave the town of Cascade after killing his assailant in a fair fight. In his escape he stumbles into the hideout of a bandit gang led by Meyer and falls in love with his daughter Susan (Beverly Garland). This interesting plot is aided by fine performances across the board. Emile Meyer's portrayal of bad man Henry Harrison Hammer is a gem.

BAD MAN, THE First National Pictures, Inc., 1930, B&W, 77 min. **Director:** Clarence Badger; **Screenplay:** Howard Eastabrook; **Cinematographer:** John F. Seitz; **Editor:** Frank Ware; **Cast:** Walter Huston, Dorothy Revier, James Rennie, O. P. Heggie, Guinn "Big Boy" Williams, Myrna Loy.

A Mexican bandit comes to the aid of a man who once saved his life when the man was about to lose his ranch. This early talkie should interest Walter Houston fans. Look for an appearance by 25-year-old Myrna Loy. An earlier silent version was filmed in 1923 by Associated First National and featured Jack Mulhall, Holbrook Binn, and Enid Bennett.

BAD MAN, THE (aka: TWO GUN CUPID, GB) MGM, 1941, B&W, 70 min. **Producer:** J. Walter Ruben;

Director: Richard Thorpe; **Screenplay:** Wells Root; **Music:** Franz Waxman; **Cinematographer:** Clyde De Vinna; **Editor:** Conrad A. Nervig; **Cast:** Lionel Barrymore, Laraine Day, Wallace Beery, Ronald Reagan, Henry Travers, Chris-Pin Martin, Tom Conway, Chill Wills.

Based on the play by Porter Emerson Browne, this is the third remake of Browne's play. This version has Wallace Beery as Pancho Lopez, the role played by Walter Huston in the 1930 film. Beery is the western outlaw and Lionel Barrymore is Uncle Henry Jones, a decent chap and former friend who has to depend on the bad man's loyalty to save his ranch from crooks. The interplay and chemistry between Beery and Barrymore, two of the era's most adept screen personalities, is a delight to see.

BAD MAN FROM BODIE See *GUNMAN FROM BODIE*.

BAD MAN FROM RED BUTTE Universal, 1940, B&W, 58 min. **Producer:** Joseph Stanley; **Director:** Ray Taylor; **Screenplay:** Sam Robins; **Music:** Everette Carter (songs), Ralph Freed (uncredited), Milton Rosen (songs), Hans J. Salter (incidental music), and Frank Skinner (incidental music); **Cinematographer:** William B. Sickner; **Editor:** Paul Landres; **Cast:** Johnny Mack Brown, Anne Gwynne, Bob Baker, Fuzzy Knight, Norman Willis, Lafe McKee, Bill Cody Jr., Lloyd Ingraham.

A cowboy (Johnny Mack Brown) arrives in town and is immediately mistaken for his twin brother, who is wanted for murder. (See also *OLD CHISHOLM TRAIL, THE*.)

BAD MAN OF BRIMSTONE, THE MGM, 1937, Color, 89 min. **Producer:** Harry Rapf; **Director:** J. Walter Ruben; **Screenplay:** Cyril Hume, Richard Maibaum, Maurice Rapf, and J. Walter Ruben (story); **Music:** William Axt, David Snell, and Herbert Stothart; **Cinematographer:** Clyde De Vinna; **Editor:** Frank Sullivan; **Cast:** Wallace Beery, Virginia Bruce, Dennis O'Keefe, Joseph Calleia, Lewis Stone, Guy Kibbee, Bruce Cabot, Cliff Edwards.

Wallace Beery stars as an outlaw who is reformed by a family revelation. Top-flight character actors help this sentimental film.

BAD MAN OF DEADWOOD Republic, 1941, B&W, 61 min, VT. **Producer:** Joseph Kane; **Director:** Kane; **Screenplay:** James R. Webb; **Music:** Cy Feuer; **Cinematographer:** William Nobles; **Editor:** Charles Craft; **Cast:** Roy Rogers, George "Gabby" Hayes, Carol Adams, Henry Brandon, Herbert Rawlinson, Sally Payne, Jay Norvello, Hal Taliaferro, Monte Blue.

Roy Rogers plays a young cowpoke named Bill Brady who tries to clear his name by helping businessmen fight a monopoly. He and his sidekick Professor Blackstone (Gabby Hayes) are forced to establish fair business practices in the town of Deadwood, currently dominated by entrepreneurs who scare off potential competitors. While many of Rogers's later films were essentially musical reviews with a few plot elements added, *Bad Man of Deadwood* has an interesting plot with the musical numbers added for support. Songs include "Call Of The Dusty Trail," "Joe Brady," and "Home on the Rangeland." Look for stuntman supreme Yakima Canutt in an uncredited role as the stage driver, as well as a supporting cast full of familiar faces. (See also *UNDER WESTERN STARS*.)

BAD MAN OF HARLEM See *HARLEM ON THE PRAIRIE*.

BAD MAN OF WYOMING See *WYOMING*.

BADMAN'S COUNTRY Warner Bros., 1958, B&W, 68 min. **Director:** Fred Sears; **Screenplay:** Orvelle Hammond; **Music:** Irving Gertz; **Cinematographer:** Benjamin H. Kline; **Editor:** Grant Whytock; **Cast:** George Montgomery, Neville Brand, Buster Crabbe, Karen Booth, Gregory Walcott, Malcolm Atterbury, Russell Johnson.

This fictionalized account has George Montgomery as sheriff Pat Garrett joining Wyatt Earp (Buster Crabbe), Bat Masterson (Gregory Walcott) and Buffalo Bill (Malcolm Atterbury) for a last-stand showdown with Butch Cassidy (Neville Brand) and his cohorts.

BADMAN'S GOLD Eagle Lion Classics, 1951, B&W, 56 min. **Producer:** Robert Emmett Tansey; **Director:** Tansey; **Screenplay:** Alyn Lockwood and Tansey; **Cast:** John Carpenter, Alyn Lockwood, Kenne Duncan, Emmett Lynn, Jack Daly.

When a series of robberies takes place on a stage line carrying gold, a marshal is called to investigate.

BADMAN'S TERRITORY RKO, 1946, B&W, 97 min. **Producer:** Nat Holt; **Director:** Tim Whelan; **Screenplay:** Jack Natteford, Luci Ward, Bess Taffell, and Clarence Upson Young; **Music:** Roy Webb; **Cinematographer:** Robert De Grasse; **Editor:** Philip Martin; **Cast:** Randolph Scott, Ann Richards, George "Gabby" Hayes, Ray Collins, James Warren, Lawrence Tierney, Tom Tyler, Steve Brodie, Phil Warren, William Moss, Nestor Paiva, Isabel Jewell, Kermit Maynard (uncredited).

Marshal Mark Rowley (Randolph Scott) comes to the town of Quinto in search of his brother, who has been wounded by the James gang. In a town notorious for its lack of law and order, he soon encounters not only Frank and Jesse James but the Daltons and Sam Bass as well. Framed on a horse-stealing charge by a corrupt marshal, Rowley is later freed and stays on to help crusading newspaper editor Henryette

Alcott (Ann Richards) in her campaign to help make Quinto part of the Oklahoma Territory.

Badman's Territory has some of the genre's most famous lawbreakers under its canopy: Jesse and Frank James (Lawrence Tierney and Tom Tyler); the Dalton brothers (Steve Brodie, James Warren, and William Moss); Sam Bass (Nestor Paiva); and Belle Star (Isabel Jewell). The film is highlighted by its strong cast, including a banner job by "Gabby" Hayes as the Coyote Kid, the windy westerner who drives getaway wagons for the James and Daltons gangs. A good movie with Randolph Scott at his lawman best, the film proved so successful that RKO drafted a sequel called *RETURN OF THE BAD MEN* (1949). The original film is also shown in a computer-colored version.

BADMEN OF ARIZONA See *ARIZONA MAHONEY.*

BAD MEN OF MISSOURI Warner Bros., 1941, B&W, 71 min. **Producer:** Harlan Thompson; **Director:** Ray Enright; **Screenplay:** Charles Grayson and Robert E. Kent; **Music:** Howard Jackson; **Cinematographer:** Arthur L. Todd; **Editor:** Clarence Kolster; **Cast:** Dennis Morgan, Jane Wyman, Wayne Morris, Arthur Kennedy, Victor Jory, Alan Baxter, Walter Catlett, Howard Da Silva, Faye Emerson, Russell Simpson.

This fictional western about the famed Younger brothers features Arthur Kennedy, Wayne Morris, and Dennis Morgan as Jim, Bob, and Cole Younger. The brothers turn to a lawless life after being enraged by the perfidy of carpetbaggers in post-Civil War Missouri.

Outlaw "heroes" became the order of the day after the popularity of Henry King's 1939 film *JESSE JAMES* started a trend of romanticizing the West's real outlaws. In an interesting sidebar, Humphrey Bogart rejected a role in this film with the words "Are you kidding!" Actually Bogie could have done worse. *Bad Men of Missouri* is a very good, often overlooked film with an excellent performance by the versatile Dennis Morgan, who distinguished himself in musical features as well as straight drama.

BAD MEN OF THE BORDER Universal, 1945, B&W, 56 min. **Producer:** Wallace Fox; **Director:** Fox; **Screenplay:** Adele Buffington; **Music:** Everette Carter (songs); **Cinematographer:** Maury Gertsman; **Editor:** Philip Cahn; **Cast:** Kirby Grant, Armida, Fuzzy Knight, John Eldredge, Barbara Sears, Edward M. Howard.

A U.S. marshal masquerading as an outlaw and a female Mexican agent investigating a counterfeiting ring join forces to bring in a gang of crooks. *BORDER BADMEN* was the first series vehicle Kirby Grant made for Universal. Generally Grant's series was a peg or two below Johnny Mack Brown's series with the same studio. Nevertheless, many of his entries made for good Saturday afternoon fun.

As a child Grant received a scholarship to the American Conservatory of Music in Chicago as a violinist and a singer.

He appeared in 17 westerns, mostly with Universal and Monogram, and gained his greatest fame as Sky King in the popular 1950s television series of the same name. His Universal series entries include *Trail to Vengeance, Code of the Lawless* (1945); *Rustler's Round-up* aka *Rustler's Hideout, Gunman's Code, Gun Town,* and *Lawless Breed* aka *Lawless Clan* (1946).

BAD MEN OF THUNDER GAP (aka: THUNDER GAP OUTLAWS) PRC, 1943, B&W, 60 min. **Producers:** Arthur Alexander and Alfred Stern; **Director:** Albert Herman; **Screenplay:** Elmer Clifton; **Music:** Lee Zahler (director); **Cinematographer:** Robert E. Cline; **Editor:** Charles Henkel Jr.; **Cast:** James Newill, Dave O'Brien, Guy Wilkerson, Janet Shaw, Jack Ingram, Charles King, Tom London, I. Stanford Jolley, Bud Osborne.

When outlaws plague a small town, the Texas Rangers set out to get them in this below-average entry in the "Texas Rangers" series. Reissued in 1947 by Eagle-Lion as *Thunder Gap Outlaws.* (See also *FIGHTING VALLEY.*)

BAD MEN OF TOMBSTONE Allied Artists, 1949, B&W, 74 min. **Producers:** Frank King, Herman King, and Maurice King; **Director:** Kurt Neumann; **Screenplay:** Arthur Strawn, Philip Yordan, and Jay Monaghan; **Music:** Roy Webb; **Cinematographer:** Russell Harlan; **Editor:** Richard Heermance; **Cast:** Barry Sullivan, Marjorie Reynolds, Broderick Crawford, Fortunio Bononova, Guinn "Big Boy" Williams, John Kellogg, Mary Newton, Morris Ankrum, Billy Gray.

During the Gold Rush days, a young man is determined to make his fortune, but he turns to a life of crime instead. In 1946 Monogram formed a wholly new subsidiary called Allied Artists to handle its higher-budget productions. In 1953 the corporate name was changed from Monogram Pictures Corporation to Allied Artists Corporation.

BAKER'S HAWK Doty-Dayton, 1976, Color, 105 min, VT, DVD. **Producer:** Lyman Dayton; **Director:** Dayton; **Screenplay:** Dan Greer and Hal Harrison Jr.; **Music:** Lex De Azevedo; **Cinematographer:** Bernie Abraham; **Editor:** Parkie L. Singh; **Cast:** Clink Walker, Burl Ives, Diane Baker, Lee Montgomery, Alan Young, Taylor Lacher, Bruce M. Fischer.

Young Billy Baker (Lee Montgomery) comes of age after befriending an older hermitlike man named Mr. McGraw (Burl Ives), while his parents (Clint Walker and Diane Baker) struggle against a band of vigilantes. Filmed on location in Utah, this is a great family film as well as a favorite for actor Clint Walker, who plays Dan Baker, a good, no-nonsense family man who pinch-hits for the sheriff in cleaning up the town. Based on a novel by Jack M. Bickham, the film features a steady performance by Clint Walker and the usual standout performance from Burl Ives.

BALLAD OF A GUNFIGHTER Parade Releasing Corporation, 1964, Color, 84 min. **Producer:** Bill Ward; **Director:** Ward; **Screenplay:** Ward; **Music:** Jaime Mendoza-Nava; **Cinematographer:** Brydon Baker; **Editor:** Jack Cornell; **Cast:** Marty Robbins, Joyce Redd, Robert Barron, Michael Davis, Laurette Luez, Charlie Aldrich, Paul McDonald, Cynthia Goodwins, Claude Aldrich.

When an outlaw plans to rob a stagecoach, another man foils him by taking not only the gold but also his girl. This film is the first starring venture for entertainer Marty Robbins, and fans will love hearing him sing "El Dorado" and "San Angelo."

BALLAD OF CABLE HOGUE, THE Warner Bros., 1970, Color, 121 min, VT. **Producers:** Phil Feldman (executive), William Faralla (coproducer), Gordon T. Dawson (associate), and Sam Peckinpah; **Director:** Peckinpah; **Screenplay:** John Crawford and Edmund Penney; **Music:** Jerry Goldsmith; **Cinematographer:** Lucien Ballard; **Editors:** Lou Lombardo and Frank Santillo; **Cast:** Jason Robards Jr., Stella Stevens, David Warner, Strother Martin, Slim Pickens, L. Q. Jones, Peter Whitney, Gene Evans.

Cable Hogue (Jason Robards) is double-crossed and left without water in the barren desert, but he is saved when he finds enough water to survive. He decides to build a new life for himself by establishing a much-needed rest stop on the local stagecoach line called Cable Spring. Stella Stevens gives a career performance as Hilly, a prostitute from a nearby town who moves in with him. Cable and Hilly even manage to sing a song together, bringing an element of romantic comedy to this drama.

Peckinpah is able to present a lyrical ode to the dying West, this time without the excessive violence employed in his highly acclaimed *THE WILD BUNCH* a year earlier. When Cable Hogue is mortally wounded after being run over by an automobile, he requests that his bed be brought out to him so he can die in the great outdoors. It is not just Cable who is dying but the ethos of rugged individualism that embodied the spirit of the "Old West" as well.

BALLAD OF JOSIE Universal, 1967, Color, 102 min. **Producers:** Norman MacDonnell and Martin Melcher; **Director:** Andrew V. McLaglen; **Screenplay:** Harold Swanton; **Music:** Frank De Vol; **Cinematographer:** Milton R. Krasner; **Editors:** Fred A. Chulack and Otho Lovering; **Cast:** Doris Day, Peter Graves, George Kennedy, Andy Devine, William Talman, David Hartman, Guy Raymond, Don Stroud, Paul Fix, Harry Carey Jr., Robert Lowery, Teddy Quinn, Karen Jenson, Elizabeth Fraser, Audrey Christie.

Doris Day plays Josie Minick, a young widow who stirs up things in a western town by raising sheep instead of cattle, then organizes the local women to demonstrate for women's suffrage. A couple of nice songs including "The Ballad of Josie" (Don Costa and Ronnie Dante) and "Wait Till Tomorrow"

(Gene de Paul and Jack Lloyd) will delight Doris Day fans. Marty Melcher produced this musical western spoof especially for wife Day.

BALLAD OF LITTLE JO, THE PolyGram Film Entertainment, 1993, Color, 121 min, VT. **Producers:** Fred Berner, Ira Deutchman (executive), Anne Dillon (associate), Brenda Goodman, and John Sloss (executive); **Director:** Maggie Greenwald; **Music:** David Mansfield; **Cinematographer:** Declan Quinn; **Editor:** Keith Reamer; **Cast:** Suzy Amis, Bo Hopkins, Ian McKellen, Heather Graham, David Chung, Carrie Snodgrass, Anthony Heald, Melissa Leo, Sam Robards.

When Josephine Monaghan (Suzie Amis) gives birth to an illegitimate child, her future is ruined. Compromised by her past, she flees the socialite world of New England and heads west. But when she discovers that the best life there can offer a single mother is that of a prostitute, she makes the bold decision to take a stab at freedom and independence by masquerading as a man. Although she has chosen to live like a man, she still yearns for her lost femininity. Amis gives an outstanding performance in the title role. But it is Bo Hopkins who delivers the film's most endearing performance as Frank Badger, the cursing, gunslinging, rough-and-tough western guy with a heart of gold.

The Ballad of Little Jo was inspired by a true story and set in 1866 during the Gold Rush. Writer/director Maggie Greenwald helmed this well-intentioned revisionist saga of frontier life with a distinctly feminist bent, somber in tone but only marginally exciting.

BANDIDO Bandido Productions/United Artists, 1956, Color, 92 min. **Producer:** Robert L. Jacks; **Director:** Richard Fleischer; **Screenplay:** Eric Felto; **Music:** Max Steiner; **Cinematographer:** Ernest Laszlo; **Editor:** Robert Golden; **Cast:** Robert Mitchum, Ursula Thiess, Gilbert Roland, Zachary Scott, Rodolfo Acosta, Jose Torvay, Henry Brandon, Douglas Fowley.

An arms dealer (Zachary Scott) and a mercenary (Robert Mitchum) clash during the 1916 Mexican Revolution. Filmed in Mexico and skillfully helmed by Richard Fleisher, *Bandido* delivers an excellent performance by Mitchum as the American soldier of fortune who sides with the rebels against the "regulares" supported by Scott. To complicate matters, he also has designs on Scott's beautiful wife, played by Ursula Thiess. Look for plenty of action and a stellar performance by Scott as the film's heavy. The good musical score was composed by the three-time Oscar-winning composer Max Steiner, who scored a record 306 films over a 30-year period.

BANDIT KING OF TEXAS Republic, 1949, B&W, 60 min. **Producer:** Gordon Kay (associate); **Director:** Fred C. Brannon; **Screenplay:** Olive Cooper; **Music:** Stanley Wilson; **Cinematographer:** John MacBurnie; **Editor:** Irving

M. Schoenberg; **Cast:** Allan Lane, Eddy Waller, Helene Stanley, Jim Nolan, Harry Lauter, Robert Bice.
See *BOLD FRONTIERSMAN, THE.*

BANDIT MAKES GOOD, THE Essanay, 1907, B&W, 2 reels. **Producer:** G. M. Anderson; **Director:** Anderson; **Screenplay:** Anderson; **Cast:** Gilbert M. "Broncho Billy" Anderson.

This highly successful two-reeler, filmed in Golden, Colorado, and lifted from a plot by Peter Tyne, is the first movie for actor G. M. Anderson (born Max Aronson), who adopted the film name "Broncho Billy." But because it was not actually part of the Broncho Billy series, Anderson himself claimed his first film to be *BRONCHO BILLY AND THE BABY* (1908). Broncho Billy is an outlaw who gives up his freedom to help a lost child and is ultimately reformed by love. Here Anderson exemplifies all the traits of the western hero: the good bad man, the rugged individual and loner who is both respected and feared.

Anderson took the lead only because he could not find anyone he felt was suitable for the part. By providing a pleasing mixture of action and sentiment, this film became so popular that the initial $1,000 investment grossed over $50,000. Until then, Anderson had considered himself more of a director and an executive for the Chicago-based Essanay Studio than an actor. More films followed, but there was no continuing theme—except the character of Broncho Billy. As Broncho Billy, Anderson would star in hundreds of one- and two-reel westerns. Subsequent films include *Broncho Billy's Christmas Dinner, Broncho Billy's Adventure* (1911); *Broncho Billy's Oath* (1913); *Broncho Billy and the Bandits, Broncho Billy and the Greaser, Broncho Billy's Bible* (1914).

Anderson turned out more than 375 one- and two-reel Broncho Billy westerns between 1908 and 1915. He offered a new film each week, with himself as writer, director, and star. This and subsequent films made Broncho Billy a popular attraction and Anderson the industry's first movie star as well as the first actor to be given screen credit. With a budget of about $800 per picture, each film grossed nearly $50,000. Eventually Anderson dropped the "h" to become Bronco Billy Anderson.

He was all but forgotten when, in 1957, he was honored by the Academy of Motion Pictures with a special Oscar "for his contributions to the development of motion pictures as entertainment." While very few of his one- and two-reelers have survived, they set the stage for such worthy Anderson successors as William S. Hart, Tom Mix, and Harry Carey. Anderson died in Little Rock, Arkansas, in 1971 at the age of 89.

BANDIT QUEEN Lippert, 1950, B&W, 71 min. **Producers:** William Berke, Jack Leewood, and Murray Lerner; **Director:** Berke; **Screenplay:** Budd Lesser, Victor West, and Orville Hampton (additional dialogue); **Music:** Albert Glasser; **Cinematographer:** Ernest Miller; **Editor:** Carl Pierson; **Cast:** Barbara Britton, Philip Reed, Willard Parker, Barton MacLane, Martin Garralaga, Jack Perin, Chuck Roberson.

When land grabbers murder her family in Old California, a girl takes the guise of a masked crusader and leads a vigilante group against the killers.

BANDIT RANGER RKO, 1942, B&W, 64 min. **Producer:** Bert Gilroy; **Director:** Leslie Selander; **Screenplay:** Bennett Cohen and Morton Grant; **Music:** Fred Rose and Ray Whitley (songs); **Cinematographer:** Nicholas Musuraca; **Editor:** Les Millbrook; **Cast:** Tim Holt, Cliff Edwards, Joan Barclay, Leroy Mason, Glenn Strange.

Rancher Clay Travis (Tim Holt) finds and brings in the body of Ranger Frank Mattison, who was murdered on the road. But it is Travers himself who is framed for the ranger's murder. He manages to escape, comes up with proof to clear his name, and eventually succeeds in bringing the real killers to justice. (See also *ALONG THE RIO GRANDE.*)

BANDIT TRAIL, THE RKO, 1941, B&W, 60 min. **Producer:** Bert Gilroy; **Director:** Edward Killy; **Screenplay:** Norton S. Parker; **Music:** Fred Rose, Paul Sawtell, and Ray Whitely (songs); **Cinematographer:** Harry J. Wild; **Editor:** Frederic Knudson; **Cast:** Tim Holt, Ray Whitely, Janet Waldo, Lee "Lasses" White, Morris Ankrum, Roy Barcroft.

BANDITS, THE (aka: *LOS BANDIDOS*, **Mexico)** Conrad-Zacharias, 1967, Color, 88 min. **Directors:** Robert Conrad and Alfred Zacharias; **Screenplay:** Edward DiLorenzo; **Cast:** Conrad, Pedro Armendáriz Jr., Roy Jenson, Jan-Michael Vincent, Manuel López Ochoa.

The story centers around three cowboys who are saved from the noose by a Mexican, then follow their rescuer across the border, where they have a series of adventures. Filmed in Mexico and distributed by Lone Star, this movie was not released in the United States until 1979.

BANDOLERO 20th Century Fox, 1968, Color, 106 min, VT. **Producer:** Robert L. Jacks; **Director:** Andrew V. McLaglen; **Screenplay:** James Lee Barrett; **Music:** Jerry Goldsmith; **Cinematographer:** William H. Clothier; **Editor:** Folmar Blangsted; **Cast:** James Stewart, Dean Martin, Raquel Welch, George Kennedy, Andrew Prine, Will Geer, Clint Richie, Denver Pyle, Sean McClory, Harry Carey Jr., Don "Red" Berry, Guy Raymond, Perry Lopez, Jock Mahoney, Dub Taylor, Big John Hamilton, Bob Adler, John Mitchum, Joseph Patrick Cranshaw, Roy Barcroft.

When Dee Bishop (Dean Martin) kills a rancher during an attempted bank robbery, Sheriff Johnson (George Kennedy) arrests the Martin's gang and sentences them to be hanged. But Bishop's older brother Mace (James Stewart) poses as the hangman and rescues the five men, who head to Mexico with Maria the rancher's widow (Raquel Welch) as their hostage. Both Dee and Mace are killed in an encounter with Sheriff Johnson and his posse, who have been following them. After the burial Maria returns to Texas with her new beau, Sheriff Johnson. She confesses, "I was a whore at thirteen and my family of twelve never went hungry."

The story goes that when Raquel Welch was signing autographs on the set for her fans, James Stewart heard her complain that she didn't like what she was doing. Stewart replied by telling her, "You better sign those, they're the ones paying your salary." The curvaceous Welch is just one of the big-name stars to appear in this unusual western, which hovers somewhere between being a serious western and a tongue-in-cheek spoof.

Bandolero marked the third teaming of Stewart and director Andrew McLaglen. According to McLaglen, it was a typical "deal" project from the start, "a Zanuck thing from the beginning." In other words, Darryl Zanuck had already determined his cast and writer when he phoned McLaglen—who was making another film at the time—suggesting that he direct the project.

Zanuck told McLaglen that had already received a six-page outline for a western titled *Mace*, and that he wanted James Lee Barrett to write it and James Stewart, Dean Martin, and Raquel Welch to be in it. "Nobody else, that's the combination I want," Zanuck decreed. McLaglen in turn showed the outline to Barrett, who agreed to write it for the people Zanuck wanted. Filmed in Pace, Arizona, and Del Rio, Texas, the picture grossed well into the millions in distributors' domestic retails despite just so-so reviews from critics. Also in the cast is B western star Don "Red" Barry, listed in the credits as Donald Barry.

BANJO HACKETT ROAMIN' FREE (aka: BANJO HACKETT) Columbia Pictures Television/NBC, 1976, Color. **Producer:** Bruce Lansbury; **Director:** Andrew V. McLaglen; **Screenplay:** Ken Trevey; **Music:** Morton Stevens; **Cinematographer:** Al Francis; **Editors:** Dann Cahn and David Wages; **Cast:** Albert Able, John Anderson, Ben Bates, Chuck Connors, Jeff Corey, Gloria DeHaven, Ike Eisenmann, Stan Haze, Anne Francis, L. Q. Jones, Don Meredith, Jan Murray, Slim Pickens, Jennifer Warren, Doodles Weaver.

This made-for-television western involves a horse trader and his young nephew traveling west in search of the boy's Arabian horse, which has been stolen by a bounty hunter. Football great Don Meredith stars as Banjo Hackett in this TV feature film, which was to be the pilot of a television series but didn't sell. In addition to being one of the best directors of western films, Andrew V. McLaglen has a television resume that is second to none. Among his numerous credits are 116 episodes of *Have Gun Will Travel*, 96 of *Gunsmoke*, and some 15 of *Rawhide*.

BANQUERO United Artists, 1970, Color, 115 min. **Producers:** Hal Klein and Aubrey Schenck; **Director:** Gordon Douglas; **Screenplay:** William Marks and George Schenck; **Music:** Dominic Frontiere; **Cinematographer:** Gerald Perry Finnerman; **Editor:** Charles Nelson; **Cast:** Lee Van Cleef, Warren Oates, Forrest Tucker, Kerwin Mathews, Mariette Hartley, Harry Lauter.

Warren Oates plays bad guy Jake Remy, who after destroying a town must deal with a feisty ferry operator (Lee Van Cleef) in order to navigate an escape. In the process we are given the rare sight of a naval battle in a western picture. The film is a spin-off on the successful spaghetti westerns that breathed new life into the genre in the 1960s and 1970s. As such it tries to merge the classic western of bygone days with the new spaghetti-oriented films of the period. Dominic Frontiere's excellent music is orchestrated with a zesty Italian flavor, and Van Cleef delivers a particularly skillful performance.

BAR 20 United Artists, 1943, B&W, 54 min. **Producers:** Lewis J. Rachmil and Harry Sherman; **Director:** Leslie Selander; **Screenplay:** Morton Grant, Norman Houston, and Michael Wilson; **Cinematographer:** Russell Harlan; **Cast:** William Boyd, Andy Clyde, George Reeves, Dustin Farnum, Victor Jory, Douglas Lowley, Robert Mitchum.

Hop-Along Cassidy (William Boyd) and pals California (Andy Clyde) and Lingo (George Reeves) try to help a girl and her mother after they lose their valuables in a holdup. The chief suspect is the girl's fiancé. Robert Mitchum broke into films in a series of Hop-Along Cassidy films such as *Bar 20*. Mitchum (listed as Bob Mitchum) appears as ranch owner Richard Adams. (See also *HOP-ALONG CASSIDY*.)

BAR 20 RIDES AGAIN Paramount, 1935, B&W, 62 min. **Producer:** Harry Sherman; **Director:** Howard Bretherton; **Screenplay:** Doris Schroeder and Gerald Geraghty; **Music:** Dave Franklin and Sam H. Stept; **Cinematographer:** Archie Stout; **Editor:** Edward Schroeder; **Cast:** William Boyd, James Ellison, Jean Rouverol, George "Gabby" Hayes, Harry Worth, Frank McGlynn, Paul Fix, Al St. John, John Merton, Frank Layton, Chill Wills and the Avalon Boys.

The boys from the Bar 20 Ranch find themselves up against a crazed land baron who thinks he is another Napoleon. Future Oscar-nominated actor Chill Wills (*The Alamo*) formed and led a singing group known as "Chill Wills and the Avalon Boys," appearing in several movies, before disbanding the group in 1938 to begin his long and versatile career as a character actor. One of the very best of the more than 65 Hop-Along Cassidy films to be released between 1935 and 1948. (See also *HOP-ALONG CASSIDY*.)

BARBAROSA Universal, 1982, Color, 90 min, VT. **Producers:** Paul Lazarus III, Martin Starger (executive), and William D. Wittliff; **Director:** Fred Schepisi; **Screenplay:** Wittliff; **Music:** Bruce Smeaton; **Cinematographer:** Ian Baker; **Editors:** David Ramirez and Don Zimmerman; **Cast:** Willie Nelson, Gary Busey, Isela Vega, Gilbert Roland, Danny De La Paz, Alma Martinez, George Voskovec, Howland Chamberlain, Sharon Compton.

Willie Nelson is Barbarosa, a grizzled, free-spirited outlaw on the run, having killed some members of his bride's Mexican family on his wedding night 30 years earlier. He meets up with Karl (Gary Busey), a country boy who leaves home after killing his brother-in-law. Karl becomes Barbarosa's protégé as the two are constantly pursued by revenge-seeking relatives. The legend of Barbarosa continues after his death, as Karl himself disappears into the desert in the guise of his mentor.

Filmed in Texas by Australian director Fred Schepisi, who carefully brings the western legend to light, Ian Baker's camera work is full of beautiful imagery and rare ethereal lighting patterns. Interestingly, Nelson and Busey, as well as producer/screenwriter William Wittliff, all hail from Texas. Nelson and Busey, who deliver endearing performances, are also both accomplished musicians.

BARBARY COAST United Artists, 1935, B&W, 91 min. **Producer:** Samuel Goldwyn; **Director:** Howard Hawks; **Screenplay:** Ben Hecht and Charles MacArthur; **Cast:** Miriam Hopkins, Edward G. Robinson, Joel McCrea, Walter Brennan, Frank Craven, Brian Donlevy, Donald Meek, Harry Carey, David Niven, Tom London.

A dance hall queen throws over a corrupt gambling house operator for an honest and broke young man in this western/drama period piece. Actor Tom London, who appears in the picture, holds a record 2,000 screen appearances, having made his debut as the locomotive driver in THE GREAT TRAIN ROBBERY (1903) and his final appearance in THE LONE TEXAN (1959). While it is mainly Hopkins's picture, Joel McCrea and Edward G. Robinson (as the town's underworld leader) turn in stellar performances, as does Harry Carey as the organizer of the vigilantes. The film received an Academy Award nomination for Best Cinematography.

BARBARY COAST GENT (aka: GOLD TOWN, THE HONEST THIEF) MGM, 1944, B&W, 87 min. **Producer:** Orville O. Dull; **Director:** Roy Del Ruth; **Screenplay:** Grant Garett, William R. Lipman, and Harry Ruskin; **Cinematographer:** Charles Salerno Jr.; **Editor:** Adrienne Fazan; **Cast:** Wallace Beery, Binnie Barnes, John Carradine, Bruce Kellogg, Frances Rafferty, Chill Wills, Noah Beery, Ray Collins, Morris Ankrum, Donald Meek, Louise Beavers.

Plush Brannon (Wallace Beery) is a con man who is thrown out of San Francisco's Barbary Coast and heads for the gold-rush region of Nevada. Once there he discovers a real gold mine, but complications follow as he tries to go straight.

BARGAIN, THE Paramount, 1914, B&W, 50 min, VT. **Producer:** Thomas H. Ince; **Director:** Reginald Barker; **Screenplay:** William H. Clifford and Ince; **Cinematographer:** Robert Newhard; **Cast:** William S. Hart, J. Frank Burke, Clara Williams, J. Barney Sherry, James Dowling.

A notorious bandit, injured while trying to rob a stagecoach, is rescued by a rancher and nursed back to health by the rancher's pretty daughter, with whom he falls in love. William S. Hart appears as the outlaw in his first film feature—a worthy silent film effort by two early screen pioneers, Thomas H. Ince and Hart. (See also HELL'S HINGES.)

BARON OF ARIZONA, THE Deputy Corporation/Lippert Pictures, Inc., 1950, B&W, 93 min. **Producers:** Carl K. Hittleman and Robert L. Lippert (executive); **Director:** Samuel Fuller; **Screenplay:** Fuller; **Cinematographer:** James Wong Howe; **Cast:** Vincent Price, Ellen Drew, Vladimir Sokoloff, Beulah Bondi, Reed Hadley, Robert Barrat, Fred Kohler Jr., Tristram Coffin, I. Stanford Jolley.

Vincent Price plays James Addison Reavis, an ambitious and polished con man (loosely based on a real person) who tries to swindle his way to ownership of most of Arizona. In attempting to do so, he forges a chain of historical evidence allowing him to make a foundling girl (Ellen Drew) the descendant of the original owners of the deed. He then marries her in order to perpetrate the swindle.

While the plot is not very exciting for a western, this is a superbly told story directed and scripted by Samuel Fuller, with Price delivering an outstanding performance in the title role. It is just too bad this fine movie is not out in video.

BARRICADE Warner Bros., 1950, Color, 77 min. **Producer:** Saul Elkins; **Director:** Peter Godfrey; **Screenplay:** William Sackheim; **Music:** William Lava; **Cinematographer:** Carl E. Guthrie; **Editor:** Clarence Kolster; **Cast:** Dane Clark, Raymond Massey, Ruth Roman, Morgan Farley, Walter Coy.

Set in a gold-mining camp, this is a classic battle of good versus evil, with Dane Clark as hero Bob Peters and Raymond Massey as sinister Boss Kruger, a tyrant who is exploiting the denizens of a mining camp. Ruth Roman, in the heyday of her beauty, provides the film's feminine allure. Clark and Massey are seasoned pros, yet despite the strong cast the film has just ordinary genre appeal.

BAT MASTERSON STORY, THE See GUNFIGHT AT DODGE CITY.

BATTLE AT APACHE PASS, THE Universal, 1952, Color, 85 min. **Producer:** Leonard Goldstein; **Director:** George Sherman; **Screenplay:** Gerald Dawson Adams; **Music:** Hans J. Salter; **Cinematographer:** Charles P. Boyle; **Editor:** Ted J. Kent; **Cast:** John Lund, Jeff Chandler, Beverly Tyler, Bruce Cowling, Susan Cabot, John Hudson, James Best, Regis Toomey, Richard Egan, Hugh O'Brien, Gregg Palmer, Jay Silverheels, Jack Elam, Jack Ingram.

Jeff Chandler again plays Cochise, the Apache warrior who tries to prevent more Indian wars but does not quite succeed. This above-average treatment of the great Apache leader benefits from Chandler's dignity and stature.

BATTLE AT ELDERBUSH GULCH (aka: BATTLE OF ELDERBUSH GULCH)

Biograph, 1914, B&W, two reels. **Director:** D. W. Griffith; **Screenplay:** Griffith; **Cinematographer:** G. W. Bitzer; **Cast:** Lionel Barrymore, Elmer Booth, Kate Bruce, Harry Carey, Lillian Gish, Robert Harren, Dell Henderson, Charles Hill Mailes, Mae Marsh, Alfred Paget, Blanche Sweet, Henry B. Walthall.

Lillian Gish and Mae Marsh play two eastern girls who come in conflict with some particularly savage Indians. As usual D. W. Griffith makes good use of facial closeups and last-minute rescues. Although America was not that far past the pioneer days as a nation, the subject of the "Old West" had become a pivotal theme in western movie making as early as 1910. Shot in the San Fernando Valley by ace cinematographer Billy Bitzer, Griffith constructed a western town especially for the picture, making advanced usage of intercutting from one action sequence to another.

The story is that the baby used in the film's opening sequences was a black child that Griffith borrowed from a foundling home nearby because of the photogenic value of the dark eyes. By time the film was released as a two-reeler by Biograph, Griffith had left the studio to begin independent productions. A landmark western of the silent era, this is one of Griffith's best genre pieces, which film historian William Everson calls "a superb action film, with savage massacre scenes and brilliantly constructed edited battle scenes."

One of the movies' true pioneers, Griffith was totally devoted to the art of film and to developing new and dynamic means of storytelling. He made westerns because they provided him with a perfect framework to build upon stories of action and suspense. Most of his outstanding one- and two-reel westerns for Biograph were made in Hollywood, where the rugged scenery gave them a tremendous scenic advantage over their eastern counterparts. His other notable westerns during the period include *FIGHTING BLOOD* (1911) and *THE LAST DROP OF WATER* (1911), a precursor of the 1923 epic *THE COVERED WAGON*. Later came *The Massacre*, (made in 1912 but not released until 1914), an austere depiction of the Custer massacre, both antiwar and sympathetic to the Indian point of view. It was also one of the first films to use a moving camera. After the inflated *Scarlet Days* (1913), Griffith and the western parted ways.

BATTLE OF POWDER RIVER   See *TOMAHAWK*.

BATTLE OF THE ROGUE RIVER, THE

Columbia, 1954, Color, 71 min. **Producer:** Sam Katzman; **Director:** William Castle; **Screenplay:** Douglas Heyes; **Music:** Mischa Bakaleinikoff, George Dunning, W. Frank Haring, and Paul Sawtell; **Cinematographer:** Henry Freulich; **Editor:** Charles Nelson; **Cast:** George Montgomery, Richard Denning, Martha Hyer, John Crawford, Emory Parnell, Michael Granger.

Oregon is trying to become a state in 1850, but Major Frank Archer has two big obstacles. He has to deal with a bevy of hostile Indians with a history of defeating the army and a group of disgruntled whites who do not want statehood and are determined to keep the Indians on the warpath.

BATTLING OUTLAW   See *BILLY THE KID IN TEXAS*.

BATTLING WITH BUFFALO BILL

Universal, 1931, B&W, 12 episodes. **Producer:** Henry MacRae; **Director:** Ray Taylor; **Screenplay:** MacRae, Ella O'Neill, George H. Plympton, and William F. Cody; **Cast:** Tom Tyler, Rex Bell, Lucille Browne, Francis Ford, William Desmond, Jim Thorpe, Yakima Canutt, Chief Thunderbird, Bud Osborne.

Based on the book *The Great West That Was*, Yakima Canutt was second unit director in this 12-episode western adventure serial. Buffalo Bill (Tom Tyler) battles gambler Jim Rodney (Francis Ford), who is trying to scare off the townspeople so he can gain possession of a gold strike discovered in the area.

BEAST OF HOLLOW MOUNTAIN, THE (aka: *BESTIA DE LA MONTANA, LA* [Mexico], MONSTRUO DE LA MONTANA HUECCA, EL; VALLEY OF THE MISFITS)

Nassour-Brothers-Peliculas Rodriguez Productions/United Artists, 1956, Color, 81 min. **Producers:** Edward Nassour and William Nassour; **Director:** Nassour and Ismael Rodriguez; **Screenplay:** Robert Hill and Jack DeWitt; **Music:** Raul Lavista; **Cinematographer:** Jorge Stahl (Jorge Stahl Jr.); **Editors:** Fernando Martinez, Holbrook N. Todd, and Maury Wright; **Cast:** Guy Madison, Patricia Medina, Carlos Rivas, Mario Navarro, Pasqual Garcia Pena.

An American cowboy living in Mexico discovers that his cattle are being eaten by a giant prehistoric dinosaur. This unusual melding of western and monster themes, based on a story by Willis O'Brien, makes for an enjoyable and entertaining movie, topped by a clever ending. It was filmed in Mexico during the "golden age" of monster movies.

BEAUTY AND THE BANDIT

Monogram, 1946, B&W, 77 min. **Producer:** Scott R. Dunlap; **Director:** William Nigh; **Screenplay:** Charles Belden; **Music:** Edward J. Kay (director); **Cinematographer:** Harry Neumann; **Editor:** Fred Maguire; **Cast:** Gilbert Roland, Vida Aldana, Ramsay Ames, Martin Garralaga, William Gould, George J. Lewis, Glenn Strange.

A young Frenchman, traveling by stagecoach in Old California, is transporting a chest full of silver to complete a complex business deal in San Marino. But the stage is ambushed by a band of men whose leader is a mysterious bandido known as Cisco (Gilbert Roland). The bandit, who claims that the money was extorted over a period of many years from the poor people of California, stays behind with the Frenchman while his men escape with the silver. Little does he know that the Frenchman is actually a lovely woman in disguise. When the truth is unveiled, the two are irresistibly drawn to each other, and the plot thickens. (See also *CISCO KID, THE.*)

BELLE LE GRANDE Republic, 1951, B&W, 90 min. **Producer:** Herbert Yates; **Director:** Allan Dwan; **Screenplay:** D. D. Beauchamp; **Music:** Victor Young; **Cinematographer:** Reggie Lanning; **Editor:** Harry Keller; **Cast:** Vera Hruba Ralston, John Carroll, Muriel Lawerence, Hope Emerson, William Ching, Grant Withers, John Qualen, Harry Morgan.

Set in Virginia City, a lady gambler (Vera Ralston) is willing to play hardball to win back her no-account guy (John Carroll), even though he has a yen for her younger sister. One of Republic's bigger productions, this uneven film does have its moments, including an epic fire scene, a happy ending, a melodic musical score, and a talented cast of supporting players. A young James Arness, *Gunsmoke's* future Matt Dillon, can be seen briefly in the great fire scene.

BELLE OF THE NINETIES Paramount, 1951, B&W, 73 min, VT, DVD. **Producer:** William Le Baron; **Director:** Leo McCarey; **Screenplay:** Mae West; **Music:** Arthur Johnson; **Cinematographer:** Karl Struss; **Editor:** Le Roy Stone; **Cast:** Mae West, Roger Pryor, Johnny Mack Brown, John Miljan, Katherine De Mille, James Donlan, Gene Austin, Benny Baker, Stuart Holmes, Harry Woods, Edward Gargan, Libby Taylor.

Mae West is an entertainer who loves men and jewelry and prefers to be looked over rather than overlooked. As usual West's witty remarks (which she also scripted) are laden with innuendo, allowing her to get around the censors and entertain her audience at the same time. Her gallery of male admirers includes Roger Pryor as boxer Tiger Kid and Johnny Mack Brown as Brooks Claybourne, a smitten young man who sends Mae a diamond necklace.

In addition to her wit and witticisms, the film's soundtrack includes "Memphis Blues," "Troubled Waters," "When a St. Louis Woman Goes Down to New Orleans" and "My American Beauty." The ever-popular standard "My Old Flame," sung by West and written by the team Arthur Johnson and Sam Coslow, was introduced in the film by West with Duke Ellington and his Orchestra. Ellington also recorded the song, as did such artists as Billie Holiday, Stan Getz, and Benny Goodman.

BELLE STARR 20th Century Fox, Color, 87 min. **Producer:** Kenneth Macgowan; **Director:** Irving Cummings; **Screenplay:** Lamar Trotti, Niven Bush (story) and Cameron Rogers (story); **Music:** Alfred Newman; **Cinematographers:** Ernest Palmer and Ray Rennahan; **Editor:** Robert L. Simpson; **Cast:** Randolph Scott, Gene Tierney, Dana Andrews, Shepperd Strudwick, Elizabeth Patterson, Chill Wills, Louise Beavers, Olin Howlin, Joe Sawyer,

Charles Trowbridge, Mae Marsh, Kermit Maynard, Charles Middleton.

An aristocratic Southern belle (Gene Tierney), whose family lost their land to Northerners during the Civil War, marries Confederate guerrilla leader Sam Starr (Randolph Scott), and the two continue their fight against Yankee carpetbaggers. A highly fictionalized and overly romanticized film, Tierney's Belle Starr is a genteel southern woman who turns to crime only out of the tragedy of the times. In reality, however, the true Belle was a disreputable woman whose claims to fame includes being the first woman to be tried in federal court for horse stealing. Nevertheless, the beautiful Tierney is a delight to behold on any screen—fictionalized or not—and Scott lends an authenticity to any film with a western label. A television version in 1980 with Elizabeth Montgomery in the title role is historically vacuous as well.

BELLE STARR'S DAUGHTER 20th Century Fox, 1948, B&W, 85 min. **Producer:** Edward L. Alperson; **Director:** Leslie Selander; **Screenplay:** W. R. Burnett; **Music:** Edward Kilenyi (director); **Cinematographer:** William A. Sickner; **Editor:** Jason H. Bernie; **Cast:** George Montgomery, Rod Cameron, Ruth Roman, Wallace Ford, Charles Kemper, Jack Lambert, Fred Libby, Isabel Jewell, Larry Johns.

The daughter of the infamous Belle (Ruth Roman) arrives at the town where her mother was murdered determined to find the killer. A marshal is blamed for the murder. Good cast and the steady direction of Leslie Selander makes this film a "sleeper" of sorts and worth seeing.

BELLE STARR STORY, THE (aka: *IL MIO CORPO PER UN POKER*, Italy) High Desert Films, 1967, Color, 90 min. **Producer:** Oscar Righini; **Director:** Lina Wertmuller (as Nathan Wich); **Teleplay:** Wertmuller (as Wich); **Music:** Charles DuMont; **Cinematographer:** Alessandro Deva; **Editor:** Renato Chinquini; **Cast:** Elsa Martinelli, Robert Woods, George Eastman, Dan Harrison, Eugene Walter, Francesca Richini.

As a young girl, Belle witnesses the brutal murder of her parents and is betrayed by her trusted uncle. She is befriended by a young bandit, and before long they become lovers. Belle's exploits quickly become the talk of the West. This dull, dreadful, and fabricated account of Belle's life is just plain bad.

BELLS OF CAPISTRANO Republic, 1942, B&W, 78 min. **Producer:** Harry Grey; **Director:** William Morgan; **Screenplay:** Lawrence Kimble; **Music:** Milton Ager, Jerry Charlton, Walter Donaldson, Thomas Holer, Sol Meyer, Jimmy Morgan, Fred Stryker, and Jack Yellen; **Cinematographer:** Reggie Lanning; **Editor:** Edward Mann; **Cast:** Gene Autry, Smiley Burnette, Virginia Grey, Lucien Littlefield, Morgan Conway, Claire Du Brey, Charles Cane, Joe Struch

Jr., Maria Shelton, Tristram Coffin (uncredited), Jay Novello (uncredited).

When her competition in the rodeo business gets too tough, rodeo owner Jennifer (Virginia Grey) asks for help. Singer Gene Autry and his crew join the rodeo, which is targeted for destruction by a rival outfit. This was Autry's last film before joining the service in 1942.

BELLS OF CORONADO   Republic, 1950, B&W, 67 min, VT. **Producer:** Edward J. White; **Director:** William Witney; **Screenplay:** Sloan Nibley; **Music:** R. Dale Butts and Stanley Wilson; **Cinematographer:** John MacBurnie; **Editor:** Tony Martinelli; **Cast:** Roy Rogers, Dale Evans, Pat Brady, Grant Withers, Leo Cleary, Clifton Young, Robert Bice, Stuart Randall, Rex Lease, Edmund Cobb.

Roy Rogers is a modern-day insurance agent who thwarts an evil gang of foreign agents headed by Grant Withers. The gang is determined to smuggle uranium to unfriendly powers. Filmed vividly in Trucolor, the film includes such songs as "Bells of Coronado," "Got No Time for the Blues," and "Save a Smile for a Rainy Day." This speedy and fast-paced Rogers entry combines good action with an entertaining story.

BELLS OF ROSARITA   Republic, 1945, B&W, 68 min, VT. **Producer:** Edward J. White (as Eddie White); **Director:** Frank McDonald; **Screenplay:** Jack Townley; **Music:** Betty Best, Jospeh Dubin, Jack Elliott, Robert Mitchell, Morton Scott, and Raymond Scott; **Cinematographer:** Ernest Miller; **Editor:** Arthur Roberts; **Cast:** Roy Rogers, George "Gabby" Hayes, Dale Evans, Adele Mara, Grant Withers, Addison Richards, Roy Barcroft, Bob Nolan and the Sons of the Pioneers, William "Wild Bill" Elliott, Allan Lane, Don "Red" Barry, Robert Livingston, Sunset Carson.

Dale Evans inherits a circus, but her dead father's partner (Grant Withers) tries to take it away. Roy Rogers and Bob Nolan are filming a movie on location at the circus, so they invite fellow movie star cowboys "Wild Bill" Elliott, Allan Lane, Don "Red" Barry, Robert Livingston, and Sunset Carson, to put on a lively show and ultimately foil the bad guys. This is a thoroughly enjoyable horse opera with lots of good music and a vintage performance by Adele Mara.

BELLS OF SAN ANGELO   Republic, 1947, B&W, 78 min, VT. **Producer:** Edward J. White; **Director:** William Witney; **Screenplay:** Sloan Nibley; **Music:** Mort Glickman and Morton Scott; **Cinematographer:** Jack K. Marta; **Editor:** Lester Orlebeck; **Cast:** Roy Rogers, Dale Evans, Andy Devine, John McGuire, Olaf Hytten, David Sharpe, Fritz Leiber, Hank Patterson, Fred "Snowflake" Toones, Eddie Acuff, Bob Nolan.

Lawman Roy joins novelist Dale in search of criminals who are smuggling silver across the Mexican border. Lots of gun-play and plenty of action makes for an exciting ride. One of Republic's best Roy Rogers efforts, the film's musical entries include the title tune, "Hot Lead," and "I Like to Get up Early in the Morning."

BELOW THE BORDER   Monogram, 1942, B&W, 57 min. **Producer:** Scott R. Dunlap; **Director:** Howard Bretherton; **Screenplay:** Jess Bowers (Adele S. Buffington); **Cinematographer:** Harry Neumann; **Editor:** Carl Pierson; **Cast:** Buck Jones, Tim McCoy, Raymond Hatton, Linda Brent, Dennis Moore, Charles King, Eva Puig, Roy Barcroft, Bud Osborne.

This exciting Rough Riders action yarn has Buck Roberts (Buck Jones) going underground as a bandit, while Tim McCall (Tim McCoy) poses as a cattle buyer. Their object is to trap and capture evil Ed Scully (Roy Barcroft), who has been rustling cattle in Border City. Sandy (Raymond Hatton) is busy collecting information by posing as a saloon janitor. (See also *ARIZONA BOUND*.)

BEND OF THE RIVER (aka: WHERE THE RIVER BENDS, UK)   Universal, 1952, Color, 91 min, VT. **Producer:** Aaron Rosenberg; **Director:** Anthony Mann; **Screenplay:** Borden Chase; **Music:** Hans J. Salter; **Cinematographer:** Irving Glassberg; **Editor:** Russell F. Schoengrath (Russell Schoengarth); **Cast:** James Stewart, Arthur Kennedy, Julie Adams, Rock Hudson, Lori Nelson, J. C. Flippen, Chubby Johnson, Royal Dano, Harry Morgan (as Henry Morgan), Frances Bavier, Howard Petrie, Stepin Fetchit.

Filmed in Mt. Hood, Oregon, *Bend on the River* marks the second teaming of director Anthony Mann and star James Stewart. With Mann at the helm, a grizzled Stewart plays a former border raider and consummate loner, a man of psychological complexities who teams with another outsider, Arthur Kennedy, after having saved him from the noose. "I just don't like hangings," Stewart tells a bewildered Kennedy, an ex-Missouri Raider himself.

Together they take on the task of leading a wagon train to central Oregon's Columbia River country. (Farmers were totally dependent on supply shipments from Portland during their first years in Oregon.) But Stewart and Kennedy clash over the supplies destined for the settlers. The discovery of gold makes Portland a boomtown, and Kennedy wants to sell the supplies to miners at inflated prices. Stewart in turn is obsessed with seeing that the farmers get what they need. The result is a climactic fight to the death between Stewart and Kennedy, the man he had earlier saved from the rope.

Based on William Gulick's novel *Bend of the Snake*, the film is faithful to history. Director Anthony Mann was fascinated with westerns and is credited with "reinventing" the genre with a string of remarkable films in the 1950s. Like his contemporary Budd Boetticher, Mann has acquired a certain cult status around the world, and his films have been examined and reexamined in cinema classes in the United States and abroad.

James Stewart (right) and Arthur Kennedy in Bend of the River (UNIVERSAL/AUTHOR'S COLLECTION)

A year earlier Mann and Stewart had scored points with *WINCHESTER '73*, Stewart's first western since *DESTRY RIDES AGAIN* (1939). While Stewart worked regularly with Mann and became the director's archetypal western "hero" in the 1950s, the two actually went back a long way together. In a 1969 interview with Christopher Wicking and Barrie Pattison, Mann related how Stewart, fresh out of college, was in a summer company at the Red Barn Theater in Locust Valley, New York, headed by Mann, who had directed the fledgling actor in a couple of plays.

However, while Stewart often talked about the directors he had worked with (Capra, Hitchcock, Ford, Stevens) he rarely mentioned Mann, the director who provided Stewart with a tougher image than he ever imagined and whose pictures more than anyone else's were responsible for making Stewart the biggest mid-century male star. Purportedly the actor and director had a major rift in the mid-50s which had not healed by the time Anthony Mann died in 1967. When Mann went into production with *THE MAN OF THE WEST*, which many consider his finest western and one suited totally for Stewart, it was with Gary Cooper in the lead.

BENEATH WESTERN SKIES Republic, 1944, B&W, 56 min. **Producer:** Louis Gray; **Director:** Spencer Gordon Bennet; **Screenplay:** Albert DeMond and Bob Williams (Robert Creighton Williams); **Cast:** Robert Livingston, Smiley Burnette, Effie Laird, Frank Jaquet, Tom London, Charles Miller.

To combat lawlessness in her town, teacher Carrie Stokes (Effie Laird) writes to her former students searching for a lawman. Johnny Revere (Robert Livingston) arrives and starts cleaning up the town, but his efforts are compromised when he loses his memory after being hit on the head. One of three "John Paul Revere" horse operas Livingston did at Republic. It's a good one.

BEST OF THE BADMEN RKO, 1951, Color, 84 min. **Producer:** Herman Schlom; **Director:** William D. Russell; **Screenplay:** Robert Hardy Andrews and John Twist; **Music:** Paul Sawtell; **Cinematographer:** Edward Cronjager; **Editor:** Desmond Marquette; **Cast:** Robert Ryan, Claire Trevor, Jack Buetel, Robert Preston, Walter Brennan, Bruce

Cabot, John Archer, Lawrence Tierney, Barton MacLane, Robert J. Wilke, Tom Tyler.

Set in post-Civil War days, Union officer Jeff Clanton (Robert Ryan) is convicted of murder by a kangaroo court. He escapes and joins a band of outlaws, including Frank and Jesse James (Tom Tyler and Lawrence Tierney) and the Younger Brothers (Bruce Cabot, Robert J. Wilke, and John Cliff). Together they declare a vendetta against Robert Preston's corrupt detective agency, which was responsible for setting up Clanton. With an excellent cast including an off-beat performance by Preston (in his pre-*Music Man* days) as bad guy Mathew Fowler and a touching performance by Claire Trevor as Lily, Preston's disgruntled wife, this over-looked film is a must for any true western fan.

BETWEEN FIGHTING MEN KBS/World Wide, 1932, B&W, 62 min, VT. **Producers:** Samuel Bischoff, Burt Kelly, and William Saal; **Director:** Forrest Sheldon; **Screenplay:** Betty Burbridge and Forrest Sheldon; **Cinematographer:** Ted D. McCord; **Editor:** David Burg; **Cast:** Ken Maynard, Ruth Hall, Josephine Dunn, Wallace MacDonald, Albert J. Smith, Walter Law, James Bradbury Jr., John Pratt, Roy Buck, Jim Corey.

Ken (Ken Maynard) fights with brother Wally (Wallace Mac-Donald) for the affections of a pretty girl while trying to fend off a conflict between cattlemen and sheepmen. Slim, hand-some, and an incredible stunt and trick rider, Ken Maynard starred in a series of 18 westerns at First National in the 1920s. With the advent of sound, Maynard fluctuated between major companies and cheap independents. He made many films with Universal, which was the one major company that maintained a full B western schedule. Although he did not take well to dialogue, Maynard's Universal westerns were colorful, unpredictable, and full of action. He also did six less-than-satisfying entries in Monogram's *The Trail Blazers* series. (See also *LUCKY LARKIN.*)

BETWEEN MEN Supreme, 1935, B&W, 59 min, VT. **Producer:** A. W. Hackel; **Director:** Robert N. Bradbury; **Screenplay:** Charles F. Royal (as Charles Francis Royal); **Cinematographer:** Bert Longenecker; **Editor:** S. Roy Luby; **Cast:** Johnny Mack Brown, Beth Marion, William Farnum, Earl Dwire, Lloyd Ingraham, Frank Ball, Barry Downing, Forrest Taylor, Horace B. Carpenter.

The complicated plot line has Johnny Wellington (Johnny Mack Brown) heading west to find the rejected granddaughter of the man who raised him. In his pursuit he also finds his real father (William Farnum), but the two men do not realize they are father and son and eventually clash. The fist fight between Brown and Farnum is a real slugfest.

Beth Marion plays Gail Winters, Johnny Mack Brown's love interest. *Between Men* was her first film, and she worked with Brown again the following year in *EVERYMAN'S LAW* before marrying stuntman Cliff Lyons. She recalls Brown, a former University of Alabama all-American football star, as a

"very nice fellow and a real gentleman. We filmed in Lone Pine, California, and conditions were quite different back then. We worked 24 hours straight one day. Remember that was before we had the Screen Actor's Guild." This well-done B western played to good reviews. (See also *GAMBLING TER-ROR, THE.*)

BEYOND THE LAST FRONTIER Republic, 1943, B&W, 60 min. **Producer:** Herbert Yates; **Director:** Howard Bretherton; **Screenplay:** John K. Butler and Morton Grant; **Music:** Mort Glickman; **Cinematographer:** Bud Thackery; **Editor:** Charles Craft; **Cast:** Eddie Dew, Smiley Burnette, Robert Mitchum (Bob Mitchum), Harry Woods, Lorraine Miller, Ernie Adams.

In this film—one of a pair Robert Mitchum made with Eddie Dew—the Texas Rangers try to stop border gunrunners by having one of their own infiltrate their gang.

Before becoming a big star, Robert Mitchum paid his dues. He worked in 15 films in 1943, including this western where, as Bob Mitchum, he plays a villain named Trigger Dolan. According to actor John Mitchum, his brother Robert had a very practical side. "Bob may have made disparaging remarks about these roles, but they were sure paying the bills."

BEYOND THE LAW Rayton Talking Pictures/Syndicate, 1930, B&W, 60 min. **Director:** J. P. McGowan; **Screenplay:** George Arthur Durlam (as G. A. Durlam); **Cinematographer:** Frank Newman; **Editor:** Arthur Brooks; **Cast:** Robert Frazer, Louis Lorraine, Jimmy Kane, Lane Chandler, Charles King, Edward Lynch.

A border saloon, half in California, half in Nevada, is a hang-out for frontier gangs in this fast-moving early sound film.

BEYOND THE PECOS (aka: BEYOND THE SEVEN SEAS, UK) Universal, 1945, B&W, 58 min. **Producer:** Oliver Drake; **Director:** Lambert Hillyer; **Screenplay:** Bennett Cohen; **Music:** Paul Sawtell; **Editor:** Ray Snyder; **Cast:** Rod Cameron, Eddie Dew, Fuzzy Knight, Jennifer Holt, Al Ferguson, Robert Homans, Frank Jacquet, Jack Rockwell.

Two men from feuding families fight over lucrative oil rights and the love of a pretty girl.

BEYOND THE PURPLE HILLS Columbia/Gene Autry Productions, 1950, B&W, 69 min. **Producer:** Armand Schaefer; **Director:** John English; **Screenplay:** Norman S. Hall; **Music:** Daniele Amfitheatrof, Mischa Bakalenikoff, R. H. Bassett, Sidney Cutner, George Duning, Paul Mertz, Heintz Roemheld, Louis Silvers, and Marlin Skiles; **Cinematographer:** William Bradford; **Editor:** Richard Fantl; **Cast:** Gene Autry, Pat Buttram, Joe Dennison, Don Beddoe, James Millican, Don Reynolds, Hugh O'Brian, Roy Gordon, Robert J. Wilke, Gregg Barton.

Gene Autry plays a hick town sheriff who must arrest Jack Beaumont (Hugh O'Brian), even though he believes Jack is innocent of his father's murder. He then sets out to prove his friend's innocence. This is an early film entry for O'Brian, who made his screen debut in 1950 and later starred as TV's Bat Masterson. (See also *TUMBLING TUMBLEWEEDS*.)

BEYOND THE RIO GRANDE Biltmore, 1930, B&W, 60 min, 6 reels. **Producer:** F. E. Douglas; **Director:** Harry S. Webb (as Harry Webb); **Music:** Henry Taylor; **Cinematographer:** William Nobles; **Editor:** Frederick Paine; **Cast:** Jack Perrin, Franklyn Farnum, Charline Burt, Emma Tansey, Jay Wilsey.

When his partner robs a bank, a man is falsely accused of the crime and forced to flee south of the border in this early talkie, interesting for fans of Jack Perrin and Franklyn Farnum. (See also *APACHE KID'S ESCAPE, THE*.)

BEYOND THE ROCKIES RKO-Pathé, 1932, B&W, 60 min. **Producer:** David O. Selznick; **Director:** Fred Allen; **Screenplay:** Oliver Drake; **Cinematographer:** Ted D. Mccord; **Editor:** William Clemens; **Cast:** Tom Keene, Rochelle Hudson, Marie Wells, Julian Rivero, Ernie Adams, Tom London, William Welsh, Hank Bell, Ted Adams.

When cattle rustling becomes a problem in a section of Texas, the government sends an undercover agent to investigate. David O. Selznick was executive producer of this early oater, which features Tom Keene at his manly best.
    RKO-Pathé, soon to be RKO Radio, began its serial westerns with Tom Keene as its star. Genuinely handsome and a reasonably good actor, he handled action well but was never totally at ease with horses. His RKO films were carefully made and notable for big-scale climaxes. Born George Duryea, he played lead roles in major productions until 1931, when he changed his name to Tom Keene and began starring in numerous westerns, starting with *Sundown Trail* in 1931, his first series feature. Other series films include *Freighters of Destiny* (1931); *PARTNERS, Ghost Valley, Come On Danger, Saddle Buster* (1932); *THE CHEYENNE KID, CROSSFIRE, Son of the Border, SCARLET RIVER* (1933).

BEYOND THE SACRAMENTO Columbia, 1940, B&W, 58 min. **Producer:** Leon Barsha; **Director:** Lambert Hillyer; **Screenplay:** George Meehan; **Editor:** James Sweeney; **Cast:** William "Wild Bill" Elliott, Evelyn Keyes, Dub Taylor, Frank LaRue, Don Beddoe, Bradley Page, Norman Willis.

Settlers in California are plagued by lawlessness until Bill Elliott rides into town and tries to change things. Helmed by the capable Lambert Hillyer, who directed films for William S. Hart, this film features a good performance by versatile Evelyn Keyes.

BEYOND THE SEVEN SEAS See *BEYOND THE PECOS*.

BIG BONANZA Republic, 1945, B&W, 68 min. **Producer:** Edward J. White; **Director:** George Archainbaud; **Screenplay:** Paul Gangelin, Dorrell McGowan, and Stuart McGowan; **Cinematographer:** Reggie Lanning; **Editor:** Tony Martinelli; **Cast:** Richard Arlen, Robert Livingston, Jane Frazee, George "Gabby" Hayes, Lynn Roberts, Bobby Driscoll.

A Union soldier wrongly accused of cowardice heads west to find a new life. Once there he meets up with an old friend who is both a gambling house proprietor and the same man who framed him on the false charge. Richard Arlen and Robert Livingston are the good and bad guys in this top-notch Republic feature.

BIG BOY RIDES AGAIN Beacon Pictures, 1935, B&W, 55 min. **Producers:** Arthur Alexander and Max Alexander; **Director:** Albert Herman; **Screenplay:** William L. Nolte; **Cinematographer:** Henry Forbes; **Editor:** Ralph Holt; **Cast:** Guinn "Big Boy" Williams, Connie Bergen, Lafe McKee, Frank Ellis, Charles K. French, Augie Gomez, Bud Osborne.

When a man who comes back to town to claim the estate of his father, who was shot by a masked killer, he also sets out to find the identity of his father's murderer.

BIG CALIBRE Supreme Pictures Corp., 1935, B&W, 58 min. **Producer:** A. W. Hackell; **Director:** Robert Bradbury; **Screenplay:** Bradbury and Perry Murdoch; **Cinematographer:** John Alton and William Hyer; **Editor:** F. Roy Luby; **Cast:** Bob Steele, Peggy Campbell, Forrest Taylor, Georgia O'Dell, William Quinn, John Elliott, Earl Dwire, Frank Ball.

A young man is intent on avenging his father's murder committed by a grotesque chemist who uses gas to kill his victims. Director Robert Bradbury cowrote the screenplay and directs son Bob Steele in this routine oater.

BIG COUNTRY, THE United Artists, 1958, Color, 166 min, VT. **Producers:** William Wyler and Gregory Peck; **Director:** Wyler; **Screenplay:** James R. Webb, Sy Bartlett, and Robert Wilder; **Music:** Jerome Moross; **Cinematographer:** Franz F. Planer; **Editor:** Robert Swink; **Cast:** Gregory Peck, Jean Simmons, Carroll Baker, Charlton Heston, Burl Ives, Charles Bickford, Alfonso Bedoya, Chuck Connors, Chuck Hayward, Buff Brady, Jim Burk, Dorothy Adams.

In *The Big Country*, Gregory Peck, who coproduced the film, provides an interesting and less-than-traditional hero. He plays an eastern sea captain who heads west to marry Patricia Terrill (Carroll Baker) and soon finds himself in the throes of a long-standing range war. Charles Bickford plays rancher Henry Terrill, who is embroiled in a murderous feud for the control of vital water rights with the Hannasseys, headed by old Rufus Hannassey, who is played by Burl Ives.

An enormously successful, large-scale western that some consider a veiled allegory of the Cold War, *The Big Country* earned over $4 million in distributors' domestic rentals and sported a big-name cast, Ives's Oscar-winning performance, stunning photography, and a brilliant musical score by Jerome Moross. Peck, Jean Simmons, Carroll Baker, and Charlton Heston (in an extremely strong role as Terrill's truculent ranch foreman) provide appealing leads, but it is longtime character actors Ives and Bickford, as two embittered patriarchs battling out a 34-year-old feud over neutral water rights, who really hold the story together.

William Wyler's aim was always to craft a good story. Ives is superb as burly Rufus Hannassey, a role that garnered him an Oscar and a Golden Globe Award; and former Major League baseball player Chuck Connors is especially convincing as Buck, Ives's uncouth and vulgar son whom Rufus is forced to kill. His grief as he cradles his dying son in his arms conveys a true sense of hopelessness and loss, before Hannassey and Terrill face off in a final encounter between the two "selfish, ruthless, vicious old men," as Jim McCay (Peck) calls them.

Director Wyler's experience in the western genre was somewhat limited before helming *The Big Country*. His only significant works in this genre were *HELL'S HEROES* (1930), his first talking film; *THE WESTERNER* (1940), with an Oscar-winning performance by Walter Brennan; and *FRIENDLY PERSUASION* (1956), which, like *The Big Country*, enforces the pacifist leanings of its hero.

Filmed in epic splendor for the big screen in a variety of locations, including Arizona's Canyon de Chelly National Park; California's Mojave Desert; Red Rock Canyon State Park; and Stockton, California, the film is an expansive visual delight. Audiences loved it; critics were divided. *Films in Review* called the story "a mass of inconsistencies" and faulted Wyler's direction. *Variety*, however, decreed that "*The Big Country* lives up to its title," while *Time* called it "a starkly beautiful, carefully written, classic western that demands comparison with *Shane*."

BIG HAND FOR THE LITTLE LADY (aka: BIG DEAL AT DODGE CITY, UK)   Warner Bros., 1966, Color, 95 min, VT. **Producer:** Fielder Cook; **Director:** Cook; **Screenplay:** Sidney Carroll; **Music:** David Raskin; **Cinematographer:** Lee Garmes; **Editor:** George R. Rohrs; **Cast:** Henry Fonda, Joanne Woodward, Jason Robards, Paul Ford, Charles Bickford, Burgess Meredith, Kevin McCarthy, Robert Middleton, John Quelan.

The wealthiest men in the territory around Laredo get together for a poker game once a year. The stakes are unlimited. They include an undertaker (Charles Bickford), a lawyer (Kevin McCarthy), and a very rich rancher (Jason Robards). Enter a newcomer (Henry Fonda) who, despite protestations from his wife (Joanne Woodward), sits in on the game. When the pot reaches $20,000 in Fonda's favor, the excitement causes him to have a heart attack—so his wife takes over his hand. "How do you play this game," she asks the boys sitting

around the table. Some pretty unusual events loom ahead as the stakes grow higher and higher.

This comedy/drama is a joy to watch, and the performances from many of the industry's top character actors are all first rate. The film's visual style reveals director Fielder Cook's television background, and cinematographer Lee Garmes makes splendid use of angled shots and facial nuances. The suspense grows as viewers are treated to a surprise ending.

BIG JACK   MGM, 1949, B&W, 85 min. **Producer:** Gottfried Reinhardt; **Director:** Richard Thorpe; **Cinematographer:** Robert Surtees; **Editor:** George Boemler; **Screenplay:** Marvin Borowsky, Gene Fowler, Ben Hecht (uncredited), Robert Thoeren, and Otto Van Eyss; **Cast:** Wallace Beery, Richard Conte, Marjorie Main, Edward Arnold, Vanessa Brown, Jack Lambert.

Marjorie Main and Wallace Beery are vagabond thieves in colonial America. Richard Conte plays Dr. Meade, a moralistic doctor who wants to reform them. Wallace Beery's last film is an average finale for the great actor, who died that same year at age 64.

BIG JAKE   National General Pictures (A Batjac Production), 1971, Color, 109 min, VT. **Producer:** Michael Wayne; **Director:** George Sherman; **Screenplay:** Harry Julian Fink and Rita Fink; **Music:** Elmer Bernstein; **Cinematographer:** William Clothier; **Editor:** Harry Gerstad; **Cast:** John Wayne, Richard Boone, Maureen O'Hara, Patrick Wayne, Chris Mitchum, Bobby Vinton, Bruce Cabot, Glenn Corbett, Harry Carey Jr., John Doucette, Jim Davis, John Agar, Gregg Palmer, Robert Warner, Jim Burke, Dean Smith, Ethan Wayne, Virginia Caspers, William Walker, Jerry Gatlin, Tom Hennesy, Don Epperson, Everett Creach, Jeff Wingfield, Hank Worden, Chuck Roberson.

In 1909 John Fain (Richard Boone) and his gang attack the Texas ranch of the McCandles family, killing 10 people and kidnapping little Jake McCandles (Ethan Wayne) for a million-dollar ransom. In desperation, the boy's grandmother Martha (Maureen O'Hara) summons her long-estranged husband Jacob (John Wayne) back from Mexico. Together with his Apache friend Sam Sharpshooter (Bruce Cabot), an old canine named Dog, and his two estranged sons (Patrick Wayne and Chris Mitchum), Big Jake takes the ransom money and sets out to retrieve the grandson he has never seen.

Wayne is just right as Big Jake McCandles in this unusually violent, sometimes funny, and always entertaining western. Boone is a worthy adversary as the evil John Fain, an arch villain deluxe. Wayne assembled a cast of western reliables, including Harry Carey Jr. (as a bad guy this time), John Agar; Jim Davis; John Doucette; Glenn Corbett; Gregg Palmer; stuntman supreme Dean Smith ("Kid" Duffy); old stalwarts Bruce Cabot, Richard Boone, and Hank Worden; popular young actors Patrick Wayne and Chris Mitchum; singer Bobby Vinton; and Wayne's favorite leading lady Maureen O'Hara (their fifth and final film together).

The banter between Big Jake and his lippy sons is priceless, and the old man is not beyond teaching the boys a lesson or two. When son James (Patrick Wayne) insists on calling him "Daddy," Big Jake gives him a lesson in elocution and manners at the short end of his fists, of course: "You can call me father, or you can call me Jacob, you can call me Jake. You can call me a dirty son of a bitch. But if you ever call me daddy again, I'll finish this fight."

After the Fain gang has finally been dispatched in a brutal climax, little Jake (Ethan Wayne) approaches the towering man who has rescued him and hesitantly says, "Grandfather!" The towering man embraces his grandson for the first time and answers, "You're damn right I am!"

While Wayne was delighted to work with his 10-year-old son Ethan, and father and son worked well together, others in the cast were far from enchanted. Christopher Mitchum, for one, recalls that young Ethan was "a real pain in the ass . . . and Duke knew it . . . Any time Duke heard him mouth off to anybody or be disrespectful, he'd grab him by the back of the coat and say, 'Now Ethan, You can't do that!' He'd straighten him out, but as soon as [Duke] turned his back, he'd get cocky again. Oh, he was a brat. People didn't know what to do, he was Duke's kid."

There is a historical bent as well. The arched courtyard utilized in the bloody climax of *Big Jake* was actually used by Pancho Villa and his men when they slaughtered 750 persons. The film marked the 11th and final pairing of John Wayne and actor Bruce Cabot. Cabot, a longtime film veteran and Wayne's good friend, died the following year from cancer. The film remains one of Wayne's most popular pictures and can be seen constantly on television.

BIG LAND, THE (aka: STAMPEDE, UK) Jaguar, 1957, Color, 92 min. **Producers:** George C. Bertholon and Alan Ladd (uncredited); **Director:** Gordon Douglas; **Screenplay:** David Dortot (story) and Martin Rackin; **Music:** David Buttolph; **Cinematographer:** John F. Seitz; **Editor:** Thomas Reilly; **Cast:** Alan Ladd, Virginia Mayo, Edmond O'Brien, Anthony Caruso, Julie Bishop, John Qualen, Don Castle, David Ladd, John Doucette.

John Wayne, Patrick Wayne, and Christopher Mitchum in Big Jake (NGP/COURTESY OF CHRISTOPHER MITCHUM)

Richard Boone as Jack Fain in Big Jake (NGP/AUTHOR'S COLLECTION)

Based on the novel *The Big Deal* by Frank Gruber, the movie's plot concerns cattle owners and grain farmers joining together to bring a railroad link to Texas. Alan Ladd plays Chad Morgan, an ex-soldier who leads a group of fellow Texans on a cattle ride to Missouri where, they heard, there was a railroad for shipping.

When Morgan takes a calculated risk and blunders, his men take off, leaving him to fend for himself. He finds shelter in a stable where he encounters a wanderer named Jagger (Edmond O'Brien), whose promising career as an architect has been defeated by alcohol. They return to Jagger's hometown, where Chad and Jagger's beautiful sister Helen (Virginia Mayo) are immediately attracted to one another. Chad and Helen encourage Jagger to give up drink and to design the new town, with funds and labor to be supplied by local farmers who need the spur to get the meat to market. Chad is sure he can persuade the Texans to lead the cattle drives to get the new spur, which would assure the railroad plenty of business—but not before a cast of villains decide they have different ideas.

An underrated actor whom costar Virginia Mayo called "the most sensitive, tender actor I ever worked with," Alan Ladd turns in his finest performance since *SHANE*, and his production company (Jaguar) came up with a solid film. Edmond O'Brien delivers an excellent portrayal as the beleaguered Jagger. Ladd's son David made his acting debut in this credible film. The following year the two would stir hearts in the touching western *THE PROUD REBEL*, making the young Ladd a sought-after child star.

BIG NORTH, THE See *WILD NORTH, THE*.

BIG SHOW, THE Republic, 1936, B&W, 70 min. **Producer:** Nat Levine; **Director:** Mack V. Wright; **Screenplay:** Dorrell McGowan and Stuart E. McGowan; **Music:** Ted Koehler, Sam H. Stept, and Ned Washington (songs); **Cinematographers:** Edgar Lyons and William Nobles; **Editor:** Robert Jahns; **Cast:** Gene Autry, Smiley Burnette, Kay Hughes, Sally Payne, William Newell, Max Terhune.

Gene Autry confuses two girls by being both himself and his stunt double during the Texas Centennial in Dallas. It begins when a stuck-up cowboy hero refuses to appear at a rodeo, and his stunt double takes his place and eventually gets mixed up with gangsters. This entertaining Autry feature, filmed at the Texas Centennial Exposition with a good number of country and western acts, marks the screen debut of Max Terhune. Before his days as "King of the Cowboys," Roy Rogers appeared in this film as a member of the uncredited Sons of the Pioneers. (See also *TUMBLING TUMBLEWEEDS*.)

BIG SKY, THE RKO, 1952, B&W, 140 min, VT. **Producer:** Howard Hawks; **Director:** Hawks; **Screenplay:** Dudley Nichols; **Music:** Dimitri Tiomkin; **Cinematographer:** Russell Harlan; **Editor:** Christian Nyby; **Cast:** Kirk Douglas, Dewey Martin, Elizabeth Threatt, Arthur Hunnicutt, Buddy Baer, Steven Geray, Hank Worden, Jim Davis, Henri Letondal, Robert Hunter, Booth Coleman, Paul Frees, Frank DeKorva, Guy Wilkerson, Don Beddoe.

Two adventurous fur traders, frontiersmen Boone Caudill (Dewey Martin) and Jim Deakins (Kirk Douglas) join up with Boone's Uncle Zeb (Arthur Hunnicutt, in an Oscar-nominated performance) for a boisterous fur-trading expedition up the Mississippi and into uncharted Blackfoot Indian territory. Both Douglas and Martin are well suited to be rugged frontiersmen. They brawl in taverns, drink heavily, and even sing together to the tune of "Whiskey Leave Me Alone" before they finally get around to the business of traveling the 2,000 miles on a riverboat to trade for valuable beaver pelts with the hostile Blackfoot. In the meantime both men vie for the affections of a Blackfoot Indian princess played by Elizabeth Threatt, while Douglas endures having his finger cut off.

One of American cinema's great storytellers, director Howard Hawks excelled in a variety of genres. In his first Western since his highly acclaimed *RED RIVER* (1948), he again plays on the theme of camaraderie and conflict, which we have come to expect from a Hawks western. A sprawling outdoor drama nominated for two Academy Awards, *The Big Sky*, although a bit too long, is a compelling film that retains a considerable amount of Americana and enables us to better understand the history and lore of the Blackfoot. Russell Harlan's marvelous black-and-white photography captures the grandeur and the majesty of the natural surroundings, much of which was shot in Grand Teton National Park.

BIG SOMBRERO, THE Columbia, 1949, Color, 82 min. **Producer:** Armand Shaefer; **Director:** Frank McDonald; **Screenplay:** Henry Batista and Clifford D. Shank; **Cinematographer:** William Bradford; **Editors:** Batista and Shank; **Cast:** Gene Autry, Elena Verdugo, Steve Dunne, George J. Lewis, Vera Marsh.

A cowboy tries to stop a crook from marrying a girl for her ranch, which the man wants to sell in this very entertaining Gene Autry offering. The soundtrack includes "My Darling Clementine" and the hit song "My Adobe Hacienda." (See also *TUMBLING TUMBLEWEEDS*.)

BIG STAMPEDE, THE Warner Bros., 1932, B&W, 54 min, VT. **Producer:** Leon Schlesinger; **Director:** Tenny Wright; **Screenplay:** Kurt Kempler; **Cinematographer:** Ted McCord; **Editor:** Frank Ware; **Cast:** John Wayne, Noah Beery, Paul Hurst, Mae Madison, Luis Alberni, Berton Churchill.

It is the early pioneer days, and Deputy Sheriff John Steel (John Wayne) must bring down an evil cattle-rustling baron (Noah Beery) who is terrorizing the countryside and bumping off local lawmen. This early Wayne horse opera is a remake of the 1927 silent film *LAND BEYOND THE LAW*, based on the novel of the same name by Marion Jackson. It was remade by Warners in 1937 under the original title with Dick Foran in the starring role.

Wayne's series at Warner Bros. was carefully patterned after a silent Ken Maynard series, using both the basic plots and extensive chunks of the same action material. Wayne even had to dress like Maynard, ride with the same kind of horse, with the same kind of sidekick. Other early Wayne oaters for Warner Bros. are *Haunted Gold, Ride Him, Cowboy, The Telegraph Trail* (1932); *Somewhere in Sonora* and *Man from Monterey* (1933). (See also *RIDE HIM, COWBOY*.)

BIG TRAIL, THE Fox Film Studio, 1930, B&W, 125 min, VT, (158 min/70 mm). **Producer:** Winfield Sheehan; **Directors:** Raoul Walsh and Louis Loeffler; **Screenplay:** Mary Boyle, Hal G. Evarts, Jack Peabody, and Florence Postal; **Music:** R. H. Bassett, Peter Brunelli, Arthur Kay (uncredited), and Jack Virgil; **Cinematographer:** Lucian N. Andriot (35 mm version) and Arthur Edeson (70 mm version); **Editor:** Jack Dennis; **Cast:** John Wayne, Marguerite Churchill, El Brendel, Tully Marshall, Tyrone Power Sr., David Rollins, Ian Keith, Frederick Burton, Russ Powell, Ward Bond, Marcia Harris, Andy Shufford, Helen Parrish.

In his first starring role, John Wayne plays an authentic American hero named Breck Coleman who leads a wagon train across the Midwest to the Northwest. This big western film portrays the hardships and challenges facing settlers moving west and a hero who shows courage, capability, and determination—an early preview of those very traits which years later helped make Wayne an American icon.

The Big Trail was to be an epic big budget project—in effect a true successor to the silent epic *THE COVERED WAGON* (1923). The story of a wagon train's struggle along the Overland Trail between Missouri and Oregon is told with a good amount of action and adventure. Like most sound directors, Walsh searched for talent with stage experience. He chose Marguerite Churchill, whose Broadway roots matched her incandescent beauty, as the female lead. The best secondary roles went to proven stage actors Ian Keith, Tyrone Power Sr., Tully Marshall, and El Brendel.

Finding a male lead was more difficult. Many silent film stars lacked the proper voice for talkies. Walsh wanted Tom Mix, but Mix was working on another film. Gary Cooper was busy making *THE VIRGINIAN* for Samuel Goldwyn. Cooper also commanded $17,000 per picture. Because Walsh knew that in

The Big Trail dialogue took a back seat to action and scenery, he agreed to go with an untested young actor named Duke Morrison, whose full name was Marion Michael Morrison.

It was John Ford who recommended 23-year-old Duke Morrison to Raoul Walsh. Walsh was one of Fox's most highly regarded directors at the time, specializing in action pictures. He had directed IN OLD ARIZONA (1929), Hollywood's first outdoor talkie. The Fox studio, however, felt that the name Duke Morrison did not sound American enough and began looking for an alternative screen name.

Walsh, a Revolutionary War buff, was a great admirer of General "Mad Anthony" Wayne. He suggested the name Anthony Wayne to production boss Winfield Sheehan, but Sheehan felt that Anthony sounded too Italian and Tony too much like a girl's name. When someone on the set suggested the name "John," Sheehan said fine. The name John was very American as well as the first name of Wayne's sponsor John Ford. So Marion Morrison, later Duke Morrison, now became John Wayne.

Wayne went into training immediately, and Walsh prescribed lessons for his new leading man. He learned to be a cowboy from real cowboys turned stuntmen and was taught how to throw a knife, draw a gun, mount a horse, and ride with the natural grace that distinguished his career. According to a 1971 interview with *Playboy* magazine, Wayne admitted to having been quite sick during the filming and to losing 18 pounds to an acute case of "Montezuma's Revenge," or "the Aztec two-step." Either way it translates into severe dysentery.

Contrary to Hollywood legend, Wayne's performance was adequate enough, and the film itself remains one of the most impressive of the early talkies. Unfortunately, many movie theaters were not equipped for the 70 mm picture designed in the Grandeur (widescreen) process and showed it instead in the standard 35 mm version. Consequently, the film was a financial failure. Wayne would have to wait another decade before becoming the big star many had hoped he would be when he made the film.

But if the impetus behind *The Big Trail* was to be a worthy successor to *The Covered Wagon*, the results were more successful. The hardships of the great wagon treks were filmed far more realistically and in greater detail than James Cruze's silent epic, and the film includes some remarkably handled action sequences, including a vicious Indian attack and an ominous buffalo hunt. Originally running 158 minutes in its 70 mm showings, it was chopped down to 125 minutes for its 35 mm release. It is a film William Everson has called "one of the most impressive of all super-Westerns." The German version, made simultaneously, was still playing commercially in German theaters in the post-World War II period, while the big Indian battle scenes were used continuously through the 1930s and '40s to pad out cheaper pictures.

BILLY'S TWO HATS (aka: LADY AND THE OUTLAW, THE)   United Artists, 1973, Color, 97 min. **Producers:** Norman Jewison and Patrick J. Palmer; **Director:** Ted Kotcheff; **Screenplay:** Alan Sharp; **Music:** John Scott; **Cinematographer:** Brian West; **Editor:** Thom Noble; **Cast:** Gregory Peck, Desi Arnaz Jr., Jack Warden, David Huddleston, Sian Barbara Allen, John Pearce.

Gregory Peck plays a middle-aged bank robber named Deans who is on the run from the law. He and his partner, a half-breed named Billy Two Hats (Desi Arnaz Jr.) try to stay one step ahead of the numerous obstacles threatening their lives and their freedom. When Deans is shot and unable to walk, Billy builds an Indian cot and proceeds to drag Deans behind his horse in hope of reaching a safe haven. Peck's offbeat portrayal of an Irish rogue piques interest.

BILLY THE KID   MGM, 1930, B&W, 90 min. **Producer:** King Vidor; **Director:** Vidor; **Screenplay:** Charles MacArthur, Laurence Stallings, and Wanda Tuchock; **Cinematographer:** Gordon Avil; **Editor:** Hugh Wynn; **Cast:** Johnny Mack Brown, Wallace Beery, Kay Johnson, Karl Dane, Wyndham Standing, Russell Simpson, Roscoe Ates, Blanche Frederici.

In the first sound version of the exploits of the legendary outlaw, Billy the Kid (Johnny Mack Brown) murders a cattle baron in revenge for the death of a pal, then gets married. But he and his bride are trailed by his friend, Sheriff Pat Gar-

Johnny Mack Brown in the 1930 production Billy the Kid *(MGM/AUTHOR'S COLLECTION)*

rett (Wallace Beery), and a posse. Filmed in 70 mm for the wide screen, Vidor took cast and crew to New Mexico, shooting his scenes on the actual locations where the Lincoln County Wars were fought and where Billy the Kid first came to prominence. The film features superb panoramic shots and an intricate use of terrain and natural lighting, most vividly in a sequence where Billy is besieged in a cave among colorful rock formations, while Pat Garrett entices him out of hiding by frying more bacon.

Director King Vidor hired William S. Hart as technical advisor to help film William Noble Burns's novel *Saga of Billy the Kid* (1927). To add to the realism of the film, Hart contributed a gun used by the real Billy, and the rickety towns and dusty streets have a definite Hart imprint. But realism halts abruptly with an ending that contradicts history. In Vidor's *Billy the Kid*, Pat Garrett allows Billy to escape over the Mexican border. Since Billy's various killings are depicted as decidedly cold-blooded, even if somewhat justified by circumstances, the sudden happy ending is a bit hard to accept. The alternate and more historically accurate ending where Garrett kills Billy was used only in the European release.

Johnny Mack Brown—later to be a leading star of B westerns but previously known mainly as a clotheshorse and society leading man to Greta Garbo, Mary Pickford, and Joan Crawford—brought an athletic ability and a pleasing personality to the role of Billy. But it is Wallace Beery as Pat Garrett who gives the best performance, in a role that the extroverted actor surprisingly underplays to great effect. Few, if any, actors have played Pat Garrett any better than Beery.

One of the three big westerns of the formidable sound period (the other two being THE BIG TRAIL [1930] and CIMARRON [1931]), King Vidor's *Billy the Kid* remains among the best of the many subsequent retellings of the story.

BILLY THE KID MGM, 1941, Color, 94 min, VT. **Producer:** Irving Asher; **Director:** David Miller; **Screenplay:** Gene Fowler; **Music:** Ormond Ruthvan and David Snell; **Cinematographers:** William V. Skall and Leonard Smith; **Editor:** Robert J. Kern; **Cast:** Robert Taylor, Brian Donlevy, Mary Howard, Gene Lockhart, Lon Chaney Jr., Henry O'Neill, Guinn "Big Boy" Williams, Cy Kendall, Ted Adams.

This MGM remake, directed by David Miller, focuses on Billy the Kid's later life. The story begins with Billy (Robert Taylor) in a small southwestern town, where he joins a gang headed by Gene Lockhart. Inadvertently he stumbles on an old boyhood pal, Jim Sherwood, who is now a U.S. marshal, while also striking up a friendship with kindly landowner Eric Keating (Ian Hunter). Billy seems to be on the straight and narrow until Keating is killed by a gang member. The Kid now retreats on a campaign of violence and revenge against the killers of his mentor. When he refuses to surrender to Sherwood (Brian Donlevy) for a legal trial, the two men draw on each other. But Billy, a left-handed gun, draws with his right hand instead and dies in his friend's arms.

Some say that Robert Taylor was too sophisticated and mature for his role, and the ending where Billy allows Pat

Robert Taylor and Brian Donlevy in the 1941 production of Billy The Kid *(MGM/AUTHOR'S COLLECTION)*

Garrett (renamed Jim Sherwood) to outdraw him, then dies with a smile on his face, defies common sense. Yet for sheer entertainment value, this *Billy the Kid* remake not only provides solid and colorful entertainment, it also established Robert Taylor as a credible action star.

Filmed in magnificent color in Monument Valley, the film benefits from a fine supporting cast, especially Gene Lockhart, who plays against type as Dan Hickey, the chief villain. Taylor himself was pleased with the film, believing that it did much to change his screen image. He told friends that in part he wished he had been born and lived in a 19th-century western milieu, but he also realized that he probably would have gotten himself "shot to death very young." *Billy The Kid* also marked the first full-scale directorial assignment for David Miller, as well as Robert Taylor's initial entry into Western films.

BILLY THE KID IN BLAZING FRONTIER See *BLAZING FRONTIER.*

BILLY THE KID IN CATTLE STAMPEDE See *CATTLE STAMPEDE.*

BILLY THE KID IN SANTA FE PRI, 1941, B&W, 64 min. **Producer:** Sigmund Neufeld; **Director:** Sam Newfield (as Sherman Scott); **Screenplay:** Joseph O'Donnell; **Cinematographer:** Jack Greenhalgh; **Editor:** Holbrook N. Todd; **Cast:** Bob Steele, Al St. John, Rex Lease, Marin Sais, Dennis Moore, Karl Hackett, Steve Clark, Hal Price, Charles King, Frank Ellis, Dave O'Brien, Keene Duncan, Curley Dresden, John Elliott.

BILLY THE KID IN TEXAS (aka: BATTLING OUTLAW) PRC, 1940, B&W, 52 min, VT. **Producer:** Sigmund Neufield; **Director:** Sam Newfield; **Screenplay:**

Joseph O'Donnell; **Cinematographer:** Jack Greenhalgh; **Editor:** Holbrook N. Todd; **Cast:** Bob Steele, Terry Walker, Al St. John, Carlton Young, Charles King, John Merton, Frank LaRue, Slim Whitaker.

Billy (Bob Steele) arrives in a lawless Texas and finds his old friend Fuzzy (Al St. John). When he stands up to a nasty gang leader, the town appoints him sheriff. Billy and Fuzzy then go out to retrieve some stolen money and clear a man falsely accused of the theft.

Bob Steele is one of many actors who portrayed Billy the Kid on the B western Saturday afternoon screen. He appeared in half a dozen Billy the Kid oaters for PRC in the early 1940s, starting with *Billy the Kid Outlawed* (1940). Other entries include *Billy the Kid's Range War, Billy the Kid's Fighting Pals,* and *Billy the Kid in Santa Fe* (1941).

BILLY THE KID RETURNS   Republic, 1938, B&W, 53 min, VT, DVD. **Producer:** Charles E. Ford; **Director:** Joseph Kane; **Screenplay:** Jack Natteford; **Cinematographer:** Ernest Miller; **Editor:** Lester Orlebeck; **Music:** Sid Robin, Alberto Colombo, and Tim Spencer; **Cast:** Roy Rogers, Smiley Burnette, Lynne Roberts, Morgan Wallace, Fred Kohler, Wade Boteler, Edwin Stanley, Horace Murphy, Joseph Crehan, Robert Emmett Keane.

Roy Rogers—who plays himself and the infamous "Kid" with whom he is confused—manages to restore the tranquility of Lincoln County after subduing the criminal element. Lots of songs are featured here, including "Born in the Saddle," "When the Sun is Setting in the Saddle," "Trail Blazing," "When I Camped Under the Stars," and "Give Me The Range." The songs are credited to Smiley Burnette and Eddie Cherkose. Look for George Montgomery in an uncredited role. (See also *UNDER WESTERN STARS.*)

BILLY THE KID RIDES AGAIN   See *KID RIDES AGAIN, THE.*

BILLY THE KID'S FIGHTING PALS (aka: TRIGGER PALS)   PRC, 1941, B&W, 59 min. **Producer:** Sigmund Neufeld; **Director:** Sam Newfield (as Sherman Scott); **Screenplay:** George Plympton; **Cinematographer:** Jack Greenhalgh; **Editor:** Holbrook N. Todd; **Cast:** Bob Steele, Al St. John, Phyllis Adair, Carleton Young, Charles King, Curley Dresden, Hal Price, George Chesebro.

BILLY THE KID'S RANGE WAR   PRC, 1941, B&W, 57 min. **Producer:** Sigmund Neufeld; **Director:** Sam Newfield (as Peter Stewart); **Screenplay:** Jack William Lively; **Music:** Lew Porter; **Cinematographer:** Jack Greenhalgh; **Editor:** Holbrook N. Todd; **Cast:** Bob Steele, Al St. John, Carleton Young, Joan Barclay, Karl Hackett, Ted Adams, Rex Lease, Milton Kibbee, Buddy Roosevelt.

BILLY THE KID'S ROUNDUP   PRC, 1941, B&W, 48 min. **Producer:** Sigmund Neufeld; **Director:** Sam Newfield (as Sherman Scott); **Screenplay:** Fred Myron; **Cinematographer:** Jack Greenhalgh; **Editor:** Holbrook N. Todd; **Cast:** Buster Crabbe, Al St. John, Carlton Young, Glenn Strange, Charles King, Slim Whitaker, John Elliott, Dennis Moore, Kenne Duncan.

BILLY THE KID TRAPPED   PRC, 1942, B&W, 59 min. **Producer:** Sigmund Neufeld; **Director:** Sam Newfield (as Sherman Scott); **Screenplay:** Oliver Drake; **Music:** Johnny Lange and Lou Porter; **Cinematographer:** Jack Greenhalgh; **Editor:** Holbrook N. Todd; **Cast:** Buster Crabbe, Al St. John, Malcolm "Bud" McTaggart, Anne Jeffreys, Glenn Strange, George Chesebro, Walter McGrail, Ted Adams, Jack Ingram.

Boss Stanton (Glenn Strange) sees that Billy and his friends, Fuzzy and Jeff, break out of jail. He wants them free so three of his men can impersonate them for the robberies and murders they are about to commit. Buster Crabbe appeared as Billy the Kid in more than a dozen B westerns for PRC between 1941 and 1943, including *Billy the Kid's Roundup, Billy the Kid Wanted* (1941); *Sheriff of Sage Valley, Law and Order, Billy the Kid's Smoking Gun* (1942); *Western Cyclone, The Kid Rides Again, Fugitive of the Plains, Cattle Stampede, Blazing Frontier* (1943).

BILLY THE KID VS. DRACULA   Embassy Pictures, 1966, Color, 89 min. **Producer:** Carroll Case; **Director:** William Boudine; **Screenplay:** Carl K. Hittleman; **Music:** Raoul Kraushaar; **Cinematographer:** Lothrop B. Worth; **Editor:** Roy V. Livingston; **Cast:** Chuck Courtney, John Carradine, Melinda Plowman, Virginia Christine, Walter Janovitz, Roy Barcroft, Olive Carey, Bing Russell, Harry Carey Jr.

Count Dracula (John Carradine) woos a ranch owner's daughter hoping to make her his mate. But her boyfriend just happens to be the notorious outlaw Billy the Kid (Chuck Courtney), who is trying to go straight. Carradine considered this to be his worst picture (his face grows red every time he sees a girl) but it is all in good fun. Look for appearances by western legends Harry Carey Jr. as the wagon master and Roy Barcroft as Sheriff Griffin. The West goes campy, and while some reviewers have found this picture to be plain fun, others have found it to be plain bad.

BITE THE BULLET   Columbia, 1975, Color, 131 min, VT. **Producer:** Richard Brooks; **Director:** Brooks; **Screenplay:** Brooks; **Music:** Alex North; **Cinematographer:** Harry Stradling Jr.; **Editor:** George Grenville; **Cast:** Gene Hackman, Candice Bergen, James Coburn, Ben Johnson, Ian Bannen, Jan-Michael Vincent, Robert Donner, Jean Willes, Mario Arteaga, Dabney Coleman, John McLiam, Robert Hoy, Jerry Gatlin, Sally Kirkland, Walter Scott Jr.

Set in the early years of the 20th century, this western drama concerns a disparate group of people engaged in a grueling 700-mile horse race. Among the nine contestants who vie for the $2,000 prize are Gene Hackman, Ben Johnson, James Coburn, Jan-Michael Vincent, and an alluring Candice Bergen, whose designer jeans don't exactly fit the Edwardian era of the film. Although each is determined to win at any cost, the protagonists develop an abiding respect for one another along the way that precipitates a surprising climax. A particularly touching moment has Ben Johnson, an old-timer they call "Mister," talking about the glory of winning, a performance that some say should have garnered the veteran actor a second Oscar or at least a nomination.

Superbly photographed in New Mexico and the recipient of two Academy Award nominations, this picture, while a bit overlong, deserves attention.

BITTER CREEK Allied Artists, 1954, B&W, 74 min. **Producer:** Vincent M. Fennel; **Director:** Thomas Carr; **Screenplay:** George Waggner; **Music:** Raoul Kraushaar; **Cinematographer:** Ernest Miller; **Editor:** Sam Fields; **Cast:** William "Wild Bill" Elliott, Carlton Young, Beverly Garland, Claude Akins, Jim Akins, Jim Hayward, John Harmon, Veda Ann Borg.

When his rancher brother is shot in the back, a man sets out to avenge the murder. A well-scripted and compact oater, the film is most notable because it marked Bill Elliott's last western picture. Although not as good as his best for Republic, it is a decent western adios for Elliott, who made two more films (both nonwesterns) before his death in 1965.

BLACK BANDIT Universal, 1938, B&W, 58 min. **Producers:** Paul Malvern and George Waggner; **Director:** Waggner; **Screenplay:** Waggner (Joseph West); **Cinematographer:** Gus Peterson; **Editor:** Carl Pierspon; **Cast:** Bob Baker, Marjorie Reynolds, Hal Taliaferro, Jack Rockwell, Forrest Taylor, Glenn Strange.

Twin brothers Bob and Don Ramsey (Bob Baker) are on opposite sides of the law. Bob is a sheriff and Don is a famous outlaw known as the Black Bandit. When the Black Bandit strikes, his look-alike sheriff brother is arrested. Refusing to implicate his brother, Bob escapes and heads after Don. Baker's costar Marjorie Reynolds became better known a few years later when she helped Bing Crosby introduce the all-time yuletide standard "White Christmas" in the film *Holiday Inn.*

Baker made a series of feature films for Universal in the late 1930s, beginning with COURAGE OF THE WEST, and SINGING OUTLAW in 1937; BORDER WOLVES, THE LAST STAND, WESTERN TRAIL, *Outlaw Express*, PRAIRIE JUSTICE, GUILTY TRAILS, GHOST TOWN RIDERS (1938); *The Phantom Stage, Honor of the West* (1939). In 1939 he joined Johnny Mack Brown for a series of seven features: *Desperate Trails, Oklahoma Frontier* (1939); *Bad Man from Red Butte, Chip of the Flying U, Riders of Pasco Basin, West of Carson City* (1940); *Ride 'Em Cowboy* (1942).

BLACK BART (aka: BLACK BART HIGHWAYMAN, UK) Universal, 1948, Color, 80 min. **Producer:** Leonard Goldstein; **Director:** George Sherman; **Screenplay:** William Bowers, Jack Natteford, and Luci Ward; **Music:** Frank Skinner; **Cinematographer:** Irving Glassberg; **Editor:** Russell F. Schoengarth; **Cast:** Yvonne De Carlo, Dan Duryea, Jeffrey Lynn, Percy Kilbride, Lloyd Gough, Frank Lovejoy, John McIntire, John Beddoe, Eddie Arcuff.

Dan Duryea plays the cheerful Charlie Boles, who leaves his partners to become the outlaw Black Bart. On the day he robs a Wells Fargo stagecoach carrying a shipment of gold, he finds his old partners Lance Hardeen (Jeffrey Lynn) and Jersey Brady (Percy Kilbride) on the same stage. Also on the stage is the enticing and notorious Lola Montez (Yvonne De Carlo), a voluptuous dancer heading to Sacramento. As outlaws Duryea and Lynn battle for her affections, she tries to thwart their attempts to overthrow the Wells Fargo Company. An interesting and well-played western that is marred by one visible gaffe: the observant viewer will find a newspaper column circa 1849 that mentions automobiles.

BLACK BOUNTY HUNTER, THE See *BOSS NIGGER.*

BLACK DAKOTAS, THE Columbia, 1954, Color, 65 min. **Producer:** Wallace MacDonald; **Director:** Ray Nazarro; **Screenplay:** Ray Buffum and De Vallon Scott; **Music:** Mischa Bakaleinikoff; **Cinematographer:** Ellis W. Carter; **Editor:** Aaron Stell; **Cast:** Gary Merrill, Wanda Hendrix, John Bromfield, Noah Beery Jr., Fay Roope, Howard Wendell, Robert F. Simon, James Griffith, Richard Webb, Jay Silverheels, George Keymas.

Two men about to steal money from the Sioux Indians start an Indian uprising to cover their escape. They do this by killing a Sioux emissary, then having one of the culprits assume his identity. This engrossing story is helped by some beautiful color photography, a good cast, and a particularly adept performance by Gary Merrill as the two-timing criminal mastermind.

BLACK HILLS PRC, 1948, B&W, 60 min. **Producer:** Jerry Thomas; **Director:** Ray Taylor; **Screenplay:** Joseph F. Poland; **Music:** Walter Greene; **Cinematographer:** Ernest Miller; **Editor:** Hugh Winn; **Cast:** Eddie Dean, Roscoe Ates, Shirley Patterson, Terry Frost, Steve Drake, Nina Bara, William Fawcett.
See *CARAVAN TRAIL, THE.*

BLACK HORSE CANYON (aka: ECHO CANYON, WILD HORSE CANYON) Universal, 1954, Color, 81 min. **Producer:** John W. Rogers; **Director:** Jesse Hibbs; **Screenplay:** Geoffrey Holmes; **Music:** Henry Mancini and Hans J. Salter; **Cinematographer:** George Robinson; **Editor:** Frank Gross; **Cast:** Joel McCrea, Mari

Blanchard, Race Gentry, Murvyn Vye, Irving Bacon, John Pickard, Ewing Mitchell, Pilar Del Rey, Henry Wills.

In this film based on Les Savage Jr.'s novel *The Wild Horse*, a longtime cowpoke and a cattle breeder's niece join forces to capture a rebellious black stallion but find themselves opposed by a neighboring rancher. Joel McCrea stands out in this appealing, easy-going oater. Along with Ben Johnson and Tim Holt, McCrea was considered one of the top three horsemen among Hollywood actors.

BLACKJACK KETCHUM, DESPERADO
Columbia, 1956, B&W, 76 min. **Producer:** Sam Katzman; **Director:** Earl Bellamy; **Screenplay:** Jack Natteford and Luci Ward; **Music:** Mischa Bakeleinkoff (supervisor); **Editor:** Saul A. Goodkind; **Cast:** Howard Duff, Victor Jory, Margaret Fields, Angela Stevens, William Tannen, Martin Garralaga.

This movie was based on the Louis L'Amour novel *Kilkenny* and filmed in the Alabama Hills of Lone Pine, California. Blackjack "Tom" Ketchum (Howard Duff) shoots a man in self-defense while doing a good deed. He is forced into hiding and must endure yet another shoot-out before returning to a life of peace. In another Hollywood attempt to transform a man of unsavory character into a victimized gunslinger, the film shares little in common with the real-life historical outlaw Duff portrays in the movie.

BLACK LASH, THE Western Adventures Co., 1952, B&W, 54 min. **Producer:** Ron Ormond; **Director:** Ormond; **Screenplay:** June Carr, Kathy McKeel, and Timothy Ormond; **Music:** Walter Greene; **Cinematographer:** Ernest Miller; **Editor:** Hugh Winn; **Cast:** Lash LaRue, Al St. John, Ray Bennett, Peggy Stewart, Byron Keith, Jim Bannon.

Marshal Lash La Rue sent "Deuce" Rago to prison in the 1948 film *Frontier Revenge*. Lash finds out that "Deuce" is now out of jail and his outlaw gang is back in business. So once again he and Fuzzy (Al St. John) must try to bring him in. (See also *LAW OF THE LASH*.)

BLACK MARKET RUSTLERS Monogram, 1943, B&W, 58 min. **Producer:** George W. Weeks; **Director:** S. Roy Luby; **Screenplay:** Patricia Harper; **Music:** Frank Sanucci; **Cinematographer:** Edward A. Kull; **Editor:** Roy Claire; **Cast:** Ray Corrigan, Dennis Moore, Max Terhune, Evelyn Finley, Steve Clark, Glenn Strange, Carl Sepulveda, George Chesebro, Hank Worden.

The setting is World War II, and the black market is rampant. This neat little Monogram venture was designed to discourage the purchase of black-market beef. This time the Range Busters (Ray Corrigan, Dennis Moore, and Max Terhune) are called on to fight cattle rustlers and a gang that strikes fast by hauling the beef away in trucks. (See also *RANGE BUSTERS, THE*.)

BLACK NOON Andrew J. Fenady Productions, 1971, Color, 74 min. **Producer:** Andrew J. Fenady; **Director:**

Bernard L. Kowalski; **Teleplay:** Fenady; **Music:** George Dunning; **Cinematographer:** Keith C. Smith; **Editor:** Dann Cahn; **Cast:** Roy Thinnes, Yvette Mimieux, Ray Milland, Gloria Grahame, Lynn Loring, Henry Silva, Hank Warden.

In the 1830s a young minister and his wife are saved from death in the desert by a group from a nearby town whose minister recently died—a town terrorized by an evil gunfighter. The minister brings luck to the town for a time, and then the unexpected, the unexplained and the unforeseen all conspire to bring about an ending that is a true nail-biter.

Following writer/producer Andrew J. Fenady's success on the big screen with *CHISUM*, CBS bigwigs Paul King and Phillip Barry approached him with an offer to do a film for television. Fenady suggested another western, but the powers at CBS were skeptical, so he countered with four words: "Witchcraft in the West." It had never been done before, and the CBS brass bought the idea. Fenady also assembled a top notch cast, including ex-Oscar winners Ray Milland (*The Lost Weekend*) and Gloria Grahame (*The Bad and the Beautiful*). Thirty years later pundits and fans are calling the film "absolutely incredible" and a must-see movie that effectively combines the western and horror genres. Unfortunately the film has not been released on video and remains largely unknown.

BLACK PATCH Warner Bros., 1957, B&W, 82 min. **Producer:** Allen H. Miner; **Director:** Miner; **Screenplay:** Leo Gordon; **Music:** Jerry Goldsmith; **Cinematographer:** Edward Colman; **Editor:** Jerry Young; **Cast:** George Montgomery, Diane Brewster, Tom Pittman, Leo Gordon, House Peters Jr., Strother Martin, Sebastian Cabot.

George Montgomery is a tough sheriff out to clear his name when he is accused of killing a bank robber who was the husband of the woman he once loved.

BLACK RODEO Cinerama Releasing Corporation, 1972, Color, 87 min. **Producer:** Jeff Kanew; **Director:** Kanew; **Screenplay:** Kanew; **Cinematographer:** High Bell, Amin O. Chaudhri, Louis San Andres, John Stevens, John Wing, and Kanew; **Cast:** Archie Wycoff, Clarence Gonzalez, Pete Knight, Marval Rogers, Reuben Heura, Joanne Eason, Cornell Fields, Moses Fields, Muhammad Ali (himself), Woody Strode (narrator).

This is an interesting documentary about a rodeo that takes place mostly in Harlem, New York City. Various black rodeo performers appear here, with comments by well-known black personalities and background music supplied and performed by such artists as B. B. King, Ray Charles, and Dee Dee Sharp.

BLACK SPURS Paramount, 1965, Color, 81 min. **Producer:** A. C. Lyles; **Director:** R. G. Springsteen; **Screenplay:** Steve Fisher; **Music:** Jimmy Haskell; **Cinematographer:** Ralph Woolsey; **Editor:** Archie Marshek; **Cast:** Rory Calhoun, Linda Darnell, Scott Brady, Lon Chaney Jr., Richard Arlen, Bruce Cabot, Terry Moore, Patricia Owens, James

Best, Jerome Courtland, De Forrest Kelley, James Brown, Chuck Roberson.

A cowboy gains the alliance of several important people in a small western town, in a scheme to make a nearby community so wild that the railroad will bypass it. Filmed in Techniscope with a cast of veteran stars assembled by producer A. C. Lyles, this standard 1960s horse opera marks the last film appearance of onetime screen beauty Linda Darnell, who perished in a house fire a short time later.

BLACK WHIP, THE (aka: MAN WITH A WHIP, THE) 20th Century Fox, 1956, B&W, 81 min. **Producer:** Robert W. Stabler; **Director:** Charles Marquis Warren; **Screenplay:** Orville H. Hampton; **Music:** Raoul Kraushaar; **Cinematographer:** Joseph F. Biroc; **Editor:** Fred W. Berger; **Cast:** Hugh Marlow, Coleen Gray, Richard Gilden, Angie Dickinson, Strother Martin, Paul Richards, Sheb Wooley, Adele Mara.

When they rescue a quartet of dance-hall girls in a small western town, two brothers find themselves up against a whip-wielding bad guy. Among the young beauties rescued by Hugh Marlow and Richard Gilden in this spicy little horse opera is 25-year-old Angie Dickinson.

BLAZING ACROSS THE PECOS Columbia, 1948, B&W, 55 min, VT. **Director:** Ray Nazarro; **Screenplay:** Norman S. Hall; **Cast:** Charles Starrett, Smiley Burnette, Charles C. Wilson, Paul Campbell, Jack Ingram, Chief Thundercloud, Pierce Lyden, Jock Mahoney.

The Durango Kid foils the efforts of a gambling czar to take over a town. Jock Mahoney doubles Starrett in the stunts. (See also *DURANGO KID, THE.*)

BLAZING ARROWS See *FIGHTING CARAVANS.*

BLAZING BULLETS Monogram, 1951, B&W, 51 min. **Producer:** Vincent M. Fennelly; **Director:** Wallace Fox; **Screenplay:** George Daniels; **Cast:** Johnny Mack Brown, Lois Hall, House Peters Jr., Stanley Price, Edmund Cobb, Dennis Moore, Milburn Morante, Forrest Taylor, Ed Cassidy, George De Normand, Carl Mathews.

A U.S. marshal tries to find a man who has been kidnapped along with his gold bullion, since the man's daughter's fiancée is suspected of the crime. This Monogram oater was one of Johnny Mack Brown's final films. After appearing in some 200 movies and being listed among the top ten money-making western stars between 1942 and 1950, he retired from the screen in 1953 to become the manager-host of a restaurant and subsequently made only occasional film appearances until his death in 1974. (See also *UNDER ARIZONA SKIES.*)

BLAZING FRONTIER (aka: BILLY THE KID IN BLAZING FRONTIER) PRC, 1943, B&W, 59 min.

Producer: Sigmund Neufeld; **Director:** Sam Newfield; **Screenplay:** Patricia Harper; **Cinematographer:** Robert E. Klein; **Editor:** Holbrook N. Todd; **Cast:** Buster Crabbe, Al St. John, Marjorie Manners, Milton Kibbee, Kermit Maynard, Frank Hagney, George Chesebro.

See *BILLY THE KID TRAPPED.*

BLAZING GUNS Kent, 1935, B&W, 55 min. **Producer:** William Kent; **Director:** Ray Heinz; **Screenplay:** Forbes Parkhill; **Cast:** Reb Russell, Marion Shilling, Lafe McKee, Joseph W. Girard, Frank McCaroll, Slim Whitaker.

Bob Grady (Reb Russell) is saved from hanging by a young woman (Marion Shilling) whose family he befriended. He recognizes the leader of the vigilantes who set him up for the hanging and proceeds to go after him. (See also *LIGHTNING TRIGGERS.*)

BLAZING GUNS Monogram, 1943, B&W, 54 min. **Producer:** Robert Emmett Tansey; **Director:** Tansey; **Screenplay:** Frances Kavanaugh; **Cinematographer:** Marcel Le Picard; **Editors:** Frederick Bain and Carl Pierson; **Cast:** Ken Maynard, Hoot Gibson, Le Roy Mason, Emmett Lynn, Weldon Heyburn, Roy Brent.

Federal marshals Ken Maynard and Hoot Gibson (The Trail Blazers) are sent to Willow Springs, where their two predecessors were killed trying to bring law and order to the town. Naturally they run into lots of trouble. (See also *DEATH VALLEY RANGERS.*)

BLAZING HILLS, THE See *BLAZING SUN, THE.*

BLAZING JUSTICE Spectrum Pictures Inc., 1936, B&W, 60 min. **Producer:** Ray Kirwood; **Director:** Albert Herman; **Screenplay:** Zarah Tazil; **Cinematographer:** Bill Hires; **Editor:** Holbrook N. Todd; **Cast:** Bill Cody, Gertrude Messinger, Gordon Griffith, Milburn Morante, Budd Buster, Frank Yaconelli.

A cowboy who captures two rustlers is given a $500 reward. He decides to take a vacation and winds up being accused for a murder he did not commit.

BLAZING SADDLES Warner Bros., 1972, Color, 93 min, VT, DVD. **Producer:** Michael Hertzberg; **Director:** Mel Brooks; **Screenplay:** Brooks, Norman Steinberg, Richard Pryor, and Andrew Bergman (story); **Music:** John Morris and Brooks (songs); **Cinematographer:** Joseph F. Biroc; **Editor:** Danford B. Greene and John C. Howard; **Cast:** Cleavon Little, Gene Wilder, Slim Pickens, Harvey Korman, Madeline Kahn, Mel Brooks, Burton Gilliam, Alex Karras, David Huddleston, Dom DeLuise, Count Basie.

To ruin a western town, a corrupt political boss (Harvey Korman) appoints a black sheriff (Cleavon Little), who promptly becomes his main adversary. Among the main characters is the Waco Kid (Gene Wilder), a prissy, alcoholic gunslinger who had once been a legend in his time; and Mongo, the dimwitted strongman played by former pro football great Alex Karras.

The film has many memorable moments, such as an Indian (Mel Brooks) speaking Yiddish; a town named Rockridge, where everyone's last name is Johnson; a cameo by Count Basie leading a jazz band in the middle of the desert; and Madeline Kahn—as Lili Von Shtupp—doing a takeoff on Marlene Dietrich. There are exercises in vulgarity aplenty: a campfire scene with beans and an accent on flatulence and a placid church congregation singing "Our Town Is Turning to Shit," among others.

The role of Bart, the black sheriff, was originally intended for Richard Pryor, but because of the controversial nature of Pryor's stand-up comedy routines, Mel Brooks couldn't secure financing for the project. So Pryor was made a cowriter of the script, and Cleavon Little took on the role. Nominated for three Academy Awards, including the film's title song (sung by Frankie Laine), the film was the most popular western of the 1970s and made a household name of Mel Brooks. This is borscht-belt shtick at its best, compromised only by an unsteady ending and some jokes in incredibly bad taste.

Irreverent, brilliant, comical, disgusting at times, Brooks's *Blazing Saddles* remains for many the ultimate western spoof. It combines burlesque with western themes, with nary an aspect of the genre left untouched.

BLAZING SIXES Warner Bros., 1937, B&W, 55 min. **Producer:** Bryan Foy; **Director:** Noel M. Smith; **Screenplay:** John T. Nevelle; **Cinematographer:** Ted D. McCord; **Editor:** Frederick Richards; **Cast:** Dick Foran, Helen Valkis, Mira McKinney, John Merton, Glenn Strange, Milton Kibbee, Kenneth Harlan, Bud Osborne.

Government agent Red Barton (Dick Foran) is sent to a small western town to find the source of a recent series of gold robberies and the methods that are used to get the gold out of the country unseen. Matters are complicated when pretty Barbara Morgan arrives to claim her inheritance. But the ranch she is about to inherit just happens to be headquarters for the outlaw gang.

Foran changed his name from John to Dick before moving to Warner Bros., where he became a singing hero in a string of low-budget western films. In this pleasing and entertaining entry, he croons three songs cowritten by M. K. Jerome and Jack Scholl: "The Prairie Is My Home," "Ridin' On to Monterrey," and "In a Little Prairie Town." (See also *MOONLIGHT ON THE PRAIRIE.*)

BLAZING SUN, THE (aka: BLAZING HILLS, THE) Columbia, 1950, B&W, 69 min. **Producer:** Armand Shaefer; **Director:** John English; **Screenplay:** Jack Townley; **Cinematographer:** William Bradford; **Editor:** James Sweeney; **Cast:** Gene Autry, Pat Buttram, Lynne Roberts, Anne Gwynne, Edward Norris, Kenne Duncan, Alan Hale, Gregg Barton, Steve Darrell, Tom London, Sandy Sanders, Frankie Marvin.

BLAZING THE OVERLAND TRAIL Columbia, 1956, B&W, 15 chapters. **Producer:** Sam Katzman; **Director:** Spencer Gordon Bennet; **Screenplay:** George Plympton; **Cast:** Lee Roberts, Dennis Moore, Norman Brooks, Gregg Barton, Don C. Harvey, Lee Mogan, Edward Coch, Pierce Lyden, Reed Howes, Al Ferguson, Pete Kellett, Kermit Maynard.

In this cliffhanger a crooked rancher organizes a gang to raid the Overland Trail but finds himself opposed by an army scout and a Pony Express agent. This 15-chapter serial is the last to be filmed in the United States and marks a sad farewell to a special genre staple.

BLAZING TRAIL, THE Columbia, 1949, B&W, 59 min. **Producer:** Colbert Clark; **Director:** Ray Nazarro; **Screenplay:** Barry Shipman; **Cinematographer:** Ira H. Morgan; **Editor:** Paul Borofsky; **Cast:** Charles Starrett, Smiley Burnette, Fred F. Sears, Margarie Stapp, Trevor Bardette, Steve Darrell, Steve Pendleton, Jock Mahoney.

BLINDMAN (aka: *CIECO II, PISTOLERO CIECO*, Italy) Abkco/20th Century-Fox, 1971, Color, 105 min. **Producers:** Tony Anthony, Saul Swimmer, and Roberto Infascelli (executive); **Director:** Ferdinando Baldi; **Screenplay:** Pier Giovanni (as Piero Anchisi), Anthony, and Vincenzo Cerami; **Music:** Selvio Cipriani; **Cinematographer:** Riccardo Pallottini; **Editor:** Roberto Perpignani; **Cast:** Tony Anthony, Ringo Starr, Lloyd Battista, Magna Konopa, Raf Baldassarre, Marisa Solinas.

A blind but deadly gunman is hired to escort 50 mail-order brides to a group of miner fiancés. However, his business partners doublecross him by selling the women to a bandit. Seeking revenge, the blind man pursues the bandits into Mexico. The most interesting aspect of this routine Italian venture is Ringo Starr as a slimy Mexican bandit named Candy and such lines as, "What kind of son of a bitch puts a snake in a man's salad?"

BLOCKED TRAIL, THE Republic, 1943, B&W, 55 min. **Director:** Elmer Clifton; **Screenplay:** John K. Butler and Jacquin Frank; **Cast:** Bob Steele, Tom Tyler, Jimmy Dodd, Helen Deverell, George J. Lewis, Walter Soderling, Charles F. Miller, Kermit Maynard.

The Three Mesquiteers are suspected of killing a man so they set out to expose the real killer. The big problem is that the man's murder was witnessed only by his horse. (See also *THREE MESQUITEERS, THE.*)

BLOOD ARROW 20th Century Fox, 1958, B&W, 76 min. **Producer:** Robert W. Stabler; **Director:** Charles Marquis Warren; **Screenplay:** Fred Freiberger; **Music:** Raoul Kraushaar; **Cinematographer:** Fleet Southcott; **Editor:** Michael Luciano; **Cast:** Scott Brady, Paul Richards, Phyllis Coates, Don Haggerty, Rocky Shahan, Des Slattery, William McGraw, Patrick O'Moore, Jeanne Bates, Robert Dierkes, Diana Darrin.

Phyllis Coates plays a Mormon girl named Bess who trudges through tough Indian territory to obtain medicine needed for her people. Predictably, she runs into the usual array of hostile Indians in her quest to obtain the serum.

BLOOD ON THE ARROW Allied Artists, 1964, Color, 91 min. **Producers:** Sam Firks and Leon Fromkess; **Director:** Sidney Salkow; **Screenplay:** Mark Hanna and Robert E. Kent; **Music:** Richard LaSalle; **Cinematographer:** Kenneth Peach; **Editor:** William Austin; **Cast:** Dale Robertson, Martha Hyer, Wendell Corey, Dandy Curran, Paul Mantee, Robert Carricart, Ted de Corsica, Elisha Cook Jr., John Mathews.

Usual histrionics about an Apache massacre and how the survivors attempt to rescue a son who is held captive.

BLOOD ON THE MOON RKO, 1948, B&W, 88 MIN. **Producers:** Sig Rogell and Theron Warth; **Director:** Robert Wise; **Screenplay:** Lillie Hayward and Harold Shumate; **Music:** Roy Webb; **Cinematographer:** Nichola Musuraca; **Editor:** Samuel E. Beetley; **Cast:** Robert Mitchum, Barbara Bel Geddes, Robert Preston, Walter Brennan, Phyllis Thaxter, Frank Faylen, Tom Tully, Charles McGraw, Clifton Young, Tom Tyler, Tom Keene.

Based on Luke Short's novel *Gunman's Chance,* Robert Mitchum portrays a strange drifter who is hired by his old pal and partner (Robert Preston) to bilk some unsuspecting landowners. But as Mitchum comes to realize the nasty nature of his buddy's plan and how deviously the homesteaders are being manipulated, the two men drift apart and become sworn enemies, culminating in a deadly knockdown, drag-out fistfight between Mitchum and Preston, after a long chase and a gun battle involving Preston and his henchmen against Mitchum.

Director Robert Wise assembled an ensemble cast for his first western, and a very good one it is, capturing the crisp style employed by Luke Short in writing his western novels. It is too bad this intelligent film, which film historian William K. Everson calls one of RKO's best films and one of the best-scripted westerns of the 1940s, has been computer-colored, negating the splendid black-and-white footage of the original.

BLOOD SEEKERS See *CAIN'S CUT THROATS.*

BLUE Paramount, 1968, Color, 113 min. **Producers:** Judd Bernard and Irwin Winkler; **Director:** Silvio Narrizzano; **Screenplay:** Meade Roberts and Ronald M. Cohen;

Music: Manos Hadjidakis; **Cinematographer:** Stanley Cortez; **Editor:** Stewart Linder; **Cast:** Terence Stamp, Joanna Pettet, Karl Malden, Ricardo Montalban, Anthony Costello, Joe De Santis.

Blue is set on the uneasy border between Texas and Mexico, across which bandits Ricardo Montalban and older brother Joe De Santis come for looting raids. "Blue," played by Terence Stamp, has been raised by Montalban but is torn between loyalty to Montalban and his own unidentified kin. So called because of the color of his eyes, Blue is actually the son of American parents slaughtered by Mexicans during the Texas Revolution. While he learns to become a cold-blooded killer like his three stepbrothers, he finds himself drawn to another, more peaceful way of life when he takes part in a raid into Texas.

The film is exceedingly violent. Even allowing for the last-minute casting of Stamp, his performance is dull, and he does not speak a word for the first 50 minutes, although he grunts a little and there are close-ups of his eyes and nostrils. Moreover, Stamp speaks no more than 200 words during the entire film. The $5 million-plus film, according to *Variety,* suffers from "poor writing, dull performances, and pretentious direction."

BLUE BLAZES RAWDEN Paramount Artcraft/ William S. Hart Productions, 1918, B&W, 15 min, VT. **Producer:** Thomas Ince; **Director:** William S. Hart; **Screenplay:** J. G. Hawks; **Cinematographer:** Joseph H. August (as Joe August); **Cast:** William S. Hart, Maude George, Gertrude Claire, Robert McKim, Robert Gordon, Jack Hoxie.

As an actor, director, and writer, William S. Hart was the first man to put poetry into the western film. The archetypal good badman, Hart plays Rawden, a north-woods lumberjack who fights with a crooked dance-hall owner for the affections of the lovely Babette DuFresne (Maude George). When the owner is killed and his mother and younger brother arrive in town, Rawden attempts to ease their suffering by creating the fiction that the dance-hall owner was really a well-loved man who died naturally. But when the owner's brother learns the truth about the death, he starts gunning for Rawden. Thomas Ince, one of the movies' early giants, produced this fine silent film, which remains among Hart's very best. (See also *HELL'S HINGES.*)

BLUE CANADIAN ROCKIES Columbia/Gene Autry Productions, 1952, B&W, 58 min, VT. **Producer:** Armand Schaefer; **Director:** George Archainbaud; **Screenplay:** Gerald Geraghty; **Cinematographer:** William Bradford; **Editor:** James Sweeney; **Cast:** Gene Autry, Pat Buttram, Gail Davis, Carolina Cotton, Ross Ford, Tom London.

Sent by his employer to stop a man's daughter from marrying a scoundrel, Gene Autry finds that the girl has turned her home into a dude ranch and game preserve, but the place has been plagued by a series of murders. This routine but interesting early 1950s Autry venture includes a backdrop of stock Canadian footage. (See also *TUMBLING TUMBLEWEEDS*.)

BLUE MONTANA SKIES Republic, 1939, B&W, 56 min. **Producers:** Harry Grey and Herbert J. Yates (executive); **Director:** B. Reeves Eason; **Screenplay:** Gerald Geraghty; **Cinematographer:** Jack A. Marta; **Editor:** Lester Orlebeck; **Cast:** Gene Autry, Smiley Burnette, June Story, Harry Woods, Tully Marshall, Al Bridge, Glenn Strange, Dorothy Granger, Robert Winkler, Edmund Cobb, Jack Ingram, Augie Gomez, John Beach, Elmo Lincoln.

Gene follows a clue written on a rock by a dead man, hoping to find a smuggling operation near the Canadian border. The film boasts good musical interludes and a well-written script. (See also *TUMBLING TUMBLEWEEDS*.)

BLUE STEEL Lone Star/Monogram, 1934, B&W, 54 min, VT. **Producer:** Paul Malvern; **Director:** Robert Bradbury; **Screenplay:** Bradbury; **Cinematographer:** Archie Stout; **Editor:** Carl Pierson; **Cast:** John Wayne, Eleanor Hunt, George "Gabby" Hayes, Edward Peil Sr., Yakima Canutt, Lafe McKee, George Cleveland, Earl Dwire.

This early John Wayne venture has the Duke playing a tough marshal named John Carruthers, who goes undercover to unmask crooked speculators. The speculators know there is gold in the soil and try to coerce the townsfolk into selling their ranches so they can steal the gold lying under them. Yakima Canutt plays a character named Danti, the Dot Bandit, and doubles Wayne in the stunts. Cinematographer Archie Stout worked with Wayne in 25 films, the same number as William Clothier and more than any other cinematographer. Director Robert Bradbury helmed Wayne in 16 films; only John Ford directed Wayne in more features. (See also *LAWLESS FRONTIER*.)

BOILING POINT, THE Allied Pictures, 1932, B&W, 62 min. **Producer:** M. H. Hofman; **Director:** George Melford; **Screenplay:** Donald W. Lee; **Cinematographers:** Tom Galligan and Harry Neumann; **Editor:** Mildred Johnson; **Cast:** Hoot Gibson, Helen Foster, Wheeler Oakman, Skeeter Bill Robbins, Billy Bletcher, Lafe McKee, Charles Bailey, G. Raymond Nye, Tom London, George "Gabby" Hayes (as George Hayes).

Hoot Gibson plays Jimmy Duncan, whose uncle George "Gabby" Hayes gives him 30 days to learn to control his temper or lose his inheritance. He gets mixed up with a gang of robbers and trouble soon comes along. Born Edmund Richard, Hoot Gibson was one of the immaculately costumed western stars of the 1930s, gaining enormous popularity on the Saturday matinee movie scene. His style combined comedy with modern story and enough action to keep audiences interested.

BOLD CABALLERO, THE (aka: BOLD CAVALIER, UK) Republic, 1936, Color, 67 min, VT. **Producer:** Nat Levine; **Director:** Wells Root; **Screenplay:**

Root; **Music:** Karl Hajos (uncredited) and Hugo Riesnfeld (uncredited); **Cinematographer:** Jack Marta; **Editor:** Lester Orlebeck; **Cast:** Robert Livingston, Heather Angel, Sig Ruman, Ian Wolfe, Robert Warwick, Charles Stevens, Emily Fitzroy, Walter Long.

While trying to help the colonials in Spanish California, Zorro (Robert Livingston) is charged with the murder of the new governor. This little-known color film is the first sound Zorro movie, and Livingston does a nice job as the masked avenger who sweeps away tyranny and oppression.

BOLD FRONTIERSMAN, THE Republic, 1948, B&W, 59 min. **Producer:** Gordon Kay; **Director:** Phillip Ford; **Screenplay:** Robert Creighton Williams; **Music:** Mort Glickman (director); **Cinematographer:** Ernest Miller; **Editor:** Arthur Roberts; **Cast:** Allan Lane, Eddy Waller, Roy Barcroft, John Alvin, Francis McDonald, Fred Graham, Ed Cassidy, Edmund Cobb.

Rocky Lane and his horse Black Jack try to protect the gold that ranchers acquired to build a new dam after being hard

Allan "Rocky" Lane (publicity shot), star of The Bold Frontiersman *and dozens of westerns for Republic (1948–53). He was one of the top ten western stars in 1951–53, but the demise of the B western compromised his popularity.* (AUTHOR'S COLLECTION)

hit by a drought. However, he must first battle the bad guys, led by a fellow called Smiling Jim (Roy Barcroft), who are up to no good.

In 1948, after appearing as Red Ryder in more than a half-dozen features, Lane added the nickname "Rocky" and became Allan "Rocky" Lane with his stallion, Black Jack. Unlike other B western stars, he never deviated from his name, appearing only as Allan "Rocky" Lane. He was one of the top ten western stars from 1951 to 1953, but as quickly as his fame came, it disappeared as the B western reign ended. His "Rocky" Lane films include *The Wild Frontier* (1947); *Carson City Raiders, Desperadoes of Dodge City, Marshal of Amarillo, Sundown in Santa Fe, Oklahoma Badlands, Renegades of Sonora, The Denver Kid* (1948); *Bandit King of Texas, Navajo Trail Raiders, Frontier Investigator, The Wyoming Bandit, Death Valley Gunfighter, Powder River Rustlers, Sheriff of Wichita* (1949); *Frisco Tornado, Gunmen of Abilene, Covered Wagon Raid, Vigilante Hideout, Code of the Silver Sage, Salt Lake Raiders, Rustlers on Horseback, Trail of Robin Hood, Desert of Lost Men* (1950); *Desert of Lost Men, Wells Fargo Gunmaster, Rough Riders of Durango, Night Riders of Montana, Fort Dodge Stampede* (1951); *Captive of Billy the Kid, Desperadoes Outpost, Black Hills Ambush, Leadville Gunslinger* (1952); *Savage Frontier, El Paso Stampede, Bandits of the West, Marshal of Cedar Rock* (1953). (See also *ADVENTURES OF RED RYDER* and *SHERIFF OF SUNDOWN*.)

BONANZA TOWN   Columbia, 1951, B&W, 56 min, VT. **Producer:** Colbert Clark; **Director:** Fred F. Sears; **Screenplay:** Bert Horswell and Barry Shipman; **Music:** Mischa Bakaleinikoff (director); **Cinematographer:** Henry Freulich; **Editor:** Paul Borofsky; **Cast:** Charles Starrett, Fred F. Sears, Luther Crockett, Myron Healey, Charles Horvath, Slim Duncan, Smiley Burnette, Vernon Dent.

BONANZA: THE RETURN   Lions Gate Entertainment, 1993, Color, 96 min, VT, DVD. **Producers:** Kent McCray and Gary Wohlleben; **Director:** Jerry Jameson; **Screenplay:** David Dortort and Michael Landon, Jr.; **Music:** Bruce Miller; **Cinematographer:** Haskell Boggs; **Cast:** Ben Johnson, Michael Landon Jr., Emily Warfield, Brian Leckner, Alistair McDougall, Richard Roundtree, Jack Elam, Dirk Blocker, Dean Stockwell, Linda Gray.

Bronc Evans (Ben Johnson), who has taken over the Ponderosa for his late friend Ben Cartwright, fights to protect the ranch from a hostile takeover by a conniving tycoon, Augustus Brandenburg (Dean Stockwell). When things get violent, newspaper reporter Walter Fenster (Dirk Blocker) comes to Virginia City to get the story. A new generation of Cartwright grandchildren whom Ben Cartwright never knew also arrive to help save the Ponderosa.

BOOM TOWN BADMEN   See *ROARING WESTWARD*.

BOOT HILL BANDITS   Monogram/Range Busters, Inc., 1942, B&W, 58 min. **Producer:** George W. Weeks;

Director: S. Roy Luby; **Screenplay:** George Arthur Durlam; **Editor:** Roy Claire; **Cast:** Charles King, John "Dusty" King, Carl Mathews, Merrill McCormick, John Merton, Milburn Morante, Tex Palmer, Glenn Strange, Max Terhune, Ray "Crash" Corrigan.

This Range Busters feature has the boys arriving in a small town plagued by a series of Wells Fargo gold shipment robberies to find out who is behind the lawlessness. Glenn Strange gives a fine performance as a psychotic killer. (See also *RANGE BUSTERS, THE*.)

BOOTHILL BRIGADE   Republic, 1937, B&W, 56 min. **Producer:** A. W. Hackel; **Director:** Sam Newfield; **Screenplay:** George Plympton; **Cinematographer:** Bert Longenecker; **Editor:** Roy Claire; **Cast:** Johnny Mack Brown, Claire Rochelle, Dick Curtis, Horace Murphy, Frank La Rue, Ed Cassidy, Bobby Nelson, Frank Ball, Steve Clark, Frank Ellis.

A rancher fires his men and uses a crooked land dealer to put the other ranchers off their own land. This is the final film in Johnny Mack Brown's series for A. W. Hackel. (See also *GAMBLING TERROR, THE*.)

BOOTHILL MAMAS   See *OUTLAW WOMEN*.

BOOTS AND SADDLES   Republic, 1937, B&W, 60 min, VT. **Producer:** Sol C. Siegal; **Director:** Joseph Kane; **Screenplay:** Oliver Drake and Jack Natteford; **Music:** Smiley Burnette (songs), Karl Hajos, Lani McIntyre, Carson Robinson, and Walter Samuels (songs); **Cinematographer:** William Nobles; **Editor:** Lester Orlebeck; **Cast:** Gene Autry, Smiley Burnette, Judith Allen, Ronald Sinclair, Guy Usher, William "Wild Bill" Elliott (as Gordon Elliott).

A young Englishman inherits a ranch and plans to sell it. However, Gene Autry is determined to make him into a real westerner by teaching him "the Code of the West." (See also *TUMBLING TUMBLEWEEDS*.)

BOOTS MALONE   Columbia, 1952, B&W, 102 min. **Producer:** Milton Holmes; **Director:** William Dieterle; **Screenplay:** Milton Holmes and Harold Buchanan (originally uncredited); **Music:** Elmer Bernstein; **Cinematographer:** Charles Lawton Jr.; **Editor:** Al Clark; **Cast:** William Holden, Stanley Clements, Basil Ruysdale, Benton Reid, Ralph Dumke, Ed Begley, Hugh Sanders, Harry Morgan (Henry Morgan) Johnny Stewart, Whit Bissell.

A 15-year-old boy who loves horses (Johnny Stewart) meets a down-and-out jockey agent (William Holden) who trains the boy to be a jockey, but for a price of his own. The nice interplay between Holden and young Stewart provides a story rich in drama and pathos.

BOOTS OF DESTINY   Grand National Pictures, 1937, B&W, 60 min. **Producer:** M. H. Hoffman; **Director:**

Arthur Rosson; **Screenplay:** Arthur Rosson and Philip Graham White; **Cinematographer:** Tom Galligan; **Editor:** Dan Milner; **Cast:** Ken Maynard, Claudia Dell, Vince Barnett, Ed Cassidy, Martin Garralaga, George Morrell.

When the Jack Harmon gang and a rival Mexican gang go after a hidden treasure on the Wilson ranch, Acey Devcy (Vince Barnett) goes to find Ken Crawford (Ken Maynard), but instead he finds Ken in jail for a crime he didn't commit. The title refers to traces of clay on the villain's boots. (See also *LUCKY LARKIN*.)

BORDER BADMEN PRC, 1945, B&W, 59 min. **Producer:** Sigmund Neufeld; **Director:** Sam Newfield; **Screenplay:** George Milton; **Music:** Frank Sanucci; **Cinematographer:** Jack Greenhalgh; **Editor:** Holbrook N. Todd; **Cast:** Buster Crabbe, Al St. John, Lorraine Miller, Charles King, Ray Bennett, Arch Hall Sr., Budd Buster, Marilyn Gladstone.

See *OUTLAW OF THE PLAINS*.

BORDER BRIGAND Universal, 1935, B&W, 56 min. Producers: Buck Jones and Irving Starr; Director: Nick Grinde; Screenplay: Stewart Anthony; Music: Mischa Bakaleinikoff (uncredited), Paul Van Loan (uncredited), and Oliver Wallace (uncredited); Cinematographers: William Sickner and Allen O. Thompson; Editor: Bernard Loftus; Cast: Buck Jones, Lona Andre, Fred Kohler, Frank Rice, Hank Bell, Gertrude Astor, J. P. McGowan, Edward Keane, Lew Meehan, Al Bridge, Slim Whitaker.

When his brother is murdered by a gang leader who escapes across the border into the United States, a Canadian Mountie goes undercover to catch the killer. In addition to appearing in nearly 200 pictures (starting in 1918), Buck Jones also produced nearly 25 movies in the 1920s and '30s. (See also *STONE OF SILVER CREEK*.)

BORDER CABALLERO Puritan Pictures, 1936, B&W, 59 min, VT. Producers: Sigmund Neufeld, Sam Newfield, and Leslie Simmonds; Director: Newfield; Screenplay: Norman S. Hall and Joseph O'Donnell; Cinematographer: Jack Greenhalgh; Editor: Holbrook N. Todd; Cast: Tim McCoy, Lois January, Ralph Byrd, J. Frank Glendon, Ted Adams, John Merton.

Tex Weaver (Ralph Byrd) is working undercover to bring a gang of bank robbers into the arms of justice. When he is killed, Tim Ross (Tim McCoy), who is working as a marksman with Doc Shaw's Traveling Show, takes over. Posing as a Mexican, he lays a trap for the gang. The handsome and dignified McCoy, who was one of the half-dozen top western stars of the 1920s, enjoyed a popularity that survived intact through and beyond the 1930s. The all-black costume he took to wearing was imitated by William Boyd for his Hopalong Cassidy roles. (See also *MAN FROM GUN TOWN*.)

BORDER CAFÉ RKO, 1937, B&W, 67 min. **Producer:** Robert Sisk; **Director:** Lew Landers; **Screenplay:**

Lionel Houser; **Cinematographer:** Nicholas Musuraca; **Editor:** Jack Hively; **Cast:** Harry Carey, John Beal, Armida, George Irving, Leona Roberts, J. Carrol Naish, Marjorie Lord, Lee Patrick, Paul Fix.

Keith Whitney (John Beal), the son of a wealthy eastern senator, heads west and gets stone drunk at a border café. After losing the money his father had given him to buy a ranch, he learns that his parent is arriving. A kindly rancher named Tex (Harry Carey) takes him in and tells the father that his son is part owner. When the father and his girlfriend are kidnapped, Tex and the now-reformed Keith set out after them. Carey, a study in naturalism and grace on the screen, would win a Best Supporting Actor nomination two years later in Frank Capra's *Mister Smith Goes to Washington*. *Border Café* was based on Thomas Gill's story "In the Mexican Quarter."

BORDER DEVILS Artclass Pictures Company, 1932, B&W, 65 min. **Producer:** Louis Weiss; **Director:** William Nigh; **Screenplay:** Harry C. Crist and Murray Leoinster; **Cinematographer:** William Dietz; **Editor:** Holbrook N. Todd; **Cast:** Kathleen Collins, Harry Carey, George "Gabby" Hayes, Niles Welch, Albert J. Smith, Merrill McCormick, Art Mix, Olive Golden.

Jim Gray (Harry Carey) is looking for a gang leader known as the General. When an associate is murdered, Jim assumes his identity and, with his pal Squint Saunders (Gabby Hayes), tries to join the gang. However, they are captured, and Jim is told that if he wants to join the gang, he must first kill his partner. This early western talkie pairs Harry Carey with his wife Olive (billed as Olive Golden); both were good friends of John Ford. Olive Carey would appear in many Western films including Ford's *THE SEARCHERS* and John Wayne's *THE ALAMO*. The mother of film star Harry Carey Jr., she died in 1988 at the age of 93.

BORDER FEUD Producer's Releasing Corp., 1947, B&W, 54 min. **Producer:** Jerry Thomas; **Director:** Ray Taylor; **Screenplay:** Patricia Harper and Joseph O'Donnell; **Cinematographer:** Milford Anderson; **Editor:** Joseph Gluck; **Cast:** Lash La Rue, Al St. John, Ian Keith, Gloria Marlen, Kenneth Ferril, Ed Cassidy, Bob Duncan, Casey MacGregor, Buster Slaven, Mike Conrad, Bud Osborne, Henry Wills.

The tag line for this film reads "Gun feud justice bows to his whip," and no western star used that whip like Lash La Rue. In this action-packed La Rue outing, Lash plays Marshal Cheyenne Davis, who is called to town to settle a feud between two families, the Condons and the Harts. He poses as an outlaw, but when the bad guys learn his true identity they issue a fake wanted poster, hoping that the townsfolk will lynch him. (See also *LAW OF THE LASH*.)

BORDER G-MEN RKO, 1938, B&W, 60 min. **Producer:** Bert Gilroy; **Director:** David Howard; **Screenplay:**

Oliver Drake; **Music:** Gene Autry and Ray Whitley (songs); **Cinematographer:** Joseph H. August; **Editor:** Frederic Knudtson; **Cast:** George O'Brien, Laraine Day (as Laraine Johnson), Ray Whitley, John Miljan, Rita Le Roy, Edgar Dearing, Edward Keane, Ethan Laidlaw, Hugh Sothern, Bob Burns.

Government agent Jim Galloway (George O'Brien) is sent undercover to investigate a shifty businessman who is violating the Neutrality Act, a law forbidding the export of troops and war material to foreign countries in the years before World War II. The film is billed both as a film noir and as a western piece. O'Brien's great screen presence adds to this action-packed oater from RKO. The rugged O'Brien made the transition from the silent screen to talkies quite smoothly, and he was an RKO staple in the 1930s. Ray Whitley sings "Back in the Saddle Again" (which he cowrote with Gene Autry, who used it as his theme song). Laraine Day is credited as Laraine Johnson. (See also *RACKETEERS OF THE RANGE*.)

BORDER GUNS   Aywon Film Corporation, 1935, B&W. **Producer:** Nathan Hirsh; **Directors:** Robert J. Horner and Jack Nelson; **Screenplay:** Ollie Milliken; **Cinematographer:** James Diamond; **Editor:** William Austin; **Cast:** Bill Cody, Blanche Mehaffey, George Chesebro, William Desmond, Jimmy Aubrey, Franklyn Farnum, Wally Wales, Fred Church.

Bill Harris (Bill Cody) is working undercover and looking for rustlers. When he rides into town, he makes friends with Fred Palmer, who is one of the rustlers. Both take a fancy to pretty Jane Wilson. When the rustlers' boss learns Bill's true identity, he exploits his attraction to Jane, hoping that Fred's friends will kill him. Aywon Film Corporation was a small film company with eight documented movie titles between 1920 and 1935.

BORDERLAND   Paramount, 1937, B&W, 82 min, VT. **Producer:** Harry Sherman; **Director:** Nate Watt; **Screenplay:** Harrison Jacobs; **Music:** Lee Zahler; **Cinematographer:** Archie Stout; **Editor:** Robert Warwick; **Cast:** William Boyd, James Ellison, George "Gabby" Hayes, Morris Ankrum, John Beach, Nora Lane, Charlene Wyatt, Trevor Bardette, Earl Hodgins.

Hoppy goes underground as an outlaw. He is hired by the Texas Rangers to track down a gang leader known as the Fox, and in order to make himself credible to the gang he becomes as disagreeable and miserable as he can be. This film allows William Boyd an opportunity to showcase some considerable acting ability. With strong characterizations, a literate script, and a great performance by Morris Ankrum as the lead outlaw, this film, based on the story by Clarence E. Mulford, ranks as one of the better Hop-Along Cassidy efforts. (See also *HOP-ALONG CASSIDY*.)

BORDER LAW   Columbia, 1931, B&W, 63 min. **Producer:** Irving Briskin; **Director:** Louis King; **Screenplay:**

Stewart Anthony; **Music:** Irving Bibo (uncredited) and Sam Perry (uncredited); **Cinematographer:** L. William O'Connell; **Editor:** Otto Meyer; **Cast:** Buck Jones, Lupita Tower, Jim Mason, Frank Rice, Don Chapman, Louis Hickus, E. R. Smith, John Wallace.

When Jim's brother is killed by Shag Smith, Jim and Thunder quit the Rangers so they can cross the border and join Smith's gang. The plan is to get the gang to cross back over the border, where the Rangers will be waiting for them. This early Buck Jones formula piece has a familiar plot. (See also *WHITE EAGLE*.)

BORDER LEGION   Paramount, 1924, B&W, 68 min. **Presenters:** Adolph Zukor and Jesse L. Lasky; **Director:** William K. Howard; **Screenplay:** George Hull; **Cinematographer:** Alvin Wycoff; **Cast:** Antonio Moreno, Helene Chadwick, Rockliffe Fellowes, Gibson Gowland, Charles Ogle, James Corey, Edward Gribbon, Luke Cosgrave.

In this version of the Zane Grey novel, Joan Randle (Helene Chadwick) tells Jim Cleve (Antonio Moreno) that he is too lazy to go bad. To prove her wrong, he goes west to join the notorious Border Legion gang. Joan regrets what she has done and follows him, but when she is captured by gang leader Jack Kells (Rockliff Fellows), she shoots him in self-defense and then nurses him back to health. In the end it is Kells who sacrifices his life to save her, while Joan and Jim manage to escape the clutches of the bad guys. This is the first of three Paramount versions of the film, and according to *Photoplay* magazine it provides "mighty good entertainment" for the silent screen.

BORDER LEGION, THE   Goldwyn, 1918, B&W, six reels. **Director:** T. Hayes Hunter; **Screenplay:** Victor de Viliers and Laurence Marston; **Cinematographer:** Abe Schlotz; **Editor:** Alex Troffey; **Cast:** Blanche Bates, Hobart Bosworth, Eugene Strong, Kewpie Morgan, Russell Simpson, Arthur Morrison, Richard Souzade, Kate Elmore.

In this six-reel silent version of the Zane Grey novel, cowhand Jim Cleve (Eugene Strong) is wrongly accused of murder and is rescued by Jack Kells (Hobart Bosworth), the leader of a band of Idaho outlaws known as the Border Legion. But when the legion takes pretty Joan Randle (Blanche Bates) prisoner, leaving Cleve to guard her, Cleve realizes he cannot be part of the gang and decides to rescue her.

In 1916 Zane Grey published the novel *The Border Legion*. Subsequently, the novel provided the raw material for five screenplays. This version, the first of the five, starred Hobart Bosworth, who achieved stardom in the *Count of Monte Cristo* (Paramount, 1913).

BORDER LEGION, THE   Paramount, 1930, B&W, 68 min. **Directors:** Otto Brower and Edwin H. Knopf; **Screenplay:** Percy Heath and Edward E. Paramore Jr.; **Cinematographer:** Max Stengler; **Editor:** Doris Drought; **Cast:**

Richard Arlen, Jack Holt, Fay Wray, Eugene Pallette, Stanley Fields, E. H. Calvert, Ethan Allen, Syd Saylor.

The first talking version of Zane Grey's novel has a bit of a twist: Jack Kells saves Jim Cleve from being hanged for a crime committed by one of his gang. In gratitude, Jim joins the Kells gang. Later, when gang member Hack Gulden kidnaps Joan Randle, Jim guards her and prevents Gulden from making advances. However, Kells fears an attack by an armed posse and orders an attack on the town of Alder Creek, Idaho. When Jim is imprisoned for attempting to warn the towns-people of the impeding attack, Kells helps him escape. As Gulden is about to confront Jim in a final showdown, Kells appears and shoots Gulden dead before perishing himself.

Made by Paramount as part of the early talkie-era craze, this film features Richard Arlen as Jim Cleve, Jack Holt as Jack Kells, and Fay Wray as Joan Randle. Arlen and Wray were big-name contract players at Paramount, while the ever-popular Jack Holt usually worked with Columbia. To capitalize on property the studio already owned, Paramount remade the film in 1934 and renamed it *The Last Round-Up*, with Randolph Scott as Jim Cleve and a plot that closely resembles the 1930 film.

BORDER LEGION, THE (aka: WEST OF THE BADLANDS) Republic, 1940, B&W, 58 min. Producer: Joseph Kane; Director: Joseph Kane; Screenplay: Olive Cooper and Louis Stevens; Music: William Lava (uncredited) and Milton Rosen (uncredited); Cinematographer: Jack A. Marta; Editor: Edward Mann; Cast: Roy Rogers, George "Gabby" Hayes, Carol Hughes, Joe Sawyer, Maude Eburne, Jay Novello, Wally Wales.

As part of the Roy Rogers series for Republic, Roy is cast as Steve Kells. The plot concerns an eastern doctor who is on the run from the authorities in New York. He heads west and comes to the aid of friends besieged by an outlaw gang known as the Border Legion. Subsequently, he is able to clear himself of any wrongdoing back east. Joseph Kane, who directed Roy Rogers in scores of films, helmed this streamlined version of *The Border Legion*, based on the novel by Zane Grey.

BORDER OUTLAWS Universal, 1950, B&W, 57 min. Producers: Jack Schwarz and Richard Talmadge; Director: Arthur Hoerl; Cast: Spade Cooley, Maria Hart, Bill Edwards, Bill Kennedy, George Slocum, John Laurenz, Douglas Wood, Bud Osburn, John Carpenter.

A mysterious masked outlaw named "The Phantom Rider" terrorizes a county and is wanted for smuggling drugs. Spade Cooley, a country swing bandleader, made a few attempts to capture the sagebrush screen with films like this one. Nicknamed the "King of Western Swing," Cooley received a life sentence for killing his wife but was released after serving several years of his time. He died of a heart attack while performing a benefit for the police department in Oakland, California. Among his more than two dozen film appearances are such sagebrush features as *Rockin' in the Rockies*, *Outlaws of the Rockies* (1945); *Tumbleweed Tempo*, *Texas Pandhandle* (1946); *Vacation Days* (1947); *Square Dance Jubilee*, *Silver Bandit*, *Kid from Gower Gulch* (1949); *I Shot Billy the Kid*, *Everybody's Dancin'* (1950); *Casa Manana* (1951); *The Big Tip Off* (1955).

BORDER PATROL United Artists, 1943, B&W, 63 min, VT. Producers: Lewis J. Rachmil and Harry Sherman; Director: Leslie Selander; Screenplay: Michael Wilson; Music: Irvin Talbot; Cinematographer: Russell Harlen; Editor: Sherman Rose; Cast: William Boyd, Andy Clyde, Bill George, Russell Simpson, Claudia Drake, George Reeves, Duncan Renaldo, Pierce Lyden, Robert Mitchum, Cliff Parkinson.

Hoppy, California, and Johnny are Texas Rangers trying to end a scheme whereby Mexicans are smuggled into the United States for the purpose of providing slaves for a corrupt silver-mine owner. Hoppy and the boys are captured and sentenced to hang, but they finally escape, free the slaves, and bring the bad guys to justice. William Boyd played Hop-Along Cassidy in 66 pictures, a Hollywood record for playing the same character on screen. (See also *HOP-ALONG CASSIDY*.)

BORDER PATROLMAN, THE 20th Century Fox, 1936, B&W, 60 min. Producer: Sol Lesser; Director: David Howard; Screenplay: Ben S. Cohen and Daniel Jarrett; Cinematographer: Frank B. Good; Editor: Robert O'Crandall; Cast: George O'Brien, Polly Ann Young, William P. Carlton, LeRoy Mason, Al Hill, Smiley Burnette, Tom London.

When a border patrolman catches a spoiled young lady smoking in a no-smoking area, her parents hire the patrol-man to watch over their daughter. But when she runs over the border and gets involved with jewel thieves, he has to go in and save her. A nice mixture of comedy and action makes for a pleasant film.

BORDER PHANTOM Republic, 1937, B&W, 60 min, VT. Producer: A. W. Hackel; Director: S. Roy Luby; Screenplay: Fred Myton; Cinematographer: Jack Greenhalgh; Editor: Roy Claire; Cast: Bob Steele, Harley Wood, Don Barclay, Horace Murphy, Perry Murdock, Mike Morita, Karl Hackett, John Peters.

Larry O'Day (Bob Steele) stumbles across and battles an Asian villain who is smuggling Chinese "picture girls" across the Mexican border for sale to wealthy Chinese bachelors. This interesting film is one of Steele's better ventures and most energetic performances. (See also *LIGHTNIN' CRANDALL*; *RIDERS OF THE DESERT*.)

BORDER RIVER Universal, 1954, Color, 80 min. Producer: Albert J. Cohen; Director: George Sherman; Screenplay: Louis Stevens and William Sackheim; Cinematographer: Irving Glassberg; Editor: Frank Gross; Cast: Joel McCrea, Yvonne De Carlo, Pedro Armendáriz, Howard

A scene from Border River (UNIVERSAL/AUTHOR'S COLLECTION)

Petrie, Erika Nordin, Alfonso Bedoya, Ivan Triesault, George J. Lewis, George Wallace, Lane Chandler, Charles Horvath, Nacho Galindo.

Joel McCrea is a Confederate officer who leads his men into Mexico for the purpose of buying guns for the Confederacy. He has $2 million in gold. The problem is, who to trust?

BORDER ROUND-UP Producers Releasing Company, 1942, B&W, 57 min, VT. **Producer:** Sigmund Neufeld; **Director:** Sam Newfield; **Screenplay:** Stephen Worth; **Cast:** George Houston, Al St. John, John Dennis Moore, Charles King, I. Stanford Jolley.

The Lone Rider (George Houston) comes to the aid of a friend who has been framed for murder. Houston, a former opera singer, found greener pastures making western films, particularly in a series of action-packed, low-budget westerns for PRC, for whom he did a more credible job than critics often accorded him. The television title is *The Lone Rider in Border Roundup*. Other features in "The Lone Rider" series include *The Lone Rider in Ghost Town* (1941) and *The Lone Rider in Cheyenne* (1942).

Director Sam Newfield (1899–1964) helmed more than 200 films, including nearly 150 westerns. He was the brother of Sigmund Neufeld, president of Producers Releasing Corporation (PRC), for whom he directed many films.

BORDER SADDLE MATES Republic, 1952, B&W, 67 min, VT. **Producer:** Edward J. White (associate); **Director:** William Witney; **Screenplay:** Albert DeMond; **Music:** John Elliott; **Cinematographer:** John MacBurnie; **Editor:** Harold Minter; **Cast:** Rex Allen, Mary Ellen Kay, Slim Pickens, Roy Barcroft, Forrest Taylor, Jimmy Moss, Bud Osburne, The Republic Rhythm Riders.

BORDER SHOOTOUT Turner Home Video, 1990, B&W, 110 min, VT. **Producer:** C. T. McIntyre; **Director:** McIntyre; **Screenplay:** McIntyre; **Music:** Coley Music Group; **Cinematographer:** Dennis Dalzell; **Cast:** Cody Glenn, Glenn Ford, Jeff Kaake, Charlene Tilton, Michael Forrest, Michael Ansara.

Honest but naïve rancher Kirby Frye (Cody Glenn) is appointed deputy in a corrupt Arizona border town, and soon all hell breaks loose. Glenn Ford plays the aging sheriff who must remain cool under pressure even though the town has given up on him. Jeff Kaake is the ruthless Phil Sundeen, who tyrannizes the town and is the son of one of the town's founders. The reviews are mixed here. Some reviewers like this action-packed film, while others find it to be an amateurish production. Either way the plot, based on Elmore Leonard's novel, is a good one.

BORDERTOWN GUNFIGHTERS Republic, 1944, B&W, 60 min. **Director:** Howard Bretherton; **Screenplay:** Norman Hall; **Cinematographer:** Jack A. Marta; **Editor:** Richard L. Van Enger; **Cast:** William "Wild Bill" Elliott, George "Gabby" Hayes, Anne Jeffreys, Ian Keith, Harry Woods, Edward Earle, Karl Hackett, Roy Barcroft.

Treasury agent Bill Elliott is sent to break up a crooked lottery game being run out of El Paso and to bring the corrupt lottery boss Cameo Shelby (Ian Keith) to justice. This was one of Bill Elliott's first films for Republic Studios after leaving Columbia in 1943 to work in the Red Ryder series. Like William S. Hart, Elliott was a perfectionist who took his acting very seriously. Experts say that his eight films with Gabby Hayes at Republic were among his very best, including *Calling Wild Bill Elliott, Death Valley Manhunt, The Man From Thunder River, Overland Mail Robbery* (1943); *Hidden Valley Outlaws, Marshal of Reno, Mojave Firebrand, Tucson Raiders, Wagon Tracks West* (1944); *Bells of Rosarita* (1945); *Wyoming* (1947).

BORDER TREASURE RKO, 1950, B&W, 60 min. **Producer:** Herman Schlom; **Director:** George Archainbaud; **Screenplay:** Norman Houston; **Music:** Paul Sawtell; **Cinematographer:** J. Roy Hunt; **Editor:** Desmond Marquette; **Cast:** Tim Holt, Richard Martin, Inez Cooper, Jane Nigh, House Peters Jr., John Doucette, Tom Monroe, Lee Fredrick, Julian Rivero, Vince Barnett.

In this RKO oater Anita Castro (Inez Cooper) is raising money for Mexican earthquake victims. But while she is transporting the valuables across the border, the Bat gang led by John Doucette attacks her. Ed Porter and Chito (Tim Holt and Richard Martin) lend a helping hand, driving off the bad guys and retrieving the loot. Any time Holt, Martin, and House Peters Jr. work together there is an element of fun. (See also *ALONG THE RIO GRANDE*.)

BORDER VENGEANCE Kent, 1935, B&W, 45 min. **Producer:** Willis Kent; **Director:** Ray Heintz; **Cast:** Reb Russell, Mary Jane Carey, Kenneth McDonald, Ben Corbett, Hank Bell, Glenn Strange, June Bupp, Norman F. Feusier, Clarence Geldart, Slim Whitaker, Fred Burns, Pat Harmon.

After discovering that 40 head of his cattle have been rustled away, a rancher is murdered. A neighboring family is unjustly accused of the crime, and they flee across the border in search of the real killers and to clear their name. Reb Russell, born Lafayette H. Russell in 1905, made nearly a dozen films, including seven features in 1935 alone. (See also *LIGHTNING TRIGGERS*.)

BORDER VIGILANTES Paramount, 1941, B&W, 63 min. **Producer:** Harry Sherman; **Director:** Derwin Abrahams; **Cinematographer:** Russell Harlan; **Editors:** Carroll Lewis and Robert B. Warwick; **Cast:** William Boyd, Russell Hayden, Andy Clyde, Victor Jory, Morris Ankrum, Frances Gifford.

A town victimized by outlaws sends for Hoppy, Lucky, and California after their own vigilante committee fails to solve the town's problems. Hoppy and his pals soon discover that the bad guys and the town vigilantes are led by the same corrupt boss. (See also *HOP-ALONG CASSIDY*.)

BORDER WOLVES Universal, 1938, B&W, 56 min. **Producer:** Paul Malvern; **Director:** Joseph H. Lewis; **Screenplay:** Norman S. Parker; **Cinematographer:** Harry Nuemann; **Cast:** Bob Baker, Constance Moore, Fuzzy Knight, Dickie Jones, Willie Fung, Glenn Strange, Frank Campeau, Oscar O'Shea, Ed Cassidy.

During the time of the California Gold Rush, a man is falsely accused of criminal activities and sets out to clear his name. Bob Baker's pleasant personality and some good songs make for an enjoyable Universal oater. Among the uncredited musical team for this little-known B western are future award-winning composers David Raskin (*Laura*) and Franz Waxman (*Sunset Boulevard, A Place in the Sun*). (See also *BLACK BANDIT*.)

BORN RECKLESS Warner Bros., 1958, B&W, 80 min. **Producer:** Aubrey Schenck; **Director:** Howard W. Koch; **Screenplay:** Richard H. Landau and Schenck; **Music:** Buddy Bregman; **Cinematographer:** Joseph F. Biroc; **Editor:** John F. Schreyer; **Cast:** Mamie Van Doren, Jeff Richards, Arthur Hunnicutt, Carol Ohmart, Tommy Duggan, Nacho Galindo, Don "Red" Barry.

Kelly Cobb (Jeff Richards) travels to one country rodeo after another hoping to make enough money to buy a piece of land. Along the way he rescues trick rider Jackie Adams, played by the vivacious Mamie Van Doren, from the clutches of an amorous sportswriter. They go off together, and Jackie begins to fall in love with Kelly. But Kelly refuses to notice, preferring instead to risk life and limb for his coveted "pot of gold" and an occasional floozy or two. The big question is, can the alluring Jackie convince the reckless Kelly to change his roaming ways? Look for Don "Red" Barry in the role of Okie.

BORN TO BATTLE Reliable Pictures Corporation, 1935, B&W, 63 min. **Producer:** Bernard B. Ray; **Director:** Harry S. Webb; **Screenplay:** Rose Gordon and Carl Krusada; **Cinematographer:** J. Henry Kruse; **Editor:** Frederick Bain; **Cast:** Tom Tyler, Jean Carmen, Earl Dwire, Julian Rivero, Nelson McDowell, William Desmond, Richard Alexander.

"Cyclone" Tom Saunders (Tom Tyler) is hired by a ranchers' association to investigate some recent cattle rustling at one of their ranches. After quickly discovering that the original suspects—a father and daughter—are incapable of rustling, he turns his attention to the swaggering foreman, Nate Lenox (Richard Alexander), who is the true culprit. (See also *MYSTERY RANCH*.)

BORN TO BUCK American National Enterprises, 1968, Color, 93 min, NTSC. **Producer:** Casey Tibbs; **Cast:** Tibbs, Henry Fonda, Rex Allen (narrators).

This is a documentary about rodeo champion Casey Tibbs breeding his own bucking broncos on the Teton Sioux Indian reservation in South Dakota, then driving his herd of some 400 horses halfway across the state and back to his ranch. Some marvelous scenic value enhances this interesting and different documentary feature.

BORN TO THE SADDLE Astor Pictures, 1957, Color, 77 min. **Producer:** Hal Shelton; **Director:** William Beaudine; **Screenplay:** Adele S. Buffington and Gordon Ray Young; **Music:** Emil Velazco; **Cinematographer:** Marcel Le Picard; **Editor:** Chester W. Schaeffer; **Cast:** Bob Anderson, Rand Brooks, Chuck Courtney, Boyd Davis, Leif Ericson, Milton Kibbee, Fred Kohler Jr., Dolores Prest, Glenn Strange, Lucille Thompson, Donald Woods.

A young boy is befriended by a man who hires him to train a horse for an important race. But the man is really a gambler, and the race is fixed.

BORN TO THE WEST (aka: HELL TOWN) Paramount, 1937, B&W, 59 min, VT. **Producer:** William T. Lackey; **Director:** Charles Barton; **Screenplay:** Stuart Anthony; **Cinematographer:** Devereaux Jennings; **Editor:** John F. Link; **Cast:** John Wayne, Marsha Hunt, Johnny Mack Brown, John Patterson, Monte Blue, James Craig.

In one of his best pre-*STAGECOACH* ventures, John Wayne plays cowboy Dare Rudd, who lands a job as a cook at the ranch of his cousin, played by Johnny Mack Brown. Assigned to deliver a herd of cattle to a railroad, he becomes involved in a crooked card game and is subsequently rescued by

Brown. The combination of Wayne, Brown, and Zane Grey's fine novel proved a winner for Paramount.

Paramount borrowed Wayne for this one—a version of a 1926 silent film starring Jack Holt in the lead role. Due to a studio clerical error Alan Ladd was credited for an appearance in this film, but he never appears.

BORROWED TROUBLE United Artists, 1948, B&W, 58 min. **Producers:** William Boyd and Lewis Rachmil; **Director:** George Archainbaud; **Screenplay:** Charles Belden; **Music:** Darrell Calker; **Cinematographer:** Mack Stengler; **Editor:** Fred W. Berger; **Cast:** Boyd, Andy Clyde, Rand Brooks, Elaine Riley, John Parrish, Cliff Clark, Helen Chapman, John Kellogg.

Hoppy rescues a kidnapped school teacher (Helen Chapman) who has been fighting against a saloon opening up next to her school. William Boyd was one of the few western stars to produce his own films. (See also *HOP-ALONG CASSIDY*.)

BOSS COWBOY Superior Talking Pictures Inc., 1936, B&W, 51 min. **Producer:** Victor Adamson; **Director:** Adamson; **Screenplay:** Betty Burbridge; **Cast:** Buddy Roosevelt, Frances Morris, Sam Pierce, George Chesebro, Fay McKenzie, Lafe McKee, Bud Osborne.

Ranchers Nolan and Kerns are both losing cattle to a team of rustlers, but a wanted poster reveals that Kerns is actually the leader of the rustlers. It remains for hero Dick Taylor (Buddy Roosevelt) to go after Kerns and bring him to justice. Roosevelt (born Kent Sanderson) appeared in more than 100 films, including 66 westerns, in a career dating back to the silent era. *Boss Cowboy* is just one of two pictures produced by Superior Talking Pictures.

BOSS NIGGER (aka: THE BLACK BOUNTY HUNTER; THE BLACK BOUNTY KILLER (UK); BOSS) Dimension Pictures, 1975, Color, 87 min. **Producers:** Jack Arnold and Fred Williamson; **Director:** Arnold; **Screenplay:** Jack Williamson; **Cinematographer:** Robert Caramico; **Cast:** Fred Williamson, D'Urville Martin, William Smith, R. G. Armstrong, Don "Red" Barry, Barbara Leigh, Carmen Hayworth, Carmen Zapata.

Fred Williamson is a bounty hunter who out-hustles and out-thinks every white man around. Produced by Williamson, the tag line reads, "White Man's Town . . . Black Man's Law!" Influenced by the blaxploitation films of the early 1970s, this cliché-ridden and overly violent picture was filmed in Santa Fe, New Mexico, in Todd-AO, 35, a special widescreen cinematographic process.

BOSS OF BOOMTOWN Universal Pictures, 1944, B&W, 56 min. **Producer:** Oliver Drake (associate); **Director:** Ray Taylor; **Screenplay:** William Lively; **Music:** Hans Salter; **Cast:** Rod Cameron, Tom Tyler, Fuzzy Knight, Vivian Austin, Ray Whitely, Jack Ingram, Robert Barron,

Marie Austin, Max Wagner, Sam Flint, Richard Alexander, Forest Taylor, Beverlee Mitchell.

Two pals ride to a brawling western town where they encounter a city boss and some genuine romance. Tom Tyler and Rod Cameron make a good duo in Cameron's first starring venture in the western genre.

BOSS OF BULLION CITY Universal, 1940, B&W, 61 min. **Producer:** Harry Sherman; **Director:** Ray Taylor; **Screenplay:** Victor McLeod and Arthur St. Claire; **Music:** Ralph Freed (uncredited), Hans J. Salter (uncredited), Frank Skinner (uncredited), and Clifford Vaughn (uncredited); **Cast:** Johnny Mack Brown, Fuzzy Knight, Nell O'Day, Maria Montez, Earle Hodgins, Harry Woods, Melvin Lang, Richard Alexander, Karl Hackett.

Johnny Mack Brown sets out to disrupt the operations of a crooked town boss. For feminine allure look for sultry seductive Maria Montez as Linda Calhoun, the film's second female lead. Billed as the "Queen of Technicolor" and "The Caribbean Cyclone" by her legions of fans, the Dominican-born beauty was found dead in her bathtub in 1951 at age 34. Cowboy hero Johnny Mack Brown made about 30 films for Universal, including this very good series piece, before moving on to Monogram in 1943. (See also *OLD CHISHOLM TRAIL, THE*.)

BOSS OF LONELY VALLEY Universal, 1937, B&W, 60 min. **Producer:** Buck Jones; **Director:** Ray Taylor; **Screenplay:** Frances Guihan; **Music:** David Klatzkin (uncredited) and Oliver Wallace (uncredited); **Cinematographer:** Allen O. Thompson; **Cast:** Buck Jones, Muriel Evans, Harvey Clark, Lee Phelps, Richard Holland, Grace Goodall, Marty Fain.

One of Hollywood's most popular cowboy stars, Buck Jones was an accomplished horseback rider since childhood, reaching the height of his popularity in the mid-1930s. Based on a novel by Forrest Brown, *Boss of Lonely Valley*, which Jones produced, deals with two investigators (Jones and Harvey Clark) and an unsavory gang leader (Walter Miller) who is taking away ranchers' land with a bunch of phony deeds. (See also *STONE OF SILVER CREEK*.)

BOSS OF RAWHIDE PRC, 1944, B&W, 57 min. **Producer:** Alfred Stern; **Director:** Elmer Clifton; **Screenplay:** Clifton; **Music:** Oliver Drake, Herbert Myers, and James Newill; **Cinematographer:** Robert E. Cline; **Editor:** Charles Henkle Jr.; **Cast:** Dave O'Brien, James Newill, Guy Wilkerson, Nell O'Day, Ed Cassidy, Jack Ingram, Billy Bletcher, Charles King, George Chesebro, Bob Hill.

The Texas Rangers are sent to an area where mysterious killings have been taking place. (See also *FIGHTING VALLEY*.)

BOSS RIDER OF GUN CREEK, THE Universal, 1936, B&W, 60 min. **Producer:** Buck Jones; **Director:** Leslie

Selander; **Screenplay:** Frances Guihan; **Music:** David Klatzkin, Milan Roder, Heintz Roemheld, and Oliver Wallace (all uncredited); **Cinematographer:** Allen O. Thompson; **Cast:** Buck Jones, Muriel Evans, Harvey Clark, Alphonse Ethier, Tom Chatterton, Josef Swickard, Iron Eyes Cody.

Buck Jones plays a dual role (Larry Day/Gary Elliott) in this 1936 film, which he also produced for Universal. The plot involves a man who impersonates his double to clear himself of a murder conviction. Jones, the most popular western star in the country in 1935, was still going strong with the Rough Riders series in 1942, when he met a tragic and heroic death attempting to rescue people trapped in the infamous Coconut Grove nightclub fire in Boston while on a campaign tour to sell U.S. bonds. Jones produced 23 films between 1928 and 1937. (See also *STONE OF SILVER CREEK*.)

BOTH BARRELS BLAZING Columbia, 1945, B&W, 57 min. **Producer:** Colbert Clark; **Director:** Derwin Abrahams; **Screenplay:** William Lively; **Cinematographer:** George Meehan; **Editor:** Henry Batista; **Cast:** Charles Starrett, Tex Harding, Dub Taylor.

Kip Allen, aka the Durango Kid, goes after an outlaw gang that is robbing the railroads. Since the Rangers cannot follow them into New Mexico, Allen decides to take a vacation, and as the Durango Kid he is able to go after them. Ironically, Charles Starrett entered the picture business as a trained dramatic actor who somehow was able to carve his niche as a B western hero. Starrett appeared in 132 western films, of which the Durango Kid pictures numbered over 60. (See also *DURANGO KID, THE*.)

BOUNTY HUNTER, THE Warner Bros., 1954, Color, 79 min. **Producer:** Samuel Bishkoff; **Director:** André De Toth; **Screenplay:** Winston Miller; **Music:** David Buttolph; **Cinematographer:** Edwin B. DuPar; **Editor:** Clarence Kolster; **Cast:** Randolph Scott, Dolores Dorn, Marie Windsor, Howard Petrie, Harry Antrim, Robert Keyes, Ernest Borgnine, Dub Taylor.

The Pinkerton Agency sends Joe Kipp (Randolph Scott) after a trio of train robbers. His job is to track down the three robbers and retrieve the $100,000 they have stolen, but he finds that all three are holding respectable positions in a small town. One is the sheriff (Howard Petrie), one is the postmaster (Dub Taylor), and one is a devious woman (played superbly by Marie Windsor). André De Toth carved his westerns on a relatively small budget, and although his low-budget films were good, they did not match the excellence of Budd Boetticher's work with Randolph Scott. Many of their films together are looked upon today as classics. Look for a brief appearance by Fess Parker as the wild cowboy in the film's finale.

BOUNTY KILLER, THE Embassy Pictures, 1965, Color, 92 min. **Producer:** Alex Gordon; **Director:** Spencer Gordon Bennet; **Screenplay:** Ruth Alexander and Leo Gor-

don; **Music:** Ronald Stein; **Cinematographer:** Frederick E. West; **Editor:** Ronald Sinclair; **Cast:** Dan Duryea, Rod Cameron, Audrey Dalton, Richard Arlen, Buster Crabbe, Fuzzy Knight, Johnny Mack Brown, Bob Steele, Gilbert L. "Broncho Billy" Anderson.

The plot involves a tenderfoot from the East who arrives in the Wild West, where violence is king. He soon discovers that there is easy money in bounty killing. He must now choose between this violent lifestyle and the love of a beautiful saloon singer. A great ensemble of old-timers makes this intelligently written film an interesting vehicle. But the film's best claim to fame is the final screen appearance of Broncho Billy Anderson as an old man seated in the saloon.

BOWERY BUCKAROOS Monogram, 1947, B&W, 66 min, VT. **Producer:** Jan Grippo; **Director:** William Beaudine; **Screenplay:** Tim Ryan, Edmond Seward, and Jerry Warner; **Cinematographer:** Marcel Le Picard; **Cast:** Leo Gorcey, Huntz Hull, Bobby Jordan, Gabriel Dell, William "Billy" Benedict, David Gorcey, Julie Gibson, Minerva Urecal, Norman Willis, Iron Eyes Cody.

When a drugstore owner is accused of murder, the popular boys from the Bowery head to the western town of Hangman's Hollow to find the real murderer.

BOY FROM OKLAHOMA Warner Bros., 1954, Color, 87 min. **Producer:** David Weisbart; **Director:** Michael Curtiz; **Screenplay:** Frank Davis and Winston Miller; **Music:** Max Steiner; **Cinematographer:** Robert Burks; **Editor:** James C. Moore; **Cast:** Will Rogers Jr., Nancy Olson, Lon Chaney Jr., Anthony Caruso, Wallace Ford, Clem Bevans, Merv Griffin, Louis Jean Heydt, Sheb Wooley, Slim Pickens.

Will Rogers Jr. plays a pacifist sheriff who manages to keep the town in line while romancing pretty Nancy Olson. This fun movie later became a spin-off for the TV series *Sugarfoot*.

BRANDED Columbia, 1931, B&W, 61 min, VT. **Director:** D. Ross Lederman; **Screenplay:** Randall Faye; **Music:** Mischa Bakaleinikoff (uncredited), Sidney Cutner (uncredited), and Sam Perry (uncredited); **Cinematographer:** Elmer Dyer and Benjamin H. Kline; **Editor:** Otto Meyer; **Cast:** Buck Jones, Ethel Kenyon, Wallace MacDonald, Philo McCullough, Albert J. Smith, John Oscar, Fred Burns.

Cuthbert Dale (Buck Jones) and his sidekick "Swede" (John Oscar) break up a stage robbery but find themselves arrested for committing the robbery. Unlike Tom Mix, behind whom he was second string at Fox in the 1920s, Jones made the successful transition into the talkies. This 1931 production for Columbia was one of his first sound pictures. (See also *WHITE EAGLE*.)

BRANDED Paramount, 1950, Color, 104 min, VT. **Producer:** Mel Epstein; **Director:** Rudolph Mate; **Screenplay:**

Sidney Boehm and Cyril Hume; **Music:** Roy Webb; **Cinematographer:** Charles B. Lang Jr.; **Editor:** Doane Harrison; **Cast:** Alan Ladd, Mona Freeman, Charles Bickford, Robert Keith, Joseph Calleia, Peter Hansen, Tom Tully, Milburn Stone, Selena Royle.

Alan Ladd plays an itinerant gunfighter known simply as Choya in this film based on a 1934 story by Max Brand. Outlaws want him to impersonate the long-missing son of a rancher named Lavory (Charles Bickford). They persuade Choya to become involved in a million-dollar scheme to gain access to the B-O-M ranch and consequently to the Lavory estate. Conflict occurs when he begins to fall for his so-called sister, played by pretty Mona Freeman. Choya admits the sham and confesses that he is indeed a "four-flushin' thief." To prove his mettle and to regain her love and respect, he sets out to find her real brother, who was kidnapped as a five-year-old, 25 years earlier.

Helmed by Rudolph Mate, this film is a visual treat. A photographer turned director, Mate and cameraman Charles B. Lang Jr. take every advantage of the Arizona scenery in each location shot. Ladd does a nice job in this smartly filmed pulp western, emerging as a true blue horse-opera hero. But it is Robert Keith as the slimy outlaw T. Jefferson Leffingwell who steals the acting credits. The film also marked the start of a long friendship between Ladd and actor Peter Hansen (making his movie debut as Tonio, the Lavorys' long-lost kidnapped son).

Alan Ladd's enormous popularity during the 1940s and early '50s is too often overlooked. He was among Paramount's biggest stars, and he had scored big two years earlier with WHISPERING SMITH. Now as the carefree outlaw with a conscience in Rudolph Mate's *Branded*, Ladd's regular appearance in westerns was assured. Three years later he would achieve definitive stature with SHANE.

Alan Ladd (right) with Charles Bickford and Mona Freeman in Branded *(PARAMOUNT/AUTHOR'S COLLECTION)*

BRANDED A COWARD Supreme, 1935, B&W, 58 min, VT. **Producer:** A. W. Hackel; **Director:** Sam Newfield; **Screenplay:** Earl Snell; **Cinematographer:** William Nobles; **Cast:** Johnny Mack Brown, Billy Seward, Syd Saylor, Lloyd Ingraham, Lee Shumway, Yakima Canutt.

Young Johnny Hume, age six or seven, witnesses the slaughter of his mother, father, and brother by a venomous gang led by a varmint known as "The Cat" (Yakima Canutt). The convoluted plot then moves ahead 20 years. Johnny (Johnny Mack Brown) has grown to manhood and has become an expert rider and target shooter, but he remains traumatized by the fearful memories of his youth. When a group of outlaws stick up the local saloon, Johnny cowers behind the bar. Consequently he hits the trail in shame accompanied by his only pal, a stuttering friend named Oscar. Along the way he encounters a stage holdup and garners enough spunk to shoot a couple of the highwaymen. He takes the stage to the town of Lawless, Arizona, where he is offered the job of marshal. His old fears are resurrected until he learns that the stagecoach robbers who have been terrorizing the town are being run by a new and unknown boss emulating—even to the use of his name—the vicious "Cat." Johnny Mack Brown's first series western for Supreme Pictures is quite good despite its low budget. (See also GAMBLING TERROR, THE.)

BRAND OF FEAR Monogram, 1949, B&W, 56 min. **Producer:** Louis Gray; **Director:** Oliver Drake; **Screenplay:** Basil Dickey; **Editor:** Carl Pierson; **Cast:** Jimmy Wakely, Dub Taylor, Gail Davis, Tom London, Marshall Reed, William Ruhl, Holly Bane, William Bailey, Boyd Stockman, Frank McCarroll, Myron Healey, Bob Woodward, Victor Adamson, Ray Jones, Ray Whitley, Bill Potter.

A cowpoke falls in love with a pretty girl, but he discovers to his dismay that she is the daughter of an ex-convict. Some good singing by Jimmy Wakely and a strong supporting cast are big assets in this otherwise average oater. (See also ACROSS THE RIO GRANDE.)

BRAND OF THE DEVIL PRC, 1944, B&W, 62 min. **Producer:** Arthur Alexander; **Director:** Harry L. Fraser; **Screenplay:** Elmer Clifton; **Cast:** Dave O'Brien, James Newill, Guy Wilkerson, Ellen Hall, I. Stanford Jolley, Charles King, Reed Howes, Budd Buster.

When Molly Dawson (Ellen Hall) sends for the Texas Rangers, Tex, Panhandle, and Jim (Dave O'Brien, Guy Wilkerson, and James Newill) arrive on the scene pretending not to know each other. But eventually their identities become known, and they are captured by a gang of rustlers known as the Devil's Brand. The last of the Texas Rangers series for James Newill. (See also FIGHTING VALLEY.)

BRAND OF THE OUTLAWS Supreme Pictures, 1936, B&W, 60 min. **Producer:** A. W. Hackel; **Director:** Robert N. Bradbury; **Screenplay:** Forbes Parkhill; **Cine-**

matographer: Bert Longenecker; **Editor:** Dan Milner; **Cast:** Bob Steele, Margaret Marquis, Jack Rockwell, Charles King, Ed Cassidy, Frank Ball.

After saving the life of a lawman, a cowboy joins up with a gang without knowing that they are cattle rustlers. When the sheriff captures him and brands him an outlaw, he sets out to prove his innocence. This excellent B western, with Robert N. Bradbury directing son Bob Steele, is a good, old-fashioned, no-frills picture, realistically filmed with taut drama and lots of action. (See also *KID COURAGEOUS*.)

BRASS LEGEND, THE   United Artists, 1956, Color, 79 min. **Producers:** Herman Cohen and Robert Goldstein; **Director:** Gerd Oswald; **Screenplay:** Don Arnold; **Music:** Paul Dunlap; **Cinematographer:** Charles Van Enger; **Editor:** Marjorie Fowler; **Cast:** Hugh O'Brien, Nancy Gates, Raymond Burr, Reba Tassell, Donald MacDonald, Robert Burton, Eddie Firestone.

When a boy aids in the capture of a vicious killer, Hugh O'Brien tries to save him from the grip of the killer now out for revenge. Plenty of action and a tremendous performance by Raymond Burr as the villainous murderer, including a gem of a death scene, make this an entertaining film.

BRAVADOS, THE   20th Century Fox, 1958, Color, 98 min, VT. **Producer:** Herbert B. Swope; **Director:** Henry King; **Screenplay:** Philip Yordon; **Music:** Lionel Newman; **Cinematographer:** Leon Shamroy; **Editor:** William Mace; **Cast:** Gregory Peck, Joan Collins, Steven Boyd, Henry Silva, Lee Van Cleef, Andrew Duggan, Gene Evans, Joe Da Rita.

This grim western tells the story of a taciturn stranger who comes to town to witness the hangings of the four men who raped and murdered his wife. When they escape, he vows to hunt them down. He manages to kill three of the four brutal bravados, showing not an inch of mercy. When he catches up with the last man, he discovers he was wrong; brutal and wicked as they were, they had nothing to do with her death. The film then explores the ironic consequences of his deed. The men Peck kills were innocent of the crime for which he killed them, but guilty of many others.

This film is one of the best of the revenge-oriented westerns, a theme that surfaced with William S. Hart's *HELL'S HINGES* in 1916 and reached its apex in the 1950s. Albert Salmi's performance as one of the pursued villains is excellent. So is the entire film, which the *Saturday Review* called "one of the better westerns in a long, long, time [with] superior direction and a thought provoking theme."

BRAVE WARRIOR   Columbia, 1952, Color, 73 min. **Producer:** Sam Katzman; **Director:** Spencer Gordon Bennet; **Screenplay:** Robert E. Kent; **Music:** Mischa Bakaleinikoff (director); **Cinematographer:** William V. Skall; **Editor:** Aaron Stell; **Cast:** Jon Hall, Christine Larson, Jay Silverheels, Michael Ansara, Harry Cording, James Seay.

Set in Indiana during the 18th century, Steve Ruddell (Jon Hall) attempts to prevent an Indian uprising being supported by the British. Jay Silverheels plays the great Tecumseh, and Michael Ansara takes the part of the Prophet.

BREAKHEART PASS   United Artists, 1975, Color, 95 min, VT. **Producers:** Jerry Gershwin and Elliott Kastner; **Director:** Tom Gries; **Screenplay:** Alistair MacLean; **Music:** Jerry Goldsmith; **Cinematographer:** Lucien Ballard; **Editor:** Byron "Buzz" Brandt; **Cast:** Charles Bronson, Ben Johnson, Richard Crenna, Jill Ireland, Charles Durning, Ed Lauter, Bill McKinney, David Huddleston, Roy Johnson, Rayford Barnes, Archie Moore, Sally Kirkland, Sally Kemp, John Mitchum, Reed Morgan, Casey Tibbs, Doug Atkins.

Charles Bronson is an undercover government agent who tries to trip up a gang of gunrunners, with the bulk of the action taking place on a train. Two of filmland's very best—cinematographer Lucien Ballard and second unit director Yakima Canutt—help make this an exciting, action-filled ride, where no one is exactly what he or she seems to be. As the train passes through snowy mountains, various characters disappear from the train or are found dead. The train is transporting crates of medicine to a small fort near a place called Breakheart Pass. One of the film's highlights is a fistfight between Bronson and ex-light-heavyweight boxing champion Archie Moore. Actor John Mitchum (Redbeard), himself a former boxer, recalled also duking it out with Bronson in the film:

> Charlie is really a street guy and carried that Depression Era attitude with him. We had a little run-in on *Breakheart Pass* . . . The director said, "John, when you slap him I want it to look so real that you really have to throw a punch at him." I threw a left hook at him with an open hand, but in a hundredth of a second I saw he wasn't rolling with it. He had this stern look and was really looking macho. Now I weigh about 215 pounds, so I had to pull the punch or hit him in the face. The director saw that and took me aside and wanted to know why I pulled the punch. I said that Bronson wasn't reacting, so rather than hit him, and I threw a hell of a punch, I had to pull it or hit him hard. Well there is Bronson behind me, now in a fighting stance. He's coming in with his left hand by his left knee. So I said, "Yes, Charlie," and I took my stance. "Here's how I do it." He took a look and backed off. The next time he took the punch beautifully and I hit him with my right hand.

Bronson and female lead Jill Ireland were real-life husband and wife for 22 years before her death in 1990. Look for fine supporting performances from Ben Johnson as a crooked marshal and Ed Lauter as an honest army colonel. The film was the first western for popular British suspense writer Alistair MacLean. Director Tom Gries had garnered unanimous critical acclaim for his 1968 western *WILL PENNY*. While *Breakheart Pass* falls short of that standard, it still remains a polished and well-crafted feature film. A top-flight cast and an intriguing tale provide enough twists and turns to satisfy genre fans of all ages.

BRECKENRIDGE STORY, THE See *RIDE CLEAR OF DIABLO*.

BREED OF THE BORDER (aka: SPEED BRENT WINS) Monogram, 1933, B&W, 58 min. **Producer:** Trem Carr; **Director:** Robert N. Bradbury; **Screenplay:** Harry O. Jones; **Cinematographer:** Faxon M. Dean and Archie Stout; **Editor:** Carl Pierson; **Cast:** Bob Steele, Marion Byron, Ernie Adams, George "Gabby" Hayes (as George Hayes), Henry Roquemore, Fred Craven.

Bob Steele is cowboy race driver Speed Brent. When he drives some shady characters to the border, they slug him and take his bonds. Brent and good friend Chuck ("Gabby" Hayes) go after the culprits. Some good fencing scenes between Steele and Fred Craven highlight this ordinary Monogram oater. Other films in which Bob Steele appeared for Monogram include *HIDDEN VALLEY* (1932); *GALLOPING ROMEO*, and *THE GALLANT FOOL* (1933).

BREED OF THE WEST National Players, 1930, B&W, 5 reels. **Producer:** F. E. Douglas; **Director:** Alvin J. Neitz; **Screenplay:** Neitz; **Cinematographer:** William Nobles; **Editor:** Ethel Davey; **Cast:** Wally Wales, Virginia Brown Faire, Buzz Barton, Hank Cole, Bobby Dunn, George Gerwin, Lafe McKee.

A ranch hand is in love with his boss's daughter, but his rival is the ranch foreman who plans to rob the old man. Actor Wally Wales—a likable and able westerner—never climbed to the top ladder of western stars in the 1920s, although his films and performances were generally enjoyable. With the advent of sound he became better known as a character actor and villain. His distinctive speaking style as well as his costuming made him an instantly recognizable player. He later renamed himself Hal Taliaferro.

BRIDE WASN'T WILLING, THE See *FRONTIER GAL*.

BRIGHAM YOUNG (aka: BRIGHAM YOUNG-FRONTIERSMAN, UK) 20th Century Fox, 1940, B&W, 114 min, VT. **Producer:** Darryl F. Zanuck; **Director:** Henry Hathaway; **Screenplay:** Louis Bromfield and Lamar Trotti; **Music:** Alfred Newman; **Cinematographer:** Arthur C. Miller; **Editor:** Robert Bischoff; **Cast:** Tyrone Power, Linda Darnell, Dean Jagger, Brian Donlevy, Jane Darwell, John Carradine, Mary Astor, Vincent Price, Ann E. Todd, Marc Lawrence, Fuzzy Knight, Dickie Jones, Tully Marshall.

Following the death of Joseph Smith in Illinois, a group of Mormons led by Brigham Young make the long trek westward to their promised land in Salt Lake, Utah. Dean Jagger takes on the title role with appropriate dignity and sensitivity, and Mary Astor is the dedicated wife who stands solidly behind her man through all avenues of adversity. Vincent Price is Mormon martyr Joseph Smith, whose murder in prison by an angry mob is the film's most compelling scene. Not to be ignored either is a visually impressive look at the panoramic vistas of the precarious trail westward. Although perhaps not a great movie, this is still a good one to be sure. Yet the impressive cast doesn't lift the film as high as it might have had the picture stuck more to historical fact and focused less on the decorative love story between Tyrone Power and Linda Darnell, two of the silver screen's best-looking stars.

BRIMSTONE Republic, 1949, B&W/Color, 90 min. **Producer:** Joseph Kane; **Director:** Kane; **Screenplay:** Thomas Williamson; **Cinematographer:** Jack A. Marta; **Editor:** Arthur Roberts; **Cast:** Rod Cameron, Lorna Gray, Walter Brennan, Forrest Tucker, Jack Holt, Jim Davis, James Brown, Guinn "Big Boy" Williams, Jack Lambert, Grant Williams, Hal Taliaferro.

Undercover agent Rod Cameron breaks up a cattle-rustling family headed by Walter Brennan. A strong cast, skillful direction, and Republic's indelible signature make this enjoyable picture with a familiar plot one of Cameron's best westerns.

BRING ME THE HEAD OF ALFREDO GARCIA Estudios Churubusco Azteca, Optimus Films/United Artists, 1974, Color, 112 min, VT. **Producer:** Martin Baum; **Director:** Sam Peckinpah; **Screenplay:** Gordon Dawson and Peckinpah; **Music:** Jerry Fielding; **Cinematographer:** Alex Phillips Jr.; **Editor:** Garth Craven; **Cast:** Warren Oates, Isela Vega, Gig Young, Robert Webber, Helmut Dantine, Emilio Fernando Fernandez, Kris Kristofferson.

Warren Oates plays an expatriate American piano bar player trying make it rich in Mexico. A family scandal prompts a wealthy and powerful rancher to put a price on the head of a man named Alfredo Garcia, who left his unwed daughter with child. Private detectives Gig Young, Robert Webber, and Helmut Dantine are commissioned for the job. They meet Oates, whose girlfriend has been intimate with Garcia and knows he is dead. Knowing that there is a price on the man's head, they set out to get it from a grave. True to form, the search results in lots of dead people and untold misery. This is vintage Sam Peckinpah with the usual blend of violence, black humor, and a cynically revisionist view of history. However, the film lacks the integrity and interest of such earlier ventures as *THE WILD BUNCH* (1969) and *RIDE THE HIGH COUNTRY* (1962).

BROADWAY TO CHEYENNE (aka: FROM BROADWAY TO CHEYENNE) Monogram, 1932, B&W, 60 min. **Producer:** Trem Carr; **Director:** Harry L. Fraser; **Screenplay:** Wellyn Totman; **Cinematographer:** Archie Stout; **Editor:** Carl Pierson; **Cast:** Rex Bell, Marceline Day, Matthew Betz, Huntley Gordon, Roy D'Arcy, Robert Ellis, George "Gabby" Hayes (George Hayes), Si Jinks.

A cowboy detective takes on a gang of big-city thugs who want to set up a protection racket out west. This film features one of the early sound appearances for the lovable "Gabby" Hayes, who appeared in more than 200 films and had an early fling at playing villains before becoming the comic sidekick to William Boyd, Roy Rogers, and other western stars.

BROKEN ARROW 20th Century Fox, 1950, Color, 93 min, VT. **Producer:** Julian Blaustein; **Director:** Delmer Daves; **Screenplay:** Albert Maltz and Michael Blankfort; **Music:** Hugo Friedhofer; **Cinematographer:** Ernest Palmer; **Editor:** J. Watson Web Jr.; **Cast:** James Stewart, Jeff Chandler, Debra Paget, Basil Ruysdael, Will Geer, Joyce McKenzie, Arthur Hunnicutt.

Based on the novel *Blood Brother* by Elliott Arnold, this film gave a big boost to Jeff Chandler, who won an Oscar nomination as Cochise, the Apache chief no white man had seen in years. James Stewart is Civil War veteran Tom Jeffords, now a scout, who is upset by the mistreatment of the Indians and tries to make peace between the settlers and the Apache so the mail can get through without the risk of an Indian attack. Aided by a compelling and ill-fated love story between the white man Jeffords and a beautiful Indian maiden named Sonseeahray, played by Debra Paget, *Broken Arrow* was nominated for three Academy Awards and was the recipient of a Golden Globe Award for Best Film Promoting International Understanding. Within a historical context, however, the subplot linking Jeffords with an Indian maiden is in error. The real Tom Jeffords remained a bachelor all his life.

Delmer Daves helmed this intelligent western film which depicts the American Indian in a compassionate and respectful manner. *Newsweek* called it "one of the most emotionally satisfying westerns since *Stagecoach*." In His *A Pictorial History Of the Western Film* (1969), William Everson notes how *Broken Arrow* manages "that rare movie trick of making a social comment without overloading the scales." While the Indian had been treated sympathetically in earlier films, no film did it in such a prevailing and enthusiastic way. In crafting this large-scale portrait of the American Indian, Daves avoids the extreme pretense and pandering "political correctness" employed 40 years later in Kevin Costner's *DANCES WITH WOLVES*.

BROKEN LANCE 20th Century Fox, 1954, Color, 96 min, VT. **Producer:** Sol C. Siegal; **Director:** Edward Dmytryk; **Screenplay:** Richard Murphy and Philip Yordan (story); **Music:** Leigh Harline; **Cinematographer:** Joe MacDonald; **Editor:** Dorothy Spencer; **Cast:** Spencer Tracy, Robert Wagner, Jean Peters, Richard Widmark, Katy Jurado, Hugh O'Brien, Eduard Franz, Earl Holliman, E. G. Marshall, Carl Benton Reid, Philip Ober, Edmund Cobb.

It's brother against brother, sons against father, in this western remake of *House of Strangers* (1949). Spencer Tracy is terrific as rancher Matt Devereaux, the obdurate patriarch of a cattle empire whose second wife (Katy Jurado) is a Comanche Indian. When Devereaux raids a copper smelter that is polluting his cattle's water, he runs afoul of the law. Youngest son Joe (Robert Wagner) takes the rap and spends three years in jail. Most of the film is told in flashbacks by Wagner, who has gone to prison to protect his father. When he is released his father is dead, his mother has returned to her people, and his three brothers from his father's first wife have turned on him and stripped him of his inheritance. The final showdown between Joe and his half-brother Ben (Richard Widmark) is tinged by cross-currents of bitterness and racial hatred.

Director Edward Dmytryk's first western, the movie won two Oscar nominations and an Academy Award for writer Philip Yordan. This excellent film showcases top-flight performances by Tracy and Widmark, whose exhilarating verbal combat with one another is acting at its best.

BROKEN LAND, THE 20th Century Fox, 1962, Color, 60 min. **Producer:** Leonard A. Schwartz; **Director:** John A. Bushelman; **Screenplay:** Edward J. Lasko; **Music:** Richard LaSalle; **Cinematographer:** Floyd Crosby; **Cast:** Kent Taylor, Diana Darrin, Jody McCrea, Robert Sampson, Jack Nicholson, Gary Sneed, Don Orlando, Helen Joseph, H. Tom Cain, Bob Pollard.

Kent Taylor plays a sadistic sheriff who delights in being nasty to just about everyone. Jody McCrea is the harassed deputy, and 25-year-old Jack Nicholson—still relegated to B pictures—plays the benign son of a notorious gunman and a patsy for the whims of the cruel sheriff. This interesting film includes an excellent performance by Kent Taylor.

BROKEN STAR Bel-Air Productions/United Artists, 1956, B&W, 82 min. **Producer:** Howard W. Koch; **Director:** Leslie Selander; **Screenplay:** John C. Higgins; **Music:** Paul Dunlap; **Cinematographer:** William Margulies; **Editor:** John Schrever; **Cast:** Howard Duff, Lita Baron, Bill Williams, Henry Calvin, Douglas Fowley.

A deputy marshal claims he killed a man in self-defense when he really murdered him for his gold.

BRONCHO BILLY AND THE BABY Essany, 1908, B&W, one reel. **Producer:** Gilbert M "Broncho Billy" Anderson; **Director:** Reginald Barker; **Screenplay:** Anderson (based on a story by Peter Tyne); **Cast:** Gilbert Anderson, Jack Totheroh.

See *BANDIT MAKES GOOD, THE*.

BRONCO BILLY Warner Bros., 1980, Color, 116 min, VT. **Producers:** Dennis Hackin and Neal Dobrofsky; **Director:** Clint Eastwood; **Screenplay:** Dennis Hackin; **Music:** Steve Dorff (conductor); **Cinematographer:** David Wort; **Editor:** Ferris Webster; **Cast:** Clint Eastwood, Sondra Locke, Geoffrey Lewis, Scatman Crothers, Bill McKinney, Sam Bottoms, Dan Vadis, Sierra Pacheur, Walter Barnes, Hank Worden.

Clint Eastwood is Bronco Billy, the owner and star attraction of a contemporary Wild West show that travels to the Midwest. But when he and his show fall on hard times and public interest starts to wane, his profits plummet greatly. Things start to change when he encounters a spoiled society girl named Antoinette Lily (Sondra Locke), who has been deserted by her husband. Billy agrees to help her, but only if she consents to act as a target for his sharp-shooting and knife-throwing act.

This was Eastwood's seventh stint as a director and his third teaming with then-girlfriend Sondra Locke, and many say that their chemistry on-screen was never any better. Shot on location in Idaho, Oregon, and New York, with some nice songs sung by Merle Haggard, Ronnie Milsap, Penny DeHaven, and by Eastwood himself, this gentle film with a good-natured theme is a welcome departure from the usually tougher Eastwood ventures.

BRONCO BUSTER Universal, 1952, Color, 80 min. **Producer:** Ted Richmond; **Director:** Budd Boetticher; **Screenplay:** Horace McCoy; **Music:** Daniele Amfitheatro, Charles Previn, Milton Rosen, Hans J. Salter, Fred Skinner, Leith Stevens and Alfred Tommasino; **Cinematographer:** Clifford Stine; **Editor:** Edward Curtiss; **Cast:** John Lund, Scott Brady, Joyce Holden, Chill Wills, Dan Poore, Jerry Ambler, Casey Tibbs, Pete Crump.

In this taut little story with great rodeo action, Tom Moody (John Lund) helps Bart Eaton (Scott Brady) learn the rodeo game. Because neither Lund nor Brady were cowboys per se, director Budd Boetticher decided to surround his two leading men with real cowboys. He went on tour to assemble the best team of rodeo riders and stuntmen he could find, including the great Casey Tibbs and stuntman supreme Bill Williams. Boetticher reported, "I brought all of them over and let them stay with me, so I would be sure they'd find their way to the studio in the morning. They were a terrific group of guys, and really helped Lund and Brady learn the tricks."

An ex-matador and an excellent horseman himself, Boetticher garnered an Oscar nomination for his first major film, *The Bullfighter and the Lady* (1951). A few years later he teamed with writer Burt Kennedy, actor Randolph Scott, and producer Harry Joe Brown to put together the "Ranown cycle." This remarkable set of films, beginning with *Seven Men From Now* (1956); *The Tall T, Decision at Sundown* (1957); *Buchanan Rides Alone* (1958); *Ride Lonesome* (1959); and *Comanche Station* (1960), are considered among the finest westerns ever made.

BRONZE BUCKAROO, THE Hollywood Productions, 1939, B&W, VT. **Producers:** Jed Buell (uncredited), Richard C. Kahn (uncredited), and Alfred N. Sack (uncredited); **Director:** Kahn; **Screenplay:** Kahn; **Music:** Lew Porter; **Cinematographer:** Roland Price and Clark Ramsey; **Cast:** Herb Jeffries (Herbert Jeffrey), Lucius Brooks, Artie Young, Lee Calmes, Rellie Harden, Spencer Williams, Earl Morris.

A cowboy and his pal go to a ranch to help a girl whose father has been bushwhacked, and the cowpoke sets out to find the culprit. In *The Bronze Buckaroo*, Herb Jeffries (who was a featured vocalist with the Duke Ellington Orchestra during the Big Band Era) plays a fellow named Bob Blake, who sings over the credits and throughout the film. Naturally he still has time to tangle with the bad guys and come out on the side of the angels at the final fadeout.

This film was part of a series of all-black westerns that appear occasionally on television and are available at video stores. They are fun to see, primarily due to the presence of Jeffries, a singing cowboy who can really sing. But according to William Everson, writing in *A Pictorial History of the Western Film*, they contain "more self-imposed racial stereotypes than 'white' Hollywood ever created." Other features include *Two Gun Man from Harlem, Harlem on the Prairie* (1938); and *Harlem Rides the Range* (1939).

BROTHERS IN THE SADDLE RKO, 1949, B&W, 60 min. **Producer:** Herman Schlom; **Director:** Leslie Selander; **Screenplay:** Norman Houston; **Music:** Paul Sawtell; **Cinematographer:** J. Roy Hunt; **Editor:** Samuel E. Beetley; **Cast:** Tim Holt, Richard Martin, Steve Brodie, Virginia Cox, Carol Foran, Tom Keene (Richard Powers), Stanley Andrews.

In this 1949 RKO venture, Tim Holt (the good brother) pulls Steve Brodie (the bad-seed brother) out of a saloon after he kills a cheating poker player in self-defense. Good brother Holt convinces him to give himself up for trial, but without the crucial testimony of a saloon girl who has fled to Mexico, Brodie is found guilty. The two brothers make their way to a secret hideout, from where Holt sets out to find the missing saloon girl. When he returns, his enthusiasm for his brother lessens when he learns someone matching Brodie's description has held up a stagecoach, killing the man who was his chief accuser at the trial.

Tim Holt was one of the few western stars with significant "A" movie credits (*The Magnificent Ambersons, The Treasure of the Sierra Madre*). Early on his dad, actor Jack Holt, gave his son some fatherly advice: "If you want to make a lasting impression with the public and in your career, then stick with the westerns." (See also *ALONG THE RIO GRANDE*.)

BROTHERS OF THE WEST Victory, 1937, B&W, 58 min. **Producer:** Sam Katzman; **Director:** Katzman; **Screenplay:** Basil Dickey; **Cinematographer:** William Hyer; **Editor:** Holbrook N. Todd; **Cast:** Tom Tyler, Lois Wilde, Dorothy Short, Lafe McKee, Bob Terry, Dave O'Brien, Roger Williams, Jim Corey.

Tom Tyler plays a range detective whose brother is accused of robbing a bank and killing the bank president. In order to prove him innocent, Tyler must decipher his only clue—an unusual set of tracks. (See also *FEUD OF THE TRAIL*.)

BROTHERS O'TOOLE, THE   American National Enterprises, 1973, Color, 95 min. **Producer:** Charles E. Sellier Jr.; **Director:** Richard Erdman; **Screenplay:** Marion Hargrove and Tim Kelly; **Music:** Don Piestrup; **Cast:** John Astin, Steve Carlson, Pat Carroll, Hans Conreid, Lee Meriwether, Allyn Joslyn, Richard Jury, Richard Erdman.

John Astin's rambling diatribes against the denizens of the little town of Molly-Be-Damn have their moments, and his dual role as O'Toole and Dangerous Ambrose provides some comic relief. Otherwise this film is flat and forgettable, a western comedy spoof that is mainly for the kids.

BUCHANAN RIDES ALONE   Columbia, 1958, Color, 78 min. **Producer:** Harry Joe Brown; **Director:** Budd Boetticher; **Screenplay:** Burt Kennedy and Charles Lang III; **Music:** Misha Bakaleinikoff, George Dunning, Heintz Roemheld, Paul Sawtell, and Fred Steiner; **Cinematographer:** Lucien Ballard; **Editor:** Al Clark; **Cast:** Randolph Scott, Craig Stevens, Barry Kelley, Peter Whitney, Manuel Rojas, L. Q. Jones.

Buchanan Rides Alone has hero Randolph Scott inadvertently riding into Agry Town on the California border. The town is controlled by the Agry brothers, who also serve as town judge, sheriff, and hotel keeper. When Buchanan (Scott) tries to help out a Mexican seeking revenge on one of the brothers, he finds himself pitted against the whole family. They also seem determined to relieve him of the money he earned fighting in the Mexican Revolution.

This picture is but one of a string of excellent films helmed by Budd Boetticher in conjunction with writer Burt Kennedy, producer Harry Joe Brown, and actor Randolph Scott. Boetticher's raw, tough, deceptively simple movies have performed the rare double treat of pleasing serious cineastes and making money at the box office, earning him worldwide acclaim.

The prototype for a Boetticher hero, Randolph Scott exudes a William S. Hart stature in the film and delivers an understated performance tempered with humor and warmth. This excellent western also boasts top performances from Craig Stevens (in his first serious role) as the mysterious heavy Abe Carbo and L. Q. Jones as the offbeat gunman Pecos Hill.

BUCK AND THE PREACHER   Columbia, 1972, Color, 102 min, VT, DVD. **Producer:** Joel Glickman; **Director:** Sidney Poitier; **Screenplay:** Ernest Kinov and Drake Walker; **Music:** Benny Carter; **Cinematographer:** Alex Phillips Jr.; **Cast:** Sidney Poitier, Harry Belafonte, Cameron Mitchell, Denny Miller, Nita Talbot.

This film is about a group of former slaves who travel west after the Civil War. Sidney Poitier plays Buck, an ex-Union cavalryman acting as the scout, and Harry Belafonte is a Bible-toting con man—a hustler preacher—who tags along and becomes Buck's partner. On their way to settle "where the stink of slavery ain't in the air," they are harassed by bad guy Cameron Mitchell and his gang of "labor recruiters," who want to force the blacks back to Louisiana.

Belafonte actually learned how to chew and spit tobacco for his part of the con-man preacher, and to give his teeth the proper stained appearance he coated them with mascara and clear nail polish. The film marks the directorial debut of Sidney Poitier.

BUCKAROO FROM POWDER RIDGE   Columbia, 1947, B&W, 55 min. **Producer:** Colbert Clark; **Director:** Ray Nazarro; **Screenplay:** Norman S. Hall; **Cinematographer:** George F. Kelley; **Editor:** Paul Borofsky; **Cast:** Charles Starrett, Smiley Burnette, Eve Miller, Forrest Taylor, Paul Campbell, The Cass County Boys, Kermit Maynard, Frank McCarroll, Roy Butler.

An outlaw gang leader plans to counterfeit the government bonds his gang stole in a bank holdup in this standard feature with Charles Starrett as the impeccably dressed Durango Kid and Smiley Burnette as his faithful sidekick. Starrett was Columbia's top western star for almost two decades and also among the B western's top 10 money-making stars almost every year between 1936 and 1954, when the *Motion Picture Herald* listed western stars separately. Most Starrett buffs consider his *DURANGO KID* films to have been at their best in the period from 1945 to 1949. (See also *DURANGO KID, THE*.)

BUCKAROO SHERIFF OF TEXAS   Republic, 1950, B&W, 60 min. **Producer:** Rudy Ralston; **Director:** Philip Ford; **Screenplay:** Arthur E. Orloff; **Cinematographer:** John MacBurnie; **Editor:** Arthur Roberts; **Cast:** Michael Chapin, Eilene Janssen, James Bell, Hugh O'Brian, Steve Pendleton, Tristram Coffin, Alice Kelley, Selmer Jackson, Ed Cassidy.

A group of young children help bring a notorious outlaw to justice. This first of four films in the "Rough Ridin' Kids" series shows that the law business in the Old West is best left to adults.

BUCK BENNY RIDES AGAIN   Paramount, 1940, B&W, 82 min. **Producer:** Mark Sandrich; **Director:** Sandrich; **Screenplay:** Edmund Beloin, William Morrow and Zion Myers; **Music:** Victor Young with Frank Loesser and Jimmy McHugh (songs); **Cinematographer:** Charles Lang; **Editor:** LeRoy Stone; **Cast:** Jack Benny, Ellen Drew, Eddie "Rochester" Anderson, Andy Devine, Phil Harris, Dennis Day, Virginia Dale, Linda Cornell, Ward Bond, Morris Ankrum, Fred Allen (voice uncredited).

In this delightful spoof Jack Benny and pal Phil Harris head west in order to win a bet with longtime nemesis Fred Allen. It seems that Jack has been boasting to Fred that he is a true cowpoke who roughs it up big-time at his Nevada ranch (fictitious, of course). When Jack falls for singer Joan Cameron (Ellen Drew), Joan's sisters maneuver her to the same Nevada town. Jack must now prove to his newfound ladylove that he is indeed 100-percent cowboy, and his radio friends (Harris, Dennis Day, and Eddie "Rochester" Anderson) provide him with cover. Crisp, witty dialogue, some fine songs by Frank Loesser and Jimmy McHugh, the scene-stealing talent of Eddie "Rochester" Anderson, and Benny's impeccable comedic timing make this one lots of fun and perhaps Benny's best film.

BUCKSKIN (aka: THE FRONTIERSMAN)
Paramount, 1968, Color, 97 min, VT. **Producer:** A. C. Lyles; **Director:** Michael Moore; **Screenplay:** Steve Fisher; **Music:** Jimmie Haskell; **Cinematographer:** W. Wallace Kelley; **Editor:** John W. Wheeler; **Cast:** Barry Sullivan, Joan Caulfield, Wendell Corey, Lon Chaney Jr., John Russell, Barbara Hale, Barton MacLane.

This A. C. Lyles film production tells the story of a heroic marshal (Barry Sullivan) battling against a domineering cattle baron (Wendell Corey) who is trying to force homesteaders out of the territory. It's a familiar plot with former big-name stars and veteran players marking Lyles's final entry for Paramount.

BUCKSKIN FRONTIER (aka: THE IRON ROAD, UK)
Harry Sherman Productions/United Artist, 1943, B&W, 65 min, VT. **Producer:** Harry Sherman; **Director:** Leslie Selander; **Screenplay:** Norman Houston, Bernard Schubert, and Harry Sinclair Drago; **Music:** Victor Young; **Cinematographer:** Russell Harlan; **Cast:** Richard Dix, Jane Wyatt, Albert Dekker, Lee J. Cobb, Victor Jory, Lola Lane, Max Baer, Joe Sawyer, George Reeves, Guinn "Big Boy" Williams.

A railroad representative (Richard Dix) and freight-line owner (Lee J. Cobb) fight over business and a crucial mountain pass. This is one of the better efforts in a good group of pictures produced by Harry Sherman and starring Dix. An interesting bit of casting has Cobb playing Jane Wyatt's father when the two stars were actually the same age.

BUFFALO BILL
20th Century Fox, 1944, Color, 90 min, VT. **Producer:** Harry Sherman; **Director:** William A. Wellman; **Screenplay:** Cecile Cramer, Eneas MacKenzie, Clements Ripley, and Frank Winch (story); **Music:** David Buttolph; **Cinematographer:** Leon Shamroy; **Editor:** James B. Clark; **Cast:** Joel McCrea, Maureen O'Hara, Linda Darnell, Thomas Mitchell, Anthony Quinn, Moroni Olson.

Director William Wellman offers a sentimental account of Buffalo Bill Cody, from his days as a cavalry scout to the time he became a famous showman and the owner of the most authentic Wild West show in the country. Joel McCrea gives his usual sturdy performance in the title role, while the focal point of the film features a head-on battle between the U.S. Cavalry and the Cheyenne at War Bonnet Gorge.

The big-name cast includes Thomas Mitchell as the eastern newspaperman who writes books about Buffalo Bill's fame in the West, then acts as his promoter when he visits the East. Two of the screen's reigning beauties vie for his affection: Maureen O'Hara as the senator's daughter who weds Bill Cody, and Linda Darnell as the Indian school teacher who also loves him. Wellman's film shows Bill Cody spending much of his later years in vigorous protest against the harsh treatment accorded the Indians in his earlier days as an Indian fighter—a rather unusual take for a mid-1940s western.

As scout, fighter and friend of the Indian, and showman, Wellman's Buffalo Bill Cody is every inch an American hero. The struggle between the Indian and the white man is explored well, and the colorful panorama of the western landscape and the great outdoors is a visual delight. While the film is a bit short on history and a little long on romance and wedded life, Wellman's *Buffalo Bill* still packs lots of grand-scale entertainment value. Despite its obvious limitations, *Variety* called it both a "super western" and a "magnificent production."

Others who have played the famed Indian scout, bison hunter, and carnival showman in film are James Ellison in *THE PLAINSMAN* (1936); Richard Arlen in *Buffalo Bill Rides Again* (1947); Louis Calhern in *ANNIE GET YOUR GUN* (1950); Charlton Heston in *PONY EXPRESS* (1952); Clayton Moore in *BUFFALO BILL IN TOMAHAWK TERRITORY* (1953); Gordon Scott in *BUFFALO BILL, HERO OF THE FAR WEST* (1964); Guy Stockwell in *THE PLAINSMAN* (1966); and Paul Newman in *BUFFALO BILL AND THE INDIANS* (1976). The character of Buffalo Bill Cody was a particular favorite of the silent screen.

BUFFALO BILL AND THE INDIANS, OR SITTING BULL'S HISTORY LESSON
De Laurentis/United Artists, 1976, Color, 123 min, VT. **Producer:** Robert Altman; **Director:** Altman; **Screenplay:** Altman and Alan Rudolph; **Music:** Richard Baskin; **Cinematographer:** Paul Lohmann; **Editors:** Peter Appleton and Dennis M. Hill; **Cast:** Paul Newman, Joel Grey, Kevin McCarthy, Harvey Keitel, Allan F. Nichols, Geraldine Chaplin, Pat McCormick, Denver Pyle, Shelley Duvall, Burt Lancaster.

Unlike William Wellman's 1944 film, Robert Altman chooses to debunk Bill Cody as little more than a hollow showman and a flamboyant fraud. Shot on location in Alberta, Canada, the action takes place at Buffalo Bill's winter arena in the 1880s and presents Sitting Bull as a true figure of heroism, while Cody, with his long flowing hair and colorful beard, is a charlatan perpetrating a deceitful myth. The film's high point is an evening performance put on by a troupe for visiting President Grover Cleveland (Pat McCormick), which prompts the nation's chief executive to declare of Buffalo Bill, "It's a man like this that's made this country what it is today."

The fact that Altman released the film in America's bicentennial year is revealing. The 1970s began a general trend in film to demean or "revise" our heroes and icons. Most interesting is that for America's bicentennial celebration, not one film was made glorifying the American Revolution. Yet the bottom line here is that despite its talented cast (including a particularly strong performance by Frank Kaquitts, who plays the part as Sitting Bull in total silence) the film is basically dull and preachy, with Paul Newman turning in one of his weakest performances in the title role. Moreover, Altman's adaptation for the screen actually uses very little from Arthur Kopit's original 1969 Broadway play *Indians*, from which the story was carved. (See also *BUFFALO BILL*.)

BUFFALO BILL, HERO OF THE FAR WEST (aka: BUFFALO BILL)

Les Films Corona, 1964, Color. **Producer:** Solly V. Bianco; **Director:** Mario Costa; **Screenplay:** Louis Agotay, Pierre Corti, Luciano Martino, and Nino Stresa; **Music:** Carlo Rustichelli; **Cinematographer:** Massimo Dallamano; **Editors:** Gordon Scott and Jolanda Benvenuti; **Cast:** Gordon Scott, Mario Brega, Jan Hendriks, Catherine Ribeiro, Ineborg Schoner.

Early imitation Italian western has former Tarzan Gordon Scott as Buffalo Bill. The general trend among these early Italian ventures was to play it safe by using legendary figures from the American West such as Bill Cody, Wyatt Earp, and Wild Bill Hickok. The familiar plot here has renegade Indians buying guns and Buffalo Bill being sent in to stop the arms trading and prevent an Indian war. This film is often presented on television as *Buffalo Bill*, which sometimes causes confusion with the Wellman film. (See also *BUFFALO BILL*; Appendix I, Spaghetti Westerns A–Z)

BUFFALO BILL IN TOMAHAWK TERRITORY

Jack Schwartz Productions/United Artists, 1952, B&W, 66 min, VT. **Producers:** Edward Finney and Bernard B. Ray; **Director:** Bernard B. Ray; **Screenplay:** Sam Neuman and Nat Tanchuck; **Cinematographer:** Elmer Dyer; **Cast:** Clayton Moore, Slim Andrews, Rodd Redwing, Chief Yowlachie, Chief Thundercloud, Charlie Hughes, Sharon Dexter.

Outlaws try to steal land from the Indians, but Buffalo Bill Cody and his sidekick come to their rescue. (See also *BUFFALO BILL*.)

BUFFALO GIRLS

CBS Entertainment, 1995, Color, 180 min. **Producers:** Sandra Saxon Brice and Suzanne Coston; **Director:** Rod Hardy; **Teleplay:** Cynthia Whitcomb; **Music:** Lee Holdridge; **Cinematographer:** David Connell; **Editor:** Richard Bracken; **Cast:** Anjelica Huston, Melanie Griffith, Sam Elliott, Jack Palance, Reba McEntire, Gabriel Byrne, Peter Coyote, Tracey Walter, Floyd "Red Crow" Westerman.

This excellent TV miniseries, based on the novel by Larry McMurtry, features outstanding performances by Anjelica Huston (Calamity Jane); Sam Elliott (Wild Bill Hickok); and Melanie Griffith as Dora DuFran, the bordello madam who specializes in domestic and romantic entanglements. During the last days of the Wild West, Calamity Jane works as a mule driver for George Custer and tries to reclaim her daughter when she travels to London with Buffalo Bill's Wild West Show. Filmed in New Mexico and in Great Britain, the miniseries garnered many honors, including an Emmy nomination for Huston (Best Actress) and Golden Globe nominations for Sam Elliott and Melanie Griffith (Best Performances in Supporting Roles).

BUFFALO GUN

Globe, 1961, B&W, 72 min. **Producer:** A. R. Milton; **Director:** Albert C. Gannaway; **Screenplay:** Milton; **Music:** Ramey Idriss; **Cinematographer:** Gerald Perry Finnerman; **Editor:** Carl Pingitor; **Cast:** Marty Robbins, Webb Price, Carl Smith, Wayne Morris, Don "Red" Barry, Mary Ellen Kay, Douglas Fowley.

Three singing government agents are sent west to investigate the thefts of shipment to the Indians. This was the last film for actor Wayne Morris, whose budding career was interrupted by World War II, in which he served with valor as a navy aviator and won four Distinguished Flying Crosses. He died in 1959. While this film was produced in 1958, its release was delayed until 1961.

BUFFALO SOLDIERS

Citadel Enterprise Productions/Turner Pictures, 1997, Color. **Producers:** Pen Densham, David R. Ginsburg, Danny Glover, Ilene Kahn, Richard B. Lewis, Carolyn McDonald, John Watson, and Gordon Wolfe; **Director:** Charles Haid; **Music:** Joel McNeely; **Cinematographer:** William Wages; **Editor:** Andrew Doerfer; **Cast:** Danny Glover, Lamont Bentley, Tom Bower, Timothy Busfield, Bob Gunton.

This is a beautifully filmed TV western about an all-black cavalry troop (under white officers) and its role in the winning of the West. Glover, who coproduced the film for cable, is superb as the taciturn NCO who bucks racism among some white officers while pursuing renegade Indians. The film provides a provocative, compelling, and often violent account of an understated and long-ignored historical event.

BUFFALO STAMPEDE, THE

See *THUNDERING HERD, THE.*

BUGLES IN THE AFTERNOON

Cagney Productions/Warner Bros., 1952, Color, 85 min, VT. **Producer:** William Cagney; **Director:** Roy Rowland; **Screenplay:** Harry Brown and Daniel Mainwaring; **Music:** Dimitri Tiomkin; **Cinematographer:** Wilfred M. Cline; **Editor:** Thomas Reilly; **Cast:** Ray Milland, Helena Carter, Hugh Marlow, Forrest Tucker, Barton MacLane, George Reeves.

Set in the Dakota Territory at the time of Custer's Last Stand, a cavalry sergeant branded a coward during the Civil War falls victim to an officer's jealousy, and old scores must be settled on the eve of the battle at Little Big Horn. Produced by William Cagney (James Cagney's brother), Sheb Wooley appears as General George Armstrong Custer in an uncredited role.

BULLDOG COURAGE Puritan Pictures, 1935, B&W, 60 min. **Producers:** Sigmund Neufeld and Leslie Simmonds; **Director:** Sam Newfield; **Screenplay:** Frances Guihan and Joseph O'Donnell; **Music:** Oliver Wallace; **Cinematographer:** Jack Greenhalgh; **Editor:** S. Roy Luby; **Cast:** Tim McCoy, Joan Woodbury, Paul Fix, Eddie Buzard, Jack Cowell, Karl Hackett.

A miner who is swindled out of his mine turns to robbing stagecoaches. After several years, when he is tracked down and killed, his son comes to town to tangle with the banker who had wronged his dad. (See also *MAN FROM GUNTOWN*.)

BULLET CODE RKO, 1940, B&W, 58 min. **Producer:** Bert Gilroy; **Director:** David Howard; **Screenplay:** Doris Schroeder; **Music:** Paul Sawtell; **Cinematographer:** Harry J. Wild; **Editor:** Frederic Knudtson; **Cast:** George O'Brien, Virginia Vale, Slim Whitaker, Howard C. Hickman, Harry Woods, William Haade, Kirby Grant (as Robert Stanton).

George O'Brien plays Steve Holden, a rancher who fends off an attack by cattle rustlers. In the process he believes he unwittingly killed young Bud Mathews, who had warned him of the impending attack. Unaware that Mathews had already been killed by rustler boss Cass Barton (Harry Woods), Holden heads to the Matthews's hometown to tell the boy's family, but then he finds out that local businessmen plan to oust the boy's father from his ranch.

In a 1993 interview with the author published in *White Hats and Silver Spurs*, Virginia Vale, George O'Brien's costar in *Bullet Code* and nearly half a dozen other features, recalls working with the actor:

> I think George always demanded a bit more . . . And he was a *good actor*. It's a shame that once he started in westerns, he ceased to be in big productions. Later, after he came back from the Navy, he worked in some bigger productions but only in feature parts. He was older and younger cowboys had taken over. That's understandable, and that is the business. I just wish he had more of an opportunity to show his real acting ability. (See also *RACKETEERS OF THE RANGE*.)

BULLET FOR A BADMAN Universal, 1964, Color, 80 min. **Producer:** Gordon Kay; **Director:** R. G. Springsteen; **Screenplay:** Mary Willingham and Willard Willingham; **Music:** Irving Gertz, William Lava, Henry Mancini, Heinz Roemheld, Hans J. Salter, Frank Skinner, and Herman Stein; **Cinematographer:** Joseph F. Biroc; **Editor:** Russell F. Schoengarth; **Cast:** Audie Murphy, Darren McGavin, Ruta Lee, Beverly Owen, Skip Homeier, George Tobias, Alan Hale Jr.

Audie Murphy plays an ex-lawman who puts his guns on again to catch his former nemesis (Darren McGavin). McGavin just happens to be the former husband of Murphy's wife and the father of the boy he believes to be his own son.

BULLETS AND SADDLES Monogram, 1943, B&W, 54 min. **Producer:** Trem Carr; **Director:** Anthony Marshall; **Screenplay:** Elizabeth Beechers; **Cinematographer:** Edward A. Kull; **Editor:** Roy Claire; **Cast:** Ray Corrigan, Max Terhune, Dennis Moore, Julie Duncan, Glenn Strange, Rose Plummer.

The last of the *Range Busters* series has the Hammond gang led by Glenn Strange going after Charlie Craig, so Craig's mother (Rose Plummer) beckons Crash, Alibi, and Denny (Ray Corrigan, Max Terhune, and Dennis Moore) to subdue the culprits. The picture was filmed at Corriganville (The Corrigan Ranch), the location point for volumes of western films. Ray "Crash" Corrigan purchased the ranch in 1935, according to his son Tom. He had worked with Clark Gable on *Mutiny on the Bounty*, and the two hunted together at the ranch site. "He thought it would be a good movie location, and as picture companies began using it for location work, they started building sets. Columbia even built a big lake," Tom Corrigan recalled in an interview with author, from *Duke We're Glad We Knew You.* By 1950 Corriganville had become a major movie ranch, with as many as seven picture companies filming there at a time. (See also *RANGER BUSTERS, THE*.)

BULLETS FOR RUSTLERS (aka: ON SPECIAL DUTY, UK) Columbia, 1940, B&W, 58 min. **Director:** Sam Nelson; **Screenplay:** John Rathmell; **Music:** Bob Nolan and Tim Spencer (songs); **Cinematographer:** George Meehan; **Editor:** Charles Nelson; **Cast:** Charles Starrett, Lorna Gray (as Adrian Booth), Bob Nolan, Ken Curtis, Kenneth McDonald, Jack Rockwell.

A cattlemen's association undercover agent pretends to be a rustler in order to join a gang he is trying to stop. In this action-packed oater Charles Starrett had the benefit of Bob Nolan and the Sons of the Pioneers while working at Columbia. He was distressed when Nolan and his group left him in 1941 to join a rising star named Roy Rogers at Republic. But Starrett's best years were fortunately in front of him, and his films remain highly regarded by collectors and fans of B westerns. (See also *GALLANT DEFENDER*.)

BULLWHIP Romson-Broidy/Allied Artists, 1958, Color, 80 min, VT. **Producer:** Helen Ainsworth; **Director:** Harmon Jones; **Screenplay:** Adele Buffington; **Music:** Leith Stevens; **Cinematographer:** John J. Martin; **Editor:** Thor Brooks; **Cast:** Guy Madison, Rhonda Fleming, James Griffith, Peter Adams, Don Beddoe, Dan Sheridan, Burt Nelson, Al Terr.

In order to control a trading post, a bad man forces a cowboy (Guy Madison) who is about to inherit the business the choice of marrying the half-Indian Cheyenne or face hanging over a false murder charge—not a bad choice when the fiery woman (the whip-wielder of the title) he is forced to wed is Rhonda Fleming. The title song is sung in superb fashion by Frankie Laine.

Guy Madison and brother Wayne Mallory in Bullwhip
(ALLIED ARTISTS/AUTHOR'S COLLECTION)

BUONO, IL BRUTTO, IL CATTIVO, IL See *GOOD, THE BAD AND THE UGLY, THE.*

BURNING HILLS, THE Warner Bros., 1956, Color, 94 min, VT. **Producer:** Richard Whorf; **Director:** Stuart Heisler; **Screenplay:** Irving Wallace; **Music:** David Buttolph; **Cinematographer:** Ted D. McCord; **Editor:** Clarence Kolster; **Cast:** Tab Hunter, Natalie Wood, Skip Homeier, Eduard Franz, Earl Holliman, Claude Akins, Ray Teal, John Doucette.

Trace Jordan (Tab Hunter) attempts to avenge the murder of his brother by a ruthless cattle baron (Ray Teal), but in pursuing the murderers he becomes pursued himself as the baron's gunslingers are hot on his trail. In the process he joins up with a half-breed Indian girl (Natalie Wood) whose father was also killed by Teal, and the two become partners in flight. The dependable Skip Homeier is outstanding as Teal's bloodthirsty son, turning in another fine villainous job. Based on the novel of the same name by Louis L'Amour, the film features Tab Hunter at the height of his screen popularity.

BURY ME NOT ON THE LONE PRAIRIE Universal, 1941, B&W, 61 min. **Director:** Ray Taylor; **Screen-**

play: Victor McLeod; **Cast:** Johnny Mack Brown, Fuzzy Knight, Nell O'Day, Kathryn Adams, Lee Shumway, Frank O'Connor, Ernie Adams, Don House, Pat O'Brien, Bud Osborne, Ed Cassidy.

A young mining engineer sets out to catch the killers of both his brother and a young girl's father. Good blend of action and music makes for one of Johnny Mack Brown's better Universal entries. (See also *OLD CHISHOLM TRAIL, THE.*)

BUSHWHACKERS, THE (aka: THE REBEL)
Realart Pictures, 1952, B&W, 70 min. **Producer:** Larry Finley; **Director:** Rodney Amateau; **Screenplay:** Amateau and Tom Gries; **Music:** Albert Glasser; **Cinematographer:** Jospeh F. Biroc; **Editor:** Francis D. Lyon; **Cast:** John Ireland, Dorothy Malone, Frank Marlowe, Wayne Morris, Lon Chaney Jr., Myrna Dell, Jack Elam, Lawrence Tierney.

John Ireland plays an ex-Confederate soldier who puts away his guns and heads home to Missouri. Predictably, he is forced to abandon his pacifist ways by a ruthless cattle baron. This was an early writing vehicle for Tom Gries before he took to directing motion pictures. Look for an excellent performance by Wayne Morris as the corrupt town sheriff and an early film appearance by western icon Jack Elam as Cree, the henchman, in this routine but entertaining range-war tale highlighted by its strong cast.

BUTCH AND SUNDANCE: THE EARLY DAYS
20th Century Fox, 1979, Color, 111 min. **Producers:** Steven Bach and Gabriel Katzka; **Director:** Richard Lester; **Screenplay:** Allan Burns; **Music:** Patrick Williams; **Cinematographer:** Laszlo Kovacs; **Editor:** George Trirogoff; **Cast:** William Katt, Tom Berenger, Jeff Corey, John Schuck, Michael C. Gwynne, Peter Weller, Brian Dennehy.

This 1979 "prequel" to *BUTCH CASSIDY AND THE SUNDANCE KID* is more a series of vignettes than a story with a sustained plot. The film recounts the comic adventures of the two young outlaws as they begin their offbeat criminal life. Although it would have been impossible to have matched the screen chemistry of Paul Newman and Robert Redford, William Katt and Tom Berenger are satisfying as Butch and Sundance.

BUTCH CASSIDY AND THE SUNDANCE KID
20th Century Fox/Campanile, 1969, B&W and Color, 110 min, VT, DVD. **Producer:** John Foreman; **Director:** George Roy Hill; **Screenplay:** William Goldman; **Music:** Burt Bacharach; **Cinematographer:** Conrad Hall; **Editors:** John C. Howard and Richard C. Meyer; **Cast:** Paul Newman, Robert Redford, Katharine Ross, Strother Martin, Henry Jones, Jeff Corey, Cloris Leachman.

George Roy Hill's film takes liberties galore by making hardworking Pinkerton detectives a bunch of flint-hearted killers, and the outlaws Butch and Sundance a couple of carefree, harmless rogues. With the Kid's girlfriend Etta Place, the two engage in a series of criminal adventures from their various robberies in the American West to their trip to Bolivia, where they are chased by law officers and meet their ultimate demise.

The real Butch Cassidy was a man named Robert Leroy Parker, one of many jobless cowhands who drifted into outlawry. He later joined forces with a gunfighter named the Sundance Kid, whose real name was Harry Longabaugh. Together Cassidy and Sundance started robbing banks in 1896, separated, then reunited as their fortunes changed. Their frequent traveling companion Etta Place may have been a prostitute rather than a schoolteacher.

A remarkable example of marvelous movie making and flawed history, this whimsical revisionist western film is a joy to watch. The film revived the career of Paul Newman, who had a small downward swing after *Cool Hand Luke* (1967), while making a front-line star of Robert Redford. With William Goldman's crisp writing and sprightly dialogue, and Burt Bacharach's Oscar-winning song "Raindrops Keep Fallin' On My Head," the film became one of the most pop-ular and highest grossing westerns ever—though some purists might argue that it is not a western in the true sense of the term. Nominated for seven Academy Award nominations, the film garnered four Oscars and reflects brilliantly the prevailing antiestablishment feeling of the late 1960s.

Warren Beatty reportedly turned down the role of Sundance in favor of a role in *Only Game in Town* (1970). Director George Roy Hill originally cast Robert Redford as Butch and Paul Newman as Sundance, and it was at Redford's suggestion that the roles were changed. Look for a young Sam Elliott as one of the card players (listed in the credits as card player #2).

BUZZY AND THE PHANTOM PINTO Ellkay Productions, 1941, B&W, 55 min. **Producer:** Richard L'Estrange; **Director:** Richard C. Kahn; **Screenplay:** E. C. Robertson; **Cast:** Robert "Buzz" Henry, Dave O'Brien, Dorothy Short, George Morrell, Sven Hugo Borg, Milburn Morante.

Paul Newman (left) and Robert Redford as Butch Cassidy and the Sundance Kid. *"Raindrops Keep Fallin' On My Head" won an Oscar for Burt Bacharach.* (20TH CENTURY FOX/AUTHOR'S COLLECTION)

BUZZY RIDES THE RANGE Ellkay Productions, 1940, B&W, 60 min. **Producer:** Richard L'Estrange; **Director:** Richard C. Kahn; **Screenplay:** E. C. Robertson; **Music:** Bob File; **Cinematographer:** Clark Ramsey; **Editor:** Adrian Weiss; **Cast:** Robert "Buzz" Henry, Dave O'Brien, Claire Rochelle, George Eldridge, George Morrell, Frank Marlo, Don Kelly, Phil Arnold.

A young boy teams with a range detective to track down outlaws. Designed to provide the first of what was to be a series for juvenile star Robert "Buzzy" Henry, the film was followed only by *Buzzy and the Phantom Pinto* (1941), later reissued in 1948 by Astor as *Western Terror*.

CAHILL: UNITED STATES MARSHAL Batjac/
Warner Bros., 1973, Color, 102 min, VT. **Producer:**
Michael Wayne; **Director:** Andrew V. McLaglen; **Screen-
play:** Harry Julian Fink and Rita M. Fink; **Music:** Elmer
Bernstein; **Cinematographer:** Joseph Biroc; **Editor:**
Robert L. Simpson; **Cast:** John Wayne, George Kennedy,
Gary Grimes, Neville Brand, Clay O'Brien, Marie Windsor,
Morgan Paul, Dan Vadis, Scott Walker, Denver Pyle, Jackie
Coogan, Royal Dano, Rayford Barnes, Dan Kemp, Harry
Carey Jr., Paul Fix, Hank Worden, Walter Barnes, Chuck
Roberson.

Tired and weary from a manhunt and shoot-out in the hills,
J. D. Cahill (John Wayne) returns to the town of Valentine,
Texas, to find that the bank has been robbed and the sheriff
and a deputy murdered. He also learns that his two young
sons, ages 12 and 17, have fallen in with the bank robbers.
The boys, feeling neglected because their dad was always
away chasing lawbreakers, had allowed smooth-talking outlaw George Kennedy to involve them in a bank robbery. But
the vicious Kennedy bedevils them when the oldest son
(Gary Grimes) double-crosses him and hides the money.
After the grizzled Wayne finally dispatches the bad guys, he
offers his sons some fatherly advice: "Don't rob banks!"

 While not of the same caliber as some later Wayne westerns (*CHISUM*, *THE COWBOYS*, *THE SHOOTIST*), this is still an
enjoyable film. By combining the twin complexities of fatherhood and law enforcement, a new theme is added to Wayne's
screen arsenal.

 The theme song, "A Man Gets to Thinking" (music by
Elmer Bernstein, lyrics by Don Black), is sung by Charlie
Rich. Marie Windsor (Mrs. Hetty Green) worked opposite
Wayne in three different decades: the '40s (*Dakota*, 1946),
the '50s (*Trouble Along the Way*, 1953), and the 1970s (*Cahill*),
a period spanning 37 years. Wayne's longtime pal Chuck
Roberson served as the film's stunt director.

**CAIN'S CUT THROATS (aka: THE BLOOD
SEEKERS; CAIN'S WAY; JUSTICE CAIN)**
Colby Productions, 1971, Color, 87 min. **Producers:** Budd
Dell and Kent Osborne; **Director:** Osborne; **Screenplay:**
Wilton Denmark; **Music:** Harley Hatcher; **Cinemato-
grapher:** Ralph Waldo; **Editor:** James C. Moore; **Cast:** John
Carradine, Scott Brady, Robert Dix, Don Epperson, Adair
Jamison, Darwin Jaston, Bruce Kimball, Teresa Thaw, Willis
Martin.

Following the Civil War, Confederate captain Justice Cain
(Scott Brady) has retired to a quiet life with his young son
and his black wife. However, the men of his old outfit, known
as Cain's Cutthroats, have turned to lives of murder, torture,
and robbery. They attempt to convince Cain to ride with
them once more. When he refuses, the Cutthroats murder
his family and leave him for dead. He is nursed back to health
by a preacher/bounty hunter (John Carradine), and the hunt
for revenge begins.

CALAMITY JANE Warner Bros., 1953, Color, 103
min, VT, CD. **Producer:** William Jacobs; **Director:** David
Butler; **Screenplay:** James O'Hanlon; **Music:** Ray Heins-
dorf; **Cinematographer:** Wilfred M. Cline; **Editor:** Irene
Morra; **Cast:** Doris Day, Howard Keel, Allyn Ann McLerie,
Philip Carey, Dick Wesson, Paul Harvey.

Perky and pretty Doris Day is a sheer delight in the title role,
although she bears no physical resemblance to the real
Calamity Jane, who was quite homely. Howard Keel plays the
reluctant Bill Hickok, who finds himself suddenly attracted
to Calamity once she takes Katy Brown's (Allyn McLerie)
advice to go feminine.

 The colorful settings and costumes add further sparkle
and flavor to the Deadwood Dakota Territory, with the team
of Sammy Fain and Paul Francis Webster providing 11 songs

Doris Day in Calamity Jane. *The song* "Secret Love" *won a Best Song Oscar and became one of the hit songs of 1953.* (WARNER BROS./AUTHOR'S COLLECTION)

including "Just Blew in from the Windy City," "The Black Hills of Dakota," and the Oscar-winning "Secret Love." Doris Day's recording of the song became the biggest hit of her career, a number-one million seller and one of top song hits of 1953.

CALAMITY JANE AND SAM BASS
Universal, 1949, Color, 85 min. **Producer:** Leonard Goldstein; **Director:** George Sherman; **Screenplay:** Maurice Geraghty and Melvin Levy; **Music:** Miklos Rozsa (uncredited); **Cinematographer:** Irving Glassberg; **Editor:** Edward Curtiss; **Cast:** Yvonne De Carlo, Howard Duff, Dorothy Hart, Willard Parker, Norman Lloyd, Lloyd Bridges, Marc Lawrence, Houseley Stevenson, Milburn Stone, Clifton Young, Ann Doran, Charles Cane.

When drifter Sam Bass (Howard Duff) shows up in Denton, Texas, looking for work, he attracts the attention of a pretty storekeeper (Dorothy Hart) and wild frontier woman Calamity Jane (a very seductive Yvonne De Carlo). His good luck with women and horses leads him astray of the law. Another physical mismatch casts the enticing De Carlo as the

plain Calamity—but that's Hollywood! The rootin' tootin' shootin' woman of the Old West has been glamorized many times for movies, notably by Jean Arthur in *THE PLAINSMAN* (1936), Evelyn Ankers in *THE TEXAN MEETS CALAMITY JANE* (1951), Judy Meredith in *THE RAIDERS* (1964), and Abbe Dalton in *The Plainsman* (1966).

CALIFORNIA
Paramount, 1946, Color, 97 min. **Producer:** Seton I. Miller; **Director:** John Farrow; **Screenplay:** Frank Butler, Miller, and Theodore Strauss; **Music:** Earl Robinson (songs) and Victor Young; **Cinematographer:** Ray Rennahan; **Editor:** Eda Warren; **Cast:** Ray Milland, Barbara Stanwyck, Barry Fitzgerald, George Coulouris, Albert Dekker, Anthony Quinn, Frank Faylen.

In this epic-style western about how California became a state, Ray Milland is an army deserter who becomes a guide for a train of covered wagons headed for the Golden State. Barry Fitzgerald plays a winegrower from Ohio who hopes to cultivate grapes in order to make wine in California. Barbara Stanwyck is a lady who has been run out of town on moral grounds and turns her venom on Milland while also becoming dangerously attracted to him. All of this makes for lots of dealing and double-dealing.

The film marks the western debut of actor Ray Milland, who took home an Oscar for *The Lost Weekend* two years earlier. The story is that Milland did this movie out of fatherly pride because his son was spending every Saturday afternoon cheering John Wayne on the big screen. Victor Young provides an excellent musical score, with six songs by the team of Earl Robinson and E. Y. Harburg included in the soundtrack. The film is an unofficial remake of James Cruze's silent epic *THE COVERED WAGON* (1923).

CALIFORNIA
AIP, 1963, B&W, 86 min. **Producer:** Hamil Petroff; **Director:** Petroff; **Screenplay:** James West; **Music:** Richard LaSalle; **Cinematographer:** Eddie Fitzgerald; **Editor:** Bert Honey; **Cast:** Jock Mahoney, Faith Domergue, Michael Pate, Susan Seaforth Hayes, Rodolfo Hoyos, Penny Santon, Jimmy Murphy.

In this film set in 1941, the people of California revolt against Mexican oppression and ask the United States for help.

CALIFORNIA CONQUEST
Columbia, 1952, Color, 78 min. **Producer:** Sam Katzman; **Director:** Lew Landers; **Screenplay:** Robert E. Kent; **Music:** Mischa Bakaleinikoff; **Cinematographer:** Ellis W. Carter; **Editor:** Richard Fantl; **Cast:** Cornel Wilde, Teresa Wright, Alfonso Bedoya, Lisa Ferraday, Eugene Iglesias, John Dehner, Ivan Lebedeff.

While California is still under Spanish control, Don Arturo Bordega thwarts a Russian attempt to confiscate the territory. The United States was in the throes of the cold war when this interesting and neglected historical sidelight was brought to the screen in 1952. This is a picture worth watching especially for its historical context.

CALIFORNIA FIREBRAND   Republic, 1948, Color, 63 min. **Producer:** Melville Tucker (associate); **Director:** Philip Ford; **Screenplay:** John K. Butler and J. Benton Cheney; **Music:** Sid Robbin and Foy Willing; **Cinematographer:** Reggie Lanning; **Editor:** Tony Martinelli; **Cast:** Monte Hale, Lorna Gray (Adrian Booth), Paul Hurst, Alice Tyrrell, Tristram Coffin.

Monte Hale finds a wounded man and assumes his identity. This helps land him the job of town marshal and puts him flush in the middle of a battle between two feuding families. Trouble arises when the wounded man arrives and exposes him as a fake. (See also HOME ON THE RANGE [1946].)

CALIFORNIA GOLD RUSH   Republic, 1946, B&W, 54 min. **Producer:** Sidney Picker (associate); **Director:** R. G. Springsteen; **Screenplay:** Bob Williams; **Cinematographer:** William Bradford; **Editor:** Charles Craft; **Cast:** Bill Elliott, Bobby Blake, Alice Fleming, Peggy Stewart, Russell Simpson, Dick Curtis, Mary Arden, Robert Blake, Dick Curtis, Dickie Dillon, Kenne Duncan.

CALIFORNIA IN 1878   See FIGHTIN' THRU.

CALIFORNIA JOE   Republic, 1943, B&W, 55 min. **Producer:** Eddy White; **Director:** Spencer Gordon Bennet; **Screenplay:** Norman S. Hall; **Cinematographer:** Ernest Miller; **Editor:** Harry Keller; **Cast:** Don "Red" Barry, Wally Vernon, Helen Talbot, Twinkle Watts, Brian O'Hara, Terry Frost, LeRoy Mason, Charles King, Pierce Lyden, Edward Earle, Edmund Cobb, Karl Hackett, Bob Kortman.

During the post-Civil War era, a trio of opportunists (Terry Frost, LeRoy Mason, and Edward Earle) have plans to make California a separate nation. Lieutenant Joe Weldon (Don "Red" Barry) masquerading under the guise of "California Joe," and sidekicks Judith Carteret (Helen Talbot) and Tumbleweed Smith (Wally Vernon) are sent west to thwart their attempts.

CALIFORNIA MAIL   Warner Bros., 1936, B&W, 56 min. **Producer:** Bryan Foy; **Director:** Noel M. Smith; **Screenplay:** Harold Buckley and Roy Chanslor; **Music:** M. K. Jerome, Jack Scholl, and Howard Jackson; **Cinematographer:** Ted D. McCord; **Editor:** Doug Gould; **Cast:** Dick Foran, Linda Perry, Edmund Cobb, Milton Kibbee, Tom Brower, Jim Farley, Edward Keane, Glenn Strange, The Sons of the Pioneers.

Cowboy singer Bill Harkins (Dick Foran) enters a bidding war with the Banton Brothers to win a U.S. mail contract for their stagecoach line. Look for an uncredited appearance by Roy Rogers as a member of the Sons of the Pioneers. (See also MOONLIGHT ON THE PRAIRIE.)

CALIFORNIAN, THE (aka: THE GENTLEMAN FROM CALIFORNIA)   20th Century Fox, 1937, B&W, 59 min. **Producer:** Sol Lesser; **Director:** Gus Meins; **Screenplay:** Gilbert Wright; **Cinematographer:** Harry Neumann; **Editors:** Arthur Hilton and Carl Pierson; **Cast:** Ricardo Cortez, Marjorie Weaver, Katherine DeMille, Maurice Black, Morgan Wallace, Nigel De Brulier, George Regas.

In 1885 a young man returns from school in Spain to his native California to find corrupt politicians stealing land from old California families. He therefore assumes the status of a Robin Hood and takes on the evil politicians.

CALIFORNIA OUTPOST   See OLD LOS ANGELES.

CALIFORNIA PASSAGE   Republic, 1950, B&W, 90 min. **Producer:** Joseph Kane; **Director:** Kane; **Screenplay:** James Edward Grant; **Music:** Jack Elliott; **Cinematographer:** John MacBurnie; **Editor:** Arthur Roberts; **Cast:** Forrest Tucker, Adele Mara, Estelita Rodriguez, Jim Davis, Peter Miles, Charles Kemper, Paul Fix.

A girl falls in love with a saloon owner, even though the man accidentally killed her brother and is being accused of robbing a stagecoach that was really held up by his crooked partner.

CALIFORNIA TRAIL, THE   Columbia, 1933, B&W, 67 min. **Director:** Lambert Hillyer; **Screenplay:** Hillyer and Jack Natteford; **Cinematographer:** Benjamin H. Kline; **Editor:** Gene Milford; **Cast:** Buck Jones, Helen Mack, Luis Alberni, George Humbert, Charles Stevens.

CALLAWAY WENT THATAWAY (aka: THE STAR SAID NO)   MGM, 1951, B&W, 81 min. **Producers:** Melvin Frank and Norman Panama; **Directors:** Frank and Panama; **Screenplay:** Frank and Panama; **Music:** Marlin Skiles; **Cinematographer:** Ray June; **Editor:** Cotton Warburton; **Cast:** Fred MacMurray, Dorothy McGuire, Howard Keel, Jesse White, Hugh Beaumont, Don Haggerty, Mae Clarke.

Two enterprising marketing people (Fred MacMurray and Dorothy McGuire) resurrect some old movies starring an ex-cowboy hero named "Smoky" Callaway and put them on television. The films prove to be a gigantic hit, and suddenly people are clamoring for the old cowboy star. The problem is nobody can find him. When a lookalike sends in a photo, MacMurray and McGuire hire him to impersonate the elusive Callaway, and he soon becomes the darling of throngs of adoring fans. Everything fits into place until the real Callaway appears in the person of a drunken womanizer who wants a piece of the action.

This is a delightful parody of the Hopalong Cassidy craze of the early 1950s; MGM stars Clark Gable, Dick Powell, Elizabeth Taylor, and Esther Williams make cameo appearances. Howard Keel is a delight in the dual role of cowboy imposter Stretch Barnes and the authentic loser "Smoky"

Callaway. This movie is just plain, old-fashioned fun and more honest than most Hollywood satires.

CALLING WILD BILL ELLIOTT Republic, 1943, B&W, 78 min, VT. **Producer:** Harry Grey; **Director:** Spencer Gordon Bennet; **Screenplay:** Anthony Coldeway; **Cinematographer:** Ernest Miller; **Cast:** William "Wild Bill" Elliott, George "Gabby" Hayes, Anne Jeffreys, Herbert Heyes, Robert "Buzz" Henry, Fred Kohler Jr., Roy Barcroft.

Ruthless, self-appointed Governor Nichols and his personal militia are driving ranchers off their land. When they go after the Culver family, Bill Elliott arrives to rally the outnumbered ranchers, who start fighting back. This film was Bill Elliott's first foray into A pictures for Republic.

CALL OF THE CANYON Republic, 1942, B&W, 71 min. **Producer:** Harry Grey; **Director:** Joseph Santley; **Screenplay:** Olive Cooper; **Cinematographer:** Reggie Lanning; **Editor:** Edward Mann; **Cast:** Gene Autry, Smiley Burnette, Ruth Terry, Thurston Hall, Joe Strauch Jr., Cliff Nazarro, Dorothea Kent, Bob Nolan and The Sons of the Pioneers, Marc Lawrence.

While in a big city, Gene Autry decides to head a group of cattlemen who have been swindled by an unscrupulous meatpacking tycoon. He becomes involved with a beautiful radio singer, and when he returns home he finds that Frog (Smiley Burnette) has rented their ranch to her. This enjoyable Autry venture combines good action and fine music. (See also *TUMBLING TUMBLEWEEDS.*)

CALL OF THE PRAIRIE Paramount, 1936, B&W, 63 min. **Producer:** Harry Sherman; **Director:** Howard Bretherton; **Screenplay:** Doris Schroeder and Vernon Smith; **Music:** Lee Lawnhurst and Tot Seymour; **Cinematographer:** Archie Stout; **Editor:** Edward Schroeder; **Cast:** William Boyd, James Ellison, Muriel Evans, George "Gabby" Hayes, Chester Conklin.

When a gang of thieves tries to pin a robbery on a foolish young man, Hoppy is convinced his young friend is innocent and sets out to prove it. In order to do that he enlists the help of sidekicks Shanghai ("Gabby" Hayes) and Johnny (James Ellison). Based on Clarence Mulford's fictional western hero, this film is one of William Boyd's earliest series efforts for Paramount. Originally one of Cecil B. DeMille's favorite actors in the 1920s, Boyd made his first appearance as Hop-Along Cassidy in 1935 and would do little else for the next 16 years, becoming one of the most successful and enduring screen characters in film history. (See also *HOP-ALONG CASSIDY.*)

CALL OF THE ROCKIES Columbia, 1938, B&W, 54 min. **Producer:** Harry L. Decker; **Director:** Alan James; **Screenplay:** Ed Earl Repp; **Music:** Bob Nolan (songs) and Morris Stoloff; **Cinematographer:** Benjamin H. Kline; **Editor:** William A. Lyon; **Cast:** Charles Starrett, Donald Grayson, Iris Meredith, Dick Curtis, Edward Le Saint, Edmund Cobb, Art Mix, John Tyrrell, George Chesebro, Glenn Strange.

CALL OF THE ROCKIES Republic, 1944, B&W, 58 min, VT. **Producer:** Lou Gray; **Director:** Leslie Selander; **Screenplay:** Bob Williams; **Cast:** Smiley Burnette, Sunset Carson, Ellen Hall, Kirk Alyn, Harry Woods, Frank Jacquet, Edmund Cobb, Robert J. Wilke, Harry Woods.

In Sunset Carson's first starring film (he takes second place to Smiley Burnette), two freight haulers lose their cargo, only to find out that a doctor and a mine owner are in cahoots to gain control of all the mines in the area.

Born Michael Harrison, Carson was a rodeo performer from his early teens. Republic changed his name to that of his fictional alter-ego, Sunset Carson, whom he portrayed in the company's films of the 1940s. These include *Bordertown Trail, Code of the Prairie, Firebrands of Arizona* (1944); *Bandits of the Badlands, The Cherokee Flash, The Oregon Trail, Bells of Rosarita, Santa Fe Saddlemates, Sheriff of Cimarron* (1945); *El Paso Kid, Alias Billy the Kid, Red River Renegades, Days of Buffalo Bill, Rio Grande Raiders* (1946); *Deadline, Sunset Carson Rides Again* (1948); *Fighting Mustang* (1949); *Battling Marshal* (1950).

CALL OF THE WILD, THE 20th Century Pictures, 1935, B&W, 89 min. **Producer:** Darryl F. Zanuck; **Director:** William Wellman; **Screenplay:** Gene Fowler and Leonard Praskins; **Music:** Alfred Newman; **Cinematographer:** Charles Rosher; **Editor:** Hanson Fritch; **Cast:** Clark Gable, Loretta Young, Jack Oakie, Reginald Owen, Frank Conroy, Sidney Toler.

Adventurers Clark Gable and Jack Oakie rescue Loretta Young, whose husband has apparently lost his way and perished in the vast Arctic region. This version of Jack London's celebrated novel was the second feature filmed for the big screen. Pathé made it as a silent feature in 1923.

While the film is more Hollywood fluff than pure Jack London, Gable and Young are able to hold an audience in romantic awe with their remarkable screen chemistry. Buck, the huge St. Bernard canine, manages to haul a 1,000-pound load over the snow while still finding time to mate with a female wolf. The vivid Alaskan panorama enhances a theme that incorporates violence, treachery, hardship, and unrequited love.

After filming this movie, Loretta Young announced her retirement and went to Paris. She returned to the United States in 1937 with a 23-month-old-baby she claimed to have adopted. Rumors abounded that the baby was also Clark Gable's, the result of a love affair they had while on location making the movie. *The Call of the Wild* was remade in 1973, with Charlton Heston starring, and again as TV movies in 1976, 1993, and 1997.

Cast members from Call of the Rockies, *Sunset Carson's first starring film. Carson was a former rodeo rider. Republic changed his name from Michael Harrison to Sunset Carson, the fictional name of the western hero he was to portray.* (REPUBLIC/AUTHOR'S COLLECTION)

CALL THE MESQUITEERS Republic, 1938, B&W, 55 min, VT. **Producer:** William A. Berke; **Director:** John English; **Screenplay:** Luci Ward; **Cinematographer:** William Nobles; **Editor:** Lester Orlebeck; **Cast:** Robert Livingston, Ray Corrigan, Max Terhune, Lynne Roberts, Sammy McKim, Earle Hodgins.

Smugglers hijack the Mesquiteers' truck, and when the police catch and kill them, they try to arrest the Mesquiteers for being part of the gang. The Mesquiteers escape, but as wanted men they must prove their innocence. Republic Pictures produced approximately 50 films in the *Three Mesquiteers* series (1935–43). Their hallmark was uncluttered action and great stunt work, usually arranged and performed by Yakima Canutt. Robert Livingston, Ray Corrigan, and Max Terhune were the original trio, but John Wayne later replaced the temperamental Livingston, who reportedly was giving Republic a lot of trouble at the time. (See also *THREE MESQUITEERS, THE*.)

CAMPBELL'S KINGDOM (UK) Rank, 1957, Color, 102 min. **Producer:** Betty E. Box; **Director:** Ralph Thomas; **Screenplay:** Robin Estridge; **Music:** Clifton Parker; **Editor:** Frederick Wilson; **Cast:** Dirk Bogarde, Stanley Baker, Michael Craig, Barbara Murray, Robert Brown, John Laurie.

Landowner Dirk Bogarde finds himself at odds with ruthless contractor Stanley Baker, who is attempting to build a dam near his property. Momentum develops because Bogarde's character is ill and has only six months to live when he arrives in the Canadian township of Come Lucky to claim his grandfather's inheritance. The film remains basically true to Hammond Innes's novel.

CANADIAN PACIFIC 20th Century Fox, 1949, Color, 95 min. **Producer:** Nat Holt; **Director:** Edwin L. Marin; **Screenplay:** Jack DeWitt and Kenneth Gamet; **Music:** Dimitri Tiomkin; **Cinematographer:** Fred Jackman Jr.; **Editor:** Philip Martin; **Cast:** Randolph Scott, Jane Wyatt, J. Carrol Naish, Victor Jory, Nancy Olson.

Randolph Scott is a surveyor for the Canadian Pacific Railroad who clashes with fur trappers led by Victor Jory. Jory and his pals try to stifle railroad building by stirring up an Indian rebellion. A superb villain, Jory manages to have Scott blown up by dynamite, although not fatally. "He was too close. If he had been just six feet away," Jory explains to explosives expert Dynamite Dawson (J. Carrol Naish). Through all the histrionics Scott is still able to romance Jane Wyatt and Nancy Olson.

CANNON FOR CORDOBA (aka: DRAGON MASTER)

The Mirisch Production Company/United Artists, 1970, Color, 104 min. **Producer:** Vincent M. Fennelly; **Director:** Paul Wendkos; **Screenplay:** Stephen Kandel; **Music:** Elmer Bernstein; **Cinematographer:** Antonio Macasoli; **Editor:** Walter A. Hannemann; **Cast:** George Peppard, Giovanna Ralli, Raf Vallone, Peter Duel, Don Gordon, John Russell.

In this film set along the Texas border during the Mexican Revolution, George Peppard leads a band of soldiers against a group of Mexican revolutionary bandits. Their job is to recover the cannons that had been stolen from General Pershing's camp. John Russell plays General John J. Pershing, an authentic and frequently ignored American hero.

CAN'T HELP SINGING

Universal, 1944, Color, 90 min, VT, CD. **Producer:** Felix Jackson; **Director:** Frank Ryan; **Screenplay:** Lewis R. Foster and Ryan; **Music:** Jerome Kern and Hans J. Salter; **Cinematographer:** Elwood Bredell and W. Howard Greene; **Editor:** Ted J. Kent; **Cast:** Deanna Durbin, Robert Paige, Akim Tamiroff, David Bruce, Leonid Kinskey.

Deanna Durbin plays the daughter of a U.S. senator who is determined to marry a cavalry officer. The problem is that the senator doesn't like the young officer and uses his influence to have him sent to a remote post in California. Durbin follows but never quite catches up with her wayward officer. Along the way she picks up an assortment of companions, including a pair of thieves and an attractive gambler (Robert Paige), whom she falls for.

Deanna Durbin sang like a nightingale and was one of the top box-office attractions of the late 1930s and early '40s. *Can't Help Singing* was her first color film and her first musical comedy vehicle. While the plot is somewhat nebulous, the sets are bright and colorful, and the costumes rich and lavish. Composer Jerome Kern (*Showboat, Roberta*) provides a score of tuneful songs, many of which Durbin sings beautifully. The production numbers are superbly staged. Set during the California Gold Rush, the film provides good escapist fun and is a must for Deanna Durbin fans.

CANYON AMBUSH (aka: GUNS ALONG THE BORDER)

Monogram, 1952, B&W, 53 min. **Producer:** Vincent M. Fennelly; **Director:** Lewis D. Collins; **Screenplay:** Joseph Poland; **Cinematographer:** Ernest Miller; **Cast:** Johnny Mack Brown, Phyllis Coates, Lee Roberts, Denver Pyle, Dennis Moore, Hugh Prosser, Marshall Reed, Pierce Lyden, Carol Henry, Stanley Price.

A government agent comes to a small town to help the local sheriff and concerned citizens in combating a gang led by a masked rider. This film marks the final Monogram series production for Johnny Mack Brown. (See also *UNDER ARIZONA SKIES.*)

CANYON CROSSROADS

United Artists, 1955, B&W, 83 min. **Producer:** William Joyce; **Director:** Alfred L. Werker; **Screenplay:** Leonard Heidman and Emmett Murphy; **Music:** George Bassman; **Cinematographer:** Gordon Avil; **Editor:** Chester W. Schaeffer; **Cast:** Richard Basehart, Phyllis Kirk, Stephen Elliott, Russell Collins.

Richard Basehart is a mining engineer who is shunned by his peers for his unorthodox beliefs. Filmed on location in Colorado, this offbeat story of uranium prospectors in the West has been extremely well received by viewers and presents an excellent modern-day western.

CANYON HAWKS

National Players, 1930, B&W, six reels. **Producer:** F. E. Douglas; **Directors:** Alan J. Neitz and J. P. McGowan; **Screenplay:** Neitz; **Cinematographer:** William Nobles; **Editor:** Fred Bain; **Cast:** Yakima Canutt, Rene Borden, Buzz Barton, Robert Walker, Bobby Dunn, Wally Wales, Cliff Lyons.

Yakima Canutt plays cattleman Jack Benson, who finds a sister and brother, Mildred and George Manning, living in one of his cabins and their sheep roaming his land. Because he is attracted to Mildred, he lets her stay and even deeds part of his land to her. This leads to problems with other cattlemen. Originally released as a six-reel feature in Cinephone, the current video release has been shortened to 39 minutes. This film should appeal to fans of Yakima Canutt because of his starring role.

CANYON PASSAGE

Universal, 1946, Color, 92 min, VT. **Producer:** Walter Wanger; **Director:** Jacques Tourneur; **Screenplay:** Ernest Pascal; **Music:** Jack Brooks and Hoagy Carmichael; **Cinematographer:** Edward Cronjager; **Editor:** Milton Carruth; **Cast:** Dana Andrews, Susan Hayward, Brian Donlevy, Patricia Roc, Ward Bond, Hoagy Carmichael, Fay Holden, Stanley Ridges, Lloyd Bridges, Andy Devine.

Set in Portland, Oregon, in the mid-1850s and based on a novel by Ernest Haycox, *Canyon Passage* tells of the trials and tribulations of a number of people in the unsettled Oregon country and of the pioneering men and women who helped build and tame the Wild West.

Dana Andrews—at the height of his screen popularity—is Logan Stuart, and Ward Bond is excellent as villain Honey Bragg. But the real scene-stealer is songwriter/actor Hoagy Carmichael. As the wandering minstrel Hi Linnet, he strums a mandolin, sings, and introduces the hit Oscar-nominated song "Ole Buttermilk Sky."

With a top-flight cast and an excellent melding of drama, romance, and action, Jacques Tourneur managed to helm a worthy western, which can be seen time and again. Ernest Haycox, who wrote *Canyon Passage*, also wrote the story for *STAGECOACH*. Walter Wanger produced both films, and both sport a strong supporting performances by Andy Devine, whose sons Tad and Dennis also appear in this film. Filmed in brilliant color, *Canyon Passage* may not be another *Stagecoach*, but in the words of the *New York Times*, it is a "whopping Western show [with] a lot of good old-fashioned thrills."

CANYON RAIDERS Monogram/Frontier, 1951, B&W, 54 min. **Producer:** Vincent M. Fennelly; **Director:** Lewis D. Collins; **Screenplay:** Jay Gilgore; **Cinematographer:** Ernest Miller; **Editor:** Richard V. Heermance; **Cast:** Whip Wilson, Phyllis Coates, I. Stanford Jolley, Fuzzy Knight, Marshall Reed, Riley Hill, Jim Bannon.

Two ranchers try to stop crooks who have rustled 500 horses and plan to sell them to the army with a forged bill of sale.

Some good action scenes can be found in this Whip Wilson Monogram venture. (See also *ABILENE TRAIL*.)

CANYON RIVER (aka: CATTLE KING) Allied Artists, 1956, Color, 79 min. **Producers:** Richard V. Heermance and Scott R. Dunlap; **Director:** Harmon Jones; **Screenplay:** Daniel B. Ullman; **Music:** Marlin Skiles; **Cinematographer:** Ellsworth Fredricks; **Editor:** George White; **Cast:** George Montgomery, Marcia Henderson, Peter Graves, Richard Eyer, Walter Sande, Robert J. Wilke, Alan Hale Jr., Jack Lambert, William Fawcett, Bud Osborne, Ray Teal.

George Montgomery leads a cattle drive from Oregon to Wyoming but must contend with both hostile Indians and ruthless rustlers in the process.

CAPTAIN APACHE (aka: THE GUNS OF APRIL MORNING) Scotia International, 1971, Color,

Dana Andrews lands a haymaker on Ward Bond in Canyon Passage. *The film features the Oscar-nominated hit song "Ole Buttermilk Sky."* (UNIVERSAL/AUTHOR'S COLLECTION)

"A whopping good Western" is how the New York Times *described* Canyon Passage. (UNIVERSAL/AUTHOR'S COLLECTION)

94 min, VT, DVD. **Producers:** Milton Sperling and Philip Yordan; **Director:** Alexander Singer; **Screenplay:** Sperling and Yordan; **Music:** Dolores Claman; **Cinematographer:** John Cabrera; **Editor:** Leigh G. Tallas; **Cast:** Lee Van Cleef, Carroll Baker, Stuart Whitman, Percy Herbert, Elisa Montes.

Lee Van Cleef is a Native American army officer who answers to the name Captain Apache. While investigating a murder he uncovers a presidential assassination plot. His dilemma occurs when he also discovers an army plot to steal land from his people. Produced in Great Britain, this picture has all the violence of the continental westerns being filmed at the time.

CAPTIVE OF BILLY THE KID Republic, 1952, B&W, 84 min. **Producer:** Harry Keller (associate); **Director:** Fred C. Brannon; **Screenplay:** M. Coates Webster and Richard Wormser; **Music:** Stanley Wilson; **Cinematographer:** John MacBurnie; **Editor:** Robert M. Leeds; **Cast:** Allan Lane, Penny Edwards, Grant Withers, Roy Barcroft, Clayton Moore.

Five people each have part of a map leading to Billy the Kid's treasure. When one of them is killed, Rocky Lane has a plan to find the killer. He poses as a crook and takes the other four pieces in the hope the killer will contact him. Unbeknownst to him, however, the killer knows that Lane is a marshal and sets a trap for him. (See also *BOLD FRONTIERSMAN, THE.*)

CAPTURE, THE RKO, 1950, B&W, 91 min. **Producer:** Niven Busch; **Director:** John Sturges; **Screenplay:** Busch; **Music:** Daniele Amfitheatrof; **Cinematographer:** Edward Cronjager; **Editor:** George Amy; **Cast:** Lew Ayres, Teresa Wright, Victor Jory, Jacqueline White, Jimmy Hunt, Barry Kelley, Duncan Renaldo.

In this early John Sturges western, Lew Ayres plays a detective who reinvestigates a robbery to learn if he might have shot an innocent man. Sturges, whose films usually involve characters in jeopardy and ensconced in a hostile environment, went on to helm such vigorous westerns as *ESCAPE FROM FORT BRAVO* (1953), *BAD DAY AT BLACK ROCK* (1955), *GUNFIGHT AT THE O.K. CORRAL* (1957), and *THE MAGNIFICENT SEVEN* (1960). This interesting and intelligent film—with much of its footage in rural Mexico—is a real sleeper.

CARAVAN TRAIL, THE PRC, 1946, Color, 53 min. **Producer:** Robert Emmett Tansey; **Director:** Tansey; **Screenplay:** Frances Kavanaugh; **Music:** Karl Hajos and Carl Hoefle; **Cinematographer:** Marcel Le Picard; **Editor:** Hugh Winn; **Cast:** Eddie Dean, Lash La Rue, Emmett Lynn, Jean Carlin, Robert Barron, Charles King, Forrest Taylor, Bud Osborne, Wylie Grant.

The leader of a wagon train of settlers needs the help of an outlaw gang leader to stop the land grabbers who have stolen the pioneers' homesteads. Eddie Dean was one of a number of western stars who worked for Producers Releasing Corporation (PRC) in the 1940s. Dean sings the popular western standard "Wagon Wheels," and the film helped launch a series of his own for costar Lash La Rue. Because of the use of Cinecolor, these colorized Eddie Dean ventures had an early edge over his other films. A lesser PRC western star, Dean was not particularly popular, and his films eventually reverted to the standard black and white. (See also *SONG OF OLD WYOMING.*)

CARIBOO TRAIL, THE 20th Century Fox, 1950, Color, 81 min. **Producer:** Nat Holt; **Director:** Edwin L. Marin; **Screenplay:** Frank Gruber and John Rhodes; **Music:** Paul Sawtell; **Cinematographer:** Fred Jackman Jr.; **Editor:** Philip Martin; **Cast:** Randolph Scott, George "Gabby" Hayes, Bill Williams, Karin Booth, Victor Jory, Douglas Kennedy, Jim Davis, Dale Robertson.

It's the standard conflict between cattlemen and settlers as gold fever sweeps the western Canadian coastline. Randolph Scott is the proverbial loner heading into the region with his herd of cattle, hoping to make more money by rearing his animals in the fine Canadian pastures. But he is betrayed by his traveling companion and a local business tycoon, and when the shooting starts a bloody gunfight ensues. Director Edwin Marin (1899–1951) helmed many effective Randolph Scott westerns, including this exciting film released one year before the director's death.

CAROLINA MOON Republic, 1942, B&W, 65 min. **Producer:** William A. Berke; **Director:** Frank McDonald; **Screenplay:** Winston Miller; **Cinematographer:** William Nobles; **Editor:** Tony Martinelli; **Cast:** Gene Autry, Smiley Burnette, June Storey, Mary Lee, Eddy Waller, Hardie Albright, Frank Dale.

CARRY ON COWBOY (aka: THE RUMPO KID, UK) Anglo-Amalgamated Productions, 1965, Color, 95 min. **Producer:** Peter Rogers; **Director:** Gerald Thomas;

Screenplay: Talbot Rothwell; **Music:** Alan Rogers and Eric Rogers; **Cinematographer:** Alan Hume; **Editor:** Rod Keys; **Cast:** Sid James, Kenneth Williams, Jim Dale, Joan Sims, Angela Douglas.

It seems that the slummy western town of Stodge City is in the grip of the Rumpo Kid and his nasty gang. The dismayed judge calls for a marshal to clean up the town. By mistake a sanitary inspector gets sent to the troubled town and is mistaken for the new marshal. Arriving on the same stage is Annie Oakley, the daughter of the sheriff who was knocked-off by the Rumpo Kid. By using his knowledge of drains to an ingenious effect, our new hero disposes of the Rumpo Kid, while taking a long walk down a deserted street in a delightful spoofing of *High Noon*. Although filmed in Surrey, England, the "western locations" here look surprisingly authentic. This Western comedy spoof from the director who gave us such series spoofs as *Carry On Constable* (1960), *Carry On Cruising* (1962), and *Carry on Doctor* (1968) packs a humorous punch.

CARSON CITY Warner Bros., 1952, Color, 87 min. **Producer:** David Weisbart; **Director:** André De Toth; **Screenplay:** Eric Jonosson and Winston Miller; **Music:** David Buttolph; **Cinematographer:** John W. Boyle; **Editor:** Robert L. Swanson; **Cast:** Randolph Scott, Lucille Norman, Raymond Massey, Richard Webb, James Millican, Larry Keating, George Cleveland, William Haade, Don Beddoe.

Set in the 1870s, Randolph Scott is a railroad engineer trying to build a railroad from Carson City to Virginia City in order to keep precious ore away from bandits. Once a cowboy himself, Hungarian-born director André De Toth crafted a solid western, making good use of Scott's screen presence.

CARSON CITY CYCLONE Republic, 1943, B&W, 55 min. **Producer:** Herbert Yates; **Director:** Howard Bretherton; **Screenplay:** Norman S. Hall; **Cinematographer:** William Bradford; **Editor:** Edward Schroeder; **Cast:** Don "Red" Barry, Lynn Merrick, Noah Berry, Bryant Washburn, Emmett Lynn, Bud Osborne, Roy Barcroft.

A night watchman at a bank is gunned down during a robbery and fingers a fellow named Barton as the gunman. When the trial comes up in neighboring Carson City, Don "Red" Barry finds a witness who says that the accused was with him that night. While Barry was not a large man physically, he handled action well, and like Alan Ladd and Bob Steele he was a dynamo on the screen. Barry's 30 westerns for Republic were among the most underrated in their entire stock. (See also *WYOMING OUTLAW.*)

CARSON CITY KID, THE Republic, 1940, B&W, 57 min, VT. **Producer:** Joseph Kane (associate); **Director:** Joseph King; **Screenplay:** Gerald Geraghty and Robert Yost; **Editor:** Helene Turner; **Cast:** Roy Rogers, George "Gabby" Hayes, Bob Steele, Noah Berry Jr., Pauline Moore, Francis McDonald, Wally Wales, Arthur Loft, George Rosener, Chester Gan.

Roy Rogers plays a bandit who is out to get the man who killed his younger brother. Roy does not play himself in this film but instead is the Carson City Kid, the proverbial "good" bad guy who must right an unjust wrong. He was not yet the hero of the singing range, and in this film he croons just one solo song, "Sonora Moon," and one other with his costar Pauline Moore. The remaining songs reflect a genuine slice of Americana: "Oh Suzanna," "Camptown Races," "Polly Wolly Doodle," and "Little Brown." The film benefits from an excellent supporting cast, including "Gabby" Hayes, Noah Beery Jr., and Bob Steele. Steele is particularly effective in the role of a villain and usually dominates his scenes. Even Yakima Canutt turns up in an uncredited role as the bartender.

CARSON CITY RAIDERS Republic, 1948, B&W, 60 min. **Producer:** Gordon Kay (associate); **Director:** Yakima Canutt; **Screenplay:** Eric Snell; **Cinematographer:** William Bradford; **Editor:** Tony Martinelli; **Cast:** Allan "Rocky" Lane, Eddy Waller, Frank Reicher, Beverly Jons, Steve Darell, Harold Goodwin.

A U.S. marshal is out to aid in the capture of a man's murderer, unaware that the man's son is out to avenge the killing himself. Lane was a particular favorite of Republic boss Herbert Yates, and he remained loyal to Yates by staying with the studio until his last film cranked through the camera. This is a better-than-average Rocky Lane venture with skilled direction from Yakima Canutt. (See also *BOLD FRONTIERSMAN, THE*.)

CASSIDY OF BAR 20 Paramount, 1938, B&W, 56 min. **Producer:** Harry Sherman; **Director:** Leslie Selander; **Screenplay:** Norman Houston; **Cinematographer:** Russell Harlan; **Editor:** Sherman Rose; **Cast:** William Boyd, Russell Hayden, Frank Darien, Nora Lane, Ralph Fiske.

Hoppy and Lucky help Hoppy's former sweetheart rid her range of rustlers and bad guys. Great photography and beautiful locations do not make up for the story, a rather bland effort for Paramount. William Boyd, who made only a couple of lower A westerns before becoming Hop-Along Cassidy, was often doubled by Cliff Lyons in his early films. Boyd learned his skills well and soon became an adept horseman and rider. (See also *HOP-ALONG CASSIDY*.)

CASTAWAY COWBOY, THE Walt Disney/Buena Vista, 1974, Color, 91 min, VT, DVD. **Producers:** Winston Hibler and Ron Miller; **Director:** Vincent McEveety; **Screenplay:** Don Tait; **Music:** Robert F. Brunner; **Cinematographer:** Andrew Jackson; **Editor:** Cotton Warburton; **Cast:** James Garner, Vera Miles, Robert Culp, Eric Shea, Elizabeth Smith, Manu Tupou.

James Garner is Texas cowpoke Lincoln Costain, who mysteriously washes up on the shore of a small Hawaiian island. Vera Miles is Henrietta MacAvoy, a widowed potato farmer who rescues Costain at a time when her farm is going under. She soon hires him with the hope of turning her wasting spread into a thriving venture. First, however, he must deal with a super cad named Bryson (Robert Culp), who holds the mortgage to the MacAvoy ranch but is willing to forget the deed if the widow MacAvoy will marry him.

This film is a tribute to the acting range of James Garner, who can exude charm with the best of them. Seven years earlier he gave a career performance as a stoic, no-nonsense Wyatt Earp in John Sturges's *HOUR OF THE GUN*.

CAST A LONG SHADOW Mirisch Company/United Artists, 1959, B&W, 82 min. **Producer:** Walter Mirisch; **Director:** Thomas Carr; **Screenplay:** John McGreevey and Martin Goldsmith; **Music:** Gerald Fried; **Cinematographer:** Wilfrid M. Cline; **Cast:** Audie Murphy, Terry Moore, John Dehner, James Best, Rita Lynn, Denver Pyle, Ann Doran.

Audie Murphy is a troubled young man because of his illegitimate birth. He turns to the bottle until he is given the responsibility of tending a ranch and the opportunity to make a new future.

CAT BALLOU Columbia, 1965, Color, 97 min, VT, DVD. **Producer:** Harold Hecht; **Director:** Elliot Silverstein; **Screenplay:** Walter Newman and Frankie Pearson; **Music:** Frank De Vol; **Cinematographer:** Jack A. Marta; **Editor:** Charles Nelson; **Cast:** Jane Fonda, Lee Marvin, Michael Callan, Dwayne Hickman, Nat "King" Cole, Stubby Kaye, Tom Nardini, John Marley, Reginald Denny, J. C. Flippen, Arthur Hunnicutt, Bruce Cabot.

In this film set in the 1890s, Catherine "Cat" Ballou (Jane Fonda) has read every western book available. When her father is killed, she decides to go out and hire the most revered gunfighter in the business: Kid Shelleen. The problem is that the Kid has become a useless drunk who has not been sober in 20 years.

Lee Marvin plays the dual role of Kid Shelleen and his evil brother Tim Strawn. Witty, crisp, and deftly written, this movie has all the ingredients: the simple farming folk terrorized by the evil land speculator, the once-heroic gunfighter with a serious drinking problem, and the final confrontation between the forces of good and evil.

Nat King Cole and Stubby Kaye turn up throughout the film, moving the story along with a series of ballads in the best western tradition. Interestingly, Roy Chanslor's original novel was a serious western; the comedy elements were added for the film.

The recipient of four Oscar nominations and an Academy Award for Marvin, *Cat Ballou* was the first big commercial hit for Jane Fonda and the last for Nat Cole, who died during the postproduction. Marvin emerged as a leading man in his own right, garnering a slew of best-actor awards from the Berlin International Film Festival, the British Academy Awards, the Golden Globe Awards, and the National Board of Review.

CATLOW (aka: *ORO DE NADIE, EL*; Spain) MGM, 1971, Color, 101 min, VT. **Producer:** Euan Lloyd;

Director: Sam Wanamaker; **Screenplay:** Scott Finch and J. J. Griffith; **Music:** Roy Budd; **Cinematographer:** Edward Scaife; **Editor:** Alan Killick; **Cast:** Yul Brynner, Richard Crenna, Leonard Nimoy, Daliah Lavi, Jo Ann Pflug, Jeff Corey, Michael Delano, David Ladd, Bessie Love.

Yul Brynner is on the run after trying to steal $2 million in gold from a pack train. He has double trouble: He has to avoid on the one hand his lawman friend (Richard Crenna) and the other a malevolent bounty hunter (Nimoy). Brynner is appealing as the carefree outlaw, and Roy Budd's musical score adds strength to the picture. Filmed in Spain and based on a novel by Louis L'Amour, this genre piece is reflective of the lighthearted violent movies of the late 1960s and early '70s.

CATTLE ANNIE AND LITTLE BRITCHES
Universal, 1981, Color, 95 min. **Producer:** Rupert Hitzig and Alan King; **Director:** Lamont Johnson; **Screenplay:** David Eyre and Robert Ward; **Music:** Sahn Berti and Tom Slouch; **Cinematographer:** Larry Pizer; **Editors:** William Haugse and Robbe Roberts; **Cast:** Burt Lancaster, Rod Steiger, John Savage, Scott Glenn, Amanda Plummer, Diane Lane, Michael Conrad.

Two teenage girls (Amanda Plummer and Diane Lane) are determined to become outlaws' groupies, so they track down the notorious Doolan-Dalton gang headed by the aging yet vigorous Burt Lancaster and his scruffy sidekick Scott Glenn. They in turn are being pursued by determined lawman Bill Tilghman (Rod Steiger). In the trivia department, Amanda Plummer, who plays "Cattle Annie," is the daughter of actors Christopher Plummer and Tammy Grimes; and lawman Bill Tilghman's deputy is played by Steve Ford, son of former President Gerald Ford. Supposedly based on a true story, this tongue-in-cheek western was filmed in Mexico.

CATTLE DRIVE
Universal, 1951, Color, 77 min. **Producer:** Aaron Rosenberg; **Director:** Kurt Neumann; **Screenplay:** Lillie Hayward and Jack Natteford; **Cinematographer:** Maury Gertsman; **Editor:** Danny B. Landres; **Cast:** Joel McCrea, Dean Stockwell, Chill Wills, Leon Ames, Henry Brandon, Howard Petrie, Bob Steele, Griff Barnett.

The pampered son of a wealthy railroad tycoon finds himself lost in the middle of nowhere when he encounters a seasoned cowboy, whom he joins on a long cattle drive across the desert to San Diego. With the cowboy's help, the young man learns life's real values and lessons in this entertaining, offbeat western with a nice message.

CATTLE EMPIRE
20th Century Fox, 1958, Color, 83 min. **Producer:** Robert Stabler; **Director:** Charles Marquis Warren; **Screenplay:** Endre Bohem and Eric Norden; **Music:** Paul Sawtell and Bert Shefter; **Cinematographer:** Brydon Baker; **Editors:** Fred Berger and Leslie Vidor; **Cast:** Joel McCrea, Gloria Talbott, Don Haggerty, Phyllis Coates, Bing Russell, Paul Brinegar, Hal K. Dawson, Richard Shannon, Charles Gray, Patrick O'Moore, Steve Raines.

Joel McCrea is John Cord, a trail boss who seeks revenge against the town of Hamilton for falsely imprisoning him. Yet when the town is in dire need of a cattle boss to lead their herd, they go to Cord, the man they once imprisoned. The well-scripted plot features numerous twists and turns, climaxed by a classic shoot-out. McCrea gives a distinguished performance as the cowboy loner who stoically rides off alone into the sunset once his business is settled.

CATTLE KING (1956)
See *CANYON RIVER*.

CATTLE KING (aka: GUNS OF WYOMING, UK)
MGM, 1963, Color, 88 min. **Producer:** Nat Holt; **Director:** Tay Garnett; **Screenplay:** Thomas Thompson; **Music:** Paul Sawtell and Bert Shefter; **Cinematographer:** William E. Snyder; **Editor:** George White; **Cast:** Robert Taylor, Robert Loggia, Joan Caulfield, Robert Middleton, Larry Gates, Malcolm Atterbury, Maggie Pierce, John Mitchum, Ray Teal.

In this film set in Wyoming during the 1880s, Robert Taylor is a successful rancher who wants to fence in his ranges, much to the dismay of his fellow cattlemen. As disputes heat up and tensions rise, President Chester A. Arthur (Larry Gates) is called on to intervene. This standard western confrontation drama is a somewhat disappointing MGM finale for Taylor, whose involvement with Metro-Goldwyn-Mayer spanned nearly three decades. The second of two films Taylor owed MGM on an option agreement, *Cattle King* reunited him with director Tay Garnett, who had guided the actor through a fine performance two decades earlier in *Bataan*.

CATTLE QUEEN OF MONTANA
RKO, 1954, Color, 88 min, VT. **Producer:** Benedict Bogeaus; **Director:** Allan Dwan; **Screenplay:** Robert Blees and Howard Estabrook; **Music:** Louis Forbes; **Cinematographer:** John Alton; **Editor:** James Leicester; **Cast:** Barbara Stanwyck, Ronald Reagan, Gene Evans, Lance Fuller, Anthony Caruso, Jack Elam, Yvette Duguay, Morris Ankrum, Myron Healey, Chubby Johnson.

Barbara Stanwyck's title role comes as a result of her father's death at the hands of villainous white man (Gene Evans) and a renegade Blackfoot Indian played by Anthony Caruso. Lance Fuller is the university-educated son of a chief who wins out over the Caruso faction of the tribe. Ronald Reagan replaced Robert Mitchum as Stanwyck's costar in this straightforward RKO western. Reagan, who made his final western the following year, plays an undercover agent trying to find the culprits who are stirring up unrest in the Blackfoot Nation. In the process he manages to become Stanwyck's self-appointed protector and good friend. Stanwyck's performance as Sierra Nevada Jones is enchanting, as is the vivid Superscope scenery of Glacier National Park.

CATTLE RAIDERS Columbia, 1938, B&W, 61 min. **Producer:** Harry L. Decker; **Director:** Sam Nelson; **Screenplay:** Joseph F. Poland and Ed Earl Repp; **Music:** Bob Nolan (songs); **Cinematographer:** John W. Boyle; **Editor:** Richard Fantl; **Cast:** Charles Starrett, Donald Grayson, Iris Meredith, Dick Curtis, Allen Brook, Edward Le Saint, Edmund Cobb, George Chesebro, Jim Thorpe, Bob Nolan and The Sons of the Pioneers.

This action-packed Charles Starrett film has Tom Reynolds (Starrett) falsely accused of murder when his gun is found at the scene of the crime. His accuser is a pal who is in debt to a crooked cattle dealer. Bob Nolan and the Sons of the Pioneers worked with Starrett before becoming a staple for Roy Rogers. Starrett would later admit that he considered quitting when he lost the Sons of the Pioneers, who at the time included Roy Rogers. Columbia was wise enough to fatten Starrett's paycheck and find him other quality musical backups. (See also *GALLANT DEFENDER, THE.*)

CATTLE STAMPEDE (aka: BILLY THE KID IN CATTLE STAMPEDE) PRC, 1943, B&W, 58 min. **Producer:** Sigmund Neufeld; **Director:** Sam Newfield; **Screenplay:** Joseph O'Donnell; **Cinematographer:** Robert E. Cline; **Editor:** Holbrook N. Todd; **Cast:** Buster Crabbe, Al St. John, Frances Gladwin, Charles King, Glenn Strange, Frank Ellis, Ed Cassidy.

CATTLE THIEF, THE Columbia, 1936, B&W, 57 min. **Producer:** Larry Darmour; **Director:** Spencer Gordon Bennet; **Screenplay:** J. A. Duff and Nate Gatzert; **Cinematographer:** Herbert Kirkpatrick; **Cast:** Ken Maynard, Geneva Mitchell, Ward Bond, Roger Williams, James Marcus, Sheldon Lewis, Edward Cecil, Jack Kirk, Edward Hearn, Glenn Strange, Al Taylor, Dick Rush, Bud McClure, Jack King.

Ken Maynard is an agent for the cattlemen's association who masquerades as a dimwit peddler in order to get the goods on an outlaw gang that is trying to cheat the ranchers out of their land. Maynard shows some real acting skill in this excellent 1930s B western. (See also *LUCKY LARKIN.*)

CATTLE TOWN Warner Bros., 1952, B&W, 71 min. **Producer:** Bryan Foy; **Director:** Noel M. Smith; **Screenplay:** Thomas W. Blackburn; **Music:** William Lava; **Cinematographer:** Ted D. McCord; **Editor:** Thomas Reilly; **Cast:** Dennis Morgan, Philip Carey, Amanda Blake, Rita Moreno, Paul Picerni, Ray Teal, Jay Novello, George O'Hanlon, Robert J. Wilke, Sheb Wooley, Charles Meredith, Merv Griffin.

The governor of Texas sends cowboy Mike McGann (Dennis Morgan) to keep peace between ranchers and a land baron. Look for a young Merv Griffin in the role of Joe in this average oater with a familiar theme.

CAUGHT Paramount, 1931, B&W, 68 min. **Director:** Edward Sloman; **Screenplay:** Agnes Brand Leahy and Keene Thompson; **Cinematographer:** Charles Lang; **Cast:** Richard Arlen, Frances Dee, Louise Dresser, Syd Saylor, Edward J. LeSaint, Tom Kennedy, Martin Burtin, Marcia Manners, Guy Oliver, Charles K. French, Jim Mason, Jack Clifford.

Louise Dresser gives a believable portrayal of Calamity Jane in this early Paramount venture. The film has Calamity as a saloon owner who is wanted for a series of crimes. This interesting movie with a different twist on the Calamity Jane legend is bolstered by a good cast and a vintage portrayal by Dresser.

CAVALIER OF THE WEST Artclass, 1931, B&W, 65 min. **Producer:** Louis Weiss; **Director:** J. P. McCarthy; **Screenplay:** McCarthy; **Cinematographer:** Frank Kesson; **Cast:** Harry Carey, Kane Richmond, Carmen Laroux, Carlotta Monte, George "Gabby" Hayes, Ted Adams, Ben Corbett, Matson Williams.

This early talkie has western screen icon Harry Carey as an army captain who sets out to restore peace when a war between Indians and whites is imminent. Two rustlers who are stealing cattle and shooting Indians try to frame Carey's brother, and Carey attempts to defend him at his murder trial.

CAVALRY Republic, 1936, B&W, 63 min. **Producer:** A. W. Hackel; **Director:** Robert N. Bradbury; **Screenplay:** George Plympton; **Cast:** Bob Steele, Frances Grant, Karl Hackett, Hal Price, Earl Ross.

CAVALRY CHARGE See *LAST OUTPOST, THE.*

CAVALRY SCOUT Monogram, 1951, Color, 78 min, VT. **Producer:** Walter Mirisch; **Director:** Leslie Selander; **Screenplay:** Thomas Blackburn and Daniel B. Ullman; **Music:** Marlin Skiles; **Cinematographer:** Harry Neumann; **Editor:** Richard B. Heermance; **Cast:** Rod Cameron, Audrey Long, Jim Davis, James Millican, James Arness, John Doucette, William Phillips.

Scout Kirby Frye (Rod Cameron) tracks down the outlaws who stole two Gatling guns among other weapons from an army arsenal. This fast-paced western should please Cameron fans.

CAVE OF OUTLAWS Universal, 1951, Color, 75 min. **Producer:** Leonard Goldstein; **Director:** William Castle; **Screenplay:** Elizabeth Wilson; **Cinematographer:** Irving Glassberg; **Editor:** Edward Curtis; **Cast:** Macdonald Carey, Alexis Smith, Edgar Buchanan, Victory Jory, Hugh O'Brian, Houseley Stevenson, Charles Horvath, Janes Van Horn, Tim Graham, Clem Fuller.

Macdonald Carey plays an ex-convict searching for gold taken 15 years earlier in a Wells Fargo holdup. Also looking for the loot is an investigator from Wells Fargo and a crooked miner. Filmed at Carlsbad Caverns in New Mexico, with some realistic stalagmites and stalactites, the film has its share of the ludicrous, such as the cave interior being brighter than the daylight and Carey's ability to overcome two armed guards after being recently shot and beaten up. Carey and Smith give steady performances, but it is Edgar Buchanan who takes the acting laurels as Dobbs, the Wells Fargo investigator.

CHALLENGE OF CHANCE, THE Continental Pictures, 1919, B&W. **Producer:** Fred L. Wilke; **Director:** Harry Revier; **Screenplay:** Roy Somerville; **Cinematographer:** Eddie James, Leo Rossi, and Arthur Todd; **Cast:** Jess Willard, Al Hart, Arline Pretty, Harry Van Meter.

Jess Willard was heavyweight champion of the world when he made this silent oater. The story deals with a ranch foreman who innocently works for a crooked horse dealer. When he discovers the truth about his boss's plans to rob a young woman, the foreman quits his job and offers his services to the woman. At 6'7" Jess Willard was the tallest heavyweight champion in history and world champ (1915–19) before losing his title to Jack Dempsey.

CHALLENGE OF THE RANGE Columbia, 1949, B&W, 54 min. **Producer:** Colbert Clark; **Director:** Ray Navarro; **Screenplay:** Ed Earl Rapp; **Music:** Smiley Burnette, Doris Fisher, and Allan Roberts (songs); **Cinematographer:** Rex Wimpy; **Editor:** Paul Borofsky; **Cast:** Charles Starrett, Paula Raymond, Billy Halop, Steve Darrell, Henry Hall, George Chesebro.

Charles Starrett attempts to sort out a slew of problems when ranchers begin accusing each other of various acts of lawlessness. Jock Mahoney is Starrett's stunt double, while the Sunshine Boys provide the songs in this excellent entry in the Durango Kid series. (See also *DURANGO KID, THE*.)

CHALLENGE TO BE FREE (aka: MAD TRAPPER OF THE YUKON) Alaska Pictures/Pacific International, 1976, Color, 88 min. **Producer:** Chuck D. Keen; **Director:** Ford Beebe and Tay Garnett; **Screenplay:** Anne Bosworth, Garnett, and Keen; **Music:** Ian Bernard; **Cinematographer:** Keen; **Editor:** Beebe; **Cast:** Mike Mazurki, Vic Christy, Fritz Ford, Tay Garnett, Jimmy Kane, John McIntire, Bob McKinnon, Patty Piper.

Made in 1972 as *Mad Trapper of the Yukon* and narrated by John McIntire, this adventure yarn deals with an animal-loving trapper who is hunted by the law after he accidentally kills a trooper. This was the final film for veteran director Tay Garnett, who also cowrote the screenplay and appears in the film as Marshal McGee. A nice film for children is bolstered by a good performance by Mike Mazurki.

CHARGE AT FEATHER RIVER, THE Warner Bros., 1953, Color, 95 min. **Producer:** David Weisbart; **Director:** Gordon Douglas; **Screenplay:** James R. Webb; **Music:** Max Steiner; **Cinematographer:** J. Peverell Marley; **Cast:** Guy Madison, Frank Lovejoy, Helen Westcott, Vera Miles, Dick Wesson, Onslow Stevens, Steve Brodie, Neville Brand, James Brown, Dub Taylor.

The story involves a group of cavalrymen, led by Guy Madison, sent to rescue two white sisters (Vera Miles and Helen Westcott), whom the Cheyenne have held captive for many years. The soldiers chosen for the mission are a group of army misfits—drunks, loafers, and boobs—a pre-"Dirty Dozen" type of brigade. When they finally rescue the sisters, Miles, who has become an Indian princess and was slated to marry an important chief named Thunder Hawk, does her best to sabotage the rescue attempt. Westcott, on the other hand, doesn't want to go back because she is afraid of how she will be treated. The problem is solved when Miles is killed and Madison and Westcott predictably fall in love.

Filmed at the height of the 3-D craze, this action-filled western has plenty of errant slings and arrows, while the air is filled with a good assortment of tomahawks, fists, knifes and bodies. In one scene a sergeant (Frank Lovejoy) sneaks up on a band of hostile Indians and is confronted by a rattlesnake. Using the one silent weapon available to him, he spits a mouthful of tobacco juice at the deadly reptile, which in pure 3-D fashion lands in the audience's lap.

CHARLIE ONE-EYE (UK) Paramount, 1973, Color, 96 min, VT. **Producers:** David Frost and James Swan; **Director:** Don Chaffey; **Screenplay:** Keith Leonard and Swan; **Music:** John Cameron; **Cinematographer:** Kenneth Talbot; **Editor:** Mike Campbell; **Cast:** Richard Roundtree, Roy Thinnes, Nigel Davenport, Jill Pearson, Aldo Sambrell, Luis Aller, Rafael Albaicin, Alexander Davion.

Filmed in Spain, this British-produced film is mainly a two-man show as a black Union Army deserter (Richard Roundtree) and an outcast Indian (Roy Thinnes) are thrown together in a desert wasteland. They soon find themselves the victims of white bounty hunters.

CHARRO! National General, 1969, Color, 98 min, VT. **Producers:** Charles Marquis Warren and Harry Caplan; **Director:** Warren; **Screenplay:** Warren; **Music:** Alan Bergman, Marilyn Bergman (songs), and Hugo Montenegro; **Cinematographer:** Elsworth Fredericks; **Editor:** Al Clark; **Cast:** Elvis Presley, Ina Balin, Victor French, Barbara Werle, Soloman Sturges, Lynn Kellog.

In this film set in a small border town, Elvis Presley plays an ex-outlaw who must face members of his former gang while attempting to romance a pretty saloon owner. This was the final film for director Charles Marquis Warren, who had not helmed a movie since 1958 and was a specialist in American western lore. Presley fans seem to find more merit to the film than the critics who generally panned it. Elvis sings just one song in this flawed attempt to change his image by casting him in a straight western.

CHATO'S LAND United Artists, 1972, Color, 92 min, VT. **Producer:** Michael Winner; **Director:** Winner; **Screenplay:** Gerald Wilson; **Music:** Jerry Fielding; **Cinematographer:** Robert Paynter; **Editor:** Winner (as Arnold Crust Jr.); **Cast:** Charles Bronson, Jack Palance, James Whitmore, Simon Oakland, Ralph Waite, Richard Jordan, Victor French, Sonia Rangan, William Watson.

Pardon Chato (Charles Bronson) is an Indian provoked into a fight by a white sheriff who taunts him incessantly with racial slurs. When Chato kills the sheriff, a local saloon keeper (Jack Palance) organizes a 13-man posse whose members are only too pleased to have an excuse to kill an Indian. The film turns to sheer vengeance when the posse captures Chato's family, kills his son, and then rapes his wife and leaves her naked in the desert. After Chato rescues his wife, he goes after the posse and eventually kills them off one by one; the hunted becomes the hunter. The film is a reworking of *The Lost Patrol* (RKO Radio, 1935). Director Michael Winner and star Bronson would repeat this general scenario two years later in the film *Death Wish*.

CHECKMATE See *DESERT HORSEMAN, THE*.

CHECK YOUR GUNS PRC, 1948, B&W, 54 min. **Producer:** Jerry Thomas; **Director:** Ray Taylor; **Screenplay:** Joseph O'Donnell; **Cinematographer:** Ernest Miller; **Editor:** Joseph Gluck; **Cast:** Eddie Dean, Roscoe Ates, Nancy Gates, George Chesebro, I. Stanford Jolley, Mike Conrad, Lane Bradford, Terry Frost, Mason Wynn, Dee Cooper, William Fawcett.

Eddie Dean wanders into the small town of Red Gap and soon becomes its sheriff. He decrees that everyone must check their guns in his office, but the forces of lawlessness continue, and a crooked judge lets the culprits go when they are caught. This is a better than average Eddie Dean musical venture.

CHEROKEE FLASH, THE Republic, 1945, B&W, 58 min. **Producer:** Bennett Cohen (associate); **Director:** Thomas Carr; **Screenplay:** Betty Burbridge; **Cinematographer:** Reggie Lanning; **Editor:** Charles Craft; **Cast:** Sunset Carson, Linda Stirling, Tom London, Roy Barcroft, John Merton, Bud Geary, Frank Jaquet, Fred Graham, Joe McGuinn, Pierce Lyden, Bud Osborne, Edmund Cobb.

When a man's adopted father—once a famous outlaw—is blamed for a robbery committed by his ex-gang, his son Sunset sets out to clear him. But the bad guys kill a witness who can clear the father, and Sunset is accused of murder. He escapes and frees his father, and the two set a trap to catch the killers. This good, action-packed Sunset Carson venture features perennial villain Roy Barcroft cast as good-guy Jeff

Carson. After the movie's release in 1945, Carson joined the ranks of the *Motion Picture Herald's* Top Ten Money-Making Western Stars for the only time the following year, finishing Number 8 in 1946. (See also *CALL OF THE ROCKIES* [1944].)

CHEROKEE KID, THE Afros & Bellbottoms Productions/HBO Video, 1996, Color, VT. **Producer:** Robin Forman; **Director:** Paris Baclay; **Screenplay:** Tim Kazurinsky and Denise DeClue; **Cinematographer:** Jack Conroy; **Editor:** Earl Watson; **Cast:** Sinbad, James Coburn, Gregory Hines, Burt Reynolds, A Martinez, Ernie Hudson, Mark Pellegrino, Herb Jeffries.

A 10-year-old lad named Isaiah sees the rest of his family killed by a man named Bloomington (James Coburn). Years later he sees Bloomington and decides to get even, but first he must get himself in the proper physical shape. He finds a worthy mentor in Otter Bob (Burt Reynolds), who trains the adult Isaiah until he is good enough to take on Bloomington. Isaiah (Sinbad) now becomes "The Cherokee Kid" and sets out to claim justice. This telefilm features a top acting job by Reynolds and an appearance by former 1930s cowboy star and big band singer Herb Jeffries (as himself).

CHEROKEE STRIP (aka: FIGHTING MARSHALL, UK) Paramount, 1940, B&W, 86 min. **Producer:** Harry Sherman; **Director:** Leslie Selander; **Screenplay:** Norman Houston and Bernard McConvill; **Music:** John Leipold; **Cinematographer:** Russell Harlan; **Editor:** Carroll Lewis and Sherman H. Rose; **Cast:** Richard Dix, Florence Rice, Victory Jory, Andy Clyde, George E. Stone, William Henry, Morris Ankrum, Douglas Fowley, Addison Richards, Hal Taliaferro, William Haade, Ray Teal, Jack Rockwell, Tex Cooper, Tom Tyler.

When Richard Dix becomes marshal of the town of Goliath in the Cherokee Strip, he hopes to get the goods on a gang led by villain Victor Jory and bring law and order to the town.

CHEROKEE STRIP, THE (aka: STRANGE LAW) Warner Bros., 1937, B&W, 55 min. **Producer:** Bryan Foy (uncredited); **Director:** Noel Smith; **Screenplay:** Joseph K. Watson and Luci Ward; **Music:** M. K. Jerome and Jack Scholl; **Cinematographer:** Lou O'Connell; **Editor:** Thomas Pratt; **Cast:** Dick Foran, Jane Bryan, Robert Paige, Joan Valerie, Edmund Cobb, Joseph Crehan, Milton Kibbee, Gordon Hart, Frank Faylen, Jack Mower, Tom Brower, Walter Soderling, Tommy Bupp.

With the opening of the Cherokee Strip, settlers are out to get free land in the Oklahoma territory. Link Carter (Edmund Cobb) moves in early and soon controls the town of Big Rock. When Carter turns to rustling and murder, his old nemesis Dick Hudson (Dick Foran) decides to take him on. This decent oater from Warner Bros. is made better with a nice selection of songs by M. K. Jerome and Jack Scholl, as well as the talented vocal pipes of Dick Foran, who sings the popular "My Little Buckaroo" at a campfire. The song was later sung by Roy Rogers in *Ridin' Down the Canyon* (1942), and again by Rogers in *Don't Fence Me In* (1945). The movie is based on Ed Earl Rapp's story "Cherokee Strip Stampeders," which originally appeared in *New Western Magazine* (October–November 1936). (See also *MOONLIGHT ON THE PRAIRIE*.)

CHEYENNE AUTUMN Warner Bros., 1964, Color, 159 min. **Producers:** John Ford and Bernard Smith; **Director:** Ford; **Screenplay:** James R. Webb; **Cinematographers:** William H. Clothier and Claude Renoir; **Editor:** Otho Lovering; **Cast:** Richard Widmark, Carroll Baker, James Stewart, Edward G. Robinson, Karl Malden, Sal Mineo, and Dolores Del Rio.

For his final western, director John Ford assembled a grand cast and took his camera out to Monument Valley, where so many of his finest films were made. Based on novels by Howard Fast and Mari Sandoz, the film tells the story of nearly 300 Cheyenne attempting to return to their ancient homelands while being pursued by the U.S. cavalry. The basic premise of the movie is to present the Indian side of the conflict, depicting the Cheyenne neither as heavies nor as misguided savages but rather as a noble and proud people. With a running time of nearly three hours, Ford presents a historical account of one of the saddest moments in the history of the American West: the 1878 flight of the Northern Cheyenne from the old Indian Territory—now the state of Oklahoma—to their ancestral lands in the Dakotas.

Lead roles were given to Richard Widmark as Captain Archer and Carroll Baker as the Quaker girl who goes along with the Indians. Ricardo Montalban and teenage heartthrob Sal Mineo were cast as Indian leaders Little Wolf and Red Shirt. Ford also made good use of such regulars as Harry Carey Jr., Ben Johnson, John Qualen, Bing Russell, Chuck Roberson, Chuck Hayward, Ken Curtis, and Patrick Wayne. George O'Brien, who starred for Ford in *THE IRON HORSE* and *THREE BAD MEN*, was given a small role as Major Braden.

To give the film more box-office clout, Warner Bros. decided to use big-name talent for the relatively small roles of Carl Schurz and Wyatt Earp, signing Spencer Tracy and James Stewart before the filming began. When Tracy was forced to cancel because of ill health, he was replaced by Edward G. Robinson.

According to Dan Ford in his book *Pappy: The Life and Times of John Ford*, problems abounded, including concerns with money and logistics. Ford also had his share of problems with some of his actors. He didn't get along with the aristocratic Ricardo Montalban, who found the director's badgering style difficult to take. The young Sal Mineo was intimidated by Ford's gruffness, and consequently his performance fell short. Ford himself became so distraught with the project that he turned the picture over to second unit director Ray Kellogg and retired to his room, taking to his bed for five days.

Some pundits have suggested that with *Cheyenne Autumn*, Ford was trying to atone for the way he had treated Indians in previous films; he admitted as much to director and film historian Peter Bogdanovich. Others claim the film reflects a pessimism and disillusionment in the director's psyche during his declining years. However, actor Harry Carey Jr., who appeared in many John Ford films during an illustrious career and had known the director for years, feels that Ford's main concern, as always, was simply to make a good picture and tell a good story.

There are some glaring flaws. The finished film was badly cut before its release, and a comedy scene set in Dodge City involving James Stewart as Wyatt Earp—while all right on its own—is significantly out of context with the rest of the film. Moreover, actor Karl Malden as a neofascist army captain is badly misplayed (unusual for the highly skilled Malden).

While far from Ford's best effort, *Cheyenne Autumn* is still a worthy endeavor. Years before the "politically correct" *DANCES WITH WOLVES*, Ford successfully dramatized the plight of the Native American far more realistically than the Oscar winner. While not as moving as Ford might have originally intended, perhaps an indication of the director's passing talent, *Cheyenne Autumn* still reflects a view of humanity far removed from the unquestioning heroics of most of his earlier films.

CHEYENNE CYCLONE (aka: RUSTLERS' RANCH) Kent, 1932, B&W, 57 min. **Producer:** Willis Kent; **Director:** Armand L. Shaefer; **Screenplay:** Oliver Drake; **Cinematographer:** William Nobles; **Editor:** Ethel Davey; **Cast:** Lane Chandler, Connie LaMont, Frankie Darro, Edward Hearn, J. Frank Glendon, Henry Rocquemore, Yakima Canutt, Marie Quillan, Jay Hunt, Charles "Slim" Whitaker, Jack Kirk, Hank Bell.

While stranded in a small town with an acting troupe, a cowboy goes to work for a cattleman who is about to lose his herd to a crook in this film based on Oliver Drake's story *Sagebrush Romeo*. Lane Chandler (who appeared in more than 120 oaters) makes for a likable western hero.

CHEYENNE KID, THE RKO, 1933, B&W, 61 min. **Director:** Robert F. Hill; **Screenplay:** Jack Curtis and Keene Thompson; **Music:** Max Steiner; **Cinematographer:** Nicholas Musuraca; **Editor:** Arthur Roberts; **Cast:** Tom Keene, Mary Mason, Alan Roscoe, Roscoe Ates, Al Bridge, Otto Hoffman, Anderson Lawler.

An easygoing cowboy is blamed for a murder he didn't commit and sets out to find the real killer. Based on W. C. Tuttle's story "Sir Piegan Passes," this is a pleasant Tom Keene series entry for RKO. (See also *BEYOND THE ROCKIES*.)

CHEYENNE KID, THE Monogram, 1940, B&W, 50 min. **Producer:** Harry S. Webb; **Director:** Robert Hill; **Screenplay:** Tom Gibson; **Cinematographer:** Edward A.

Kull; **Editor:** Robert Golden; **Cast:** Addison Randall, Louise Stanley, Kenne Duncan, Frank Yaconelli, Reed Howes, Charles King, George Chesebro, Forrest Taylor.

A notorious outlaw attempting to go straight goes to work for a cattleman, but crooks try to frame him on a murder and rustling charge.

CHEYENNE RIDES AGAIN Victory Pictures Corporation, 1937, B&W, 56 min. **Producer:** Sam Katzman; **Director:** Robert F. Hill; **Screenplay:** Basil Dickey; **Cinematographer:** William Hyer; **Editor:** Charles Henkel, Jr.; **Cast:** Tom Tyler, Lucille Brown, Carmen Laroux, Lon Chaney Jr. (as Creighton Chaney), Jimmy Fox, Roger Williams.

Tom Tyler is a detective for the cattlemen's association who poses as an outlaw after stealing $10,000 from a cattle thief in order to infiltrate his gang and get the real goods on their unlawful activities. (See also *FEUD OF THE TRAIL*.)

CHEYENNE ROUNDUP Universal, 1943, B&W, 59 min. **Producer:** Oliver Drake; **Director:** Ray Taylor; **Screenplay:** Elmer Clifton and Bernard McConville; **Music:** Hans J. Salter; **Cinematographer:** William A. Sickner; **Editor:** Otto Ludwig; **Cast:** Johnny Mack Brown, Tex Ritter, Fuzzy Knight, Jennifer Holt, Harry Woods, Roy Barcroft, Robert Barron, Budd Buster, Gil Patric.

When a bad man tries to kill a pursuing lawman and is killed himself, his good twin brother infiltrates the gang and poses as his outlaw brother. The film is a decent remake of Johnny Mack Brown's 1940 western *Bad Man from Red Butte*. (See also *OLD CHISHOLM TRAIL, THE*.)

CHEYENNE SOCIAL CLUB, THE National Central Pictures, 1970, Color, 103 min. **Producers:** Gene Kelly and James Lee Barrett (executive); **Director:** Kelly; **Screenplay:** Barrett; **Music:** Joel Hirschorn and Al Kasha (songs) and Walter Scharf; **Cinematographer:** William H. Clothier; **Editor:** Adrienne Fazan; **Cast:** James Stewart, Henry Fonda, Shirley Jones, Sue Ane Langdon, Elaine Devrey, Robert Middleton, Arch Johnson, Dabbs Greer, Jackie Russell, Jackie Joseph, Robert J. Wilke, Carl Reindel, Myron Healey, Dean Smith, John Dehner (uncredited).

John O'Hanlan and Harley Sullivan (James Stewart and Henry Fonda) are working as cowpokes with very little money when O'Hanlan gets word that his uncle died, leaving him an establishment called the Cheyenne Social Club. The two cowpokes ride nearly a thousand miles to claim the inheritance. When they arrive, O'Hanlan finds that he is now the owner of a first-class brothel, and the fun and adventure begins. One memorable scene has Stewart and Fonda riding the thousand-mile trail from Texas to Wyoming as the seasons change. With each seasonal change Fonda is still gabbing away without missing a beat.

Sue Ane Langdon, who plays Opal Ann, one of the Social Club's ladies of the evening, worked with director Gene Kelly in *A Guide For the Married Man*, and she insists that the original take of *Cheyenne Social Club* was even funnier than the tamed-down version that played to the public.

In an interview with the author, Langdon said, "Gene actually wanted me to do the Shirley Jones part in *Social Club*. But Jimmy wanted Shirley in the role. He didn't think the role should be a perky brassy lady, but a more subdued one. When we went out to Utah for the premier, it was one of the funniest movies I have ever seen. The premier audience was rolling on the floor. When I saw it the next time something was missing. Gene told me it had been re-edited, because it didn't fit the Jimmy Stewart image. It was still funny and still cute, but it was not as raucous, wild and funny as it had been before. More folksy—in the Jimmy Stewart tradition."

Cheyenne Social Club marks the final teaming of lifelong pals Jimmy Stewart and Henry Fonda who had worked together earlier in *FIRECREEK* (1968). Both actors appeared in a good number of westerns over their long careers: 20 for Fonda and 19 for Stewart. One final postscript is deserving of mention: Stewart had hoped to use his horse Pie in the film, but unfortunately the horse had gotten too old, and for the first time in years Stewart had to use a new horse.

CHEYENNE TAKES OVER Eagle Lyon, 1947, B&W, 56 min. **Producer:** Jerry Thomas; **Director:** Ray Taylor; **Screenplay:** Arthur E. Orloff; **Music:** Walter Greene; **Cinematographer:** Ernest Miller; **Editor:** Joseph Gluck; **Cast:** Lash La Rue, Al St. John, Nancy Gates, George Chesebro, Lee Morgan, John Merton, Steve Clark, Bob Woodward, Marshall Reed, Budd Buster, Carl Mathews, Dee Cooper, Buster Slaven, Hank Bell.

CHEYENNE WILDCAT Republic, 1944, B&W, 56 min. **Producer:** Louis Gray; **Director:** Leslie Selander; **Screenplay:** Randall Faye; **Cinematographer:** Bud Thackery; **Editor:** Charles Craft; **Cast:** William "Wild Bill" Elliott, Robert Blake, Alice Fleming, Peggy Stewart, Francis McDonald, Roy Barcroft, Tom London, Tom Chatterton, Kenne Duncan.

Bill Elliott and Bobby Blake (as Red Ryder and Little Beaver) come to the aid of the citizens of Cheyenne, whose life savings in bonds have been replaced by forgeries engineered by a banker. "Wild Bill" Elliott and Robert "Bobby" Blake appeared as Red Ryder and Little Beaver in 14 films between 1944 and 1946. (See also *ADVENTURES OF RED RYDER, THE*.)

CHIEF CRAZY HORSE (aka: VALLEY OF FURY, UK) Universal, 1955, Color, 86 min. **Producer:** William Alland; **Director:** George Sherman; **Screenplay:** Gerald Drayson Adams and Franklin Coen; **Music:** Frank Skinner; **Cinematographer:** Harold Lipstein; **Editor:** Al Clark; **Cast:** Victor Mature, Suzan Ball, John Lund, Ray Danton, Keith Larsen, Paul Guilfoyle, Davis Janssen, Robert

Warwick, James Millican, Morris Ankrum, Henry Willis, Dennis Weaver.

Filmed at the Badlands National Monument in South Dakota and told from an Indian perspective, director George Sherman adds a strong measure of dignity to the chief who was revered as the Sioux's greatest leader. The movie departs from history when Crazy Horse is killed by Little Big Man, a renegade half-caste played by Ray Danton. In reality Crazy Horse was imprisoned in September 1877 after a false rumor was spread that he was planning a revolt; he was then stabbed to death in a scuffle. Whether he was killed by his own knife or by a prison guard's bayonet is still not clear.

Victor Mature plays the famed Lakota Sioux war chief with verve, vigor, and the intuition of a visionary who must lead his people to ultimate triumph against the white man—a vision that came true with the defeat of General Custer at the Little Big Horn. Suzan Ball plays his wife Black Shaw.

CHILD OF THE PRAIRIE, A Aywon, 1924, B&W, 45 min. **Director:** Tom Mix; **Screenplay:** Tom Mix; **Cast:** Tom Mix, Louella Maxam, Baby Norma, Edward J. Brady, Leo Maloney, Fay Robinson, Frank Campeau.

A gambler steals a rancher's wife and child, and the little girl grows up to be reunited with her father, who wants revenge on the bad man. This fairly interesting silent Tom Mix film was made from two his early Selig two-reelers.

CHINA 9, LIBERTY 37 Europea Cinemagraphica, 1978, Color, 102 min. **Producers:** Gianni Bozzaacchi, Valario De Polis, and Monte Hellman; **Director:** Hellman; **Screenplay:** Jerry Harvey, Douglas Venturelli, Ennio De Concini, and Vicente Soriano; **Music:** Pino Donaggio; **Cinematographer:** Giuseppe Rotunno; **Editor:** Cesare D'Amico; **Cast:** Fabio Testi, Warren Oates, Jenny Agutter, Sam Peckinpah, Isabel Mestres.

A man is saved from hanging by corrupt railroad tycoons when he agrees to kill a former gunfighter for his land, then finds the victim's young wife is eager to help him. Sam Peckinpah has a cameo role as a writer who hopes to pulp the legend rather than the reality of the Old West. This is another strange film by American director Monte Hellman, who also helmed THE SHOOTING (1971). The unusual title refers to a signpost giving the distance to two nearby towns. Ronee Blakley sings the title theme in this exceedingly violent film.

CHINO (aka: VALDEZ HORSES, Spain) Cinema International Corporation, 1973, Color, 97 min, VT, DVD. **Producers:** Duilo Coletti, Dino De Laurentis, and John Sturges; **Director:** Sturges; **Screenplay:** Massimo De Rita, Clair Huffaker, Arduino Maiuri, and Rafael J. Salvia; **Music:** Guido De Angelis and Maurizio De Angelis; **Cinematographer:** Armondo Nannuzzi and Godofredo Pacheco; **Editors:** Vanio Amici, Peter Zinner, and Luis Alverez; **Cast:** Charles Bronson, Jill Ireland, Vincent Van Patten, Marcel Bozzuffi, Fausto Tozzi, Ettore Manni, Adolfo Thous.

In this film set in the 1880s, a half-breed horse raiser befriends a teenage boy who helps him on his ranch. Their lives are interrupted when the man falls in love with the sister of a neighbor who vows to destroy him. Based on the Lee Hoffman novel *The Valdez Horse* and filmed in Spain, the movie was first issued abroad in 1973 under the title *Valdez Horses*. This is a surprisingly low-key western trimmed of the usual violence that viewers tend to expect from a Bronson film.

CHIP OF THE FLYING U Selig, 1914, B&W, 2 reels. **Producer:** William Selig; **Director:** Colin Campbell; **Screenplay:** B. M. Bower; **Cast:** Tom Mix, Wheeler Oakman, Bessie Eyton, Frank Clark, Kathlyn Williams, Fred Huntly.

Based on B. M. Bower's original story, the plot of this film has had a number of reworkings over the years. This early silent version helmed by Colin Campbell was one of Tom Mix's best early westerns. In 1920 Canyon Pictures, an independent company, released his version of *Chip of the Flying U*, entitled *The Galloping Devil*. It was reissued in 1925 as *The Galloping Dude*.

CHIP OF THE FLYING U Universal, 1926, B&W, 6596 feet. **Director:** Lynn Reynolds; **Screenplay:** Reynolds and Harry Ditmar; **Cinematographer:** Harry Neumann; **Cast:** Hoot Gibson, Virginia Brown Faire, Philo McCullough, Nora Cecil, Pee Wee Holmes, Mark Hamilton, Willie Fung, Steve Clements.

Lynn Reynolds, who had directed many of Tom Mix's features for Fox, cowrote and directed the third version of this story for Universal. This time Hoot Gibson plays Chip Bennett, a ranch hand who falls for a woman doctor who is also the owner of the Flying U ranch. Chip fakes an accident so he can come under her care, and predictably they fall in love and are married. Mainly free of violence, this version utilizes comedy sequences instead.

CHIP OF THE FLYING U Universal, 1940, B&W, 55 min. **Director:** Ralph Staub; **Screenplay:** Andrew Bennison and Larry Rhine; **Cast:** Johnny Mack Brown, Bob Baker, Fuzzy Knight, Doris Weston, Forrest Taylor, Anthony Warde, Karl Hackett, Henry Hall, Claire Whitney.

The 1939 version of B. M. Bower's story has nothing to do with the original premise, except for the use of its title. In this version Johnny Mack Brown plays Chip Bennett, the foreman of the Flying U ranch who is accused of robbing a bank and shooting the bank president. His new boss believes him to be guilty, and Chip sets out to prove otherwise. The real culprits, he discovers, are foreign agents dealing in munitions. (See also OLD CHISHOLM TRAIL, THE.)

CHISHOLMS, THE CBS TV/Alan Landsburg Productions, 1979, Color, 270 min. **Producers:** David Dortort (executive), Paul Freeman, and Alan Landsburg (executive);

Director: Mel Stuart; **Teleplay:** Evan Hunter; **Music:** Elmer Bernstein; **Cinematographer:** Jacques R. Marquett; **Editor:** Corky Ehlers; **Cast:** Robert Preston, Rosemary Harris, Ben Murphy, Brian Kerwin, Jimmy Van Patten, Stacey Nelkin, Susan Swift, Charles Frank, Glynnis O'Connor, Sandra Griego, David Hayward.

Robert Preston plays Hadley Chisholm and Rosemary Harris is wife Minerva, the patriarch and the matriarch of the Chisholm clan. After being cheated out of their land in Virginia, they pack their belongings and head on to Oregon Territory. Along the way they must deal with hostile Indians, rough travel conditions, and family strife. Set in the 1840s, this well-done miniseries was originally broadcast in three parts. It was issued theatrically in a shorter version in 1979 by New Line International Releasing.

CHISUM Batjac Productions/Warner Bros., 1970, Color, 111 min, VT. **Producers:** Andrew J. Fenady and Michael Wayne (executive); **Director:** Andrew V. McLaglen;

Screenplay: Fenady; **Music:** Dominic Frontiere and Fenady (lyrics); **Cinematographer:** William H. Clothier; **Editor:** Robert Simpson; **Cast:** John Wayne, Forrest Tucker, Ben Johnson, Glenn Corbett, Andrew Prine, Bruce Cabot, Patric Knowles, Lynda Day George, Geoffrey Deuel, Richard Jaeckel, Pamela McMyler, John Agar, Lloyd Battista, Robert Donner, Ray Teal, Edward Faulkner, Ron Soble, John Mitchum, Glenn Langan, Alan Baxter, Alberto Morin, Pedro Armendáriz Jr., Christopher Mitchum, Gregg Palmer, Hank Worden.

In this film based on producer A. J. Fenady's story "Chisum and the Lincoln County Cattle War," John Wayne stars as cattle baron John Simpson Chisum, the largest ranch owner in the area of Lincoln County, New Mexico. As Chisum, Wayne dominates the screen with his usual vigor, warmth, and a largely avuncular manner. Yet when he finally deals with the vicious Lawrence Murphy (Forrest Tucker), it is with the grit, honor, and uncompromising toughness worthy of John Wayne at his best.

Chip of the Flying U (1940), *starring Johnny Mack Brown (not pictured), Bob Baker (left), Fuzzy Knight (center) and Doris Weston (right), was originally filmed in 1914 with Tom Mix in the starring role.* (UNIVERSAL/AUTHOR'S COLLECTION)

John Wayne and Ben Johnson in Chisum (WARNER
BROS./BATJAC/COURTESY OF A. J. FENADY)

Director Andrew V. McLaglen assembled an all-star cast
and a group of actors well at home in westerns. The story is
based around the bloody Lincoln County cattle war and all
the main players are here: Billy the Kid (Geoffrey Deuel), Pat

Garrett (Glenn Corbett), and Henry Tunstill (Patric
Knowles), the real-life Englishman who befriends Billy the
Kid and is murdered by his nemesis Murphy, the power-hun-
gry newcomer who was one of the principals in the infamous
Lincoln County Cattle War.

Producer/writer Andrew J. Fenady was already steeped
in western lore when he reread Zane Grey's *Nevada* and
again came across the name John Simpson Chisum. Fenady
recalls:

> It ignited a spark in me and I immediately felt this would be
> an ideal role for Duke. I called Michael Wayne at Batjac and
> he liked the title. However, he originally thought I was talk-
> ing about the old Chisholm Trail. I told him "No, the story
> is about a fellow named John Simpson Chisum, an all too
> often ignored historical figure." He told me to bring a treat-
> ment over and he'd give it to Duke. I met with Duke and
> Michael on Duke's boat "The Wild Goose." I told the story
> and read all the parts myself. Duke listened then walked sud-
> denly to the door and said "turn him loose." I was perplexed.
> All of a sudden Michael gave me a big hit on the shoulder—
> I mean a haymaker. I looked over at Michael, he smiled and
> said "It's OK. You're In!"

John Wayne and Forrest Tucker in Chisum (WARNER BROS./BATJAC/COURTESY OF A. J. FENADY)

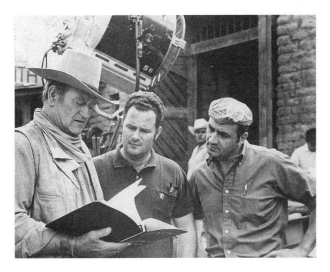

John Wayne, Michael Wayne, and A. J. Fenady on location for Chisum (COURTESY OF A. J. FENADY)

What separates this film from many genre pieces of the late 1960s and early '70s is its deft balance of story, humor, drama, conflict, and a selection of characters we actually care about. Wayne and Ben Johnson (who shines as Pepper, Chisum's grumbling foreman and friend) are great together, showing a remarkable chemistry based on nearly three decades of working with each other (Johnson was a wrangler and stuntman before he made his acting debut in Ford's *Three Godfathers* in 1948.) According to Fenady, John Wayne originally wanted Ben Johnson for the role of Pat Garrett: "I reminded Duke that Pat Garrett was twenty-eight years old when he shot Billy the Kid, and that Ben was now in his early fifties. Duke couldn't get over the fact that it had been more than twenty years since they worked together in those great John Ford Westerns. 'God, has it really been that long.' he chided me."

The film was also a reunion for John Wayne, John Agar, Forrest Tucker, and Richard Jaeckel, all of whom worked together 20 years earlier in *Sands of Iwo Jima*, the film that garnered Wayne his first Oscar nomination. Fenady's fine script, McLaglen's steady helming, Bill Clothier's superb camera work, and Dominic Frontiere's stirring music all help in making *Chisum* one of Wayne's better screen efforts. Actor William Conrad narrated this thoroughly enjoyable picture. Wayne must have thought so too. When the picture was completed he told Fenady, "This is the most pleasant picture I ever made."

CHRISTMAS MOUNTAIN Gold Coast, 1980, Color, 90 min. **Director:** Pierre De Moro; **Cast:** Slim Pickens, Mark Miller, Barbara Stanger, Fran Ryan, John Hart.

An aging cowboy learns the true meaning of Christmas when he is caught in the mountains and finds shelter with a widow and her children.

CHUKA Paramount, 1967, Color, 105 min, VT. **Producers:** Jack Jason and Rod Taylor; **Director:** Gordon Douglas; **Screenplay:** Richard Jessup; **Music:** Leith Stevens; **Cinematographer:** Harold E. Stein; **Editor:** Robert Wyman; **Cast:** Rod Taylor, Ernest Borgnine, John Mills, Luciana Paluzzi, James Whitmore, Louis Hayward, Michael Hugh O'Reilly, Barry O'Hara, Joseph Sirola, Marco Antonio, Gerald York, Lucky Carson.

A gunman comes to a small fort to tell its Indian-hating soldiers that unless the Indians are given food there will be war. Rod Taylor (who coproduced the film) stars in the title role. However, he must deal with the post commander, a nasty and mean fellow played by John Mills, who is detested by his troops.

CIMARRON RKO, 1931, B&W, 131 min, VT. **Producers:** William LeBaron and Wesley Ruggles; **Director:** Ruggles; **Screenplay:** Howard Estabrook; **Music:** Max Steiner; **Cinematographer:** Edward Cronjager; **Editor:** William Hamilton; **Cast:** Richard Dix, Irene Dunne, Estelle

Richard Dix and Irene Dunne both won Oscar nominations for Cimarron, *the Oscar-winning picture for 1930. It would be 60 years until another western,* Dances with Wolves, *would win an Academy Award for Best Picture.* (RKO/AUTHOR'S COLLECTION)

Taylor, William Collier Jr., Roscoe Ates, George E. Stone, Stanley Fields, Robert McWade, Edna Mae Oliver, Nancy Dover, Eugene Jackson.

Based on Edna Ferber's best-selling novel, *Cimarron* is the third big western to come out of the early formidable sound period; THE BIG TRAIL (1930), and King Vidor's BILLY THE KID (1930) are the other two. It was also the most commercially successful, grossing $2 million, and the only western to win an Academy Award for best picture until DANCES WITH WOLVES (1990).

Combining action, sentiment, sympathy, comedy, and lots of thrills, this landmark film begins in 1889 with the great Oklahoma land rush and concludes 40 years later in 1930. The sweeping story concerns a young Kansas girl (Irene Dunne) who weds a wanderer (Richard Dix). They move to the Oklahoma Territory to take part in the great land rush, and the subsequent history of Oklahoma as experienced by one family follows. The hero of the film, Yancey Cravat (Dix), personifies the true pioneer spirit. His proficiency as a pistoleer, a poet, a lawyer, and a crusader for unpopular causes make him the ideal hero to settle and tame the West.

Critics applauded the picture as being one of the few talkies to approach the visual sweep of the silents. It made big stars of Richard Dix, a handsome leading man from the silents; and Irene Dunne, who was just starting out in pictures after her success on Broadway in *Showboat*. At the Academy Awards for 1930–31, *Cimarron* led all entries with seven nominations and won three Academy Awards, making it the evening's biggest winner. The Oscar, however, eluded director Wesley Ruggles, who was a bit miffed and didn't mind telling folks after the awards ceremony, "I wonder where I

was when the picture was made, as it was given the award for sets, production and adaptation, which possibly I had something to do with."

Cimarron was the last big-budget epic western for quite a while as the Great Depression began to set in. While attacked by some critics today as being stilted and outdated, this graphic and engrossing film has an epic sweep and a story that continues to impress. Especially well-done is the skillful aging of the main players as they pass through a period of 40 years on the screen.

Edna Mae Oliver gives an excellent comedy performance in her role as an eccentric woman. The opening Cherokee land strip sequence set the standard for future films and deserves to be seen again and again. It is a film well worth watching, one which the *New York Daily News* called "magnificent in scope . . . one of the few talking pictures which inspires rather than awes." Mordaunt Hall in the *New York Times* praised the film as "a stupendous undertaking in view of the time . . . it gives a wonderful impressive idea of the early days of the territory. . . ."

CIMARRON MGM, 1960, Color, 131 min, VT. **Producer:** Edmund Grainger; **Director:** Anthony Mann; **Screenplay:** Arnold Schulman; **Music:** Franz Waxman; **Cinematographer:** Robert Surtees; **Editor:** John Dunning; **Cast:** Glenn Ford, Maria Schell, Anne Baxter, Arthur O'Connell, Russ Tamblyn, Mercedes McCambridge, Vic Morrow, Robert Keith, Charles McGraw, Henry Morgan, David Opatosshu.

For his final western, director Anthony Mann took to the epic screen. Like the 1931 original, the second film translation of Edna Ferber's novel begins with a bang. Thousands of land seekers are lined up in Conestoga wagons, and buckboards are ready to dash into the new Oklahoma territory at high noon, April 22, 1889. This time it is Glenn Ford who portrays Yancey Cravat, the likeable, adventurous, restless rover; and Maria Schell as his wife Sabra, who makes a transition from adoring loveable bride to an embittered, abandoned, and bigoted wife (a departure from the Irene Dunne portrayal in the earlier film). While *Variety* called the film "grand-scale action in spades," most reviews were lukewarm at best. It was also a major disappointment to director Mann, who denigrated the whole picture as "a mistake." He explains why in a 1969 interview with Christopher Wicking and Barry Pattison reprinted in *The Western Reader*.

Irene Dunne and Edna Mae Oliver in Cimarron, *based on a novel by Edna Ferber about the great 1889 Oklahoma land rush and its 40-year aftermath.* (RKO/AUTHOR'S COLLECTION)

After I had been shooting for twelve days, they [the Metro executives] decided to take the whole company indoors, so it became an economic disaster and a fiasco and the whole project was destroyed. . . . The executives panicked. We had a couple of storms—which I shot in anyway—but they thought we'd have floods and so on, so they dragged us in and everything had to be duplicated on the set. The story had to be changed, because we couldn't do the things we wanted to. So I don't consider it a film. I just consider it a disaster.

Glenn Ford and Maria Schell star in Anthony Mann's 1960 version of Cimarron. (MGM/AUTHOR'S COLLECTION)

CIMARRON KID, THE Universal, 1951, Color, 84 min. **Producer:** Ted Richmond; **Director:** Budd Boetticher; **Screenplay:** Louis Stevens; **Cinematographer:** Charles P. Boyle; **Editor:** Frank Gross; **Cast:** Audie Murphy, Beverly Tyler, James Best, Yvette Duguay, Leif Ericson, Noah Beery Jr., Hugh O'Brian, John Hubbard, Gregg Palmer, Rand Brooks, William Reynolds, Roy Roberts, David Wolfe, John Bromfield, Frank Silvera, Richard Garland.

The story concerns a young man with former ties to the Dalton gang who is wrongly accused by crooked railroad officials of aiding in a heist headed by the Daltons. He joins their gang only to be betrayed by a fellow gang member before becoming a fugitive himself. A significant western first for director Budd Boetticher, this film was released the same year as *The Bullfighter and the Lady* and garnered Boetticher an Oscar nomination for writing. It was also Boetticher's first for Universal, a studio for whom he helmed nine pictures in two years. Under Boetticher's steady direction, Audy Murphy came into his own as a western star.

CIRCLE CANYON Superior Talking Pictures, 1934, B&W, 48 min. **Directors:** Victor Adamson and Lester F. Scott; **Screenplay:** B. R. Tuttle; **Cast:** Buddy Roosevelt, June Mathews, Clarie Wood, Bob Williamson, Allen Holbrook, Harry Leland, George Hazel, Clyde McClary, Mark Harrison, John Tyke.

A cowboy arrives in an area where two outlaw gangs are fighting with each other.

CIRCLE OF DEATH Kent, 1935, B&W, 60 min. **Producer:** Willis Kent; **Director:** J. Frank Glendon; **Screenplay:** Roy Claire and Kent; **Cinematographer:** James Diamond; **Cast:** Monte Montana, Tove Linden, Yakima Canutt, Henry Hall, Ben Corbett, Steve Pendleton, John Ince, J. Frank Glendon, Slim Whitaker.

A young boy who is the lone survivor of an Indian massacre is raised by an Indian tribe. Years later he has to choose between the Indians who raised him and the whites to whom he belongs. This film was the only starring western for Monte Montana.

CISCO KID, THE Fox Film Corporation, 1931, B&W, 60 min. **Director:** Irving Cummings; **Screenplay:** Alfred A. Cohn; **Cinematographer:** Barney McGill; **Editor:** Alex Troffey; **Cast:** Warner Baxter, Edmund Lowe, Conchita Montenegro, Nora Lane, Chris-Pin Martin, Charles Stevens, Frederick Burt.

In this film set in the 1880s, the Cisco Kid comes to the aid of a girl who once saved his life. To help her he steals $5,000 from a bank to pay the impending foreclosure of her ranch. The bank decides to put the same amount of money in the hands of the person who can capture the Kid, and Mickey Dunn, his perennial nemesis, vows to win the award. At the final fadeout Dunn is sympathetic to the Kid's tale of woe and allows Cisco to ride across the border into the sunset.

Star Warner Baxter played the Cisco Kid for the first time in the enormously successful *In Old Arizona* (1929), earning an Academy Award as Best Male Actor. He repeated the role in *The Arizona Kid* (1930), then again in *Return of the Cisco Kid* (1939). The theme song, "My Tonia," from the first film can be heard here as well. Irving Cummings, who codirected the first film, helmed this endeavor, and Edmond Lowe repeated his part as Mickey Dunn.

Based on a character in a story by O. Henry, the Cisco Kid has appeared on-screen more than two dozen times. In addition to Warner Baxter, actors who have played the Kid include Cesar Romero in *CISCO KID AND THE LADY* (1939); *LUCKY CISCO KID, VIVA CISCO KID. The Gay Caballero* (1940); *RIDE ON VAQUERO, ROMANCE OF THE RIO GRANDE* (1941). Gilbert Roland played the Cisco Kid six times in 1946–47; *BEAUTY AND THE BANDIT, The Gay Cavalier, SOUTH OF MONTEREY* (1946); *KING OF THE BANDITS, RIDING THE CALIFORNIA TRAIL, ROBIN HOOD OF MONTEREY* (1947).

Duncan Renaldo played the Cisco Kid on the popular television show (1950–56) as well as in feature films, including *THE CISCO KID IN NEW MEXICO, SOUTH OF THE RIO GRANDE, THE CISCO KID RETURNS* (1945); *VALIANT HOMBRE* (1948); *THE DARING CABALLERO, The Gay Amigo, SATAN'S CRADLE* (1949); *THE GIRL FROM SAN LORENZO* (1950). The last actor to play the part was Jimmy Smits in the 1994 TV movie *The Cisco Kid*.

CISCO KID, THE Turner Pictures, 1994, Color, 91 min. **Producers:** Moctesuma Esparza and Gary Goodman; **Director:** Luis Valdez; **Screenplay:** Valdez and Michael Kane; **Music:** Joseph Julián González; **Cinematographer:** Guillermo Navarro; **Editor:** Zach Staenberg; **Cast:** Jimmy Smits, Cheech Marin, Sadie Frost, Bruce Payne, Ron Perlman, Tony Amendola, Pedro Armendáriz Jr.

This made-for-TV movie revises the classic O. Henry character from many films and a previous 1950s' TV series of the same name, so that Cisco (Jimmy Smits) and Pancho (Cheech Marin) are now "anti-gringo" Mexican revolutionaries rather than wanderers of the Old West. The son of veteran western character actor Pedro Armendáriz has a featured role.

CISCO KID AND THE LADY, THE 20th Century Fox, 1940, B&W, 74 min. **Producer:** John Stone; **Director:** Herbert L. Leeds; **Screenplay:** Frances Hyland; **Cinematographer:** Barney McGill; **Editor:** Nick DeMaggio; **Cast:** Cesar Romero, Marjorie Weaver, Chris-Pin Martin, George Montgomery, Robert Barrat, Virginia Field, Harry Green, Gloria Ann White, John Beach, Ward Bond, Harry Hayden.

An orphan whose father has been killed by bandits inherits a mine. The Cisco Kid saves the mine and finds the child's mother as well. This is the first of a half-dozen "Cisco Kid" adventures with Cesar Romero in the title role. It also marks the feature debut of actor George Montgomery in a leading role. Previously Montgomery had appeared in low-budget action films as an extra, stuntman, and bit player under his real name George Letz. (See also *CISCO KID, THE*.)

CISCO KID IN NEW MEXICO, THE (aka: IN OLD NEW MEXICO) Monogram, 1945, B&W, 62 min. **Producer:** Philip N. Krasne; **Director:** Phil Rosen; **Screenplay:** Betty Burbridge; **Music:** David Chudnow; **Cinematographer:** Arthur Martinelli; **Cast:** Duncan Renaldo, Martin Garralaga, Norman Willis, Gwen Kenyon, Lee "Lasses" White, Aurora Roche, Ken Terrell, Dick Gordon, Donna Dax, Pedro de Cordoba, Harry Depp.

Cisco and Pancho come to the aid of a nurse accused of murder. This is one of the films where Cisco and Pancho are redubbed as Chico and Pablo in TV prints. (See also *CISCO KID, THE*.)

CISCO KID RETURNS, THE Monogram, 1945, B&W, 64 min. **Producers:** Philip N. Krasne and Richard L'Estrange; **Director:** John P. McCarthy; **Screenplay:** Betty Burbridge; **Cinematographer:** Harry Neumann; **Editor:** Marty Cohen; **Cast:** Duncan Renaldo, Martin Garralaga, Cecilia Callejo, Roger Pryor, Anthony Warde, Fritz Leiber, Vicki Lane, Jan Wiley, Sharon Smith, Cy Kendall, Eva Puig, Emmett Lynn, Bud Osborne.

In Duncan Renaldo's first appearance as The Cisco Kid, Cisco and Pancho suspect a respected businessman of being behind a series of crimes. The TV title of this appealing entry for Cisco Kid fans is *Daring Adventure*. (See also *CISCO KID, THE*.)

CITY OF BADMEN, THE 20th Century Fox, 1953, Color, 81 min. **Producer:** Leonard Goldstein; **Director:** Harmon Jones; **Screenplay:** George W. George and George F. Slavin; **Music:** Lionel Newman; **Cinematographer:** Charles G. Clark; **Editor:** George A. Gittens; **Cast:** Jeanne Crain, Dale Robertson, Richard Boone, Lloyd Bridges, Carole Mathews, Carl Betz, Joanne Dru, Whitfield Connor,

Hugh Sanders, Rodolfo Acosta, Harry Carter, Robert Adler, John Doucette, Don Haggerty, James Best, Alan Dexter, Leo Gordon.

It's the Gentleman Jim Corbett/Bob Fitzsimmons heavyweight championship fight, and a group of robbers attempt to steal the prizefight gate. This western with a hook has an excellent restaging of the Corbett/Fitzsimmons heavyweight contest held in Carson City, Nevada, in 1897. An excellent cast, plenty of romance, and an original story adds some sparkle to this interesting western/crime melodrama.

CITY SLICKERS Columbia/Castle Rock, 1991, Color, 114 min, VT, CD. **Producers:** Billy Crystal and Irby Brown; **Director:** Robert Underwood; **Screenplay:** Lowell Ganz, Babaloo Mandel, and Billy Crystal (uncredited); **Music:** Hummie Mann and Marc Shaiman; **Cinematographer:** Dean Semler; **Editor:** O. Nicholas Brown; **Cast:** Billy Crystal, Daniel Stern, Bruno Kirby, Patricia Wettig, Helen Slater, Jack Palance, Nobel Willingham, Tracey Walter, Josh Mostel, David Paymer, Bill Henderson, Jeffrey Tambor, Phil Lewis, Jayne Meadows, Alaan Charoff.

Billy Crystal, Daniel Stern, and Bruno Kirby are three boyhood pals approaching middle age in a state of uncertainty. To honor Crystal's 39th birthday, they decide to take off for two weeks on a ranch trip driving cattle across New Mexico and into Colorado. There they meet other cowboy wannabes and a pretty young woman making the trip on her own. By time they are through they have rediscovered themselves and have learned about each other with lots of laughs and pathos along the way. A great soundtrack includes "Young at Heart," "Tumbling Tumble Weeds," and the themes from *Rawhide* and *Bonanza*.

This western comedy with a heart garnered veteran actor Jack Palance a Best Supporting Actor Oscar. As Curly, the gritty and gnarled trail boss, Palance had waited 39 years since his last nomination as the evil gunman Jack Wilson in *SHANE* (1953). Upon accepting his long-awaited Oscar, he commented, "You know, there's a time when you attain a certain age plateau when producers say, 'Well, what do you think? Can we risk it?'" Then to demonstrate his virility, the 72-year-old actor suddenly moved away from the podium, got down on the floor, and started doing pushups. By the time he was doing them one-handed, the audience was roaring its approval.

Helen Slater (left) and Jack Palance (right) in City Slickers. *As Curly, the grizzled ranch hand, the 72-year-old Palance won a Best Supporting Actor Oscar and astonished audiences with a series of one-armed pushups at the awards ceremony.* (COLUMBIA/CASTLEROCK/AUTHOR'S COLLECTION)

CITY SLICKERS II: CURLY'S REVENGE Castle Rock/Face/Columbia, 1994, color, 116 min, VT. **Producer:** Billy Crystal; **Director:** Paul Weiland; **Screenplay:** Crystal, Lowell Ganz, and Balaboo Mandel; **Music:** Marc Shaiman; **Cinematographer:** Adrian Biddle; **Editor:** William M. Anderson; **Cast:** Billy Crystal, Daniel Stern, Jon Lovitz, Jack Palance, Patricia Wettig, Pruitt Taylor Vince, Bill McKinney, Lindsey Crystal, Nobel Willingham, Jayne Meadows.

The pals (minus Bruno Kirby) return to the West to find Curly's lost treasure. This time they must contend with Duke Washburn (Jack Palance), Curly's nasty twin brother, when they hit the sagebrush in this better-than-average sequel. The soundtrack includes "The Godfather Waltz," and the theme from *Treasure of the Sierra Madre*.

CLAIM JUMPERS See *DUEL AT SILVER CREEK*.

CLANCY OF THE MOUNTED Universal, 1933, B&W, 12 chapters. **Director:** Ray Taylor; **Screenplay:** Basil Dickey, Harry O. Hoyt, and Ella O'Neill; **Cast:** Tom Tyler, Jacqueline Wells (Julie Bishop), Earl McCarthy, William Desmond, Rosalie Roy, W. L. Thomas, Leon Duval, Francis Ford, Tom London, Edmund Cobb, William Thorne, Al Ferguson, Fred Humes, Frank Lackteen, Steve Clementee.

Crooks who are after a dead man's gold mine frame a Mountie's brother on a murder charge. This action-packed cliffhanger will delight Tom Tyler fans.

CLASH OF THE WOLVES Warner Bros., 1925, B&W. **Director:** Noel Mason Smith; **Screenplay:** Charles A. Logue; **Cinematographer:** Joe Walker; **Editor:** Clarence Kolster; **Cast:** Rin Tin Tin, June Marlow, Charles Farrell, Will Walling, Pat Hartigan.

A fire in the mountains brings a wolf pack into the nearby desert. The leader of the pack—who is half-dog, half-wolf—has a price on his head, but he is befriended by a borax prospector whom he aids against a rival in this good, solid Rin Tin Tin adventure piece.

CLEARING THE RANGE Allied Pictures, 1931, B&W, 61 min. **Producer:** M. H. Hoffman Jr.; **Director:** Otto Brower; **Screenplay:** Jack Natteford; **Cinematographer:** Ernest Miller; **Cast:** Hoot Gibson, Sally Ellers, Robert Homans, Edward Peil Sr., George Mendoza, Edward Hearn, Maston Williams, Eva Grippon.

When Jim Freemont is murdered, his brother Curt (Hoot Gibson) arrives and poses as a coward in public, but he sneaks out privately to become the daring El Capitan and searches for the killer. Good photography and some well-staged fight scenes compensate for the slow pace of the film.

CLUE, THE See *OUTCASTS OF BLACK MESA*.

COCKEYED COWBOYS OF CALICO COUNTY (aka: A WOMAN FOR CHARLIE, UK) Universal, 1970, Color, 99 min. **Producer:** Ranald MacDougall; **Director:** Anton Leader and MacDougall; **Screenplay:** MacDougall; **Music:** Lyn Murray; **Cinematographer:** Richard L. Rawlings; **Editor:** Richard G. Wray; **Cast:** Dan Blocker, Nanette Fabray, Jim Backus, Wally Cox, Jack Elam, Henry Jones, Stubby Kaye, Mickey Rooney, Noah Beery Jr., Marge Champion, Don "Red" Barry, Hamilton Camp, Tom Basham, Iron Eyes Cody, James McCallion, Byron Foulger, Ray Ballard, Jack Cassidy.

A town that fears losing its blacksmith decides to send for a mail-order bride to keep him from leaving town. However, when the bride doesn't arrive, they set out to find a replacement. Old-line movie fans will enjoy seeing B western hero Don "Red" Barry, *Bonanza's* Dan Blocker, villain Jack Elam, and talented dancer Marge Champion on the same movie screen. This Western comedy was originally made for television but was issued to the theaters first.

CODE OF THE CACTUS Victory, 1939, B&W, 56 min. **Producer:** Sam Katzman; **Director:** Sam Newfield; **Screenplay:** Edward Halperin; **Music:** Johnny Lange (songs) and Lew Porter (songs); **Cinematographer:** Marcel Le Pickard; **Editor:** Holbrook N. Todd; **Cast:** Tim McCoy, Ben Corbett, Dorothy Short, Ted Adams, Alden "Stephen" Chase, Forrest Taylor, Bob Terry, Slim Whitaker, Frank Wayne, Dave O'Brien, Kermit Maynard.

Lawman "Lightnin'" Bill Carson (Tim McCoy) is enlisted by a group of ranchers to help stop a gang of rustlers who use trucks to steal their cattle. Well-paced action oater that should appeal to Tim McCoy fans. (See also *RIDING TORNADOS, THE*.)

CODE OF THE FEARLESS Spectrum, 1939, B&W, 56 min. **Producer:** C. C. Burr; **Director:** Raymond K. Johnson; **Screenplay:** Fred Myton; **Music:** Johnny Lange, Lew Porter, and Ian Sadlow; **Cinematographer:** Elmer Dyer; **Editor:** Charles Henkel Jr.; **Cast:** Fred Scott, John Merton, Harry Harvey, George Sherwood, Don Gallaher, William Wood, Walter McGrail, Frank La Rue, Phil Dinham.

A Texas Ranger (Fred Scott) is drummed out of the service in order to infiltrate an outlaw gang. Scott was one of many would-be Gene Autry successors. While his voice was pleasant enough, the songs in this film are pedestrian, and he was not able to benefit from a production studio like Republic Pictures. (See also *MOONLIGHT ON THE RANGE*.)

CODE OF THE LAWLESS Universal, 1945, B&W, 60 min. **Producer:** Wallace Fox; **Director:** Fox; **Screenplay:** Patricia Harper; **Cinematographer:** Maury Gertsman; **Editor:** Saul A. Goodkind; **Cast:** Kirby Grant, Jane Adams (Poni Adams), Fuzzy Knight, Hugh Prosser, Barbara Sears, Edward Howard, Rune Holtman, Pierce Lyden, Roy Bent, Budd Buster, Rex Lease.

See *BAD MEN OF THE BORDER*.

CODE OF THE MOUNTED Ambassador, 1935, B&W, 60 min. **Producers:** Maurice Conn and Sigmund Neufeld; **Director:** Sam Newfield; **Screenplay:** George Wallace Sayre; **Cinematographer:** Edgar Lyons; **Editor:** John English; **Cast:** Kermit Maynard, Robert Warwick, Syd Saylor, Lillian Miles, Wheeler Oakman, Roger Williams, Dick Curtis, Stanley Blystone, Artie Ortego, Eddie Phillips, Jim Thorpe.

When a thug robs and kills a fur trapper, he is caught and locked up by the Mounties, but with his partner's help he manages to break out. The Mounties launch an investigation and discover that the two are part of a ruthless crime ring run by a female gangster. This movie's interesting concept is based on the novel *Wheels of Fate* by James Oliver Curwood. (See also *FIGHTING TEXAN*.)

CODE OF THE OUTLAW (aka: RIDERS OF THE SUNSET TRAIL) Republic, 1942, B&W, 57 min. **Producer:** Louis Gray; **Director:** John English; **Screenplay:** William Colt MacDonald and Barry Shipman; **Cinematographer:** Reggie Lanning; **Cast:** Bob Steele, Tom Tyler, Rufe Davis, Weldon Heyburn, Benny Bartlett, Melinda Leighton, Donald Curtis, John Ince, Kenne Duncan, Phil Durham, Hank Worden, Bud Osborne, Cactus Mack.

This later *Three Mesquiteers* entry for Republic has Bob Steele as Tucson, Tom Tyler as Stoney, and Rufe Davis as Lullaby. The Mesquiteers hunt down an outlaw who is responsible for the theft of bank payroll. While we may miss the old guard, these three are likable and the action is fast-paced. This trio made 20 "Three Mesquiteers" westerns, beginning with *Under Western Skies* (1940) and *Santa Fe Scouts* (1943). (See also *THREE MESQUITEERS, THE*.)

CODY OF THE PONY EXPRESS Columbia, 1950, B&W, 15 chapters. **Producer:** Sam Katzman; **Director:** Spencer Gordon Bennett; **Screenplay:** Lewis Clay, Charles R. Condon, David Mathews, George Plympton, and Joseph F. Poland; **Cast:** Jock Mahoney, Dickie Moore, Peggy Stewart, William Fawcett, Tom London, Helena Dare, George J. Lewis, Pierce Lyden, Jack Ingram, Rick Vallin, Frank Ellis.

The army sends an undercover agent to find out who is behind a series of stagecoach raids. The usual cliffhangers have the audience coming back for more.

CODE OF THE PRAIRIE Republic, 1944, B&W, 56 min, VT. **Director:** Spencer Gordon Bennet; **Screenplay:** Anthony Coldway and Albert DeMond; **Cinematographer:** Bud Thackery; **Editor:** Harry Keller; **Cast:** Sunset Carson, Smiley Burnette, Peggy Stewart, Weldon Heyburn, Tom Chatterton, Roy Barcroft, Bud Geary, Tom London, Jack Kirk, Tom Steele, Robert J. Wilke, Frank Ellis, Rex Lease, Henry Wills, Ken Terrell, Charles King.

Sunset Carson and photography pal Smiley Burnette come to the aid of a girl and her father, who want to start a newspaper in a small town. But they are opposed by a gang of thugs who are led by the town barber. The interesting plot is well acted by Carson as himself and Peggy Stewart as the girl. (See also *CALL OF THE ROCKIES* [1944].)

CODE OF THE RANGE Columbia, 1936, B&W, 55 min. **Producer:** Peter B. Kyne; **Director:** Charles C. Coleman; **Screenplay:** Ford Beebe; **Cinematographer:** George Meehan; **Cast:** Charles Starrett, Mary Blake, Edward Coxen, Alvin Cavan, Albert Smith, Edward Peil Sr., Edmund Cobb, Edward Le Saint, Ralph McCullough, George Chesebro, Art Mix.

Cattlemen are odds with each other over allowing sheepmen to use the range for grazing their herds. A crooked saloon owner tries to exploit the situation for his own gain. (See also *GALLANT DEFENDER*.)

CODE OF THE RANGERS Monogram, 1938, B&W, 1938. **Producer:** Maurice Conn; **Director:** Sam Newfield; **Screenplay:** Stanley Roberts; **Cinematographer:** Jack Greenhalgh; **Cast:** Tim McCoy, Rex Lease, Judith Ford, Wheeler Oakman, Roger Williams, Kit Guard, Frank McCarroll, Jack Ingram, Loren Riebe, Budd Buster, Edward Peil Sr., Hal Price, Herman Hack, Frank La Rue.

This Tim McCoy oater concerns two brothers who belong to the Texas Rangers. When one of the brothers joins forces with a group of outlaws, the other is called upon to bring him to justice. (See also *RIDING TORNADO, THE*.)

CODE OF THE SADDLE Monogram, 1947, B&W, 53 min. **Producer:** Barney A. Sarecky; **Director:** Thomas Carr; **Screenplay:** Eliot Gibbons; **Cinematographer:** Harry Neumann; **Editor:** Fred Maguire; **Cast:** Johnny Mack Brown, Raymond Hatton, Riley Hill, Kay Morley, William Bailey, Zon Murray, Ted Adams, Bud Osborne, Ken Duncan Jr., Gary Garrett.

When a rancher is killed, the two cowboys who are visiting him and his daughter set out to find the killer. Although a neighbor is accused, John (Johnny Mack Brown) and Winks (Raymond Hatton) soon discover that the sheriff is the real culprit. (See also *UNDER ARIZONA SKIES*.)

CODE OF THE SILVER SAGE Republic, 1950, B&W, 60 min. **Producer:** Gordon Kay (associate); **Director:** Fred Brannon; **Screenplay:** Arthur E. Orloff; **Music:** Stanley Wilson; **Cinematographer:** Joan MacBurnie; **Editor:** Irving M. Schoenberg; **Cast:** Allan Lane, Eddy Waller, Roy Barcroft, Kay Christopher, Lane Bradford, William Ruhl, Richard Emory, Kenne Duncan, Rex Lease, Hank Patterson, John Butler, Forrest Taylor.

A deranged man plans to become the dictator of the Arizona Territory, and U.S. cavalry lieutenant Rocky Lane is sent to stop him. Roy Barcroft plays the mad villain with his usual aplomb in this action-packed and exciting Rocky Lane adventure. (See also *BOLD FRONTIERSMAN, THE.*)

CODE OF THE WEST RKO, 1947, B&W, 57 min. **Producer:** Herman Schlom; **Director:** William Berke; **Screenplay:** Norman Houston; **Music:** Harry Harris (song), Lew Pollack (song), and Paul Sawtell; **Cinematographer:** Jack MacKenzie; **Editor:** Ernie Leadlay; **Cast:** James Warren, Debra Alden, John Laurenz, Raymond Burr, Rita Lynn, Robert Clark, Carol Forman, Harry Woods, Steve Brodie, Emmett Lynn, Harry Cheshire, Budd Buster, Jason Robards Sr.

Two men come to the aid of a man and his daughter when they try to open a bank and are opposed by a corrupt town boss.

COLE YOUNGER, GUNFIGHTER Allied Artists, 1958, Color, 78 mn. **Producer:** Ben Schwalb; **Director:** R. G. Springsteen; **Screenplay:** Daniel Mainwaring; **Music:** Marlin Skiles; **Cinematographer:** Harry Neumann; **Editor:** William Austin; **Cast:** Frank Lovejoy, James Best, Abby Dalton, Jan Merlin, Douglas Spencer, Ainslie Pryor, Frank Ferguson, Myron Healey, George Keymas, Dan Sheridan, John Mitchum, Stanley Andrews.

Set in Texas during the 1870s and filmed in CinemaScope, this film depicts the most famous of the Younger brothers developing a reputation as a gunfighter because of his opposition to corrupt lawmen. More than 20 actors have played gunfighter Cole Younger on film. This time the always-reliable Frank Lovejoy portrays the eldest Younger brother as a gunfighter with a big heart who fights corruption. Although the film is historically flawed, the story is well told and Lovejoy handles the role well.

COLORADO Republic, 1940, B&W, 54 min, VT. **Producer:** Joseph Kane; **Director:** Kane; **Screenplay:** Harrison Jacobs and Louis Stevens; **Cinematographer:** Jack A. Marta; **Editor:** Edward Mann; **Cast:** Roy Rogers, George "Gabby" Hayes, Pauline Moore, Milburn Stone, Maude Eburne, Wally Wales (as Hal Taliaferro), Vester Pegg, Fred Burns, Lloyd Ingraham, Iron Eyes Cody.

Roy Rogers is Lt. Jerry Burke, a Union officer who is sent to Denver with sidekick "Gabby" to find out what is causing trouble with the Indians. This routine shoot-'em-up Rogers vehicle is enhanced by an exciting finale.

COLORADO AMBUSH Monogram, 1951, B&W, 52 min. **Producer:** Vincent F. Fenelly; **Director:** Lewis D. Collins; **Screenplay:** Myron Healey; **Cinematographer:** Gilbert Warrenton; **Editor:** Fred Maguire; **Cast:** Johnny Mack Brown, Myron Healey, Lois Hall, Tommy Farrell, Christine McIntyre, Marshall Bradford, Lyle Talbot.

Written by actor Myron Healey, who also plays villain Chet Murdock, the plot deals with a ranger who investigates the murder of three Wells Fargo men. Lois Hall and Tommy

Farrell offer strong support to this above-average Johnny Mack Brown venture for Monogram. Healey was recently awarded a Golden Boot for his enormous contributions to western films. (See also *UNDER ARIZONA SKIES.*)

COLORADO KID, THE Republic, 1937, B&W, 56 min. **Producer:** A. W. Hackel; **Director:** Sam Newfield; **Screenplay:** Harry F. Olmsted and Charles F. Royal; **Cinematographer:** Robert E. Cline; **Editor:** S. Roy Luby; **Cast:** Bob Steele, Marian Weldon, Karl Hackett, Ernie Adams, Ted Adams, Frank La Rue, Horace Murphy, Keene Duncan, Budd Buster, Frank Ball, John Merton.

When a murder is committed, the Colorado Kid (Bob Steele) is arrested and jailed for the crime. With the help of a pal he breaks out of jail and goes after the real culprit. (See also *LIGHTNIN' CRANDALL.*)

COLORADO PIONEERS Republic, 1945, B&W, 57 min. **Producer:** Sidney Picker; **Director:** R. G. Springsteen; **Screenplay:** Fred Harman and Earle Snell; **Cinematographer:** Bud Thackery; **Cast:** Bill Elliott, Robert Blake (Bobby Blake), Alice Fleming, Roy Barcroft, Bud Geary, Billy Cummings, Freddie Chapman, Tom London, Monte Hale, Billie "Buckwheat" Thomas, Frank Jacquet, George Chesebro, Emmett Vogan, Tom Chatterton.

A group of tough city kids who are sent west to be "reformed" help Red Ryder (Bill Elliott) and Little Beaver (Robert Blake) stop a malevolent rancher intent on taking some valuable land. This feature with a different twist is a worthy addition to the Red Ryder series. (See also *ADVENTURES OF RED RYDER, THE.*)

COLORADO RANGER (aka: GUNS OF JUSTICE) Lippert Pictures, 1950, B&W, 59 min. **Producers:** Murray Lerner, Robert Lippert (executive), and Ron Ormond; **Director:** Thomas Carr; **Screenplay:** Ormond and Maurice Tombragel; **Cinematographer:** Ernest Miller; **Editor:** Hugh Winn; **Cast:** James Ellison, Julie Adams (Betty Adams), John L. Cason, Russell Hayden, Raymond Hatton, Fuzzy Knight, Tom Tyler, Dennis Moore, George Chesebro, Stanley Price, Stephen Carr.

Two pals (James Ellison and Russell Hayden) go to collect an inheritance left by Ellison's mother. When they arrive at the Shamrock family ranch, they find that his stepfather has been kidnapped.

COLORADO SERENADE PRC, 1946, Color, 68 min. **Director:** Robert Emmett Tansey; **Screenplay:** Frances Kavanaugh; **Music:** Sam Armstrong (songs), H. L. Canova (songs) and Carl Hoefle (songs); **Cinematographer:** Robert Shackelford; **Editor:** Hugh Winn; **Cast:** Eddie Dean, Roscoe Ates, David Sharpe, Mary Kenyon, Forrest Taylor.

This Eddie Dean action yarn has two cowboys saving a judge who is about to be ambushed. They later discover that one of

Eddie Dean stars in Colorado Serenade, *one of Dean's better entries in his PRC/Eagle Lion Series.* (PRC/AUTHOR'S COLLECTION).

the would be-killers is actually the judge's son, who refuses to believe that the judge is really his father. The interesting plot line helps make this entry one of Dean's better ventures for his PRC/Eagle Lion series.

COLORADO SUNDOWN Republic, 1952, B&W, 67 min, VT, DVD. **Producer:** Edward J. White; **Director:** William Witney; **Screenplay:** William Lively and Eric Taylor; **Music:** D. Dale Butts; **Cinematographer:** John MacBurnie; **Editor:** Tony Martinelli; **Cast:** Rex Allen, Mary Ellen Kay, Slim Pickens, June Vincent, Fred Graham, John Daheim, Louise Beavers, Chester Clute, Clarence Straight, Ed Cassidy, Rex Lease, Harry Harvey, Bud Osborne, Hal Price.

A rancher helps a friend claim a spread he has inherited, but soon finds himself involved with a murder instead. This exciting oater is one of the better entries in Rex Allen's Republic series. (See also *ARIZONA COWBOY.*)

COLORADO SUNSET Republic, 1939, B&W, 61 min. **Producer:** Herbert Yates; **Director:** George Sherman; **Screenplay:** Betty Burbridge and Stanley Roberts; **Cinematographer:** William Nobles; **Cast:** Gene Autry, Smiley Burnette, June Story, Barbara Pepper, Larry "Buster" Crabbe, Robert Barrat, William Farnum, Patsy Montana, Frankie Marvin, Purnell B. Pratt, Kermit Maynard, Jack Ingram, Elmo Lincoln, Ethan Laidlaw, Fred Burns, Jack Kirk, Budd Buster, Ed Cassidy, Slim Whitaker, Murduck McQuarie, Ralph Peters, the CBS-KMBC Texas Rangers.

In this Gene Autry entry, a musical group buys a cattle ranch, but the herd turns out to be milk cows and they find themselves pressured to join a combine run by a band of crooks. By 1939 Gene Autry was the number-one box office draw among all western stars. Autry employed and maintained his own stock company of directors, cameramen, musicians, and actors, including the lovely June Story, his leading lady in *Colorado Sunset.* (See also *TUMBLING TUMBLEWEEDS.*)

COLORADO TERRITORY Warner Bros., 1949, B&W, 94 min. **Producer:** Anthony Veiller; **Director:** Raoul Walsh; **Screenplay:** Edmund H. North and John Twist; **Music:** David Buttolph; **Cinematographer:** Sidney Hickox; **Editor:** Owen Marks; **Cast:** Joel McCrea, Virginia Mayo, Dorothy Malone, John Archer, James Mitchell, Morris Ankrum, Basil Ruysdael, Frank Puglia, Ian Wolfe, Harry Woods, Housley Stevenson.

Joel McCrea is Wes McQueen, an outlaw who is sprung from jail by his gang. After meeting "nice" girl Dorothy Malone, he decides to pull one last heist in order to secure a better future. But the girl betrays him, and the train he is slated to rob is full of lawmen. Wes and his half-breed companion Colorado Carson, played by blond and barefooted Virginia Mayo, head to the hills, where they both die on the high ledge of a canyon wall.

In this excellent and underrated western adapted from W. R. Burnett's novel and the film *High Sierra* (1941), which was also directed by Raoul Walsh. McCrea, Malone, and Mayo take the roles that originally belonged to Humphrey Bogart, Joan Leslie, and Ida Lupino in the earlier film. Warner Bros. would reuse the plot a third time with the 1955 gangster film *I Died a Thousand Times*.

COLORADO TRAIL Columbia, 1938, B&W, 55 min. **Producer:** Harry L. Decker; **Director:** Sam Nelson; **Screenplay:** Charles F. Royal; **Music:** Bob Nolan (songs) and Morris Stoloff; **Cinematographer:** Benjamin H. Klien; **Editor:** William A. Lyon; **Cast:** Charles Starrett, Iris Merrith; Edward Le Saint, Al Bridge, Robert Fiske, Dick Curtis, Bob Nolan, Hank Bell, Edward Peil Sr., Edmund Cobb, Jack Clifford.

A young man joins cattlemen in a range war, with his father on the opposite side. This is yet another typically high-quality Charles Starrett entry in Columbia's B western stable before his more famous Durango Kid days. In 1936 Starrett signed with Columbia, where he would star in 115 westerns over the next 16 years. (See also *GALLANT DEFENDER*.)

COLT COMRADES United Artists, 1943, B&W, 67 min, VT. **Producers:** Lewis J. Rachmil and Harry Sherman; **Director:** Leslie Selander; **Screenplay:** Michael Wilson; **Cinematographer:** Russell Harlan; **Editor:** Sherman A. Rose; **Cast:** William Boyd, Andy Clyde, Bill George, Teddi Sherman, Jay Kirby, Victor Jory, George Reeves, Douglas Fowley, Herbert Rawlinson, Earle Hodgins, Robert Mitchum.

When Hoppy and his pals discover an underground well, which is a potential threat to Jeb Hardin's monopoly on regional water, Hardin retaliates by framing Hoppy and accusing him of cattle rustling. Hoppy, of course, sets out to prove his innocence in this average Hop-Along Cassidy venture that features a young Robert Mitchum. (See also *HOP-ALONG CASSIDY*.)

COLT .45 (aka: THUNDERCLOUD) Warner Bros., 1950, Color, 70 min. **Producer:** Saul Elkins; **Director:** Edwin Marin; **Screenplay:** Thomas Blackburn; **Music:** William Lava; **Cinematographer:** Wilfred M. Cline; **Editor:** Frank Magee; **Cast:** Randolph Scott, Zachary Scott, Ruth Roman, Lloyd Bridges, Alan Hale, Ian MacDonald, Chief Thundercloud, Walter Coy, Charles Evans, Lute Crockett, Buddy Roosevelt, Hal Taliaferro, Art Miles, Barry Reagan, Franklyn Farnum.

Another taut Edwin Marin/Randolph Scott western has Scott as a salesman heading west with a pair of demonstration Colt 45s. While Scott is showing the guns to a local sheriff, bad man Zachary Scott seizes the weapons, shoots the sheriff, and takes off with the prized pistols on a robbery spree. Randolph Scott is held as an accomplice, but once released he takes after the villain, retrieves the pistols, and establishes his innocence.

COLUMN SOUTH Universal, 1953, Color, 82 min. **Producer:** Ted Richmond; **Director:** Frederick De Cordova; **Screenplay:** William Sacheim; **Music:** Herman Stein and Henry Mancini (uncredited); **Cinematographer:** Charles Boyle; **Editor:** Milton Carruth; **Cast:** Audey Murphy, Robert Sterling, Ray Collins, Gregg Palmer, Ralph Moody, Dennis Weaver, Johnny Downs, Russell Johnson, Bob Steele, Jack Kelly, Ray Montgomery, Richard Garland, James Best, Ed Rand.

In order to prevent fighting between the Indians and the U.S. cavalry, a young lieutenant tries to help the Navajo before they are forced into war by an intolerant army captain. Two future television icons, *Gunsmoke's* Dennis Weaver and *Maverick's* Jack Kelly, appear in supporting roles.

COMANCHE United Artists, 1956, Color, 87 min. **Producer:** Carl Krueger; **Director:** George Sherman; **Screenplay:** Carl Krueger; **Music:** Herschel Burke Gilbert; **Cinematographer:** George Stahl Jr.; **Editor:** Charles L. Kimball; **Cast:** Dana Andrews, Kent Smith, Linda Cristal, Lowell Gilmore, Nestor Paiva, Stacy Harrris, Mike Mazurki, Henry Brandon, Reed Sherman, John Litel, Iron Eyes Cody.

Filmed in Durango, Mexico, this action-laden oater has two scouts assigned to find the Comanche chief and offer him the promise of a lasting peace. But good intentions don't always work, and the land becomes a setting for gunplay and killing.

COMANCHEROS, THE 20th Century Fox, 1961, 107 min, VT. **Producer:** George Sherman; **Director:** Michael Curtiz; **Screenplay:** James Edward Grant and Clair Huffaker; **Music:** Elmer Bernstein; **Cinematographer:** William H. Clothier; **Editor:** Louis R. Loefler; **Cast:** John Wayne, Stuart Whitman, Ian Balin, Nehemiah Persoff, Lee Marvin, Michael Ansara, Patrick Wayne, Joan O'Brien, Jack Elam, Edgar Buchanan, Guinn "Big Boy" Williams, John Dierkes, Roger Mobley, Bob Steele, Aissa Wayne, Gregg Palmer, Don Bodie.

Texas Ranger John Cutter (John Wayne) brings in gambler Paul Regret (Stuart Whitman) on a dueling charge. When Regret helps him subdue an Indian attack, the Rangers ask him to join their ranks. Together Cutter and Regret are assigned the job of penetrating an outlaw group supplying guns and liquor to the Comanche, by the deranged and evil Graile (Nehemiah Persoff). This big, brash, humorous western adventure was the final film for director Michael Curtiz, who died the following year. Look for appealing cameos by Bob Steele as the harried rancher about to become a father again and Guinn "Big Boy" Williams as a slow-witted gunrunner who is jailed and doesn't know why. This was Wayne's 125th movie over a 33-year period. *Variety* called it " . . . a likeable piece of high adventure escape entertainment . . . the production is as big as all outdoors, and action-packed to boot."

COMANCHE STATION   Columbia, 1960, Color, 74 min, VT. **Producers:** Budd Boetticher, Harry Joe Brown, and Randolph Scott; **Director:** Boetticher; **Screenplay:** Burt Kennedy; **Cinematographer:** Charles Lawton Jr.; **Editor:**

Randolph Scott stars in Budd Boetticher's Comanche Station, *the last in a string of outstanding Boetticher westerns starring Scott as the taciturn hero.* (COLUMBIA/ COURTESY OF BUDD AND MARY BOETTICHER)

Randolph Scott and Nancy Gates in Comanche Station (COLUMBIA/COURTESY OF BUDD AND MARY BOETTICHER).

Randolph Scott enters Comanche territory to try to bring back a woman being held prisoner in Comanche Station. (COLUMBIA/COURTESY OF BUDD AND MARY BOETTICHER)

Edwin H. Bryant; **Cast:** Randolph Scott, Nancy Gates, Claude Akins, Skip Homeier, Richard Rust, Rand Brooks, P. Holland, Foster Hood, Joe Molina, Vince St. Cyr.

Randolph Scott arguably did his best work in the seven westerns helmed by Budd Boetticher and written by Burt Kennedy in the late 1950s. In the last of these excellent films, Scott enters Comanche territory to try to bring back a white woman being held prisoner by the Indians. His own wife had been captured years earlier. On his way back, a trio of outlaws join him. Unbeknownst to him the woman's husband had put a price on her head—to the tune of $5,000 dead or alive. The outlaws want the money, and the Indians

Randolph Scott and Claude Akins in Comanche Station (COLUMBIA/COURTESY OF BUDD AND MARY BOETTICHER)

are braced to attack. *Variety* called this typically well-made and fast-paced Boetticher venture a good western "by any standard."

Filmed in Lone Pine, California, the film benefits from cameraman Charles Lawton's superb exterior shots of the rugged locations and screenwriter Burt Kennedy's crisp dialogue. Randolph Scott retired from the screen after making this picture. Two years later he and Joel McCrea would both come out of retirement and team for the first time in Sam Peckinpah's *RIDE THE HIGH COUNTRY.*

COMANCHE TERRITORY Universal, 1950, Color, 76 min, VT. **Producer:** Leonard Goldstein; **Director:** George Sherman; **Screenplay:** Oscar Brodney and Lewis Meltzer; **Music:** Frank Skinner; **Cinematographer:** Maury Gertsman; **Editor:** Frank Gross; **Cast:** Maureen O'Hara, Macdonald Carey, Will Geer, Charles Drake, Pedro de Cordoba, Ian MacDonald, Rick Vallin, Parley Baer, Edmund Cobb, James Best, Glenn Strange.

When outlaws try to steal land belonging to the Indians because of rich silver deposits, Jim Bowie comes to the aid of the Indians. Macdonald Carey plays a highly fictionalized Bowie in this overly romanticized story highlighted by magnificent scenery.

COME ON COWBOYS Republic, 1937, B&W, 58 min, VT. **Producer:** Sol C. Siegal; **Director:** Joseph Kane; **Screenplay:** Betty Burbridge; **Cinematographer:** Ernest Miller; **Editor:** Lester Orlebeck; **Cast:** Robert Livingston, Ray Corrigan, Max Terhune, Maxine Doyle, Willie Fung, Edward Peil Jr., Horace Murphy, Anne Bennett, Ed Cassidy, Roger Williams, Yakima Canutt, George Burton.

When an old circus pal gets mixed up with crooks, the Three Mesquiteers come to his rescue. Action under the big top abounds in this adventurous Mesquiteers series entry. The trio of Ray Corrigan, Robert Livingston, and Max Terhune made 14 *Three Mesquiteers* features for Republic Pictures. (See also *THREE MESQUITEERS, THE.*)

COME ON DANGER RKO, 1932, B&W, 54 min. **Director:** Robert F. Hill; **Screenplay:** Lester Ilfeld and David Lewis; **Cinematographer:** Nicholas Musuraca; **Cast:** Tom Keene, Julie Haydon, Roscoe Ates, Robert Ellis, William Scott, Frank Lackteen, Wade Boteler.

Ranger Larry Madden (Tom Keene) and a pal set out to capture the murderer of the ranger's brother. He soon finds out that the gang leader he wants is a woman who has been framed for the crime. This is an intelligent and well-scripted early B western from RKO. Keene was RKO's first series star in the 1930s. One of the genuinely handsome western stars of the period, he was also a decent actor who could handle action well. RKO would continue to make series westerns until the early 1950s. (See also *BEYOND THE ROCKIES.*)

COME ON DANGER RKO, 1942, B&W, 58 min. **Producer:** Bert Gilroy; **Director:** Edward Killy; **Screenplay:** Norton S. Parker; **Music:** Fred Rose and Ray Whitley (songs); **Cinematographer:** Harry J. Wild; **Editor:** Frederic Knudson; **Cast:** Tim Holt, Frances E. Neal, Ray Whitley, Lee "Lasses" White, Karl Hackett, Malcott "Bud" McTaggart, Glenn Strange, Slim Whitaker, Kate Harrington, Buzz Barton.

A Texas Ranger is assigned to bring in the female leader of a band of outlaws. When she is wounded, he discovers that a crooked tax collector is actually behind all the trouble. After 10 years, RKO remade *Come On Danger* with top star Tim Holt in the role that was Tom Keene's in 1932. Although an enjoyable B western, this film does not rise to the level of the 1932 production. (See also *ALONG THE RIO GRANDE*.)

COME ON RANGERS Republic, 1938, B&W, 57 min, VT. **Producer:** Charles E. Ford; **Director:** Joseph Kane; **Screenplay:** Gerald Geraghty and Jack Natteford; **Cinematographer:** Al Wilson; **Editor:** Edward Mann; **Cast:** Roy Rogers, Lynne Roberts, Raymond Hatton, J. Farrell MacDonald, Harry Woods, Purnell Pratt, Bruce MacFarland, Lane Chandler, Chester Gunnels, Lee Powell, George Montgomery, Robert J. Wilke.

The Texas Rangers are disbanded because of a lack of money, but they gather together again to help the U.S. Cavalry deal with marauding outlaws pouring into the state. This exciting and well-made Roy Rogers venture includes such songs as "A Western Love Song," "I've Learned a Lot About Women," and "Tenting Tonight."

COME ON, TARZAN World Wide Pictures, 1932, B&W, 61 min. **Producers:** Samuel Bischoff, Burt Kelly, William Saal, and E. W. Hammons (executive); **Director:** Alan James; **Screenplay:** E. W. Hammonds; **Cast:** Ken Maynard, Merna Kennedy, Niles Welch, Roy Stewart, Kate Campbell, Bob Kortman, Nelson McDowell, Jack Rockwell.

COMES A HORSEMAN United Artists, 1978, Color, 118 min, VT. **Producers:** Gene Kirkwood and Dan Paulson; **Director:** Alan J. Pakula; **Screenplay:** Dennis Lynton Clark; **Music:** Michael Small; **Cinematographer:** Gordon Willis; **Editor:** Marion Rothman; **Cast:** James Caan, Jane Fonda, Jason Robards, George Grizzard, Richard Farnsworth, Jim Davis, Mark Harmon.

In this modern-day western set in the 1940s, James Caan plays an independent rancher recently returned from World War II who teams up with ranch owner Jane Fonda after his partner is killed—presumably by Jason Robards (as nasty as he has been in any role). The story is simple and at times painfully slow, despite a heavyweight cast. Gordon Willis's stunning photography and a superb performance by Richard Farnsworth are the strongest elements of this film.

Ex-stuntman Farnsworth is thoroughly at home with his role as Dodger, Fonda's aging ranch hand. The critics thought so too. Farnsworth was awarded both the National Board of Review and the National Society of Film Critics Awards as Best Supporting Actor, in addition to a well-deserved Oscar nomination. The title comes from a song by Gordon Lightfoot, "Don Quixote," which contains the line, "Comes a horseman, wild and free." The film was not without personal tragedy. Stuntman Jim Sheppard was killed when a horse he was dragging veered from its course and caused him to hit his head on a fence post.

COMIN' ROUND THE MOUNTAIN Republic, 1936, B&W, 60 min. **Producer:** Nat Levine; **Director:** Mack V. Wright; **Screenplay:** Charles Drake, Dorrell McGowan, and Stuart E. McGowan; **Music:** Arthur Kay; **Cinematographer:** William Nobles; **Cast:** Gene Autry, Ann Rutherford, Smiley Burnette, LeRoy Mason, Raymond Brown, Ken Cooper, Tracy Layne, Robert McKenzie, Laura Puente.

Gene Autry plays an express driver who is robbed and left to die in the desert. He is saved when he captures and then rides a wild horse to safety. When the story begins to center on a horse race that is being played for big stakes, it's his horse Champion who steals the show. (See also *TUMBLING TUMBLEWEEDS*.)

COMMAND, THE Warner Bros., 1954, Color, 94 min. **Producer:** David Weisbart; **Director:** David Butler; **Screenplay:** Samuel Fuller and Russell S. Hughes; **Music:** Dimitri Tiomkin; **Cinematographer:** Wilfred M. Cline; **Editor:** Irene Morra; **Cast:** Guy Madison, Joan Weldon, James Whitmore, Carl Benton Reid, Harvey Lembeck, Ray Teal, Robert Nichols, Don Shelton, Gregg Barton, Boyd "Red" Morgan.

Guy Madison plays an army doctor with no combat experience who is forced to take command of a cavalry troop after the commanding officer dies. This requires him to lead a wagon train through hostile Indian territory and battle the scourge of smallpox. He manages to improvise battle tactics, allowing him to defeat the Indians and win the respect of his recalcitrant troops, while saving a wagon train and two infantry companies as well. Based on James Warner Bellah's novel *Rear Guard*, the picture was originally filmed—although not released—in 3-D. This was the first feature western filmed in CinemaScope, and it features one of Guy Madison's best performances.

COMPANY OF COWARDS See *ADVANCE TO THE REAR*.

CONAGHER TNT, 1991, Color, 118 min, VT. **Producer:** Sam Elliott and John A. Kuri; **Director:** Reynaldo Vilalobos; **Teleplay:** Elliott, Katharine Ross, and Jeffrey M. Meyer; **Music:** J. A. C. Redford; **Cinematographer:** James R. Bagdonas; **Editor:** Zach Staenberg; **Cast:** Sam Elliott,

Katherine Ross, Barry Corbin, Billy Green Bush, Paul Koslo, Ken Curtis, Gavan O'Herlihy, Buck Taylor, Dub Taylor.

Sam Elliott gives arguably his finest performance as Con Conagher, an honest and hard-working cowboy who, in the best cowboy tradition, works the herds to market over great cattle trails. His ethos is always true to the Cowboy Code: "I take a man's money, I ride the brand—I don't know no other way."

Katharine Ross is Evie Teale, a struggling widow stranded with two children on a remote homestead after her husband dies in an accident. Their lives are intertwined as they fight the elements, Indians, outlaws, and a pervading loneliness. Ross is outstanding as Mrs. Teale. Barry Corbin, who plays stage driver Charlie McCloud, a man steeped in decency and integrity, also delivers a fine performance.

Sam Elliott received a Golden Globe nomination for Best Performance by an Actor in a Miniseries or a Motion Picture Made for Television. Extremely well done and historically accurate, this faithful adaptation of Louis L'Amour's novel is a visual treat and artistically first rate. Beautifully helmed by ace cinematographer Vilalobos in his directorial debut, it is among the finest westerns to appear on any screen during the 1990s.

CONCENTRATION KID, THE Hoot Gibson Productions/Universal, 1930, B&W, 57 min. **Producer:** Hoot Gibson; **Director:** Arthur Rosson; **Screenplay:** Harold Tarshis; **Cinematographer:** Harry Neumann; **Editor:** Gilmore Walker; **Cast:** Hoot Gibson, Kathryn Crawford, Duke R. Lee, Jim Mason, Robert Homans, Fred Gilman.

The Concentration Kid (Hoot Gibson) is in love with a radio singer he has never met, so he makes a bet that he can meet her and win her over. Just as it looks like he will be able to do so, she learns of the bet and decides to leave. Gibson, who also produced the film, was a genuine cowboy, winning the title "Champion Cowboy of the World" in 1912 and becoming one of Hollywood's best and most daring stuntmen before emerging as a top-flight western film star. (See also *SPURS*.)

CONQUERING HORDE, THE Paramount, 1931, B&W, 76 min. **Director:** Edward Sloman; **Screenplay:** Grover Jones and William McNutt; **Cinematographer:** A. J. Stout; **Cast:** Richard Arlen, Fay Wray, George Mendoza, Ian MacLaren, Claude Gillingwater, James Durkin.

A Texan returns home after the Civil War to help in the rebuilding of the state, but he finds he must first deal with a group of northern carpetbaggers. This early talkie, originally made by Paramount in 1924 as *North of 36*, is a staple for fans of Richard Arlen.

CONQUERORS, THE RKO, 1932, B&W, 86 min. **Producer:** David O. Selznick; **Director:** William Wellman; **Screenplay:** Robert Lord; **Music:** Max Steiner; **Cinematographer:** Edward Cronjager; **Editor:** William Hamil-

ton; **Cast:** Richard Dix, Ann Harding, Guy Kibbee, Edna Mae Oliver, Julie Haydon, Donald Cook, Walter Walker, Wally Albright, Marilyn Knowlden, Harry Holman, Jason Robards, E. H. Calvert.

Newlyweds Richard Dix and Ann Harding move west to Fort Allen, Nebraska, during the tumultuous days of the post–Civil War era. They encounter many hardships, including the death of their little son in an accident as the crowds are lining up to welcome the first locomotive. Dix builds the town's first bank, which collapses in the financial crisis of 1893, but he rises from the ashes and builds his bank once again. The story closes with the family's grandson (also played by Dix) becoming a World War I hero and a member of the famed Lafayette Escadrille.

Eager to capitalize on the success of *CIMARRON* (1931), RKO sought to repeat the formula the following year. The studio cast its stalwart star Richard Dix as hero Roger Standish, and the popular Ann Harding—whose character ages decades during the course of the film's 80-plus minutes—as his wife Caroline. The cinematography was handled by Edward Cronjager, who had also photographed *Cimarron*.

By balancing rugged outdoor action with a proper blend of drama, story development, and romance, the film succeeded in appealing to all audiences, not just western aficionados. Helmed by 36-year-old William Wellman, *The Conquerors* has been praised by film historian William Everson for containing "some unusually powerful sequences, including . . . a grim mass of lynching episodes so starkly designed and lit and so casually underplayed, that it quite outshines the more carefully and lengthily constructed lynching scenes in Wellman's much later *The Ox Bow Incident*."

CONQUEST OF CHEYENNE Republic, 1946, B&W, 54 min. **Director:** R. G. Springsteen; **Screenplay:** Earle Snell; **Cinematographer:** William Bradford; **Editor:** Charles Craft; **Cast:** William "Wild Bill" Elliott, Robert Blake, Alice Fleming, Peggy Stewart, Bill George, Milton Kibbee, Tom London, Emmett Lynn, Keene Duncan, George Sherwood.

CONQUEST OF COCHISE Columbia, 1953, Color, 70 min. **Producer:** Sam Katzman; **Director:** William Castle; **Screenplay:** Henry Freulich; **Editor:** Al Clark; **Cast:** John Hodiak, Robert Stack, Joy Page, Rico Alaniz, Fortunio Bonanova, Edward Colmans, Alex Montoya, Steven Ritch.

In this film set in the Southwest during the 1950s, cavalry major Burke (Robert Stack) and his troops try to keep a lid on an explosive situation where Cochise (John Hodiak) is being prodded into starting a war.

COPPER CANYON Paramount, 1950, Color, 84 min, VT. **Producer:** Mel Epstein; **Director:** John Farrow; **Screenplay:** Jonathan Latimer; **Music:** Daniele Amfitheatrof and Jay Livingston (songs); **Cinematographer:** Charles

Lang; **Editor:** Eda Warren; **Cast:** Ray Milland, Hedy Lamarr, Macdonald Carey, Mona Freeman, Harry Carey Jr., Frank Faylen, Hope Emerson.

In this western set in post–Civil War Nevada, Ray Milland is a stage-show marksman who appears in town and is recognized by ex-Confederate soldiers as Colonel Desmond, their beloved officer who reportedly had escaped from a Yankee prison. The ex-rebels had gone west after the war to work in the copper mines, but the local smelters, who are former Yankees, refuse to smelt the rebel ore. Milland denies his real identity but is eventually forced to end the dispute by leading his men on one final charge. Hedy Lamarr plays Lisa Roselle, a lovely gambler whom the miners refuse to trust—especially since she has eyes for Milland. Former B western stars Rex Lease and Buddy Roosevelt appear in uncredited roles.

COPPER SKY 20th Century Fox, 1957, B&W, 77 min. **Producers:** Robert W. Stabler and Charles Marquis Warren; **Director:** Charles Marquis Warren; **Screenplay:** Eric Norden and Robert S. Stabler; **Music:** Raoul Kraushaar; **Cinematographer:** Brydon Baker; **Editor:** Fred W. Berger; **Cast:** Jeff Morrow, Coleen Gray, Strother Martin, Paul Brinegar, John Pickard, Patrick O'Moore, Jack Lomas.

A drunken ex-soldier (Jeff Morrow) and a prim and prissy schoolteacher (Coleen Gray) survive an Indian massacre in a small town and trek across the desert to the nearest outpost. Along the way the two opposites develop an attraction and a caring for one another.

CORNER CREEK Columbia, 1948, Color, 90 min, VT. **Producer:** Harry Joe Brown; **Director:** Ray Enright; **Screenplay:** Kenneth Gamel; **Music:** Rudy Schrager; **Cinematographer:** Fred Jackman Jr.; **Editor:** Harvey Manger; **Cast:** Randolph Scott, Marguerite Chapman, George Macready, Sally Eilers, Edgar Buchanan, Barbara Reed, Wallace Ford, Forrest Tucker, William Bishop, Joe Sawyer, Russell Simpson.

Randolph Scott is a loner bent on taking revenge on the people responsible for his fiancé's mysterious death in this adaptation of Luke Short's novel of the same name. He finds help from pretty hotel owner Marguerite Chapman. Some great fisticuffs between Scott and Forrest Tucker add to the excitement.

CORNERED Columbia, 1932, B&W, 58 min. **Director:** B. Reeves Eason; **Screenplay:** Wallace MacDonald; **Cinematographer:** John Stumar; **Editor:** Otto Meyer; **Cast:** Tim McCoy, Raymond Hatton, Noah Beery, Shirley Grey, Niles Welch, Claire McDowell.

After Moody Pierson (Niles Welch) saves the life of Sheriff Tim Laramie (Tim McCoy), he is arrested for murder. Believing that Moody is innocent, Sheriff Tim allows him to escape. The townsfolk promptly fire the sheriff, who now goes after the real killer. McCoy's performance is always a

delight, and Noah Beery's portrayal of deranged villain Red Slavins is compelling. This very good McCoy venture for Columbia is made more interesting by an early uncredited appearance by Walter Brennan as the court clerk. (See also *RIDING TORNADO, THE.*)

CORPUS CHRISTI BANDITS Republic, 1945, B&W, 56 min. **Producer:** Stephen Auer; **Director:** Wallace Grissell; **Screenplay:** Norman S. Hall; **Cinematographer:** Bud Thackery; **Editor:** Charles Craft; **Cast:** Allan "Rocky" Lane, Helen Talbot, Jack Kirk, Twinkle Watts, Roy Barcroft, Tom London, Keene Duncan.

Through scenes told in flashback, a man relates the story of his grandfather, Corpus Christi Jim ("Rocky" Lane), who became an outlaw due to the activities of carpetbaggers. After grand dad and two partners rob a stagecoach, they decide to go straight and return the money. When a fourth gang member refuses and leaves, the two former partners find themselves on the opposite side of the law. (See also *BOLD FRONTIERSMAN, THE.*)

COUNT THREE AND PRAY Columbia, 1955, Color, 102 min. **Producer:** Ted Richmond; **Director:** George Sherman; **Screenplay:** Herb Meadow; **Music:** George Duning; **Cinematographer:** Burnett Guffey; **Editor:** William A. Lyon; **Cast:** Van Heflin, Joanne Woodward, Philip Carey, Raymond Burr, Allison Hayes, Myron Healey, Nancy Culp.

A pastor (Van Heflin) with a shady past moves into a small town and becomes enamored with an orphaned girl. Raymond Burr plays the villain with a patented degree of nastiness. Filmed in CinemaScope with good performances by everyone, this forgotten western marks the film debut of actress Joanne Woodward.

COUNT YOUR BLESSINGS See *FACE TO THE WIND.*

COURAGE OF THE WEST Universal, 1937, B&W, 56 min. **Producer:** Paul Malvern; **Director:** Joseph H. Lewis; **Screenplay:** Norton Parker; **Cinematographer:** Virgil Miller; **Editor:** Charles Craft; **Cast:** Bob Baker, J. Farrell MacDonald, Lois January, Fuzzy Knight, Harry Woods, Carl Stockdale, Buddy Cox.

The Texas Rangers are assigned to stop a group of outlaws who are robbing Wells Fargo messengers. This film marked Bob Baker's first starring role in a series venture. A singing cowboy, Baker was employed by Universal in its aim to attract a family audience. His films were among the most relaxed and easy-going westerns ever made and were designed to limit or maximize action—despite the fact that Baker was a rugged fellow and an expert horseman who often did his own stunts. Universal discontinued the unpopular series at the end of the 1930s and reverted back to the more action-packed and hard-hitting Johnny Mack Brown series. (See also *BLACK BANDIT.*)

COURAGEOUS AVENGER, THE Supreme, 1935, B&W, 58 min, VT. **Producer:** A. W. Hackel; **Director:** Robert Bradbury; **Screenplay:** Charles F. Royal; **Cinematographer:** E. M. MacManigal; **Editor:** S. Roy Luby; **Cast:** Johnny Mack Brown, Helen Ericson, Warner P. Richmond, Eddie Parker, Ed Cassidy, Frank Bell, Forrest Taylor, Earl Dwire.

An agent who is sent to investigate the thefts of gold bullion shipments discovers that the mine owner is behind it. He also discovers that the owner has his gang capture travelers to use them as slave labor in the mine. (See also *GAMBLING TERROR, THE.*)

COURTIN' TROUBLE Monogram, 1948, B&W, 58 min. **Director:** Ford Beebe; **Screenplay:** Ronald Davidson; **Cast:** Jimmy Wakely, Dub Taylor, Virginia Belmont, Leonard Penn, Steve Clark, Marshall Reed, House Peters, Frank LaRue, Bob Woodward, Bud Osborne, Boyd Stockman, Bill Bailey, Bill Hale, Carol Henry, Louis Armstrong, Arthur Smith.

COVERED WAGON, THE Paramount, 1923, B&W, 98 min, VT. **Director:** James Cruze; **Screenplay:** Jack Cunningham; **Music:** Hugo Riesenfeld; **Cinematographer:** Karl Brown; **Editor:** Dorothy Arzner; **Cast:** J. Warren Kerrigan, Lois Wilson, Alan Hale, Ernest Torrence, Tully Marshall, Ethel Wales, Charles Ogle, Guy Oliver, Johnny Fox, Frank Albertson.

Two wagon trains consisting of 300 vehicles leave Kansas City for Oregon. Along the way one of the trains gets cut off from the main convoy and heads for the California Gold Rush. Emerson Hough wrote "The Covered Wagon" for the *Saturday Evening Post* and chose as his subjects those pioneers who left their farms and the security of life east of Ohio for

James Cruze's The Covered Wagon, *a landmark epic from the silent era and one of the era's most influential pictures* (PARAMOUNT/AUTHOR'S COLLECTION)

the vagaries of the American West. However, the discovery of gold in the California hills provided these pioneers with a new and exciting lure.

Set in 1848, this landmark film from the silent era ushered in the beginning of the western epic, which marked a retreat from the overly melodramatic film and concentrated instead on the historical aspects of filmmaking. While James Cruze's 1923 film is still decidedly romantic and somewhat sentimental, it is also more authentic historically than the movies which preceded it. Moreover, its semidocumentary style and Karl Brown's excellent camera work make it a must for students and pundits of the genre.

Three months in the making, the film is estimated to have cost $800,000, a significant amount of money for that time. It was the only epic film to date not made by D. W. Griffith. The public response was enormous, and the film is single-handedly credited with revitalizing the western film. The year it was released (1923), only 50 Westerns were made. One year after its release, the number of westerns produced jumped threefold, paving the way for the two other great westerns of the silent era: John Ford's THE IRON HORSE (1924) and Henry King's THE WINNING OF BARBARA WORTH (1926).

The silent westerns are unique in that they operate so close to history; the last of the "real" cowboys and railroad builders were often hired as consultants for such films. The great cattle drives were only a decade or two in the past and remembered well by many who made movies back then. Moreover, the credits of *The Covered Wagon* are illuminating. Actor Jack Albertson, who had a small uncredited role, would go on to win a Best Supporting Actor Oscar 45 years later for the film *The Subject Was Roses* (1968); while director/writer Delmer Daves (BROKEN ARROW; 3:10 TO YUMA) began his film career as a 19-year-old prop boy for James Cruze in *The Covered Wagon*. Tim McCoy is listed as the Indian liaison. The film's editor, Dorothy Arzner, also cut another famous historical epic produced by Paramount during the 1920s, *Old Ironsides*, and later became a director herself, one of the very few women to hold this position at the time.

Director Cruze grew up in Utah, where the picture was filmed, and remembered his grandfather talking about his own travels during the period. Some critics argue over the total merit of the film, many finding it dull by today's standards. Even William S. Hart found flaw in its authenticity, most notably having its wagon master inviting an open attack by Indians in a box canyon. Nevertheless, as William K. Everson points out in his *Pictorial History of the Western Film*, Cruze's epic remains a milestone in western filmmaking, "supremely important in that by being made at all it introduced the epic tradition to the western, and gave it scale, and poetic and documentary values."

COVERED WAGON DAYS Republic, 1940, B&W, 56 min, VT. **Producer:** Harry Grey; **Director:** George Sherman; **Screenplay:** Earle Snell; **Music:** Cy Feuer; **Cinematographer:** William Nobles; **Editor:** Bernard Loftus; **Cast:** Robert Livingston, Raymond Hatton, Duncan

Renaldo, Kay Griffith, George Douglas, Ruth Robinson, Paul Marion, John Merton, Tom Chatterton, Tom London, Guy D'Ennery.

The Three Mesquiteers become involved with silver smugglers when a crooked businessman tries to force one of their uncles to sell his silver mines. (See also *THREE MESQUITEERS, THE.*)

COVERED WAGON RAID Republic, 1950, B&W, 60 min. **Producer:** Gordon Kay; **Director:** R. C. Springsteen; **Screenplay:** M. Coates Webster; **Cinematographer:** John MacBurnie; **Editor:** Harry Keller; **Cast:** Allan "Rocky" Lane, Eddie Waller, Alex Gerry, Lyn Thomas, Dick Curtis, Pierce Lyden, Sherry Jackson, Rex Lease.

COVERED WAGON TRAILS Syndicate Pictures, 1930, B&W, 51 min. **Director:** J. P. McGowan; **Screenplay:** Sally Winters; **Cinematographer:** Hap Depew; **Cast:** Bob Custer, Phyllis Bainbridge, Perry Murdock, Charles Brinley, Martin Cichy, J. P. McGowan.

Lawman "Smoke" Sanderson (Bob Custer) is trailing a gang of crooks working along the Mexican border. In the process he falls in love with one of the gang member's sisters. A good musical score keeps the action moving.

COVERED WAGON TRAILS Monogram, 1940, B&W, 52 min. **Producer:** Harry S. Webb; **Director:** Raymond K. Johnson; **Screenplay:** Tom S. Gibson; **Cinematographer:** Edward A. Kull; **Editor:** Robert Golden; **Cast:** Jack Randall, Sally Cairns, David Sharpe, Lafe McKee, Budd Buster, Glenn Strange.

A cowboy opposes corrupt cattlemen who are trying to stop settlers from farming the range. The song "Under Texas Skies" was written by Johnny Lange and Lew Porter.

COWBOY Columbia, 1958, Color, 92 min, VT. **Producer:** Julian Blaustein; **Director:** Delmer Daves; **Screenplay:** Dalton Trumbo and Edmund H. North; **Music:** George Dunning; **Cinematographer:** Charles Lawton Jr.; **Editors:** Al Clark and William A. Lyon; **Cast:** Glenn Ford, Jack Lemmon, Anna Kashfi, Brian Donlevy, Dick York, Victor Manuel Mendoza, Richard Jaeckel, King Donovan, Vaughn Taylor, Robert "Buzz" Henry, Strother Martin.

The year before he died Frank Harris published his memoirs entitled *My Reminiscences as a Cowboy*, an account of his experiences on the cattle trails in 1871. The film adaptation begins with Harris (Jack Lemmon) working as a clerk at a Chicago hotel. Soft and somewhat diffident, he meets a tough cattleman named Tom Reese (Glenn Ford). He convinces the leathery Reese to take him on the next drive, a 2,000-mile trek from Chicago to the Rio Grande. He starts out a tenderfoot, dismayed and shocked at watching a man die from a snakebite—the result of a practical joke that went wrong. En route Harris toughens up and becomes a force in his own right, dealing with a cattle stampede, an Indian attack, and a bang-up fistfight. Most important, he wins the respect of the gritty Reese. The film ends with both men taking a bath in a Chicago hotel, as they joyously shoot cockroaches off the wall.

How much of Harris's memoirs is solid truth and how much is exaggeration and distortion is open to question. What is certain is that this is a fine film with good performances. Lemmon succeeds in creating a believable cowboy, and Ford is excellent as the solid cattleman. The film marked the third time Delmer Daves helmed Ford in a western, with director and actor working together in *JUBAL* and *3:10 TO YUMA*.

COWBOY AND THE BANDIT, THE International Pictures, 1935, B&W, 57 min. **Producer:** Louis Weiss; **Director:** Albert Herman; **Screenplay:** Jack Jevne; **Cinematographer:** Arthur Reed; **Editor:** Carl Himm; **Cast:** Rex Lease, Bobby Nelson, Blanche Mehaffey, Richard Alexander, Bill Patton, Wally Wales, William Desmond.

A gang of crooks is after a pretty lady's land, but a fun-loving cowboy comes to her aid and succeeds in busting up the ornery gang of gamblers and killers.

COWBOY AND THE BLONDE, THE 20th Century Fox, ·1941, B&W, 68 min. **Producer:** Ralph Dietrich; **Director:** Ray McCarey; **Screenplay:** William Brent and William Bullock; **Music:** Cyril J. Mockridge; **Cinematographer:** Charles G. Clark; **Editor:** Harry Reynolds; **Cast:** Mary Beth Hughes, George Montgomery, Alan Mowbray, Robert Conway, Richard Lane, John Miljan, Fuzzy Knight.

Rodeo star George Montgomery tries his hand at moviemaking, but diva Mary Beth Hughes's temper tantrums and poor attitude are more than he can handle. By the final fadeout, however, she proves easy fodder for Montgomery's manly charms. The film has been called *Taming of the Shrew* country style.

COWBOY AND THE GIRL, THE See *LADY TAKES A CHANCE, THE*.

COWBOY AND THE INDIANS, THE Columbia, 1949, B&W, 68 min. **Producer:** Armond Shaefer; **Director:** John English; **Screenplay:** Dwight Cummins and Dorothy Yost; **Cinematographer:** William Bradford; **Editor:** Henry Batista; **Cast:** Gene Autry, Sheila Ryan, Frank Richards, Hank Patterson, Jay Silverheels, Claudia Drake, George Nokes, Charles S. Evens, Clayton Moore, Frank Lackteen.

An evil Indian agent is cheating the Indians into starvation. Gene Autry's job is to show that a series of Indian raids is based on sheer survival rather than malevolence toward the whites. When a young brave is blamed for the murder of a Navajo chief actually committed by the agent and his gang of thugs, Gene sets out to prove his innocence. A good story and a good script highlight this picture, which features a

quartet of songs including "Here Comes Santa Claus." (See also *TUMBLING TUMBLEWEEDS*.)

COWBOY AND THE KID, THE Universal, 1936, B&W, 68 min. **Producer:** Buck Jones; **Director:** Ray Taylor; **Screenplay:** Frances Guihan; **Cinematographer:** Allen O. Thompson; **Editor:** Bernard Loftus; **Cast:** Buck Jones, Bill Burrud, Dorothy Revier, Harry Worth, Oliver Eckhardt, Mary Mersch, Burr Caruth, Kernan Cripps, Lafe McKee.

A drifter down on his luck encounters a young boy just after the boy's father has been murdered. The two become good friends, and the drifter decides to raise the orphaned lad. Based on a story written by Buck Jones, this excellent Jones venture is replete with drama, comedy, and pathos. (See also *STONE OF SILVER CREEK*.)

COWBOY AND THE LADY, THE United Artists, 1938, B&W, 91 min. **Producer:** Samuel Goldwyn; **Director:** H. C. Potter; **Screenplay:** Sonya Levien and S. N. Behrman; **Music:** Alfred Newman and Lionel Newman; **Cinematographer:** Gregg Toland; **Editor:** Sherman Todd; **Cast:** Gary Cooper, Merle Oberon, Patsy Kelly, Walter Brennan, Fuzzy Knight, Mabel Todd, Henry Kolker, Harry Davenport.

Gary Cooper plays a lanky cowboy named "Stretch" Willoughby, who catches the attention of the snobbish and fun-loving Mary Smith (Merle Oberon). When Mary and her uncle Hanibal are picked up in a nightclub raid, her senator father, who is running for president, whisks her off to a Florida estate. Once there she decides to join her maid and cook on a blind date with three cowboys who are appearing in a local rodeo show. She is paired with Cooper and wins him over with a phony story that she is supporting four sisters and a drunken father. Soon they are in love. Nominated for three Academy Awards, this snappy little comedy makes

Gary Cooper and Merle Oberon in The Cowboy and the Lady (UNITED ARTISTS/AUTHOR'S COLLECTION)

good use of Cooper's astonishing screen personality: the nice fellow who remains whimsical until he is made fun of, then proves his courage.

COWBOY AND THE PRIZEFIGHTER, THE
Eagle-Lion, 1949, Color, 59 min. **Producer:** Jerry Thomas; **Director:** Lewis D. Collins; **Screenplay:** Fred Harman and Thomas; **Music:** Raoul Kraushaar; **Cinematographer:** Gilbert Warrenton; **Editor:** Frank Baldridge and Joseph Gluck; **Cast:** Jim Bannon, Don Haggerty, Don Key Reynolds, Emmett Lynn, Marin Sais, John Hart, Karen Randle, Lou Nova.

This is the fourth and last of the "Red Ryder" series distributed by Eagle-Lion, filmed in Cinecolor, with Jim Bannon in the title role. Red teams with Steve Stevenson (Don Haggerty) to prevent the takeover of Ryder's ranch, foiling a fixed fight between Steve, who had been a boxer in college, and the bad man's hired pugilist (Lou Nova, who lost a heavyweight championship fight against Joe Louis in 1941). (See also *ADVENTURES OF RED RYDER, THE*.)

COWBOY AND THE SENORITA, THE
Republic, 1944, B&W, 52 min, VT. **Producer:** Harry Grey; **Director:** Joseph Kane; **Screenplay:** Gordon Kahn; **Music:** Phil Ohman, Walter Scharf, and Ned Washington; **Cinematographer:** Reggie Lanning; **Editor:** Tony Martinelli; **Cast:** Roy Rogers, Mary Lee, Dale Evans, John Hubbard, Guinn "Big Boy" Williams, Fuzzy Knight, Wally Wales, Bob Nolan and the Sons of the Pioneers.

This feature marks the first of the 27 films Dale Evans made with Roy Rogers. Dale plays a headstrong young woman who tries to save her 17-year-old cousin from having her gold mine taken over by a greedy town boss (John Hubbard). Roy and pal Guinn "Big Boy" Williams play two cowpokes who go to work for the young women but then are accused of kidnapping her. Songs include "She Wore a Yellow Ribbon," "Bunk House Bugle Boy," and "Enchilada Man."

With diminished action and a reliance on music and big production numbers, Roy Rogers's ventures came to be regarded as mere musicals by critics. William Everson wrote that the costumes employed by Roy, Dale, and the Sons of the Pioneers were "more reminiscent of uniforms or Broadway chorus line costumes than of authentic Western regalia." Later in the decade the trend started to change again, and the emphasis of Roy's films moved away from music and toward action and bloodshed. (See also *UNDER WESTERN STARS*.)

COWBOY CANTEEN
Columbia, 1944, B&W, 72 min. **Producer:** Jack Fier; **Director:** Lew Landers; **Screenplay:** Felix Adler and Paul Gangelin; **Music:** Irving Bibo (songs); **Cinematographer:** George Meehan; **Editor:** Aaron Stell; **Cast:** Charles Starrett, Jane Frazee, Barbara Jo Allen, Roy Acuff and his Smokey Mountain Boys and Girls, Dick Curtis, Jeff Donnell, Edythe Elliott, Dub Taylor, Max Terhune, The Mills Bothers, Jimmy Wakely and his Saddle Pals.

A ranch owner enlists in the army and finds his newly hired hands are all female, so the service sends him back home to help establish a cowboy canteen. This cute little wartime western musical is in tune with the patriotism of its day.

COWBOY CAVALIER
Monogram, 1948, B&W, 57 min. **Producer:** Louis Gray; **Director:** Derwin Abrahams; **Screenplay:** J. Benton Cheney and Ronald Davidson; **Editor:** Carl Pierson; **Cast:** Jimmy Wakely, Dub Taylor, Louis Armstrong, Jan Bryant, Steve Clark, Douglas Evans, Milburn Morante, Bud Osborne, Carol Henry.

COWBOY COMMANDOS
Monogram, 1943, B&W, 55 min. **Producer:** George W. Weeks; **Director:** S. Roy Luby; **Screenplay:** Elizabeth Beecher; **Cinematographer:** Edward A. Kull; **Editor:** Roy Claire; **Cast:** Ray Corrigan, Dennis Moore, Max Terhune, Evelyn Finley, Johnny Bond, Budd Buster, John Merton.

The westerns go wartime as the Range Busters uncover a band of Nazis who are attempting to sabotage the production of a magnesium mine. Johnny Bond sings "I'll Shoot (Get) the Führer, Sure as Shootin'." This good Range Busters series entry features Ray Corrigan, Dennis Moore, and Max Terhune as appealing heroes. (See also *RANGE BUSTERS, THE*.)

COWBOY COUNSELLOR
Allied Pictures, 1932, B&W, 62 min. **Producer:** M. H. Hoffman Jr.; **Director:** George Melford; **Screenplay:** Jack Natteford; **Cinematographer:** Tom Galligan, Benjamin H. Kline, and Harry Neumann; **Editor:** Mildred Johnson; **Cast:** Hoot Gibson, Sheila Bromley, Jack Rutherford, Skeeter Bill Robbins, Al Bridge, Fred Gilman, Bobby Nelson.

A con man poses as a lawyer to sell copies of a phony law book, but things start getting hot when he has to defend a young fellow falsely accused of robbery.

COWBOY FROM BROOKLYN (aka: ROMANCE AND RHYTHM, UK)
Warner Bros., 1938, B&W, 77 min. **Producers:** Lou Edelman and Hal B. Wallis; **Director:** Lloyd Bacon; **Screenplay:** Earl Baldwin; **Music:** Johnny Mercer, Harry Warren, and Richard A. Whiting; **Cinematographer:** Arthur Edeson; **Editor:** James Gibbon; **Cast:** Dick Powell, Pat O'Brien, Priscilla Lane, Dick Foran, Ann Sheridan, Johnnie Davis, Ronald Reagan, Emma Dunn, Jeffrey Lynn.

Dick Powell plays Elly Jordan, an actor who can only get a radio job if he proves he is an authentic cowboy. A singer from Flatbush, Jordan is sponsored as a crooning cowboy by a couple of fast-talking smoothies played by Pat O'Brien and Ronald Reagan. Reagan received seventh billing in the film and was paired with Ann Sheridan as the film's secondary love interest. Four years later Reagan and Sheridan would be paired again in Sam Wood's *Kings Row*, arguably Reagan's finest film effort. Legendary composers Harry Warren,

Richard Whiting, and Johnny Mercer provide a number of songs, including "I've Got a Heartful of Music," "I'll Dream Tonight," and "Ride Tenderfoot Ride." Based on the play *Howdy Stranger* by Louis Pelletier and Robert Sloane, the film was later remade as *Two Guys from Texas*. Clayton Moore appears in the credits as Jack Moore.

COWBOY FROM LONESOME RIVER Columbia, 1944, B&W, 55 min. **Producer:** Jack Fier; **Director:** Benjamin Kline; **Screenplay:** Luci Ward; **Cinematographer:** Dave Ragin; **Editor:** Aaron Stell; **Cast:** Charles Starrett, Vi Athens, Dub Taylor, Jimmy Wakley, Kenneth MacDonald, Ozie Waters.

COWBOY FROM SUNDOWN Monogram, 1940, B&W, 57 min. **Producer:** Edward Finney; **Director:** Spencer Gordon Bennett; **Screenplay:** Robert Emmett Tansey and Roland Lynch; **Music:** Frank Harford, Johnny Lange, Tex Ritter (songs), and Frank Sanucci; **Cinematographer:** Marcel Le Picard; **Editor:** Russell Schoengarth; **Cast:** Tex Ritter, Pauline Haddon, Chick Hannon, Roscoe Ates, Carlton Young, George Pembroke, Dave O'Brien, Patsy Moran, Tristram Coffin, Slim Andrews, Bud Osborne, Glenn Strange.

When a sheriff is forced to quarantine a cattle area due to hoof and mouth disease, anger is aroused in ranchers who have to get their herds to market or lose their ranches to a local banker who holds their mortgages. With this film, star Tex Ritter helped build a new Monogram image for westerns. He looked like an authentic cowboy, he could handle fights, he was excellent in action scenes, and he could sing. (See also *SONG OF THE GRINGO*.)

COWBOY HOLIDAY Beacon, 1934, B&W, 56 min. **Producers:** Arthur Alexander and Max Alexander; **Director:** Robert F. Hill; **Screenplay:** Rock Hawley (Robert F. Hill); **Music:** Sam Perry; **Cinematographer:** Gilbert Warrenton; **Editor:** Holbrook N. Todd; **Cast:** Guinn "Big Boy" Williams, Janet Chandler, Julio Rivero, Richard Alexander, John Elliott, Alma Chester.

A cowboy tries to help his lawman pal who will lose his job if he doesn't bring in a bandit known as the Juarez Kid. There are a few laughs here but little else.

COWBOY IN MANHATTAN Universal, 1943, B&W, 56 min. **Producer:** Paul Malvern; **Director:** Frank Woodruff; **Screenplay:** Maxwell Shane, William C. Thomas, and Warren Wilson; **Music:** Everett Carter and Milton Rosen (songs), and Hans J. Salter; **Cinematographer:** Elwood Bredell; **Editor:** Fred R. Feitshans Jr.; **Cast:** Frances Langford, Robert Paige, Leon Errol, Walter Catlett, Joe Sawyer, Jennifer Holt.

In order to win over Broadway star Babs Lee (Frances Langford), struggling cowboy Bob Allen (Robert Paige) poses as a millionaire cowboy. This is a remake of the 1937 film *You're a Sweetheart*.

COWBOY IN THE CLOUDS Columbia, 1943, B&W, 54 min. **Director:** Benjamin H. Kline; **Screenplay:** Elizabeth Beecher; **Cinematographer:** George Meehan; **Editor:** Aaron Stell; **Cast:** Charles Starrett, Dub Taylor, Julie Duncan, Jimmy Wakely, Davison Clark, Hal Taliaferro, Dick Curtis, Ed Cassidy, Paul Conrad.

A cowboy joins the Civil Air Patrol to serve his country and combat its enemies. Musical help from Jimmy Wakley and his backup group plus some fine comedy by Dub Taylor make this film one of the better Starrett efforts. (See also *GALLANT DEFENDER*.)

COWBOY MILLIONAIRE 20th Century Fox, 1935, B&W, 65 min. **Producer:** Sol Lesser; **Director:** Edward F. Cline; **Screenplay:** Daniel Jarrett and George Waggner; **Music:** Abe Meyer; **Cinematographer:** Frank B. Good; **Editor:** W. Donn Hayes; **Cast:** George O'Brien, Evalyn Bostock, Edgar Kennedy, Maude Allen, Alden "Stephen" Chase, Daniel Jarrett, Lloyd Ingraham, Dean Benton, Thomas Curran.

George O'Brien is a cowboy who falls in love with an aristocratic young lady from England who is vacationing at a dude ranch. After many a misunderstanding they finally get together. O'Brien excels in this tender and romantic western, which is a must for his fans.

COWBOY ROUNDUP See *RIDE 'EM COWBOY*.

COWBOYS, THE Warner Bros., 1972, Color, 128 min, VT, DVD. **Producer:** Mark Rydell; **Director:** Rydell; **Screenplay:** Irving Ravetch, Harriet Frank Jr., and William Dale Jennings; **Music:** John Williams; **Cinematographer:** Robert Surtees; **Editors:** Robert Swink and Neil Travis; **Cast:** John Wayne, Roscoe Lee Browne, Bruce Dern, Colleen Dewhurst, Alfred Barker Jr., Slim Pickens, Steve Benedict, Robert Carradine, Norman Howell Jr., A Martinez, Sean Kelly, Clay O'Brien, Sam O'Brien, Jerry Gatlin, Richard Farnsworth.

John Wayne gives one of his best performances as Wil Anderson, an aging rancher who trains and relies on a group of 11 youngsters to help him on a huge cattle drive, taking 1,200 head of cattle from his Double-O Ranch to the railroad 400 miles away. Once the trail drive starts, the boys slowly become men under Wil's fatherly guidance. Rustler Bruce Dern and his gang fight with Wayne, and eventually Dern shoots him dead. The foul deed prompts the boys to seek revenge, and a plan to retaliate is established under the leadership of Roscoe Lee Browne, the urbane African-American wagon-train cook who previously had exchanged some pithy comments with Wayne and the kids.

Youngsters learn the ropes from aging rancher Wil Anderson in The Cowboys. (WARNER BROS./AUTHOR'S COLLECTION)

Bruce Dern is excellent as Asa Watts, the psychotic "Long Hair," who has the dubious distinction of killing Wayne in the film—the first time the Duke died on-screen since *Wake of the Red Witch* in 1948. Wayne is tough and gritty as ever, having told Dern, "I'm 30 years older than you are. I've had my back busted once, my hip twice, and on my worst day I could beat the hell out of you." Dern reportedly received some death threats for the foul deed.

The violent ending where the boys dispatch the villains met with controversy. Leonard Maltin for one has faulted the film for positively depicting "violent revenge" and called the film itself "disappointing." But most reviews were far more positive. Arthur B. Clarke in *Films in Review* wrote that "*The Cowboys* is the kind of folk story you want to believe; hence indictments of it for not being realistic are irrelevant and/or tendentious."

Rex Reed was impressed and wrote in the *New York Daily News* that " . . . in *The Cowboys* all the forces that have made [John Wayne] a dominant personality as well as a major screen presence seem to combine in an unusual way,

Bruce Dern and Roscoe Lee Browne. Dern would long be remembered as the villain who killed John Wayne in The Cowboys. (WARNER BROS./AUTHOR'S COLLECTION)

providing him with the best role of his career. Old Dusty britches can really act. . . ." Similarly, Arthur Knight wrote in *The Saturday Review* that " . . . while the sight of a dozen or so kids wiping out a band of rustlers has its sanguinary aspects, it is a model of restraint compared to the wholesale slaughter in Kurosawa's *The Seven Samurai*, long considered a classic. . . ."

Wayne thoroughly enjoyed working with the young cast and the director. Yet things were not entirely cut and dry, and he ran into some differences with Mark Rydell concerning the ending. According to Luster Bayless, Wayne's friend and wardrobe man, while Wayne liked Rydell and respected his work, the two had a different opinion on how the story should end: "Duke didn't believe the boys should take the law into their own hands. He thought they should lasso Dern and bring him in. He didn't think there should be all that violence. Duke left an option. Since he didn't believe he should die in the end when he was shot in the back, he made a bit of a movement in the final scene just in case they decided he shouldn't die. He left them an option, but Rydell did it his way."

Blending comedy, tragedy, and the ambience of the Old West, *The Cowboys* opened at Radio City Music Hall and eventually grossed over $4 million domestically. The film is bolstered by a stirring musical overture written and conducted by John Williams. A teleseries based upon the film had a brief run on ABC-TV in 1974.

COWBOY SERENADE (aka: SERENADE OF THE WEST, UK) Republic, 1942, B&W, 66 min. **Producer:** Harry Grey; **Director:** William Morgan; **Screenplay:** Olive Cooper; **Music:** Raoul Kraushaar; **Cinematographer:** Jack A. Marta; **Editor:** Lester Orlebeck; **Cast:** Gene Autry, Smiley Burnette, Fay McKenzie, Cecil Cunningham, Rand Brooks, Addison Richards, Tristram Coffin, Slim Andrews, Hank Worden.

COWBOYS FROM TEXAS, THE Republic, 1939, B&W, 57 min. **Producer:** Harry Gray; **Director:** George Sherman; **Screenplay:** Oliver Drake; **Cinematographer:** Ernest Miller; **Editor:** Tony Martinelli; **Cast:** Robert Livingston, Raymond Hatton, Duncan Renaldo, Carole Landis, Ivan Miller, Charles Middleton, Betty Compson, Ethan Laidlaw, Yakima Canutt.

Cattle ranchers and homesteaders are at war over the open range, so the Three Mesquiteers try to bring the matter to a peaceful solution. Future leading lady Carole Landis is one of a few select young actresses to appear in a "Three Mesquiteers" feature and later make her mark in A-level movies. (See also *THREE MESQUITEERS, THE*.)

COWBOY STAR Columbia, 1936, B&W, 56 min. **Producer:** Harry L. Decker; **Director:** David Selman; **Screenplay:** Frances Guihan; **Music:** Howard Jackson, Raffaello Penso, and Louis Silvers; **Cinematographer:** Allen G.

Siegler; **Editor:** William A. Lyon; **Cast:** Charles Starrett, Iris Meredith, Si Jenks, Marc Lawrence, Edward Peil Sr., Wally Albright, Ralph McCullough, Richard Terry, Landers Stevens, George Chesebro.

Tired of being a cowboy movie star, Spencer Yorke (Charles Starrett) quits the film business and buys a ranch so that he can be a real cowboy. But like it is with his movies, he soon finds out that trouble on the ranch is not far behind. (See also *GALLANT DEFENDER*.)

COW COUNTRY Monogram/Allied Artists, 1953, B&W, 82 min. **Producer:** Scott R. Dunlap; **Director:** Leslie Selander; **Screenplay:** Adele Buffington; **Music:** Edward J. Kay; **Cinematographer:** Harry Neumann; **Editor:** John C. Fuller; **Cast:** Edmond O'Brien, Helen Westcott, Robert Lowery, Barton MacLane, Peggie Castle, Robert Barrat, James Millican, Don Beddoe, Robert J. Wilke, Raymond Hatton, Tom Tyler, Chuck Courtney.

In the Texas Panhandle during the 1880s, ranchers attempt to keep their spreads despite depression and drought. The debt-ridden ranchers show grit and determination in overcoming numerous obstacles. Well made and well acted, this lesser-known film is worth watching.

COW TOWN Columbia, 1950, B&W, 70 min. **Producer:** Armond Schaefer; **Director:** John English; **Screenplay:** Gerald Geraghty; **Cinematographer:** William Bradford; **Editor:** Henry Batista; **Cast:** Gene Autry, Gail Davis, Harry Shannon, Jock Mahoney, Clark "Buddy" Burroughs, Harry Harvey, Steve Darrell, Chuck Roberson, House Peters Jr.

Gene Autry responds to cattle rustling by stringing barbed wire all around the range. However, he soon finds himself disliked by a pretty female rancher and in the middle of a huge range war. This action-packed Autry entry for Columbia is sprinkled with such songs as "Down in the Valley," and "Powder Your Face With Sunshine." (See also *TUMBLING TUMBLEWEEDS*.)

COYOTE TRAILS Reliable, 1935, B&W, 60 min. **Producer:** Bernard B. Ray; **Director:** Ray; **Screenplay:** Rose Gordon and Carl Krusada; **Cinematographer:** J. Henry Kruse; **Editor:** Frederick Bain; **Cast:** Tom Tyler, Ben Corbett, Alice Dahl, Lafe McKee, Richard Alexander, Slim Whitaker, George Chesebro.

Tom Tyler and sidekick Ben Corbett attempt to capture a stallion, which they believe has been falsely accused of rustling a rancher's horses. (See also *MYSTERY RANCH*.)

CRASHING BROADWAY Monogram, 1933, B&W, 55 min. **Producer:** Paul Malvern; **Director:** John P. McCarthy; **Screenplay:** Wellyn Totman; **Cast:** Rex Bell, Doris Hill, Harry Bowen, George "Gabby" Hayes, Charles King, Henry Roquemore, Ann Howard, Blackie Whiteford, Perry Murdock.

Heading east for the first time, cowpoke Tad Wallace (Rex Bell) runs into trouble with big-city hoodlums when his act flops on Broadway.

CRASHING THRU Grand National, 1939, B&W, 65 min. **Producer:** Philip N. Krasne; **Director:** Elmer Clifton; **Screenplay:** Sherman Lowe; **Music:** Jack Brooks (songs) and Jules Loman (lyricist); **Cinematographer:** Edward Linden; **Editor:** S. Roy Luby; **Cast:** James Newill, Warren Hull, Jean Carmen, Dave O'Brien, Milburn Stone, Walter Byron, Stanley Blystone, Robert Frazer.

Six people, including a brother and sister, are in on a gold robbery. Three of them double-cross the others. Mountie Renfrew (James Newell) goes after them alone when his partner Kelly (Warren Hull) is wounded. This is the final entry in the "Renfrew of the Mounted" series for Grand National. Newill was one of the many would-be Gene Autry successors who tried to capitalize on Autry's popularity in the late 1930s.

CRASHING THRU Monogram, 1949, B&W, 57 min. **Producer:** Barney A. Sarecky; **Director:** Ray Taylor; **Screenplay:** Adele S. Buffington; **Music:** Edward J. Kay; **Cinematographer:** Harry Neumann; **Editor:** John C. Fuller; **Cast:** Whip Wilson, Andy Clyde, Christine Larsen, Tristram Coffin, Steve Darrell, George J. Lewis, Jan Bryant, Kenne Duncan.

When a Ranger is killed during a stage holdup, an undercover Wells Fargo agent assumes his identity and sets out to capture the gang that is responsible for the killing in Whip Wilson's first Monogram series entry.

CRIME'S HIGHWAY See DESERT JUSTICE.

CRIMSON TRAIL, THE Universal, 1935, B&W, 56 min. **Director:** Al Rabock; **Screenplay:** Jack Natteford; **Cast:** Buck Jones, Polly Ann Young, Carl Stockdale, Charles K. French, Ward Bond, Robert Kortman, Bud Osborne, Paul Fix.

Two rival ranchers are running against each other in an election. When one of them is killed, his nephew searches for the culprits but falls in love with the other man's daughter. Buck Jones was signed by Universal to follow Tom Mix as its main series star. One of the exceptional early Jones entries for the studio, *The Crimson Trail* combined good scripts with top action content. (See also STONE OF SILVER CREEK.)

CRIPPLE CREEK Columbia, 1952, Color, 78 min. **Producer:** Edward Small; **Director:** Ray Nazzaro; **Screenplay:** Richard Schaver; **Music:** Mischa Bakaleinikoff; **Cinematographer:** William V. Skall; **Editor:** Richard Fantl; **Cast:** George Montgomery, Karin Booth, Jerome Courtland, William Bishop, Richard Egan, Don Porter, John Dehner.

George Montgomery, Jerome Courtland, and Richard Egan are undercover agents in the Old West trying to break a gold-smuggling ring working out of the town of Cripple Creek. This solid western has some interesting plot twists and a cast of familiar faces.

CRIPPLE CREEK BARROOM Edison Company, 1898, B&W, 25'.

This pre-1900 effort is a brief tabloid showing tophatted dandies lounging in a tough western bar presided over by an apparently Indian female barkeeper. While there is no plot per se, this short vignette, running less than 10 seconds, is usually regarded as the first western in the sense that it depicts a western scene.

CROOKED RIVER (aka: THE LAST BULLET) Lippert, 1950, B&W, 85 min. **Producer:** Robert L. Lippert; **Director:** Thomas Carr; **Screenplay:** Ron Ormond and Maurice Tombragel; **Music:** Walter Greene; **Cinematographer:** Ernest Miller; **Editor:** Hugh Winn; **Cast:** James Ellison, Julie Adams, Russell Hayden, John L. Cason, Russell Hatton, Fuzzy Knight, Tom Tyler, Dennis Moore.

This last James Ellison/Russell Hayden series effort from Lippert is laden with stock footage from an old Bob Steele film. Its good cast does not compensate for the weak production. The title was changed to *The Last Bullet* when it aired on television.

CROOKED TRAIL, THE Supreme, 1936, B&W, 1936. **Producer:** A. W. Hackel; **Director:** S. Roy Luby; **Screenplay:** George Plympton; **Cinematographer:** Jack Greenhalgh; **Editor:** Roy Claire; **Cast:** Johnny Mack Brown, Lucille Browne, John Merton, Charles King, Ted Adams, John Van Pelt, Ed Cassidy, Horace Murphy.

A man is saved by two others from thirst in the desert. When he later becomes sheriff, he refuses to believe that one of his rescuers is a thief who has reverted to his old outlaw ways. (See also GAMBLING TERROR, THE.)

CROSSED TRAILS Monogram, 1948, B&W, 53 min. **Producer:** Louis Gray; **Director:** Lambert Hillyer; **Screenplay:** Adele Buffington (as Colt Remington); **Cinematographer:** Harry Nuemann; **Editor:** Fred Maguire; **Cast:** Johnny Mack Browne, Lynne Carver, Raymond Hatton, Douglas Evans, Steve Clark, Bud Osborne, Ted Adams, Henry Hall.

CROSSFIRE RKO, 1933, B&W, 55 min. **Producer:** David O. Selznick; **Director:** Otto Brower; **Screenplay:** Tom McNamara; **Cinematographer:** Nicholas Musuraca; **Editor:** Frederic Knudtson; **Cast:** Tom Keene, Betty Furness, Edgar Kennedy, Eddie Phillips, Lafe McKee, Nick Cogley, Jules Cowles, Tom Brown.

A soldier returns west after serving in World War I and finds gangsters working the range. This picture was Tom Keene's final film for RKO and based on a story by Harold Shumate. (See also *BEYOND THE ROCKIES*.)

CROSSFIRE TRAIL Turner Network Television, 2001, Color, 92 minutes, VHS, DVD. **Producers:** Michael Brandman, Steven J. Brandman, Thomas John Kane, Tom Selleck (executive producer), Simon Wincer (coexecutive producer); **Director:** Wincer; **Teleplay:** Charles Robert Carner; **Music:** Eric Colvin; **Cinematographer:** David Eggby; **Editor:** Terry Blyth; **Cast:** Tom Selleck, Virginia Madsen, Wilfred Brimley, David O'Hara, Christian Kane, Barry Corbin, Mark Harmon.

Tom Selleck is Rafe Covington, a sea- and land-going drifter who promises a dying friend that he will look after his Wyoming ranch and his friend's widow, Anne Rodney (Virginia Madsen). For Covington, a man is only as good as his word, and he is determined to keep his promise no matter what obstacles he might encounter. He acknowledges that his whole life "never had roots deeper than top soil"; yet behind the strong no-nonsense demeanor, there is a man of obvious breeding—a rather uncommon drifter with a penchant for Beethoven's "Moonlight Sonata" and an appreciation of the classical poetic word.

To compound matters, the widow Rodney has some early doubts as to Rafe's intentions. Moreover, she is tied closely to an unscrupulous land grabber, Bruce Barkow, played superbly against type by Mark Harmon. The plot unfolds briskly. The absorbing story benefits from crisp, economical dialogue and escalating drama as Rafe and Anne are drawn closer together. The battle lines are drawn between Rafe and the duplicitous Barkow and evolve to a full-scale rage, culminating in an exciting and well-crafted shoot-out—a fight to the finish.

Crossfire Trail is based on a book by Louis L'Amour, and is a prime example of how good westerns can be made when all the necessary ingredients are integrated intelligently. Selleck delivers a fine performance and wears his Western spurs like a real pro. The film also reteams the actor with Simon Wincer, who directed *Quigley Down Under* and helmed the award-winning *Lonesome Dove*. Moreover, audiences loved it. *Crossfire Trail* made a big splash in the ratings. The film produced the highest ratings for an original movie ever shown on cable. According to the Turner network, the film drew a 9.6 cable rating, representing 7.3 million homes.

CRY BLOOD, APACHE Golden Eagle, 1970, Color, 82 min, VT. **Producer:** Jody McCrea and Harold Roberts; **Director:** Jack Starrett; **Screenplay:** Sean MacGregor; **Music:** Elliott Kaplan; **Cinematographer:** Bruce Scott; **Cast:** Andy Anza, Marie Gahva, Don Henley, Carol Kemp, Don Kemp, Jody McCrea, Joel McCrea.

A gang of sadistic cowboys let nothing stand in their way in their search for gold. Only an appearance by Joel McCrea, father of producer/actor Jody McCrea, saves this anemic western from being a total bomb.

CRY FOR ME, BILLY See *FACE TO THE WIND*.

CULPEPPER CATTLE COMPANY, THE 20th Century Fox, 1972, Color, 92 min, VT. **Producer:** Paul Helmick; **Director:** Dick Richards; **Screenplay:** Eric Bercovici and Gregory Prentiss; **Music:** Tom Scott; **Cinematographer:** Lawrence Edward Williams and Ralph Woolsey; **Editor:** John F. Burnett; **Cast:** Gary Grimes, Billy Green Bush, Luke Askew, Bo Hopkins, Geoffrey Lewis, Wayne Sutherlin, John McLiam, Matt Clark, Raymond Guth, Royal Dano, Jerry Gatlin.

A teenage boy becomes part of a cattle drive to Colorado and learns how unromantic and grim the real West can be. Frank Culpepper (Billy Green Bush) is a hard-nosed range boss who hires teenager Grimes and watches as he matures during the hard, bloody, and violent drive.

Reviews were mixed. Charles Champlin of the *Los Angeles Times* called the picture "a considerably better-than-average western with a real feeling for place, and time." However, *Time* dismissed it as "episodic and rather punchy," while *Variety* called it "an unsuccessful attempt to mount a poetic and stylistic ballet of death in the environment of a period western."

The film marked the directorial debut of Dick Richards—previously a still photographer and TV commercial director—who had spent more than three years researching the American West.

CURSE OF THE UNDEAD (aka: MARK OF THE WEST) Universal, 1959, B&W, 79 min, VT. **Producer:** John Gershenson; **Director:** Edward Dein; **Screenplay:** Dein and Mildred Dein; **Music:** Irving Gertz; **Cinematographer:** Ellis W. Carter; **Editor:** George A. Gittens; **Cast:** Eric Fleming, Michael Pate, Kathleen Crowley, John Hoyt, Bruce Gordon.

A mysterious gunslinger for hire is really a vampire. As young women in a small western town are dying one by one, it is up to Preacher Dan (Eric Fleming) to save the town and his girlfriend (Kathleen Crowley). Perhaps the first vampire western, this is a genre piece with a twist.

CURTAIN CALL AT CACTUS CREEK (aka: TAKE THE STAGE, UK) Universal, 1950, Color, 86 min. **Producer:** Robert Arthur; **Director:** Charles Lamont; **Screenplay:** Oscar Brodney and Howard Dimsdale; **Music:** Walter Scharf; **Cinematographer:** Russell Metty; **Editor:** Frank Gross; **Cast:** Donald O'Connor, Gale Storm, Walter Brennan, Vincent Price, Eve Arden, Chick Chandler, Joe Sawyer, Rex Lease, I. Stanford Jolley, Hank Worden.

A traveling entertainer (Donald O'Connor) gets mixed up with bank robbers in the Old West. Veteran genre players Rex Lease, I. Stanford Jolley, and Hank Worden add to the plot, and the outstanding cast provides an ample amount of good-natured laughs. A superb song-and-dance man, O'Connor proves he can entertain in any venue. Two years later he would achieve enduring fame in the film favorite, *Singing in the Rain.*

CUSTER MASSACRE, THE   See *GREAT SIOUX MASSACRE, THE.*

CUSTER OF THE WEST (aka: GOOD DAY FOR FIGHTING) Cinerama Security, 1967, Color, 143 min, VT, DVD. **Producer:** Philip Yordan; **Director:** Robert Siodmak; **Screenplay:** Benard Gordon and Julian Halevy; **Music:** Bernado Segall; **Cinematographer:** Cecilio Paniagua; **Editors:** Peter Parasheles and Maurice Rootes; **Cast:** Robert Shaw, Mary Ure, Ty Hardin, Jeffrey Hunter, Robert Ryan, Lawrence Tierney, Kieron Moore, Marc Lawrence.

Filmed in Spain, Robert Siodmak's *Custer of the West* presents Custer's contribution to military history in a manner compatible with the revisionist views of the 1960s. The flamboyant Civil War hero was given command of the Seventh Cavalry in the West, then was forced to deal with warring Indians and army rivals. He tells the Cheyenne, "Right or wrong, for better or worse, that's the way things get done. That's history. I'm talking about history. You are paying the price for being backward."

Few episodes of the American West have been more subject to controversy than the career of General George Armstrong Custer and his demise at the hands of the Cheyenne at the Battle of Little Big Horn. Robert Siodmak took over the direction of this 1967 biography after both Akira Kurosawa and Fred Zinnemann reportedly withdrew from the project. He presents Custer as neither a brave hero nor a self-serving incompetent blunderer, but rather as a complex man at odds with the changing tide of history.

In the United States this film was a financial and critical bust, although in Europe it made an acceptable—if not a large—commercial showing. Custer is efficiently portrayed by actor Robert Shaw, and there is a forceful cameo by Robert Ryan as a gold-hungry soldier who deserts the army. The film was shown originally in wide-screen Cinerama then later released in conventional screen projection size by MGM.

CUSTER'S LAST FIGHT Bison, 1912, B&W, 55 min. **Director:** Thomas Ince and Francis Ford; **Screenplay:** Richard V. Spencer; **Cast:** Francis Ford, Anna Little, Grace Cunard, William Eagleshirt, J. Barney Sherry.

This early Thomas Ince silent production is considered one of the first very good westerns. Depicting the final showdown between Custer and Sitting Bull, it was originally a three-reeler that was expanded to feature length when it was reissued in 1925. Actor Francis Ford was the older brother of famed director John Ford.

CUSTER'S LAST STAND Weiss Productions/Stage & Screen, 1936, B&W, 65 (91) min. **Producer:** Louis Weiss; **Director:** Elmer Clifton; **Screenplay:** George A. Durlam, Eddy Graneman, and Bob Lively; **Cast:** Rex Lease, Jack Mulhall, Ruth Mix, Dorothy Gulliver, William Farnum, Lona Andre, Reed Howes, Bobby Nelson, Budd Buster, Iron Eyes Cody, George Chesebro, Helen Gibson, Alan Greer, Franklin Farnum, William Farnum.

A scout for General Custer tries to aid settlers who are being attacked by a renegade Indian. The talented veteran cast is the best thing this generally dull film has to offer. George Chesebro does particularly well as a dishonest soldier who turns good. This feature version was originally a 15-chapter serial, and consequently it offers lots of stock footage.

CYCLONE FURY Columbia, 1951, B&W, 53 min. **Producer:** Colbert Clark; **Director:** Ray Nazarro; **Screenplay:** Edward Earl Repp and Barry Shipman; **Cinematographer:** Harry Freulich; **Editor:** Paul Borofsky; **Cast:** Charles Starrett, Smiley Burnette, Fred F. Sears, Clayton Moore, Robert J. Wilke, George Chesebro, Louis Lettieri, Merle Travis & His Bronco Busters.

When a rancher is murdered, an agent who is sent by the government to ensure the delivery of a herd of horses becomes suspicious. (See also *DURANGO KID, THE.*)

CYCLONE KID Big 4, 1931, B&W, 60 min. **Producer:** Burton L. King; **Director:** J. P. McGowan; **Screenplay:** George Morgan; **Editor:** Frederick Bain; **Cast:** Buzz Barton, Ralph Bushman, Caryl Lincoln, Lafe McKee, Ted Adams, Blackie Whiteford, Silver Harr.

A ranch foreman who is in love with his boss's daughter is aided by a young boy when opposing a band of outlaws.

CYCLONE KID, THE Republic, 1942, B&W, 56 min. **Producer:** George Sherman (associate); **Director:** Sherman; **Screenplay:** Richard Murphy; **Cinematographer:** Bud Thackery; **Editor:** Edward Schroeder; **Cast:** Don "Red" Barry, John James, Lynn Merrick, Alex Callam, Joel Friedkin, Slim Andrews, Rex Lease.

A gunman changes his tune and turns against his crooked cattle boss when his lawyer brother comes out west. After his association with the "Red Ryder" serial, Don "Red" Barry starred in a number of films as other characters such as the Cyclone Kid and the Tulsa Kid. (See also *ADVENTURES OF RED RYDER, THE; WYOMING OUTLAW.*)

CYCLONE OF THE SADDLE Argosy, 1935, B&W, 53 min. **Producer:** Lewis Weiss; **Director:** Elmer Clifton; **Screenplay:** Clifton and George M. Merrick; **Cinematographer:** Edward Linden; **Cast:** Rex Lease, Janet Chandler, Bobby Nelson, William Desmond, Yakima Canutt, Art Mix, Chief Thundercloud, George Chesebro.

The army assigns an officer to intercede when an outlaw gang causes trouble with settlers and Indians.

CYCLONE ON HORSEBACK RKO, 1941, B&W. **Producer:** Bert Gilroy; **Director:** Edward Killy; **Screenplay:** Norton S. Parker; **Music:** Fred Rose and Ray Whitley; **Cast:** Tim Holt, Marjorie Reynolds, Ray Whitley, Lee "Lasses" White, Harry Worth, Dennis Moore, Eddie Dew.

Three cowpokes come to the aid of a pretty girl and her brother, who are attempting to string a telegraph wire but are thwarted by a band of hoodlums. Tim Holt is the appealing hero in this well-paced, action-packed western with an exciting finale. (See also *ALONG THE RIO GRANDE*.)

CYCLONE PRAIRIE RANGERS Columbia, 1944, B&W, 55 min. **Producer:** Jack Fier; **Director:** Benjamin H. Kline; **Screenplay:** Elizabeth Beecher; **Cinematographer:** Fayte M. Browne; **Editor:** Aaron Stell; **Cast:** Charles Starrett, Dub Taylor, Constance Worth, Jimmy Wakely, Ray Bennett, Edmund Cobb, I. Stanford Jolley.

Saboteurs are out to destroy a rancher's food crop during World War II. This wartime plot serves up plenty of action. (See also *DURANGO KID, THE*.)

CYCLONE RANGER Spectrum, 1935, B&W, 60 min. **Producer:** Ray Kirkwood; **Director:** Robert F. Hill; **Screenplay:** Oliver Drake; **Cinematographer:** Donald Biddle Keyes; **Cast:** Bill Cody, Nina Quartero, Eddie Gribbon, Soledad Jimenez, Earl Hodgins, Zarah Tazil, Donald Reed, Colin Chase.

An outlaw is befriended by a blind woman and pretends to be her son, who was killed by a posse.

D

DAKOTA Republic, 1945, B&W, 82 min, VT. **Producer:** Herbert Yates; **Director:** Joseph Kane; **Screenplay:** Lawrence Hazard; **Music:** Walter Scharf; **Cinematographer:** Jack Marta; **Editor:** Fred Allen; **Cast:** John Wayne, Vera Hruba Ralston, Walter Brennan, Ward Bond, Ona Munson, Hugo Haas, Mike Mazurki, Olive Blakeney, Paul Fix, Grant Withers, Robert Barrat.

John Wayne plays John Devlin, an ex-soldier who elopes with a railroad heiress (Vera Hruba Ralston). They head west to Dakota, where she owns land and where a railroad line is to be built. Along the way they encounter two men, Jim Bender (Ward Bond) and Bigtree Collins (Mike Mazurki), who own the town of Fargo and are burning out the homesteaders and blaming the Indians.

When Devlin arrives in town and sees what is happening, he sides with the wheat farmers and the land war begins. Several unsuccessful attempts on Devlin's life are made by Bender and his gang. In a battle of the dishonorable, Collins kills Bender before Devlin puts Collins away in a fight-to-the-finish finale.

John Wayne's final film for Republic during the war years was not one of his better ventures. Female lead Vera Hruba Ralston was the girlfriend of Republic boss Herb Yates, and her acting skills were limited at best. Yates was grooming the Czech-born actress to be one of Republic's new leading ladies and had hoped to use Wayne to help advance her career.

Jeanette Mazurki Linder was a 25-year-old Hollywood journalist in 1945 before becoming the movie and TV editor for Copley News Service. Then the wife of actor Mike Mazurki, she spent a lot of time on the set. In a 1999 interview she recalled the filming of *Dakota* and wove an intriguing tale of Herbert Yates and the much younger, foreign-born Ralston. It was a situation that provided more than a few problems for John Wayne as well:

Vera was a skating champion and "Papa" Yates was a married man and had children. He saw her and imported her over here, like Darryl Zanuck did with Sonja Henie. He had seen Vera skating in the newsreels and fell very much in love with her. She was a nice person and everybody liked her. She just wasn't a very good actress. Each day Yates would be on the set every minute of every hour. It was an open thing everybody knew this but you didn't print those things back then. Wayne just hated to work with her. If there was a love scene Yates was all over the place. Duke mentioned this on the side to Mike. It was uncomfortable for Duke. There was no real love lost between Duke and Herb Yates. Duke would just do his job. The less they had to do with each other the better.

Despite a high-quality supporting cast, plenty of fisticuffs, and an epic fire scene, this big brawling oater is not as good as it could have been. The song "Coax Me" was written by Andrew Sterling and Harry Von Tiber.

DAKOTA INCIDENT Republic, 1956, Color, 88 min, VT. **Producer:** Michael Baird; **Director:** Lewis R. Foster; **Screenplay:** Frederick Lewis Fox; **Music:** R. Dale Butts; **Cinematographer:** Ernest Haller; **Editor:** Howard A. Smith; **Cast:** Dale Robertson, Linda Darnell, John Lund, Ward Bond, Regis Toomey, Skip Homeier, Irving Bacon, John Doucette, Whit Bissell, William Fawcett, Malcolm Atterbury, Diane DuBoise, Charles Horvath.

A stagecoach is attacked by Indians, and the passengers on the stage must both defend themselves and deal with their own private disputes. This overlooked western with a surrealistic bent and outstanding color design benefits from Dale Robertson's authentic western presence.

Dale Robertson (right) stars in Dakota Incident. (REPUBLIC/AUTHOR'S COLLECTION)

DAKOTA KID, THE   Republic, 1951, B&W, 70 min. **Producer:** Rudy Ralston; **Director:** Philip Ford; **Screenplay:** William Lively; **Cinematographer:** John MacBurnie; **Editor:** Harry Keller; **Cast:** Michael Chapin, Eilene Janssen, James Bell, Dean Norton, Margaret Field, Robert Shayne, Roy Barcroft, Mauritz Hugo, House Peters Jr.

A group of youngsters aid the law in rounding up an outlaw gang. This feature is one of a quartet of films in Republic's *Rough Ridin' Kids* series.

DAKOTA LIL   20th Century Fox, 1950, Color, 88 min. **Producer:** Edward L. Alperson; **Director:** Leslie Selander; **Screenplay:** Maurice Geraght; **Music:** Dimitri Tiomkin; **Cinematographer:** Jack Greenhalgh; **Editor:** Francis D. Lyon; **Cast:** George Montgomery, Marie Windsor, Rod Cameron, John Emery, Wallace Ford, Jack Lambert, James Flavin, J. Farrell MacDonald.

George Montgomery plays a young Tom Horn before he supposedly went bad. Montgomery is good as the legendary Horn, but it is Marie Windsor, as the dance-hall girl who helps the lawman trap a band of railroad thieves, who gives a genuinely excellent performance in the title role. The film is based on a story by Frank Gruber.

DALLAS   Warner Bros., 1950, Color, 94 min, VT. **Producer:** Anthony Veiller; **Director:** Stuart Heisler; **Screenplay:** John Twist; **Music:** Max Steiner; **Cinematographer:** Ernest Haller; **Editor:** Clarence Kolster; **Cast:** Gary Cooper, Ruth Roman, Steve Cochran, Raymond Massey, Barbara Payton, Leif Ericson, Jerome Cowan, Reed Hadley.

Blayde Hollister (Gary Cooper), is an ex-Confederate officer who comes to Dallas seeking revenge on the three brothers who had plundered his land and murdered his family. Once in Dallas he finds that the outlaws who wronged him are now respectable and wealthy citizens. Wild Bill Hickok appears in a minor part in the person of actor Reed Hadley. Despite a good cast, vigorous action, an excellent musical score by Max Steiner, Ernest Haller's stunning photography, and the presence of Ol' Coop himself, the film is at best a standard western melodrama.

DALTON GANG, THE (aka: THE OUTLAW GANG)
Lippert, 1949, B&W, 58 min, VT. **Producers:** Robert Lippert and Ron Ormond; **Director:** Ford Beebe; **Screenplay:** Beebe; **Music:** Walter Greene; **Cinematographer:** Archie R. Dalzell; **Editor:** Hugh Winn; **Cast:** Don "Red" Barry, Robert Lowery, James Millican, Julie Adams, Byron Foulger, J. Farrell MacDonald, Greg McClure, George J. Lewis.

Two lawmen set out to capture the infamous Dalton gang in this routine Don "Red" Barry venture for Lippert. The title became *The Outlaw Gang* for television airings.

DALTON GIRLS, THE
United Artists, 1957, B&W, 71 min. **Producer:** Howard W. Koch; **Director:** Reginald La Borg; **Screenplay:** Herbert Purdom and Maurice Tombragel; **Music:** Les Baxter; **Cinematographer:** Carl E. Guthrie; **Editor:** John F. Schreyer; **Cast:** Merry Anders, Penny Edwards, Sue George, John Russell, Lisa Davis, Malcom Atterbury.

After the Dalton gang is rounded up by the law, several female relatives set out to preserve the infamous family tradition.

DALTONS RIDE AGAIN, THE
Universal, 1945, B&W, 70 min. **Producer:** Howard Welsch; **Director:** Ray Taylor; **Screenplay:** Henry Blankfort, Roy Chanslor, and Paul Gangelin; **Music:** David Buttolph, Paul Sawtell, and Frank Skinner; **Cinematographer:** Charles Van Enger; **Editor:** Paul Landres; **Cast:** Alan Curtis, Kent Taylor, Lon Chaney Jr., Noah Beery Jr., Martha O'Driscoll, Jess Barker, Thomas Gomez, Milburn Stone, John Litel.

The story of the Dalton brothers is told by the only surviving member of the notorious Coffeyville, Kansas, shoot-out where many died, including Bob and Grat Dalton, and where Emmett Dalton survived and was sentenced to life in prison.

Universal originally assigned Ford Beebe to direct the project. When Beebe turned it down after the shooting schedule was reduced from 32 to 16 days, Ray Taylor came on board to helm the film. Alan Curtis, Kent Taylor, Lon Chaney Jr., and Noah Beery Jr. are excellent as the four Dalton Brothers (Emmett, Bob, Grat, Ben). Despite the film's brevity it is a fine picture enhanced by good acting and an exciting shoot-out at film's end. It is a western that the *New York Post* called "lively, lusty, and full of surprises."

DALTONS' WOMEN, THE
Western Adventures, 1950, B&W, 80 min. **Producer:** Ron Ormond; **Director:** Thomas Carr; **Screenplay:** Ron Orland and Maurice Tombragel; **Music:** Walter Greene; **Cinematographer:** Ernest Miller; **Editor:** Hugh Winn; **Cast:** Lash La Rue, Al St. John, Jack Holt, Tom Neal, Pamela Blake, Raymond Hat-ton, Jacqueline Fontain, Tom Tyler, J. Farrell MacDonald, Terry Frost, Bud Osborne.

When the Dalton gang moves west and assumes new identities, marshals Lash and Fuzzy go after them. They receive help from Pinkerton agent Joan Talbot (Pamela Blake) as they try to sort out who the bad guys really are. (See also *LAW OF THE LASH*.)

DAN CANDY'S LAW (aka: ALIEN THUNDER)
Cinerama Releasing Corporation/American-International, 1974, Color, 95 min. **Producer:** Marie-Jose Raymond; **Director:** Claude Fournier; **Screenplay:** George Malko; **Music:** George Delerue; **Cinematographer:** Claude Fournier; **Editors:** Jacques Gagne and Yves Langlois; **Cast:** Donald Sutherland, Jack Creley, Jean Duceppe, Chief Dan George, Kevin McCarthy, Gordon Tootoosis.

Mountie Donald Sutherland chases a Cree Indian accused of murdering a sergeant. However, he soon finds himself to be the hunted rather than the hunter. The picture was released into theaters under the title *Alien Thunder*. Produced in Canada and filmed in Saskatchewan, the beautiful scenery enhances a rather tepid plot. The video title is *Alien Thunder*.

DANCES WITH WOLVES
Tig/Majestic, 1990, Color, 183 min, VT, DVD, CD. **Producers:** Jim Wilson and Kevin Costner; **Director:** Costner; **Screenplay:** Michael Blake; **Music:** John Barry; **Cinematographer:** Dean Semler; **Editor:** Neil Travis; **Cast:** Kevin Costner, Mary McDonnell, Graham Greene, Rodney Grant, Floyd "Red Crow" Westerman, Tantoo Cardinal, Robert Pastorelli, Charles Rockett, Wes Studi.

In his directorial debut, Kevin Costner stars as Lieutenant John Dunbar, a Union officer in the Civil War who finds peace and self-discovery among the Sioux Indians on the pristine Dakota plains of the 1860s. He discovers a culture so refreshing and a life so appealing to the spirit that by the time the U.S. Army decides to look for him, he has become a Sioux whose name is Dances With Wolves.

The film has merit: a fine performance by Wes Studi as the "toughest Pawnee," a beautifully choreographed buffalo hunt, stunning location photography, and a sterling musical score by mega-Oscar winner John Barry. Praised by some as a brilliant piece of filmmaking and dismissed by others as little more than a grandiose ode to political correctness, *Dances With Wolves* became the first western to win an Academy Award as Best Picture since *CIMARRON* 39 years earlier. Filmed in Dakota over a period of 17 weeks, the film runs three hours in length, and one-third of the dialogue is subtitled in the Lakota (Sioux) language. In December 1991 a 232-minute "extended version" premiered in Great Britain and was later released on home video.

Critical reviews were quite mixed. Leonard Maltin calls it an extraordinary film, "simply and eloquently told, with every element falling into place." For critic Roger Ebert it was a "simple story, magnificently told," with the sweep and clarity of a western by John Ford.

On the other hand, Costner's film has been widely criticized for pandering to the politically correct and for being historically inaccurate. Every white in the film is either insane (the officer who posts Costner to the Sioux territory), is obnoxious and foolish (the muleskinner who takes them there), or are murderers (soldiers and cavalrymen), all of which led one critic to label it an "overlong picture-postcard, politically correct horse opera."

Critics poked fun at Costner's New Age consciousness. In *Time*, Richard Schickel lampooned the actor for coming across as a "1990s Yuppie who suddenly decides to take his Sierra Club membership seriously." Pauline Kael of the *New Yorker* was even more scathing: "Costner has feathers in his hair and feathers in his head. . . . This epic was made by a bland megalomaniac."

Historical inaccuracies are sprinkled everywhere. Costner's chief villains, for example, are the merciless Pawnee killers intent on slaughtering the Sioux and stealing everything they own, while historically the opposite is true. The Sioux and their allies outnumbered the Pawnee 25 to 1 and would have exterminated them had the need arisen. Joseph Roquemor was particularly rough in his assessment in *History Goes to the Movies*:

> Bent on demolishing vintage stereotypes of American Indians as childish savages, director Costner substitutes fashionable new Hollywood platitudes for ole Hollywood cliches . . . it [replaces] old distorted notions about Indians with equally warped 1990s cant . . . [leaving] three hours of pretentious, invincible ignorance on film—not a better understanding of 19th-Century Native Americans.

Nevertheless, the film was a major success for Costner, winning six Academy Awards (including Best Picture and Best Director) and 11 Oscar nominations. Costner himself was inducted into the Sioux Nation and the National Cowboy Hall of Fame. *Dances With Wolves* was the fourth highest-grossing film of 1990 at $81.5 million.

DANGER AHEAD Monogram, 1940, B&W, 60 min. **Producer:** Philip N. Krasne; **Director:** Ralph Staub; **Screenplay:** Edward Halperin; **Music:** Betty Laidlaw, Johnny Lange (songs), Lew Porter (songs) and Robert Lively (title theme); **Cinematographer:** Mack Stengler; **Editor:** Martin G. Cohn; **Cast:** James Newell, Dave O'Brien, Dorothy Kent, Dick Rich, Guy Usher, John Dilson, Harry Depp, David Sharpe, Lester Dorr, Bob Terry.

Renfrew (James Newell) and the Mounties are at odds with an obstinate young woman who refuses to help the Mounties capture an outlaw.

DANGEROUS VENTURE United Artists, 1947, B&W, 59 min. **Producers:** William Boyd, Lewis J. Rachmil, and Harry Sherman; **Director:** George Archainbaud; **Screenplay:** Doris Schroeder; **Music:** David Chudnow; **Cinematographer:** Mack Stengler; **Editor:** Fred W. Berger; **Cast:** William Boyd, Andy Clyde, Rand Brooks, Fritz Leiber, Harry Cording, Betty Alexander, Francis McDonald.

Hoppy and the boys search for a tribe of Indians who are presumed to be descendants of the Aztecs. However, a band of outlaws tries to discredit the tribe by committing crimes while dressed as Indians. An archaeologist finds gold in the Indian burial grounds and hooks up with the bad guys. (See also *HOP-ALONG CASSIDY*.)

DANGER PATROL RKO, 1937, B&W, 59 min. **Director:** Lew Landers; **Screenplay:** Sy Bartlett; **Cinematographer:** Nicholas Musuraca; **Editor:** Ted Cheesman; **Cast:** Sally Eilers, John Beal, Harry Carey, Frank M. Thomas, Crawford Weaver, Lee Patrick, Edward Gargen.

While working as a nitro shooter in the oil fields, a young medical student falls in love with the daughter of the man who is training him. Harry Carey delivers a good performance as the mentor-father.

DANGERS OF THE CANADIAN MOUNTED (aka: R.C.M.P. AND THE TREASURE OF GENGHIS KHAN) Republic, 1948, B&W, 156 min, 12 episodes, VT. **Producer:** Mike Frankovich; **Directors:** Fred C. Brannon and Yakima Canutt; **Screenplay:** Franklin Adreon, Basil Dickey, Sol Shor, and Robert G. Walker; **Cinematographer:** John MacBurnie; **Editor:** Cliff Bell Sr. and Sam Starr; **Cast:** Jim Bannon, Virginia Belmont, Anthony Warde, L. Stanford Jolley, Lee Morgan, Phil Warren, Dorothy Granger.

The Canadian Mounties are on the trail of a gang of crooks going after a hidden Chinese treasure on the Canada-Alaska border. The television feature title is *R.C.M.P. and the Treasure of Genghis Khan*.

DANGER TRAILS Beacon, 1935, B&W, 62 min. **Producers:** Arthur Alexander and Max Alexander; **Director:** Robert F. Hill; **Screenplay:** Hill (as Rock Hawkey); **Cinematographer:** William Hyer; **Editor:** Holbrook N. Todd; **Cast:** Guinn "Big Boy" Williams, Marjorie Gordon, John Elliott, Steve Clark, Edmund Cobb, Wally Wales, Ace Cain, George Chesebro.

A football star returns from the East to find his long-lost father. On his way three bandits, who turn out to be his brothers, hold up his stagecoach. He must now choose between his outlaw family and the law. Guinn "Big Boy" Williams wrote the original story for this entertaining venture.

DANGER VALLEY Monogram, 1937, B&W, 58 min. **Producer:** Robert Bradbury; **Director:** Bradbury; **Screenplay:** Robert Emmett Tansey (as Robert Emmett); **Music:** Johnny Lange and Fred Stryker (songs); **Cinematographer:** Bert Longenecker; **Editor:** Howard Dillinger; **Cast:** Addison Randall (as Jack Randall), Lois Wilde, Hal Price, Charles King, Earl Dwire, Ernie Adams, Jimmy Aubrey, Edward Brady, Sherry Tansey, Bud Osborne.

Two cowboys come upon a ghost town where an old man has discovered gold. But an outlaw gang who wants the loot is harassing the old man, so Jack and sidekick Lucky help him fight back.

DANIEL BOONE RKO, 1936, B&W, 75 min. **Producer:** George A. Hirliman; **Director:** David Howard; **Screenplay:** Daniel Jarrett; **Music:** Jack Stern and Harry Tobias (songs); **Cinematographer:** Frank Good; **Editor:** Ralph Dixon; **Cast:** George O'Brien, Heather Angel, John Carradine, Ralph Forbes, George Regas, Dickie Jones, Clarence Muse.

In 1775 frontiersman Daniel Boone leads 30 settler families from North Carolina to Kentucky, facing threats by hostile Indians on the one hand and renegade whites on the other. Although not heavily budgeted, this is a solid production with an outstanding performance by George O'Brien in the title role and a strong supporting performance by John Carradine as the infamous Simon Girty, the white renegade who sells rifles to the Wyandot tribe. O'Brien's performance was not overlooked by the *New York Times*, which commented that "For all his physical prowess, George O'Brien manages to project Daniel Boone as a shy, unassuming adventurer, which is presumably what the man was."

DANIEL BOONE, TRAIL BLAZER Republic, 1956, Color, 76 min, VT. **Producer:** Albert C. Gannaway; **Directors:** Gannaway and Ismael Rodriguez; **Screenplay:** Tom Hubbard and John Patrick; **Music:** Raul Lavista; **Cinematographer:** Jack Draper; **Editor:** Fernando Martinez; **Cast:** Bruce Bennett, Lon Chaney Jr., Faron Young, Ken Dibbs, Jacqueline Evans, Freddy Fernandez, Fred Kohler Jr.

Bruce Bennett is Daniel Boone and Lon Chaney Jr. is Chief Black Fish in this familiar story of the famous frontiersman who leads his people from North Carolina to Boonesville, Kentucky.

DAREDEVILS OF THE WEST Republic, 1943, B&W, 196 min, 12 episodes. **Producers:** Herbert J. Yates and William J. O'Sullivan; **Director:** John English; **Screenplay:** Ronald Davidson, Basil Dickey, William Lively, Joseph O'Donnell, and Joseph F. Poland; **Music:** Mort Glickman; **Cinematographer:** Bud Thackery; **Editors:** Wallace Grissell, Tony Martinelli, and Edward Todd; **Cast:** Allan Lane, Kay Aldridge, Robert Frazer, William Haade, Eddie Acuff, Ted Adams, Stanley Andrews.

A young man comes to the aid of a girl whose stagecoach lines are being threatened by mysterious attacks in this exciting and well-done serial western from Republic Studio.

DARING ADVENTURER, THE See *THE CISCO KID RETURNS.*

DARING CABALLERO, THE United Artists, 1949, B&W, 60 min. **Director:** Wallace Fox; **Screenplay:** Betty Burbridge and Frances Kavanaugh; **Music:** Albert Glasser; **Cinematographer:** Lester White; **Editor:** Martin G. Cohn; **Cast:** Duncan Renaldo, Leo Carillo, Alden "Stephen" Chase, Edmund Cobb, Pedro de Cordoba, Charles Halton.

Cisco and Pancho (dubbed as Chico and Pablo) come to the aid of a banker who is falsely accused of robbery and murder. (See also *CISCO KID, THE.*)

DARING DANGER Columbia, 1932, B&W, 57 min. **Director:** D. Ross Lederman; **Screenplay:** William Colt MacDonald and Michael Trevellian; **Cinematographer:** Benjamin H. Kline; **Editor:** Otto Meyer; **Cast:** Tim McCoy, Alberta Vaughn, Wallace MacDonald, Robert Ellis, Richard Alexander, Murdock MacQuarrie.

A cowboy and a cattlemen's agent help an old man and his daughter who are being harassed by a crook trying to starve them off their land.

DARK COMMAND Republic, 1940, B&W, 94 min, VT. **Producers:** Herbert J. Yates and Sol Siegal (associate); **Director:** Raoul Walsh; **Screenplay:** F. Hugh Herbert, Lionel Houser, and Grover Jones; **Music:** Victor Young; **Cinematographer:** Jack Marta; **Editor:** William Morgan; **Cast:** Claire Trevor, John Wayne, Walter Pidgeon, Roy Rogers, George "Gabby" Hayes, Porter Hall, Marjorie Main, Raymond Walburn, Joe Sawyer, Helen MacKellar.

In this film set in Lawrence, Kansas, just before the Civil War, disgruntled schoolteacher Will Cantrell (Walter Pidgeon) tries for the office of Federal Marshal and is embittered when cowboy Bob Seton (John Wayne) wins the election. "I'm better at smelling than spelling," Seton tells the townfolk before winning. Matters grow worse when Cantrell realizes that Seton is making advances to the girl he loves, Mary McCloud (Claire Trevor). But when Mary's hotheaded brother Fletch (Roy Rogers) is tried for murder at Seton's insistence, Cantrell takes advantage of the rift by threatening violence to the jury to assure a not-guilty verdict and win his way into Mary's heart.

Feeling the exhilaration of power, Cantrell organizes a band of guerrillas who raid and pillage the Kansas countryside. Fletch, who is grateful to Cantrell for saving his life, joins the renegades, while the distraught Mary reluctantly agrees to marry Cantrell. A ruthless attack on Lawrence and the slaughter of innocent women and children provide fodder for the an exciting climax. Seton kills the treacherous Cantrell, and amidst the ashes of a burning city, he wins over Mary.

Dark Command marked the first time John Wayne and Raoul Wash worked together since Walsh directed the then-fledgling Wayne in *THE BIG TRAIL* 10 years earlier. Considered at the time to be Republic's finest A-level western, it was also the studio's most expensive project at a cost of $700,000.

Republic capitalized on the screen chemistry between Wayne and Trevor, displayed so successfully in *STAGECOACH* (United Artists, 1939), then repeated again the same year in

RKO's *ALLEGHENY UPRISING*. The studio garnered an extraordinary cast. Walter Pidgeon was borrowed from MGM for the important role of Will Cantrell (based on the real-life leader of the infamous Quantrill Raiders); and 29-year-old Roy Rogers, still a couple of years from replacing Gene Autry as the acknowledged "King of the Cowboys," was cast as young firebrand Fletch McCloud. Western fans still delight in seeing John Wayne, Roy Rogers, and the irascible "Gabby" Hayes (in perhaps his best role) sharing the same screen for the only time.

Based on the novel by W. R. Burnett, *Dark Command* is a dynamic shoot-'em-up adventure with an excellent score by Victor Young; solidly constructed scenes, particularly the burning of Lawrence; skillful stunt work choreographed by Yakima Canutt; and good performances by all, especially Pidgeon and Marjorie Main as Cantrell's beleaguered and stoic mother.

DARK VIOLENCE   See *ANGEL IN EXILE*.

DAUGHTER OF THE WEST, THE   Film Classics, 1949, Color, 77 min. **Producer:** Martin Mooney; **Director:** Harold Daniels; **Screenplay:** Irwin Franklyn and Raymond L. Schrock; **Music:** Juan Duval and Victor Granados; **Cinematographer:** Henry Sharp; **Editor:** Doug Bagler; **Cast:** Martha Vickers, Phillip Reed, Donald Woods, Marion Carney, William Farnum, James Griffith, Luz Alba, Tony Barr, Pedro de Cordoba, Tommy Cook.

A young woman working on an Indian reservation tries to help the Navajo when a corrupt agent attempts to steal their copper mines.

DAVY CROCKETT, INDIAN SCOUT (aka: INDIAN SCOUT)   United Artists, 1950, B&W, 71 min. **Producer:** Edward Small; **Director:** Lew Landers; **Screenplay:** Richard Schayer; **Music:** Paul Sawtell; **Cinematographers:** George E. Diskant and John J. Mescall; **Editors:** Kenneth G. Crane and Stewart S. Frye; **Cast:** George Montgomery, Ellen Drew, Philip Reed, Noah Beery Jr., Paul Guilfoyle, Addison Richards, Ray Teal.

Davy Crockett (not the hero of the Alamo, but his cousin) guides a wagon train through hostile territory and rescues the cavalry from ambushing Indians. The film has little to do with the legendary hero.

DAVY CROCKETT, KING OF THE WILD FRONTIER   Walt Disney/Buena Vista, 1955, Color, 81 min, VT. **Producer:** Bill Walsh; **Director:** Norman Foster; **Screenplay:** Tom Blackburn; **Music:** George Bruns; **Cinematographer:** Charles Boyle; **Editor:** Chester Schaeffer; **Cast:** Fess Parker, Buddy Ebsen, Basil Ruysdael, Hans Conried, William Bakewell, Kenneth Tobey, Pat Hogan, Nick Cravat, Mike Mazurki, Don Megowan.

The film opens with Davy Crockett (Fess Parker) winning the respect of an Indian leader and defeating badman Bigfoot Mason (Mike Mazurki). He becomes a local hero in the Tennessee frontierland and is sent to Congress, where he becomes friends with his former general, Andrew Jackson (Basil Ruysdael). A series of articles written by his friend George Russell (Buddy Ebsen) helps to make him a plain-talking hero who tells the truth. When Davy and Jackson disagree over an Indian bill, he and Russell head for Texas, where they die gloriously at the Alamo.

Shown originally as three parts on the "Frontierland" segment of the *Disneyland* television series, this film was issued theatrically to cash in on the mid-50s TV craze. The series had made a national hero of actor Fess Parker, and the title song became the number one song in the country. Merchandising was excessive; coonskin caps, toy guns, records, and lunch boxes became the order of the day, all bearing a Davy Crockett logo. Despite the fact that the original Davy Crockett miniseries ended with the hero's death, Disney took good advantage of the national craze and filmed a sequel entitled *Davy Crockett and the River Pirates* (1956), showing it first on television and then in theaters.

Directed by Norman Foster, the sequel emphasized the character of Mike Fink, who was first Crockett's enemy and then became his friend. Interestingly, while the Davy Crockett character made Fess Parker into a big-time star, it was Buddy Ebsen who had been Disney's first choice for the role of the famed frontier hero.

DAWN AT SOCORRO   Universal, 1954, Color, 80 min. **Producer:** William Alland; **Director:** George Sherman; **Screenplay:** George Zuckerman; **Cinematographer:** Carl E. Guthrie; **Editor:** Edward Curtiss; **Cast:** Rory Calhoun, Piper Laurie, David Brian, Kathleen Hughes, Alex Nicol, Edgar Buchanan, Mara Corday, Roy Roberts, Skip Homeier, James Millican, Lee Van Cleef.

In this 1954 western, Brett Wade (a gunfighter, gambler, and classical pianist) is wounded in a gunfight. When the doctor finds Wade has signs of tuberculosis, he encourages him to find an environment with pure air. En route to Colorado, Wade tries hard to leave his former life behind, but while helping out a young woman he finds himself faced with the real prospect of one last shoot-out.

DAWN ON THE GREAT DIVIDE   Monogram, 1942, B&W, 63 min, VT. **Producer:** George W. Weeks; **Director:** Howard Bretherton; **Screenplay:** William L. Nolte; **Cinematographer:** Harry Neumann; **Editor:** Carl Pierson; **Cast:** Buck Jones, Mona Barrie, Raymond Hatton, Robert Lowery, Rex Bell, Maude Eburne, Christine McIntyre, Tristram Coffin, Roy Barcroft, Steve Clark, Bud Osborne.

Three pals lead a wagon train of supplies for the railroad, but two brothers planning to hijack the train hire an outlaw gang to dress as Indians, conduct a raid, and place the blame on a local tribe. Buck Jones is the tough, two-fisted leader of the wagon train in this above-average shoot-'em-up oater with more than its share of plot twists. This was Buck Jones's final film. Late in the year he perished in the tragic Boston Coconut Grove Nightclub fire while on a campaign tour to sell U.S. War Bonds.

DAWN RIDER, THE Monogram, 1935, B&W, 56 min, VT, DVD. **Producer:** Paul Malvern; **Director:** Robert Bradbury; **Screenplay:** Bradbury; **Cinematographer:** Archie Stout; **Editor:** Carl Pierson; **Cast:** John Wayne, Marion Burns, Dennis Moore, Reed Howes, Joseph De Grasse, Yakima Canutt, Earl Dwire, Nelson McDowell.

John Wayne plays John Mason, a man who sees his father shot down in an express office holdup and eventually brings the desperadoes to justice. However, it turns out that the woman who nurses him back to health after being shot is the daughter of the man who gunned down his father.

Lest anyone think that John Wayne did not pay his proper dues, try to imagine making nine films in one year. This vehicle was one of nine Wayne features released in 1935, and it was the next to the last in the Monogram/Lone Star series before Republic took over the Paul Malvern releases. A copyrighted version of the film was reissued in 1985 with a new original score composed and orchestrated by William Barber. Distributed by Fox/Lorber, it ran 48 minutes. It is also available in a computer-colorized version.

DAWN TRAIL, THE Columbia, 1930, B&W, 66 min. **Producer:** Sol Lesser; **Director:** Christy Cabanne; **Screenplay:** John T. Neville; **Cinematographer:** Ted D. McCord; **Editor:** James Sweeney; **Cast:** Buck Jones, Miriam Seeger, Charles Morton, Erville Alderson, Edward Le Saint, Charles King, Hank Mann, Inez Gomez.

Buck Jones is a sheriff who must hold his girl's brother for murder as the result of a range war between cattlemen and sheepmen. Remade as *Tracy Rides* (1935) and again as *Texas Stampede* (1939). (See also *WHITE EAGLE*.)

DAY OF FURY, A Universal, 1956, Color, 78 min. **Producer:** Robert Arthur; **Director:** Harmon Jones; **Screenplay:** Oscar Brodney and James Edmiston; **Music:** Henry Mancini; **Cinematographer:** Ellis W. Carter; **Editor:** Sherman Todd; **Cast:** Dale Robertson, Mara Corday, Jock Mahoney, Carl Benton Reid, Jan Merlin, John Dehner, Dee Carroll, Sheila Bromley, James Bell, Dani Crayne.

A young rebel in the Old West tries to terrorize a small town. The interesting plotline is helped by the presence of TV western staples Dale Robertson and Jock Mahoney and a fine performance by Jan Merlin.

DAY OF THE BADMAN Universal, 1958, Color, 82 min. **Producer:** Gordon Kay; **Director:** Harry Keller; **Screenplay:** Lawrence Roman; **Music:** Hans Salter; **Cinematographer:** Irving Glassberg; **Editor:** Sherman Todd; **Cast:** Fred MacMurray, Joan Weldon, John Ericson, Robert Middleton, Marie Windsor, Edgar Buchanan, Edward Franz, Skip Homeier, Peggy Converse, Robert Foulk, Ann Doran, Lee Van Cleef, Eddy Waller, Chris Alcaide, Don Haggerty, Christopher Dark.

Fred MacMurray plays Judge Jim Scott, a man with a double dilemma. He must contend with the relatives of the man he is about to hang and also deal with his unfaithful fiancée, who has fallen in love with the town's good-looking sheriff. MacMurray, at the height of his popularity, was about to embark on the long-running TV sitcom *My Three Sons*. Excellent performances by villains Robert Middleton and Skip Homeier move this film along.

DAY OF THE EVIL GUN MGM, 1968, Color, 95 min. **Producer:** Jerry Thorpe; **Director:** Thorpe; **Screenplay:** Charles Marquis Warren and Eric Bercovici; **Music:** Jeff Alexander; **Cinematographer:** W. Wallace Kelley; **Editor:** Alex Beaton; **Cast:** Glenn Ford, Arthur Kennedy, Dean Jagger, John Anderson, Paul Fix, Nico Minardos, Harry Dean Stanton, Royal Dano.

Professional gunman Glenn Ford returns home after a long absence to find that his wife and daughter have been kidnapped by some Chiricahua Apache. When he takes off after them, he is joined by a neighbor (Arthur Kennedy) who has been courting Ford's wife in his absence. Along the way the two men encounter Indians, Mexican bandits, army deserters, and a town ravaged by a cholera epidemic. The gunfighter (Ford) uses his weapons reluctantly, while the benign farmer (Kennedy) starts to enjoy the killing. "It gets easier all the time, doesn't it," Ford chides. When they retrieve the women and get them home, the now trigger-happy and jealous Kennedy insists on shooting it out with Ford.

DAY OF THE OUTLAW United Artists, 1959, B&W, 92 min. **Producer:** Sidney Harmon; **Director:** André De Toth; **Screenplay:** Philip Yordan; **Music:** Alexander Courage; **Cinematographer:** Russell Harlan; **Editor:** Robert Lawrence; **Cast:** Robert Ryan, Burl Ives, Tina Louise, Alan Marshal, Venitia Stevenson, David Nelson, Nehemiah Persoff, Jack Lambert, Frank DeKova, Lance Fuller, Elisha Cook Jr., Dabbs Greer, Helen Westcott.

Cowboys and ranchers put their differences aside when a blizzard forces an outlaw gang to spend the night in a little Wyoming mountain town. Burl Ives is excellent as Captain Jack Bruhn, the outlaw leader who proves to be a more decent man than one might expect. Robert Ryan plays a townsman who is in love with Tina Louise (one of only four females in the town). Because she is married, he plans to kill her husband and lead the outlaw gang out of town himself. This is a well-acted film with an interesting plot line based on the novel by Lee Wells.

DAYS OF BUFFALO BILL Republic, 1946, B&W, 56 min. **Producers:** Herbert Yates and Bennett Cohen; **Director:** Thomas Carr; **Screenplay:** William Lively and Doris Schroeder; **Cinematographer:** Alfred S. Keller; **Edi-**

tor: Tony Martinelli; **Cast:** Sunset Carson, Peggy Stewart, Tom London, James Craven, Rex Lease, Edmund Cobb, Eddie Parker, Michael Sloane, Bill George (as Jay Kirby), George Chesebro.

A cowboy and his pal who are framed for murder run from a posse in order to prove their innocence. Interestingly, despite the title, Buffalo Bill Cody never appears in the movie. (See also *CALL OF THE ROCKIES* [1944].)

DAYS OF JESSE JAMES Republic, 1939, B&W, 63 min, VT, DVD. **Producer:** Joseph Kane; **Director:** Kane; **Screenplay:** Earle Snell; **Cinematographer:** Reggie Lanning; **Editor:** Tony Martinelli; **Cast:** Roy Rogers, George "Gabby" Hayes, Don "Red" Barry, Pauline Moore, Harry Woods.

An opportunistic sheriff and a crooked banker commit a series of robberies and blame them on Jesse James. Roy Rogers is the railroad detective who is on the trail of the famed outlaw but meets up with the sheriff and the crooked banker instead.

DAYS OF OLD CHEYENNE Republic, 1943, B&W, 55 min. **Producer:** Edward J. White; **Director:** Elmer Clifton; **Screenplay:** Norman S. Hall; **Music:** Mort Glickman; **Cinematographer:** Reggie Lanning; **Editor:** Harry Keller; **Cast:** Don "Red" Barry, Lynn Merrick, William Haade, Emmett Lynn, Herbert Rawlinson, Charles F. Miller.

Don "Red" Barry accepts the job of town marshal in the belief that the town is interested in his maintaining law and order. He is mistaken and soon finds himself battling a corrupt political leader instead. (See also *ADVENTURES OF RED RYDER, THE; WYOMING OUTLAW.*)

DEAD DON'T DREAM, THE United Artists/Hop-Along Cassidy Productions, 1948, B&W, 55 min. **Producers:** William Boyd and Lewis J. Rachmil; **Director:** George Archainbaud; **Screenplay:** Francis Rosenwald; **Music:** Ralph Stanley; **Cinematographer:** Mack Stengler; **Editor:** Fred W. Berger; **Cast:** William Boyd, Andy Clyde, Rand Brooks, John Parish, Leonard Penn, Mary Tucker, Francis McDonald, Dan Haggerty.

Hoppy's partner Lucky finally decides to get himself married, but his wedding plans are dashed when his fiancée's father is murdered before the ceremony. Hoppy tries to get to the bottom of the killing. An atmosphere of mystery makes this one of the best of the later *HOP-ALONG CASSIDY* ventures.

DEADLINE Astor, 1948, B&W, 57 min. **Producers:** Oliver Drake and Walt Maddox; **Director:** Drake; **Screenplay:** Drake (as C. O. Drake); **Music:** Frank Sanucci; **Cinematographer:** James S. Brown Jr.; **Editor:** Mary Cohn; **Cast:** Sunset Carson, Pat Starling, Lee Roberts, Stephen Keyes, Frank Ellis, Forrest Mathews, Al Terry, Pat Gleason, Bob Curtis, Phil Arnold, Joe Hiser, Donald Gray.

DEADLINE, THE Columbia, 1931, B&W, 60 min. **Producer:** Irving Briskin; **Director:** Lambert Hillyer; **Screenplay:** Hillyer; **Cinematographer:** Byron Haskin; **Editor:** Maurice Wright; **Cast:** Buck Jones, Loretta Sayers, Robert Ellis, Raymond Nye, Ed Brady, Knute Ericson, George Ernest, Jack Curtis, James Farley, Harry Todd, Robert Kortman.

A hot-tempered cowboy is released from jail, only to find himself in trouble with area outlaws. A good script and Hillyer's capable direction puts this Buck Jones vehicle a notch or two above the ordinary early sound oater. (See also *WHITE EAGLE.*)

DEADLY COMPANIONS, THE Pathé America, 1961, Color, 90 min. **Producer:** Charles B. Fitzsimmons; **Director:** Sam Peckinpah; **Screenplay:** A. S. Fleischman; **Music:** Marlin Skiles; **Cinematographer:** William Clothier; **Editor:** Stanley E. Rabjohn; **Cast:** Maureen O'Hara, Steve Cochran, Brian Keith, Chill Wills, Strother Martin, Will Wright, Jim O'Hara, Chuck Hayward.

An ex-army officer (Brian Keith) accidentally kills a woman's son. To make amends he agrees to escort the woman (Maureen O'Hara) across the desert so her son may be buried alongside his father. Their journey is complicated by unfriendly Indians and by Keith's two unsavory partners, played by Steve Cochran and Chill Wills.

Brian Keith, who starred in TV's *The Westerner*, suggested that Peckinpah helm this modest little western for the big screen after working with him on his popular television series. Filmed in Panavision, Peckinpah's first full-length movie is a credible, well-crafted, and understated film. His second feature film, *RIDE THE HIGH COUNTRY* (1962), would be a great one.

DEADLY PEACEMAKER See *MAN WITH THE GUN.*

DEADLY RECTOR Action International Pictures, 1989, Color. **Producer:** Fritz Matthews; **Director:** David Heavener; **Screenplay:** Heavener; **Music:** Brian Scott Bennett; **Cast:** David Heavener, Alyson Davis, Darwyn Swalve, Stuart Whitman.

In a futuristic world inhabited by the Amish, a roving gang led by a corpulent leader is making life unbearable for the townspeople. The only one to stand in their way is a lone gunfighter who never draws first. He's the rector!

DEADLY TRACKERS, THE Warner Bros., 1973, Color, B&W, 110 min, VT. **Producer:** Fouad Said; **Director:** Barry Shear; **Screenplay:** Lukas Heller; **Music:** Jerry Fielding; **Cinematographer:** Gabriel Torres; **Editors:** Michael Economou and Carl Pingitore; **Cast:** Richard Harris, Rod Taylor, Al Letierri, Neville Brand, William Smith.

Richard Harris plays a peaceful man whose wife and son are killed by a band of brutal thugs led by Rod Taylor (playing against type). He sets out on a mission of revenge against the perpetrators that quickly deteriorates into an orgy of vile ugliness. Based on the story "Riata" by Samuel Fuller, this poorly directed film is downbeat, violent, and, despite its credible plot line, a waste of good talent.

DEAD MAN Miramax, 1995, B&W, 121 min, VT, DVD, CD. **Producer:** Deetra J. MacBride; **Director:** Jim Jarmusch; **Screenplay:** Jarmusch; **Music:** Neil Young; **Cinematographer:** Robby Miller; **Editor:** Jay Rabinowitz; **Cast:** Johnny Depp, Gary Farmer, Lance Henriksen, Michael Wincott, John Hurt, Billy Bob Thornton, Robert Mitchum.

Bill Blake (Johnny Depp), a mild-mannered Ohio accountant, finds his life completely transformed as he evolves into a notorious gunman. Blake leaves his job in Cleveland for the remote frontier of the West only to find that the job is filled by the time he gets there. Before long he runs afoul of an ornery factory boss named Dickinson (Robert Mitchum), and then kills for the first time when Dickinson's son shoots his woman after finding her in bed with Blake. Taking to the hills, he is pursued by three bounty hunters, led by the sadistic man in black, Cole Wilson (Lance Henriksen), and a few more folks who are trying to track him down.

DEAD MAN'S GOLD Screen Guild, 1948, B&W, 60 min. **Producer:** Ron Ormond; **Director:** Ray Taylor; **Screenplay:** Moree Harding and George Welsch; **Music:** Walter Greene; **Cinematographer:** Ernest Miller; **Editor:** Hugh Winn; **Cast:** Lash La Rue, Al St. John, Peggy Stewart, Terry Frost, John L. Cason, Pierce Lyden, Lane Bradford.
See *LAW OF THE LASH.*

DEAD MAN'S GULCH Republic, 1943, B&W, 55 min. **Producer:** Edward J. White; **Director:** John English; **Screenplay:** Norman S. Hall and Robert Creighton Williams; **Music:** Morton Glickman; **Cinematographer:** Ernest Miller; **Editor:** Arthur Roberts; **Cast:** Don "Red" Barry, Lynn Merrick, Clancy Cooper, Emmett Lynn, Malcom "Bud" McTaggart, Jack Rockwell, John Vosper, Pierce Lyden, Lee Shumway, Rex Lease, Al Taylor.

A former Pony Express rider discovers that crooks are using him to cheat ranchers on freight rates. (See also *WYOMING OUTLAW.*)

DEAD MAN'S TRAIL Monogram, 1952, B&W, 59 min. **Producer:** Vincent Fennelly; **Director:** Lewis D. Collins; **Screenplay:** Joseph F. Poland and Melville Shyer; **Cinematographer:** Ernest Miller; **Editor:** Sam Fields; **Cast:** Johnny Mack Brown, Barbara Allen, I. Stanford Jolley, Terry Frost, Lane Bradford, Gregg Barton, James Ellison.

The brother of an outlaw who has been killed by his own gang assists a sheriff in tracking down the outlaws and helps recover the stolen money. This is the last pairing of Johnny Mack Brown and James Ellison in the Monogram series. (See also *DEAD MAN'S TRAIL.*)

DEAD OR ALIVE PRC, 1944, B&W, 56 min, VT. **Producer:** Arthur Alexander; **Director:** Elmer Clifton; **Cinematographer:** Robert E. Cline; **Editor:** Hugh Winn; **Cast:** Tex Ritter, Dave O'Brien, Guy Wilkerson, Marjorie Clements, Rebel Randall.

Tex and two lawmen buddies help out a judge who asks them to take on an outlaw gang that is trying to snag a girl's ranch. This formula Tex Ritter oater is packed with action and limited in plot. Among the songs he sings are "I'm Gonna Leave You Like I Found You," and "Don't Care Since You Said Goodbye." (See also *SONG OF THE GRINGO.*)

DEADWOOD DICK Columbia, 1940, B&W, 15 chapters. **Producer:** Larry Darmour; **Director:** James W. Horne; **Screenplay:** Wyndham Gittens, Morgan B. Cox; George Morgan, and John Cutting; **Cinematographer:** James S. Brown Jr.; **Editors:** Dwight Caldwell and Earl Turner; **Cast:** Don Douglas, Lorna Gray (Adrian Booth), Harry Harvey, Marin Sais, Lane Chandler, Jack Ingram, Charles King, Yakima Canutt, Edmund Cobb, Franklyn Farnum.

Deadwood Dick is a mysterious figure of the prairie who is aided by Wild Bill Hickok. Together they try to thwart the nefarious activities of "The Skull" and his evil gang who are terrorizing the area in and around Deadwood, South Dakota. This well-received and popular Columbia cliffhanger has the black-clad title character chasing evildoers with flying mounts and superb horsemanship.

DEADWOOD PASS Gotham Pictures/Gothic, 1933, B&W, 62 min. **Producers:** John R. Freuler (executive) and Burton I. King; **Director:** J. P. McGowan; **Screenplay:** Oliver Drake; **Cinematographer:** Edward A. Kull; **Editor:** Frederick Bain; **Cast:** Tom Tyler, Lafe McKee, Alice Dahl, Edmund Cobb, Slim Whitaker, Merrill McCormick, Carlotta Monti.

A government agent poses as the notorious outlaw "The Hawk" in order to find out where his gang has hidden the stolen loot.

DEADWOOD '76 Fairway-International, 1965, Color, 94 min. **Producer:** Arch Hall Jr. (as Nicholas Merriweather); **Director:** James Landis; **Screenplay:** Hall Jr. and Arch Hall Sr. (as William Watters); **Music:** Paul Sawtell and Harper MacKay; **Cinematographer:** William Zsigmond; **Editor:** Anthony M. Lanza; **Cast:** Arch Hall Jr., Jack Lester, La Donna Cottier, Arch Hall Sr., Liz Renay, Robert Dix.

A young drifter heading to the Dakotas to take part in the gold rush is mistaken for Billy the Kid. The consequences prove deadly. Wild Bill Hickok, Calamity Jane, Sam Bass, and Chief Crazy Horse are some of the historical figures that appear in this low-budget, overstated, and outdated oater.

DEAF SMITH AND JOHNNY EARS (aka: LOS AMIGOS) MGM, 1972, Color, 91 min. **Producers:** Joseph Janni and Luciano Perugia; **Director:** Paolo Carava; **Screenplay:** Lucia Brudi, Cavara, Harry Essex, Augusto Finocchi, and Oscar Saul; **Music:** Daniele Patucchi; **Cinematographer:** Tonio Delli Colli; **Editor:** Mario Morra; **Cast:** Anthony Quinn, Franco Nero, Pamela Tiffin, Franco Graziosi, Ira von Furstenberg, Renzo Moneta, Renato Romano, Cristina Airoldi, Mario Carra.

Filmed in Italy and originally titled *Los Amigos*, this macho western has two pals attempting to prevent a would-be dictator from taking over the new Republic of Texas. The opening scene is excessively violent, with the bad guys wiping out a family of innocent people including a number of women and children. The rest of this beautifully photographed film shows great interplay between Anthony Quinn and Franco Nero as the two protagonists and features an enjoyable musical score by Daniele Patucchi.

DEATH GOES NORTH Columbia, 1939, B&W, 56 min. **Producer:** Kenneth J. Bishop; **Director:** Frank McDonald; **Screenplay:** Edward R. Austin; **Cinematographer:** Harry Forbes; **Editor:** William Austin; **Cast:** Edgar Edwards, Sheila Bromley, James McGrath, Jameson Thomas, Walter Byron, Arthur Kerr, Dorothy Bradshaw, Reginald Hincks, Vivian Combe.

In this film set in the Canadian Northwest, a Mountie and his dog attempt to bring in a killer. Produced in Canada, the movie was issued there by Columbia Pictures.

DEATH OF A GUNFIGHTER Universal, 1969, Color, 100 min. **Producer:** Richard E. Lyons; **Director:** Allen Smithee (Robert Totten and Don Siegel); **Screenplay:** Joseph Calvelli; **Music:** Carol Hall and Oliver Nelson; **Cinematographer:** Andrew Jackson; **Editor:** Robert Shugrue; **Cast:** Richard Widmark, Lena Horne, Carroll O'Connor, David Opatoshu, Kent Smith, Jacqueline Scott, Morgan Woodward, Larry Gates, Dub Taylor, John Saxon, Darlene Carr, Royal Dano, Jimmy Lyden, Kathleen Freeman.

Richard Widmark plays Marshal Frank Patch, an aging lawman who still rides a horse and wears a gun even though he is considered an anachronism as the 20th century approaches. Years earlier he had tamed the town, but time has passed him by, and the townsfolk, with an eye to the future, want him out. When the marshal refuses to resign, the same people who had once deplored violence choose to use violence against the man who had brought them peace. The only person to help him is his longtime mistress (Lena Horne), whom he marries on the last day before he is due to face a showdown with the well-armed townspeople.

Don Siegel took over directing from Robert Totten for the final four days of shooting *Death of a Gunfighter* after a long-standing feud between Totten and star Richard Widmark led to Totten's removal. Universal had given Widmark creative control of the picture, and the actor was under the impression that Siegel would helm the project. Universal, however, wanted Siegel to direct Clint Eastwood, who was to film *TWO MULES FOR SISTER SARA* in Mexico. Because both pictures were coming up for production at the same time, Siegel suggested that the multitalented Totten should helm *Death of a Gunfighter*. Since Siegel and Totten were good friends and had a mutual respect for each other's work, they decided that the fictitious name of Allen Smithee would appear on the credits.

Totten also directed the award-winning *Huckleberry Finn* and *The Red Pony* as well as a slew of *Gunsmoke* episodes for television. Shortly before his unexpected death in 1997, he discussed his work with Siegel in an interview with the author.

> When the picture was finished, Don and I were sitting in the projection room, a little cutting room, looking at the picture. Don Siegel said, "I'm not going to put my name on this picture, these people are full of crap." He asked me how I felt about it and I said I thought he was right. It was my picture except for the four sequences he did. Don said, "I'll tell you what, Tot, let's go to the DGA (Directors' Guild of America) and have them hash it out for us."
>
> So we went down there and they brought out every name guy on the council. Every one had something to say. One of the guys who was sitting quietly in the background reminded us that it was past eleven o'clock, and that the since Don and I had the deepest respect for each other, and that the film meant a lot to both of us, we were not going to have our names in the credits and no one was going to force us to do it. So I suggested that we have a *nom de plume*. Let's come up with a name that is no name. A name that can't be found in the U.S. Census. A name that doesn't exist. So we wrote down the name 'Allen Smithee.' Now the picture was "directed by the fictitious Allen Smithee."

This compelling western, bolstered by Widmark's superb performance, provides a sad commentary on human nature. Lena Horne sings the song "Sweet Apple Wine" (Carol Hall and Oliver Nelson). Originally slated for television, the film was instead released theatrically.

DEATH RIDES THE PLAINS PRC, 1943, B&W, 53 min. **Producer:** Sigmund Neufeld; **Director:** Sam Newfield; **Screenplay:** Joseph O'Donnell; **Cinematographer:** Robert E. Cline; **Editor:** Holbrook N. Todd; **Cast:** Robert Livingston, Al St. John, Patti McCarty, Ray Bennett, John Elliott, Slim Whitaker, I. Stanford Jolley, Kermit Maynard, George Chesebro, Karl Hackett.

Rocky Cameron (The Lone Rider) attempts to stop a rancher who is offering to sell his land so he can then kill the buyers for their money in this entry to PRC's Lone Rider series. Robert Livingston succeeded George Houston as the Lone Rider, appearing in three series entries: *Overland Stage* (1942); *Death Rides the Plains* (1943); *Law of the Saddle* (1944). (See also *LONE RIDER AMBUSHED, THE*.)

DEATH RIDES THE RANGE Colony Pictures, 1940, B&W, 58 min. **Producers:** Arthur Alexander and Max Alexander; **Director:** Sam Newfield; **Music:** Colin Mac-Donald; **Cinematographer:** Arthur Reed; **Editor:** Holbrook N. Todd; **Cast:** Ken Maynard, Fay McKenzie, Ralph Peters, Julian Rivero, Charles King, John Elliott, William Costello.

Bad guy Joe Larkin (Charles King) knows there is helium on the Morgan ranch. He tries to steal the ranch so he can sell the helium to a foreign agent. But hero Ken Maynard finds the mine and the helium and sets out to help the Morgans hold on to their ranch.

DEATH VALLEY Screen Guild Productions, 1946, B&W/Color, 72 min. **Producer:** William David; **Director:** Lew Landers; **Screenplay:** Doris Schroeder; **Music:** Carl Hoefle; **Cinematographer:** Marcel Le Picard; **Editor:** George McGuire; **Cast:** Robert Lowery, Nat Pendleton, Helen Gilbert, Sterling Holloway, Barbara Read, Russell Simpson, Paul Hurst, Dick Scott.

A man buys a fake gold-claim map in Death Valley, but the lure of gold drives him mad.

DEATH VALLEY GUNFIGHTER Republic, 1949, B&W, 60 min. **Producer:** Gordon Kay; **Director:** R. G. Springsteen; **Screenplay:** Robert Creighton Williams; **Music:** Stanley Wilson; **Cinematographer:** Ernest Miller; **Editor:** Arthur Roberts; **Cast:** Allan "Rocky" Lane, Gail Davis, Eddy Waller, Jim Nolan, William Henry.

"Rocky" Lane is a peace officer who is attacked by outlaws while investigating a payroll robbery. (See also *BOLD FRONTIERSMAN, THE*.)

DEATH VALLEY MANHUNT Republic, 1943, B&W, 55 min. **Producer:** Edward J. White; **Director:** John English; **Screenplay:** Anthony Coldeway and Norman S. Hall; **Music:** Mort Glickman; **Cinematographer:** Ernest Miller; **Editor** Harry Keller; **Cast:** William "Wild Bill" Elliott, George "Gabby" Hayes, Anne Jeffreys, Weldon Heyburn, Herbert Hayes, Davison Clark, Pierce Lyden.

Unbeknownst to an oil company president, one of his men is pulling a swindle on independent drillers. But when the crooked marshal is accidentally killed, "Wild Bill" Elliott is brought in as the new marshal, and things begin to change.

DEATH VALLEY OUTLAWS Republic, 1941, B&W, 54 min. **Producer:** Herbert Yates; **Director:** German Sherman; **Screenplay:** Jack Lait Jr. and Don Ryan; **Music:** Cy Feuer; **Cinematographer:** Edgar Lyons; **Editor:** Tony Martinelli; **Cast:** Don "Red" Barry, Lynn Merrick, Milburn Stone, Robert McKenzie, Karl Hackett, Rex Lease, Jack Kirk, Michael Owen, Fred "Snowflake" Toones.

See *WYOMING OUTLAW.*

DEATH VALLEY RANGERS Monogram, 1943, B&W, 59 min. **Producer:** Robert Emmett Tansey; **Director:** Tansey; **Screenplay:** Elizabeth Beecher; **Cinematographer:** Edward E. Kull; **Editor:** Carl Pierson; **Cast:** Ken Maynard, Hoot Gibson, Bob Steele, Weldon Heyburn, Linda Brent, Glenn Strange, Karl Hackett, Charles King, Lee Roberts.

The Trail Blazers (Ken Maynard, Hoot Gibson, and Bob Steele) come to the aid of a local businessman who has been losing gold shipments to stage robbers. They try to halt the robberies and to find out how the perpetrators manage to get the stolen gold out of town without a trace.

A rather lame imitation of Monogram's successful "Rough Rider" series, which halted after a year due to Buck Jones's tragic death, "The Trail Blazers" suffered from poor production values; repetitious, unmelodic musical scores; and paper-thin plots. Nevertheless the features were fast-paced and deliberately designed to exploit the spectacular stunt-work. While studio publicists insisted that the veteran stars were still scorning doubles, it was apparent that Cliff Lyons and other stuntmen were in many action scenes. The six features in the series include *Wild Horse Stampede, Blazing Guns, Death Valley Rangers, Law Rides Again* (1943); *Arizona Whirlwind, Westward Bound* (1944).

DECISION AT SUNDOWN Columbia, 1957, Color, 77 min. **Producers:** Harry Joe Brown and Randolph Scott; **Director:** Budd Boetticher; **Screenplay:** Charles Lang Jr.; **Music:** Mischa Bakaleinikoff and Heinz Roemheld; **Editor:** Al Clark; **Cast:** Randolph Scott, John Carroll, Karen Steele, Valerie French, Noah Beery Jr., John Archer, Andrew Duggan, James Westerfield, Ray Teal.

Randolph Scott rides into the town of Sundown searching for the man who supposedly killed his wife. He finds him just as he is about to marry a local girl. Look for an outstanding performance from perennial bad guy Ray Teal, on the side of good in this film, appearing as a rancher who helps Scott get even with villain John Carroll. The film is yet another excellent teaming of Scott and Boetticher, with Scott delivering one of his best performances.

DEEP IN THE HEART OF TEXAS Universal, 1942, B&W, 62 min. **Producer:** Oliver Drake; **Director:** Elmer Clifton; **Screenplay:** Drake and Grace Norton; **Music:** Hans Salter; **Cinematographer:** Harry Neumann; **Cast:** Roy Brent, Johnny Mack Brown, Budd Buster, Edmund Cobb, Frank Ellis, William Farnum, Kenneth Harlan, Earle Hodgins, Jennifer Holt, Ray Jones, Fuzzy Knight, The Jimmy Wakely Trio.

A man returns home as the commissioner of public affairs and finds himself at odds with his father, who is now the leader of a guerrilla band. Good action, good drama, and good music combine for an appealing Johnny Mack Brown feature. (See also *OLD CHISHOLM TRAIL, THE*.)

DEERSLAYER, THE Republic, 1943, B&W, 67 min. **Producers:** E. B. Derr, P. S. Harrison, and John W. Kraft; **Director:** Lew Landers; **Screenplay:** Derr, Harrison, and Kraft; **Cinematographer:** Arthur Martinelli; **Editor:** George McGuire; **Cast:** Bruce Kellogg, Jean Parker, Larry Parks, Warren Ashe, Wanda McCay, Yvonne De Carlo, Addison Richards.

The Deerslayer comes to the aid of an Indian tribe whose beautiful princess is being coveted by a rival Huron brave. The Huron burn their village and kidnap the princess. Republic Pictures issued this independent production based on the J. Fenimore Cooper novel from the producers P. S. Harrison and E. B. Derr, who also wrote the script.

DEERSLAYER, THE 20th Century Fox, 1957, Color, 78 min. **Producer:** Kurt Neumann; **Director:** Neumann; **Screenplay:** Carroll Young; **Music:** Paul Sawtell and Bert Shefter; **Cinematographer:** Karl Struss; **Editor:** Jodie Copelan; **Cast:** Lex Barker, Rita Moreno, Forrest Tucker, Cathy O'Donnell, J. C. Flippen, Carlos Rivas.

The Deerslayer (Lex Barker) and his Mohican blood brother Chingachgook (Carlos Rivas) rescue an ornery hunter and his two daughters who are living in an isolated island fort. They try to prevent an Indian war when they find that the ornery man they rescued is actually a scalp hunter. This colorful adaptation of the J. Fenimore Cooper novel was filmed in Kinescope.

In 1978 NBC-TV ran a remake of Cooper's novel for the small screen as part of its "Classic Illustrated" series. It was a follow-up to the previous year's highly regarded *The Last of the Mohicans*. The script was written in part by an uncredited Dalton Trumbo, who was still feeling the effect of the Hollywood Blacklist.

Cooper's *Deerslayer* has had a long film trail, being filmed as early as 1913. A silent version, originally issued in Germany in 1920, was released in the United States in 1923 and remains most notable for an appearance by Bela Lugosi as Chingachgook.

DELIVER US FROM EVIL See *RUNNING WILD*.

DEMON FOR TROUBLE, A Supreme, 1934, B&W, 58 min. **Producer:** A. W. Hackel; **Director:** Robert F. Hill; **Screenplay:** Jack Natteford; **Cinematographer:** William C. Thompson; **Editor:** William Austin; **Cast:** Bob Steele, Don Alvarado, Gloria Shea, Nick Stuart, Walter McGrail, Carmen Laroux, Lafe McKee, Perry Murdock, Blackie Whitford, Jimmy Aubrey.

DENVER AND THE RIO GRANDE Paramount, 1952, Color, 89 min, VT. **Producer:** Nat Holt; **Director:** Byron Haskin; **Screenplay:** Frank Gruber; **Music:** Paul Sawtell; **Cinematographer:** Ray Rennahan; **Editor:** Stanley E. Johnson; **Cast:** Edmond O'Brien, Sterling Hayden, Dean Jagger, Laura Elliott, Lyle Bettger, ZaSu Pitts, Paul Fix, Tom Powers, Dan Haggerty, James Burke.

This fictionalized account of the building of the Denver and Rio Grande Railroad in the Colorado Mountains centers on the rivalry between two competent and competing companies who hope to complete the line. The climax features an actual head-on collision between two steam locomotives. Filmed in Durango, Mexico, the film includes lots of landslides, robberies, and shootings to complement good performances.

DENVER KID, THE Republic, 1948, B&W, 60 min. **Producer:** Gordon Kay (associate); **Director:** Philip Ford; **Screenplay:** Bob Williams; **Cinematographer:** John MacBurnie; **Editor:** Harold Minter; **Cast:** Allan "Rocky" Lane, Eddy Waller, William Henry, Douglas Fowley, Rory Mallinson, George Lloyd, George Meeker, Emmett Vogan, Hank Patterson.

DEPUTY MARSHAL Lippert Pictures, 1949, B&W, 60 min. **Producer:** Robert L. Lippert; **Director:** William A. Berke; **Screenplay:** Berke and Charles Heckelmann; **Music:** Irving Bibo and John Stephens (songs); **Cinematographer:** Carl Berger; **Editor:** Edward Mann; **Cast:** Jon Hall, Frances Langford, Dick Foran, Julie Bishop, Joe Sawyer, Russell Hayden.

A deputy marshal fights against a pair of gangster brothers who want to take land from the farmers to build a railroad. The formula plot is highlighted by a strong cast, some decent songs by Irving Bibo and John Stevens, and the ever-pleasing voices of Frances Langford and Dick Foran.

DESERT BANDIT Republic, 1941, B&W, 56 min. **Producer:** George Sherman; **Director:** Sherman; **Screenplay:** Eliot Gibbons and Bennett Cohen; **Music:** Cy Feuer; **Cinematographer:** William Nobles; **Editor:** Ray Snyder; **Cast:** Don "Red" Barry, Lynn Merrick, William Haade, James Gillette, Dick Wessel, Tom Chatterton, Tom Ewell, Robert Strange, Charles R. Moore, Ernie Stanton.

DESERTER, THE Paramount, 1971, Color, 99 min, VT. **Producers:** Norman Baer, Dino De Laurentiis, and Ralph B. Serpe; **Director:** Burt Kennedy; **Screenplay:** Clair Huffaker; **Music:** Piero Piccioni; **Cinematographer:** Aldo Tonti; **Editor:** Frank Santillo; **Cast:** Bekim Fehmiu, Richard Crenna, Chuck Connors, Ricardo Montalban, Ian Bannen, Brandon De Wilde, Slim Pickens, Woody Strode, Albert Salmi, Patrick Wayne, John Huston.

This film, a U.S.-Italian-Yugoslavian coproduction, deals with an army officer who deserts and disappears into the Southwest because he believes his wife's death was due to army negligence. With a band of specially trained soldiers he wages war against the Apache for mutilating his wife.

Director Burt Kennedy assembled a big-name cast and shot on location in Italy and Spain. However, he was beset with a slew of problems almost from the start. A fierce rain-storm early in the production washed out the road to the shooting location, and the cast had to spend six hours travel-ing there together by car. Then, Kennedy's star Bekim Fehmiu refused to work. Two dogs in the picture had a fight, and one had to go to the hospital. The next day two actors had a fight, and one had to go to the hospital. Three weeks later a horse fell off a bridge and lived. Kennedy attests that the crew was the worst he ever worked with.

DESERT GOLD (aka: AFTER THE STORM)

Kay Bee, 1914, B&W, two reels. **Director:** Scott Sidney; **Screenplay:** Thomas H. Ince and Richard Spencer; **Cast:** Charles Ray, Frank Borsage, Clara Williams, Robert Korman.

DESERT GOLD

W. W. Hodkinson, 1919, B&W, seven reels. **Producer:** Benjamin Hampton; **Director:** T. H. Hunter; **Screenplay:** Fred Myton; **Cinematographers:** Abraham Scholtz and A. L. Todd; **Cast:** E. K. Lincoln, Edward Coxen, Eileen Percy, Margerie Wilson, William H. Bainbridge, Laura Winston, Walter Long, Russell Simpson, Arthur Morrison, Mrs. Dark Cloud, Frank Lanning, Mary Jane Irving.

DESERT GOLD

Paramount, 1926, B&W, 70 min, VT. **Producers:** Adolph Zukor and Jesse L. Lasky; **Director:** George B. Seitz; **Screenplay:** Lucien Hubbard; **Cinematographer:** Charles Edgar Schoenbaum; **Cast:** Neil Hamilton, Shirley Mason, Robert Frazer, William Powell, Josef Swickard, George Irving, Eddie Gribbon, Frank Lackteen, Bernard Siegel, George Regas, Ralph Yearsley, Aline Goodwin.

DESERT GOLD

Paramount, 1936, B&W, 58 min. **Producer:** Harold Hurley; **Director:** James P. Hogan; **Screenplay:** Stuart Anthony and Robert Yost; **Cinematographer:** George T. Clemens; **Editor:** Chandler House; **Cast:** Tom Keene, Marsha Hunt, Monte Blue, Robert Cummings, Raymond Hatton, Buster Crabbe, Frank Mayo, Walter Miller, Leif Ericson.

In 1914, one year after the publication of Zane Grey's *Desert Gold*, Thomas Ince turned out the first of four screen ver-sions of the novel. At the height of the silent picture era, Paramount produced two versions of the Grey work, the first in 1919 and the second in 1926. The 1926 entry, directed by George Seitz, concerns an easterner (Robert Frazer) who travels west with pal Neil Hamilton. An outlaw killer (William Powell) plunders a border town and tries to kidnap Hamilton's daughter in this worthy silent picture with a fine cast.

In 1936 James Hogan directed the only talkie version of the Zane Grey novel. Paramount made ample use of stock footage from the 1926 film as well as appealing young studio players Robert Cummings, Buster Crabbe, and Marsha Hunt. Tom Keene took the role of Dick Gale (Robert Frazer's part in the 1926 feature). The plot centers on the leader of an outlaw gang who tries to kidnap a girl who is loved by a soldier and his eastern friend. This is an interest-ing film and one well worth seeing.

DESERT GUNS

Beaumont, 1936, B&W, 58 min. **Producer:** Mitchell Leichter; **Director:** Charles Hutchison; **Screenplay:** C. C. Chin; **Cast:** Conway Tearle, Margaret Morris, Charles K. French, Budd Buster, William Gould, Marie Werner, Kaye Brinker, Duke Lee.

A lawman pretends to be the long-lost brother of a young girl in order to save her inheritance from a band of crooks.

DESERT HORSEMAN, THE (aka: CHECK-MATE, UK)

Columbia, 1946, B&W, 57 min, VT. **Producer:** Colbert Clark; **Director:** Ray Nazarro; **Screenplay:** Sherman L. Lowe; **Music:** Mischa Bakaleinikoff, Paul Sawtell, and Marlin Skiles; **Cinematographer:** L. William O'Connell; **Editor:** Paul Borofsky; **Cast:** Charles Starrett, Adele Roberts, Richard Bailey, Smiley Burnette, John Merton, Walt Shrum, George Morgan.

When he is falsely accused of robbing an army payroll, Steve Godfrey (Charles Starrett) sets out to clear his name by taking on the alias of the Durango Kid. (See also *DURANGO KID, THE.*)

DESERT JUSTICE (aka: CRIME'S HIGHWAY, UK)

Atlantic, 1936, B&W, 58 min. **Producer:** William A. Berke; **Director:** Lester Williams (Berke); **Screenplay:** Lewis Kingdon and Gordon Phillips; **Cinematographer:** Robert E. Cline; **Editor:** Arthur A. Brooks; **Cast:** Jack Perrin, Warren Hymer, Maryan Downing, Roger Williams, David Sharpe, Budd Buster, William Gould, Fred "Snowflake" Toones, Earl Dwire, Dennis Moore.

A band of bank robbers take refuge at a cowboy's ranch. One of the robbers turns out to be the cowboy's brother. When the brother is killed by the gang, the cowboy tracks them across the desert.

DESERT MAKING

See *DESERT WOOING, A.*

DESERT OF LOST MEN

Republic, 1951, B&W, 54 min. **Producer:** Harry Keller; **Director:** Keller; **Screenplay:** M. Coates Webster; **Music:** Stanley Wilson; **Cinematographer:** John A. MacBurnie; **Editor:** Harold Minter; **Cast:** Allan "Rocky" Lane, Irving Bacon, Mary Ellen Kay, Roy Barcroft, Ross Elliott, Cliff Clark, Boyd "Red" Morgan, Leo Clary.

A deputy marshal sets out to track down and capture a noto-rious outlaw gang made up of bad men from all over the West. A zesty "Rocky" Lane vehicle, well written and with an interesting plot. (See also *BOLD FRONTIERSMAN, THE.*)

DESERT PASSAGE (aka: STARLIGHT CAN-YON) RKO, 1952, B&W, 62 min. **Producer:** Herman Schlom; **Director:** Leslie Selander; **Screenplay:** Norman Houston; **Music:** Paul Sawtell; **Cinematographer:** J. Roy Hunt; **Editor:** Paul Weatherwax; **Cast:** Tim Holt, Joan Dixon, Walter Reed, Dorothy Patrick, John Dehner, Clayton Moore, Lane Bradford, Michael Mark, Richard "Chito" Martin.

Recent parolee John Carver (Walter Reed) returns to town to collect some stolen goods he had hidden there. He hires stagecoach owners Tim Holt and Chito Rafferty (Richard Martin) to take him to Mexico, but the pair soon discovers that almost everyone Carver knows is after the loot as well. Holt delivers a fine effort in his last B-level film, alongside a top-notch performance by veteran character actor Reed as the paroled Carver. (See also *ALONG THE RIO GRANDE*.)

DESERT PATROL Republic, 1938, B&W, 56 min. **Producer:** A. W. Hackel; **Director:** Sam Newfield; **Screenplay:** Fred Myton; **Cinematographer:** Robert E. Cline; **Editor:** Robert O. Crandall; **Cast:** Bob Steele, Marion Weldon, Rex Lease, Ted Adams, Forrest Taylor, Budd Buster, Steve Clark, Jack Ingram.

Texas Ranger Dave Austin (Bob Steele) sets out to get the smuggling gang who killed a fellow Ranger in this good reworking of the revenge theme. (See also *LIGHTNIN' CRANDALL*.)

DESERT PHANTOM Supreme, 1936, B&W, 60 min, VT. **Producer:** A. W. Hackel; **Director:** S. Roy Luby; **Screenplay:** Earle Snell; **Cinematographer:** Bert Longenecker; **Editor:** Roy Claire; **Cast:** Johnny Mack Brown, Sheila Bromely, Ted Adams, Karl Hackett, Hal Price, Nelson McDowell.

DESERT PURSUIT Monogram, 1952, B&W, 71 min. **Producer:** Lindsley Parsons; **Director:** George Blair; **Screenplay:** Scott Darling; **Cinematographer:** William Sickner; **Editor:** Leonard W. Herman; **Cast:** Wayne Morris, Virginia Grey, George Tobias, Anthony Caruso, Emmett Lynn, John Doucette, Gloria Talbott.

A prospector and a girl are pursued by an outlaw gang while searching the California desert for gold in this adaptation of the novel *Starlight Canyon* by Kenneth Perkins.

DESERT TRAIL, THE Monogram/Lone Star, 1935, B&W, 54 min, VT, DVD. **Producer:** Paul Malvern; **Director:** Cullen Lewis (Lewis D. Collins); **Screenplay:** Lindsley Parsons; **Music:** Norman Spencer; **Cinematographer:** Archie Stout; **Editor:** Carl Pierson; **Cast:** John Wayne, Mary Korman, Paul Fix, Eddy Chandler, Carmen Laroux, Lafe McKee, Al Ferguson, Henry Hall, Frank Brownlee.

John Wayne is a star rodeo performer who clashes with his friend over a girl and brings a band of holdup bandits to jus-tice. This B Wayne western, which is also available in a computer-colorized version, features some exciting rodeo sequences. Writer Lindsley Parsons, who worked with Wayne on a number of films, recalled these early days at Monogram.

> His [Duke's] problem was that he didn't feel he was an actor. We'd be out on location, and he'd do a dialogue sequence and he'd just cuss himself out terribly. He would go behind a rock and talk about how lousy he was. I think I kept the dialogue simple and easy to speak. I didn't try to write long speeches for him. I think that's one of the reasons we became very good friends.

DESERT VENGEANCE Columbia, 1931, B&W, 65 min. **Producers:** Irving Briskin, Harry Cohn, and Sol Lesser; **Director:** Louis King; **Screenplay:** Stuart Anthony; **Cinematographer:** Ted D. McCord; **Editor:** Ray Snyder; **Cast:** Buck Jones, Barbara Bedford, Douglas Gilmore, Edward Brady, Bob Fleming, Slim Whitaker.

A bandit who runs a remote town stronghold falls for a girl who deceives him. He then saves her when her partner leaves her to die in the desert as the two fight off an attack by a rival gang. The feature is one of the very best early Buck Jones talkies. (See also *WHITE EAGLE*.)

DESERT VIGILANTE Columbia, 1949, B&W, 56 min. **Producer:** Colbert Clark; **Director:** Fred Sears; **Screenplay:** Earle Snell; **Music:** Smiley Burnette and Jimmy Wakely; **Cinematographer:** Rex Wimpy; **Editor:** Paul Borofsky; **Cast:** Charles Starrett, Peggy Stewart, Tristram Coffin, Mary Newton, George Chesebro, Smiley Burnette.

A government agent is on the trail of a band of silver smugglers near the Mexican border. He meets a pretty girl whose uncle has been killed by the band, and the Durango Kid goes into action. (See also *DURANGO KID, THE*.)

DESERT WOOING, A (aka: DESERT MAKING) Paramount, 1918, B&W, 55 min. **Producer:** Thomas Ince; **Director:** Jerome Storm; **Screenplay:** J. G. Hawks; **Cinematographer:** Edwin Willat; **Cast:** Enid Bennett, Jack Holt, Donald MacDonald, J. P. Lockney, Charles Spere, Elinor Hancock.

A woman in need of money sells her pretty daughter in marriage to a rugged rancher, and the girl eventually learns to love her husband. This Thomas Ince silent feature will be pleasing to Jack Holt fans.

DESPERADO, THE Allied Artists, 1954, B&W, 80 min. **Producer:** Vincent M. Fennelly; **Director:** Thomas Carr; **Screenplay:** Geoffrey Homes (Daniel Mainwaring); **Music:** Raoul Kraushaar; **Editor:** Sam Fields; **Cast:** Wayne Morris, Jimmy Lydon, Beverly Garland, James Lyden, Dabbs Greer, Rayford Barnes, Lee Van Cleef, Nestor Paiva, Roy Barcroft, John Dierkes, I. Stanford Jolley, Florence Lake.

In 1810 Texas, a young lawman teams with an outlaw to oppose the carpetbagger government of the Lone Star State. This was one of the last westerns of the 'B' era.

DESPERADOES, THE Columbia, 1943, Color, 86 min, VT. **Producer:** Harry Joe Brown; **Director:** Charles Vidor; **Screenplay:** Robert Carson; **Music:** Morris Stoloff (director); **Cinematographers:** Allen M. Davey and George Meehan; **Editor:** Gene Havlick; **Cast:** Randolph Scott, Glenn Ford, Claire Trevor, Evelyn Keyes, Edgar Buchanan, Raymond Walburn, Guinn "Big Boy" Williams, Bernard Nedell, Irving Bacon, Glenn Strange, Slim Whitaker, Edward Pawley, Chester Clute, Francis Ford, Charles King.

Randolph Scott and Glenn Ford team as a sheriff and an outlaw who find themselves on the same side of the law, with Ford attempting to go straight and Scott trying to clean up the town. The exciting climax has the reformed Ford stampeding a herd of horses to free Scott, who has been falsely accused of assisting in a robbery. Briskly directed by Charles Vidor, this solid and underrated adaptation of a story by Max Brand includes a pleasant musical score orchestrated by Morris Stoloff (with strains of old folk favorites "Red River Valley" and "Speak to Me of Love") and fine performances, particularly by Ford as the repentant outlaw Cheyenne Rogers. Edgar Buchanan also shines as the popular mail-coach driver Uncle Willie McCloud, who unbeknownst to all is in league with the town's crooked banker. *The Desperadoes* was the first color feature for Columbia Pictures.

DESPERADOES, THE Columbia, 1969, Color, 90 min. **Producer:** Irving Allen; **Director:** Henry Levin; **Screenplay:** Walter Brough; **Music:** David Whitaker; **Cinematographer:** Sam Leavitt; **Editor:** Geoffrey Foote; **Cast:** Vince Edwards, Sylvia Syms, Benjamin Edney, Jack Palance, Sheila Burrell, George Maharis, Kate O'Mara.

Following the Civil War, a father and his sons head west to lead an outlaw gang. Things unravel when one of the sons deserts and decides to marry and settle down. Soon he finds that his own family has pillaged his land.

DESPERADOES ARE IN TOWN, THE 20th Century Fox, 1956, B&W, 73 min. **Producer:** Kurt Neumann; **Director:** Neumann; **Screenplay:** Neumann and Earle Snell; **Music:** Paul Sawtell and Bert Shefter; **Cinematographer:** John J. Mescall; **Cast:** Robert Arthur, Kathleen Nolan, Rhys Williams, Rhodes Reason, Mae Clark.

A former outlaw befriends a young man in this film based on Bennett Foster's story *The Outlaws Are in Town*. When the ex-outlaw is killed by his former partners, the young man seeks to revenge his friend's death.

DESPERADOES OF DODGE CITY Republic, 1948, B&W, 60 min. **Producer:** Gordon Kay; **Director:** Philip Ford; **Screenplay:** Bob Williams; **Music:** Morton

Scott (director); **Cinematographer:** John MacBurnie; **Editor:** Harold Minter; **Cast:** Allan "Rocky" Lane, Eddy Waller, Mildred Coles, Roy Barcroft, Tristram Coffin, William Phipps, James Craven, House Peters Jr.

In this "Rocky Lane" venture, Rocky must deliver an important message to an army post. The message is stolen by one of four men riding on the stagecoach with him. When Rocky and the four get trapped in a shack by an outlaw gang, he learns that one of them is the gang leader. Rocky now has to retrieve the message and find the identity of the true culprit. (See also *BOLD FRONTIERSMAN, THE*.)

DESPERADOES OF THE WEST Republic, 1950, B&W, 167 min, 12 episodes. **Producer:** Herbert J. Yates; **Director:** Fred Brannon; **Screenplay:** Ronald Davidson; **Cinematographer:** John MacBurnie; **Editor:** Cliff Bell, Sr. and Sam Starr; **Cast:** Tom Keene (as Dick Powers), Judy Clark, I. Stanford Jolley, Roy Barcroft, Lee Phelps, Cliff Clark.

A crook and his outlaw gang attempt to thwart ranchers from successfully drilling on their oil-rich land in order to get a lease on their oil properties to turn over to his eastern syndicate bosses. This standard and competent Republic serial has all the requisites: saloon brawls, gunfights, explosions, wagons falling from cliffs, split-second escapes, and great stuntwork. Included as well is extensive stock footage from earlier productions, so it is not unusual to see hero and villains alike, for no apparent reason, changing their costumes many times in order for them to match earlier footage. Tom Keene (credited here as Dick Powers) is an appealing hero, while I. Stanford Jolley and the ever-present Roy Barcroft make for excellent villains.

DESPERATE TRAIL, THE Fidelity Studios, 1994, Color, 93 min, VT. **Producer:** Brad Krevoy; **Director:** P. J. Pesce; **Screenplay:** Pesce and Tom Abrams; **Music:** Stephen Endleman; **Cinematographer:** Michael Bonvillain; **Editor:** Bill Johnson; **Cast:** Sam Elliott, Craig Sheffer, Linda Fiorentino, John Furlong, Robin Westphal, Boots Sutherland.

Sam Elliott plays an unforgiving marshal in this original western saga released directly for video. It was filmed on location in Bonanza Creek Ranch and Tesuque, New Mexico. Elliott goes against type as a lawman obsessed with catching his fugitive daughter-in-law (Linda Fiorentino), who killed her abusive husband and fled. She manages to break away from Elliott's grasp and eventually allies herself with a dandified highwayman (Craig Sheffer). Elliott's apprehending tactics now become increasingly brutal. This well-written and well-acted western sports interesting characters, a "Bonnie and Clyde" scenario, and enough surprises to provide an exciting ride until the very end.

DESPERATE TRAILS Universal, 1939, B&W, 60 min. **Producer:** Albert Ray; **Director:** Ray; **Screenplay:** Andrew Bennison; **Music:** Charles Previn; **Cinematographer:**

Jerome Ash; **Cast:** Johnny Mack Brown, Frances Robinson, Baker Bob, Fuzzy Knight, Russell Simpson.

A crooked lawyer and a banker are behind a group of night riders who are trying to rustle a girl's horses. Johnny Mack Brown's first film for Universal is a good one. (See also *OLD CHISHOLM TRAIL, THE.*)

DESTRY Universal, 1954, Color, 95 min. **Producer:** Stanley Rubin; **Director:** George Marshall; **Screenplay:** Felix Jackson; **Music:** Henry Mancini, Frank Skinner, and Herman Stein; **Cinematographer:** George Robinson; **Editor:** Ted J. Kent; **Cast:** Audie Murphy, Mari Blanchard, Lyle Bettger, Thomas Mitchell, Edgar Buchanan, Lori Nelson, Mary Wickes, Alan Hale Jr.

Based on the Max Brand story *Destry Rides Again*, this film portrays a small town in the Old West controlled by a ruthless mob boss named Decker. When the local sheriff dies under mysterious circumstances, Decker arranges to have the town drunk appointed sheriff. Instead of being ineffectual, the new sheriff sends for Tom Destry, son of a famous two-fished lawman, to be his deputy.

This is a reworking of the 1932 version of *Destry Rides Again* with Tom Mix and the 1939 classic with Jimmy Stewart and Marlene Dietrich. Genre purists often argue that while Audie Murphy had many fine screen moments, he was a pale successor to James Stewart and not up to the part of Tom Destry. Other sources disagree. *Variety*, for one, praised Murphy's performance, calling it one of the actor's best screen efforts and insisting that Murphy "tackles the role, and probably better fits the original [Max] Brand conception than his predecessors." George Marshal who helmed the 1939 film, also directed this later version. *Destry* is a well-crafted and worthwhile film, but not an improvement on the 1939 feature.

DESTRY RIDES AGAIN (aka: JUSTICE RIDES AGAIN) Universal, 1932, B&W, 55 min. **Producer:** Stanley Bergerman; **Director:** Ben Stoloff; **Screenplay:** Isadore Bernstein and Robert Keith; **Cinematographer:** Daniel B. Clark; **Editors:** Maurice Pivar and Arthur Hilton; **Cast:** Tom Mix, Claudia Dell, ZaSu Pitts, Stanley Fields, Earle Foxe, Edward Piel Sr., Francis Ford, Tony the Wonder Horse (himself).

None of the three versions of Max Brand's 1930 novel has ever followed the book very closely, yet two of the versions—in 1932 and 1939—have managed to become genre classics. The 1932 film starred Tom Mix, the most popular cowboy of his era and one of the most popular of all time. The feature was made as part of a deal Mix had with Universal, which required the studio to pay him $10,000 per week during the production of six films. Universal also gave Mix total control of casting and story, and he was allowed to use his favorite Fox cameraman, Daniel B. Clark.

Mix plays Tom Destry, part owner of a stagecoach line, but his partner is working hand-in-hand with a dishonest sheriff. When Destry decides to run for sheriff himself, he is framed on a murder charge and sentenced to prison. He vows revenge, and when pardoned he dispatches two of the outlaws, killing them directly. Later he captures the crooked Sheriff Wendell, and in an exciting finale he saves his girl from the clutches of his two-timing partner.

Despite the plot change, the film did well at the box office and was well received by critics and audiences alike. An appealing romantic interlude between Mix and heroine Claudia Dell works nicely too. With the exception of his vigorous fight scenes, Tom Mix did most of his own stunts. On the other hand, Tony the Wonder Horse was used only in close-ups; the popular steed had a double for most of the hard riding. This was Mix's first talking picture and is ample proof why he has remained one of the great genre stars. The feature was reissued as *Justice Rides Again* in order not to conflict with the 1939 remake.

DESTRY RIDES AGAIN Universal, 1939, B&W, 94 min, VT. **Producer:** Joe Pasternak; **Director:** George Marshall; **Screenplay:** Felix Jackson, Henry Myers, and Gertrude Purcell; **Music:** Frank Skinner and Charles Previn (director); **Cinematographer:** Hal Mohr; **Editor:** Milton Carruth; **Cast:** Marlene Dietrich, James Stewart, Charles Winniger, Mischa Auer, Brian Donlevy, Allen Jenkins, Una Merkel.

Released in that extraordinary film year of 1939, *Destry Rides Again* marked a revival of the western spoof, which had remained dormant since the satires of Mack Sennett and the levity of Douglas Fairbanks during the 1920s. A youthful James Stewart plays pacifist sheriff Tom Destry with wit and style, arriving on the stagecoach carrying a canary and a parasol (which are not really his), then strutting over to the Last Chance Saloon, unarmed, and ordering a glass of milk. The plot involves a young tenderfoot (Stewart) who is drafted into becoming marshal of a rough town, then falls under the spell of Frenchy (Marlene Dietrich), the seductive saloon singer.

This version of *Destry* is a rowdy comical western that revived Dietrich's faltering film career and proved to be a big moneymaker as well. Dietrich's role is pivotal. For the first time we have hints that women in westerns were about to cease being simply objects of respect and future motherhood. Dietrich's Frenchy is a raucous saloon girl who spends her time destroying men in the Last Chance Saloon, which is owned by a villain named Kent (played superbly by Brian Donlevy). As Parkinson and Jeavons note in their *A Pictorial History of Westerns*, Dietrich transforms "her *Blue Angel* sexuality to the wild frontier, devastating cowboy and audience alike with her inimitable rendering of 'See What the Boys in the Back Room Will Have,' and retaining her allure even at the end of an unladylike brawl with Una Merkel when both have been drenched with water."

The sexy humor did not please everyone. The Hays Office, which was in charge of maintaining decency in film, had been around since 1922. In 1939 it had received a large number of complaints from religious groups and started a policy of getting tough. David Selznick fought strongly for *Gone With the Wind* to keep the "damn" in Rhett Butler's "Frankly, my dear, I don't give a damn." While the Hays Office permitted Dietrich to push money into her ample cleavage, it censored her accompanying line, "There's gold in them thar' hills."

Among the pundits who were not so effusive was William Everson. In his *Pictorial History of the Western Film* he writes, "*Destry Rides Again* worked a peculiar kind of chemistry in its teaming of Marlene Dietrich and James Stewart. It was actually a dull and uneventful Western, weak on both story and drama, full of cliché; yet the dynamic Dietrich personality, plus a memorable musical score and a cast full of enjoyable character players somehow held it all together and turned it into a freak box-office smash."

Yet with the possible exception of Mel Brooks's BLAZING SADDLES some 35 years later, no western spoof has approached *Destry Rides Again* in popularity or lasting genre lore. It has some of the best barroom scenes ever put on film, a marvelous musical score by Frank Skinner, and a plethora of lively dialogue. After more than six decades, *Destry Rides Again* remains an appealing film and one not unreasonably credited with introducing sex to the western. The film might not be the landmark western some have claimed, but it is still a delightful slice of entertainment punctuated with action, laughs, and lots of human sentiment.

DEVIL HORSE, THE Pathé, 1926, B&W, 50 min. **Producer:** Hal Roach; **Director:** Frank Jackman; **Screenplay:** Hal Roach; **Cinematographers:** Floyd Jackman and George Stevens; **Cast:** Yakima Canutt, Gladys Morrow, Bob Kortman, Roy Clements, Master Fred Jackson.

A man who as a young lad saw his family wiped out by an Indian massacre enlists the help of a wild stallion to rescue a major's daughter who has been kidnapped by a renegade Indian. Filmed on location at Little Big Horn River in Montana and in Newhall, California, this action-packed silent western was produced and written by Hal Roach. *The Devil Horse* is also Yakima Canutt's most worthy silent effort. Canutt would gain fame in the talkie period, first as a stuntman/villain in a number of Monogram and Republic westerns, then later as a director and organizer of mass-action sequences in genre and nongenre films. Future award-winning director George Stevens (*SHANE, Giant*) was the film's second cameraman. This is a gem of a silent film, which William K. Everson has called " . . . a large-scale programmer with excellent mass as well as individual stunting and some superior photography of excellent locations. . . ."

DEVIL HORSE, THE Mascot, 1932, B&W, 12 chapters. **Producer:** Nat Levine; **Director:** Otto Brower; **Screenplay:** George Morgan, Barney A. Sarecky, George H. Plympton, and Wyndham Gittens; **Music:** Lee Zahler; **Cinematographers:** Ernest Miller, Victor Schurich, and Carl Wester; **Editors:** Victor Schurich, Ray Snyder, and Gilmore Walker; **Cast:** Harry Carey, Noah Beery, Frankie Darro, Greta Granstedt, Barrie O'Daniels, Jack Mower, Al Bridge.

Harry Carey in the serial The Devil Horse (MASCOT/AUTHOR'S COLLECTION)

A remake of the 1926 silent feature, this 1932 serial has Harry Carey in a dual role as a murdered ranger and the dutiful brother who is determined to find the killer. He gets help from a boy (Frankie Darro) who has run with a wild horse herd since he was a child. Noah Beery makes an effective villain as Canfield, the respected rancher who is involved in crooked horse racing while leading an outlaw gang. Yakima Canutt's stuntwork is superb as he literally fights a horse dangling by his feet from its neck. This fast-paced action serial was filmed in Phoenix, Arizona.

DEVIL RIDERS PRC, 1943, B&W, 56 min, VT. **Producer:** Sigmund Neufeld; **Director:** Sam Newfield; **Screenplay:** Joseph O'Donnell; **Cinematographer:** Robert E. Cline; **Editor:** Robert O. Crandell; **Cast:** Buster Crabbe, Al St. John, Patti McCarty, Charles King, John Merton, Kermit Maynard, Frank La Rue, Jack Ingram, George Chesebro.

See *OUTLAWS OF THE PLAINS*.

DEVIL'S BEDROOM (aka: FURY OF VENGEANCE) Allied Artists, 1964, B&W, 78 min. **Producers:** George Gunter and L. Q. Jones; **Director:** Jones (as Justus McQueen); **Screenplay:** Morgan Woodward and Claude Hall; **Music:** Emil Cadkin and Maitland Stewart;

Cast: John Lupton, Valerie Allen, Dickie Jones, Ken Ariola, Bill Buckner, Thomas Commack, L. Q. Jones, Morgan Woodward.

When a valuable oil deposit is found on a local man's property, a couple tries to drive the poor fellow insane in order to obtain his ranch. Small-town prejudice leads to the tragic persecution of this ordinary fellow, whose worst "crime" is being a loner. Actor L. Q. Jones and partner Alvy Moore produced this obscure film, with Jones helming the production under his original name Justus McQueen. Actor Morgan Woodward, who gained notoriety as the infamous "Man With No Eyes" in *Cool Hand Luke*, cowrote the screenplay and, like Jones, also appears in the cast.

As Justus McQueen, Jones made his screen debut in Raoul Walsh's popular World War II film *Battle Cry*, in which he played a soldier named L. Q. Jones. He liked the name so much that he took it as his own. He subsequently became one of the busiest actors in the picture business.

DEVIL'S CANYON RKO, 1953, Color, 92 min. **Producer:** Edmund Grainger; **Director:** Alfred L. Werker; **Screenplay:** Frederick Hazlitt and Harry Essex; **Music:** Daniele Amfitheatrof; **Cinematographer:** Nicholas Musaraca; **Cast:** Virginia Mayo, Dale Robertson, Stephen McNally, Arthur Hunnicutt, Robert Keith, J. C. Flippen, Paul Fix.

A former marshal is put in prison for shooting two men in self-defense, but he soon learns that the brother of the men he shot is in the same prison and plotting revenge. Before long he becomes involved in a full-scale prison riot. Dale Robertson's authentic western presence makes this oater, originally filmed in 3-D, an enjoyable genre piece.

DEVIL'S DOORWAY MGM, 1950, B&W, 84 min. **Producer:** Nicholas Nayfack; **Director:** Anthony Mann; **Screenplay:** Guy Trosper; **Music:** Daniele Amfitheatrof; **Cinematographer:** John Alton; **Editor:** Conrad A. Nervig; **Cast:** Robert Taylor, Louis Calhern, Paula Raymond, Marshall Thompson, James Mitchell, Edgar Buchanan.

In an interesting departure from type, Robert Taylor plays Lance Poole, a Shoshone Indian who wins the Congressional Medal of Honor while fighting with the Union forces at Gettysburg. He returns home to his tribal lands in Wyoming with great hope and the intent of becoming a peaceful farmer. Instead he finds that sheepherders covet his father's land and the land of his fellow tribesmen, whom an Indian-hating lawyer (Louis Calhern) has stirred up. As injustices to his people escalate, he is forced to take up arms and refuses any compromise suggested by sympathetic lawyer Orrie Masters (Paula Raymond). Ultimately, a bloody and violent battle ensues between the Indians and the sheepherders that results in Lance's death. There is a supreme irony in seeing Poole face the cavalry dressed in his military uniform. Mortally wounded, he salutes the cavalry commander before falling dead.

In 1950 Anthony Mann began his western cycle with three films that offered interesting variations of the frontier theme: *Devil's Doorway*, THE FURIES, and WINCHESTER 73. In *Devil's Doorway* he took up the plight of the American Indian, a theme not handled sympathetically for some time. Shot in the manner of a film noir, Mann's first western remains an amazingly radical departure from the ordinary genre piece of its day and a prelude to a series of fine westerns that would appear in the 1950s. While it was actually made before BROKEN ARROW, it was held for release by MGM until Fox's movie had proven the popularity of a strongly pro-Indian film.

The plotline for the film is said to have been drawn from the real-life account of Chief Joseph of the Nez Perce nation. The critics were mixed. Most agreed that with help from a little skin darkener, the Nebraska-born Taylor looked the part of an Indian, but some found his portrayal of a Shoshone wanting and less than convincing. The real acting laurels belong instead to Calhern as the Indian-hating attorney and Edgar Buchanan as the kindly lawyer.

Yet in spite of the uneven reviews and poor box-office results, both the film and Taylor's performance play out surprisingly well today. Mann's forceful direction, especially in the climactic battle scenes, was a portent of things to come from this fine filmmaker. It is a film that the *New York Times* called " . . . a whopping action film . . . [which] does speak out against the red man's sad plight as a mistreated ward of the government. *Devil's Doorway* is a western with a point of view that rattles some skeletons in our family closet. . . ."

DEVIL'S MISTRESS, THE Emerson, 1966, Color, 66 min. **Producer:** Wes Moreland; **Director:** Orville Wanzer; **Screenplay:** Wanzer; **Music:** Billy Allen and Douglas Warren; **Cinematographer:** Teddy Gregory; **Cast:** Joan Stapleton, Robert Gregory, Forrest Westmoreland, Douglas Warren, Oren Williams, Arthur Resley.

A female vampire preys on unsuspecting cowboys while four cowpokes murder a man.

DEVIL'S PLAYGROUND, THE United Artists, 1946, B&W, 65 min. **Producers:** William Boyd and Lewis J. Rachmil; **Director:** George Archainbaud; **Screenplay:** Doris Schroeder; **Music:** David Chudnow; **Cinematographer:** Mack Stengler; **Editor:** Fred W. Berger; **Cast:** William Boyd, Andy Clyde, Rand Brooks, Elaine Riley, Robert Elliott, Joseph J. Greene, Francis McDonald, Nedrick Young.

Hoppy, California, and Lucky help protect a young lady against a corrupt sheriff and a crooked judge who are after her friend's gold. Good action sequences, a well-written story, and scenic locations make this entry one of Hop-Along Cassidy's best later ventures. (See also *HOP-ALONG CASSIDY*.)

DEVIL'S SADDLE LEGION, THE Warner Bros., 1937, B&W, 57 min. **Producer:** Bryan Foy; **Director:**

Bobby Connolly; **Screenplay:** Edward Earle Rapp; **Music:** M. K. Jerome, Jack Scholl, and Howard Jackson; **Cinematographer:** Ted McCord; **Editor:** Frank Magee; **Cast:** Dick Foran, Anne Nagel, Willard Parker, Eddie Stanton, Max Hoffman Jr., Jeff York.

A young man is blamed for his father's murder and framed for another killing. He is sentenced to 10 years hard labor, building a dam that is used to divert water needed by ranchers. This project was conceived by a gang of crooks who need convict workers to build the dam. They find a way to convict innocent people so they can get the cheap labor. (See also *MOONLIGHT ON THE PRAIRIE*.)

DEVIL'S TRAIL Columbia, 1942, B&W, 61 min. **Producer:** Leon Barsha; **Director:** Lambert Hillyer; **Screenplay:** Robert Lee Johnson and Philip Ketchum; **Editor:** Charles Nelson; **Cast:** Bill Elliott, Tex Ritter, Eileen O'Hearn, Noah Beery, Frank Mitchell, Ruth Ford, Art Mix, Tristram Coffin.

In this story set in pre-Civil War Kansas at a time when the slavery question was rife, a federal marshal tries to aid his pal Wild Bill Hickok, who has been falsely accused of murder. This first-rate entry in Columbia's Bill Elliott/Tex Ritter series delivers an outstandingly villainous performance from Noah Beery as Bull McQuade. Robert Lee Johnson adapted the screenplay from his story "The Town in Hell's Backyard."

DIRTY DINGUS MAGEE MGM, 1970, Color, 91 min, VT, CD. **Producer:** Burt Kennedy; **Director:** Kennedy; **Screenplay:** Tom Waldman, Frank Waldman, and Joseph Heller; **Music:** Jeff Alexander, Mack David, and Billy Strange; **Cinematographer:** Harry Stradling Jr.; **Editor:** William B. Gulick; **Cast:** Frank Sinatra, George Kennedy, Anne Jackson, Lois Nettleton, Jack Elam, Michelle Carey, John Dehner, Henry Jones, Harry Carey Jr., Paul Fix, Don "Red" Barry (as Donald Barry).

Frank Sinatra plays a scruffy rascal with no morals or conscience who steals anything he gets his hands on. George Kennedy is a dimwitted sheriff who gets more than his share of bops on the head. Dingus (Sinatra) is a sly con man operating around the town of Yerkey's Hole, New Mexico. Served by a stageline called the Jackass Mail, the town has only one industry, a bordello that caters to the troopers from nearby Fort Horner and does a booming business.

Produced and directed by Burt Kennedy and scripted in part by Joseph Heller of *Catch 22* fame, this western was based on the novel *The Ballad of Dingus Magee* by David Markson. The film has seen mixed reviews. *Variety* called it " . . . a good period western comedy, covering the spectrum from satire, through double entendre, to low slapstick"; while Leonard Maltin praised it as a "broad, bawdy spoof . . . fast paced and amusing especially for Western buffs" in his *Video & Movie Guide*. However, Joe Hyams in *The Life and Times of the Western Movie* slaps the film for being "full of the worst kind of humor." As an example he cites a scene where

a girl holding a chicken calls out to a soldier on his way out of the brothel, "Wait, you forgot your cock."

In his autobiography *Hollywood Trail Boss*, Burt Kennedy praises Frank Sinatra for his overall talent and hard work. While not as good as Kennedy's earlier spoof *SUPPORT YOUR LOCAL SHERIFF* (1969) nor his robust *THE ROUNDERS* (1965), *Dirty Dingus Magee* has a good share of laughs; some fine performances from a talented cast, especially from Sinatra and Kennedy as double-crossing buddies; and a gratuitous assortment of whores, Indians, and cavalry soldiers to make things interesting. The picture has been badly cut for TV release.

DIRTY LITTLE BILLY Columbia, 1972, Color, 93 min. **Producer:** Jack L. Warner; **Director:** Stan Dragoti; **Screenplay:** Dragoti and Charles Moss; **Music:** Sascha Burland; **Cinematographer:** Ralph Woolsey; **Editor:** David Wages; **Cast:** Michael E. Pollard, Lee Purcell, Richard Evans, Charles Aidman, Dran Hamilton, Willard Sage, Josip Elic.

Michael Pollard plays Billy the Kid as a dimwitted murderous psychopath who turns to crime in his early years. This is not a normal western by any turn of the imagination, and genre fans will probably find it wanting. It is worth noting that by the end of the 1960s, a newer generation weaned on and molded by Vietnam found it difficult to accept the standard heroic conventions of the westerns that had been sanctified by the "establishment."

DISCIPLE, THE Ince/Triangle, 1915, B&W, 60 min, VT. **Producer:** Thomas Ince; **Director:** William S. Hart; **Screenplay:** Ince and Barret McCormick; **Music:** Wedgewood Nowell; **Cinematographer:** Joe August; **Cast:** William S. Hart, Dorothy Dalton, Thelma Salter, Robert McKim, Charles K. French.

A parson new to the town of Barren Gulch denounces God when he loses his wife to the seductions of a gambler named Doc Hardy. Forsaking his ministry, he takes his little daughter to live alone in the mountains. He returns to his faith only when his daughter becomes ill, and the only one who can save her is the same man who took his wife away from him. (See also *HELL'S HINGES*.)

DISTANT DRUMS Warner Bros., 1951, Color, 101 min, VT. **Producer:** Milton Spirling; **Director:** Raoul Walsh; **Screenplay:** Martin Rackin and Niven Busch; **Music:** Max Steiner; **Cinematographer:** Sidney Hickox; **Editor:** Folmar Blangsted; **Cast:** Gary Cooper, Mari Aldon, Richard Webb, Ray Teal, Arthur Hunnicutt, Robert Barrett, Clancy Cooper, Larry Carper, Gregg Barton, Sheb Wooley.

Gary Cooper plays Captain Quincy Wyatt, an experienced Indian fighter who leads a small force of swamp fighters deep into the Florida Everglades to put down a Seminole uprising. During the difficult journey they come upon a beautiful captive girl who, with her servant, joins the men on their mission. Filmed on location in the Florida Everglades, with superb photography by Sid Hickox and a lush musical score by Max Steiner, the film is a standard Gary Cooper vehicle. As Bosley Crowther noted in his *New York Times Review,* "Don't look for surprises . . . Raoul Walsh, who directed, did so precisely the same way that he has been directing such pictures for a matter of some twenty-five years. That is to say that Mr. Cooper is kept steady and laconic throughout, the action is serio-comic, and the pace is conventionally maintained."

In his next film Cooper would score big with his Oscar-winning performance as Will Kane in Stanley Kramer's *HIGH NOON.*

DISTANT TRUMPET, A Warner Bros., 1964, Color, 117 min. **Producer:** William H. Wright; **Director:** Raoul Walsh; **Screenplay:** Albert Beich and Richard Fielder; **Music:** Max Steiner; **Editor:** David Wages; **Cast:** Troy Donahue, Suzanne Pleshette, Diane McBain, James Gregory, William Reynolds, Claude Akins, Kent Smith, Judson Pratt, Bartlett Robinson, Richard X. Slattery.

An officer (Troy Donahue) falls in love with a lieutenant's wife at a frontier cavalry post. But when the man is killed, the officer's fiancée arrives on the scene just as an Indian attack is about to commence. This was Raoul Walsh's final film. While not his best work, the film benefits from the stunning location terrain of New Mexico's and Arizona's pictorial Painted Desert as well as a vintage big battle sequence.

DJANGO B.R.C./Tecisa, 1965, Color, 91 min, DVD. **Producers:** Manolo Bolognini and Sergio Corbucci; **Director:** Corbucci; **Screenplay:** Franco Rossetti, Jose G. Maesso, Piero Vivarelli, Bruno Corbucci, Sergio Corbucci, and Geoffrey Copleston; **Music:** Luis Enriquez Bacalov; **Cinematographer:** Enzo Barboni; **Editor:** Nino Baragli and Sergio Montanari; **Cast:** Rafael Albaicin, Franco Nero, Jose Bodalo, Angel Alvarez, Simon Arriaga, Loredana Nusciak.

A mysterious stranger arrives in a small border town during a battle between Mexican and American soldiers and takes off with gold belonging to the Mexican army. The first of the very violent Italian-produced "Django" series, this film was helmed by Sergio Corbucci, one of the most able directors of Italian spaghetti westerns. His other works include *Minnesota Clay,* (1965); *Navajo Joe, Ringo and His Golden Pistol* (1966); *The Hellbinders* (1967); *A Professional Gun* (1968); and *Compañeros* (1970).

DOC United Artists, 1971, Color, 96 min, VT. **Producer:** Frank Perry; **Directors:** Frank D. Gilroy and Perry; **Screenplay:** Pete Hamill; **Music:** Jimmy Webb; **Cinematographer:** Gerald Hirschfeld; **Editor:** Alan Heim; **Cast:** Stacy Keach, Faye Dunaway, Harris Yulin, Michael Witney, Denver John Collins.

This time it's Stacy Keach as the tubercular Doc Holliday. He joins forces with prostitute Katie Elder (Faye Dunaway),

and they end up aiding Wyatt Earp in his battle with the Clanton clan. Pete Hamill's original screenplay gives Doc Holliday the dominant treatment over his lawman partner, Wyatt Earp. Doc is depicted as little more than a weak-willed drunk, while Earp is presented as a diminished and corrupt opportunist whose sleazy opportunism was responsible for the gunfight at the O.K. Corral.

The role of Ike Clanton's nephew "The Kid" is played by Denver John Collins, the brother of popular folksinger Judy Collins. Reportedly many of the people director Frank Perry used to inhabit his fictionalized Tombstone were found in New York City. A bartender in the film is played by an official from then-mayor John Lindsay's administration, while Mr. Clum, the editor of *The New Tombstone Epitaph,* is played by Dan Greenberg, author of *How to be a Jewish Mother.* Greenberg, it seems, was sitting next to Perry at a dinner party and was surprised to hear Perry exclaim, "That face— I've got to have that face in my film." The manure-littered streets of Tombstone as visually depicted by Perry were actually filmed in Spain.

In yet another attempt to "demythologize" the American West, one partisan antiestablishment reviewer went so far as to proclaim that "even Viet Nam has its roots in the blood drenched turf of the O.K. Corral."

DODGE CITY Warner Bros., 1939, Color, 104 min, VT. **Producers:** Robert Lord and Hal B. Wallis; **Screenplay:** Robert Buckner; **Music:** Max Steiner; **Cinematographer:** Sol Polito; **Editor:** George Amy; **Cast:** Errol Flynn, Olivia de Havilland, Ann Sheridan, Bruce Cabot, Frank McHugh, Alan Hale, John Litel, Henry Travers, Henry O'Neill, Victor Jory, William Lundigan, Guinn "Big Boy" Williams, Gloria Holden, Ward Bond, Monte Blue.

Wade Hutton (Errol Flynn), an Irish soldier of fortune who had fought in India and Cuba, comes to the United States to join Jeb Stuart's greycoats before heading west. When he reaches Dodge City, Kansas, he finds a wide-open cattle town "with no ethics but cash and killing." Dodge is the northernmost shipping point to St. Louis and Chicago for longhorn cattle being brought up the Old Chisholm Trail from Texas.

Corruption, graft, and lawlessness are running rampant, and the town is controlled mainly by Jeff Surrett (Bruce Cabot). Surrett's gambling saloon typifies the wickedness and lawlessness that was Dodge City, Kansas, which provides the excuse for Wade Hutton to take over the sheriff's post when a young boy is killed in the crossfire of a shoot-out. Ever the romancer, he also captures the hearts of saloon girl Ruby Gilman (Ann Sheridan) and good girl Abbie Irving (Olivia de Havilland), finally winning over the latter. By thwarting Surrett and his wicked thugs, Hutton cleans up the town, making it safe for further migration.

An exciting Technicolor extravaganza, this was Warner Bros.' answer to the revival of the A western in 1939, a year that also included such films as *STAGECOACH, DESTRY RIDES AGAIN, JESSE JAMES, UNION PACIFIC,* and *MAN OF CONQUEST.* This captivating and energetic film moves quickly and is full of action; the superbly staged saloon brawl in *DODGE CITY* has been used in countless films and TV shows as stock footage. Although short on historical fact, the film has withstood the test of time and was reissued in black and white in 1951 along with *VIRGINIA CITY* as a popular double bill.

Directed by Michael Curtiz, *Dodge City* marks Errol Flynn's entry into the western genre. Two more Curtiz/Flynn westerns would follow: *Virginia City* (1940) and *THEY DIED WITH THEIR BOOTS ON* (1941). The film also reunited Flynn with costar and leading lady Olivia de Havilland. The two had worked together in *The Adventures of Robin Hood* (1938) a year earlier and would be seen together again in *SANTA FE TRAIL* in 1940. Despite his British manners, Flynn proved himself an ideal western film hero through the sheer force of his screen presence, and he made eight Warner westerns.

The film received good reviews. *Variety* called it "a lusty western packed with action, including some of the dandiest melee stuff screened," while the *New York Times* called it "... an exciting thriller for the kiddies, or, for grown folks with an appetite for the wild and wooly."

DOLLAR A HEAD, A   See *NAVAJO JOE*.

DOMINO KID, THE   Columbia, 1957, B&W, 74 min. **Producers:** Rory Calhoun and Victor M. Orsatti; **Director:** Ray Nazarro; **Screenplay:** Hal Biller and Kenneth Gamet; **Music:** Mischa Bakaleinikoff; **Cinematographer:** Irving Lippman; **Editor:** Gene Havlick; **Cast:** Rory Calhoun, Kristine Miller, Andrew Duggan, Yvette Duguay, Peter Whitney, Eugene Iglesias, Roy Barcroft, Denver Pyle, Ray Corrigan.

A man returning home to Texas finds his father and brother have been murdered, and he sets out to find the killers. Rory Calhoun wrote the original story for this fairly entertaining film.

DON DAREDEVIL RIDES AGAIN   Republic, 1951, B&W, 167 min, 12 episodes, VT. **Producer:** Herbert Yates; **Director:** Fred C. Brannon; **Screenplay:** Ronald Davidson; **Music:** Gerald Roberts (director) and Stanley Wilson (supervisor); **Cinematographer:** Ellis W. Carter; **Editor:** Cliff Bell Sr.; **Cast:** Ken Curtis, Aline Towne, Roy Barcroft, Robert Einer, Lane Bradford, John L. Cason, I. Stanford Jolley.

A homesteader disguises himself as the masked Don Daredevil to combat a political boss who is trying to run settlers off their land by claiming an old land grant is a fake. There is lots of stock footage in this cliffhanger serial with a good plot.

DON'T FENCE ME IN   Republic, 1945, B&W, 71 min. **Producer:** Donald H. Brown; **Director:** John English; **Screenplay:** Dorrell McGowan, Stuart McGowan, and John K. Butler; **Music:** R. Dale Butts, Bob Nolan (songs), Cole Porter, and Morton Scott; **Cinematographer:** William Bradford; **Editor:** Scott; **Cast:** Roy Rogers, George "Gabby" Hayes, Dale Evans, Robert Livingston, Moroni Olsen, Marc Lawrence, Lucile Gleason, Paul Harvey, Douglas Fowley, Tom London, Steve Barclay, Edgar Dearing, Helen Talbot, Bob Nolan and The Sons of the Pioneers.

Dale Evans is an undercover reporter from the East hoping to discover the true story of ex-outlaw named Wildcat Kelly. She travels to a dude ranch run by Roy Rogers, Gabby Hayes, and the Sons of the Pioneers. It so happens that Gabby has some mysterious knowledge about "Wildcat" Kelly, who supposedly has been dead and buried for many years. Many Roy Rogers fans consider this Saturday matinee treat to be among his very best features, but it's Gabby Hayes who manages to steal most of the laughs and laurels. One hilarious sequence has Gabby in a funeral parlor pretending to be dead while the Sons of the Pioneers are singing "The Last Roundup." Nolan and his Pioneers also sing the western classic "Tumbling Tumbleweeds."

The title song "Don't Fence Me In" was written by Cole Porter and introduced in this film by Roy Rogers and the Sons of the Pioneers. Basing it on a poem by Robert Fletcher, Porter had originally written the song 10 years earlier for an unproduced film. It immediately became one of the biggest hits for 1945, spending 16 weeks on "Your Hit Parade"—and eight times as number one. Bing Crosby and the Andrews Sisters made the hit recording for Decca Records. Gene Autry, Sammy Kaye, and Kate Smith also had popular recordings of the tune.

DOOLINS OF OKLAHOMA, THE   Columbia, 1949, B&W, 90 min. **Producers:** Harry Joe Brown and Randolph Scott; **Director:** Gordon Douglas; **Screenplay:** Kenneth Gamet; **Music:** George Dunning and Paul Sawtell; **Cinematographer:** Charles Lawton Jr.; **Editor:** Charles Nelson; **Cast:** Randolph Scott, Louise Albritton, George Macready, John Ireland, Virginia Huston, Charles Kemper, Noah Beery Jr., Dona Drake, Robert Barrat, Jock Mahoney.

Randolph Scott, the head of the Doolin gang, attempts to go straight, but when his brothers continue their lawless ways, a sheriff and his posse hunts his entire family. This action-packed, well-staged Scott western, coproduced with Harry Joe Brown, is tailor-made for genre fans.

DOUBLE IDENTITY   See *HURRICANE SMITH*.

DOWN DAKOTA WAY   Republic, 1949, Color, 67 min, VT. **Producer:** Edward J. White; **Director:** William Witney; **Screenplay:** John Butler and Sloan Nibley; **Music:** R. Dale Butts, Sid Robbin, Foy Willing, and Stanley Wilson; **Cinematographer:** Reggie Lanning; **Editor:** Tony Martinelli; **Cast:** Roy Rogers, Dale Evans, Pat Brady, Monte Montana, Roy Barcroft.

A crooked businessman tries to sell cattle infected with deadly hoof and mouth disease. To cover up his plans he has the local veterinarian murdered. There is lots of good action in this enjoyable Roy Rogers feature.

DOWN IN OLD SANTA FE   See *IN OLD SANTA FE.*

DOWN MEXICO WAY   Republic, 1941, B&W, 77 min. **Producer:** Harry Grey (associate); **Director:** Joseph Saintly; **Screenplay:** Olive Cooper, Albert Duffy, Dorell McGowan, and Stuart E. McGowan; **Cinematographer:** Jack A. Marta; **Editor:** Howard O'Neill; **Cast:** Gene Autry, Smiley Burnette, Fay McKenzie, Harold Huber, Sidney Blackmer, Joe Sawyer, Andrew Tombes, Murray Alper, Arthur Loft, Duncan Renaldo, Paul Fix, Eddie Dean, the Herrera sisters.

Bad guys swindle the good folk of Sage City on the pretext of producing a movie in their community. Gene and Frog chase them to Mexico, where they plan to rob a rich Mexican ranchero. This film has a good script and some great songs, including "South of the Border," which was first introduced and recorded by Autry in 1939 and became the number one sheet-music seller of the year as well as a top record seller; and "Maria Elena," which spent 22 weeks on "Your Hit Parade." (See also *TUMBLING TUMBLEWEEDS.*)

DRAGON MASTER   See *CANNON FOR CORDOBA.*

DRAGOON WELLS MASSACRE   Allied Artists, 1957, Color, 88 min. **Producer:** Lindsley Parsons; **Director:** Harold Schuster; **Screenplay:** Warren Douglas; **Music:** Paul Dunlap; **Cinematographer:** William H. Clothier; **Editor:** Maurice Wright; **Cast:** Dennis O'Keefe, Barry Sullivan, Mona Freeman, Katy Jurado, Sebastian Cabot, Max Showalter, Jack Elam, Trevor Bardette, Warren Douglas, Hank Worden, Judy Stranges, Alma Beltran, John War Eagle.

Actor turned writer Warren Douglas scripted this western about a diverse group of people, including outlaws and lawmen, who are cornered in a fort about to be attacked by Indians. In his autobiography *The Light's Getting Yellow,* published posthumously, Douglas recalls an entertaining screen fight between stars Mona Freeman and Katy Jurado while on location in Kanob, Utah.

> Katy and Mona took on one another in a beautiful, slam bam, rough and tumble fight. The stunt girls did the long shots but Katy and Mona did all the mayhem in the medium and close shots. It was one of the best female fights I have ever seen and one would have sworn they were going to kill one another. They were just so intent upon their work that they never heard the director call "Cut!" So we just let them go on enjoying themselves until they couldn't swing another punch.
>
> They tore into one another in hundred degree heat, under blazing sun, wearing heavy skirts with a half dozen petticoats beneath for another three or four minutes until Katy looked out of the corner of her eye and saw us standing in a smiling circle, all sipping upon a glass of lemonade. When she shrieked an obscenity and a threat, the circle evaporated and disappeared. It was the wise thing to do.

Douglas was especially fond of the film and considered *Dragoon Wells Massacre* and THE RETURN OF JACK SLADE (1955) his two favorite scripts. As usual, he found a small part for himself as Jud, the prison driver, who gets killed by Sebastian Cabot halfway through the picture. All in all, this neat little oater boasts a strong cast, good direction by Harold Schuster, and a compelling script by the multitalented Douglas, whom friend and colleague Clint Walker has called "one of the sleeping giants of the picture business."

DRANGO   United Artists, 1957, B&W, 92 min. **Producers:** Hall Bartlett, Jules Bricken, and Jeff Chandler; **Director:** Bartlett; **Screenplay:** Bartlett; **Music:** Elmer Bernstein; **Cinematographer:** James Wong Howe; **Cast:** Jeff Chandler, John Lupton, Joanne Dru, Morris Ankrum, Ronald Howard, Julie London, Donald Crisp, Parley Baer, Milburn Stone.

Jeff Chandler is Major Clint Drango, a Yankee Civil War veteran assigned to restore order to a southern town that his command had plundered.

DRIFT FENCE   Paramount, 1936, B&W, 56 min. **Producer:** Harold Hurley; **Director:** Otto Lovering; **Screenplay:** Robert Yost and Stuart Anthony; **Cinematographer:** Virgil Miller; **Editor:** C. A. Hisserich; **Cast:** Tom Keene, Benny Baker, Larry "Buster" Crabbe, Katherine DeMille, Leif Erickson, Stanley Andrews, Richard Carle, Irving Bacon.

A young dude named Jim Traft (Benny Baker) comes west to take over a ranch he has inherited. Because he does not welcome the challenge, he hires a veteran wrangler (Tom Keene) to assume his identity. The wrangler upsets things when he strings a drift fence at the ranch, which is anathema to the cattle ranchers who demand an open range. Tom Keene's restrained performance is indication of how good he really was in his prior RKO western series, while Benny Baker's presence lends a nice slice of comedy relief.

Remarkably, Buster Crabbe, who in the same year would enjoy enormous popularity in Universal's *Flash Gordon* cliffhanger serial, was limited to but a small role. He plays Slinger Dunn, a young rancher who falls under the influence of crooked Clay Jackson. When he discovers that his sister (Katherine DeMille) is coveted by Jackson, he eventually helps the ranchers combat the villains.

While most Zane Grey works have been filmed more than once and some several times, *Drift Fence* was filmed only once. An excellent 1936 B western, this picture benefits from a steady interpretation of Zane Grey's novel, plenty of action, and good performances by all.

DRUM BEAT   Warner Bros., 1954, Color, 111 min, VT. **Producer:** Delmer Daves; **Director:** Daves; **Screenplay:** Daves; **Music:** Victor Young; **Cinematographer:** J. Peverell Marley; **Editor:** Clarence Kolster; **Cast:** Alan Ladd, Audrey Dalton, Marisa Pavan, Robert Keith, Rodolfo Acosta,

Charles Bronson, Warner Anderson, Elisha Cook Jr., Anthony Caruso, Perry Lopez, Peter Hansen.

Alan Ladd is frontiersman Johnny Mace, who is sent by President Ulysses S. Grant to negotiate a peace treaty with the Modoc Indians. President Grant wants to accomplish this without the use of force, but that is impossible because Modoc leader "Captain Jack" (Charles Bronson) is a fearless warrior, a formidable foe, and a driven man who had murdered General Edward R. S. Canby and led the Modoc in their 1872–73 war with the U.S. government.

The historical perspective is important. Edward Canby (Warner Anderson) was the only general ever killed in the field during the 400-year conflict between whites and Native Americans, and the event that precipitated this tragic occurrence is the theme for this film. (George Custer was a lieutenant colonel when he died fighting the Sioux and the Cheyenne.)

Filmed in Arizona in color and CinemaScope, this auspicious debut for Jaguar Productions was coanchored by Alan Ladd and Delmer Daves. The film also features such Ladd "regulars" as Anthony Caruso, Perry Lopez, and Peter Hansen. Daves, who helmed and scripted the film, was descended from pioneer stock himself and took pride in the realism of his western films and in dealing soberly with relations between whites and Native Americans during the settlement of the frontier. The film was a personal favorite for Daves, who had laid new groundwork with his highly acclaimed BROKEN ARROW (1950) a few years earlier.

A good action film with a scene-stealing performance from Bronson, *Drum Beat* was his first picture after ridding himself of his surname Buchinsky. The role of Captain Jack gave his film career a definite boost up from the bit roles and minor heavies he had been playing since 1951. Alan Ladd gives his best performance since *SHANE*.

DRUMS ACROSS THE RIVER
Universal, 1954, Color, 78 min. **Producer:** Melville Tucker; **Director:** Nathan Juran; **Screenplay:** John K. Butler and Lawrence Roman; **Music:** Henry Mancini; **Cinematographer:** Harold Lipstein; **Editor:** Virgil Vogel; **Cast:** Audie Murphy, Walter Brennan, Lyle Bettger, Lisa Gaye, Hugh O'Brian, Mara Corday, Jay Silverheels, Emile Meyer, Regis Toomey, Morris Ankrum, Bob Steele, Gregg Barton, Lane Bradford.

A young man joins a group of gold hunters who go into the Indian territory. When he comes to realize he is the victim of his own bigotry and sees what his compatriots are really up to, he joins with his father in trying to restore peace. This Audie Murphy vehicle serves up a good share of twists and turns but makes the revealing mistake of having the stirrups visible beneath the Indians' horses.

DRUMS ALONG THE MOHAWK
20th Century Fox, 1939, Color, 103 min, VT. **Producers:** Raymond Griffith and Darryl F. Zanuck (executive); **Director:** John Ford; **Screenplay:** Walter D. Edmunds and Sonya Levien; **Music:** Alfred Newman; **Cinematographers:** Bert Glennon and Ray Rennahan; **Editor:** Robert Simpson; **Cast:** Claudette Colbert, Henry Fonda, Edna Mae Oliver, Eddie Collins, John Carradine, Dorris Bowden, Arthur Shields, Robert Lowery, Roger Imhof, Francis Ford, Ward Bond, Jack Pennick (as J. Ronald Pennick).

Set at the dawn of the Revolutionary War, Gil and Lana Martin (Henry Fonda and Claudette Colbert) move to the Mohawk Valley and face immediate hardships. Their farm is burned by Indians, they lose their first child, Gil Martin goes to war, another baby is born, and then Indians attack again. The villagers are forced into a fort where the Indians almost overrun the stockade. Gil returns just in the nick of time with reinforcements, and the film ends on a high note with the young couple confident that a better future looms ahead.

This big picture with a huge cast and crew was shot at a remote location in Utah's Wasatch Mountains. According to Dan Ford—John Ford's grandson and author of *Pappy: The Life of John Ford*—the picture was beset with problems from the start. Not least was difficulty between director Ford and leading lady Colbert. "Froggy," as they called her, was a perfectionist who fretted and complained about everything from her wardrobe to her lines, and Ford, who was never known for his patience with women, resented having to accommodate her.

Another problem was the weather. Summer storms hit the location, and the skies were overcast day after day, inhibiting the shooting schedule. Finally, there was some disagreement and animosity between Ford and producer Darryl Zanuck on the form and pace the picture should take.

Ford had just completed *Young Mr. Lincoln* (1939), and many of the same people who worked with him on that film were also involved with *Drums Along the Mohawk*. Lamar Trotti did both screenplays, and Bert Glennon was the cinematographer for both projects. Most striking, Henry Fonda was cast in the lead role opposite Colbert. Fonda had been working with Ford for a period of months, and a close personal and professional bond had developed between them. *Young Mr. Lincoln*, in fact, had opened to outstanding reviews while they were still shooting *Drums Along the Mohawk*. Just a short time later Ford would cast Fonda as Tom Joad in *The Grapes of Wrath* (1940), the film that garnered the Ford the second of his record-setting four Oscars as Best Director.

In *The Western Films of John Ford*, author/historian J. A. Place suggests that in the traditional sense, *Drums Along the Mohawk* is not a true western because the Revolutionary War time frame predates the post-Civil War period we tend to associate with westerns. Then, paradoxically, she argues that not only is *Drums Along the Mohawk* a western but even more specifically a John Ford western, because Ford's ideas about white civilization and its mission in the West has its "purest expression in this film." It should not be surprising that footage from the movie was later used in *Buffalo Bill* (1944) and *Mohawk* (1956).

This was John Ford's first color feature, and his imprint is pervasive. A poet among directors, his lingering romanticism was incorporated in both story and character and magnified by the vast expanse of his glorious landscapes. With a script based on the book by Walter D. Edmonds, the final cut of *Drums Along the Mohawk* presents a sound historical study and one basically faithful to the author's intent. Wounded in battle, Fonda tells Colbert of the historic moment fighting the Indians in upstate New York: "I remember thinking how hot it was and wondering how long we'd been away—when it happened . . . I heard a crack—like a stick breaking—and all of a sudden the fellow next to me stopped talking and fell over on his side. . . ."

Interestingly, relatively few Hollywood films have dealt with the period surrounding the American Revolution. One of the few, and one of the very best, is *Drums Along the Mohawk*. The fact that it was released in 1939, the same year as Ford's landmark western *Stagecoach*, is a testimony to this director's prolific artisanship. Although it was nominated for two Academy Awards, *Drums Along the Mohawk* received good but not outstanding reviews. *Variety* praised the "colorful backgrounding" and "unusually good photography," noting it was an outdoor spectacle which highly pleased the eye, "even if the story [from the novel by Edmonds], on occasion, gets a bit slow and some incidents fail to excite." *The New York Herald Tribune* found the film lacking in unity, but because of its direction and its playing, described it as "a genuinely distinguished historical film." *The New York Times* called it "a first rate historical film, as rich atmospherically as it is in action."

DRUMS IN THE DEEP SOUTH RKO, 1951, Color, 87 min, VT. **Producers:** Frank King and Maurice King; **Director:** William Cameron Menzies; **Screenplay:** Sidney Harmon and Phillip Yordan; **Music:** Dimitri Tiomkin; **Cinematographer:** Lionel Lindon; **Editor:** Richard Heermance; **Cast:** James Craig, Barbara Payton, Guy Madison, Barton MacLane, Robert Osterloh, Robert Easton, Louis Jean Heydt, Myron Healey, Craig Stevens.

As General Sherman marches through Georgia, James Craig and Guy Madison are best pals who graduated from West Point together and now find themselves on opposite sides in the Civil War.

DUCHESS AND THE DIRTWATER FOX, THE 20th Century Fox, 1976, Color, 103 min, VT. **Producer:** Melvin Frank; **Director:** Frank; **Screenplay:** Frank, Jack Rose, and Barry Sandler; **Music:** Charles Fox and Sammy Cahn (additional songs); **Cinematographer:** Joseph F. Biroc; **Editors:** Frank Bracht and Bill Butler; **Cast:** George Segal, Goldie Hawn, Conrad Janis, Thayer David, Jennifer Lee, Richard Farnsworth, Pat Ast.

A crooked gambler is forced to join forces with a dance-hall woman as they head for the desert with some stolen loot. This slapstick comedy may be of interest to fans of the two stars. Goldie Hawn received a Golden Globe nomination (Best Motion Picture Actress in a Musical or Comedy) for her work in this film, which also features a stellar character performance from Richard Farnsworth as the stage driver.

DUCK YOU SUCKER See *FISTFUL OF DYNAMITE.*

DUDE BANDIT Allied Pictures, 1933, B&W, 62 min. **Producer:** M. J. Hoffman Jr.; **Director:** George Melford; **Screenplay:** Jack Natteford; **Music:** Sam Perry; **Cinematographers:** Tom Galligan and Harry Neumann; **Cast:** Hoot Gibson, Gloria Shea, Hooper Atchley, Skeeter Bill Robbins.

A man investigates the murder of a friend by pretending to be a dimwit. When he finds out a crooked banker is responsible, he takes on the guise of a bandit to stop him. Hoot Gibson's character is similar to the one he did in *Spirit of the West* a year earlier.

DUDE COWBOY RKO, 1941, B&W, 59 min. **Producer:** Bert Gilroy; **Director:** David Howard; **Screenplay:** Morton Grant; **Music:** Fred Rose and Ray Whitley; **Cinematographer:** Harry J. Wild; **Editor:** Frederic Knudtson; **Cast:** Tim Holt, Marjorie Reynolds, Ray Whitley, Lee "Lasses" White, Louise Currie, Helen Holmes, Eddie Kane, Eddie Dew, Tom London, Glenn Strange.

DUDE GOES WEST Allied Artists, 1948, B&W, 86 min. **Producers:** Frank King and Maurice King; **Director:** Kurt Neumann; **Screenplay:** Mary Loos and Richard Sale; **Music:** Dimitri Tiomkin; **Cinematographer:** Karl Strauss; **Editor:** Richard V. Heermance; **Cast:** Eddie Albert, Gale Storm, James Gleason, Gilbert Roland, Binnie Barnes, Barton MacLane, Douglas Fowley, Tom Tyler.

Daniel Bone, an eastern sharpshooting gunsmith fresh out of the Bowery, heads west to ply his trades. Along the way he encounters a girl looking for the murderer of her father, and consequently he finds himself at odds with an outlaw gang.

DUDE RANCH Paramount, 1931, B&W, 71 min. **Director:** Frank Tuttle; **Screenplay:** Lloyd Corrigan, Percy Heath, and Grover Jones; **Cinematographer:** Henry W. Gerrard; **Cast:** Eugene Pallette, June Collier, James Crane, Stuart Erwin, Mitzie Green, Jack Oakie, Guy Oliver.

To impress a girl, an actor goes to a dude ranch, where he poses as a cowboy. This cute little antique talkie has a plot similar to Jack Benny's BUCK BENNY RIDES AGAIN (1940), but it lacks the overall production merit of Benny's outstanding spoof.

DUDE RANGER, THE Fox, 1934, B&W, 68 min, VT. **Producers:** Sol Lesser and John Zanft; **Director:** Edward F. Cline; **Screenplay:** Barry Barringer; **Cinematographer:** Frank B. Good; **Editor:** W. Don Hayes; **Cast:** George O'Brien, Irene Hervey, Le Roy Mason, Henry Hall, Syd Saylor, Lloyd Ingraham.

After inheriting a ranch in Arizona from his uncle, a young man finds out it is being plagued by rustlers in this strong adaptation of the Zane Grey story. George O'Brien's early westerns for Fox had good scripts, many based on Zane Grey novels, and are important because of their capable direction, excellent photography, and picturesque locations. They also served as a useful training ground for new stars whom Fox was grooming, including Humphrey Bogart, George Brent, Maureen O'Sullivan, and Myrna Loy. While not major westerns, O'Brien's entries for Fox were well above the standard B western programmers.

DUDE WRANGLER, THE World Wide Pictures, 1930, B&W, 60 min. **Director:** Richard Thorpe; **Screenplay:** Robert N. Lee; **Cast:** Lina Basquette, George Duryea (Tom Keene/Richard Powers), Francis Bushman, Clyde Cook, Ethel Wales, Sojin, Wilfrid North.

A young man borrows money to buy a dude ranch, but one of the guests plots to sabotage the operation so he can impress the girl they both want. This is an interesting early talkie for Tom Keene, who is billed here as George Duryea. Keene appeared in numerous features for varied studios and was also sometimes credited as Dick Powers and Richard Powers. (See also *BEYOND THE ROCKIES.*)

DUEL AT APACHE WELLS Republic, 1957, B&W, 69 min. **Producer:** Joseph Kane; **Director:** Kane; **Screenplay:** Bob Williams; **Music:** Gerald Roberts; **Cinematographer:** Jack Marta; **Editor:** Richard L. Van Enger; **Cast:** Anna Maria Alberghetti, Ben Cooper, Jim Davis, Harry Shannon, Frances McDonald, Bob Steele, Frank Puglia, Ian MacDonald, John Dierkes, Ric Roman.

A young man returns home and must confront the crook who murdered his father and stole his lands. The familiar theme is made better by Jim Davis as the villain and Bob Steele as his henchman.

DUEL AT DIABLO United Artists, 1966, Color, 103 min, VT. **Producers:** Fred Engel and Ralph Nelson; **Director:** Nelson; **Screenplay:** Michael M. Grilikhes and Marvin H. Albert; **Music:** Neal Hefti; **Cinematographer:** Charles F. Wheeler; **Editor:** Fredric Steinkamp; **Cast:** James Garner, Sidney Poitier, Bibi Andersson, Dennis Weaver, Bill Travers, William Redfield, John Hoyt, John Crawford, John Hubbard, Ralph Nelson, Bill Hart, Eddie Little Sky.

James Garner is a scout seeking revenge for the murder of his Indian wife. Sidney Poitier is a dandified cynic and former cavalry officer who makes his living breaking in horses for the army and must show that courage knows no color. Bibi Andersson is a white woman who is taken captive by the Apache and gives birth to a half-breed child, much to her husband's disgust.

Distinguished by its excellent cast, this compelling, violent, and touching film deals with a range of issues, including racism and bigotry. With a haunting musical score by Neal Hefti, this 1966 western (by the producer, director, and star who gave us *Lilies of the Field* [1963] a few years earlier) deserves to be seen. Dennis Weaver gives a wonderfully solid performance as Andersson's tormented husband, who can't

come to grips with his wife's malfeasance due to his belief that any decent woman would prefer to die rather than be an Apache squaw.

DUEL AT SILVER CREEK (aka: CLAIM JUMPERS) Universal, 1952, Color, 77 min. **Producer:** Leonard Goldstein; **Director:** Don Siegel; **Screenplay:** Joseph Hoffman and Gerald Drayson Adams; **Music:** Hans J. Salter; **Cinematographer:** Irving Glassberg; **Editor:** Russell F. Schoengarth; **Cast:** Audie Murphy, Faith Domergue, Stephen McNally, Susan Cabot, Gerald Mohr, Lee Marvin, Eugene Iglesias, Kyle James, Walter Sande.

The Silver Kid comes to town to do some gambling, but he soon finds himself in an unholy alliance with the sheriff to stop a gang of murdering claim jumpers. The first full-length western for ace director Don Siegel (*TWO MULES FOR SISTER SARA* (1969), *THE SHOOTIST* (1976)) is a fast-paced action film. The picture also marks one of the first-screen appearances for actor Lee Marvin, who hitherto had been acting on the Broadway stage and that the same year had landed a part in the Broadway production of *Billy Budd*.

DUEL IN DURANGO See *GUN DUEL IN DORADO.*

DUEL IN THE MISSISSIPPI Columbia, 1955, Color, 72 min. **Director:** William Castle; **Screenplay:** Gerald Grayson Adams; **Cinematographer:** Henry Freulich; **Editor:** Edwin H. Bryant; **Cast:** Lex Barker, Patricia Medina, Warren Steven, John Dehner, Ian Keith, Chris Alcaide, John Mansfield.

In this film set in New Orleans in the 1820s, a young man goes into bondage so his father will not have to go to jail and eventually stops raids on sugar plantations by bayou renegades.

DUEL IN THE SUN Selznick Releasing, 1946, Color, 138 min, VT. **Producer:** David O. Selznick; **Directors:** King Vidor, Otto Brower, William Dieterle, Sidney Franklin, William Cameron Menzies, and Josef von Sternberg; **Screenplay:** Selznick; **Music:** Dimitri Tiomkin; **Cinematographers:** Lee Garmes, Hal Rosson, and Ray Rennahan; **Editors:** Hal C. Kern, William Ziegler, John D. Faure, and Charles Freeman; **Cast:** Jennifer Jones, Joseph Cotten, Gregory Peck, Lionel Barrymore, Lillian Gish, Walter Huston, Herbert Marshall, Charles Bickford, Harry Carey, Joan Tetzel, Otto Kruger, Sidney Blackmer, Scott McKay, Butterfly McQueen.

At its most basic, this film tells the story of crusty cattle baron Senator McCandles (Lionel Barrymore), the lord and master of a ranch called Spanish Bit. His wife Laura Belle (Lillian Gish) lives with a past indiscretion that has haunted their tenuous marriage and the upbringing of their two sons.

The sons are poles apart in character and temperament. Jesse (Joseph Cotten) is an honorable and decent man;

brother Lewt (Gregory Peck) is a swaggering, undisciplined, and lecherous charmer who understands neither boundaries nor limits. Into this scenario comes Pearl Chavez (Jennifer Jones), a tempestuous and voluptuous half-breed girl whose father (Herbert Marshall) has been hanged for murdering his half-breed wife and her lover. Pearl becomes irresistibly drawn to Lewt to the detriment of all, including a kindly rancher named Sam Pierce (Charles Bickford), who wants to marry Pearl. Lewt, however, dispatches Sam permanently by putting a bullet through him. Before the lovers die in each other's arms in the steamy climax, Lewt also manages to wreck a train and attempts to murder his brother Jesse in the process.

Novelist-screenwriter Nevin Busch favored themes of interfamilial relationships in western settings. This is seen in two other films based on Busch's work, PURSUED (1947), and THE FURIES (1950). To make the film, Selznick set aside a then-astronomical advertising budget of more than $1 million for his $7 million epic western. Teaser ads appeared as early as June 1945, a year and a half before the movie was released. But due to a labor strike against Technicolor, it was uncertain that the film could open in time to qualify for the Oscars.

Contemporary pundits and critics have diminished David O. Selznick's attempt to create a western *Gone With the Wind* as an overblown, overlong, and exploitive piece of visual pulp fiction. To do so, however, ignores some salient facts. First, *Duel in the Sun* was the top box-office hit of 1947 (no other western can make that claim for any other year) and won immediate praise from filmmakers such as Frank Capra and Mervyn LeRoy. Second, nearly every scene in the film deals with high-powered emotion and intensity, and among the outstanding big-name cast, Jennifer Jones and Lillian Gish both received Oscar nominations.

There was also a bout with censorship. The passionate love affair between Jennifer Jones and Gregory Peck, partic-

ularly their death scene where they shoot each other and die in an "orgasmic embrace," did not sit well with the Catholic Church. The archbishop of Los Angeles, for one, directed priests to warn their parishioners that "pending classification by the Legion of Decency, they may not, with a free conscience, attend the motion picture *Duel in the Sun* which appears to be morally offensive and spiritually depressing." Local censor boards in Memphis, Tennessee, and Hartford also banned the movie—at least at first.

A torrent of complaints caused the management of the Egyptian Theater on Hollywood Boulevard to replace the posters advertising the picture in order to protect the public from Jennifer Jones's ample cleavage. Could this be the same actress who had won an Oscar for playing Saint Bernadette in the *The Song of Bernadette* (1943)?

Yes, she was! But she was also Selznick's protégée, love interest, and soon-to-be wife. Moreover, Selznick took over almost every aspect of the film, writing the screenplay, making sure that Jones received maximum attention, and sending memorandums to almost everyone connected with the production. Although King Vidor receives sole credit as director, he left the project after disagreements with Selznick, and Josef von Sternberg, among others, directed some further scenes.

Duel in the Sun has a quality cast and a rich array of supporting players, which helped it get by censorship difficulties. Its use of color and lighting effects is imaginative, and the mass riding sequences where the ranchers gather to oppose the intruding railroad is King Vidor at his best. Dimitri Tiomkin's musical score is thumping and passionate, and an intimate final scene between Barrymore and a dying Gish reminds us of how much the modern screen misses such presences.

A flawed film to be sure, yet at times a compelling one, *Duel in the Sun* is surely no *Gone with the Wind*. But it remains entertaining and illuminating, a groundbreaker of sorts, in that overt sexuality in a western had never been so apparent, so passionate, and at times so silly as in this expansive, steamy, and controversial epic saga.

DURANGO KID, THE Columbia, 1940, B&W, 61 min. **Producer:** Jack Fier; **Director:** Lambert Hillyer; **Screenplay:** Paul Franklin; **Cinematographer:** John Stumer; **Editor:** Richard Fantl; **Cast:** Charles Starrett, Pat Brady, Luana Walters, Steve Clark, Frank La Rue, Melvin Lang, Kenneth MacDonald, Bob Nolan, Jack Rockwell, Forrest Taylor.

Charles Starrett appears as the Durango Kid in this 1940 film, but not until 1944 did he regularly play the western Robin Hood. A former football star at Dartmouth, Starrett made his first appearance as an extra in a silent feature called *The Quarterback* (1926).

Starting in the mid-1940s, Starrett made 64 features as the Durango Kid, the role for which he is best remembered. During that time he achieved a degree of popularity reserved for only a few cowboy heroes, as he continued to receive fan mail long after hanging up his screen spurs—despite the fact that most of his westerns have not played on TV. His

Harry Carey and unidentified actor in Duel in the Sun
(SELZNICK INTERNATIONAL/AUTHOR'S COLLECTION)

Durango Kid entries for Columbia include *COWBOY CAN-TEEN, Cowboy from Lonesome River, CYCLONE PRAIRIE RANGERS*, (1944); *RETURN OF THE DURANGO KID, RUSTLERS OF THE BADLANDS, Rough Ridin' Justice, BOTH BARRELS BLAZING, OUTLAWS OF THE ROCKIES, LAWLESS EMPIRE, Blazing the Western Trail* (1945); *Two Fisted Stranger, Song of the Sierras, ROARING RANGERS, Land Rush, HEADING WEST, GUNNING FOR VENGEANCE, GALLOPING THUNDER, The Frontier Gunlaw, Fighting Frontiersman, TERROR TRAIL, THE DESERT HORSEMAN* (1946); *WEST OF DODGE CITY, Law of the Canyon, PRAIRIE RAIDERS, STRANGER FROM PONCA CITY, RIDERS OF THE LONE STAR, SOUTH OF THE CHISHOLM TRAIL, LONE HAND TEXAN, THE LAST DAYS OF BOOT HILL* (1947); *WHIRLWIND RAIDERS, WEST OF SONORA, Trail to Laredo, SIX GUN LAW, PHANTOM VALLEY, BUCKAROO FROM POWDER RIDGE, BLAZING ACROSS THE PECOS* (1948); *CHALLENGE OF THE RANGE, SOUTH OF DEATH VALLEY, Bandits of El Dorado, RENEGADES OF THE SAGE, QUICK ON THE TRIGGER, LARAMIE, HORSEMEN OF THE SIERRAS, EL DORADO PASS, DESERT VIGILANTE, THE BLAZING TRAIL* (1949); *TRAIL OF THE RUSTLERS, Texas Dynamo, STREETS OF GHOST TOWN, ACROSS THE BADLANDS, RAIDERS OF TOMAHAWK CREEK, LIGHTNING GUNS, OUTCASTS OF BLACK MESA, FRONTIER OUTPOST* (1950); *PRAIRIE ROUNDUP, Fort Savage Raiders, SNAKE RIVER DESPERADOES, PECOS RIVER, Kid from Amarillo, CYCLONE FURY, BONANZA TOWN* (1951); *THE ROUGH TOUGH WEST, LARAMIE MOUNTAINS, SMOKY CANYON, Kid from Broken Gun, JUNCTION CITY, HAWK OF THE WILD RIVER* (1952).

In 1953 actor Wally Cassell played the Durango Kid in Universal's *Law and Order*.

DURANGO VALLEY RAIDERS Republic, 1938, B&W, 55 min, VT. **Producer:** A. W. Hackel; **Director:** Sam Newfield; **Screenplay:** George H. Plympton; **Cinematographer:** Robert E. Cline; **Editor:** Roy Claire; **Cast:** Bob Steele, Louise Stanley, Karl Hackett, Ted Adams, Forrest Taylor, Steve Clark, Horace Murphy, Jack Ingram.

A young cowboy becomes involved with people trying to fight an outlaw gang. He discovers that the gang is led by the corrupt local sheriff, "The Shadow," who has control of the Durango Valley.

DYNAMITE CANYON Republic, 1941, B&W, 58 min. **Producer:** Robert Emmett Tansey; **Director:** Frances Kavanaugh; **Screenplay:** Tansey; **Cinematographer:** Jack Young; **Editor:** Frederick Bain; **Cast:** Tom Keene, Evelyn Finley, Stanley Price, Kenne Duncan, Slim Andrews.

When a gang of outlaws murder two men over a copper deposit, a ranger who is sent to investigate masquerades as an outlaw named Trigger Jones in order to join the gang. This is an average entry for Tom Keene's last Monogram series. (See also *WHERE TRAILS DIVIDE*.)

DYNAMITE PASS RKO, 1950, B&W, 61 min, VT. **Producer:** Herman Schlom; **Director:** Lew Landers; **Screenplay:** Norman Houston; **Music:** Paul Sawtell; **Cinematographer:** Nicholas Musuraca; **Editor:** Robert Swink; **Cast:** Tim Holt, Richard Martin, Lynne Roberts, Regis Toomey, John Dehner, Robert Shayne, Don C. Harvey, Denver Pyle, Ross Elliott, Don Haggerty.

E

EACH ONE FOR HIMSELF See *RUTHLESS FOUR, THE.*

EAGLE AND THE HAWK Paramount, 1950, Color, 104 min. **Producers:** William H. Pine and William C. Thomas; **Director:** Lewis R. Foster; **Screenplay:** Foster and Geoffrey Homes (Daniel Manwaring); **Music:** Rudy Schrager; **Cinematographer:** James Wong Howe; **Editor:** Howard A. Smith; **Cast:** John Payne, Rhonda Fleming, Dennis O'Keefe, Thomas Gomez, Fred Clark, Frank Faylen, Eduardo Noriega, Grandon Rhodes, Walter Reed.

The U.S. government sends two law enforcers to Mexico to make Maximillian the emperor of Mexico. This average piece of historical screen fiction is brightened by an entertaining performance by the often underrated John Payne.

EAGLE'S BROOD, THE Paramount, 1935, B&W, 61 min. **Producer:** Harry Sherman; **Director:** Howard Bretherton; **Screenplay:** Harrison Jacobs and Doris Schroeder; **Music:** Sidney D. Mitchell and Sam H. Stept; **Cinematographer:** Archie Stout; **Editor:** Edward Schroeder; **Cast:** William Boyd, James Ellison, William Farnum, George "Gabby" Hayes, Addison Richards, Joan Woodbury.

When outlaws murder a young couple and kidnap their child, Hop-Along Cassidy comes to the rescue. The second entry in the *HOP-ALONG CASSIDY* series is a good one and a portent of things to come. (See also *HOP-ALONG CASSIDY.*)

EL CONDOR National General, 1970, Color, 102 min, VT. **Producer:** André De Toth; **Director:** John Guillermin; **Screenplay:** Stephen Carabatsos and Larry Cohen; **Music:** Maurice Jarre; **Cinematographer:** Henri Persin; **Editors:** Walter Hannemann and William Ziegler; **Cast:** Jim Brown, Lee Van Cleef, Patrick O'Neal, Marianna Hill, Iron Eyes Cody, Imogen Hassall, Elisha Cook Jr.

Made in Spain, this spaghetti western features Jim Brown and Lee Van Cleef as two soldiers of fortune who enlist the aid of an Apache chief named Santana (Iron Eyes Cody) to go after a fortune in gold located in a Mexican fortress called El Condor. Hungarian-born André De Toth, who helmed a number of American westerns (*Springfield Rifle*, 1952; *Man in the Saddle*, 1951; *The Last of the Comanches*, 1952), took to producing westerns in Europe late in his career.

EL DORADO Paramount, 1967, Color, 126 min, VT. **Producer:** Howard Hawks; **Director:** Howard Hawks; **Screenplay:** Leigh Brackett; **Music:** Nelson Riddle; **Cinematographer:** Harold Rossen; **Editor:** John Woodcock; **Cast:** John Wayne, Robert Mitchum, James Caan, Charlene Holt, Michele Carey, Arthur Hunnicutt, R. G. Armstrong, Edward Asner, Paul Fix, Johnny Crawford, Christopher George, Robert Rothwell, Adam Roarke, Chuck Courtney, Robert Donner, John Mitchum.

Aging gunfighter Cole Thornton (John Wayne) comes to the aid of his pal J. D. Harrah (Robert Mitchum) in opposing a corrupt land baron (Ed Asner) and his gang of thugs. This film combines the screen presence of two outstanding and dominant film personalities, Wayne and Mitchum. Paramount did not want the film to conflict with the opening of *NEVADA SMITH* in the summer of 1966, so the studio did not release the film until June 1967.

This was the fourth teaming of Wayne and Howard Hawks, with actor and director having worked together previously in *RED RIVER* (1948), *Hatari* (1962), and *RIO BRAVO* (1959). While many have claimed that *El Dorado* was a recycled *Rio Bravo*, Hawks always denied such a contention. Yet the plots are similar. Once again an aging gunfighter played by Wayne helps out his drunken sheriff pal (Mitchum instead of Dean Martin). Replacing "Colorado," the deadly juvenile with a gun played by Ricky Nelson in *Rio Bravo*, is a more realistic, and virile James Caan—in an early significant role—is "Mississippi," a dapper young fellow handy with a knife but painfully inept with a gun. Veteran character actor Arthur Hunnicutt plays the feisty old jailer, a role similar to Walter Brennan's "Stumpy" in the earlier movie.

As he did in *Rio Bravo* (1959) and would do once more with RIO LOBO (1973), Hawks effectively employs the theme of a disparate trio of men bonding together to bring down the bad guys. As gunfighter Cole Thornton, Wayne is still every bit the master. He knows he is up against a hired gun with a hefty temper but is not overly disturbed. The odds are now in his favor because, as he reasons, "a fella in this business hasn't got the right to get mad. If he gets mad, he's not so good. So the madder he gets, the better I like it." And when he finally dispatches adversary Dan McLeod (Christopher George) by a ruse and a bullet, he explains to the dying man, "You're too good to give a chance to."

But the real joy is watching Wayne and Mitchum work together. Both were masters of underplaying a part. Both were very subtle actors who could accomplish much more with simple response to a situation than with a huge reaction. In *Duke, We're Glad We Knew You*, John Mitchum reflected on working with his brother Bob and with Wayne in *El Dorado*: "To see the two of them together was really marvelous, because they are both legends of the screen. It came across that the two really respected each other. At the end of the picture when the two of them walk down the street together, each one being wounded in the opposite leg, these two on one leg are better than most people on two legs. It was a good picture. They did a beautiful job."

El Dorado was one of the first films for actor Robert Donner. He recalled meeting and working with John Wayne for the first time: "We were down in old Tucson making 'El Dorado.' Basically Howard Hawks was the one who introduced me to him. When I first looked at him, he had recently come back from lung surgery. I looked at him and saw the moves he was making with his shoulder, the way he turned around. I said, 'My God, this man is a caricature of himself.' You see him on a twenty-five foot screen and he moves so largely. Then all of a sudden you see him in person and you realize that this is the way he really moves and it works."

Arthur Hunnicutt and John Wayne in Howard Hawks's El Dorado (PARAMOUNT/AUTHOR'S COLLECTION)

James Caan and Michele Carey in El Dorado (PARAMOUNT/AUTHOR'S COLLECTION)

James Caan's "Mississippi" offers an oblique explanation for the title of the film by frequently quoting lines from Edgar Allan Poe's poem "El Dorado," a tale about a knight who grows old and tired in search of El Dorado. Few directors have been as adept at telling a good story on his own terms as Howard Hawks. If one accepts the old adage that nothing succeeds like a good story well told, then this film with a familiar plot is as enjoyable today as it was when it first hit the screen some 35 years ago.

EL DORADO PASS Columbia, 1949, B&W, 55 min. **Producer:** Colbert Clark; **Director:** Ray Navarro; **Screenplay:** Earl Snell; **Cinematographer:** Rex Wimpy; **Editor:** Burton Kramer; **Cast:** Charles Starrett, Smiley Burnette, Steve Darrell, Elena Verdugo, Rory Mallinson, Ted Mapes, Stanley Blystone, Shorty Thompson.

Charles Starrett stars as the Durango Kid in El Dorado Pass. (COLUMBIA/AUTHOR'S COLLECTION)

EL PASO Paramount, 1949, Color, 91 min. **Producers:** William H. Pine and William C. Thomas; **Director:** Lewis R. Foster; **Screenplay:** Foster; **Music:** Darrell Calker; **Cinematographer:** Ellis W. Carter; **Editor:** Howard A. Smith; **Cast:** John Payne, Gail Russell, Sterling Hayden, George "Gabby" Hayes, Dick Foran, Eduardo Noriega, Henry Hull, Mary Beth Hughes, H. B. Warner.

In Texas after the Civil War, a young lawyer realizes that the gun is the only way to rid the area of lawlessness. Actress Gail Russell was at the peak of her incredible beauty when this unpretentious and action-filled oater was filmed. It became a commercially successful venture for Paramount.

EL PASO STAMPEDE Republic, 1953, B&W, 53 min. **Director:** Harry Keller; **Screenplay:** Arthur E. Orloff; **Cast:** Allen "Rocky" Lane, Phyllis Coates, Eddy Waller, Stephen Chase, Roy Barcroft, Edward Clark, Tom Monroe.

EL RANCH GRANDE   See *RANCHO GRANDE.*

EL SALVEJO   See *MACHISMO.*

ELECTRIC HORSEMAN, THE   Columbia, 1979, Color, 120 min, VT. **Producer:** Ray Stark; **Director:** Sydney Pollack; **Screenplay:** Robert Garland; **Music:** Dave Grusin; **Cinematographer:** Owen Roizman; **Editor:** Sheldon Kahn; **Cast:** Robert Redford, Jane Fonda, Valerie Perrine, John Saxon, Nicolas Coster, Allan Arbus, Wilford Brimley.

Robert Redford plays a five-time all-around rodeo champion named Sonny Steele, who has fallen on hard times and taken to drink. His former fame allows him to take a job promoting a breakfast cereal called Ranch Breakfast for aspiring rodeo riders. He and his horse are wired and covered up with light bulbs, and as they ride around the ring his horse rears up and the "Electric Horseman" doffs his hat. However, when a new horse is shot full of harmful drugs by the sponsors, Sonny decides to save it by stealing the horse and setting it free in the wild. This creates media attention, causing reporter Jane Fonda to seek him out. By the final fadeout, the two have fallen in love, and she comes to understand what the lone cowboy is trying to do.

Compared unfavorably with *LONELY ARE THE BRAVE* (1962), the David Miller/Kirk Douglas film, Sydney Pollack's *The Electric Horseman* marks the film debut of Willie Nelson as Redford's business manager Wendall, who tries to keep the horseman sober from event to event. Some nice Nelson songs give an edge to yet another attempt to show how big companies have ruined and/or corrupted the best in the American West. The film captured an Oscar nomination for Best Sound, losing out to Francis Ford Coppola's *Apocalypse Now* (1979).

EMPTY HOLSTERS Warner Bros., 1937, B&W, 62 min. **Director:** B. Reeves Eason; **Screenplay:** John T.

Neville; **Music:** M. K. Jerome and Jack Scholl; **Cinematographer:** Ted D. McCord; **Editor:** Clarence Kolster; **Cast:** Dick Foran, Patricia Walthall, Emmett Vogan, Glenn Strange, Anderson Lawler, Wilfred Lucas, Tom Brower, George Chesebro, Charles Le Moyne, Edmund Cobb, Art Mix.

A cowboy released from prison after being falsely convicted of murder and robbery sets out to clear his name and capture the real culprit. This familiar story benefits from plenty of fast-paced action.

EMPTY SADDLES Universal, 1936, B&W, 67 min. **Producer:** Buck Jones; **Director:** Leslie Selander; **Screenplay:** Frances Guihan; **Music:** David Klatzkin, Charles Previn, and Oliver Wallace (all uncredited); **Cinematographer:** Herbert Kirkpatrick and Allen O. Thompson; **Editor:** Bernard Loftus; **Cast:** Buck Jones, Louise Brooks, Harvey Clark, Charles Middleton, Lloyd Ingraham, Frank Campeau, Claire Rochelle.

A cowboy tries to stop a war between cattle ranchers and sheepmen that has been instigated by a gang of crooks. This routine Buck Jones venture is made more notable by the casting of Louise Brooks as his leading lady. (See also STONE OF SILVER CREEK.)

END OF THE TRAIL Columbia, 1932, B&W, 61 min. **Producer:** Irving Briskin; **Director:** D. Ross Lederman; **Screenplay:** Stuart Anthony; **Cinematographer:** Benjamin H. Kline; **Editor:** Ottom Meyer; **Cast:** Tim McCoy, Luana Walters, Wheeler Oakman, Wade Botler, Lafe McKee, Wally Albright, Chief White Eagle, Henry Hall.

Captain Tim Travers (Tim McCoy) is forced out of the army after being falsely accused of giving guns to the Indians. He goes to live with the Arapaho after his adopted son is killed, and eventually he thwarts a massacre. The film has no villain in the normal sense of the term, but it does possess a surprising sense of tragedy. In the original version Travers's son is killed by the cavalry, and McCoy himself dies at the end. However, a last-minute happy ending was tacked on before the film went into release. Fans of McCoy consider this film to be among actor's very best efforts, one which film historian William Everson calls a "... genuinely poetic study of the white man's betrayal of the Indians." (See also RIDING TORNADO, THE.)

END OF THE TRAIL Columbia, 1936, B&W, 70 min. **Producer:** Irving Briskin; **Director:** Erle C. Kenton; **Screenplay:** Harold Shumate; **Cinematographer:** John Stumar; **Cast:** Jack Holt, Louise Henry, Douglas Dumbrille, Guinn "Big Boy" Williams, George McKay, John McGuire, Edward LeSaint, Frank Shannon, Art Mix, Blackie Whiteford, Black-Jack Ward, Edgar Dearing.

Two friends who have grown up together find themselves on opposite sides of the law. To complicate matters they are both in love with the same girl. Based on the novel *Outlaws of Palouse* by Zane Grey, this fine Jack Holt venture is handled in an adult manner.

ENEMY OF THE LAW PRC, 1945, B&W, 55 min. **Producer:** Arthur Alexander; **Director:** Harry L. Fraser; **Screenplay:** Fraser and Jack Greenhalgh; **Editor:** Holbrook Todd; **Cast:** Tex Ritter, Dave O'Brien, Guy Wilkerson, Kay Hughes, Jack Ingram, Charles King, Frank Ellis, Kermit Maynard, Henry Hall.

The Texas Rangers track down a gang who years earlier had robbed a safe and hid the loot. While Tex Ritter made some 70 movies, his "Texas Ranger" series for PRC (1944–45) is generally considered among his weakest work. Ritter appeared as Ranger Tex Haines in eight series features: *Dead or Alive, Whispering Skull, Gangsters of the Frontier* (1944); *Three in the Saddle, Frontier Fugitives, Flaming Bullets, Marked for Murder, Enemy of the Law* (1945).

ESCAPE FROM FORT BRAVO MGM, 1953, Color, 98 min, VT. **Producer:** Nicholas Nayfack; **Director:** John Sturges; **Screenplay:** Frank Fenton; **Music:** Jeff Alexander; **Cinematographer:** Robert Surtees; **Editor:** George Boemler; **Cast:** William Holden, Eleanor Parker, John Forsythe, William Demarest, William Campbell, Polly Bergen, Richard Anderson, Carl Benton Reid, John Lupton.

Based on a story by Phillip Rock and set in 1863 during the Civil War, *Escape from Fort Bravo* tells the tale of a woman who helps her Confederate fiancé escape from a Yankee prison camp in Arizona. The problem is that she falls in love with the very Union officer who had captured her fiancé and delivered him to Fort Bravo. Matters are further complicated when they all find themselves under attack by a hostile Indians. Most of the men—Union and Confederate—perish in a well-staged Indian attack before being saved from extermination by the fortuitous arrival of the cavalry.

This was William Holden's first western since STREETS OF LAREDO in 1949. The underrated Eleanor Parker is ravishing as the woman who captures the hearts of both Confederate officer John Forsythe and Union officer Holden. Originally shot in 3D, the film was released in the regular format because the initial popularity of the three-dimensional gimmick had been already greatly diminished.

ESCAPE FROM RED ROCK 20th Century Fox, 1958, B&W, 75 min. **Producer:** Bernard Glasser; **Director:** Edward Bernds; **Screenplay:** Bernds; **Music:** Lex Baxter; **Cinematographer:** Brydon Baker; **Editor:** John F. Link, Sr.; **Cast:** Brian Donlevy, Eileen Janssen, Gary Murray, J. C. Flippen, William Phipps, Myron Healey, Nesdon Booth, Dan White, Andre Adoree, Tina Menard, Courtland Shepard.

In order to save his brother's life, a young rancher is forced to take part in a robbery with his brother's gang. He then flees into the desert with his girlfriend while hostile Indians are on the warpath. Brian Donlevy as the gang leader and Myron Healey as a vicious gang member are cast standouts.

ESCORT WEST United Artists, 1958, B&W, 75. **Producers:** Nate H. Edwards and Robert E. Morrison; **Director:** Francis D. Lyon; **Screenplay:** Leo Gordon and Fred Hartsook; **Music:** Henry Vars; **Cinematographer:** William H. Clothier; **Editor:** Otto Ludwig; **Cast:** Victor Mature, Elaine Stewart, Faith Domergue, Reba Waters, Noah Beery Jr., Rex Ingram, John Hubbard, Harey Carey Jr., Slim Pickens, Roy Barcroft, Ken Curtis, Chuck Hayward.

An ex-Confederate officer and his daughter traveling west are snubbed by a Union wagon train. Later they find two women who are survivors of the wagon train after it has been attacked by Indians. The film was made in association with Batjac Productions (John Wayne is the uncredited producer), and producer Robert Morrison (listed in the credits) was John Wayne's younger brother.

EUREKA STOCKADE (aka: MASSACRE HILL) British-Pathé, 1949, B&W, 103 min. **Producer:** Leslie Norman (associate); **Director:** Harry Watt; **Screenplay:** Walter Greenwood and Harry Wyatt; **Music:** John Greenwood; **Cinematographer:** George Heath; **Editor:** Leslie Norman; **Cast:** Chips Rafferty, Jane Barrett, Jack Lambert, Peter Illing, Gordon Jackson, Ralph Truman, Peter Finch.

This well-received drama about the Australian gold rush is set in the 1850s, when gold was discovered in Australia. The story chronicles the conflict between working men intent on panning for gold and their former employers plus the government intent on restricting their freedom. This exciting and well-produced frontier saga came from the J. Arthur Rank Studio.

EVERYBODY'S DANCIN' Lippert, 1950, B&W, 67 min. **Producer:** Robert Nunes; **Director:** Will Jason; **Screenplay:** Dorothy Raison; **Cast:** Spade Cooley, Richard Lane, Hal Derwin, James Millican, Lyle Talbot, Roddy McDowell, Adele Jergens, Sterling Hayden, James Ellison, Russell Hayden, Michael Whalen, Sid Melton, The Sons of the Pioneers, Barbara Woodell, Ginny Jackson, Chuy Reyes Orchestra, Tex Cromer, Ginny Jackson, Bobby Hyatt.

When crooks set out to take over a ballroom owner's business, several show business stars come to his rescue. Lively musical numbers with a distinctly western twang and some big-name stars enliven this feature from Lippert Studio.

EVERY MAN FOR HIMSELF See *RUTHLESS FOUR, THE.*

EVERYMAN'S LAW Supreme, 1936, B&W, 62 min. **Producer:** A. W. Hackel; **Director:** Albert Ray; **Cinematographer:** Jack Greenhalgh; **Editor:** Leete Renick Brown; **Cast:** Johnny Mack Brown, Beth Marion, Frank Campeau, Roger Gray, John Beck, Lloyd Ingraham, Horace Murphy, Richard Alexander, Slim Whitaker, Ralph Bucko, Budd Buster, Ed Cassidy.

Three lawmen pretend to be hired guns in order to get the goods on a rancher who is harassing homesteaders. (See also *GAMBLING TERROR, THE.*)

EVIL ROY SLADE Universal, 1972, Color, 67 min, VT. **Producer:** Jerry Belson, Garry Marshall, and Howie Horowitz (executive); **Director:** Jerry Paris; **Screenplay:** Belson and Marshall; **Music:** Stuart Margolin, Murray MacLeod, Jerry Riopelle, and James Prigmore; **Cinematographer:** Sam Leavitt; **Editor:** Richard R. Sprague; **Cast:** John Astin, Mickey Rooney, Dick Shawn, Dom DeLuise, Pamela Austin, Edie Adams, Henry Gibson, Milton Berle.

This is a zany and often hilarious spoof about a rascal and scoundrel by the name of Evil Roy Slade (John Astin). The only surviving infant of a wagon train attack, he sent out such bad vibes that even wolves and hostile Indians wanted no part of him, leaving the infant to fend for himself in the wilderness.

But can he ever become an honest man, even with the love of wholesome and beautiful Betsy Potter (Pamela Austin)? That remains to be seen. The film boasts great character performances by Milton Berle as Betsy's shoe salesman cousin, Mickey Rooney as a thumbless scoundrel with a dog named Custer, Dom DeLuise as the "funny boy" psychiatrist, and Dick Shawn as Bing Bell, the spangle-drenched singing ex-marshal who comes out of retirement gunnin' and strummin' for Evil Roy Slade.

EYE FOR AN EYE, AN (aka: TALLION) Embassy, 1966, Color, 106 VT. **Producer:** Carroll Case; **Director:** Michael Moore; **Screenplay:** Bing Russell and Summer Williams; **Music:** Raoul Kraushaar; **Cinematographer:** Lucien Ballard; **Editor:** William Austin and Bob Wyman; **Cast:** Robert Lansing, Patrick Wayne, Slim Pickens, Gloria Talbott, Paul Fix, Strother Martin, Henry Wills, Jerry Gatlin, Rance Howard, Clint Howard.

An ex-bounty hunter is out to get the men who murdered his wife and son and enlists the aid of another man to help him. Both men are physically handicapped, providing for an interesting oater with a different plot twist.

EYES OF TEXAS Republic, 1948, Color, 54 min, VT. **Producer:** Edward J. White; **Director:** William Witney; **Screenplay:** Sloan Nibley; **Music:** R. Dale Butts and Morton Scott; **Cinematographer:** Jack A. Marta; **Editor:** Tony Martinelli; **Cast:** Roy Rogers, Lynne Roberts, Andy Devine, Nana Bryant, Roy Barcroft, Danny Morton, Francis Ford, Pascale Perry, Stanley Blystone, Bob Nolan.

Evil lady Nana Bryant is eager to acquire valuable ranch land at any cost, including using vicious killer dogs to discourage prospective landowners. One of the top directors of B westerns, the talented William Witney brought a harder and tougher edge to the Roy Rogers films in the late 1940s, after many had stagnated into overblown musicals by the mid '40s. This film is among Roy Rogers's best entries for Republic.

FABULOUS TEXAN, THE Republic, 1947, B&W, 95. **Producer:** Edmund Grainger; **Director:** Edward Ludwig; **Screenplay:** Lawrence Hazard and Horace McCoy; **Music:** Anthony Collins; **Cinematographer:** Reggie Lannin; **Editor:** Richard L. Van Enger; **Cast:** William Elliott, Ruth Donnelly, John Carroll, Stanley Andrews, Catherine McLeod, Andy Devine, Albert Dekker, Jim Davis, Russell Simpson, James Brown, George Beban, Johnny Sands, Harry Davenport, John Miles, Reed Hadley.

When returning Confederate officers Wild Bill Elliott and John Carroll find their part of Texas under the dictatorial rule of carpetbagger Albert Dekker, a man is forced to become a bandit in order to defend himself and his rights. This well-crafted story is told with a top-notch cast, featuring the strong presence of Bill Elliott.

FACE OF A FUGITIVE Columbia, 1957, Color, 81 min. **Producer:** David Heilweil; **Director:** Paul Wendkos; **Screenplay:** David T. Chantler and Daniel B. Ullman; **Music:** Jerry Goldsmith; **Cinematographer:** Wilfred M. Cline; **Editor:** Jerome Thoms; **Cast:** Fred MacMurray, Lin McCarthy, Dorothy Green, Alan Baxter, Myrna Fahey, James Coburn, Francis DeSales, Gina Gillespie, Ron Hayes, Danny Larson, Paul Burns, Buzz Henry.

In one of a string of western pictures he made during the late 1950s, Fred MacMurray plays a man falsely accused of murder who changes his identity and rides to a new location, hoping to begin life over again. However, his past keeps cropping up, and he can not settle down in peace until he wins a few more battles and complete vindication.

Between 1957 and 1960, the versatile MacMurray made a string of six western pictures. The 49-year-old actor, who had begun his career nearly three decades earlier on the musical stage, was getting a little bored with the genre and was considering returning to his ranch with wife June Haver. He was quoted as saying, "I'm getting a little saddle sore. I wish I could get a good comedy again for a change." Before long his fear of becoming a Hollywood typecast was allayed when Disney approached him for a role in their film hit *The Shaggy Dog* (1959). A whole new career opened up for the veteran actor, including a top supporting role in the Oscar-winning film *The Apartment* (1960) and lasting TV fame in the popular television series *My Three Sons* (1960–72).

FACE TO THE WIND (aka: CRY FOR ME, BILLY; APACHE MASSACRE; COUNT YOUR BLESSINGS; THE LONG TOMORROW) Warner Bros., 1974, Color, 93 min. **Producers:** Elliott Kastner and Harvey Matofsky; **Director:** William A. Graham; **Screenplay:** David Markson; **Music:** Michael Franks and Richard Markowitz; **Cinematographer:** Jordan Croenweth; **Editor:** Jim Benson; **Cast:** Cliff Potts, Xochitl del Rosiaro, Harry Dean Stanton, Don Wilbanks, Woody Chamblis, William Carstems.

When a young drifter meets and falls in love with an Indian maiden, the two find themselves the object of hate and violence. This obscure and exceedingly violent little genre piece was first released in 1972 under the title *Cry for Me Billy*.

FAIR WARNING Fox, 1931, B&W, 74 min. **Director:** Alfred L. Werker; **Screenplay:** Ernest Pascal; **Cinematographer:** Ross Fisher; **Editor:** Ralph Dietrich; **Cast:** George O'Brien, Louise Huntington, Mitchell Harris, George Brent, Nat Pendelton, Willard Robertson.

A cowboy tries to prove that two cowboys are responsible for the robbing of a saloon. This entertaining early talkie for the athletic George O'Brien was based on the novel *The Untamed* by Max Brand.

FALCON OUT WEST, THE   RKO, 1944, B&W, 64 min. **Producer:** Maurice Geraghty; **Director:** William Clemens; **Screenplay:** Morton Grant and Billy Jones; **Cinematographer:** Harry J. Wild; **Editor:** Gene Milford; **Cast:** Tom Conway, Carole Gallagher, Barbara Hale, Joan Barclay, Cliff Clark, Edward Gargan, Minor Watson, Donald Douglas.

The famed detective, Falcon, heads west to catch the killer of a millionaire rancher who died in a New York City nightclub. Learning that the victim was slipped rattlesnake venom, Falcon follows the trail to Texas, where his own life is placed in jeopardy.

FALSE COLORS   United Artists, 1943, B&W, 65 min. **Producers:** Lewis J. Rachmil and Harry Sherman; **Director:** George Archainbaud; **Screenplay:** Bennett Cohen; **Cinematographer:** Russell Harlan; **Editor:** Fred W. Berger; **Cast:** William Boyd, Andy Clyde, Jimmy Rogers, Tom Seidel, Claudia Drake, Douglas Dumbrille, Robert Mitchum, Glenn Strange, Pierce Lyden, Roy Barcroft.

One of the Bar 20 wranglers inherits a ranch. When he is killed, Hoppy agrees to look after the place and the dead man's sister. However, a crooked banker who was behind the murder is determined to get the land for himself. This series entry is bolstered by excellent photography, a solid plot, and some fast action. (See also *HOP-ALONG CASSIDY.*)

FALSE HERO   See *ROARING RANGERS.*

FALSE PARADISE   United Artists, 1948, B&W, 59 min. **Producers:** William Boyd and Lewis J. Rachmil; **Director:** George Archainbaud; **Screenplay:** Harrison Jacobs and Doris Schroeder; **Music:** Ralph Stanley; **Cinematographer:** Mack Stengler; **Editor:** Fred W. Berger; **Cast:** William Boyd, Andy Clyde, Rand Brooks, Joel Friedkin, Elaine Riley, Kenneth MacDonald, Don Harrerty, Cliff Clark.

Hoppy and the boys learn that a banker who is trying to cheat people out of their silver-rich land is in league with an outlaw gang. The last entry in the "Hop-Along Cassidy" series is little more than an average vehicle. (See also *HOP-ALONG CASSIDY.*)

FANCY PANTS   Paramount, 1950, Color, 92 min, VT. **Producer:** Robert L. Welch; **Director:** George Marshall; **Screenplay:** Edmund L. Hartmann, Robert O'Brien, and Harry Leon Wilson; **Music:** Van Cleave; **Cinematographer:** Charles Lang; **Editor:** Archie Marshek; **Cast:** Bob Hope, Virginia Kelley, Percy Hudson, Lucille Ball, Bruce Cabot, Lea Penman, Hugh French, John Alexander, Colin Keith-Johnston.

Bob Hope stars as a hammy American actor masquerading as an English lord among rough and tough westerners seeking statehood in New Mexico. The real fun starts when President Theodore Roosevelt decides to pay a visit to the troubled territory and Hope has to continue his ruse.

Hope is at his best as the high-class British butler who is hired by a newly rich wildcat western girl (Lucille Ball) to bring some culture to her frontier community in this adaptation of "Ruggles of Red Gap" by Harry Leon Wilson. Ball matches Hope gag for gag. At film's end, she plants a kiss on his lips, to which Hope replies, "A kiss like that could kill a guy!" Hope was a talented comic actor and the film was a huge commercial success, ranking number 18 in box-office receipts for 1950. Popular with audiences, the movie was described by *Variety* as ". . . a bright bouncy farce with never a serious moment, played in broadest slapstick by Bob Hope, Lucille Ball and fine cast of comedy characters."

FANGS OF THE ARCTIC   Monogram, 1953, B&W, 62 min. **Producer:** Lindsley Parsons; **Director:** Rex Bailey; **Screenplay:** William Raynor and Warren Douglas; **Cinematographer:** William A. Sickner; **Editor:** Leonard W. Herman; **Cast:** Kirby Grant, Lorna Hanson, Robert Sherman, Warren Douglas, Leonard Penn, Richard Avonde, John Close, Phil Tead, Roy Gordon.

A Mountie and his husky dog are on the trail of crooks engaged in illegal trapping. Scripted by William Raynor and Warren Douglas, the film is a credible adaptation of the James Oliver Curwood story.

FANGS OF THE WILD (aka: FOLLOW THE HUNTER)   Lippert, 1954, B&W, 71 min. **Producer:** Robert L. Lippert; **Director:** William Claxton; **Screenplay:** Orville H. Hampton; **Cinematographer:** Paul Ivano; **Editor:** Monica Collington; **Cast:** Charles Chaplin Jr., Onslow Stevens, Margia Dean, Fred Ridgeway, Phil Tead, Robert Stevenson.

A young man witnesses a murder in the north woods, but he cannot convince his father what he saw and soon becomes the target of the murderer.

FAR COUNTRY, THE   Universal, 1954, Color, 97 min, VT. **Producer:** Aaron Rosenberg; **Director:** Anthony Mann; **Screenplay:** Borden Chase; **Cinematographer:** William H. Daniels; **Editor:** Russell F. Schoengarth; **Cast:** James Stewart, Ruth Roman, Corinne Calvet, Walter Brennan, John McIntire, Jay C. Flippen, Harry Morgan, Steve Brodie, Connie Gilchrist, Robert Wilke, Chubby Johnson, Royal Dano, Jack Elam, Kathleen Freeman, Connie Van, Gregg Barton, John Doucette.

James Stewart's portrayal of the lonely and alienated loner reaches its apex in *The Far Country*—the fifth collaborative effort between director and star, which began with *WINCHESTER '73* (1950). The film begins with Stewart and sidekick Walter Brennan taking a herd of cattle to Alaska. In Skagway they lose their herd to a corrupt sheriff (John McIntire) when Stewart accidentally busts up a hanging. They manage to steal the cattle back and get the herd to Dawson, where they sell the herd to a group of corrupt bidders who want to take over the area. Only when his pal Brennan is killed does Stewart decide to go along with the citizenry and begin his fight.

Anthony Mann specialized in taut, violent, and realistic westerns, and Stewart frequently portrayed the stumbling, brutalized, and reluctant hero pursuing a personal mission with a grim determination. As Parkinson and Jeavons point out in their *Pictorial History of Westerns*, if Mann's heroes are neurotic and cynical, "it is because they have been forced into hysterical violence by their need to avenge a wrong or to blot out the past." Because Stewart's Jeff Webster was once hurt in a love affair, he does not want to be responsible for anyone and shuns all human involvement.

For his big bold outdoor adventure, skillfully scripted by Bordon Chase, Mann took his cast and crew on location around the Columbia Icefields and to Jasper National Park to get an authentic chilly northern atmosphere of the pioneer days of 1896. In one particularly violent scene Stewart, shot full of bullets, is thrown into the icy water. With fine performances, an authentic portrayal of mining camps and boomtowns, breathtaking location filming, and remarkable historical accuracy, critics generally applaud *The Far Country* and consider it a must for anyone interested in top-flight filmmaking and the western genre. The song "Pretty Little Primrose" (Milton Rosen and Frederick Herbert) is performed by Connie Gilchrist, Kathleen Freeman, and Connie Van.

FAR FRONTIER, THE Republic, 1948, Color, 67 min, VT. **Producer:** Edward J. White; **Director:** William Witney; **Screenplay:** Sloan Nibley; **Music:** R. Dale Butts; **Cinematographer:** Jack A. Marta; **Cast:** Roy Rogers, Gail Davis, Andy Devine, Francis Ford, Roy Barcroft, Clayton Moore, Robert Strange, Holly Bane, Lane Bradford, Edmund Cobb.

Desperadoes smuggle deported gangsters back to the United States in oil drums. Border patrolman Roy Rogers makes sure the scheme does not work. This top-quality Roy Rogers venture, with a hard-edged touch by director William Witney, has plenty of action and is unusual in that the villains and supporting cast dominate the film.

FARGO Monogram, 1952, Color, 69 min. **Producer:** Vincent M. Fennelly; **Director:** Lewis D. Collins; **Screenplay:** Jack DeWitt and Joseph F. Poland; **Music:** Raoul Kraushaar; **Cinematographer:** Ernest Miller; **Editor:** Sam Fields; **Cast:** William "Wild Bill" Elliott, Myron Healey, Fuzzy Knight, Jack Ingram, Arthur Space, Robert J. Wilke, Terry Frost, I. Stanford Jolley, House Peters Jr., Denver Pyle.

After his brother is murdered by a cattleman, a man returns to North Dakota and begins helping small ranchers in fencing off the range, thus starting a range war. With Monogram in the process of changing itself into Allied Artists, it began concentrating on a higher-bracket product. Consequently, the studio started a new and intelligent series with Bill Elliott, such as *Fargo*, which provided a satisfying mixture of good action and good scripts. (See also *WACO*.)

FARGO KID, THE RKO, 1940, B&W, 63 min. **Producer:** Bert Gilroy and Lee S. Marcus (executive); **Director:** Edward Killy; **Screenplay:** Morton Grant and Arthur V. Jones; **Music:** John Leipold; **Cinematographer:** Harry Wild; **Editor:** Frederic Knudtson; **Cast:** Tim Holt, Ray Whitely, Emmett Lynn, Jane Drummond, Cy Kendall, Ernie Adams, Paul Fix, Glenn Strange.

The Fargo Kid (Tim Holt) rides into town on an outlaw's horse. When he is mistaken for the outlaw, two crooked businessmen try to hire him to kill a man so they can get his ore-rich land from the intended victim's wife. Filmed in Kanob, Utah, and based on W. C. Tuttle's *Sir Piegan Passes*, this well-made remake of *The Cheyenne Kid* (RKO's 1933 film with Tom Keene) features the songs "Twilight on the Prairie," and "Crazy Ole Trails Ahead," played and sung in the saloon by Ray Whiteley's band and reprised as background music at film's end. (See also *ALONG THE RIO GRANDE*.)

FAR HORIZONS, THE (aka: UNTAMED WEST) Paramount, 1955, Color, 108 min. **Producer:** William H. Pine; **Director:** Rudolph Mate; **Screenplay:** Winston Miller and Edmund North; **Music:** Hans J. Salter; **Cinematographer:** Daniel L. Fapp; **Editor:** Frank Bracht; **Cast:** Fred MacMurray, Charlton Heston, Donna Reed, Barbara Hale, William Demarest, Alan Reed.

Fred MacMurray and Charlton Heston play famed American explorers Meriwether Lewis and William Clark in the early 1800s, when the United States had just acquired the Louisiana Territory from France. Filmed in 1955, the picture is based on the Lewis and Clark expedition to discover a water route from St. Louis to the Pacific Ocean. Along the way from St. Louis to Oregon, they enlist the help and talents of a beautiful Indian girl named Sacajawea (Donna Reed).

Based on the novel *Sacajawea of the Shoshones* by Della Gould Emmons, the film is a nice vehicle for the three big-name stars. However, despite being shot on or near the original Lewis and Clark trail, it defies historical accuracy. For example, the husband of Sacajawea, who also accompanied the expedition, was omitted from the screenplay altogether, while the 34-year-old Donna Reed playing the teenage Sacajawea is a bit of a stretch.

Fred MacMurray, who had already made some 70 movies, went on to star in the TV series *My Three Sons* (1960–72). Likewise, Reed, who two years earlier had garnered an Oscar as Best Supporting Actress (*From Here to Eternity* [1953]), achieved TV stardom on *The Donna Reed Show;* while 30-year-old Charlton Heston would soon become an industry superstar in a series of biblical and historical epics such as *The Ten Commandments* (1956) and *Ben Hur* (1959).

FAST BULLETS Reliable, 1936, B&W, 58 min. **Producer:** Bernard B. Ray; **Director:** Henri Samuels; **Screenplay:** Karl Krusada and Rose Gordon; **Cinematographer:** Pliny Goodfriend; **Editor:** Fred Bain; **Cast:** Tom Tyler, Rex Lease, Margaret Nearing, Al Bridge, William Gould, Robert Walker.

Tim Holt (right) as The Fargo Kid (RKO/AUTHOR'S COLLECTION)

FASTEST GUITAR ALIVE, THE MGM, 1967, Color, 87 min. **Producer:** Sam Katzman; **Director:** Michael Moore; **Screenplay:** Robert E. Kent; **Cinematographer:** W. Wallace Kelley; **Editor:** Ben Lewis; **Cast:** Roy Orbison, Sammy Jackson, Maggie Pierce, Joan Freeman, John Doucette, Patricia Donahue, Ben Cooper, Bem Lessy, Iron Eyes Cody.

Near the end of the Civil War, Confederate spies steal gold from the U.S. mint in San Francisco. Whey they find out the war is over, they have to replace the money without being detected. At the time of its release, Roy Orbison's fellow Sun Studios crooner Elvis Presley had been making profitable movies for nearly a decade. But Sam Katzman's effort to capitalize on Orbison (whose hit records included "Pretty Woman" and "Only the Lonely") did not work out. The best that the movie can claim is eight songs, seven cowritten and performed by the singer himself. Leonard Maltin noted that this effort has "the dumbest title imaginable for a Civil War espionage story."

FASTEST GUN ALIVE, THE MGM, 1956, B&W, 95 min. **Producer:** Clarence Greene; **Director:** Russell Rouse;

Screenplay: Rouse and Frank Gilroy; **Music:** Andre Previn; **Cinematographer:** George J. Folsey; **Editors:** Harry V. Knapp and Ferris Webster; **Cast:** Glenn Ford, Jeanne Crain, Broderick Crawford, Russ Tamblyn, Allyn Joslyn, Leif Ericson, John Dehner, Noah Beery Jr., John Doucette.

Glenn Ford plays a peace-loving storekeeper in the small town of Cross Creek who just happens to be the fastest gun in the West. His strong distaste for gunplay results from watching his lawman father shot down and killed. He only shows off his considerable skills to his wife (Jeanne Crain), as he drills bullets through two coins he flips in the air before they fall to the ground. It isn't long before word gets out, and a dangerous gunslinger played by Broderick Crawford threatens to tear the town apart unless Ford faces him in a dramatic showdown. Ford's portrayal of the fastest gun was reprised 11 years later in Richard Thorpe's *THE LAST CHALLENGE* (1967).

FAST ON THE DRAW (aka: SUDDEN DEATH) Lippert, 1950, B&W, 57 min. **Producers:** Robert L. Lippert and Ron Ormond; **Director:** Thomas Carr; **Screenplay:**

Ormond and Maurice Tombragel; **Cinematographer:** Ernest Miller; **Editor:** Hugh Winn; **Cast:** James Ellison, Russell Hayden, Julie Adams, John L. Cason, George Chesebro.

Texas Rangers are after a dishonest landowner and one of them poses as an outlaw in order to get the goods on him.

FENCE RIDERS Monogram, 1950, B&W, 57 min. **Producer:** Walter Fox; **Director:** Fox; **Screenplay:** Eliot Gibbons; **Cinematographer:** Harry Neumann; **Editor:** John C. Fuller; **Cast:** Whip Wilson, Andy Clyde, Reno Browne, Myron Healey, Holly Bane, Riley Hill, Ed Cassidy, John Merton.

See *ABILENE TRAIL.*

FEUD MAKER Republic, 1938, B&W, 60 min. **Producer:** A. W. Hackel; **Director:** Sam Newfield; **Screenplay:** George Plympton; **Cinematographer:** Robert Cline; **Editor:** Roy Claire; **Cast:** Bob Steele, Marion Weldon, Karl Hackett, Frank Ball, Budd Buster, Lew Meeehan.

A cowpoke tries to stop a crook who has instigated a feud between ranchers and homesteaders. Another typical action-packed Bob Steele venture in A. W. Hackel's series done at Republic.

FEUD OF THE RANGE (aka: FEUD ON THE RANGE) Metropolitan, 1939, B&W, 55 min. **Producer:** Harry Webb; **Director:** Webb; **Screenplay:** Karl Krusada; **Cast:** Bob Steele, Victor Adamson, Robert Burns, Budd Buster, Richard Cramer, Jean Cranford, Jack Ingram, Charles King.

A bad guy instigates a feud on the range in order to obtain land, and a cowboy sets out to stop him. Bob Steele made five features for short-lived Metropolitan Pictures in 1939–40. Most were cheaply made with lots of stock footage. Other Bob Steele Metropolitan ventures include *Mesquite Buckaroo, El Dorado Rides, Smoky Trail* (1939); and *Pinto Canyon* (1940).

FEUD OF THE TRAIL Victory, 1937, B&W, 56 min. **Director:** Robert Hill; **Screenplay:** Basil Dickey; **Cast:** Tom

Tom Tyler stars in Feud of the Trail. *An independent production company, Victory, produced a series of Tom Tyler oaters in the early 1930s.* (VICTORY/AUTHOR'S COLLECTION)

Tyler, Harley Wood, Milburn Morante, Roger Williams, Lafe McKee.

Cowboys set out to recover gold that has been stolen from a family and belongs to the Grange (a regional agricultural cooperative). An independent production company that cranked out B westerns during the 1930s, Victory produced a series of Tom Tyler features, including *Phantom of the Range, Rip Roarin' Buckaroo* (1936); *Cheyenne Rides Again, Feud of the Trail, Lost Ranch, Mystery Range, Brothers of the West, Orphan of the Pecos* (1937).

FEUD OF THE WEST Diversion, 1936, B&W, 62 min. **Producer:** Walter Futter; **Director:** Harry Fraser; **Screenplay:** Phil Dunham; **Cinematographer:** Ted D. McCord; **Editor:** Carl Himm; **Cast:** Hoot Gibson, Buzz Barton, Bob Kortman, Ed Cassidy, Joan Barclay, Nelson McDowell.

A rodeo rider is hired by a rancher to get evidence on the gang who killed his son and nephew, but he is framed for murder and has to head for the hills. A superb rodeo rider himself, Hoot Gibson made six features for the independent Diversion Pictures in 1935–36. The other five include *Cavalcade of the West, Frontier Justice, Lucky Terror, The Riding Avenger* (1936); and *Swifty* (1935).

FIDDLIN' BUCKAROO Universal, 1933, B&W, 63 min. **Producer:** Ken Maynard; **Director:** Maynard; **Screenplay:** Nate Gatzert; **Cast:** Ken Maynard, Gloria Shea, Fred Kohler, Frank Rice, Jack Rockwell, Jack Mower, Bob McKenzie, Roy Bucko, Buck Bucko.

Produced and directed by star Ken Maynard, the film deals with an undercover agent who is arrested for supposedly aiding an outlaw gang in a robbery. But he breaks out of jail when the gang kidnaps a rancher's pretty daughter.

Ken Maynard (right) stars in Fiddlin' Buckaroo.
(UNIVERSAL/AUTHOR'S COLLECTION)

FIEND WHO WALKED THE WEST, THE 20th Century Fox, 1958, B&W, 101 min. **Producer:** Herbert B. Swope Jr.; **Directors:** Gordon Douglas, Harry Brown, and Philip Yordan; **Music:** Bernard Herrmann; **Cinematographer:** Joseph MacDonald; **Editor:** Hugh S. Fowler; **Cast:** Robert Evans, Hugh O'Brian, Linda Cristal, Stephen McNally, Edward Andrews, Ron Ely, Ken Scott, Emile Meyer, Gregory Morton, Georgia Simmons.

A madman escapes from jail and goes on a violent killing spree. His cellmate is then allowed to escape from the same prison in order to stop him. In the course of its long history, the western has incorporated a variety of elements and themes into its basic format, including this exceedingly brutal genre piece.

FIGHTERS OF THE SADDLE (aka: FIGHTERS IN THE SADDLE) Davis, 1929, B&W, 50 min. **Producer:** J. Charles Davis; **Cinematographer:** Paul H. Allen; **Cast:** Art Acord, Peggy Montgomery, John Lowell, Tom Bay, Betty Carter, Lynn Sanderson, Cliff Lyons, Jack Ponder.

The owner of a land company wants a ranch for a country road expansion and frames a young girl and her brother who have leased the property. This was one of the last films for actor Art Acord. For years his reputation was sustained almost solely by his legions of loyal fans. Almost nothing is left of his work today, although in his big Universal serials and western specials he was major rival to Tom Mix.

FIGHTING BILL FARGO Universal, 1941, B&W, 58 min. **Producer:** Will Cowan; **Director:** Ray Taylor; **Screenplay:** Dorcas Cochran, and Arthur V. Jones; **Music:** Everett B. Jones, Milton Rosen, and Hans J. Salter; **Cast:** Johnny Mack Brown, Fuzzy Knight, Nell O'Day, Ted Adams, James Blaine, Al Bridge, The Eddie Dean Trio, Robert Kortman, Kermit Maynard, Bud Osborne.

A man who returns home to help his sister run his late father's newspaper becomes involved with crooks attempting to fix the results of an election. Good Johnny Mack Brown venture with songs provided by Eddie Dean and his trio. (See also *OLD CHISHOLM TRAIL, THE*.)

FIGHTING BLOOD Biograph, 1911, B&W, 18 min. **Producer:** D. W. Griffith; **Director:** Griffith; **Cinematographer:** G. W. Bitzer; **Cast:** Lionel Barrymore, Clara Bracy, Kate Bruce, William J. Butler, Robert Harron.

After the Civil War, an ex-soldier and his family settle in the Dakota Territory. The son quarrels with his father and leaves home, and while riding in the hills he spots a band of Indians attacking a neighborhood homestead. He races back to warn his family with the Indians in close pursuit.

D. W. Griffith's genius is reflected by how he instantly wins audience sympathy: two children cowering under the bed, as excited as they are frightened; another pantomimes that she cannot shoot the guns because the noise hurts her ears, but she'll do her bit by loading them for the others. What Griffith could accomplish in such a short time span—an overall theme, subplots, superb action, and audience sympathy—is ample proof of just how far advanced he was in his ideas and how little he was understood by his contemporaries. Some of the same orchestrated action sequences were repeated in his 1924 epic *America*. *Fighting Blood* was filmed at Lookout Mountain, Sierra Madre, and San Fernando, California. (See also *BATTLE AT ELDERBUSH GULCH*.)

FIGHTING CARAVANS (aka: BLAZING ARROWS) Paramount, 1931, B&W, 91 min. **Directors:** Otto Brower and David Burton; **Screenplay:** Edward G. Paramour Jr., Keene Thompson, and Agnes and Brand Leahey; **Music:** John Leipold, Oscar Potoker, Emil Bierman, Max Burgunker, Emil Hilb, Herman Hand, Karl Hajos, and Sigmund Krumgold; **Cinematographer:** Lee Garmes and Henry Gerrard; **Editor:** William Shea; **Cast:** Gary Cooper, Lily Damita, Ernest Torrence, Fred Kohler, Tully Marshall, Eugene Pallette, Roy Stewart, May Boley, James Farley, James Marcus, Eve Southern.

By 1931 Gary Cooper was Paramount's most prized and versatile leading man, outdistancing such other studio leads as Frederic March, Jack Oakie, Maurice Chevalier, and Richard Arlen. In this western adventure of epic proportion, the 30-year-old Cooper plays Clint Belmet, a guide for a cross-country caravan, who is arrested in Missouri for disturbing the peace. His two older partners persuade orphaned French girl (Lily Damita), whose wagon train has just arrived, to join the caravan and pose as Clint's wife so the marshal will let him go. She agrees because she thinks she is saving his life. Another member of the caravan is Lee Murdock, an unsavory frontiersman in league with the Indians who plans to betray the members of the caravan for his own gain.

Clint reveals the ruse to Lily and apologizes to her; they become good friends. His two pals begin to fear that their young friend, whom they raised, will want to settle down and get married, and their attempts to break off the blossoming romance are effective for a time. However, a big Indian attack occurs as the caravan is attempting to cross the river. Clint swims to a wagon loaded with kerosene and after dumping the oil into the water sets it afire. This demoralizes the Indian attack, but not before his older partners Bill and Jim are killed along with the villain Murdoch. The remnants of the train pushes westward with Clint as its sole guide and Lily beside him.

Although *Fighting Caravans* was based on a Zane Grey novel (1929), it bears a strong resemblance to *THE COVERED WAGON*, James Cruze's 1923 silent epic. Paramount put enormous effort into producing westerns, which always were good box office for the studio. This particular production warranted two directors, two photographers, and no fewer than nine composers to assemble the musical score (which was not all that unusual in the early days of sound). So much footage was used, in fact, that when William Shea finished his editing chores, there was enough background for another film—*WAGON WHEELS*, released in 1934 by Paramount with

Randolph Scott in the lead role. Whenever *Fighting Caravans* is shown on television, which is not often, the title has been changed to *Blazing Arrows*.

FIGHTING CHAMP, THE Monogram, 1932, B&W, 56 min. **Producer:** Trem Carr; **Director:** J. P. McCarthy; **Screenplay:** Wellyn Totman; **Cinematographer:** Archie Stout; **Editor:** Carl Pierson; **Cast:** Bob Steele, Arletta Duncan, Kit Guard, George Chesebro, George "Gabby" Hayes, Charles King, Henry Rocquemore, Lafe McKee, Frank Ball, Si Jenks.

A cowboy who foils a stage holdup is drafted into fighting a traveling boxer. A well-staged boxing match highlights this Bob Steele action-packed film, which includes a good performance by George Chesebro as the unctuous fight manager.

FIGHTING CODE, THE Columbia, 1933, B&W, 65 min. **Director:** Lambert Hillyer; **Screenplay:** Hillyer; **Cinematographer:** Allen G. Siegler; **Editor:** Clarence Kolster; **Cast:** Buck Jones, Diane Sinclair, Ward Bond, Richard Alexander, Alfred P. James, Erville Alderson, Gertrude Howard, Louis Natheaux, Charles Brinley.

A detective is trying to discover who killed a girl's father when he is mistaken for the the girl's long-lost brother. Soon he is a target for murder himself. This routine Buck Jones entry is improved by its mystery motif. (See also *WHITE EAGLE*.)

FIGHTING FOOL Columbia, 1932, B&W, 58 min. **Director:** Lambert Hillyer; **Screenplay:** Frank Clark; **Cinematographer:** Benjamin H. Kline; **Editor:** Otto Meyer; **Cast:** Tim McCoy, Marceline Day, Mary Carr, Robert Ellis, Ethel Wales, Dorothy Granger, Robert Kortman.

See *RIDING TORNADO, THE*.

FIGHTING FOR JUSTICE Columbia, 1932, B&W, 60 min. **Director:** Otto Brower: **Screenplay:** Robert Quigley; **Editor:** Otto Meyer; **Cast:** Tim McCoy, Joyce Compton, Walter Brennan, Robert Frazer, William V. Mong, Hooper Atchley, Henry Sedley, Harry Todd, Lafe McKee.

Crooks kill a man who has just bought a cattle ranch belonging to another man, who must then clear himself of the charge of murder. A good script and good action adventure make for an effective early Tim McCoy talkie. (See also *RIDING TORNADO, THE*.)

FIGHTING FRONTIER RKO, 1943, B&W, 57 min. **Producer:** Bert Gilroy; **Director:** Lambert Hillyer; **Screenplay:** J. Benton Cheney, Bernard McConville, and Norton S. Parker; **Music:** Paul Sawtell, and Fred Rose and Ray Whitely (songs); **Cinematographer:** Jack Greenhalgh; **Editor:** Less Milbrook; **Cast:** Tim Holt, Cliff Edwards, Ann Summers,

Eddie Dew, William Gould, Davison Clark, Slim Whitaker, Tom London.

Special agent Kit Russell (Tim Holt) is appointed by the governor to infiltrate an outlaw gang and get the goods on its leader in this high-quality entry to Holt's fine and long-standing RKO series. (See also *ALONG THE RIO GRANDE*.)

FIGHTING GRINGO, THE   RKO, 1939, B&W, 59 min. **Producer:** Bert Gilroy; **Director:** David Howard; **Screenplay:** Oliver Drake; **Cinematographer:** Harry J. Wild; **Editor:** Frederic Knudtson; **Cast:** George O'Brien, Lupita Tovar, Lucio Villegas, William Royal, Glenn Strange, Slim Whitaker, Leroy Mason.

The leader of a band of hired guns finds himself involved in the rescue of a gold shipment and in helping a man save his ranch from a group of bandits. (See also *RACKETEERS OF THE RANGE*.)

FIGHTING HERO   Reliable, 1934, B&W, 55 min. **Producer:** Bernard B. Ray; **Director:** Harry Webb; **Screen-play:** Carl Krusada and Rose Gordon; **Cast:** Tom Tyler, Renee Borden, Edward Hearn, Richard Bottiller, Ralph Lewis, Tom London, George Chesebro.

FIGHTING KENTUCKIAN, THE   Republic, 1949, B&W, 100 min, VT. **Producer:** John Wayne; **Director:** George Waggner; **Screenplay:** Waggner; **Music:** George Anthiel; **Cinematographer:** Lee Garmes; **Editor:** Richard L. Van Enger; **Cast:** John Wayne, Vera Hrube Ralston, Philip Dorn, Oliver Hardy, Marie Windsor, John Howard, Hugo Haas, Grant Withers, Odette Myrtil, Paul Fix, Mae Marsh, Jack Pennick, Mickey Simpson.

Set in the post-Napoleonic era, when many French officers and their families were exiled from France, this film tells of a little-known slice of American history when the U.S. Congress granted four townships of land in the territory of Alabama to officers of Napoleon's defeated army.

Fleurette Marchand (Vera Hrube Ralston), the daughter of one such officer, is on a shopping trip to Mobile when she has a romantic introduction to a rugged Kentucky rifleman

George O'Brien (dressed in black) stars in The Fighting Gringo. (RKO/AUTHOR'S COLLECTION)

The popular George O'Brien first worked for Fox before becoming RKO's resident cowboy in the 1930s. A former boxing champion, he left RKO to serve his country during World War II. (AUTHOR'S COLLECTION)

named John Breen (John Wayne), who with his fellow troopers is returning home from the final battle of the War of 1812. Captivated by her beauty, Breen detours his regiment so he can continue to woo the young woman. However, her father (Hugo Haas) and his fellow exiles are at the mercy of the wealthy and powerful Blake Randolph (John Howard), who is determined to marry the lovely Fleurette.

Along the way, Breen discovers evidence of a scheme to evict French settlers from their land by switching the stakes set by the surveyors. The plot thickens as a pitched battle ensues between the French forces and a group of corrupt rivermen led by the wily George Hayden (Grant Withers) and Beau Merritt (Paul Fix). All ends well when Breen dispatches the vicious Hayden with a gunshot, and then, with help from the Second Kentucky Riflemen led by Andrew Jackson, the rivermen are routed and the French colony is saved. Predictably, Breen marries Fleurette, and the Fighting Kentuckians take to the trail once more.

Sandwiched between two of John Wayne's best films, SHE WORE A YELLOW RIBBON and *Sands of Iwo Jima*, this ordinary Wayne venture is perhaps most notable for the casting of comedian Oliver Hardy, better known as the rotund half of the Laurel and Hardy slapstick team, as Wayne's sidekick and pal Willie Paine. Although it is far from being one of Wayne's better efforts, the film benefits from the performance of Marie Windsor as the scheming seductive Ann Logan

and a fine bit of work by Hardy as the bumbling yet tough backwoods fighter.

The Fighting Kentuckian was the first of three films Windsor made with John Wayne. While their professional association spanned more than three decades (she also appeared with Wayne in *Trouble Along the Way* [1953] and *Cahill: U.S. Marshal* [1973]), she didn't know till years later that Wayne had produced the film. "When I went on the interview he was there," she recalled. "But I didn't realize at the time that he was one of the producers."

FIGHTING LAWMAN, THE Allied Artists, 1953, B&W, 71 min. **Producer:** Vincent M. Fennelly; **Director:** Thomas Carr; **Screenplay:** Daniel B. Ullman; **Music:** Raoul Kraushaar; **Cinematographer:** Gilbert Warrenton; **Editor:** Sam Fields; **Cast:** Wayne Morris, Virginia Grey, John Kellogg, Harry Lauter, John Pickard, Rick Vallin, Myron Healey.

A woman determined to recover loot stolen by a quartet of robbers is pursued by a sheriff who is determined to see her fail.

FIGHTING LEGION, THE Universal, 1930, B&W, 75 min. **Producer:** Ken Maynard; **Director:** Harry J. Brown; **Screenplay:** Bennett Cohen; **Cast:** Ken Maynard, Dorothy Dwan, Ernie Adams, Stanley Blystone, Frank Rice, Harry Todd, Robert Walker.

FIGHTING MAN OF THE PLAINS 20th Century Fox, 1949, Color, 94 min. **Producer:** Nat Holt; **Director:** Edwin L. Marin; **Screenplay:** Frank Gruber; **Music:** Paul Sawtell; **Cinematographer:** Fred Jackman; **Editor:** Philip Martin; **Cast:** Randolph Scott, Jane Nigh, Bill Williams, Victory Jory, Dale Robertson, Douglas Kennedy, Joan Taylor, J. Farrell McDonald, Paul Fix.

Randolph Scott plays a notorious gunman who sets out to find his brother's killer. He kills the wrong man and ends up as the sheriff of a lawless Kansas town. With some help from his old pal Jesse James, (Dale Robertson) he manages to set the town straight and clean things up. This solid Scott western is notable for the presence of Robertson in his first significant role.

FIGHTING MARSHAL, THE Columbia, 1931, B&W, 58 min. **Director:** D. Ross Lederman; **Screenplay:** Frank Howard Clark; **Cinematographer:** Benjamin H. Kline; **Editor:** Otto Meyer; **Cast:** Tim McCoy, Dorothy Gulliver, Matthew Betz, Mary Carr, Pat O'Malley, Edward Le Saint, Lafe McKee.

FIGHTING MUSTANG Astor, 1948, B&W, 60 min. **Producer:** Walt Maddox; **Director:** Oliver Drake; **Screenplay:** Rita Ross; **Cast:** Sunset Carson, Al Terry, Steven Ceves, Pat Stirling, Polly McKay, Joe Hiser, Forrest Mathews, Bob Curtis.

Two rangers stationed near the badlands try to stop an outlaw gang that is stealing wild horses.

FIGHTING PARSON   Allied, 1933, B&W, 70 min. **Producer:** M. H. Hoffman Jr.; **Director:** Harry L. Fraser; **Screenplay:** Fraser and Ed Weston; **Cinematographer:** Henry Kohler and Harry Neumann; **Editor:** Mildred Johnston; **Cast:** Hoot Gibson, Marceline Carr, Skeeter Bill Robbins, Ethel Wales, Stanley Blystone, Robert Frazer.

FIGHTING RANGER, THE   Columbia, 1934, B&W, 60 min. **Producer:** Irving Briskin; **Director:** George B. Seitz; **Screenplay:** Harry O. Hoyt; **Cinematographer:** Sidney Wagner; **Editor:** Leon Barsha; **Cast:** Buck Jones, Dorothy Revier, Frank Rice, Bradley Page, Ward Bond, Frank La Rue, Paddy O'Flynn.

In this action-packed remake of Buck Jones's BORDER LAW (1931), a ranger quits the service in order to round up a murderous outlaw gang. Before turning to full-length feature films director George Seitz was also known as the serial king, helming and writing many cliffhangers including *The Perils of Pauline* (1914) and all subsequent Pearl White serials. He made some 40 features between 1927 and 1933. (See also *WHITE EAGLE*.)

FIGHTING RANCH   See *FIGHTIN' THRU*.

FIGHTING RANGER, THE   Monogram, 1948, B&W, 57 min. **Producer:** Barney Sarecki; **Director:** Lambert Hillyer; **Screenplay:** Ronald Davidson; **Music:** Edward J. Kay; **Cinematographer:** Harry Neumann; **Editor:** Carl Pierson; **Cast:** Johnny Mack Brown, Raymond Hatton, Marshall Reed, Christine Larson, I. Stafford Jolley, Milburn Morante.

Johnny Mack Brown is a ranger who finds out that a man framed his cousin for murder in order to inherit his ranch, so he gets a job on the spread in order to capture the culprit. This average Brown entry for his Monogram series was helmed by Lambert Hillyer, whose body of work had declined since the days when he wrote and directed for William S. Hart. (See also *UNDER ARIZONA SKIES*.)

FIGHTING REDHEAD, THE   Eagle Lion, 1949, Color 55 min. **Producer:** Jerry Thomas; **Director:** Lewis D. Collins; **Screenplay:** Paul Franklin and Jerry Thomas; **Music:** Darrell Calker and David Chudnow; **Cinematographer:** Gilbert Warrenton; **Editor:** Joseph Gluck; **Cast:** Jim Bannon, Don Kay Reynolds, Peggy Stewart, John Hart, Emmett Lynn, Lane Bradford.

In this feature Red Ryder (Jim Bannon) helps a girl capture the cattle rustlers who murdered her homesteader followers. The always capable Peggy Stewart and John Hart deliver nice performances. Hart understudied Clayton Moore as The Lone Ranger in 52 episodes of the TV series, then starred in the TV series *Hawkeye and The Last of the Mohicans*. (See also *ADVENTURES OF RED RYDER, THE*.)

FIGHTING RENEGADE   Victory, 1939, B&W, 60 min. **Producer:** Sam Katzman; **Director:** Sam Newfield; **Screenplay:** William Lively; **Cinematographer:** Arthur Reed; **Editor:** Holbrook N. Todd; **Cast:** Tim McCoy, Joyce Bryant, Ben Corbett, Ted Adams, Budd Buster, Dave O'Brien, Forrest Taylor.

FIGHTING SEVENTH, THE   See *LITTLE BIG HORN*.

FIGHTING SHADOWS   Columbia, 1935, B&W, 60 min. **Director:** David Selman; **Screenplay:** Ford Beebe; **Cinematographer:** George Meehan; **Editor:** Al Clark and Gene Milford; **Cast:** Tim McCoy, Robert Allen, Geneva Mitchell, Ward Bond, Si Jenks, Otto Hoffman, Jim Mason, Bud Osborne.

See *RIDING TORNADO, THE*.

FIGHTING SHERIFF, THE   Columbia, 1931, B&W, 67 min. **Producer:** Sol Lesser; **Director:** Louis King; **Screenplay:** Stuart Anthony; **Cast:** Buck Jones, Loretta Sayers, Robert Ellis, Harlan Knight, Paul Fix, Tom Bay, Lillian Worth, Clarence Muse, Lafe McKee, Slim Whitaker.

FIGHTING TEXAN   Ambassador, 1937, B&W, 58 min. **Producer:** Maurice Caan; **Director:** Charles Abbott; **Screenplay:** Joseph O'Donnell; **Cinematographer:** Jack Greenhalgh; **Editor:** Richard G. Wray; **Cast:** Kermit Maynard, Elaine Shepard, Frank La Rue, Budd Buster, Ed Cassidy.

A rancher finds that his stock of horses is mysteriously being depleted, while a nearby ranch has had a sudden upsurge in its horse population. Few independent series of the mid-1930s matched the relative quality of this Kermit Maynard series produced by Ambassador Films. Simple but with decent plots, they utilized effective musical scores, camera tricks for running inserts, elaborate opticals, and other technical niceties. They also had a generous supply of action, and in Kermit Maynard they had a star with a naturalistic breezy style who was also an accomplished stuntman and rider.

In addition to *Fighting Texan*, Ambassador Pictures produced 16 other features with Kermit Maynard between 1935 and 1937. These include *THE RED BLOOD OF COURAGE, CODE OF THE MOUNTED, HIS FIGHTING BLOOD, WILDERNESS MAIL, NORTHERN FRONTIER, TRAILS OF THE WILD* (1935); *PHANTOM PATROL, SONG OF THE TRAIL, TIMBER WAR, WILDCAT TROOPER* (1936); *ROARING SIX GUNS, ROUGH RIDING RHYTHM, GALLOPING DYNAMITE, VALLEY OF TERROR, WHISTLING BULLETS,*

WILD HORSE ROUND-UP (1937). Nearly all were based on stories by James Oliver Curwood.

FIGHTING THROUGH Willis Kent, 1934, B&W, 55 min. **Producer:** Willis Kent; **Director:** Harry Fraser; **Screenplay:** Fraser; **Cast:** Reb Russell, Lucille Lund, Yakima Canutt, Edward Hearn, Chester Gan, Steve Colanto, Bill Patton.

Two cowpokes become friends when one saves the other's life after a framed card game. The two get a job on a girl's ranch and save her from kidnappers. (See also *LIGHTNING TRIGGERS*.)

FIGHTING VALLEY PRC, 1943, B&W, 62 min. **Producer:** Arthur Alexander; **Director:** Oliver Drake; **Screenplay:** Drake; **Cinematographer:** Ira K. Morgan; **Cast:** Dave O'Brien, James Newill, Guy Wilkerson, Patti McCarty, Jimmy Aubrey, Robert Bice, Budd Buster, Jess Cavin.

The Texas Rangers help a man whose ore is being stolen from his smelting mine by hijackers. PRC produced this pedestrian series starring Dave O'Brien, James Newill, and Guy Wilkerson. Other entries include *Rangers Take Over*, BAD MEN OF THUNDER GAP aka *Thunder Gap Outlaws* (recut version, 1947), *West of Texas* aka *Shooting Irons, Border Buckeroos, Trail of Terror, Return of the Rangers* (1943); BOSS OF RAWHIDE, Gunsmoke Mesa, Outlaw Roundup. *Guns of the Law, The Pinto Bandit, Spook Town*, BRAND OF THE DEVIL (1944).

FIGHTING VIGILANTES, THE PRC, 1947, B&W, 61 min. **Producer:** Jerry Thomas; **Director:** Ray Taylor; **Screenplay:** Robert B. Churchill; **Music:** Walter Greene; **Cinematographer:** Ernest Miller; **Editor:** Hugh Winn; **Cast:** Lash LaRue, Al St. John, Jennifer Holt, George Chesebro, Lee Morgan, Marshall Reed.

See *LAW OF THE LASH*.

FIGHTING WESTERNER, THE See *ROCKY MOUNTAIN MYSTERY*.

FIGHTING WITH KIT CARSON Mascot, 1933, B&W, 12 chapters. **Producer:** Nat Levine; **Directors:** Colbert Clark and Armand Schaefer; **Screenplay:** Clark, Wyndham Gittens, Jack Natteford and Barney A. Sarecky; **Music:** Lee Zahler; **Cinematographer:** Ernest Miller, William Nobles, and Alvin Wyckoff; **Editor:** Earl Turner; **Cast:** Johnny Mack Brown, Betsy King Ross, Noah Beery, Noah Beery Jr., Tully Marshall, Edmund Breese, Al Bridge, Edward Hearn, Lafe McKee, Jack Mower.

A pack train led by Kit Carson is attacked by Kraft and his Mystery Riders, a gang that wants a government shipment of gold the train is carrying. This rather slow-moving venture was Johnny Mack Brown's first serial.

FIGHTIN' THRU (aka: CALIFORNIA IN 1878, FIGHTING RANCH, FIGHTING THRU) Tiffany, 1930, B&W, 61 min. **Producer:** Phil Goldstone; **Director:** William Nigh; **Screenplay:** Jack Natteford; **Cinematographer:** Arthur Reed; **Editor:** Earl Turner; **Cast:** Ken Maynard, Jeanette Loff, Wallace MacDonald, Carmelita Geraghty, William L. Thorne, Charles King.

A gold miner is accused of killing his partner but finds out a gambler and a saloon girl are the real culprits. This oater, bereft of a soundtrack, is one of Ken Maynard's earliest talkies.

FINGER ON THE TRIGGER (aka: BLUE LIGHTNING and EL DEDO EN EL GATILLO) Allied Artists, 1965, Color, 87 min. **Producer:** Sidney W. Pink; **Director:** Pink; **Screenplay:** Pink and Luis de los Arcos; **Music:** José Solá; **Cinematographer:** Antonio Macasoli; **Editor:** Margarita de Ochoa; **Cast:** Rory Calhoun, Aldo Sambrell, James Philbrook, Leo Anchóriz, Todd Martin, Georges Rigaud, Silvia Solar.

Calhoun and his band of Yankee Civil War veterans find themselves on a border town vying with a group of ex-Confederate soldiers for a legendary treasure of Spanish gold.

FIREBRANDS OF ARIZONA Republic, 1944, B&W, 55 min. **Producer:** Louis Gray; **Director:** Leslie Selander; **Screenplay:** Randall Faye; **Cinematographer:** Bud Thackery; **Editor:** Harry Keller; **Cast:** Smiley Burnette, Sunset Carson, Earl Hodgins, Roy Barcroft, LeRoy Mason, Tom London, Jack Kirk, Rex Lease, Robert Wilke, Fred "Snowflake" Toones, Pierce Lyden, Budd Buster.

Sunset Carson and his pal Frog Milhouse, a hypochondriac, are on their way to see a doctor when the law mistakes Frog for a look-alike outlaw named Beefsteak Disco. This Sunset Carson venture is better than average mainly due to the dual role played by Smiley Burnette. (See also *CALL OF THE ROCKIES* [1944].)

FIRECREEK Warner Bros., 1968, Color, 104 min, VT. **Producers:** Philip Leacock and John Mantley; **Director:** Vincent McEveety; **Screenplay:** Calvin Clements; **Music:** Alfred Newman; **Cinematographer:** William H. Clothier; **Editor:** William Ziegler; **Cast:** James Stewart, Henry Fonda, Inger Stevens, Gary Lockwood, Dean Jagger, Ed Begley, J. C. Flippen, Jack Elam, James Best, Barbara Luna, Jacqueline Scott, Brooke Bundy, J. Robert Porter, Morgan Woodward, John Qualen, Louise Latham, Athena Lorde, Harry "Slim" Duncan.

The calm of a small western town is threatened by the arrival of four drifters led by the laconic Larkin, played by Henry Fonda in his first fully villainous role. James Stewart plays Cobb, a timid, part-time sheriff who prefers tending his farm to engaging in fisticuffs or violence. But when Larkin's gang (including Gary Lockwood, Jack Elam, and Morgan

Woodward) terrorize the town and hang a simple-minded young deputy, Cobb, against the advice of almost all the town folk, takes it upon himself to challenge Larkin and his cronies. When the storekeeper and elder (played by Dean Jagger) reminds Stewart of the futility of his act, telling him that "We are a town of failures and losers," Stewart stoically replies, "The day a man decides not to face the world is the day he better step out of it."

In many ways the film is a play on the *HIGH NOON* (1952) theme. The final duel alone shows several parallels, including four villains against the protagonist, the killing of the second villain in the stable, the crucial assistance of a woman in dispatching yet another (Inger Stevens puts a bullet into Fonda's back, just in time to save Stewart's life), and finally the arrival of a buckboard to take the wounded hero out of town.

While James Stewart came to the western rather late in his career, he embraced it so wholeheartedly that he has earned a special place in the genre. Director Vincent McEveety, making his film debut on the big screen, was well familiar with westerns, having helmed numerous television oaters. He was also able to get a remarkably layered performance out of the 60-year-old Stewart, which in many ways matches the actor's very best efforts.

As noted above, *Firecreek* marked Henry Fonda's first major foray as a villain. Due to a decision by Warner Bros. to pump the picture directly into neighborhood theaters, it was not seen by too many people, making his impact all the greater a short time later when he played the vicious, cold-blooded killer in Sergio Leone's *ONCE UPON A TIME IN THE WEST* (1969). *Firecreek* marks the first teaming of long-time pals Stewart and Fonda and offers a profound character study of a group of protagonists who are not what they initially seem to be. The final showdown and shoot-out between Stewart and Fonda is as compelling as it is novel and merits further attention. The two big stars would later appear together in the far more convivial and lighthearted western *THE CHEYENNE SOCIAL CLUB* (1970).

This underrated western touches every element of the human condition without the flash and pomp of bigger productions.

FIRST REBEL, THE   See *ALLEGHENY UPRISING*.

FIRST TEXAN, THE   Allied Artist, 1956, Color, 82 min. **Producer:** Walter Mirisch; **Director:** Byron Haskin; **Screenplay:** Daniel B. Ullman; **Music:** Roy Webb; **Cinematographer:** Wilfred M. Cline; **Editor:** George White; **Cast:** Joel McCrea, Felicia Farr, Jeff Morrow, Wallace Ford, Abraham Sofaer, Jody McCrea, Chubby Johnson, Myron Healey, Carl Benton Reid.

Joel McCrea plays Sam Houston, who defeats the forces of Santa Ana at the Battle of San Jacinto six weeks after the fall of the Alamo. This is an excellent study of the life and times of Sam Houston, a reluctant hero who wanted no part of the Texas fight until President Andrew Jackson urged him to take the lead in making Texas independent of Mexican rule.

Joel McCrea (with stick) as Sam Houston in The First Texan *(ALLIED ARTISTS/AUTHOR'S COLLECTION)*

FIRST TRAVELING SALESLADY, THE   RKO, 1956, Color, 92 min. **Producer:** Arthur Lubin; **Director:** Lubin; **Screenplay:** Devery Freeman and Stephen Longstreet;; **Music:** Irving Gertz (song), and Hal Levy; **Cinematographer:** William E. Snyder; **Editor:** Otto Ludwig; **Cast:** Ginger Rogers, Barry Nelson, Carol Channing, David Brian, James Arness, Clint Eastwood, Dan White, Robert F. Simon, Frank Wilcox, Tristram Coffin, Pierce Lyden.

When a Broadway show is closed because some of her corsets are used in a number, designer Rose Gilroy (Ginger Rogers) and her secretary Molly Wade (Carol Channing) head west to sell barbed wire, but they soon find themselves in all kinds of trouble. Originally written for Mae West, this trite comedy also features 24-year-old Clint Eastwood as Lieutenant Jack Rice, whose romantic pairing with Carol Channing, according to Leonard Maltin, makes for "one of the oddest couples in screen history."

Eastwood had recently seen his contract dropped by Universal and consequently went to work for RKO, a longtime haven for low-budget productions. He was given his largest role to date and a promise for a separate byline reading "And introducing Clint Eastwood." The soundtrack song "A Corset Can Do a Lot for a Lady" pretty much says it all.

FISTFUL OF DOLLARS, A   United Artists, 1964, Color, 96 min, VT. **Producer:** Harry Colombo and George

Papi; **Director:** Sergio Leone; **Screenplay:** Leone and Duccio Tessari: **Music:** Ennio Morricone; **Cinematographer:** Massimo Dallamaro and Frederico G. Larraya; **Editor:** Bob Quintle (Roberto Cinquinil); **Cast:** Clint Eastwood, Marianne Koch, John Wells, Wolfgang Lucschy, S. Rupp, Antonio Prieto.

Produced in 1964 and released in the United States in 1967, this film startled viewers by reversing the mythology of the American western. Though not the first Italian-made western, *A Fistful of Dollars* established the pattern followed in scores of films for the balance of the decade and into the next. A mysterious laconic drifter—"The Man with No Name"— rides into a trouble-ridden town and puts himself in the middle of a conflict between two families. With no other motive other than profit, he hires himself out to two warring families, then sets one against the other. "We spend our time here between funerals and burials," a townsman tells the mysterious stranger.

Writer/director Sergio Leone, who as a youth watched Hollywood movies with reverence, took one of the most prominent symbols of American freedom and optimism, the cowboy, and turned him into a ruthless profiteer. But there is also admiration for a character like Eastwood's Man with No Name for his bravery, resourcefulness, pragmatism, and consummate survival skills.

The film made an international star of Eastwood and a major film icon of Leone. *A Fistful of Dollars* started the popular "spaghetti" western craze of the 1960s and was noted for its explicit brutality, flamboyant visual style, and abundant use of extreme close-ups. It gave an enormous boost to the stagnant career of Clint Eastwood, who was perfectly cast as the laconic Man with No Name. In fact, Eastwood was so influenced by Leone's filmmaking style that he paid tribute to his mentor at the end of his Academy Award-winning western *UNFORGIVEN* (1992).

Leone's spaghetti westerns, born out of the cynicism and amorality of the 1960s, bred a new type of hero, one motivated by greed, not altruism, in a world where heroes and villains were harder to tell apart and where the good guys seemed to lose more battles than they won. The tall-in-the-saddle lawman exemplified in the traditional western was suddenly deemed out of step with the turbulence of a troubled era—an America which had endured civil unrest, a presidential assassination, an unpopular war in Southeast Asia, and a youth movement that rallied around the change to "Question Authority."

Leone financed the modestly budgeted film by raising the necessary $200,000 from German, Spanish, and Italian interest groups. Of this total, Eastwood received a $15,000 salary and a chance to see Europe for free. Once there he found that he was the only one on the set who could speak English. Despite this obstacle, the film was wrapped up in a very short time, and Eastwood returned to America to continue filming the *Rawhide* series (1959–66).

Eastwood himself had initial reservations about a project that would be financed by a German-Italian-Spanish production company with an Italian director. He was sure that no

European studio could make a successful, realistic western. However, when he read the script he was impressed and recognized the story as a remake of Japanese director Akira Kurosawa's masterpiece *Yojimbo* (1961). He was well aware that a few years earlier a remake of Kurosawa's *Seven Samurai* (1954) had resulted in *THE MAGNIFICENT SEVEN* (1960), which helped launched the careers of superstars Steve McQueen, Charles Bronson, and James Coburn.

While Eastwood learned to respect his director, he was also confident that the film would never be shown in the United States. He reasoned that the character he played, that of a ruthless, mercenary drifter, was too offbeat to be accepted as a hero in his native land. At the time Eastwood was far from obscure, but he was hardly famous either. His role as Rowdy Yates on television's *Rawhide*, while significant, had not made him a star. Leone had tried to get many American actors for the lead role of The Man with No Name, including Henry Fonda, Charles Bronson, and James Coburn. But Eastwood turned out to be what Leone wanted, and he even altered the role somewhat to accommodate the actor. In turn, Eastwood too had to adapt, learning to smoke, which was difficult for him, but he accomplished the feat so well that the smoking cheroot became an integral part of his persona in the spaghetti westerns.

The film was more international than Italian, having been filmed in Spain and coproduced with Spain and West Germany. Leone followed the success of *A Fistful of Dollars* with two more films *FOR A FEW DOLLARS MORE* (1965) and *THE GOOD, THE BAD AND THE UGLY* (1966). Then came his most ambitious work, *ONCE UPON A TIME IN THE WEST*, first conceived in 1967 but not released until 1983. Each became a big hit and revitalized the western in the United States and around the world.

FISTFUL OF DYNAMITE (aka: DUCK, YOU SUCKER) Rafran/Euro International, 1972, Color, 157 min, VT, DVD. **Producer:** Fulvio Morsella; **Director:** Sergio Leone; **Screenplay:** Luciano Vincenzoni, Sergio Donati, and Leone; **Music:** Ennio Morricone; **Cinematographer:** Guiseppe Ruzzolini; **Editor:** Nino Baragli; **Cast:** Rod Steiger, James Coburn, Ramolo Valli, Jean Michael Antoine, Vivienne Chandler, David Warbeck.

After his success with Clint Eastwood's "Man With No Name" in *A FISTFUL OF DOLLARS*, Sergio Leone made this sprawling, excessive film set during the Mexican Revolution. Rod Steiger plays a simple bandit who wants to rob a bank in a Mexican town but instead gets mixed up in a revolution in which he has no interest. He meets James Coburn, an IRA terrorist and expert with explosives (dynamite). Together they become involved in a peasant revolt. Reviewed originally as *Duck, You Sucker*, the film's English title was changed soon after to *A Fistful of Dynamite*. In the United States it was released in a 138-minute version. Although Leone inserts some occasional light touches, action dominates the film— firing squads and lots of shooting, a blown-up bridge when troops are crossing, and a train collision at the climax.

FIVE BLOODY GRAVES (aka: FIVE BLOODY DAYS TO TOMBSTONE, GUN RIDERS, LONELY MAN) Independent International, 1970, Color, 88 min. **Producers:** Al Adamson and Samuel M. Sherman; **Director:** Adamson; **Screenplay:** Robert Dix; **Cinematographer:** Vilmos Zsigmond; **Editors:** William Faris and Peter Perry; **Cast:** Robert Dix, Scott Brady, Jim Davis, John Carradine, Paula Raymond, John "Bud" Carlos, Gene Raymond.

Narrated by the voice of death (Gene Raymond), this extremely violent film tells of an odd mix of travelers pursued across the desert by a savage band of Indians.

FIVE CARD STUD Paramount, 1968, Color, 103 min, VT. **Producer:** Hal. B. Wallis; **Director:** Henry Hathaway; **Screenplay:** Marguerite Roberts; **Music:** D. H. Doane, Maurice Jarre, E. C. Van, Al Styne, and Ned Washington (lyrics); **Cinematographer:** Daniel L. Fapp; **Editor:** Warren Lowe; **Cast:** Dean Martin, Robert Mitchum, Inger Stevens, Roddy McDowall, Katharine Justice, Yaphet Kotto, Denver Pyle, Whit Bissell, Ted de Corsica, Jerry Gatlin.

An interesting plot based on a novel by Ray Gaulden has the players in an ongoing poker game being mysteriously killed off one by one. All this begins when seven men sit down to a game of poker, and one player, a stranger, is caught cheating and is hanged. It seems like a clear-cut case of revenge, as the remaining members of the poker game meet with interesting and untimely deaths. One is suffocated in a barrel of flour, another is strangled with barbed wire, a third is hanged from the bell rope in the church, and a fourth is strangled by hand. Robert Mitchum plays an itinerant preacher who arrives in town after the hanging, and Dean Martin, the only card player not present at the hanging, sets out to solve the crime. Martin also sings the title song.

This is not one of director Henry Hathaway's best efforts, but it is still an enjoyable slice of entertainment for folks who like a good murder mystery with a western backdrop. Hathaway scored big a year later with *TRUE GRIT* (1969), the film that garnered John Wayne his long-awaited Oscar.

FIVE GUNS TO TOMBSTONE United Artists, 1961, B&W, 71 min. **Producer:** Robert E. Kent; **Director:** Edward L. Cahn; **Screenplay:** Jack DeWitt, Arthur E. Orloff, and Richard Shayer; **Music:** Paul Sawtell and Bert Shefter; **Cinematographer:** Maury Gertzman; **Editor:** Bernard Small; **Cast:** Willis Bouchey, James Brown, Wally Coy, Jeff De Benning, John Eldredge, Joe Hayworth, Robert Karnes, Jon Locke, Boyd "Red" Morgan.

A reformed gunslinger discovers his outlaw brother is trying to lure him back to lawlessness by framing him for a crime he didn't commit.

FIVE GUNS WEST Palo Alto Productions, 1955, Color, 73 min, VT. **Producer:** Roger Corman; **Director:** Corman; **Screenplay:** R. Wright Campbell; **Music:** Buddy Bergman; **Cinematographer:** Floyd Crosby; **Editor:** Ronald Sinclair; **Cast:** John Lund, Mike Connors, Jonathan Haze, R. Wright Campbell, Paul Birch, Dorothy Malone.

Roger Corman's first directorial effort has five murderers released from prison to join the Confederate army. They are assigned to steal gold from a Union stagecoach, but after they steal the loot they decide to keep it themselves.

FIVE SAVAGE MEN See *ANIMALS, THE.*

FLAME OF SACRAMENTO See *IN OLD SACRAMENTO.*

FLAME OF THE BARBARY COAST Republic, 1945, B&W, 91 min, VT. **Producer:** Joseph Kane; **Director:** Kane; **Screenplay:** Borden Chase; **Music:** Morton Scott; **Cinematographer:** Robert de Grasse; **Editor:** Richard L. van Enger; **Cast:** John Wayne, Ann Dvorak, Joseph Schildkraut, William Frawley, Virginia Grey, Russell Hicks, Jack Norton, Paul Fix, Manart Kippen, Eve Lynne, Marc Lawrence, Butterfly McQueen, Rex Lease, Hank Bell, Al Murphy.

A strapping Montana cattleman (John Wayne) fleeced of his money by a San Francisco gambling house owner returns to the City by the Bay to set up a rival saloon. He also romances the gambler's singer-sweetheart, a beautiful woman who has earned the name "The Flame of the Barbary Coast" (Ann Dvorak).

The story follows a predictable path until all goes asunder with the disastrous 1906 San Francisco earthquake. The film features a great performance by Joseph Schildkraut as gambler Tito Morell. The film received an Oscar nomination for Best Scoring of a Dramatic Picture and for Best Sound Recording.

FLAME OF THE WEST Monogram, 1945, B&W, 70 min. **Producer:** Scott R. Dunlap; **Director:** Lambert Hillyer; **Screenplay:** Adele Buffington; **Cinematographer:** Harry Neumann; **Editor:** Dan Millner; **Cast:** Johnny Mack Brown, Raymond Hatton, Joan Woodbury, Ray Bennett, Horace B. Carpenter, Lynne Carver, Douglas Dumbrille, Bob Duncan.

Johnny Mack Brown plays a mild-mannered, pacifist doctor. He angers his girlfriend, who thinks he is a coward for not opposing a gang of local outlaws. But when the town sheriff is killed by a dishonest gambler, he is goaded into stopping the outlaw gang. Helmed by Lambert Hillyer, this series oater is an interesting departure from Brown's run-of-the-mill entries. The feature also spotlights Pee Wee King (co-composer of "Tennessee Waltz" and "Slow Polk") and his Golden West Cowboys, who provide the musical interludes which by now were firmly established in series westerns. This is also one of Johnny Mack Brown's very best westerns. (See also *UNDER ARIZONA SKIES*.)

FLAMING FEATHER Paramount, 1951, Color, 77 min. **Producer:** Nat Holt; **Director:** Ray Enright; **Screenplay:** Gerald Greyson Adams; **Music:** Paul Sawtell; **Cinematographer:** Ray Rennahan; **Editor:** Elmo Billings; **Cast:** Sterling Hayden, Forrest Tucker, Arleen Whelan, Barbara Rush, Victory Jory, Richard Arlen, Edgar Buchanan, Ray Teal.

A band of renegade Ute led by a treacherous white man pillage across the Southwest, causing excessive carnage. A group of vigilantes set out to rescue a girl who has been captured by them and is being held in Montezuma Castle.

FLAMING FRONTIER, THE Universal, 1926, B&W, 8, 828'. **Director/story:** Edward Sedgwick; **Screenplay:** Edward J. Montagne, Charles Kenyon, and Raymond Schrock; **Cinematographer:** Virgil Miller; **Cast:** Hoot Gibson, Anne Cornwall, Dustin Farnum, Ward Crane, Kathleen Key, Eddie Gribbon, Harry Todd, Harold Goodwin, George Fawcett, Noble Johnson, Charles K. French, William Steele, Walter Rodgers, Ed Wilson, Joe Bonomo.

Hoot Gibson plays Pony Express rider Bob Langdon, who wins an appointment to West Point with the help of a U.S. senator (George Fawcett). He soon succumbs to the charms of the senator's pretty daughter (Ann Cornwall), so much so that the good-natured Bob even protects her brother from a scandal involving another woman. Eager to please the young lady, he accepts the guilt for her brother's misdeeds and consequently is expelled from the academy. He returns to the West to serve with Custer (Dustin Farnum) at the Battle of Little Big Horn. He rides for help but arrives too late to save the troops. Nevertheless he is able to bring a crooked Indian agent to justice. With his reputation now restored, he returns to West Point.

Prior to the sound era, Hoot Gibson was Universal's most popular western star, earning as much as $14,000 a week in the late 1920s. Directed and written by Edward Sedgwick, *The Flaming Frontier* was one of Gibson's most popular and well-received ventures and typical of the light but action-packed films that delighted audiences of the silent screen. One of the more memorable sequences within the film is where the Indians attack buffalo hunters in order to protect their herds from being further slaughtered. The picture also included footage of a number of fine battle scenes that were later used in Universal's first all-talking serials, *The Indians Are Coming* (1930). But as William Everson points out in his *Pictorial History of the Western Film*, Universal's *The Flaming Frontier*, while dealing with Custer's Last Stand, was sold not on its epic qualities but rather on its star cast (Gibson, Farnum, and others) and on its spectacular action scenes.

FLAMING FRONTIER 20th Century Fox, 1958, B&W, 70 min. **Producer:** Sam Newfield; **Director:** Newfield; **Screenplay:** Louis Stevens; **Music:** John Bath; **Cinematographer:** Frederick Ford; **Editor:** Douglas Robertson; **Cast:** Bruce Bennett, Jim Davis, Don Girrard, Paisley Maxwell, Cecil Linder.

When trouble develops between whites and the Sioux Indians, a half-breed Sioux cavalry officer tries to intervene, but predictably he runs into a wall of prejudice.

FLAMING FRONTIERS Universal, 1938, B&W, 15 episodes, VT. **Producer:** Henry MacRae; **Directors:** Alan James and Ray Taylor; **Screenplay:** Basil Dickey, Wyndham Gittens, Paul Perez, and Ella O'Neill; **Music:** Sam Perry, Charles Previn, Henry Roemheld, Clifford Vaughn, Edward Ward, and Franz Waxman; **Cast:** Johnny Mack Brown, Ralph Bowman, Eleanor Hansen, Charles Middleton, James Blaine, Charles Stevens, Chief Thundercloud, Roy Barcroft, Iron Eyes Cody.

Johnny Mack Brown plays Tex Houston, a famous Indian scout who comes to the aid of a young woman being wooed by a crook who wants to marry her for her father's gold mine. The plot line in the 15-chapter serial, based on Peter B. Tyne's story "The Tie That Binds," is a bit thin, but nonstop action helps keep this cliffhanger honest.

FLAMING GOLD RKO, 1933, B&W, 54 min. **Producers:** Merian C. Cooper and Sam Jaffe; **Director:** Ralph Ince; **Screenplay:** Malcom Stuart Boylan; **Cinematographer:** Charles Rosher; **Cast:** William Boyd, Mae Clark, Pat O'Brien, Robert McWade, Rollo Lloyd.

William Boyd (in his pre-Hop-Along Cassidy days) and pal Pat O'Brien are drilling for oil in the jungle. However, when Boyd goes to the city to get financing he meets working girl Mae Clark. They hit it off and get married without Boyd knowing that she is a working girl. When O'Brien discovers the truth, he assumes that she tricked his pal, and the film becomes a dated melodrama about the friendship/love triangle.

FLAMING GUNS Universal, 1932, B&W, 57 min. **Director:** Arthur Rosson; **Screenplay:** Jack Cunningham; **Music:** Alfred Newman, Sam Perry, and Heintz Roemheld; **Cinematographer:** Jerome Ash; **Editor:** Philip Cahn; **Cast:** Tom Mix, Ruth Hall, William Farnum, George Hackathorne, Clarence Wilson, Bud Osborne, Duke R. Lee, Gilbert "Pee Wee" Holmes.

A ranch foreman falls in love with a banker's daughter, but when he and the girl's parents have a falling out, foreman and girl flee across the border to Mexico. A remake of Hoot Gibson's silent feature *The Buckaroo Kid* (1929) and based on the novel by Peter B. Kyne, this oater is one of the weaker Tom Mix series entries for Universal. (See also *FOURTH HORSEMAN, THE*.)

FLAMING LEAD Colony, 1939, B&W, 57 min. **Producers:** Arthur Alexander and Max Alexander; **Director:** Sam Newfield; **Screenplay:** Joseph O'Donnell; **Cinematographer:**

Arthur Reed; **Editor:** Holbrook N. Todd; **Cast:** Ken Maynard, Eleanor Stewart, Reed Howes, Carlton Young, Walter Long, Tom London, Dave O'Brien.

A cowboy comes to the aid of a rancher who is about to lose an army contract due to the constant rustling which is depleting his stock. A good story and lots of movement make this oater one of Ken Maynard's better later films.

FLAMING STAR 20th Century Fox, 1960, Color, 101 min. **Producer:** David Weisbart; **Director:** Don Siegel; **Screenplay:** Nunnally Johnson and Clair Huffaker; **Music:** Cyril Mockbridge, Sherman Edwards, and Sid Wayne (songs); **Cinematographer:** Charles G. Clarke; **Editor:** Hugh S. Fowler; **Cast:** Elvis Presley, Barbara Eden, Steve Forrest, Dolores Del Rio, John McIntyre, Rodolfo Acosta, Karl Swenson, Ford Rainey, Richard Jaeckel, L. Q. Jones.

A tightly knit family comprised of a white settler (Pa Burton), his Kiowa Indian wife, his white son by a previous marriage, and his half-Indian son is caught in midst of an Indian uprising. The plot unfolds when the Kiowa massacre a white family in the vicinity, and the settlers demand that the Burtons prove their loyalty to the white folk. Meanwhile, Netty Burton (Dolores del Rio) and Pacer Burton (Elvis Presley) go to the Kiowa camp hoping to arrange a truce. They fail in their attempt, and on the way home a crazed settler fatally wounds Netty. Before she dies she sees the "flaming star" of death. She leaves her deathbed and wanders into the wind-swept fields where she dies. Rampaging Kiowa kill Pa Burton a short time later. When his half-brother Clint (Steve Forrest) is wounded by the Kiowa, Pacer leaves the tribe to help. He staves off some marauding Indians and after the skirmish goes to town to say goodbye to Clint. But he too follows the "flaming star" to his death.

Don Siegel, who 16 years later would direct John Wayne's final film, THE SHOOTIST (1976), helmed what most critics and reviewers consider to be Elvis Presley's finest film entry. In a part originally written for Marlon Brando, Presley is excellent as the half-breed Indian who must choose sides when his mother's people go on the warpath. As with most Don Siegel films, the picture packs plenty of excitement.

The British publication *Films and Filming* called the production a "minor western classic," while Arthur Knight in *Saturday Review* praised Presley's dramatic performance as being "singularly effective." *Variety* was less effusive, calling the film "disturbingly familiar, and not so convincing, [yet] attractively mounted and consistently diverting." Interestingly, no songs occur after the first 10 minutes of the film, with Elvis singing only the title song and another offering, "A Cane and a High Starched Collar."

FLAP (aka: THE LAST WARRIOR, UK) Warner Bros., 1970, Color, 105 min. **Producer:** Jerry Adler; **Director:** Carol Reed; **Screenplay:** Clair Huffaker; **Music:** Marvin Hamlisch; **Cinematographer:** Fred J. Keonekamp; **Editor:** Frank Bracht; **Cast:** Anthony Quinn, Claude Akins, Tony Bill, Shelley Winters, Victor Jory, Rodolfo Acosta, Anthony Caruso.

A renegade Paiute Indian (Anthony Quinn) claims that the city of Phoenix belongs to him. The second most decorated Indian veteran of World War II, Flapping Eagle (Quinn) becomes frustrated with life on the reservation, even more so when he discovers a plot to construct a superhighway trough his tribal homeland. He organizes the tribe, attempts to attract public attention to the plight of the Paiute, and takes part in a number of comic antics. He becomes a martyr to the cause when he is gunned down by a half-breed police sergeant. The film ends with the Indians taking over the city of Phoenix, basing their claim on treaties dating back to 1832.

This so-called comic western was directed by Sir Carol Reed, the distinguished British director who helmed such gems as *Odd Man Out* (1947), *Fallen Idol* (1948), *The Third Man* (1949), and *Oliver* (1968). While Reed embraced no ideological cause and never intended to be a message filmmaker, this picture became tinged by the political sensitivities of the day. Clair Huffaker wrote the screenplay based on his novel *Nobody Loves a Drunken Indian*, his story about modern-day Paiute Indians in Arizona, with the title of the novel originally slated to be used for the film.

However, in an effort to avoid offending anyone, it was changed to *Nobody Loves Flapping Eagle*. Then a group of Indians who read the script wanted the title to be changed back, because they felt the film contained an important message. The final result does little justice to Huffaker's original novel and was poorly received by critics and audiences alike. The theme song, "If Nobody Loves," written by Marvin Hamlisch with words by Estelle Levitt, is sung in the film by Kenny Rogers and the First Edition.

FLESH AND THE SPUR American International, 1956, B&W, 80 min. **Producers:** Mike Connors (as Touch Connors) and Alex Gordon; **Director:** Edward Cahn; **Screenplay:** Charles B. Griffith and Mark Hanna; **Music:** Ronald Stein and Ross Bagdasarian (title song); **Cinematographer:** Frederick West; **Editor:** Robert S. Eisen; **Cast:** John Agar, Marla English, Mike Connors, Raymond Hatton, Joyce Meadows, Maria Monay, Keene Duncan, Buddy Roosevelt.

A cowboy searching for the killer of his twin brother meets a girl and a gunfighter who help lead him into outlaw territory. This well-paced and little known Western is skillfully scripted and features a fine performance by John Agar in a dual role.

FOLLOW THE HUNTER See *FANGS OF THE WILD*.

FOOL'S GOLD United Artists, 1946, B&W, 82 min. **Producer:** Lewis J. Rachmil; **Director:** George Archainbaud; **Screenplay:** Doris Schroeder; **Music:** David Chudnow; **Cinematographer:** Mack Stengler; **Editor:** Fred W. Berger; **Cast:** William Boyd, Andy Clyde, Rand Brooks, Jane

Randolph, Robert Emmet Keane, Stephen Barclay, Forbes Murray, Harry Cording, Earle Hodgins.

An army lieutenant who deserted when summoned for a court-martial is captured by outlaws, and Hop-Along Cassidy agrees to help his colonel father rescue him. This is an entertaining entry in the long-running *HOP-ALONG CASSIDY* series as well as one of his better entries.

FOR A FEW DOLLARS MORE United Artists, 1965, Color, 125 min, VT, DVD. **Producer:** Alberto Grimaldi; **Director:** Sergio Leone; **Screenplay:** Luciano Vincenzoni; **Music:** Ennio Morricone; **Cinematographer:** Massimo Dallamano; **Editors:** Adriana Novelli, Eugenio Alabiso, and Georgio Serralonga; **Cast:** Clint Eastwood, Lee Van Cleef, Gian Maria Volonte, Mara Krup, Luigi Pistilli, Klaus Kinski.

Two bounty hunters (Clint Eastwood and Lee Van Cleef) race for the reward money riding on the head of a brutal bandit named Indio (Gian Maria Volonte). First separately and then in a shaky and untrusting alliance, the pair manages to set the stage for the killing of the bandido with a usual menu of murder, violence, and carnage.

The first of two sequels to *A FISTFUL OF DOLLARS* (1964), *A Few Dollars More* is actually a more interesting film, due largely to the presence of Lee Van Cleef as weapons-obsessed bounty hunter Colonel Mortimore, whose interest in killing the villain is personal revenge for having raped his sister and not for monetary gain or profit. The climax comes when the colonel confronts the bandit Indio and kills him in revenge for his sister's death. Satisfied with vengeance, he allows "The Man With No Name" to keep the reward money. The Man quickly agrees and leaves town with a gruesome cargo, the bodies of dozens of wanted men, on the back of his wagon. The Spanish countryside and the Italo studio interiors combine for a realistic southwestern effect.

Unlike its trend-setting predecessor, *For a Few Dollars More* was given a working budget of $600,000, three times more than *A Fistful of Dollars*. For his second appearance as The Man With No Name, Clint Eastwood received $50,000, a modest sum by today's standards, but $35,000 more than he received for *A Fistful of Dollars*. The film was enormously popular and reviewed well by *Variety*, who called it a "hard-hitting western" and a "top action entry." However, others were appalled by the excessive violence and carnage. "A treat for necrophiliacs. The rest of us can get our kicks for free at the butcher store," commented Judith Crist for the NBC *Today Show*. Veteran critic Bosley Crowther in the *New York Times* called Eastwood "a fearless killing machine," with director Leone "piling violence upon violence and charges the screen with hideous fantasies of sudden death." The English dubbed version was released in the United States in 1967 and in the United Kingdom in 1968.

FORBIDDEN TRAILS Monogram, 1941, B&W, 60 min. **Producer:** Scott R. Dunlap; **Director:** Robert N. Bradbury; **Screenplay:** Jesse Bowers (Adele Buffington); **Cinematographer:** Harry Neumann; **Editor:** Carl Pierson; **Cast:**

Buck Jones, Tim McCoy, Raymond Hatton, Christine McIntyre, Dave O'Brien, Tristram Coffin, Charles King, Bud Osborne.

Trapped in a burning cabin by a couple of ex-cons, Buck Roberts (Buck Jones) has his horse drag him to safety. He joins pals Tim McCall (Tim McCoy) and Sandy Hopkins (Raymond Hatton) and the Rough Riders to take after the villains while helping a mine owner who is being forced to sign a hauling contract. (See also *ARIZONA BOUND* [1941].)

FORBIDDEN VALLEY Universal, 1938, B&W, 67 min. **Producers:** Henry MacRae and Elmer Tambert; **Director:** Wyndham Gittens; **Screenplay:** Gittens; **Cast:** Noah Beery Jr., Frances Robinson, Robert Barrat, Fred Kohler, Henry Hunter, Samuel S. Hinds, Stanley Andrews.

After growing up in a secret canyon, a young man sets out to round up a herd of wild horses and take them to market, but rustlers steal the herd.

FOREST RANGERS, THE Paramount, 1942, Color, 87 min. **Producer:** Robert Sisk; **Director:** George Marshall; **Screenplay:** Harold Scumate; **Music:** Victor Young; **Cinematographers:** Charles Lang and William V. Skall; **Editor:** Paul Weatherwax; **Cast:** Fred MacMurray, Paulette Goddard, Susan Hayward, Lynne Overman, Albert Dekker, Eugene Pallette, Regis Toomey, Rod Cameron, Clem Bevans, James Brown, Kenneth Griffith, Keith Richards, William Cabanne.

A forest ranger (Fred MacMurray) marries a wealthy girl (Paulette Goddard), much to the chagrin of lumber owner Susan Hayward, who tries to prove to him that he made a mistake. In one humorous encounter, the three protagonists (MacMurray, Goddard, and Hayward) are stranded in the woods and have to spend the night with only one blanket to share among the three of them. Director George Marshall orchestrated a superb forest fire scene where arson is suspected and the culprit is surprisingly revealed in the climactic final scenes.

The picture was actually filmed during a real forest fire outside Lakeview, Oregon. Although the camera crew was provided with heat-resistant film, the crew was forced to quit shooting when their film began to melt. When the movie came out in 1942, Technicolor was still a novelty, and consequently the color is gorgeous. While the plot is a bit trite, the scope of the production (cast, sets, costumes, and scenery) would be hard to replicate even today.

But the film's biggest winner was the hit song "Jingle, Jangle, Jingle" (words by Frank Loesser, music by Joseph J. Lilley), which became the country's number one song in radio performances, sheet music, and record sales. It made 14 appearances on "Your Hit Parade," five times as number one. Gene Autry (Okeh records) was one of many stars who recorded the song.

FORLORN RIVER Famous Players-Lasky/Paramount, 1926, B&W, 6 reels. **Producers:** Jesse L. Lasky and

Adolph Zukor; **Director:** John Waters; **Screenplay:** George C. Hull; **Cinematographer:** C. Edgar Schoenbaum; **Cast:** Jack Holt, Raymond Hatton, Arlette Marchal, Edmund Burns, Tom Santschi, Joseph W. Girard, Christian Frank, Al Hart, Nola Luxford, Chief Yowlachie, Jack Moore. See *FORLORN RIVER* (1937).

FORLORN RIVER (aka: RIVER OF DESTINY)

Paramount, 1937, B&W, 56 min. **Producer:** Harold Hurley; **Director:** Charles Barton; **Screenplay:** Stuart Anthony and Robert Yost; **Music:** Borris Morros; **Cinematographer:** Harry Hallenberger; **Editor:** John F. Link Sr.; **Cast:** Buster Crabbe, June Martel, John Patterson, Harvey Stephens, Chester Conklin, Lew Kelly, Syd Saylor.

Buster Crabbe is a cowboy on the trail of a wily outlaw who has framed him for a crime he didn't commit. Based on a story by Zane Grey, the film is a well done adaptation of the author's work. It was also made as a silent film by Paramount in 1929, under the direction of John Waters, with Jack Holt in the leading role.

FORT APACHE

RKO, 1948, B&W, 127 min, VT, DVD. **Producers:** John Ford and Merian C. Cooper; **Director:** Ford; **Screenplay:** Frank S. Nugent; **Music:** Richard Hageman; **Cinematographer:** Archie Stout; **Editor:** Jack Murray; **Cast:** John Wayne, Henry Fonda, Shirley Temple, John Agar, Ward Bond, George O'Brien, Victor McLaglen, Pedro Armendáriz, Anna Lee, Irene Rich, Guy Kibbee, Grant Withers, Miguel Inclan, Dick Foran, Frank Ferguson, Francis Ford.

The first of John Ford's celebrated cavalry trilogy, *Fort Apache* tells the story of former Civil War general Owen Thursday (Henry Fonda), demoted to the rank of lieutenant colonel and shipped west to a desert outpost, Fort Apache. The veteran soldiers at the outpost resent their new commander because he knows nothing about fighting Indians. They include Captain York (John Wayne); Captain Collingwood (George O'Brien); Lieutenant O'Rourke (John Agar), son of Sergeant-Major O'Rourke (Ward Bond); and sergeants Beaufort, Mulcahy, and Quincannon (Pedro Armendáriz, Victor McLaglen and Dick Foran). Before long they come to realize that Thursday's main concern is fame, glory, and the

John Wayne (third from left) and Henry Fonda (third from right) in Fort Apache, *the first of John Ford's celebrated cavalry trilogy* (RKO/AUTHOR'S COLLECTION)

John Agar and Shirley Temple in Fort Apache. *Agar and Temple had been real-life husband and wife.*
(RKO/AUTHOR'S COLLECTION)

restoration of his former rank. His continued insistence on rigid discipline further antagonizes his men.

Colonel Thursday's burning ambition to seek fame reaches fruition when Cochise, chief of the Apache, resenting the corrupt tactics of the local agent, attracts national attention by leading his tribe into Mexico. Thursday figures that if he can bring them back into the fold, his reputation will be made and the glory he seeks will be his. Because Cochise trusts Captain York, Colonel Thursday sends his executive officer and Sergeant Beauford to arrange a meeting. Trusting York's word, Cochise brings his people back over the line. But instead of arriving with a small bodyguard as he had promised, Thursday appears with his entire command and arrogantly orders Cochise to start back toward the reservation or face the consequences. When Captain York protests, Thursday accuses him of cowardliness.

In defiance, Cochise throws his thousand warriors against a smaller cavalry force, wiping it out save for Captain York's small detail guarding a commissary cache. Returning to Fort Apache, York puts his personal feelings aside, covers his superior's blunder, and allows Thursday's name to live on in the army's annals of heroism. "No one died more gallantly—or earned more honor for his regiment," Captain York tells a throng of hungry reporters. He knows better, of course, but refuses to besmirch the regiment and its brave men.

To enhance the film's romantic theme, Ford chose an adult Shirley Temple to play Philadelphia Thursday. Temple still had great box-office appeal and was paid the same amount of money ($100,000) as Fonda and Wayne. Ford also cast Temple's tall, handsome, athletic husband John Agar (in his screen debut) as Lieutenant O'Rourke, her romantic interest in the film. Romance between the colonel's daughter and young O'Rourke develops instantly, but the colonel frowns upon the idea of his daughter marrying the son of a noncommissioned officer.

Since Ford usually had a whipping boy, his principal target for this film was the 26-year-old Agar, whom he delighted in calling "Mr. Temple" in front of cast and crew. According to Dan Ford, the director's grandson, Agar rebelled at one point, stormed off the set, and threatened to quit the picture, but John Wayne took him aside and convinced him to stick it out. Before his death in 2002, John Agar recalled his screen debut in an interview and reflected on his debt of gratitude to John Wayne whom he speaks of with the fondest of awe.

> I was really flabbergasted when I first met Mr. Ford and he put me in *Fort Apache*. It was my first movie, and remember I was working with what I considered all the big stars—guys like Ward Bond, Victor McLaglen, Henry Fonda, George O'Brien, and of course John Wayne. It was such a thrill to work with these same guys whom I had admired as a kid. What a wonderful feeling, and more important they were all so helpful to me. They were behind me all the way. Instead of looking down their noses and saying this is a beginner who doesn't know a thing, they always tried to help me out.
>
> It's no secret that Ford was pretty tough on people at times. I thought he was a kidder of sorts, but he got rough with me a couple of times. Duke would come over, put his hand on my shoulder and say, "Don't worry about it. He's done that to me. He's done that to Fonda. He's done that to everybody."

With a script suggested by the story "Massacre" by James Warner Belch, the film called for a generous $2.5 million budget. To assure adequate payback, Ford chose his actors with uncanny precision. Wayne and Fonda were proven Ford staples. Other roles went to Ford regulars Anna Lee, Ward Bond, Victor McLaglen, Jack Pennick, and Pedro Armendáriz. Ford's old friend George O'Brien, who starred for him many years earlier in the silent film *The Iron Horse* (1924), was given a strong supporting role as Captain Collingwood.

Ford skillfully delineates the lifestyles and personalities that make up the storyline. The camaraderie and bonding that mil-

Victor McLaglen, Jack Pennick, and Dick Foran in Fort Apache (RKO/AUTHOR'S COLLECTION)

John Wayne as Captain Kirby York, John Agar as Second Lieutenant Michael O'Rourke, Shirley Temple as Philadelphia Thursday, and Henry Fonda as Colonel Owen Thursday in Fort Apache (RKO/AUTHOR'S COLLECTION)

itary life entails is superbly presented. Moreover, through the female cast (Temple, Lee, Irene Rich) the viewer gains a concept of domestic life on the frontier and sees how the wives and family members of the troop dealt with grief and survival.

Generally considered a classic today—perhaps the ultimate foray of the U.S. cavalry into the cinematic battlefield—the early reviews were somewhat mixed. *Newsweek* caustically noted that the film succeeds "in bringing back the time-honored business of making redskins bite the dust as first rate entertainment," a theme certain "progressive" critics today still embrace. On the other hand, Bosley

Crowther in the *New York Times* called *Fort Apache* "a rootin' tootin', Wild West Show," elaborating that "John Wayne is powerful, forthright, and exquisitely brave." Similarly, Harold Barnes in the *New York Herald Tribune* stated that "John Wayne is excellent as a captain who escapes the slaughter and protects his superior's name for the sake of the service." *Variety* praised the integration of Richard Hageman's "superb musical score," effusively noting that "mass action, humorous by-play in the western cavalry outpost, deadly suspense, and romance are masterfully combined in this productions."

FORT BOWIE United Artists, 1958, B&W, 80 min. **Producer:** Aubrey Scheneck; **Director:** Howard W. Koch; **Screenplay:** Maurice Tombragel; **Music:** Les Baxter; **Cinematographer:** Carl E. Guthrie; **Editor:** John H. Bushelman; **Cast:** Ben Johnson, Jan Harrison, Kent Taylor, Jana Davi, Peter Mamakos, Larry Chance.

Colonel Garrett (Kent Taylor) is the fort commander who suspects his wife of having an affair with Captain Thompson (Ben Johnson) while they face the danger of an Indian attack. He therefore sends his junior officer on a dangerous mission to try to persuade a renegade Indian leader to cease his attacks against the settlers and his soldiers. Although the plot is somewhat standard, the film benefits from Johnson's authentic western stature.

FORT COURAGEOUS 20th Century Fox, 1965, B&W, 72 min. **Producer:** Hal Klein; **Director:** Leslie Selander; **Screenplay:** Richard H. Landau; **Music:** Richard LaSalle; **Cinematographer:** Gordon Avil; **Editor:** John F. Schrever; **Cast:** Fred Beir, Don "Red" Barry, Hanna Landy, Harry Lauter, Cheryl MacDonald, Michael Carr, Fred Krone, Joe Partridge, Walter Reed, George Sawaya, Kent Taylor.

A fort is beleaguered by Indian attacks, and a court-martialed sergeant is forced to take over the command.

FORT DEFIANCE United Artists, 1951, Color, 82 min. **Producer:** Fred Melford; **Director:** John Rawlins; **Screenplay:** Louis Lantz; **Music:** Paul Sawtell; **Cinematographer:** Stanley Cortez; **Editor:** Thomas Pratt; **Cast:** Dane Clark, Ben Johnson, Peter Graves, Tracey Roberts, George Cleveland, Ralph Sanford, Iron Eyes Cody, Dennis Moore, Craig Woods, Dick Elliott.

As a group of people at a fort prepare for an impending Navajo attack, they must first come to grips with their feelings toward one another.

FORT DOBBS Warner Bros., 1958, B&W, 93 min. **Producer:** Martin Rackin; **Director:** Gordon Douglas; **Screenplay:** George W. George and Burt Kennedy; **Music:** Max Steiner; **Cinematographer:** William H. Clothier; **Editor:** Clarence Kolster; **Cast:** Clint Walker, Virginia Mayo, Brian Keith, Richard Eyer, Russ Conway, Michael Dante.

A widow and her young son are escorted through Indian country by a man who the woman believes killed her husband. Clint Walker makes a believable hero as he fights all obstacles to make life decent for himself and for the woman. The original title of the film was *Fifteen Bullets from Fort Dobbs*, a reference to the repeating rifles that someone is selling to the Indians. This was Clint Walker's first film, but he was already well known from his popular television series *Cheyenne* (1955).

FORT DODGE STAMPEDE Republic, 1951, B&W, 60 min. **Producer:** Harry Keller (associate); **Director:** Keller; **Screenplay:** Richard Wormer; **Music:** Stanley Wilson; **Cinematographer:** John MacBurnie; **Editor:** Irving M. Schoenberg; **Cast:** Allan "Rocky" Lane, Mary Ellen Kay, Roy Barcroft, Chubby Johnson, Trevor Bardette, Bruce Edwards, Jack Ingram, Kermit Maynard.

FOR THE LOVE OF MIKE 20th Century Fox, 1960, Color, 87 min. **Producers:** Robert B. Radnitz and George Sherman; **Director:** Sherman; **Screenplay:** D. D. Beauchamp; **Music:** Raul Lavista; **Cinematographer:** Alex Phillips; **Editor:** Fredrick Y. Smith; **Cast:** Richard Basehart, Stuart Erwin, Arthur Shields, Danny Zaidivar, Armondo Silvestrie, Elsa Cardenas, Rex Allen, Michael Steckler, Danny Bravo.

A young Indian boy nurses an injured colt back to health then trains the horse for an important race, hoping to win enough money to build a shrine for his village. Filmed in CinemaScope, this intelligently produced film features B western star Rex Allen as himself and provides good clean family fun.

FOR THE SERVICE Universal, 1936, B&W, 65 min. **Producer:** Buck Jones; **Director:** Jones; **Screenplay:** Isadore Bernstein; **Cast:** Buck Jones, Beth Marion, Fred Kohler, Clifford Jones, Edward Keene, Frank McGlynn, Ben Corbett, Chief Thundercloud.

While in Indian territory, a government agent tries to outwit an outlaw gang. This action-packed oater was also produced and directed by its star, Buck Jones. (See also *STONE OF SILVER CREEK*.)

FOR THOSE WHO DARE See *LUST FOR GOLD*.

FORT MASSACRE United Artists, 1958, Color, 89 min. **Producer:** Walter Mirisch; **Director:** Joseph M. Newman; **Screenplay:** Martin Goldsmith; **Music:** Marlin Skiles; **Cinematographer:** Carl E. Guthrie; **Editor:** Richard V. Heermance; **Cast:** Joel McCrea, Forrest Tucker, Susan Cabot, John Russell, George N. Neise, Anthony Caruso, Denver Pyle.

Joel McCrea is the leader of a cavalry troop that finds itself under constant attack by the Indians. A deft combination of action and characterization adds up to a well-done western.

FORT OSAGE Monogram, 1952, Color, 72 min. **Producer:** Walter Mirisch; **Director:** Leslie Selander; **Screenplay:** Daniel Ullman; **Music:** Marlin Skiles; **Cinematographer:** Harry Neumann; **Editor:** Richard V. Heermance; **Cast:** Rod Cameron, Jane Nigh, Morris Ankrum, Douglas Kennedy.

A scout is hired to lead a wagon train into the West, but he soon finds out that the people who hired him are responsible for an Indian uprising.

FORT TI Columbia, 1953, Color, 73 min. **Producer:** Sam Katzman; **Director:** William Castle; **Screenplay:** Robert E. Kent; **Music:** Joseph Dubin, George Dunning, Hugo Friedhofer, Paul Mertz, Heinz Roemheld, Hans J. Salter, and Marlin Skiles; **Cinematographer:** Lester White and Lothrop B. Worth; **Editor:** William A. Lyon; **Cast:** George Montgomery, Joan Vohs, Irving Bacon, James Seay, Ben Astor, Phyliss Fowler.

In this film set against the backdrop of the French and Indian War in colonial America, British soldiers attempt to rout the French army from Fort Ticonderoga. There are lots of arrows, spears, and tomahawks to dodge in this routine period piece originally filmed in 3D.

FORTUNE HUNTER, THE See *OUTCAST, THE*.

FORT UTAH Paramount, 1967, Color, 84 min. **Producer:** A. C. Lyles; **Director:** Lesley Selander; **Screenplay:** Steve Fisher and Andrew Craddock; **Music:** Jimmy Haskell; **Cinematographer:** Lothrop B. Worth; **Editor:** John F. Schreyer; **Cast:** John Ireland, Virginia Mayo, Scott Brady, John Russell, Robert Strauss, Richard Arlen, James Craig, Jim Davis, John "Red" Barry.

An Indian agent and a cowboy are forced to defend a wagon train from an Indian attack. This standard formula piece from A. C. Lyles again features former big-name stars at the twilight of their careers.

FORT VENGEANCE Allied Artists, 1953, Color, 75 min. **Producer:** Walter Wanger; **Director:** Leslie Selander; **Screenplay:** Daniel B. Ullman; **Music:** Paul Dunlap; **Cinematographer:** Harry Nuemann; **Editor:** Walter Hannemann; **Cast:** James Craig, Rita Moreno, Keith Larson, Reginald Denny, Morris Ankrum.

On the run from the law, a man and his pal go to Canada, where they join the Mounties. They become involved with fur thieves. Indians, and romance in this colorful oater from Allied Artists.

FORT WORTH Warner Bros., 1951, Color, 80 min. **Producer:** Anthony Veiller; **Director:** Edwin L. Marin; **Screenplay:** John Twist; **Music:** David Buttolph; **Cinematographer:** Sidney Hickox; **Editor:** Clarence Kolster; **Cast:** Randolph Scott, David Brian, Phyllis Thaxter, Helena Carter, Dickie Jones, Ray Teal, Michael Tolan.

Randolph Scott plays an ex-gunfighter who now runs a small-town newspaper. However, he soon learns that the pen is not mightier than the sword when he is forced to confront a group of outlaws with his six-shooter again. The script pro-

vides a balance of action and romance suited to adult western fans, with well-rounded characters and an intriguing plot. Scott gives his usually solid performance, and Phyllis Thaxter makes a charming western heroine, thanks mainly to John Twist's deft screenplay, which allows her to be a more able prairie femme than most of her contemporaries.

FORTY GRAVES FOR FORTY GUNS See *MACHISMO*.

FORTY GUNS 20th Century Fox, 1957, B&W, 79 min. **Producer:** Samuel Fuller; **Director:** Fuller; **Screenplay:** Fuller; **Music:** Harry Suckman; **Cinematographer:** Joseph F. Biroc; **Editor:** Gene Fowler; **Cast:** Barbara Stanwyck, Barry Sullivan, Dean Jagger, John Ericson, Gene Barry, Robert Dix, Jidge Carroll.

Barbara Stanwyck is Jessica Drummond, a rough and tough woman who appoints herself baroness of Tombstone, Arizona. The trouble starts when she encounters opposition from an ex-gunfighter (Barry Sullivan) now working for the U.S. attorney general and his brothers. This wildly dramatic Sam Fuller opus, filmed in CinemaScope, is a must for his fans and is mentioned briefly in "A Personal Journey Through American Movies" by Martin Scorsese. The songs "High Ridin' Woman" and "God Has His Arms Around Me," composed and written by Harold Adamson, Harry Suckman, and Victor Young, are sung by guitar-playing Jidge Carroll.

Samuel Fuller's two primal themes, sex and death, are in this wildly stylized story of a lady rancher's affair with a gunman. William Everson calls *Forty Guns* Fuller's most violent and extreme film, "a western that takes place not in the familiar landscape, but in a strange, grotesquely distorted Ur-world located in the lower depths of the director's mind."

Top-flight performances by Stanwyck, Sullivan, and John Ericson as Stanwyck's brawling brother and a would-be killer, combined with Fuller's triple capacity as producer-scriptwriter-director, makes for a film that provides a solid piece of entertainment and is a worthy and unique addition to the western genre.

40 GUNS TO APACHE PASS Columbia, 1966, Color, 95 min. **Producer:** Grant Wytock; **Director:** William Witney; **Screenplay:** Willard Willingham and Mary Willingham; **Music:** Richard LaSalle; **Cinematographer:** Jacques Marquette; **Editor:** Grant Whytock; **Cast:** Audie Murphy, Michael Burns, Kenneth Tobe, Laraine Stevens, Robert Brubaker, Kay Stewart.

With the Apache on the warpath, the U.S. Army must defend itself. After leading a group of settlers to safety, cavalry captain Bruce Coburn (Audie Murphy) hunts for the traitor who sold stolen rifles to the Indians.

FORTY NINERS Allied Artists, 1954, B&W, 71 min. **Producer:** Vincent Fennelly; **Director:** Thomas Carr;

Screenplay: Dan Ullman; **Music:** Raoul Kraushaar; **Cinematographer:** Ernest Miller; **Editor:** Sam Fields; **Cast:** William "Wild Bill" Elliot, Virginia Grey, Harry Morgan, John Doucette, Lane Bradford, I. Stanford Jolley, Harry Lauter, Earle Hodgins, Dean Cromer, Ralph Sanford.

In order to find out the identities of three men involved in a killing, a marshal takes on the guise of a murderer.

FORT YUMA United Artists, 1955, Color, 75 min. **Producer:** Howard Koch; **Director:** Leslie Selander; **Screenplay:** Danny Arnold; **Music:** Paul Dunlap; **Cinematographer:** Gordon Avil; **Editor:** John F. Schreyer; **Cast:** Peter Graves, Joan Vohs, Joan Taylor, Abel Fernandez, Stanley Clements, John Pickard, Addison Richards.

A homesteader kills an Apache chief and the Indians go on the warpath in this fast-paced melodrama.

FOUR FACES WEST United Artists, 1948, B&W, 89 min. **Producer:** Harry Sherman; **Director:** Alfred E. Green; **Screenplay:** C. Graham Baker and Teddi Sherman; **Music:** Paul Sawtell; **Cinematographer:** Russell Harlan; **Editor:** Edward Mann; **Cast:** Joel McCrea, Frances Dee, Charles Bickford, Joseph Calleia, William Conrad, Martin Garralaga.

Ross McEwen (Joel McCrea) steals $2,000 from a New Mexico bank in order to save his father's ranch. With honest lawman Pat Garrett (Charles Bickford) in hot pursuit, McEwen escapes by boarding a train. He is aided by a pretty railroad nurse (Frances Dee) who wants him to return and face justice and by a decent saloon keeper and gambler played by Joseph Calleia. What becomes increasingly clear is that McEwen is a very decent man, and the more Garrett chases him, the more the lawman comes to respect the man he is chasing. However, Garrett is not alone on the chase. The banker puts out an award of $3,000 (more money than was actually stolen), and others soon join the hunt—despite the fact that McEwen has left the bank an IOU.

When McCrea, Dee, and Calleia leave the train for a stagecoach, the gambler takes the other two to visit Inscription Rock, on which "adventurers and scoundrels, brave men who leave their imprint" have carved their names and the words *paso por aqui* ("He passed this way.") The words are cut in stone and are the only traces of the brave men who came west to the new land; there are more than 500 inscriptions dating back to 1605.

As he continues on his own, McCrea comes upon a ranch where everyone is suffering from diphtheria. Instead of continuing his flight, he stops to care for the ailing family. He manages to save their lives, but in doing so he uses up all his bullets to make a smudge of sulfur. In a state of exhaustion, he collapses just as the marshal, the nurse, and the gambler arrive. Garrett agrees to use his influence on the judge and jury if McEwen will turn himself in. It is the gambler who bestows the final judgment on McEwen: he is a "valiant gentleman!"

For this remarkable film where not one person is killed nor one gunshot fired, Graham Baker wrote a screenplay based on a story by Nebraska-born writer Eugene Manlove Rhodes. The film was shot on location in New Mexico, where Pat Garrett chased Billy the Kid and where the author lived. Rhodes had a keen sense of the West and an integral and steadfast fondness for the brave, selfless, and honest individuals who settled it. When he died he was buried in the San Andres mountains of New Mexico near his ranch. Not surprisingly, the epitaph on his gravestone reads *"Paso por Aqui."*

This surprisingly nonviolent western was greeted well by the critics. *Newsweek* praised its upbeat style as "the same old wine in the same old bottle [with] a pleasantly new flavor," while *Time* called it "pleasing on the eyes and ears." Given today's proclivity for perverse western protagonists with long coats and evil souls, *Four Faces West* brings joy to the heart with McCrea's Ross McEwen, a true western hero for all seasons.

FOUR FAST GUNS Universal, 1959, B&W, 72 min. **Producer:** William J. Hole Jr.; **Director:** Hole Jr.; **Screenplay:** James Edmiston and Dallas Gautois; **Cinematographer:** John M. Nickolaus Jr.; **Editors:** Reginald Brown, Henry F. Salerno, and Harold E. Wooley; **Cast:** James Craig, Martha Vickers, Edgar Buchanan, Brett Halsey, Paul Richards, Blu Wright, Richard Martin, John Swift, Paul Raymond.

This standard shoot-out western pits brother against brother when a gunman is hired to rid a town of its lawless elements.

FOUR FOR TEXAS Warner Bros., 1963, Color, 124 min, VT. **Producers:** Robert Aldrich and Howard W. Koch (executive); **Director:** Aldrich; **Screenplay:** Aldrich and Teddi Sherman; **Music:** Nelson Riddle; **Cinematographer:** Ernest Laszlo; **Editor:** Michael Luciano; **Cast:** Frank Sinatra, Dean Martin, Anita Ekberg, Ursula Andress, Victor Buono, Richard Jaeckel, Mike Mazurki, Jack Elam.

Frank Sinatra and Dean Martin battle each other for control of a town's gambling casinos, with the two stars exchanging a never-ending array of quips. They portray soldiers of fortune who ultimately have to join forces in vanquishing the threat of their mutual enemies, a treacherous banker (Victor Buono) and his irresponsible, hapless hitman (Charles Bronson). The female contingent consists of Anita Ekberg, a former Miss Sweden; and Ursula Andress, who had recently appeared in the James Bond hit *Dr. No.* (1962). The cleavage is plentiful, and the producers of *Four for Texas* reportedly made sure that the measurements were just right, holding Hollywood's first nude screen tests for the film. (The nude scenes were cut by the censors before the film was released.) This weak and disjointed film also includes appearances by Arthur Godfrey and The Three Stooges.

FOUR GUNS TO THE BORDER (aka: SHADOW VALLEY) Universal, 1954, Color, 83 min. **Producer:** William Alland; **Director:** Richard Carlson; **Screenplay:** George Van Marter and Franklin Coen; **Music:** Henry Mancini and Hans J. Salter; **Cinematographer:** Russell Metty; **Editor:** Frank Gross; **Cast:** Rory Calhoun,

Colleen Miller, George Nader, Walter Brennan, Nina Foch, John McIntire, Charles Drake, Jay Silverheels, Nestor Paiva, Robert F. Hoy.

After holding up a bank, an outlaw gang comes to the aid of an ex-gunman and his daughter, who are being attacked by Indians. Based on a story by Louis L'Amour, the film offers a morality lesson of sorts at the finale and provides a better-than-average handling of the outlaw vs. Indian theme.

FOURTH HORSEMAN, THE Universal, 1932, B&W, 63 min. **Producer:** Carl Laemmle; **Director:** Hamilton MacFadden; **Screenplay:** John Cunnington and Nina Wilcox Putnam; **Music:** Sam Perry and Heintz Roemheld; **Cinematographer:** Daniel B. Clark; **Editor:** Philip Cahn; **Cast:** Tom Mix, Margaret Lindsay, Fred Kohler, Donald Kirke, Raymond Hatton, Buddy Roosevelt.

A cowboy tries to help a girl save her ghost-town property using irrigation, which will recultivate the area, but he learns outlaws are using it as a hideaway. Tom Mix finished out the silent era with a brief series of lackluster films for the FBO studio controlled by Joseph Kennedy. He returned to the screen to make a series of nine talking films for Universal. The first two entries, *Destry Rides Again* (with no resemblance to the 1939 James Stewart version) and *Rider of Death Valley*, were among his best pictures. He retired after 1933's *Rustler's Roundup*, his final picture in the Universal series. His other Universal series features include *Texas Badman, My Pal, The King, Hidden Gold, Flaming Guns* (1932); and *Terror Trail* (1933).

FOXFIRE Universal, 1955, Color, 87 min. **Producer:** Aaron Rosenberg; **Director:** Joseph Pevney; **Screenplay:** Kerri Frings; **Music:** Henry Mancini and Frank Skinner; **Cinematographer:** William Daniels; **Editor:** Ted J. Kent; **Cast:** Jane Russell, Jeff Chandler, Dan Duryea, Mara Corday, Barton MacLane, Frieda Inescort.

Jane Russell and Jeff Chandler are well matched as a pretty socialite vacationing in Arizona and the Indian (half-Apache) mining engineer whom she impulsively marries. Before long they encounter cultural barriers endemic to the times, while the engineer's quest for gold almost destroys their marriage. Chandler wrote the lyrics for the title film's title song, which he sings in the movie, while Russell is still a "knockout" in short hair. Moreover, the cultural and racial matters are handled quite well.

FRANK AND JESSE Trimark, 1994, Color, 105 min, VT, DVD. **Producers:** Cassian Elwes, Elliott Kastner, and Mark Amin; **Director:** Robert Boris; **Screenplay:** Boris; **Music:** Mark McKenzie; **Cinematographer:** Walt Lloyd; **Editor:** Christopher Greenbury; **Cast:** Rob Lowe, Bill Paxton, Randy Travis, Dana Wheeler-Nicholson, Maria Pitallo, Luke Askew, Sean Patrick Flanery, Alexis Arquette.

At the end of the Civil War, Frank and Jesse James, along with other former guerrillas who rode with Quantrill, take an oath of allegiance to the Union. But they become increasingly alienated by a Chicago railroad company that is trying to buy up Missouri land. After their father is murdered, the brothers seek revenge and begin their life of crime. They assemble a gang, which includes Cole Younger and Bob and Charlie Ford, and start robbing banks, trains, and coaches—with Pinkerton detectives always on their trail.

This 1994 venture stars Rob Lowe as Jesse and Bill Paxton as Frank, with country singer Randy Travis as gunman Cole Younger. *Frank and Jesse* may not be of the same calibre as many earlier films, but Lowe and Paxton come off surprisingly well as the infamous brothers. Like many earlier endeavors, such as the Tyrone Power/Henry Fonda 1939 film *JESSE JAMES*, the brothers are depicted more as sympathetic figures than the emotionally disturbed killers and borderline psychopaths portrayed in films like *THE GREAT NORTHFIELD, MINNESOTA RAID* (1972).

FRANK JAMES RIDES AGAIN See *GUNFIRE* (1950).

FREIGHTERS OF DESTINY RKO, 1931, B&W, 60 min. **Director:** Fred Allen; **Screenplay:** Adele Buffington; **Cinematographer:** Ted D. McCord; **Editor:** William Clemens; **Cast:** Tom Keene, Barbara Kent, Frank Rice, Mitchell Harris, Fred Burns, Slim Whitaker.

FRENCHIE Universal, 1950, Color, 81 min. **Producer:** Michael Kraike; **Director:** Louis King; **Screenplay:** Oscar Brodney; **Music:** Hans J. Salter; **Cinematographer:** Maury Gertsman; **Editor:** Ted J. Kent; **Cast:** Joel McCrea, Shelley Winters, Paul Kelly, Elsa Lanchester, Marie Windsor, John Russell, John Emery, George Cleveland, Regis Toomey, Paul E. Burns.

When her father is murdered, a woman returns home, opens a saloon, and plans revenge. The film is a mediocre remake of Max Brand's *DESTRY RIDES AGAIN* (1939), with the heroine (Shelley Winters) stopping a bullet meant for the hero.

FRIENDLY PERSUASION Allied Artists, 1956, B&W, 137 min, VT, DVD. **Producer:** William Wyler; **Director:** Wyler; **Screenplay:** Michael Wilson and Jessamyn West; **Music:** Dimitri Tiomkin; **Cinematographer:** Ellsworth Fredericks; **Editors:** Robert Belcher, Edward A. Biery, and Robert Swink; **Cast:** Gary Cooper, Dorothy McGuire, Anthony Perkins, Richard Eyer, Robert Middleton, Phyllis Love, Mark Richman.

A family of pacifist Quakers are faced with problems of conscience when the Confederate Army begins burning down nearby towns. Gary Cooper is Jeff Birdwell, Dorothy McGuire is his wife Eliza, and Anthony Perkins is their son Josh, who finally decides that he has to fight. While it is a simple story, based on a novel by Jessamyn West, the footage is filled with just about everything in the way of comedy and drama, suspense and action, complemented by warm, beguiling vignettes of family life.

Producer/director William Wyler had the project in mind for eight years and brought the property to Allied Artists from Paramount. The production cost was in excess of $3 million, and the picture was the 20th top-grossing film for 1956, taking in $74 million. No screenplay credit appears on the film because writer Michael Wilson pleaded the Fifth Amendment when he was summoned, in 1951, as a witness before the House Un-American Activities Committee. A week before the nominations were released, the Academy Board of Governors passed a new rule that anybody who refused to talk to a congressional committee could not receive an Oscar.

Friendly Persuasion was nominated for six Academy Awards, including Best Picture, Best Director, Best Supporting Actor (Anthony Perkins), and Best Adapted Screenplay—although Michael Wilson was declared to be ". . . ineligible for nomination under Academy bylaws." A rumored drive to honor the blacklisted writer apparently fizzled when Deborah Kerr announced the Best Adapted Story Oscar to the writers of *Around the World in 80 Days* (1956). Dimitri Tiomkin was nominated for Best Song, "Friendly Persuasion (Thee I Love)," and conducted his own musical score.

FRISCO KID, THE Warner Bros., 1979, Color, 122 min, VT. **Producer:** Howard W. Koch Jr.; **Director:** Robert Aldrich; **Music:** Frank De Vol; **Cinematographer:** Robert B. Hauser; **Editors:** Jack Horger, Dennis E. Lew, Irving Rosenblom, Saul Saladow, and Maury Weintrobe; **Cast:** Gene Wilder, Harrison Ford, Ramon Bieri, Val Bisoglio, George Ralph DiCenzo.

In the 1850s, a penniless and bungling Orthodox rabbi named Avram Belinski (Gene Wilder) is packed off by a Polish yeshiva to a leaderless congregation in San Francisco. His money is stolen in Philadelphia, so rather than take a steamship to California he has to set off on foot. After a series of comical vignettes, he teams up with a good-hearted cowboy outlaw (Harrison Ford), who proves a perfect foil for Belinski's many gaffes. As is his practice, director Robert Aldrich inserts a goodly amount of action among the comedy and drama. Wilder and Ford work surprisingly well together in this western spoof.

FRISCO TORNADO Republic, 1950, B&W, 60 min. **Producer:** Gordon Kay; **Director:** R. G. Springsteen; **Screenplay:** M. Coates Webster; **Cinematographer:** John MacBurnie; **Editor:** Robert M. Leeds; **Cast:** Allan Lane, Eddy Waller, Martha Hyer, Alden "Stephen" Chase, Ross Ford, Lane Bradford, Hal Price, Rex Lease, George Chesebro, Edmund Cobb.

FROM BROADWAY TO CHEYENNE See *BROADWAY TO CHEYENNE.*

FROM HELL TO TEXAS (aka: HELL BENT KID) 20th Century Fox, 1958, Color, 100 min. **Producer:** Robert Buckner; **Director:** Henry Hathaway; **Screenplay:**

Buckner and Wendell Maves; **Music:** Daniele Amfitheatrof; **Cinematographer:** Wilfred Cline; **Editor:** Johnny Erin; **Cast:** Don Murray, Diane Varsi, Chill Wills, Dennis Hopper, R. G. Armstrong, J. C. Flippen, Margo, John Larch, Ken Scott, Harry Carey Jr., Rodolfo Acosta, Salvador Acosta.

Director Henry Hathaway skillfully visualizes the inevitable course of events when a ruthless, wealthy rancher (R. G. Armstrong) loses two of his three sons. A peaceful, wandering cowboy named Tod Lohman (Don Murray) has the misfortune to accidentally kill one of the rancher's sons, a situation made even worse when Lohman is also blamed for a second son's death in a horse stampede. He only escapes the rancher's vengeance when he saves the life of the third son, played by Dennis Hopper, who is caught in the middle of a deadly blaze. This gunfight, a maelstrom of fire and flame, is one of the most violent and exciting confrontations in the history of the genre.

This is a big, colorful western, which Bosley Crowther of the *New York Times* called a "good solid pictureful of continually lively action and pegged on a cogent character," and a first-rate performance by Armstrong as the villain. The film was similarly praised by the *New York Herald Tribune*, which stated that "If flames and movie gunplay don't distress you, you'll find this Western big enough, lively enough and sufficiently pictorial to give you extraordinary enjoyment." The aspect of the family of killers—direct descendants of the evil Clantons in John Ford's *MY DARLING CLEMENTINE* (1946)—is a notable change in the genre after World War II.

Chill Wills gives a superb performance as a sympathetic rancher with a big heart and a tomboy daughter (Diane Varsi) whom Don Murray's character wants to romance. Reportedly, Dennis Hopper required 85 retakes for one scene, causing director Henry Hathaway to tell him "you'll never work in this town again!" It was 10 years before Hopper obtained another major role.

FROM NOON TILL THREE United Artists, 1976, Color, 99 min, VT. **Producers:** M. J. Frankovich and William Self; **Director:** Frank Gilroy; **Screenplay:** Gilroy; **Music:** Elmer Bernstein; **Cinematographer:** Lucien Ballard; **Editor:** Maury Winetrob; **Cast:** Charles Bronson, Jill Ireland, Douglas Fowley, Stan Haze, Don "Red" Barry, Bert Williams.

Adapted for the screen by Frank Gilroy (from his novel), this offbeat spoof deals with a two-bit robber who has a brief tryst with a woman. When the woman later thinks he is dead, she fictionalizes their romances and turns him into a legendary hero. Her love story becomes the subject of plays and stories—there is even a song. When the outlaw returns and is very much alive, no one—not even the widow who has come to believe her own fabulous tale—believes he is who he claims to be. The song "Hello and Goodbye" was written by Elmer Bernstein, with lyrics by Alan and Marilyn Bergman.

FRONTIER BADMEN Universal, 1943, B&W, 73 min. **Producer:** Ford Beebe; **Directors:** Beebe and Frank

Skinner; **Screenplay:** Morgan Cox and Gerald Geraghty; **Music:** Hans J. Salter; **Cinematographer:** William A. Sickner; **Editor:** Fred R. Feitshans; **Cast:** Robert Paige, Anne Gwynne, Noah Beery Jr., Diana Barrymore, Leo Carrillo, Lon Chaney Jr., Andy Devine, Thomas Gomez, Tex Ritter, William Farnum, Robert Homans, Kermit Maynard.

In 1869 two cattlemen (Robert Paige and Noah Beery Jr.) drive their herd on the Old Chisholm Trail to Abilene. Once there they find that a syndicate has taken over the cattle trade and the dealings between cattle owners and buyers.

Although made on a medium budget, this western holds a great deal of authenticity and boasts a fine cast, including Universal's monster lead, Lon Chaney Jr.; romantic lead Robert Paige; cowboy star Tex Ritter; silent lead William Farnum; and Diana Barrymore, daughter of the celebrated John Barrymore. Good direction by Ford Beebe, some nice songs from Tex Ritter, and a well-orchestrated cattle stampede make for an exciting and skillfully made feature, which Hoot Gibson called one of the finest westerns he had ever seen.

FRONTIER CRUSADER PRC, 1940, B&W, 62 min. **Producers:** Sigmund Neufeld and Peter Stewart (Sam Newfield); **Screenplay:** Arthur Durlam and William Lively; **Cinematographer:** Jack Greenhalgh; **Editor:** Holbrook N. Todd; **Cast:** Tim McCoy, Dorothy Short, Forrest Taylor, Ted Adams, Joan Merton, Kenne Duncan, George Chesebro.

A mysterious rider arrives on the scene as outlaws plan to rob a mine payroll in order to get control of the mine.

FRONTIER DAYS Spectrum, 1934, B&W, 61 min. **Producer:** Al Alt; **Director:** Robert F. Hill; **Screenplay:** Jimmy Hawkey (Hill); **Cinematographer:** Byrdon Baker; **Editor:** S. Roy Luby; **Cast:** Bill Cody, Ada Ince, Wheeler Oakman, Bill Cody Jr., Franklyn Farnum, Lafe McKee.

The Pinto Kid (Bill Cody) is blamed for a murder when the town's leading citizen kills a man whose ranch he wants. The Kid must now clear his name and prove his innocence.

FRONTIER FEUD Monogram, 1945, B&W, 54 min. **Producer:** Charles Bigalow; **Director:** Lambert Hillyer; **Screenplay:** Jess Bowers (Adele Buffington); **Cinematographer:** Harry Neumann; **Editor:** Dan Milner; **Cast:** Johnny Mack Brown, Raymond Hatton, Dennis Moore, Christine McIntyre, Jack Ingram, Frank La Rue, Edmund Cobb.

FRONTIER FIGHTERS See *WESTERN CYCLONE*.

FRONTIER FURY Columbia, 1943, B&W, 55 min. **Producer:** Jack Fier; **Director:** William A. Berke; **Screenplay:** Betty Burbridge; **Cinematographer:** Benjamin H. Kline; **Editor:** Jerome Thoms; **Cast:** Charles Starrett,

Arthur Hunnicutt, Roma Aldrich, Clancy Cooper, I. Stanford Jolley, Edmund Cobb, Bruce Bennett.

When funds belonging to Indians are stolen, the agent is fired and tries to find the real robbers. (See also *GALLANT DEFENDER*.)

FRONTIER GAL (aka: THE BRIDE WASN'T WILLING) Universal, 1945, B&W, 92 min. **Producers:** Howard Benedict, Michael Feissier, and Ernest Pagano; **Director:** Charles Lamont; **Screenplay:** Fessier and Pagano; **Editor:** Ray Snyder; **Cast:** Yvonne De Carlo, Rod Cameron, Andy Devine, Fuzzy Knight, Sheldon Leonard, Andrew Tombes, Jan Wiley.

After a one-night honeymoon with a fiery French woman, a man returns from prison to find that his wife is now a saloon owner and he is the father of a little girl. The plot has Johnny Hart (Rod Cameron) riding into the tough town of Red Gulch with a posse in hot pursuit. At the local saloon he takes a fancy to saloon singer Lorena Dumont (Yvonne De Carlo) and forces the reluctant lass to marry him at gunpoint. After one glorious night together, she turns her new spouse over to the sheriff. Six years later he returns to Red Gulch, and the remainder of the film has the two lovers constantly sparring in anger, much to the dismay of Johnny's new flame, Sheila Winthrop (Jan Wiley). Eventually their young daughter brings the two tempestuous souls to a reconciliation.

De Carlo and Cameron are well matched in this fun western with lots of good old-fashioned humor. Budgeted at $4.1 million (a hefty sum for Universal), this color project was originally slated for the popular team of Maria Montez and Jon Hall, but the duo had already lost much of their box-office appeal. Relative newcomers De Carlo and Cameron just happened to be on the lot and were given the assignment, which helped greatly in establishing the careers of both future stars. William Everson calls this movie a "piquant sex farce . . . and underrated Western comedy."

FRONTIER GUN 20th Century Fox, 1969, B&W, 70 min. **Producer:** Richard E. Lyons; **Director:** Paul Landres; **Screenplay:** Stephen Kandel; **Music:** Paul Dunlap; **Cinematographer:** Walter Strenge; **Editor:** Robert Fritch; **Cast:** John Agar, Joyce Meadows, Barton MacLane, Robert Strauss, Morris Ankrum, Doodles Weaver.

A young man rides into a small town and soon finds himself appointed an unwilling sheriff. He must now stand up to the town bosses, a gambler and a saloon keeper, neither of whom look upon him in a friendly way.

FRONTIER HORIZON See *NEW FRONTIER*.

FRONTIER INVESTIGATOR Republic, 1949, B&W, 60 min. **Producer:** Gordon Kay; **Director:** Fred C. Brannon; **Screenplay:** Robert Creighton Williams; **Music:** Stanley Wilson; **Cinematographer:** Ernest Miller; **Editor:**

Arthur Roberts; **Cast:** Allan "Rocky" Lane, Roy Barcroft, Gail Davis, Francis Ford, Robert Emmett Keane, Harry Lauter, George Lloyd, Tom London, Clayton Moore, Marshall Reed.

FRONTIER JUSTICE Diversion/Grand National, 1936, B&W, 58 min. **Producer:** Walter Futter; **Director:** Robert F. McGowan; **Screenplay:** Scott Darling; **Cinematographer:** Arthur Reed; **Editor:** Carl Himm; **Cast:** Hoot Gibson, Jane Barnes, Richard Cramer, Roger Williams, John Elliott, Franklyn Farnum, Fred "Snowflake" Toones, George Yeoman, Lafe McKee.

FRONTIER LAW Universal, 1943, B&W, 55 min. **Producer:** Oliver Drake; **Director:** Elmer Clifton; **Screenplay:** Clifton; **Cast:** Russell Hayden, Jennifer Holt, Dennis Moore, Fuzzy Knight, Jack Ingram, Wally Wales, I. Stanford Jolley, Johnny Bond and His Red River Valley Boys.

Two cowboys ride into an area plagued by cattle rustling only to find that one of their pals is working for the villain in charge of the rustling.

FRONTIER MARSHAL Fox, 1934, B&W, 66 min. **Producer:** Sol Lesser; **Director:** Lewis Seiler; **Screenplay:** Stuart Anthony and William Counselman; **Cinematographer:** Robert H. Planck; **Cast:** George O'Brien, Irene Bentley, George E. Stone, Alan Edwards, Ruth Gillette, Berton Churchill, Ward Bond.

In Tombstone, Arizona, a crooked mayor is responsible for a series of stage holdups and gambling and dance hall activities. Shortly after he kills his banking partner, law enforcer Michael Wyatt (Wyatt Earp with a different name) arrives in town. He is attracted to Mary Reid (Irene Bentley), the daughter of the murdered man, and rejects Queenie La Verne (Ruth Gillette). In the ensuing conflict he joins forces with Doc Warren (the Doc Holiday character, played by Alan Edwards) and a crusading newspaper editor named Pickett in a classic battle of good versus evil.

The real Wyatt Earp spent much of his later years hanging around movie lots and became friends with both Tom Mix and William S. Hart. Earp was convinced that the public would be interested in his life story. He put together a long manuscript, but publishers turned a deaf ear. Then in 1928—one year before his death—he met author Stuart N. Lake. Lake listened to Earp's story, took it all down, and in 1931 published Earp's memoirs under the title *Wyatt Earp: Frontier Marshal.*

This 1934 film was the first talking version of Lake's book, which was later used for Allan Dwan's 1939 film with the same title, and then by John Ford in his classic *MY DARLING CLEMENTINE* (1946). Fox used one of its most appealing contract players, George O'Brien, in the starring role. The cast also includes Berton Churchill as the corrupt mayor. Five years later Churchill performed a similar role as the crooked banker in Ford's *STAGECOACH* (1939). Writ-

ing in the *New York Times*, Mordant Hall had this to say: "*Frontier Marshal*, being a frank melodrama, does not bother about plausibility. And one gathers that it was produced with the adapter and the director having their tongue in their cheek."

FRONTIER MARSHAL 20th Century Fox, 1939, B&W, 70 min. **Producer:** Sol Wertzel; **Director:** Allan Dwan; **Screenplay:** Sam Hellman; **Cinematographer:** Charles G. Clarke; **Editor:** Robert Bishoff; **Cast:** Randolph Scott, Nancy Kelly, Cesar Romero, Binnie Barnes, John Carradine, Edward Norris, Eddie Foy Jr., Ward Bond, Lon Chaney Jr., Cris-Pin Martin, Joe Sawyer.

In this 1939 version of Stuart Lake's book, Randolph Scott is Wyatt Earp, who brings law and order to Tombstone with the help of Doc Holliday (Cesar Romero). A very popular film, it was also Allan Dwan's first sound western. Because studio head Darryl F. Zanuck insisted that the lead character be called Wyatt Earp, even though the film could have been about any frontier marshal, the studio had to pay $5,000 to a relative of Earp's living in San Francisco. After the picture was released she sued the studio, claiming that the romance between Earp and Sarah Allen (Nancy Kelly) was fictitious.

Scott is just fine as the laconic lawmaker, while Romero's Doc Holliday is a more glamorous figure. Instead of a dentist with a tubercular cough, Doc is a former obstetrician and is plagued with a bad heart. Many scenes and bits of dialogue were later used in John Ford's *MY DARLING CLEMENTINE* (1946). *Frontier Marshal*, in fact, was used by Ford for his interpretation of the Earp-Holliday saga. Some interesting casting has Eddie Foy Jr. impersonating his famous vaudevillian dad. Ward Bond, who plays Earp's brother in *My Darling Clementine*, appears briefly in this film as a cowardly town marshal. Moreover, actor Charles Stevens, who plays a drunken Indian in *Frontier Marshal*, repeats the role in Ford's remake. This is colorful retelling of the events leading to the gunfight at the O.K. Corral, with an excellent recreation of the shootout itself.

FRONTIER OUTLAWS PRC, 1944, B&W, 58 min, VT. **Producer:** Sigmund Neufeld; **Director:** Sam Newfield; **Screenplay:** Joseph O'Donnell; **Cinematographer:** Robert E. Cline; **Editor:** Holbrook N. Todd; **Cast:** Buster Crabbe, Al St. John, Frances Gladwin, Marin Sais, Charles King, Jack Ingram.

FRONTIER OUTPOST Columbia, 1950, B&W, 55 min. **Producer:** Colbert Clark; **Director:** Ray Nazarro; **Screenplay:** Barry Shipman; **Cinematographer:** Fayte M. Brown; **Editor:** Paul Borofsy; **Cast:** Charles Starrett, Smiley Burnette, Lois Hall, Paul Campbell, Steve Darrell, Slim Duncan, Jock Mahoney, Chuck Roberson.
See *DURANGO KID, THE.*

FRONTIER PHANTOM, THE Western Adventure/Realart, 1952, B&W, 56 min. **Producer:** Ron Ormond;

Director: Ormond; **Screenplay:** June Carr and Maurice Tombragel; **Cinematographer:** Ernest Miller; **Editor:** Hugh Winn; **Cast:** Lash La Rue, Al St. John, Archie Twitchell, Virginia Herrick, Kenne Duncan, Sandy Sanders, Clarke Stevens, Cliff Taylor, Bud Osborne.

Two U.S. marshals attempt to uncover the ringleader of a counterfeiting outfit, with one of them assuming the guise of his outlaw brother, The Frontier Phantom. This exciting and action-packed outing marks the final starring series western for Lash La Rue. The picture also marks the end of Al St. John's (Fuzzy Q. Jones) 40-year movie career.

FRONTIER PONY EXPRESS Republic, 1939, B&W, 58 min, VT. **Producer:** Joseph Kane; **Director:** Kane; **Screenplay:** Norman S. Hall; **Cinematographer:** William Nobles; **Editor:** Gene Milford; **Cast:** Roy Rogers, Lynn Roberts, Raymond Hatton, Edward Keane, Noble Johnson, Monte Blue.

In 1861 a crooked senator schemes to establish his own republic in California by pretending to aid the Confederacy in getting hold of the state via the Pony Express. Future genre star George Montgomery appears in an uncredited role. This entertaining Roy Rogers entry includes such songs as "Rusty Spurs" and "My Old Kentucky Home."

FRONTIER REVENGE Screen Guild/Western Adventure, 1948, B&W, 58 min. **Producer:** Ron Ormond; **Director:** Ray Taylor; **Screenplay:** Taylor; **Music:** Walter Greene; **Cinematographer:** James S. Brown Jr.; **Editor:** Hugh Winn; **Cast:** Lash La Rue, Al St. John, Peggy Stewart, Jim Bannon, Ray Bennett, George Chesebro, Kermit Maynard.

FRONTIER SCOUT Grand National, 1938, B&W, 61 min. **Producers:** Maurice Conn and Franklyn Warner; **Director:** Sam Newfield; **Screenplay:** Francis Guihan; **Music:** Joseph Nussbaum; **Cinematographer:** Jack Greenhalgh; **Editor:** Richard G. Wray; **Cast:** George Houston, Beth Marion, Al St. John, Dave O'Brien, Guy Chase, Jack Ingram, Jack C. Smith.

Wild Bill Hickok aids local ranchers plagued by cattle rustlers and Indian raids. This 1938 film marks the western debut of George Houston in the role of Bill Hickok.

FRONTIERSMAN, THE Paramount, 1939, B&W, 74 min. **Director:** Leslie Selander; **Screenplay:** Norman Houston and Harrison Jacobs; **Cast:** William Boyd, George "Gabby" Hayes, Russell Hayden, Evelyn Venable, William Duncan, Clara Kimball.

FRONTIERSMAN, THE (1968) See BUCKSKIN.

FRONTIERS OF '49 Columbia, 1939, B&W, 54 min. **Producer:** Larry Darmour; **Director:** Joseph Levering; **Screenplay:** Nate Gatzert; **Music:** Lee Zahler; **Cinematographer:** James S. Brown Jr.; **Editor:** Dwight Caldwell; **Cast:** William "Wild Bill" Elliott, Luana Alcaniz, Hal Taliaferro, Charles King, Slim Whitaker, Al Furguson, Jack Walters, Ed Cassidy.

Two government men are sent to California in 1848 to stop the dictatorial activities of a crook who has forced Spanish ranches off their lands. The film is yet another compact and action-packed Bill Elliott venture. (See also LAW COMES TO TEXAS, THE.)

FRONTIER TOWN Grand National, 1938, B&W, 59 min. **Producer:** Edward Finney; **Director:** Ray Taylor; **Screenplay:** Edmond Kelso; **Cinematographer:** Gus Peterson; **Editor:** Frederick Bain; **Cast:** Tex Ritter, Ann Evers, Horace Murphy, Hank Worden.

FRONTIER UPRISING United Artists, 1961, B&W, 68 min. **Producer:** Robert E. Kent; **Director:** Edward L. Cahn; **Screenplay:** Owen Harris; **Music:** Paul Sawtell and Bert Shefter; **Cinematographer:** Maury Gertzman; **Editor:** Kenneth G. Crane; **Cast:** Jim Davis, Nancy Hadley, Ken Mayer, Nestor Paiva, Don O'Kelly, Addison Richards.

A trail guide leading a wagon train to the West in the 1840s discovers that the United States and Mexico are at war and that the Mexicans who control California have made an alliance with the local Indians. Jim Davis delivers a fine performance as the frontier scout heading the wagon train.

FRONTIER VENGEANCE Republic, 1939, B&W, 54 min. **Producer:** George Sherman; **Director:** Nate Watt; **Screenplay:** Barry Shipman; **Cinematographer:** Reggie Lanning; **Editor:** Edward Mann; **Cast:** Don "Red" Barry, Betty Moran, George Offerman Jr., Ivan Miller, Yakima Canutt, Kenneth MacDonald.

FUGITIVE, THE Monogram, 1933, B&W, 56 min. **Producers:** Trem Carr and Paul Malvern; **Director:** Harry L. Fraser; **Screenplay:** Harry Q. Jones (Fraser); **Cinematographer:** Archie Stout; **Cast:** Rex Bell, Cecilia Parker, George "Gabby" Hayes, Bob Kortman, Tom London.

A cowboy is falsely accused of a crime and is forced to run from the law until he can prove his innocence. Cowboy star Rex Bell left Hollywood after making more than 25 westerns to become lieutenant governor of Nevada.

FUGITIVE FROM SONORA Republic, 1943, B&W, 57 min. **Producer:** Herbert J. Yates; **Director:** Howard Bretherton; **Screenplay:** Norman S. Hall; **Music:** Mort Glickman; **Cinematographer:** William Bradford; **Editor:** Richard L. Van Eager; **Cast:** Don "Red" Barry,

Wally Vernon, Lynn Merrick, Harry Cording, Ethan Laidlaw, Pierce Lyden.

FUGITIVE OF THE PLAINS PRC, 1943, B&W, 56 min. **Producer:** Sigmund Neufeld; **Director:** Sam Newfield; **Screenplay:** George Wallace Sayre; **Music:** Leo Erdody; **Cinematographer:** Jack Greenhalgh; **Cast:** Buster Crabbe, Al St. John, Maxine Leslie, Jack Ingram, Kermit Maynard.

FUGITIVE SHERIFF, THE Columbia, 1936, B&W, 58 min. **Producer:** Larry Darmour; **Director:** Spencer Gordon Bennet; **Screenplay:** Nate Gatzert; **Cinematographer:** James H. Brown Jr.; **Editor:** Dwight Caldwell; **Cast:** Ken Maynard, Beth Marion, Walter Miller, Hal Price, John Elliott, Edmond Cobb.

FUGITIVE VALLEY Monogram, 1941, B&W, 60 min. **Producer:** George W. Weeks; **Director:** S. Roy Luby; **Screenplay:** John Vlahos and Robert Finkle; **Music:** Frank Sanucci; **Cinematographer:** Robert E. Cline; **Editor:** Roy Claire; **Cast:** Ray Corrigan, John King, Max Terhune, Julie Duncan, Glenn Strange, Roger Kortman, Tom London.

An outlaw gang led by the "Whip" terrorizes the countryside, and the Range Busters get into the gang in order to stop them. Glenn Strange and Roger Kortman are outstanding in their villainous roles. (See also *RANGE BUSTERS, THE*.)

FURIES, THE Paramount, 1950, B&W, 109 min. **Producer:** Hal Walis; **Director:** Anthony Mann; **Screenplay:** Charles Schnee; **Music:** Franz Waxman; **Cinematographer:** Victor Milner; **Editor:** Archie Marshek; **Cast:** Barbara Stanwyck, Wendell Corey, Walter Huston, Judith Anderson, Gilbert Roland, Thomas Gomez, Beulah Bondi, Albert Dekker, John Bromfield.

T. C. Jeffords (Walter Huston) is a self-made cattle baron who controls a vast stretch of New Mexico called the Furies, riding herd with his strong-willed daughter Vance (Barbara Stanwyck). When Jeffords decides to wed Washington society matron Flo Burnett (Judith Anderson), Vance's love/hate relationship with her father erupts and she hurls a pair of scissors at Flo, disfiguring her face. As punishment Jeffords banishes Vance from his spread. When her father spitefully hangs Juan Herrara (Gilbert Roland), a Mexican friend and former lover of Vance's whose family has dwelled for ages on the ranch, Vance plots revenge and tries to overthrow her father with the help of a gambler named Rip Darrow (Wendell Corey). Her all-consuming love for her father turns to unabashed hatred. "You're in love with hate," Rip tells her.

This big-scale western, well put together by Hal Wallis, was based on a novel by Niven Busch, whose penchant for interfamilial relationships in western settings can also be seen in his *DUEL IN THE SUN* (1947) and the screenplay for *PURSUED* (1947). Critical reviews were mixed. The *New York*

Mirror termed it "a taut and stirring drama . . . [a] superior film." *Newsweek*, however, judged *The Furies* "a pretentious exercise in Freudian dramatics." This was the final film for actor Walter Huston, who died of a heart attack on April 7, 1950. When the picture premiered in Tucson later that year, Barbara Stanwyck offered a moving speech of tribute to the late, great star. The song "T.C. Roundup Time" was written by the team of Ray Evans and Jay Livingston.

FURY AT FURNACE CREEK 20th Century Fox, 1948, B&W, 88 min. **Producer:** Fred Kohlmar; **Director:** H. Bruce Humberstone; **Screenplay:** Charles G. Booth and Winston Miller; **Music:** David Raskin; **Cinematographer:** Harry Raskin; **Editor:** Robert L. Simpson; **Cast:** Victor Mature, Coleen Gray, Glenn Langan, Reginald Gardiner, Albert Dekker, Fred Clark, Ray Teal, Jay Silverheels.

A young man tries to prove that his father was not the cause of a massacre and sets out to clear his name by uncovering proof that three saddle bums were the real culprits.

FURY AT GUNSIGHT PASS Columbia, 1956, B&W, 68 min. **Producer:** Wallace McDonald; **Director:** Fred F. Sears; **Screenplay:** David Lang; **Music:** Mischa Bakaleinikoff; **Cinematographer:** Fred Jackman Jr.; **Editor:** Saul A. Goodkind; **Cast:** David Brian, Neville Brand, Richard Long, Lisa Davis, Kathleen Warren, Percy Helton, Wally Vernon, George Kemas.

A wedding halts their attempt to rob a bank, so an outlaw gang decides to take over the town. This low-budget oater helmed by Fred Sears has some interesting subplots and is bolstered by a talented group of character actors, including David Brian and Neville Brand.

FURY AT ROCK RIVER See *QUIET GUN, THE*.

FURY AT SHOWDOWN United Artists, 1957, B&W, 75 min. **Producer:** John Beck; **Director:** Gerd Oswald; **Screenplay:** Lucas Todd; **Music:** Harry Suckman; **Cinematographer:** Joseph Lashelle; **Editor:** Robert Golden; **Cast:** John Derek, John Smith, Carolyn Craig, Nick Adams, Gage Clark.

A peace-loving man is branded a coward and forced into a shoot-out to rescue his girl.

FURY OF VENGEANCE See *DEVIL'S BEDROOM*.

FUZZY SETTLES DOWN PRC, 1944, B&W, 60 min. **Producer:** Sigmund Neufeld; **Director:** Sam Newfield; **Screenplay:** Louise Rousseau; **Cinematographer:** Jack Greenhalgh; **Editor:** Holbrook N. Todd; **Cast:** Buster Crabbe, Al St. John, Patty McCarthy, Charles King, John Merton, Frank McCarrol.

See *OUTLAWS OF THE PLAINS*.

GALLANT DEFENDER Columbia, 1935, B&W, 60 min. **Producer:** Harry L. Decker; **Director:** David Selman; **Screenplay:** Ford Beebe; **Cinematographer:** Benjamin H. Kline; **Editor:** Al Clark; **Cast:** Charles Starrett, John Perry, Harry Woods, Edward LaSaint, Jack Clifford, Bob Chesebro, Bob Nolan, Roy Rogers, Tim Spencer and the Sons of the Pioneers.

Charles Starrett comes to the aid of homesteaders being harassed by cattlemen who don't want them to homestead their range. Roy Rogers appears in an uncredited role as a member of the Sons of the Pioneers. This film is the first of more than 100 oaters Starrett made for Columbia between 1935 and 1952. His earlier works are generally considered better than his Durango Kid entries, for which he is best known. Among these better early offerings are THE COWBOY STAR (1936), *Outlaws of the Prairie* (1938), *Texas Stagecoach* (1940) and *Bad Men of the Hills* (1942).

Before the Durango Kid became Starrett's film identity in 1945—he made THE DURANGO KID in 1940, but it did not become a series until 1945 with RETURN OF THE DURANGO KID—his pre-series features for Columbia include: CODE OF THE RANGE, *The Cowboy Star*, STAMPEDE, *Mysterious Avenger, Secret Patrol*, (1936); OUTLAWS OF THE PRAIRIE, WESTBOUND MAIL, *Trapped*, TWO FISTED SHERIFF, ONE MAN JUSTICE, *Two-Gun Law, Old Wyoming Trail* (1937); WEST OF CHEYENNE, SOUTH OF ARIZONA, CATTLE RAIDERS, *Laws of the Plains, Call of the Rockies, Start Cheering*, COLORADO TRAIL, RIO GRANDE, *West of Santa Fe* (1938); THE THUNDERING WEST, RIDERS OF BLACK RIVER, *Outpost of the Mounties*, WESTERN CARAVANS, TEXAS STAMPEDE, SPOILERS OF THE RANGE, NORTH OF THE YUKON, *The Man from Sundown* (1939); *Blazing Six Shooters*, TEXAS STAGECOACH, WEST OF ABILENE, TWO FISTED RANGERS, THUNDERING FRONTIER, THE STRANGER FROM TEXAS, The Durango Kid, BULLETS FOR RUSTLERS (1940); *The Pinto Kid*, PRAIRIE STRANGER, THUNDER OVER THE PRAIRIE, *The Royal Mounted*

Patrol, RIDERS OF THE BADLANDS, OUTLAWS OF THE PANHANDLE, THE MEDICO OF PAINTED SPRINGS (1941); WEST OF TOMBSTONE, LAWLESS PLAINSMAN, *Riding Through Nevada, Riders of the Northland, Down Rio Grande Way, Bad Man of the Hills* (1942); *Robin Hood of the Range*, COWBOY IN THE CLOUDS, PARDON MY GUN, LAW OF THE NORTHWEST, *Hail to the Rangers*, FRONTIER FURY, *The Fighting Buckaroo* (1943); RIDING WEST (1944); ROUGH RIDIN' JUSTICE (1945).

GALLANT FOOL, THE Monogram, 1933, B&W, 60 min. **Producer:** Trem Carr; **Director:** Robert Bradbury; **Screenplay:** Bradbury and Harry O. Jones (Harry L. Fraser); **Cinematographer:** Faxon M. Dean; **Editor:** Carl Pierson; **Cast:** Bob Steele, Arletta Duncan, George "Gabby" Hayes, Theodore Lorch, John Elliott, Perry Murdoch.

GALLANT LEGION, THE Republic, 1948, B&W, 88 min. **Producer:** Joseph Kane (associate); **Director:** Kane; **Screenplay:** Gerald Drayson Adams; **Cinematographer:** Jack Marta; **Editor:** Richard L. Van Enger; **Cast:** William "Wild Bill" Elliott, Adrian Booth (Lorna Gray), Joseph Shildkraut, Bruce Cabot, Andy Devine, Jack Holt, Grant Withers, Adele Mara, James Brown.

A crooked politician tries to split Texas in half by disbanding the Texas Rangers, but a rancher moves to stop him with the help of a woman reporter. This A-level western from Republic is among its very best and most underappreciated films. Bill Elliott heads a fine cast in this realistic and respectful portrait of the Texas Rangers.

GALLOPING DYNAMITE Ambassador, 1937, B&W, 58 min. **Producer:** Maurice Conn; **Director:** Harry Fraser; **Screenplay:** Sherman Lowe and Charles Condon;

Music: Connie Lee; **Cinematographer:** Jack Greenlight; **Editor:** Robert Jahns; **Cast:** Kermit Maynard, Arien Allen, John Merton, John Ward, Stanley Blystone.

GALLOPING ROMEO Monogram, 1933, B&W, 60 min. **Producers:** Trem Carr and Paul Malvern; **Director:** Robert N. Bradbury; **Screenplay:** Harry O. Jones (Harry L. Fraser); **Cinematographer:** Archie Stout; **Cast:** Bob Steele, Doris Hill, George "Gabby" Hayes, Edward Brady, Frank Ball, Lafe McKee.

GALLOPING THUNDER Columbia, 1946, B&W, 54 min. **Producer:** Colbert Clark; **Director:** Ray Nazzaro; **Screenplay:** Ed Earl Rapp; **Cast:** Charles Starrett, Smiley Burnette, Merle Travis and His Bronco Busters, Richard Bailey, Edmund Cobb.

See *DURANGO KID, THE.*

GAL WHO TOOK THE WEST, THE Universal, 1949, Color, 84 min. **Producer:** Robert Arthur; **Director:** Frederick De Cordova; **Screenplay:** William Bowers and Oscar Brodney; **Music:** Hans J. Salter and Frank Skinner; **Cinematographer:** William H. Daniels; **Editor:** Milton Carruth; **Cast:** Yvonne De Carlo, Charles Coburn, Scott Brady, John Russell, Myrna Dell, James Millican, Clem Bevans.

An opera singer comes to Arizona in the 1890s and two feuding brothers vie for her affections.

GAMBLER, THE See *KENNY ROGERS AS THE GAMBLER.*

GAMBLER FROM NATCHEZ 20th Century Fox, 1954, Color, 88 min. **Producer:** Leonard Goldstein; **Director:** Henry Levin; **Screenplay:** Irving Wallace and Gerald Grayson Adams; **Music:** Lionel Newman; **Cinematographer:** Lloyd Newman; **Editor:** William Murphy; **Cast:** Dale Robertson, Debra Paget, Thomas Gomez, Lisa Daniels, Kevin McCarthy, Douglas Dick, Woody Stroud.

When a trio of men gun down his father after falsely accusing him of cheating at cards, a young man (Dale Robertson) sets out to avenge the murder. Set in New Orleans in the

Dale Robertson (front row, second from left) stars in Gambler from Natchez. (20TH CENTURY FOX/AUTHOR'S COLLECTION)

1840s, this entertaining frontier drama is filled with action, romance, humor, handsome men, beautiful women, and some clear-cut boundaries between good and evil.

GAMBLER WORE A GUN, THE   United Artists, 1961, B&W, 64 min. **Producer:** Robert E. Kent; **Director:** Edward L. Cahn; **Screenplay:** Owen Harris; **Cinematographer:** Floyd Crosby; **Editor:** Kenneth G. Crane; **Cast:** Jim Davis, Mark Allen, Merry Anders, Addison Richards, Boyd "Red" Morgan.

An honest gambler buys a ranch but is prevented from taking it over because the owner died before signing the proper papers. When he tries to help the man's children, the gambler discovers that a gang of crooks is hiding stolen goods at the ranch.

GAMBLING MAN   See OUTLAW'S SON.

GAMBLING TERROR, THE   Republic, 1937, B&W, 53 min, VT. **Producer:** A. W. Hackel; **Director:** Sam Newfield; **Screenplay:** Fred Myton and George H. Plympton; **Cinematographer:** Bert Longnecker; **Editor:** Roy Claire; **Cast:** Johnny Mack Brown, Iris Meredith, Charles King, Dick Curtis, Ted Adams, Horace Murphy.

Jeff Hayes (Johnny Mack Brown) pretends to be a gambler so he can stop a crook who is running a cattle protection racket. This interesting oater is one of 16 features Brown made with producer A. W. Hackel between 1935 and 1937 for Supreme and Republic. The others include BRANDED A COWARD, BETWEEN MEN, COURAGEOUS AVENGER (1935); *Valley of the Lawless, Desert Phantom, Rogue of the Range, EVERYMAN'S LAW, THE CROOKED TRAIL, Undercover Man* (1936); *Trail of Vengeance, Lawless Land, Bar-Z Bad Men, Guns in the Dark, A LAWMAN IS BORN, BOOTHILL BRIGADE* (1937).

GANGBUSTERS   See ARIZONA GANGBUSTERS.

GANGS OF SONORA   Republic, 1941, B&W, 56 min. **Producer:** Louis Gray (associate); **Director:** John English; **Screenplay:** Albert DeMond, William Colt Macdonald, and Doris Schroeder; **Music:** Cy Feuer; **Cinematographer:** Robert Livingston; **Cast:** Bob Steele, Rufe Davis, June Johnson, Bud Buster, Bud McTaggart, Jack Kirk, Hal Price.

GANGSTERS OF THE FRONTIER (aka: RAIDERS OF THE FRONTIER, UK)   PRC, 1944, B&W, 56 min, VT. **Producer:** Arthur Alexander; **Director:** Elmer Clifton; **Screenplay:** Clifton; **Music:** Lee Zahler; **Cinematographer:** Robert E. Cline; **Editor:** Charles Henkle Jr.; **Cast:** Dave O'Brien, Tex Ritter, Guy Wilkerson, Betty Miles, I. Stanford Jolley, Marshal Reed, Patti McCarty.
See ENEMY OF THE LAW.

GARDEN OF EVIL   20th Century Fox, 1954, Color, 100 min. **Producer:** Charles Brackett; **Director:** Henry Hathaway; **Screenplay:** Frank Fenton; **Music:** Bernard Herrmann; **Cinematographer:** Milton R. Krasner and Jorge Stahl Jr.; **Editor:** James B. Clark; **Cast:** Gary Cooper, Susan Hayward, Richard Widmark, Hugh Marlow, Cameron Mitchell, Rita Moreno, Victor Manuel Mendoza.

A former Texas sheriff (Gary Cooper), a philosophical cardsharp (Richard Widmark), and a spineless killer (Cameron Mitchell) are three American soldiers of fortune en route to the gold fields of California when they are stranded in a Mexican fishing village. They are hired by a woman (Susan Hayward) to rescue her husband from the cave-in of a gold mine located in an area that the Indians call the Garden of Evil. To get there they have to travel through ominous terrain full of bandits and hostile Indians. Their return journey is just as arduous, as passions and tension begin to erupt.

This was Gary Cooper's 81st film and his first in CinemaScope. It was also a reunion for Cooper and Susan Hayward, who had only begun her career in films when she first appeared with Cooper in *Beau Geste* (1939). Director Henry Hathaway as usual provides lots of adventure, interesting characters, and good location film from Uruarpan Micholan, Mexico. In a particularly pleasant scene set in a village café, Rita Moreno sings two songs, "La Negra Noche" by Emilio D. Uranga and "Aqui" by Ken Darby and Lionel Neumann. The combination of big-name stars, vivid technicolor, and wide-screen CinemaScope (still in its infancy) worked well for audiences. But the critics, always more concerned with scripts than ancillary aspects of filmmaking, remained only lukewarm at best.

GATLING GUN (1954)   See SIEGE AT RED RIVER.

GATLING GUN, THE (aka: KING GUN)   Universal, 1973, Color, 93 min. **Producer:** Oscar Nichols; **Director:** Robert Gordon; **Screenplay:** Mark Hannah and Joseph Van Winkle; **Music:** Paul Sawtell and Bert Shefter; **Cinematographer:** Jacques R. Marquette; **Cast:** Guy Stockwell, Woody Strode, Barbara Luna, Robert Fuller, Patrick Wayne, Pat Buttram, John Carradine, Phil Harris, Judy Jordan, Carlos Rivas.

A cavalry officer and his men must protect a Gatling gun and a westward-bound family from marauding Indians in this action-packed oater. Woody Strode turns in a good performance and handles most of the stunt bow-and-arrow work in his scenes.

GAUCHO SERENADE (aka: KEEP ROLLIN)   Republic, 1940, B&W, 66 min. **Producer:** William Berke; **Director:** Frank McDonald; **Screenplay:** Betty Burbridge and Bradford Ropes; **Cinematographer:** Reggie Lanning; **Cast:** Gene Autry, Smiley Burnette, June Storey, Duncan Renaldo, Mary Lee.

A group of businessmen is out to kidnap a former partner's son so he won't squeal on them, but Gene and Frog intervene to stop them. Along the way they get involved with a group of show girls and a pompous singing cowboy. (See also *TUMBLING TUMBLEWEEDS*.)

GAUCHOS OF EL DORADO Republic, 1941, B&W, 56 min. **Director:** Lester Orlebeck; **Screenplay:** Albert DeMond; **Cinematographer:** Reggie Lanning; **Editor:** Charles Craft; **Cast:** Bob Steele, Tom Tyler, Rufe Davis, Lois Collier, Duncan Renaldo, Yakima Canutt, Eddie Dean.

See *THREE MESQUITEERS, THE*.

GAY AMIGO, THE United Artists, 1949, B&W, 60 min. **Producer:** Philip N. Krasne; **Director:** Walter Fox; **Screenplay:** Doris Schroeder; **Music:** Albert Glasser; **Cinematographer:** Ernest Miller; **Editor:** Martin G. Cohn; **Cast:** Duncan Renaldo, Leo Carrillo, Joe Sawyer, Armida, Fred Kohler Jr., Clayton Moore, Helen Servis.

See *CISCO KID, THE*.

GAY BUCKAROO, THE Allied Pictures, 1932, B&W, 66 min. **Producer:** M. H. Hoffman Jr.; **Director:** Phil Rosen; **Screenplay:** Philip Graham White; **Cinematographer:** Henry Neumann; **Editor:** Mildred Johnston; **Cast:** Hoot Gibson, Roy D'Arcy, Merna Kennedy, Edward Peil Sr., Lafe McKee, Charles King, The Hoot Gibson Cowboys.

A rancher and a gambler are rivals for the love of a pretty girl in this early Hoot Gibson talkie.

GAY CABALLERO, THE Fox Films, 1932, B&W, 60 min. **Producer:** Edmund Granger; **Director:** Alfred Werker; **Screenplay:** Barry Conners and Philip Klein; **Cinematographer:** George Schniederman; **Editor:** Alfred DeGaetano; **Cast:** George O'Brien, Victor McLaglen, Conchita Montenegro, Linda Watkins.

Ted Radcliffe, a college football hero, returns to his ranch in the west to find that a crooked Mexican cattle baron has taken control of his family and its money. (See also *DUDE RANGER, THE*.)

GENTLEMAN FROM CALIFORNIA See *CALIFORNIAN, THE*.

GENTLEMAN FROM TEXAS Monogram, 1946, B&W, 55 min. **Producer:** Scott R. Dunlap; **Director:** Lambert Hillyer; **Screenplay:** J. Benton Chaney; **Cinematographer:** Harry Neumann; **Editor:** Fred Maguire; **Cast:** Johnny Mack Brown, Raymond Hatton, Reno Browne, Ted Adams, Tristram Coffin, Pierce Lyden.

GERONIMO Paramount, 1939, B&W, 89 min. **Director:** Paul Sloane; **Screenplay:** Sloane; **Music:** Gerard Carbonara and John Leipold; **Cinematographer:** Henry Sharp; **Editor:** John F. Link Sr.; **Cast:** Preston Foster, Ellen Drew, Andy Devine, William Henry, Ralph Morgan, Gene Lockhart, Monte Blue, Chief Thundercloud.

The great Apache warrior is depicted here as a one-dimensional, bloodthirsty, and evil adversary to army captain Starrett (Preston Foster), who is attempting to stop an Indian war. Composed largely from stock footage including *THE TEXAS RANGERS* (1936), *WELLS FARGO* (1937), and some silents as well, the film actually gives Geronimo (Chief Thundercloud) a very small part. Similarly, second-billed Ellen Drew as Alice Hamilton has just a few scenes herself. Once she becomes involved in a stagecoach wreck borrowed from *Wells Fargo*, she remains in a coma for the rest of the story.

Film historian William Everson has called the film "particularly inept." In essence it was an attempt by Paramount to cash in on *STAGECOACH* (1939). Moreover, no one had the nerve to claim credit for the story, so it was allocated to director Paul Sloane, who probably deserved it for his cunning in maneuvering around the old footage. The plot itself, and even much of the dialogue, was a reworking of the 1933 *Lives of a Bengal Lancer*. The best this film can offer is an excellent performance by Gene Lockhart, whose duplicity as the evil gunrunner results in a particularly gory death.

GERONIMO United Artists, 1962, Color, 101 min, VT. **Producers:** Arthur Gardner and Jules Levy; **Director:** Arnold Laven; **Screenplay:** Pat Fielder; **Music:** Hugo Friedhofer; **Cinematographer:** Alex Phillips; **Editor:** Marsh Hendry; **Cast:** Chuck Connors, Kamala Devi, Amanda Ames, John Anderson, Pat Conway, Adam West.

Chuck Connors in the title role portrays Geronimo in the leaner days of his career. Denied the humanitarian treatment promised him by white supervisors on the reservation, Geronimo and some 50 tribesmen escape to Mexico, where they wage a war against the U.S. cavalry to focus attention on their plight. A U.S. senator (Denver Pyle) is sent west to investigate the situation, arriving just in time to prevent the massacre of Geronimo and his surviving warriors. A fine physical production, the picture was filmed in Mexico with former big-league baseball player Connors surprisingly solid as the famed Apache warrior.

The real Geronimo and his people surrendered in 1886 and eventually settled in Fort Sill, Oklahoma. In 1903 the subdued warrior was taken to the St. Louis World's Fair, where he sold pictures of himself for 25 cents each.

GERONIMO: AN AMERICAN LEGEND Columbia, 1993, Color, 115 min. **Producers:** Walter Hill and Neil Canton; **Director:** Hill; **Screenplay:** John Milius and Larry Gross; **Music:** Rye Cooder; **Cinematographer:** Lloyd Ahern; **Editors:** Donna Aron, Carmel Davies, and

Freeman A. Davies; **Cast:** Jason Patric, Gene Hackman, Robert Duvall, Matt Damon, Wes Studi, Rodney A. Grant.

This epic feature, based on a screen story by John Milius, concentrates on 1885–86, when the U.S. Army devoted 5,000 men, or one-quarter of its troop strength, to stamp out Indian resistance once and for all. While director Walter Hill's respect for Geronimo is certainly apparent, he does not resort to the same sentimentality or overly simplistic moral preaching that is found in SOLDIER BLUE and DANCES WITH WOLVES. Physically impressive and with fine performances, the picture captured an Oscar nomination for Best Sound. Hill's film, it might be added, works much better on the big screen, where the vast expanse of the drama can be fully played out. Wes Studi makes a sturdy and commanding Geronimo, while young actors Jason Patric and Matt Damon do well and hold their own with character greats Gene Hackman and Robert Duvall. *Variety* has called this 1993 film a "sad, stately . . . physically impressive, well-acted picture whose slightly stodgy literary quality holds it back from an even greater impact."

GHOST CITY   Monogram, 1932, B&W, 60 min. **Producer:** Trem Carr; **Director:** Wellyn Turner; **Cinematographer:** Archie Stout; **Editor:** L. Logan Pearson; **Cast:** Bill Cody, Andy Shepherd, Helen Forrest, Walter Miller, Thomas A. Curran.

Bill Temple (Bill Cody) comes to the aid of a girl who is attempting to gain her rightful goldfield inheritance from a crook who is trying to thwart her of her efforts.

GHOST GUNS   Monogram, 1944, B&W, 60 min. **Producer:** Charles Bigelow; **Director:** Lambert Hillyer; **Screenplay:** Frank H. Young; **Cinematographer:** Marcel Le Picard; **Editor:** Pierre Janet; **Cast:** Johnny Mack Brown, Raymond Hatton, Evelyn Finley, Ernie Adams, Bob Cason, Marshall Reed.

GHOST OF HIDDEN VALLEY   PRC, 1946, B&W, 56 min. **Producer:** Sigmund Neufeld; **Director:** Sam Newfield; **Screenplay:** Ellen Coyle; **Cinematographer:** Arthur Reed; **Editor:** Holbrook N. Todd; **Cast:** Buster Crabbe, Al St. John, Jean Carlin, John Meredith, Charles King, Jimmy Aubrey.

GHOST OF ZORRO   Republic, 1959, B&W, 72 min. **Producer:** Herbert J. Yates; **Director:** Fred C. Brannon; **Screenplay:** Royal K. Cole, William Lively, and Sol Shor; **Cinematographer:** John MacBurnie; **Editors:** Cliff Bell Sr. and Harold Minter; **Cast:** Clayton Moore, Pamela Blake, Roy Barcroft, George J. Lewis, Gene Roth, John Crawford, I. Stanford Jolley, Tom Steele.

When crooks try to stop the construction of a telegraph line, a descendant of Don Diego decides to stop them. This is the

feature version of a 12-chapter 1939 serial by the same name. Clayton Moore's role as the masked hero was the casting inspiration for his tenure as the Lone Ranger in the subsequent TV series.

GHOST PATROL   Puritan, 1936, B&W, 56 min, VT. **Producers:** Sigmund Neufeld and Leslie Simmonds; **Director:** Sam Newfield; **Screenplay:** Wyndham Gittens; **Cinematographer:** Jack Greenhalgh; **Editor:** John English; **Cast:** Tim McCoy, Claudia Dell, Walter Miller, James Burtis, Lloyd Ingraham, Wheeler Oakman.

A professor invents a radium tube that makes internal combustion engines stop running, and when he and his invention are captured by a gang of crooks, federal agent Tim Cavalry (Tim McCoy) is sent to the rescue. (See also MAN FROM GUN-TOWN.)

GHOST RIDER, THE   Superior/First Division, 1935, B&W, 56 min. **Producer:** Louis Weiss; **Director:** Jack Levine; **Screenplay:** Jack West (Jack Levine); **Cast:** Rex Lease, Bobby Nelson, Ann Carol, Franklyn Farnum, Lloyd Ingraham, Eddie Parker, Lafe McKee.

A deputy sheriff on the trail of a band of outlaws finds himself being aided by a ghostly masked phantom.

GHOST RIDER, THE   Monogram, 1943, B&W, 58 min. **Producer:** Scott R. Dunlap; **Director:** Wallace Fox; **Screenplay:** Jess Bowers (Adele Buffington); **Cast:** Johnny Mack Brown, Edmund Cobb, Raymond Hatton, Charles King, Bud Osburn.

A marshal joins forces with an outlaw gang in order to find the man who murdered his father. This 1943 venture was the first of the Johnny Mack Brown/Raymond Hatton series for Monogram. (See also UNDER ARIZONA SKIES.)

GHOST TOWN   Commodore, 1936, B&W, 56 min. **Producer:** William Berke; **Directors:** Harry Carey and Harry L. Fraser; **Screenplay:** Weston Edwards (Fraser) and Monro Talbot; **Music:** Lee Zahler; **Cinematographer:** Robert E. Cline; **Editor:** Arthur A. Brooks; **Cast:** Harry Carey, David Sharpe, Ruth Findlay, Lee Shumway.

When claim jumpers try to take a mine, a cowboy comes to the aid of the owner. Western star Harry Carey codirected this routine little oater for William Berke. Other Carey/Berke ventures include *Wild Mustang, Wagon Trail, Rustler's Paradise, Last of the Clintons* (1935); *Aces Wild* (1937).

GHOST TOWN   United Artists, 1955, B&W, 75 min. **Producers:** Howard W. Koch and Aubrey Schenck; **Director:** Allen Miner; **Screenplay:** Jameson Brewer; **Music:** Paul Dunlap; **Cinematographer:** Joseph S. Biroc; **Editor:** Mike

Pozen; **Cast:** Kent Taylor, John Smith, Marian Carr, John Doucette, William "Bill" Phillips.

Passengers on a stagecoach are forced to reveal their true characters when they find themselves about to be attacked by Indians.

GHOST-TOWN GOLD Republic, 1936, B&W, 55 min, VT. **Producer:** Nat Levine; **Director:** Joseph Kane; **Screenplay:** Oliver Drake and Jack Rathmell; **Cinematographer:** Jack Marta and William Nobles; **Editor:** Lester Orlebeck; **Cast:** Robert Livingston, Ray Corrigan, Max Terhune, Kay Hughes, LeRoy Mason, Yakima Canutt, Bob Kortman, Milburn Mirante, I. Stanford Jolley, Bud Osborne, Hank Worden.

GHOST TOWN LAW United Artists, 1942, B&W, 77 min. **Producer:** Scott Dunlap; **Director:** Howard Bretherton; **Screenplay:** Jess Bowers (Adele Buffington); **Cinematographer:** Harry Neumann; **Editor:** Carl Pierson; **Cast:** Buck Jones, Tim McCoy, Raymond Hatton, Virginia Carpenter, Charles King, Tom London.

GHOST TOWN RENEGADES PRC, 1947, B&W, 58 min. **Producer:** Jerry Thomas; **Director:** Ray Taylor; **Screenplay:** Patricia Harper; **Music:** Walter Greene; **Cinematographer:** Ernest Miller; **Editor:** Jack Gluck; **Cast:** Lash LaRue, Al St. John, Jennifer Holt, Jack Ingram, Terry Frost, Steve Clark.

GHOST TOWN RIDERS Universal, 1938, B&W, 54 min. **Producer:** Trem Carr; **Director:** George Waggner; **Screenplay:** Joseph West (Waggner); **Cast:** Bob Baker, Fay Shannon, Hank Worden, Forrest Taylor, Glenn Strange, Jack Kirk, Reed Howes.

Two cowboys with a herd of horses come across a ghost town which a gang is planning to take over by faking a gold boom. This pleasant Bob Baker entry for Universal was helmed by George Waggner and predated his later horror ventures for the same studio. (See also *BLACK BANDIT.*)

GHOST VALLEY RKO, 1932, B&W, 54 min. **Producer:** Harry Joe Brown (associate); **Director:** Fred Allen; **Screenplay:** Adele Buffington; **Cinematographer:** Ted D. McCord; **Editor:** William Clemens; **Cast:** Tom Keene, Myrna Kennedy, Mitchell Harris, Ted Adams.

GHOST VALLEY RAIDERS Republic, 1940, B&W, 57 min. **Producer:** George Sherman; **Director:** Sherman; **Cinematographer:** Ernest Miller; **Editor:** Lester Orlebeck; **Cast:** Don "Red" Barry, Lona Andre, LeRoy Mason, Tom London, Jack Ingram, Ralph Peters.

While attempting to capture a notorious stagecoach robber, a cowboy assumes a phony identity. This fast-paced action oater helped establish Don "Red" Barry as one of the premier and most popular B western cowboy stars. (See also *WYOMING OUTLAW.*)

GIANTS A'FIRE See *ROYAL MOUNTED PATROL.*

GIRL AND THE GAMBLER, THE RKO, 1939, B&W, 63 min. **Producer:** Cliff Reid; **Director:** Lew Landers; **Screenplay:** Joseph Fields and Clarence Upson Young; **Music:** Aaron Gonzalez; **Cinematographer:** Russell Metty; **Editor:** Desmond Marquette; **Cast:** Leo Carrillo, Tim Holt, Steffi Duna, Donald MacBride, Chris-Pin Martin, Edward Raquello, Paul Fix.

GIRL FROM SAN LORENZO, THE United Artists, 1950, B&W, 58 min. **Producer:** Philip Krasne; **Director:** Derwin Abrahams; **Screenplay:** Ford Beebe; **Music:** Albert Glasser; **Cinematographer:** Kenneth Peach; **Editor:** Martin G. Cohn; **Cast:** Duncan Renaldo, Leo Carrillo, Jane Adams, Edmund Cobb, David Sharpe.

GIRL OF THE GOLDEN WEST Paramount, 1915, B&W, five reels. **Producer:** Cecil B. DeMille; **Director:** DeMille **Screenplay:** DeMille; **Cinematographer:** Alvin Wyckoff; **Editor:** DeMille; **Cast:** Mabel Van Buren, Theodore Roberts, House Peters, Anita King, Sydney Keane, Billy Elmer.

This was the first screen version of David Belasco's 1905 play about life and love in a California mining camp in 1849, later the subject of Giacomo Puccini's 1910 opera of the same name, the first such production with an American theme. The film follows the original story fairly closely: An outlaw and sheriff love the same woman, but she wins his freedom in a dramatic poker game (at which she cheats). One of several silent-era adaptations of frontier-themed plays or novels (including *Rose of the Rancho* and *The Virginian* [1914]) directed by DeMille for Paramount during its early years.

GIRL OF THE GOLDEN WEST Associated First National, 1923, B&W, 6,800 feet. **Producer:** Robert North; **Director:** Edwin Carewe; **Screenplay:** Adelaide Heilbron; **Cinematographer:** Sol Polito and Thomas Story; **Editor:** Robert De Lacey; **Cast:** Sylvia Breamer, J. Warren Kerrigan, Russell Simpson, Rosemary Theby, Wilfred Lucas, Nelson McDowell.

The second silent version of the Belasco play and Puccini opera (this time by Associated First National) starred as Ramerrez, the outlaw, J. Warren Kerrigan, fresh from his success as the dashing hero of the blockbuster western epic *The Covered Wagon* (1923).

GIRL OF THE GOLDEN WEST First National, 1930, B&W, 81 min. **Producer:** Robert North; **Director:** John Francis Dillon; **Screenplay:** Waldemar Young; **Cinematographer:** Sol Polito; **Cast:** Ann Harding, James Rennie, Harry Bannister, Ben Hendricks Jr., J. Farrell MacDonald.

Filmed twice earlier as a silent film, this first sound version of David Belasco's 1905 play and Puccini's 1910 opera features Ann Harding, one of the silver screen's first major female stars (on loan from Pathé Pictures) as the female lead, and her then-husband Harry Bannister as Sheriff Jack Rance. A pretty saloon owner (Harding) falls in love with a notorious bandit (James Rennie) and wins his freedom in a poker game with a lawman (Bannister). Harding's performance is good, but the rest of the film is limited due mainly to the early constraints of setting a stage play to the screen. As *Variety* noted in its review, "The dialogue version is practically the stage piece in unchanged transcription even to the arrangement of scenes . . . such an arrangement only emphasizes the limitations of the stage and calls attention to the artificiality of the whole affair." Unlike the later 1938 version, this treatment has no songs.

GIRL OF THE GOLDEN WEST MGM, 1938, Color, 121 min, VT. **Producer:** William Anthony McGuire; **Director:** Robert Z. Leonard; **Screenplay:** Isabel Dawn and Boyce DeGaw; **Music:** Herbert Stoddard (director); Sigmund Romberg and Gus Kahn (songs); **Cinematographer:** Oliver T. Marsh; **Editor:** W. Donn Hayes; **Cast:** Jeanette MacDonald, Nelson Eddy, Walter Pidgeon, Leo Carrillo, Buddy Ebsen, Cliff Edwards, Monte Woolley, Priscilla Lawson.

David Belasco's play becomes a star-studded MGM musical with Jeanette MacDonald as the girl who runs the mining town's lone saloon and Nelson Eddy as the Mexican bad man. The storyline here is Hollywood fluff and dramatically unconvincing, with Eddy far too soft as the hearty hero. Yet Walter Pidgeon makes a sturdy sheriff, and a supporting cast of excellent players, including Leo Carrillo, Buddy Ebsen, Cliff Edwards, and Noah Beery, prove quite credible.

However, the picture is mainly a musical, and although the team of Sigmund Romberg and Gus Kahn produced no big-time hit song here, MacDonald's golden voice is splendid, and Nelson Eddy, whatever his limitations as an actor, most certainly can sing. While their rendering of the interlude song "Who Are We to Say" is charming, they perform only one other duet, "Dance with Me My Love," a ballad with a tango beat. Buddy Ebsen chimes in with a vigorous "The West Ain't Wild Anymore," and "Mariachie" provides a robust production number set in the Governor's Spanish courtyard as part of the annual Rancho Fiesta Celebration.

MacDonald also sings "Ave Maria" (Bach/Gounod) and "Liebestraum," with Gus Kahn providing lyrics to Franz Liszt's classical piece. Though far from MacDonald and Eddy's best offering and suffering from a stilted and dated plot, *Girl of the Golden West* pleased legions of the famous duo's fans and provide some good entertainment.

GIT ALONG LITTLE DOGIES (aka: SERENADE OF THE WEST, UK) Republic, 1937, B&W, 60 min. **Producers:** Joseph Kane and Armand Schaefer; **Director:** Kane; **Screenplay:** Dorrell McGowan and Stuart E. McGowan; **Music:** Flemming Allen, Smiley Burnette, Sidney Mitchell, Sam H. Stept; **Cinematographer:** Guy Peterson; **Editor:** Tony Martinelli; **Cast:** Gene Autry, Smiley Burnette, Judith Allen, Weldon Heyburn, William Farnum.

GLORY GUYS, THE United Artists, 1965, Color, 112 min. **Producers:** Arthur Gardner, Arnold Laven, and Jules Levy; **Director:** Laven; **Screenplay:** Sam Peckinpah; **Music:** Riz Ortlani; **Cinematographer:** James Wong Howe; **Editor:** Ernst R. Rolf; **Cast:** Tom Tryon, Harve Presnell, Senta Berger, Michael Anderson Jr., James Caan, Andrew Duggan, Slim Pickens, Peter Breck.

A cavalry troop with untrained recruits is ordered by its superior officer to battle with rampaging Sioux. The all-too-familiar love triangle has been thrown in for glitter. The picture garnered a Golden Globe nomination for actor James Caan in the category of Most Promising Male Newcomer. Filmed in Durango, Mexico, this routine '60s western was scripted by Sam Peckinpah.

GLORY TRAIL, THE Crescent, 1936, B&W, 65 min. **Producer:** E. B. Derr; **Director:** Lynn Shores; **Screenplay:** John T. Neville; **Cinematographer:** Arthur Martinelli; **Editor:** Donald Barratt; **Cast:** Tom Keene, Joan Barclay, James Busch, Frank Melton, E. H. Calvert, Walter Long.

After the Civil War a cowboy takes part in the settlement of the West and events that result in the Bozeman Massacre. Tom Keene starred in eight films for Crescent Pictures in 1936–37. The others include *Rebellion* (aka *Lady From Frisco*, 1936); *Raw Timber, The Law Commands, Drums of Destiny, Battle of Greed, Old Louisiana, Under Strange Flags* (1937).

GODDESS OF SAGEBRUSH GULCH Biograph, 1912, B&W, 17 min, one reel. **Producer and Director:** D. W. Griffith; **Screenplay:** Griffith and G. W. "Billy" Bitzer; **Cast:** Blanche Sweet, Dorothy Bernard, Charles West.

D. W. Griffith often used the Old West for his one-reelers. This one-reel feature, filmed in California in January 1912, concerns a young girl, who is beloved by all in a mining camp, and her sister, who attracts the one man she loves. Subtitled *A Story of the Golden West*, this appealing entry showed a great improvement in Griffith's filming techniques, particularly in his camera setups and the utilization of lighting for close-ups.

GOD'S COUNTRY Action Pictures, 1946, Color, 64 min. **Producer:** William B. David; **Director:** Robert Emmett Tansey; **Screenplay:** Tansey; **Cinematographer:** Carl Wester; **Cast:** Robert Lowery, Helen Gilbert, William Farnum, Buster Keaton, Stanley Andrews, Al Ferguson.

On the run from the law, a man and his pals head to the north country, where they get involved in helping a young woman and her father save their forest from a crooked lumber boss. This little-known film based on a story by James Oliver Curwood is a real sleeper and provides some good solid entertainment.

GOD'S COUNTRY AND THE MAN (aka: ROSE OF THE RIO GRANDE, TRAIL OF THE LAW) Syndicate Pictures, 1931, B&W, 59 min. **Producer:** John P. McCarthy; **Director:** McCarthy; **Screenplay:** Wellyn Totman; **Cinematographer:** Archie Stout; **Editor:** Charles J. Hunt; **Cast:** Tom Tyler, Betty Mack, Al Bridge, Ted Adams, George "Gabby" Hayes, John Rivero, John Elliott, William Bertram.

A government agent is sent to a tough frontier town to bring back one of the most ruthless criminals in the business. This decent early Tom Tyler talkie based on a story by Al Bridge also features Bridge as the fiddle-playing villain and "Gabby" Hayes (listed as George Hayes) sporting a short beard.

GOD'S COUNTRY AND THE MAN Monogram, 1937, B&W, 56 min. **Producer:** Robert N. Bradbury; **Director:** Bradbury; **Screenplay:** Robert Emmett (Robert Emmett Tansey); **Cinematographer:** Bert Longnecker; **Editor:** Howard Dillinger; **Cast:** Tom Keene, Betty Compson, Charlotte Henry, Charles King, Billy Bletcher, James Sheridan.

A cowboy and his friends set out to track down his father's killer, and on the way they discover a vein of gold. The killer finds out about it and returns to try to take it from them. Despite the stock footage, Tom Keene's first Monogram film (a remake of the 1931 feature) is a good one. (See also *WHERE TRAILS DIVIDE*.)

GOIN' SOUTH Paramount, 1978, Color, 105 min, VT. **Producers:** Harry Gittes and Harold Schneider; **Director:** Jack Nicholson; **Screenplay:** Al Ramrus, Charles Shyer, Alan Mandel, and John Herman Shaner; **Music:** Perry Botkin Jr., Van Dyke Parks, and Ken Lauter (additional music); **Cinematographer:** Nestor Almendros; **Editors:** John Fitzgerald Beck and Richard Chew; **Cast:** Jack Nicholson, Mary Steenburgen, Christopher Lloyd, John Belushi, Veronica Cartwright, Richard Bradford, Jeff Morris, Danny De Vito, Ed Begley Jr.

Set in Texas in the 1866, Henry Moon (Jack Nicholson) is a horse thief on the verge of being hanged. He is saved by a local ordinance providing that any male guilty of a crime other than manslaughter can escape the rope if a woman of property agrees to marry him. (Because the Civil War had just ended there was a serious shortage of able men.) The woman who rescues him (Mary Steenburgen) is not interested in a husband; what she wants is a laborer to work her gold mine. Once they marry she turns out to be a pretty stern taskmaster, and marital problems abound.

The film marks the second directorial assignment for Jack Nicholson, (who helmed *Drive, He Said* in 1972). It is also the movie debut of Mary Steenburgen, who captured a Golden Globe nomination for Best Motion Picture Debut (female); and of John Belushi (though his second film *Animal House* [1978] was released first.) *Goin' South* played to very mixed reviews. Leonard Maltin called it "an amusing Western comedy, not for all tastes." *Variety*, on the other hand is less than enthusiastic, especially with the totality of Nicholson's performance as the bearded dirty horse thief who acts more like the widow's grandfather than a handsome rogue out to compromise her virginity: "Jack Nicholson playing 'Gabby' Hayes is interesting, even amusing at times, but Hayes was never a leading man which *Goin' South* desperately needs."

GOLD Majestic Pictures, 1932, B&W, 58 min. **Producers:** Henry L. Goldstone; **Director:** Otto Brower; **Screenplay:** Scott Darling; **Cinematographer:** Charles Marshall and Arthur Reed; **Editor:** S. Roy Luby; **Cast:** Jack Hoxie, Alice Day, Hooper Atchley, Mathew Betz, Jack Clifford, Lafe McKee.

A cowboy turned miner fights a gang that buys miners' claims and then murders them. When the man he shares a claim with is murdered, the man's daughter blames him, and he sets out to find the real killer. The ending depicts the villain tied to a wagon disguised as an intended victim being gunned down by his own men.

Actor/cowboy Jack Hoxie (born John F. Stone) was raised in Indian Territory and became a cowboy star in numerous silent oaters. He made seven talking features for Majestic Pictures in the early 1930s before leaving the movie business to star in his own western-style circus. In the late 1930s he retired to a ranch in Oklahoma, where he lived out his days in relative obscurity. He died in Kansas in 1965 at the age of 80. In addition to *Gold*, he made six more oaters for the soon-to-be-defunct Majestic Pictures. They include *Phantom Express, Outlaw Justice, Law and Lawless* (1932); *Via Pony Express, Gun Law, Trouble Busters* (1933).

GOLDEN GIRL 20th Century Fox, 1951, Color, 108 min. **Producer:** George Jessel; **Director:** Lloyd Bacon; **Screenplay:** Gladys Lehman; **Music:** Lionel Newman; **Cinematographer:** Charles G. Clarke; **Editor:** Louis R. Loeffler; **Cast:** Mitzi Gaynor, Dale Robertson, Dennis Day, James Barton, Una Merkle, Kermit Maynard.

This musical western set in California during the Civil War finds actress Lotta Crabtree (Mitzi Gaynor) falling in love with a man who turns out to be a Confederate spy (Dale Robertson). The song "Never" (music by Lionel Newman, lyrics by Eliot Daniel) gained an Oscar nomination as Best Song.

GOLDEN STALLION, THE Republic, 1949, Color, 67 min, VT. **Producer:** Edward J. White; **Director:** William

Witney; **Screenplay:** Sloan Nibley; **Music:** Nathan Scott, Stanley Wilson, Eddie Cherkose, Nathan Gluck, Sol Meyers, Ann Parentean, and Sid Robbin (songs), Jule Styne (uncredited), Foy Willing; **Cinematographer:** Jack Marta; **Editor:** Tony Martinelli; **Cast:** Roy Rogers, Dale Evans, Estelita Rodriguez, Pat Brady, Douglas Evans.

GOLDEN TRAIL, THE   Monogram, 1940, B&W, 52 min. **Producer:** Edward Finney; **Director:** Albert Herman; **Screenplay:** Roland Lynch, Roger Merton, Robert Emmett Tansey; **Music:** Jack Frost, Frank Harford, Johnny Lange, Lew Porter, Tex Ritter (songs), and Frank Sanucci; **Cinematographer:** Marcel Le Picard; **Editor:** Robert Golden; **Cast:** Tex Ritter, Slim Andrews, Stanley Price, Chuck Morrison, Warner Richmond.

GOLDEN WEST, THE   Fox, 1932, B&W, 74 min. **Director:** David Howard; **Screenplay:** Gordon Rigby; **Cast:** George O'Brien, Janet Chandler, Marion Burns, Arthur Pierson, Onslow Stevens, Emmett Corrigan, Chief Big Tree, John War Eagle.

A young man (George O'Brien) becomes a member of the Indian tribe that killed his father and grows up hating whites. He subsequently leads an attack on settlers in this excellent screen adaptation of the Zane Grey novel. (See also *DUDE RANGER, THE.*)

GOLD IS WHERE YOU FIND IT   First National, 1938, Color, 90 min. **Producers:** Samuel Bishoff and Hal B. Wallis; **Director:** Michael Curtiz; **Screenplay:** Robert Buckner and Warren Duff; **Music:** Max Steiner; **Cinematographer:** Allen M. Davey and Sol Polito; **Editor:** Clarence Kolster; **Cast:** George Brent, Olivia de Havilland, Claude Raines, Margaret Lindsay, John Litel, Tim Holt, Barton MacLane, Sidney Toler, George "Gabby" Hayes.

Gold is discovered on California farmland, and a terrible feud erupts between farmers and miners. Predictably, Olivia de Havilland, the daughter of the most prominent wheat growers, and George Brent, who is employed by the mining syndicate, fall in love. Off-screen narration at the beginning and end lends a documentary aura to a rather conventional story bolstered by a solid cast and a first-rate production team.

GOLD MINE IN THE SKY   Republic, 1938, B&W, 60 min. **Producer:** Charles E. Ford (associate); **Director:** Joseph Kane; **Screenplay:** Betty Burbridge and Jack Natteford; **Music:** Alberto Columbo; **Cinematographer:** William Nobles; **Editor:** Lester Orlebeck; **Cast:** Gene Autry, Smiley Burnette, Carol Hughes, Craig Reynolds, Cupid Ainsworth.

Gene Autry is made executor for a young spendthrift, whose father had not wanted her to marry without his approval. When Gene refuses to turn the place into a dude ranch, the girl's crooked boyfriend hires Chicago gangsters to knock him

off. George Montgomery (as George Letz) appears in an uncredited role as one of the ranch hands. A good plot, sturdy action and some nice music help make this one of Gene Autry's better ventures. (See also *TUMBLING TUMBLEWEEDS.*)

GOLD OF THE SEVEN SAINTS   Warner Bros., 1961, B&W, 88 min. **Producer:** Leonard Freeman; **Director:** Gordon Douglas; **Screenplay:** Leigh Brackett, Steve Freeze, and Leonard Freeman; **Music:** Howard Jackson; **Cinematographer:** Joseph F. Biroc; **Editor:** Folmar Blangsted; **Cast:** Clint Walker, Roger Moore, Leticia Romain, Robert Middleton, Chill Wills, Gene Evans, Roberto Contreas, Arthur Stewart.

Two trappers (Clint Walker and Roger Moore) find a gold strike but end up being chased across the desert by marauders. Some great location shooting in Utah and the convincing presence of Clint Walker (TV's *Cheyenne*, 1955) constitute the film's main interest. In a particularly galling torture scene, Roger Moore is stripped to the waist and bound inside a skin of wet rawhide, which will shrink in the sun and slowly crush him.

GOLD RAIDERS   United Artists, 1951, B&W, 56 min. **Producers:** Bernard Glasser and Jack Schwartz; **Director:** Edward Bernds; **Screenplay:** William Lively and Elwood Ullman; **Music:** Alexander Starr; **Cinematographer:** Paul Ivano; **Editor:** Fred Allen; **Cast:** George O'Brien, Moe Howard, Larry Fine, Shemp Howard, Lyle Talbot, Sheila Ryan, Clem Bevans, John Merton, Monte Blue, Fuzzy Knight.

An ex-marshal sells insurance to miners in order to protect their gold shipments, while three loonies with a traveling variety store end up chasing the crooks. Needless to say it is the Three Stooges who save the day in this amusing western, which features a vintage performance by Clem Bevans as the old man with a few problems of his own. Director Ed Bernds managed to put this film together in little more than a week, and did so on a tiny budget. Three Stooges fans will love it.

GOLD TOWN, THE   See *BARBARY COAST GENT.*

GOLDTOWN GHOST RIDERS   Columbia, 1953, B&W, 59 min. **Producer:** Arnold Schaefer; **Director:** George Archainbaud; **Screenplay:** Gerald Geraghty; **Music:** Mischa Bakaleinikoff; **Cinematographer:** William Bradford; **Editor:** John Sweeney; **Cast:** Gene Autry, Smiley Burnette, Gale Davis, Kirk Riley, Carlton Young, Denver Pyle, John Doucette.

Circuit Judge Gene Autry must pass judgment on a man who claims he has already done time for the killing he is accused of committing. (See also *TUMBLING TUMBLEWEEDS.*)

GONE WITH THE WEST   See *LITTLE MOON AND JUD MCGRAW.*

GOOD DAY FOR A HANGING Columbia, 1958, Color, 85 min, VT. **Producer:** Charles Schneer; **Director:** Nathan Juran; **Screenplay:** Daniel Ullman and Maurice Zimm; **Music:** Mischa Bakaleinikoff, George Duning, George Greeley, Heinz Roemheld, and Leith Stevens; **Cast:** Fred MacMurray, Maggie Hayes, Robert Vaughn, Joan Blackman, James Drury, Wendell Holmes, Emile Meyer, Bing Russell, Denver Pyle, Gregg Barton.

Fred MacMurray plays an ex-lawman who captures a debonair killer (Robert Vaughn), then to his dismay discovers that the townsfolk do not care because they do not believe he is guilty. This well-done movie is too often neglected by fans of the genre and shows the versatile MacMurray at his best.

GOOD DAY FOR FIGHTING See *CUSTER OF THE WEST.*

GOOD GUYS AND BAD GUYS Warner Bros., 1969, Color, 91 min, VT. **Producers:** Ronald M. Cohen, Robert Goldstein, and Dennis Shryack; **Director:** Burt Kennedy; **Screenplay:** Cohen and Shryack; **Music:** William Lava; **Cinematographer:** Harry Stradling Jr.; **Editors:** Howard Deane and Otho Lovering; **Cast:** Robert Mitchum, George Kennedy, Martin Balsam, David Carradine, Tina Louise, Douglas Fowley, Lois Nettleton, John David Chandler, John Carradine, Marie Windsor, Buddy Hackett, Christopher Mitchum.

Robert Mitchum spoofs his tough guy image as a marshal who insists that bad guy George Kennedy, an over-the-hill outlaw, is still a dangerous villain. For all his trouble Mitchum gets a surprise retirement party. When Kennedy, his long-time foe, is discarded by his outlaw gang, the two join forces to thwart a train robbery led by group of young outlaws headed by David Carradine. Burt Kennedy, who helmed many of the most amusing western spoofs of the 1960s and '70s, got his money's worth by teaming the sardonic Mitchum with the burly Kennedy and an energetic supporting cast. This fanciful and enjoyable western comedy ends in a frivolous and robust chase scene befitting Mack Sennett's Keystone Kops.

GOOD, THE BAD AND THE UGLY, THE United Artists, 1968, Color, 155 min. **Producer:** Alberto Grimaldi; **Director:** Sergio Leone; **Screenplay:** Luciano Vincenzon and Leone; **Music:** Ennio Morricone; **Cinematographer:** Tonio Delli Colli; **Editors:** Nino Baragli and Eugenio Alabiso; **Cast:** Clint Eastwood, Eli Wallach, Lee Van Cleef, Aldo Giuffre, Mario Brega, Luigi Pistilli, Rada Rassimony, Enzo Petito.

At the height of the Civil War, a Mexican bandit named Tuco (Eli Wallach) is nearly captured by two bounty hunters. His life is saved by a mysterious stranger (Clint Eastwood), who kills both bounty hunters. It soon becomes clear why the stranger saved the life of the Mexican. He hopes to form a

Clint Eastwood (left) and Eli Wallach star in The Good, the Bad and the Ugly, *considered to be the best of Sergio Leone's spaghetti trilogy.* (UNITED ARTISTS/AUTHOR'S COLLECTION)

partnership in which he will collect the reward money for the bandit and then rescue him before he can be hanged. The plan works, and the act is repeated again and again, with the reward loot on Tuco's head growing by the day. At the same time a terrifying bounty hunter played superbly by Lee Van Cleef is following up on information that he hopes will lead him to a fortune of buried Confederate gold. He recruits a band of thugs who begin to menace and torture all who have come into contact with the money. In time the three men form an uneasy alliance that is soon compromised by betrayal and counterbetrayal. Along the way they taunt and torture each other and contribute to a total of 20 dead bodies sprawled across the western landscape. When they finally reach the cemetery where the gold is buried, the three stare each other down, and it is clear that only a showdown will decide who gets the riches.

For the third and best of his offbeat trilogy, Leone had little trouble putting together a hefty budget of $1 million—far more than had been spent on *A FISTFUL OF DOLLARS* (1964) and *FOR A FEW DOLLARS MORE* (1967) combined. Eastwood received $250,000 for the film, having become one of the industry's highest paid actors. Predictably, the film is excessively violent, with lots of gratuitous blood and gore. While Eastwood is vintage as the mysterious stranger, it is the villainous Van Cleef (in his second trilogy film) and the hammy yet virtuoso performance by Wallach as the backstabbing Tuco that truly elevates this "spaghetti" venture far above the ordinary.

The Good, the Bad and the Ugly opened to huge audiences in early 1968 and solidified Eastwood's standing as an industry superstar. While far from enthusiastic, critics generally treated the film more generously than its two forerunners. Yet they were far from praiseworthy. *Variety* called the film ". . . a curious amalgam of the visually striking, the dramatically feeble, and the offensively sadistic." *Time* wrote that *The*

Good, the Bad and the Ugly "might serve as the film's own capsule review. The good lies in Sergio Leone's skillful camera work. Bad is the word for the wooden acting . . . and Ugly is his insatiable appetite for beatings." In the *New York Times*, Renata Adler suggested that "the film must be the most expensive, pious and repellent movie in the history of its peculiar genre. . . ."

Yet this should not obviate the fact that among the new breed of "spaghetti westerns" that came to dominate the genre, this film stands up remarkably well. The art decoration and the sets are extremely realistic, and the battle scenes with hundreds of men engaged in combat are of epic proportion. The music is haunting, and some scenes—particularly the one when Eastwood frantically attempts to load an empty pistol before assassins break into his room—are memorable cinematic moments laden with suspense.

This was to be Clint Eastwood's last film with Sergio Leone. He returned to the United States and began making his own films, at first working with other directors and then directing his own films. Whatever one might think of spaghetti westerns, and controversy most certainly prevails, the western film and the direction of the genre had been permanently altered to complement the grim reality of the times. Conversely, it gave new impetus to a fading genre which had been losing its popularity with moviegoers.

GORDON OF GHOST CITY
Universal, 1933, B&W, 12 chapters. **Producer:** Henry MacRae; **Director:** Ray Taylor; **Screenplay:** Basil Dickey, Harry O. Hoyt, Het Mannheim, Ella O'Neill, and George Plympton; **Cinematographer:** John Hickson; **Editors:** Frank Gross and Alvin Todd; **Cast:** Buck Jones, Madge Bellamy, Walter Miller, Craig Reynolds, William Desmond, Tom Ricketts, Francis Ford.

A mysterious masked figure and an outlaw gang try to gain control of a gold strike in a small town, and the town decides to hire a man to bring peace to the area. Based on the novel *Oh, Promise Me* by Peter Tyne, this fast-paced and entertaining serial was Buck Jones's initial serial entry.

While at Universal in the 1930s, Jones made four serials including the above entry. The others include *The Roaring West* (1935), which was all action and no plot; *The Phantom Rider* (1936), which was all plot and little action; and *The Red Rider* (1934), which is generally considered the best of the lot.

GO WEST
MGM, 1925, B&W, 69 min, VT, DVD. **Producer:** Joseph M. Schneck; **Director:** Buster Keaton; **Screenplay:** Keaton; **Cinematographer:** Bert Haines and Elgin Lessley; **Cast:** Buster Keaton, Kathleen Myers, Howard Truesdale, Ray Thompson.

The title card introducing the film's hero says it all. "Some people go through life making friends wherever they go, while others just travel through life." Buster Keaton plays Homer Holiday, a friendless drifter who heads westward and endures a number of misfortunes until he lands a job at the Thompson spread, run by a stern ranch owner (Howard Truesdale). Here he befriends a cow, Brown Eyes, who saves his life. Later he goes along with her on the train when she is included in a shipment for market. When a rival rancher attacks the train, "Friendless" (Keaton) takes control and gets the shipment safely to market.

As a reward, Thompson offers Friendless his choice of reward, and he chooses Brown Eyes. The film concludes with Friendless, Thompson, the man's daughter Gloria, and Brown Eyes driving away in a car. Although perhaps not Keaton's best silent effort, this is a good film which highlights the actor's enormous talent and comic skills. His best laughs come at the end, when the herd reaches Los Angeles and becomes embroiled in a stampede through the city streets, befuddling the inhabitants.

GO WEST
MGM, 1940, B&W, 80 min, VT. **Producer:** Jack Cummings; **Director:** Edward Buzzell; **Screenplay:** Irving Brecher; **Music:** Charles Wakefield Cadman, Roger Edens, Bronislau Kaper (songs), and Gus Kahn; **Cinematographer:** Leonard Smith; **Editor:** Blanch Sewell; **Cast:** Groucho Marx, Chico Marx, Harpo Marx, John Carroll, Diana Lewis.

S. Quentin Quale (Groucho Marx) arrives at the railroad station with a line of porters carrying his luggage. When they don't have change for a dime, he glibly insists, "Well, keep the baggage." He soon meets up with the Panello brothers (Harpo and Chico) and fleeces them out of the price of a train ticket to go west. Once out west, the trio concentrates on getting back a land deed presently in the clutches of a villain named Red Baxter. The fun culminates when the three fellows from the East (Groucho, Harpo, and Chico) race after the villains while aboard a train. It's a bumpy ride. "Break the brake," screams Joe Panello (Chico). The good-natured Rusty (Harpo) obliges by smashing the brake and throwing it away. The train smashes through a house, which it pulls along to the breakneck finale.

It was almost inevitable that at one time or another every screen comedy team would spoof the western genre, and the Marx Brothers were no exception. There is the bill-changing routine in Grand Central Station, a wild melee and clowning in a rolling stagecoach, and the climactic zany train chase. While not the Marx Brothers' zaniest romp nor the best spoof to be seen on a western screen, Groucho, Harpo, and Chico handle their parts well. Pure fun with its share of hilarious moments, the feature is more suited to fans of the Marx Brothers than fans of westerns, many of whom refuse to treat it as a significant genre piece.

GO WEST YOUNG LADY
Columbia, 1941, B&W, 70 min. **Producer:** Robert Sparks; **Director:** Frank R. Strayer; **Screenplay:** Karen DeWolf and Richard Flournoy; **Music:** Sammy Cahn and Saul Chaplin; **Cinematographer:** Henry Freulich; **Editor:** Gene Havlick; **Cast:** Penny Singleton, Glenn Ford, Ann Miller, Allen Jenkins, Jed Prouty, Bob Wills.

A saloon keeper sends for his nephew, who turns out to be a pretty young lady, and the misadventures begin. This tepid western comedy marks one of the first leading roles for 25-year-old Glenn Ford, whose credits include 25 westerns during his long tenure as one of the industry's top leading men. Penny Singleton and Bob Wills and His Texas Playboys provide for some lively music, and talented actress/dancer Ann Miller steals the show by hoofing to the tune "I Wish I Could Be a Singing Cowboy."

GRAND CANYON TRAIL Republic, 1948, Color, 67 min, VT. **Producer:** Edward J. White; **Director:** William Witney; **Screenplay:** Gerald Geraghty; **Music:** Jack Elliott and Foy Willing (songs); **Cinematographer:** Reggie Lanning; **Editor:** Tony Martinelli; **Cast:** Roy Rogers, Jane Frazee, Andy Devine, Robert Livingston, Roy Barcroft, Charles Coleman, James Finlayson.

Roy Rogers and pal Cookie Bullfincher (Andy Devine) take on a crook who is trying to locate a vein of silver. Willam Witney deftly directs this above-average series entry, which provides a good blend of action, suspense, and comedy. Robert Livingston changes hats to make a fine villain, and James Finlayson provides good comic relief as the befuddled sheriff. (See also UNDER WESTERN STARS.)

GRANNY GET YOUR GUN Warner Bros., 1940, B&W, 56 min. **Director:** George Army; **Screenplay:** Kenneth Gamet; **Music:** Howard Jackson; **Cinematographer:** L. William O'Connell; **Editor:** Jack Killifer; **Cast:** May Robson, Harry Davenport, Margot Stevenson, Hardie Albright, Clem Bevans, Clay Clement.

Based on a story by mystery writer Erle Stanley Gardner, a woman returns to Nevada after making a fortune as a gold miner to help her granddaughter, who has been falsely accused of murder. She then sets out to find the real culprit in this fun-filled B feature with nice performances by May Robson and Harry Davenport in the lead roles and an assorted group of familiar character actors for support.

GRAYEAGLE AIP, 1978, Color, 104 min, VT. **Producer:** Charles Pierce; **Director:** Pierce; **Screenplay:** Pierce; **Music:** James Mendoza-Nava; **Cinematographer:** Jim Roberson; **Editor:** Roberson; **Cast:** Ben Johnson, Alex Cord, Lana Wood, Iron Eyes Cody, Jack Elam, Paul Fix, Jacob Daniels.

Ben Johnson plays a rancher who sets out to track an Indian named Grayeagle (Alex Cord), who has kidnapped his daughter, but he is forced to face a shocking truth. This overlong and laconic genre piece is bolstered by Johnson's sturdy and sympathetic screen presence.

GREAT ADVENTURES OF WILD BILL HICKOK (aka: WILD BILL HICKOK) Columbia, 1938, B&W, 15 chapters. **Producer:** Jack Fier; **Directors:** Sam Nelson and Mack V. Wright; **Screenplay:** George Arthur Durlam, Dalls M. Fitzgerald, Tom Gibson, L. Ron Hubbard, Charles Arthur Powell, and George Rosener; **Editor:** Richard Fantl; **Cast:** William "Wild Bill" Elliott, Monte Blue, Carole Wayne, Frankie Darro, Dickie Jones, Sammy McKim, Kermit Maynard, Roscoe Ates, Reed Hadley, Chief Thundercloud, George Chesebro, Art Mix.

As marshal of Abilene, Wild Bill Hickok organizes a group of youngsters into a group called "Flaming Arrows" to help him combat a renegade group of "phantom riders" who are trying to stop a cattle drive from Texas over the old Chisholm Trail. This well-made 15-chapter Columbia serial helped propel actor Gordon Elliott to genre stardom under the name "Wild Bill" Elliott. The serial also goes under the title of *Wild Bill Hickok*.

GREAT BANK ROBBERY, THE Warner Bros.-Seven Arts, 1969, Color, 98 min. **Producer:** Malcolm Stuart; **Director:** Hy Averback; **Screenplay:** William Peter Blatty; **Music:** Nelson Riddle; **Cinematographer:** Fred J. Koenekamp; **Editor:** Gene Milford; **Cast:** Zero Mostel, Kim Novak, Clint Walker, Claude Akins, Akim Tamiroff, Larry Storch, Sam Jaffe, Mako, Elisha Cook Jr., Bob Steele.

A bogus preacher, a Mexican gang, and the local sheriff all compete for control of the town of Friendly. Two decent songs by the team of Sammy Cahn and Jimmy Van Heusan and Panavision are about the best this nebulous western spoof has to offer.

GREAT DAY IN THE MORNING RKO, 1956, Color, 92 min. **Producer:** Edward Grainger; **Director:** Jacques Tourneur; **Screenplay:** Lesser Samuels; **Music:** Leith Stevens; **Cinematographer:** William E. Snyder; **Editor:** Harry Marker; **Cast:** Virginia Mayo, Robert Stack, Ruth Roman, Alex Nicol, Raymond Burr, Leo Gordon.

Separatist sentiments and gold-rush fever clash in pre-Civil War Colorado. Beautiful color photography, a strong cast (particularly good emotional interaction between Robert Stack and Ruth Roman), and some good action scenes are the strongest elements in this ordinary oater based on a story by Robert Hardy Andrews.

GREAT DIVIDE, THE First National Pictures, 1929, B&W, 72 min. **Producer:** Robert North; **Director:** Reginald Barker; **Screenplay:** Fred Myton and Paul Perez; **Cinematographer:** Lee Garmes and Alvin Knechtel; **Cast:** Dorothy Mackaill, Ian Keith, Myrna Loy, Lucien Littlefield, George Fawcett.

A young woman from the East who is vacationing in the West with her friends and her fiancé finds herself being courted by a mine owner. The film features 24-year-old Myrna Loy, who appeared in six genre films between 1925 and 1930.

The Great Divide was released in both a sound and silent version, allowing it to be distributed to theaters not yet equipped with sound systems. This picturesque early talkie, based on William Vaughn Moody's 1909 play, was first filmed in 1925 by MGM with Alice Terry, Conway Tearle, and Wallace Beery.

GREAT GUNDOWN, THE See *MACHISMO*.

GREAT JESSE JAMES RAID, THE Lippert, 1953, Color, 73 min. **Producer:** Robert Lippert; **Director:** Reginald La Borg; **Screenplay:** Richard Lippert; **Music:** Lou Hersher and Bert Shefter; **Cinematographer:** Gilbert Warrenton; **Editor:** Carl Pearson; **Cast:** Willard Parker, Barbara Payton, Tom Neal, Wallace Ford, James Anderson, Jim Bannon.

Jesse James is coaxed out of retirement to join Bob Ford for one last bank heist. Lippert Studios hoped to get some box office punch by capitalizing on the tawdry romance between Tom Neal and Barbara Payton, which had been one of Hollywood's major scandals in the early 1950s. Willard Parker stars as the famed outlaw.

GREAT K & A TRAIN ROBBERY, THE Fox, 1926, B&W, 4,800'. **Producer:** Jesse Lasky; **Director:** Lewis Seiler; **Screenplay:** John Stone; **Cinematographer:** Dan Clark; **Cast:** Tom Mix, Dorothy Dawn, William Walling, Harry Grippe, Carl Miller, Edward Piel, Curtis McHenry.

The K & A Railroad undergoes a series of robberies, and Tom Gordon (Tom Mix) is hired to solve the case. He assumes the guise of a bandit and boards a train owned by Eugene Cullen (William Walling). However, he is discovered by Cullen's daughter, who soon falls in love with him. With the help of his wonder horse Tony, Gordon unmasks the culprits, captures the outlaws, and wins the heart of the heroine.

Based on Paul Leicester Ford's 1897 novel, the film, which uses the Denver and Rio Grande Railroad for background, was shot on location at Royal Gorge, Colorado. It also contains some of Tom Mix's most elaborate stunt work. Few of Mix's best westerns have survived due to the ravages of fire and decomposition. Among his other superior 1920s Fox westerns, always with an emphasis on stuntwork, are *The Lone Star Ranger* (1923), *The Rainbow Trail* (1925), *Sky High* (1922), and *Just Tony* (made in 1922 as a tribute to his horse).

GREAT MAN'S LADY, THE Paramount, 1942, B&W, 90 min, VT. **Producer:** William Wellman; **Director:** Wellman; **Screenplay:** W. L. River; **Music:** Victor Young; **Cinematographer:** William C. Mellor; **Editor:** Thomas Scott; **Cast:** Barbara Stanwyck, Joel McCrea, Brian Donlevy, K. T. Stevens, Thurston Hall, Lloyd Corrigan, Etta McDaniel.

Hannah Sempler (Barbara Stanwyck), a 109-year-old woman, tells the story of her life in a series of flashbacks, including her romance with Ethan Hoyt (Joel McCrea), the heroic pioneer who carved the town of Hoyt City out of the wilderness. The story begins in 1941 with the town celebrating the birthday of Hoyt, its founder and namesake.

The flashbacks start back in 1848 as Hannah relates how she eloped with Hoyt, suffered with him through the hardships of frontier life, and pushed him into success. When, through a series of misunderstandings, jealousies, and secrets, he comes to believe she is dead, he decides to remarry. Rather than blemish his career (as a senator by returning), Hannah fades into obscurity, only to finally relate the true story of the great man and the founding of the city nearly a century later.

Joel McCrea and Barbara Stanwyck were a familiar film team, appearing together in six motion pictures. The film's theme of self-sacrifice was not lost on wartime audiences; it was released as part of a double bill with John Huston's *Our Russian Front*, a wartime documentary about the heroism of the Russians against Nazi Germany. Well aware of McCrea's heroic potential on the screen, Wellman directed him two years later in *BUFFALO BILL* (1944).

GREAT MEADOW, THE MGM, 1931, B&W, 75 min. **Director:** Charles Brabin; **Screenplay:** Brabin and Edith Ellis; **Music:** William Axt; **Cinematographer:** William H. Daniels and Clyde de Vinna; **Editor:** George Hively; **Cast:** Johnny Mack Brown, Eleanor Boardman, Lucille La Verne, Anita Louise, Gwen Gordon, Guinn "Big Boy" Williams.

In 1777 pioneers in a little Virginia village are lured by a speech from Daniel Boone to undertake a mountainous 500-mile trek to settle new land in Kentucky. However, the dream soon fades into a grim reality as they are forced to endure Indian raids, bad weather, hunger, and death. Filmed in Real-ife 70mm, this early genre role for Johnny Mack Brown boasts some good action scenes and conveys a basic sense of authenticity to the dangers heaped upon these pioneer men and women.

GREAT MISSOURI RAID, THE Paramount, 1951, Color, 84 min. **Producer:** Nat Holt; **Director:** Gordon Douglas; **Screenplay:** Frank Gruber; **Music:** Paul Sawtell; **Cinematographer:** Ray Rennahan; **Editor:** Philip Martin; **Cast:** Wendell Corey, Macdonald Carey, Ellen Drew, Ward Bond, Bruce Bennett, Bill Williams, Ann Revere, Tom Tyler, Paul Fix, Jim Bannon.

Frank and Jesse James (Wendell Corey and Macdonald Carey) are forced into outlawry by a vindictive northerner (Ward Bond) who becomes a detective for the bankers association and sets out to hunt them down. Along the way they join forces with Cole and Jim Younger (Bruce Bennett and Bill Williams) in this familiar but colorful treatment of the James saga.

GREAT NORTHFIELD, MINNESOTA RAID, THE Universal, 1972, Color, 91 min, VT. **Producer:** Jennings Lang; **Director:** Philip Kaufman; **Screenplay:** Kaufman; **Music:** Dave Grusin; **Cinematographer:** Bruce Surtees; **Editor:** Douglas Stewart; **Cast:** Cliff Robertson,

Robert Duvall, Luke Askew, R. G. Armstrong, Dana Elcar, Elisha Cook Jr., Royal Dano.

When the State of Missouri decides to grant amnesty to Jesse James (Robert Duvall) and Cole Younger (Cliff Robertson), Cole wants to accept the offer, but Jesse is skeptical and feels that railroad companies will continue to misappropriate their land even if freedom from arrest is guaranteed. The plot unfolds as the railroad executives pay off the legislative leaders to drop the amnesty bill, prompting Cole and Jesse to engage in an ingenious plan to rob the Northfield, Minnesota, bank, reputed to be the biggest one west of the Mississippi.

While outlaws had long been portrayed as folk heroes in Hollywood, a particular strain of antiestablishment films appeared in the late 1960s, then flourished in the early 1970s, when concession to authority was generally considered unworthy of merit. Duvall's Jesse James is a far cry from the romantic hero portrayed by Tyrone Power in Henry King's popular 1939 movie and subsequent films of the 1940s and '50s. Jesse is portrayed here as a half-crazed, Bible-thumping southern zealot who can't accept that the war is over—basically the unsavory character he actually was.

Yet the true villains here are the Pinkerton detectives who will stop at nothing in their attempts to crush the James and the Younger brothers. In order for audiences to better sympathize with the robbers, the authorities at all times are made to look bad. The proprietor of the Northfield bank emerges as a two-timing charlatan, and the town's posse is even crueler and dumber than the gang they are pursuing.

This was the 25th picture about Jesse James, and it boasts excellent performances from both Duvall and Robertson, whose Cole Younger emerges as the film's real hero, hailed by the mob "as the greatest outlaw ever." With little concession to glamour, the picture's popularity was mainly contingent on word of mouth rather than critical approval or broad audience appeal. Like so many 1970s westerns, the film's plot is largely obscured by the director's determination to depict in minute detail the symbols of modernization in a changing America.

Among the film's major flaws is an overstated baseball game where the fielders are inappropriately clumsy and the game far too long. As Cole Younger happens upon a baseball game being played in Northfield, one of the townspeople explains, "It's our new national pastime." Cole blasts the ball with his shotgun and retorts, "Our national pastime is shooting and always will be."

Time called *The Great Northfield, Minnesota Raid*, ". . . a lovely, odd sort of middle Western . . . neither conventional western fiction nor completely documented fact." But *Variety* was far more critical, suggesting it was at best a valiant attempt at filmmaking that failed to come off, while faulting the film's "utter lack of sustained narrative, confused and inept writing . . . apparent indecision whether to make this drama or comedy, and a mishmash of irrelevant sequences."

GREAT SCOUT AND CATHOUSE THURSDAY (aka: WILDCAT) American International, 1976, Color, 102 min. **Producers:** Jules Buck, David Korda, and Samuel Z. Arkoff (executive); **Director:** Don Taylor; **Screenplay:** Richard Shapiro; **Music:** John Cameron; **Cinematographer:** Alex Phillips Jr.; **Editor:** Sheldon Kahn; **Cast:** Lee Marvin, Oliver Reed, Robert Culp, Elizabeth Ashley, Strother Martin, Kay Lenz, Sylvia Miles.

Set in Colorado during the presidential campaign of William Jennings Bryant and William Howard Taft (1908), this western comedy spoof finds old sidekicks Lee Marvin and Oliver Reed joining together to get revenge on the partner (Robert Culp), who after cheating them out of their gold mine shares went on to gain newfound respectability. They kidnap his wife (Elizabeth Ashley) hoping to force his hand, but the problem is he doesn't want her back. Cathouse Thursday (Kay Lenz) is a young prostitute and half-breed Harvard grad who spreads venereal disease across the West as revenge against white society, yet manages to have a touching romantic interlude with the crusty and far older Marvin.

GREAT SIOUX MASSACRE, THE (aka: THE CUSTER MASSACRE; THE GREAT SIOUX RAID; MASSACRE AT THE ROSEBUD) Columbia, 1965, Color, 91 min. **Producer:** Leo Fromkess; **Director:** Sidney Salkow; **Screenplay:** Fred C. Dobbs (Melvin Gluck); **Music:** Emil Newman and Edward B. Powell; **Cinematographer:** Irving Lippman; **Editor:** William Austin; **Cast:** Joseph Cotten, Darren McGavin, Philip Carey, Julie Summers, Nancy Kovack, Michael Pate, Iron Eyes Cody, House Peters Jr.

The events leading up to Custer's Last Stand is the main focus of this above-average western with Philip Carey in the role of George Armstrong Custer. Filmed in CinemaScope, alternate titles include *The Custer Massacre, The Great Sioux Raid*, and *Massacre at the Rosebud.*

GREAT SIOUX UPRISING Universal, 1953, Color, 80 min. **Producer:** Albert J. Cohen; **Director:** Lloyd Bacon; **Screenplay:** Melvin Levy, J. Robert Bren, and Gladys Atwater; **Music:** Henry Mancini, Milton Rosen, and Herman Stein; **Cinematographer:** Maury Gertzman; **Editor:** Edward Curtiss; **Cast:** Jeff Chandler, Faith Domergue, Lyle Bettger, Peter Whitney, Stacy Harris, Walter Sandee, Lane Bradford, Jack Ingram.

A doctor who poses as a veterinarian to track down two horse thieves prevents a Sioux uprising by befriending Chief Red Cloud. Jeff Chandler gives his usual fine performance as the ex-army officer in this average low-budget oater filmed in Pendleton, Oregon.

GREAT STAGECOACH ROBBERY Republic, 1945, B&W, 56 min. **Producer:** Louis Gray; **Director:** Leslie Selander; **Screenplay:** Randall Faye; **Cinematographer:** Bob Thackery; **Editor:** Charles Craft; **Cast:** William "Wild Bill" Elliott, Robert Blake, Sylvia Arslan, Hank Bell, Horace Carpenter, Tom London.

GREAT TRAIN ROBBERY, THE Edison, 1903, B&W, 12 min. **Director:** Edwin Porter; **Screenplay:** Porter; **Cinematographer:** Porter; **Cast:** A. C. Abadie, Gilbert M. "Broncho Billy" Anderson, George Barnes, Walter Cameron, Frank Hanaway, Morgan Jones, Tom London, Marie Murray, Mary Snow.

The clerk at a train station is assaulted and tied up by four men who threaten the operator and rob the train. They take the money and shoot a passenger before a little girl discovers the assaulted clerk and informs the sheriff. The sheriff and his men set off to capture the bandits.

Although this 12-minute silent feature is credited with establishing the western genre, it is not, strictly speaking, the very first western. Earlier film vignettes had shown scenes of cattle roundups and buffalo herds, while the Edison Company had already produced *Cripple Creek* (1898), replete with cowboys, dudes, barmaids, and booze. But *The Great Train Robbery* undoubtedly was the first western with a recognizable form, and it established the essential formula that became the matrix of the genre: crime, pursuit, showdown, and justice. Included as well are fistfights, horse chases, and gunplay. The appeal of a small child character was added, as was the oft-repeated saloon bully forcing the dude to dance. Most important perhaps is that it is a remarkably sophisticated film that became a huge commercial success as well. Even though it was filmed in the East, the New Jersey locations were intelligently employed, despite some tell-tale modern telegraph lines that parallel the railroad tracks. The editing was remarkable, and the story has a compelling sense of drama and suspense.

The commercial success of *The Great Train Robbery* prompted more than just sequels; it also prompted outright imitation. The following year (1904), the Lubin Company in Philadelphia remade the picture nearly scene for scene except for an occasional detail, such as a different calendar. *The Great Train Robbery* (1904) was directed by Siegmund Lubin, with Jack Frawley behind the camera and Emily Lubin as the little girl. In fact, imitations became so apparent that a couple of years later Edison itself made a parody of the picture, calling it *The Little Train Robbery* (1905).

Despite the topical interest (train robberies were not uncommon in 1903) and the film's enormous popularity, the growth of the western genre remained rather slow. In 1906 another Edison film, *A Race for Millions*, went so far as to conclude with a gun duel on the main street (very obviously a painted set). The trend now moved away from "goodies and baddies" toward individual heroes and villains, paving the way for the star-hero, such as "Broncho Billy" Anderson (who had a small role in *The Great Train Robbery*) and later western heroes William S. Hart and Tom Mix. Tom London, who played the railroad operator in *The Great Train Robbery*, had been a railroad operator in real life, and he would go on to appear in more films than any actor in the history of the motion picture business.

GREAT TRAIN ROBBERY, THE Republic, 1941, B&W, 61 min. **Producer:** Joseph Kane; **Director:** Kane;

Screenplay: Olive Cooper, Robert L. Shannon, and Garnett Weston; **Music:** Cy Feuer; **Editor:** Lester Orlebeck; **Cast:** Bob Steele, Claire Carlton, Milburn Stone, Helen MacKellar, Monte Blue, Yakima Canutt.

A train carrying a shipment of money disappears en route to its destination, and a railroad detective is assigned to find it. While the film bears no relation to the 1903 classic, it packs a good blend of mystery and action, with Steele quite good in the lead role.

GREEN GRASS OF WYOMING 20th Century Fox, 1948, Color, 89 min. **Producer:** Robert Bassler; **Director:** Louis King; **Screenplay:** Martin Berkeley; **Music:** Cyril J. Mockridge; **Cinematographer:** Charles G. Clarke; **Editor:** Nick DeMaggio; **Cast:** Peggy Cummins, Charles Coburn, Robert Arthur, Lloyd Nolan, Burl Ives.

Two rival families breed and raise trotting horses, while the boy and girl from each family (Robert Arthur and Peggy Cummins) find romance together. This Technicolor outing is an endearing and well-crafted production, appealing to juvenile and adult audiences alike. It showcases some adept horse work and a pair of horses (a beautiful white stallion and a glorious black mare) who actually steal the show from a capable cast headed by Charles Coburn, Lloyd Nolan, and Burl Ives. Cinematographer Charles G. Clark won an Oscar nomination for his color cinematography, and Martin Berkeley was accorded a nomination by the Writer's Guild of America for Best Written American Western.

GREY FOX, THE United Artists, 1982, Color, 110 min, VT. **Producer:** Peter O'Brien; **Director:** Phillip Boros; **Screenplay:** John Hunter; **Music:** Michael Conway Baker; **Cinematographer:** Frank Tidy; **Editor:** Frank Irvine; **Cast:** Richard Farnsworth, Jackie Burroughs, Ken Pogue, Wayne Robson, David Peterson, Timothy Webber.

Richard Farnsworth plays Bill Miner, an aging but gentlemanly stagecoach robber at the turn of the 20th century who, when released from San Quentin after 30-plus years in prison, decides to go to Canada to become a train robber. Miner lives a quiet life in a frontier town, passing himself off as a gold digger in between train robberies, and he has a tender love affair with a cultured woman who works as a photographer in town.

A longtime actor and stuntman, Farnsworth was suggested by Francis Coppola to star in this $3 million production, and his performance is superb. But while the film provides great entertainment, it is also terrible history. The real Miner, who spent time in San Quentin at a time when prisoners were routinely flogged and beaten, committed at least 27 major crimes, including armed robbery, horse stealing, smuggling, and burglary. He robbed more stagecoaches than the James and Younger Brothers combined, and at the date of his last arrest by Pinkerton detectives, he had stolen a grand total of $370,000 in cash and securities.

Farnsworth flawlessly captures all the charisma and folksy sense of humor of the real Bill Miner, a man able to pass himself off as an aging, good-natured, free-spirited, and rather benign soul, incapable of hurting anyone. The press, especially, fell under Miner's charming spell. The day after his death on September 2, 1913, one newspaper described him as a "kindly, lovable old man . . . whose manner was that of a friend to all mankind."

The real Miner was quite different. He was a hypocritical, self-proclaimed socialist, born to a middle-class family, who lived like a king in 1880 while his mother lived in poverty after his father's death. He never gave her a cent. While the movie provides top-quality entertainment and a compelling story, it distorts and omits many facts and gives a glowing endorsement of Miner's way of life.

GROOM WORE SPURS, THE
Universal, 1951, B&W, 80 min. **Producer:** Howard Welsch; **Director:** Richard Whorf; **Screenplay:** Frank Burt, Robert Carson, and Robert Libott; **Music:** Arthur Lange and Charles Maxwell; **Cinematographer:** J. Peverell Marley; **Editor:** Otto Ludwig; **Cast:** Ginger Rogers, Jack Carson, Joan Davis, Stanley Ridges, Richard Whorf.

Ginger Rogers is a lawyer hired to keep dumb cowboy Jack Carson out of trouble. She marries and then divorces him, and later she comes to his defense in a criminal case. Actor Richard Whorf plays himself in this zesty comedy spoof, which also takes a look at the fantasy of cowboy movie making.

GUILTY TRAILS
Universal, 1938, B&W, 57 min. **Producer:** Trem Carr; **Director:** George Waggner; **Screenplay:** Joseph West (Waggner); **Music:** Flemming Allen and Frank Sanucci; **Cinematographer:** Gus Peterson; **Editor:** Carl Pierson; **Cast:** Bob Baker, Marjorie Reynolds, Hal Taliaferro (Wally Wales), Georgia O'Dell, Glenn Strange, Forrest Taylor, Tom London.

GUN BATTLE AT MONTEREY
Allied Artists, 1957, B&W, 74 min. **Producer:** Carl K. Hittleman; **Directors:** Sidney A. Franklin Jr. and Hittleman; **Screenplay:** Jack Leonard and Lawrence Resner; **Music:** Robert Wiley Miller; **Cinematographer:** Harry Neumann; **Editor:** Harry Coswick; **Cast:** Sterling Hayden, Ted de Corsia, Pamela Duncan, Mary Beth Hughes, Lee Van Cleef, I. Stanford Jolley.

Two outlaws named Reno and Turner rob the express in Monterey. But when Turner (Sterling Hayden) wants to leave the partnership, Reno (Ted de Corsia) shoots him and leaves him for dead. Turner is found and nursed back to health by a young woman, and later he begins searching for Reno across California before finding him running a bar in Del Ray.

GUN BELT
United Artists, 1953, Color, 77 min. **Producer:** Edward Small: **Director:** Ray Nazarro; **Screenplay:** Jack DeWitt and Richard Schayer; **Music:** Irving Gertz; **Cinematographer:** W. Howard Greene; **Editor:** Grant Whytock; **Cast:** George Montgomery, Tab Hunter, Helen Westcott, John Dehner, Douglas Kennedy, Jack Elam, Rex Lease.

A notorious outlaw tries to go straight but is implicated in a crime by his old gang. George Montgomery gives a particularly good performance as the ex-outlaw in this above-average and lesser-known oater. The film also marked the western debut of 22-year-old Tab Hunter in the role of Chip Ringo.

GUN BROTHERS
United Artists, 1956, B&W, 79 min. **Producer:** Grand Productions, Inc.; **Director:** Sidney Salkow; **Screenplay:** Gerald Drayson Adams and Richard Schayer; **Music:** Irving Gertz; **Cinematographer:** Kenneth Peach; **Editor:** Arthur Hilton; **Cast:** Buster Crabbe, Ann Robinson, Neville Brand, Michael Ansara, Walter Sande, Roy Barcroft, Slim Pickens.

An ex-outlaw trying to go straight joins his brother who is setting up his own homestead. However, they are soon attacked by his former partner and a gang of thugs.

GUN CODE
PRC, 1940, B&W, 57 min. **Producer:** Sigmund Neufeld; **Director:** Peter Stewart (Sam Newfield); **Screenplay:** Joseph O'Donnell; **Cinematographer:** Jack Greenhalgh; **Editor:** Holbrook N. Todd; **Cast:** Tim McCoy, Inna Gest, Robert Winkler, Jack Richardson, Dave O'Brien, George Chesebro.

A federal agent is sent to a small town to stop a protection racket. Tim McCoy is well cast as the stern agent in this low-budget PRC entry.

GUN DUEL IN DORADO (aka: DUEL IN DURANGO)
United Artists, 1957, B&W, 73 min. **Producer:** Robert E. Kent; **Director:** Sidney Salkow; **Screenplay:** Louis Stevens; **Music:** Paul Sawtell and Bert Shefter; **Cinematographer:** Maury Gertsman; **Editor:** Robert Golden, George Montgomery, Ann Robinson, Steve Brodie, Bobby Clark, Frank Ferguson, Don "Red" Barry, Boyd "Red" Morgan, Roy Barcroft.

While attempting to go straight, an ex-outlaw is forced to shoot it out with his former gang before being able to reform for good. The TV title is *Duel in Durango*.

GUN FEVER
United Artists, 1958, B&W, 83 min. **Producers:** Harry Jackson and Sam Weston (Anthony Spinelli); **Director:** Mark Stevens; **Screenplay:** Stanley H. Silverman and Stevens; **Music:** Paul Dunlap; **Cinematographer:** Charles Van Enger; **Editor:** Lee Gilbert; **Cast:** Mark Stevens, John Lupton, Larry Storch, Aaron Saxon, Jerry Barclay, Dean Fredericks, Iron Eyes Cody.

When his father is murdered, a young man sets out to find the killer only to discover that it is a close family friend.

GUN FIGHT   United Artists, 1961, B&W, 67 min. **Producer:** Robert E. Kent; **Director:** Edward L. Cahn; **Screenplay:** Gerald Drayson Adams and Richard Schayer; **Music:** Paul Sawtell and Bert Shefter; **Cinematographer:** Walter Strenge; **Editor:** Robert Carlisle; **Cast:** James Brown, Joan Staley, Gregg Palmer, Ron Soble, John Locke.

A former soldier heads west to join his brother in a ranching venture and finds out that his brother is really an outlaw.

GUNFIGHT, A   Paramount, 1971, Color, 90 min. **Producers:** A. Roland Lubin and Harold Jack Bloom; **Director:** Lamont Johnson; **Screenplay:** Bloom; **Music:** Laurence Rosenthal; **Cinematographer:** David Walsh; **Editor:** Bill Mosher; **Cast:** Kirk Douglas, Johnny Cash, Jane Alexander, Raf Vallone, Karen Black, Eric Douglas.

In this film set in Texas circa 1855, Kirk Douglas and Johnny Cash are two aging gunfighters who devise a novel scheme to make money. Because the two legendary quick-draw artists are always asked who is the faster gun, they decide to stage a gunfight in a bull ring and sell tickets. The one left standing is to claim all the proceeds. The event is staged by a bullfight promoter named Alverez (Raf Vallone), who has a real yen for Douglas's wife, played by Jane Alexander. In the big showdown, Cash kills Douglas with a single shot, but the victory and the money are bittersweet and tainted—because he knows that one day he will have to face a deadly contest with a younger and faster gun.

This offbeat film was produced and financed by American Indians, the Jicarilla Apache of New Mexico, who raised $2 million to invest in the project. Helmed by Lamont Johnson, the picture has nothing to do with Indians. Rather, it serves as a morality tale on guns, guts, and greed, although it engendered little audience interest.

Reviews were mixed. *Variety* praised both the stars and the director's handling of the "ruggedly sensitive script . . . a depiction in allegorical form of the darker sides of human nature." Conversely, *Cue* found the story "too contrived to be taken as seriously as it should," with stars Kirk Douglas, Johnny Cash, Jane Alexander, and Karen Black approaching "every scene as if it were their big moment."

GUNFIGHT AT COMANCHE CREEK   Allied Artists, 1964, Color, 90 min. **Producer:** Ben Schwalb; **Director:** Frank McDonald; **Screenplay:** Edward Bernds; **Music:** Marlin Skiles; **Cinematographer:** Joseph Biroc; **Editor:** William Austin; **Cast:** Audie Murphy, Ben Cooper, Colleen Miller, DeForest Kelly, Jan Merlin, Adam Williams.

In Comanche Creek, Colorado, in 1875 a gang helps a man break out of jail and then use him to commit a robbery. When the reward is high enough they shoot him and proceed to collect the reward money. To stop a repetition of this nefarious scam, the National Detective Agency arranges to have one of its agents (Audie Murphy) jailed for train robbery, and the gang falls for the bait. This taut and surprisingly effective Murphy venture boasts an excellent low-key

performance by Jan Merlin as National Detective Agent Nielson.

Merlin recalled his long-standing association with Audie Murphy in a 1993 interview: "I did a lot of work with Audie. We played in the TV series *Whispering Smith* together. He was usually the hero and I was the villain when we worked together. It was Audie who felt that maybe I shouldn't play the heavy all the time. So in a film we did together called *Gunfight at Comanche Creek* he insisted that I be cast as his best friend. So I got killed very early in the picture. I really preferred being the heavy. That way you lasted throughout the picture."

GUNFIGHT AT DODGE CITY (aka: BAT MASTERSON STORY, THE)   United Artists, 1959, Color, 81 min. **Producer:** Walter Mirisch; **Director:** Joseph M. Newman; **Screenplay:** Martin Goldsmith and Daniel B. Ullman; **Music:** Hans J. Salter; **Cinematographer:** Carl Guthrie; **Cast:** Joel McCrea, Julie Adams, John McIntire, Nancy Gates, Richard Anderson, James Westerfield, Don Haggerty, Wright King.

Bat Masterson seeks revenge against the murder of his brother and becomes sheriff of Dodge City. He soon discovers that the citizens do not approve of his trying to clean up the town. Joel McCrea made the film at the same time that Randolph Scott made COMANCHE STATION (1960) for Budd Boetticher. Both men then retired from films before being teamed, for the first time, in Sam Peckinpah's RIDE THE HIGH COUNTRY in 1962.

GUNFIGHT AT THE O.K. CORRAL   Paramount, 1957, Color, 122 min, VT. **Producer:** Hal B. Wallis; **Director:** John Sturges; **Screenplay:** Leon Uris; **Music:** Dimitri Tiomkin; **Cinematographer:** Charles Lang Jr.; **Editor:** Warren Lowe; **Cast:** Burt Lancaster, Kirk Douglas, Rhonda Fleming, Jo Van Fleet, John Ireland, Lyle Bettger, Frank Faylen, Earl Holliman, Ted De Corsia, Dennis Hopper, De Forrest Kelley, Martin Milner, Kenneth Tobey, Lee Van Cleef, Olive Carey, Jack Elam.

Burt Lancaster and Kirk Douglas enact the roles of Wyatt Earp and Doc Holliday, respectively, as they prepare to battle the Clanton clan at the historic O.K. Corral. The story opens in Fort Griffith, Texas, when Earp, the celebrated lawman, saves Holliday, the alcoholic gambler, from a lynch mob. The action moves to Dodge City, Kansas, where Holliday, at first ordered to leave town and then permitted to stay, helps Earp gun down three outlaws. When Wyatt's brother, the marshal of Tombstone, seeks his help in handling the dangerous Clanton gang, Holliday accompanies him to the Arizona frontier town. The film culminates in a five-minute gun battle in which the Earps and Holliday wipe out the Clanton crew at the O.K. Corral on October 26, 1881.

Although clearly not the best of the Earp/Holliday/Clanton screen depictions (it does not approach John Ford's MY DARLING CLEMENTINE, 1944), the film benefits mainly from the dominant presence of Lancaster and Douglas, both at the height of their popularity as dynamic leading men. Actress Jo Van Fleet delivers a stellar performance as Kate, Holliday's former girlfriend who is now a burned-out saloonkeeper. A further plus is the Vista Vision location shooting (Tucson, Phoenix, Fort Griffith, and Tombstone), which provides a sound but historically inaccurate reconstruction of the famous gunfight. The five-minute gunfight lensed in Old Tucson took director John Sturges 44 hours to film but bears little resemblance to what really happened at the famous stockyard.

Based on the magazine article "The Killer" by George Scullin, with a screenplay by Leon Uris, the film garnered two Oscar nominations (sound and film editing) and was a big commercial success, grossing $4.7 million in distributors' rentals in the United States and Canada alone, making it the ninth highest-grossing film of 1957. Frankie Laine sings the title song written by Dimitri Tiomkin and Ned Washington, the team who provided the Oscar-winning title song from *HIGH NOON* five years earlier. Actor John Ireland, who plays Johnny Ringo, the Clanton's hired gun, was also on the losing side of the O.K. Corral skirmish years earlier, appearing as the fallen Billy Clanton in *My Darling Clementine*.

Opinions vary as to the film's overall merit. Some genre fans and students find it overblown and less than satisfying. In his *Great Hollywood Westerns*, Ted Sennett calls it "a fairly perfunctory film, which, at least, enshrined its cliches in bright Technicolor." Despite such limitations and a strong historical rebuke from *History Goes to the Movies*, the picture found favorable reviews in *Variety*, which called it "an absorbing yarn"; and from the *Saturday Review*'s Hollis Alpert, who found it "original and refreshing." Sturges would treat the Earp/Holliday/Clanton story quite differently a decade later in *HOUR OF THE GUN* (1967) with James Garner, Jason Robards Jr., and Robert Ryan in the lead roles.

GUNFIGHTER, THE 20th Century Fox, 1950, B&W, 85 min, VT. **Producer:** Nunnally Johnson; **Director:** Henry King; **Screenplay:** William Sellers and William Bowers; **Music:** Alfred Newman and Dimitri Tiomkin; **Cinematographer:** Arthur C. Miller; **Editor:** Barbara McLean; **Cast:** Gregory Peck, Helen Westcott, Millard Mitchell, Jean Parker, Karl Malden, Skip Homeier, Anthony Ross, Verna Felton, Richard Jaeckel, Alan Hale, Mae Marsh, Jack Elam.

Gregory Peck plays Jimmy Ringo, a tough but worn-out gunfighter who comes to a small western town hoping to escape his past. But he finds that there is always one more gun-happy punk lurking in the wings trying to earn his spurs by killing the daunted Ringo. The film is set almost entirely in a saloon, where Peck is awaiting a meeting with his estranged wife that has been set up by Marshal Mark Strett (played superbly by Millard Mitchell), a lawman who once rode with him. Meanwhile, the town bustles with gossip and speculation as to who will eventually kill the aging gunman. Eventually a younger gun (Skip Homeier) kills the older man, only to discover that he is now the one to be hunted.

This sophisticated western has grown in stature over the years, and for some time now it has been considered a genre classic—the representative post-World War II western that paved the way for the likes of *HIGH NOON* two years later. It is the first film of any consequence to present the now familiar theme of the mature outlaw unable to settle down and live his life out peaceably, becoming instead a man hunted in perpetuity.

The dark, brooding setting takes on the aura of a Greek tragedy, with the conclusion preordained and the audience sympathetic to the morally flawed protagonist or antihero. To date no other western had been able to present such a true sense of tragedy to its climax.

Gregory Peck, for years King's favorite actor, had recently supplanted Tyrone Power as 20th Century Fox's top leading man. Yet despite near-flawless performances by Peck and Millard Mitchell, the film only enjoyed moderate critical and public success at the time of its release. It remained for too long a misunderstood and commercially unsuccessful film, forgotten by many and relegated to being a "connoisseur's piece."

In his *Pictorial History of the Western Film*, William Everson lauds the year 1950 for three of the finest A westerns Hollywood ever produced: Delmer Daves's *BROKEN ARROW*; John Ford's *THE WAGONMASTER*; and Henry King's *The Gunfighter*, which he considers a far better film than *High Noon*. Everson notes, "*The Gunfighter* creates such a mood of inexorable Greek Tragedy that no matter how many times one sees it, one is always hoping subconsciously for that accidental change of circumstance or timing that will bring about a happy ending. . . ."

King's landmark film marked the evolution of the gunfighter into an alienated hero and set the trend for the slew of psychological westerns that would dominate much of the genre during the 1950s. Over the years, the theme of the gunfighter loner trying to live down his reputation would be filmed many times over.

GUNFIGHTERS, THE (aka: THE ASSASSIN, UK) Columbia, 1947, Color, 87 min. **Producer:** Harry Joe Brown; **Director:** George Waggoner; **Screenplay:** Alan Le May; **Music:** Rudy Schrager; **Cinematographer:** Fred Jakeman Jr.; **Editor:** Harvey Manger; **Cast:** Randolph Scott, Barbara Britton, Dorothy Hart, Bruce Cabot, Forrest Tucker, Grant Withers, Griff Barnett.

A gunfighter vows not to spill blood again, but circumstances obviate his good intentions. Even though the plot and theme have been repeated often, this is a fine adaptation of Zane Grey's *Twin Sombreros* with good work by Randolph Scott as he returns to the author whose material gave him screen stardom more than a decade earlier.

GUNFIGHTERS OF THE NORTHWEST Columbia, 1954, B&W, 15 episodes. **Producer:** Sam Katzman; **Director:** Spencer Gordon Bennet; **Screenplay:** Royal K. Cole, Arthur Hoerl, and George H. Plympton; **Cast:** Jock Mahoney, Phyllis Coates, Clayton Moore, Don C. Harvey, Marshall Reed, Rodd Redwing, Lyle Talbot, Tom Farrell, Lee Roberts, Chief Yowlachie, Gregg Barton, Pierce Lyden.

Marauding Indians and an avalanche face a Mountie in the great Northwest.

GUNFIGHT IN ABILENE Universal, 1967, Color, 86 min. **Producer:** Howard Christie; **Director:** William Hale; **Screenplay:** John D. Black and Berne Giler; **Music:** Bobby Darin; **Cinematographer:** Maury Gertsman; **Editor:** Gene Palmer; **Cast:** Bobby Darin, Emily Banks, Leslie Nielsen, Donnelly Rhodes, Don Dubbins.

Set in the post-Civil War era, Bobby Darin plays a gun-shy sheriff who is forced to take up arms against a gang of outlaws upon his return to Abilene. Pop singer Darin performs convincingly in this full-scale dramatic role.

GUNFIRE Resolute, 1935, B&W, 56 min. **Producer:** Alfred T. Mannon; **Director:** Harry Fraser; **Screenplay:** Harry C. Crist (Fraser); **Cast:** Rex Bell, Ruth Mix, Buzz Barton, Milburn Morante, William Desmond.

GUNFIRE (aka: FRANK JAMES RIDES AGAIN) Lippert, 1950, B&W, 59 min. **Producer:** William A. Berke; **Director:** Berke; **Screenplay:** Berke; **Cinematographer:** Ernest Miller; **Editor:** Carl Pierson; **Cast:** Don "Red" Barry, Robert Lowery, Pamela Blake, Wally Vernon, Steve Pendleton.

A man who looks like Frank James starts a series of holdups, and the real Frank James comes out of seclusion to search for him. The film boasts some fine work by Don "Red" Barry in a dual role.

GUNFIRE AT INDIAN GAP Republic, 1958, B&W, 69 min. **Producer:** Rudy Ralston; **Director:** Joseph Kane; **Screenplay:** Barry Shipman; **Cinematographer:** Jack A. Marta; **Editor:** Frederic Knudston; **Cast:** Vera Ralston, Anthony George, George Macready, Barry Kelley, John Doucette, George Keymas, Chubby Jackson, Glenn Strange.

Three outlaws are after a shipment of gold and a half-breed girl ensconced at a remote relay station.

GUN FOR A COWARD Universal, 1956, Color, 88 min. **Producer:** William Alland; **Director:** Abner Biberman; **Screenplay:** R. Wright Campbell; **Cinematographer:** George Robinson; **Editor:** Edward Curtiss; **Cast:** Fred Mac-Murray, Jeffrey Hunter, Janice Rule, Chill Wills, Dean Stockwell, Iron Eyes Cody, Robert F. Hoy, Bob Steele.

A successful rancher has trouble with two sons who are remarkably different. One is a hothead, while the other is reputed to be coward. This routine oater with a psychological bent is yet another entry in Fred MacMurray's "western sojourn" during the mid- to late 1950s, which found the actor making seven westerns in five years (1955–59).

GUN FURY Columbia, 1953, Color, 83 min. **Producer:** Lewis Rachmil; **Director:** Raoul Walsh; **Screenplay:** Roy Huggins and Irving Wallace; **Music:** Mischa Bakaleinikoff; **Cinematographer:** Lester White; **Editors:** James Sweeny and Jerome Thoms; **Cast:** Rock Hudson, Donna Reed, Philip Carey, Roberta Haynes, Leo Gordon, Lee Marvin, Neville Brand, John Dierkes.

In this movie originally shot in 3D, Rock Hudson plays a former Yankee who is weary of violence. However, his pacifist bent changes when fiancée Donna Reed is kidnapped by an outlaw gang led by an embittered southerner, played by Philip Carey. Based on the novel *Ten Against Caesar* by K. R. G. Granger, the screenplay was written by Roy Huggins, and by best-selling author Irving Wallace. The film helped Hudson solidify his stature as a major star and genuine heartthrob. By the end of 1953, Hudson's fan mail had increased to nearly 4,000 letters per month, a far cry from the 14 he had received after the release of *Peggy* in 1950, his first substantial role.

GUN GLORY MGM, 1957, Color, 89 min, VT. **Producer:** Nicholas Nayfack; **Director:** Roy Rowland; **Screenplay:** William Ludwig; **Music:** Jeff Alexander; **Cinematographer:** Harold J. Marzorita; **Editor:** Frank Santillo; **Cast:** Stewart Granger, Rhonda Fleming, Chill Wills, Steve Rowland, James Gregory.

A gunfighter defends his town when cattlemen threaten to destroy it by stampeding cattle through the farmlands. The best ingredient in this average genre piece is the commanding presence of the British actor Stewart Granger, who made eight westerns (including foreign-made films), starting with *THE WILD NORTH* (1952).

The movie was filmed in El Centro near the Mexican border, and MGM brought in actor Paul "Kelo" Henderson, a real-life cowboy and former ranch foreman, to help the British-born Granger learn the mechanics of gunwork and horsemanship. "Granger was just enamoured with the American West," Henderson recalls. "He had bought a ranch of his own and brought his own horse on the set with him. While he never became an expert with the guns he learned to draw and shoot fairly well. He was a pretty regular guy and very appreciative of my help. The first day I met him he made it a point to introduce me to his wife, actress Jean Simmons, who was filming close by."

GUN HAWK, THE Allied Artists, 1963, Color, 92 min. **Producer:** Richard Bernstein; **Director:** Edward Ludwig; **Screenplay:** Jo Heims; **Music:** Jimmie Haskell; **Cinematographer:** Paul Vogel; **Editor:** Rex Lipton; **Cast:** Rory Calhoun, Rod Cameron, Ruta Lee, Rod Lauren, Morgan Woodward, Robert J. Wilke, Gregg Barton.

A gunslinger who is being chased by lawmen for a killing makes his way to an outlaw hideout called Sanctuary. Along the way he teams up with a young punk who yearns for "a good fight and a bad woman." The savvy older man tries to dissuade the younger fellow from continuing his wild ways. Rory Calhoun and Rod Cameron make the film work fairly well. Throughout their respective film careers Calhoun and Cameron made a combined total of 80 westerns.

GUN JUSTICE Universal, 1934, B&W, 59 min. **Producer:** Ken Maynard; **Director:** Alan James; **Screenplay:** Robert Quigley; **Music:** Sam Perry; **Cinematographer:** Ted D. McCord; **Editor:** Charles Harris; **Cast:** Ken Maynard, Cecilia Parker, Hooper Atchley, Walter Miller, William Gould.

GUN LAW Majestic, 1933, B&W, 59 min. **Producer:** Larry Darmour; **Director:** Lewis D. Collins; **Screenplay:** Collins and Oliver Drake; **Cinematographer:** William Nobles; **Editor:** S. Roy Luby; **Cast:** Jack Hoxie, Betty Boyd, Mary Carr, Paul Fix, Harry Todd, Edmund Cobb.

GUN LAW RKO, 1938, B&W, 60 min. **Producer:** Bert Gilroy; **Director:** David Howard; **Screenplay:** Oliver Drake; **Cinematographer:** Joseph H. August; **Editor:** Frederic Knudtson; **Cast:** George O'Brien, Rita Oehmen, Ray Whitley, Ward Bond, Paul Everton, Robert Gleckler, Paul Fix.

When a series of stagecoach robberies occur, a U.S. marshal assumes the guise of an outlaw to capture the culprits. This exciting George O'Brien entry for RKO is a remake of *West of the Law* (Film Bookings Office, 1928) starring Tom Tyler and *The Reckless Rider* (Willis Kent, 1932) with Lane Chandler. (See also *RACKETEERS OF THE RANGE.*)

GUN LAW JUSTICE Monogram, 1949, B&W, 55 min. **Producer:** Louis Gray; **Director:** Lambert Hillyer; **Screenplay:** Basil Dickey; **Cinematographer:** Harry Neumann; **Editor:** John C. Fuller; **Cast:** Jimmy Wakely, Dub Taylor, Jane Adams, Tex Atchinson, Tom Chatterton, Edmund Cobb.

GUN LORDS OF STIRRUP BASIN Republic, 1937, B&W, 53 min. **Producer:** A. W. Haeckel; **Director:** Sam Newfield; **Screenplay:** Fred Myton and George H. Plympton; **Cinematographer:** Bert Longenecker; **Editor:** S. Roy Luby; **Cast:** Bob Steele, Louise Stanley, Karl Hackett, Ernie Adams, Frank La Rue.

GUNMAN FROM BODIE (aka: BAD MAN FROM BODIE) Monogram, 1941, B&W, 62 min. **Producer:** Scott Dunlap; **Director:** Spencer Gordon Bennett; **Screenplay:** Jess Bowers (Adele Buffington); **Cinematographer:** Harry Neumann; **Editor:** Carl Pierson; **Cast:** Buck Jones, Tim McCoy, Raymond Hatton, Christine McIntyre, Dave O'Brien.

GUNMAN'S CODE Universal, 1946, B&W, 55 min. **Producer and Director:** Wallace Fox; **Screenplay:** William

Lively; **Cast:** Kirby Grant, Fuzzy Knight, Jane Adams, Danny Morton, Bernard Thomas, Karl Hackett, Charles Miller.

GUNMAN'S WALK Columbia, 1958, Color, 97 min. **Producer:** Fred Kohlmar; **Director:** Phil Karlson; **Screenplay:** Ric Hardman and Frank Nugent; **Music:** George Dunning, Fred Karger, and Richard Quine; **Cinematographer:** Charles Lawton Jr.; **Editor:** Jerome Thoms; **Cast:** Van Heflin, Tab Hunter, James Darren, Kathryn Grant, Mickey Shaugnessy, Ray Teal.

Van Heflin is a rancher who tries to raise his two sons (Tab Hunter and James Darren) to be respectable citizens with regard to the law. However, he is slow to notice that one of his sons has become a cold-blooded killer. This interesting and well-knit western with a psychological bent has rarely received its proper attention. Heflin and Hunter are excellent in their respective roles as the rancher and his wayward son.

GUNMEN FROM LAREDO Columbia, 1959, Color, 67 min. **Producer:** Wallace Macdonald; **Director:** MacDonald; **Screenplay:** Clarke Reynolds; **Music:** George Dunning and Paul Sawtell; **Cinematographer:** Irving Lippman; **Editor:** Al Clark; **Cast:** Robert Knapp, Jane Davi, Walter Coy, Paul Birch.

An Indian girl helps a man who has escaped from jail track the four outlaws who framed him for the killing of his brother.

GUNMEN OF ABILENE Republic, 1950, B&W, 60 min. **Producer:** Gordon Kay; **Director:** Fred Frannon; **Screenplay:** M. Coates Webster; **Music:** Stanley Wilson; **Cinematographer:** Ellis W. Carter; **Editor:** Irving M. Schoenberg; **Cast:** Allan "Rocky" Lane, Eddy Waller, Roy Barcroft, Donna Hamilton, George Chesebro.

GUNNERS AND GUNS See *RACKETEER ROUND-UP.*

GUNNING FOR JUSTICE Monogram, 1948, B&W, 55 min. **Producer:** Barney A. Sarecky; **Director:** Ray Taylor; **Screenplay:** J. Benton Cheney; **Music:** Edward B. Kay; **Cinematographer:** Harry Neumann; **Editor:** John C. Fuller; **Cast:** Johnny Mack Brown, Raymond Hatton, Ted Adams, Dee Cooper, Evelyn Finley, Carol Henry, I. Stanford Jolley, Bud Osborne, Max Terhune.

GUNNING FOR VENGEANCE Columbia, 1946, B&W, 56 min. **Producer:** Colbert Clark; **Director:** Ray Nazarro; **Screenplay:** E. Earl Rapp; **Cast:** Charles Starrett, Smiley Burnette, Marjean Neville, Curt Barrett and The Trailsmen, Lane Chandler, Frank La Rue.

GUN PACKER Monogram, 1938, B&W, 51 min. **Producer:** Robert Emmett Tansey; **Director:** Wallace Fox; **Screenplay:** Robert Emmett (Tansey); **Cinematographer:** Bert Longenecker; **Cast:** Jack Randall, Louise Stanley, Charles King, Barlow Borland, Glenn Strange, Lloyd Ingraham.

GUN PLAY (aka: LUCKY BOOTS) First Division Pictures, 1935, B&W, 59 min. **Producer:** Arthur Alexander; **Director:** Albert Herman; **Screenplay:** William L. Nolte; **Cinematographer:** William Hyer; **Cast:** Guinn "Big Boy" Williams, Marion Shilling, Wally Wales, Frank Yaconelli, Tom London.

Two cowboys comes to the aid of a lady who believes there is a treasure buried on her land after a Mexican bandit leader is killed, and one of the cowboys finds the dead man's boots. Guinn "Big Boy" Williams sings "Home on the Range" in this above-average oater from a Poverty Row (very low budget) studio.

GUNPLAY RKO, 1951, B&W, 61 min. **Producer:** Herman Schlom; **Director:** Leslie Selander; **Screenplay:** Ed Earl Repp; **Music:** Paul Sawtell; **Cinematographer:** J. Roy Hunt; **Editor:** Douglas Biggs; **Cast:** Tim Holt, Richard Martin, Joan Dixon, Harper Carter, Mauritz Hugo, Robert Bice, Marshall Reed, Robert Wilke.

GUNPOINT Universal, 1965, Color, 1965. **Producer:** Gordon Kay; **Director:** Earl Bellamy; **Screenplay:** Mary Willingham and William Willingham; **Music:** Hans J. Salter; **Cinematographer:** William Margulies; **Editor:** Russell F. Schoengarth; **Cast:** Audie Murphy, Joan Staley, Warren Stevens, Edgar Buchanan, Denver Pyle, Morgan Woodward, Royal Dano.

A Colorado sheriff pursues a gang of train robbers into New Mexico, where he has no official jurisdiction. He is aided by a motley posse that includes a sharpshooting gambler whose fiancée has been kidnapped by the gang.

GUN RANGER, THE Republic, 1937, B&W, 56 min, VT. **Producer:** A. W. Hackel; **Director:** Robert N. Bradbury; **Screenplay:** George H. Plympton; **Cinematographer:** Bert Longnecker; **Editor:** S. Roy Luby; **Cast:** Bob Steele, Eleanor Stewart, John Merton, Ernie Adams.

A girl's father is killed and a ranger tries to find the murderer. This exciting and fast-paced entry was produced by A. W. Hackel and helmed by Robert N. Bradbury. (See also *RIDER OF THE LAW; RIDERS IN THE DESERT*.)

GUN RUNNER Monogram, 1949, B&W, 56 min. **Director:** Lambert Hillyer; **Screenplay:** J. Benton Chaney; **Cast:** Jimmy Wakely, Dub Taylor, Noel Neill, Mae Clarke, Kenne Duncan, Steve Clark, Marshall Reed.
See *ACROSS THE RIO GRANDE*.

GUNS ALONG THE BORDER See *CANYON AMBUSH*.

GUNS AND GUITARS Republic, 1936, B&W, 58 min. **Producer:** Nat Levine; **Director:** Joseph Kane; **Screenplay:** Dorrell McGowan and Stuart E. McGowan; **Cinematographer:** Ernest Miller; **Editor:** Lester Orlebeck; **Cast:** Gene Autry, Smiley Burnette, Dorothy Dix, Earl Hodgins, Tom London.

After he is framed for murdering the sheriff, Gene proves his innocence, gets himself elected sheriff, and sets out after the real culprit. (See also *TUMBLING TUMBLEWEEDS*.)

GUNS FOR HIRE (aka: BLAZING TRAIL) Kent, 1932, B&W, 58 min. **Producer:** Willis Kent; **Director:** Lewis D. Chandler; **Screenplay:** Oliver Drake; **Cinematographer:** James Diamond; **Editor:** S. Roy Luby; **Cast:** Lane Chandler, Sally Darling, Neal Hart, Yakima Canutt, John Ince.

A gunman and a rancher join forces to fight a gang of crooks. This low-budget Lane Chandler venture also features silent-screen star Neal Hart in a major role as the rival gunman.

GUNSIGHT RIDGE United Artists, 1957, B&W, 85 min. **Producer:** Robert Bassler; **Director:** Francis D. Lyon; **Screenplay:** Elizabeth Jennings and Talbot Jennings; **Music:** David Raskin; **Cinematographer:** Ernest Laszlo; **Cast:** Joel McCrea, Mark Stevens, Joan Weldon, Addison Richards, I. Stanford Jolley, George Chandler, Slim Pickens, L. Q. Jones.

In this film set in the Arizona territory, the citizens hire a deputy marshal to stop a series of robberies. Eventually he discovers that some supposedly respectable citizens are responsible for the crimes.

GUNS IN THE AFTERNOON See *RIDE THE HIGH COUNTRY*.

GUNS IN THE DARK Republic, 1937, B&W, 56 min, VT. **Producer:** A. W. Hackel; **Director:** Sam Newfield; **Screenplay:** Charles F. Royal; **Cinematographer:** Bert Longnecker; **Editor:** Roy Claire (S. Roy Luby); **Cast:** Johnny Mack Brown, Claire Rochelle, Syd Saylor, Ted Adams, Dick Curtis.

GUNSLINGER (aka: YELLOW ROSE OF TEXAS, THE) American Releasing Corporation, 1956, Color, 71 min. **Producer:** Roger Corman; **Director:** Corman; **Screenplay:** Charles B. Griffith and Mark Hanna; **Music:** Ronald Stein; **Cinematographer:** Frederick E. West; **Editor:** Charles Gross; **Cast:** Beverly Garland, John Ireland, Allison Hayes, Jonathan Haze, Martin Kingsley, Margaret Campbell, Chris Alcaide.

When the town's sheriff is gunned down, his wife pins on a badge and takes his place. Hired killer John Ireland is sent to do her in, but instead he falls in love with her. Unfortunately, the promising plot deteriorates rapidly, and what remains is a routine western, one of Corman's early six-day cheapies.

GUNSLINGERS Monogram, 1950, B&W, 55 min. **Producer:** Wallace Fox; **Director:** Fox; **Screenplay:** Adele Buffington; **Music:** Edward Kay; **Cinematographer:** Harry Neumann; **Cast:** Whip Wilson, Andy Clyde, Reno Browne, Dennis Moore, Hank Bell.

GUN SMOKE Paramount, 1931, B&W, 64 min. **Director:** Edward Sloman; **Screenplay:** Grover Jones and William Slavens McNutt; **Cinematographer:** Archie Stout; **Cast:** Richard Arlen, Mary Brian, Eugene Pallette, Louise Fazenda, Charles Winninger, William Boyd, Anne Shirley (as Dawn O'Day).

Gangsters take over a small western town but are opposed by a cowboy and his pal. This interesting interplay of the western and gangster genres has Richard Arlen as the hero and William Boyd in a rare role as the main villain.

GUN SMOKE (aka: GUNSMOKE ON THE GUADALUPE) Kent, 1935, B&W. **Producer:** Willis Kent and Monte Montana; **Director:** Bartlett A. Carre; **Screenplay:** Paul Evan Lehman; **Music:** David Broekman; **Editor:** S. Roy Luby; **Cast:** Gene Alsace, Marion Shilling, Henry Hall, Roger Williams, Lafe McKee.

A man seeking revenge on a cattleman brings in a herd of sheep.

GUN SMOKE Monogram, 1945, B&W, 57 min. **Producer:** Charles J. Bigelow; **Director:** Howard Bretherton; **Screenplay:** Frank K. Young; **Cinematographer:** Marcel Le Picard; **Editor:** J. M. Foley; **Cast:** Johnny Mack Brown, Raymond Hatton, Roy Butler, Jennifer Holt, Riley Hill, Wen Wright, Ray Bennett.

GUNSMOKE (AKA: MAN'S COUNTRY, A; ROUGHSHOD) Universal, 1953, Color, 79 min, VT. **Producer:** Aaron Rosenberg; **Directors:** Bartlett A. Carre, Nathan Juran, and Richard Whorf; **Screenplay:** D. D. Beauchamp; **Cinematographer:** Charles P. Boyle and Harvey Gould; **Editor:** Ted J. Kent; **Cast:** Audie Murphy, Susan Cabot, Paul Kelly, Charles Drake, Mary Castle, Jack Kelly.

Audie Murphy is an outlaw who is hired to chase a family off their ranch, but he has a change of heart and decides to run the ranch after falling for the rancher's daughter. Murphy makes a convincing hero in this above-average oater based on Norman A. Fox's novel *Roughshod*.

GUNSMOKE IN TUCSON Allied Artists, 1958, Color, 79 min. **Producer:** William D. Coates and Igo Kantor; **Director:** Thomas Carr; **Screenplay:** Robert L. Joseph and Paul Leslie Peil; **Music:** Sidney Cutner; **Cinematographer:** William P. Whitley; **Editor:** George White; **Cast:** Mark Stevens, Forrest Tucker, Gail Robbins, Kevin Hagen, Bill Henry, Richard Reeves, George Keymas.

Two young brothers watch the hanging of their father and are forced to grow up on their own. One becomes a sheriff and the other becomes an outlaw. The plot thickens as the two brothers are forced to face off against one another when turbulence between a cattle baron and settlers in the Arizona territory comes to a head. Filmed in CinemaScope, this familiar brother vs. brother tale works surprisingly well due to good performances by the two stars.

GUNSMOKE MESA PRC, 1944, B&W, 59 min. **Producer:** Arthur Alexander; **Director:** Harry L. Fraser; **Screenplay:** Elmer Clifton; **Music:** Lee Zahler; **Cinematographer:** Ira H. Morgan; **Editor:** Charles Henkel Jr.; **Cast:** James Newill, Dave O'Brien, Guy Wilkerson, Patti McCarty, Richard Alexander, Jack Ingram, Kermit Maynard, Michael Vallon.

GUNSMOKE RANCH Republic, 1937, B&W, 59 min, VT. **Producer:** Sol C. Siegel (associate); **Director:** Joseph Kane; **Screenplay:** Oliver Drake; **Music:** Drake (song); **Cinematographer:** Gus Peterson; **Editor:** Russell F. Schoengarth; **Cast:** Robert Livingston, Ray Corrigan, Max Terhune, Kenneth Harlan, Sammy McKim.

GUNSMOKE TRAIL Monogram, 1938, B&W, 57 min. **Producer:** Maurice Conn; **Director:** Sam Newfield; **Screenplay:** Fred Myton; **Editor:** Martin G. Conn; **Cast:** Addison Randall (as Jack Randall), Louise Stanley, Al St. John, Henry Roquermore, Ted Adams, John Merton.

GUN SMUGGLERS RKO, 1948, B&W, 61 min. **Producer:** Herman Schlom; **Director:** Frank McDonald; **Screenplay:** Norman Houston; **Cinematographer:** J. Roy Hunt; **Editor:** Les Millbrook; **Cast:** Tim Holt, Richard Martin, Martha Hyer, Gary Gray, Paul Hurst, Dan Haggerty.

GUNS OF APRIL MORNING, THE See *CAPTAIN APACHE*.

GUNS OF A STRANGER Universal, 1973, Color, 91 min. **Producer:** Robert Hinkle; **Director:** Hinkle; **Screenplay:** Charles Aldrich; **Cast:** Marty Robbins, Chill Wills, Steve Tackett, Ronny Robins, Bill Coontz.

Marty Robbins is a drifter and a singer in this subpar family film.

GUNS OF FORT PETTICOAT Columbia, 1957, Color, 82 min. **Producer:** Audie Murphy; **Director:** George Marshall; **Screenplay:** Walter Doniger and C. William Harrison; **Cinematographer:** Ray Rennahan; **Editor:** Al Clark; **Cast:** Audie Murphy, Kathryn Grant, Hope Emerson, Jeff Donnell, Jeanette Nolan, Sean McClory, Nestor Paiva, Ray Teal, John Dierkes.

Audie Murphy stars as an Army deserter who whips a group of women into shape to help them fight off an impending Indian attack. This exciting, well-cast film is one of Audie Murphy's best and features one of his most enjoyable performances.

GUNS OF HATE RKO, 1948, B&W, 61 min. **Producer:** Herman Schlom; **Director:** Leslie Selander; **Screenplay:** Norman Houston and Ed Earl Rapp; **Music:** Paul Sawtell; **Cinematographer:** George E. Diskant; **Editor:** Desmond Marquette; **Cast:** Tim Holt, Nan Leslie, Richard Martin, Steve Brodie, Myrna Dell, Jason Robards Sr.

GUNS OF JUSTICE See COLORADO RANGER.

GUNS OF SONORA See OUTLAWS OF SONORA.

GUNS OF THE LAW PRC, 1944, B&W, 56 min. **Producer:** Arthur Alexander; **Director:** Elmer Clifton; **Screenplay:** Clifton; **Music:** Aleth "Speed" Hanson, James Newill, and Dave O'Brien; **Cinematographer:** Edward A. Kull; **Editor:** Charles Henkel Jr.; **Cast:** James Newill, Dave O'Brien, Guy Wilkerson, Jennifer Holt, Budd Buster, Charles King, Jack Ingram.

GUNS OF THE MAGNIFICENT SEVEN United Artists/Mirish Company, 1969, Color, 105 min, VT. **Producer:** Vincent M. Fennelly; **Director:** Paul Wendkos; **Screenplay:** Herman Hoffman; **Music:** Elmer Bernstein; **Cinematographer:** Antonio Macasoli; **Editor:** Walter Hannemann; **Cast:** George Kennedy, James Whitmore, Monte Markham, Reni Santoni, Bernie Casey, Joe Don Baker, Michael Ansara.

A gunslinger and six cohorts agree to help spring a Mexican revolutionary leader from prison so he can continue to work for his cause. George Kennedy takes the role of Chris, played by Yul Brynner in the two earlier *Seven* films: John Sturges's *THE MAGNIFICENT SEVEN* (1960) and Burt Kennedy's *THE RETURN OF THE SEVEN* (1966). While this sequel is not nearly as good as Sturges's original, there is still enough action here to satisfy diehard fans.

GUNS OF THE PECOS Warner Bros./First National, 1937, B&W, 56 min. **Producers:** Bryan Foy, Hal B. Wallis, and Jack L. Warner; **Director:** Noel Smith; **Screenplay:** Harold Buckley; **Music:** M. K. Jerome and Jack

Scholl; **Cinematographer:** Ted D. McCord; **Editor:** Frank DeWar; **Cast:** Dick Foran, Anne Nagel, Gordon Hart, Joseph Crehan, William "Wild Bill" Elliott (as Gordon Elliott), Eddie Acuff.

Rustlers murder an army major who is buying horses for the service, and the Texas Rangers are assigned to track down the murderers. Foran's pleasing personality is always a plus, even though this series entry for Warner Bros. is rather ordinary. A capable actor and a fine singer, Foran sings "When the Cowboy Takes a Wife" and "The Prairie Is My Home," music and lyrics by M. K. Jerome and Jack Scholl. (See also *MOONLIGHT ON THE PRAIRIE*.)

GUNS OF THE TIMBERLAND Warner Bros., 1959, Color, 91 min. **Producer:** Aaron Spelling; **Director:** Robert D. Webb; **Screenplay:** Joseph Petracca and Spelling; **Music:** David Buttolph; **Cinematographer:** John F. Seitz; **Editor:** Tom McAdoo; **Cast:** Alan Ladd, Jeanne Crain, Gilbert Roland, Frankie Avalon, Lyle Bettger, Noah Beery Jr., Alana Ladd, Johnny Seven.

Alan Ladd plays lumberjack Jim Hadley, leading his crew of men in search of a new forest to cut. The plot thickens as ranchers and townspeople oppose the loggers, who are intent on clearing the land with the aid of a government grant. This colorful feature with an interesting plot also features then-teen heartthrob Frankie Avalon in his movie debut and Ladd's daughter Alana as Jane Peterson. Even with his personal and professional life in marked decline, Alan Ladd still delivered a punch in his final western.

GUNS OF WYOMING See *CATTLE KING* (1963).

GUN STREET United Artists, 1962, B&W, 67 min. **Producer:** Robert Kent; **Director:** Edward L. Cahn; **Screenplay:** Sam C. Freedle; **Music:** Richard La Salle; **Cinematographer:** Gilbert Warrenton; **Editor:** Kenneth G. Crane; **Cast:** James Brown, Jean Willes, John Clark, Med Flory, John Pickard, Peggy Stewart.

A sheriff tries to stop a convict from murdering the man who sent the convict to prison and married his wife.

GUN THAT WON THE WEST Columbia, 1955, Color, 71 min. **Producer:** Sam Katzman; **Director:** William Castle; **Screenplay:** James B. Gordon; **Cinematographer:** Henry Freulich; **Editor:** Al Clark; **Cast:** Dennis Morgan, Paula Raymond, Richard Denning, Chris O'Brien, Robert Morgan.

In this film set in Wyoming, the cavalry and its scouts use the Springfield Rifle (the title weapon) to restore the peace with the Indians.

GUN THE MAN DOWN (aka: ARIZONA MISSION) United Artists/Batjac, 1956, B&W, 74 min. **Pro-**

ducers: Robert E. Morrison and John Wayne; **Director:** Andrew McLaglen; **Screenplay:** Burt Kennedy; **Music:** Henry Vars; **Cinematographer:** William Clothier; **Editor:** A. Edward Sutherland; **Cast:** James Arness, Angie Dickinson, Robert J. Wilke, Emile Meyer, Don Megowan, Michael Emmet, Harry Carey Jr.

A wounded man swears vengeance on cohorts who left him during a holdup. James Arness plays the outlaw out for revenge when his pals and his girl leave him behind. He catches up with them in a town near the border.

GUN TOWN Universal, 1946, B&W, 55 min. **Producer:** Wallace Fox; **Director:** Fox; **Screenplay:** William Lively; **Music:** Norman Berens and Milton Rosen (songs); **Cinematographer:** Maury Gertsman; **Editor:** Ray Snyder; **Cast:** Kirby Grant, Louise Currie, Fuzzy Knight, Claire Carleton, Lyle Talbot.

HAIL TO THE RANGERS (aka: ILLEGAL RIGHTS, UK) Columbia, 1943, B&W, 58 min. **Producer:** Jack Fier; **Director:** William Berke; **Screenplay:** Gerald Geraghty; **Cinematographer:** Benjamin H. Kline; **Editor:** William F. Claxton; **Cast:** Charles Starrett, Leota Archer, Arthur Hunnicutt, Bob Archer, Lloyd Bridges, Ted Adams, Tom London.

An ex-ranger comes to the aid of rancher pal whose range is about to be lost to an influx of homesteaders. The twist here is that the homesteaders are the bad guys for a change. This Charles Starrett venture marks one of the early screen appearances for actor Lloyd Bridges, who had been signed to a Columbia Studio contract in 1941.

HAIR TRIGGER Atlantic, 1936, B&W, 59 min. **Producer:** William A. Berke; **Director:** Harry L. Fraser; **Screenplay:** Weston Edwards (Fraser); **Cinematographer:** Robert E. Cline; **Editor:** Arthur A. Brooks; **Cast:** Jack Perrin, Wally Wales, Ed Cassidy, Robert Walker, Fred "Snowflake" Toones, Betty Mack.

A cowboy tries to stop a gang of smugglers working along the U.S.-Mexican border. Perrin's character is named Jack "Hair Trigger" Casey.

HALF BREED, THE RKO, 1952, Color, 81 min. **Producers:** Harold Shumate and Herman Schlom; **Director:** Stuart Gilmer; **Screenplay:** Shumate and Richard Wormser; **Cinematographer:** William V. Skall; **Editor:** Samuel E. Beetley; **Cast:** Robert Young, Janice Carter, Jack Buetel, Barton MacLane, Reed Hadley, Porter Hall, Connie Gilchrist.

A half-breed Apache is goaded by a group of crooked profiteers into leading his tribe against white settlers in Arizona.

HALLELUJAH TRAIL, THE United Artists/The Mirisch Corporation, 1965, Color, 165 min, VT, DVD. **Producer:** John Sturges; **Director:** Sturges; **Screenplay:** John Gay; **Cinematographer:** Robert Surtees; **Editor:** Ferris Webster; **Cast:** Burt Lancaster, Lee Remick, Jim Hutton, Pamela Tiffin, Donald Pleasence, Brian Keith, Martin Landau, John Anderson, Dub Taylor, Whit Bissell.

John Dehner narrates this western comedy, based on a Bill Gullick novel, about a rambunctious female temperance leader (Lee Remick) out to stop a cavalry-guarded whisky shipment en route to thirsty Denver miners. The strongest points in this overlong yet fun-filled film are its ensemble cast and the impeccable timing and interplay between Burt Lancaster and Jim Hutton as soldiers assigned to escort the alcohol to its final destination. But the real scene stealer is Martin Landau as Chief Walks-Stooped-Over, one of the Indians trying to intercept and steal the firewater. Filming took place in Lone Pine, California, and in McKinley County, New Mexico. The New Mexico crew was confronted with the heaviest rainfall in the region in 50 years, and both the tents and the set decorations were washed away.

HALLIDAY BRAND, THE United Artists, 1957, B&W, 77 min. **Producer:** Collier Young; **Director:** Joseph H. Lewis; **Screenplay:** George W. George and George F. Slavin; **Music:** Stanley Wilson; **Cinematographer:** Ray Rennahan; **Editor:** Michael Luciano and Stuart O'Brien; **Cast:** Joseph Cotten, Viveca Lindfors, Betsy Blair, Ward Bond, Bill Williams, J. C. Flippen, Christopher Dark, Jeanette Nolan, Glenn Strange, John Dierkes, I. Stanford Jolley.

Sheriff and rancher Big Dan Halliday (Ward Bond) has two sons, played by Joseph Cotten and Bill Williams. Halliday so dominates his family and his workers that his sons take different paths, while his intent on preserving the untainted family name leads him to refuse protection from a lynch mob that hangs his daughter's half-breed lover. Cotten delivers an excellent performance in this interesting psychological treatment of the father/son theme. Ward Bond as the father was only two years older than Cotten, his son in the film, and just 13 years older than second son Williams.

HANDS ACROSS THE BORDER
Republic, 1943, B&W, 72 min, VT, DVD. **Producer:** Harry Grey; **Director:** Joseph Kane; **Screenplay:** J. Benton Cheney and Bradford Ropes; **Music:** Hoagy Carmichael, Phil Ohman, and Ned Washington; **Cinematographer:** Reggie Lanning; **Editor:** Tony Martinelli; **Cast:** Roy Rogers, Ruth Terry, Guinn "Big Boy" Williams, Onslow Stevens, Mary Breen, Duncan Renaldo.

Roy is forced to ride Trigger in a race to help an honest rival who has been duped by crooks to win a cavalry contract. The plot of the film is subordinate to the musical numbers, and the picture ends with a grand musical finale. (See also *UNDER WESTERN STARS*.)

HANDS ACROSS THE ROCKIES
Columbia, 1941, B&W, 55 min. **Producer:** Leon Barsha; **Director:** Lambert Hillyer; **Screenplay:** Paul Franklin; **Cast:** Bill Elliott, Mary Daily, Dub Taylor, Kenneth MacDonald, Frank La Rue, Donald Curtis.

Wild Bill Hickok and his pal Cannonball look for the murderer of Cannonball's father. They arrive in a small town where a girl who is a witness to the crime is being forced to marry the man who did the deed. Bill Elliott played Wild Bill Hickok in 11 films for Columbia. (See also *WILDCAT OF TUCSON, THE*.)

HANG 'EM HIGH
United Artists, 1968, Color, 101 minutes, VT. **Producer:** Leonard Freeman; **Director:** Ted Post; **Screenplay:** Leonard Freeman and Mel Goldberg; **Music:** Dominic Frontiere; **Cinematographer:** Richard Kline and Leonard South; **Editor:** Gene Fowler; **Cast:** Clint Eastwood, Inger Stevens, Ed Begley, Pat Hingle, Arlene Golonka, Ben Johnson, James MacArthur, Bruce Dern, Dennis Hopper, Bob Steele, Alan Hale Jr., Charles McGraw.

Clint Eastwood is Jed Cooper, who purchases a herd of cattle from a local rancher and is driving them across the Rio Grande en route to his own land. Suddenly he is surrounded by a group of vigilantes who tell him they have just found the cattle baron dead. Because he has the herd, he is the prime suspect, and although he struggles bitterly they hang him by the neck and leave him for dead. Just before he is about to die, he is rescued by a passing lawman (Ben Johnson) and taken to Judge Fenton (Pat Hingle), the local magistrate, where he is deputized and authorized to track down his assailants. He ignores the judge's warning to bring them in alive, and when he finds them he kills them one by one.

Along the way he romances Inger Stevens, a widow who is searching for her husband's killers; their love scenes provide a rare and touching tenderness. Not so tender nor so rare are scenes of group hangings, with as many as six men lined up along a huge scaffolding, their heads hooded, as they are dropped in unison to their doom. The film ends in a blazing gun battle between Cooper and vigilante leader Wilson (Ed Begley) and his cohorts. As the gunfight ensues and only Cooper and Wilson are left alive, Cooper enters the house and finds that the terrified Wilson has committed suicide—ironically, by hanging himself.

The film was Eastwood's first significant American effort following the *Dollar* trilogy with Sergio Leone. To give the film a more American imprint, he cast many well-known actors in supporting roles, including old-time B western star Bob Steele, who is excellent as Jenkins, the one man in the vigilante group who is opposed to the hanging and voluntarily turns himself in to the law. Eastwood also engaged former *Rawhide* (1959–66) director and pal Ted Post to helm the picture, thus providing a continuity to his days on the popular TV series. The film, which cost $1.7 million to produce, grossed more than $17 million worldwide and $5 million domestically. For his efforts, Clint Eastwood's salary rose to $400,000 plus a percentage of the profits.

Reviews, while mixed, were generally on the positive side. *Film Weekly* called it "one of the best western films of this year," while Archie Winsten in the *New York Post* commented that it is "a Western of quality, courage, danger, and excitement which places itself squarely in the procession of old fashioned westerns made with the latest techniques. . . ." *Variety* notes that while "Eastwood projects a likable image . . . the part is only a shade more developed over his Sergio Leone Italoaters. . . ."

HANGING JUDGE, THE   See *NAKED GUN*.

HANGING TREE, THE
Warner Bros., 1959, Color, 106 min, VT. **Producers:** Martin Jurow and Richard Shepherd; **Director:** Delmer Daves; **Screenplay:** Wendell Maves and Halstead Welles; **Music:** Max Steiner; **Cinematographer:** Ted McCord; **Editor:** Owen Marks; **Cast:** Gary Cooper, Maria Schell, Karl Malden, George C. Scott, John Dierkes, Virginia Gregg, Ben Piazza.

Gary Cooper plays Joe Frail, a frontier doctor running away from personal tragedy who drifts into a Montana gold-mining town. Here he proves himself as adept with a gun, a scalpel, and a poker game as he is in his kindly medical practice. His first action has him saving an accused thief (Ben Piazza) from a posse. After he nurses the lad back to health, the two become good friends. Frail then takes on the recovery of Maria Schell, a Swiss immigrant who is ill and has been blinded by exposure. Karl Malden plays Frenchie, an all-purpose villain who wants Piazza's life, Cooper's money, and Schell's body.

The script is based on Dorothy M. Johnson's novelette, which won the Western Writers of America's Spur Award.

Cooper is superb in what *Variety* called one of his best roles, while Delmer Daves's direction is straight and steady. The exteriors were filmed some 40 miles from Yakima, Washington, in a mining camp in the mountains specially built on location by art director Daniel B. Cathcart. Mark David and Jerry Livingston's title song, sung by Marty Robbins, garnered an Oscar nomination. A real "sleeper" at the time of its release, *The Hanging Tree* holds up very well today. The critic for the *London Observer* commented that as a "psychiatric doctor Mr. Cooper is still one of the most reliable cowboy heroes on the screen." The film marked the screen debut of actor George C. Scott.

HANGMAN, THE Paramount, 1959, B&W, 87 min. **Producer:** Frank Freeman Jr.; **Director:** Michael Curtiz; **Screenplay:** Dudley Nichols; **Music:** Harry Sukman; **Cinematographer:** Loyal Griggs; **Editor:** Terry O. Morse; **Cast:** Robert Taylor, Fess Parker, Tina Louise, Jack Lord, Shirley Harmer, Mickey Shaughnessy, Gene Evans.

Robert Taylor is a deputy marshal searching for a man involved in a holdup. He offers the man's former girlfriend (Tina Louise) $500 if she will come to the town of North Creek and identify him. She declines to help at first, even though she has been reduced to working as a laundress. The wanted man (Jack Lord) now lives in North Creek as a respected citizen with a wife and a child. He is well loved by the townsfolk for rehabilitating several men away from crime, and the town is in no mood to turn him over to Taylor. Nor does Taylor get much help from resident sheriff Fess Parker. By the time Tina Louise shows up unexpectedly and agrees to track down Lord, Taylor has been so softened that he eventually departs from his rigidly held views of law and justice. He turns in his badge and opts for retirement in California. Tina Louise, moved by his decision and by his confession of a childhood tragedy in which a relative was killed by outlaws, is won to his side.

This was Robert Taylor's first film as an independent after a 24-year association with MGM. It opened in Brooklyn in August 1959 on a double bill with Danny Kaye's *The Five Pennies*. While initial reviews were mixed, the film has held up surprisingly well, largely due to the imprint of celebrated director Michael Curtiz.

HANGMAN'S KNOT Columbia, 1952, Color, 81 min, VT. **Producer:** Harry Joe Brown; **Director:** Roy Huggins; **Screenplay:** Huggins; **Cinematographer:** Charles Lawton Jr.; **Editor:** Gene Havlick; **Cast:** Randolph Scott, Donna Reed, Lee Marvin, Claude Jarman Jr., Frank Faylen, Richard Denning, Clem Bevans, Monte Blue, Ray Teal, Guinn "Big Boy" Williams.

Randolph Scott plays a Confederate officer who learns that the Civil War is over only after his soldiers have successfully taken a gold shipment from a Union troop. He and his soldiers decide to return home, each with a share of the booty. However, they run into a band of outlaws who corner them at a way station then lay siege to them. This fine and neg-

lected western film is well worth watching, especially for those enamored by the Randolph Scott/Budd Boetticher films later in the decade. As with the Boetticher pictures, Scott coproduced the film with Harry Joe Brown, combining a strong cast with an interesting plot and a deft story line.

HANNAH LEE (aka: OUTLAW TERRITORY) Realart, 1953, Color, 75 min. **Producer:** Jack Broder; **Directors:** Lee Garmes and John Ireland; **Screenplay:** MacKinlay Kantor and Rip Von Ronkel (Alfred); **Music:** Paul Dunlap; **Cinematographer:** Garmes; **Editor:** Chester W. Schaeffer; **Cast:** John Ireland, Joanne Dru, Macdonald Carey, Stuart Randall, Frank Ferguson, Don Haggerty, Tristram Coffin.

Professional killer Ben Crow (Macdonald Carey) is hired by some cattlemen to eliminate squatters. When Marshal Sam Rochelle (John Ireland) is sent to bring him in, pretty saloon owner Haille (Hannah) Lee (Joanne Dru) becomes a reluctant witness. This interesting film, loosely based on MacKinlay Kantor's novel *Wicked Water*, marked actor Ireland's only stab at directing. The original release in 3D proved fuzzy and blurred, and the film was rereleased flat and in black and white in 1954. The title song was written by Stan Jones and sung in the movie by Ken Curtis.

HANNIE CAULDER Paramount/Curtwell Productions, 1971, Color, 85 min, VT. **Producer:** Patrick Curtis; **Director:** Burt Kennedy; **Screenplay:** Z. X. Jones (Kennedy) and David Haft; **Cinematographer:** Edward Scaife; **Editor:** Jim Connock; **Cast:** Raquel Welch, Robert Culp, Ernest Borgnine, Christopher Lee, Jack Elam, Strother Martin, Diana Dors.

Raquel Welch plays a woman who is widowed, raped, and left homeless after an attack by a trio of violent bad men: Ernest Borgnine, Jack Elam, and Strother Martin. In desperation, she hires a bounty hunter (Robert Culp) to teach her to shoot so she can seek vengeance. Much of the time Welch's body is on display. Over tight, shrink-to-fit pants, she wears only a loose fitting poncho, which is susceptible to prevailing breezes and her own movements. But she learns how to shoot and shoot well, with a special weapon designed by a master gunsmith named Bailey (Christopher Lee). This bizarre and mystical western leaves the audience somewhat puzzled, but it boasts good performances, especially by the trio of demented villains who display a bent for humor, and an excessive amount of gore and slime.

HARD HOMBRE Allied Pictures, 1931, B&W, 65 min, VT. **Producer:** M. H. Hoffman; **Director:** Otto Brower; **Screenplay:** Jack Natteford; **Cinematographer:** Harry Neumann; **Editor:** Mildred Johnston; **Cast:** Hoot Gibson, Lina Basquette, Mathilde Comont, G. Raymond Nye, Jessie Arnold, Jack Byron.

Peaceful Patton (Hoot Gibson) goes to work at the Martini ranch and is mistaken for the notorious outlaw Hard Hombre. This fanciful little oater is a rather typical early Gibson entry.

HARD MAN, THE Columbia, 1957, Color, 80 min. **Producer:** Helen Ainsworth; **Director:** George Sherman; **Screenplay:** Leo Katcher; **Music:** Mischa Bakaleinikoff; **Cinematographer:** Henry Freulich; **Editor:** William A. Lyon; **Cast:** Guy Madison, Valerie French, Lorne Greene, Barry Atwater, Robert Burton, Myron Healey.

A deputy marshal investigating the murder of a rancher who had refused to sell out to a cattle baron finds himself falling in love with the murdered man's wife. This interesting oater with a psychological twist has been long neglected.

HARLEM ON THE PRAIRIE (aka: BAD MAN OF HARLEM) Associated Features, 1938, B&W, 54 min. **Producer:** Jed Buell; **Director:** Sam Newfield; **Screenplay:** Fred Myton and Flourney E. Miller; **Music:** Lew Porter; **Cinematographer:** William Hyer; **Editor:** Robert Jahns; **Cast:** Herb Jeffries, F. E. Miller, Manton Moreland, Connie Harris, Maceo Sheffield, William Spencer Jr.

A black cowboy tries to prevent a crooked Los Angeles cop from fleecing club owners. This is an interesting curio among the three all-black features starring Herb Jeffries. It is always lots of fun to see the comedic talent of Manton Moreland who gained fame as Birmingham Brown in a number of Charlie Chan movies. (See also *BRONZE BUCKAROO, THE.*)

HARLEM RIDES THE RANGE Hollywood Productions, 1939, B&W, 56 min. **Producers:** Richard C. Kahn and Clark Ramsey; **Director:** Kahn; **Screenplay:** F. E. Miller and Spencer Williams; **Music:** Lew Porter; **Cinematographer:** Roland Price and Clark Ramsey; **Cast:** Herb Jeffries, Lucius Brooks, F. E. Miller, Artie Young, Clarence Brooks.

HARRY TRACY, DESPERADO IMC/Isram, 1982, Color, 107 min. **Producer:** Ronald I. Cohen; **Director:** William A. Graham; **Screenplay:** David Lee Henry and R. Lance Hill; **Music:** Mickey Erbe and Maribeth Solomon; **Cinematographer:** Allen Daviau; **Editor:** Ron Wisman; **Cast:** Bruce Dern, Helen Shaver, Michael C. Gwynne, Gordon Lightfoot, Jacques Hubert, Daphne Goldrick, Lynne Kolber.

Known as a friend of the poor and a gallant knight to the ladies, Harry Tracy finds himself becoming a legendary outlaw who is relentlessly hunted by the law. The picture was filmed in Canada and sports a nice performance from Bruce Dern.

HARMONY TRAIL (aka: WHITE STALLION) Meridian Pictures, 1944, B&W, 57 min. **Producer:** Walt Maddox; **Director:** Robert Emmett Tansey; **Screenplay:** Frank Simpson; **Cinematographer:** Edward A. Kull; **Editor:** Frederick Bain; **Cast:** Ken Maynard, Eddie Dean, Gene Alsace, Max Terhune, Glenn Strange, Ruth Roman, Charles King.

Agent Rocky Camron (Gene Alsace) is investigating a payroll robbery when he encounters old friends Ken Maynard, Eddie Dean, and Max Terhune (as themselves), who help him capture the gang that robbed the local bank. This low-budget but entertaining little oater was Ken Maynard's last B western. Eddie Dean sings "On the Banks of the Sunny San Juan," which he cowrote with Glenn Strange. In 1947 the picture was reissued by Astor as *White Stallion*.

HARVEY GIRLS, THE MGM, 1946, Color, 102 min, VT, DVD, LD. **Producer:** Arthur Freed; **Director:** George Sidney; **Screenplay:** Edmund Beloin; Nathaniel Curtis, Harry Crane, James O. Hanlon, Samson Raphaelson, and Kay Van Riper; **Music:** Harry Crane and Lennie Hayton (director); **Cinematographer:** George Folsey; **Editor:** Albert Akst; **Cast:** Judy Garland, John Hodiak, Ray Bolger, Angela Lansbury, Marjorie Main, Cyd Charisse, Chill Wills, Kenny Baker, Jack Lambert, Morris Ankrum, Ray Teal.

The old-style railroad train has always played a crucial role in western films, sometimes as a setting for colorful musical numbers. And as the West expanded, so did Fred Harvey's railroad stations with assorted restaurants and a bevy of proper young waitresses called Harvey girls, who even managed to have a civilizing effect on local town rowdies. This entertaining George Sidney musical features top performances by Judy Garland and legendary hoofer Ray Bolger; a manly performance by John Hodiak as the irascible Ned Trent, who wins the heart of alluring and innocent Susan Bradley (Garland); and a vintage supporting cast, including Angela Lansbury, Cyd Charisse, and Chill Wills. Some skillfully staged musical numbers include the Oscar-winning "On the Atchison, Topeka, and the Santa Fe" by Harry Warren and Johnny Mercer.

All the lighthearted ingredients are here: saloon brawls, romance, singing, dancing, and some decent action scenes. Based on the novel by Samuel Hopkins Adams and filmed in Monument Valley, the picture also garnered an Oscar nomination for Best Scoring of a Musical Picture (Lennie Hayton). Cyd Charisse's voice is dubbed by Marion Doenges.

HAUNTED GOLD MGM, 1932, B&W, 58 min, VT. **Producer:** Leon Schlesinger; **Director:** Mack V. Wright; **Screenplay:** Adele S. Buffington; **Music:** Leo F. Forbstein; **Cinematographer:** Nicholas Musuraca; **Editor:** William Clemens; **Cast:** John Wayne, Sheila Terry, Harry Woods, Erville Alderson, Otto Hoffman, Martha Mattox, Blue Washington.

John Wayne and Sheila Terry receive a letter requesting them to go to a ghost town with an abandoned mine. When they contend with a band of villains who are looking for the gold, they receive some unexpected help from a mysterious figure called "The Phantom," who wears a mask and black cape and supposedly haunts the mine. Wayne manages to defeat the outlaw and to "unmask" the Phantom.

After working briefly at Columbia, Wayne switched in 1932–33 to Warner Bros., where he appeared in a number of films, including his first western series. These films helped establish him as a young and likable sagebrush hero. With capable production values and good casts and directors, they found great audience appeal.

Haunted Gold was reissued to theaters as late as 1962. Like most series it was filmed in roughly a week. A remake of Ken Maynard's silent feature *Phantom City* (1928), it combined new footage with action shots from Maynard's 1920s entries.

HAUNTED MINE, THE Monogram, 1946, B&W, 51 min. **Producer:** Scott R. Dunlap; **Director:** Derwin Abrahams; **Screenplay:** Frank H. Young; **Cinematographer:** Harry Neumann; **Editor:** Fred Maguire; **Cast:** Johnny Mack Brown, Raymond Hatton, Linda Johnson, Ray Bennett, Riley Hill, Claire Whitney, John Merton.

HAUNTED RANCH Monogram, 1943, B&W, 57 min. **Producer:** George W. Weeks; **Director:** Robert Emmett Tansey; **Screenplay:** Elizabeth Beecher; **Cast:** John "Dusty" King, David Sharpe, Max Terhune, Julie Duncan, Glenn Strange, Charles King, Bud Osborne, Rex Lease, Fred "Snowflake" Toones, Bud Buster.

The Range Busters come to the aid of girl whose ranch is being besieged by a gang of crooks. Some spooky happenings add interest to this series entry. (See also *RANGE BUSTERS, THE.*)

HAUNTED TRAILS Monogram, 1949, B&W, 58 min. **Producer:** Eddie Davis; **Director:** Lambert Hillyer; **Screenplay:** Adele S. Buffington; **Cinematographer:** Harry Neumann; **Editor:** John C. Fuller; **Cast:** Whip Wilson, Andy Clyde, Reno Browne, William Ruhl, John Merton, Dennis Moore, Mary Gordon.

HAWK, THE See *RIDE HIM COWBOY.*

HAWK OF THE WILD RIVER Columbia, 1952, B&W, 53 min. **Producer:** Colbert Clark; **Director:** Fred F. Sears; **Screenplay:** Howard J. Green; **Music:** Mischa Bakaleinikoff; **Cinematographer:** Fayte M. Browne; **Editor:** Paul Borofsky; **Cast:** Charles Starrett, Smiley Burnette, Jock Mahoney, Clayton Moore, Eddie Parker, Jim Diehl, Lane Chandler, Syd Saylor.

HEADIN' EAST Columbia, 1937, B&W, 67 min. **Producer:** L. G. Leonard; **Director:** Ewing Scott; **Screenplay:** Paul Franklin, Joseph Hoffman, and Ethel La Blanche; **Cinematographer:** Allen O. Thompson; **Editor:** Robert O. Crandall; **Cast:** Buck Jones, Ruth Coleman, Shemp Howard, Donald Douglas, Elaine Arden.

When gangsters try to take advantage of lettuce growers, a rancher heads to the big city to help them. This out-of-the-ordinary Buck Jones venture should be of interest to his fans. (See also *LAW OF THE TEXAN.*)

HEADIN' FOR THE RIO GRANDE Grand National, 1936, B&W, 60 min. **Producer:** Edward Finney; **Director:** Robert N. Bradbury; **Screenplay:** Lindsley Parsons and Robert Emmett (Tansey); **Music:** Tex Ritter (songs) and Frank Sanucci; **Cinematographer:** Gus Peterson; **Editor:** Frederick Bain; **Cast:** Tex Ritter, Eleanor Stewart, Syd Saylor, Warner P. Richmond, Budd Buster, Bud Osborne.

HEADING WEST Columbia, 1946, B&W, 54 min. **Producer:** Colbert Clark; **Director:** Ray Nazarro; **Screenplay:** Ed Earl Rapp; **Cast:** Charles Starrett, Smiley Burnette, Doris Houck, Norman Willis, John Merton, Hal Taliaferro, Hank Penny and His Plantation Boys.

HEADIN' NORTH Tiffany, 1930, B&W, 60 min. **Producer:** Trem Carr; **Director:** J. P. McCarthy; **Screenplay:** McCarthy; **Music:** Irving Bibo; **Cinematographer:** Archie Stout; **Editor:** Fred Allen; **Cast:** Bob Steele, Barbara Luddy, Perry Murdock, Walter Shumray, Eddie Dunn, Fred Burns.

Jim Curtis (Bob Steele) and his pal Snicker (Perry Murdock) escape the law with the marshal in hot pursuit. To elude him they change clothes with two actors, forcing them to do vaudeville skits for cover.

HEARTLAND Filmhouse, 1979, Color, 96 min, VT, DVD. **Producers:** Beth Harris and Michael Hausman; **Directors:** Richard Pearce and Beth Ferris; **Music:** Charles Gross; **Cinematographer:** Fred Murphy; **Editor:** Bill Yahraus; **Cast:** Rip Torn, Conchata Ferrell, Barry Primus, Megan Folsom, Lilia Skala, Amy Wright.

In 1910 a woman and her daughter come to a small Wyoming town so she can work as a housekeeper for a Scottish rancher. Rip Torn is absolutely excellent as the stoic and rugged rancher who marries the woman for mutual convenience but learns to love her deeply. This outstanding depiction of the lonely rugged frontier is based on letters written by Eleanor Stewart. The letters, dated from April 1909 to November 13, 1910, were first printed in *The Atlantic Monthly*. It is a realistic and touching movie made with a high degree of integrity and decency, and it offers a well-rounded picture of frontier life and the role of frontier women.

HEART OF ARIZONA (aka: GUNSMOKE) Paramount, 1938, B&W, 68 min. **Producer:** Harry Sherman; **Director:** Leslie Selander; **Screenplay:** Norman Houston and Harrison Jacobs; **Cinematographer:** Russell Harlen; **Editor:** Sherman A. Rose; **Cast:** William Boyd,

George "Gabby" Hayes, Russell Hayden, John Elliott, Billy King, Lane Chandler.

HEART OF THE GOLDEN WEST Republic, 1942, B&W, 65 min, VT. **Producer:** Joseph Kane; **Director:** Kane; **Screenplay:** Earl Felton; **Music:** Mort Glickman, William Lava, and Paul Sawtell; **Editor:** Richard Van Enger; **Cast:** Roy Rogers, Smiley Burnette, Ruth Terry, George "Gabby" Hayes, Bob Nolan, Walter Catlett, Paul Harvey.

This extremely good entry in Republic's Roy Rogers series has Roy and his pals trying to convince a man to use his steamboat to transport his cattle by boat when ranchers refuse to pay unjust shipping charges to haul their cattle to market. It provides a neat blending of song and action and is a pleasant digression from Roy's more inflated musicals of a few years later. (See also *UNDER WESTERN STARS*.)

HEART OF THE NORTH Warner Bros., 1938, Color, 85 min. **Producers:** Bryan Foy, Hal B. Wallis, and Jack L. Warner; **Director:** Lewis Seiler; **Screenplay:** William Byron Mowery; **Cast:** Dick Foran, Gloria Dickson, Patric Knowles, Allen Jenkins, Janet Chapman, James Peterson, Gale Page.

A Mountie is dismissed from the service but redeems himself and proves his innocence when he saves a man from being lynched. This rugged Technicolor outdoors adventure is an A entry for Dick Foran and not considered a part of his B western series for Warner Bros.

HEART OF THE RIO GRANDE Republic, 1942, B&W, 68 min. **Producer:** Harry Grey; **Director:** William Morgan; **Screenplay:** Lillie Hayward and Winston Miller; **Cinematographer:** Harry Neumann; **Editor:** Lester Orlebeck; **Cast:** Gene Autry, Smiley Burnette, Fay McKenzie, Edith Fellows, Pierre Watkin, William Haade, Edmund Cobb, Milton Kibbee, Jean Porter.

HEART OF THE ROCKIES Republic, 1937, B&W, 67 min. **Producer:** Sol C. Siegel; **Director:** Joseph Kane; **Screenplay:** Oliver Drake and Jack Natteford; **Cinematographer:** Jack A. Marta; **Editor:** Lester Orlebeck; **Cast:** Robert Livingston, Ray Corrigan, Max Terhune, Lynne Roberts, Sammy McKim, J. P. McGowan, Yakima Canutt.

HEARTS OF THE WEST (aka: HOLLYWOOD COWBOY) MGM, 1975, Color, 102 min, VT. **Producer:** Tony Bill; **Director:** Howard Zieff; **Screenplay:** Rob Thompson; **Music:** Ken Lauber; **Cinematographer:** Mario Tosi; **Editor:** Edward Warschilka; **Cast:** Jeff Bridges, Andy Griffith, Donald Pleasence, Blythe Danner, Alan Arkin, Richard B. Shull, Herb Edelman, Marie Windsor.

Jeff Bridges stars as fledgling writer Lewis Tater, who enrolls in a correspondence school in Nevada in the early 1930s, only to discover that the school is run by a trio of crooks. After a series of misadventures pursuing the correspondence crooks through the desert, he ends up starring in cheaply made B westerns after being rescued by a quickie oater company.

This thoroughly enjoyable film was praised by critics but failed at the box office. There are great performances by Bridges; Andy Griffith; Blythe Danner as Bridges's curvaceous love interest; and especially Alan Arkin, who received the New York Film Critics Circle Award as Best Supporting Actor for his role as Kessler, the beleaguered director. *The Hollywood Reporter* called the film "an entertainment which tickles the funnybone without insulting the mind." Similarly the *New York Daily News* enjoyed Bridges's work, praising his "naïve comic style and unaffected warmth. . . ."

HEAVEN ONLY KNOWS United Artists, 1947, B&W, 1947. **Producer:** Seymour Nebenzal; **Director:** Albert Rogell; **Screenplay:** Art Arthur, Ernest Haycox, and Rowland Leigh; **Music:** Heinz Roemheld; **Cinematographer:** Karl Struss; **Editor:** Edward Mann; **Cast:** Robert Cummings, Ray Bennett, Brian Donlevy, Stuart Erwin, Marjorie Reynolds, Bill Goodwin, Edgar Kennedy, John Litel.

An angel named Mike visits earth to rectify a heavenly bookkeeping error. He had permitted a soulless man to run loose because his destiny had not been entered properly in the heavenly book. He finds him in the person of a murderous Montana saloon owner and gambler (Brian Donlevy). This amusing comedy/fantasy is pure delight, with Cummings refreshingly naïve as the angel set loose in a tough western town. His mission is to bring the killer and the lovely schoolmarm together because according to the books they should have been married for two years. The film's straightforward manner lends a lightness to what otherwise might have been a sugar-sweet or even a heavily melodramatic film. Viewers who have seen this oft-forgotten film have been as a rule totally impressed.

HEAVEN'S GATE United Artists, 1980, Color, 210 min, VT, DVD. **Producer:** Joanne Carelli; **Director:** Michael Cimino; **Screenplay:** Cimino; **Music:** David Mansfield; **Cinematographer:** Vilmos Zsigmond; **Editors:** Lisa Fruchtman, Gerald Greenberg, William Reynolds, and Tom Rolf; **Cast:** Kris Kristofferson, Christopher Walken, John Hurt, Sam Waterston, Brad Dourif, Isabelle Huppert, Joseph Cotten, Jeff Bridges.

Based on the Johnson County wars which took place in the 1890s in Wyoming, the film deals with a group of cattlemen led by Sam Waterston who are convinced that their herds are being looted by immigrant settlers. With the state's approval, the operators of the large cattle ranches draw up a hit list of 125 poor immigrants in Johnson County whom they deem responsible for the rustling. The immigrants are eastern Europeans who arrived in Wyoming clinging to train cars. In *Heaven's Gate* the Johnson County wars become the symbol of class struggle in America, the ethos being that the rich kill the poor.

Kris Kristofferson is James Averill, a wealthy Bostonian who somehow becomes marshal of Johnson County 20 years after graduating from Harvard. In the West he meets a classmate, a member of the Stock Growers Association who tells him, "It's getting dangerous to be poor in this country."

"Always was," Kristofferson replies as he eventually turns against his class.

The Johnson County wars provided the background for Owen Wister's landmark 1902 novel *The Virginian.* To Wister, a wealthy easterner, the big cattlemen were in the right and the small ranchers were thieves. To director Michael Cimino they were revolutionary heroes.

Yet despite an energetic, rousing opening, beautifully photographed—as was the whole film—by Vilmos Zsigmond, this $35 million epic was roundly criticized as an overlong and disjointed saga, so confusing and ponderous that it fails to work at a number of levels. In fact, the initial reviews were so bad that the film was withdrawn and rereleased five months later with 70 minutes cut from the original 210. Considered a disaster once more, it was again withdrawn.

With its floundering mix of historical accuracy and ridiculous error as well as a nebulous and incoherent storyline, the film was an enormous disappointment for director Michael Cimino, who had won an Academy Award in 1988 for helming *The Deer Hunter* and had spent two years on *Heaven's Gate.* Moreover, many now felt that with the film's enormous failings the western as a genre was finished for good. *Heaven's Gate* proved such a financial disaster that it led to the sale of United Artists to MGM. Among its few public accolades are a 1981 Oscar nomination for Best Art Direction (Tambi Larson). *Variety* sums up the collective reviews by stating that "Cimino's attempts to draw a portrait of the plight of the immigrants in the West in that period are so impersonal that none of the victims ever get beyond patented stereotypes."

HEAVEN WITH A GUN   MGM, 1969, Color, 97 min. **Producers:** Frank King and Martin King; **Director:** Lee H. Katzin; **Screenplay:** Richard Carr; **Music:** Johnny Mandel; **Cinematographer:** Fred J. Koenekamp; **Editor:** Dann Cahn; **Cast:** Glenn Ford, Carolyn Jones, Barbara Hershey, John Anderson, David Carradine, J. D. Cannon, Noah Beery Jr., Harry Townes.

A conflict between cattle ranchers and sheep breeders escalates in the small western town of Vinagaroon. When a stranger (Glenn Ford) arrives in town, the ranchers suspect that he is a gunman hired by sheep breeders. Actually he is a peace-loving man attempting to escape his violent past. As the conflict grows he is forced to return to the world of violence that he once knew. Ford offers a sturdy performance in what increasingly became a familiar role for him—a man seeking inner peace who cannot quite escape his violent past. The team of Johnny Mandel (music) and Paul Francis (lyrics) wrote the title song "Heaven with a Gun."

HEIR TO TROUBLE   Columbia, 1935, B&W, 59 min. **Producer:** Larry Darmour; **Director:** Spencer Gordon Bennet; **Screenplay:** Nate Gatzert and Ken Maynard; **Cinematographer:** Herbert Kirkpatrick; **Editor:** Dwight Caldwell; **Cast:** Ken Maynard, Joan Perry, Harry Woods, Martin Faust, Harry Bowen.

When a cowboy adopts the young son of a late saddle pal, he encounters trouble from a rival who wants to steal both his girl and his mining property.

HELDORADO   Republic, 1946, B&W, 70 min. **Producer:** Edward J. White (associate); **Director:** William Witney; **Screenplay:** Gerald Geraghy and Julian Zimet; **Music:** R. Dale Butts and Bob Nolan (songs); **Cinematographer:** William Bradford; **Editor:** Lester Orlebeck; **Cast:** Roy Rogers, Dale Evans, George "Gabby" Hayes, Paul Harvey, Brad Dexter, Paul Harvey, Rex Lease, Bob Nolan and The Sons of the Pioneers, Clayton Moore, Steve Darrell, John Bagni.

HELL BENT FOR LEATHER   Universal, 1960, Color, 82 min. **Producer:** Gordon Kay; **Director:** George Sherman; **Screenplay:** Christopher Knopf; **Music:** Irving Gertz and William Lava; **Cinematographer:** Clifford Stine; **Editor:** Milton Carruth; **Cast:** Audie Murphy, Felicia Farr, Stephen McNally, Robert Middleton, Allan Lane, Bob Steele, John Qualen, Eddie Little Sky.

Audie Murphy is a horse trader who is falsely accused of murder. Corrupt sheriff Stephen McNally knows he is innocent but still leads a posse against him to collect a reward.

HELL BENT KID   See *FROM HELL TO TEXAS.*

HELL CANYON OUTLAWS (aka: THE TALL TROUBLE)   Republic, 1957, B&W, 72 min. **Producer:** T. Frank Woods; **Director:** Paul Landres; **Screenplay:** Max Glanbard and Allan Kaufman; **Music:** Irving Gertz; **Cinematographer:** Floyd Crosby; **Editor:** Elmo Williams; **Cast:** Dale Robertson, Brian Keith, Rosanna Rory, Dick Kalman, Don Megowan, Mike Lane, Buddy Baer.

A sheriff is forced to take on an outlaw gang that has taken over a small town. This action-packed Dale Robertson venture was produced during the last days of Republic Studios.

HELLER IN PINK TIGHTS   Paramount, 1960, Color, 100 min, VT. **Producers:** Marcello Girosi and Carlo Ponti; **Director:** George Cukor; **Screenplay:** Walter Bernstein and Dudly Nichols; **Music:** Daniele Amfitheatrof; **Cinematographer:** Harold Lisptein; **Editor:** Howard Smith; **Cast:** Sophia Loren, Anthony Quinn, Margaret O'Brien, Steve Forrest, Eileen Heckart, Ramon Novarro, Edmond Lowe.

Based on Louis L'Amour's novel *Heller with a Gun,* the film's story concerns a theatrical troupe traveling throughout the

Old West with a posse in hot pursuit and bill collectors and Indians not far behind. George Cukor's curious casting has Sophia Loren donning a blond wig as she plays an actress with a constant bent for getting into difficult situations. Silent screen great Ramon Navarro as a sinister banker is worth the price of admission, while child star Margaret O'Brien has a chance to show her mettle as an adult actress. This tongue-in-cheek, turn-of-the-century spoof has its share of gleeful touches, and although far from a masterpiece it still manages to entertain.

HELLFIRE Republic, 1949, Color, 90 min, VT. **Producer:** William J. O'Sullivan; **Director:** R. G. Springsteen; **Screenplay:** Dorrell McGowan and Stuart E. McGowan; **Music:** R. Dale Butts; **Cinematographer:** Jack A. Marta; **Editor:** Terry Martinelli; **Cast:** William Elliott, Marie Windsor, Forrest Tucker, Jim Davis, H. B. Warner, Paul Fix, Grant Withers, Harry Woods, Emery Parnell, Denver Pyle.

Bill Elliott play a cardsharp whose life is saved when a preacher takes a bullet meant for him. He promises to complete the dying preacher's mission and collect money to build a church, but he must do it only in a way compatible with the teachings of the Bible. Elliott delivers one of his best performances in this exceptional B western from Republic, while Marie Windsor is equally superb as Doll Brown, the mysterious woman outlaw whom Elliott tries to reform.

HELL FIRE AUSTIN Tiffany, 1932, B&W, 90 min. **Producer:** Phil Goldstone; **Director:** Forrest Sheldon; **Screenplay:** Betty Burbridge; **Cinematographer:** Ted D. McCord and Joe Novak; **Cast:** Ken Maynard, Ivy Merton, Nat Pendleton, Alan Roscoe, Jack Perrin, Lafe McKee.

When two men return from the trenches of World War I and receive a poor welcome in their Texas town, they eventually wind up in jail. They are paroled when one of them agrees to ride a horse in a cross-country race. This well-written early Ken Maynard talkie packs a solid punch.

HELLGATE Lippert, 1952, B&W, 87 min. **Producer:** John C. Champion; **Director:** Charles Marquis Warren; **Screenplay:** Warren; **Music:** Paul Dunlap; **Cinematographer:** Ernest Miller; **Editor:** Elmo Williams; **Cast:** Sterling Hayden, Joan Leslie, Ward Bond, James Arness, Peter Coe, John Pickard, Robert J. Wilke.

Sterling Hayden plays a man wrongly accused of fighting with a covert guerrilla group during the Civil War. He is sent to New Mexico's notorious Hellgate Prison, where the warden (Ward Bond) nurses a grudge against the guerrillas because his family was killed in one of their raids. Bond treats Hayden with excessive sadistic cruelty in an effort to force an escape attempt and provide an excuse to legitimately kill him.

When Hayden tries to launch his escape plan, he is recaptured and sentenced to solitary confinement. He redeems himself by helping to halt the spread of a plague epidemic that engulfs the prison, and eventually he receives a

full pardon for his heroism. The movie is a refashioning of the story of Dr. Samuel Mudd, which was first filmed by 20th Century Fox in 1936 as *The Prisoner of Shark Island.*

HELLO TROUBLE Columbia, 1932, B&W, 67 min. **Director:** Lambert Hillyer; **Screenplay:** Hillyer; **Cinematographer:** Benjamin H. Kline; **Editor:** Gene Milford; **Cast:** Buck Jones, Lina Basquette, Russell Simpson, Otto Hoffman, Wallace MacDonald, Alan Roscoe, Ward Bond, Walter Brennan.

A Texas Ranger on the trail of a trio of cattle rustlers quits the service when he kills one of the trio, then finds out that the fellow he killed had been one of his friends.

HELL'S HEROES Universal, 1930, B&W, 68 min. **Producer:** Carl Laemmle Jr.; **Director:** William Wyler; **Screenplay:** C. Gardner Sullivan and Tom Reed; **Music:** David Brockman; **Cinematographer:** George Robinson; **Editor:** Harry Marker; **Cast:** Charles Bickford, Raymond Hatton, Fred Kohler, Fritz Ridgeway, Joe De La Cruz.

After robbing a bank, the three surviving outlaws escape into the desert, where they lose their horses in a storm. As they make their way through the sweltering and windswept desert with only a limited supply of water, they stumble upon a dying woman who is about to give birth. They decide to honor their promise to the baby's mother to take the child to his father, unaware that one of the men they killed during the robbery was that same father.

This superb but virtually forgotten early western was the first sound version of Peter B. Kyne's 1913 novel *The Three Godfathers.* Included in the soundtrack is Stephen Foster's "Oh Susanna," played on a harmonica by Raymond Hatton; and the Christmas carol favorite "Silent Night," sung by a choir. *Hell's Heroes* was director William Wyler's first western and his first talking picture. In 1936, the story was remade again as THE THREE GODFATHERS by Richard Boleslawski and by John Ford in 1948 as a tribute to Harry Carey. Years earlier, in 1916, Ford made a silent version of the story entitled *MARKED MEN.*

Shot on location in the Mojave Desert and the Panamint Valley and closely following Tyne's book, the film was enormously successful both with critics and audiences. *Variety* praised it as "gripping, real, and convincingly out of the ordinary."

HELL'S HINGES Triangle, 1916, B&W, 55 min. **Producer:** Thomas Ince; **Directors:** William S. Hart and Charles Swickhard; **Screenplay:** C. Gardner Sullivan; **Cinematographer:** Joseph H. August; **Cast:** William S. Hart, Clara Williams, Jack Standing, Louise Glaum, Alfred Hollingsworth.

A crooked gambler hires a bad man to stop the work of the new town minister, but the gunman (William S. Hart) falls for the clergyman's sister and tries to help his cause. This top-notch silent with Hart as the reformed bad man combines action, violence, and a faithful recreation of the Old West. The bad man's conversion to the side of the angels is best reflected by a typical G. Gardner Sullivan title card for the film: "I reckon God ain't wantin' me much, ma'am, but when I look at you, I feel I've been ridin' the wrong trail."

William S. Hart was the original screen cowboy. Hart's "good bad man" persona was fully developed for the screen by writers like C. Gardner Sullivan, his favorite scribe. In 1914 he signed a contract with Thomas Ince and joined Ince's Triangle Film Company. Along with his last film *TUMBLEWEEDS* (1925), *Hell's Hinges* is considered a true masterpiece, a beautifully made picture that contains some of the silent cinema's most evocative and best titles. It also contains many adept individual touches, such as Hart's character Bill Tracey reading the Bible for the first time while he smokes and keeps his whiskey handy. Hart gave the screen its first classic westerns, and like nearly all of his westerns this film contains a good deal of footage of the star with his horse Fritz. The movie itself was admitted into the National Film Registry in 1994.

William S. Hart made more than 50 westerns. While *THE ARYAN* (1916) and *Hell's Hinges* represent outstanding examples of his Triangle work, he also scored big with films like *THE BARGAIN* (1914), and *On the Night Stage* (1915), both for Paramount. Other outstanding films include *The Disciple*

(1915), a typical Hart morality tale; *The Narrow Trail* (1917), which contains some of his best riding shots; *The Aryan*, which was his own personal favorite; *BLUE BLAZES RAWDEN* (1918); *Branding Broadway* (1918), a lighthearted western set in New York in which he lassoes the villain in Central Park, something he tried in 1915 in *BETWEEN MEN*; *THE TOLL GATE* (1920); and *WILD BILL HICKOK* (1923), a pleasant and accurate biography of the famed lawman, despite Hart's lack of physical likeness.

HELL'S OUTPOST Republic, 1954, B&W, 89 min. **Producer:** Joseph Kane; **Director:** Kane; **Screenplay:** Kenneth Gamet; **Music:** R. Dale Butts; **Cinematographer:** Jack Marta; **Editor:** Richard L. Van Enger; **Cast:** Rod Cameron, Joan Leslie, Chill Wills, John Russell, Oliver Blake, Ben Cooper.

Based on Luke Short's novel *Silver Rock*, this film tells the story of a war hero (Rod Cameron) who returns home determined to work his mining claim but instead finds himself having to battle a crooked banker. The film boasts sturdy performances by Cameron as the hero and Russell as a very nasty bad man.

HELL TOWN See *BORN TO THE WEST*.

HEMP BROWN See *SAGA OF HEMP BROWN*.

HENRY GOES TO ARIZONA (aka: SPATS TO SPURS) MGM, 1940, B&W, 67 min. **Director:** Edwin L. Marin; **Screenplay:** Milton Merlin; **Music:** David Snell; **Cinematographer:** Sidney Wagner and Lester White; **Editor:** Conrad Nervig; **Cast:** Frank Morgan, Virginia Weidler, Guy Kibbee, Slim Summerville, Douglas Fowley.

A destitute New York actor named Henry inherits his murdered brother's ranch just outside Tonto City, Arizona, but quickly discovers there is a nefarious outlaw gang eager to do him in as well. This lighthearted western comedy benefits from its cast of appealing character actors.

HE RIDES TALL Universal, 1964, B&W, 84 min. **Producer:** Gordon Kaye; **Director:** R. G. Springsteen; **Screenplay:** Charles W. Irwin and Robert Creighton Williams; **Music:** Irving Gertz; **Cinematographer:** Ellis W. Carter; **Cast:** Tony Young, Dan Duryea, Jo Morrow, R. G. Armstrong, Madlyn Rhue, Bob Steele.

On his wedding night a marshal must tell his foster father that he was forced to gun down his son. This realistic dramatic western has a fine performance by Duryea as the villain.

HERITAGE OF THE DESERT (aka: WHEN THE WEST WAS YOUNG) Paramount, 1932, B&W, 60 min. **Producer:** Harold Hurley; **Director:** Henry Hathaway; **Screenplay:** Frank Partos and Harold Shumate; **Cinematographer:** Archie Stout; **Cast:** Randolph Scott,

William S. Hart in Hell's Hinges (TRIANGLE/ AUTHOR'S COLLECTION)

Sally Blane, David Landau, J. Farrell MacDonald, Gordon Wescott, Guinn "Big Boy" Williams, Charles Sevens, Jack Pennick.

Based on a story by Zane Grey, the plot concerns a young man raised by a desert rancher who tries to stop a claim jumper from taking his property. Paramount first filmed this picture as a silent feature in 1924 with a cast that included Bebe Daniels, Lloyd Hughes, Ernest Torrence, and Noah Beery. The reissue title of the film is *When the West Was Young*.

HERITAGE OF THE DESERT Paramount, 1939, B&W, 73 min. **Producer:** Harry Sherman; **Director:** Leslie Selander; **Screenplay:** Norman Houston; **Music:** Victor Young; **Cinematographer:** Russell Harlen; **Editor:** Sherman A. Rose; **Cast:** Donald Woods, Evelyn Venable, Russell Hayden, Robert Barrat, Sidney Toler, C. Henry Gordon, Willard Robertson, Paul Fix, Paul Guilfoyle, Rod Cameron.

Easterner John Abbott heads west to investigate trouble on the ranch he owns. The culprit, however, is his own manager, who arranges for Abbott to be shot and then leaves him for dead. When Abbott recovers he starts working with guns in anticipation of a final showdown. The third and final film adaptation of this Zane Grey work is a genuine winner.

HEROES OF THE ALAMO Sunset/Columbia, 1937, B&W, 75 min. **Producer:** Anthony J. Xydias; **Director:** Harry L. Fraser; **Screenplay:** Roby Wentz; **Cinematographer:** Robert E. Cline; **Editor:** Arthur A. Brooks; **Cast:** Bruce Warren, Ruth Findlay, Lane Chandler, Rex Lease.

Stephen Austin fights for the independence of Texas from Mexico and Texans battle General Santa Anna at the Alamo in this decent independent film. Originally issued by Sunset Pictures in 1937, it was picked up by Columbia the following year.

HEROES OF THE SADDLE Republic, 1940, B&W, 56 min. **Producer:** Harry Grey; **Director:** William Witney; **Screenplay:** Jack Natteford; **Music:** Cy Feuer and Karl Hajos; **Cinematographer:** William Nobles; **Editor:** Lester Orlebeck; **Cast:** Robert Livingston, Raymond Hatton, Duncan Renaldo, Loretta Weaver, Patsy Lee Parsons.

HEROES OF THE WEST Universal, 1932, B&W, 12 chapters. **Producer:** Henry MacRae; **Director:** Ray Taylor; **Screenplay:** Basil Dickey, Ella O'Neill, George Plympton, and Joe Roach; **Cast:** Noah Beery Jr., Julie Bishop, Onslow Stevens, William Desmond, Martha Mattox, Philo McCullough, Edmund Cobb, Francis Ford.

Efforts to build a transcontinental railroad are resisted by crooks and hostile Indians as a contractor moves to Wyoming with his daughter and son to fulfill his contract obligations. The cast in this Universal serial is more interesting than the plot.

HERO OF PINE RIDGE See *YODELIN' KID FROM PINE RIDGE*.

HE WORE A STAR See *STAR PACKER, THE*.

HIDDEN DANGER Monogram, 1948, B&W, 55 min. **Producer:** Barney A. Sarecky; **Director:** Ray Taylor; **Screenplay:** J. Benton Cheney and Eliot Gibbons; **Cinematographer:** Harry Neumann; **Editor:** John Fuller; **Cast:** Johnny Mack Brown, Raymond Hatton, Steve Clark, Kenne Duncan, Bill Hale, Myron Healey, Carol Henry, Christine Larson.

HIDDEN GOLD (aka: OH, PROMISE ME) Universal, 1932, B&W, 55 min. **Producer:** Karl Laemmle Jr.; **Director:** Arthur Rosson; **Screenplay:** James Mulhauser and Jack Natteford; **Music:** Sam Perry and Heinz Roemheld; **Cinematographer:** Daniel B. Clark; **Cast:** Tom Mix, Judith Barrie, Raymond Hatton, Eddie Gribbon, Donald Kirke.

A cowboy goes to jail to get in good with the outlaw gang that has hidden the loot from a robbery. (See also *FOURTH HORSEMAN, THE*.)

HIDDEN GOLD Paramount, 1940, B&W, 60 min, VT. **Producer:** Harry Sherman; **Director:** Leslie Selander; **Screenplay:** Gerald Geraghty and Jack Merserveau; **Cinematographer:** Russell Harlan; **Editors:** Lewis J. Rachmil and Caroll Lewis; **Cast:** William Boyd, Russell Hayden, Minor Watson, Ruth Rogers, Britt Wood.

HIDDEN GUNS Republic, 1956, B&W, 90 min. **Producers:** Albert G. Gannaway and Samuel Roeca; **Director:** Gannaway; **Screenplay:** Gannaway; **Music:** Ramey Idress; **Cinematographer:** Clark Ramsey; **Editor:** Leo Barsha; **Cast:** Bruce Bennett, Richard Arlen, John Carradine, Faron Young, Lloyd Corrigan, Angie Dickinson, Guinn "Big Boy" Williams.

A sheriff and his deputized son try to curtail the outrages of an outlaw who has the town so intimidated that no one will speak out against him. When the sheriff heads to a nearby town to find an available witness, the outlaw hires a gunman to deal with the sheriff and his witness. Good performances by a trio of veteran actors—Richard Arlen as the sheriff, Bruce Bennett as the outlaw, and John Carradine as the hired gun—help make this a suspenseful little oater.

HIDDEN VALLEY Monogram, 1932, B&W, 60 min. **Producer:** Trem Carr; **Director:** Robert N. Bradbury;

Cinematographer: Archie Stout; **Editor:** Carl Pierson; **Cast:** Bob Steele, Gertrude Messinger, Francis McDonald, Ray Hallor, George "Gabby" Hayes.

HIDDEN VALLEY OUTLAWS Republic, 1944, B&W. **Producer:** Louis Gray; **Director:** Howard Bretherton; **Screenplay:** John K. Butler; **Cast:** William "Wild Bill" Elliott, George "Gabby" Hayes, Anne Jeffreys, Roy Barcroft, Kenne Duncan, Charles Miller, Yakima Canutt.

An outlaw gang terrorizes a small southwestern town, but a marshal ("Wild Bill" Elliott) comes to its rescue.

HIGH LONESOME Eagle Lion, 1950, Color, 81 min. **Producer:** Alan Le May; **Director:** Le May; **Screenplay:** Le May; **Music:** Rudy Schraeger; **Cinematographer:** W. Howard Greene; **Editor:** Jack Ogilvie; **Cast:** John Drew Barrymore, Chill Wills, John Archer, Lois Butler, Kristine Miller, Jack Elam.

John Barrymore Jr. is a moody brooding youth who becomes involved with two escaped convicts about to commit a murder. Chill Wills wrote the song "Twenty Miles from Carson."

HIGH NOON United Artists, 1952, B&W, 84 min, VT, DVD. **Producer:** Stanley Kramer; **Director:** Fred Zinnemann; **Screenplay:** Carl Foreman; **Music:** Dimitri Tiomkin; **Cinematographer:** Floyd Crosby; **Editor:** Elmo Williams; **Cast:** Gary Cooper, Grace Kelly, Thomas Mitchell, Lloyd Bridges, Katy Jurado, Otto Kruger, Lon Chaney Jr., Harry Morgan, Ian MacDonald, Lee Van Cleef, Sheb Wooley.

On an otherwise quiet morning in the town of Hadleyville, ex-marshal Will Kane has just married Amy, a pretty young Quaker girl. They are just about to leave town when word is received that Frank Miller, whom Kane helped send to prison five years earlier, has been pardoned and is heading back to Hadleyville to settle the score with the former marshal. Will and Amy leave town with honeymoon thoughts and hopes of opening a general store in a nearby community. But Kane's strong sense of honor and duty compels him to turn back and face Miller, much to Amy's dismay.

Frank Miller is scheduled to arrive on the noon train. Waiting at the station are three of the old gang: James Pierce, Jack Colby, and Ben Miller, Frank's brother. In the meantime, the middle-aged Kane sets out to get support from the townspeople, but one by one they turn their backs on him. Even a plea to the congregation during a morning service fails. Left alone, Will Kane is forced to face the four men alone as the deserted streets of Hadleyville become his personal battlefield. When the final shot is mounted and the four outlaws lie dead on the street, the pious citizens of Hadleyville rush out to congratulate their victorious marshal. In disdain, Kane removes his badge and throws it on the ground, and without looking back or saying a word, Kane and Amy leave Hadleyville for good.

High Noon made a two-time Oscar winner out of Gary Cooper. While the picture was not without some slight

Gary Cooper won a second Oscar as Will Kane in High Noon. *The title song sung by Tex Ritter in the film won an Oscar for composer Dimitri Tiomkin and lyricist Ned Washington. The movie was also nominated for Best Picture, Best Director, and Best Screenplay.* (UNITED ARTISTS/AUTHOR'S COLLECTION)

faults, Cooper's performance was flawless. As so often happens with a film production, the filmmaker's first choice for a leading man proved unavailable, and his second choice became a far more perfect pick. Originally Gregory Peck, who had recently replaced Tyrone Power as 20th Century Fox's top leading man, was offered the pivotal role of Will Kane. He rejected the offer, mainly because he felt it was too much like his role in *THE GUNFIGHTER* two years earlier. Cooper agreed to accept the role on the condition that he receive a percentage of the profits, a salary tradition pioneered by Cooper's good friend Jimmy Stewart.

There has been a great deal of literature on the movie itself, including the fact that few involved ever thought it would become a genre classic. The chosen footage (85 minutes) was considered too episodic, but then Dimitri Tiomkin and Ned Washington composed the title song. Tex Ritter sang it at different points in the soundtrack, lending a needed cohesion to the film and enshrining it in box-office history. Because the movie's scenario was written by Carl Foreman, a victim of the prevailing McCarthy communist hearings, many viewers saw this chronicle as a parallel to the hearings themselves; they were intrigued by a picture whose hero was human enough to be flawed. Director Fred Zinnemann allowed cinematographer Floyd Cooper to use extreme close-ups of Cooper, registering every crease and wrinkle of the star's famous face in moments of contemplation, anxiety, and final resolution.

While purists have at times found fault in this landmark western, some even criticizing the impact of the title song, the response to *High Noon* was tremendous. No longer was the cowboy hero rendered in stereotype dimensions. Instead he became the aging lawman fighting for his principles against all odds. *Life* thought that "although *High Noon* has some defects, few recent Westerns have gotten so much tension and excitement into the classic struggle between good and evil." In *The New Yorker*, John McCarton commented, "Gary Cooper, who stalked desperadoes down many a deserted cowtown street, never took a more effective stroll than he does in *High Noon*."

Based on the story "Tin Star" by John W. Cunningham, the film captured four Academy Awards: Best Actor (Cooper), Song (Tiomkin and Washington), Scoring (Tiomkin), and Editing (Elmo Williams and Harry Gerstad). The film garnered three more Oscar nominations, including Best Picture, Screenplay, and Director. *High Noon* also won the prestigious New York Film Critics Award as Best Picture for 1952. While the picture was in production, screenwriter Carl Foreman was subpoenaed by the House Un-American Activities Committee and pleaded the Fifth Amendment. By the time the film was winning the New York Film Critics Award, Foreman had moved to England.

The title song also took on a life all its own. Introduced in the film by Tex Ritter and recorded by Ritter on the Capital label, it was Frankie Laine's recording for Columbia that became a huge best-seller. Then-president Dwight Eisenhower admitted to whistling the song for hours on end.

The film also became the first western to be nominated as Best Picture since William Wellman's THE OX BOW INCIDENT in 1943. It was the ninth top-grossing picture for 1952. The American Film Institute named *High Noon* number 33 in its list of the century's top 100 movies (the highest listing for a western). It was also named the second best western film of the 20th century (behind SHANE, 1953) by the Western Writers of America. A multihonored film, it has been selected for the National Film Registry.

HIGH PLAINS DRIFTER   Universal, 1972, Color, 105 min, VT, DVD. **Producer:** Robert Daley; **Director:** Clint Eastwood; **Screenplay:** Ernest Tidyman; **Music:** Dee Barton: **Cinematographer:** Bruce Surtees; **Editor:** Ferris Webster; **Cast:** Clint Eastwood, Verna Bloom, Marianna Hill, Mitch Ryan, Jack Ging.

When a mysterious stranger arrives in the town of Lago in the 1870s, there is reason for suspicion and concern. Upon his arrival he is harassed and goaded into a gunfight by three bullies. Before long the three lie dead, but the stranger shows not an ounce of emotional feeling, and it becomes clear that he is in Lago for revenge. In a recurring dream scene we see a hapless man (the former sheriff) being whipped to death by three shrouded men, while a cowardly group of citizens stands by helplessly. The stranger never says who he is, and the audience is left to wonder: Is he the sheriff returned from death? Is he a relative of the beaten sheriff out to settle a score? Is the whole scenario a surrealistic ploy? He renames the town "Hell," paints the whole town red, and ultimately burns the place to the ground.

High Plains Drifter was the first western directed by Clint Eastwood. To emphasize the individuality of his effort, a publicity still was taken of a graveyard and two tombstones; on one is written "S. Leone," on the other "Don Siegel." Eastwood was first attracted to the project when he read a nine-page idea for a screenplay at Universal. Believing that it would make a memorable and offbeat film, he enlisted the help of Ernest Tidyman, who had recently won an Oscar for writing the screenplay for *The French Connection* (1971). Universal tried to shoot the film on the studio lot. Eastwood, however, was determined to build an entire western town in the desert near Lake Mono in the California Sierras. It took a large crew almost 18 days to construct the town, which would be burned down during the film's climax.

Critical reviews were mixed. The *Los Angeles Times* called it "a stylized, allegorical Western of much chilling paranoid atmosphere and considerable sardonic humor. . . ." The *London Observer* commented that the film "shows Clint Eastwood to be a genuinely talented filmmaker . . . Not at all a likable film, but an impressive one." Rex Reed was not nearly as affirming in his *New York Daily News* review, calling *High Plains Drifter* "one of the year's most hysterical comedies. The acting is a riot, the direction (by Eastwood) is as interesting (and as mobile) as the rear end of Eastwood's horse. I've seen better westerns at the Pepsi Cola Saloon at Disneyland."

Either way the film was an enormous success, taking in more than $7 million in distributors' domestic rentals and solidifying Eastwood's role as one of the major influences in the western genre in the 1970s, as he had been in the 1960s.

HIGH VENTURE   See *PASSAGE WEST*.

HIGH VERMILION   See *SILVER CITY*.

HIGH, WIDE, AND HANDSOME   Paramount, 1937, B&W, 110 min. **Producer:** Arthur Hornblow Jr.; **Director:** Rouben Mamoulian; **Screenplay:** Oscar Hammerstein and George O'Neil; **Music:** Hammerstein and Jerome Kern; **Cinematographers:** Victor Milner and Theodore Sparkuhl; **Editor:** Archie Marshek; **Cast:** Irene Dunne, Randolph Scott, Dorothy Lamour, Elizabeth Patterson, Charles Bickford, Akim Tamiroff, Raymond Walburn.

Randolph Scott is a tough oil prospector who strikes it rich in the booming town of Titusville, Pennsylvania. In an attempt to push Scott off his land, an evil cattle baron refuses to ship oil to his refinery. Scott in turn organizes the other prospectors to build a pipeline that will carry the oil to the refinery without the help of the railroad. He finds unlikely help in Dorothy Lamour, a sideshow performer who drafts several circus elephants to aid in the construction of the pipeline. This $1.9 million picture boasts an energetic cast and six songs by the team of Jerome Kern and Oscar Hammerstein, including the ever-popular "The Folks who Live on the Hill," sung by Irene Dunne.

HILLS OF OKLAHOMA Republic, 1950, B&W, 67 min. **Producer:** Franklin Aldreon; **Director:** R. G. Springsteen; **Screenplay:** Victor Arthur and Olive Cooper; **Music:** Stanley Wilson; **Cinematographer:** Ellis W. Carter; **Editor:** Arthur Roberts; **Cast:** Rex Allen, Elizabeth Fraser, Elizabeth Risdon, Robert Karnes, Fuzzy Knight, Roscoe Ates.

HILLS OF OLD WYOMING Paramount, 1937, B&W, 78 min, VT. **Producer:** Harry Sherman; **Director:** Nate Watt; **Screenplay:** Maurice Geraghty; **Music:** Ralph Rainger and Leo Robin; **Cinematographer:** Archie Stout; **Editor:** Robert Warwick; **Cast:** William Boyd, George "Gabby" Hayes, Morris Ankrum, Russell Hayden, Gail Sheridan, John Beach, George Chesebro.

HILLS OF THE BRAVE See *PALOMINO, THE.*

HILLS OF UTAH, THE Columbia, 1951, B&W, 70 min. **Producer:** Armond Schaefer; **Director:** John English; **Screenplay:** Gerald Geraghty and Les Savage Jr.; **Cinematographer:** William Bradford; **Editor:** James Sweeney; **Cast:** Gene Autry, Pat Buttram, Elaine Riley, Donna Martell, Onslow Stevens, Denver Pyle.

Gene intercedes in a long-standing battle between cattle ranchers and copper miners in this enjoyable oater with more of an emphasis on drama than on song.

HIRED GUN, THE MGM, 1957, B&W, 63 min. **Producers:** Rory Calhoun and Victor M. Orsatti; **Director:** Ray Nazarro; **Screenplay:** Buckley Angell and David Lange; **Music:** Albert Glasser; **Cinematographer:** Harold J. Marzoratti; **Editor:** Frank Santillo; **Cast:** Rory Calhoun, Anne Francis, Vince Edwards, John Litel, Chuck Connors, Guinn "Big Boy" Williams.

A lawman brings a young woman back to a small town where she is to be hung for murder, but he becomes convinced of her innocence and tries to find the real killer. This compact and compelling little western filmed in CinemaScope boasts a fine performance by the underrated Anne Francis.

HIRED HAND, THE Universal, 1971, Color, 90 min, VT. **Producer:** William Hayward; **Director:** Peter Fonda; **Screenplay:** Alan Sharp; **Music:** Bruce Langhorne; **Cinematographer:** Vilmos Zsigmond; **Editor:** Frank Mazzola;

Cast: Peter Fonda, Warren Oates, Verna Bloom, Robert Pratt, Severn Darden, Ann Doran.

Harry Collings (Peter Fonda) returns home to his farm after years of drifting with his pal Arch Harris (Warren Oates). His hope is to make up for lost time with his wife and daughter by working the farm for them. The family appears to be putting their lives together when duty and loyalty beckons Harry to go to the aid of his buddy Arch, now being held hostage by a deranged villain played by Severn Darden.

This overlooked film benefits from Vilmos Zsigmond's beautiful camera work, Alan Sharp's intelligent screenplay, and outstanding performances by Fonda and Oates as two buddies locked in a bond of friendship.

HIS BROTHER'S GHOST PRC, 1945, B&W, 58 min, VT. **Producer:** Sigmund Neufeld; **Director:** Sam Newfield; **Screenplay:** Milton Raison and George Wallace Sayer; **Cinematographer:** Jack Greenhalgh; **Editor:** Holbrook N. Todd; **Cast:** Buster Crabbe, Al St. John, Charles King, Karl Hackett, Arch Hall Sr.

After being ambushed by outlaws, a man sends for his lookalike brother. After his death the bad guys see the impersonator and think it is the man's ghost. Al St. John does a good job in a dual dramatic role in this entry for PRC's Billy Carson Series, with Buster Crabbe as Carson.

HIS FATHER'S SON See *OUTLAW'S SON.*

HIS NAME WAS MADRON See *MADRON.*

HIT THE SADDLE Republic, 1937, B&W, 57 min, VT. **Producer:** Nat Levin; **Director:** Mack V. Wright; **Screenplay:** Oliver Drake; **Music:** Alberto Columbo; **Cinematographer:** Jack A. Marta; **Editor:** Tony Martinelli and Lester Orlebeck; **Cast:** Robert Livingston, Ray Corrigan, Max Terhune, Rita Hayworth (as Rita Cansino), J. P. McGowan, Ed Cassidy, Sammy McKim, Yakima Canutt.

HITTIN' THE TRAIL (aka: HITTIN' THE TRAIL FOR HOME) Grand National, 1937, B&W, 58 min, VT. **Producer:** Edward Finney; **Director:** Robert N. Bradbury; **Screenplay:** Robert Emmett (Tansey); **Music:** Frank Sanucci; **Cinematographer:** Gus Peterson; **Editor:** Frederick Bain; **Cast:** Tex Ritter, Jerry Berth, Tommy Bupp, Earl Dwire.

HOEDOWN Columbia, 1950, B&W, 64 min. **Producer:** Colbert Clark; **Director:** Ray Nazarro; **Screenplay:** Barry Shipman; **Music:** Eddy Arnold, Francis Clark, Bob Hilliard, Edward G. Nelson, Steve Nelson, and Fred Stryker; **Cinematographer:** Fayte M. Browne; **Editor:** Paul Borofsky; **Cast:** Eddy Arnold, Jeff Donnell, Jock Mahoney, Guinn

"Big Boy" Williams, Carolina Cotton, Fred Sears, The Pied Pipers, The Oklahoma Wranglers.

A cowboy film star comes to a dude ranch and finds that bank robbers are hiding there. This fun-filled country musical western sports a top job by hero Jock Mahoney, with country singing stars Eddy Arnold and Carolina Cotton appearing as themselves.

HOLLYWOOD COWBOY (aka: WINGS OVER WYOMING) RKO, 1937, B&W, 64 min. Producer: George A. Hirliman; Director: Ewing Scott; Screenplay: Daniel Jarrett and Scott; Cinematographer: Frank B. Good; Editor: Robert O. Crandall; Cast: George O'Brien, Cecilia Parker, Maude Eburne, Joe Caits, Charles Middleton.

While vacationing in a small western town, a cowboy film star discovers that local ranchers are being cheated by the legal protection agency and decides to help them. This fine George O'Brien vehicle for RKO blends comedy and action nicely. (See also RACKETEERS OF THE RANGE.)

HOLLYWOOD COWBOY (1975) See HEARTS OF THE WEST.

HOLLYWOOD ROUND-UP Columbia, 1937, B&W, 54 min. Producer: L. G. Leonard; Director: Ewing Scott; Screenplay: Joseph Hoffman, Ethel La Blanche, and Monroe Shaff; Cinematographer: Allen Q. Thompson; Editor: Robert O. Crandall; Cast: Buck Jones, Helen Twelvetrees, Grant Withers, Dickie Jones, Shemp Howard.

Because of a film's star jealousy, a stuntman is fired. He gets a job with another film company but becomes the fall guy when a local bank is robbed. (See also LAW OF THE TEXAN.)

HOLY TERROR, A Fox, 1931, B&W, 53 min. Producer: Edmund Grainger (associate); Director: Irving Cummings; Screenplay: Myron C. Fagan; Cinematographer: George Schniederman; Editor: Ralph Dixon; Cast: George O'Brien, Sally Eilers, Rita La Roy, Humphrey Bogart, Stanley Fields.

A polo-playing playboy heads west to Wyoming after his father is murdered. This rather routine George O'Brien effort for Fox is perhaps most notable for an early screen appearance by Humphrey Bogart as Steve Nash, the ranch foreman who is pursuing one woman while another is pursuing him.

HOMBRE 20th Century Fox, 1967, Color, 111 min, VT. Producers: Irving Ravetch and Martin Ritt; Director: Ritt; Screenplay: Ravetch and Harriet Frank Jr.; Music: David Rose; Cinematographer: James Wong Howe; Editor: Frank Bracht; Cast: Paul Newman, Fredric March, Richard Boone, Diane Cilento, Cameron Mitchell, Barbara Rush, Martin Balsam.

This is a stark character study of a white man named John Russell (Paul Newman), also called Hombre, who was raised among the Apache. While he cannot fully identify with either race, his sympathies lie with the oppressed Indians. The story unfolds on a stagecoach in which his fellow passengers are Fredric March, an Indian agent turned thief; Barbara Rush, his disillusioned wife; Diane Cilento, a tough-talking tainted woman; and Richard Boone, a disgusting and treacherous bandit. Martin Balsam plays their Mexican driver. When they are forced to take refuge in a mining camp, Hombre's values are fatally tested as he ironically gives up his life to save an Indian-hating woman (Rush).

Filmed in Arizona, with a plot modeled on STAGECOACH, the picture is darkly pessimistic, yet engaging and compelling, with beautiful photography by James Wong Howe and particularly strong performances by Rush and Martin Balsam. Generally viewed as one of the best traditional westerns of the 1960s, the picture's reviews were quite positive. Variety called it "a handsome production, about greed and survival in the Old West." The Christian Science Monitor's Frederick H. Guidey found it to be "an engrossing exploration of mankind's obligations and frailties," while Bosley Crowther, writing in the New York Times, called it "a first rate cooking of a Western recipe . . . not a great Western film nor a creation, but an excellent putting of heat to a fine selected blend."

Directed by Martin Ritt, who helmed Newman in Hud (1963), and based on a novel by Elmore Leonard, the film was a critical and box-office success. It grossed $6.5 million in domestic rentals, making it the 12th leading box-office hit of 1967 and the highest-grossing western of the year.

HOME IN OKLAHOMA Republic, 1946, B&W, 72 min. Producer: Edward J. White; Director: William Witney; Screenplay: Gerald Geraghty; Music: Joseph Dubin and Morton Scott; Cinematographer: William Bradford; Editor: Lester Orlebeck; Cast: Roy Rogers, George "Gabby" Hayes, Dale Evans, Carol Hughes, George Meeker, Lanny Rees.

HOME IN WYOMIN' Republic, 1942, B&W, 67 min. Producers: Harry Grey and Edward Mann; Director: William Morgan; Screenplay: Robert Tasker and M. Coates Webster; Music: Raoul Kraushaar; Cinematographer: Ernest Miller; Cast: Gene Autry, Smiley Burnette, Fay McKenzie, Olin Howlin, Chick Chandler, Forrest Tayler.

Radio cowboy Gene comes to the aid of a former employer who is in trouble with his failing rodeo. This good Gene Autry venture, based on a story by detective fiction writer Stuart Palmer, is enhanced by its mystery aura. (See also TUMBLING TUMBLEWEEDS.)

HOME ON THE PRAIRIE (aka: RIDIN' THE RANGE) Republic, 1939, B&W, 58 min. Producer: Harry Grey; Director: Jack Townley; Screenplay: Paul Franklin and Charles Arthur Powell; Music: Alberto

Columbo and William Lava; **Cinematographer:** Reggie Lanning; **Editor:** Lester Orlebeck; **Cast:** Gene Autry, Smiley Burnette, June Storey, George Cleveland, Jack Mulhall.

HOME ON THE RANGE   Paramount, 1935, B&W, 54 min. **Producer:** Harold Hurley; **Director:** Arthur Jacobson; **Screenplay:** Ethel Doherty, Grant Garett, Charles Logue, and Harold Shumate; **Music:** Jay Gorney, E. Y. Harburg, Arthur Johnston, and John Leipold; **Cinematographer:** William Mellor; **Editor:** John Dennis; **Cast:** Randolph Scott, Ann Sheridan, Dean Jagger, Jackie Coogan, Fuzzy Knight.

Randolph Scott and ex-child star Jackie Coogan are brothers who own a stable of racing ponies in this film based on Zane Gray's novel *Code of the West*. One of their horses is scheduled to appear in a big race with a strong likelihood of winning. But a band of sharpshooters try to victimize the brothers and thwart their hopes by fixing the race. Actress Ann Sheridan—in one of her earliest roles—provides the film's love interest.

Paramount had already filmed Zane Grey's story as a silent under the title *Code of the West*, with Owen Moore and Constance Bennett in starring roles. In 1929 FBO issued a film titled *Code of the West* not based on Grey's work. However, RKO did a remake in 1947 that used the novel's original title and featured James Warren, Debra Alden, and Harry Woods.

HOME ON THE RANGE   Republic, 1946, Color, 55 min. **Producer:** Louis Gray (associate); **Director:** R. G. Springsteen; **Screenplay:** Betty Burbridge and Bernard McConville; **Music:** R. Dale Butts; **Cinematographer:** Marcel Le Picard; **Editor:** Charles Craft; **Cast:** Monte Hale, Lorna Gray (as Adrian Booth), Bob Nolan and the Sons of the Pioneers, Tom Chatterton, Robert Blake, LeRoy Mason, Roy Barcroft.

A rancher who wants to protect the wildlife in his area has his ideas challenged by local cattlemen. This average oater was actor Monte Hale's first starring role for Republic. Other Hale ventures in which he starred under his own name include *Out California Way* (1946); *Last Frontier Uprising, Under Colorado Skies, Along the Oregon Trail* (1947); *The Timber Trail, Son of God's Country, California Firebrand* (1948). Hale's other films for Republic include *Law of the Golden West, South of Rio, Pioneer Marshal, San Antone Ambush, Ranger of Cherokee Strip, Prince of the Plains* (as Bat Masterson), *Outcasts of the Trail* (as Pat Garrett) (1949); *The Vanishing Westerner, The Old Frontier, The Missourians* (1950).

HOMESTEADERS, THE   Allied Artists, 1953, B&W, 62 min. **Producer:** Vincent Fennelly; **Director:** Lewis D. Collins; **Screenplay:** Milton Raison and Sid Theil; **Music:** Raoul Kraushaar; **Cinematographer:** Ernest Miller; **Editor:** Sam Fields; **Cast:** William "Wild Bill" Elliott, Robert Lowery, Emmett Lynn, George Wallace, Robert "Buzz" Henry.

Crooks are after a wagon train carrying dynamite for the army, but two Oregon homesteaders aboard the train try to stop them. This Allied Artists venture with Bill Elliott in the lead is among the last top-grade B westerns made as the genre was fading out of existence.

HOMESTEADERS OF PARADISE VALLEY   Republic, 1947, B&W, 59 min. **Producer:** Sidney Picker; **Director:** R. G. Springsteen; **Screenplay:** Earle Snell; **Music:** Mort Glickman; **Cinematographer:** Alfred S. Keller; **Editors:** Charles Craft and Alfred S. Keller; **Cast:** Allan Lane, Robert Blake, Ed Cassidy, George Chesebro, Edyth Elliott, Tom London.

HONDO   Warner Bros., 1953, Color, 84 min, VT. **Producer:** Robert Fellows; **Director:** John Farrow; **Screenplay:** James Edward Grant; **Music:** Emil Newman and Hugo Friedlander; **Cinematographers:** Robert Burks and Archie Stout; **Editor:** Ralph Dawson; **Cast:** John Wayne, Geraldine Page, Ward Bond, Michael Pate, Lee Aaker, James Arness, Rodolfo Acosta, Leo Gordon, Tom Irish, Paul Fix, Rayford Barnes.

John Wayne is Hondo Lane, a half-Indian cavalry scout with a dog companion who happens upon a woman and her son living on an isolated ranch in hostile Apache territory. During his stay he learns that the woman's husband has deserted her in the wake of an impending Apache uprising. However, Angie Lowe (Geraldine Page) is determined to protect her home, a trait that Hondo deeply admires.

When Hondo leaves Mrs. Lowe and her son Johnny (Lee Aaker) and rides into town, the Apache do attack. Their chief, Vittorio (Michael Pate), is impressed when young Johnny shoots one of his braves in defense of his mother. Prompted by the lad's courage, Vittorio adopts the boy and makes him a blood brother.

While in town, Hondo gets into an argument with a stranger. When he leaves, the stranger ambushes him, and Hondo is forced to kill him in self-defense. Matters are complicated when he learns that the man he felled is Ed Lowe, Angie's wayward husband. The Apache capture Hondo, but because he displays great courage in the face of torture, Vitorrio orders him to fight Silva, a particularly cruel Apache warrior. Hondo defeats Silva but decides to spare the Indian's life. When Hondo and Angie finally meet again their romantic attachment grows stronger. He decides to tell Angie the whole truth, even at the risk of compromising their relationship. Angie understands, and she and her son Johnny, who has bonded with Hondo, all leave for California. After Vittorio dies, Silva begins a murdering rampage but is killed while attacking the wagon train that Hondo is leading westward.

Reportedly Wayne was less than enchanted with his costar Geraldine Page, who was plucked fresh from the Broadway stage. According to most accounts Wayne wasn't too high on what he called "New York" actors. Yet their romantic scenes together are believable and tender, and Page garnered an Oscar nomination for her film debut.

Lee Aacker, Geraldine Page, John Wayne, and Ward Bond in Hondo, *originally shot in 3D. Page won an Oscar nomination in her screen debut.* (WARNER BROS./AUTHOR'S COLLECTION)

Lee Aaker, who played young Johnny, was just 10 years old when *Hondo* was made: "I recall that in one scene he [Wayne] picks me up and throws me in the water. I have a nice eight by ten-inch autographed picture that says, 'Lee, some day I'll give you a real swimming lesson.' He remains a hero to me and I still cherish that picture."

For the late Leo Gordon, who played Ed Lowe, *Hondo* was his very first western. Trained on the New York stage, with lifetime experiences dating back to actually serving time in prison, Gordon recalled filming a few sequences with Wayne:

I was born in Brooklyn and was not a trained cowboy when we made *Hondo*. I was doing a stage play with Edward G. Robinson when this artist fellow saw me and thought I would be a good prospect and signed me up. A couple of weeks later I got a call and one of the questions was "Do you ride?" The only horses I had ever been close to were those pulling the Borden milk wagon. "Hell yes, I can ride." So the following day I rented a horse in Central Park and rode for eight hours. I spent the next couple of days in a bath with Epsom salt.

My agent told me I had a couple of weeks on a picture with John Wayne which was going to be shot in Mex-

ico. This was the first time I met John Wayne. I had a couple of run-ins with him, nothing of great importance. In the fight scene at the bar, I grabbed his shirt and he said, "Hey, easy on that! These shirts are not easy to come by." I threw a sharp right at his jaw and he said, "Cut, cut, cut. Don't you know how to throw a punch?" And he demonstrated by dropping his right arm way back and making a roundhouse. I said, "Hell, you can do that and I'll nail you three times before you can get it up there."

The next run-in was my death scene where he shoots me at the waterhole. He shoots me and I'm lying on my right hip and I just buckled forward, and he says, "Jeeze Christ, don't you know when you get hit with a damn slug, you fly backwards?" So this time I was a little pissed off and I pulled up my shirt and indicated where I had once been shot. I told him I had caught two in the gut once and that I fell forward. "Well it looks better for the camera," he shot back at me.

Hondo Lane is one of John Wayne's vintage roles. His entry on the screen is perhaps his most impressive since *STAGECOACH* (1939). Yakima Canutt did some doubling for

Wayne just as he had done two decades earlier. Shot originally in 3D and filmed in Caramongo, Mexico, the film is based on a *Colliers* magazine story by Louis L'Amour. Offset by the gimmicky 3D process, the film has only recently gained the stature it richly deserves. One of its major liabilities is that it was released the same year (1953) as George Steven's western masterpiece *SHANE*, with a stunning career performance by Alan Ladd in the title role. *Hondo* is an excellent picture, *Shane* a superb one, and the latter film stole the western thunder that year.

In 1967 *Hondo* was remade by MGM under the direction of Lee Katzin and produced by John Wayne and Andrew J. Fenady. With Ralph Taeger in the title role, and scripted by Fenady, it contracted to ABC-TV as a telefeature. That fall it became the opening segment of a teleseries that had only a limited run. It was issued in Europe in 1967 under the title *Hondo and the Apaches*.

HONEST THIEF, THE   See *BARBARY COAST GENT.*

HONKERS, THE   United Artists, 1972, Color, 102 min. **Producers:** Arthur Gardner and Stephen Lodge; **Director:** Steve Ihnat; **Screenplay:** Ihnat and Stephen Lodge; **Music:** Jimmie Haskell; **Cinematographer:** James Crabe **Cast:** James Coburn, Lois Nettleton, Slim Pickens, Joan Huntington, Richard Anderson.

A once-famous rodeo star (James Coburn) seeks a comeback to impress his son and to win over his estranged wife. The film covers three days in his life, and from dawn of the first day till dusk of the third day, he manages to both win and lose all that is important to him. He gains the affections of his estranged wife, only to lose her again because of his philandering. He tries to win back his young son by teaching him to cheat and lie, but instead he loses the boy's respect. He also loses his best pal (Slim Pickens), a rodeo clown who dies saving his life. He has one special day, winning a considerable sum of money only to end up alone.

This was the only film for director Steve Inhat, who died shortly after it was completed. In 1972 there was a spate of rodeo films in which the heroes were not big-money winners but fellows who were deemed to be past their primes. Similar themes were dealt with by Sam Peckinpah in *JUNIOR BONNER* (1972) and by Cliff Robertson in *J. W. COOP* (1972), both of which are regarded as better films.

HONKY TONK   MGM, 1941, B&W, 105 min, VT. **Producer:** Pandro S. Berman; **Director:** Jack Conway; **Screenplay:** Marguerite Roberts and John Sanford; **Music:** Franz Waxman; **Cinematographer:** Harold Rossen; **Editor:** Blanche Sewell; **Cast:** Clark Gable, Lana Turner, Frank Morgan, Claire Trevor, Marjorie Main, Albert Dekker, Chill Wills, Veda Ann Borg.

Clark Gable plays Candy Johnson, a slick con artist who arrives in Yellow Creek, Nevada. Once there he gives up his crass saloon girl (Claire Trevor) and marries the daughter of the local justice of the peace (Lana Turner) to expand his illicit activities. When the judge is later shot by the owner of a gambling saloon, the shock causes Johnson's wife to suffer a miscarriage. Candy has a change of heart, pursues the straight and narrow, and sets out to settle the score with the gambler and his gang.

The obvious chemistry between Gable and Turner (their first pairing) and MGM's ability to turn out a glossy western were harbingers for success. While the screenplay is padded to accommodate more interplay between the stars, this familiar story of the western rascal tamed by the eastern lady boasts lots of action, an outstanding supporting cast, and Clark Gable at his two-fisted and virile best.

HONOR OF THE RANGE   Universal, 1934, B&W, 61 min. **Producer:** Ken Maynard; **Director:** Alan James; **Screenplay:** Nate Gatzert; **Cinematographer:** Ted D. McCord; **Cast:** Ken Maynard, Cecilia Parker, Fred Kohler, Frank Hagney, Jack Rockwell.

See *LUCKY LARKIN.*

HONOR OF THE WEST   Universal, 1939, B&W, 60 min. **Producer:** Trem Carr; **Director:** George Waggoner; **Screenplay:** Joseph West (Waggoner); **Music:** Fleming Allen; **Cinematographer:** Harry Neumann; **Editor:** Charles Craft; **Cast:** Bob Baker, Marge Champion, Carleton Young, Jack Kirk.

HOP-ALONG CASSIDY (aka: HOP-ALONG CASSIDY ENTERS)   Paramount, 1935, B&W, 60 min, VT. **Producer:** Harry Sherman; **Director:** Howard Bretherton; **Screenplay:** Doris Schroeder; **Music:** Dave Franklin and Sam H. Stept; **Cinematographer:** Archie Stout; **Editor:** Edward Schroeder; **Cast:** William Boyd, Jimmy Ellison, Paula Stone, George "Gabby" Hayes, Kenneth Thomson.

After returning to the Bar 20 ranch, Bill Cassidy tries to find out who is behind a series of rustling attempts as his boss tries to keep his water rights. During the course of the storyline Cassidy is slightly injured in a gun battle, giving him a temporary limp and a new moniker, "Hop-Along." A well-made western with a plethora of fine outdoor locations, a strong plot, and minimal use of stock footage, this film proved so popular that it would lead to 65 other Cassidy screen adventures and assure William Boyd a slice of genre immortality.

In 1935 Paramount initiated this new series based on Clarence E. Mulford's Hop-Along Cassidy books. Uncertain at first that this initial venture would even warrant a follow-up, Paramount had no idea that it would develop into one of the most popular series of all, sustaining itself through the 1940s, then becoming a television staple during the 1950s. Interestingly, the screen character created for Cassidy had little resemblance to Mulford's literary protagonist. In the Mulford books, Hop-Along was a heavy-drinking, heavy-smoking, cussing, and not too pristine character. Boyd only agreed to play the part if Hoppy was made into the clean-living hero his fans came to know and love, the noble hero who rarely kissed the girl (Boyd was already 40 when the series started), and let the bad guy draw first. In fact, Boyd's characterizations became so popular that when Mulford's novels were later reissued, they were partially rewritten to accommodate this new image.

According to film historian William Everson, the early Cassidy westerns were in many ways the best. They made up for their lack of polish with good scripts, good casts, and "a realistic picture of ranch life with the humdrum chores and boisterous horseplay." Moreover, the first dozen or so Hop-Along Cassidy films made up for their generally slow pace with "climaxes of astonishing vigor and scope." The buildup was methodical, and the large-scale action climaxes would suddenly hit the screen with an equally sudden introduction of background music, which hitherto had been largely muted.

By 1943 Boyd had made 54 Hop-Along Cassidy features for original producer Harry Sherman. After Sherman quit the projects, Boyd made 12 more on his own for a total of 66 Hop-Along Cassidy westerns. All the movies made a 100 percent profit or better.

The "Hoppies" also launched the "Trio Western." Because Boyd was over 40, he got younger partners to play the romantic leads—Jimmy Ellison, Russell Hayden, Brad King—and a second partner for comic relief—"Gabby" Hayes, Britt Wood, Andy Clyde. The immediate follow-ups to the original series entry were also well received. Among the best are *Hop-Along Cassidy Returns* (1936), *Texas Trail* (1937), *In Old Mexico* (1938), *Three Men from Texas* (1940), and *Hoppy Serves a Writ* (1943).

A complete listing of Boyd's Hop-Along Cassidy features follows in chronological order: *Hop-Along Cassidy, The Eagle's Brood* (1935); *Call of the Prairie, Heart of the West, Hop-Along Cassidy Returns, Three on the Trail, Trail Dust* (1936); *Borderland, Hills of Old Wyoming, Hop-Along Rides Again, North of the Rio Grande, Rustlers' Valley, Texas Trail* (1937); *Cassidy of Bar 20, The Frontiersmen, Heart of Arizona, In Old Mexico, Pride of the West, Sunset Trail, Partners of the Plains, Bar 20 Justice* (1938); *Law of the Pampas, Range War, Renegade Trail, Silver on the Sage* (1939); *Showdown, Hidden Gold, Santa Fe Marshal, Stagecoach War, Three Men from Texas* (1940); *Border Vigilantes, Doomed Caravan, In Old Colorado, Outlaws of the Desert, Pirates on Horseback, Secrets of the Wasteland, Riders of the Timberline, Stick to Your Guns, Twilight on the Trail, Wide Open Town* (1941); *Undercover Man, Lost Canyon* (1942); *Bar 20, Border Patrol, Colt Comrades, False Colors, Hoppy Serves a Writ, The Leather Burners* (1943); *Forty Thieves, Lumberjack, The Mystery Man, Riders of the Deadline, Texas Masquerade* (1944); *The Devil's Playground, Fools Gold* (1946); *Dangerous Venture, Hoppy's Holiday, The Marauders, Unexpected Guest* (1947); *Borrowed Trouble, The Dead Don't Dream, False Paradise, Silent Conflict, Sinister Journey, Strange Gamble* (1948); *The Greatest Show on Earth* (1952)`.

In 1998 Chris Lybbert played Hop-Along Cassidy in the film *Gunfighter*. Director Leslie Selander helmed 29 Hop-Along Cassidy features during the years 1939–43.

`Boyd made a cameo appearance as Hop-Along Cassidy in Cecil B. DeMille's Oscar-winning film *The Greatest Show on Earth* (1952).

HOP-ALONG CASSIDY RETURNS
Paramount, 1936, B&W, 71 min. **Producer:** Harry Sherman; **Director:** Nate Watt; **Screenplay:** Harrison Jacobs; **Music:** John Leipold; **Cinematographer:** Archie Stout; **Editor:** Robert Warwick Jr.; **Cast:** William Boyd, George "Gabby" Hayes, Gail Sheridan, Evelyn Brent, Morris Ankrum, William Janney.

After his editor friend is killed in an ambush, Hoppy becomes sheriff of a small town. He finds himself at odds with a woman who wants to take control of the town for the gold in a nearby mine. In this movie William Boyd kissed Evelyn Brent on the forehead as she lay dying. His fans found this act to be unmanly, so all future romance was left to his partners, with a different leading lady in each picture. (See also *HOP-ALONG CASSIDY*.)

HOP-ALONG RIDES AGAIN
Paramount, 1937, B&W, 65 min. **Producer:** Harry Sherman; **Director:** Leslie Selander; **Cinematographer:** Russell Harlan; **Editor:** Robert Warwick; **Cast:** William Boyd, George "Gabby" Hayes, Russell Hayden, Nora Lane, Harry Worth.
See *HOP-ALONG CASSIDY*.

HOPPY SERVES A WRIT
Paramount, 1943, B&W, 69 min, VT. **Producers:** Lewis J. Rachmil and Harry Sherman;

William Boyd as Hop-Along Cassidy. *Boyd appeared in 66 Hop-Along Cassidy films.* (AUTHOR'S COLLECTION)

Director: George Archainbaud; **Screenplay:** Gerald Geraghty; **Music:** Irvin Talbot; **Cinematographer:** Russell Harlan; **Editor:** Sherman A. Rose; **Cast:** William Boyd, Andy Clyde, Bill George, Victor Jory, George Reeves, Jan Christy, Forbes Murray, Robert Mitchum, Roy Barcroft.

Sheriff Hoppy must find a way to bring a group of bad guys to justice in Texas. His big problem is that they are now hiding across state lines in Oklahoma. A good script and an excellent performance by Victor Jory as the villain makes this one of the better series features. Also took for Robert Mitchum (listed in the credits as Bob Mitchum) and future TV Superman George Reeves. (See also *HOP-ALONG CASSIDY.*)

HOPPY'S HOLIDAY   United Artists, 1947, B&W, 60 min. **Producers:** William Boyd, Lewis J. Rachmil, and Harry Sherman; **Director:** George Archainbaud; **Screenplay:** J. Benton Cheney, Bennett Cohen, and Ande Lamb; **Music:** David Chudnow; **Cinematographer:** Mack Stengler; **Editor:** Fred W. Berger; **Cast:** William Boyd, Andy Clyde, Rand Brooks, Andrew Tombes, Jeff Corey, Mary Ware.

HORIZONS WEST   Universal, 1952, Color, 81 min. **Producer:** Albert J. Cohen; **Director:** Budd Boetticher; **Screenplay:** Louis Stevenson; **Music:** Herman Stein; **Cinematographer:** Charles P. Boyle; **Editor:** Ted J. Kent; **Cast:** Robert Ryan, Rock Hudson, Julie Adams, Judith McIntire, Raymond Burr, James Arness, Dennis Weaver, Rodolfo Acosta, Walter Reed.

Brothers Dan and Neil Hammond return to Texas after the Civil War. Dan (Robert Ryan) turns to cattle rustling in an attempt to build a one-man empire, while Neil (Rock Hudson) eventually becomes a lawman and marshal. After Ryan kills rival overlord Raymond Burr and turns his affections on Burr's widow, his destiny leads him to the inevitable showdown with his brother. The interesting cast features up-and-coming stars Hudson, Burr, James Arness, and Dennis Weaver before they hit it big in the industry.

HORSEMEN OF THE SIERRAS (aka: REMEMBER ME)   Columbia, 1949, B&W. **Producer:** Colbert Clark; **Director:** Fred F. Sears; **Screenplay:** Barry Shipman; **Cinematographer:** Fayte M. Browne; **Editor:** Paul Borofsky; **Cast:** Charles Starrett, Smiley Burnette, Lois Hall, Tommy Ivo, John Dehner, Jason Robards Sr., Jock Mahoney, George Chesebro.

HORSE SOLDIERS, THE   United Artists, 1959, Color, 115 min, VT, DVD. **Producers:** Lee Mayhin and Martin Rankin; **Director:** John Ford; **Screenplay:** Mahin and Rankin; **Music:** David Buttolph; **Cinematographer:** William Clothier; **Editor:** Jack Murray; **Cast:** John Wayne, William Holden, Constance Towers, Judson Pratt, Hoot Gibson, Ken Curtis, Bing Russell, Hank Worden, Chuck Hayward, Denver Pyle, Strother Martin, Walter Reed, Anna Lee, Althea Gibson.

It is April 1863, and the Civil War is going badly for the Union. The key stumbling block is Vicksburg, high on a bluff over the Mississippi River. General Ulysses S. Grant calls in Colonel Marlow (John Wayne) and dispatches him 300 miles into enemy territory. Marlow takes off on his "horse ride" with a brigade of depleted Union cavalry troops. His men think they are on the way north and find out their true destination only at daybreak, when they find the sun rising over their left shoulders.

The journey is compromised from the start by friction between Marlow, a realistic authoritarian, and his surgeon, Major Kendall (William Holden), a more liberal-minded and compassionate man. Among other things, Marlow resents Kendall for not carrying arms and because Kendall asserts his right as an officer in the Medical Corp to declare any soldier unfit for combat, much to Marlow's dismay. Matters are further complicated by the presence of Hannah Hunter (Constance Towers), a southern belle who is scheming to sabotage their plans but falls in love with Marlow instead.

The film is based on an actual raid led by Colonel Benjamin H. Grierson, a former Illinois music teacher who was sent by General Grant with a force of 1,700 mounted men on a raid, tearing up railroad tracks and checking enemy troop strength around Vicksburg. Grierson's name was changed to Marlow in the film; some have suggested that this is because it would have been difficult to envisage John Wayne as a music teacher.

The pairing of Holden and Wayne is interesting. Both had production companies of their own, while both had great respect—personal and professional—for one another. Veteran actor Walter Reed, who played a cavalry scout in the film, shared some interesting observations on Wayne, Holden, and John Ford.

> Wayne always wanted to be a director. When we did *The Horse Soldiers*, he'd try to second-guess Ford. Right before a scene he'd say, "Walter, why don't we do it this way? You do this . . ." I'd say, "Duke, if the old man . . ." He'd look at me and say, "Shhh!" He didn't want the old man to hear anything. He didn't want me to say to Ford, "Well, Mr. Wayne wanted me to do it this way, or something to the effect."
>
> It was funny because Duke didn't do it maliciously. He had ideas—a lot of good ideas. Duke would kind of smile at me and say, "Don't tell him." Ford was the only guy who could tell Wayne anything. He had a lot of respect for the old man. But some of Duke's ideas were so good that if Ford called me on it, I'd tell the old man something like "I thought you wanted it that way." I liked Ford, but he was a tough man. In the days I did *The Horse Soldiers* for him we were on horses every day, even Saturdays and Sundays for fourteen weeks.

Reed also related an amusing anecdote concerning Holden and Ford: "When we did *The Horse Soldiers* we were in this great big trailer. We were the Horse Soldiers and when they said something, we'd yell, 'Yo!' Well once Ford yelled in that rapsy voice of his, 'Bill Holden!' So Holden runs to the door and says, 'Yo!' like that. Then he turns around to us and says with a puzzled look. 'What the hell am

I doing that for? I'm making a million dollars on this picture and he's only making five-hundred-thousand [laughing]. What am I going 'Yo' for?'"

At first look *The Horse Soldier* seemed to be a surefire winner. It had a top director in John Ford and two big-name stars in Wayne and Holden. But the deal that consummated the picture was one of the most complicated ever put together in Hollywood. It was a joint operation between six corporations, including United Artists, the Mirisch Company, John Ford Productions, Wayne's Batjac Productions, and William Holden Productions. Six sets of agents, lawyers, and accountants spent six months drawing up one of the most complex contracts ever written. To compound matters, haggling continued over completion bonds, cost overruns, annuities, and so on. Filming took place in Louisiana under less than favorable climate and conditions, and the work was arduous and at times difficult to endure.

According to Dan Ford in *Pappy: The Life of John Ford*, his grandfather had problems dealing with racial segregation in the South, and a personal tragedy blighted the entire project. John Ford blamed himself for the death of stuntman Fred Kennedy, who, although overweight and out of shape, pleaded with Ford to allow him to take one more fall. At first Ford was adamant in his refusal, but he recanted when the stuntman insisted he needed extra money to help his family. He landed the wrong way on his fall and broke his neck. The tragedy sickened Ford and destroyed what little enthusiasm he may have had for the project.

The Horse Soldiers was Ford's first western since THE SEARCHERS, and except for a segment of HOW THE WEST WAS WON (1962), it was Ford's only sound film to deal with the Civil War. Though the film falls short of his best work, Ford's mastery for military ritual and William Clothier's stunning picture-postcard photography work extremely well. Despite the occasionally muddled script and a nebulous love story, some of the scenes show outstanding merit. One scene in particular stands out for its rare emotional purity. A column of peach-fuzzed boys marches out to face the Union cavalry and almost certain death. The mother of one of the drummer boys (Anna Lee) comes out and begs the headmaster not to take her boy. She had already lost her husband and three sons in the war and begs that her last son be spared. The boy is dismissed and is dragged kicking from the ranks.

In another scene Confederate soldiers pour from a train to engage the Union troops in battle while their colonel, seen in reflection in the window, watches in gleeful pride. Later we see this colonel wounded and staggering with a Confederate flag in his grasp.

The film was mildly received by critics, and while some reviewers were kind, it died at the box office and barely covered its cost. The bridge used in the climax of *The Horse Soldiers* was 200 feet long and was constructed at a cost of more than $50,000.

HOSTILE GUNS Paramount, 1967, Color, 91 min, VT. **Producer:** A. C. Lyles; **Director:** R. C. Springsteen; **Screenplay:** Steve Fisher; **Music:** Jimmie Haskell; **Cine-**matographer: Lothrop B. Worth; **Editor:** John F. Schreyer; **Cast:** George Montgomery, Yvonne De Carlo, Tab Hunter, Brian Donlevy, John Russell, Leo Gordon, James Craig, Richard Arlen, Emile Meyer, Don "Red" Barry, Fuzzy Knight.

A good cast highlights this A. C. Lyles production of a sheriff and his deputy who lead a prison wagon through hostile country while they are being stalked by an outlaw gang with a score to settle.

HOUR OF THE GUN United Artists, 1967, Color, 100 min, VT. **Producer:** John Sturges; **Director:** Sturges; **Screenplay:** Edward Anhalt; **Music:** Jerry Goldsmith; **Cinematographer:** Lucien Ballard; **Editor:** Ferris Webster; **Cast:** James Garner, Jason Robards Jr., Robert Ryan, Albert Salmi, Charles Aidman, Steve Ihnat, William Windom, William Shallert, Jon Voight.

John Sturges's Earp/Holliday/Clanton saga begins with the famous gunfight at the O.K. Corral and follows Wyatt Earp in his quest for personal revenge. Sturges produced and directed this film 10 years after his highly successful GUN-FIGHT AT THE O.K. CORRAL (1957) with a bitter Earp (James Garner) more concerned with avenging the death of his brother than enforcing and enforcing law and order in Tombstone.

In the cynical 1960s it became increasingly the fashion to probe deeply into the character and psyche of the nation's folk heroes. In keeping with the revisionist attitudes of the decade, the film focuses on the demythification rather than the creation of a legend. Consequently, as Garner's Earp becomes a harbinger for cold revenge and moral decline, Jason Robard's Doc Holliday, an admitted gambler and boozer who operates outside the law for much of his life, becomes the more substantial moral force of the two.

Garner delivers a remarkably solid performances as the obsessed Wyatt Earp—an interesting departure from the more glib and likeable roles expected from this fine actor. The interaction between Garner and Robards plays out well on screen, and Robert Ryan as Ike Clanton makes a perfect villain.

HOW THE WEST WAS WON MGM, 1962, Color, 165 min. **Producer:** Bernard Smith; **Directors:** Henry Hathaway, John Ford, and George Marshall; **Screenplay:** James R. Webb; **Music:** Alfred Newman and Ken Darby; **Cinematographer:** William H. Daniels, Milton Krasner, Joseph LaShelle, and Charles B. Lange Jr.; **Cast:** Carroll Baker, Lee J. Cobb, Henry Fonda, Gregory Peck, John Wayne, Karl Malden, Debbie Reynolds, James Stewart, Eli Wallach, George Peppard, Robert Preston, Richard Widmark, Brigid Bazlen, Walter Brennan, Raymond Massey, Agnes Moorehead, Harry Morgan, Thelma Ritter.

This grand panoramic saga follows the fortunes of a New England farm family for three generations and covers a 60-year time span, from 1839 to 1899. The film covers the western pioneering through the Civil War, Indian violence, buffalo stampedes, the Gold Rush, outlaws, the arrival of the railroads, and finally law and order, with nearly every avenue of the western trek at least superficially explored. The enormity of the project was so demanding that three of Hollywood's top directors of westerns helmed different segments: John Ford, the Civil War episode; Henry Hathaway, the outlaw chases and, plains and river sequences; and George Marshall, the building of the first transcontinental railroad and the buffalo stampede.

Of the three directors, however, only Ford's section on the Civil War truly succeeds. Eve Rawling's (Carroll Baker) farewell to her son Zeb (George Peppard) as he goes to war and the prayer to her dead father (Karl Malden) has the genuine touch of sentiment that Ford handles so well. He stages the 1862 Battle of Shiloh with master strokes, skillfully conveying all its brutality and horror, sickening General Grant (Harry Morgan) to such an extent that he threatens to give up his command. Other historical luminaries who appear in the picture are Abraham Lincoln (Raymond Massey) and General William Tecumseh Sherman (John Wayne).

Narrated by Spencer Tracy and filmed in Cinerama, *How the West Was Won* plays far better in theaters and movie houses than it does on the small screen. Yet despite Academy Awards for film editing, sound, and story and screenplay; and additional Oscar nominations for best picture, color cinematography, color costume design, color art direction, and original music score, critical reviews were mixed at best. *Variety* called the film a "magnificent, exciting spectacle . . . some of the best lensing ever seen." Affirmative as well was the *New York Herald Tribune*, which praised it as "not only a tribute to the American past, but to American movie making." On the other hand, most serious film scholars panned the effort. In his *A Pictorial History of the Western Film*, William Everson writes that "Cinerama's *How the West Was Won*, far from being the 'definitive' Western it set out to be, was merely a superficial circus, notable for its fine location, superb photography, and exciting stunt action sequences, but somehow never achieving even conviction, let alone poetry or the genuine epic stature it sought."

HUD Paramount, 1963, B&W, 112 min, VT. **Producers:** Irving Ravetch and Martin Ritt; **Director:** Ritt; **Screenplay:** Ravetch and Harriet Frank Jr.; **Music:** Elmer Bernstein; **Cinematographer:** James Wong Howe; **Editor:** Frank Brachi; **Cast:** Paul Newman, Melvyn Douglas, Patricia Neal, Brandon De Wilde, Whit Bissell, Crahan Denton.

During the early 1960s some of the most interesting and entertaining westerns had contemporary settings. Martin Ritt's *Hud* depicts three generations of a modern-day western family, with the boisterous and self-serving Paul Newman poisoning the honest values of his father, Melvyn Douglas.

Douglas won an Oscar for Best Supporting Actor as Homer Bannon, a longtime Texas rancher with an innate pride in conquering the wilderness and an abiding love for the land. Paul Newman is his son Hud, a new breed of westerner: mean-spirited, unprincipled, cynical, and arrogant.

Hud's credo is, "You don't look out for yourself, the only hand you'll ever get is when they lower the box."

Brandon De Wilde, in his strongest performance since *SHANE* (1953), in Lon, Hud's teenage nephew, whose feelings for his father change from idolizing to loathing as he watches Hud's loutish behavior toward Alma, the family's housekeeper (Patricia Neal in an Oscar-winning role) and Hud's value war against the noble Homer. When Homer dies, Lon decides to leave the ranch forever, vowing to the unrepentant Hud that he will never return.

Based on the novel by Larry McMurtry with a screenplay by Harriet Frank Jr. and Irving Ravetch, the film successfully shows the transition and passing of the baton from the Old West, with its code of honor, to the New West, with its accent on greed and indifference.

There is no discounting the fine performances by all four leads. Patricia Neal and Melvyn Douglas garnered well deserved Academy Awards, while Paul Newman received a Best Actor nomination. The film also captured an Oscar for black and white cinematography and nominations for adapted screenplay and black and white art direction.

HUNTING PARTY United Artists, 1971, Color, 108 min. **Producer:** Lou Morheim; **Director:** Don Medford; **Screenplay:** William W. Norton and Morheim; **Music:** Riz Ortolani; **Cast:** Oliver Reed, Gene Hackman, Candice Bergen, Simon Oakland, Ronald Howard, L. Q. Jones, Mitch Ryan, Rayford Barnes, Dean Selmier.

Gene Hackman is a cruel and obsessive rancher. While he is on a hunting trip with four cohorts, a gruff outlaw (Oliver Reed) kidnaps his disenchanted young wife (Candice Bergen), thinking she is a teacher who can teach him to read. Hackman's special train is replete with a bordello and a series of high-powered rifles with telescopic lenses. However, after Bergen is roughed up and raped by Reed, she inexplicably develops feelings for her abductor and decides to stay with him. When Hackman finds out, he sets out to kill Reed and his gang one by one.

The worst of the spaghetti western influence, which permeated the genre in the 1970s, can be seen in this unnecessarily violent and basically obscene picture. Serious students of the genre find no redeeming features here, just a blatant waste of good talent. In their *Pictorial History of Westerns*, Michael Parkinson and Clyde Jeavons aptly call it an "entirely repellent" film. *Variety* points out that "seldom has so much fake blood been splattered for so little reason," while Leonard Maltin called it a total bomb. The only question that remains is why actors like Hackman and Reed and such credible supporting players as Mitch Ryan, Simon Oakland, L. Q. Jones, and Dean Selmier accepted such employment.

HUNT TO KILL See *WHITE BUFFALO*.

HURRICANE SMITH (aka: DOUBLE IDENTITY) Republic, 1941, B&W, 68 min. **Producer:** Robert North; **Director:** Bernard Vorhaus; **Screenplay:** Robert

Presnell; **Cinematographer:** Ernest Miller; **Editor:** Edward Mann; **Cast:** Ray Middleton, Jane Wyatt, Harry Davenport, J. Edward Bromberg, Henry Brandon.

Rodeo rider Hurricane Smith is wrongly convicted of robbery and murder, but he escapes and creates a happy new life for himself. Things turn sour when a criminal shows up to claim the loot he thinks Smith is hiding. Republic's one attempt to make a western star out of handsome Ray Middleton, a fine actor and excellent singer, fizzled because of the film's weak script. Middleton went on to a distinguished career on the Broadway musical stage, appearing in the original stage production of Irving Berlin's *Annie Get Your Gun.* He later appeared on Broadway in *South Pacific* and the original stage production of *Man of La Mancha.*

I

IDAHO Republic, 1943, B&W, 70 min. **Producer:** Harry Grey; **Director:** Joseph Kane; **Screenplay:** Roy Chanslor and Olive Cooper; **Music:** Morton Scott; **Cinematographer:** Reggie Lanning; **Editor:** Arthur Roberts; **Cast:** Roy Rogers, Smiley Burnette, Bob Nolan and the Sons of the Pioneers, Virginia Grey, Harry Shannon, Ona Munson, Dick Purcell, Onslow Stevens, Roy Barcroft, Tom London, Rex Lease, Jack Ingram.

A former outlaw who is now a respected judge finds himself blackmailed by two hoodlums and a female gambling house operator when he refuses to help them rob a bank. Roy sets things straight.

   With Gene Autry in military service by 1943, Roy Rogers was now the country's number one cowboy star. Bigger budgets and Autry's old sidekick Smiley Burnette made Rogers films like *Idaho* become more like musical extravaganzas than standard Westerns. (See also *UNDER WESTERN STARS.*)

IDAHO KID, THE Colony, 1936, B&W, 59 min. **Producer:** Arthur Alexander; **Director:** Robert F. Hill; **Screenplay:** George H. Plympton; **Cinematographer:** Robert E. Cline; **Editor:** Charles Henkel Jr.; **Cast:** Rex Bell, Marion Shilling, David Sharpe, Earl Dwire, Lafe McKee, Charles King, Lane Chandler.

Todd Hollister aka The Idaho Kid (Rex Bell) returns home in time to stop a long-standing feud between his real father and the man who raised him in this film based on the story "Idaho" by Paul Evan Lehman.

   Rex Bell made four films for Colony Pictures in 1936, the other three being *Law and Lead*, *Stormy Trails*, and *West of Nevada*. His other four features for Colony include *Phantom Rider* (1938) *Flaming Lead* (1939); *Death Rides the Range* and *Lightning Strikes West* (1940), each starring Ken Maynard.

I KILLED GERONIMO Eagle Lion, 1950, B&W, 62 min. **Producer:** Jack Swartz; **Director:** John Hoffman; **Screenplay:** Sam Neuman and Nat Tanchuck; **Cast:** James Ellison, Virginia Herrick, Chief Thundercloud, Smith Balleu, Myron Healey.

An army captain sets out to find the gang that is supplying guns to the Indians but instead ends up in hand-to-hand combat with the menacing Geronimo, aptly played by Chief Thundercloud. Too much stock footage and a weak script limit this effort.

I KILLED WILD BILL HICKOK Associated Artists/Wheeler Company, 1956, Color, 63 min. **Producer:** Johnny Carpenter; **Director:** Richard Talmadge; **Screenplay:** Carpenter; **Cinematographer:** Virgil Miller; **Editor:** Maurice Wright; **Cast:** Johnny Carpenter (as John Forbes), Denver Pyle, Virginia Gibson, Helen Westcott, Tom Brown, I. Stanford Jolley, Frank Carpenter.

The film tells in flashback the story of "Johnny Rebel" Savage, the man who shot the legendary Wild Bill, by trying to prove that Hickok was really a bad fellow and that his killing was fully justified.

   In the 1950s Hickok's heroic film stature underwent a strange metamorphosis, and he became accepted, without any buildup or explanation, as a villain. The one redeeming feature of this movie is the appearance of Helen Westcott, whose talents are fully wasted in a weak attempt at revisionist history.

ILLEGAL RIGHTS See *HAIL TO THE RANGERS.*

INCIDENT AT PHANTOM HILL Universal, 1966, Color, 88 min. **Producer:** Harry Tatelman; **Director:**

Earl Bellamy; **Screenplay:** Frank Nugent and Ken Pettus; **Music:** Hans J. Salter; **Cinematographer:** William Margulies; **Editor:** Gene Milford; **Cast:** Robert Fuller, Jocelyn Lane, Dan Duryea, Tim Simcox, Linden Chiles, Claude Akins.

As two men and a girl trek through the desert in search of a shipment of gold that was hijacked at the end of the Civil War, they are forced to fight the elements, hostile Indians, and one another. Good performances by Dan Duryea and Robert Fuller highlight this suspenseful Earl Bellamy western.

INDIAN AGENT RKO, 1948, B&W, 63 min. **Producer:** Herman Schlom; **Director:** Leslie Selander; **Screenplay:** Norman Houston; **Music:** C. Bakaleinikoff; **Cinematographer:** J. Roy Hunt; **Editor:** Les Millbrook; **Cast:** Tim Holt, Noah Beery Jr., Richard Martin, Nan Leslie, Harry Woods, Tom Keene (as Dick Powers), Iron Eyes Cody.

INDIAN FIGHTER United Artists, 1955, Color, 1955. **Producer:** William Schorr; **Director:** André De Toth; **Screenplay:** Frank Davis and Ben Hecht; **Music:** Franz Waxman; **Cinematographer:** Wilfred M. Cline; **Editor:** Richard Cahoon; **Cast:** Kirk Douglas, Elsa Martinelli, Walter Matthau, Diana Douglas, Walter Abel, Lon Chaney Jr., Elisha Cook Jr., Ray Teal, Hank Warden.

Kirk Douglas plays Johnny Hawks, a tough scout sent from Fort Laramie to lead a wagon train of settlers through the dangerous Dakota Sioux territory into Oregon. He tries to make peace with a Sioux leader, while romancing the chief's beautiful daughter (Elsa Martinelli). Walter Matthau and Lon Chaney Jr. do a fine job as the villains in this grand CinemaScope western scripted by Ben Hecht. *Variety* notes that the film should satisfy the "demands of outdoor fans," while André De Toth's direction "reaches a high point in a refreshing novel Indian attack on a frontier fort, and in the death duel, Sioux style, between Kirk Douglas and Harry Landers."

INDIAN LOVE CALL See *ROSE MARIE.*

INDIAN MASSACRE, THE (aka: HEART OF AN INDIAN, THE) Bison, 1912, B&W, silent, 2 reels. **Producer and Director:** Thomas H. Ince; **Cast:** Francis Ford, Ann Little, Grace Cunard, William Eagle Shirt, J. Barney Sherry, Charles K. French, Lillian Christy, Art Acord.

Thomas Ince's highly regarded silent film goes a long way in documenting the Indian way of life, establishing them as human beings of nobility and feeling while presenting both sides of a complex problem: the courage of the pioneering white settlers and the tragedy of reckless extermination of the Indian. The closing scene of an Indian woman's silhouette, praying beneath the burial pyre of her dead child, is meticulously filmed and tugs at the heart.

INDIAN SCOUT See *DAVY CROCKETT, INDIAN SCOUT.*

INDIAN TERRITORY Columbia/Gene Autry Productions, 1950, B&W, 70 min. **Producer:** Armand Shaefer; **Director:** John English; **Screenplay:** Norman S. Hall; **Music:** Mischa Bakaleinikoff; **Cinematographer:** William Bradford; **Editor:** John Sweeney; **Cast:** Gene Autry, Pat Buttram, Gail Davis, Kirby Grant, James Griffith.

After leaving the Confederate cavalry, Gene Autry becomes an undercover man for the Union army.

INDIAN UPRISING Columbia, 1952, Color, 75 min. **Producer:** Bernard Small; **Director:** Ray Nazarro; **Screenplay:** Kenneth Gamet and Richard Schayer; **Music:** Ross DiMaggio; **Editor:** Richard Fantl; **Cast:** George Montgomery, Audrey Long, Carl Benton Reid, Eugene Iglesias, John Baer, Joe Sawyer, Robert Foster Dover, Robert Shayne.

George Montgomery is a cavalry captain whose troops are caught in the middle of a dispute between white settlers and distrustful Indians. When greedy speculators take hold of the reservation's rich gold deposits, Geronimo and his tribe declare war. While in the process of facing a court-martial, Montgomery is called upon to stop the attack.

IN EARLY ARIZONA Columbia, 1938, B&W, 53 min. **Producer:** Larry Darmour; **Director:** Joseph Levering; **Screenplay:** Nate Gatzert; **Cinematographer:** James S. Brown Jr.; **Editor:** Dwight Caldwell; **Cast:** William "Bill" Elliott, Dorothy Gulliver, Harry Woods, Jack Ingram, Franklyn Farnum.

A peaceful fellow takes up guns and a badge to clean up a town controlled by screen. Bill Elliott's first starring series oater is a gem, well written and with plenty of action.

IN OLD AMARILLO Republic, 1951, B&W, 67 min. **Producer:** Edward J. White; **Director:** William Witney; **Screenplay:** Sloane Nibley; **Music:** R. Dale Butts; **Cinematographer:** Jack A. Marta; **Editor:** Tony Martinelli; **Cast:** Roy Rogers, Estelita Rodriguez, Penny Edwards, Pinky Lee, Roy Barcroft.
See *UNDER WESTERN STARS.*

IN OLD ARIZONA Fox, 1929, B&W, 95 min. **Directors:** Irving Cummings and Raoul Walsh; **Screenplay:** Tom Barry; **Cinematographer:** Arthur Edeson and Alfred Hansen; **Editor:** Louis R. Loeffler; **Cast:** Warner Baxter, Edmund Lowe, Dorothy Burgess, J. Farrell MacDonald, Joe Brown.

In the first talkie filmed outdoors and the first important sound western, Tonia (Dorothy Burgess), an alluring Mexican vixen, soon finds herself in the middle of a jam between the dashing Cisco Kid (Warner Baxter) and the army sergeant who is pursuing him. *In Old Arizona* introduces Warner Baxter as the colorful bandit the Cisco Kid, who seems less inclined to ply his lawless trade than battle Texas Ranger Mickey Dunn (Edmund Lowe) for the affections of the lovely Tonia.

Director Raoul Walsh was set to play the role of the Cisco Kid himself, but he lost an eye in a freak accident. While heading back from a location in Utah, a jackrabbit jumped through the windshield of his car, leaving Walsh permanently blind in one eye and accounting for the patch he wore all his life. As a result he turned over much of his directing chores on the film to Irving Cummings. Actor Warner Baxter inherited the Cisco Kid role and won an Oscar as the year's best actor. Moreover, his good looks and deep voice brought lots of dollars and an abundance of fan mail to the studio. Baxter would repeat his role in two more features: THE CISCO KID and THE RETURN OF THE CISCO KID.

Based on a story by O. Henry, *In Old Arizona* was a major breakthrough in filmmaking and most specially the western genre. By the late 1920s, westerns were facing a dilemma. Because of the advent of sound, the floundering between too much silent action and too much static dialogue had become troublesome. But sound brought some limitations in that western fans had to do without the usual genre conventions. Because sound recording equipment was stored in stationary soundproof booths, genre staples like the chase scene were dropped, and a third of the movie took place indoors. Yet by taking the camera outdoors and by picking up gunshots, hoofbeats, and natural noises as mundane as frying bacon, *In Old Arizona* proved for all time that the western could more than cope with sound.

It has been too easy for modern pundits and critics to make light of this film and demean its overall value. Not so for *Variety*, which recognized its true merit: "It's the first outdoor talkie and a Western, with a climax twist to make the story stand out from the usual hill and dale thesis. It's outdoors, it talks and it has a great performance by Warner Baxter. That it's long and that it moves slowly is also true, but the exterior sound revives the novelty angle again."

In addition to a Best Actor award for Baxter, the film was nominated for four additional Academy Awards: Best Picture, Best Director, Cinematographer, and Writing. (See also *CISCO KID, THE.*)

IN OLD CALIENTE   Republic, 1939, B&W, 55 min, VT. **Producer:** Joseph Kane; **Director:** Kane; **Screenplay:** Gerald Geraghty and Norman Houston; **Cinematographer:** William Nobles; **Editor:** Edward Mann; **Cast:** Roy Rogers, Lynne Roberts, George "Gabby" Hayes, Jack La Rue, Katharine DeMille.

IN OLD CALIFORNIA   Republic, 1942, B&W, 88 min, VT, DVD. **Producer:** Robert North (associate); **Director:** William McGann; **Screenplay:** Gladys Atwater; **Music:** Don Buttolph; **Cinematographer:** Jack A. Marta; **Editor:** Howard O'Neill; **Cast:** John Wayne, Binnie Barnes, Albert Dekker, Helen Parish, Patsy Kelly.

In this film set during the California Gold Rush, Tom Craig (John Wayne), a handsome and tough Bostonian, heads to the West, where he sets up business as a pharmacist. On the way he meets lovely saloon singer Lacy Miller (Binnie Barnes), who is engaged to Britt Dawson (Albert Dekker), the crooked political overlord of Sacramento. Craig endears himself to the community by curing minor aches and pains in the absence of a physician. He stays away from Lacy because of her engagement and instead finds himself involved with a scheming society woman. Things change abruptly when Lacy learns that her fiancée Dawson has obtained his wealth by forcing tribute from neighboring ranchers, and Tom now finds himself in the midst of a romantic triangle. Disturbed at the ranchers' lack of grit, he asks, "Doesn't anybody fight back around here? Angry men defending their home," he continues, "can never be defeated." When Tom decides to lead the ranchers in a successful revolt, Dawson sets out to kill him. But Dawson, in turn, is mortally wounded by his own brother.

Minus its star appeal, *In Old California* is a basic Republic Pictures formula piece. Without John Wayne, *New York Times* critic Bosley Crowther wrote, "the film would be down with the usual run of strays." The film may also be seen in computerized color.

IN OLD CALIFORNIA (1948)   See *OLD LOS ANGELES.*

IN OLD CHEYENNE   Republic, 1941, B&W, 58 min. **Producer:** Joseph Kane; **Director:** Kane; **Screenplay:** Olive Cooper; **Cinematographer:** William Nobles; **Editor:** Charles Craft; **Cast:** Roy Rogers, George "Gabby" Hayes, Joan Woodbury, J. Farrell MacDonald, Sally Payne, George Rosener.

IN OLD COLORADO   Paramount, 1941, B&W, 66 min. **Producer:** Harry Sherman; **Director:** Howard Bretherton; **Screenplay:** J. Benton Cheney, Russell Hayden, and Norton S. Parker; **Editor:** Carroll Lewis; **Cast:** William Boyd, Russell Hayden, Andy Clyde, Margaret Hayes, Morris Ankrum, Sarah Padden, Cliff Nazarro.

IN OLD MEXICO   Paramount, 1938, B&W, 67 min, VT. **Producer:** Harry Sherman; **Director:** Edward D. Venturini; **Screenplay:** Harrison Jacobs; **Cinematographer:** Russell Harlan; **Editor:** Robert Warrick; **Cast:** William Boyd, George "Gabby" Hayes, Russell Hayden, Paul Sutton, Al Ernest Garcia, Jan Clayton, Trevor Bardette.

When an old friend is in trouble, Hoppy, Windy, and Lucky head south of the border and find themselves caught in a murder, a setup, and a conspiracy to frame Hoppy. (See also *HOP-ALONG CASSIDY.*)

IN OLD MONTEREY   Republic, 1939, B&W, 74 min. **Producer:** Armond Schaefer; **Director:** Joseph Kane;

Screenplay: Gerald Geraghty, Dorrell McGowan, and Stuart E. McGowan; **Music:** Walter Donaldson and Billy Rose; **Cinematographer:** Ernest Miller; **Editor:** Edward Mann; **Cast:** Gene Autry, Smiley Burnette, June Storey, George "Gabby" Hayes, Stuart Hamblen, Jonathan Hale.

Gene runs into opposition from a group of ranchers when the U.S. Army sends him to buy up land for bombing maneuvers. The most interesting feature about this 1930s Autry venture is its ambiguous title. The ultramodern setting takes us nowhere near Monterey. The only bearing here is the title song sung somewhere along the way. (See also *TUMBLING TUMBLEWEEDS*.)

IN OLD NEW MEXICO See *CISCO KID IN OLD NEW MEXICO, THE*.

IN OLD OKLAHOMA (aka: WAR OF THE WILDCATS) Republic, 1943, B&W, 102 min, VT. **Producer:** Robert North; **Director:** Albert S. Rogell; **Screenplay:** Eleanore Griffith and Ethel Hill; **Music:** Walter Scharf; **Cinematographer:** Jack A. Marta; **Editor:** Ernest J. Nims; **Cast:** John Wayne, Martha Scott, Albert Dekker, George "Gabby" Hayes, Marjorie Rambeau, Dale Evans, Grant Withers, Sidney Blackmer, Yakima Canutt.

Attractive and independent Cathy Allen (Martha Scott) writes a daring book and is obliged to leave the small town where she has been living. She goes to Sapula, Oklahoma, where she meets prosperous oil operator Jim Gardner (Albert Dekker) and attractive cowboy Dan Somers (John Wayne). Predictably the two men become rivals for Cathy's affection and for oil contracts.

In Old Oklahoma was Republic's only picture to break into the top grossers for 1943, and it helped solidify Wayne's image as the hard moral man. His Dan Sommers was a former sergeant in the U.S. Army who was the first American to reach the top on San Juan Hill and continued to fight for his country in the Philippines after the Spanish-American War. The picture thus touched a patriotic wartime nerve and also scored well with most critics, including the federal government, which praised it as an "excellent example of successful cooperation" between the government and studio. The *Hollywood Reporter* called it "a picture that cannot fail. . . . It has no aim except entertainment and that it hits with uncanny accuracy . . ." A good, no-nonsense action film, *In Old Oklahoma* received Oscar nominations for Best Scoring of a Dramatic or Comedy Picture and for Best Sound Recording.

IN OLD SACRAMENTO (aka: FLAME OF SACRAMENTO) Republic, 1946, B&W, 89 min. **Producer:** Joseph Kane (associate); **Director:** Kane; **Screenplay:** Frank Gruber and Frances Hyland; **Music:** Will D. Cobb, Gus Edwards, Fred Gilbert, Jean Lenoir, and Bruce Siever; **Cinematographer:** Jack A. Marta; **Editor:** Fred Allen; **Cast:** William "Wild Bill" Elliott, Constance Moore, Hank Daniels, Ruth Donnelly, Eugene Pallette, Lionel Stander, Jack LaRue.

Bill Elliott has a double identity. By day he is dashing Johnny Barrett, who romances women; and by night he is Spanish Jack, a masked bandit who is always one step ahead of the law. However, when the woman he loves begins to suspect him and a young man he befriends is arrested for being him, he begins to rethink his style of life and sets out to clean up the town. This rather expensive Republic effort marks Elliott's first A western, and a good one it is. Featured in the soundtrack are strains of the ever-beautiful "Speak to Me of Love" by Jean Lenoir and Bruce Siever.

IN OLD SANTA FE (aka: DOWN IN OLD SANTA FE) Mascot, 1934, B&W, 64 min. **Producer:** Nat Levine; **Director:** David Howard; **Screenplay:** Colbert Clark and James Gruen; **Music:** Gene Autry, Harold C. Lewis, Howard Jackson, and Heinz Roemheld; **Cinematographer:** Ernest Miller and William Nobles; **Editor:** Thomas Scott; **Cast:** Ken Maynard, Evelyn Knapp, Kenneth Thompson, George "Gabby" Hayes, George Chesebro, Gene Autry, Smiley Burnette.

When big-city gangsters arrive at a dude ranch, trouble begins for ranch hand Ken Maynard, who loses his horse Tarzan in a crooked race and gets framed for murder. This film marks the screen debut of Gene Autry in an uncredited role as the square dance caller/singer who sings a couple of songs at the dude ranch.

INSIDE INFORMATION See *LONE PRAIRIE, THE*.

INVITATION TO A GUNFIGHTER United Artists, 1964, Color, 92 min, VT. **Producer:** Richard Wilson; **Director:** Wilson; **Screenplay:** Elizabeth Wilson and Richard Wilson; **Music:** David Raskin; **Cinematographer:** Joseph MacDonald; **Editor:** Robert C. Jones; **Cast:** Yul Brynner, Janice Rule, George Segal, Alfred Ryder, Clifford David.

A former Confederate soldier (George Segal) returns to his hometown of Pecos, New Mexico, to discover that his farm has been sold as "enemy property" and his girl (Janice Rule) has married a maimed Union soldier. Distraught, he goes on a rampage and starts to terrorize the town, not a difficult undertaking since all the men in town were either killed or injured during the war.

A gunfighter claiming to be the "fastest gun in the West" is given $500 to kill Segal. Fast though he may be, he turns out to be a cultured and erudite Creole who quotes poetry and plays music. When he takes his time with the hit, the town eventually turns on him with surprising results.

IRON HORSE, THE Fox, 1924, B&W, 133 min, 11 reels. **Producer:** John Ford; **Director:** Ford; **Screenplay:** Charles Darnton and Charles Kenyon; **Music:** John Lanchbery; **Cinematographer:** George Schneiderman; **Cast:** George O'Brien, Madge Bellamy, Cyril Chadwick, Fred Kohler, Gladys Hulette, James A. Marcus, J. Farrell MacDonald.

A true epic of the silent era, John Ford's massive frontier drama tells the story of the building of the transcontinental railroad while paying full tribute to the nation's pioneering past. The film was made almost entirely on location in Nevada, and the cast and crew worked under conditions similar to the pioneer laborers, practically building the Union Pacific Railroad all over again. Complete towns were constructed, and a massive train of 56-coaches was used for transportation.

Ford was nearly 29 when he made *The Iron Horse*, and he had already directed nearly 40 westerns. Well over two hours in length (his longest film up to that time was about 80 minutes), it became the model for all subsequent railroad westerns. Even at this early stage of his career, Ford's editing skills and fluid camera work are superb, as evidenced by his climactic action scenes, where hordes of Indians attack one locomotive while others race to the rescue and at the same time the hero and the villain are each staging his own personal battle.

For the lead role of Davy Brandon, Ford chose 24-year-old George O'Brien, a former assistant cameraman and stuntman who had been an all-around athlete at Santa Clara College and heavyweight boxing champion of the Pacific Fleet during World War I. O'Brien delivers a top-grade performance as the youthful scout and lover who romances Madge Bellamy. He subsequently became one of the major western stars of the 1920s and '30s.

The opening credits pronouncing the film to be "accurate and faithful in every particular" are an obvious exaggeration. But on the whole it is remarkably accurate. Ford's rendition of crews building Cheyenne, Wyoming, is also faithful to history. In 1867 mounted Indians actually tried to stop a locomotive with a 40-foot hand-held rope, and "Hell on Wheels" saloon/brothels did follow crews westward.

IRON MISTRESS, THE   Warner Bros., 1952, Color, 110 min. **Producer:** Henry Blanke; **Director:** Gordon Douglas; **Screenplay:** James R. Webb; **Music:** Max Steiner; **Cinematographer:** John F. Seitz; **Editor:** Alan Crosland Jr.; **Cast:** Alan Ladd, Virginia Mayo, Joseph Calleia, Phyllis Kirk, Douglas Dick, Anthony Caruso.

Alan Ladd's first effort for Warner Bros. is a loosely based account of the life of Jim Bowie before he reached enduring fame at The Alamo. Ladd's Bowie is a backwoods guy who is introduced to the fashionable society of New Orleans by painter John Audubon. After falling in love with fickle Virginia Mayo, a beautiful but manipulative woman, he manages to build up a fortune of his own by gambling and speculating, while building his reputation with the knife which would soon bear his name. When his romance with Mayo fails, he gives up the society world and heads for Texas.

Ignoring the fluff and the largely fabricated storyline, Ladd's sheer charisma and screen presence makes this an appealing film—a pleasing costume piece with lots of good action and a nice performance by Mayo as the scheming siren.

IRON ROAD, THE   See *BUCKSKIN FRONTIER*.

IROQUOIS TRAIL, THE   United Artists, 1950, B&W, 85 min. **Producers:** Bernard Small and Edward Small; **Director:** Phil Karlson; **Screenplay:** Richard Shayer; **Cinematographer:** Henry Freulich; **Editor:** Kenneth G. Crane; **Cast:** George Montgomery, Brenda Marshall, Glenn Langdon, Reginald Denny, Sheldon Leonard, John Doucette, Monte Blue.

Based on the Leatherstocking Tales by James Fenimore Cooper, this film tells the tale of Hawkeye, an American scout, and his Indian blood brother Sagamore. Together the two help the British wrest control of the St. Lawrence/Hudson River valleys from the French during the French and Indian War.

I SHOT BILLY THE KID   Lippert, 1950, B&W, 58 min. **Producer:** William A. Berke; **Director:** Berke; **Screenplay:** Ford Beebe and Orville H. Hampton; **Cinematographer:** Ernest Miller; **Editor:** Carl Pierson; **Cast:** Don "Red" Barry, Robert Lowery, Spade Cooley, Richard Farmer, Jack Geddes, Bill Kennedy, Wendy Lee.

The story of Billy the Kid (Don Barry) is told by Pat Garrett (Robert Lowery), who explains why he killed the famed outlaw. The film claims to be based on fact, which is a bit of a stretch considering that, except for the basic outline of his life, scholars seem to agree on very little about Billy the Kid, including his name or whether or not he was really left-handed. Although in this film Don "Red" Barry is about twice the age of Billy when the outlaw was killed by Pat Garrett, he is extremely good in the title role, and the film makes for action-packed entertainment.

I SHOT JESSE JAMES   Lippert, 1949, B&W, 81 min. **Producer:** Carl K. Hittleman; **Director:** Samuel Fuller; **Screenplay:** Fuller; **Cinematographer:** Ernest Miller; **Editor:** Paul Landres; **Cast:** Preston Foster, Barbara Britton, John Ireland, Reed Hadley, J. Edward Bromberg, Tom Tyler.

Samuel Fuller's treatment of the Jesse James saga focuses on Bob Ford (John Ireland) and explains why Ford shot Jesse. The film then follows Ford's life as it begins to unravel piece by piece. It seems Ford kills Jesse so he can win a pardon and be free to marry his childhood sweetheart, but as things start falling apart, he loses her as well. Reed Hadley plays Jesse, and Tom Tyler delivers a fine performance as Frank James.

IVORY-HANDLED GUN, THE   Universal, 1935, B&W, 58 min, VT. **Producer:** Buck Jones; **Director:** Ray Taylor; **Screenplay:** John T. Nevelle; **Cinematographer:** Allen Thompson; **Editor:** Bernard Loftus; **Cast:** Buck Jones, Charlette Wynters, Walter Miller, Frank Rice, Carl Stockdale.

JACKASS MAIL MGM, 1942, B&W, 80 min. **Producer:** John W. Considine; **Director:** Norman McLoud; **Screenplay:** Lawrence Hazzard; **Music:** Earl K. Brent; **Cinematographer:** Clyde De Vinna; **Editor:** Gene Roggiero; **Cast:** Wallace Beery, Marjorie Main, J. Carroll Naish, Darryl Hickman, William Haade, Dick Curtis.

Wallace Beery is Marmaduke "Just" Baggot, an old-time bad man being pursued by the woman owner of a mail wagon team and a saloon girl (Marjorie Main). After escaping from a hanging party, he stops a robbery and becomes a local hero. Fans of Beery and Main should appreciate this whimsical adventure.

JACK MCCALL DESPERADO Columbia, 1953, Color, 76 min. **Producer:** Sam Katzman; **Producer:** Sidney Salkow; **Screenplay:** John O'Dea; **Cinematographer:** Henry Freulich; **Editor:** Aaron Stell; **Cast:** George Montgomery, Angela Stevens, Douglas Kennedy, James Seay, Jay Silverheels.

A Southerner joins the Union army during the Civil War but is framed on the charge of giving information to the enemy. Convicted of treason and sentenced to die, he escapes to find the man who framed him. In a true assault on the Bill Hickok legend, McCall justifiably shoots and kills a cowardly and murderous Hickok in a fair fight and is acquitted in court. No attempt is made to mention the fact that McCall was retried by a different court and promptly hanged.

JACK SLADE (aka: JACK SLADE DESPERADO) Allied Artists, B&W, 1953, 89 min. **Producer:** Lindsley Parsons; **Director:** Harold D. Schuster; **Screenplay:** Warren Douglas; **Music:** Paul Dunlap; **Cinematographer:** William A. Sickner; **Editor:** Leonard W. Herman;

Cast: Mark Stevens, Dorothy Malone, Barton MacLane, John Litel, Paul Langton, Lee Van Cleef.

A 12-year-old boy sees his father gunned down in front of him. He later becomes a lawman and the West's reputed fastest gun. Disillusioned with his work, he leaves his girl and his law enforcement career behind and turns instead to a life of crime. Mark Stevens delivers an unusual performance as the morose Jack Slade in this offbeat but well-made little western.

In his autobiography writer Warren Douglas tells how his good friend, producer Lindsley Parsons, found a character named Jack Slade in Mark Twain's book *Roughing It*. Slade was a hard-riding, fast-shooting alcoholic, a fascinating fellow whose persona Douglas adapted to his screenplay. Douglas presents a detailed and full account of a screenplay's evolution from its inception through the finished film product in Herb Fagen's book *White Hats and Silver Spurs*.

JAMES BROTHERS, THE See *TRUE STORY OF JESSE JAMES, THE*.

JAYHAWKERS, THE Paramount, 1959, Color, 100 min, VT. **Producer:** Melvin Frank and Norman Panama; **Director:** Frank; **Screenplay:** A. I. Bezzerides, Frank Fenton, Frank, and Joseph Petracca; **Music:** Jerome Moross; **Cinematographer:** Loyal Griggs; **Editor:** Everette Douglas; **Cast:** Jeff Chandler, Fess Parker, Nicole Maurey, Henry Silva, Herbert Rudley.

Prior to the Civil War, when Kansas was divided between proslave and antislave forces, two men (Jeff Chandler and Fess Parker) battle for power, control of the territory, and the affections of beautiful Nicole Maurey. In one of his rare roles as a heavy, Jeff Chandler delivers an interesting performance as the leader of the abolitionist Jayhawkers, a man who has dreams of building an empire and becoming the Napoleon of the plains. Fess Parker is convincing as a wily farmer who is spurred on by revenge.

JEEPER CREEPERS (aka: MONEY ISN'T EVERYTHING, UK) Republic, 1939, B&W, 69 min. **Producer:** Armand Schaefer; **Director:** Frank McDonald; **Screenplay:** Dorrell McGowan; **Cinematographer:** Ernest Miller; **Editor:** Ernest J. Nimms; **Cast:** Roy Rogers, the Weavers (Leon, Frank, June, and Loretta), Maris Wrixon, Billy Lee, Dan White, Lucien Littlefield.

A backwoods family is being fleeced out of their land by a rich industrialist, but they decide to win it back by trying to humanize the culprit. Roy Rogers plays an empathetic sheriff. (See also UNDER WESTERN STARS.)

JEREMIAH JOHNSON Warner Bros., 1972, Color, 108 min, VT, DVD. **Producer:** Joe Wizan; **Director:** Sydney Pollack; **Screenplay:** John Millius and Edward Anhalt; **Music:** Tim McIntire and John Rubenstein; **Cinematographer:** Duke Callaghan; **Editor:** Thomas Stanford; **Cast:** Robert Redford, Will Geer, Delle Bolton, Josh Albee, Allyn Ann McLerie.

Robert Redford is Jeremiah Johnson, a man whose personal journey and search for solitude in the wilderness produces a slew of hardships and challenges. Disgusted with civilization, Johnson becomes a mountain man in the Rockies, where he meets up with an old trapper named Griz (Will Geer) and an Indian woman (Allyn Ann McLerie).

John Milius employed two sources for his screenplay: *Mountain Man*, a novel by Vardis Fisher; and *Crow Killer*, a short nonfiction biography by Raymond W. Thorp and Robert Bunker. Johnson, an historical figure, was to become a legend in his own time.

Most have praised this film as a true work of art, exquisitely photographed, with an uplifting theme that a person can find spiritual peace in the battle against nature. The main criticism, and a valid one, is that the film doesn't seem to know where and when to quit. Much of the film's unnecessary ramblings lead to an ending void of finality.

According to author Joe Hyams in *The Life and Times of the Great Western Movie*, the film was so popular that it inspired a class of seventh graders in Lancaster, California, to do research on Johnson. They discovered in their research that when Johnson died in 1900, he was buried in a veteran's cemetery in Los Angeles near the San Diego Freeway, even though Johnson's expressed desire had been to be buried in the mountains. The students eventually saw his wish fulfilled. Johnson's body was disinterred and flown to Wyoming, where it was laid to rest. Robert Redford attended the ceremony.

JESSE JAMES 20th Century Fox, 1939, Color, 105 min, VHS. **Producer:** Darryl F. Zanuck; **Director:** Henry King; **Screenplay:** Nunnally Johnson; **Music:** Louis Silvers; **Cinematographer:** George Barnes and W. Howard Green; **Editor:** Barbara McLean; **Cast:** Tyrone Power, Henry Fonda, Nancy Kelly, Randolph Scott, Brian Donlevy, Henry Hull, Jane Darwell, John Carradine, Donald Meek.

With the Civil War over, Jesse James returns home to take up his life as a peaceful farmer. But unscrupulous bankers and railroad men take away his land and kill his mother, prompting Jesse and brother Frank into a life of outlawry. The brothers commence their infamous careers as outlaws by robbing trains owned by the railroad. These acts lead to an escalation of further crimes. While Frank escapes the law, Jesse is shot in the back by Bob Ford (John Carradine) in the honeymoon cottage he shares with Nancy Kelly.

This 1939 western started a new vogue for romanticizing the West's real outlaws. Director Henry King at least kept one foot in the historical past, even though star Tyrone Power has ample opportunity to overindulge his interpretation as a handsome, noble, charming, and misunderstood Robin Hood of the West. *Time* noted that writer Nunnally Johnson's screenplay presents the famed outlaw ". . . as an amiable brigand, genuinely devoted to his aged mother and generally more sinned against than sinning."

Tyrone Power and Henry Fonda provide big-name sympathetic portrayals of the James Brothers. It was a turnabout for Fox, which had not made a major Western between the advent of the talkies and Henry King's 1939 film. With the huge success and popularity of *Jesse James*, Fox came back to the western fold with a fury, although it should be added that most were in the "biography" category.

Fox lavished a huge budget to produce this $2 million Technicolor blockbuster. Authentic on-location sites in Pineville, Missouri, were utilized for a time, with throngs of tourists and locals often at hand. Following the Hollywood premier of the picture, Ms. Jo Frances James of Los Angeles, a descendant of the film's subjects said, "About the only connection it had with fact is that there once was a man named James, and he did ride a horse."

The film was a breakthrough in shaping the film career of Henry Fonda. Bosley Crowther in the *New York Times* lauded Fonda "as the tobacco-chewing Frank James . . . [for] a beautiful characterization."

JESSE JAMES AT BAY Republic, 1941, B&W, 56 min. **Producer:** Joseph Kane; **Director:** Kane; **Screenplay:** James R. Webb; **Cinematographer:** William Nobles; **Editor:** Tony Martinelli; **Cast:** Roy Rogers, George "Gabby" Hayes, Sally Payne, Gale Storm, Roy Barcroft, Hal Taliaferro.

JESSE JAMES, JR. Republic, 1942, B&W, 56 min. **Producer:** George Sherman (associate); **Director:** Sherman; **Screenplay:** Taylor Caven, Richard Murphy, and Doris Schroeder; **Music:** Cy Feuer; **Cinematographer:** John MacBurnie; **Editor:** William P. Thompson; **Cast:** Don "Red" Barry, Lynn Merrick, Al St. John, Douglas Walton, Karl Hackett, George Chesebro.

A young man tries to thwart crooks who are trying to destroy a telegraph headquarters. Hero Johnny Barrett (Don "Red" Barry) gets some help from the bicycle-riding Pop Sawyer (Al St. John). (See also *WYOMING OUTLAW.*)

JESSE JAMES' WOMEN   United Artists, 1954, Color, 83 min, VHS. **Producers:** Donald Barry, Tom Garraway, and Lloyd Royal; **Director:** Don "Red" Barry; **Screenplay:** Barry and William Cox; **Music:** Walter Greene; **Cinematographer:** Walter Greene; **Editor:** Barton E. Hayes; **Cast:** Don "Red" Barry, Peggy Castle, Jack Buetel (as Jack Beutel), Lita Baron, Mike Carr, Sam Keller.

Jesse James and his gang are on the run and holding up in a small Mississippi town. Before long the famed outlaw is complicating the lives of several women—most of them in low-cut gowns. Don "Red" Barry's only stab at directing also features two songs: "Careless Lover" (music and lyrics by George Anthiel) and "In the Shadow of My Heart" by the prolific Stan Jones.

JOE KIDD   Universal, 1972, Color, 88 min, VHS, DVD. **Producer:** Sidney Bickerman; **Director:** John Sturges; **Screenplay:** Elmore Leonard; **Music:** Lalo Schifrin; **Cinematographer:** Bruce Surtees; **Editor:** Ferris Webster; **Cast:** Clint Eastwood, Robert Duvall, John Saxon, Stella Garcia, James Wainwright, Paul Koslo, Gregory Walcott, Dick Van Patten, Lynn Marta.

In this film set in New Mexico after the turn of the century, Clint Eastwood is Joe Kidd, a town malcontent who is hired by powerful landowner Frank Harlan (Robert Duvall) to help track down a Mexican revolutionary named Louis Chama (John Saxon). But after a series of run-ins with Harlan, Kidd eventually becomes convinced that he is on the wrong side of the battle. He changes sides after Harlan lures Chama into a trap in a cowardly attempt to destroy the revolutionary leader. A heated range war follows, concluding with Kidd dramatically driving a locomotive off the track and into the buildings housing Harlan's men.

Based on an original screenplay by Elmore Leonard called "Sinola" and directed by John Sturges (*The Magnificent Seven*, [1960] *Bad Day at Black Rock*, [1955] *The Great Escape* [1963]), the film falls far short of Eastwood's better film endeavors. On the other hand, it ranks among his more successful films, having outgrossed many of his other efforts.

JOE DAKOTA   Universal, 1957, Color, 79 min. **Producer:** Howard Christie; **Director:** Richard Bartlett; **Screenplay:** Norman Jolley and William Talman; **Music:** Joseph Gershenson, Henry Mancint, and Hans J. Salter; **Cinematographer:** George Robinson; **Editor:** Fred McDowell; **Cast:** Jock Mahoney, Luana Patten, Charles McGraw, Barbara Lawrence, Claude Akins, Lee Van Cleef, Anthony Caruso, Steve Darrell, Rita Lynn, Gregg Barton.

Jock Mahoney is a stranger who arrives in a town that is down on itself and where the people are cold and unfriendly.

He successfully restores their pride and self respect by getting them to come to terms with a long-held secret. Stuntman turned actor Mahoney delivers a solid performance in this suspenseful life oater, which at the same time is sweet and touching.

JOHNNY CONCHO   United Artists, 1956, B&W, 84 min. **Producer:** Frank Sinatra; **Director:** Don McGuire; **Music:** Nelson Riddle; **Cinematographer:** William C. Mellor; **Editor:** Eda Warren; **Cast:** Frank Sinatra, Phyllis Kirk, Keenan Wynn, Wallace Ford, William Conrad, Leo Gordon, Claude Akins, John Qualen.

Frank Sinatra plays a skinny, cowardly bully who lives in the glory of his gunman brother Red Concho. But when Red is gunned down, the cowardly Johnny is forced to stand up against another gunman on his own, and by film's end he displays some surprising grit. This movie was Frank Sinatra's first and only serious western (*The Kissing Bandit*, 1948, was a musical).

JOHNNY GUITAR   Republic, 1954, Color, 110 min, VHS, CD. **Producer:** Herbert J. Yates; **Director:** Nicholas Ray; **Screenplay:** Philip Yordan; **Music:** Victor Young; **Cinematographer:** Harry Stradling Jr.; **Editor:** Richard L. Van Enger; **Cast:** Joan Crawford, Sterling Hayden, Mercedes McCambridge, Scott Brady, Ward Bond, Ben Cooper, Ernest Borgnine, John Carradine, Royal Dano, Paul Fix.

In her first western since *Montana Moon* (1930), Joan Crawford plays Vienna, the strong-willed owner of a plush gambling saloon standing in the middle of the Arizona wilderness. Knowing that the railroad is coming through, she plans to build a new town and become rich. She is opposed by Mercedes MacCambridge, the frustrated leader of a nearby community.

The women wear the pants in this unusual film helmed by Nicholas Ray. The men generally show themselves to be characters of dubious distinction, with Sterling Hayden as Johnny Guitar, Vienna's former paramour and now protector; and Scott Brady as the Dancin' Kid, who hangs around Vienna long enough to incur the wrath of the neurotic and unstable Emma (McCambridge).

The themes of love, hate, violence, jealousy, and treachery envelop this film, which concludes with a violent showdown between Vienna and Emma. Because of its strong psychological and metaphysical overtones, the picture at various times has been called an anti-McCarthy western, a marxist western, and even a lesbian western. The Europeans in general and the French critics in particular love this film and have elevated it to cult status. Certainly its sexual concerns, memorable dialogue, and heavily symbolic scenes make for a unique movie. As author Danny Peary notes "a male dancer and male guitarist vie for the love of a gun toting woman."

Yet despite the many platitudes, critics remain divided. Because of the overdose of passions and sexuality, there is little room for conventional western action. In his *Video Guide,*

Leonard Maltin calls the film "simply fascinating." Conversely, *Variety* finds Crawford's performance to be flawed, noting that "Johnny Guitar . . . proves the actress should leave saddles and Levis to someone else and stick to city lights for the background," while pointing out that ". . . scriptor [Phillip] Yordan and director [Nicholas] Ray became so involved with character nuances and neuroses that *Johnny Guitar* never has enough chance to rear up in the saddle and ride at an acceptable outdoor pace."

Author Jennifer Peterson presents an interesting perspective on the lingering *Johnny Guitar* controversy in an article "The Competing Tunes of Johnny Guitar: Liberalism, Sexuality, Masquerade," which appears in Jim Kitses and Gregg Rickman's *The Western Reader.* The movie was filmed in Sedona, Arizona. The title song is sung by Peggy Lee but does not always appear on the CD soundtrack.

JOHNNY RENO   Paramount, 1966, Color, 83 min, VHS. **Producer:** A. C. Lyles; **Director:** R. G. Springsteen; **Screenplay:** Steve Fisher; **Music:** Jimmy Haskell; **Cinematographer:** Harold E. Stine; **Editor:** Bernard Matis; **Cast:** Dana Andrews, Jane Russell, Lon Chaney Jr., John Agar, Lyle Bettger, Tom Drake, Richard Arlen, Robert Lowery.

A sheriff brings in the accused killer of an Indian chief's son for trial, but he finds that most of the townspeople support the accused. Good performances by a veteran cast makes for an enjoyable A. C. Lyles oater.

JORY   Avco-Embassy, 1972, Color, 97 min. **Producer:** Howard Minsky; **Director:** Jorge Fons; **Screenplay:** Gerald Herman and Robert Irving; **Music:** Al De Lory; **Cinematographer:** Jorge Stahl; **Editors:** Fred Chulak and Sergio Ortega; **Cast:** John Marley, B. J. Thomas, Robby Benson, Brad Dexter, Claudio Brook, Ben Baker, Ted Markland.

A 15-year-old boy grows up fast when he sets out to take revenge on the men who murdered his father and his friends. This surprisingly effective western features a fine performance by young Robby Benson in his screen debut. Filmed in Mexico, the movie was issued theatrically only on an experimental basis. Singer B. J. Thomas plays an expert gun handler who is unable to fire at another human being even in his own defense.

JOURNEY TO SHILOH   Universal, 1968, Color, 101 min. **Producer:** Howard Christie; **Director:** William Hale; **Screenplay:** Gene Coon; **Music:** David Gates; **Cinematographer:** Enzo Martinelli; **Editor:** Edward W. Williams; **Cast:** James Caan, Michael Sarrazin, Brenda Scott, Don Stroud, Paul Peterson, Michael Burns, Jan-Michael Vincent, Harrison Ford, John Doucette, Noah Beery Jr., Myron Healey, Bing Russell, Rex Ingram.

In 1862 a group of young Texans march off to join the Confederate army without knowing what they are fighting for or the real meaning of war. Despite a good cast, including a young Harrison Ford, the film failed to generate much positive interest.

JUBAL   Columbia, 1956, Color, 100 min, VHS. **Producer:** William Fadiman; **Director:** Delmer Daves; **Screenplay:** Daves and Russell S. Hughes; **Music:** David Raksin; **Cinematographer:** Charles Lawton Jr.; **Editor:** Al Clark; **Cast:** Glenn Ford, Ernest Borgnine, Rod Steiger, Valerie French, Felicia Farr, Noah Beery Jr., Charles Bronson, John Dierkes, Jack Elam.

Glenn Ford plays Jubal Troop, a ranch hand who is an object of lust on the part of his boss's promiscuous wife in this adaptation of Paul Wellman's novel *Jubal Troop.* Jubal is rescued by friendly rancher Shep Horgan (Ernest Borgnine), a big-hearted and coarse man who claims that there are only three things worth fighting for: "a woman, a full belly, and a roof over your head." However, when Shep makes Jubal his foreman, he incurs the wrath of Pinky (Rod Steiger), a cowardly bully who had previously been the lover of Shep's unfaithful wife Mae. Pinky's hatred for Jubal soon becomes as strong as his sexual desire for Mae (Felicia Farr in her screen debut). The aftermath is a torrid fuse of emotions: sex, passion, killing, and revenge, as Steiger makes Borgnine think that Jubal is fooling around with his wife.

A gripping dramatic story set in pioneer Wyoming and filmed in the majestic Grand Tetons, the film exudes mounting suspense as tensions and passions increase steadily. The characters are fully developed and the performances are top grade, with Borgnine delivering an excellent performance as the kindly yet flawed rancher; and a fine, low-key performance by Charles Bronson as Reb Haslipp, the young ranch hand who befriends Jubal Troop. Bronson had delivered well for Delmer Daves two years earlier as Modoc chief Captain Jack in Daves's *DRUM BEAT* (1954).

Reportedly, the role of Pinky was originally slated to go to Aldo Ray, who was enormously popular at the time. It would have been Ray's first western and his first role as a heavy. According to studio brass he had given his okay to Delmer Daves to rewrite the script and build up his part. When he subsequently changed his mind and turned the role down, Columbia put Ray under suspension.

One of the screen's most underrated western directors, Delmer Daves brilliantly plays out the Othello theme with a western setting. While others portrayed the West as they would have liked it to be, Daves's penchant was to portray it as it was, and he came to be considered the documentarian of the western film. His own family had pioneer roots. Daves's grandfather himself made covered-wagon crossings, had been a Pony Express rider, and for a time lived among the Hopi and Navajo Indians. Although Delmer Daves never helmed a Western epic among his many outstanding genre films, he began his film career as a property assistant on James Cruze's silent epic *THE COVERED WAGON* (1923).

JUBILEE TRAIL   Republic, 1954, Color, 103 min, VHS. **Producer:** Joseph Kane (associate); **Director:** Kane;

Screenplay: Bruce Manning; **Music:** Victor Young; **Cinematographer:** Jack A. Marta; **Editor:** Richard L. Van Enger; **Cast:** Vera Hruba Ralston, Joan Leslie, Forrest Tucker, John Russell, Ray Middleton, Pat O'Brien, Buddy Baer, Jim Davis, Barton MacLane, Richard Webb.

A woman wanted for murder heads west with her young daughter and a baby. She finds herself having to pick among an assortment of men who are pursuing her. This big-budget film with some big-name stars somehow fails to rise above the ordinary.

JUNCTION CITY Columbia, 1952, B&W, 54 min. **Producer:** Colbert Clark; **Director:** Ray Nazzaro; **Screenplay:** Barry Shipman; **Cinematographer:** Henry Freulich; **Editor:** Paul Borofsky; **Cast:** Charles Starrett, Smiley Burnette, Jock Mahoney, Kathleen Case, John Dehner, George Chesebro, Chris Alacide.

JUNIOR BONNER Cinerama Releasing/ABC, 1972, Color, 100 min, VHS, DVD. **Producer:** Joe Wizan; **Director:** Sam Peckinpah; **Screenplay:** Jeb Rosebrook; **Music:** Jerry Fielding; **Cinematographer:** Lucien Ballard; **Editor:** Robert L. Wolfe; **Cast:** Steve McQueen, Robert Preston, Ida Lupino, Ben Johnson, Joe Don Baker, Barbara Leigh, Mary Murphy, Donald "Red" Barry.

Over-the-hill rodeo rider Junior Bonner (Steve McQueen) has trouble adjusting to the complexities of modern life. Bonner returns to his home in Prescott, Arizona, to take part in the July 4 Frontier Days Rodeo. While he is still trying to beat the eight-second clock, his younger brother Curly (Joe Don Baker) is on the way to making his first million by buying up land to make mobile home developments. Eventually Junior proves himself in front of a hometown crowd, riding a bull that had never been ridden and that had defeated him before. He takes the money he wins and gives it to his father Ace, a veteran rodeo rider, whose desire and dream is to move to Australia. Robert Preston and Ida Lupino are outstanding as Bonner's parents.

This picture is often labeled as director Sam Peckinpah's most gentle film, and like most of the director's work it is concerned with human dignity. Interestingly, it was released the same year as Peckinpah's extremely violent nonwestern *The Getaway*. According to McQueen biographer Marshall Terrill, the actor more or less backed into the role. At the time Robert Redford was looking for a rodeo picture, but when an outline of the film was sent to him he turned it down. Producer Joe Wizan had thought all along that it was better suited for McQueen, who read the script and loved it.

Reviewers were kind, and the actor received some of his best reviews to date. The *Los Angeles Times* wrote that "Steve McQueen is explosive and gives one of his finest performances." Kathleen Carroll in the *New York Daily News* called the movie "a nice easygoing rodeo picture" and noted that "McQueen has met with a role that fits him like a glove." *Variety* was equally awed: "The later-day film genre of mis-understood-rodeo-drifter-gets one of its best expositions in *Junior Bonner*. Steve McQueen stars handily in the title role."

Yet despite the plethora of fine reviews and critical acclaim, the film died at the box office and was a financial failure. It grossed a mere $2 million worldwide, and ABC lost $4 million in the process. Of course, in summer 1972 Hollywood produced more than its share of rodeo films, with *J. W. Coop*, *The Honkers*, *When Legends Die*, and *Junior Bonner* all being released within the same three-month period.

JUSTICE CAIN See *CAIN'S CUT THROATS*.

JUSTICE OF THE RANGE Columbia, 1935, B&W, 58 min. **Producer:** Irving Briskin; **Director:** David Selman; **Screenplay:** Ford Beebe; **Cinematographer:** George Meehan; **Editor:** Al Clark; **Cast:** Tim McCoy, Billie Seward, Ward Bond, Guy Usher, George "Gabby" Hayes, Jack Rockwell.

JUSTICE RIDES AGAIN See *DESTRY RIDES AGAIN*.

JUST PALS Fox, 1920, B&W, 50 min. **Director:** John Ford (as Jack Ford); **Screenplay:** Paul Schofield; **Cinematographer:** George Schneiderman; **Cast:** Buck Jones, Helen Ferguson, George Stone, Duke R. Lee, William Buckley, Eunice Murdock.

A small-town vagabond is turned into a hero and he-man when he befriends a young boy. This good silent oater melding the talents of John Ford and Buck Jones makes for an interesting film and one of the better earlier Jones efforts.

JUST TONY Fox, 1922, B&W, 58 min. **Director:** Lynn Reynolds; **Screenplay:** Reynolds; **Cinematographer:** Daniel B. Clark; **Cast:** Tom Mix, Claire Adams, J. P. Lockney, Duke R. Lee, Frank Campeau, Walt Robbins.

A cowboy seeks revenge against the man who shot him in a barroom brawl. While he is searching for him, he befriends a wild stallion and inadvertently falls in love with the daughter of the man who shot him. The horse demonstrates his gratitude by saving the cowboy and the rancher's daughter when they are captured by villains. Not only did Tom Mix find his faithful horse Tony in this classic silent, he also displays some of his best and most elaborate stunts.

In the silent era Tom Mix and Tony were Fox's top money-making asset, with Mix earning up to $17,500 per week. While William S. Hart's horse Fritz was the first equine star of American film, Mix's white mount Tony became the best-known and most popular horse in cowboy films. In fact, Mix made this picture as a tribute to his mount and to please the countless fans who enjoyed the camaraderie between star and horse.

The top cowboy star of the 1920s, Mix propelled himself to stardom with *The Untamed* in 1920, a film adaptation of the popular Max Brand novel. Other popular Mix features during the 1920s include *Sky High* (1921); *Soft Boiled, North of the Hudson Bay, The Lone Star Ranger* (1923); *Riders of the Purple Sage,* THE RAINBOW TRAIL, *The Best Badman* (1925); THE GREAT K & A TRAIN ROBBERY (1926); and *The Last Trail* (1927).

J. W. COOP Columbia, 1972, Color, 112 VT. **Producer:** Cliff Robertson; **Director:** Robertson; **Screenplay:** Gary Cartwright, Bud Shrake, and Robertson; **Music:** Don Randi and Louis Shelton; **Cinematographer:** Frank Stanley; **Editor:** Alex Beaton; **Cast:** Cliff Robertson, Geraldine Page, Cristina Ferrare, R. G. Armstrong, R. L. Armstrong, John Crawford.

Rodeo star J. W. Coop gets out of prison after 10 years (he had passed bad checks and roughed up a sheriff), and he is determined to become a champion once more. Things have changed in a decade, as society seems to now value only one goal: financial success. Described as the "guy with the greatest heart ever seen in rodeo," he tries to set things straight by again becoming the greatest rodeo rider on the circuit while also trying to cope with a world he no longer seems to understand very well.

Cliff Robertson received nearly unanimous critical acclamation for his skillful "hat trick" of producing, directing, scripting, and starring in this extremely well-done film, creating a vivid and strong character study that is a testimony to Robertson's too often-ignored artistic skills. *Variety* noted that "Robertson's sensitive treatment and savvy direction has created a character at once heroic and tragic."

KANSAN, THE (aka: WAGON WHEELS, UK)
United Artists, 1943, B&W, 79 min, VHS. **Producer:** Harry
Sherman; **Director:** George Archainbaud; **Screenplay:**
Harold Shumate; **Music:** Gerard Carbonara, Foster Carling,
and Phil Ohman; **Cinematographer:** Russell Harlan; **Editor:** Carroll Lewis; **Cast:** Richard Dix, Jane Wyatt, Albert
Dekker, Victor Jory, Robert Armstrong, Beryl W. Wallace,
Rod Cameron, George Reeves.

John Bonniwell (Richard Dix) cleans up the town of Broken
Lance, which is overrun by outlaws. In doing so he becomes
an instant hero to the honest citizenry, only to find himself
betrayed by corrupt city officials. The story ends with an old
fashion showdown on Main Street.

Helmed by George Archainbaud, one of Hollywood's
most prolific and least remembered directors of B pictures,
the film boasts a nice performance by Dix as the heroic marshal and Victor Jory as the suave villain. With an Oscar-nominated musical score by Gerald Carbona, this archetypal
1940s western was applauded by Theodore Strauss in the
New York Times as a "whooping-hollering . . . cloud of dust
headed by granite faced Richard Dix on the side of law and
order." The song "Lullaby of the Herd" by Foster Carling
(words) and Phil Ohman (music) is sung in the film by The
King's Men. George Reeves (TV's future Superman) appears
in an uncredited role as Jesse James. The film was based on
the novel *Peace Marshal* by Frank Gruber.

KANSAS CYCLONE Republic, 1941, B&W, 57 min.
Producer: George Sherman; **Director:** Sherman; **Screenplay:** Oliver Drake and Doris Schroeder; **Cinematographer:** William Nobles; **Editor:** Charles Craft; **Cast:** Don
"Red" Barry, Lynn Merrick, William Haade, Milton Kibbee,
Harry Worth, Eddie Dean.

KANSAS RAIDERS Universal, 1950, Color, 80 min.
Producer: Ted Richmond; **Director:** Ray Enright; **Screenplay:** Robert L. Richards; **Cinematographer:** Irving Glassberg; **Editor:** Milton Carruth; **Cast:** Audie Murphy, Brian
Donlevy, Marguerite Chapman, Scott Brady, Tony Curtis,
Richard Arlen, Richard Long, John Kellog, Dewey Martin,
George Chandler.

The James Brothers (Audie Murphy and Richard Long) join
Quantrill's Raiders during the Civil War. However, they discover that Quantrill (Brian Donlevy) is a megalomaniac and
that the Raiders are more concerned with killing and looting
than they are with fighting Northern soldiers. World War
II's most decorated GI, Murphy makes an appealing Jesse
James, portraying him as the proverbial good boy gone bad.
Kansas Raiders marked one of the earliest screen appearances
for actor Tony Curtis, who, like Murphy, made his screen
debut in the late 1940s.

KANSAS TERRITORY Monogram, 1952, B&W, 65
min. **Producer:** Vincent Fennally; **Director:** Lewis D.
Collins; **Screenplay:** Daniel B. Ullman; **Cinematographer:**
Ernest Miller; **Editor:** Richard V. Heermance; **Cast:**
William "Wild Bill" Elliott, Peggy Stewart, Lane Bradford,
John Hart, William Fawcett, Pierce Lyden.

A man who has been wrongfully accused of a crime returns
home to avenge the death of his brother. This later-day
Monogram oater is more than a cut above average, with a
good performance by John Hart as the marshal. (See also
WACO.)

KEEP ROLLIN' See *GAUCHO SERENADE.*

KENNY ROGERS AS THE GAMBLER (aka: THE GAMBLER) CBS-TV, 1980, Color, 94 min. **Producer:** Jim Byrnes; **Director:** Dick Lowry; **Teleplay:** Byrnes and Cort Casady; **Music:** Larry Cansler: **Cinematographer:** Joseph F. Biroc; **Editor:** Jerrold L. Ludwig; **Cast:** Kenny Rogers, Christine Belford, Harold Gould, Clu Gallager, Lance LeGault, Lee Purcell, Neil Summers.

A gambler named Brady Hawks returns to the town where his son and the woman he never married reside—even though an enemy waits there for him to arrive. The narrative springboard for this TV movie, written by Don Schlitz, is based on Rogers's hit song, which is sung by Rogers in the film. A popular television western, it was followed by two sequels: *The Gambler, Part II—The Adventure Continues*, and *Part III—The Legend Continues*.

KENTUCKIAN, THE United Artists, 1955, Color, 104 min, VHS, DVD. **Producers:** Harold Hecht and James Hill; **Director:** Burt Lancaster; **Screenplay:** A. B. Guthrie and Felix Holt; **Cinematographer:** Ernest Laszlo; **Music:** Bernard Hermann; **Editors:** George E. Luckenbacher and William B. Murphy; **Cast:** Burt Lancaster, Dianne Foster, Diana Lynn, John McIntire, Una Merkel, John Carradine, Walter Matthau, Donald MacDonald.

In his first directorial effort, Burt Lancaster plays a rugged frontiersman who travels to Texas with his son in search of a place to start a new life. Based on the novel *The Gabriel Horn* by Felix Holt, the film also marks the screen debut of Walter Matthau as the whip-wielding heavy.

This slow-moving western adventure drama has a few tense moments, such as Lancaster's frantic dash across a shallow lake while the villain tries assiduously to reload his musket. Another plus is the title song, written by Irving Gordon and recorded by The Hilltoppers, which became a Top 20 recording.

KENTUCKY RIFLE Howco-International, 1956, Color, 84 min. **Producer:** Carl K. Hittleman; **Director:** Hittleman; **Screenplay:** Frank Chase Jr., Lee Hewitt, and Hittleman; **Music:** Irving Gertz; **Cinematographer:** Paul Ivano; **Editor:** Hugh Winn; **Cast:** Chill Wills, Lance Fuller, Cathy Downs, Jess Parker, Jeanne Cagney.

When a wagon train breaks down, the passengers are forced to travel through Comanche territory but are impeded by Indians who want their cargo and rifles. Chill Wills sings the folk standard "Sweet Betsy from Pike."

KID BLUE 20th Century Fox, 1973, Color, 100 min. **Producer:** Marvin Schwartz; **Director:** James Frawley; **Screenplay:** Edwin Shrake; **Music:** Tom McIntire and John Rubenstein; **Cinematographer:** Billy Williams; **Editor:** Stefan Arnsten; **Cast:** Dennis Hopper, Warren Oates, Peter Boyle, Ben Johnson, Janice Rule.

Dennis Hopper is a train robber and general hooligan who decides to settle down in a small Texas town at the turn of the 20th century. He runs into trouble, however, when his friend's wife tries to seduce him. This so-so genre spoof was filmed in Mexico.

KID COURAGEOUS Supreme, 1935, B&W, 62 min. **Producer:** A. W. Hackel; **Director:** Robert N. Bradbury; **Screenplay:** Bradbury; **Cinematographer:** William Hyer; **Editor:** S. Roy Luby; **Cast:** Bob Steele, Rene Borden, Arthur Loft, Jack Cowell, Kit Guard, Lafe McKee.

When a man travels west to discover the identity of a robber responsible for a series of thefts, he ends up saving a pretty girl from a marriage she does not want. This fast-moving and entertaining little oater is one of a series of westerns Bob Steele made for Supreme Pictures between 1934 and 1936. Others in the series include: *A Demon for Trouble, Brand of Hate* (1934); *Rider of the Law, The Kid Ranger, Smokey Smith, Trail of Terror, Alias John Law, Western Justice, Big Calibre, Sundown Saunders, Tombstone Terror* (1935); *Brand of the Outlaws, Last of the Warrens* (1936).

KID FROM BROKEN GUN, THE Columbia, 1952, B&W, 55 min. **Producer:** Colbert Clark; **Director:** Fred F. Sears; **Screenplay:** Ed Earl Rapp and Barry Shipman; **Cinematographer:** Fayte M. Browne; **Editor:** Charles Clague; **Cast:** Charles Starrett, Smiley Burnette, Jock Mahoney, Angela Stevens, Tristram Coffin, Myron Healey, Chris Alcaide.

Two men arrive in a small town to help a pal, an ex-prizefighter who has been falsely accused of robbery and murder. This film ended the seven-year-long *DURANGO KID* series for Columbia with Charles Starrett as The Durango Kid.

KID FROM SANTA FE, THE Monogram, 1940, B&W, 57 min. **Producer:** Harry S. Webb; **Director:** Bernard B. Ray (as Raymond K. Johnson); **Screenplay:** Carl Krusada; **Cinematographer:** William Hyer and Edward A. Kull; **Editor:** Robert Golden; **Cast:** Addison Randall, Clarene Curtis, Forrest Taylor, Claire Rochelle, Tom London, George Chesebro, Dave O'Brien, Jimmy Aubrey, Kenne Duncan.

See *RIDERS OF THE DAWN*.

KID FROM TEXAS, THE MGM, 1939, B&W, 71 min. **Producer:** Edgar Selwyn; **Director:** S. Sylvan Simon; **Screenplay:** Milton Merlin; **Music:** William Axt; **Cinematographer:** Sidney Wagner; **Editor:** Fredrick Y. Smith; **Cast:** Dennis O'Keefe, Buddy Ebsen, Jack Carson, Tully Marshall, Virginia Dale, Iron Eyes Cody, John Hubbard, J. M. Kerrigan.

A polo-playing cowboy goes to the East, where he becomes the manager of a Long Island estate and falls in love with the daughter of the owner of a Wild West show.

KID FROM TEXAS, THE (aka: TEXAS KID OUTLAW, UK) Universal, 1950, Color, 78 min. **Pro-**

ducer: Paul Short; **Director:** Kurt Neumann; **Screenplay:** Karl Kamb; **Cinematographer:** Charles Van Enger; **Editor:** Frank Gross; **Cast:** Audie Murphy, Gale Storm, Albert Dekker, Shepperd Strudwick, Will Geer, William Talman.

Audie Murphy's first starring role has him playing Billy the Kid in this action-packed but none-too-accurate production from Universal. In this one young Billy is hired by a kindly rancher, but upon the rancher's death he becomes an outlaw bent on revenge. The exteriors of this picture were filmed in New Mexico.

KID RANGER, THE Supreme, 1935, B&W, 57 min. **Producer:** A. W. Hackel; **Director:** Robert N. Bradbury; **Screenplay:** Bradbury; **Cinematographer:** E. M. MacManigal; **Editor:** S. Roy Luby; **Cast:** Bob Steele, William Franum, Joan Barclay, Earl Dwire.

KID RIDES AGAIN, THE (aka: BILLY THE KID RIDES AGAIN) PRI, 1943, B&W, 55 min. **Producers:** Sigmund Newfield and Burt Sternbach; **Director:** Sam Newfield; **Screenplay:** Fred Myton; **Cinematographer:** Jack Greenhalgh; **Editor:** Holbrook N. Todd; **Cast:** Buster Crabbe, Al St. John, Iris Meredith, Edward Peil, I. Stanford Jolley, Glenn Strange, Ted Adams.

KID'S LAST RIDE Monogram, 1941, B&W, 55 min, VHS. **Producer:** George W. Weeks; **Director:** S. Roy Luby; **Music:** Harry Tobias; **Cinematographer:** Robert E. Cline; **Editor:** S. Roy Luby; **Cast:** Ray Corrigan, John "Dusty" King, Max Terhune, Luana Walters, Edwin Brian, Al Bridge.

This Range Busters series entry has the Range Busters pretending to help a crook who has blackmailed a young man into telling him where there is a supply of money belonging to a rancher. In reality they intend to expose the gang of crooks. (See also *RANGE BUSTERS, THE*.)

KID VENGEANCE (aka: TAKE ANOTHER HARD RIDE) Cannon, 1977, Color, 94 min, VHS. **Producers:** Yoram Globus, Menahem Golan, and Frank Johnson; **Director:** Joseph Manduke; **Screenplay:** Ken Globus, Bud Robbins, and Jay Tefler; **Music:** Francesco De Masi; **Cinematographer:** David Gurfunkle; **Cast:** Lee Van Cleef, Jim Brown, Leif Garrett, Glynnis O'Connor.

This overly violent and gory oater made in Israel has a young man teaming up with a prospector to avenge the killing of his parents and the kidnapping of his sister.

KILLER AND 21 MEN, THE See *PARSON AND THE OUTLAW, THE*.

KILLER ON A HORSE See *WELCOME TO HARD TIMES*.

KING AND FOUR QUEENS, THE United Artists, 1956, Color, 86 min, VHS. **Producer:** David Hempstead; **Director:** Raoul Walsh; **Screenplay:** Richard Allen Simmons and Margaret Fitts; **Music:** Alex North; **Cinematographer:** Lucien Ballard; **Editors:** David Bretherton and Louis R. Loeffler; **Cast:** Clark Gable, Eleanor Parker, Jean Willes, Barbara Nichols, Sara Shane, Jo Van Fleet, J. C. Flippen.

Smooth cowboy Dan Kehoe (Clark Gable) rides into a ghost town inhabited by the mother of four bandits (supposedly deceased) and the bandits' supposed widows. In order to find the treasure that originally lured him into town, he starts to woo each of the women, using every trick available in his book in an attempt to bilk them of a share of the money the outlaws had hidden before their capture. Eventually he settles down with Eleanor Parker, the prettiest of the young widows. Gable's manly presence still dominates in this Raoul Walsh venture that was made near the end of the director's great career and filmed in St. George, Utah, in CinemaScope.

KING GUN See *GATLING GUN, THE*.

KING OF DODGE CITY Columbia, 1941, B&W, 63 min. **Producer:** Leon Barsha; **Director:** Lambert Hillyer; **Screenplay:** Gerald Geraghty; **Cinematographer:** Benjamin H. Kline; **Editor:** Jerome Thoms; **Cast:** Tex Ritter, William "Wild Bill" Elliott, Judith Linden, Dub Taylor, Guy Usher, Pierce Lyden, George Chesebro, Tristram Coffin.

An ex-lawman and an itinerant sheriff combine to oppose a crook and his gang who are trying to take over a Kansas town in 1861. This steady Bill Elliott/Tex Ritter venture for Columbia is one of eight joint efforts the two cowboy stars made together. (See also *VENGEANCE OF THE WEST*.)

KING OF THE ARENA (aka: KING OF THE RANGE) Universal, 1933, B&W, 59 min. **Producer:** Ken Maynard; **Director:** Alan James; **Screenplay:** James; **Cinematographer:** Ted D. McCord; **Editor:** Charles Harris; **Cast:** Ken Maynard, Lucile Browne, John St. Polis, Bob Kortman, Michael Visaroff.

KING OF THE BANDITS Monogram, 1947, B&W, 66 min, VHS. **Producer:** Jeffrey Bernerd; **Director:** Christy Cabanne; **Screenplay:** Bennett Cohen and Gilbert Roland; **Cinematographer:** William A. Sickner; **Editor:** Roy V. Livingston; **Cast:** Gilbert Roland, Angela Greene, Chris-Pin Martin, Anthony Warde, Laura Treadwell.

KING OF THE BULLWHIP Western Adventure, 1951, B&W, 59 min, VHS. **Producer:** Ron Ormond; **Director:** Ormond; **Screenplay:** Jack Lewis and Ira Webb; **Cinematographer:** Ernest Miller; **Editor:** Hugh Winn; **Cast:**

Lash La Rue, Al St. John, Anne Gwynne, Tom Neal, Dennis Moore.

Two U.S. marshals are summoned to a town by a bank president in order to combat a mysterious masked bandit called El Azote. This interesting and exciting Lash La Rue venture features some brutal fight sequences, especially at the start and finish when whips are brandished.

KING OF THE COWBOYS Republic, 1943, B&W, 67 min, VHS, DVD. **Producer:** Harry Grey; **Director:** Joseph Kane; **Screenplay:** J. Benton Cheney and Olive Cooper; **Cinematographer:** Reggie Lanning; **Editor:** Harry Keller; **Cast:** Roy Rogers, Smiley Burnette, Bob Nolan, Peggy Moran, Gerald Mohr, Dorothea Kent, Lloyd Corrigan.

Roy goes undercover to capture a group of saboteurs fronted by a phony psychic and a governor's assistant. (See also *UNDER WESTERN STARS*.)

KING OF THE MOUNTIES Republic, 1942, B&W, 196 min, 12 episodes. **Producer:** Herbert J. Yates; **Director:** William Witney; **Screenplay:** Taylor Caven, Ronald Davidson, William Lively, Joseph O'Donnell, and Jospeh Poland; **Cinematographer:** Bud Thackery; **Editor:** Tony Martinelli and Edward Todd; **Cast:** Allan Lane, Gilbert Emery, Russell Hicks, Peggy Drake, George Irving, Abner Biberman, Nestor Paiva.

A Mountie uncovers a plot by three enemy agents who are devising the Axis invasion of North America. This good Allan Lane cliffhanger for Republic provides a worthy follow-up to Lane's 12-chapter *King of the Royal Mounted* two years earlier, which was codirected by William Witney.

KING OF THE PECOS Republic, 1936, B&W, 54 min, VHS. **Producer:** Paul Malvern; **Director:** Joseph Kane; **Screenplay:** Dorrell McGowan, Stewart E. McGowan, and Bernard McConiville; **Cinematographer:** Jack A. Marta; **Editor:** Joseph H. Lewis; **Cast:** John Wayne, Muriel Evans, Cy Kendall, Jack Clifford, Arthur Aylesworth, Herbert Heywood.

John Clayborn (John Wayne) seeks revenge on a Texas cattle baron named Stiles, who killed his parents 10 years earlier. He tries to break up Stiles's water monopoly and rustling operation legally, but when his efforts fail he turns to force. Character actor Cy Kendall is the prototypical villain who is felled by his own greed. In this film he is crushed by his own safe.

KING OF THE RANGE See *MARAUDER, THE* (1947).

KING OF THE WILD HORSES Columbia, 1947, B&W, 79 min. **Producer:** Ted Richmond; **Director:** George Archainbaud; **Screenplay:** Brenda Weisberg; **Music:** Mischa Bakaleinikoff; **Cinematographer:** George Meehan and

Philip Tannura; **Editor:** Henry Batista; **Cast:** Preston Foster, Gail Patrick, Billy Sheffield, Guinn "Big Boy" Williams, Patti Brady, Ruth Warren, Grant Withers, Charles Kemper.

A young boy tames and befriends a wild stallion in this appealing, well-cast little film which provides good family viewing.

KING OF THE WILD STALLIONS Allied Artists, 1959, Color, 76 min. **Producer:** Ben Schwalb; **Director:** R. G. Springsteen; **Screenplay:** Ford Beebe; **Music:** Marlin Skiles; **Cinematographer:** Carl E. Guthrie; **Editor:** George White; **Cast:** George Montgomery, Diane Brewster, Edgar Buchanan, Emile Meyer, Jerry Hartleben, Denver Pyle.

A woman and her son who are fighting to save their ranch from a crooked rival get some help from a cowboy and his horse in this charming family yarn.

KISSING BANDIT, THE MGM, 1948, Color, 102 min. **Producer:** Joe Pasternak; **Director:** Laslo Benedek; **Screenplay:** Isobel Lennart and John Briard Harding; **Music:** Earl K. Brent, Nacio Herb Brown, and Edward Heyman; **Cinematographer:** Robert Surtees; **Editor:** Adrienne Fazan; **Cast:** Frank Sinatra, Kathryn Grayson, J. Carrol Naish, Mildred Natwick, Ricardo Montalban, Ann Miller, Cyd Charisse.

The son of a Mexican bandit becomes a bandit himself against his will. To complicate matters he falls in love with the daughter of the governor, who is expecting tax collectors from Spain. Frank Sinatra is Ricardo, the title character, who persistently romances a series of fair ladies until he falls under the spell of the beautiful Theresa (Kathryn Grayson). Pure fluff and light on plot, the most engaging feature of this lesser MGM musical is a production dance, "The Dance of Fury," with Ricardo Montalban, Ann Miller, and Cyd Charisse as the three specialty dancers. The song "Love Is Where You Find It" (words by Earl Brent, music by Nacio Herb Brown), which enjoyed more than modest success, was introduced in the film by Grayson, who also recorded it.

KIT CARSON United Artists, 1940, B&W, 97 min. **Producer:** Edward Small; **Director:** George B. Seitz; **Screenplay:** George Bruce; **Music:** Edward Ward; **Cinematographer:** John J. Mescall and Robert Pittack; **Editors:** William F. Claxton and Fred R. Feitshans Jr.; **Cast:** Jon Hall, Lynn Bari, Dana Andrews, Harold Huber, Ward Bond, Renie Riano, Clayton Moore.

In this rousing tale about the conquest of California, famed trapper Kit Carson (Jon Hall) and his supporters join ranks with army captain John C. Fremont (Dana Andrews) as they battle against Mexican troops and hostile Indians. Moreover, the two men compete for the affections of pretty Delores Murphy (Lynn Bari). While the film is loose historically, the action and excitement it renders can stir many a heart. A particularly memorable sequence has marauding Indians surrounding an enclosed circle of covered wagons, forcing settlers to fight for their life. This scene prompted the *New York Times* to call it "a straight old-fashioned action picture with more violent mayhem per linear foot of celluloid than we've seen in recent weeks."

In 1928 Lloyd Ingraham and Alfred L. Lerker helmed *Kit Carson* for Paramount as a silent feature, with Fred Thomson as the famed trapper and frontiersman. Like Buffalo Bill Cody, Billy the Kid, and Daniel Boone, Christopher "Kit" Carson (1809–68) has been fodder for the silver screen. In the 1930s there were several films featuring the character of Kit Carson, including many serials. Other Carson features include Johnny Mack Brown in *Fighting with Kit Carson* (1933), Sammy McKim in *The Painted Stallion* (1938), and Bill Elliott in *Overland With Kit Carson* (1939).

KLONDIKE KATE Columbia, 1943, B&W, 64 min. **Director:** William Castle; **Screenplay:** M. Coates Webster; **Music:** Harry Revel; **Cinematographer:** John Stumar; **Editor:** Mel Thorsen; **Cast:** Ann Savage, Tom Neal, Glenda Farrell, Constance Worth, Sheldon Leonard, Lester Allen.

Set during the Alaska gold rush in the late 1890s, a young hotel owner is nearly lynched for a murder he did not commit. This film was based on the reminiscences of real-life saloon owner Kate Rockwell Matson and features the exceptional Ann Savage in the title role.

KNIGHTS OF THE RANGE Paramount, 1940, B&W, 70 min, VHS. **Producer:** Harry Sherman; **Director:** Lesley Selander; **Screenplay:** Norman Houston; **Music:** John Leipold and Victor Young; **Cinematographer:** Russell Harlan; **Editor:** Carroll Lewis; **Cast:** Russell Hayden, Jean Parker, Victor Jory, J. Farrell MacDonald, Morris Ankrum, Britt Wood, The King's Men.

In Oklahoma's Cimarron territory a young man gets involved with a gang of outlaws but switches sides to come to the aid of a girl and her father. This lesser-known oater is an entertaining adaptation of the Zane Grey novel.

KONGA, THE WILD STALLION Columbia, 1940, B&W, 65 min. **Producer:** Wallace MacDonald; **Director:** Sam Nelson; **Screenplay:** Harold Shumate; **Music:** Mischa Bakaleinikoff, Ben Oakland, and George Parrish; **Cinematographer:** Benjamin H. Kline; **Editor:** Charles Nelson; **Cast:** Fred Stone, Rochelle Hudson, Richard Fiske, Robert Warrick, Don Beddoe.

A rancher kills the man who shot his favorite horse, then goes to jail for the deed. Years later he is reunited with the horse, which has been cared for by his daughter. Fred Stone does a nice job as the beleaguered rancher in this somewhat obscure film.

LADY AND THE OUTLAW, THE See *BILLY'S TWO HATS.*

LADY FROM CHEYENNE, THE Universal, 1941, 88 min. **Producer:** Frank Lloyd; **Director:** Lloyd; **Screenplay:** Warren Duff and Kathryn Scala; **Music:** Frank Skinner; **Cinematographer:** Milton Krasner; **Editor:** Edward Curtiss; **Cast:** Susan Hayward, Robert Preston, Edward Arnold, Frank Craven, Gladys George.

Susan Hayward plays Annie Morgan, a liberated schoolteacher who brings women's suffrage to Wyoming by leading her own campaign for the right to sit on a jury and by starting up a school in this wild and woolly town. This fictionalized account of the early women's suffrage movement boasts a nifty performance by Hayward in one of her earliest starring roles and still makes for an interesting film. The soundtrack includes "Willie of the Valley" (words by Milton Drake, music by Ben Oakland) which was first introduced in *MY LITTLE CHICKADEE* (1940).

LADY FROM FRISCO See *REBELLION.*

LADY FROM TEXAS, THE Universal, 1951, Color, 78 min. **Producer:** Leonard Goldstein; **Director:** Joseph Pevney; **Screenplay:** Gerald Grayson Adams and Connie Lee Bennett; **Cinematographer:** Charles P. Boyle; **Editor:** Virgil W. Vogel; **Cast:** Howard Duff, Mona Freeman, Josephine Hull, Gene Lockhart, Craig Stevens, Ed Begley, Chris-Pin Martin, Jay C. Flippen, Barbara Knudson.

When an eccentric widow whose husband had been killed in the Civil War is accused of being insane by a bunch of crooks, a cowboy and a girl come to her aid. This entertaining little western comedy is surprisingly well done and a joy to watch.

LADY TAKES A CHANCE, THE (aka: THE COWBOY AND THE GIRL) RKO, 1943, B&W, 86 min, VHS. **Producer:** Frank Ross; **Directors:** Henry Hathaway and William A. Seiter; **Screenplay:** Robert Ardrey; **Music:** Roy Webb; **Cinematographer:** Frank Redman; **Editor:** Theron Warth; **Cast:** Jean Arthur, John Wayne, Charles Winninger, Phil Silvers, Mary Field, Grant Withers.

Jean Arthur is Molly Truesdale, a city gal from New York who heads west by bus. On the way she encounters a handsome rodeo cowboy named Duke Hudkins (John Wayne). They share lots of fun and frolic until Mary discovers that the thought of marriage and commitment is not what the handsome cowboy has in mind. In one particularly funny scene, Duke even flees in terror when he catches a glimpse in the mirror of himself wearing an apron. In the end she manages to hook her cowboy as Duke follows her to New York, rescues her from three unsuitable suitors, and brings her back to the West.

An enjoyable well-written comedy in which John Wayne proves he can deliver some authentic comic dialogue, the film played to good reviews and was RKO's third leading grosser for 1943. James Agee, America's leading critic, praised Wayne's performance; while the *New York Times* in its September 16, 1943, review called the picture "a plain, ordinary good time."

LAND BEYOND THE LAW Warner Bros., 1937, B&W, 54 min. **Producer:** Bryan Foy; **Director:** B. Reeves Eason; **Screenplay:** Luci Ward and Joseph K. Watson; **Music:** M. K. Jerome and Jack Scholl; **Cinematographer:** Ted D. McCord and L. William O'Connell; **Editor:** Frederick

Richards; **Cast:** Dick Foran, Linda Perry, Wayne Morris, Harry Woods, Irene Franklin.

Warner's resident singing cowboy, Dick Foran (who is billed as "Dick Foran, the Singing Cowboy" in this one) finds himself in trouble with the law when he mistakenly gets mixed up with a band of outlaws. This good series entry has the crooning cowboy singing "The Prairie is My Home" during the opening credits and again at the end of the film. (See also *MOONLIGHT ON THE PRAIRIE.*)

LAND OF FIGHTING MEN Monogram, 1938, B&W, 53 min. **Producer:** Maurice Cohn; **Director:** Alan James; **Screenplay:** Joseph O'Donnell; **Music:** Eddie Cherkose, Connie Lee, and Charles Rosoff; **Cinematographer:** Robert E. Cline; **Editor:** Richard G. Wray; **Cast:** Addison Randall (as Jack Randall), Bruce Bennett, Louise Stanley, Dickie Jones, Wheeler Oakman.

See *RIDERS OF THE DAWN.*

LAND OF HUNTED MEN Monogram, 1943, B&W, 58 min. **Producer:** William L. Nolte; **Director:** S. Roy Luby; **Screenplay:** Elizabeth Beecher; **Cinematographer:** James S. Brown Jr.; **Editor:** Luby (as Roy Claire); **Cast:** Ray Corrigan, Dennis Moore, Max Terhune, Phyllis Adair, John Merton.

An outlaw gang is terrorizing the countryside, and the Range Busters are hot on their trail. Ray Corrigan returns to the Range Buster series in this entry, and Dennis Moore joins the trio as its third member. (See also *RANGE BUSTERS, THE.*)

LAND OF MISSING MEN Tiffany, 1930, B&W, 60 min. **Producer:** Trem Carr; **Director:** John P. McCarthy; **Screenplay:** McCarthy and Bob Quigley; **Cinematographer:** Harry Neumann; **Cast:** Bob Steele, Al St. John, Eddie Dunn, Caryl Lincoln, Al Jennings.

In one of his first sound films, a youthful Bob Steele is on the run heading south toward the Mexican border with pal Al "Fuzzy" St. John. When they stop at a supposedly friendly saloon, they find the piano roll playing and everyone inside dead. Fuzzy fears the obvious; they had better clear out fast before they are blamed for the dead bodies. The unique plot makes for an exciting and engrossing early sound western adventure.

LAND OF THE LAWLESS Monogram, 1947, B&W, 64 min. **Producer:** Barney Sarecky; **Director:** Lambert Hillyer; **Screenplay:** J. Benton Cheney; **Cinematographer:** William A. Sickner; **Editor:** Robert O. Crandall; **Cast:** Johnny Mack Brown, Raymond Hatton, Steve Clark, Edmund Cobb, Tristram Coffin, Virginia Cox.

A man arrives in a small town to find that his best pal has been murdered, so he joins a prospector in ridding the town of a corrupt female saloon boss and her henchmen. (See also *UNDER ARIZONA SKIES.*)

LAND OF THE OPEN RANGE, THE RKO, 1941, B&W, 60 min. **Producer:** Bert Gilroy; **Director:** Edward Killy; **Screenplay:** Morton Grant; **Cinematographer:** Harry J. Wild; **Editor:** Frederic Knudtson; **Cast:** Tim Holt, Ray Whitely, Janet Waldo, Lee "Lasses" White, Robert Cavanaugh, Roy Barcroft, Lee Bonnell.

An unusual plot line to this Tim Holt RKO series entry has a dying outlaw stating in his will that the large tract of land he owns can only be homesteaded by ex-convicts. (See also *ALONG THE RIO GRANDE.*)

LAND OF THE OUTLAWS Monogram, 1944, B&W, 56 min. **Producer:** Charles Bigalow; **Director:** Lambert Hillyer; **Screenplay:** Joseph O'Donnell; **Cinematographer:** Harry Neumann; **Editor:** John C. Fuller; **Cast:** Johnny Mack Brown, Raymond Hatton, John L. Cason, Ray Elder, Art Fowler, Chick Hannon.

LAND OF THE SIX GUNS Monogram, 1940, B&W, 54 min. **Producer:** Harry S. Webb; **Director:** Raymond K. Johnson (Bernard B. Ray); **Cinematographers:** William Hyer and Edward A. Kull; **Editor:** Robert C. Golden; **Cast:** Addison Randall, Steve Clark, Richard Cramer, Kenne Duncan, Carl Mathews, Bud Osborne, Jack Perrin, Louise Stanley, Glenn Strange.

LARAMIE Columbia, 1949, B&W, 55 min. **Producer:** Colbert Clark; **Director:** Ray Nazarro; **Screenplay:** Barry Shipman; **Cinematographer:** Rex Wimpy; **Editor:** Paul Borofsky; **Cast:** Charles Starrett, Smiley Burnette, Fred F. Sears, Tommy Ivo, Myron Healey, Robert J. Wilke, Jay Silverheels.

LARAMIE MOUNTAINS Columbia, 1952, B&W, 54 min. **Producer:** Colbert Clark; **Director:** Ray Nazarro; **Screenplay:** Barry Shipman; **Cinematographers:** Fayte M. Browne and Rex Wimpy; **Editor:** Paul Borofsky; **Cast:** Charles Starrett, Smiley Burnette, Fred F. Sears, Jock Mahoney, Marshall Reed, Robert J. Wilke, Myron Healey.

LARAMIE TRAIL, THE Republic, 1944, B&W, 55 min. **Producer:** Louis Gray; **Director:** John English; **Screenplay:** J. Benton Cheney; **Music:** Mort Glickman; **Cinematographer:** Bud Thackery (as Ellis Thackerey); **Editor:** Harry Keller; **Cast:** Robert Livingston, Smiley Burnette, Linda Brent, Martin Garralaga, John James, Slim Whitaker, Roy Barcroft.

In this final entry in the Johnny Revere series (the previous two, also released in 1944, were *Pride of the Plains* and *Beneath Western Skies*), a man and his pal arrive at a Spanish hacienda to help a young man who is falsely accused of murder. This little series from Republic scores a point or two, largely due to a good script and Robert Livingston's charismatic presence.

LASCA OF THE RIO GRANDE Universal, 1931, B&W, 60 min. **Producer:** Samuel Bishoff; **Director:** Edward Laemmle; **Screenplay:** Randall Faye; **Music:** Charles Speidel; **Cinematographer:** Harry Neumann; **Editor:** Ted Kent; **Cast:** Johnny Mack Brown, Leo Carrillo, Dorothy Burgess, Tom London, Slim Summerville, Chris-Pin Martin, Frank Campeau.

In this film based on the poem "Lasca" by Frank Deprez, a Texas Ranger and a Mexican bandit are both in love with a dance-hall girl. When she kills a man in self-defense, the Ranger must bring her in. This early curio oater was filmed at a time when former football all-American Johnny Mack Brown was an up-and-coming star with Universal.

LASH, THE (aka: ADIOS) First National Pictures, 1930, B&W, 75 min. **Producer:** Frank Lloyd; **Director:** Lloyd; **Screenplay:** Lanier Bartlett and Bradley King; **Cinematographer:** Ernest Haller; **Editor:** Harold Young; **Cast:** Richard Barthelmess, Mary Astor, James Rennie, Marian Nixon, Fred Kohler.

Popular actor Richard Barthelmess is Don Francisco Defina, a southern California nobleman who disguises himself as El Puma in order to lead a revolt against a tyrannical land agent. This neat early talkie features a young Mary Astor as Rosita Garcia.

LAST BANDIT, THE Republic, 1949, Color, 80 min. **Producer:** Joseph Kane; **Director:** Kane; **Screenplay:** Jack Natteford, Luci Ward, and Thames Williamson; **Music:** R. Dale Butts; **Cinematographer:** John J. Martin; **Editor:** Arthur Roberts; **Cast:** William "Wild Bill" Elliott, Lorna Gray (as Adrian Booth), Forrest Tucker, Andy Devine, Jack Holt, George Chesebro.

A reformed outlaw attempting to go straight (Bill Elliott) runs into problems with an errant no-good brother (Forrest Tucker), who is planning a big gold heist by robbing the local railroad. Plenty of action, plenty of color, and that patented Elliott persona makes for an enjoyable, fast-paced, and adventurous Republic ride.

LAST BULLET, THE See *CROOKED RIVER.*

LAST CHALLENGE, THE (aka: PISTOLERO OF RED RIVER) MGM, 1967, Color, 105 min. **Producer:** Richard Thorpe; **Director:** Thorpe; **Screenplay:** Albert Maltz (as John Sherry) and Robert Emmett Ginna; **Music:** Richard Shores; **Cinematographer:** Elsworth Fredericks; **Editor:** Richard Farrell; **Cast:** Glenn Ford, Angie Dickinson, Chad Everett, Gary Merrill, Jack Elam, Delphi Lawrence, Royal Dano.

Glenn Ford plays Marshal Dan Blaine, the West's fastest gun, who has finally settled down to the leisurely life. His tranquility is broken, however, when young gunslinger Lot McGuire (Chad Everett) arrives in town to challenge the marshal. Ford gives his usual steady performance in this thematic western, which is bolstered by a good supporting cast and a nice performance by Angie Dickinson as Lisa Denton, the woman who tries to prevent the impending shoot-out.

LAST COMMAND Republic, 1955, Color, 110 min, VHS. **Producer:** Frank Lloyd (associate); **Director:** Lloyd; **Screenplay:** Warren Duff; **Music:** Max Steiner; **Cinematographer:** Jack Marta; **Editor:** Tony Martinelli; **Cast:** Sterling Hayden, Anna Maria Alberghetti, Richard Carlson, Arthur Hunnicutt, Ernest Borgnine, J. Carrol Naish, Ben Cooper, John Bell, Virginia Grey, Jim Davis, Otto Kruger.

Arthur Hunnicutt gives a different physical and emotional portrayal of Davy Crockett and Sterling Hayden stars as Jim Bowie in this 1955 account of the siege at the Alamo. What is unique about this well-cast quality film is that the story is told through the eyes of Jim Bowie, the maker of the infamous knife, who emerges as the main protagonist. The battle scenes are top-notch and brilliantly realistic. Moreover, the plot is engrossing, with drama and romance skillfully woven into the script. While the 40-year-old Hayden and the 19-year-old Anna Maria Alberghetti seem at times to be a generational mismatch, they manage to pull off their romantic interlude rather convincingly.

The story has it that John Wayne had often pitched Republic chief Herbert Yates about a film on the Alamo, but Yates insisted he had already done a small budget Alamo film called *MAN OF CONQUEST* (1939). Then, perhaps to spite Wayne, Yates proceeded to make *The Last Command.* The song "Jim Bowie" is sung by Gordon MacRae.

LAST DAYS OF BOOT HILL, THE Columbia, 1947, B&W, 55 min. **Producer:** Colbert Clark; **Director:** Ray Nazarro; **Screenplay:** Norman Hall; **Cinematographer:** George F. Kelley; **Editor:** Paul Borofsky; **Cast:** Charles Starrett, Smiley Burnette, Al Bridge, Paul Campbell, Bill Free.

LAST DROP OF WATER, THE Biograph, 1911, B&W, one reel. **Director:** D. W. Griffith; **Screenplay:** Griffith; **Cinematographer:** G. W. Billy Blitzer; **Cast:** Blanche Sweet, Joseph Greybill, Charles West, W. Christie Miller, William J. Butler, Jeannie McPherson, Robert Herron, Dell Henderson.

This is an important silent feature mainly because it was the precursor to James Cruze's *THE COVERED WAGON* (1923). It was shot on location in San Fernando's Topanga Canyon and Lookout Mountain, California, with prairie schooners and livestock used for authenticity. The film opens before the wagon train heads westward and proceeds to tell of the trials and tribulations of a group of settlers, three of whom are involved in a romantic triangle. (See also *BATTLE AT ELDER-BUSH GULCH.*)

LAST FRONTIER, THE Columbia, 1955, Color, 98 min. **Producer:** William Fadiman; **Director:** Anthony Mann; **Screenplay:** Russell S. Hughes and Philip Yordan; **Music:** Leigh Harline; **Cinematographer:** William C. Mellor; **Editor:** Al Clark; **Cast:** Victor Mature, Guy Madison, Robert Preston, James Whitmore, Anne Bancroft, Russell Collins.

One hundred rookie soldiers commanded by a vicious officer nicknamed "The Butcher of Shiloh" are forced to hold out against besieging Indians until troops can arrive from Fort Laramie in the spring. Robert Preston is the unsavory commanding officer, while Victor Mature is the virile and uncouth army scout who has eyes for Preston's wife (Anne Bancroft) as matters worsen.

The film is one of many westerns helmed by Anthony Mann in the 1950s. The director was quite critical of Victor Mature's western work, unlike that of James Stewart and Gary Cooper, who generally scored high marks from Mann. In a 1969 interview with Christopher Wicking and Barrie Pattison, Mann was quoted as saying, "Mature can't get near a horse. It's a curse when they don't learn when they are adept at the art of writing, fencing, swimming and the other things that are necessary, which they must learn, if they don't know." The title song with music by Lester Lee and words by Ned Washington is sung by Rusty Draper.

A silent film, *The Last Frontier* (Metropolitan, 1926) was directed by George Seitz and marked the first western appearance by an actor named William Boyd, who a decade later would embark upon a historic role as Hop-Along Cassidy. This adaptation of Courtney Ryley Cooper's 1923 novel tells of a wagon train that is attacked by Indians while on its way to Salinas, Kansas. When her entire family is killed, the one surviving daughter blames her fiancée, scout Tom Kirby (Boyd), who had suggested the trip. Originally conceived by Thomas Ince, the project was sold to producer Hunt Stromberg, who in turn sold it to Metropolitan Pictures.

LAST FRONTIER UPRISING Republic, 1947, Color, 67 min. **Producer:** Louis Grey; **Director:** Leslie Selander; **Screenplay:** Harvey Gates; **Music:** Mort Glickman; **Cinematographer:** Bud Thackery; **Editor:** Charles Craft; **Cast:** Monte Hale, Lorna Gray, James Taggart, Philip Van Zandt, Edmund Cobb.

Singing cowboy Monte Hale plays himself in this story of a young fellow who buys horses for the government, then finds himself pitted against a gang of horse thieves. Hale made some 30 westerns for Republic between 1945 and 1954. (See also HOME ON THE RANGE.)

LAST HARD MEN, THE 20th Century Fox, 1976, Color, 98 min. **Producers:** William Seltzer and Russell Thacher; **Director:** Andrew V. McLaglen; **Screenplay:** Guerdon Trueblood; **Music:** Jerry Goldsmith; **Cinematographer:** Duke Callaghan; **Editor:** Fred A. Chulack; **Cast:** Charlton Heston, James Coburn, Barbara Hershey, Jorge Rivero, Robert Donner, Christopher Mitchum.

In this film set in the American Southwest in the early 20th century, James Coburn stars as a half-breed convict who escapes from a chain gang with several of his fellow convicts. In search of revenge, he and his gang kidnap the daughter of the retired lawman (Charlton Heston) who not only had put him behind bars, but whom he holds responsible for the death of his young Navajo wife. Consequently, the lawman is forced out of retirement and begins tracking the outlaws in a bloody attempt to rescue his daughter.

Solid performances by Coburn and Heston and good directing by Andrew V. McLaglen elevate this handsomely produced western punctuated with revenge and violence. Moreover, the details of a crucial transition period in American history (such as references to many early 20th-century appliances and inventions that quite puzzle the previously incarcerated Coburn) are well captured in the film's script and art direction.

LAST HORSEMAN, THE Columbia, 1944, B&W, 58 min. **Producer:** Leon Barsha; **Director:** William Berke; **Screenplay:** Ed Earl Repp; **Music:** Cindy Walker and Bob Willis; **Editor:** Jerome Thoms; **Cast:** Russell Hayden, Dub Taylor, Ann Savage, Bob Wills, John Maxwell, Ted Mapes.

Russell Hayden stars in this little oater about a ranch foreman who is out to get the crooks who bilked him. His plan is that he and his pals will dress as women to fool the culprits, who had used an innocent woman to help them rob a bank. This little oater boasts a good mixture of action and music. It is interesting to see Hayden (best remembered as Hop-Along Cassidy's sidekick Lucky) in a starring role of his own. He later went on to produce the successful television series *26 Men* (1957–59), starring Tris Coffin and Paul "Kelo" Henderson.

LAST HUNT, THE MGM, 1956, Color, 108 min, VHS. **Producer:** Dore Schary; **Director:** Richard Brooks; **Screenplay:** Brooks; **Music:** Daniele Amfitheatrof; **Cinematographer:** Russell Harlan; **Editor:** Ben Lewis; **Cast:** Robert Taylor, Stewart Granger, Lloyd Nolan, Debra Paget, Russ Tamblyn, Constance Ford.

In one of his finest screen roles, Robert Taylor plays a vicious buffalo hunter named Charles Gilson, who has a pathological hatred for both the buffalo and the Indian. His credo is to destroy the bison herds because "one less buffalo means one less Indian." He teams up with fellow buffalo hunter Sandy McKenzie (Stewart Granger), who quickly learns that Gilson delights in killing not only animals but destitute Indians as well.

Others who join the hunting party are Lloyd Nolan as a drunken buffalo skinner and Russ Tamblyn as a half-breed. Debra Paget is the Indian girl who is the lone survivor of one of Gilson's killing sprees. Tensions build to the inevitable climax where Gilson and McKenzie clash, with Gilson stalking McKenzie and the Indian girl. While he waits for them to emerge from their refuge, the elements intervene and he dies from exposure, to no one's dismay. A striking scene has

Granger and Paget walking past Taylor's frozen body, barely looking at the deathly stillness of his frozen face.

Shot on location at Custer State Park in South Dakota and filmed in CinemaScope, this solid western benefits from the utilization of Frederic Remington's paintings as illustrations behind the title credit. Remington drawings are also incorporated into the actual buffalo-killing episodes.

LAST MUSKETEER, THE Republic, 1952, B&W, 67 min. **Producer:** Edward J. White (associate); **Director:** William Witney; **Screenplay:** Arthur E. Orloff; **Music:** Nathan Scott; **Cinematographer:** John MacBurnie; **Editor:** Harold Minter; **Cast:** Rex Allen, Mary Ellen Kay, Slim Pickens, James Anderson, Boyd "Red" Morgan, Monte Montague, Michael Hall, Stan Jones, The Republic Rhythm Riders.

LAST POSSE, THE Columbia, 1953, B&W, 73 min. **Producer:** Harry Joe Brown; **Director:** Alfred L. Werker; **Screenplay:** Kenneth Gamet; **Music:** stock music/uncredited; **Cinematographer:** Burnett Guffey; **Editor:** Gene Havlick; **Cast:** Broderick Crawford, John Derek, Charles Bickford, Wanda Hendrix, Warner Anderson, Henry Hull.

A sheriff sends a posse after the culprits who supposedly stole a rancher's money. The posse, however, returns to town with neither the money nor any captives. An excellent and tightly knit little film told largely through a series of flashbacks. John Derek delivers a fine performance, showing that he was far more than just another Hollywood "pretty face."

LAST OF THE BADMEN Allied Artists, 1957, Color, 79 min. **Producer:** Vincent Fennelly; **Director:** Paul Landress; **Screenplay:** David T. Chantler and David B. Ullman; **Music:** Paul Sawtell; **Cinematographer:** Ellsworth Fredericks; **Editor:** William Austin; **Cast:** George Montgomery, Keith Larson, James Best, Douglas Kennedy, Michael Ansara, John Doucette, Walter Reed.

In the 1880s, Chicago detectives head out west to find the killers of one of their colleagues. The urban/western connection makes for an enjoyable little film, with George Montgomery delivering well in the kind of role that was made for him.

LAST OF THE CLINTONS Ajax Pictures, 1935, B&W, 59 min, VHS. **Producer:** William A. Berke; **Director:** Harry L. Fraser; **Screenplay:** Fraser (as Weston Edwards); **Cinematographer:** Robert E. Cline; **Editor:** Arthur A. Brooks; **Cast:** Harry Carey, Betty Mack, Del Gordon, Victor Potel, Earl Dwire, Ruth Findley.

Trigger Carsen (Harry Carey) infiltrates an outlaw gang in order to expose their rackets. But when the gang orders him to kidnap a young girl, they find out his real identity. Carey fans should enjoy this oater, but otherwise this low-budget production is less than routine.

LAST OF THE COMANCHES (aka: THE SABRE AND THE ARROW, UK) Columbia, 1952, Color, 85 min. **Producer:** Buddy Adler; **Director:** André De Toth; **Screenplay:** Kenneth Gamet; **Music:** George Duning; **Cinematographers:** Ray Cory and Charles Lawton Jr.; **Editor:** Al Clark; **Cast:** Broderick Crawford, Barbara Hale, Johnny Stewart, Lloyd Bridges, Mickey Shaughnessy, Martin Milner, Milton Parsons, Steve Forrest, Jay Silverheels, George Chesebro.

In this reworking of the 1943 film *Sahara* (Warner Bros.), Broderick Crawford leads a group of survivors from an Indian raid to safety, as the six surviving members of a cavalry unit join the passengers of a stagecoach in staving off Comanche attack.

LAST OF THE DESPERADOS, THE Associated Film Distributors, 1955, B&W, 75 min. **Producer:** Sigmund Neufeld; **Director:** Sam Newfield; **Screenplay:** Orville Hampton; **Music:** Paul Dunlap; **Cinematographer:** Edward Linden; **Editor:** Holbrook N. Todd; **Cast:** James Craig, Margia Dean, Jim Davis, Barton MacLane, Bob Steele, Donna Martell.

After killing Billy the Kid, Pat Garrett (James Craig) is pursued by members of Billy's gang. Forced to hide out in another town, he falls for a woman who just happens to be Billy's ex-girlfriend. There is lots of good action in this low-budget production with a different plot twist.

LAST OF THE DUANES, THE Fox, 1930, B&W, 55 min. **Producers:** Edward Butcher and Harold B. Lipsitz; **Director:** Alfred L. Werker; **Screenplay:** Ernest Pascal; **Music:** Cliff Friend; **Cinematographer:** Daniel B. Clark; **Editor:** Ralph Dietrich; **Cast:** George O'Brien, Lucile Browne, Myrna Loy, Walter McGrail, James Bradbury Jr., Nat Pendleton.

Buck Duane (George O'Brien) avenges his father's murder by gunning down the killer. He flees from the law, only to complicate matters by getting himself entangled with two women. The first he rescues from the clutches of a bad man; the second is the bad man's wife, who falls for Duane.

The cinematic evolution of this Zane Grey novel is particularly interesting, with four versions spanning the years 1919-41. In this early sound version, songs were added, and David Howard, who usually directed the popular O'Brien's Fox westerns, directed a Spanish-language version simultaneously with the Werker film, entitled *El Ultimode Los Vargas*.

Grey's 1914 novel was first filmed in 1919 with William Farnum, one of the most popular stars in the silent era, in the lead. *The Last of the Duanes* was remade by Fox in 1924 with the ever-popular Tom Mix as Buck Duane and with the plot line remaining much as it had been before.

LAST OF THE DUANES 20th Century Fox, 1941, B&W, 57 min. **Producer:** Sol M. Wurtzel; **Director:** James Tingling; **Screenplay:** William H. Councilman Jr. and Irving Cummings Jr.; **Music:** Cyril J. Mockridge; **Cinematographer:** Charles G. Clarke; **Editor:** Nick Demaggio; **Cast:** George Montgomery, Lynne Roberts, Eve Arden, Francis Ford, George F. Stone.

George Montgomery, one of the 20th Century Fox's rising young stars, plays Buck Duane in the 1941 adaptation of Zane Grey's work. As in the 1930 version, Texas-born Buck Duane returns home to find that his father was murdered. He trails the killer until he discovers that the outlaw is part of a gang; he then calls in the Texas Rangers.

Montgomery had recently scored well in a remake of Zane Grey's *Riders of the Purple Sage* 1941 and soon was promoted to being a studio leading man. Directed by James Tingling, this film provides a decent entry to the western genre and is an excellent example of how the same story can be replayed over and over again, each time with a different emphasis.

LAST OF THE FAST GUNS Universal, 1958, Color, 82 min. **Producer:** Howard Christie; **Director:** George Sherman; **Screenplay:** David P. Harmon; **Cinematographer:** Alex Phillips Jr.; **Editor:** Patrick McCormick; **Cast:** Jock Mahoney, Gilbert Roland, Linda Cristal, Eduard Franz, Lorne Greene, Carl Benton Reed.

A gunman heads to Mexico hoping to find the missing brother of the man who hired him. There is lots of action in this neat oater in which stuntman Jock Mahoney proves himself a viable leading man.

LAST OF THE MOHICANS, THE Associated Producers, 1920, B&W, 6 reels. **Directors:** Maurice Tourneur and Clarence Brown; **Screenplay:** Robert Dillon; **Cast:** Wallace Beery, Barbara Bedford, Albert Roscoe, Lillian Hall, Henry Woodward, James Gordon, Harry Lorraine.

The first cinematic version of the James Fenimore Cooper novel dates back to 1909, when D. W. Griffith produced a loose adaptation entitled *Leatherstocking* as one of his first films for Biograph. In 1911, two more films, each a reel long, were released by the Powers and the Thanhouser production companies. The latter was filmed at Lake George, the actual site of the Fort William Henry massacre in 1757, which occurred during the French and Indian Wars. After the fort was captured, French officers promised safe passage for all those remaining British forces, but they could not control the Hurons under their command, who killed nearly everyone trying to escape.

The Associated Producer's version of the Cooper story was the first feature-length adaptation. It focused more on Magua (Wallace Beery), making Hawkeye a secondary character, and employed a highly stylized approach in its cinematography. Particularly well-staged and strikingly photographed scenes include the Fort Henry massacre and the final fight to the death between Magua and Uncas.

LAST OF THE MOHICANS, THE United Artists, 1936, B&W, 91 min. **Producers:** Harry M. Goetz and Edward Small; **Director:** George Seitz; **Screenplay:** Phillip Dunne, John Balderson, Paul Perez, and Daniel Moore; **Cinematographer:** Robert Planck; **Editor:** Jack Dennis; **Cast:** Randolph Scott, Binnie Barnes, Heather Angel, Hugh Buckler, Henry Wilcoxon, Bruce Cabot, Robert Barrat, Phillip Reed.

Randolph Scott is excellent as Hawkeye, the frontier hero of Cooper's oft-filmed novel. Set during the French and Indian War, Hawkeye and two Mohican friends escort sisters Alice and Cora Monroe through the hostile wilderness. Alice Monroe (Binnie Barnes) is in love with Hawkeye, while her sister Cora (Heather Angel) falls in love with Uncas, the sturdy and sensitive Mohican brave.

Adapted for the screen by John Balderston, Paul Perez, and Daniel Moore, this is arguably the best movie treatment of Cooper's *The Last of the Mohicans*. The balanced combination of drama, action, and romance culminates in one of the most touching death scenes ever put on film: Cora and Uncas, aware of the futility of their love, tragically plunging together off a cliff to their death. In addition to Scott's stalwart performance, the film boasts outstanding supporting performances by Binnie Barnes and Henry Wilcoxon (as Duncan Hayward, the priggish British major) and a career performance by Bruce Cabot as the sinister Huron warrior Magua.

This movie continues to play amazingly well, given all the changes in film technology over the past 60 years. Moreover, for history buffs it covers the often ignored pre-Revolutionary era, when the American colonists were still loyal subjects of the British crown and the French and British were vying for control of the North American continent.

The first talking version of *The Last of the Mohicans* was a 12-chapter Mascot serial in 1932, starring Harry Carey and Edwina Booth. Carey reportedly was paid $10,000 for his role as Hawkeye. Among the most memorable scenes is the opening sequence, in which the Mohican tribe is massacred.

LAST OF THE MOHICANS, THE 20th Century Fox, 1992, Color, 122 min, VHS, DVD, CD. **Producers:** Hunt Lowry and Michael Mann; **Director:** Mann; **Screenplay:** Mann and Christopher Lowe; **Cinematographer:** Dante Spinotti; **Editors:** Dov Hoenig and Arthur Schmidt; **Cast:** Daniel Day-Lewis, Madeleine Stowe, Russell Means, Wes Studi, Eric Schweig, Jodhi May.

Daniel Day-Lewis brings a dashing mane of hair into his role as Hawkeye, this time a courageous woodsman at peace with nature. Sisters Alice and Cora Munro (Jodhi May and Madeleine Stowe) are escorted through hostile country to join their father, the British commander of forces that are under French siege. Handsomely produced, Michael Mann's film was shot in South Carolina and includes well-staged and bloody battle scenes, good performances, and lots of romance and action. The film garnered an Oscar for Best Sound.

LAST OF THE PONY RIDERS Columbia, 1953, B&W, 59 minutes. **Producer:** Armand Schaefer; **Director:** George and Archainbaud; **Screenplay:** Ruth Woodman; **Music:** George Duning, Heintz Roemheld, and Paul Sawtell; **Cinematographer:** William Bradford; **Editor:** James Sweeney; **Cast:** Gene Autry, Smiley Burnette, Kathleen Case, Dickie Jones, John Downey, Howard Wright.

The final Gene Autry theatrical feature has Gene as an ex-Pony Express rider attempting to protect his U.S. mail franchise. This is a pleasant film finale for the legendary Autry. (See also *TUMBLING TUMBLEWEEDS.*)

LAST OF THE REDMEN Columbia, 1947, Color, 79 min, VHS. **Producer:** Sam Katzman; **Director:** George Sherman; **Screenplay:** Herbert Delmas and George H. Plympton; **Cinematographer:** Ray Fernstrom; **Editor:** James Sweeney; **Cast:** Jon Hall, Evelyn Ankers, Michael O'Shea, Julie Bishop, Buster Crabbe, Rick Vallin, Robert "Buzz" Henry.

This 1947 adaptation of *The Last of the Mohicans* has an Indian, the last of his Mohican tribe, risking his life to save the lives of white settlers. This time it's Jon Hall as the scout Hawkeye, who attempts to escort the Munro sisters through hostile Indian territory, and Buster Crabbe—against type—as the evil Magua. Evelyn Ankers and Julie Bishop play Alice and Cora Munro.

LAST OF THE WARRENS, THE Supreme, 1936, B&W, Color, 60 min. **Producer:** A. W. Hackel; **Director:** Robert N. Bradbury; **Screenplay:** Bradbury; **Cinematographer:** Bert Longnecker; **Editor:** S. Roy Luby; **Cast:** Bob Steele, Margaret Marquis, Charles King, Horace Murphy, Lafe McKee.

Directed by his dad Robert N. Bradbury, Bob Steele plays Ted Warren, a World War I veteran who returns home only to find that everyone thinks he's dead. Charles King plays the culprit who has rustled Ted's cattle stock, taken over the Warren ranch, and is now after Ted's girlfriend. When Kent shoots Ted's father and mistakenly leaves him for dead, the Warrens' plan is to have the wounded appear as a ghost in order to gain a confession from Kent.

LAST OUTLAW, THE RKO, 1936, B&W, 62 min, VHS. **Producer:** Robert Sisk (associate); **Director:** Christy Cabanne; **Screenplay:** Jack Townley and John Twist; **Music:** Alberto Columbo and Max Steiner; **Cinematographer:** Jack MacKenzie; **Editor:** George Hively; **Cast:** Harry Carey, Hoot Gibson, Tom Tyler, Henry B. Walthall, Margaret Callahan, Ray Mayer, Frank Jenks.

Harry Carey is Dean Payton, an aging outlaw who is released from prison after serving a 25-year sentence. Hoping now for a life of peace, he finds instead that there is a gang of crooks on his range and that his daughter is now the mistress of gangster Al Goss, played by Tom Tyler.

One of the silent screen's western icons, Harry Carey's taciturn stoic presence lent a rare authenticity to yet more heroic roles in the 1930s, including a trio of fine westerns for RKO in the late 1930s (*Powdersmoke Range*, 1935; *The Last Outlaw*, 1936; and *The Law West of Tombstone*, 1938). The film was cowritten by E. Murray Campbell and John Ford, who had previously directed a silent version of *The Last Outlaw* for Universal in 1919. It costars Hoot Gibson, who got his start in Carey's early John Ford westerns; and Henry B. Walthall, who worked with Carey during his Biograph days with D. W. Griffith. Actor Fred Scott represented the new fad of the singing cowboy.

Many pundits claim that this was one of Harry Carey's very best films, with the *New York Times* calling *The Last Outlaw* "a thoroughly enjoyable Western melodrama, deftly streamlined and softly satiric. . . ." Ford himself requested that the rights to the film be conveyed to Carey for a proposed remake in the post–World War II period, but with Carey's death in 1947 the project never materialized.

LAST OUTPOST, THE (aka: CAVALRY CHARGE) Paramount, 1951, Color, 89 min. **Producers:** William H. Pine and William C. Thomas; **Director:** Lewis R. Foster; **Screenplay:** Daniel Mainwaring (as Geoffrey Homes), Winston Miller, and George Worthing Yates; **Music:** Lucien Cailiet; **Cinematographer:** Loyal Griggs; **Editor:** Howard A. Smith; **Cast:** Ronald Reagan, Rhonda Fleming, Bruce Bennett, Bill Williams, Noah Beery Jr., Peter Hanson, Hugh Beaumont.

Two brothers (Ronald Reagan and Bruce Bennett) who fought on opposite sides during the Civil War mend their mutual hard feelings in order to defend themselves against an Indian attack. Matters are complicated, though, because they are in love with the same beautiful woman (Rhonda Fleming).

Reagan was allowed to use his own personal horse in filming his role of the Confederate cavalry officer who rescues a federal garrison from an Indian attack. Shot in Technicolor in Tucson, Arizona, the film benefits from beautiful scenery and Rhonda Fleming's alluring looks as well as one of the most exciting charges ever filmed. The film was rereleased in 1962 under the title *Cavalry Charge*.

LAST REBEL Columbia, 1970, Color, 90 min. **Producer:** Larry G. Spangler; **Director:** Denys McCoy; **Screenplay:** Warren Keefer (Lorenzo Sabatini); **Music:** Tony Ashton and Jon Lord; **Cinematographer:** Carlo Carlini; **Cast:** Joe Namath, Jack Elam, Woody Strode, Ty Hardin, Victoria George, Renato Ramono.

After the Civil War, a veteran attempts to stop a small Missouri town from lynching some ex-slaves. This insipid, poor Italian production is of interest only because it stars Hall of Fame pro football star Joe Namath.

LAST ROUND-UP, THE Paramount, 1934, B&W, 60 min. **Producer:** Harold Hurley; **Director:** Henry

Hathaway; **Screenplay:** Jack Cunningham; **Music:** Herman Hand; **Cinematographer:** Archie Stout; **Cast:** Randolph Scott, Barbara Fritchie, Fred Kohler, Monte Blue, Fuzzy Knight, Charles Middleton.

In this second sound adaptation of Zane Grey's novel *The Border Legion*, Randolph Scott and Barbara Fritchie are the imperiled lovers for whom Monte Blue, a good-natured outlaw, sacrifices his life. The film uses stock footage from the silent version (1924) and the first sound version (1930) to enhance fight scenes.

LAST ROUND-UP, THE   Columbia, 1947, B&W, 77 min. **Producer:** Armand Schaefer; **Director:** John English; **Screenplay:** Edward Snell and Jack Towney; **Cinematographer:** William Bradford; **Editor:** Aaron Stell; **Cast:** Gene Autry, Jean Heather, Ralph Morgan, Carol Thurston, Mark Daniels, Russ Vincent, Robert Blake.

In this modern-day western, Gene is assigned to round up a tribe of Indians squatting on barren land. However, the real culprit is a crooked land baron who stirs up trouble among the Indians in order to stop an aqueduct project that would hinder his takeover of the land.

Gene Autry's first films for Columbia were different from his Republic ventures. With more sobering plots and restrained music, films like *The Last Roundup* were among the better B westerns of the period, according to film historian William Everson. Autry would eventually go on to suppress most of the musical content of his films and concentrate on more serious themes such as this film, which in part is a commentary on the poor lot of the American Indian.

This picture should not be confused with a 1934 film bearing the same title, Henry Hathaway's *The Last Round-Up*, which was based on the novel *Border Legion* by Zane Grey and starred Randolph Scott. (See also *TUMBLING TUMBLEWEEDS*.)

LAST STAGECOACH WEST   Republic, 1957, B&W, 87 min. **Producer:** Rudy Ralston; **Director:** Joseph Kane; **Screenplay:** Barry Shipman; **Cinematographer:** Jack A. Marta; **Cast:** Jim Davis, Mary Castle, Victor Jory, Lee Van Cleef, Grant Withers, Roy Barcroft, John Alderson, Glenn Strange.

When the railroad replaces the stagecoach as the best means for delivering the mail, a man loses his stage business. With what money he has left he buys a ranch and some cattle, then recruits a gang to rob the railroad express offices as a means for revenge. As usual Victor Jory delivers a good performance as the ex-stagecoach owner turned gang leader.

LAST STAND, THE   Universal, 1938, B&W, 56 min. **Producers:** Trem Carr and Paul Malvern; **Director:** Joseph H. Lewis; **Screenplay:** Harry O. Hoyt and Norton S. Parker; **Cinematographer:** Harry Neumann; **Editor:** Charles Craft; **Cast:** Bob Baker, Constance Moore, Fuzzy Knight, Earl Hodgins, Forrest Taylor.

LAST STAND AT SABER RIVER   Turner Television Network, 1997, Color, 96 min, VHS. **Producers:** Michael Brandman (executive), Stephen J. Brandman, Mary Ann Braubach, Thomas John Kane, Tom Selleck (executive); **Director:** Dick Lowry; **Teleplay:** Ronald M. Cohen; **Music:** David Shire; **Cinematographer:** Ric Waite; **Editor:** William Stitch; **Cast:** Tom Selleck, Suzy Amis, Rachel Duncan, Haley Joel Osment, Keith Carradine, David Carradine, Harry Carey Jr.

Paul Cable (Tom Selleck), returns home in the waning days of the Civil War, to a wife (Suzy Amis) who hasn't forgiven him for leaving his family behind for the sheer adventure of war, and to his children who hardly remember him at all. Emotionally scarred, Cable makes one last attempt to protect his homestead and his family caught up in the middle of power struggle in the Arizona territory.

Tom Selleck emerged as a major force in the western genre in this 1997 made-for-TV western based on the book by Elmore Leonard. David Lowry's direction makes excellent use of the magnificent landscapes, with Selleck delivering his most multidimensional performance to date. As executive producer, Selleck also emerges as a filmmaker of inordinate skill, particularly in regard to characters and the casting of performers in those roles. His characters belong. Suzy Amis (*The Ballad of Little Jo*) is excellent as Selleck's forlorn wife. David and Keith Carradine are convincing as two Union wranglers consumed with hate against Cable, a Confederate veteran. Old-line fans can appreciate the casting of Harry Carey Jr., one of the industry's most noble character actors, as James Sanford.

Last Stand at Saber River won the Western Heritage Bronze Wrangler Award. Haley Joel Osment garnered the Young Stars award for Best Performance by a Young Actor in a Made for TV Movie.

LAST SUNSET   Universal, 1961, Color, 112 min. **Producers:** Eugene Frenke and Edward Lewis; **Director:** Robert Aldrich; **Screenplay:** Dalton Trumbo; **Music:** Ernest Gold; **Cinematographer:** Ernest Laszlo; **Editor:** Michael Luciano; **Cast:** Rock Hudson, Kirk Douglas, Dorothy Malone, Joseph Cotten, Carol Lynley, Neville Brand, Regis Toomey, Jack Elam.

Scripted by the formerly blacklisted writer Dalton Trumbo and helmed by Robert Aldrich, this offbeat western pits philosophical outlaw Kirk Douglas against upstanding sheriff Rock Hudson. Hudson pursues Douglas (who had killed his brother-in-law) on a trail that eventually leads to Douglas's ex-paramour, played by Dorothy Malone. She has a daughter (Carol Lynley) who attracts Douglas's eye, while Hudson conveniently falls for Malone. When Malone's husband (Joseph Cotten) dies after a successful cattle drive, Douglas tells Malone he intends to run off with her daughter. Matters reach a pitch when Malone tells him that Lynley is actually his daughter—a clear implication of incest. The film culminates with the expected showdown between Hudson and Douglas. When the dust clears, Douglas is dead.

The twist here is that when Hudson examines the fallen man, he discovers that Douglas had entered the shoot-out with an empty gun.

Filming began in Mexico in 1960, although the picture was not released until 1961. Hudson was so popular at the time that he received top billing in the credits over the more accomplished Douglas. The result was a complicated western that includes a menagerie of sordid and pathological themes.

LAST TRAIL, THE Fox, 1933, B&W, 59 min. **Director:** James Tinling; **Screenplay:** Stuart Anthony; **Music:** Arthur Lange; **Cinematographer:** Arthur C. Miller; **Editor:** Barney Yates; **Cast:** George O'Brien, Claire Trevor, El Brendel, Lucille La Verne, Matt McHugh, Edward Le Saint.

A man discovers that gangsters have taken control of the family's ranch and sets out to stop them in this enjoyable version of the Zane Grey novel with a blend of action and comedy. A fast-moving silent version of Grey's *The Last Trail*, released by Fox in 1927, starred Tom Mix and was directed by Louis Seiler. Fox first filmed the story in a 1921 silent feature starring Maurice Flynn, Eva Novak, and Wallace Beery.

LAST TRAIN FROM GUN HILL Paramount, 1959, Color, 98 min. **Producer:** Hal B. Wallis; **Director:** John Sturges; **Screenplay:** James Poe; **Music:** Dimitri Tiomkin; **Cinematographer:** Charles Lang Jr.; **Editor:** Warren Low; **Cast:** Kirk Douglas, Anthony Quinn, Henry Fonda, Carolyn Jones, Earl Holliman, Brad Dexter, Brian Hutton.

Mort Morgan's (Kirk Douglas) Indian wife is raped and killed by two young thugs (Earl Holliman and Brian Hutton). Douglas, who happens to be the marshal of Pauley, discovers a clue that leads him to the neighboring community of Gun Hill. Here he discovers that one of his wife's killers is the son of his old friend Craig Beldon (Anthony Quinn), who is the literal "Boss" of Gun Hill. The inevitable tragedy occurs when Douglas, after holding the lad in a hotel room, tries to bring Holliman to justice on that last train from Gun Hill to Pauley and is challenged by Quinn and his henchmen, who are determined to thwart him.

This excellent western steeped in action includes a psychological bent that rarely impedes the story line. Douglas and Quinn deliver strong performances laced with tension and drama, with Quinn torn between fidelity to the friend who had once saved his life and to his only son, whom he had raised alone. The underrated Holliman is excellent as Rick Beldon, Quinn's brutal and cowardly son, whose only apology to Douglas is: "It ain't my fault you married a damn squaw." The time element that is key to HIGH NOON 1952 and 3:10 TO YUMA 1957 is well employed here.

LAST WAGON, THE 20th Century Fox, 1956, 98 min. **Producer:** William Hawks; **Director:** Delmer Daves; **Screenplay:** Daves and James Edward Grant; **Music:** Lionel Newman; **Cinematographer:** Wilfred M. Cline; **Editor:**

Hugh S. Fowler; **Cast:** Richard Widmark, Felicia Farr, Susan Kohner, Tommy Rettig, Stephanie Griffin, Nick Benton Reid, James Drury, Ray Strickland.

Richard Widmark is Comanche Todd, a convicted murderer who is chained to a wagon train for killing three brothers in revenge for the murder of his Indian wife. He is then entrusted with leading the six surviving children of an Apache attack to safety through hostile Indian territory.

Helmed by Delmer Daves, one of the most skilled yet unheralded directors of westerns in the early and mid-1950s (*BROKEN ARROW* [1950], *DRUM BEAT* [1954], *3:10 TO YUMA* [1957], *COWBOY* [1958]), the film never received the critical acclaim it deserved. But those who might have a chance to watch it on television should take the opportunity to do so. Set in the Arizona territory in 1873, the film provides the talented Widmark with a vintage role, while Tommy Rettig delivers an exceptional performance as the youngster who admires Widmark's grit and savvy.

LAST WARRIOR, THE See *FLAP*.

LAW AND JAKE WADE, THE MGM, 1958, Color, 86 min, VHS. **Producer:** William Hawks; **Director:** John Sturges; **Screenplay:** William Bowers; **Cinematographer:** Robert Surtees; **Editor:** Ferris Webster; **Cast:** Robert Taylor, Richard Widmark, Patricia Owens, Robert Middleton, Henry Silva, De Forrest Kelley, Burt Douglas, Eddie Fireston.

Robert Taylor is outlaw Jake Wade, who decides to go straight but must still battle his old partner Clint Holister (Richard Widmark), the leader of an outlaw band. Holister wants to find some stolen money, the location of which only Jake Wade knows.

This film was Taylor's second MGM western of 1958, the other being *Saddle in the Wind*. As with *Saddle in the Wind*, Taylor plays the reformed outlaw; he had deserted Widmark's predatory gang, taking along the proceeds from a bank robbery. After many years he has now settled in as the highly respected marshal of a small New Mexico town. When he learns that Widmark is facing the noose on a murder charge, Taylor decides he owes his old partner a favor and decides to rescue him. Much to his regret, the ungracious Widmark starts rehashing the old bank robbery and begins thinking about the missing money.

Not a great western, albeit a good one, much of the picture was filmed on glossy MGM exterior sets. The High Sierra and Death Valley scenery is brilliantly photographed in CinemaScope by Robert Surtees; the wily Widmark is superb as the twisted Holister; and the supporting cast of Henry Silva, Robert Middleton, De Forrest Kelley, Burt Douglas, and Eddie Fireston offer praiseworthy performances.

LAW AND LAWLESS Majestic, 1932, B&W, 59 min. **Producers:** Larry Damour and Harry L. Goldstone; **Director:** Armand Schaefer; **Screenplay:** Oliver Drake;

Cinematographer: William Nobles; **Editor:** S. Roy Luby; **Cast:** Jack Hoxie, Hilda Moreno, Julian Rivero, Yakima Canutt, Jack Mower. See *GOLD.*

LAW AND ORDER Universal, 1932, B&W, 75 min. **Director:** Edward L. Cahn; **Screenplay:** John Huston and Tom Reed; **Music:** David Brockman, David Klatzman, and Sam Perry; **Cinematographer:** Jackson Rose; **Editors:** Milton Carruth and Philip Cahn; **Cast:** Walter Huston, Harry Carey, Russell Hopton, Raymond Hatton, Ralph Ince, Harry Woods, Andy Devine, Walter Brennan.

In this atmosphere saga based on the novel *Saint Johnson* by W. R. Burnette, four lawmen (modeled after the Earps and Doc Holliday) clean up a tough town; the film ends in a brutal gunfight at the O.K. Corral. Walter Huston is Frame Johnson, the hard-nosed marshal who tames Tombstone with the help of Ed Brandt (Harry Carey), a Doc Holliday surrogate. Andy Devine appears as an accidental killer whom the lawmen are forced to hang.

This uncompromising film, helmed by Edward L. Cahn (his directional debut), is a rare movie in which realism and austerity are never compromised, as men grow tired of the endless killing that was part and parcel of cleaning up the lawlessness and disorder of unruly frontier towns like Tombstone. Moreover, this somewhat obscure western has been unanimously hailed by genre experts as a superb piece of filmmaking, a vintage motion picture that recaptures the grim West in the best tradition of William S. Hart.

In his *Pictorial History of the Western Film (1969)*, William E. Everson called *Law and Order* "the finest reconstruction yet of the famous gun duel at the O.K. Corral." Scripted in part by John Huston, who in 1948 would direct his father Walter to an Oscar-winning performance in *Treasure of the Sierra Madre*, the film sees the weary marshal riding out of town as the only survivor of the famous gunfight, knowing that "other such towns wait him and his guns." Unlike *High Noon* (1952) many years later, Everson concludes that this 1932 film "achieves a sense of Greek tragedy, without consciously striving for it." Director Edward Cahn never again came close to replicating what was an early sound era near-masterpiece.

Universal made the most out of Burnette's novel as a property, developing it into a 1937 serial entitled *Wild West Days* starring Johnny Mack Brown, and then producing

Johnny Mack Brown (center) in the 1940 remake of Law and Order *(UNIVERSAL/AUTHOR'S COLLECTION)*

another *Law and Order* in 1940, also with Brown. This latter version is a formula B western which bears little resemblance to the original. Comedy and musical sequences dilute this adaptation even further.

LAW AND ORDER Universal, 1953, Color, 80 min, VHS. **Producer:** John Rogers; **Director:** Nathan Juran; **Screenplay:** Gwen Bagni, John Bagni, and J. D. Beauchamp; **Music:** Henry Mancini; **Cinematographer:** Clifford Stein; **Editor:** Ted J. Kent; **Cast:** Ronald Reagan, Dorothy Malone, Preston Foster, Alex Nichol, Ruth Hampton, Russell Johnson, Jack Kelly, Dennis Weaver, Wally Cassell.

This color remake of W. R. Burnette's story has Ronald Reagan as Frame Johnson, who after cleaning up the raucous Tombstone wants nothing more than to settle down in nearby Cottonwood and live out the rest of his life in peace. However, his wish is thwarted when he is forced to take on bad guy Kurt Durling, and must return to his old profession once more in the pursuit of justice. The result is an action-packed Technicolor western designed to appeal to audiences of the day.

Reagan's natural ease in front of a camera demonstrates the fact that he was a solid screen star who handled his roles rather well. Moreover, his natural bent for the West is easily apparent. According to James Robert Parish and Don Stanke's *The All Americans*, Reagan told Howard McClay of the *Los Angeles Daily News*, "I've been itching to sling a six-gun ever since I first put on grease paint. Never could swing it. Now at long last I made the grade and I'd like to keep doing it as long as they let me.

"Western stories are pure Americana—something everybody can know and understand. Their history is recent enough to be real, old enough to be romantic. Mix that up with horses, action, a little love, and lots of money and you've found a real strike."

Nevertheless, this 1953 remake is little more than a standard period piece, and it falls far short of the 1932 original. In the original there were no women other than the brief appearance of a rather dowdy lady of the night. In the remake beautiful Dorothy Malone provides the obligatory love interest that Reagan hopes to marry once justice is achieved. Moreover, the poignant and gut-wrenching hanging scene of the original 1932 film, where the victim is a dimwitted Andy Devine, is reduced here to a routine lynching party by a gang of nasty thugs.

LAW BEYOND THE RANGE Columbia, 1935, B&W, 60 min. **Director:** Ford Beebe; **Screenplay:** Beebe and Lambert Hillyer; **Music:** Mischa Bakaleinikoff and Louis Silvers; **Cinematographer:** Benjamin H. Kline; **Editor:** Ray Snyder; **Cast:** Tim McCoy, Robert Allen, Billie Seward, Guy Usher, Harry Todd, Walter Brennan, Si Jenks, James B. "Pop" Kenton.
See *RIDING TORNADO, THE*.

LAW COMES TO TEXAS, THE Columbia, 1939, B&W, 61 min. **Producer:** Larry Darmour; **Director:** Joseph

Levering; **Screenplay:** Nate Gatzert; **Cinematographer:** James S. Brown Jr.; **Editor:** Dwight Caldwell; **Cast:** William "Wild Bill" Elliott, Veda Borg, Bud Osborne, Charles King, Slim Whitaker.

Texas is plagued by outlaws and murder, so a man trying to restore law and order establishes the Texas Rangers. This action-packed oater is one of a series Bill Elliott did for producer Larry Darmour. The others include *In Early Arizona* (1938), *Frontiers of '49* (1939), and *The Valley of Vanishing Men* (1942).

LAW COMMANDS, THE Crescent, 1937, B&W, 60 min. **Producer:** E. B. Derr; **Director:** William Nigh; **Screenplay:** Bennett Cohen; **Cinematographer:** Arthur Martinelli; **Editor:** Donald Barratt; **Cast:** Tom Keene, Lorraine Randall, Budd Buster, Mathew Betz, Robert Fiske, John Merton.

LAW FOR TOMBSTONE, THE Universal, 1937, B&W, 59 min, VHS. **Producer:** Buck Jones; **Directors:** B. Reeves Eason and Jones; **Screenplay:** Frances Guihan; **Cinematographer:** John Hickson and Allen Q. Thompson; **Editor:** Bernard Loftus; **Cast:** Buck Jones, Muriel Evans, Harvey Clark, Carl Stockdale, Earl Hodgins, Alexander Gross, Chuck Morrison.

LAWLESS BREED (aka: LAWLESS CLAN) Universal, 1946, B&W, 58 min. **Producer:** Wallace Fox; **Director:** Fox; **Screenplay:** Bob Williams; **Music:** Milton Rosen; **Cinematographer:** Maury Gertsman; **Editor:** Otto Ludwig; **Cast:** Kirby Grant, Jane Adams, Fuzzy Knight, Dick Curtis, Karl Hackett, Harry Brown.
See *BAD MEN OF THE BORDER*.

LAWLESS BREED, THE Universal, 1952, Color, 83 min. **Producer:** William Alland; **Director:** Raoul Walsh; **Screenplay:** Bernard Gordon; **Music:** Joseph Gershenson; **Cinematographer:** Irving Glassberg; **Editor:** Frank Gross; **Cast:** Rock Hudson, Julie Adams, Mary Castle, John McIntyre, Hugh O'Brien, Dennis Weaver, Forrest Lewis, Lee Van Cleef, Glenn Strange.

Rock Hudson is John Wesley Hardin, who returns home after spending 16 years in prison to find that his teenage son simply worships him. He has preserved his six-gun, looks up to him as a sterling gunman, and is obsessed with emulating his father and following in his gunman footsteps. To teach his son the pitfalls of being a gunslinger, Hardin joins a gang for one final violent showdown and dies in an act of self-sacrifice to ensure that his son will no longer be attracted to his violent ways.

Directed by Raoul Walsh, the film has plenty of action and is supposedly based on the actual story of Hardin's career, published after his release from prison—although the sentimental ending is questionable, and the film is basically a whitewash job, since Wes Hardin was in reality one of the West's more unsavory outlaws.

Hudson received top billing for the first time, and his performance is top-notch and deserving of leading man status. At the screening for *The Lawless Breed*, Oscar-winning actress Jane Wyman, unfamiliar with Hudson's screen work at that time, was impressed enough with his performance to agreed to have him cast as her leading man in the 1954 blockbuster *Magnificent Obsession*. But acting laurels really belong to veteran actor John McIntyre, who shows his versatility by playing both Hudson's father and uncle—one puritanical and cruel, the other rough but sympathetic.

LAWLESS CODE Monogram, 1949, B&W, 58 min. **Producer:** Louis Gray; **Director:** Oliver Drake; **Screenplay:** Basil Dickey; **Cinematographer:** Harry Neumann; **Editor:** Carl Pierson; **Cast:** Jimmy Wakely, Dub Taylor, Ellen Hall, Tristram Coffin, Riley Hill, Kenne Duncan, Myron Healey.

See *ACROSS THE RIO GRANDE.*

LAWLESS COWBOYS Monogram, 1951, B&W, 58 min. **Producer:** Vincent M. Fennelly; **Director:** Lewis D. Collins; **Screenplay:** Maurice Tombragel; **Cinematographer:** Ernest Miller; **Editor:** Samuel Fileds; **Cast:** Whip Wilson, Jim Bannon, Lane Bradford, Pamela Duncan, Bruce Edwards, I. Stanford Jolley, Fuzzy Knight, Stanley Price, Marshall Reed.

See *ABILENE TRAIL.*

LAWLESS EIGHTIES Republic, 1957, B&W, 70 min. **Producer:** Rudy Ralston; **Director:** Joseph Kane; **Screenplay:** Kenneth Gamet; **Music:** Gerald Roberts; **Cinematographer:** Jack A. Marta; **Editor:** Joseph Harrison; **Cast:** Buster Crabbe, John Smith, Marilyn Saris, Ted de Corsia, Anthony Caruso, John Doucette, Walter Reed, Frank Ferguson.

A gunfighter comes to the aid of a circuit rider who has been beaten by outlaws because he has seen them mistreating Indians.

LAWLESS EMPIRE Columbia, 1945, B&W, 58 min. **Producer:** Colbert Clark; **Director:** Vernon Keays; **Screenplay:** Bennett Cohen; **Music:** Tommy Duncan and Bob Wills; **Cinematographer:** George Meechan; **Editor:** Paul Borofsky; **Cast:** Charles Starrett, Tex Harding, Dub Taylor, Mildred Law, Johnny Walsh, Ethan Laidlaw.

Steve Ranson, aka The Durango Kid, assumes the role of town marshal to help a minister and his wife aid a group of settlers who are being harassed by a gang of raiders. There is lots of fast-paced action in this series entry as well as a lot of good, old-fashioned cowboy music supplied by the Texas Playboys. (See also *THE DURANGO KID*.)

LAWLESS FRONTIER, THE Monogram, 1934, B&W, 59 min. **Director:** Robert N. Bradbury; **Screenplay:** Bradbury; **Cinematographer:** Archie Stout; **Editor:** Charles Hunt; **Cast:** John Wayne, Sheila Terry, George "Gabby" Hayes, Earl Dwire, Yakima Canutt, Jack Rockwell, Gordon B. Woods.

A crooked sheriff tries to pin some crimes on John Tobin (John Wayne), but Wayne proves him wrong once the gang is rounded up. Producer Paul Malvern churned out a large number of John Wayne westerns for Monogram (1933–35), many of them helmed by Robert N. Bradbury. Other Malvern and Wayne films includes *Riders of Destiny* (1933); *Sagebrush Trail, The Lucky Texan, West of the Divide, Blue Steel, The Man from Utah, Randy Rides Alone, The Star Packer, The Trail Beyond* (1934); *'Neath Arizona Skies, Texas Terror, Rainbow Valley, The Desert Trail,* and *Paradise Canyon* (1935). According to Randy Roberts and James Olson in their book *John Wayne, American,* Wayne finished one eight-picture contract with Monogram and then signed on and completed another.

LAWLESS LAND Republic, 1937, B&W, 60 min. **Producer:** A. W. Hackel; **Director:** Albert Ray; **Screenplay:** Andrew Bennison; **Cinematographer:** Jack Greenhalgh; **Editor:** S. Roy Luby; **Cast:** Johnny Mack Brown, Louise Stanley, Ted Adams, Julian Rivero, Horace Murphy, Frank Bell.

LAWLESS NINETIES, THE Republic, 1936, B&W, 55 min, VHS. **Producer:** Paul Malvern; **Director:** Joseph Kane; **Screenplay:** Joseph P. Poland; **Cinematographer:** William Nobles; **Cast:** John Wayne, Ann Rutherford, Harry Woods, George "Gabby" Hayes, Al Bridge, Fred "Snowflake" Toones, Land Chandler, Tom London, Charles King, Cliff Lyons.

John Wayne is an undercover agent who is sent to break up a gang. The action in this Wayne venture concludes with a pitched battle at the edge of a barricaded town in which Wayne cleans up the gang and captures the gang leader.

This was the first film in Wayne's series for Republic for which the entire film had musical scoring. In his previous Republic ventures only the chase scenes were scored. With increased production values at Republic, Wayne now began reaching more of an urban audience for the first time. Bosley Crowther, the lead reviewer for the *New York Times*, viewed the film from the upscale Rialto Theater in New York and liked what he saw. He especially enjoyed the film's energy, noting in his review of June 29, 1936: "It is rare that a Western screen story affords so many legitimate and even logically necessary pretexts for action."

LAWLESS PLAINSMEN (aka: ROLL ON, UK) Columbia, 1942, B&W, 59 min. **Producer:** Jack Fier; **Director:** William Berke; **Screenplay:** Luci Ward; **Cinematographer:** Benjamin H. Kline; **Editor:** William A. Lyon; **Cast:** Charles Starrett, Russell Hayden, Cliff Edwards, Luana Walters, Ray Bennett, Gwen Kenyon.

Indians kill the leader of a wagon train, and the man's daughter persuades another man to take over the train. He discovers that a crook is behind the attacks and deals with him appropriately. There is lots of action in this fast-paced Charles Starrett/Russell Hayden venture for Columbia. (See also *GALLANT DEFENDER*.)

LAWLESS RANGE   Monogram, 1935, B&W, 53 min, VHS. **Producers:** Trem Carr and Paul Malvern; **Director:** Robert N. Bradbury; **Screenplay:** Lindsley Parsons; **Music:** Sam Perry and Clifford Vaughan; **Cinematographer:** Archie Stout; **Editor:** Carl Pierson; **Cast:** John Wayne, Sheila Bromley, Frank McGlynn, Jack Curtis, Yakima Canutt, Earl Dwire.

John Wayne is an undercover agent sent by the governor to discover the motive behind a series of mysterious raids in isolated Pequino Valley, where the villain is a ruthless banker. The film marks John Wayne's final venture as a singing cowboy. Although his voice was most likely dubbed, he retired from the genre completely and without any remorse.

LAWLESS STREET, A (aka: MARSHALL OF MEDICINE BEND)   Columbia, 1955, Color, 78 min, VHS. **Producers:** Harry Joe Brown and Randolph Scott; **Director:** Joseph H. Lewis; **Screenplay:** Kenneth Gamet; **Music:** Paul Sawtell; **Cinematographer:** Ray Rennahan; **Editor:** Gene Havlick; **Cast:** Randolph Scott, Angela Lansbury, Warner Anderson, Jean Parker, Wallace Ford, Michael Pate, John Emery.

A doctor discovers that a local businessman has him marked for murder because he loves the physician's estranged wife. Randolph Scott delivers his usual solid performance as the prototype loner hero. For those accustomed to seeing Angela Lansbury only as a female TV writer/detective in *Murder She Wrote*, she shines here as a leggy and seductive showgirl. Warner Anderson and Michael Pate perform well as villains—Anderson as an unscrupulous womanizing businessman and Pate as a treacherous gloved gunman.

Based on Brad Ward's story, *"Marshal of Medicine Bend"* and coproduced by Randolph Scott and Harry Joe Brown, the film builds in suspense, culminating in a barroom showdown where the boundaries between the forces of good and evil are all too clearly defined.

LAWLESS VALLEY, THE   RKO, 1939, B&W, 59 min. **Producer:** Bert Gilroy; **Director:** David Howard; **Screenplay:** Oliver Drake; **Cinematographer:** Harry Wild; **Editor:** Frederic Knudtson; **Cast:** George O'Brien, Kay Sutton, Walter Miller, Fred Kohler Sr., Fred Kohler Jr., Lew Kelly, George Chesebro, Kirby Grant.

George O'Brien is a prison parolee who returns home to clear his name and to establish the guilt of the parties who put him behind bars. This series entry boasts yet another sturdy performance by O'Brien, RKO's resident cowboy before the advent of Tim Holt. The film is also unusual in that father-and-son actors Fred Kohler and Fred Kohler Jr. play father-and-son villains. (See also *RACKETEERS OF THE RANGE*.)

LAW MAN (1956)   See *STAR IN THE DUST*.

LAWMAN   United Artists, 1971, Color, 99 min, VHS, DVD. **Producer:** Michael Winner; **Director:** Winner; **Screenplay:** Gerald Wilson; **Music:** Jerry Fielding; **Cinematographer:** Robert Paynter; **Editor:** Frederic Wilson; **Cast:** Burt Lancaster, Robert Ryan, Lee J. Cobb, Robert Duvall, Sheree North, Joseph Wiseman, J. D. Cannon, Albert Salmi, John McGiver.

Jarred Maddox (Burt Lancaster), a stoic and philosophical marshal, rides into an unfamiliar town determined to hunt down the seven men who accidentally killed an old man during a drunken rage. He learns that each of the men work for local rancher Vincent Bronson. Even when the entire town turns against him, Maddox continues his pursuit determined to bring the men to justice. When a storekeeper inquires into his motive, suggesting that the man they killed must have been his kin and that his unyielding pursuit of them is a matter of personal revenge, Maddox responds, "No, just a lawman." Robert Ryan again turns in a marvelous performance as the town's timid sheriff, which can only make pundits wonder why he never gained the enormous industry stature he so richly deserved.

LAWMAN IS BORN, A   Republic, 1937, B&W, 58 min. **Producer:** A. W. Hackel; **Director:** Sam Newfield; **Screenplay:** George H. Plympton; **Cinematographer:** Bert Longnecker; **Editor:** S. Roy Luby; **Cast:** Johnny Mack Brown, Iris Meredith, Warner P. Richmond, Mary MacLaren, Dick Curtis.

An outlaw who is falsely accused of murder realizes that the only way to clear himself is to become a lawman. Despite a rather complex plot, this Johnny Mack Brown entry for Republic boasts a lot of action. (See also *GAMBLING TERROR, THE*.)

LAW MEN   Monogram, 1944, B&W, 58 min, VHS. **Producer:** Charles J. Bigelow; **Director:** Lambert Hillyer; **Screenplay:** Glenn Tryon; **Cinematographer:** Harry Neumann; **Editor:** John C. Fuller; **Cast:** Johnny Mack Brown, Raymond Hatton, Robert Frazer, Edmund Cobb, Kirby Grant, Jan Wiley, Isabel Withers.

See *UNDER ARIZONA SKIES*.

LAW OF THE BADLANDS   RKO, 1950, B&W, 59 min. **Producer:** Herman Schlom; **Director:** Leslie Selander; **Screenplay:** Ed Earl Repp; **Music:** Paul Sawtell; **Cast:** Tim Holt, Richard Martin, Joan Dixon, Robert Livingston, Leonard Penn, Harry Woods.

LAW OF THE .45s (aka: THE MYSTERIOUS MR. SHEFFIELD, UK)   Normandy Pictures/Grand

National, 1935, B&W, 56 min. **Producer:** Arthur Alexander; **Director:** John P. McCarthy; **Screenplay:** Robert Emmett Tansey; **Cinematographer:** Robert E. Cline; **Editor:** Holbrook N. Todd; **Cast:** Guinn "Big Boy" Williams, Molly O'Day, Al St. John, Ted Adams, Lafe McKee.

Guinn "Big Boy" Williams is Tucson and Al St. John is Stoney in this first adaptation of William Colt MacDonald's Mesquiteers story. Still minus a third Mesquiteer, Tucson and Stoney are hot on the trail of an outlaw gang that is terrorizing the territory. (See also *THREE MESQUITEERS, THE.*)

LAW OF THE GOLDEN WEST Republic, 1949, B&W, 60 min. **Producer:** Melville Tucker (associate); **Director:** Philip Ford; **Screenplay:** Norman Hall; **Music:** Stanley Wilson and Ernest Miller; **Editor:** Richard L. Van Enger; **Cast:** Monte Hale, Gail Davis, Roy Barcroft, Lane Bradford, John Hurst.

Monte Hale is young Buffalo Bill Cody in this Republic oater about a young man who hunts down the murderer of his father and discovers a land-grab conspiracy. (See also *HOME ON THE RANGE.*)

LAW OF THE LASH PRC, 1947, B&W, 53 min. **Producer:** Jerry Thomas; **Director:** Ray Taylor; **Screenplay:** William L. Nolte; **Music:** Albert Glasser; **Cinematographer:** Robert E. Cline; **Editors:** Norman A. Cerf and Hugh Winn; **Cast:** Lash La Rue, Lee Roberts, Mary Scott, Jack O'Shea, Charles King.

U.S. Marshal Cheyenne Davis (Lash La Rue) and his pal Fuzzy (Al St. John) go undercover to clean up a town run by bandits. After playing second fiddle to Eddie Dean in several PRC westerns, in 1947 the studio gave La Rue a series of his own, in which he enjoyed brief success. Other series films include *Stage to Mesa City, Return of the Lash, Cheyenne Takes Over, Border Feud, The Fighting Vigilantes, Ghost Town Renegades, Pioneer Justice* (1947); *Dead Man's Gold, Frontier Revenge* (1948); *Son of Billy the Kid, Son of a Badman, Outlaw Country* (1949); *The Dalton's Women* (1950); *The Thundering Trail, King of the Bullwhip, The Vanishing Out* (1951); and *The Frontier Phantom* and *The Black Lash* (1952).

LAW OF THE LAWLESS Paramount, 1964, Color, 87 min. **Producer:** A. C. Lyles; **Director:** William Claxton; **Screenplay:** Steve Fisher; **Music:** Paul Dunlap; **Cinematographer:** Lester Shorr; **Editor:** Otho Lovering; **Cast:** Dale Robertson, Yvonne De Carlo, William Bendix, Bruce Cabot, Barton MacLane, John Agar, Richard Arlen, Don "Red" Barry, Lorraine Bendix, George Chandler, Lon Chaney Jr.

Hanging Judge Clem Rogers (Dale Robertson) rides into a Kansas town to preside over the trial of his onetime friend Pete Stone (John Agar). Big Tom Stone, Pete's father, hires gunman Joe Rile (Bruce Cabot), the same man who killed Roger's father, to now kill the judge, while a sexy saloon singer (Yvonne de Carlo) is used as bait to seduce the judge.

However, she becomes enamored with him instead and is beaten up by the chief henchman Lon Chaney Jr. The film culminates in a trial where it is discovered that Pete Stone murdered his victim because he was having an affair with the victim's wife. He is found guilty and sentenced to hang. When gunman Joe confronts Rogers and admits that it was he who had killed the judge's father, Rogers refuses to take the bait and fight. Joe rides out of town, a beaten and humiliated man. Big Tom then tries to kill Rogers, who makes quick work of him as justice prevails.

This film was the first of 11 low-budget westerns produced by A. C. Lyles, and some say it is the best. While these quick production pieces have usually been fodder for serious critics, they have found favor among fans of the genre, largely because of the former big-name stars Lyles employed among his staple of actors. Look for onetime star and leading man Richard Arlen as the bartender.

LAW OF THE NORTHWEST Columbia, 1943, B&W, 57 min. **Producer:** Jack Fiuer (associate); **Director:** William Berke; **Screenplay:** Luci Ward; **Cinematographer:** Benjamin H. Kline; **Editor:** Jerome Thoms; **Cast:** Charles Starrett, Shirley Patterson, Arthur Hunnicutt, Stanley Brown, Davison Clark, Johnny Mitchell, Donald Curtis.
See *GALLANT DEFENDER.*

LAW OF THE PAMPAS Paramount, 1939, B&W, 72 min. **Producer:** Harry Sherman; **Director:** Nate Watt; **Screenplay:** Harrison Jacobs; **Music:** Victor Young; **Cinematographer:** Russell Harlan; **Editor:** Carrol Lewis; **Cast:** William Boyd, Russell Hayden, Sidney Toler, Steffi Duna, Sidney Blackmer, Eddie Dean.
See *HOP-ALONG CASSIDY.*

LAW OF THE PANHANDLE Monogram, 1950, B&W, 55 min. **Producer:** Jerry Thomas; **Director:** Lewis D. Collins; **Screenplay:** Joseph F. Poland; **Cinematographer:** Harry Neumann; **Editor:** William Austin; **Cast:** Johnny Mack Brown, Jane Adams, Myron Healey, Ted Adams, Kermit Maynard.
See *UNDER ARIZONA SKIES.*

LAW OF THE PLAINS Columbia, 1938, B&W, 96 min. **Producer:** Harry L. Decker; **Director:** Sam Nelson; **Screenplay:** Maurice Geraghty; **Music:** Bob Nolan; **Cinematographer:** Benjamin H. Kline; **Editor:** Gene Havlick; **Cast:** Charles Starrett, Iris Meredith, Bob Nolan, Robert Warick, Dick Curtis, The Sons of the Pioneers, Art Mix, George Chesebro.
See *GALLANT DEFENDER.*

LAW OF THE RANGE Universal, 1941, B&W, 59 min. **Producer:** Wil Cowan; **Director:** Ray Taylor; **Screenplay:** Sherman Lowe; **Music:** Everett Carter, Gomer Cool, and Milton Rosen; **Cinematographer:** Charles Van Enger;

Cast: Johnny Mack Brown, Fuzzy Knight, Nell O'Day, Wally Wales.

See *OLD CHISHOLM TRAIL.*

LAW OF THE RANGER Columbia, 1937, B&W, 58 min. **Producer:** Larry Darmour; **Director:** Spencer Gordon Benet; **Screenplay:** Nate Gatzert and Joseph Levering; **Music:** Mischa Bakaleinikoff and Lee Zahler; **Cinematographer:** James S. Brown; **Editor:** Dwight W. Caldwell; **Cast:** Robert Allen, Elaine Shepard, John Merton, Wally Wales (as Hal Taliaferro), Lafe McKee, Tom London, Slim Whitaker (as Charles Whitaker).

Rangers Bob and Wally (Robert Allen and Wally Wales) go undercover to investigate the intimidation of settlers by a crook and his gang, who are trying to get control of all the water rights in the area.

This entertaining entry is one of nine western actor Robert Allen made for Columbia between 1935 and 1937. A multitalented actor who graduated from Dartmouth in 1929 with a degree in literature, Allen (born Irvine E. Theodore Baehr) appeared in a number of films of different genres, but his main claims to fame are these Columbia westerns, which he did with aplomb and efficiency. Since he could not sing or play the guitar, however, Columbia decided to challenge Gene Autry by signing a new cowboy star named Roy Rogers. With Allen's western career over, he spent much of his remaining acting years on the stage. When he died at age 92 in 1998, he may well have been the oldest living cowboy star to date.

Allen's first western films—*Fighting Shadow, Law Beyond the Range,* and *The Revenge Rider*—all starred Tim McCoy and were filmed in 1935. In addition to *Law of the Ranger,* his popular "Ranger Bob" films for Columbia in 1936–37 include *The Unknown Ranger, Rio Grande Ranger* (1936); *Reckless Ranger, The Rangers Step In,* and *Ranger Courage* (1937).

LAW OF THE RIO GRANDE Syndicate Pictures, 1931, B&W, 50 min. **Producers:** F. E. Douglas and Harry S. Webb; **Directors:** Bennett Cohen and Forrest Sheldon; **Screenplay:** Betty Burbridge and Cohen; **Cinematographer:** Herbert Kirkpatrick; **Editor:** Frederick Bain; **Cast:** Bob Custer, Betty Mack, Edmund Cobb, Harry Todd, Carlton S. King.

When an ex-outlaw tries to go straight and becomes a ranch foreman, his plans are thwarted by a former cohort who tries to coax him back to the wrong side of the law.

Kentucky-born Bob Custer was a real cowboy who left the range to perform on the rodeo circuit. In the 1920s he gained some stature in a series of medium-budget westerns. He branched out into other genres under his real name, Raymond Glenn, and then returned to the western fold in the 1930s, mainly working with low-budget independent film companies like Syndicate Pictures. His other Syndicate oaters include *The Fighting Terror, Headin' Westward* (1929); *Under Texas Skies* (1930); *Riders of the North,* and *Son of the Plains* (1931).

LAW OF THE SADDLE (aka: THE LONE RIDER IN THE LAW OF THE SADDLE) PRC,

1943, B&W, 59 min. **Producer:** Sigmund Neufeld; **Director:** Melville De Lay; **Screenplay:** Fred Myton; **Cinematographer:** Robert E. Cline; **Editor:** Holbrook N. Todd; **Cast:** Robert Livingston, Al St. John, Betty Miles, Lane Chandler, John Elliott, Reed Howes.

The Lone Rider goes after an outlaw gang that travels from town to town electing one of its members as sheriff. Robert Livingston as "Rocky Cameron" replaced George Huston as The Lone Rider in 1943. All told, Livingston played the character in four other Lone Rider features for PRC: *Wild Horse Rustlers, Death Rides the Plains, Wolves of the Range,* and *Raiders of Red Gap* (1943).

LAW OF THE TEXAN Columbia, 1938, B&W, 54 min. **Producer:** Monroe Shaff; **Director:** Elmer Clifton; **Screenplay:** Arthur Hoerl and Shaff; **Cinematographer:** Edward Linden; **Editor:** Charles R. Hunt; **Cast:** Buck Jones, Dorothy Fay, Kenneth Harlan, Donald Douglas.

The leader of the Texas Rangers discovers that a cattle-rustling attempt is nothing but a ruse to hide the theft of some precious ore. The mysterious figure who is responsible for this is called El Coyote, and Jones is determined to find him. Jones made a series of films for Columbia in 1937–38. They include *Hollywood Round-up, Boss of Lonely Valley, Headin' East* (1937); *Overland Express, The Stranger from Arizona,* and *California Frontier* (1938).

LAW OF THE VALLEY Monogram, 1944, B&W, 59 min. **Producer:** Charles J. Bigelow; **Director:** Howard Bretherton; **Screenplay:** Joseph O'Donnell; **Music:** Edward J. Kay; **Cinematographer:** Marcel Le Picard; **Editor:** Pierre Janet; **Cast:** Johnny Mack Brown, Raymond Hatton, Lynne Carver, Edmund Cobb, George De Normand, Charles King.

See *UNDER ARIZONA SKIES.*

LAW OF THE WEST Trem Carr Productions, 1932, B&W, 58 min. **Producer:** Trem Carr; **Director:** Robert Bradbury; **Screenplay:** Bradbury; **Music:** Maurice Abrahams, Grant Clarke, and Lewis F. Muir; **Cinematographer:** Will Cline and Archie Stout; **Editor:** Charles Hunt; **Cast:** Bob Steele, Nancy Drexel, Edward Brady, Hank Bell, Charles West, Rose Plummer, Earl Dwire.

Having been kidnapped as a baby, a young man grows up thinking that his father is the gang leader who kidnapped him. When the unsuspecting young man is ordered to kill his real father (now a town marshal), the plot thickens. This engrossing western melodrama also features the song "Ragtime Cowboy Joe."

LAW OF THE WEST Monogram, 1949, B&W, 54 min. **Producer:** Barney A. Sarecky; **Director:** Ray Taylor; **Screenplay:** J. Benton Cheney; **Music:** Edward J. Kay; **Cinematographer:** Harry Neumann; **Editor:** John C. Fuller; **Cast:** Johnny Mack Brown, Max Terhune, Bill Kennedy, Jack Ingram, Riley Hill.

Ken Maynard, Jack La Rue, and Hoot Gibson star in The Law Rides Again. (MONOGRAM/AUTHOR'S COLLECTION)

LAW RIDES AGAIN, THE
Monogram, 1943, B&W, 58 min. **Producer:** Robert Tansey; **Director:** Alan James; **Screenplay:** Tansey (as Robert Emmett) and Frances Cavanaugh; **Cinematographer:** Marcel Le Picard; **Editor:** Carl Pierson; **Cast:** Ken Maynard, Hoot Gibson, Jack LaRue, Betty Miles, Emmett Lynn, Kenneth Harlan, Chief Thundercloud, Chief Many Treaties.

See *DEATH VALLEY RANGERS.*

LAW VS. BILLY THE KID, THE
Columbia, 1954, Color, 72 min. **Producer:** Sam Katzman; **Director:** William Castle; **Screenplay:** John T. Williams; **Cinematographer:** Henry Fruelich; **Editor:** Aaron Snell; **Cast:** Scott Brady, Betta St. John, James Griffith, Alan Hale Jr., Paul Cavanagh.

Billy the Kid is on the run when he is befriended by a rancher. He falls in love with the rancher's pretty daughter, and when he is forced to kill a man for her love, he is brought to justice by his old friend Pat Garrett.

Scott Brady becomes just one more actor to portray the infamous outlaw in this historically flawed film, which provides average entertainment.

LAW WEST OF TOMBSTONE
RKO, 1938, B&W, 72 min. **Producer:** Cliff Reed; **Director:** Glenn Tyron; **Screenplay:** John W. Twist and Clarence Upson Young; **Music:** Robert Russell Bennett and Roy Webb; **Cast:** Harry Carey, Tim Holt, Evelyn Brent, Jean Rouverol, Clarence Kolb, Allan Lane.

Harry Carey plays a spinoff of Judge Roy Bean named Bill Parker, who sets up court in a small town where his rules with a six-shooter. When his daughter, believing he is dead, shows up in town to marry an unsavory man, he is forced to oppose the marriage. Tim Holt costars as "The Tonto Kid," the town's young gunslinger, who dispatches her good-for-

nothing fiance then falls in love with her (and the feeling is mutual). Together with the judge, who lets the crime go unpunished, the Tonto Kid rids the town of the evil McQuinn gang.

This top-notch B western takes a good look at the career of Judge Roy Bean, albeit by a different name. Set in Arizona in the 1880s, the film incorporates the legends of several famous western legends into one feature. In addition to the Roy Bean analogy, there are similarities between the Tonto Kid and Billy the Kid, and between the McQuinn gang and the infamous Clantons of O.K. Corral fame. Genre fans loved this picture, which, along with *Powdersmoke Range* (1935) and *The Last Outlaw* (1936), is one of the trio of superb B westerns that Harry Carey did for RKO in the mid/late 1930s.

LEATHER BURNERS, THE
United Artists, 1943, B&W, 58 min. **Producer:** Harry Sherman; **Director:** Joseph Henabury; **Screenplay:** Blix Lomax; **Music:** Samuel Kaylin; **Cinematographer:** Russell Harlan; **Editor:** Carroll Lewis; **Cast:** William Boyd, Andy Clyde, Bill George, Victor Jory, George Givot, Bobby Larson, George Reeves, Wally Wales, Forbes Murray, Robert Mitchum, Bob Burns.

A calculating cattle rustler (Victor Jory) frames Hoppy and California for murder, and it remains for junior detective Bobby Larson to prove his heroes are innocent. Robert Mitchum appears as Randall in an uncredited role. (See also *HOP-ALONG CASSIDY.*]

LEFT HANDED GUN, THE
Warner Bros., 1958, Color, 99 min, VHS. **Producer:** Fred Coe; **Director:** Arthur Penn; **Screenplay:** Leslie Stevens; **Music:** Alexander Courage; **Cinematographer:** J. Peverell Marley; **Editor:** Folmar Blangsted; **Cast:** Paul Newman, Lita Milan, John Dehner, Hurd Hatfield, James Congdon, James Best, Lane Chandler.

Paul Newman employs his Method training in presenting William Bonney, aka Billy the Kid, as a petulant and disturbed young man. When his mentor Henry Tunstill offers young Billy a new start, Billy is appreciative and loyal. But when Tunstill is killed, Billy swears revenge on the four men who ambushed and killed his boss. As Jay Hyams points out in *The Life and Times of the Western Movie*, Newman's "Method acting leads to wild, uncontrolled body movements: when Billy nods his head in assent, his chin strikes his chest."

Once Tunstill is killed, Billy starts shooting lots of people, and everything he does is reported in the eastern newspapers. An interesting twist has Billy followed about by an eastern drummer who is a true believer of the myth. But once he sees that Billy has feet of clay and the myth is a falsehood, in true Judas fashion he turns Billy in to the law, and the Kid—he dies in essence a victim of his own publicity.

Based on a 1955 NBC television play by Gore Vidal entitled "The Death of Billy the Kid," starring a young Paul Newman, the story was transferred to the screen by director Arthur Penn. Newman, who was rapidly reaching his peak as a major Hollywood star in 1958, portrays the outlaw as a man to be pitied rather than scorned, a fellow too illiterate and too jaded to deal with his numerous hang-ups and problems.

Four decades after its release the film still swims in controversy. Some critics praise the strong psychological overtones, even its religious symbolism, which seems to liken Billy to a Christlike "figure of glory." *Variety*, for example, calls the film "a smart exciting western paced by Paul Newman's intense portrayal." Others find the film far too artsy, with Newman's Billy more like a "Dead End Kid out West." As James Parish and Michael Pitts put it in *The Great Western Movies*, "One could not conceive of Johnny Mack Brown, Robert Taylor, Buster Crabbe, etc. ever portraying the famed Billy in such an introspective, sullen manner as that offered by Newman."

In the final analysis, the film is generally unconvincing and historically flawed. While boasting fine performances, especially by James Best as one of Billy's young cohorts, the film offers little of historical value for even amateur historians to grasp. For the record, Billy was not even left-handed. Nevertheless, like it or not, *The Left Handed Gun*, was not just Arthur Penn's first picture but an indication of the direction the western movie would travel in future years.

LEFT-HANDED LAW Universal, 1937, B&W, 62 min. **Producer:** Buck Jones; **Director:** Leslie Selander; **Screenplay:** Frances Guihan; **Cinematographer:** William Sickner and Allen Q. Thompson; **Editor:** Bernard Loftus; **Cast:** Buck Jones, Noel Francis, Matty Fain, George Regas, Robert Frazer, Lee Phelps.

In this excellent Buck Jones venture for Universal, an army colonel named Alamo Bowie tries to bring peace to a town plagued by lawlessness. His efforts lead to a final showdown with gang leader One Shot Brady, who is reputed to be the fastest gun in the territory. (See also *STONE OF SILVER CREEK*.)

LEGAL LARCENY See *SILVER CITY RAIDERS*.

LEGEND OF NIGGER CHARLEY, THE (aka: THE LEGEND OF BLACK CHARLEY) Paramount, 1972, Color, 98 min. **Producer:** Larry G. Spangler; **Director:** Martin Goldman; **Screenplay:** Goldman and Spangler; **Music:** John Bennings; **Cinematographer:** Peter Eco; **Editor:** Howard Kuperman; **Cast:** Fred Williamson, D'Urville Martin, Don Pedro Colley, Gertrude Jeanette, Marcia McBroom, Alan Gifford.

Fred Williamson plays Charley, a 21-year-old blacksmith who is freed from slavery following the death of his master. The late owner's overseer is determined to revoke the declaration of freedom and sell Charley at an auction, but Charley kills him in a fight and runs off with two other slaves. As the three fugitives head west, they are pursued by a slave catcher and a posse. There is a showdown in a saloon where Fowler, the slave catcher, and his cohorts are killed. Charley now goes to work for a homesteader named Dewey Lyons, who

needs protection from a gang of bandits. In a final assault many of Charley's pals are killed, and the bandits are either killed or dispersed.

One of the black exploitation films that first appeared in the gangster arena during the late 1960s, this western take-off is little more than an orgy of violence. Judith Crist in *New York* Magazine called it "the blaxploitation flick of the week." The *Washington Post* poked a little fun, saying, "Trash, bless its heart, knows no discrimination."

Fred Williamson played professional football for a decade before making his film debut in *M*A*S*H* (1970). *The Legend of Nigger Charley* did well enough to warrant a sequel, *The Soul of Nigger Charley* (1973), written and directed by Larry Spangler and also starring Williamson and D'Urville Martin. The true irony of both projects is that after 40 years of trying to eradicate the word *nigger* from serious discourse, southerners in particular were befuddled to see it on their billboards when the film previewed in Atlanta. So when it was first released in Atlanta, Georgia in the early 1970s, many local newspapers altered the title to *The Legend of Black Charley*. Yet the fame of the films somehow manage to rest in large part on the titles of both movies.

LEGEND OF THE LONE RANGER Universal/Associated Film Distribution, 1981, Color, 98 min, VHS. **Producers:** Walter Conlenz, Lew Grade, and Jack Wrather; **Screenplay:** Ivan Goff and William Roberts; **Music:** John Barry; **Cinematographer:** Laszlo Kovacs; **Editor:** Thomas Stanford; **Cast:** Klinton Spilsbury, Michael Horse, Christopher Lloyd, Matt Clark, Juanin Clay, Jason Robards Jr., John Hart, Richard Farnsworth, Buck Taylor, Chuck Hayward.

A Texas Ranger who is the sole survivor of an attack arranged by the Butch Cavandish gang returns to fight back as the masked hero. Even the presence of Richard Farnsworth as Buffalo Bill and Jason Robards Jr. as a frequently inebriated President Ulysses S. Grant cannot lift this 1981 feature above the level of mediocrity. The best the film can offer is some great scenery, decent action, and a rousing rendition of "The William Tell Overture." It is an excellent example of the old adage that it is unwise to fool around with a classic and makes viewers wish for the "good old days" when Clayton Moore and Jay Silverheels rode the range together and thwarted legions of bad guys.

A 1952 title, *The Legend of the Lone Ranger*, which is available on VHS and DVD, consists of three episodes of the long-running TV series starring Clayton Moore and Jay Silverheels. This combined film chronicles how the Lone Ranger and Tonto first met and how the Lone Ranger found his horse Silver while avenging the death of his brother.

LEGEND OF TOM DOOLEY, THE Columbia, 1959, B&W, 79 min, VHS. **Producer:** Stanley Shpetner; **Director:** Ted Post; **Screenplay:** Shpetner; **Music:** Ronald Stein; **Cinematographer:** Gilbert Warrenton; **Editor:** Robert S. Eisen; **Cast:** Michael Landon, Jo Morrow, Jack Hogan, Richard Rust, Dee Pollock, Ken Lynch.

Tom Dooley (Michael Landon) is a young Confederate soldier unaware that the war is over who is unjustly pursued after attacking a Union stage. The film is basically a vehicle for the popular Landon, who was riding a high wave at the time, and an obvious attempt to capitalize on the popularity of the Kingston Trio song hit.

LEGENDS OF THE FALL Tri Star, 1994, Color, 134 min. **Producer:** Edward Zwick; **Director:** Zwick; **Screenplay:** Susan Shilliday and Bill Wittliff; **Music:** James Horner; **Cinematographer:** John Toll; **Editor:** Steven Rosenblum; **Cast:** Brad Pitt, Anthony Hopkins, Aiden Quinn, Julia Ormond, Henry Thomas, Karina Lombardi.

Set in the early 20th century, the story focuses on the three sons of a retired cavalry officer and how their lives are affected by history, war, love, and changing times. What begins as an interesting family saga becomes a little more than an overblown melodrama as the film continues. Nevertheless the cast is excellent and well suited for their roles. Based on the novella *Legends of the Fall* by Jim Harrison, the film captured an Oscar for Best Cinematography and Oscar nominations for Best Art Direction and Best Sound.

LEGION OF THE LAWLESS RKO, 1940, B&W, 59 min. **Producer:** Bert Gilroy; **Director:** David Howard; **Screenplay:** Doris Schroeder; **Cinematographer:** Harry J. Wild; **Editor:** Frederic Knudtson; **Cast:** George O'Brien, Virginia Vale, Herbert Haywood, Hugh Southern, William "Billy" Benedict, Eddy Waller.

George O'Brien is a young lawyer leading homesteaders and ranchers against a group out to steal land wanted for a railroad. O'Brien and Virginia Vale make an attractive romantic couple in this good, action-filled RKO outing. (See also *RACKETEERS OF THE RANGE*.)

LIFE AND TIMES OF JUDGE ROY BEAN, THE First Artists, 1972, Color, 120 min, VHS. **Producer:** John Foreman; **Director:** John Huston; **Screenplay:** John Milius; **Cinematographer:** Richard Moore; **Editor:** Hugh S. Fowler; **Cast:** Paul Newman, Victoria Principal, Anthony Perkins, Ned Beatty, John Huston, Ava Gardner, Stacy Keach, Jacqueline Bisset, Dean Smith, Bill McKinney, Tab Hunter, Neil Summers.

The film opens with a title card stating: "Maybe this isn't the way it was . . . it is the way it should have been." Then in a series of vignettes we see Paul Newman arrive in the Texas badlands. He draws a moustache on his wanted poster, then enters the saloon and announces who he is. The saloon crowd doesn't take kindly to the intruder. They beat him up, rob him, tie him to a horse, and let the horse run through the prairie until Newman is presumably dead. The only snafu is that he is saved by a Mexican town girl (Victoria Principal), returns to the saloon, and massacres everyone in sight.

Another myth-breaker from the 1970s, this film imaginatively depicts the life of Roy Bean, a Confederate irregular who later opened a saloon in west Texas between the Pecos and Rio Grande rivers. Styling himself the "law west of the Pecos," Bean dispensed a highly idiosyncratic if effective mode of justice. Like its subject, *The Life and Times of Judge Roy Bean* still stirs controversy. It has pleased many filmmakers and critics for its idiosyncratic approach to the lore of the West and its blending of action, comedy, sentiment, and satire. Conversely, many consider it a profound travesty of the Old West, with Bean a vengeful enforcer with no respect for law and order.

Yet Ted Sennett in his *Great Hollywood Westerns* calls *The Life and Times of Judge Roy Bean* "one of the best Western films of the seventies." Certainly director John Huston helmed some of filmland's very best productions, such as *The Maltese Falcon*, *The Treasure of the Sierra Madre*, and *The African Queen*. It is therefore easy to understand why many pundits and critics found fault with this $4 million revisionist production about Judge Bean—a character played to the hilt by Walter Brennan in the far more satisfying THE WESTERNER (1940), for which he won an Oscar.

As noted in *The Great Western Movies*, *Newsday* termed the film a "revisionist western that makes fun of its own characters and the heroic legends of manifest destiny . . . the film is not only anti-heroic, it is anti-dramatic." The *San Francisco Chronicle* was even tougher. "It is a string of sequences, some for the sake of a gag which isn't worth the footage, some for a grotesque but hearty laugh, some to bridge the gap between Blood and Guts and Hearts and Flowers."

Nevertheless the cast should be applauded, and some big-name stars like Paul Newman, Roddy McDowell, Jacqueline Bisset, and Anthony Perkins were strong selling points. But the price for admission might be well spent for the appearance of Ava Gardner as Lillie Langtry, an object of Judge Roy Bean's magnificent obsessions. In one scene, some years after Bean dies in a hail of bullets, Langtry arrives at the Judge Roy Bean Museum (once a saloon) in the town the judge has named for her. Miss Lillie examines the memorabilia, and as she departs she offers a comment on her patron, the late departed judge. "He must have been some man," she exclaims.

Huston, who also appears in the film as Grizzly Adams, joins the ranks of the revisionists who reexamined our national mythology during the Vietnam era following the success of George Roy Hill's BUTCH CASSIDY AND THE SUNDANCE KID and Robert Altman's MCCABE AND MRS. MILLER. The success of his effort is debatable, but perhaps in the final analysis writer Joseph Roquemore says it best. In his book *History Goes to the Movies*, he examines the quality and historical accuracy of a number of films, and he had this to say about Huston's film: "Just how bad is *The Life and Times of Judge Roy Bean*? One critic labeled the film outlandish enough to convince viewers unschooled in Texas history that Roy Bean and Lillie Langtry were purely fictional characters. Worst of all: the movie is boring, and Huston's sporadic lapses into slapstick and farce fall absolutely flat."

LIFE IN THE RAW Fox, 1933, B&W, 59 min. **Director:** Lewis King; **Screenplay:** Stuart Anthony; **Cinematog-**

rapher: Robert H. Planck; **Cast:** George O'Brien, Claire Trevor, Warner P. Richmond, Francis Ford, Greta Nilsen.

When a cowboy falls for a pretty girl, he sets out to reform her no-good brother in this adaptation of a story by Zane Grey. This fun-packed George O'Brien venture marks the screen debut of Claire Trevor, who is listed in the credits only as "the girl."

LIGHT IN THE FOREST Walt Disney/Buena Vista, 1958, Color, 93 min. **Producer:** Walt Disney; **Director:** Hershel Daugherty; **Screenplay:** Lawrence Edward Watkin; **Music:** Gil George and Paul Smith; **Cinematographer:** Ellsworth Fredericks; **Editor:** Stanley Johnson; **Cast:** Fess Parker, Wendell Corey, Joanne Dru, James MacArthur, Jessica Tandy, John McIntyre, Joseph Calleia.

As a result of a 1764 peace treaty, a young white boy who has been raised by Indians is returned home. However, he finds it difficult to adjust to his new surroundings. An excellent cast and a pleasant story makes for an enjoyable, fun-filled Disney venture.

LIGHTNIN' BILL CARSON Puritan Pictures, 1936, B&W, 75 min. **Producers:** Sigmund Neufeld and Leslie Simmonds; **Director:** Sam Newfield; **Screenplay:** Joseph O'Donnell; **Cinematographer:** Jack Greenhalgh; **Editor:** John English; **Cast:** Tim McCoy, Lois January, Rex Lease, Harry Worth, Karl Hackett, Lafe McKee.

Tim McCoy is a U.S. marshal after the outlaw brother of the girl he loves while a notorious bandit is pursuing him at the same time. This decent B venture from Puritan Pictures introduced the character of G-man Lightnin' Bill Carson, a role in which McCoy would continue for Victory Pictures in 1938–39. (See also *MAN FROM GUNTOWN*.)

LIGHTNIN' CARSON RIDES AGAIN Victory, 1938, B&W, 58 min. **Producer:** Sam Katzman; **Director:** Sam Newfield; **Screenplay:** Joseph O'Donnell; **Cinematographer:** Marcel Le Picard; **Editor:** Holbrook N. Todd; **Cast:** Tim McCoy, Joan Barclay, Ted Adams, Bob Terry, Forrest Taylor, Slim Whitaker.

Carson's nephew is accused of murder. To find the real culprit Carson poses as a Mexican so he may better infiltrate the gang that he suspects of being responsible for the murder. McCoy, who appears as Colonel Tim McCoy in the credits, assumes the role of "Lightnin' Bill Carson" in his first Victory series effort for producer Sam Katzman in 1938–39. The others were *Six Gun Trail*, (1938), *Code of the Cactus*, *Texas Wildcats*, *Outlaw's Paradise*, *Straight Shooter*, *Fighting Renegade*, and *Trigger Fingers* (1939).

LIGHTNIN' CRANDALL Republic, 1937, B&W, 60 min. **Producer:** A. W. Hackel; **Director:** Sam Newfield; **Screenplay:** Charles F. Royal; **Cinematographer:** Bert Longnecker; **Editor:** S. Roy Luby; **Cast:** Bob Steele, Lois January, Charles King, Earl Dwire, Ernie Adams, Frank La Rue.

To escape his reputation as the fastest gun in Texas, Bob "Lightnin" Crandall (Bob Steele) leaves the Lone Star State for Arizona. He poses as a tenderfoot until he finds himself in the middle of a range war and is forced to use his guns once more.

Bob Steele made pictures for a number of independent studios. Among those he starred in for Republic in the 1930s are *CAVALRY* (1936); *BORDER PHANTOM, THE COLORADO KID, LIGHTNIN' CRANDALL, GUN LORDS OF STIRRUP BASIN, THE RED ROPE, THE TRUSTED OUTLAW* (1937); *DESERT PATROL, FEUD MAKER* (1938).

LIGHTNING GUNS (aka: TAKING SIDES) Columbia, 1950, B&W, 55 min. **Producer:** Colbert Clark; **Director:** Frank F. Sears; **Screenplay:** Fayte M. Browne; **Editor:** Charles Clark; **Cast:** Charles Starrett, Smiley Burnette, Gloria Henry, William Bailey, Edgar Dearing, Raymond Bond.

LIGHTNING JACK Village Roadshow Productions, 1994, Color, 98 min, VHS, DVD. **Producers:** Greg Coote and Simon Wincer; **Director:** Wincer; **Screenplay:** Paul Hogan; **Music:** Bruce Rowland; **Cinematographer:** David Eggby; **Editor:** O. Nicholas Brown; **Cast:** Paul Hogan, Cuba Gooding Jr., Beverly D'Angelo, Kamala Lopez-Dawson, Pat Hingle, L. Q. Jones, Ben Cooper, Sandy Ward.

This comedy western stars Paul Hogan as Lightning Jack Kane, an Australian outlaw in the Wild West. A failed outlaw, he tries to make a name for himself with one big heist, with his only sidekick being a young black shop assistant (Cuba Gooding Jr.).

The film culminates with a perfect heist, so perfect that nobody knows about it, which robs Hogan of any fame he meant to achieve. Hogan's Lightning Jack is similar to his far more famous Crocodile Dundee, and while the film has sparks of humor and some cute vignettes, it faltered at the box office. Nevertheless, it is always good to see veterans L. Q. Jones (as the sheriff) and Ben Cooper (as a shopkeeper in the bank) once again.

LIGHTNING RAIDERS PRC, 1945, B&W, 61 min. **Producer:** Sigmund Neufeld; **Director:** Sam Newfield; **Screenplay:** Elmer Clifton; **Cinematographer:** Jack Greenhalgh; **Editor:** Holbrook N. Todd; **Cast:** Buster Crabbe, Al St. John, Mady Lawrence, Henry Hall, Steve Darrell, I. Stanford Jolley, Karl Hackett.

LIGHTNING STRIKES WEST Colony, 1940, B&W, 55 min. **Producer:** Arthur Alexander; **Director:** Harry L. Fraser; **Screenplay:** Martha Chapin; **Music:** Lew Porter; **Cinematographer:** Elmer Dyer; **Editor:** Charles Henkel Jr.; **Cast:** Ken Maynard, Claire Rochelle, Bob Terry, Michael Vallon.

U.S. Marshal Lightning Ken Morgan goes under cover, posing as a vagrant to capture an escaped convict who has rejoined his old gang in search of some government loot stolen from a dam project. This entertaining oater was the last solo series entry for Ken Maynard, who made four films for Colony Pictures from 1938 to 1940. In addition to this film, they include *Phantom Ranger* (1938), *Flaming Lead* (1939), and *Death Rides the Range* (1940).

LIGHTNING TRIGGERS   Willis Kent Productions, 1935, B&W, 58 min. **Producer:** Willis Kent; **Director:** S. Roy Luby; **Cast:** Reb Russell, Yvonne Pelletier, Jack Rockwell, Fred Kohler, Edmond Cobb, Lillian Castle.

An interesting twist in this Reb Russell oater has a cowboy joining a gang to get the goods on them and then learning that the gang leader is his father. Willis Kent Productions made 19 films between 1932 and 1935; Reb Russell appeared in eight of them. Others include *Fightin' Through, Man from Hell* (1934); *Arizona Badman, Blazing Guns, Border Vengeance, Cheyenne Tornado, Outlaw Rule, Range Warfare* (1935).

LIGHT OF WESTERN STARS, THE   Paramount, 1930, B&W, 70 min. **Producer:** Harry Sherman; **Directors:** Otto Brower and Edwin H. Knopf; **Screenplay:** Grover Jones and William Slavens McNutt; **Music:** Charles Midgely; **Cinematographer:** Charles Lange; **Cast:** Richard Arlen, Mary Brian, Harry Green, Regis Toomy, Fred Kohler, William Le Maire, George Chandler.

A cowboy (Richard Arlen) falls for an easterner (Mary Brian), the sister of his murdered friend. But when a local lawman, in cahoots with the killer, tries to take her ranch for back taxes, the cowboy stages a robbery and steals the gold that was stolen from his friend in order to pay off the ranch.

This early sound version of Zane Grey's novel of the same name is pleasant fare with a strong accent on action. It was first brought to the silent screen in 1919 by United Pictures, with Dustin Farnum in the starring role. Paramount produced two other adaptations: one in 1925, with Jack Holt in the lead role, directed by William A. Howard; and one in 1940, a version that is less faithful to its source than the others.

LIGHT OF WESTERN STARS, THE   Paramount, 1940, B&W, 64 min. **Producer:** Harry Sherman; **Director:** Leslie Selander; **Screenplay:** Norman Houston; **Music:** Victor Young; **Cinematographer:** Russell Harlan; **Editor:** Sherman A. Rose; **Cast:** Victor Jory, Jo Ann Sayers, Russell Hayden, Morris Ankrum, Tom Tyler, Alan Ladd, Esther Estrella, Eddie Dean, J. Farrell MacDonald.

Two years before he achieved screen stardom in *This Gun for Hire* (1942), Alan Ladd had a small part in the fourth version of Zane Grey's *Light of the Western Stars*, playing a cowhand named Danny who hangs around the saloon, dances with the cantina girl (Esther Estrella), and becomes involved in the shooting of the sheriff. The story concerns a ranch foreman (Victor Jory in one of his few good guy roles) who is on the verge of becoming an outlaw when he is helped by a pretty girl who has faith in his decency. Although the film does not faithfully follow the Zane Grey novel, it does provide good, fast-paced action and is helmed skillfully by Leslie Selander.

LIGHTS OF OLD SANTA FE   Republic, 1944, B&W, 56 min, VHS. **Producer:** Harry Grey; **Director:** Frank McDonald; **Screenplay:** Gordon Kahn and Robert Creighton Williams; **Music:** Morton Scott; **Cinematographer:** Reggie Lanning; **Editor:** Ralph Dixon; **Cast:** Roy Rogers, Dale Evans, George "Gabby" Hayes, Lloyd Corrigan, Tom Keene, Roy Barcroft, Bob Nolan and the Sons of the Pioneers.

With time out for lots of music and songs, Roy and the Sons of the Pioneers work for a rodeo that a rival company is threatening. A big rodeo finale supplants the usual dramatic climax. (See also *UNDER WESTERN STARS*.)

LION AND THE HORSE   Warner Bros., 1952, Color, 83 min. **Producer:** Bryan Foy; **Director:** Louis King; **Screenplay:** Crane Wilbur; **Music:** Max Steiner; **Cinematographer:** Edwin DuPar; **Editor:** William H. Ziegler; **Cast:** Steve Cochran, Ray Teal, Bob Steele, Harry Antrim, George O'Hanlon, Sherry Jackson, House Peters Jr., Lane Chandler.

A cowboy who tries to save his stallion from an uncaring new owner takes the horse into the wilds and seeks sanctuary with an old rancher and his little granddaughter. The horse emerges as a hero when it kills a cattle-killing lion at film's end. Unfortunately this excellent and overlooked family film has yet to appear on video.

LION'S DEN, THE   Puritan, 1936, B&W, 59 min. **Producers:** Sam Katzman, Sigmund Neufeld, and Leslie Simmonds; **Director:** Sam Neufeld; **Screenplay:** John T. Neville; **Cinematographer:** Jack Greenhalgh; **Editor:** John English; **Cast:** Tim McCoy, Joan Woodbury, Don Barclay, J. Frank Glendon, John Merton, Dick Curtiss.

LITTLE BIG HORN (aka: THE FIGHTING SEVENTH, UK)   Lippert, 1951, B&W, Color. **Producer:** Carl T. Hittleman; **Director:** Charles Marquis Warren; **Screenplay:** Warren, Harold Shumate; **Music:** Paul Dunlap; **Cinematographer:** Ernest Miller; **Editor:** Carl Pierson; **Cast:** Lloyd Bridges, John Ireland, Marie Windsor, Reed Hadley, Jim Davis, Wally Cassell, Hugh O'Brien, King Donovan.

A small band of the U.S. Cavalry tries to warn George Armstrong Custer of the impending massacre at Little Big Horn. Their mission is compromised when the patrol commander suspects that his wife is having an affair with a subordinate.

This grim, neatly scripted western is a real sleeper that continues to hold up well after 50 years and may be one of the best films to come out of Lippert Pictures. Good performances from a convincing cast more than compensate for an allegedly small budget. A fairly popular film when it was released in 1951, little is heard about it today. Maurice Sigler and Larry Stock wrote the song "On the Little Big Horn," with lyrics by Stanley Adams. Charles Marques Warren received a nomination from The Writers Guild of America for Best Written American Low-Budget Film (1952).

LITTLE BIG MAN National General Pictures, 1970, Color, 147 min, VHS. **Producer:** Stuart Millar; **Director:** Arthur Penn; **Screenplay:** Calder Willingham; **Music:** John Hammond; **Cinematographer:** Harry Stradling, Jr.; **Editors:** Dede Allen and Richard Marks; **Cast:** Dustin Hoffman, Faye Dunaway, Chief Dan George, Martin Balsam, Richard Mulligan, Jeff Corey, Aimee Eccles.

Little Big Man recounts the life of a 121-year-old frontiersman who was brought up by the Cheyenne and claims to have been, among other things, the only survivor of Custer's Last Stand. Jack Crabb (Dustin Hoffman) ages from a young man in the wild West to a venerable episodic storyteller. Whether his tales are true or not is moot because what he is really doing is recreating the myth of the West in his old age. His various incarnations find him as a gunfighter, medicine show huckster, adopted Indian, and an intimate of the likes of George Custer and Wild Bill Hickok.

Custer (Richard Mulligan) is portrayed as a demented, overly vain leader who leads his troops to certain death, completing the cycle of what had become the debunking of the military icon once treated so heroically in film and legend. Wild Bill Hickok (Jeff Corey) emerges as a benign fellow who becomes Jack Crabb's good drinking buddy.

As for Crabb himself, he was given the name "Little Big Man" by an Indian chief named Old Lodge Skins, played to perfection by Chief Dan George, a performance worthy of the Oscar nomination he received. Crabb's story, to cite author Jay Hyams in his *The Life and Times of the Western Movie*, "is like the West itself—a mixture of history and fictional inventiveness, pure fable and dramatic accounts of human tragedy and courage." The story goes that Dustin Hoffman (Method actor that he is) sat in his dressing room for an hour, screaming at the top of his lungs, in order to get the raspy voice of a man who is supposed to be more than 120 years old.

Based on the novel of the same name by Thomas Berger, the film is historical revisionism to be sure, and the content and characters are somewhat ambiguous. Nevertheless, critics remain greatly impressed with the film. Unlike Penn's earlier film western, THE LEFT HANDED GUN (1958), which received mixed critical reviews, *Little Big Man* has been almost unanimously well received. Moreover, while *The Left Handed Gun* failed to make a big box-office dent or crack the top 20 films in gross income for 1958, at $17 million *Little Big Man* was the ninth top-grossing film for 1971 and the number one western. (The only other western to make the top 20 that year was BIG JAKE with John Wayne, at $7.5 million).

The film also captured its share of awards and nominations. Dustin Hoffman won a nomination for Best Actor by the BAFTA (British Academy Awards), and John Hammond was nominated for the Anthony Asquith Award for Film Music by the BAFTA. But the major share of laurels went to Chief Dan George for his role of Old Lodge Skins, chief of the Cheyenne. He received an Academy Award nomination for Best Supporting Actor (the Oscar went to John Mills in *Ryan's Daughter*), a Best Supporting Actor nomination by the BAFTA, and a Golden Globe nomination in the same category. Chief Dan George did win both the prestigious New York Film Critics Award and The National Society of Film Critics Award as Best Supporting Actor.

LITTLE JOE, THE WRANGLER Universal, 1942, B&W, 60 min. **Producer:** Oliver Drake; **Director:** Lewis D. Collins; **Screenplay:** Elizabeth Beecher and Sherman L. Lowe; **Cinematographer:** William A. Sickner; **Editor:** Russell F. Schoengarth; **Cast:** Johnny Mack Brown, Evelyn Cook, James Craven, Robert F. Hill, Jennifer Holt, Fuzzy Knight, Ethan Laidlaw.

LITTLE MOON AND JUD MCGRAW (aka: GONE WITH THE WEST) International Cinefilm, 1975, Color, 95 min. **Director:** Bernard Girrard; **Screenplay:** Marcus Demian, Monroe Manning, and Douglas Day Stewart; **Cast:** James Caan, Stefanie Powers, Sammy Davis Jr., Aldo Ray, Pepper Martin, Robert Walker Jr., Barbara Werle, Michael Conrad.

When a newspaper reporter and his girlfriend visit a ghost town, they are told a story about a young man and an Indian girl who team up to get revenge on the town boss and his gang. Filmed originally in 1969 by Cinema Releasing Corporation under the title *Man Without Mercy*, the film, by all available accounts, has absolutely nothing to recommend it.

LLANO KID, THE Paramount, 1939, B&W, 70 min. **Producer:** Harry Sherman; **Director:** Edward D. Venturini; **Screenplay:** Wanda Tuchock; **Music:** Victor Young; **Cinematographer:** Russell Harlan; **Editor:** Sherman Rose; **Cast:** Tito Guizar, Gale Sondergaard, Alan Mowbray, Jan Clayton, Emma Dunn, Minor, Chris-Pin Martin, Glenn Strange, Harry Worth, Eddie Dean.

Based on the O. Henry story "Double Dyed Deceiver" and set on the Texas-Mexican border, this oater follows a dashing highwayman named the Llano Kid who has a habit of robbing stagecoaches. Fast forward to a husband-and-wife team of adventurers, John and Lora Travers, who are looking for a fellow named Enrique Ibarra, the lost heir to a vast fortune south of the border. Fate intervenes when the Llano Kid robs their stagecoach, and the couple contemplates having the Kid pose as the elusive Enrique.

This pleasant little film benefits from a grand performance by Oscar-winning actress Gale Sondergaard (*Anthony Adverse*, 1936), as the beautiful and devious Lora, who falls for the Kid in vain. The O. Henry story was first filmed in 1930 as THE TEXAN, with Gary Cooper in the starring role.

LOADED PISTOLS Columbia, 1949, B&W, 70 min. **Producer:** Armand Schaefer; **Director:** John English; **Screenplay:** Dwight Commins and Dorothy Yost; **Music:** Mischa Bakaleinikoff; **Cinematographer:** William Bradford; **Editor:** Aaron Snell; **Cast:** Gene Autry, Barbara Britton, Chill Wills, Jack Holt, Russell Arms, Robert Shayne, Clem Bevans, Fred Kohler Jr., Leon Weaver.

When the lights go out at a craps game, a man is killed by a gunshot. Another man is blamed for the crime, but Gene Autry believes he is innocent and helps hide him from the law. To find the real killer, Gene decides to reenact the crime, and this time when the lights go off, someone takes a shot at him. The aura of mystery, a top-flight cast, and plenty of action make for an enjoyable Autry vehicle.

LOCAL BAD MAN, THE Allied Pictures, 1932, B&W, 59 min. **Producer:** M. H. Hoffman Jr.; **Director:** Otto Brower Jr.; **Cinematographer:** Tom Galligan and Harry Neumann; **Editor:** Mildred Johnston; **Cast:** Hoot Gibson, Sally Blaine, Edward Peil Sr., Hooper Atchley, Milton Brown.

When two crooked bankers rob their own express shipment, they set out to blame their driver.

LONE AVENGER, THE Allied Pictures, 1933, B&W, 61 min, VHS. **Producers:** Samuel Bischoff, Burt Kelly, and William Saal; **Director:** Alan James; **Screenplay:** Betty Burbridge, James and Forrest Sheldon; **Cinematographer:** Tom Galligan and Harry Neumann; **Editor:** Mildred Johnston; **Cast:** Ken Maynard, Muriel Gordon, James A. Marcus, Al Bridge, Charles King.

This top-notch Ken Maynard oater has a cowboy trying to stop an outlaw gang from taking over a town and causing a bank panic.

LONE COWBOY Paramount, 1934, B&W, 64 min. **Director:** Paul Sloane; **Screenplay:** Agnes Brand Leahy, Paul Sloane, and Bobby Vernon; **Cinematographer:** Theodor Sparkuhl; **Cast:** Jackie Cooper, Lila Lee, Barton MacLane, Addison Richards, Charles Middleton, Gavin Gordon.

A juvenile delinquent from Chicago is sent to live with his dad's cowboy pal. The boy and the man become good friends, and together they take on a band of outlaws in this charming and different genre piece.

LONE GUN, THE United Artists, 1954, Color, 76 min. **Producer:** Edward Small; **Director:** Ray Nazarro; **Screenplay:** Don Martin and Richard Schayer; **Cinematographer:** Lester White; **Editor:** Bernard Small and Edward Small; **Cast:** George Montgomery, Dorothy Malone, Frank Faylen, Neville Brand, Skip Homeier, Robert Wilke.

A lawman on the trail of a gang of cattle thieves in Texas falls in love with a rancher's pretty daughter. By this time in his career the sturdy and capable George Montgomery had become a staple in the western genre. Good performances by Montgomery and Dorothy Malone make for a better than routine low-budget western.

LONE HAND, THE Universal, 1953, Color, 80 min. **Producer:** Howard Christie; **Director:** George Sherman; **Screenplay:** Joseph Hoffman; **Music:** Henry Mancini; **Cinematographer:** Maury Gertzman; **Editor:** Paul Weatherwax; **Cast:** Joel McCrea, Barbara Hale, Alex Nicol, Charles Drake, Jimmy Hunt, James Arness, Roy Roberts, Frank Furguson, Wesley Morgan.

A young boy who has great admiration for his father is miffed when he learns that his dad is an outlaw. The caveat, however, is that the father is actually a spy on the side of the law, and his job is to discover who is the head of an outlaw gang. This is a fine and touching father/son film with the usual good performance by Joel McCrea, whose natural ease in front of a western camera is always a pleasure to behold.

LONE HAND TEXAN, THE Columbia, 1947, B&W, 54 min. **Producer:** Colbert Clark; **Director:** Ray Nazarro; **Screenplay:** Ed Earl Repp; **Cinematographer:** George F. Kelley; **Editor:** Paul Borofsky; **Cast:** Charles Starrett, Smiley Burnette, Fred Sears, Mary Newton, George Chesebro, Frank Rice.

LONELY ARE THE BRAVE Universal, 1962, B&W, 107 min. **Producer:** Edward Lewis; **Director:** David Miller; **Screenplay:** Dalton Trumbo; **Music:** Jerry Goldsmith; **Cinematographer:** Philip Lathrop; **Editor:** Leon Barsha; **Cast:** Kirk Douglas, Gena Rowlands, Michael Kane, Carroll O'Connor, Walter Matthew, William Shallert, George Kennedy, Bill Bixby.

The alienation of the cowboy in a modern, mechanized society provides the theme for David Miller's *Lonely Are the Brave*. In Albuquerque, New Mexico, Jack Burns (Kirk Douglas), a wandering cowboy and independent man determined to go where he wants and to do what he pleases, finds it difficult to live in the wide-open spaces that are now being invaded by the future. When his best and only pal is jailed for helping Mexicans cross the border illegally, Burns deliberately causes a disorder so he too will be jailed and can help spring his buddy. However, his friend decides not to escape because he has a wife and kids and does not want to risk a longer sentence. Burns therefore escapes on his own and takes off with his horse to the Mexican border.

A true anachronism, Burns is now pursued by a modern-day posse that has walkie-talkies, jeeps, helicopters, and rifles with telescopic lenses at its disposal. While the sheriff (Walter Matthau) has a degree of respect and sympathy for Burns, his inept deputy (William Shallert) has none. Even with all the odds against him, Burns outwits the authorities and almost makes it to freedom. However, when crossing a wet highway in the dark, he is run over by a huge truck carrying, of all things, 56 toilets to Drake City, New Mexico. Burns's horse is quickly shot, and in a last quest for freedom the cowboy is fatally wounded.

This unique film, while generally applauded by critics, fell short at the box office and with popular audiences more in tune to the shoot-'em-up, action-packed westerns that dominated the early 1960s. Dalton Trumbo based his screenplay on Edward Abbey's novel *Brave Cowboy*. Kirk Douglas commented that "*Spartacus* had the same theme. This is about enslavement in modern times."

In *The Great Western Pictures*, James Parish and Michael Pitts cite *The Saturday Review*'s critique by Arthur Knight: ". . . Dalton Trumbo has fashioned for him [Knight] the finest western script since *High Noon* [1952] and *The Gunfighter* [1950]." *Variety*, on the other hand, felt that the filmmakers settled on surface rather than substance: "The failure of the Dalton Trumbo screenplay . . . is that it does not provide viewers with a sustained probing of the hero's perplexity." In *A Pictorial History of the Western Film*, William Everson calls it "an interesting, if not wholly successful effort . . . pretentious and forced in the face of the simplicity and naturalistic quality of *Ride the High Country*, which came out the same year."

Taken in its entirety, *Lonely Are the Brave* is a film commentary that allows the viewer to think and rethink, and in the final analysis it succeeds in leaving its mark on the audience. It is not an easy film to forget.

LONELY MAN, THE Paramount, 1957, B&W, 88 min. **Producer:** Pat Duggan; **Director:** Henry Levin; **Screenplay:** Harry Essex and Robert Smith; **Music:** Van Cleve; **Cinematographer:** Lionel Lindon; **Editor:** William Murphy; **Cast:** Jack Palance, Anthony Perkins, Neville Brand, Robert Middleton, Elisha Cook Jr., Lee Van Cleef, Denver Pyle, John Doucette.

Jack Palance delivers a solid performance as an aging outlaw hoping to retire and win back the affection of his estranged son (Anthony Perkins), whom he hasn't seen in 17 years. Matters are complicated by the fact that he is going blind and members of his former gang are after him. Moreover, his son holds him responsible for the death of his mother because Palance deserted her years earlier. Filmed in Vista-Vision, the film features fine performances that compensate for a somewhat tired plot.

LONELY TRAIL, THE Republic, 1936, B&W, 56 min, VHS. **Producer:** Nat Levine; **Director:** Joseph Kane; **Screenplay:** Jack Natteford; **Music:** Heinz Roemfeld; **Cinematographer:** William Nobles; **Editor:** Robert Johns; **Cast:** John Wayne, Ann Rutherford, Cy Kendall, Bob Kortman, Fred "Snowflake" Toones, Yakima Canutt, Dennis Moore (as Denny Meadows).

In post-Civil War Texas, carpetbaggers seek to exploit the people of the South. Enter John Wayne, who helps the governor of Texas rid the state of the hated carpetbaggers. At the time of this film's release, with the country in the throes of the Great Depression, a popular theme in B westerns had the hero (Wayne), a true man of the people, taking on the corrupt money interests, as exemplified by evil bankers, lawyers, and outlaws. The ethos of these populist westerns could be found in the prevailing saying, "If you put a banker, a lawyer, and a businessman in a barrel and roll it down a hill, there will always be a son-of-a-bitch on top." Included in the film soundtrack are two Stephen Foster songs, "De Camptown Races" (1850) and "Swanee River" (1851), played on a banjo, danced to by Eugene Jackson, and sung by Etta McDaniel. Also featured is the traditional spiritual "Swing Low, Sweet Chariot," arranged by Henry Thacker Burleigh.

LONE PRAIRIE, THE (aka: INSIDE INFORMATION) Columbia, 1942, B&W, 58 min. **Producer:** Leon Barsha; **Director:** William A. Berke; **Screenplay:** Fred Myton; **Cast:** Russell Hayden, Lucille Lambert, John Merton, John Maxwell, Dub Taylor, Bob Wills, Edmund Cobb.

Crooks go after a man's ranch because a railroad is going through it. They try to steal his cattle, until a cattle buyer comes to the man's rescue. This pleasant fare stars Russell Hayden (Lucky of Hop-Along Cassidy fame) in the lead role. There is plenty of good music here as well, with Bob Wills and His Texas Playboys involved in musical interludes.

LONE RANGER, THE Republic, 1938, B&W, 264 min, 15 episodes. **Producers:** Robert M. Beche and Sol C. Siegel; **Directors:** John English and William Witney; **Screenplay:** Franklyn Adreonn, Ronald Davidson, Lois Eby, Barry Shipman, Fran Striker, and George Worthing Yates; **Music:** Alberto Colombo, Karl Hajos, and William Lava; **Cinematographer:** William Nobles; **Editors:** Edward Todd and Helene Turner; **Cast:** Lee Powell, Chief Thundercloud, Lynne Roberts, Hal Taliaferro (Wally Walls), Herman Brix (Bruce Bennett), Lane Chandler, George Letz (George Montgomery), Stanley Andrews.

After the Civil War, five lawmen (Lee Powell, Herman Brix, Lane Chandler, Hal Taliaferro, and George Letz) unite to fight the nefarious Jeffries gang, aided by a masked man and his Indian friend (Chief Thundercloud as Tonto). It becomes apparent that one of the lawmen is the Lone Ranger, as one by one they are killed off until only one of their number is left to combat Jeffries and his gang alone. You really do not know who the Lone Ranger is until the last chapter.

This landmark western serial helped build the careers of Herman Brix (who later became Bruce Bennett) and George Letz (who became George Montgomery at 20th Century Fox). Lee Powell, who continued to be a serial lead, later died in combat during World War II.

The famous masked man, his horse Silver, and his Indian pal Tonto began their radio careers in 1932, with the first film format being this 1938 serial. It was later released in 1940 as a 69-minute feature film called *Hi-Yo-Silver*. The serial proved so popular that Republic followed with another 15-chapter serial, *The Lone Ranger Rides Again*, the following year. The second series was also directed by English and

Witney and starred Robert Livingston as the Masked Man, with Chief Thundercloud again as Tonto.

After *The Lone Ranger*, the B western serial had reached its peak, and henceforth it entered a period of permanent decline.

The chapters in this serial are: (1) Heigh-Yo-Silver! (2) Thundering Earth; (3) The Pitfall; (4) Agents of Treachery; (5) The Steaming Cauldron; (6) Red Man's Courage; (7) Wheels of Disaster; (8) Fatal Treasure; (9) The Missing Spur; (10) Flaming Fury; (11) The Silver Bullet; (12) Escape; (13) The Fatal Plunge; (14) Messengers of Doom; (15) The Last of the Rangers.

LONE RANGER, THE   Warner Bros., 1956, Color, 86 min. **Producers:** Willis Goldbeck and Jack Wrather; **Director:** Stuart Heisler; **Screenplay:** Herb Meadow; **Music:** David Buttolph; **Cinematographer:** Edwin Dupar; **Editor:** Clarence Kolster; **Cast:** Clayton Moore, Jay Silverheels, Lyle Bettger, Bonita Granville, Perry Lopez, Robert J. Wilke, John Pickard, Beverly Washburn, Michael Ansara, Frank DeKova, Lane Chandler.

The governor of a territory hires the Lone Ranger and Tonto to find out why trouble is brewing between Indians and whites. When they rescue a cowboy from some Indians, he tells them that the trouble is the fault of a rancher who wants to prevent the territory from becoming a state because it would ruin his chances of obtaining valuable iron ore from Indian land. The Masked Man and Tonto stop a settler march into an Indian village by dynamiting the trail, and a short time later the rancher is arrested for murder. Their good deeds done, the Lone Ranger and his faithful Indian companion ride off into the sunset to a hearty "Hi-ho Silver."

Brace Beemer, who played the Lone Ranger on radio, wanted the job when the show became a television series. But the role went to Republic serial hero Clayton Moore, a talented actor in his own right. When Moore took leave of the series for two years, he was replaced by John Hart, who later starred in his own series, *Hawkeye and the Last of the Mohicans* (1957). Moore then returned to the series. Bonita Granville, the onetime Warner Bros. star who plays Welcome Kilgore, the villain's wife, was married to Jack Wrather, the producer of the *Lassie* (1954–74) series on television and executive supervisor of this film. Beverly Washburn, who played her daughter Lila, is best remembered as the young girl in the film favorite *Old Yeller* (1957).

LONE RANGER AND THE LOST CITY OF GOLD, THE   United Artists, 1958, Color, 80 min. **Producer:** Sherman A. Harris; **Director:** Leslie Selander; **Screenplay:** Robert Shaefer and Eric Freiwald; **Music:** Lee Baxter and Lenny Adelson; **Cinematographer:** Kenneth Peach; **Editor:** Robert S. Golden; **Cast:** Clayton Moore, Jay Silverheels, Douglas Kennedy, Charles Watts, Noreen Nash, Lisa Montell.

The clue to an Indian tribe's lost gold mine rests with a combination of five medallions, each being held by friends of the chief. The leader of a gang of hooded raiders and his girlfriend manage to kill off the medallion holders, thus obtaining three disks. The Lone Ranger and Tonto are called in to thwart the plot, but not before a fourth person is killed. The gang leader is then killed by his girlfriend, who is finally captured by the Lone Ranger. This exciting follow-up to the very successful 1956 feature was helmed by veteran western director Leslie Selander, and it still makes for enjoyable viewing.

LONE RIDER AMBUSHED, THE   PRC, 1941, B&W, 63 min. **Producer:** Sigmund Neufeld; **Director:** Sam Newfield; **Screenplay:** Oliver Drake; **Music:** Johnny Lange and Lew Porter; **Cinematographer:** Jack Greenhalgh; **Editor:** Holbrook N. Todd; **Cast:** George Houston, Al St. John, Maxine Leslie, Frank Hagney, Jack Ingram, Hal Price, Ted Adams.

The Lone Rider assumes the identity of the former outlaw Keno Harris to try to learn where the gold from his last big heist is hidden. His hope is to clear an innocent bank teller who has been accused of robbing the bank.

The Lone Rider first appeared in a silent film in 1922, with Victor Adamson in the title role. In 1941 George Houston began a series of films for Producers Releasing Corporation that included eight pictures featuring Tom Cameron/The Lone Rider. Each feature was produced by Sigmund Neufeld and directed by Sam Newfield. They generally were entertaining B series features, the best being *The Lone Rider in Ghost Town* (1941), with a strong story scripted by William Lively and a cast of genre veterans: Budd Buster, Alden Chase, Reed Howes, Charles King, Jack Ingram, and Lane Bradford. Each feature also included sidekick Al St. John, who as Fuzzy Jones was the Lone Rider's partner.

Other films in the series include *The Lone Rider Crosses the Rio* aka *Across the Border, The Lone Rider Fights Back, The Lone Rider Rides On* (1941); *The Lone Rider in Texas Justice, Outlaws of Boulder Pass* (1942). Upon Houston's premature death at age 44, Robert Livingston succeeded him as Rocky Cameron/the Lone Rider for five films, also with Al St. John: *Overland Stagecoach* (1942); *Death Rides the Plains, Raiders of Red Gap, Wild Horse Rustlers, Wolves of the Range, Law of the Saddle* (1943).

In 1994 Luke Askew played a character named The Lone Rider in the film *Frank and Jesse*.

LONE RIDER CROSSES THE RIO, THE   See *ACROSS THE BORDER*.

LONE RIDER IN THE LAW OF THE SADDLE   See *LAW OF THE SADDLE*.

LONESOME DOVE   Motown/Cabin Fever Entertainment, 1989, Color, 384 min, VHS, DVD, CD. **Producer:** Robert Halmi Jr.; **Director:** Simon Wincer; **Teleplay:** Bill Witliff; **Music:** Basil Poledouris; **Cinematographer:** Douglas

Milsome; **Editor:** Corky Ehlers; **Cast:** Robert Duvall, Tommy Lee Jones, Anjelica Huston, Danny Glover, Diane Lane, Robert Urich, Frederic Forrest, D. B. Sweeney, Rick Schroder.

Based on Larry McMurtry's novel of the same name, this superb TV miniseries relates the tale of two former Texas Rangers, Woodrow Call (Tommy Lee Jones) and Augustus McCrea (Robert Duvall), who manage a comfortable but modest living running a cattle company just outside the run-down town of Lonesome Dove, Texas. When a third Ranger, Jack Spoon (Robert Urich), arrives on the scene he perks Call's interest in becoming the first company to take their herd to the mostly unsettled northern region of Montana, deemed to be perfect cattle country. Call, in turn, convinces the less than enthusiastic and more complacent Gus McCrea to join him for the thrill of recapturing their old Texas Ranger days just one last time. The long journey results in a slew of problems and a catalogue of numerous casualties—and a story that never ceases to compel. The story line is intriguing, the characters well defined, the scenery panoramic and rich, and the casting outstanding, although reportedly Larry McMurtry's work was originally written as a screenplay for John Wayne, Jimmy Stewart, and Henry Fonda.

Named the all-time best television miniseries by *Roundup Magazine* (published by the Western Writers of America), this legendary epic won Emmy nominations for Tommy Lee Jones (Outstanding Lead Actor in a Miniseries or Special), Anjelica Huston (Outstanding Lead Actress in a Miniseries or Special), Diane Lane (Outstanding Supporting Actress in a Miniseries or Special), and Danny Glover (Outstanding Supporting Actor in a Miniseries or Special).

Among many other awards and nominations, *Lonesome Dove* won two Golden Globe Awards, one for Best Miniseries or Motion Picture Made for TV and one to Robert Duvall for Best Performance by an Actor in a Miniseries or Motion Picture Made for TV. Golden Globe nominations also went to Tommy Lee Jones (Best Performance by an Actor in a Supporting Role) and Anjelica Huston (Best Performance in a Supporting Role).

A sequel, *Return to Lonesome Dove* (1993), appeared as an NBC miniseries with Jon Voight as Woodrow Call and only Rick Schroder of the earlier cast repeating his role as Newt Dobbs, the youngest member of the original team.

LONESOME TRAIL (aka: ON THE CHEROKEE TRAIL) Monogram, 1945, B&W, 57 min. **Producer:** Oliver Drake; **Director:** Drake; **Screenplay:** Louise Rousseau; **Cinematographer:** William Sickner; **Editor:** Fred Maguire; **Cast:** Jimmy Wakely, Lee "Lasses" White, John James, Iris Cliff, Lorraine Miller.

LONE STAR MGM, 1951, B&W, 94 min, VHS. **Producer:** Z. Wayne Griffin; **Director:** Vincent Sherman; **Screenplay:** Borden Chase; **Music:** David Buttolph; **Cinematographer:** Harold Rosson; **Editor:** Ferris Webster;

Cast: Clark Gable, Ava Gardner, Broderick Crawford, Lionel Barrymore, Beulah Bondi, Ed Begley.

Texas independence is the theme in this MGM western as good guy Clark Gable enters Texas on orders from the president to talk Sam Houston into changing his thinking about Mexico. Among other things he finds himself pitted against bad man Broderick Crawford and involved in a torrid romance with Ava Gardner. Lionel Barrymore plays Andrew Jackson and Moroni Olson is Sam Houston.

LONE STAR BULLETS See *NIGHT RIDERS, THE.*

LONE STAR TRAIL Universal, 1943, B&W, 58 min. **Producer:** Oliver Drake (associate); **Director:** Ray Taylor; **Screenplay:** Drake; **Music:** Hans Salter; **Cinematographer:** William A. Sickner; **Editor:** Ray Snyder; **Cast:** Johnny Mack Brown, Tex Ritter, Fuzzy Knight, Jennifer Holt, Jimmy Wakely and the Jimmy Wakely Trio, Earl Hodgins, Jack Ingram, Robert Mitchum, George Eldridge.

Johnny Mack Brown is framed for robbery and takes to the trail. With the aid of a marshal he sets out to find who framed him. This was one of the first films to give real notice to Robert Mitchum, and his fight scene with Brown is a real gem. This was the last of the Johnny Mack Brown/Tex Ritter series for Universal. (See also *OLD CHISHOLM TRAIL, THE.*)

LONE STAR VIGILANTES Columbia, 1942, B&W, 58 min. **Producer:** Leon Barsha; **Director:** Wallace Fox; **Screenplay:** Luci Ward; **Cinematographer:** Benjamin H. Kline; **Editor:** Mel Thorsen; **Cast:** William "Wild Bill" Elliott, Tex Ritter, Frank Mitchell, Virginia Carpenter, Luana Walters, Budd Buster, Forrest Taylor.

Two Civil War veterans return to their home in Texas find their town under the rule of bandits who are masquerading as army troopers. Tex Ritter sings a couple of songs in this Columbia teaming of Bill Elliott and Tex Ritter. The film was reissued in 1950.

LONE TEXAN, THE 20th Century Fox, 1959, B&W, 71 min. **Producer:** Jack Leewood; **Director:** Paul Landres; **Screenplay:** James Landis and Jack W. Thomas; **Music:** Paul Dunlap; **Cinematographer:** Walter Strenge; **Editor:** Robert Fritch; **Cast:** Willard Parker, Grant Williams, Audrey Dalton, Douglas Kennedy, Dabs Greer, Rayford Barnes, Barbara Heller.

This interesting low-budget venture has a Union cavalry officer returning home to find that he is considered a traitor and that his younger brother is accused of being a corrupt sheriff.

LONE TEXAS RANGER, THE Republic, 1945, B&W, 56 min. **Producer:** Louis Grey; **Director:** Spencer Gordon Bennet; **Screenplay:** Bob Williams; **Editor:** Charles Craft; **Cast:** Bill Elliott, Robert Blake, Roy Barcroft, Budd

Buster, Alice Flemming, Rex Lease. See *ADVENTURES OF RED RYDER, THE.*

LONGHORN, THE Monogram, 1951, B&W, 70 min. **Producer:** Vincent Fennally; **Director:** Lewis D. Collins; **Screenplay:** Daniel B. Ullman; **Cinematographer:** Ernest Miller; **Editor:** Richard Heermance; **Cast:** William "Wild Bill" Elliott, Myron Healey, Phyllis Coates, John Hart, I. Stanford Jolley, Lane Bradford, Marshall Reed.

A cowpoke organizes a cattle drive for the purpose of cross-breeding stock, but a good-for-nothing friend and his gang plan to rustle the herd along the way. Bill Elliott is at his best in this fine B western, which benefits from a well-written script, a good cast, and lots of old-fashioned action. In the late 1940s and early 1950s, Elliott enjoyed a brief reputation as the initial proponent of a new "realism" in series westerns that attempted to hark back to the austerity of William S. Hart. (See also *WACO.*)

LONG RIDERS, THE United Artists, 1980, Color, 99 min, VHS, DVD, CD. **Producer:** Tim Zinnemann; **Director:** Walter Hill; **Screenplay:** Bill Bryden, Steven Smith, James Keach, Stacy Keach, and Hill; **Music:** Ry Cooder; **Cinematographer:** Ric Waite; **Editors:** Freeman A. Davies and David Holden; **Cast:** David Carradine, Keith Carradine, Robert Carradine, James Keach, Stacy Keach, Dennis Quaid, Randy Quaid, Christopher Guest, Nicholas Guest, Harry Carey Jr., Pamela Reed.

The Great Northfield Raid in Minnesota emerges as a central sequence in this gritty Walter Hill western which depicts outlaw life in frontier America, not with romantic nostalgia but rather as treacherous and brutal. It explores the life of these young outlaw riders and the bonds that they form. The film covers about 15 years of the career of the

Phyllis Coates, Bill Elliott, Myron Healey, in The Longhorn (MONOGRAM/AUTHOR'S COLLECTION)

James gang, with an interesting bit of casting as brothers play brothers: James and Stacy Keach as Jesse and Frank James; David, Keith, and Robert Carradine as Cole, Jim, and Bob Younger; Dennis and Randy Quaid as Ed and Quell Miller; and Christopher and Nicholas Guest as Charlie and Bob Ford.

The biggest drawback, however, is that Walter Hill never takes the time to investigate the motivation or psychology behind his characters, leading to a film that glorifies violence for its own sake and contains barely an iota of emotional content or historical significance.

LONG TOMORROW, THE See *FACE TO THE WIND.*

LOOK-OUT SISTER Astor Pictures, 1947, B&W, 63 min, VHS. **Producer:** Berle Adams; **Director:** Bud Pollard; **Screenplay:** John E. Gordon and Will Morrisey; **Music:** Dallas Bartley, Water Bishop, Benny Carter, Jeff Dane, Irving Gordon, Louis Jordan, Dick Miles, Fleecie Moore, and Sid Robbin; **Cinematographer:** Carl Berger; **Editor:** Pollard; **Cast:** Louis Jordan, Suzette Harbin, Monte Hawley, Bob Scott, Glen Aaron Izenhall, Tom Southern, Maceo Sheffield, Jack Clisby.

Made for the African-American market of the 1940s, this film is more of a movie revue featuring Louis Jordan, his band, and 11 decent tunes than it is a picture with any sustained plot or character development. The story concerns a bandleader at a dude ranch who tries to save it from foreclosure. Two of the actors, Tom Southern and Maceo Sheffield, also appeared in the Herb Jeffries black westerns of the 1930s.

LOS AMIGOS See *DEAF SMITH AND JOHNNY EARS.*

LOST CANYON United Artists, 1942, B&W, 61 min. **Producer:** Harry Sherman; **Director:** Leslie Selander; **Screenplay:** Harry O. Hoyt; **Cinematographer:** Russell Harlan; **Editor:** Sherman A. Rose; **Cast:** William Boyd, Andy Clyde, Bill George, Lola Lane, Douglas Fowley.

LOST TRAIL, THE Monogram, 1945, B&W, 53 min. **Producer:** Scott R. Dunlap; **Director:** Lambert Hillyer; **Screenplay:** Adele Buffington (Jess Bowers); **Cinematographer:** Marcel Le Picard; **Editor:** Dan Milner; **Cast:** Johnny Mack Brown, Raymond Hatton, Jennifer Holt, Riley Hill, Kenneth MacDonald.

LOUISIANA GAL See *OLD LOUISIANA.*

LOVE ME TENDER 20th Century Fox, 1956, B&W, 89 min, VHS. **Producer:** David Weisbart; **Director:** Robert D. Webb; **Screenplay:** Robert Geraghty; **Music:** Vera Matson, Lionel Newman, and Elvis Presley; **Cinematographer:** Lee Tover; **Editor:** Hugh S. Fowler; **Cast:** Richard Egan,

Debra Paget, Elvis Presley, Robert Middleton, William Campbell, Neville Brand, Mildred Dunnock, Bruce Bennett, James Drury, L. Q. Jones, Barry Coe.

Elvis Presley plays young Clint Reno, who stays on to help run the family farm while his three older brothers march off to fight in the Civil War. When his eldest sibling (Richard Egan) fails to return home and word is received that he has been killed in combat, Elvis marries pretty Debra Paget, the gal his older brother had left behind. But Egan unexpectedly returns, and he brings with him some valuable pilfered items, which he and his two other brothers start squabbling over. He is also miffed by his youngest brother's marriage to the girl he still loves, and the resulting triangle leads to tragic consequences.

Presley does a respectable job in his screen debut. In an obvious attempt to capitalize on Elvis's enormous popularity, the film allocates ample time for him to sing a few songs including the title number, which became a number one seller on the RCA label. Presley and Vera Matson wrote the song using a melody based on the Civil War song "Aura Lee, or the Maid with the Golden Hair." Other songs include "Poor Boy," "We're Gonna Move," and "Let Me." A big box-office success, *Love Me Tender* grossed $4.5 million, making it the seventh biggest money-maker for 1957.

LUCKY BOOTS   See *GUN PLAY*.

LUCKY CISCO KID   20th Century Fox, 1940, B&W, 68 min. **Producer:** Sol M. Wurtzel; **Director:** H. Bruce Humberstone; **Screenplay:** Robert Ellis and Helen Logan; **Music:** Cyril J. Mockridge; **Cinematographer:** Lucien N. Andriot; **Editor:** Fred Allen; **Cast:** Cesar Romero, Mary Beth Hughes, Dana Andrews, Evelyn Venable, Chris Pin-Martin, Willard Robertson, Johnny Sheffield, Joe Sawyer, Francis Ford.

LUCKY LARKIN   Universal, 1930, B&W, 66 min. **Producers:** Harry Joe Brown and Ken Maynard; **Director:** Brown; **Screenplay:** Marion Jackson and Leslie Mason (titles); **Cinematographer:** Ted D. McCord; **Editor:** Fred Allen; **Cast:** Ken Maynard, Nora Lane, Jim Farley, Harry Todd, Paul Hurst, Blue Washington, Charles Clary.

Ken Maynard is a cowboy who agrees to ride in a big race to save the ranch of the man whose daughter he loves. This basically silent film makes use of a musical score and sound effects. After a series of superior westerns for Great National, Maynard came to Universal in 1929 for series of sound westerns, including *Senior Americano* (part talkie), *The Wagon Master* (part talkie, 1929); *Lucky Larkin, Mountain Justice, Song of the Saddle, The Fighting Legion,* and *Parade of the West* (1930).

Released by the studio when, surprisingly, it dropped western productions, Maynard spent a short time with independent companies until returning to Universal in 1933 for eight fairly lavish westerns, including *King of the Arena, Strawberry Roan, The Trail Drive* (1933); *Smoking Guns, Gun Justice, Wheels of Destiny,* and *Honor of the Range* (1934).

LUCKY TERROR   Grand National, 1936, B&W, 61 min. **Producer:** Walter Fudder; **Director:** Alan James; **Screenplay:** James; **Cinematographer:** Arthur Reed; **Editor:** Carl Himm; **Cast:** Hoot Gibson, Charles Hill, Lona Andre, George Chesebro, Charles King.

LUCKY TEXAN, THE   Monogram/Lone Star, 1934, B&W, 55 min, VHS. **Producer:** Paul Malvern; **Director:** Robert N. Bradbury; **Screenplay:** Bradbury; **Cinematographer:** Archie Stout; **Editor:** Carl Pierson; **Cast:** John Wayne, Barbara Sheldon, Lloyd Whitlock, George "Gabby" Hayes, Yakima Canutt, Eddie Parker.

John Wayne and "Gabby" Hayes discover a vein of gold. When Hayes is accused of murder, Wayne sets out to prove his innocence and manages to find out that the real culprit is the sheriff's son.

LUST FOR GOLD (aka: FOR THOSE WHO DARE)   Columbia, 1949, B&W, 90 min. **Producer:** S. Sylvan Simon; **Director:** Simon; **Screenplay:** Richard English and Tod Sherdman; **Cinematographer:** Archie Stout; **Editor:** Gene Havlick; **Cast:** Ida Lupino, Glenn Ford, Gig Young, William Prince, Edgar Buchanan, Will Geer, Paul Ford.

Based on Barry Storm's book *Thunder God's Gold,* the film tells the tale of how immigrant Jacob Walz, the Dutchman of Arizona's Lost Dutchman legend, found his treasure. The story starts and ends in 1948, with long flashback sequences describing the period between 1880 and 1887. The plot unfolds when the grandson of the original discoverer of the richest gold mine in America decides to search for the mine, which is worth $20 million. The result is an orgy of mystery, action, romance, murder, and double-dealing. Glenn Ford is Walz, who discovers the mine and is willing to kill to keep it. Ida Lupino is the beguiling woman who attempts to seduce Ford in order to gain control of the fortune for herself and her no-good husband.

George Marshal was slated to helm this film, but he was replaced by S. Sylvan Simon. More problems loomed when novelist Barry Storm, from whose book the screenplay was derived, sued Columbia Pictures for a number of things, including plagiarism. Storm's work, which was based on fact, concerned the Lost Dutchman Gold Mine, which according to legend is still hidden somewhere in Arizona.

LUST IN THE DUST   Fox Run, 1984, Color, 87 min, VHS, DVD. **Producers:** Allan Glaser and Tab Hunter; **Director:** Paul Bartel; **Screenplay:** Philip John Taylor; **Music:** Peter Matz; **Cinematographer:** Paul Lohmann; **Editor:** Alan Toomayan; **Cast:** Tab Hunter, Divine, Geoffrey

Lewis, Henry Silva, Cesar Romero, Gina Gallego, Woody Strode.

This campy R-rated satire has dance-hall girl Rosie Valdez, played by transvestite performer Divine, stranded in the desert after an outlaw gang attacks her. A mysterious gunman appears on the scene, and together they go to a small town where the population is after a hidden treasure. Some might find this movie humorous, even outlandish. Leonard Maltin calls it "a bomb"; and Divine was nominated for a 1986 Razzie Award as Worst Actress.

LUST TO KILL, A Barjul International/Emerson, 1959, 69 min. **Producers:** Patrick Betz and A. R. Milton; **Director:** Oliver Drake; **Screenplay:** Tom Hubbard and Samuel Roeca; **Cinematographer:** Glen MacWilliams; **Editor:** Everett Dodd; **Cast:** Jim Davis, Don Megowan, Allison Hayes, Claire Carleton.

A cowboy who escapes from jail with the help of his girlfriend goes after the men he holds responsible for his brother's shooting by lawmen.

LUSTY MEN RKO, 1952, B&W, 113 min. **Producers:** Norman Krasna and Jerry Wald; **Director:** Nicholas Ray; **Screenplay:** David Dortort and Horace McCoy; **Music:** Roy Webb; **Cinematographer:** Lee Garmes; **Editor:** Ralph Dawson; **Cast:** Susan Hayward, Robert Mitchum, Arthur Kennedy, Frank Faylen, Walter Cox, John Mitchum.

Robert Mitchum plays aging rodeo star Jeff McCloud in one of the first and surely one of the best films about rodeo. Broke and down on his luck, McCloud returns home to Oklahoma, where he meets a young cowboy (Arthur Kennedy) and his wife (Susan Hayward). His tales of past glories inspire Kennedy, who wants to learn to rodeo, and Mitchum agrees to teach Kennedy the tricks of the rodeo trade for half the take. Kennedy does well and makes a killing, but instead of putting his earnings away toward the ranch he had always wanted, he too starts spending it on women and booze. Mitchum warns him: "Either you beat the money or the money beats you."

Directed by Nicholas Ray, this modern-day western employs a lot of actual rodeo footage. According to John Mitchum in his book *Them Ornery Mitchum Boys*, Robert Mitchum dubbed Nicholas Ray "The Mystic" because "Ray would sit in his director's chair in such deep concentration that nothing could penetrate it. Suddenly he would leap up and go into action with every detail straight in his mind." John Mitchum, who also had a part in the film as a wrangler, recalls that Ray was exceedingly pleased with Bob Mitchum's performance, saying for the record that "Bob's portrayal of the worn-out cowboy was the best, most poignant ever." Novelist Horace McCoy (*They Shoot Horses, Don't They?*) and David Dortort, who went on to produce and create the popular *Bonanza* (1959–73) series on television, share the writing credits. The picture is a beautifully filmed western melodrama deserving of attention.

MACHISMO (aka: FORTY GRAVES FOR FORTY GUNS; EL SALVEJO; THE GREAT GUNDOWN) Box Office International, 1971, Color, 95 min. **Producers:** Ronald Victor Garcia, Paul Nobert, and Harry H. Novack; **Director:** Paul Hunt; **Screenplay:** Garcia, Steve Fisher, Hunt, and Robert Padilla; **Music:** Alan Caddy, Ronald Fallon, and Jack Preisner; **Cinematographer:** Garcia; **Editors:** Mike Bennett, Ronald Victor Garcia, Paul Hunt, and Tony de Zarraga; **Cast:** Robert Padilla, Malilia Saint Duval, Richard Rust, Steve Oliver, Royal Dano.

A jailed Mexican bandit is offered a pardon to cross the border into Mexico and bring back a gang of murderous gold thieves in this violent low-budget picture filmed in Arizona. Originally filmed as *El Salvejo (The Savage)*, the film was reissued in 1977 by Sun Production as *The Great Gundown*.

MACKENNA'S GOLD Columbia, 1969, Color, 128 min, VHS, DVD. **Producers:** Carl Foreman and Dimitri Tiomkin; **Director:** J. Lee Thompson; **Screenplay:** Foreman; **Music:** Quincy Jones; **Cinematographer:** Joseph MacDonald; **Editors:** Bill Lenny and John F. Link; **Cast:** Gregory Peck, Omar Sharif, Camilla Sparv, Keenan Wynn, Julie Newmar, Ted Cassidy, Raymond Massey, Burgess Meredith, Anthony Quayle, Edward G. Robinson, Lee J. Cobb, Eli Wallach, Robert Phillips.

In this adaptation of Will Henry's novel, after Marshall Sam Mackenna (Gregory Peck) kills an old Apache in self-defense, he memorizes the content of the old man's map, which legend decrees will lead to a fabled Canyon of Gold. The gold belongs to the Apache, and the gods have decreed that it is to remain untouched. However, a short time later Mackenna is kidnapped by a brutal Mexican outlaw named Colorado (Omar Sharif), whose entourage includes a murderous Apache strongman named Monkey and a dangerous Apache woman, Hesh-Ke. Hesh-Ke's passion and desire for Mackenna, a former lover, is ravenous and obsessive, and her histrionics include some underwater aqua-dynamics which come perilously close to murder.

What keeps Mackenna alive is the fact that only he can lead Colorado to the elusive canyon. But word of the gold has already spread, and the outlaw band is now joined by an assortment of vengeful Apache, renegade soldiers, and the "honest citizens" of the nearby town whose desire for a piece of the golden rock defies all sense of reason. "You can't keep gold a secret, it travels through the air," one of the citizens explains, as greed and gold fever take a stronger hold.

Yet danger looms ahead as the "good citizens" and the outlaws meet untimely deaths one by one, until only Mackenna, Colorado, and lovely Inga Bergmann (Camilla Sparv) remain alive. Mackenna and Colorado engage into a dramatic fight to the finish atop the fabulous Canon del Oro, until the mountain itself starts crumbling to the ground.

Despite the top-quality cast, a superb musical score by Quincy Jones, and some deft photography, the film failed to excite critics, many of whom saw it as just another overblown and overlong western adventure yarn. The film is narrated by Victor Jory, and the song "Old Turkey Buzzard" is sung by Jose Feliciano, whose career was in high gear back then. Despite tepid reviews, this movie still makes a mark on fans of the genre who are willing to ignore some blatant flaws—including a number of pre-release cuts—and who find enough action and excitement here to satisfy. Interestingly, one of George Lucas's projects while still a film student was documenting the making of this film.

MACKINTOSH AND T.J. Penland Productions, 1975, Color, 96 min. **Producer:** Tim Penland; **Director:** Marvin J. Chomsky; **Screenplay:** Paul Savage; **Music:** Waylon Jennings; **Cinematographer:** Terry K. Meade; **Editor:**

Howard E. Smith; **Cast:** Roy Rogers, Clay O'Brien, Billy Green Bush, Andrew Robinson, Joan Hackett, James Hampton, Luke Askew, Dean Smith, Larry Mahan.

This is an old-fashioned modern-day western with Roy Rogers as an aging ranch hand who has a positive influence on a young boy. Together they fight a rabies epidemic and search for a madman who is hiding on a large ranch. A must for all true Roy Rogers fans, and his last full-length starring feature, this entertaining film was largely overlooked when it came out in 1975. It was reissued in 1984. The music was supplied by Waylon Jennings, Willie Nelson, and the Waylors.

MAD DOG MORGAN (aka: MAD DOG) Cinema Shores International, 1976, Color, 102 min, VHS. **Producer:** Jeremy Thomas; **Director:** Phillipe Mora; **Screenplay:** Mora; **Music:** Patrick Flynn; **Cinematographer:** Mike Molloy; **Editor:** John Scott; **Cast:** Dennis Hopper, Jack Thompson, David Gulpilil, Michael Pate.

Produced in Australia under the above title, this brutal tale tells the story of the famous 19th-century outlaw "Mad Dog" Morgan in the rough-and-ready world of the 1800s. This R-rated Australian film won the John Ford Memorial Award as the best western of the Year for 1976. The TV print of this extremely violent film runs 93 minutes and has been retitled *Mad Dog*.

MADRON (aka: HIS NAME WAS MADRON, UK) Four Star/Excelsior, 1971, Color, 92 min, VHS, DVD. **Producers:** Emmanuel Heningman and Rick Weaver; **Director:** Jerry Hopper; **Screenplay:** Edward Chappel; **Music:** Riz Ortolani; **Cinematographer:** Adam Greenberg and Marcel Grignon; **Editor:** Renzo Lucidi; **Cast:** Richard Boone, Leslie Caron, Paul Smith, Mosko Alkalai, Gabi Amrani.

A nun who survives a wagon-train attack and a cantankerous old gunfighter try to ward off warring Apache. The strongest element in this extremely violent film shot in Israel's Negev Desert is the Oscar-nominated song "Till Love Touches Your Life" (words by Arthur Hamilton, music by Riz Ortolani), which is sung on the soundtrack by Richards Wiliams.

MAD TRAPPER OF THE YUKON See CHALLENGE TO BE FREE.

MAGNIFICENT SEVEN, THE United Artists, 1960, Color, 128 min, VHS, DVD, CD. **Producer:** John Sturges; **Director:** Sturges; **Screenplay:** William Roberts; **Music:** Elmer Bernstein; **Cinematographer:** Charles Lang; **Editor:** Ferris Webster; **Cast:** Yul Brynner, Steve McQueen, Eli Wallach, Horst Buchholz, Charles Bronson, Robert Vaughn, Brad Dexter, James Coburn, Robert Wilke, Bing Russell, Whit Bissell.

When the inhabitants of a small Mexican town are harassed and devastated by a ruthless bandit gang headed by Eli Wallach, they decide to hire a diverse group of paid gunslingers to take up their cause. Considering that this is not the type of work each gunslinger would normally accept (the times have passed them by), and the pay is paltry at best, each gunman's reason to help becomes a personal mission. In time the meager pay becomes less and less important, as the gunslingers develop a fondness and loyalty to the wretched Mexican farmers they are training to fight and have pledged to protect.

Based on Akira Kurosawa's masterpiece *The Seven Samurai* (1954), the real strength of *The Magnificent Seven* resides in the characterizations of the seven gunmen. Led by Yul Brynner as Chris, the mysterious black-clad loner, the six other recruits include Steve McQueen as the laconic Vin; Horst Buchholz as Chico, the insecure wannabe; Charles Bronson as O'Reilly, the half-breed who understands the plight of the farmers; James Coburn as Britt, the mellow but deadly knife-thrower, a study in concentration; Robert Vaughn as Lee, a man in search of his lost courage; and Brad Dexter as Harry, a down-and-out gunslinger convinced that the farmers must have a hidden treasure.

A tremendously exciting film which philosophizes about the nature of power and violence, the film benefits greatly from Elmer Bernstein's Oscar-nominated musical score, so stirring and inspirational that the theme song was used in ads for Marlboro cigarettes. *The Magnificent Seven* also established the unique screen identities of McQueen, Bronson, and Coburn, who were reunited with director John Sturges three years later in *The Great Escape* (1963).

For McQueen especially, *The Magnificent Seven* was his first real shot at stardom. Originally the movie was designed to center around its star, Yul Brynner, and funding was based solely on his appearance in the film. Sturges was to handpick Brynner's costars, to make sure that all of them would complement rather than upstage him. However, according to author Marshall Terrill in *Steve McQueen, Portrait of an American Rebel*, McQueen made sure that someway, somehow, he would manage to steal scenes away from Brynner, which he did quite successfully. Consequently, the relationship between the two stars was far from amiable, and "the tension between the two stars crackled."

While some critics carped at the idea of a Japanese masterpiece being updated to the Old West, *Variety* reflected on the mood of American moviegoers, calling the film ". . . a rip roaring rootin' tootin' Western with lots of bite and tang and old fashion abandon." Yet perhaps the greatest legacy of Sturges's *The Magnificent Seven* is that after 40 years it has stood the test of time. It also strongly influenced the later spaghetti westerns from Italy. The film proved so successful that six years later United Artists produced a sequel, THE RETURN OF THE SEVEN (1966). It followed suit with yet another sequel, THE GUNS OF THE MAGNIFICENT SEVEN (1969); then one more, THE MAGNIFICENT SEVEN RIDE (1972).

MAGNIFICENT SEVEN RIDE, THE United Artists/Mirish Co., 1972, Color, 100 min. **Producer:** William A. Caliham; **Director:** George McCowan; **Screenplay:** Arthur Rowe; **Music:** Elmer Bernstein; **Cinematogra-**

pher: Fred J. Koenecamp; **Editor:** Walter Thompson; **Cast:** Lee Van Cleef, Stephanie Powers, Mariette Hartley, Luke Askew.

In the Seven's fourth ride, Marshal Chris Adams (Lee Van Cleef) is asked to chase down a gang of bandits, but he has since married and settled down and is not interested in further gunplay. When his wife is killed he heads south and joins with a bunch of cutthroats, and a new seven ride again. Even with its decidedly "spaghetti" bent—a pulsating musical score, six-guns blazing, rising dust, and a whole lot of meanness and violence—many *Magnificent Seven* aficionados consider this 1972 outing to be the best of the sequels.

MAIL ORDER BRIDE (aka: WEST OF MONTANA, UK) MGM, 1964, Color, 83 min. **Producer:** Richard E. Lyons; **Director:** Burt Kennedy; **Screenplay:** Kennedy; **Music:** George Bassman; **Cinematographer:** Paul Vogel; **Editor:** Frank Sintello; **Cast:** Buddy Ebsen, Keir Dullea, Lois Nettleton, Warren Oates, Barbara Luna, Paul Fix, Marie Windsor.

When an irresponsible young fellow (Keir Dullea) inherits a ranch, his guardian (Buddy Ebsen) feels he is not yet ready to assume such a responsibility. He determines that what the boy needs is a good wife. Looking through the ads in a Montgomery Ward catalogue, he sets out to Kansas City to pick up the mail order bride (Lois Nettleton), who turns out to be a young widow with a child. Director Burt Kennedy turns out a nice little western with this deft comedy, which is tempered with enough action to keep things interesting.

MAJOR DUNDEE Columbia, 1965, Color, 134 min, VHS. **Producer:** Jerry Bresler; **Director:** Sam Peckinpah; **Music:** Daniele Amfitheatrof; **Cinematographer:** Sam Leavitt; **Editors:** William A. Lyon, Don Starling, and Howard Kunin; **Cast:** Charlton Heston, Richard Harris, Jim Hutton, James Coburn, Michael Anderson Jr., Senta Berger, Warren Oates, Ben Johnson, Mario Adorf, Brock Peters, R. G. Armstrong, L. Q. Jones, Dub Taylor.

In this film set near the end of the Civil War, a band of renegade Apache massacre a cavalry post in New Mexico. In a nearby area, Major Amos Dundee (Charlton Heston) is the commandant of an outpost with 400 Confederate prisoners, Union deserters, desperadoes, and convicted thieves. Dundee adds a number of volunteers to his command and sets out to retaliate against the Apache.

Another major adversary is Confederate captain Benjamin Tyreen (Richard Harris), a former friend of Dundee's who is the ranking officer of the Confederate prisoners but agrees to assist Dundee in leading his expedition against the savage Apache. As the force is dispatched toward the border, they are a command divided against itself.

Once they enter Mexico the conflict between the two officers intensifies, the more so because they both become attracted to the same beautiful widow (Senta Berger). The battle now won, Dundee is forced to fight against French

troops supporting the "puppet government" of Maximilian in Mexico. When Dundee finally returns across the river, all that is left of his regiment are 11 survivors.

Unfortunately, the film was bogged down by many problems. Although the climactic battle scene ranks among the best ever filmed, two other key scenes were deleted amid a harangue of wrangling and ill will. Director Sam Peckinpah disowned the film, which was cut by others, while Heston reportedly found Peckinpah so obnoxious and abusive toward his actors that he physically threatened the director.

Heston later remarked that this was the only time he ever threatened anybody on a movie set. In his 1978 book *The Actor's Life*, Heston wrote, "I think we all wanted to make a different film. Columbia wanted a cowboy and Indian story, I wanted a picture that dealt with some basic issues of the Civil War, and Sam [Peckinpah] wanted . . . It was called *The Wild Ones*."

Despite a bevy of critical shortcomings, the film benefits greatly from a superb cast. According to *Variety*, "Charlton Heston delivers one of his regulation hefty portrayals, and gets solid backing from a cast including Richard Harris as the rebel captain who presents a dashing figure. . . ."

MAN ALONE, THE Republic, 1955, Color, 96 min, VHS. **Producer:** Herbert J. Yates; **Director:** Ray Milland; **Screenplay:** John Tucker Battle; **Music:** Victor Young; **Cinematographer:** Lionel Lindon; **Editor:** Richard L. Van Enger; **Cast:** Ray Milland, Mary Murphy, Ward Bond, Raymond Burr, Arthur Space, Lee Van Cleef, Alan Hale Jr., Douglas Spencer.

In his first directorial attempt, Ray Milland also stars as a fugitive who escapes a lynch mob and finds refuge with the sheriff's daughter (Mary Murphy), who is quarantined in her Arizona home where her father is recovering from yellow fever. A compelling love story develops between Milland and Murphy, leading to the eventual uncovering of the real culprits who were responsible for the murders Milland had been accused of perpetrating. This above-average western combines good drama with a hefty degree of suspense and action.

MAN AND BOY (aka: RIDE A DARK HORSE) Levitt-Pickman, 1972, Color, 82 min, VHS. **Producer:** Marvin Miller; **Director:** E. W. Swackhamer; **Screenplay:** Harry Essex and Oscar Saul; **Music:** J. J. Johnson; **Cinematographer:** Arnold R. Rich; **Editor:** John A. Martinelli; **Cast:** Bill Cosby, Gloria Foster, Leif Ericson, George Spell, Douglas Turner Ward, John Anderson, Henry Silva, Dub Taylor, Yaphet Kotto, Shelley Morrison.

In his film debut, Bill Cosby plays a former U.S. cavalryman named Caleb Revers, who lives on a 14-acre ranch with his wife and son. His horse is stolen by an aging black outlaw named Lee Christmas, who is on his way to Mexico because "It's warm across the border. I hear tell the arthritis just melts away." Father and son set out to capture the thief in this average film that was one of a slew of predominantly black films to appear in the early 1970s. Cosby does a nice job in a strictly dramatic role.

MAN BEHIND THE GUN, THE Warner Bros., 1952, Color, 82 min. **Producer:** Robert Sisk; **Director:** Felix E. Feist; **Screenplay:** Robert Buckner and John Twist; **Music:** David Buttolph; **Cinematographer:** Bert Glennon; **Editor:** Owens Marks; **Cast:** Randolph Scott, Patrice Wymore, Dick Wesson, Philip Carey, Lina Romay, Roy Roberts, Maurice Ankrum, Alan Hale Jr., Anthony Caruso, Douglas Fowley.

Randolph Scott is an undercover army officer who is sent to investigate a southern California secessionist movement that wants to split the territory into slave- and nonslave-holding areas.

MAN CALLED GANNON, A Universal, 1969, Color, 105 min. **Producer:** Howie Christie; **Director:** James Goldstein; **Screenplay:** D. D. Beauchamp, Borden Chase, and Gene R. Kearney; **Music:** Alan Bergman, Marilyn Bergman, and Dave Grusin; **Cinematographer:** William Margulies; **Editors:** Gene Palmer and Richard M. Sprague; **Cast:** Anthony Franciosa, Michael Sarrazin, Judi West, Susan Oliver, John Anderson, Harry Davis.

A seasoned cowpoke takes a young tenderfoot under his wing, but when a range war begins they find themselves on opposite sides. Based on Dee Linford's novel *Man Without a Gun*, this film is a poor remake of the 1955 original starring Kirk Douglas.

MAN CALLED HORSE, A National General, 1969, Color, 114 min, VHS. **Producer:** Sandy Howard; **Director:** Elliot Silverstein; **Screenplay:** Jack DeWitt; **Music:** Lloyd One Star and Leonard Rosenman; **Cinematographer:** Robert B. Houser and Gabriel Torres; **Editors:** Phillip W. Anderson and Michael Kahn; **Cast:** Richard Harris, Judith Anderson, Jean Gascon, Manu Tupou, Dub Taylor.

English aristocrat John Morgan (Richard Harris) survives a brutal Indian attack on his hunting party. Taken prisoner, he is brutally tortured by his captives and finally adopted by them. He is claimed by an old woman who treats him as a beast of burden until he decides to prove his courage by submitting to the brutal Sun Vow Ceremony.

A cliché-laden attempt to authentically present Native American history at the twilight of the Hollywood western, the film is best remembered for its graphic depiction of the Sioux Sun Vow ceremony. Harris's chest is pierced, ropes are threaded through his wounds, and he is suspended from the ceiling of a hut as a test of his courage and endurance before being accepted in the tribe. He eventually marries an Indian woman, although in true Hollywood fashion she is killed for marrying a white man. In time he becomes chief, but by film's end he leaves the tribe and returns to England.

More than 500 Sioux Indians appear in the film, and 80 percent of the spoken dialogue is in the Sioux language. While the film was praised by critics for its blunt reality, the truth is that the ritual conveyed in the film was not used in such an extreme way by the Sioux, although they were cer-

tainly capable of extreme brutality. Harris later appeared in two sequels: *THE RETURN OF A MAN CALLED HORSE* (1976) and *TRIUMPHS OF A MAN CALLED HORSE* (1983).

MAN CALLED SLEDGE, A Columbia/Dino de Laurentiis, 1970, Color, 93 min, VHS. **Producers:** Harry Bloom and Dino De Laurentiis; **Director:** Vic Morrow; **Screenplay:** Morrow and Frank Kowalski; **Music:** Gianni Ferrio; **Cinematographer:** Lucidi Kuveiller; **Editor:** Renzo Lucidi; **Cast:** James Garner, Laura Antonelli, Dennis Weaver, Claude Akins, John Marley.

A wanted outlaw joins with three other men in stealing half a million dollars from a prison, but once they obtain the loot they begin falling out among themselves.

MAN FROM BITTER RIDGE, THE Universal, 1955, Color, 80 min. **Producer:** Howard Pine; **Director:** Jack Arnold; **Screenplay:** Lawrence Roman and Teddi Sherman; **Music:** Henry Mancini; **Cinematographer:** Russell Metty; **Editor:** Milton Carruth; **Cast:** Lex Barker, Mara Corday, Stephen McNally, John Dehner, Trevor Bardette, Ray Teal, Myron Healey.

A special agent who is trying to uncover the source of a series of robberies is himself accused of the crimes he is investigating.

MAN FROM CHEYENNE Republic, 1942, B&W, 60 min. **Producer:** Joseph Kane; **Director:** Kane; **Screenplay:** Winston Miller; **Cinematographer:** Reggie Lanning; **Editor:** William P. Thompson; **Cast:** Roy Rogers, George "Gabby" Hayes, Sally Payne, Gale Storm, Lynne Carver, William Hadde, Bob Nolan and the Sons of the Pioneers.

MAN FROM COLORADO, THE Columbia, 1948, Color, 100 min, VHS. **Producer:** Jules Shermer; **Director:** Henry Levin; **Screenplay;** Robert Andrews and Ben Maddow; **Music:** George Duning; **Cinematographer:** William E. Snyder; **Editor:** Charles Nelson; **Cast:** Glenn Ford, William Holden, Ellen Drew, Ray Collins, Edgar Buchanan, Jerome Courtland.

At the close of the Civil War, two officers return from battle to their home town of Yellow Mountain. Owen Devereaux (Glenn Ford) is a former colonel and war hero who is appointed federal district judge. Del Stewart (William Holden), the town marshall, served as a captain under Devereaux's command during the war. But he is forced to turn against his former friend and commanding officer when Ford's emotional facilities deteriorate to the point of insanity.

Glenn Ford delivers what is arguably his finest performance as a man battling an escalating madness—all the more disturbing because he is aware of what is happening. At first he is a sympathetic figure verging on the edge. But as his madness increases he becomes thoroughly brutal, terrorizing both the town and his former soldiers. When all is lost, he burns the town to the ground in a final act of defiance. A fine cast and excellent performances show the extent to which mental anguish associated with war can transform a human being into a killing machine.

MAN FROM DAKOTA MGM, 1940, B&W, 74 min, VHS. **Producer:** Edward Chodorov; **Director:** Leslie Fenton; **Screenplay:** Laurence Stallings; **Music:** Daniele Amfitheatrof and David Snell; **Cinematographer:** Ray June; **Editor:** Conrad A. Nervig; **Cast:** Wallace Beery, John Howard, Dolores Del Rio, Donald Meek, Robert Barrat, Addison Richards.

A Union prisoner of war with a checkered past tries to redeem himself by stealing Confederate plans. He escapes from jail with another man and heads north to deliver the plans to General Grant. In their attempt to cross Confederate lines, they receive help from pretty Dolores Del Rio.

MAN FROM DEATH VALLEY Monogram, 1931, B&W, 61 min. **Director:** Lloyd Nosler; **Screenplay:** George Arthur Durlam (Arthur Durlam); **Cinematographer:** Archie Stout; **Cast:** Tom Tyler, Betty Mack, John Oscar, Si Jenks, John Oscar, Gino Corrado, Stanley Blystone.

MAN FROM DEL RIO United Artists, 1956, B&W, 82 min. **Producer:** Robert L. Jacks; **Director:** Harry Horner; **Screenplay:** Richard Carr; **Music:** Fred Steiner; **Cinematographer:** Stanley Cortez; **Editor:** Robert Golden; **Cast:** Anthony Quinn, Katy Jurado, Peter Whitney, Douglas Fowley, John Larch, Whit Bissell, Douglas Spencer.

Anthony Quinn is Dave Robles, a Mexican gunfighter who wins respect for himself when he tries to save a town from a brutal outlaw gang. When he outdraws the outlaw sheriff, the town invites him to assume the role of sheriff, tin star and all. To his dismay, once he starts taking his job seriously, everybody turns against him. Whit Bissell gives a fine performance as Breezy Morgan, the town drunk.

MAN FROM GALVESTON, THE Warner Bros., 1963, B&W, 57 min. **Producer:** Michael Meshekoff; **Director:** William Conrad; **Screenplay:** Dean Riesner and Michael S. Zagor; **Music:** David Buttolph; **Cinematographer:** Bert Glennon; **Editor:** Bill Wiard; **Cast:** Jeffrey Hunter, Preston Foster, James Coburn, Joanna Cook Moore, Edward Andrews, Kevin Hagen.

Attorney Timothy Higgins (Jeffrey Hunter) comes to a small Texas town to defend a former girlfriend accused of murder. Issued theatrically, this was originally a pilot to the TV series *Temple Houston* (NBC TV, 1963–64).

MAN FROM GOD'S COUNTRY Allied Artists, 1958, Color, 1958. **Producer:** Scott R. Dunlap; **Director:** Paul Landres; **Screenplay:** George Waggner; **Music:** Gerald Fried and Marlin Skiles; **Cinematographer:** Harry Neumann; **Editor:** George White; **Cast:** George Montgomery, Randy Stuart, Kim Charney, Susan Cummings, James Griffith, House Peters Jr.

A group of Montana ranchers work together to obtain land needed for the railroad in this rather bland George Montgomery vehicle.

MAN FROM GUNTOWN Puritan Pictures, 1935, B&W, 61 min. **Producer:** Nat Ross; **Director:** Ford Beebe; **Screenplay:** Beebe and Thomas Ince Jr.; **Cinematographer:** James Diamond; **Editor:** Robert Jahns; **Cast:** Tim McCoy, Billie Seward, Wheeler Oakman, Robert McKenzie, Rex Lease, Eva McKenzie, Jack Clifford, George Chesebro.

When a man is falsely accused of a crime, the town marshal helps him to escape from jail so he can get the goods on the real culprit. As usual, Tim McCoy stands tall with style and dignity. Wheeler Oakman is perfectly cast as the slimy villain, and Robert McKenzie is hilarious as Oakman's inept attorney.

Man from Guntown is generally considered the best of Tim McCoy's 1935–36 above-average westerns for Puritan Pictures. Other McCoy Puritan oaters include *Outlaw Deputy*, BULLDOG COURAGE (1935); *GHOST PATROL, ACES AND EIGHTS, BORDER CÁBALLERO, LIGHTNIN' BILL CARSON, Roaring Guns, The Traitor*; and *The Lion's Den* (1936).

MAN FROM HELL, THE Kent, 1934, B&W, 55 min. **Producer:** Willis Kent; **Director:** Lewis D. Collins; **Screenplay:** Melville Shyer; **Cinematographer:** William Nobles; **Editor:** S. Roy Luby; **Cast:** Reb Russell, Fred Kohler, Ann Darcy, George "Gabby" Hayes, Jack Rockwell, Slim Whitaker.

See *LIGHTNING TRIGGERS*.

MAN FROM LARAMIE, THE Columbia, 1955, Color, 104 min, VHS, DVD. **Producer:** William Gietz; **Director:** Anthony Mann; **Music:** George Duning; **Cinematographer:** Charles Lang; **Editor:** William Lyon; **Cast:** James Stewart, Arthur Kennedy, Donald Crisp, Cathy O'Donnell, Alex Nicol, Aline MacMahon, Wallace Ford, Jack Elam, Gregg Barton.

Will Lockhart (James Stewart) is an army officer on a military mission who also has a revenge vendetta with personal overtones. Someone has been selling repeating rifles to the Apache, and one of those guns killed his brother. Lockhart's duty as an army officer is to find who was responsible. Along the way his trail crosses with a number of warped, sadistic characters. An ancillary plot involves a feud about two ranch owners, Kate Canady (Aline MacMahon) and Lec Waggoman (Donald Crisp), whose respective son and foremen (Alex Nicol and Arthur Kennedy) are the ones who have been selling the rifles. Matters are compounded when the sadistic Nicol is killed by Kennedy and Stewart is framed for the murder. A particular chilling scene has Nicol ordering his men to hold out Stewart's palm so he can fire a bullet into it.

The film reflects Anthony Mann's fascination with families exploding from within, a favorite theme for the director.

In the 1950s, James Stewart became Mann's prototype loner hero, a disenchanted protagonist seeking a private mission of redemption or an avenue for personal revenge. At the start of the picture Lockhart (Stewart) explains, "I can't rightly say any place is my home. I belong where I am." *The Man from Laramie* was the final Mann/Stewart film collaboration, and the director admittedly wanted to recapitulate his five years with the actor by reprising themes and situations used in their other pictures.

Stewart's performance was praised by *Saturday Review* (July 30, 1955), which stated, "Stewart, through his gangling charm and innate honesty, never lets the hero become simply a stock figure." Appropriately, Stewart insisted on doing his own riding down treacherous slopes. According to Stewart biographer Donald Dewey the actor always considered *The Man from Laramie* his favorite western. This CinemaScope production helped to make him the biggest Hollywood box office star of the year. Stewart seemed bemused by his newfound popularity. When he tried to figure out how he had unseated the previous year's premier attraction, he could only suggest to an interviewer: "Maybe that's what it is . . . people identify with me, but dream of being John Wayne."

The movie was based on a *Saturday Evening Post* story by Thomas T. Flynn, and the credits acknowledge appreciation to the people of New Mexico, where the picture was filmed in CinemaScope.

MAN FROM MONTANA (aka: MONTANA JUSTICE)
Universal, 1941, B&W, 59 min. **Producer:** Will Cowan (associate); **Director:** Ray Taylor; **Screenplay:** Bennett Cohn; **Music:** Ralph Freed, Milton Rosen, Frank Skinner, and Franz Waxman; **Cinematographer:** Charles Van Enger; **Editor:** Paul Landres; **Cast:** Johnny Mack Brown. Fuzzy Knight, Nell O'Day, Jean Brooks, Billy Lenhart.

MAN FROM MONTEREY
Warner Bros., 1933, B&W, 57 min, VHS. **Producer:** Leon Schlesinger; **Director:** Mack V. Wright; **Screenplay:** Lesley Mason; **Music:** Leo F. Forbstein; **Cinematographer:** Ted D. McCord; **Editor:** William Clemens; **Cast:** John Wayne, Ruth Hall, Luis Alberni, Donald Reed, Nina Quartero.

John Wayne is John Holmes, an army officer sent to Monterey to advise Mexican landholders to record their property under Spanish land grants or lose them to the public domain. Interestingly, most of Wayne's early Warner Bros. films combined light humor and romance and were patterned on Ken Maynard films. Moreover, in most of of these the first name of Wayne's film character is John.

MAN FROM MUSIC MOUNTAIN
Republic, 1938, B&W, 58 min. **Producer:** Charles Ford; **Director:** Joseph Kane; **Cinematographer:** Jack Marta; **Editor:** Lester Orlebeck; **Cast:** Gene Autry, Smiley Burnette, Carol Hughes, Sally Payne, Ivan Miller.

This excellent blend of action, story, and music highlights Gene Autry as a singing cowboy who stymies a gang of crooks bent on swindling a group of settlers by trying to revamp a ghost town rich in gold deposits belonging to the settlers. This feature contains six songs, including "There's a Little Deserted Town on the Prairie" (Gene Autry, Johnny Marvin, Fred Rose); "I'm Beginning to Care" (Autry, Marvin, Rose); and "The Man from Music Mountain" (Peter Tinturin, Jack Lawrence, Eddie Cherkose). (See also *TUMBLING TUMBLEWEEDS.*)

MAN FROM MUSIC MOUNTAIN (aka: TEXAS LEGIONNAIRES)
Republic, 1943, B&W, 71 min. **Producer:** Harry Grey; **Director:** Joseph Kane; **Screenplay:** J. Benton Cheney and Bradford Ropes; **Cinematographer:** William Bradford; **Editor:** Tony Martinelli; **Cast:** Roy Rogers, Ruth Terry, Paul Kelly, Ann Gillis, George Cleveland, Pat Brady.

Roy returns to his hometown to make a radio appearance as a singing cowboy, but he soon finds himself in the middle of a war between sheep raisers and cattlemen. By combining a neat blend of song and action, this Roy Rogers western is one of the best before Roy was thrust in his more inflated musicals. (See also *UNDER WESTERN STARS.*)

MAN FROM NEVADA, THE
See *NEVADAN, THE.*

MAN FROM OKLAHOMA, THE
Republic, 1945, B&W, 68 min. **Producer:** Louis Gray (associate); **Director:** Frank McDonald; **Screenplay:** John K. Butler; **Music:** Al Cameron, June Carroll, Duke Ellington, Don George, Sanford Green, Johnny Hodges, Harry James, Morton Scott, Milo Sweet, Nat Vincent, and Ted Weems; **Cinematographer:** William Bradford; **Editor:** Tony Martinelli; **Cast:** Roy Rogers, George "Gabby" Hayes, Dale Evans, Roger Pryor, Arthur Loft, Maude Eburne, Edmund Cobb, Bob Nolan.

Roy becomes involved in a feud between rival ranchers instigated by a supposed friend of one of the ranchers. This picture has some great songs, including the hit standard "I'm Beginning to See the Light" (Harry James, Duke Ellington, Don George, Johnny Hodges), sung in the film by Dale Evans. (See also *UNDER WESTERN STARS.*)

MAN FROM RAINBOW VALLEY
Republic, 1946, Color, 56 min. **Producer:** Louis Gray; **Director:** R. G. Springsteen; **Screenplay:** Betty Burbridge; **Music:** Mort Glickman; **Cinematographer:** Bud Thackery; **Editor:** Edward Mann; **Cast:** Monte Hale, Lorna Gray, Jo Anne Marlowe, Ferris Taylor.

Monte Hale is a cowboy who comes to the aid of a rancher/comic strip writer whom a crooked rodeo owner is swindling.

MAN FROM SONORA
Monogram, 1951, B&W, 54 min. **Producer:** Vincent Fennelly; **Director:** Lewis D.

Collins; **Screenplay:** Maurice Trombragel; **Cast:** Johnny Mack Brown, Phyllis Coates, Lyle Talbot, House Peters Jr., Lee Roberts, John Merton, Pierce Lydon.

MAN FROM SNOWY RIVER, THE   20th Century Fox, 1982, Color, 95 min. **Producer:** Geoff Burrows; **Director:** George Miller; **Screenplay:** Fred Cullen and John Dixon; **Music:** Bruce Rowland; **Cinematographer:** Keith Wagstaff; **Editor:** Adrian Carr; **Cast:** Kirk Douglas, Jack Thompson, Tom Burlison, Sigrid Thornton, Lorraine Bayly, Chris Haywood, Terence Donovan.

In early 20th-century Australia, a young man grows into manhood working for a cattle baron, with whose daughter he falls in love. This beautifully photographed Australian film—shot in the spectacularly rugged terrain in the Great Divide Ranges in Victoria—features Kirk Douglas in dual roles as twin brothers who haven't spoken to each other for years due to an altercation which is explained later in the narrative. This film was inspired by a legendary poem by A. B. "Banjo" Patterson which nearly every Australian has drummed into him or her as a child.

MAN FROM TEXAS   Eagle-Lion, 1948, B&W, 71 min, VHS. **Producers:** Joseph Fields and Bryan Foy; **Director:** Leigh Jason; **Screenplay:** Jerome Chodorow and Fields; **Music:** Earl Robinson; **Cinematographer:** Jackson Rose; **Editors:** Jackson Rose, Norman Colbert, and Alfred DeGaetano; **Cast:** James Craig, Lynn Bari, Johnnie Johnston, Harry Davenport, Una Merkel, Wallace Ford, Clancy Cooper.

The El Paso Kid, a onetime notorious outlaw, marries and tries to lead a peaceful life. His past, however keeps following him. James Craig does a particularly good job in this otherwise average oater from Eagle-Lion, which is based on the play "Missouri Legends" by Elizabeth B. McGinty.

MAN FROM THE ALAMO, THE   Universal, 1953, Color, 79 min, VHS. **Producer:** Aaron Rosenberg; **Director:** Budd Boetticher; **Screenplay:** D. D. Beauchamp and Steve Fisher; **Music:** Frank Skinner; **Cinematographer:** Russell Metty; **Editor:** Virgil Vogel; **Cast:** Glenn Ford, Julie Adams, Chill Wills, Hugh O'Brien, Victor Jory, Neville Brand.

Men inside the Alamo draw lots so that one man can escape and warn their families about the danger. The man is Glenn Ford, and he is deemed a deserting coward by most people because they do not know the reason for his survival. When the families are massacred by renegades disguised as Mexican soldiers, Ford is forced to join the gang in order to expose the villains.

This film is a prime example of how an A western with a big-name star and a skilled director can meld with the action-packed pace of the Bs to produce an economical and effective western with loads of audience appeal. The polished stunt work, staged and performed by David Sharpe, compares with the best of the Republic westerns. Budd Boetticher's imprint combining violent but believable action with an excellent script based on a story by Niven Busch and Oliver Crawford is apparent everywhere.

MAN FROM THE BLACK HILLS   Monogram, 1952, B&W, 51 min. **Producer:** Vincent Fennally; **Director:** Thomas Carr; **Screenplay:** Joseph O'Donnell; **Music:** Raoul Kraushaar; **Cinematographer:** Ernest Miller; **Editor:** Sam Fields; **Cast:** Johnny Mack Brown, James Ellison, Joel Allen, Stanley Andrews, Ray Bennett, Lane Bradford, Rand Brooks.

MAN FROM TUMBLEWEEDS, THE   Columbia, 1940, B&W, 59 min. **Producer:** Leon Barsha; **Director:** Joseph H. Lewis; **Screenplay:** Charles F. Royal; **Cinematographer:** George Meehan; **Editor:** Charles Nelson; **Cast:** William "Wild Bill" Elliott, Ernie Adams, Ray Bennett, Stanley Brown, Buel Bryant, Edward Cecil.

Bill Elliott enlists the aid of paroled prisoners to help him bring law and order to a town controlled by a ruthless outlaw gang.

MAN FROM UTAH, THE   Monogram, 1934, B&W, 57 min, VHS. **Producer:** Paul Malvern; **Director:** Robert N. Bradbury; **Screenplay:** Lindsley Parsons; **Music:** Lee Zahler; **Cinematographer:** Archie Stout; **Editor:** Carl Pierson; **Cast:** John Wayne, Polly Ann Young, Anita Campillo, Edward Peil, George "Gabby" Hayes, Yakima Canutt, George Cleveland.

John Wayne tries to expose a gang that is making a racket out of the rodeo. He enters a horse-riding rodeo contest, but suspicious gang members put a poisoned needle under his saddle. This action-packed Monogram/Lone Star oater is loaded with stock rodeo footage.

MAN IN THE SADDLE   Columbia, 1951, Color, 87 min. **Producer:** Harry Joe Brown; **Director:** André De Toth; **Screenplay:** Kenneth Gamet; **Music:** George Duning; **Cinematographer:** Charles Lawton Jr.; **Editor:** Charles Nelson; **Cast:** Randolph Scott, Joan Leslie, Ellen Drew, Alexander Knox, Richard Rober, John Russell, Alfonso Bedova, Guinn "Big Boy" Williams, Clem Bevans, Cameron Mitchell, Richard Crane, Frank Sully.

Once again Randolph Scott is the taciturn hero who swallows his pride when the woman he loves marries another man for money. But when her new husband threatens Scott's ranch and hires gunmen to intimidate him, Scott is forced to strike back. This entertaining, romantic, and action-filled western coproduced by Scott is bolstered by Tennessee Ernie Ford's singing of the title song throughout the picture.

MAN IN THE SHADOW   Universal, 1957, B&W, 81 min, VHS. **Producer:** Albert Zugsmith; **Director:** Jack

Arnold; **Screenplay:** Gene L. Coon; **Music:** Hans J. Salter and Herman Stein; **Cinematographer:** Arthur E. Arling; **Editor:** Edward Curtiss; **Cast:** Jeff Chandler, Orson Welles, Colleen Miller, Ben Alexander, Barbara Lawrence, John Larch.

Sheriff Ben Saddler (Jeff Chandler) investigates the murder of a Mexican ranch hand, and increasingly he comes to believe that Virgil Renshler, the tyrannical owner of the Golden Empire Ranch (Orson Welles), is responsible for the murder. But because the town needs Renshler's business, the sheriff finds the entire county against him, and more than one attempt is made on his life. The tensions build until the inevitable final showdown between Saddler and Renshler.

This modern-day, atmospheric western filmed in black and white provides all the ingredients of a taut mystery as it depicts the lonely battle of one man against a corrupt and venal power structure. Chandler and Welles deliver subtle but powerful performances, with Chandler engaged in what is arguably his best work since winning an Oscar nomination for *BROKEN ARROW* (1950) seven years earlier. At the same time the film deals with some profound social issues without hitting the audience with lots of verbiage—thus making its point in a more direct and sincere manner.

MAN IN THE WILDERNESS Warner Bros., 1971, Color, 104 min, VHS. **Producer:** Sandy Howard; **Director:** Richard C. Sarafian; **Screenplay:** Jack DeWitt; **Music:** Johnny Harris; **Cinematographer:** Gerry Fisher; **Editor:** Geoffrey Foot; **Cast:** Richard Harris, John Huston, Henry Wilcoxon, Percy Herbert, Dennis Watterman.

A group of explorers trying to sell treasured beaver pelts struggle through the winter to find the Missouri River. This film is based on the true story of a fur trapper named Hugh Glass, who was mauled by a bear and left for dead by his companions. This fine survivalist movie also involved the producer (Sandy Howard), screenwriter (Jack DeWitt), and star (Richard Harris) who collaborated on *A MAN CALLED HORSE* (1970) one year earlier.

MAN OF ACTION Columbia, 1933, B&W, 60 min. **Director:** George Melford; **Screenplay:** Robert Quigley; **Cinematographer:** John H. Boyle; **Editor:** Otto Meyer; **Cast:** Tim McCoy, Caryl Lincoln, Julian Rivero, Wheeler Oakman, Walter Brennan.

When a ranger (Tim McCoy) and his pal try to discover who robbed a local bank, they uncover a scheme to steal a girl's ranch. Based on a story by William Colt McDonald, this entertaining McCoy vehicle has Julian Rivero singing a few love songs.

MAN OF CONQUEST Republic, 1939, B&W, 105 min. **Producer:** Sol C. Siegel (associate producer); **Director:** George Nichols Jr.; **Screenplay:** Jan Fortune, Wells Root, and E. E. Paramore Jr.; **Music:** Victor Young; **Cinematographer:** Joseph H. August; **Editor:** Edward Mann; **Cast:** Richard Dix, Gail Patrick, Edward Ellis, Joan Fontaine, Ralph Morgan, Robert Barrat, Victor Jory, Robert Armstrong, George "Gabby" Hayes, Max Terhune, Pedro de Cordoba.

An outstanding film biography tells the story of Sam Houston from his early days in Tennessee through his leadership role in the battle for Texas independence. This is considered by most films historians to be the best cinematic biography of Houston and the best depiction for Texas's fight for independence against the forces of Mexico's General Santa Ana.

Richard Dix makes a splendid, nearly perfect Sam Houston. According to film historian William Everson, the film makes "the development and birth of a great state understandable as no similar movie. . . . Its climactic Battle of Jacinto, staged by stunt maestro Reeves Eason and Yakima Cannutt, was relatively brief and small scale, yet far more vigorous than the long sustained battle scenes in *The Alamo.*"

MAN OF THE FOREST Paramount, 1933, B&W, 62 min. **Producer:** Harold Hurley; **Director:** Henry Hathaway; **Screenplay:** Jack Cunningham and Harold Shumate; **Cinematographer:** Ben F. Reynolds; **Editor:** Jack Dunn; **Cast:** Randolph Scott, Verna Hillie, Harry Carey, Noah Beery, Barton MacLane, Buster Crabbe, Guinn "Big Boy" Williams, Vince Barnett.

In one of his earliest screen westerns—his second with director Henry Hathaway—Randolph Scott tries to stop a crook (Noah Beery) who wants to steal an ex-convict's (Harry Carey) land and to kidnap the man's niece so the land can not be turned over to her. However, when Carey tries to retrieve his niece, Beasley (Beery) kills him and frames Scott, who is arrested for murder. This exciting adaptation of the Zane Grey story benefits from stunning photography by Ben F. Reynolds. The film was one of many 1930s westerns that Paramount made and remade in its highly popular Zane Grey series. Interestingly, the footage was built around silent versions, a practice made easier by hiring many of the same players so that footage a decade later could be intercut more easily.

MAN OF THE FRONTIER See *RED RIVER VALLEY* (1936).

MAN OF THE WEST, THE United Artists, 1958, Color, 100 min, VHS. **Producer:** Walter Mirisch; **Director:** Anthony Mann; **Screenplay:** Reginald Rose; **Music:** Leigh Harline; **Cinematographer:** Ernest Haller; **Editor:** Richard Heermance; **Cast:** Gary Cooper, Julie London, Lee J. Cobb, Arthur O'Connell, Jack Lord, John Dehner, Royal Dano, Robert J. Wilke, Neville Brand.

Gary Cooper is Link Jones, a reformed bandit and killer who has since married, settled down, and gone straight. Entrusted with the savings of his community, of which he is now a respected member, he sets out on a mission to get his town a schoolteacher. However, members of his former gang rob him quite by accident, and in order to ensure the safety of fellow passengers Julie London and Arthur O'Connell, he pretends to rejoin his former cronies, who are led by the venal Dock Tobin (Lee J. Cobb), a particularly repulsive villain.

Largely dismissed by critics in 1958 for its strong undertones of sex and violence, the film has gained in stature over the years, with some film historians now proclaiming it among the best of the Anthony Mann westerns. As in Mann's earlier westerns, the film not only has a strong action base but also deals with the psychological marrow of its main protagonist. In commenting on *The Man of the West* in his *Great Hollywood Westerns*, Ted Sennett calls it, "An unusually harsh and unsparing Western, with a blistering screenplay by Reginald Rose [which] drew fire for some of its boldest scenes (especially one in which the woman [Julie London] is forced to strip for the gang), yet its primal force could hardly be denied." The film thus underlines the violence and sex that had become increasingly more prevalent in western movies.

MAN OR GUN Republic, 1958, B&W, 79 min. **Producer:** Albert Gannaway; **Director:** Gannaway; **Screenplay:** James Cassity and Vance Skarstedt; **Music:** Gene Garf and Ramey Idriss; **Cinematographer:** Jack A. Marta; **Editor:** Merrill G. White; **Cast:** Macdonald Carey, Audrey Totter, James Craig, James Gleason, Warren Stevens, Harry Shannon.

A drifter (Macdonald Carey) arrives in a small town ruled by a ruthless family and tries to free the townsfolk from this tyranny. A good cast and some solid acting compensates for what is otherwise a dreary, dank film.

MAN'S COUNTRY Monogram, 1938, B&W, 53 min. **Producer:** Robert Emmett Tansey; **Director:** Robert Hill; **Screenplay:** Tansey; **Cinematographer:** Bert Longnecker; **Editor:** Howard Dillinger; **Cast:** Addison Randall (as Jack Randall), Marjorie Reynolds, Walter Long, Ralph Peters, Forrest Taylor, Charles King, Bud Osborne.

MAN TRAILER, THE Columbia, 1934, B&W, 59 min. **Producer:** Irving Briskin; **Director:** Lambert Hillyer; **Screenplay:** Hillyer; **Cinematographer:** Benjamin H. Kline; **Editor:** Gene Milford; **Cast:** Buck Jones, Cecilia Parker, Arthur Vinton, Clarence Geldart, Steve Clark.

Dan Lee (Buck Jones) is a Texas fugitive who has been unjustly accused of murder during a recent cattle war. While on the move he catches a stagecoach and prevents a robbery, saving the daughter of the local sheriff in the process. As a reward he is made sheriff of a nearby small town, and he promptly wins the heart of Sally, the sheriff's daughter.

The plot develops as the outlaw gang leader warns Dan Lee that if he attempts to prevent the robbery of nearby Wells Fargo station, the outlaw will expose Lee's past. Dan admits his past to Sally, who stands by him. After being captured by the outlaws, Lee escapes and leads the posse to the outlaw hideout, where a shoot-out takes place and the outlaws are overrun. Dan, now exonerated completely, retains both his job as marshal and Sally's affection.

The Man Trailer was made late in Buck Jones's first series for Columbia. The plot was borrowed by director/writer Lambert Hillyer from his old boss William S. Hart, who had used the same premise in *The Return of Draw Egan* (1916). Generally considered one of the best B westerns ever, the film benefits from Lambert Hillyer's well-written script and an outstanding performance from the ever-capable Buck Jones.

MAN WHO LOVED CAT DANCING, THE MGM, 1973, Color, 114 min, VHS. **Producers:** Eleanor Perry and Martin Poll; **Director:** Richard Sarfian; **Screenplay:** Perry; **Music:** John Williams; **Cinematographer:** Harry Stradling; **Editor:** Tom Rolf; **Cast:** Burt Reynolds, Sarah Miles, Lee J. Cobb, Jack Warden, George Hamilton, Bo Hopkins, Robert Donner, Jay Silverheels.

A defiant woman (Sarah Miles) leaves her husband (George Hamilton). Along the way she accidentally witnesses a train robbery, is kidnapped by the outlaw gang, and winds up riding with them. The gang is led by Jay Grobard (Burt Reynolds), who once loved an Indian woman named Cat Dancing. Since Cat Dancing is now dead, Grobard wants to buy back their children from the Shoshone and plans to obtain the money needed by robbing the train. The plot moves on when Hamilton joins a posse led by Lee J. Cobb to retrieve his wife. By then Miles has already become intimate with Reynolds and has emerged as a self-assured woman.

Written by Eleanor Perry and based on a novel by Marilyn Durham, an Indiana housewife turned author, the film is a flawed adaptation of the Durham novel. *Variety* pointed out that the film was "supposedly a period western from a woman's viewpoint [but it] emerges as a steamy, turgid meller, uneven in dramatic focus and development."

MAN WHO SHOT LIBERTY VALANCE, THE Paramount, 1962, B&W, 123 min, VHS. **Producer:** Willis Goldbeck; **Director:** John Ford; **Screenplay:** James Warner Bellah and Goldbeck; **Music:** Cyril Mockridge; **Cinematographer:** William H. Clothier; **Editor:** Otho Levering; **Cast:** John Wayne, James Stewart, Vera Miles, Lee Marvin, Edmond O'Brien, Andy Devine, Ken Murray, Woody Strode, Jeanette Nolan, John Qualen, John Carradine, Strother Martin, Lee Van Cleef.

U.S. Senator Ransom "Ranse" Stoddard (James Stewart) and his wife Hallie (Vera Miles) return to the town of Shinbone for the funeral of their old friend Tom Doniphon (John Wayne). While in town Stoddard decides to tell his story to a young newspaper editor; the tale is seen through flashbacks dating to the time he first arrived in Shinbone as an idealistic young lawyer.

In those days, the town was harassed by the sadistic Liberty Valance (Lee Marvin). Valance's major obstacle is the stoic presence of Tom Doniphon, which alone seems to keep a modicum of peace in the town. Despite Valance's brutality to him, Stoddard still hopes to eliminate the gunman through legal measures. His chief ally is newspaper editor Dutton Peabody (played superbly by Edmond O'Brien). However, it appears that Stoddard (after some marksmanship training by Doniphon) has changed his mind, and he finally guns down Valance. With this shooting, he becomes a local hero and eventually is elected a U.S. senator.

However, in a key scene Doniphon tells Stoddard the truth: It was he, Doniphon, who shot Liberty Valance in the darkness of the street. But for Hallie's sake—she is no longer Tom's girl but has fallen in love with Ranse—as well as to help establish law and order in the territory, Ranse must continue to take credit for the killing and accept the nomination for senator. Thus Stoddard becomes a public hero as "The Man Who Shot Liberty Valance." Doniphon, his usefulness compromised by the fact that he has become a relic in a changing world, sinks increasingly into a damaging melancholy.

At the conclusion of Ranse's story, the reporter slowly tears up his notes. A surprised Stoddard asks, "You're not going to use the story?" The reporter replies, "No sir. As our late great editor, Dutton Peabody, used to say: 'It ain't news. This is the West. When legend becomes fact, print the legend!'"

The Man Who Shot Liberty Valance has gained in great stature since the modest reviews it received upon its release—so much so that many film historians and fans now consider it to be among Ford's very best westerns. Certainly it is one of the most talked about. While *Variety* reported in 1962 that the film "falls distinctly shy of its innate story . . . ," by 1986 film critic Tag Gallagher was hailing it as a "masterpiece" with Ford at the "apex of his career."

What is also certain is that *The Man Who Shot Liberty Valance* represents a personal statement, even a lament, on the part of the director for the waning of the Old West as he saw it. Over the years, students of John Ford's work have pointed out that his vision of the West grew progressively darker and that there was less of a spirit of hope and optimism that characterized his earlier films.

According to Dan Ford in his biography *Pappy: The Life of John Ford*, the film was an *auteur* project all the way. Ford found the property, developed the script with Willis Goldbeck and Jim Bellah, raised half of the $3.2 million budget, and personally brought together the all-star cast, "perhaps the best he ever had."

In their comprehensive biography *John Wayne: American*, authors Randy Roberts and James Olson attest that Wayne was unforgettable in the role of Tom Doniphon, giving a particularly strong performance. Tom Doniphon was out of step with his time, and Wayne played the part perfectly.

Actor Ken Murray was quoted as saying that "Ford was a monster on the set" and was particularly nasty to Wayne, because he was upset that Wayne had not used him more in *The Alamo*. Years later Wayne complained to Dan Ford how difficult the film had been for him: "He [Ford] had Jimmy Stewart for the shitkicker hero. He had Edmond O'Brien for the quickwitted humor. Add Lee Marvin for a flamboyant heavy, and shit, I've got to walk through the goddamned picture."

The movie was filmed in black and white, and Ford wanted it to be highly focused on drama. As such he eschewed the more expansive style he usually employed in favor of a constricted style with an unusually large number of close-ups. Wilfred Mifflin commented in *Films in Review:* ". . . I had a wonderful time watching Ford switching his cast from sentiment to valor and back again."

MAN WITH A WHIP, THE   See *BLACK WHIP, THE.*

MAN WITHOUT A STAR   Universal, 1955, Color, 89 min, VHS. **Producer:** Aaron Rosenberg; **Director:** King Vidor; **Screenplay:** Borden Chase and D. D. Beauchamp; **Music:** Joseph Gershenson; **Cinematographer:** Russell Metty; **Editor:** Virgil Vogel; **Cast:** Kirk Douglas, Jeanne Crain, Claire Trevor, William Campbell, Richard Boone, Jay C. Clinton, Myrna Hansen, Mara Corday, Eddie Waller, Sheb Wooley.

Kirk Douglas is a free-spirited drifter named Dempsey Rae, who escapes civilization by moving further and further westward. Along the way he encounters and befriends young Jeff Jimson (William Campbell) and mentors him in the ways of manhood and the western cowboy. The two accept work from an attractive but duplicitous woman rancher named Reed Bowman (Jeanne Crain). Reed and Dempsey share some intimacy, but when Reed becomes involved in a range war, Dempsey wants no part of her double-dealing and leaves for town. Here he joins a group of local ranchers and becomes involved with Idonee, a madam with a heart of gold (Claire Trevor). Meanwhile, Reed hires a malevolent thug named Steve Miles (Richard Boone) to take Dempsey's place, and Dempsey is forced to fight him.

Director King Vidor provided raw passion and desire in his steamy *DUEL IN THE SUN* (1946), and sparks fly here as well as Douglas and Crain stir up some sexual heat—a departure from Crain's perpetual girl-next-door image. Douglas surprises as well by playing a banjo and singing a song in this worthwhile western with a good amount of flair and flavor. The title song is sung by Frankie Laine.

MAN WITH THE GUN (aka: DEADLY PEACE-MAKER; THE TROUBLE SHOOTER, UK)
United Artists, 1955, B&W, 83 min, VHS. **Producer:** Samuel Goldwyn; **Director:** Richard Wilson; **Screenplay:** N. B. Stone and Wilson; **Music:** Alex North; **Cinematographer:** Lee Garmes; **Editor:** Gene Milford; **Cast:** Robert Mitchum, Jan Sterling, Karen Sharpe, Henry Hull, Emile Meyer, John Lupton, Barbara Lawrence, Ted de Corsia, Leo Gordon.

An alienated Clint Tollinger (Robert Mitchum) rides into town in search of his estranged wife (Jan Sterling). Sheridan City is a lawless town, so the folk there hire him as town gunman, paying him $500 for his services. He is remarkably successful, managing to shoot up a band of outlaws, establish a curfew, and push the outlaws and their guns out of town. While the good townsfolk applaud his endeavors, they start to castigate him for being too violent. Finally, once the threat is gone, they no longer want him around. Mitchum is superb in this slow-moving film with a familiar and standardized theme. Look for Angie Dickinson in the uncredited role of Kitty.

MANY RIVERS TO CROSS MGM, 1955, Color, 94 min. **Producer:** Jack Cummings; **Director:** Roy Rowland; **Screenplay:** Harry Brown and Guy Trosper; **Music:** Cyril J. Mockridge; **Cinematographer:** John F. Seitz; **Editor:** Ben Lewis; **Cast:** Robert Taylor, Eleanor Parker, Victor McLaglen, Jeff Richards, Russ Tamblyn, James Arness, Alan Hale Jr.

An aggressive Kentucky frontier woman (Eleanor Parker) is determined to land a reluctant buckskin-clad bachelor (Robert Taylor). She marries him in a shotgun wedding, but Taylor prefers to hunt, trap, and fish—all the prerogatives of a free man. This seasoned western frontier spoof has Taylor on the run from his angry bride, returning to the fold just in time to save Parker from the clutches of angry Indians. Russ Tamblyn, Victor McLaglen, John Hudson, and Jeff Richards provide a strong cadre of supporting players.

Many Rivers to Cross was the third teaming of Robert Taylor and Eleanor Parker. There is an irony here as well: It was in the middle of film that Taylor married Ursula Thiess. Reportedly Parker took the news very hard, since she was in love with Taylor and had hoped to marry him herself.

MARAUDERS, THE (aka: KING OF THE RANGE) United Artists, 1947, B&W, 63 min. **Producers:** William Boyd, Lewis J. Rachmil, and Harry Sherman; **Director:** George Archainbaud; **Music:** David Chudnow; **Cinematographer:** Mack Stengler; **Editors:** Fred W. Berger and McClure Capps; **Cast:** William Boyd, Andy Clyde, Rand Brooks, Ian Wolfe, Dorinda Clifton, Mary Newton.

MARAUDERS, THE MGM, 1955, Color, 81 min. **Producer:** Arthur M. Lowe Jr.; **Director:** Gerald Mayer; **Screenplay:** Earl Felton, Jack Leonard, and Alan Marcus; **Music:** Paul Sawtell; **Cinematographer:** Harold J. Marzorati; **Editor:** Russell Selwyn; **Cast:** Dan Duryea, Jeff Richards, Keenan Wynn, Jarma Lewis, John Hudson.

A small rancher fights to save his spread when a greedy land baron hires gunmen to drive him away.

MARKED FOR MURDER PRC, 1945, B&W, 58 min. **Producer:** Arthur Alexander; **Director:** Elmer Clifton; **Screenplay:** Clifton; **Music:** Frank Hartford, Tex Ritter, and Don Weston; **Cinematographer:** Edward A. Kull; **Editor:** Holbrook N. Todd; **Cast:** Tex Ritter, Dave O'Brien, Guy Wilkerson, Marilyn McConnell, Charles King, Ed Cassidy.

MARKED MEN Universal, 1919, B&W, 5 reels. **Producer:** P. A. Powers; **Director:** Jack (John) Ford; **Screen-play:** H. Tipton Steck; **Cinematographer:** John W. Brown; **Cast:** Harry Carey, Joe Harris, Ted Brooks, David Kirby, J. Farrell MacDonald, Winifred Westover.

The third film version of Peter Kyne's book *The Three Godfathers* has Harry Carey as Cheyenne Harry, who escapes from jail with two outlaw pals. They meet up at a mining camp, where they make plans to rob a bank. After executing the robbery, they are chased into the Mojave. As they make their way in the blazing heat, they encounter a dying mother and her infant and agree to carry the child to safety. Of the three bandits, only Cheyenne arrives safely with the baby. This five-reeler silent film was John Ford's (billed as Jack Ford) favorite among his early films.

Peter Kyne was the first western writer whose works were regularly purchased for the screen. Other film versions of his story include *Broncho Billy and the Baby* (1909); Edward Le Saint's *THE THREE GODFATHERS* (1916); *HELL'S HEROES* (1930); *THE THREE GODFATHERS* (1936); and John Ford's *THREE GODFATHERS* (1948), which is dedicated to the memory of Harry Carey.

MARKED TRAILS Monogram, 1944, B&W, 58 min. **Producer:** William Strobach; **Director:** John P. McCarthy; **Screenplay:** Victor Hammond and McCarthy; **Cinematographer:** Harry Neumann; **Cast:** Bob Steele, Hoot Gibson, Veda Ann Borg, Lynton Brent, Steve Clark, Ben Corbett.

Two lawmen are on the trail of a notorious outlaw gang, with one of them posing as a bad man to infiltrate the gang.

MARK OF THE LASH Screen Guild, 1948, B&W, 60 min. **Producer:** Ron Ormond; **Director:** Ray Taylor; **Screenplay:** Ormond and Ira Webb; **Music:** Walter Greene; **Cinematographer:** Ernest Miller; **Editor:** Hugh Winn; **Cast:** Lash La Rue, Al St. John, Suzi Crandall, Marshall Reed, John L. Cason, Tom London, Jimmy Martin.

Lash and Fuzzy try to rid the Red Rock area of an outlaw gang in this fast-paced Lash La Rue actioner.

MARK OF THE WEST See *CURSE OF THE UNDEAD*.

MARK OF ZORRO, THE 20th Century Fox, 1940, B&W, 94 min, VHS. **Producers:** Raymond Griffith and Darryl Zanuck; **Director:** Rouben Mamoulian; **Screenplay:** John Taintor Foote; **Music:** Alfred Newman; **Cinematographer:** Arthur Miller; **Editor:** Robert Bishoff; **Cast:** Tyrone Power, Linda Darnell, Basil Rathbone, Gale Sondergaard, Eugene Pallette, J. Edward Bromberg.

Tyrone Power doubles up as the foppish California nobleman Don Diego and the swashbuckling masked avenger Zorro. After an extensive education in the Spanish army in Madrid, Don Diego returns to California to find that his father has been replaced as the alcalde of Los Angeles, so he embarks on a one-man Robin Hood-style crusade against the new power structure. His two-minute sword duel with the evil Esteban Pasquale (Basil Rathbone) is one of the most exciting examples of swordplay ever put on screen, and it leaves ample time for Don Diego to romance beautiful Lolita Quintero (Linda Darnell), the niece of the man who is his avowed enemy.

This popular 1940 film is a remake of a seven-reel silent endeavor starring and produced by Douglas Fairbanks (*The Mark of Zorro*, United Artists, 1920). The film is based on Johnston McCulley's novel *The Curse of Capistrano*, in which a Robin Hood type of character named Zorro avenges evil and fights for justice. The 1920 adaptation proved so successful with critics and audiences that in 1925 Fairbanks made a sequel, *Don Q. Son of Zorro*.

Zorro appeared again in Republic's 1936 film THE BOLD CABALLERO, with Robert Livingston playing the masked hero. The following year Republic released a 12-chapter serial *Zorro Rides Again*, directed by William Witney and John English, with John Carroll as James Vega/Zorro and Noah Beery, who had appeared in the 1920 film as the villain. One year later (1938) Republic used Witney and English once again to direct a second 12-chapter serial, *Zorro's Fighting Legion*, with Reed Hadley in the hero's role. In 1949 Republic followed with yet another 12-chapter serial GHOST OF ZORRO, this time with Clayton Moore (soon to be TV's *The Lone Ranger*) as an engineer and descendant of Zorro. This was later reedited and issued as a feature film in 1959, under the same title. In 1998 Antonio Banderas appeared as the title character in THE MASK OF ZORRO, introducing the masked hero to a new generation of viewers and audiences.

MARSHAL OF AMARILLO Republic, 1948, B&W, 60 min. **Producer:** Gordon Kay; **Director:** Philip Ford; **Screenplay:** Bob Williams; **Music:** Morton Scott; **Cinematographer:** John MacBurnie; **Editor:** Harold Minter; **Cast:** Allan Lane, Eddy Waller, Mildred Coles, Clayton Moore, Roy Barcroft, Trevor Bardette, Minerva Urecal, Denver Pyle.

MARSHAL OF CEDAR ROCK Republic, 1953, B&W, 54 min. **Producer:** Herbert J. Yates; **Director:** Harry Keller; **Screenplay:** Albert DeMond and M. Coates Webster; **Cinematographer:** John MacBurnie; **Editor:** Tony Martinelli; **Cast:** Allan Lane, Roy Barcroft, William Henry, Phyllis Coates, Eddy Waller, Robert Shayne, John Crawford, John Hamilton.

MARSHAL OF CRIPPLE CREEK Republic, 1947, B&W, 54 min. **Producer:** Sidney Pickner; **Director:** R. G. Springsteen; **Screenplay:** Earle Snell; **Cinematographer:** William Bradford; **Editor:** Harold Minter; **Cast:** Allan Lane, Robert Blake, Gene Roth, Trevor Bardette, William Self, Roy Barcroft, Tom London.

With the discovery of gold, a small settlement is turned into a boom town. A band of crooks try to scam the situation, but they find themselves having to contend with Red Ryder. This

film is Allan Lane's last entry in his "Red Ryder" series for Republic. (See also ADVENTURES OF RED RYDER, THE.)

MARSHAL OF GUNSMOKE (aka: SHERIFF OF GUNSMOKE) Universal, 1944, B&W, 59 min. **Producer:** Oliver Drake; **Director:** Vernon Kesys; **Screenplay:** William Lively; **Music:** Hans J. Salter; **Cinematographer:** Harry Neumann; **Editor:** Alvin Todd; **Cast:** Tex Ritter, Jennifer Holt, Russell Hayden, Fuzzy Knight, Harry Woods, Johnny Bond.

A marshal and his lawyer brother obtain the aid of a saloon singer to get the goods on her crooked boss and stop him from taking over the town. This above-average Tex Ritter/Russell Hayden venture has Jennifer Holt singing a couple of songs and Tex himself singing "Git Along Little Dogies."

MARSHAL OF LAREDO Republic, 1945, B&W, 56 min. **Producer:** Sidney Picker; **Director:** R. G. Springsteen; **Screenplay:** Bob Williams; **Cinematographer:** Bud Thackery; **Editor:** Charles Craft; **Cast:** William "Wild Bill" Elliott, Robert Blake, Alice Fleming, Roy Barcroft, Lane Bradford, George Chesebro.

MARSHAL OF MEDICINE BEND See LAWLESS STREET, A.

MARSHAL OF MESA CITY RKO, 1939, B&W, 62 min. **Producer:** Bert Gilroy; **Director:** David Howard; **Screenplay:** Jack Lait Jr.; **Music:** Paul Sawtell; **Cinematographer:** Harry J. Wild; **Editor:** Frederic Knudston; **Cast:** George O'Brien, Virginia Vale, Leon Ames, Henry Brandon, Harry Cording.

When a man saves a girl from the unwanted advances of a nearby city's sheriff, he is made marshal of a lawless town and sets out to bring about law and order. George O'Brien and Virginia Vale make an attractive screen couple in this enjoyable yet somewhat complicated RKO venture. (See also RACKETEERS OF THE RANGE.)

MARSHAL OF RENO Republic, 1944, B&W, 54 min. **Producer:** Louis Grey; **Director:** Wallace Grissell; **Screenplay:** Anthony Coleway; **Music:** Joseph Dubin; **Cinematographer:** Reggie Lanning; **Editor:** Charles Craft; **Cast:** William "Wild Bill" Elliott, Robert Blake, Roy Barcroft, Fred Burns, Edmund Cobb, Tom Chatterton.

MASKED RAIDERS RKO, 1949, B&W, 65 min. **Producer:** Herman Schlom; **Director:** Leslie Selander; **Screenplay:** Norman Houston; **Cinematographer:** George E. Discant; **Editor:** Les Millbrook; **Cast:** Tim Holt, Richard Martin, Marjorie Lord, Gary Gray, Frank Wilcox, Tom Tyler, Clayton Moore, Jason Robards Sr.

MASKED RIDER, THE Universal, 1941, B&W, 58 min. **Producer:** Will Cowan; **Director:** Ford Beebe; **Screenplay:** Sherman L. Lowe and Victor McLeod; **Music:** Everett Carter, C. Fernandez, and Milt Rosen; **Cinematographer:** Charles Van Enger; **Editor:** Paul Landres; **Cast:** Johnny Mack Brown, Fuzzy Knight, Nell O'Day, Grant Withers, Roy Barcroft.

MASK OF ZORRO, THE Amblin/Tri Star, 1998, Color, 136 min, VHS, DVD. **Producer:** Douglas Claybourne; **Director:** Martin Campbell; **Screenplay:** John Escrow, Ted Elliott, and Terry Rossio; **Music:** James Horner; **Cinematographer:** Phil Meheux; **Editor:** Thom Noble; **Cast:** Antonio Banderas, Anthony Hopkins, Catherine Zeta Jones, Stuart Wilson, Matt Letscher, Maury Chaykin.

Zorro (Anthony Hopkins) is the aristocratic Don Diego de la Vega. With his battle against colonial Spanish rule won, he decides to hang up his mask and tend to his wife and baby daughter. But the outgoing Spanish governor Montero (Stuart Wilson) kidnaps his daughter and throws Don Diego into a dungeon. Fast-forward 20 years and Montero is back with a scheme to buy Alta, California. Now old and gray, Don Diego is on the verge of assassinating Montero when he spots his daughter Elena (Catherine Zeta Jones), who has been raised to believe that Montero is her father. Don Diego thereupon recruits dashing outlaw Alejandro Murrieta (Antonio Banderas) and teaches him all that he knows, the idea being that Murrieta will appear as the reincarnation of Zorro.

This movie was filmed in Mexico and boasts good acting by the major protagonists. *Variety* called it ". . . closer in spirit to a vintage Errol Flynn or Tyrone Power swashbuckler than anything that's come out of Hollywood in quite some time. . . ."

MASSACRE Warner Bros., 1934, B&W, 70 min. **Producer:** Robert Presnell Sr.; **Director:** Alan Crosland; **Screenplay:** Ralph Block and Sheridan Gibney; **Music:** Bernhard Kaun; **Cinematographer:** George Barnes; **Editor:** Terry O. Morse; **Cast:** Richard Barthelmess, Ann Dvorak, Dudley Digges, Claire Dodd, Henry O'Neill, Robert Barrat, Sidney Toler.

A college-educated Sioux chief tries to combat discrimination and injustice against the people of his reservation and to remove the crooked officials who are cheating them. Richard Barthelmess is excellent as the caring Indian leader in a film that Leonard Maltin calls an "interesting attempt to show an enlightened view of contemporary Indians, in the context of typical Warner Bros. melodramatic fodder."

MASSACRE 20th Century Fox/Lippert, 1956, Color, 76 min. **Producers:** Robert L. Lippert Jr., Robert Lippert, and Olallo Rubio Gandara; **Director:** Louis King; **Screenplay:** D. D. Beauchamp; **Music:** Gonzalo Curie; **Cinematographer:** Gilbert Warrenton; **Editor:** Carl Pierson; **Cast:** Dan Clark, James Craig, Martha Roth, Jaime Fernandez, Jose Munoz, Enrique Zambrano.

Filmed in Mexico, the film concerns a group of crooked traders who sell guns to the Indians, which results in the needless killing of settlers.

MASSACRE, THE See *BATTLE AT ELDERBUSH GULCH, THE.*

MASSACRE AT THE ROSEBUD See *GREAT SIOUX MASSACRE, THE.*

MASSACRE HILL See *EUREKA STOCKADE.*

MASSACRE RIVER Allied Artists, 1949, B&W, 78 min. **Producers:** Julian Lesser and Frank Melford; **Director:** John Rawlins; **Screenplay:** Louis Stevens; **Music:** John Leipold and Lucien Moraweck; **Cinematographer:** Jack MacKenzie; **Editors:** Richard Cahoon and William B. Murphy; **Cast:** Guy Madison, Rory Calhoun, Carole Mathews, Cathy Downs, Steve Brodie, Art Baker, Iron Eyes Cody, Emory Parnell, Queenie Smith.

A trio of cavalry officers who are sent to the West after the Civil War find their friendship compromised over a colonel's pretty daughter and the activities of a gambling establishment owner. Based on a novel by Harold Bell Wright, this routine western benefits from charismatic star appeal.

MASTERSON OF KANSAS Columbia, 1954, Color, 73 min. **Producer:** Sam Katzman; **Director:** William Castle; **Music:** Mischa Bakaleinikoff; **Cinematographer:** Henry Freulich; **Editor:** Henry Batista; **Cast:** George Montgomery, Nancy Gates, James Griffith, Jean Willes, Benny Rubin, Gregg Barton.

George Montgomery is Bat Masterson, who, along with Wyatt Earp (Bruce Cowling) and Doc Holliday (James Griffith), saves a negotiator who is responsible for making a treaty that gives grazing lands to the Indians rather than a group of cattlemen. Even the trio of Masterson, Earp, and Holliday fails to lift this standard oater above the ordinary.

MAVERICK Icon/Warner, 1994, Color, 129 min, VHS, DVD, CD. **Producers:** Bruce Davey and Richard Donner; **Director:** Donner; **Screenplay:** William Goldman; **Music:** Randy Newman; **Cinematographer:** Vilmos Zsigmond; **Editors:** Stuart Baird and Michael Kelly; **Cast:** Mel Gibson, Jodie Foster, James Garner, Graham Greene, James Coburn, Alfred Molina, Leo Gordon, Dub Taylor, Robert Fuller, Denver Pyle.

Though James Garner has a prominent role in the film version of the famed TV series, it is Mel Gibson who assumes the role of feisty Brett Maverick, the wily cardsharp who takes on the biggest and best in the world of big-game poker.

The first part of the film is told in flashback, as Brett Maverick arrives in a small scenic town to find a card game and stumbles on a table where the players include demure but sometimes treacherous temptress Annabelle Bransford (Jodie Foster). Some other card-playing principals include Angel (Alfred Molina), who likes to shoot people who win money from him; Chief Joseph (Graham Greene), an Indian with a future in public relations; and The Commodore (James Coburn), a con man supreme.

As good and winsome as Gibson is in the title role, it is Garner as retired lawman Zane Cooper whose personal charm carries the somewhat thin plot. Included are a bevy of familiar cameo appearances from the world of TV westerns, contemporary country music, and even Gibson's *Lethal Weapon* (1987) partner Danny Glover as an uncredited bank robber.

Sharing a stagecoach, Gibson, Foster, and Garner take turns fleecing each other, endangering each other, and rescuing each other before taking part in a climactic poker game that culminates with a surprise ending. Gibson's Icon production company produced the film, and his *Lethal Weapon* director Richard Donner helmed the project. William Goldman, who scripted *Butch Cassidy and the Sundance Kid* (1969), wrote the screenplay.

In his review of May 20, 1994, the *Washington Post*'s Joe Brown called *Maverick* "affectionate, amiable, eager-to-please in a TV movieish sort of way. . . . *Mav* makes grand use of its wide-screen western locations—pastel canyons, dusty frontier towns, and riverboats churning down muddy rivers." Roger Ebert in his May 5, 1994, review called the film "the first lighthearted, laugh-oriented family Western in a long time. . . ."

Interestingly, Meg Ryan had been the original choice for the role of Annabelle, not Jodie Foster. The name of James Garner's character Zane Cooper was taken from novelist Zane Grey and actor Gary Cooper, both of whom worked largely in the western genre. Among those making cameo appearances are Carlene Carter (playing a waitress on the riverboat), Hal Ketchum (as a bank robber), Clint Black (as a gambler who gets thrown off the boat for cheating); Waylon Jennings and Kathy Mattea (two people with guns on the riverboat), Will Hutchins (TV's *Sugarfoot*) in an uncredited role, and Reba McEntire (as an uncredited spectator). April Ferry won an Oscar nomination for Best Costume Design.

MAVERICK, THE   Allied Artists, 1952, B&W, 71 min. **Producer:** Vincent Fennelly; **Director:** Thomas Carr; **Screenplay:** Fennelly; **Music:** Raoul Kraushaar; **Cinematographer:** Ernest Miller; **Editor:** Sam Fields; **Cast:** William "Wild Bill" Elliott, Phyllis Coates, Myron Healey, Richard Reeves, Terry Frost, Rand Brooks, Gregg Barton, Denver Pyle, Robert J. Wilke.

A group of cattlemen hire gunslingers to force settlers off the range, so the government sends in the cavalry to halt the lawlessness. The film is another fine entry in Bill Elliott's final starring western film series.

MAVERICK QUEEN, THE   Republic, 1956, Color, 90 min, VHS. **Producer:** Herbert J. Yates; **Director:** Joseph Kane; **Screenplay:** Kenneth Gamet and De Vallon Scott; **Music:** Victor Young; **Cinematographer:** Jack A. Marta; **Editor:** Richard L. Van Enger; **Cast:** Barbara Stanwyck, Barry Sullivan, Scott Brady, Mary Murphy, Wallace Ford, Howard Petrie, Jim Davis, Emile Meyer, Walter Sande, George Keymas, John Doucette, Tristram Coffin.

Barbara Stanwyck is Kit Banion, the leader of an outlaw gang called the Wild Bunch, who can draw and shoot with the best of them—outlaws and lawmen alike. As owner and proprietor of a saloon, she has visitors who include the likes of Butch Cassidy and a very nasty Sundance Kid (Scott Brady). But her outlaw days become numbered when she falls in love with Pinkerton man Barry Sullivan, who infiltrates the gang, and eventually she dies in his arms.

A relatively big-budget production based on the writings of Zane Grey, *The Maverick Queen* was the first picture in Naturama, Republic's widescreen process. Stanwyck shines as the iron-willed western woman, a role she plied in a series of 1950s westerns, including *CATTLE QUEEN OF MONTANA* (1954), *THE VIOLENT MEN* (1955), and *FORTY GUNS* (1957). The title song, written by Victor Young and Ned Washington, is sung by Joni James.

McCABE AND MRS. MILLER   Warner Bros., 1971, Color, 120 min, VHS. **Producers:** Mitchell Brower and David Foster; **Director:** Robert Altman; **Screenplay:** Altman and Brian McKay; **Music:** Leonard Cohen; **Cinematographer:** Vilmos Zsigmond; **Editor:** Lou Lombardo; **Cast:** Warren Beatty, Julie Christie, Rene Auberjonois, William Devane, John Schuck, Corey Fischer, Bert Remsen, Shelley Duvall, Keith Carradine.

At the turn of the 20th century, a small-time wandering gambler, John Q. McCabe (Warren Beatty), opens a bordello in a western boom town on the Canadian border. Mrs. Constance Miller (Julie Christie), a professional madam, arrives in town and offers to use her experience to help McCabe run his business. They share the profits as the business begins to thrive. However, a corporation soon hears about the saloon's financial success and sends representatives to try to buy him out. When he refuses, the corporation sends gunmen to kill him, and the unsuspecting McCabe becomes the foil to those determined to break the power of the hated trusts. These events culminate in a deadly gunfight in the snow-filled streets of Presbyterian Church (the name of the town), where McCabe dies knee-deep in a blizzard.

Ever the iconoclast, Altman created a film that elicited either awed enthusiasm or harsh rebuke. Pauline Kael was among the film's most passionate admirers, writing that "*McCabe and Mrs. Miller* is a beautiful pipe dream of a movie—a fleeting, almost diaphanous vision of what frontier life might have been." Gary Arnold of the *Washington Post* found it "the best American movie since *Bonnie and Clyde*," while John Huston called the picture "the greatest forgotten movie of our time."

Altman attempts to give his audience the sense of western life by employing his usual stylistic tricks, with an abounding amount of detail, overlapping dialogue, use of the zoom lens, and editing that jumps from scene to scene. But for many genre enthusiasts, especially those with a more purist bent, the film is just another a stylistic attempt to demythify the American West and one that is consistent with the revisionist themes of the late 1960s and early '70s, a time when nary a hero nor a legend remained unscathed.

Unlike John Ford and Howard Hawks, Altman provides no golden frontier in his work. Few, if any, characters in this movie are even likeable. *Variety* found the film to be a "disappointing mixture . . . a confused comedy-drama plot line which is repeatedly shoved aside in favor of bawdiness." Even Vilmos Zsigmond's muted color photography, brilliant and beautiful at times, "backfires into pretentiousness."

The corporation emerges as an American evil, a villainous entity that preys on those who have the ingenuity and temerity to become successful while the town's pathetic citizenry is forced to live out a wretched existence. Unfortunately, director Altman persists in having all his actors talk at once, leaving the viewer to get lost in a maze of detail and overlapping sequences. *McCabe and Mrs. Miller* is also one of the first westerns to display frontal nudity in a series of unrelated and arguably unnecessary sequences.

The *Los Angeles Times* declared Julie Christie's Oscar-nominated performance to be the best performance of her career. While praising Christie as "excellent," *Variety* found Beatty to be either miscast or misdirected: "His own youthful looks cannot be concealed by a beard, makeup, a grunting voice, and jerky physical movements; the effect resembles a high school thesp playing Rip Van Winkle. . . ."

Despite its cinematic boldness and praise from a selected array of critics for its offbeat, surreal, and impressionistic qualities, *McCabe and Mrs. Miller* fizzled at the box office, leaving contemporary audiences for the most part unimpressed and divided. But it remains a film that must be seen by serious students of the genre.

McLINTOCK   United Artists/Batjac Productions, 1963, Color, 127 min, VHS, DVD. **Producer:** Michael Wayne; **Director:** Andrew V. McLaglen; **Screenplay:** James Edward Grant; **Music:** Frank Duval; **Cinematographer:** William Clothier; **Editor:** Otho Lovering; **Cast:** John Wayne, Maureen O'Hara, Stephanie Powers, Yvonne De Carlo, Patrick Wayne, Jack Kruschen, Chill Wills, Jerry Van Dyke, Edgar Buchanan, Bruce Cabot, Edward Faulkner, Leo Gordon, Perry Lopez, Michael Pate, Strother Martin, Gordon Jones, Robert Lowery, H. W. Ginn, Aissa Wayne.

John Wayne is George Washington McLintock, a bigger-than-life ranch owner (the town is named after him) who is asked by the Comanche to represent them when the government attempts to put them under the control of an Indian agent. His tranquility is further compromised when his estranged wife (Maureen O'Hara) returns to the McLintock ranch determined to get his consent for a divorce and to gain custody of their 17-year-old daughter Becky (Stephanie

Powers), who is attending college in the East. Becky is currently being courted by two suitors, ranch hand Dev Warren (Patrick Wayne) and Harvard-educated Matt Douglas Jr. (Jerry Van Dyke).

Arriving with O'Hara on the train are formerly imprisoned Comanche chiefs whom McLintock has helped set free. When the chiefs refuse to be taken to Fort Sill, the Indians are herded into the stockade by the other ranchers, who do not want them around. The film culminates with a raucous Fourth of July celebration and some of the most humorous and fun-filled fisticuffs in John Wayne's entire film ledger. When the tumult ceases, McLintock has finally had enough of his wife's stubbornness. In a hilarious finale, he chases her around the house (stuntman Dean Smith took the tumble out the window in O'Hara's clothes), through the town, and into a mud puddle, where he proceeds to give her an old-fashioned spanking, revealing her pantaloons—after which he agrees to the divorce. But true love wins out. She throws herself into G.W.'s arms, and the battling McLintocks are together once more.

An enormously popular film which thrives on action, humor, civic pride, just the right slice of slapstick, and a proper amount of drawing-room comedy, this remains one of John Wayne's most widely watched westerns and a genre favorite. Son Michael Wayne (age 29) produced the film; son Patrick (age 24), already a seasoned actor, was cast as Dev Warren; and Aissa Wayne (age seven) is seen as little Alice Warren. Wayne's good pal and favorite screen writer James Earl Grant, who had scripted *HONDO* (1954), did the writing here as well. Andrew V. McLaglen, who had worked as an assistant director to John Farrow on *Hondo*, was handpicked by Wayne to helm *McLintock*. He also had worked as a production assistant to John Ford in *The Quiet Man* (1952), and after *McLintock* he went on to direct three more John Wayne westerns: *THE UNDEFEATED* (1969); *CHISUM* (1970); and *CAHILL, U.S. MARSHAL* (1973).

The fact that many cast members—such as Bruce Cabot, Hank Worden, and Chill Wills—were off-camera pals of Wayne helps to lighten the mood of the picture and results in a warm interplay among the characters. As Robert Parish and Michael Pitts point out while critiquing the film in *The Great Western Pictures*, "There is a jaunty air which allows scripters, directors and players to kid the genre while showing respect for it."

A clear case in point is the mudhole scene, which was one of Wayne's very favorites and still stands out for film fans of all ages. The script called for a bombastic brawl at the edge of a mudhole, with dozens of people sliding down the hill into the muck during the fight. This free-for-all sequence, which cost $50,000, begins when Wayne takes a poke at troublemaker Leo Gordon. Wayne's challenge to Gordon after taking his shotgun from him provides perhaps the film's most enduring moment and prompts one of Wayne's most unforgettable lines: "I haven't lost my temper in forty years, but pilgrim, you caused a lot of trouble this morning, mighta got somebody killed and somebody should belt you in the mouth. But I won't. The hell I won't!"

The late Leo Gordon remembered shooting that scene in a 1995 interview with the author: "I recall that day well. John Ford came down and was visiting one day, and you would have thought the real big mucky-muck of the world was there the way Wayne catered to him. I was Pilgrim in that classic scene . . . the guy he knocks down after he says, 'The hell I won't!' The interesting thing about it is that they used a drilling material called bentonite in the construction of the hill, making it slippery as hell. It's a clay derivative used in drilling oil wells and making chocolate syrup. They needed two tons, which they mixed with water, and the bentonite was constantly reheated.

"So the first guy to go down there was my double. He cracked the hell out of his head and was bleeding all over the place. So I had to do the next shot. And before it was over they had everybody doing it, including Maureen O'Hara. No doubles at all. We spent a week in that goddamed thing. It was cold as hell!"

MEANWHILE, BACK AT THE RANCH
Curtco, 1997, Color, 70 min. **Producer:** Patrick Curtis; **Director:** Richard Patterson; **Screenplay:** Patterson; **Music:** Leslie Bricusse; **Editors:** Wil Godby and Patterson; **Cast:** Eilene Janssen.

The nefarious "Rattler," head of an outlaw band, has been terrorizing the residents of Peaceful Valley with a wave of rustling, killing, and robbery. The federal government sends 25 of its best agents to clear up the problem. They meet at the Dirty Dog saloon, and there is a monumental shoot-out, with the "Rattler" meeting his just reward. The 25 agents just happen to consist of such western heroes as Gene Autry, Roy Rogers, George O'Brien, Tim McCoy, Bob Steele, and a slew of others. This innovative effort to amalgamate on film the cinematic heroes of the Wild West provides lots of fun.

MEDICO OF PAINTED SPRINGS, THE
Columbia, 1941, B&W, 58 min. **Producer:** Jack Fier; **Director:** Lambert Hillyer; **Screenplay:** Wyndham Gittens and Winston Miller; **Cinematographer:** Benjamin H. Kline; **Editor:** Mel Thorsen; **Cast:** Charles Starrett, Terry Walker, Ben Taggart, Ray Bennett, Wheeler Oakman, Richard Fiske, Edmund Cobb.

MELODY OF THE PLAINS
Spectrum, 1937, B&W, 55 min. **Producer:** Jed Buell; **Director:** Sam Newfield; **Screenplay:** Bennett Cohen; **Music:** June Hershey and Don Swander; **Cinematographer:** Robert E. Cline; **Editor:** William Hess; **Cast:** Fred Scott, Al St. John, Louis Small, David Sharpe, Lafe McKee, Slim Whitaker.

A cowboy (Fred Scott) who thinks he has killed a man goes to work for the fellow's father, whose ranch is being sought by the crooks who were really responsible for the killing. Scott was one of the better western screen crooners. (See also *MOONLIGHT ON THE RANGE.*)

MELODY RANCH
Republic, 1940, B&W, 84 min. **Producer:** Sol C. Siegal; **Director:** Joseph Santley; **Screenplay:** Sid Culler, Ray Golden, F. Hugh Herbert, and Jack Moffitt; **Music:** Jule Styne; **Cinematographer:** Joseph H. August; **Editor:** Murray Seldeen; **Cast:** Gene Autry, Jimmy Durante, Ann Miller, Barton MacLane, Barbara Jo Allen, George "Gabby" Hayes, Jerome Cowan, William "Billy" Benedict, Veda Ann Borg.

Radio star Gene Autry's hometown of Torpedo, Arizona, invites him back to be honorary sheriff of the Frontier Days Celebration. However, he finds the place is loaded with racketeers headed by a menacing Barton MacLane, who is intent on running the honorary sheriff out of town. For this curio Republic's creative forces decided to team Gene Autry with Jimmy Durante and hoofer Ann Miller, while replacing Smiley Burnette with "Gabby" Hayes. Among the musical numbers is Miller dancing to the Paul Dresser song "My Gal Sal."

A radio motif was added in order to give the film a wider audience interest. Thus there is the comedy patter of Jimmy Durante and an array of musical numbers as well as the presence of Ann Miller, one of filmland's finest dancers ever. The careful observer might note that in the film's trolley car crash stunt, the stuntman doubling Gene Autry is John Wayne. (See also *TUMBLING TUMBLEWEEDS.*)

MELODY TRAIL
Republic, 1935, B&W, 60 min, VHS. **Producer:** Nat Levine; **Director:** Joseph Kane; **Screenplay:** Sherman L. Lowe; **Cinematographer:** Ernest Miller; **Editor:** Lester Orlebeck; **Cast:** Gene Autry, Ann Rutherford, Smiley Burnette, William Castello, Wade Boteler, Al Bridge.

See *TUMBLING TUMBLEWEEDS.*

MEN OF TEXAS (aka: MEN OF DESTINY, UK)
Universal, 1942, B&W, 82 min. **Producer:** George Waggner; **Director:** Ray Enright; **Screenplay:** Richard Brooks and Harold Shumate; **Music:** Edward Ward; **Cinematographer:** Milton R. Krasner; **Editor:** Clarence Kolster; **Cast:** Robert Stack, Broderick Crawford, Jackie Cooper, Anne Gwynne, Ralph Bellamy, Jane Darwell, Leo Carrillo, John Litel, William Farnum.

At the end of the Civil War, a young newspaperman (Robert Stack) is sent to Texas to look into reports that an uprising is pending as well as to do an investigative story on Sam Houston. Broderick Crawford is the villain who has designs of his own and tries to stop him. Lots of action is mixed with some uplifting patriotism here, as the tragedy of Pearl Harbor was still in the recent past.

MEN OF THE TIMBERLAND
Universal, 1941, B&W, 62 min. **Producer:** Bert Pivar; **Director:** John Rawlins; **Screenplay:** Griffin Jay and Maurice Tombragel; **Music:** Hans J. Salter and Maurice Wright; **Cinematographer:** John W. Boyle; **Editor:** Milton Carruth; **Cast:** Richard Arlen, Andy Devine, Linda Hayes, Francis McDonald, Willard Robertson.

A timberman discovers an illegal scheme to cut timber over a large natural area. The big problem is that the perpetrators were successfully able to bribe government officials. This action-packed B oater from Universal is from their popular Richard Arlen/Andy Devine series of pictures.

MESQUITE BUCKAROO Metropolitan, 1939, B&W, 55 min. **Producer:** Harry S. Webb; **Director:** Webb; **Screenplay:** George Plympton; **Cinematographer:** Edward A. Kull; **Editor:** Frederick Bain; **Cast:** Bob Steele, Carolyn Curtis, Frank La Rue, Charles King.

MEXICALI KID, THE Monogram, 1938, B&W, 51 min. **Producer:** Robert Emmett Tansey; **Director:** Wallace Fox; **Screenplay:** Tansey; **Cinematographer:** Bert Longnecker; **Editor:** Howard Dillinger; **Cast:** Addison Randall (as Jack Randall), Wesley Barry, Eleanor Stewart, Wilhelm von Brincken, Glenn Strange.

MEXICALI ROSE Republic, 1939, B&W, 60 min, VHS. **Producer:** Harry Grey; **Director:** George Sherman; **Screenplay:** Gerald Geraghty; **Music:** Gene Autry; **Cinematographer:** William Nobles; **Editor:** Tony Martinelli; **Cast:** Gene Autry, Smiley Burnette, Noah Beery, Luana Walters, William Farnum.

Radio singer Gene Autry discovers that an oil company sponsoring his radio shows is involved in a stock promotion fraud and is out to cheat the public and their stockholders. Noah Beery is outstanding as a lovable bandit leader in this Republic entry, which ranks among Gene Autry's very best.

MICHIGAN KID, THE Universal, 1947, B&W, 69 min. **Producer:** Howard Welsch; **Director:** Ray Taylor; **Screenplay:** Roy Chanslor and Robert Presnell Sr.; **Music:** Hans J. Salter; **Cinematographer:** Virgil Miller; **Editor:** Paul Landres; **Cast:** Jon Hall, Rita Johnson, Victor McLaglen, Andy Devine, Byron Foulger, Milburn Stone, Ray Teal, Robert Wilke.

Four strangers come to the aid of a young woman whose ranch is being threatened by corrupt town officials. This pleasant adaptation of the Rex Beach novel first appeared as a 1928 silent feature from Universal, directed by Irvin Willat and starring Renee Adoree and Conrad Nagel.

MIRACLE IN THE SAND See *THREE GODFATHERS, THE* (1936).

MIRACLE OF THE HILLS 20th Century Fox, 1959, B&W, 73 min. **Producer:** Richard E. Lyons; **Director:** Paul Landres; **Screenplay:** Charles Hoffman; **Music:** Paul Sawtell and Bert Shefter; **Cinematographer:** Floyd Crosby; **Editor:** Betty Steinberg; **Cast:** Rex Reason, Nan Leslie, Betty Lou Gerson, Jay North, June Vincent.

When a young minister tries to bring spiritual revival to an 1880s mining town, he meets with resistance from the wealthy former dance-hall hostess who is running the town. This pleasant, low-key little western is filmed in CinemaScope.

MIRACLE RIDER, THE Mascot, 1935, B&W, 306 min, 15 episodes, VHS. **Producer:** Nat Levine; **Directors:** B. Reeves Eason and Armond Schaefer; **Screenplay:** John Rathmell; **Music:** Lee Zahler; **Cinematographer:** Ernest Miller and William Nobles; **Editors:** Richard Fantl and Joseph H. Lewis; **Cast:** Tom Mix, Joan Gale, Charles Middleton, Robert Frazer, Niles Welch, Jason Robards Sr., Bob Kortman, Tom London.

Tom Mix, in his only serial and final film performance, is Captain Tom Morgan of the Texas Rangers. He is also known as The Miracle Rider, a man considered a blood brother to the Indians because of the many times he has come to their aid. His adversary is a crook named Zaroff (Charles Middleton), who wants to occupy Indian land because he knows there are deposits of powerful explosives in the soil. Moreover, a traitorous Indian named Longboat (Bob Kortman) tries to convince the present chief that Morgan is their enemy, a treacherous betrayal that results in the chief's death in an attack. However, the chief's daughter (Joan Gale) falls in love with Morgan, and together they expose Zaroff and his gang.

By 1935 Tom Mix had hoped to end his remarkably popular film career, and he had no real interest in returning to the screen. However, Mascot owner/producer Nat Levine realized that a serial starring the ever-popular Mix could mean big money and convinced the star that the proposed project would provide great entertainment value to kids. The serial was made in one month's time at a cost of $80,000, half of which went to pay Mix's salary. It paid off in a big way. The serial grossed more than $1 million dollars, and its feature version was in release throughout the 1940s and well into the 1960s in some countries. Yet for all the fanfare and dollars, the serial falls short of being among the best in Mascot's catalogue of fine serial productions.

MISFITS, THE United Artists, 1961, B&W, 124 min, VHS. **Producer:** Frank E. Taylor; **Director:** John Huston; **Screenplay:** Arthur Miller; **Music:** Alex North; **Cinematographer:** Russell Metty; **Editor:** George Tomasini; **Cast:** Clark Gable, Marilyn Monroe, Montgomery Clift, Thelma Ritter, Eli Wallach, James Barton, Kevin McCarthy.

Aging cowboy Gay Langland (Clark Gable) and recently divorced Roslyn Tabor (Marilyn Monroe) fall in love and decide to move in with his buddy Guido (Eli Wallach) at Guido's ranch house. Guido persuades Gay to allow a has-been rodeo performer named Perce Howard (Montgomery Clift) to join him in rounding up "misfits," wild horses too small for riding, to be sold for dog food. The idealistic Roslyn, who "deplores all the shootin' and killin'," convinces Perce to let the horses go, but Gay balks at the idea and overtakes the four-legged leader, taming him after a fierce battle. In a compassionate turnabout, he now decides to let the horses go their own way, and he and Roslyn reconcile.

However, the film's title also suggests a cast of characters who are themselves as much a group of "misfits" in the modern West as the undersized horses they are dealing with. Thus, in a larger sense *The Misfits* epitomized the sad and bitter end of the western dream and paved the way for a slew of movies about the displaced modern cowboy, a theme that became a focal point for many later westerns. Even today critics disagree whether the film is a flawed masterpiece or a supreme failure, with critics of all stripes having their own rationale as to why the film went astray.

As author James Goode noted in *The Story of the Misfits* (1963), a diary history of the making of the film, it was the most expensive film ever made in black and white and remained so for many years. The movie production cost over $4 million and barely grossed that much in its U.S. and Canadian releases. It was adapted for the screen by Arthur Miller (his first scenario) from his own short story as a tribute to his then wife Marilyn Monroe. Upon its release, the film was quickly panned by *Time* Magazine, which called it "terrible . . . clumsy . . . obtuse . . . nauseous . . . ponderous . . . woolly . . . glum . . . rambling . . . banal . . . and fatuously embarrassing." *Variety* was somewhat more charitable but not by too much, commenting that "the film is somewhat uneven in pace and not entirely sound in dramatic structure [with] character development . . . choppy in several instances."

The Misfits was the final film for two of the industry's all-time great movie stars, Clark Gable and Marilyn Monroe. Gable died in November 1960 from a heart attack, which some suggest came from an abundance of physical work making the picture. At age 59 he was due to become a father for the first time, but he did not live long enough to see the birth of his son, John Clark Gable.

Marilyn Monroe was a psychological mess and hard to work with. She found it difficult arriving on time for her shooting sessions and seemed incapable of delivering her lines without constant retakes. She was fired from her next film, *Something's Gotta Give*. On August 5, 1962, she was found naked and dead in her home; her death has been the source of heated controversy for 40 years.

Montgomery Clift, himself one of the movie's most troubled souls, died in 1966. Reportedly, when asked if he wanted to see *The Misfits* on late-night television, his last words ever were, "Absolutely not." Nevertheless, despite a plethora of critical disclaimers, *The Misfits* deserves another concentrated viewing. The acting is first-rate, especially Gable's, and pundits and critics are beginning to find increasing merit in the film.

MISSOURIANS, THE Republic, 1950, B&W, 60 min. **Producer:** Melville Tucker; **Director:** George Blair; **Screenplay:** Arthur Orloff; **Music:** Stanley Wilson; **Cinematographer:** John MacBurnie; **Editor:** Robert M. Leeds; **Cast:** Monte Hale, Paul Hurst, Roy Barcroft, Lyn Thomas, Lane Bradford, Robert Neil.

MISSOURI BREAKS, THE United Artists, 1976, Color, 126 min. **Producers:** Elliott Kastner and Robert M. Sherman; **Director:** Arthur Penn; **Screenplay:** Thomas McGuane; **Music:** John Williams; **Cinematographer:** Michael Butler; **Editors:** Jerry Greenberg, Stephen Rotter, and Dede Allen; **Cast:** Marlon Brando, Jack Nicholson, Kathleen Lloyd, Harry Dean Stanton.

The "breaks" in the title of this excessively violent film refers to the badlands of Montana, where the rapids of the Missouri break up the land. David Braxton (John McLiam), an early pioneer of the land, is a wealthy range boss with enough political muscle to master most of the territory. Trouble ensues when Tom Logan (Jack Nicholson), leader of the area's horse thieves, buys a ranch near the McLiam property to be a rest stop for stolen horses. McLiam responds by employing a hired gunman named Robert E. Lee Clayton (played by a 240-pound Marlon Brando) to ferret out the Logan gang, which he proceeds to do by wiping them out one by one, often in personally vicious ways—one is killed in the outhouse, another is shot while making love, and so on.

Scriptwriter Thomas McGuane was forced to let the two stars rewrite the script to suit their own tastes. Critics blasted the film for making no sense and doing so in an offensive way. In his *TV and Video Guide*, Leonard Maltin called this film a total "bomb," while *Variety* concluded that, "As a film achievement it's corned beef and hash." It is generally considered thorough waste of talent encumbered by enormous egos; author Joe Hyams calls Brando's Clayton "the most comically terrifying hired gun in any Western." An enormous amount of money was spent on salary alone. Brando was paid $1.25 million and Nicholson a hefty $1 million to do the film—an excessive amount, considering the picture was a box-office and critical bust.

MOHAWK 20th Century Fox, 1956, Color, 80 min, DVD. **Producer:** Edward L. Alperson; **Director:** Kurt Neumann; **Screenplay:** Maurice Geraghty and Milton Krims; **Music:** Edward L. Alperson; **Cinematographer:** Karl Strauss; **Cast:** Scott Brady, Rita Gam, Neville Brand, Lori Nelson, Allison Hayes, Barbara Jo Allen, Rhys Williams.

Scott Brady is an eastern artist in the West who attempts to thwart an Iroquois uprising through his involvement with Iroquois woman Rita Gam, as greedy landowners try to stop further settlements in the Mohawk Valley by inciting the Indians to war. This barely average film benefits by footage from John Ford's *Drums Along the Mohawk* (1939).

MOJAVE FIREBRAND Republic, 1944, B&W, 55 min. **Director:** Gordon Spencer Bennet; **Screenplay:** Norman Hall; **Music:** Mort Glickman; **Cinematographer:** Ernest Miller; **Editor:** Harry Keller; **Cast:** William "Wild Bill" Elliott, George "Gabby" Hayes, Anne Jeffreys, LeRoy Mason, Jack Ingram.

In this film set in 1877, "Gabby" Hayes is a mule prospector who accidentally knocks over a rock filled with silver. He hopes to build a peaceful town with the strike, but the new-found wealth brings outlaws who quickly overrun the town. Just as things look very bleak, lawman Bill Elliott happens to pass through town and brings the matter to rest. This film is yet another well-made and fast-moving Elliott venture for Republic, and it helps audiences to realize what a commanding screen presence "Wild Bill" Elliott actually was for yesteryear's B western fans.

MOLLY AND LAWLESS JOHN Producers Distributing Corporation, 1972, Color, 98 min, VHS. **Producer:** Dennis Durney; **Director:** Gary Nelson; **Screenplay:** Terry Kingsley-Smith; **Music:** Johnny Mandel; **Cinematographer:** Charles P. Wheeler; **Editor:** Gene Fowler Jr.; **Cast:** Vera Miles, Sam Elliott, Clu Galager, John Anderson, Cynthia Meyers, Charles Pinney.

The underappreciated and shy wife of an arrogant frontier sheriff is cajoled by a smooth-talking jail inmate into helping him escape from prison. Their developing relationship as they cross the desert together provides the film's nexus. In time her dissatisfaction with the abusive young prisoner increases. In an ultimate act of liberation, she kills him, returns home, tells her husband she had been kidnapped, and collects the reward money. Vera Miles lends some depth to her role as Molly, the repressed older woman, with Sam Elliott (early in his career) properly menacing as lawless John, the devious prison escapee.

MONEY ISN'T EVERYTHING See *JEEPERS CREEPERS*.

MONTANA Warner Bros., 1950, Color, 76 min, VHS. **Producer:** William Jacobs; **Director:** Ray Enright; **Screenplay:** Borden Chase, Charles O'Neill, and Richard Webb; **Music:** David Buttolph; **Cinematographer:** Karl Freund; **Editor:** Frederick Richards; **Cast:** Errol Flynn, Alexis Smith, S. Z. Sakall, Douglas Kennedy, James Brown, Ian MacDonald.

Sparks fly when an Australian sheepman (Errol Flynn) who comes to Montana to search for grazing space and to sell sheep finds a roadblock in the person of a pretty and wealthy cattle rancher played by Alexis Smith. Raoul Walsh was an uncredited codirector of this film, which is based on a story by Ernest Haycox. Jock Mahoney was a stunt double for Flynn in this slow-moving but colorful genre piece bolstered by the magnetic presence of Errol Flynn.

MONTANA BELLE RKO, 1952, Color, 80 min. **Producer:** Howard Welsch; **Director:** Allan Dwan; **Screenplay:** Horace McCoy and Norman S. Hall; **Music:** Portia Nelson and Nathan Scott; **Cinematographer:** Jack Marta; **Editor:** Arthur Roberts; **Cast:** Jane Russell, George Brent, Scott Brady, Forrest Tucker, Andy Devine, Jack Lambert, John Litel, Ray Teal.

In this fictionalized biography of Belle Starr, the female outlaw dazzles the Dalton brothers with her chicanery and superb outlaw skills before striking out on her own with outlaws Mac (Forrest Tucker) and Ringo (Jack Lambert). She further enriches herself by seducing wealthy saloon owner Tom Bradfield (George Brent), who had enlisted in a bankers scheme to trap the Daltons.

Jane Russell's Belle Starr, equal to her male counterparts in skill and grit, winds up being killed by the Daltons. Scott Brady plays Bob Dalton, the beguiled brother who falls for Belle after rescuing her from a lynch mob.

In 1948 RKO boss Howard Hughes lent Jane Russell to Columbia to make the picture, then bought it back from Columbia, and put it on the shelf for four years, hoping that the buxom Russell would become an even bigger star than she was at the time.

MONTANA DESPERADO Monogram, 1951, B&W, 51 min. **Producer:** Johnny Mack Brown; **Director:** Wallace Fox; **Screenplay:** Daniel B. Ullman; **Cinematographer:** Vincent Fennelly; **Editor:** Fred Maguire; **Cast:** Johnny Mack Brown, Virginia Herrick, Marshal Reed, Steve Clark.

MONTANA INCIDENT Monogram, 1952, B&W, 54 min. **Producer:** Vincent M. Fennelly; **Director:** Lewis D. Collins; **Screenplay:** Daniel B. Ullman; **Cast:** Whip Wilson, Rand Brooks, Noel Neill, Peggy Stewart, Hugh Prosser.

MONTANA JUSTICE See *MAN FROM MONTANA*.

MONTANA MOON MGM, 1930, B&W, 89 min. **Producer:** Malcom St. Clair; **Director:** St. Clair; **Screenplay:** Frank Butler and Sylvia Thalberg; **Music:** Nacio Herb Brown and Arthur Freed; **Cinematographer:** William H. Daniels; **Editor:** Carl Pierson; **Cast:** Joan Crawford, Johnny Mack Brown, Dorothy Sebastian, Benny Rubin, Cliff Edwards.

Joan Crawford is a spoiled heiress who meets and marries ragged cowboy Johnny Mack Brown. Although the story is dated and stilted, the film is notable for being Brown's first sound western. He and Crawford even sing "The Moon Is Low" a cappella; Cliff Edwards later strums on the banjo.

MONTANA TERRITORY Columbia, 1952, Color, 64 min. **Producer:** Colbert Clark; **Director:** Ray Nazarro; **Screenplay:** Barry Shipman; **Cinematographer:** Henry Freulich; **Editor:** Paul Borofsky; **Cast:** Lon McCallister, Wanda Hendrix, Preston Foster, Hugh Sanders, Jack Elam, Clayton Moore, Myron Healey, Robert Griffin.

An idealistic young man (Lon McCallister) comes to the Montana territory and becomes a deputy sheriff in hopes of cleaning up the area, which is infested with killers and crooks. Instead he is duped into aiding the very men he wants to apprehend. This film was the second to last for onetime child star Lon McCallister. He retired from the screen in 1953 at age 30.

MONTE WALSH National General, 1970, Color, 98 min, VHS. **Producers:** Hal Landers and Bobby Roberts; **Director:** William Fraker; **Screenplay:** David Zelag Goodman and Lucas Heller; **Music:** John Barry; **Cinematographer:** David M. Walsh; **Editors:** Richard K. Brockway, Ray Daniels, Gene Fowler, and Robert L. Wolfe; **Cast:** Lee Marvin, Jack Palance, Jeanne Moreau, Mitch Ryan, Jim Davis, Bo Hopkins, John McLiam.

Lee Marvin and Jack Palance are itinerant aging cowboys who witness the last days of old-style ranching as the big city combines from the East roll in. In his directorial debut, William Fraker delivers a realistic and serious account of the decline of the cowboy as civilization moves across the continent. "You damned accountants! *We* did it!" Walsh exclaims when a moneyman from the East takes credit for western progress.

Marvin and Palance are excellent as the two cowpokes who eventually seek separate roads. "Nobody gets to be a cowboy forever," Chet Rollins (Palance) tells Monte in sad recognition of the truth. Marvin in the title role is determined to push ahead even if he is the last cowboy standing, and he scrambles to stay afloat financially while watching everything he cares about (including aging saloon girl Jeanne Moreau) die or disappear. Chet, meanwhile, decides to give up the range for a wife and a hardware store, only to be killed by a former cowboy pal (Mitch Ryan) who has turned to robbery in order to survive.

Moving and somber, the film is based on the novel by Jack Schaefer (who also wrote *SHANE*, 1953). Joseph Roquemore in his *History Goes to the Movies* calls *Monte Walsh* a "grimly realistic film, authentic in every detail. . . ." While Schaefer's novel follows the life of Monte Walsh from his birth to his death, the movie deals only with a period in 1889 when all the big ranches were bought up and all the land fenced in, leaving numerous cowboys without work or any livelihood.

The major problem with the film is its episodic plot line, which somehow does not allow it to become a cohesive entity. That being said, there are moments of genuine pathos, such as Walsh's farewell to "The Countess" (Moreau) as he gazes at her dead body and cuts off a lock of her hair as a remembrance (one of Lee Marvin's finest screen moments); and Walsh's inordinate pride in taming a wild horse as the rest of his world is crashing down. The main song "The Good Times are Coming," incorporated into John Barry's stirring musical score, is sung by Cass Elliott. Jack Schaefer's novel was named one of the top 10 western novels of the 20th century by the Western Writers of America.

MOONLIGHTER, THE Warner Bros., 1953, B&W, 77 min. **Producer:** Joseph Bernhard; **Director:** Roy Rowland; **Screenplay:** Nevin Busch; **Music:** Heinz Roemheld and Carl Sigman; **Cinematographer:** Bert Glennon; **Editor:** Terry O'Morris; **Cast:** Barbara Stanwyck, Fred MacMurray, Ward Bond, William Ching, John Dierkes, Morris Ankrum, Jack Elam.

A cattle rustler (Fred MacMurray) returns to his western hometown and runs into his former flame (Barbara Stanwyck), who seems to hate him. However, their hate turns to love as they both are forced to contend with town villain Ward Bond. Originally shot as a 3-D black and white feature, the *New York Times* queried shortly after its release: "Exactly why the protagonists of *Double Indemnity* should have elected to participate in such a cowtown petty larceny is a mystery." It was Stanwyck's and MacMurray's third teaming together.

MOONLIGHT ON THE PRAIRIE Warner Bros., 1935, B&W, 63 min. **Director:** D. Ross Lederman; **Screenplay:** William Jacobs; **Music:** Howard Jackson, Joan Jasmyn, M. J. Jerome, Bob Nolan, and Vernon Spencer; **Cinematographer:** Fred Jackman Jr.; **Editor:** Thomas Pratt; **Cast:** Dick Foran, Sheila Bromley (as Sheila Manners), George E. Stone, Joe Sawyer, Joe King.

Dick Foran brings his mellow voice into this pleasant outing about a singing cowboy who is led to believe that he will be unjustly accused of murder at the show's next stop. The handsome Foran was to be Warner Bros.' answer to Gene Autry, and he made 12 B westerns for the studio in the 1930s. He sings "Covered Wagon Days" in this film. His character name might be different from film to film, but the "singing cowboy" tag was always the same. Other series entries include: *Treachery Rides the Range, TRAILIN' WEST, CALIFORNIA MAIL, SONG OF THE SADDLE* (1936); *GUNS OF THE PECOS, BLAZING SIXES, PRAIRIE THUNDER, LAND BEYOND THE LAW, THE DEVIL'S SADDLE LEGION, THE CHEROKEE STRIP* (1937).

MOONLIGHT ON THE RANGE Spectrum, 1937, B&W, 59 min. **Producers:** Jed Buell and George Callaghan; **Director:** Sam Newfield; **Screenplay:** Fred Myton; **Music:** June Hershey and Don Swander; **Cinematographer:** Robert E. Cline; **Editor:** William Hess; **Cast:** Fred Scott, Al St. John, Lois January, Dick Curtis, Frank La Rue, Jimmy Aubrey.

Singing cowboy Fred Scott hits the trail for revenge when his lookalike half-brother murders his best pal. Scott plays both the hero and the villain in this Spectrum venture, which includes plenty of action and four songs to boot. Scott, Spectrum's resident singing cowboy during its five-year existence, made a number of films for the short-lived studio. Others include *Romance Rides the Range* (1936); *The Singing Buckaroo, MELODY OF THE PLAINS, Roaming Cowboys, The Fighting Deputy* (1937); *Knights of the Plains, Songs and Bullets, The Ranger's Round-Up* (1938); *In Old Montana, Code of the Fearless* (1939); *Ridin' the Trail* (1940).

MOONLIGHT OVER TEXAS See *STARLIGHT OVER TEXAS*.

MOON OVER MONTANA Monogram, 1946, B&W, 56 min. **Producer:** Oliver Drake; **Director:** Drake; **Screenplay:** Betty Burbridge and Earle Snell; **Cast:** Jimmy Wakely, Jennifer Holt, Stanley Blystone, Jack Ingram, Lee 'Lesses' White.

MOUNTAIN MEN Columbia, 1980, Color, 102 min. **Producers:** Andrew Scheinman and Martin Shafer; **Director:** Richard Lang; **Screenplay:** Fraser Clarke Heston; **Music:** Michel Legrand; **Cinematographer:** Michel Hugo; **Editor:** Eva Ruggiero; **Cast:** Charlton Heston, Brian Keith, David Ackroyd, Don "D. G." Banning, Victor Jory.

Charlton Heston and Brian Keith play aging trappers battling Blackfeet Indians and a wicked chief named Heavy Eagle, who would like to see Heston's head at the top of his spear. At the same time they try to scratch out a meager existence during the final years of the fur trade. Scripted by Frazer Clarke Heston, Charlton Heston's son, this is a better film than some critics give it credit for. The Grand Tetons are unmatched in their grandeur and provide marvelous scenic backdrops that compensate for some extremely bloody battle scenes.

MOUNTAIN RHYTHM Republic, 1939, B&W, 61 min. **Producer:** Harry Grey; **Director:** B. Reeves Eason; **Screenplay:** Gerald Geraghty; **Cinematographer:** Ernest Miller; **Editor:** Lester Orlebeck; **Cast:** Gene Autry, Smiley Burnette, June Storey, Maude Eburne, Jack Pennick.
See *TUMBLING TUMBLEWEEDS*.

MULE TRAIN Columbia, 1950, B&W, 70 min. **Producer:** Armand Schaefer; **Director:** John English; **Screenplay:** Gerald Geraghty and Alan James; **Music:** Fred Glickman, Hy Heath, Johnny Lange, and Heinz Roemfeld; **Cinematographer:** William Bradford; **Editor:** Richard Fantl; **Cast:** Gene Autry, Pat Buttram, Sheila Ryan, Frank Jacquet.

Gene Autry comes to the aid of two prospectors who claim a natural cement deposit has been stolen by a contractor in cahoots with a crooked female sheriff. This interesting Autry entry—loosely based on Frankie Laine's popular record with the same title—has a slew of good songs, including "Room Full of Roses," "Cool Water," and "The Old Chisholm Trail." The title song became a number one million-seller for Frankie Laine, with whom it is most closely associated. Others who made popular recordings of the song include Bing Crosby, Ernie Ford, and Vaughn Monroe, who sang it in the 1950 film *Singing Guns*. Interestingly, it received an Oscar nomination for being in but not introduced in *Singing Guns*.

MURDER ON THE YUKON Monogram, 1940, B&W, 58 min. **Producer:** Philip N. Krasne; **Director:** Louis J. Gasnier; **Screenplay:** Milton Raison; **Music:** Vick Knight, Johnny Lange, and Lew Porter; **Cinematographer:** Elmer Dyer; **Editor:** Guy V. Thayer; **Cast:** James Newill, Dave O'Brien, Al St. John, Polly Ann Young, William Royle, Chief Thundercloud, Budd Buster, "Snub" Pollard, Kenne Duncan, Karl Hackett.

MUSTANG COUNTRY Universal, 1976, Color, 79 min. **Producer:** John Champion; **Director:** Champion; **Screenplay:** Champion; **Music:** Lee Holdridge; **Cinematographer:** J. Barry Herron; **Editor:** Douglas Robertson; **Cast:** Joel McCrea, Robert Fuller, Patrick Wayne, Nika Mina.

A former rodeo star comes across a runaway Indian boy while hunting a wild stallion in this film sleeper. Joel McCrea at age 70 proved he was still quite the master of the genre. This good, clean family film is highly entertaining but unfortunately has not been released on video. It was McCrea's first film since 1962, when he starred with Randolph Scott in *RIDE THE HIGH COUNTRY*. The song "Follow Your Restless Dreams" (Joe Henry and Lee Holdridge) is sung by Denny Brooks.

MY DARLING CLEMENTINE 20th Century Fox, 1946, B&W, 97 min, VHS. **Producers:** Samuel G. Engel and Darryl F. Zanuck; **Director:** John Ford; **Screenplay:** Engel, Sam Hellman, and Winston Miller; **Music:** David Buttolph and Cyril J. Mockridge; **Cinematographer:** Joseph MacDonald; **Editor:** Dorothy Spencer; **Cast:** Henry Fonda, Linda Darnell, Victor Mature, Cathy Downs, Walter Brennan, Tim Holt, Alan Mowbray, John Ireland, Roy Roberts, Jane Darwell, Grant Withers, J. Farrell MacDonald, Don Garner.

Based on Stuart Lake's biography *Wyatt Earp, Frontier Marshal*, the story begins with Wyatt Earp (Henry Fonda) and brothers Virgil, Morgan, and James (Tim Holt, Ward Bond, and Don Garner) driving a herd through Monument Valley. They stop near the town of Tombstone, where Wyatt, Virgil, and Morgan go into town for a shave, leaving James to watch the herd. When a drunken Indian interrupts Wyatt's shave by shooting up the town, Wyatt subdues him and berates the townsfolk for selling liquor to an Indian. (In an interesting sidebar, this scene was repeated from the 1939 version of the story, *The Federal Marshal*, and the drunken Indian, called Indian Joe, was played by the same actor, Charles Stevens, in both films.) An instant hero in Tombstone, Wyatt is offered the job of marshal but refuses.

Wyatt, Virgil, and Morgan return to camp only to find their brother James dead and their cattle stolen. The culprits, of course, are Ike Clanton (Walter Brennan) and his sons. Tensions build in a measured pace as Wyatt takes the job in Tombstone, and after an initial clash he befriends Doc Holliday (Victor Mature), a onetime talented surgeon turned gambler and killer. With Doc's help Wyatt eventually squares off against the evil Clantons at the O.K. Corral in an extremely well-staged and intelligent version of the famed gunfight.

The female leads belongs to Linda Darnell as the Mexican firebrand and dance-hall belle Chihuahua; and Cathy Downs in the lesser role of Clementine Carter, a cultured Bostonian gal in love with Doc Holliday but becomes attracted to Earp in the process.

If the story is familiar and the historical accuracy somewhat flawed, the film itself is a superb piece of craftsmanship. Certainly John Ford is at his best with a film steeped in his ideas about the civilizing of the West. Concentrating on characterization and photography, Ford reworks the well-known story of Wyatt Earp to the terms of his own lyric style.

Central to the story is Fonda's portrayal of the famed and legendary western icon. His Wyatt Earp is a taciturn, nomadic cowboy whose primary ties are with his three brothers—the mythic loner who wears his proud isolation like a badge of honor and only reluctantly assumes the role of lawman. When he visits the grave of his dead brother, he promises him that Tombstone some day will be a place "where boys like you can grow up safe."

Victor Mature delivers a sound, sympathetic, and well-controlled performance as the consumption-laden, cough-prone Doc Holliday. Yet according to Dan Ford in his excellent biography *Pappy: The Life of John Ford*, Mature had to endure such epithets as "Greaseball" and "Liverlips" from the cantankerous director. Moreover, Ford and veteran actor Walter Brennan had a series of spats on the set, and after one particularly bitter exchange, the three-time Oscar-winning actor said under no circumstances would he ever work with Ford again. And he never did.

Released in 1946, *My Darling Clementine* was John Ford's first western since *STAGECOACH* (1939). Moreover, it began a period when Ford would make his most endearing, idyllic, and optimistic westerns, culminating with *THE WAGONMASTER* in 1950. It was an era when Ford, who had already garnered three Oscars for nonwesterns, cemented his imprint as the master poet and sentimentalist of the cinematic West.

Rarely has a film, especially a western, received such top critical acclaim. *My Darling Clementine* won the Silver Ribbon Award by the Italian National Syndicate for Best Foreign Film (1948). The *New York Times* wrote, "The gentlemen are perfect. Their humors are earthly. Their activities taut. The mortality rate is simply terrific. And the picture goes off with several bangs."

The *New York Herald-Tribune* called it "a smooth and superior motion picture, wild and wooly western, though, it certainly is." William Everson calls the film "superlative . . . easily one of Ford's best Westerns . . . and quite certainly the best of all the Wyatt Earp films." Filmed in Kayenta, Arizona, and Monument Valley, Utah, *My Darling Clementine* was selected for the National Film Registry in 1991.

MY FRIEND FLICKA 20th Century Fox, 1943, Color, 89 min, VHS. **Producer:** Ralph Dietrich; **Director:** Harold D. Schuster; **Screenplay:** Francis Edward Faragoh and Lillie Hayward; **Music:** Alfred Newman; **Cinematographer:** Dewey Wrigley; **Editor:** Robert Fritch; **Cast:** Roddy McDowall, Preston Foster, Rita Johnson, James Bell, Diana Hale, Arthur Loft.

A daydreaming youngster played by Roddy McDowall longs for a colt of his own. When his rancher father fulfills the wish, the youngster must tame the rebellious horse, eventually nursing the animal back to health. This sentimental story, beautifully filmed in color, deals with the influence of the wild pony (Flicka) on the lives and philosophy of a small family as well as the personal impact the pony makes on a young boy's life.

MY HEROES HAVE ALWAYS BEEN COWBOYS Gaylord-Poll, 1991, Color, 106 min, VHS. **Producers:** Martin Poll and E. K. Gaylord; **Director:** Stuart Rosenberg; **Screenplay:** Joe Don Humphreys; **Music:** James Horner; **Cinematographer:** Bernd Heinl; **Editor:** Dennis M. Hill; **Cast:** Scott Glenn, Kate Capshaw, Ben Johnson, Balthazar Getty, Tess Harper, Gary Busey, Mickey Rooney, Clarence Williams, Dub Taylor, Clu Gulager.

Scott Glenn and Ben Johnson are superb in this contemporary western about a bull-riding cowboy plagued by bad times and the father whom he has always loved and idolized and who is languishing in a rest home until his son rescues him. Together back at home, father and son renew their lifelong bickering, while Glenn renews his relationship with his former girlfriend (Kate Capshaw). When his sister and brother-in-law (Tess Harper and Gary Busey) become intent on selling off the family property, Glenn, with Johnson's careful mentoring, begins training for his big comeback in the hope of winning the cash prize necessary to fight off Harper and Busey.

This uplifting western melodrama, rife with brilliant interplay between Glenn and Johnson, presents a gritty and realistic portrayal of contemporary rodeo life, culminating with Glenn's one last ride on the ferocious bull that almost killed him. An all-star country soundtrack features hits by Willie Nelson, Keith Whitley, Alabama, Lorrie Morgan, Clint Black, Roger Miller, and the Oak Ridge Boys. Forget some modest reviews; this is a film that should be seen and enjoyed by all true fans of the genre, with wonderful performances and a strong degree of character development.

MY LITTLE CHICKADEE Universal, 1940, B&W, 83 min. **Producer:** Lester Cowan; **Director:** Edward F. Cline; **Screenplay:** W. C. Fields and Mae West; **Music:** Frank Skinner; **Cinematographer:** Joseph Valentine; **Editor:** Ed Curtiss; **Cast:** Mae West, W. C. Fields, Joseph Calleia, Dick Foran, Ruth Donnelly, Margaret Hamilton, Donald Meek, Fuzzy Knight, Gene Austin.

W. C. Fields is a roving snake-oil vendor named Cuthbert J. Twillie, who has the misfortune to encounter a naughty lady named Flower Belle Lee (Mae West). Run out of town by the good ladies of Little Bend, she heads to the Greasewood City by train, on which she spots con man Twillie with a bag full of money (actually worthless). Believing he is rich, she seduces him and then persuades a cardsharp (Donald Meek) to marry them in a fake marriage ceremony. Once they reach Greasewood City, she refuses to consummate her vows, and a befuddled Cuthbert is seen wooing a goat in the wedding bed, thinking it is Flower Belle. "The child's afraid of me—she's all a 'twit,'" opines the chagrined Cuthbert.

The adventures and misadventures (including Fields nearly being hanged by mistake and West's uncanny marksmanship during an Indian attack on the train) find West and Fields exchanging rapid barbs, though not always to each other. As Flower Belle says when she gives an arithmetic lesson to a group of school children, "Two and two are four and five will give you ten if you play your cards right."

In what is at times a hilarious farce, Mae West lends a certain credibility to the coarse, promiscuous women who filled the parlor houses of the West where the miners and cowboys sought out a good time. Unlike the usual cinematic bighearted, good-natured saloon gals who hovered over cowboys and card players for a hug, a drink, and some fun, only a brazen comedienne like Mae West could get away with expressing the truly carnal aspects of such characters.

Although West and Fields are given credit for the screenplay, the bulk was written by West, with Fields scripting only some individual scenes. Reportedly West forbade Fields to smoke or drink on the set (a monumental task), which accounts for the fact that Fields appears to be in better physical condition than in his other Universal ventures of that period. *My Little Chickadee* matched two competing egos and temperaments in Fields and West, never in total harmony and with a slice of mutual jealousy. Nevertheless it remains the most widely shown of the two stars' feature films.

MY PAL, THE KING Universal, 1932, B&W, 74 min. **Producer:** Carl Laemmle Jr.; **Director:** Kurt Neumann; **Screenplay:** Thomas J. Crizer and Jack Natteford; **Cinematographer:** Daniel B. Clark; **Cast:** Tom Mix, Mickey Rooney, Paul Hurst, Noel Francis, Jim Thorpe, Finis Barton.

The boy king of a European country is threatened by plotters who are trying to steal his throne, but he receives some unexpected help from a cowboy who has taken his frontier show to the boy's kingdom. This unusual and interesting film is worth seeing, especially for the chance to watch Mickey Rooney (as the young king) and Tom Mix (as the frontier cowboy) working together. A particularly amusing scene has Mix teaching young Rooney American western slang.

The film was made as part of Tom Mix's final series at Universal. Although he had aged a few years, Mix is still very adept at his stunt sequences. A number of good cameo appearances includes the great American Indian athlete Jim Thorpe as a performer in Mix's troupe. As quoted in *The Great Western Movies* (Parish and Pitts), Mordaunt Hall in *The New York Times* called *My Pal, The King* "... good entertainment for children, who not only have the opportunity of following a melodramatic story, but also seeing crack riders from the Far West in action in a circus arena." (See also *FOURTH HORSEMAN, THE.*)

MY PAL TRIGGER Republic, 1946, B&W, 79 min, VHS. **Producer:** Armand Schaefer; **Directors:** Yakima Canutt and Frank McDonald; **Screenplay:** Jack Townley; **Music:** R. Dale Butts and Morton Scott; **Cinematographer:** William Bradford; **Editor:** Harry Keller; **Cast:** Roy Rogers, George "Gabby" Hayes, Dale Evans, Jack Holt, Bob Nolan, LeRoy Mason, Roy Barcroft.

Gabby Kendrick ("Gabby" Hayes) refuses to breed his horse, the Golden Sovereign, with Roy's. When the Sovereign and Roy's horse both escape, the Golden Sovereign is shot by mistake, and Roy is blamed and sent to jail. A year later Roy returns with Trigger, the son of the Golden Sovereign, and is able to clear himself when the real culprit slips up and reveals that he was present when the horse was shot. A full slice of top entertainment with a superb performance by Jack Holt as Scoville, the crooked rancher, *My Pal Trigger* is considered by many to be Roy Rogers' finest film. It is certainly one of his most popular and most beloved. It was remade as a Rex Allen oater, *Rodeo King and the Senorita*, in 1951. (See also *UNDER WESTERN STARS.*)

MYSTERIOUS AVENGER Columbia, 1936, B&W, 54 min. **Producer:** Harry L. Decker; **Director:** David Selman; **Screenplay:** Ford Beebe and Peter B. Kyne; **Cinematographer:** George Meehan; **Editor:** Richard Cahoon; **Cast:** Charles Starrett, Joan Perry, Wheeler Oakman, Edward Le Saint, Lafe McKee.

See *GALLANT DEFENDER.*

MYSTERIOUS DESPERADO, THE RKO, 1949, B&W, 61 min. **Producer:** Herbert Schlom; **Director:** Leslie Selander; **Screenplay:** Norman Houston; **Music:** Paul Sawtell; **Cinematographer:** Nicholas Musuraca; **Editor:** Less Millbrook; **Cast:** Tim Holt, Richard Martin, Frank Wilcox, Edward Norris, Robert Livingston.

MYSTERIOUS MR. SHEFFIELD, THE See *LAW OF THE .45S.*

MYSTERIOUS STRANGER See *WESTERN GOLD.*

MYSTERY MAN, THE United Artists, 1944, B&W, 58 min. **Producer:** Harry Sherman; **Director:** George Archainbaud; **Screenplay:** J. Benton Cheney; **Music:** Irvin Talbot; **Cinematographer:** Russell Harlan; **Editor:** Fred W. Berger; **Cast:** William Boyd, Andy Clyde, Jimmy Rogers, Don Costello, Eleanor Stewart, John Merton, Pierce Lyden.

See *HOP-ALONG CASSIDY.*

MYSTERY MOUNTAIN Mascot, 1934, B&W, 223 min, VHS. **Producer:** Nat Levine; **Directors:** Otto Brower and B. Reeves Eason; **Screenplay:** Bennett Cohen, Eason,

Sherman L. Lowe, Barney Sarecky, and Armond Schaefer; **Music:** Lee Zahler; **Cinematographers:** Ernest Miller and William Nobles; **Editor:** Earl Turner; **Cast:** Ken Maynard, Verna Hillie, Syd Saylor, Edward Earle, Hooper Atchley, Al Bridge.

Ken Williams (Ken Maynard) is determined to discover the identity of the mysterious Rattler, an all-purpose villain who preys upon railroads and transportation companies. But the Rattler is extremely difficult to capture because of his skill in disguising himself as other people. This interesting serial, a solid mystery as well as an adept cliffhanger, always keeps the viewer wanting for more. A relatively unknown Gene Autry appears in an uncredited role as a man named Thomas in Chapter 6. The Rattler remains unknown until finally unmasked, and his identity will not be revealed here either.

MYSTERY OF THE HOODED HORSEMAN

Grand National, 1937, B&W, 60 min. **Producer:** Edward Finney; **Director:** Ray Taylor; **Screenplay:** Edmond Kelso; **Music:** Michael David, Ritter, Fred Rose, and Frank Sanucci; **Cinematographer:** Gus Peterson; **Editor:** Frederick Bain; **Cast:** Tex Ritter, Iris Meredith, Horace Murphy, Charles King, Hank Warden, Ray Whitley & His Range Ramblers.

A band of hooded horsemen kill a man for his mine, and a cowboy and his pal go after the culprits. When Tex Ritter kills one of hooded horsemen, he uses his victim's hood to infiltrate the gang. He later escapes only to be captured by the sheriff, who thinks he really is one of them. Ritter sings a trio of good songs, including "Ride, Ride, Ride," and "Ridin' Old Paint," in this better-than-average venture from Grand National.

MYSTERY RANCH

Fox, 1932, B&W, 56 min. **Producer:** Sol M. Wurtzel; **Director:** David Howard; **Screenplay:** Alfred A. Cohn; **Cinematographers:** Joseph H. August and George Schneiderman; **Editor:** Paul Weatherwax; **Cast:** George O'Brien, Cecilia Parker, Charles Middleton, Forrestor Harvey, Charles Stevens, Noble Johnson.

MYSTERY RANCH

Reliable, 1934, B&W, 56 min. **Producer:** Bernard B. Ray; **Director:** Ray; **Screenplay:** Rose Gordon and Carl Krusada; **Cinematographer:** J. Henry Kruse; **Editor:** Frederick Bain; **Cast:** Tom Tyler, Roberta Gale, Louise Cabo, Jack Perrin, Frank Hall Crane.

The famous western fiction writer Bob Morris (Tom Tyler) arrives at the Henderson ranch, where he encounters a series of practical jokes. Thus, when a real robbery takes place, Morris thinks it is just another ruse. Tom Tyler made a series of movies for Reliable Pictures Corporation in the mid-1930s. The others include: *Ridin' Thru, Fighting Hero* (1934); *Coyote Trails, Terror of the Plains, Born to Battle, The Unconquered Bandit, Tracy Rides, Rio Rattler, Silver Bullet, Trigger Tom, The Laramie Kid* (1935); *Fast Bullets, Ridin' On, Roamin' Wild, Pinto Rustlers, Santa Fe Bound* (1936).

NAKED DAWN, THE Universal, 1955, Color, 82 min. **Producer:** James O. Radford; **Director:** Edgar G. Ulmer; **Screenplay:** Nina Schneider; Herman Schneider; **Music:** Hershal Berke Gilbert; **Cinematographer:** Frederick Gately; **Editor:** Dan Milner; **Cast:** Arthur Kennedy, Betta St. John, Eugene Iglesias, Charlita, Roy Engel, Tony Martinez, Francis McDonald.

Arthur Kennedy is Santiago, a Mexican bandit who robs a freight train and must hire a young farmer (Eugene Iglesias) to help him collect the money. The farmer's wife (Betta St. John) falls for Kennedy and plans to run off with him. Matters are complicated, however, when the farmer, sufficiently seduced by the money, plans to kill Kennedy.

NAKED GUN (aka: THE HANGING JUDGE) Associated Film Releasing Corp., 1956, B&W, 69 min. **Producer:** Ron Ormond; **Director:** Edward Dew; **Screenplay:** Ormond and Jack Lewis; **Music:** Walter Greene; **Cinematographers:** John M. Nickolaus Jr. and Gilbert Warrenton; **Editor:** Carl Pierson; **Cast:** Willard Parker, Mara Corday, Barton MacLane, Billy House, Veda Ann Borg.

An insurance agent who attempts to deliver valuable jewels to the heir of an estate becomes involved with a group of crooks determined to find an Aztec treasure. Director Edward Dew is the same Eddie Drew who starred in B westerns for Republic and Universal in the 1940s.

NAKED HILLS, THE Allied Artists, 1956, Color, 72 min. **Producer:** Josef Shaftel; **Director:** Shaftel; **Music:** Hershal Berke Gilbert; **Cinematographer:** Frederick Gately; **Editor:** Gene Fowler Jr.; **Cast:** David Wayne,

Keenan Wynn, James Barton, Marcia Henderson, Jim Backus, Denver Pyle.

The familiar gold fever theme finds David Wayne as an Indiana farmer who deserts his wife and family to prospect for gold in California. James Barton sings the song "The Four Seasons."

NAKED IN THE SUN Allied Artists, 1957, Color, 78 min. **Producer:** R. John Hugh; **Director:** Hugh; **Screenplay:** John Cresswell; **Music:** Laurence Rosenthal; **Cinematographer:** Charles T. O'Rork; **Editor:** William A. Slade; **Cast:** James Craig, Lita Milan, Barton MacLane, Robert Wark, Jim Boles.

In the 1830s, when white settlers were moving into what is now Florida, an unscrupulous slave trader captures the wife of Chief Osceola, setting off a war between the Seminole and the U.S. Army.

NAKED SPUR, THE MGM, 1953, Color, 91 min, VHS. **Producer:** William H. Wright; **Director:** Anthony Mann; **Screenplay:** Sam Rolfe and Harold Jack Bloom; **Music:** Bronislau Kaper; **Cinematographer:** William Mellor; **Editor:** George White; **Cast:** James Stewart, Janet Leigh, Robert Ryan, Ralph Meeker, Millard Mitchell.

As in his other films with director Anthony Mann, James Stewart is again a man with a bitter past. After his wife leaves him he becomes a bounty hunter and begins tracking down Robert Ryan, a murderous outlaw with a $5,000 reward on his head; Stewart hopes to use the money to start a ranch. Along the way he encounters an aging, grizzled prospector (Millard Mitchell) and a dangerous gunman dishonorably discharged from the army (Ralph Meeker). When they finally capture Ryan and a beautiful companion (Janet Leigh), Ryan employs his knowledge of human nature to turn his captors against one another. The film ends in a dramatic three-way shoot-out between Stewart, Ryan, and Meeker.

Stewart delivers a gem of a performance as Howard Kemp, a tormented man at war with himself and the outside world. Both Stewart and Ryan were deserving of Oscar consideration, which neither received; roles like theirs were often ignored at Oscar time. With only five characters to occupy the screen, Mann was able to develop their personas fully, aided by a superb, Oscar-nominated script by Sam Rolfe and Harold Jack Bloom and the director's innate sense for the visual expression of man's inner conflicts. Filmed on location in Durango, Colorado, in the Rocky Mountains, *The Naked Spur* further benefits from William Mellor's stunning color photography. Well reviewed across the board, it was selected for the National Film Registry in 1997 by the National Film Preservation Board.

NAVAJO JOE (aka: A DOLLAR A HEAD) United Artists, 1967, Color, 93 min, VHS, CD. **Producers:** Luigi Carpentieri and Emmanno Donati; **Director:** Sergio Corbucci; **Screenplay:** Fernando Di Leo and Piero Regnoli; **Music:** Ennio Morricone; **Cinematographer:** Silvano Ippoliti; **Editor:** Alberto Gallitti; **Cast:** Burt Reynolds, Aldo Sambrell, Nicoletta Machiavelli, Simon Arriaga.

The sole survivor of a bloody massacre vows revenge on the attackers who killed his wife. Burt Reynolds is the memorable loner Navajo Joe, who dispenses his own brand of justice. Arguably, the best component of Sergio Corbucci's spaghetti oater is Ennio Morricone's rousing musical score. (See also Appendix I, Spaghetti Westerns A–Z.)

NEAR THE RAINBOW'S END Tiffany, 1930, B&W, 60 min. **Producer:** Trem Carr; **Director:** J. P. McGowan; **Screenplay:** Charles A. Post and Sally Winters; **Music:** Murray Mencher, Billy Moll, and Harry Richman; **Cinematographer:** Hap Depew and T. E. Jackson; **Cast:** Bob Steele, Lafe McKee, Al Ferguson, Alfred Hewston, Louise Lorraine.

A rancher and his son fence off range to prevent cattle thefts, but when a sheepman is murdered the son is blamed. Bob Steele made his first sound screen appearance in this 1930 Tiffany oater. Steele, who made more than 160 Westerns dating back to 1925, also starred in a few of Tiffany Production features such as *Near The Trail's End, Oklahoma Cyclone* (1930); *Nevada Buckaroo, and The Ridin' Fool* 1931.

'NEATH ARIZONA SKIES Lone Star/Monogram, 1943, B&W, 52 min, VHS. **Producer:** Paul Malvern; **Director:** Harry Fraser; **Screenplay:** Burl Tuttle; **Music:** Paul Van Loan; **Cinematographer:** Archie Stout; **Editors:** Charles Hunt and Charles Pierson; **Cast:** John Wayne, Sheila Terry, Shirley Jean Rickert, Yakima Canutt, Harry L. Fraser (as Weston Edwards), George "Gabby" Hayes.

Chris Morrell (John Wayne) is the guardian of a little Indian girl who is the heiress to oil lands. When an outlaw gang plans to kidnap the girl and kill her father, Morrell foils the attempt. "Gabby" Hayes appears in an uncredited role as Matt Downing. The film is one of a series of westerns John Wayne did for producer Paul Malvern in the mid-1930s.

NEBRASKAN, THE Columbia, 1953, Color, 68 min. **Producer:** Wallace MacDonald; **Director:** Fred F. Sears; **Screenplay:** David Lang and Martin Berkeley; **Cinematographer:** Henry Freulich; **Editors:** Al Clark and James Sweeney; **Cast:** Philip Carey, Roberta Haynes, Wallace Ford, Richard Webb, Lee Van Cleef, Jay Silverheels, Dennis Weaver.

Set in 1867, when Nebraska first achieved statehood, Frontier Scout Wade Harper (Philip Carey) tries to make peace with the Nebraska Sioux. When he is falsely accused of murder, an Indian war almost breaks out. This film was originally issued in 3-D.

NED KELLY (aka: NED KELLY, OUTLAW) United Artists, 1970, Color, 101 min, VHS, CD. **Producer:** Neil Hartley; **Director:** Tony Richardson; **Screenplay:** Richardson and Ian Jones; **Music:** Shel Silverstein; **Cinematographer:** Gerry Fisher; **Editor:** Charles Rees; **Cast:** Mick Jagger, Allen Bickford, Diane Craig, Clarissa Kaye, Frank Twing, Mark McManus.

Mick Jagger stars as Ned Kelly, Australia's most famous outlaw. The son of an Irishman deported to Australia for stealing two pigs, Ned tries to lead a peaceful life, going so far as to open a sawmill. But circumstances intervene, and Ned and his brothers take up horse stealing and different brands of robbery. Sometimes they wear armor, including steel helmets that cover their faces. Eventually surrounded in a saloon, Ned's brothers commit suicide. Ned surrenders, is tried, and is sentenced to hang.

The Story of Ned Kelly, made in 1960, was Australia's first feature film. Tony Richardson's 1970 film boasts some good songs, with the Rolling Stones' Mick Jagger surprisingly effective as the legendary Aussie outlaw. *Variety* had this to say about Jagger's work: "Mick Jagger is a natural actor and performer with a wide range of expressions and postures at his instinctive command. Given whiskers, that gaunt, tough pop hero face takes on a classic hard-bitten frontier look that is totally believable for the role. . . ."

NEVADA Paramount, 1927, B&W, 67 min. **Producer:** B. P. Schulberg (associate); **Director:** John Waters; **Screenplay:** John Stone and L. G. Rigby; **Cinematographer:** C. Edgar Schoenbaum; **Editor:** Louis D. Lighton; **Cast:** Gary Cooper, Thelma Todd, Philip Strange, Ernie Adams, William Powell, Christian J. Frank, Ivan Christy, Guy Oliver.

NEVADA Paramount, 1935, B&W, 58 min. **Producer:** Harold Hurley; **Director:** Charles Barton; **Screenplay:** Garnett Weston and Stuart Anthony; **Cinematographer:** Archie Stout; **Editor:** Jack Dennis; **Cast:** Buster Crabbe, Kathleen Burke, Monte Blue, Glenn Erickson, Raymond Hatton, Stanley Andrews, Syd Saylor.

NEVADA RKO, 1944, B&W, 62 min. **Producer:** Herman Schlom; **Director:** Edward Killy; **Screenplay:** Herman Schlom; **Music:** Paul Sawtell; **Cinematographer:** Harry J. Wild; **Editor:** Roland Gross; **Cast:** Robert Mitchum, Anne Jeffreys, Guinn "Big Boy" Williams, Nancy Gates, Richard Martin, Craig Reynolds, Harry Woods, Edmund Glover.

In the third screen treatment of the Zane Grey novel, Robert Mitchum is Nevada Lacy, a young man nearly lynched for a crime he did not commit. He sets out to prove that the real culprits are a gang of claim jumpers. According to John Mitchum in his informative book *Them Ornery Mitchum Boys*, "Bob's portrayal of a cowboy named Nevada, his first starring role, earned picture makers' attention. From then on his roles began to take on greater significance."

Paramount made the first screen version of Grey's novel in 1927 and released the first sound version in 1935.

NEVADA BADMEN Monogram, 1951, B&W, 58 min. **Producer:** Vincent M. Fennally; **Director:** Lewis D. Collins; **Screenplay:** Joseph O'Donnell; **Cinematographer:** Ernest Miller; **Editor:** Richard Heermance; **Cast:** Whip Wilson, Fuzzy Knight, Jim Bannon, Phyllis Coates, I. Stanford Jolley.

NEVADA CITY Republic, 1941, B&W, 58 min. **Producer:** Joseph Kane; **Director:** Kane; **Screenplay:** James R. Webb; **Music:** Cy Feuer; **Cinematographer:** William Nobles; **Editor:** Lester Orlebeck; **Cast:** Roy Rogers, George "Gabby" Hayes, Sally Payne, George Cleveland, Joseph Crehan.

NEVADAN, THE (aka: THE MAN FROM NEVADA) Columbia, 1950, Color, 81 min. **Producers:** Harry Joe Brown and Randolph Scott; **Director:** Gordon Douglas; **Screenplay:** George W. George and George F. Slavin; **Music:** Arthur Morton; **Cinematographer:** Charles Lawton Jr.; **Editor:** Richard Fantl; **Cast:** Randolph Scott, Dorothy Malone, Forrest Tucker, Frank Faylen, George Macready, Charles Kemper.

Randolph Scott is an undercover lawman who teams with an outlaw to retrieve gold stolen by the outlaw's gang. There is plenty of action in this 1950 Columbia venture, with Scott stoic and strong and enough romance left for beautiful Dorothy Malone.

NEVADA SMITH Paramount, 1966, Color, 128 min, VHS. **Producer:** Henry Hathaway; **Director:** Hathaway; **Screenplay:** John Michael Hayes; **Music:** Alfred Newman; **Cinematographer:** Lucien Ballard; **Editor:** Frank Bracht; **Cast:** Steve McQueen, Karl Malden, Brian Keith, Arthur Kennedy, Suzanne Pleshette, Raf Vallone, Janet Margolin, Pat Hingle, Howard Da Silva, Martin Landau, Paul Fix, Gene Evans, Josephine Hutchinson, John Doucette.

Based on a character from Harold Robbin's novel *The Carpetbaggers*, Max Sand (Steve McQueen) is a young half-breed whose mother and father are brutally murdered by three men (Karl Malden, Arthur Kennedy, and Martin Landau). While setting out for revenge, he has the good fortune to meet with a traveling gunsmith named Jonas Cord (Brian Keith), who teaches him the tools of the gunman's trade. After learning his lessons well, Max—who changes his name to Nevada Smith—goes to great lengths to track down the killers. He dispatches them one by one, going so far as to land himself in a Louisiana jail so he can have access to one of the perpetrators.

McQueen lends his manly presence to the title role, but as author Jay Hyams notes in his *The Life and Times of the Western Movie*, McQueen—like halfbreed screen contemporaries Audrey Hepburn, Elvis Presley, and Paul Newman—does not really look like a Native American. Moreover, director Henry Hathaway, who helmed such top-notch Westerns as FROM HELL TO TEXAS (1958), and TRUE GRIT (1969), has an uneven hand in this film, with some scenes quite exciting and others extremely dull.

A prequel rather than a sequel, *Nevada Smith* was scripted by Michael Hayes, who also wrote the screenplay for *The Carpetbaggers* (1964), where the more adult Nevada Smith was played by Alan Ladd, who died shortly after the completion of the film. The film was shot on location in Bishop and Line Pine, California; and in Port Vincent, Louisiana, on the banks of the Amite River. McQueen, whose behavior gave Hathaway fits on the set, was paid $500,000 from Paramount Pictures (the film's budget was $4.5 million). Moreover, both Hathaway and Paramount bent over backwards to make sure that their irascible star was comfortable, with Paramount going to the extreme of giving him his own motor home.

NEWCOMERS, THE See *WILD COUNTRY* (1971).

NEW FRONTIER (aka: FRONTIER HORIZON) Republic, 1939, B&W, 57 min, VHS. **Producer:** William A. Berke (associate); **Director:** George Sherman; **Screenplay:** Betty Burbridge and Luci Ward; **Cinematographer:** Reggie Lanning; **Editor:** Tony Martinelli; **Cast:** John Wayne, Ray Corrigan, Raymond Hatton, Jennifer Jones (as Phyllis Isley), Eddie Waller.
See *THREE MESQUITEERS, THE.*

NEW MEXICO United Artists, 1951, B&W, 78 min, VHS. **Producers:** Irving Allen and Joseph Justman; **Director:** Irving Reis; **Screenplay:** Max Trell; **Music:** Lucian Moraweck; **Cinematographers:** Jack Greenhalgh and William E. Snyder; **Cast:** Lew Ayres, Marilyn Maxwell,

Andy Devine, Raymond Burr, Robert Hutton, Jeff Corey, John Hoyt, Ted de Corsia.

President Abraham Lincoln (Hans Conried) officiates at a peace settlement between the United States and Indian chief Acoma (Ted de Corsia), while members of the U.S. cavalry headed by Captain Hunt (Lew Ayers) look on. But hopes for peace are vanquished when Captain Hunt's superior officer breaks the provisions of the settlement following Lincoln's assassination. When two braves are killed by cavalry fire, Acoma swears vengeance, and Captain Hunt must go after the chief and his followers to prevent an all-out war.

The strongest element here is the film's capable cast, which includes Marilyn Maxwell as Cherry the dance-hall entertainer—although one must wonder why she is singing, dancing, and entertaining the troops in the dead of night with an Indian attack pending. While some credits list this as a color film, the video copy obtained for this 1951 film is in black and white, with "Filmed in Black and White" clearly indicated on the video jacket.

NIGHT OF THE GRIZZLY Paramount, 1966, Color, 102 min, VHS. **Producer:** Bill Dunne; **Director:** Joseph Pevney; **Screenplay:** Warren Douglas; **Music:** Leith Stevens; **Cinematographer:** Loyal Griggs and Harold Lipstein; **Editor:** Philip W. Anderson; **Cast:** Clint Walker, Martha Hyer, Keenan Wynn, Nancy Kulp, Kevin Brodie, Ellen Corby, Jack Elam, Ron Ely, Leo Gordon.

Jim Cole (Clint Walker) inherits land in Wyoming, so he trades his dangerous life as a lawman for the comparatively sedate life of a rancher. However, he has barely gotten settled when he has to face a menacing foe of a different sort: a treacherous grizzly on a murderous rampage. Compounding matters are angry neighbors who covet his property and the appearance of an outlaw he once sent to prison.

A genuinely fine film written by Warren Douglas, whom star Clint Walker called "a sleeping giant among the industry's top writers," *Night of the Grizzly* packs lots of action and adventure into a film that provides entertainment for the whole family. It remains the personal favorite for veteran actor Clint Walker.

NIGHT PASSAGE Universal, 1957, Color, 90 min. **Producer:** Aaron Rosenberg; **Director:** James Neilson; **Screenplay:** Bordon Chase; **Music:** Dimitri Tiomkin; **Cinematographer:** William Daniels; **Editor:** Sherman Todd; **Cast:** James Stewart, Audie Murphy, Dan Duryea, Dianne Foster, Elaine Stewart, Brandon De Wilde, Jay C. Flippen, Robert J. Wilke.

James Stewart and Audie Murphy are brothers on the opposite side of the law. Stewart is Grant McLaine, a frontier veteran who makes a living wandering from one construction camp to the next, entertaining crowds with his accordion. He can't get steady work because five years earlier, as a lawman, he let his outlaw brother escape after a holdup. Brother Audie Murphy is "The Utica Kid," whose career as a bandit

has been on the upswing during the intervening years. When Stewart takes a job protecting the railroad payroll, a showdown between the two brothers becomes inevitable.

Anthony Mann, who directed Stewart in a series of outstanding westerns, reportedly bailed out helming this picture after the first day of shooting, and the director's chair was given to James Neilson, a TV producer making his screen debut as a director. A solid western dealing with a brother vs. brother theme, the film benefits from its superb Colorado location shots and Dimitri Tiomkin's first-rate musical score. Brandon De Wilde (as Joey Adams) makes his second screen appearance since his spectacular success in George Stevens's *SHANE* (1953) four years earlier. Just to allay doubts, it really is Jimmy Stewart playing the accordion and singing two Dimitri Tiomkin/Ned Washington songs, "Follow the River" and "You Can't Get Far Without a Railroad."

NIGHT RAIDERS Monogram, 1952, B&W, 52 min. **Producer:** Vincent Fennally; **Director:** Howard Bretherton; **Screenplay:** Maurice Tombragel; **Cinematographer:** Ernest Miller; **Editor:** Sam Fields; **Cast:** Whip Wilson, Fuzzy Knight, Lois Hall, Marshal Bradford.

NIGHT RIDERS, THE (aka: LONE STAR BULLETS) Republic, 1939, B&W, 57 min. **Producer:** William A. Berke (associate); **Director:** George Sherman; **Screenplay:** Betty Burbridge and Stanley Roberts; **Music:** William Lava; **Cinematographer:** Jack A. Marta; **Editor:** Lester Orlebeck; **Cast:** John Wayne, Ray Corrigan, Max Terhune, Doreen McKay, Ruth Rogers George Douglas, Tom Tyler, Kermit Maynard.

NIGHT RIDERS OF MONTANA Republic, 1951, B&W, 60 min. **Producer:** Gordon Kay (associate); **Director:** Fred C. Brannon; **Screenplay:** M. Coates Webster; **Music:** R. Dale Butts, Nathan Scott, and Stanley Wilson; **Cinematographer:** John MacBurnie; **Editor:** Irving M. Schoenberg; **Cast:** Allan Lane, Chubby Jackson, Myron Healey, Claudia Barrett, Arthur Space.

NIGHT STAGE TO GALVESTON Columbia/ Gene Autry Productions, 1952, B&W, 61 min. **Producer:** Armand Schaefer; **Director:** George Archainbaud; **Screenplay:** Norman Hall; **Music:** Mischa Bakaleinikoff; **Cinematographer:** William Bradford; **Editor:** James Sweeney; **Cast:** Gene Autry, Pat Buttram, Virginia Huston, Thurston Hall, Judy Nugent, Robert Livingston.

When Gene Autry discovers that some Texas law officers are corrupt, he decides to put on his old Texas Ranger uniform and set things straight. A good story highlights this entertaining Autry venture produced by his own production company.

NIGHT TIME IN NEVADA Republic, 1948, Color, 67 min. **Producer:** Edward J. White; **Director:** William

Witney; **Screenplay:** Sloan Nibley; **Music:** R. Dale Butts; **Cinematographer:** Jack A. Marta; **Editor:** Tony Martinelli; **Cast:** Roy Rogers, Adele Mara, Andy Devine, Grant Withers, Marie Harmon, Bob Nolan.

See UNDER WESTERN STARS.

NO NAME ON THE BULLET   Universal, 1959, Color, 77 min, VHS. **Producers:** Jack Arnold and Howard Christie; **Director:** Arnold; **Screenplay:** Gene L. Coon; **Music:** Herman Stein; **Cinematographer:** Harold Lipstein; **Editor:** Frank Gross; **Cast:** Audie Murphy, Charles Drake, Joan Evans, Virginia Grey, Warren Stevens, R. G. Armstrong.

A hired assassin named John Gant rides into town. While his identity is known, the identity of the person he is after is not. Certain citizens with shady pasts and guilty consciences become increasingly concerned. One by one they start falling apart, eventually killing themselves or each other in one of Audie Murphy's best films. The ending holds quite a surprise.

NOOSE FOR A GUNMAN   United Artists, 1960, B&W, 90 min. **Producer:** Robert E. Kent; **Director:** Edward L. Cahn; **Screenplay:** Kent; **Music:** Paul Sawtell and Bert Shefter; **Cinematographer:** Walter Strenge; **Editor:** Michael Minth; **Cast:** Jim Davis, Barton MacLane, Lyn Thomas, Leo Gordon, Harry Carey Jr., John Hart, Kermit Maynard.

A gunslinger named Case Britton (Jim Davis) rides into town to meet his future bride, stop a stagecoach robbery, and get even with the man who killed his brother. Jim Davis, always an underappreciated performer, does a fine job as the honest gunman who was banished from town for killing a land baron's two sons, then returns to settle some old scores.

NORTHERN FRONTIER   Ambassador, 1935, B&W, 57 min. **Producer:** Maurice Conn; **Director:** Sam Newfield; **Screenplay:** Barry Barringer; **Cinematographer:** Edgar Lyons; **Editor:** Lyons; **Cast:** Kermit Maynard, Eleanor Hunt, Russell Hopton, J. Farrell MacDonald, LeRoy Mason, Walter Brennan, Tyrone Power, Dick Curtis, Lafe McKee.

NORTH FROM LONE STAR   Columbia, 1941, B&W, 58 min. **Producer:** Leon Barsha; **Director:** Lambert Hillyer; **Screenplay:** Charles F. Royal; **Cinematographer:** Benjamin H. Kline; **Editor:** Mel Thorsen; **Cast:** William "Wild Bill" Elliott, Richard Friske, Dorothy Fay, Dub Taylor, Arthur Loft.

When a crook takes over the town of Deadwood and makes Wild Bill Hickok its marshal, Hickok decides to clean up the town in this action-packed oater featuring a brawling saloon fight. (See also WILDCAT OF TUCSON, THE.)

NORTH OF '36   Paramount, 1924, B&W, 78 min. **Producer:** Jesse Lasky; **Director:** Irvin Willat; **Screenplay:** James Shelley Hamilton; **Cinematographer:** Alfred Gilks; **Cast:** Jack Holt, Lois Wilson, Ernest Torrence, Noah Beery, David Dunbar, Guy Oliver, George Irving.

This is Paramount's first adaptation of the Emerson Hough story, published originally as a serial in The Saturday Evening Post, about the first post-Civil War cattle drive from Texas to Abilene. Dan McMasters (Jack Holt) and Jim Nabours (Ernest Torrence) join Taisie Lockhart (Lois Wilson) on a thousand-mile journey across Indian country to get her longhorns to the railroad in Kansas. At the same time, Dan fights to prevent ex-outlaw and treasurer of Texas Sim Rudabaugh (Noah Beery) from amassing a fortune in stolen land scrip, including that to Taisie's ranch. Considered a sequel to Paramount's hugely popular western epic, The Covered Wagon (1923), North of '36 was well received but not nearly as critically nor commercially successful as the first film.

Paramount later made two sound versions of the story, The Conquering Horde in 1931 and The Texans in 1938.

NORTH OF THE GREAT DIVIDE   Republic, 1950, Color, 67 min, VHS. **Producer:** Edward J. White; **Director:** William Witney; **Screenplay:** Eric Taylor; **Music:** R. Dale Butts; **Cinematographer:** Jack A. Marta; **Editor:** Tony Martinelli; **Cast:** Roy Rogers, Penny Edwards, Gordon Jones, Roy Barcroft, Jack Lambert.

NORTH OF THE RIO GRANDE   Paramount, 1937, B&W, 70 min, VHS. **Producer:** Harry Sherman; **Director:** Nate Watt; **Screenplay:** Jack O'Donnell; **Cinematographer:** Russell Harlan; **Editor:** Robert Warwick; **Cast:** William Boyd, George "Gabby" Hayes, Russell Hayden, Morris Ankrum, Lee J. Cobb, Cliff Lyons, Lafe McKee.

NORTH OF THE YUKON   Columbia, 1939, B&W, 59 min. **Director:** Sam Nelson; **Screenplay:** Bennett Cohen; **Cinematographer:** George Meehan; **Editor:** William A. Lyon; **Cast:** Charles Starrett, Dorothy Comingore, Bob Nolan, Paul Sutton, Robert Fiske.

See GALLANT DEFENDER.

NORTH TO ALASKA   20th Century Fox, 1960, Color, 122 min, VHS. **Producers:** Henry Hathaway and John Lee Mahin; **Director:** Hathaway; **Screenplay:** John Lee Mahin, Martin Rakin, and Claud Binyon; **Music:** Lionel Newman; **Cinematographer:** Leon Shamroy; **Editor:** Dorothy Spencer; **Cast:** John Wayne, Stewart Granger, Ernie Kovacs, Fabian, Capucine, Mickey Shaughnessy, Karl Swenson.

Sam McCord (John Wayne) and George Pratt (Stewart Granger) are two partners who strike gold in Alaska. Now wealthy, George sends Sam to Seattle to bring back his fiancée, while he stays in Alaska to build a honeymoon cabin for his bride. Meanwhile, con man Frankie Canon (Ernie Kovacs) schemes to steal their claim. Back in Seattle, Sam is surprised to learn that his partner's beloved is already married. Bemused, he takes refuge in a honky-tonk, where he meets the alluring Michelle (Capucine), who is only too eager to take advantage of Sam's golden generosity.

When Sam is about to return to Alaska, he hits on an idea. He will take Michelle back with him as compensation. The problem is that she believes she is going to Alaska to be with Sam. Once there, she is taken to a hotel owned by Frankie, whom we are surprised to learn was her former lover. Frankie is determined to revive the relationship, but by now Michelle is hopelessly in love with Sam.

Reviewers generally liked the film. *The Hollywood Reporter* said the picture "plays for laughs, and in its purely male, boisterous way, it gets a good many of them. It is a thoroughly enjoyable film." *Variety* was in a similar frame of mind, calling the film the "sort of easy going, slap-happy entertaining that doesn't come around often anymore in films." *North to Alaska* grossed more than $10 million and turned in a substantial profit for 20th Century Fox. As he had done for previous films, Wayne suggested a reigning teen heartthrob to appear in the movie. This time it's pop singing star Fabian as Billy Pratt, George's younger brother. He followed Ricky Nelson in *RIO BRAVO* (1959) and Frankie Avalon in *THE ALAMO* (1960). The hit song "North to Alaska" was introduced on the soundtrack by Johnny Horton, who also recorded it for Columbia.

NORTHWEST MOUNTED POLICE Paramount, 1940, Color, 125 min. **Producer:** Cecil B. DeMille; **Directors:** DeMille, Arthur Rossen, and Eric Stacy; **Screenplay:** Alan LeMay, Jesse Lasky Jr., and G. Gardner Sullivan; **Music:** Victor Young; **Cinematographer:** Victor Milner and W. Howard Greene; **Editor:** Ann Bauchens; **Cast:** Gary Cooper, Madeleine Carroll, Preston Foster, Paulette Goddard, Robert Preston.

A 1940s film extravaganza, Cecil B. DeMille's *Northwest Mounted Police* has Gary Cooper as a Texas Ranger heading north into Canada in search of a murderer. In the process he stumbles on an insurrection waged by discontented settlers against Canadian troops. Into the plot are woven two love stories, which play out simultaneously and are neatly integrated into the exciting Northwest tapestry in pure DeMille grandeur.

Northwest Mounted Police was not only the first Cecil B. DeMille film to be shot entirely in Technicolor; it was also Gary Cooper's first color feature film. Yet in spite of Cooper's presence, a first-rate veteran cast, one Oscar (Best Editing), four other Academy Award nominations (Best Color Cinematography, Color Art Direction, Original Score, Sound), and strong audience appeal, reviews have been wanting. Film historian William Everson calls it DeMille's slowest and dullest western. This opinion is shared by Michael Parkinson and Clyde Jeavons in *A Pictorial History of Westerns*, calling it "a crashingly dull picture with minimal action. . . ."

Particularly lacking were the types of performances one would come to expect from an all-star cast that includes Cooper, Madeleine Carroll, Preston Foster, Robert Preston, and an incredibly sensuous Paulette Goddard as Lovette, the half-breed Indian girl who leads Mountie Preston down the road to deceit and destruction.

Yet contemporary reviewers were not as hard on the film as Everson and others, as is seen in review excerpts offered by James Parish and Michael Pitts in their *Great Western Pictures*. *Time* magazine was pleased, calling *Northwest Mounted Police* " . . . a movie in the grand style . . ."; while the *New York Journal American* found it to be "bang-up entertainment, a large-scale outdoor melodrama, with exciting soldier-and-Injun fights and boasting gorgeous Technicolored shots off Canada's mountains, lakes and forests. . . ."

NORTHWEST PASSAGE MGM, 1940, Color, 125 min, VHS. **Producer:** Hunt Stromberg; **Director:** King Vidor; **Screenplay:** Talbot Jennings and Laurence Stallings; **Music:** Herbert Stoddard; **Cinematographer:** William V. Skall and Sidney Wagner; **Editor:** Conrad Nurvig; **Cast:** Spencer Tracy, Robert Young, Walter Brennan, Ruth Hussey, Nat Pendleton, Robert Barrat.

Two years after winning successive Oscars (*Captains Courageous*, 1937; and *Boys Town*, 1938), Spencer Tracy stars as Major Robert Rogers, the commander of the famed Rogers Rangers. Based on the book by Kenneth Roberts and set in colonial America during the French and Indian War, the film faithfully tells the story of a group of Rangers sent up to the French-Canadian woods to wipe out a village of enemy-aiding Indian warriors amid a series of hardships and strife. Nominated for an Oscar for Best Color Cinematography, this excellent film scores high points on almost all levels: casting, musical score, photography, and audience interest, including a river-fording sequence that is brilliantly staged. While some may say it is not of the western genre per se, *Northwest Passage*, like *DRUMS ALONG THE MOHAWK* (1939) and *THE LAST OF THE MOHICANS* (1936), incorporates so much of our forgotten frontier heritage that it makes for a viable entry in any collection of western cinematic endeavors.

NORTHWEST STAMPEDE Eagle Lion, 1948, Color, 79 min. **Producer:** Albert S. Rogell; **Director:** Rogell; **Screenplay:** Art Arthur and Lillie Hayward; **Music:** Paul Sawtell; **Cinematographer:** John W. Boyle; **Editor:** Philip Cahn; **Cast:** Joan Leslie, James Craig, Jack Oakie, Chill Wills.

Female rancher Joan Leslie and rodeo champion foreman James Craig battle over whether to corral a wild stallion. No longer at the peak of their star appeal, Leslie and Craig do what they can to keep this average oater moving, with some help from a good supporting cast and some fine color scenery.

OATH OF VENGEANCE PRC, 1944, B&W, 57 min. **Producer:** Sigmund Neufeld; **Director:** Sam Newfield; **Screenplay:** Fred Myton; **Cinematographer:** Robert E. Cline; **Cast:** Buster Crabbe, Al St. John, Mady Laurence, Jack Ingram, Charles King.

Billy Carson (Buster Crabbe) and Fuzzy Knight (Al St. John) try to prove that a young man is innocent of murder. (See also *OUTLAW OF THE PLAINS*.)

OH, PROMISE ME See *HIDDEN GOLD* (1932).

OH, SUSANNA Republic, 1936, B&W, 59 min, VHS. **Producer:** Nat Levine; **Director:** Joseph Kane; **Screenplay:** Oliver Drake; **Music:** Gene Autry, Smiley Burnette, Oliver Drake, and Sam H. Step; **Cinematographer:** William Nobles; **Editor:** Lester Orlebeck; **Cast:** Gene Autry, Smiley Burnette, Frances Grant, Earle Hodgins, Donald Kirke, Boothe Howard.

OH, SUSANNA Republic, 1951, Color, 84 min. **Producer:** Joseph Kane; **Director:** Kane; **Screenplay:** Charles Marquis Warren; **Music:** R. Dale Butts; **Cinematographer:** Jack A. Marta; **Editor:** Arthur Roberts; **Cast:** Rod Cameron, Lorna Gray, Forrest Tucker, Chill Wills, John Compton, William Haade, Jim Davis.

Rod Cameron is a cavalry commander with a duty to defend settlers from a Sioux attack, but tensions increase when a rivalry with another officer threatens the unity of his command.

OKLAHOMA! Magna, 1955, Color, 143 min, VHS. **Producer:** Arthur Hornblow Jr.; **Director:** Fred Zinnemann; **Screenplay:** Sonya Levien and William Ludwig; **Music:** Richard Rodgers and Oscar Hammerstein II; **Cinematographer:** Robert Surtees; **Editor:** Gene Ruggerio; **Cast:** Gordon MacRae, Shirley Jones, Gloria Grahame, Gene Nelson, Eddie Albert, Charlotte Greenwood, Rod Steiger, James Whitmore, J. C. Flippen, Roy Barcroft.

Rodgers and Hammerstein's landmark Broadway musical was brought to the screen in 1955 with Gordon MacRae as Curly and 20-year-old Shirley Jones (in her film debut) as Laurie. A completely joyful musical with a decidedly western bent, the film, like the stage production, features some of Richard Rodgers's and Oscar Hammerstein's most beautiful and lyrical songs—"People Will Say We're in Love," "Oh What a Beautiful Mornin'," "The Surrey with the Fringe on Top"; two marvelous production numbers—"Everything's Up To Date in Kansas City" (with superb hoofing by Gene Nelson as Will Parker) and "The Farmer and the Cowman"; and the rousing title song, to celebrate the fact that the Oklahoma Territory is soon to become a state.

When Gordon MacRae was cast as Curly, he brought all the necessary ingredients to the role—except the ability to handle a horse. Consequently he enlisted the help of Ben Johnson, the man considered the best horseman in the movie business, who was working as a wrangler on the set. Well-publicized newcomer Shirley Jones, a former Miss Pittsburgh, won raves as Laurie, the alluring "girl next door." Their musical magic worked so well that MacRae and Jones would be teamed together once more as the romantic lovers in the screen version of Rodgers and Hammerstein's *Carousel* (1956).

The incomparable Agnes de Mille choreographed the dance numbers, and the sprightly cast included Method actor Rod Steiger as Judd, the crazed hired hand; and sultry, Oscar-winning dramatic actress Gloria Grahame as Ado Annie, "the girl who "can't say no." With these ingredients the film grossed $7.1 million in distributors' domestic rentals. Filmed in Eastman color and the Todd-AO widescreen process, *Oklahoma!* won Academy Awards for Best Sound Recording and Best Scoring of a Musical Picture; and two additional Oscar nominations for Best Color Cinematography and Best Editing.

As a point of reference, the 1943 stage production was based on Lynn Riggs's play *Green Grow the Lilacs*. It had a Broadway run of 2,212 performances, with Alfred Drake cast as the original Curly, Joan Roberts as Laurie, and future Oscar-winning actress Celeste Holm as Ado Annie.

OKLAHOMA ANNIE Republic, 1952, Color, 90 min, VHS. **Producers:** Sidney Picker and R. G. Springsteen; **Screenplay:** Charles E. Roberts; **Cinematographer:** Jack A. Marta; **Editor:** Richard L. Van Enger; **Cast:** Judy Canova, John Russell, Grant Withers, Roy Barcroft, Emmett Lynn, Frank Furguson.

Judy Canova (playing herself) becomes involved in cleaning up corruption in her town. This fun-packed little venture has Judy as a backwoods girl who runs a gunshop. But when she falls for the town's new sheriff, he tries to get her out of his hair by making her his deputy. Inept as she is, she still manages to corral a robbery suspect.

OKLAHOMA BADLANDS Republic, 1948, B&W, 59 min, VHS. **Producer:** Gordon Kay; **Director:** Yakima Canutt; **Screenplay:** Bob Williams; **Cinematographer:** John MacBurnie; **Editor:** Arthur Roberts; **Cast:** Allan Lane, Eddy Walker, Mildred Coles, Roy Barcroft, Gene Roth, Earl Hodgins, House Peters Jr.

OKLAHOMA BLUES Monogram, 1948, B&W, 56 min. **Producer:** Louis Gray; **Director:** Lambert Hillyer; **Screenplay:** Bennett Cohen; **Cinematographer:** Harry Neumann; **Editor:** Fred Maguire; **Cast:** Jimmy Wakely, Dub Taylor, Virginia Belmont, Steve Clark, I. Stanford Jolley.

OKLAHOMA FRONTIER Universal, 1939, B&W, 59 min. **Producer:** Albert Ray; **Director:** Ford Beebe; **Screenplay:** Beebe; **Cinematographer:** Jerome Ash; **Editor:** Louis Sackin; **Cast:** Johnny Mack Brown, Bob Baker, Fuzzy Knight, Anne Gwynne, James Blaine, Bob Kortman.

OKLAHOMA KID, THE Warner Bros., 1939, B&W, 85 min. **Producers:** Hal B. Wallis and Jack L. Warner; **Director:** Lloyd Bacon; **Screenplay:** Warren Duff and Edward E. Paramour Jr.; **Music:** Max Steiner; **Cinematographer:** James Wong Howe; **Editor:** Owen Marks; **Cast:** James Cagney, Humphrey Bogart, Rosemary Lane, Donald Crisp, Harvey Stephens.

Although James Cagney and Humphrey Bogart are better associated with the gangster films of the 1930s, this Warner Bros. western still satisfies. Cagney is Jim Kincaid, aka the Oklahoma Kid, a rebel turned outlaw who is bent on aveng-

ing the lynching death of his father, a judge. Humphrey Bogart, dressed all in black, is the nefarious Whip McCord, leader of the bandit group responsible for the death of the Kid's father.

The film was Cagney's first western and his third pairing with Bogart. In all three films, a gunfight determined the victor. Cagney, the bigger star at the time, was always the winner. Critics questioned the wisdom of transferring Cagney and Bogart from the milieu of city streets to the dusty plains of the Old West. Yet in a paradoxical way, the two screen legends wear their spurs and Stetsons surprisingly well.

The film has plenty of action as well as a slice or two of mirth and sentiment, not least a scene where Cagney lulls a Mexican baby to sleep while singing a lullaby in Spanish. (Cagney, it should be noted, started his career as a song-and-dance man, with his personal motto always being "once a song and dance man, always a song and dance man.") After dispatching an adversary with his gun, he even blows smoke out of his revolver barrel, homage to one of the most basic western clichés.

Warner Bros. had not produced many grand epics in the 1930s, the closest being the lackluster *GOLD IS WHERE YOU FIND IT* (1938). It suddenly embraced the genre the following year with *The Oklahoma Kid*, which William K. Everson calls "one of the most enjoyable of all good badman movies"; and with *DODGE CITY* (1939), the first of the big Errol Flynn outdoor epics.

Interestingly, *The Oklahoma Kid* plays better today than it did to movie audiences when it was first released. This was because 1939 was arguably the most vintage of all film years, and when compared to *STAGECOACH*, a John Ford masterpiece released the same year, this movie was seen initially as little better than a pedestrian entry in the genre.

OKLAHOMAN, THE Allied Artists, 1957, Color, 80 min. **Producer:** Walter Mirisch; **Director:** Francis D. Lyon; **Screenplay:** Daniel B. Ullman; **Music:** Hans J. Salter; **Cinematographer:** Carl E. Guthrie; **Editor:** George White; **Cast:** Joel McCrea, Barbara Hale, Brad Dexter, Gloria Talbott, Verna Felton, Michael Pate, Douglas Dick, Anthony Caruso, Ray Teal.

Joel McCrea is Dr. John Brighton, a hard-working physician whose wife dies in childbirth. He settles in a small western town where he becomes a respected member of the community. When cattle barons Cass and Mel Dobie (Brad Dexter and Douglas Dick) discover oil on Indian Charlie's (Michael Pate) land, they try to take over his small spread. Indian Charlie is forced to kill Mel Dobie in self-defense, and Doc comes to his defense, eventually thwarting Cass Dobie's ploy to have Charlie tried and hung for murder.

In the meantime the town gossips start suspecting that Doc is romantically involved with the 18-year-old Indian girl (Gloria Talbott) who works as his housekeeper and happens to be Indian Charlie's daughter. (In 1957 Talbott also played the title role in *Daughter of Dr. Jekyll*.) While the Indian girl is in love with Doc, he thinks of her only as a sweet vulnerable young lady. His true lady love is Annie Barnes (Barbara

Hale), who owns one of the biggest ranches in town. Unfortunately for a time Annie prefers to believe the insidious rumors about Doc and the girl.

As usual, McCrea is made for the western saddle, and the film itself is a classy low-budget venture with something for the whole family and where the line between good and evil, right and wrong, is clearly defined.

OKLAHOMA RAIDERS Universal, 1944, B&W, 57 min. **Director:** Lewis D. Collins; **Screenplay:** Betty Burbridge; **Music:** Johnny Bends; **Cinematographer:** William A. Sickner; **Editor:** Norman A. Cerf; **Cast:** Tex Ritter, Fuzzy Knight, Jennifer Holt, Dennis Moore, Jack Ingram.

Steve Nolan (Tex Ritter), a lieutenant in the Union army, is sent to Oklahoma disguised as a drifter. His mission is to stop a masked bandit known as El Vengador, who has been leading a series of raids against the cavalry. Featuring one of Ritter's very best starring roles, this outing combines plenty of action, a good story, a fine supporting cast, and five nice songs including "Cowboy's Dream" and "Starlight on the Prairie." It is an excellent entry to the B western catalogue.

OKLAHOMA RENEGADES Republic, 1940, B&W, 57 min. **Producer:** Harry Grey (assistant); **Director:** Nate Watt; **Screenplay:** Doris Schroeder and Earle Snell; **Cinematographer:** Reggie Lanning; **Editor:** Tony Martinelli; **Cast:** Robert Livingston, Raymond Hatton, Duncan Renaldo, Lee "Lesses" White, Florine McKinney.

OKLAHOMA TERRITORY United Artists, 1960, B&W, 67 min. **Producer:** Robert E. Kent; **Director:** Edward L. Cahn; **Screenplay:** Orville H. Hampton; **Music:** Albert Glasser; **Cinematographer:** Walter Strenge; **Editor:** Grant Whytock; **Cast:** Bill Williams, Gloria Talbott, Ted de Corsia, Grant Richards, Walter Sande.

A local Indian commissioner is murdered, and an Indian chief is charged with the crime. However, District Attorney Temple Houston (Bill Williams), believing the chief to be innocent, sets out to find the real killer.

OKLAHOMA WOMAN American Releasing Corp, 1956, B&W, 73 min. **Producer:** Roger Corman; **Director:** Corman; **Screenplay:** Lou Rusoff; **Music:** Ronald Stein; **Cinematographer:** Frederick E. West; **Editor:** Ronald Sinclair; **Cast:** Peggie Castle, Richard Denning, Cathy Downs, Tudor Owens.

An ex-gunfighter, released from prison after seven years, returns to his Oklahoma ranch, where his former girlfriend tries to frame him for murder. The tag line "Queen of the Outlaws, Queen of Sin" pretty much says it all. There is little that appeals in this early Roger Corman venture, except for diehard fans of the producer/director.

OLD BARN DANCE, THE Republic, 1938, B&W, 60 min, VHS. **Producer:** Sol C. Siegal; **Director:** Joseph Kane; **Screenplay:** Bernard McConville and Charles Royal; **Cinematographer:** Ernest Miller; **Editor:** Lester Orlebeck; **Cast:** Gene Autry, Smiley Burnette, Joan Valerie, Sammy McKim, Roy Rogers (as Dick Weston), Ivan Miller, George Montgomery, Bob Nolan.

OLD CHISHOLM TRAIL, THE Universal, 1942, B&W, 61 min. **Director:** Elmer Clifton; **Screenplay:** Clifton; **Music:** Hans Salter; **Cinematographer:** William A. Sickner; **Editor:** Ray Snyder; **Cast:** Johnny Mack Brown, Tex Ritter, Fuzzy Knight, Jennifer Holt, Mady Correll, Earle Hodgins, Roy Barcroft, Edmund Cobb, Budd Buster, Jimmy Wakely and his trio.

The female owner of a trading post challenges a woman gambler after the latter succeeds in running a cowboy out of town over water rights. Two strong male leads, Johnny Mack Brown and Tex Ritter, vie for Jennifer Holt, who is at odds with other woman Mady Correll.

Johnny Mack Brown's likable personality, acting style, and athletic prowess made him a natural for B westerns. From 1938 through 1943, he made some 30 films for Universal. After his initial series, which costarred Bob Baker, he was presented solo and then finally teamed with Tex Ritter before signing on with Monogram. His sidekick was mainly Fuzzy Knight, and his leading lady was often Nell O'Day, a fine stunt rider in her own right and a real asset to the series.

Brown's series of films with Universal were more concerned with a fast-action format than with plot, a departure from the studio's prior series with Buck Jones and Ken Maynard. Because of his tremendous athletic ability, Johnny Mack used fewer doubles than most stars in his fights and his leaps. After he departed for Monogram, Universal's final group of B westerns with Rod Cameron, Eddie Dew, and Kirby Grant were of a far lesser quality.

Johnny Mack Brown's series films for Universal include *FLAMING FRONTIERS* (1938); *DESPERATE TRAILS, OKLAHOMA FRONTIER, THE OREGON TRAIL* (1939); *CHIP OF THE FLYING U, BOSS OF BULLION CITY, RIDERS OF PASCO BASIN, BAD MAN FROM RED BUTTE, RAGTIME COWBOY JOE, Law and Order, PONY POST, WEST OF CARSON CITY, SON OF ROARING DAN* (1940); *BURY ME NOT ON THE LONE PRAIRIE, Rawhide Rangers, MAN FROM MONTANA, THE MASKED RIDER, ARIZONA CYCLONE, FIGHTING BILL FARGO, LAW OF THE RANGE* (1941); *STAGECOACH BUCKAROO, THE SILVER BULLET, RIDE 'EM COWBOY, LITTLE JOE THE WRANGLER, DEEP IN THE HEART OF TEXAS, Boss of Hangman Mesa, THE OLD CHISHOLM TRAIL,* (1942); *TENTING TONIGHT ON THE OLD CAMP GROUND, CHEYENNE ROUNDUP, RAIDERS OF SAN JOAQUIN, LONE STAR TRAIL* (1943).

OLD CORRAL, THE (aka: TEXAS SERENADE, UK) Republic, 1936, B&W, 55 min. **Producer:** Nat Levine; **Director:** Joseph Kane; **Screenplay:** Sherman L. Lowe and Joseph F. Poland; **Music:** Fleming Allen, Gene Autry, and Oliver Drake; **Cinematographer:** Edgar Lyons; **Editors:** Lyons and Lester Orlebeck, **Cast:** Gene Autry, Smiley Burnette, Irene Manning (as Hope Manning), Cornelius Keefe, Lon Chaney Jr.

Irene (Hope) Manning is a Chicago singer who witnesses a gangland murder. Fearing for her life, she heads west to a small town where a local gambler recognizes her and informs the gangsters who are out to silence her. However, Gene Autry is the sheriff, and he immediately sets out to help her.

Young Irene Manning went on to a distinguished career as a singer, stage actress, and film star, later appearing in *Yankee Doodle Dandy* (1942) with Jimmy Cagney, and costarring with Dennis Morgan in the 1944 film adaptation of *The Desert Song* (1943). In an interview with the author, Manning, who was trained in opera, remembered her screen debut in Gene Autry's *The Old Corral* more than 65 years ago.

> Gene [Autry] was very nice and gave me a kiss at the end of the movie. The boys all laughed like crazy. He never did it again. Smiley Burnette was fun. Roy Rogers was there and so were the Sons of the Pioneers. I was a student of serious music, so a western setting was a bit shocking. But I received some very good advice from the musical director Harry Grey. When I started improvising with my trained voice, he came over to me and said three words, "Keep It Simple." It was the best bit of advice I could have gotten, and I heeded those three words throughout my career.

OLD FRONTIER, THE Republic, 1950, B&W, 60 min. **Producer:** Melville Tucker; **Director:** Philip Ford; **Screenplay:** Bob Williams; **Cinematographer:** Ellis W. Carter; **Editor:** Harold Minter; **Cast:** Monte Hale, Paul Hurst, Claudia Barrett, William Henry, Tristram Coffin, Denver Pyle, Lane Bradford.

OLD LOS ANGELES (aka: CALIFORNIA OUTPOST; IN OLD CALIFORNIA) Republic, 1948, B&W, 87 min. **Producer:** Joseph Kane; **Director:** Kane; **Screenplay:** Gerald Drayson Adams and Clements Ripley; **Music:** Ernest Gold and Nathan Scott; **Cinematographer:** William Bradford; **Editor:** Richard L. Van Enger; **Cast:** William "Wild Bill" Elliott, John Carroll, Catherine McLeod, Joseph Shildkraut, Andy Devine, Estelita Rodriguez, Grant Withers, Roy Barcroft.

A lawman from Missouri heads to Los Angeles to prospect for gold but finds that his brother and several miners have been murdered. This action-packed Bill Elliott western is one of his fine A-level westerns with Republic. Unfortunately, adult audiences never quite took to Bill Elliott as the kids had, and by 1950 he was back to making B westerns, this time for Monogram.

OLD LOUISIANA (aka: LOUISIANA GAL) Crescent, 1937, B&W, 60 min. **Producer:** E. R. Derr; **Director:** Irwin Willat; **Screenplay:** Mary Ireland; **Music:** Abe Meyer; **Cinematographer:** Arthur Martinelli; **Editor:** Donald Barratt; **Cast:** Tom Keene, Rita Hayworth (as Rita Cansino), Robert Fiske, Ray Bennett, Budd Buster.

OLD OVERLAND TRAIL, THE Republic, 1953, B&W, 60 min. **Director:** William Witney; **Screenplay:** Milton Raison; **Music:** R. Dale Butts; **Cinematographer:** John MacBurnie; **Editor:** Harold Mintner; **Cast:** Rex Allen, Slim Pickens, Roy Barcroft, Virginia Hall, Gil Herman.

OLD TEXAS TRAIL, THE Universal, 1944, B&W, 60 min. **Producer:** Oliver Drake; **Director:** Lewis D. Collins; **Screenplay:** William Lively; **Music:** Paul Sawtell; **Cinematographer:** William Sickner; **Editor:** Saul A. Goodkind; **Cast:** Rod Cameron, Virginia Christine, Marjorie Clements, Jack Clifford, Edmund Cobb.

Three cowboys come to the aid of a young girl who is about to lose the option rights to her stagecoach line, and they thwart the efforts of the crooked gang that is after her contract. This strong entry in Universal's slate of B westerns features the underrated Rod Cameron providing a sturdy hero.

OLD WEST, THE Columbia, 1952, B&W, 61 min. **Producer:** Armond Schaefer; **Director:** George Archainbaud; **Screenplay:** Gerald Geraghty; **Music:** Mischa Bakaleinikoff; **Cinematographer:** William Bradford; **Editor:** James Sweeney; **Cast:** Gene Autry, Pat Buttram, Gail Davis, Lyle Talbot, Louis Jean Heydt, House Peters, House Peters Jr., Dickey Jones.

This somewhat offbeat Gene Autry entry has a horse wrangler helping a sky pilot who is trying to bring religion to a small town. A traveling minister comes to his aid following an attack.

OLD WYOMING TRAIL Columbia, 1937, B&W, 56 min. **Producer:** Harry L. Decker; **Director:** Folmer Blangsted; **Screenplay:** Ed Earl Repp; **Cast:** Charles Starrett, Donald Grayson, Barbara Weeks, Dick Curtis, George Chesebro, Edward Le Saint, Guy Usher.

OLD YELLER Walt Disney Pictures, 1957, Color, 83 min, VHS, DVD. **Producers:** Walt Disney and Bill Anderson (associate producer), Simon Wincer (coexecutive producer); **Director:** Robert Stevenson; **Screenplay:** Fred Gipson and William Tunberg (novel by Gipson); **Music:** Oliver Wallace; **Cinematographer:** Charles P. Boyle; **Editor:** Stanley Johnson; **Cast:** Fess Parker, Dorothy McGuire, Chuck Connors, Jeff York, Tommy Kirk, Beverly Washburn, Kevin Corcoran.

Living on the frontier in the 1860s, a teenager whose father is away on a cattle drive adopts a stray dog that wanders into the homestead. Reluctantly accepted at first, the dog soon proves its loyalty and becomes a vital member of the family. This warm-hearted classic was adapted from the novel by Fred Gipson.

OMAHA TRAIL, THE MGM, 1942, B&W, 61 min. **Producer:** Jack Chertok; **Director:** Edward Buzzell; **Screenplay:** Hugo Butler and Jesse Lasky Jr.; **Music:** David Snell; **Cinematographer:** Sidney Wagner; **Editor:** Conrad B. Nervig; **Cast:** James Craig, Pamela Blake, Dean Jagger, Edward Ellis, Chill Wills, Donald Meek, Howard da Silva, Harry Morgan, Morris Ankrum.

A crew of men who are hauling a locomotive by freight wagon to Omaha find themselves defenseless in the wake of an impending Indian attack because a band of crooks has confiscated all their guns. Despite a fine cast, especially excellent supporting players, this mediocre oater with lots of stock footage falls far short of the film one might expect.

O'MALLEY OF THE MOUNTED 20th Century Fox, 1936, B&W, 59 min. **Producer:** Sol Lesser; **Director:** David Howard; **Screenplay:** Frank Howard Clark and Daniel Jarrett; **Cinematographer:** Frank B. Good; **Editor:** Arthur Hilton; **Cast:** George O'Brien, Irene Ware, Stanley Fields, James Bush, Victor Potel, Reginald Barlow.

George O'Brien is a Mountie who infiltrates an outlaw gang terrorizing the U.S. border towns. He originates a plan to lure the bad men into committing a robbery, the result of which will lead to their arrest and capture. (See also *BULLET CODE*.)

ONCE UPON A HORSE Universal, 1958, B&W, 85 min. **Producer:** Hal Kantor; **Director:** Kantor; **Screenplay:** Kantor; **Music:** Frank Skinner; **Cinematographer:** Arthur E. Arling; **Editor:** Milton Carruth; **Cast:** Dan Rowan, Dick Martin, Martha Hyer, Leif Ericson, Nita Talbot, James Gleason, John McGiver, Max Baer, Buddy Baer.

Before they achieved television fame in the 1960s, Dan Rowan and Dick Martin appeared in this film. They play two hapless cattle rustlers who steal a herd, drive it into town, and then can't sell it. Every time they try to abandon the herd and leave town, they find themselves further and further in debt as they accrue more and more charges for feed and care. While there are still a few laughs here, the most interesting aspect of this film is seeing old-time western stars Tom Keene, Robert Livingston, Kermit Maynard, and Bob Steele playing themselves. Also featured are some decent songs by the Oscar-winning team of Ray Evans and Jay Livingston.

ONCE UPON A TIME IN THE WEST Paramount, 1969, Color, 165 min, VHS, CD. **Producer:** Fulvio Morsella; **Director:** Sergio Leone; **Screenplay:** Sergio Donati, Bernardo Bertolucci, Dario Argento, and Leone; **Music:** Ennio Morricone; **Cinematographer:** Tonino Delli Colli; **Editor:** Nico Baragli; **Cast:** Henry Fonda, Claudia Cardinale, Charles Bronson, Jason Robards Jr., Frank Wolfe, Jack Elam, Woody Strode, Lionel Stander.

Henry Fonda is brilliantly cast against type as one of the coldest villains in screen history, a man able to kill without blinking an eye. We see this at the start, when he first appears after the cold-blooded killing of a family of settlers. When the shooting stops, all that is left alive of the victimized family is young Timmy McBain. When one of the killers asks Fonda, "What should we do with this one, Frank?" he responds with, "Since you call me by my name," as he points his gun directly at the child, smiles, spits out tobacco, and calmly blasts the little boy away, his blue eyes shining like ice.

Also cast somewhat against type is Charles Bronson. Often the heavy during the 1950s, Bronson is the hero here, a mysterious figure we know only as The Man with the Harmonica. Mysterious too is Jason Robards Jr. as a heroic outlaw named Cheyenne. All three men seem to have more than a passing interest in ex-prostitute Jill McBain (Claudia Cardinale), who is unaware that Fonda has been sent to kill her.

Considered by many to be the high point of the "spaghetti" westerns, *Once Upon a Time in the West* has generated a number of serious critiques of various lengths and merit too numerous to analyze here. Certainly it boasts the most impressive list of credits of any spaghetti ventures, and it has achieved a cult following. Directed by Sergio Leone, it was partly scripted by Bernardo Bertolucci and the music was written by Ennio Morricone, the genre's most prolific composer. Particularly graphic is the sight of Jack Elam as one of the killers in the opening scene, his sinister left eye staring out sideways like a chameleon's, dominating the opening sequence as a doomed fly buzzes around the eye in close-up.

There are some interesting sidebars as well. For example, Al Murlock, one of the three gunmen in the opening scene, committed suicide on the set. "Harmonica," portrayed so well by Charles Bronson, was originally intended for Clint Eastwood. Most interesting is the fact that Henry Fonda originally turned down a role in the picture, so Sergio Leone flew to the United States to meet with him. Fonda asked the director why he was wanted for the movie. Leone reportedly replied, "Picture this: the camera shows a gunman from the waist down pulling his gun and shooting a running child. The camera pans up to the gunman's face and . . . it's Henry Fonda."

Released in the United States in a severely truncated version, the film was rereleased later in its original form. It has elicited kudos from some esteemed critics, not least Andrew Sarris, who considers this to be Leone's masterpiece, stating in his *Village Voice* review that "Sergio Leone is the only living director who can do justice to the baroque elaboration of revenge and violence in *The Godfather*." But what most separates this film from others of the spaghetti vintage is composer Morricone's linking of musical themes to characters, even though the score was written before production was started.

ONE EYED JACKS Paramount, 1961, Color, 141 min, VHS, DVD. **Producer:** Frank P. Rosenberg; **Director:** Marlon Brando; **Screenplay:** Guy Trosper and Calder Willingham; **Music:** Hugo Friedhofer; **Cinematographer:** Charles Lang; **Editor:** Archie Marshek; **Cast:** Marlon Brando, Karl

Malden, Katy Jurado, Ben Johnson, Slim Pickens, Elisha Cook Jr., Rodolfo Acosta, Ray Teal, Hank Warden.

Rio (Marlon Brando) and Dad Longworth (Karl Malden) are a couple of bank robbers. Escaping from the law after a robbery in Mexico, they find themselves with just one horse and a fortune in stolen gold. However, Dad finds a chance to take the money on horseback, leaving Rio to be captured by the law and spend five years in a rat-infested prison.

When Rio escapes from confinement, chained to another man, he sets out to track down Dad. He finally finds his quarry, now a respected sheriff of a small California town, married to a Mexican woman and stepfather to her beautiful daughter. Rio sets out on his plan for sweet revenge, first luring Dad into a false sense of trust and friendship, then seducing and impregnating his willing stepdaughter.

One of the most offbeat and complex westerns of the period, this film marks Brando's first—and to date only—directing endeavor. The Monterey seascapes provide a novel setting, and Brando's Method acting delineates a revenge-seeking protagonist who seems to be in more need of a psychiatrist than a gunfight. Reportedly the movie was scheduled to be filmed in 60 days, but in fact it took six months to complete, largely because of Brando's self-indulgence. A case in point is a scene where Rio sits on a rock and gazes out at the surf; Brando apparently spent hours "waiting for the right wave."

Stanley Kubrick was originally set to direct the film, but when he encountered problems with Brando, he left the project. The title itself refers to the jack in a pack of cards. In a revealing line, Rio says to Dad, "You're a one-eyed jack in this town, but I see the other side of your face." Brando and Malden, it should be mentioned, worked particularly well together. The two actors went back a long time, first working together in 1946 in Maxwell Anderson's *Truckline Cafe*. Then in 1951 Malden won a Best Supporting Actor Oscar for his role in *A Streetcar Named Desire*, the film that catapulted Brando's famed acting career. "We work like two jazz musician who have been improvising in the same small band for years," Malden has said.

Another bit of interesting casting has Ben Johnson as Bob Amory, an ornery villain. Johnson, a former wrangler and World Rodeo Champion, was a fine Oscar-winning actor—in fact the only real cowboy to ever win an Academy Award. In a 1996 interview with the author, veteran character actor Harry Carey Jr. discussed the film career of Ben Johnson, his long-standing friend and many-times movie colleague. "Ben is not a one-dimensional artist. He can go many ways. For instance, he can play one of the scariest villains you could ever want to encounter but it's all cowboy inside. Nobody ever looked better on a horse."

Supposedly in the original version of *One Eyed Jacks*, the footage ran some five hours and had no real hero or villain. Bent on salvaging some commercial value, Paramount took the project away from Brando and recut it to a feasible 141 minutes. In this version, Brando becomes the hero and Malden the villain. But what started out with a slated $1.8 million budget ended up costing the studio some $6 million,

and in its U.S. and Canadian releases it made only $4.3 million in distributors' grosses.

ONE FOOT IN HELL 20th Century Fox, 1960, Color, 90 min. **Producer:** Sydney Boehm; **Director:** James B. Clark; **Screenplay:** Boehm and Aaron Spelling; **Music:** Dominic Frontière; **Cinematographer:** William C. Mellor; **Editor:** Eda Warren; **Cast:** Alan Ladd, Don Murray, Dan O'Herlihy, Dolores Michaels, Barry Coe, Larry Gates.

Alan Ladd is a hate-crazed ex-Confederate soldier plotting revenge against the townspeople of Blue Springs, Arizona, whose indifference to his wife's pregnancy resulted in her dying during childbirth when they first arrived in town. The townsfolk attempt to make amends by making him deputy sheriff, but Ladd (very convincing in a villain's role) is far from finished. While hunting for rustlers, he murders the sheriff in cold blood, returns with the body, and tells the townsfolk that the man had been killed by the outlaws.

As the newly appointed sheriff, Ladd begins forming a gang in nearby Royce City to help him rob the Blue Springs bank of $100,000, then kill the people he holds responsible for his wife's death, and ultimately burn the town to the ground. However, two of his gang recruits, Don Murray and Dolores Michaels, fall in love and want no part of his evil plans. After the bank heist, the vengeful Ladd guns down the two remaining members of the gang and then sets out to kill the two lovers. A fight to the finish between Ladd and Murray results in Ladd's death. Hoping the town will forgive them, Murray and Michaels take the stolen money back to Blue Springs.

His onetime screen appeal in decline, Alan Ladd delivers an excellent performance against type. Had he not been fighting personal demons of his own, there are good indications that he might well have evolved as a first-rate character actor—an argument made even more convincing by his fine work as Nevada Smith in *The Carpetbaggers* (1964), his final screen role.

Cowritten by Aaron Spelling and shot in CinemaScope, this underrated and forgotten film boasts a haunting musical score by Dominic Frontière.

100 RIFLES 20th Century Fox, 1969, Color, 110 min, VHS. **Producer:** Marvin Schwartz; **Director:** Tom Gries; **Screenplay:** Gries and Clair Huffaker; **Music:** Jerry Goldsmith; **Cinematographer:** Cecilio Paniagua; **Editor:** Robert L. Simpson; **Cast:** Jim Brown, Raquel Welch, Burt Reynolds, Fernando Lamas, Dan O'Herlihy.

A tribe of Yacqui Indians led by Raquel Welch and a half-breed called Yacqui Joe (Burt Reynolds) take on an evil Mexican general (Fernando Lamas) and his army of cutthroats, who are rounding up the Yacqui and shooting them three at a time. To combat this, Reynolds robs a bank in Phoenix and uses the $6,000 to buy rifles for his people. An Arizona lawman (Jim Brown) pursues the half-breed all the way to Mexico, where he gets involved with the voluptuous Welch. The sight of a black man and a white woman embraced in passion was considered scandalous at the time.

ONE MAN JUSTICE Columbia, 1937, B&W, 59 min. **Producer:** Harry L. Decker; **Director:** Leon Barsha; **Screenplay:** Paul Perez; **Cinematographer:** Allen G. Siegler and John Stumar; **Editor:** William A. Lyon; **Cast:** Charles Starrett, Barbara Weeks, Wally Wales, Jack Clifford, Al Bridge, Walter Downing.

See *GALLANT DEFENDER, THE.*

ONE MAN'S LAW Republic, 1940, B&W, 57 min. **Producer:** George Sherman; **Director:** Sherman; **Screenplay:** Bennett Cohen and Jack Natteford; **Cinematographer:** Reggie Lanning; **Editor:** Lester Orlebeck; **Cast:** Don "Red" Barry, Janet Waldo, George Cleveland, Dub Taylor, Rex Lease, Carlton Young.

ONE MORE TRAIN TO ROB Universal, 1971, Color, 108 min. **Producer:** Robert Arthur; **Director:** Andrew V. McLaglen; **Screenplay:** William Roberts, Don Tait, and Dick Nelson; **Music:** Davis Shirre; **Cinematographer:** Alric Edens; **Editor:** Robert Simpson; **Cast:** George Peppard, Diana Muldaur, John Vernon, France Nuyen, Steve Sandor, Richard Loo, C. K. Yang, John Douchette, Robert Donner, George Chandler, Marie Windsor, Harry Carey Jr., Ben Cooper, Merlin Olsen, Pamela McMyler.

A man is released from prison and sets out to find the partner who double-crossed him. When he finds him he discovers that his former partner is the leading citizen of a small town who is trying to cheat a group of Chinese out of a fortune of gold. George Peppard is a strong lead, and an excellent supporting cast helps make this Andrew McLaglen western a cut above the ordinary 1970s genre piece.

ON SPECIAL DUTY See *BULLETS FOR RUSTLERS.*

ON THE CHEROKEE TRAIL See *LONESOME TRAIL.*

ON THE OLD SPANISH TRAIL Republic, 1947, Color, 75 min. **Producer:** Edward J. White; **Director:** William Witney; **Screenplay:** Sloan Nibley; **Music:** Bob Nolan and Morton Scott; **Cinematographer:** Jack A. Marta; **Editor:** Tony Martinelli; **Cast:** Roy Rogers, Tito Guizar, Jane Frazee, Andy Devine, Estelita Rodriguez.

ON TOP OF OLD SMOKEY Columbia, 1953, B&W, 59 min. **Producer:** Armand Schaeffer; **Director:** George Archainbaud; **Screenplay:** George Gerald Geraghty; **Music:** Mischa Bakaleinikoff; **Cinematographer:** William Bradford; **Editor:** James Sweeney; **Cast:** Gene Autry, Smiley Burnette, Gail Davis, Grandon Rhodes, Sheila Ryan, Kenne Duncan.

Mistaken for a Texas Ranger, singing star Gene Autry and the Cass County Boys come to the aid of a young woman whose ranch is being threatened by a gang of crooks because of its rich mica deposits.

OREGON PASSAGE Allied Artists, 1957, Color, 80 min. **Producer:** Lindsley Parsons; **Director:** Paul Landres; **Screenplay:** Jack DeWitt; **Music:** Paul Dunlap; **Cinematographer:** Ellis Carter; **Editor:** Maury Wright; **Cast:** John Ericson, Lola Albright, Toni Gerry, Edward Platt, Harvey Stephens.

When a cavalry officer innocently rescues an Indian girl from a tribal ceremony, he incurs the wrath of a Shoshone chief. Shot in CinemaScope and helmed by Lindsley Parsons, this otherwise bland film benefits from some brutal hand-to-hand combat between the cavalry officer and the Indian chief at film's end.

OREGON TRAIL, THE Republic, 1936, B&W, 59 min. **Producer:** Paul Malvern; **Director:** Scott Pembroke; **Screenplay:** Jack Natteford; **Cinematographer:** Gus Peterson; **Editor:** Carl Pierson; **Cast:** John Wayne, Ann Rutherford, Joseph W. Girard, Yakima Canutt.

Captain John Delmont (John Wayne) is a U.S. Army officer who takes a leave of absence to find out what has happened to his missing father. He leads a wagon train to California, where he goes after the bad men involved in his father's disappearance. Along the way he falls in love with Ann Rutherford, and with the help of some Spanish soldiers he defeats and captures the culprits. The film is one of the least seen among Wayne's early Republic B western ventures.

OREGON TRAIL, THE Universal, 1939, B&W, 15 chapters. **Producer:** Henry MacRae (associate); **Director:** Ford Beebe and Saul A. Goodkind; **Screenplay:** Basil Dickey, Edmund Kelso, George W. Plympton, and W. W. Watson; **Cinematographer:** Jerome Ash and William A. Sickner; **Editors:** Joseph Gluck, Louis Sackin, and Alvin Todd; **Cast:** Johnny Mack Brown, Louise Stanley, Bill Cody Jr., Fuzzy Knight, James Blaine, Roy Barcroft.

The last of the four Johnny Mack Brown serials for Universal in the 1930s covers the trials and tribulations of a wagon train headed west to Oregon's "promised land." Johnny Mack Brown is again clad in black as he leads the wagon train, which encounters large-scale Indian attacks, cavalry charges, and hair-raising escapes. Directed by serial expert Ford Beebe, lots of stock footage from the silent era is employed here. Roy Barcroft, in later films a perennial B western bad guy, is cast in the heroic person of General George Custer.

Back in 1923, Universal also produced an 18-chapter silent serial of *The Oregon Trail*, directed by Edward Laemmle and starring Art Accord and Louise Lorraine. (See also *OLD CHISHOLM TRAIL, THE.*)

OREGON TRAIL, THE Republic, 1945, B&W, 55 min. **Producer:** Bennett Cohen; **Director:** Thomas Carr; **Screenplay:** Betty Burbridge; **Cinematographer:** Bud Thackery; **Editor:** Richard L. Van Enger; **Cast:** Sunset Carson, Peggy Stewart, Frank Jaquet, Mary Carr, Kenne Duncan, Si Jenks, Tom London, John Merton.

OREGON TRAIL, THE 20th Century Fox, 1959, Color, 86 min. **Producer:** Richard Einfeld; **Director:** Gene Fowler, Jr.; **Screenplay:** Fowler Jr. and Louis Vittes; **Music:** Charles Devlan, Paul Dunlap, and Will Miller; **Cinematographer:** Kay Norton; **Editor:** Betty Steinberg; **Cast:** Fred MacMurray, William Bishop, Nina Shipman, Gloria Talbott, Henry Hull, John Carradine, John Dierkes.

In his last western before making *The Shaggy Dog* (1959) for Disney, Fred MacMurray is Neal Harris, a *New York Herald* writer, who is sent west via a wagon train. His mission is to find out whether President James Polk has sent soldiers disguised as pioneers to Oregon to aid in the U.S.-British dispute over the territory. He is also to investigate Indian attacks against the settlers. Not surprisingly Harris finds himself involved in the usual romantic triangle, courting pretty Prudence Cooper (Nina Shipman) to the chagrin of army captain George Wayne (William Bishop). This film was usually part of the fading double bills in theaters across the country, and according to Howard Thompson's review in the *New York Times*, it "manages to include most of the standard wagon-train cliches of the past twenty-five years."

OREGON TRAIL SCOUTS Republic, 1947, B&W, 58 min. **Producer:** Sidney Picker; **Director:** R. G. Springstein; **Screenplay:** Earle Snell; **Cinematographer:** Alfred Keller; **Editor:** Harold Minter; **Cast:** Allan Lane, Robert Blake, Martha Wentworth, Roy Barcroft, Emmett Lynn, Edmund Cobb.

OUT CALIFORNIA WAY Republic, 1946, Color, 67 min. **Producer:** Louis Grey; **Director:** Leslie Selander; **Screenplay:** Betty Burbridge; **Music:** Nathan Scott; **Cinematographer:** Bud Thackery; **Editor:** Charles Craft; **Cast:** Monte Hale, Lorna Gray (as Adrian Booth), Robert Blake, Don "Red" Barry, George "Gabby" Hayes, Allan Lane, Roy Rogers, Riders of the Purple Sage.

When a young cowboy comes to Hollywood hoping to become a film star, he finds that he has incurred the jealousy of a fading western hero. This fun-packed B oater is made for Monte Hale fans, with appearances by top B western stars Roy Rogers, Allan Lane, Don "Red" Barry, and so on, adding to the enjoyment. (See also *HOME ON THE RANGE*.)

OUTCAST, THE (aka: THE FORTUNE HUNTER, UK) Republic, 1954, Color, 90 min. **Director:** William Witney; **Screenplay:** John K. Butler and Richard Wormser; **Music:** Dale Butts; **Cinematographer:** Reggie Lanning; **Editor:** Tony Martinelli; **Cast:** John Derek, Joan Evans, Jim Davis, Catherine McLeod, Ben Cooper, Bob Steele, Harry Carey Jr., "Buzz" Henry, Hank Warden.

Handsome John Derek is Jeff Cosgrave, a young man returning home to reclaim a ranch from an evil cattle baron, who had stolen it from him after his father's death. With taut, skillful direction from William Witney and an excellent supporting cast, there is plenty of action and just enough romance to satisfy any genre fan. Unfortunately for the talented Derek, his darkly handsome features were rapidly leading to his being typecast as yet another Hollywood pretty boy. Dissatisfied with the direction his career was taking, he developed an interest in photography, eventually giving up most screen roles and becoming an accomplished still photographer.

OUTCASTS OF BLACK MESA (aka: THE CLUE) Columbia, 1950, B&W, 54 min. **Producer:** Colbert Clark; **Director:** Ray Nazarro; **Screenplay:** Barry Shipman; **Cinematographer:** Fayte M. Browne; **Editor:** Paul Borofsky; **Cast:** Charles Starrett, Smiley Burnette, Martha Hyer, Richard Bailey, Stanley Andrews, Lane Chandler.
See *DURANGO KID, THE*.

OUTCASTS OF POKER FLAT, THE RKO, 1937, B&W, 68 min. **Producer:** Robert Sisk; **Director:** Christy Cabanne; **Screenplay:** Harry Segall and John Twist; **Cinematographer:** Robert De Grasse; **Editor:** Ted Shipman; **Cast:** Preston Foster, Jean Muir, Van Heflin, Virginia Weidler, Margaret Irving, Monte Blue.

In this film based on two stories by Bret Harte—"The Outcasts" and "The Luck of Roaring Camp"—a group of people are snowbound in a cabin, with many finding a new meaning to life during their confinement. In one of his earliest screen roles, 27-year-old Van Heflin plays the young reverend who succeeds in curing gambler John Oakhurst (Preston Foster) of his drinking and gambling problem (although in the Hart stories Oakhurst was not a drinker).

The story was first filmed as a silent feature by John Ford in 1919, one of number of films Ford made with actor Harry Carey and one that was extremely well reviewed for its visual excellence. Interestingly, the Heflin role in the 1937 film was a condensed character and one not included as a separate entity in Ford's silent film for Universal. The movie was remade again in 1952 as *THE OUTCASTS OF POKER RIDGE*.

OUTCASTS OF POKER RIDGE, THE 20th Century Fox, 1952, B&W, 81 min. **Producer:** Julian Blaustein; **Director:** Joseph M. Newman; **Screenplay:** Edmund H. North; **Music:** Hugo Friedhofer; **Cinematographer:** Joseph Lashelle; **Editor:** William Reynolds; **Cast:** Anne Baxter, Dale Robertson, Miriam Hopkins, Cameron Mitchell, Craig Hill, Barbara Bates.

In this 1952 remake of *THE OUTCASTS OF POKER FLAT*, a group of social rejects take shelter in a snowbound cabin after a futile robbery attempt. This time it is Dale Robertson as gambler John Oakhurst. Also ensconced in the cabin are thief Cameron Mitchell, his wife Anne Baxter, and shady lady Miriam Hopkins. Tensions mount when sparks begin to fly between Robertson and Baxter, culminating in a fight to the finish between Robertson and Mitchell. Bret Harte's story seems to take a decline in this later movie version, although old-line screen siren Miriam Hopkins turns in a gem of a job as the "Duchess."

OUTCASTS OF THE TRAIL Republic, 1949, B&W, 60 min. **Producer:** Melville Tucker; **Director:** Philip Ford; **Screenplay:** Olive Cooper; **Music:** Stanley Wilson; **Cinematographer:** Bud Thackery; **Editor:** Tony Martinelli; **Cast:** Monte Hale, Jeff Donnell, Paul Hurst, Roy Barcroft, John Gallaudet, Tommy Ivo.

OUTLAW, THE RKO, 1943, B&W, 116 min, VHS, DVD. **Producer:** Howard Hughes; **Director:** Hughes; **Screenplay:** Jules Furthman; **Cinematographer:** Gregg Toland; **Editor:** Wallace Grissell; **Cast:** Jack Buetel, Jane Russell, Thomas Mitchell, Walter Huston, Mimi Agulia, Joe Sawyer.

One of the most publicized pictures of all time, Howard Hughes's *The Outlaw* was the first blatant introduction of the element of sex into the American western. Hughes reportedly engaged in a nationwide search for a buxom actress to play his female lead, Rio, before settling on 20-year-old Jane Russell, a former receptionist who had studied acting at Max Reinhardt's Acting Workshop. For the role of Billy the Kid, Hughes chose Jack Buetel, a 24-year-old actor with limited stage experience who had been working as an insurance clerk and, like Russell, was making his screen debut.

While publicized as a limited study in erotica, the film deals much more with the complex relationships between men, specifically, Doc Holliday (Walter Huston) and Pat Garrett (Thomas Mitchell). Buetel's Billy is not steeped in historical accuracy, although he makes for a refreshing and realistically unpleasant sort of character, capable of both cruelty and decency. The plot of the film, moreover, is a mixture of the convoluted, the complex, and the sensuous.

Initially, Billy is shot at by the half-breed Rio, Doc Holliday's mistress, whose brother Billy once killed in a gunfight. When Pat Garrett tries to arrest Billy, the young gunman won't draw, and Garrett is forced to wing him with a bullet. The injured Billy is taken to Doc Holliday's ranch, where Rio nurses him back to health. After they fall in love and are secretly wed, Doc helps Billy escape into the desert, with Pat Garrett in hot pursuit, although they discover that Rio, angry at being deserted, has filled their water canteens with sand. Garrett eventually captures Doc and shoots him. Billy captures Rio but later frees her. In perhaps one of the most flagrant departures from historical reality, Billy and Rio leave town together.

All said, the film is often quite effective. The action scenes and gunfights are first-rate, and Beutel is realistic with his gunwork. In one memorable scene, Doc is forced to shoot notches in Billy's ears in order to get The Kid to draw his gun. While Buetel was an actor of limited range, he was strangely effective in the role; and both Walter Huston and Thomas Mitchell turned in fine, steady performances.

Howard Hawks, originally slated to direct the film, left early on once he realized he could not work compatibly with Hughes, who then opted for total control of the project. Although its content is modest by today's standards, the censors had a field day with the film. After a screening in San Francisco, 20 minutes were deleted, and *The Outlaw* was denounced immediately by the Legion of Decency. Consequently, it wasn't until 1943 that it received limited release in theaters, with minor concessions made to satisfy the censors—that is, having Billy and Rio wed somewhere offscreen. But more controversy ensued over the steamy love scenes between Billy and Rio, prompting Hughes to take the picture out of circulation until 1947, when he issued a new and titillating advertising campaign.

As a postscript, it should be noted that after Hughes's death in 1976, *The Outlaw* was reissued with a G rating, meaning that it was suitable for a general audience—an indication of how much morality has changed in the intervening years. Jane Russell went on to prove herself to be more than just a voluptuous screen siren, emerging as quite a capable actress in the following years. Jack Buetel was not as fortunate. The long delay between the production and its ultimate release to the public, as well as the years he spent in service during World War II, lessened his public visibility. Howard Hawks had hoped to get Buetel to play a key role opposite John Wayne in his 1948 western *RED RIVER*. However, Hughes, who owned Buetel's contract, would not agree. The role instead went to a New York stage actor named Montgomery Cliff.

OUTLAW BRAND Monogram, 1948, B&W, 58 min. **Producer:** Louis Grey; **Director:** Lambert Hillyer; **Screenplay:** J. Benton Cheney; **Cinematographer:** Harry Neumann; **Editor:** Carl Pierson; **Cast:** Jimmy Wakely, Dub Taylor, Louis Armstrong, Tom Chatterton, Jay Kirby, Ray Whitely.

OUTLAW DEPUTY Puritan, 1935, B&W, 59 min. **Producer:** Nat Ross; **Director:** Otto Brower; **Screenplay:** Del Andrews and Ford Beebe; **Music:** Sam Perry and Lee Zahler; **Cinematographer:** James Diamond; **Editor:** Robert Jahns; **Cast:** Tim McCoy, Nora Lane, Hooper Atchley, George Offerman.

OUTLAWED GUNS Universal, 1935, B&W, 62 min. **Producer:** Buck Jones; **Director:** Ray Taylor; **Screenplay:** John T. Neville; **Cinematographer:** William A. Sickner and Allen O. Laemmle; **Editor:** Bernard Luftus; **Cast:** Buck Jones, Ruth Channing, Frank McGlynn Sr., Roy D'Arcey, Pat J. O'Brien.

Jimmy Wakely in Outlaw Brand (MONOGRAM/AUTHOR'S COLLECTION)

OUTLAW EXPRESS Universal, 1938, B&W, 56 min.
Producer: Trem Carr; **Director:** George Waggner; **Screenplay:** Norton S. Parker; **Music:** Fleming Allen (songs); **Cinematographer:** Harry Neumann; **Editor:** Charles Craft; **Cast:** Bob Baker, Cecilia Callejo, Don Barclay, LeRoy Mason, Nina Compana.

OUTLAW GANG, THE See *DALTON GANG, THE.*

OUTLAW GOLD Monogram, 1950, B&W, 56 min.
Producer: Vincent Fennelly; **Director:** Wallace Fox; **Screenplay:** Myron Healey, Jack Lewis, and Daniel B. Ullman; **Cinematographer:** Gilbert Warrenton; **Editor:** Fred Maguire; **Cast:** Johnny Mack Brown, Jane Adams, Myron Healey, Milburn Morante, Marshall Reed, Bud Osborne, Hugh Prosser.

OUTLAW JOSEY WALES, THE Warner Bros., 1976, Color, 135 min, VHS, DVD. **Producer:** Robert Daley; **Director:** Clint Eastwood; **Screenplay:** Sonia Chernus and Phil Kaufman; **Music:** Jerry Fielding; **Cinematographer:** Bruce Surtees; **Editor:** Ferris Webster; **Cast:** Clint Eastwood, Chief Dan George, Sondra Locke, John Vernon, Bill McKinney, Bruce Trueman, Sam Bottoms, Geraldine Keams, Sheb Wooley, Royal Dano.

In one of the last major studio westerns (until *PALE RIDER* in 1985), Clint Eastwood is Josey Wales, a Missouri farmer who joins a Confederate guerrilla unit after finding that his family has been murdered by errant Union soldiers. When the Confederate commander (John Vernon) dupes his men into a peaceful surrender to the Union, Wales is further alienated when the Union leader (Bill McKinney), who was also responsible for the deaths of Josey's family, executes most of the Confederate troops.

Driven to murderous revenge, Josey escapes. In time he slowly starts to show a human side again. After years of war and killing, he rescues an Indian friend (Chief Dan George) and a farm family, including Sondra Locke, from a gang of bandits dressed like Indians. In time Josey comes full circle, having been given a new chance by the man who has pursued him throughout the film and returning to farming a redeemed man as well as a redeemer.

Clint Eastwood originally agreed to star in the film with the provision that someone else would direct. He had been favorably impressed with Phil Kaufman, whose credits included THE GREAT NORTHFIELD, MINNESOTA RAID (1972). However, after several rewrites of the script and a week's work of footage, he found Kaufman's work lacking the epic quality he envisioned. He removed Kaufman from the project and took over the directing chores himself.

Filming took eight and a half weeks as the movie was shot in Utah, Arizona, and California. Like most of Eastwood's previous films, there is an excess of violence. *Variety* called *The Outlaw Josey Wales* a "Formula Clint Eastwood slaughter film for regular market . . . nothing more than a prairie *Death Wish*." Nevertheless, the film remains one of the most popular and profitable in the entire Eastwood film ledger.

The violence aside, Bruce Surtees's camera work is first-rate, and Jerry Fielding's musical score is well deserving of the Oscar nomination it received. Except for Don Siegel's exceptional film THE SHOOTIST, which marked John Wayne's final screen appearance, Clint Eastwood's *The Outlaw Josie Wales* was the only western to show a profit for the year 1976.

OUTLAW OF THE PLAINS PRC, 1946, B&W, 1946. **Producer:** Sigmund Neufeld; **Director:** Sam Newfield; **Screenplay:** A. Frederic Evans; **Music:** Lee Zahler; **Cinematographer:** Jack Greenhalgh; **Editor:** Holbrook N. Todd; **Cast:** Buster Crabbe, Al St. John, Patti McCarty, Charles King, Jack O'Shea, Bud Buster.

When crooks convince Fuzzy (Al St. John) that his worthless land contains gold, and he persuades others to join him in purchasing it, Billy Carson comes to his rescue. Following his stint as Billy the Kid for PRC, Buster Crabbe assumed the role of hero Billy Carson in more than 20 PRC features (1943–46). These include *Devil Riders* (1943); *Frontier Outlaws, Valley of Vengeance, Fuzzy Settles Down, Wild Horse Phantom, Oath of Vengeance, Thundering Gunslingers, The Drifter* (1944); *Lightning Raiders, His Brother's Ghost, Gangster's Den, Stagecoach Outlaws, Rustler's Hideout, Border Badmen, Fighting Billy Carson, Prairie Rustlers, Shadows of Death* (1945); *Gentlemen With Gun, Terrors on Horseback, Ghost of Hidden Valley, Prairie Badmen, Overland Riders* (1946).

OUTLAW ROUNDUP PRC, 1944, B&W, 56 min. **Producer:** Alfred Stern; **Director:** Harry L. Fraser; **Screenplay:** Elmer Clifton; **Music:** Aleth "Speed" Hanson; **Cinematographer:** Ira H. Morgan; **Editor:** Charles Henkle Jr.; **Cast:** Dave O'Brien, James Newill, Guy Wilkerson, Helen Stanford, I. Stanford Jolley.

OUTLAW'S DAUGHTER 20th Century Fox, 1954, Color, 75 min. **Producer:** Wesley Barry; **Director:** Barry; **Screenplay:** Sam Rocca; **Music:** Raoul Kraushaar; **Cinematographer:** Gordon Avil; **Editor:** Ace Herman; **Cast:** Jim Davis, Bill Williams, Kelly Ryan, George Cleveland, Elisha Cook Jr., Guinn "Big Boy" Williams.

This pleasant, low-budget entry has a young girl being implicated in a stagecoach holdup when robbers leave a trail to her grandfather's ranch. Gramps, it seems, was once a famous bad man who has seen the light.

OUTLAWS OF BOULDER PASS PRC, 1942, B&W, 61 min. **Producer:** Sigmund Neufeld; **Director:** Sam Newfield; **Screenplay:** Steve Braxton; **Music:** Johnny Lange and Lew Porter; **Cinematographer:** Jack Greenhalgh; **Editor:** Holbrook N. Todd; **Cast:** George Houston, Al St. John, Marjorie Manners, Charles King, I. Stanford Jolley.

OUTLAWS OF THE CHEROKEE TRAIL Republic, 1941, B&W, 56 min. **Producer:** Louis Grey (associate); **Director:** Les Orlbeck; **Screenplay:** Albert DeMond; **Cinematographer:** Ernest Haller; **Editor:** Murray Seldeen; **Cast:** Bob Steele, Tom Tyler, Rufe Davis, Lois Collier, Tom Chatterton, Iron Eyes Cody, Eddie Dean.

OUTLAWS OF PINE RIDGE Republic, 1942, B&W, 62 min. **Director:** William Witney; **Screenplay:** Norman S. Hall; **Music:** Mort Glickman; **Cinematographer:** Bud Thackery; **Editor:** William P. Thompson; **Cast:** Don "Red" Barry, Noah Beery, Jess Cavin, Roy Brent, Horace B. Carpenter, Clayton Moore, Francis Ford, Wheaton Chambers.

See *WYOMING OUTLAW.*

OUTLAWS OF SANTA FE Republic, 1944, B&W, 56 min. **Producer:** Herbert J. Yates; **Director:** Howard Bretherton; **Screenplay:** Norman S. Hall; **Music:** Mort Glickman; **Cinematographer:** John MacBurnie; **Editor:** Charles Craft; **Cast:** Don "Red" Barry, Helen Talbot, Wally Vernon, Le Roy Mason, Herbert Heyes.

OUTLAWS OF SONORA (aka: GUNS OF SONORA) Republic, 1938, B&W, 55 min, VHS. **Producer:** William A. Berke; **Director:** George Sherman; **Screenplay:** Betty Burbridge and Edmond Kelso; **Music:** Harold Peterson and Carlos Ruffino (songs); **Cinematographer:** William Nobles; **Editor:** Tony Martinelli; **Cast:** Robert Livingston, Ray Corrigan, Max Terhune, Jack Mulhall, Otis Harlan, Jean Joyce.

OUTLAWS OF THE PANHANDLE Columbia, 1941, B&W, 60 min. **Producer:** Jack Fier; **Director:** Sam Nelson; **Screenplay:** Paul Franklin; **Music:** Bob Nolan and Tim Spencer; **Cinematographer:** George Meehan; **Editor:** Arthur Seid; **Cast:** Charles Starrett, Frances Robinson, Stanley Brown, Norman Willis, Ray Teal, Bob Nolan.

OUTLAWS OF THE PRAIRIE Columbia, 1937, B&W, 59 min. **Producer:** Harry L. Decker; **Director:** Sam

Don "Red" Barry in Outlaws of Santa Fe (REPUBLIC AUTHOR'S COLLECTION)

Nelson; **Screenplay:** Harry Olmsted and Ed Earl Repp; **Music:** Bob Nolan (songs); **Cinematographer:** John W. Boyle; **Editor:** William A. Lyon; **Cast:** Charles Starrett, Donald Grayson, Iris Meredith, Norman Willis, Dick Curtis, Edward Le Saint, Edmund Cobb, Art Mix.

OUTLAWS OF THE ROCKIES (aka: ROVING ROGUE, UK) Columbia, 1945, B&W, 54 min. **Producer:** Colbert Clark; **Director:** Ray Nazarro; **Screenplay:** J. Benton Cheney; **Music:** Marlin Skyles; **Cinematographer:** George Kelley; **Editor:** Aaron Stell; **Cast:** Charles Starrett, Tex Harding, Dub Taylor, Carole Mathews, Philip Van Zandt, I. Stanford Jolley, George Chesebro.

OUTLAW'S SON (aka: GAMBLING MAN; HIS FATHER'S SON) United Artists, 1957, B&W, 88 min. **Producer:** Howard Koch; **Director:** Leslie Selander; **Screenplay:** Richards Alan Simmons; **Music:** Les Baxter; **Cinematographer:** William Marguiles; **Editor:** John F. Schreyer; **Cast:** Dane Clark, Ben Cooper, Lori Nelson, Ellen Drew, Charles Watts, Eddie Foy.

A young man (Ben Cooper) comes to the aid of his estranged father (Dane Clark), who had deserted him years earlier after being falsely accused of committing a robbery. Dane Clark and Ben Cooper deliver good performances in this modest father-son yarn.

OUTLAW STALLION, THE Columbia, 1954, Color, 64 min. **Producer:** Wallace MacDonald; **Director:** Fred Sears; **Screenplay:** David Lang; **Music:** Mischa Bakaleinikoff; **Cinematographer:** Lester White; **Editor:** Aaron Stell; **Cast:** Philip Carey, Dorothy Patrick, Billy Gray, Roy Roberts, Gordon Jones, Morris Ankrum, Chris Alcaide.

A band of thieves befriends a young woman and her son because they hope to steal her herd of horses.

OUTLAW TERRITORY See *HANNAH LEE.*

OUTLAW WOMEN (aka: BOOTHILL MAMAS) Lippert, 1952, Color, 75 min. **Producer:** Ron Ormond; **Director:** Sam Newfield; **Screenplay:** Orville Hampton; **Music:** Walter Greene; **Cinematographer:** Ellis W. Carter and Harry Neumann; **Editor:** Hugh Winn; **Cast:** Marie Windsor, Richard Rober, Allan Nixon, Carla Balenda, Jackie Coogan, Billy House, Tom Tyler, Kermit Maynard.

Marie Windsor's talent is wasted in this tale about a western town controlled by a woman gambler and her gang of female hellions—a town where men are forbidden to enter. But as tough as she is (she answers to the name of Iron Mae McLeod), she eventually succumbs to the charms of a handsome cowboy. The U.S. video title is *Booth Hill Mamas.*

OUTRAGE, THE MGM, 1964, B&W, 92 min, VHS. **Producer:** A. Ronald Lubin; **Director:** Martin Ritt; **Screenplay:** Michael Kanin; **Music:** Alex North; **Cinematographer:** James Wong Howe; **Editor:** Frank Santillo; **Cast:** Paul Newman, Laurence Harvey, Claire Bloom, Edward G. Robinson, William Shatner, Howard da Silva, Albert Salmi, Thomas Chalmers, Paul Fix.

Martin Ritt's *The Outrage* is based on the Akira Kurosawa's film *Rashomon* (1950). A husband and wife (Laurence Harvey and Claire Bloom) encounter a Mexican bandit (Paul Newman) who apparently rapes the wife and kills the husband. An investigation ensues, and in a series of flashbacks the misdeed is related from several points of view, with each version of the story using the same events to tell a very different account of what happened.

Among those involved in relating these episodes are a preacher (William Shatner), a prospector (Howard da Silva), and a con man (Edward G. Robinson), all of whom happen to meet at a deserted train station. The first two men tell the con man about the trial they have just witnessed, where three different variations of the facts were told, each related to the apparent crimes.

The film, which boasts superb photography by James Wong Howe, is taken from the 1959 stage adaptation of *Rashomon* by Fay and Michael Kanin. Yet Ritt's attempt to blend a philosophical point with conventional western action, though commendable, is riddled with flaws. There is little in the way of a cohesive story and little to link the various vignettes into a coherent theme. They never pull together as one might hope from such a production with its wide array of acting talent.

Reportedly Paul Newman spent two weeks in Mexico studying Mexican accents and voice qualities for the role of Juan Carrasco, but according to James Parish and Michael Pitts in *The Great Western Pictures*, "... neither swarthy make up, a beard, nor raggedy clothes could disguise Newman as anything other than an American movie star on a Sunday school outing." In the same source, Judith Crist in her *New York Herald Tribune* review is quoted as commenting: "What should have been a cogent, almost ritualistic examination and re-examination of the many facets of truth emerges as little more than a story told and thrice re-told simply to provide three performers with exercises in acting."

OUTRIDERS, THE MGM, 1950, Color, 93 min. **Producer:** Richard Goldstone; **Director:** Roy Roland; **Screenplay:** Irving Ravetch; **Music:** Andre Previn; **Cinematographer:** Charles Edgar Schoenbaum; **Editor:** Robert Kern; **Cast:** Joel McCrea, Arlene Dahl, Barry Sullivan, Claude Jarman Jr., James Whitmore, Ramon Navarro, Jeff Corey, Ted de Corsia.

Three Confederate spies join a wagon train going to Santa Fe during the Civil War. Their plans are to hijack its million dollars in gold for the Confederate cause. This average early 1950s western is elevated, as usual, by Joel McCrea's authentic presence.

OVERLAND EXPRESS Columbia, 1938, B&W, 55 min. **Producer:** L. G. Leonard; **Director:** Drew Eberson; **Screenplay:** Monroe Shaff; **Music:** Edward Kilenvi; **Cinematographer:** Allen O. Thompson; **Editor:** Gene Milford; **Cast:** Buck Jones, Marjorie Reynolds, Caryle Moore Jr., Maston Williams.

OVERLAND MAIL Monogram, 1939, B&W, 51 min. **Producer:** Robert Emmett Tansey; **Director:** Robert F. Hill; **Screenplay:** Tansey; **Cinematographer:** Bert Longenecker; **Editor:** Robert Golden; **Cast:** Jack Randall, George Cleveland, Tristram Coffin, Joe Garcia, Jean Joyce.

OVERLAND MAIL ROBBERY Republic, 1943, B&W, 56 min. **Director:** John English; **Screenplay:** Bob Williams and Robert Yost; **Music:** Mort Glickman; **Cinematographer:** John MacBurnie; **Editor:** Charles Craft; **Cast:** William "Wild Bill" Elliott, George "Gabby" Hayes, Anne Jeffreys, Alice Fleming, Tom London.

Another fast-paced entry into the Republic catalogue has Bill Elliott and "Gabby" Hayes helping out a young man from the East who comes west to claim an inheritance but is about to be thwarted by a crook. Bill therefore assumes the identity of the young man and is eventually framed for murder. Escaping the sheriff's grasp, he and Gabby go after the real culprits.

OVERLAND PACIFIC (aka: SILVER DOLLAR) United Artists, 1954, Color, 73 min. **Producer:** Edward Small; **Director:** Fred F. Sears; **Screenplay:** Gladys Atwater, J. Robert Bren, and Martin Goldsmith; **Music:** Irving Gertz; **Cinematographer:** Lester White; **Editor:** Buddy Small; **Cast:** Jock Mahoney (as Jack Mahoney), Peggie Castle, William Bishop, Chubby Johnson, Walter Sande.

A believable Jock Mahoney is Ross Granger, an insurance investigator who goes underground to determine the source of a series of constant Indian attacks on the railroad.

OVERLAND RIDERS PRC, 1946, B&W, 53 min. **Producer:** Sigmund Neufeld; **Director:** Sam Newfield; **Screenplay:** Ellen Coyle; **Cinematographer:** Jack Greenhalgh; **Editor:** Holbrook N. Todd; **Cast:** Buster Crabbe, Al St. John, Patti McCarty, Slim Whitaker, Bud Osborne, Jack O'Shea, Frank Ellis.

OVERLAND STAGECOACH PRC, 1942, B&W, 61 min. **Producer:** Sigmund Neufeld; **Director:** Sam Newfield; **Music:** Leo Erode; **Cinematographer:** Jack Greenhalgh; **Editor:** Holbrook N. Todd; **Cast:** Robert Livingston, Al St. John, Dennis Moore, Julie Duncan, Glenn Strange, Budd Buster, Art Mix.

OVERLAND STAGE RAIDERS Republic, 1938, B&W, 58 min, VHS. **Producer:** William Berke (associate); **Director:** George Sherman; **Screenplay:** Luci Ward; **Cinematographer:** William Nobles; **Editor:** Tony Martinelli; **Cast:** John Wayne, Louise Brooks, Ray Corrigan, Max Terhune, Frank LaRue.

OVERLAND TELEGRAPH RKO, 1951, B&W, 60 min. **Producer:** Herbert Schlom; **Director:** Lesley Selander; **Screenplay:** Adele Buffington; **Music:** Paul Sawtell; **Cinematographer:** L. Roy Hunt; **Editor:** Samuel E. Beetley; **Cast:** Tim Holt, Gail Davis, Hugh Beaumont, Mari Blanchard, George Nader, Robert J. Wilke, Cliff North, Russell Hicks, Robert Bray.

OVERLAND TRAILS Monogram, 1948, B&W, 58 min. **Producer:** Barney A. Sarecky; **Director:** Lambert Hillyer; **Screenplay:** Adele Buffington (as Jess Bowers); **Cast:** Johnny Mack Brown, Raymond Hatton, Virginia Belmont, Bill Kennedy, Virginia Carroll, Holly Bane.

OVERLAND WITH KIT CARSON Columbia, 1939, B&W, 15 chapters. **Producer:** Jack Fier; **Directors:** Sam Nelson and Norman Demming; **Screenplay:** Morgan Cox, Joseph Poland, and Ned Dandy; **Music:** Mischa

Bakaleinikoff, Sidney Cutner, and George Parish; **Cinematographer:** Benjamin H. Kline; **Editor:** Richard Fantl; **Cast:** William "Wild Bill" Elliott, Iris Meredith, Richard Fiske, Bobby Clack, James Craig, Hal Taliaferro, Dick Curtis.

Bill Elliott discards his Wild Bill Hickok moniker for frontier hero Kit Carson in this 15-chapter serial for Columbia. As the famed frontier scout, he attempts to locate a mysterious outlaw called Pegleg and his gang of Black Raiders, who are raiding settlements west of the Mississippi in order to rid the area of settlers and set an empire under Pegleg's control.

OVER THE BORDER
Monogram, 1950, B&W, 58 min. **Producer:** Wallace Fox; **Director:** Fox; **Screenplay:** J. Benton Cheney; **Cinematographer:** Harry Neumann; **Editor:** John C. Fuller; **Cast:** Johnny Mack Brown, Wendy Waldron, Myron Healey, Pierre Watkin, Frank Jaquet, House Peters Jr.

OX BOW INCIDENT, THE (aka: STRANGE INCIDENT)
20th Century Fox, 1943, B&W, 75 min. **Producer:** Lamar Trotti; **Director:** William Wellman; **Screenplay:** Trotti; **Music:** Cyril Mockridge; **Cinematographer:** Arthur C. Miller; **Editor:** Allen McNeil; **Cast:** Henry Fonda, Dana Andrews, Mary Beth Hughes, Anthony Quinn, William Eythe, Harry Morgan, Jane Darwell, Matt Briggs, Frank Conroy, Victor Kilian, Chris-Pin Martin, Willard Robertson, Ted North, Francis Ford, Margaret Hamilton.

"Hanging is any man's business who's around." So says Gil Carter (Henry Fonda) when challenging the questionable hanging of three suspected rustlers. William Wellman's classic western opens as drifters Fonda and Harry Morgan ride into a Nevada frontier town shortly before a lynch mob sets out to find the three men who allegedly were responsible for cattle rustling and the murder of a nearby rancher.

Led by a paranoid ex-Confederate officer and an assortment of brutes and bullies, the posse corners three men making camp for the night. With a strong case of circumstantial evidence to back them up, the leaders of the posse are determined to hang the three suspects (Dana Andrews, Anthony Quinn, and Francis Ford) without the formality of a trial. Only seven men, including Fonda and Morgan, attempt to stand up to the mob, but they lack the will and resources to succeed.

Based on the novel by Walter Van Tilburg Clark, *The Ox Bow Incident* is a dimly realistic ode to the dual themes of mob rule and lynch frenzy. During a memorable campfire scene, strains of "Red River Valley" help to deliver a somber tone as the camera scans the faces of posse members and victims, capturing the collective mood as they wait pensively through the silent night. In the morning the three men, protesting their innocence to the end, are summarily hanged.

With the deed done, the posse heads back to town. They intersect with the sheriff, who informs them that they made a horrible mistake. The rancher was alive, and the men who had shot and robbed him were under arrest in another town. All but seven had been responsible for the hanging of three innocent men. "God better have mercy on ya," the sheriff admonishes. "You won't get any from me." Not only had the perpetrators denigrated the rule of law, but they had also devoured the legal conscience that embodies all civilized societies—a matter brought clearly to focus when Fonda reads a touching letter that one of the victims (Andrews) wrote to his wife before his execution.

Henry Fonda delivers a brilliantly understated performance as Gil Carter, the cowboy who pursues the event with an escalating aversion. Almost as compelling is Dana Andrews as the doomed victim Donald Martin. Moreover, Wellman's superb direction delivers an uncompromising statement with blunt authority. Sometimes called the "first psychological western" (which it is not), *The Ox Bow Incident* is arguably the first film to possess a deeply vivid social conscience and to tackle a serious theme in a decidedly literate manner.

One of the most quietly powerful westerns ever put on film, *The Ox Bow Incident* was nominated for Best Picture of 1943 (losing to *Casablanca*) and was selected for the National Film Registry by the National Film Preservation Board in 1998. Immediately after completing the picture, the 37-year-old Fonda enlisted in the U.S. Navy; as an air combat intelligence officer he was later awarded a Bronze Star and a presidential citation. *The Ox Bow Incident* is the only western to have received an Academy Award nomination as Best Picture during the entire decade of the 1940s, sandwiched between *STAGECOACH* (1939) and *HIGH NOON* (1952).

PACK TRAIN Columbia, 1953, B&W, 57 min. **Producer:** Armand Schaefer; **Director:** George Archainbaud; **Screenplay:** Norman S. Hall; **Music:** Gene Autry; **Cinematographer:** Norman Hall; **Editor:** James Sweeney; **Cast:** Gene Autry, Smiley Burnette, Gail Davis, Kenne Duncan, Sheila Ryan, Tom London, Harry Lauter.

PAINTED DESERT RKO, 1931, B&W, 79 min. **Producer:** E. B. Derr; **Director:** Howard Higgin; **Screenplay:** Tom Buckingham and Higgin; **Music:** Francis Gromon; **Cinematographer:** Edward Snyder; **Editor:** Clarence Kolster; **Cast:** William Boyd, Helen Twelvetrees, William Farnum, J. Farrell MacDonald, Clark Gable, Charles Sellon, Hugh Adams.

This film is most notable for the presence of Clark Gable in his first major role as well as his talkie debut. The story concerns two partners (J. Farrell MacDonald and William Farnum) who find a baby boy in a deserted emigrant camp and clash over who should raise the boy and be its father. However, the partners eventually start to feud, and the former best friends become the worst of enemies, with the feud continuing for nearly three decades. The plot is complicated when the boy (a pre-Hop-Along Cassidy Bill Boyd), who was raised by Farnum and now owns a mining business, tries to put an end to the feud after falling in love with MacDonald's daughter.

Early talkies such as *The Painted Desert* tended to rely too much on words and too little on deeds. Nevertheless, the film has much merit, especially its beautiful scenery. Even at this early stage of his career, the 30-year-old Gable, minus his mustache, displays a remarkable stature, this time in the unlikely role of a villain. His presence in the film has been called "dynamic" by William Everson, who goes on to say that Gable plays the villain "with such force and animal magnetism that he [steals] the film away from the placid and stereotyped heroics of William Boyd." The film was also praised by *Variety*, which complimented "the excellent camera views of the fatalistic beauty of the bleak California desert." *Photoplay* insisted that this early sound western was "far above the average, . . . [making] no pretense other than entertainment."

PAINTED DESERT RKO, 1938, B&W, 59 min. **Producer:** Bert Gilroy; **Director:** David Howard; **Screenplay:** Oliver Drake; **Music:** Drake and Ray Whitley; **Cinematographer:** Harry J. Wild; **Editor:** Frederic Knudtson; **Cast:** George O'Brien, Laraine Day (as Laraine Johnson), Ray Whitley, Stanley Fields, Maude Allen.

In this remake of RKO-Pathé's 1931 film, George O'Brien inherits the William Boyd role as a young man returning to his feuding home, only to discover that a crook is trying to steal his tungsten mine. Ray Whitley sings the title song and Stanley Fields and Maude Allen provide some comic relief in this good O'Brien series entry, which makes fine use of stock footage from the earlier picture. (See also *RACKETEERS OF THE RANGE*.)

PAINTED HILLS, THE MGM, 1951, Color, 65 min, VHS. **Producer:** Charles M. Franklin; **Director:** Harold R. Kress; **Screenplay:** True Boardman; **Music:** Daniele Amfitheatrof; **Cinematographer:** Alfred Gilks and Harold Lipstein; **Editor:** Newell P. Kimlin; **Cast:** Paul Kelly, Bruce Cowling, Gary Gray, Art Smith, Ann Doran, Chief Yowlachie, Andrea Virginia Lester, Brown Jug Reynolds.

Based on a story by Alexander Hull and set in California in the 1880s, this pleasant family yarn has our favorite canine Lassie remaining ever loyal to her prospector/owner when crooks try to gain access to his gold strike.

PAINT YOUR WAGON Paramount, 1969, Color, 166 min, VHS, DVD, CD. **Producers:** Alan J. Lerner and Tom Shaw; **Director:** Joshua Logan; **Screenplay:** Paddy Chayefsky and Alan J. Lerner; **Music:** Frederick Loewe, Andre Previn, and Nelson Riddle; **Cinematographer:** William A. Fraker; **Editor:** Robert C. Jones; **Cast:** Lee Marvin, Clint Eastwood, Jean Seberg, Harve Presnell, Ray Walston, John Mitchum, Sue Casey, H. W. Gim.

Lerner and Loewe's 1951 rousing Broadway musical was brought to the silver screen in 1969 by Josh Logan. Lee Marvin stars as grizzled prospector Ben Rumson with Clint Eastwood as Pardner, the injured stranger whom Rumson saves from a runaway wagon accident. The story takes place during the Gold Rush days in the California town of No Name, where prospectors Marvin and Eastwood form a partnership and share almost everything, including a common wife (Jean Seberg) who was bought at an auction. This *ménage à trois* was not part of the original Broadway version but was added in the Paddy Chayefsky screenplay to give the movie an appeal to younger audiences.

The lure of gold finds the town of No Name rapidly increasing in population, swelling until it becomes a lawless pit of vice and debauchery, with an endless supply of gambling halls, prostitutes, and whiskey peddlers. The contrived tranquility of the Rumson household is compromised when Elizabeth (Seberg) and Pardner become increasingly attracted to each other. Even so, Elizabeth is unwilling to give up Ben. Eventually, overrun by feelings of guilt over her lifestyle, she throws them both out. When the underground caverns supposedly hoarding deposits of gold collapse due to faulty construction and excessive greed, Rumson decides to search elsewhere for more adventures, leaving Pardner and Elizabeth to work out a life together.

Paint Your Wagon is certainly not the best screen version of a Broadway musical, but it does have its share of memorable moments. Lerner and Loewe's delightful songs underscore a genuine flavor of Americana. Some songs seem not to belong to a Broadway show at all but rather are like authentic folk ballads handed down by miners from one generation to the next. The booming theme song "Wand'rin' Star" is done quite well by Lee Marvin and serves as an appropriate

A busy scene from Paint Your Wagon, *the screen adaptation of the Lerner and Loewe Broadway musical* (PARAMOUNT/AUTHOR'S COLLECTION)

frame for such numbers as Rumson's stirring "I'm On My Way"; and the classic "They Call the Wind Maria," which is performed beautifully by Harve Presnell in the role of "Rotten Luck" Willie. Clint Eastwood even chimes in with pleasant renditions of two songs, including the melodic "I Talk to the Trees." The singers were members of the Robert Wagner Chorale, and many of the extras were resident Oregon hippies.

What is particularly appealing here is the sight of manly men singing manly songs, as well as a genuinely fine performance by Lee Marvin as Ben Rumson—a risky one, to say the least, from an actor with limited or no musical experience. When Ben and Pardner go their separate ways, it is done with a proper slice of bonding, true friendship, and genuine respect.

Actor John Mitchum had a nice supporting role as Jacob Woodling, the Mormon miner who sold Elizabeth (Jean Seberg) to Rumson. In a 1995 interview with the author, he reminisced about the film.

> We did *Paint Your Wagon* in Baker, Oregon, and you had to go 52 miles into the mountains from Baker. The road was so treacherous that it took the buses three hours to go 52 miles. It was a very awesome location. Things went smoothly, except the first two weeks old Lee [Marvin] was drunk out of his mind. He pulled himself together and did a real good job. His singing surprised me. His "Wand'rin Star" was very effective.

In his autobiography *Movie Stars, Real People, and Me*, director Josh Logan also mentions Lee Marvin's heavy drinking, which he was able to work around. A bigger problem was posed by Alan J. Lerner, the gifted lyricist but fledgling producer, who showed up regularly on the set and, to everyone's dismay and annoyance, started telling the actors how to read their lines and what to do.

Paint Your Wagon is hardly the poor movie some critics have contended. It benefits strongly from its lavish sets, deft cinematography, and impressive musical numbers. The *New York Daily News* called it "a big, bawdy, rip-roaring Western musical of the gold rush in California."

PALE ARROW   See *PAWNEE*.

PALEFACE   Paramount, 1948, Color, 91 min, VHS.
Producer: Robert L. Welch; **Director:** Norman Z. McLeod; **Screenplay:** Edmund Hartman and Frank Tashlin; **Music:** Victor Young; **Cinematographer:** Ray Ranahan; **Editor:** Ellsworth Hoagland; **Cast:** Bob Hope, Jane Russell, Robert Armstrong, Iris Adrian, Jasper Martin.

Curvaceous Calamity Jane (Jane Russell) is released from prison in order to hunt down a notorious gang of outlaws who are selling guns to the Indians. For cover, she seduces then weds a bumbling correspondence school dentist, "Painless" Peter Potter (Bob Hope), who becomes her traveling companion. Replete with a litany of humorous Hope wisecracks, the teaming of Hope and Russell was a stroke of

genius, with Hope playing his usual cowardly buffoon role to perfection.

Called by *Variety* ". . . a smart-aleck travesty on the west, told with considerable humor and bright gags," *Paleface* was nominated by the Writer's Guild of America for a WGA Screen Award in two categories: Best Written American Comedy and the Best Written American Western. As popular with audiences as it was with critics, it grossed an impressive $4.5 million in distributors' domestic rental and was among the top 10 most popular movies of 1948. Its popularity prompted Paramount to make a sequel with Hope and Russell, *Son of Paleface*, which was released in 1952.

A totally delightful western spoof that time has not diminished, *Paleface* includes Ray Evans's and Jay Livingston's 1948 Academy Award-winning song "Buttons and Bows," introduced in the film by Bob Hope and made into a million-seller recording by Dinah Shore on the Columbia label.

PALE RIDER   Warner Bros., 1985, Color, 115 min.
Producer: Clint Eastwood; **Director:** Eastwood; **Screenplay:** Michael Butler and Dennis Schryack; **Music:** Lennie Niehaus; **Cinematographer:** Bruce Surtees; **Editor:** Joel Cox; **Cast:** Clint Eastwood, Michael Moriarty, Carrie Snodgress, Christopher Penn, Richard Dysart, Sydney Penny, Richard Keil, Doug McGrath, John Russell.

In California in 1850, Coy LaHood, the head of a powerful strip-mining corporation, terrorizes some independent gold miners and their families. Because the future success of the corporation depends on securing the land held by the independents, LaHood starts resorting to violence. Leading the homesteaders in peaceful protest is Hull Barrett (Michael Moriarty), a man hoping for a better life for himself, his girlfriend Sarah (Carrie Snodgress), and her 14-year-old daughter from a previous marriage, Megan (Sydney Penny). Suddenly a mysterious stranger known only as "The Preacher" (Clint Eastwood), who says little but obviously has a strong penchant for handling weapons, arrives in town. He unites the miners and gives them confidence to defy LaHood and his gang in the face of increasing violence.

Sarah and her daughter both become attracted to The Preacher, but he rejects their advances, allowing both to see that while Hull might be a less capable man, he is still the better man. After defeating LaHood's gang repeatedly, The Preacher finds himself pitted against an evil marshal (John Russell) and his army of deputies, a group that seems to include all his past adversaries. The Preacher kills them all, while Hull succeeds in killing LaHood. The Preacher then rides away as mysteriously as he arrived, suggesting perhaps an avenger with some mystic or supernatural powers—though the viewer never knows for sure.

Few can deny that *Pale Rider*, if not inspired by *SHANE* (1953), might well be a remake of the George Stevens's classic, with perhaps the most marginal difference being the Brandon De Wilde role, which here is filled by a teenage girl. What is most apparent, however, is that *Pale Rider* is a darker film, lacking the decency of spirit that exemplified *Shane*.

Nevertheless, Eastwood comes up with a worthy piece of filmmaking, skillfully produced and directed, with outstanding photography and an array of good performances, especially Moriarty in a role akin to Van Heflin's Joe Starrett in *Shane*. Eastwood obviously pays homage to his mentor Sergio Leone, with his outlaws wearing the same long coats that the villainous Henry Fonda wore in Leone's ONCE UPON A TIME IN THE WEST (1969).

Despite its craftsmanship, *Pale Rider* did not produce the spate of quality westerns that many had hoped would follow, though it did better than expected at the box office and outgrossed SILVERADO, the other big western of 1985. Critical reviews, while mixed, bordered on the positive. Andrew Sarris, in *The Village Voice*, commented that ". . . Eastwood has managed to keep the genre alive . . . through the ghostly intervention of his heroic persona." Similarly, Jeffrey Lyons in *Sneak Previews* called *Pale Rider* "easily one of the best films of the year, and one of the best Westerns in a long, long time."

Not quite as enthusiastic was Rex Reed in his *New York Post* review. Although lauding the strong cast, he carefully reminds his readers that ". . . *Pale Rider* owes such a nostalgic debt to George Stevens' *Shane* that the similarities, scene by scene, become almost a parody."

PALOMINO, THE (aka: HILLS OF THE BRAVE, UK) Columbia, 1950, Color, 73 min. **Producer:** Robert Cohn; **Director:** Ray Nazarro; **Screenplay:** Tom Kilpatrick; **Music:** Mischa Bakaleinikoff and John Leipold; **Cinematographer:** Vincent J. Farrar; **Editor:** Aaron Stell; **Cast:** Jerome Courtland, Beverly Tyler, Joseph Calleia, Roy Roberts, Gordon Jones, Robert Osterloh, Tom Trout.

After crooks steal a girl's prize horse so she will lose her ranch, a cattle buyer tries to help her retrieve the animal. This pleasant but modest little Technicolor film should appeal to the younger juvenile audience.

PALS OF THE GOLDEN WEST Republic, 1951, B&W, 68 min. **Producer:** Edward J. White; **Director:** William Witney; **Screenplay:** Albert DeMonde and Eric Taylor; **Music:** Stanley Wilson; **Cinematographer:** Jack A. Marta; **Editor:** Harold Minter; **Cast:** Roy Rogers, Dale Evans, Estelita Rodriguez, Pinky Lee, Anthony Caruso, Roy Barcroft.

Roy Rogers is assigned by the Border Patrol to investigate the smuggling of diseased cattle into the United States in his final series film for Republic. (See also UNDER WESTERN STARS.)

PALS OF THE PECOS Republic, 1941, B&W, 56 min. **Producer:** Louis Grey; **Director:** Lester Orlebeck; **Screenplay:** Herbert Dalmas and Oliver Drake; **Cinematographer:** Reggie Lanning; **Editor:** Ray Snyder; **Cast:** Robert Livingston, Bob Steele, Rufe Davis, June Johnson, Robert Winkler, Pat O'Malley.

See THREE MESQUITEERS, THE.

PALS OF THE SADDLE Republic, 1938, B&W, 60 min, VHS. **Producer:** William A. Berke (associate); **Director:** George Sherman; **Screenplay:** Betty Burbridge and Stanley Roberts; **Cinematographer:** Reggie Lanning; **Editor:** Tony Martinelli; **Cast:** John Wayne, Ray Corrigan, Max Terhune, Doreen McKay, Joseph Forte.

John Wayne's first entry in Republic's popular *Three Mesquiteers* series has him involved with a female government agent on the trail of foreign agents who are smuggling a secret chemical out of the country. (See also THREE MESQUITEERS, THE.)

PALS OF THE SILVER SAGE Monogram, 1940, B&W, 52 min. **Producer:** Edward Finney; **Director:** Albert Herman; **Screenplay:** Robert Emmett Tansey; **Music:** Johnny Lange and Lou Porter; **Cinematographer:** Marcel Le Picard; **Editor:** Robert Golden; **Cast:** Tex Ritter, Sugar Dawn, Slim Andrews, Clarissa Curtis, Glenn Strange, Carlton Young.

See SONG OF THE GRINGO.

PANAMINT'S BAD MAN 20th Century Fox, 1938, B&W, 60 min. **Producer:** Sol Lesser; **Director:** Ray Taylor; **Screenplay:** Charles Arthur Powell and Luci Ward; **Cinematographer:** Allen Thompson; **Editor:** Albert Jordan; **Cast:** Smith Ballew, Evelyn Daw, Noah Beery, Stanley Fields, Harry Woods, Pat J. O'Brien, Armand "Curly" Wright.

"Your singin', fist-swingin', cowboy favorite!" That's the tag line for this Smith Ballew oater, with Ballew as a marshal who goes undercover to Panamint (a mining town) disguised as a bad man to get the goods on a band of robbers.

PANCHO VILLA Scotia International, 1972, Color, 92 min, VHS, DVD. **Producer:** Bernard Gordon; **Director:** Eugenio Martin; **Screenplay:** Julian Zimet; **Music:** Anton Garcia Abril; **Cinematographer:** Alejandro Ulloa; **Cast:** Telly Savalas, Clint Walker, Chuck Connors, Anne Francis, Angel del Pozo.

Telly Savalas makes an unlikely Pancho Villa in this routine "spaghetti"-type European western filmed in Spain and released in the United States in 1974. Clint Walker (in a good performance) and Anne Francis are a couple of arms smugglers who aid Pancho Villa, the Mexican revolutionary who remains the only foreigner to invade American soil. Chuck Connors plays a polo-playing and obsessive military martinet. Look for an exciting climax where two trains engage in a head-on collision. However, the scenery far exceeds a rather banal story line.

PANHANDLE Allied Artists, 1948, B&W, 85 min. **Producer:** John C. Champion and Blake Edwards; **Director:**

Leslie Selander; **Screenplay:** Champion and Edwards; **Music:** Rec Dunn; **Cinematographer:** Harry Neumann; **Editor:** Richard V. Heermance; **Cast:** Rod Cameron, Cathy Downs, Reed Hadley, Anne Gwynne, Blake Edwards, J. Farrell MacDonald, Henry Hall.

An ex-gunman (Rod Cameron) packs his six-guns once more to get revenge on the murderer of his brother in this action-packed western. Cameron turns in a top-notch heroic performance, and Blake Edwards (who coproduced and cowrote the film) plays the heavy.

PARADE OF THE WEST Universal/Ken Maynard Productions, 1930, B&W, 66 min. **Producer:** Maynard; **Director:** Harry Joe Brown; **Screenplay:** Bennett Cohen; **Cinematographer:** Ted D. McCord; **Editor:** Fred Allen; **Cast:** Ken Maynard, Gladys McConnell, Otis Harlan, Frank Rice, Bobby Dunn.

Ken Maynard is a cowboy who joins a Wild West show, for which he has to ride a horse called Mankiller. However, when he begins to romance one of the performers, the owner's righthand man becomes jealous and sets out to sabotage his ride on the wild horse. This part-talkie, which should be of interest to Maynard fans, is one of eight features he produced under the banner Ken Maynard Productions. The others include: *Senor Americano, The Wagon Master* (1929), *Song of the Caballero, Sons of the Saddle, Mountain Justice* aka *Kettle Creek* (1930), *Gun Justice, Honor of the Range* (1934).

PARADISE CANYON (aka: PARADISE RANCH) Lone Star/Monogram, 1935, B&W/Color, 52 min, VHS. **Producer:** Paul Malvern; **Director:** Carl Pierson; **Screenplay:** Lindsley Parsons and Robert Emmett (Tansey); **Cinematographer:** Archie Stout; **Editor:** Jerry Roberts; **Cast:** John Wayne, Marion Burns, Reed Howes, Earl Hodgins, Gino Corrado, Yakima Canutt.

John Wayne is an undercover agent for the government sent to round up a gang of counterfeiters operating near the Mexican border. The soundtrack includes the songs "When We Were Young and Foolish" and "Snap Those Old Suspenders Once Again."

PARDNERS Paramount, 1956, Color, 90 min, VHS. **Producer:** Paul Jones; **Director:** Norman Taurog; **Screenplay:** Sidney Sheldon; **Music:** Sammy Cahn and Jimmy Van Heusen; **Cinematographer:** Daniel L. Fapp; **Editor:** Archie Marchek; **Cast:** Dean Martin, Jerry Lewis, Lori Nelson, Jeff Morrow, Agnes Moorehead, Lon Chaney Jr., Lee Van Cleef, Jack Elam, Bob Steele.

A loose remake of the Bing Crosby hit *RHYTHM ON THE RANGE* (1936) has Wade (Jerry Lewis) and Slim (Dean Martin) killed by the vicious Hollister gang. Their parting words before expiring is a wish that their respective sons avenge their deaths. Fast forward 25 years. Wade Jr. heads west to avoid an unwelcome marriage and a nagging mother, while

Slim Jr. falls for a pretty ranch owner (Lori Nelson) and tries to protect her against a group of masked outlaws, led, of course, by descendants of the Hollisters. In predictable fashion Wade Jr. and Slim Jr. bungle their way to victory over the Hollisters, thus avenging their fathers' dying wishes.

There is lots of fun here, with some charming songs from the team of Sammy Cahn and Jimmy Van Heusen. While the film ends happily with Dean and Jerry addressing the audience at film's end, "You keep comin' to see us, 'cause we sure like seein' you," the legendary comedy team was actually in the throes of splitting up, and by time the film was released their famed partnership had about come to an end. To their credit, and despite an escalating mutual hostility, their screen moments work out quite well. *Pardners* provides some good escapist fun and an opportunity to see one of cinema's great comedy teams engaged—as others before them—in spoofing the Wild West.

PARDON MY GUN Columbia, 1943, B&W, 56 min. **Producer:** Jack Fier; **Director:** William Berke; **Screenplay:** Wyndham Gittens; **Music:** Mischa Bakaleinikoff; **Cinematographer:** George Meehan; **Editor:** Mel Thorsen; **Cast:** Charles Starrett, Alma Carroll, Victor Adamson, Noah Beery, Lloyd Bridges, Dick Curtis, Arthur Hunnicutt, Jack Kirk.

PARK AVENUE LOGGER (aka: TALL TIMBER) RKO, 1937, B&W, 67 min. **Producer:** George A. Hirliman; **Director:** David Howard; **Screenplay:** Danile Jarrett and Ewing Scott; **Cinematographer:** Frank B. Good; **Editor:** Robert O. Crandall; **Cast:** George O'Brien, Beatrice Roberts, Willard Robertson, Ward Bond, Bert Hanlon. Gertrude Short.

George O'Brien, RKO's resident B western star in the 1930s, is an arrogant playboy who is sent to work in a lumber camp. Once there he discovers that the camp foreman is a crook. The TV title for this well produced series entry is *Tall Timber.*

PARSON AND THE OUTLAW, THE (aka: THE KILLER AND 21 MEN; RETURN OF THE OUTLAW) Columbia, 1957, Color, 71 min. **Producer:** Charles "Buddy" Rogers; **Director:** Oliver Drake; **Screenplay:** Drake and John Mantley; **Music:** Joe Sodia; **Cinematographer:** Clark Ramsey; **Editor:** Warren Adams; **Cast:** Anthony Dexter, Sonny Tufts, Marie Windsor, Charles "Buddy" Rogers, Jean Parker, Robert Lowery, Bob Steele.

Billy the Kid (Dexter) escapes death at the hands of Pat Garrett and decides to lead a peaceful life. But his tranquility is challenged when he becomes involved with a minister trying to fight a corrupt land baron and his henchman. This otherwise stagnant production is of curio interest due to the presence of "Buddy" Rogers who coproduced the film and appears as the Rev. Jericho Jones.

PARSON OF PANAMINT, THE   Paramount, 1941, B&W, 84 min. **Producer:** Harry Sherman; **Director:** William C. McGann; **Screenplay:** Adrian Scott and Harold Shumate; **Music:** Sam Coslow, Thomas Hastings, John Leipold, Frank Loesser, Ralph Rainger, Ann Ronell, Manning Sherman, James Thornton, and Augustus Montague Toplady; **Cinematographer:** Russell Harlan; **Editors:** Carroll Lewis and Sherman A. Rose; **Cast:** Charles Ruggles, Ellen Drew, Phillip Terry, Joseph Schildkraut, Porter Hall, Clem Bevans, Janet Beecher, Henry Kolker, Rod Cameron.

A young preacher (Philip Terry) comes to the brawling mining town of Panamint to try to reform it, but instead he finds himself involved in a murder in this adaptation of a story by Peter Kyne. Among the composers providing songs for this pleasant offbeat little Western is future movie and Broadway great Frank Loesser (*Guys and Dolls*, *The Most Happy Fella*). Paramount had previously filmed Kyne's story twice before as silent features in 1916 with Dustin Farnum, and in 1922 with Jack Holt. The film also boasts an early uncredited appearance by Rod Cameron.

PARTNERS   RKO, 1932, B&W, 58 min. **Director:** Fred Allen; **Screenplay:** Donald W. Lee; **Cinematographer:** Harry Jackson; **Editor:** Walter Thompson; **Cast:** Tom Keene, Nancy Drexel, Otto Harlan, Victor Potel.

Rancher Dick Barstow (Tom Keene) is arrested for the murder of his young partner's grandfather, who had loaned him the money to buy a ranch. He escapes from jail and sets out to find the real killer and prove his innocence. Keene makes a personable hero in this early oater from RKO-Pathé. "Home on the Range," reputed to be the favorite song of President Franklin Delano Roosevelt, is performed on-screen by an uncredited quartet. (See also *BEYOND THE ROCKIES*.)

PARTNERS OF THE PLAINS   Paramount, 1938, B&W, 70 min. **Producer:** Harry Sherman; **Director:** Lesley Selander; **Screenplay:** Harrison Jacobs; **Music:** Ralph Freed and Burton Lane; **Cinematographer:** Russell Harlan; **Editor:** Robert B. Warwick Jr.; **Cast:** William Boyd, Russell Hayden, Harvey Clark, Gwen Gaze, Hilda Plowright, Al Bridge.

PARTNERS OF THE SUNSET   Monogram, 1948, B&W, 53 min. **Producer:** Louis Gray; **Director:** Lambert Hillyer; **Screenplay:** J. Benton Cheney; **Music:** Edward J. Kay; **Cinematographer:** Harry Neumann; **Editor:** John C. Fuller; **Cast:** Jimmy Wakely, Dub Taylor, Steve Darrell, Bill George, Ray Whitley.

PARTNERS OF THE TRAIL   Monogram, 1944, B&W, 57 min. **Producer:** Scott R. Dunlap; **Director:** Lambert Hillyer; **Screenplay:** Frank H. Young; **Music:** Edward J. Kay; **Cinematographer:** Harry Neumann; **Editor:** Karl Heim; **Cast:** Johnny Mack Brown, Raymond Hatton, Lynten Brent, Steve Clark, Ben Corbett, Lloyd Ingraham, Jack Ingram, Ted Mapes.

PASSAGE WEST (aka: HIGH VENTURE, UK)   Paramount, 1951, Color, 76 min. **Producers:** William H. Pine and William C. Thomas; **Director:** Lewis R. Foster; **Screenplay:** Foster; **Music:** Mahlon Merrick; **Cinematographer:** Loyal Griggs; **Editor:** Howard A. Smith; **Cast:** John Payne, Dennis O'Keefe, Arleen Whelan, Frank Faylen, Mary Anderson, Peter Hanson, Dooley Wilson.

Six escaped convicts take refuge in a wagon train belonging to a religious sect heading west. An average early 1950s oater, the picture benefits from the presence of John Payne and Dennis O'Keefe, longtime Hollywood veterans. Look for Dooley Wilson, the piano player in *Casablanca* (1942) who sang "As Time Goes By," in the role of Rainbow.

PASSION   RKO, 1954, Color, 84 min. **Producer:** Benedict Bogeaus; **Director:** Allan Dwan; **Screenplay:** Joseph Leytes, Beatrice A. Dresher, and Howard Eastabrook; **Music:** Louis Forbes; **Cinematographer:** John Alton; **Editor:** James Leicester and Carlo Lodato; **Cast:** Cornel Wilde, Yvonne De Carlo, Raymond Burr, Lon Chaney Jr., Rodolfo Acosta, John Quelan, Anthony Caruso.

In this film set in Spanish California, a man's wife and daughter are murdered by a land-hungry army officer and his gang of thugs. The man joins forces with his pretty sister-in-law and sets out to revenge the murder of his loved ones. A violent period piece, the film boasts an interesting plot and a fine performance by Yvonne De Carlo in a dual role. Chaney and Burr lend splendid support as a moronic thug and a corrupt lawman. Of particular interest is an action-packed gunfight sequence in the snowy Sierra.

PAT GARRETT AND BILLY THE KID   MGM, 1973, Color, 122 min, VHS. **Producer:** Gordon Carroll; **Director:** Sam Peckinpah; **Screenplay:** Rudy Wurlitzer; **Music:** Bob Dylan; **Cinematographer:** John Coquillon; **Editor:** David Berlatsky, Garth Craven, Richard Halsey, Roger Spottiswoode, Robert L. Wolfe, and Tony de Zarraga; **Cast:** James Coburn, Kris Kristofferson, Richard Jaeckel, Katy Jurado, Chill Wills, Barry Sullivan, Jason Robards, Bob Dylan, R. G. Armstrong, Luke Askew, Jack Elam, Rita Coolidge, Paul Fix, L. Q. Jones, Slim Pickens.

Sam Peckinpah takes a revisionist look at Pat Garrett (James Coburn) and his pursuit of ex-cohort Billy the Kid (Kris Kristofferson) in New Mexico during the 1880s. Peckinpah touches a familiar theme. It's the last days of the western frontier, and things are changing fast. Coming to a close is the time-tested battle between law and outlaw, age and youth, corruption and freedom—the last hurrah for the vanishing free soul. Garrett, the former outlaw who now wears a sheriff's badge, tracks down his old saddlemate, finally catching up with him in Old Fort Sumner, New Mexico.

Along the way there are many blood-splattered killings, usually depicted in lazy, almost lyrical slow motion. Many scenes depict various characters' rough use of women (both Peckinpah trademarks), as well as an unpleasant chicken-shooting scene. Peckinpah also makes ample use of freeze-frames to break up action scenes and create a feeling of the melancholy of the times, which were soon to be irrevocably lost. When Billy asks Garrett how it feels to now wear a badge, Garrett's answer is clear: "It feels that times have changed."

The end comes during the night when Garrett and his band sneak up to Billy's house and kill the outlaw. Peckinpah himself appears toward the end of the film to push Garrett toward the inevitable. The next morning Garrett rides out of town with his conscience his only companion. The future has run over the past. Two decades after killing Billy, Garrett is murdered, his death paid for by the same business interests that originally hired him to shoot Billy.

The appearance of counterculture icon Bob Dylan in the role of a drifter named Alias is hardly significant and only serves to enhance the iconoclasm of the film. His musical score has questionable merit, but it does include the hit song "Knocking on Heaven's Door." Accordingly, *Variety* found Dylan's dramatic debut ". . . so peripheral . . . as to make his appearance a trivial cameo. His acting is limited to an embarrassing assortments of tics, shrugs, winks, and smiles."

For its original release the film was massively recut by MGM without consulting the director—a move not well received by Peckinpah, who had the same problem with Columbia upon the release of *MAJOR DUNDEE* (1965). Subsequently, editor Roger Spottiswoode restored it in a manner closer to Peckinpah's intentions. The Peckinpah/Spottiswoode version introduced several scenes not in the original release, most prominently a framing narrative showing Garrett's death 25 years later. The director's version, which was never released to theaters, now appears on home video and cable.

Reviews and general appeal varied greatly, especially when gauged against the prevailing counterculture westerns that seemed to dominate the late 1960s and 1970s. Some critics such as *Time's* Jay Cocks affirmed the film as a near-masterpiece, with "whole sequences here [standing] among the best Peckinpah has ever achieved." Others have found this revisionist telling of a familiar American legend to be one big misfire. The British *Monthly Film Bulletin*, for example, called the film "a paralyzed epic, an impenetrable mood piece."

Among Peckinpah's harshest critics were some of the genre's old guard, including director Howard Hawks, who had dismissed *THE WILD BUNCH* (1969) four years earlier with the oft-quoted line, "I can kill four men, take 'em to the morgue, and bury 'em before he gets one down to the ground in slow motion." John Wayne was another who found Peckinpah's violence to be too graphic. "Pictures go too far," he told *Playboy* in 1971, "when they use that kind of realism

[and] have shots of blood spurting out and teeth flying, and when they throw liver to make it look like people's insides."

PATHFINDER, THE Columbia, 1953, Color, 78 min. **Producer:** Sam Katzman; **Director:** Sidney Salkow; **Screenplay:** Robert Kent; **Cinematographer:** Henry Freulich; **Editor:** Jerome Thoms; **Cast:** George Montgomery, Helena Carter, Jay Silverheels, Walter Kingsford, Rodd Redwing.

George Montgomery is a white man raised by the Mohican Indians in this film set during the French and Indian Wars and based on a story by James Fenimore Cooper. When his people are pillaged and murdered, he joins forces with the British army as revenge against the Mingo warriors and French troops he holds responsible for the attack on his people. His mission is to retrieve secret plans from within the French fort at St. Vicente.

PAWNEE (aka: PALE ARROW, UK) Republic, 1957, Color, 80 min. **Producers:** Jack J. Gross and Philip N. Krasne; **Director:** George Waggner; **Screenplay:** Waggner, Endre Bohem, and Louis Vittes; **Music:** Paul Sawtell; **Cinematographer:** Hal McAlpin; **Editor:** Kenneth G. Crane; **Cast:** George Montgomery, Bill Williams, Lola Albright, Francis McDonald, Robert Griffin, Dabs Greer.

Once again George Montgomery is a white man raised by the Indians, this time the Pawnee. The plot develops when he has to decide whether to remain an Indian and become chief of the Pawnee nation or return to his white roots and save a wagon train from an Indian attack. The strong cast includes Bill Williams, Dabbs Greer, and Lola Albright as the white woman who falls in love with Montgomery (and the feeling is mutual). The almost obligatory love triangle, which includes wagon master Williams, adds sparkle to this routine 1950s western.

PEACEMAKER, THE United Artists, 1956, Color, 82 min. **Producer:** Hal R. Makelim; **Director:** Ted Post; **Screenplay:** Hal Richards; **Music:** George Greeley; **Cinematographer:** Lester Shorr; **Editor:** William Shea; **Cast:** James Mitchell, Rosemary Stack, Jan Merlin, Jess Barker, Hugh Sanders, Taylor Homes.

An ex-gunman, now a preacher, arrives in a small western town and finds himself in the middle of a feud between settlers and ranchers.

PECOS RIVER Columbia, 1951, B&W, 56 min. **Producer:** Colbert Clark; **Director:** Fred F. Sears; **Screenplay:** Barry Shipman; **Music:** George Duning, John Leipold, Arthur Morton, Heinz Roemheld, Hans J. Salter, Paul Sawtell, Marlin Skiles, and Paul J. Smith; **Cinematographer:** Fayte M. Browne; **Editor:** Paul Bofofsky; **Cast:** Charles Starrett, Jock Mahoney, Delores Sidener, Steve Darrell, Smiley Burnette, Frank Jenks.

See *DURANGO KID, THE.*

PERILOUS JOURNEY Republic, 1953, B&W, 90 min. **Producer:** William J. O'Sullivan; **Director:** R. G. Springsteen; **Screenplay:** Vingie E. Roe and Richard Wormser; **Music:** Victor Young; **Cinematographer:** Jack A. Marta; **Editor:** Richard L. Van Enger; **Cast:** Vera Hruba Ralston, David Brian, Scott Brady, Charles Winninger, Hope Emerson, Eileen Christy, Leif Ericson, Veda Ann Borg, Ben Cooper, Denver Pyle, Kathleen Freeman, John Dierkes.

A woman eager to locate her gambler husband joins four dozen mail-order brides on a ship headed to California. An unusual plot and a top-flight performance by Hope Emerson as the stern-willed chaperone make for an interesting little film.

PERSUADER, THE Allied Artists, 1957, B&W, 72 min. **Producer:** Dick Ross; **Director:** Ross; **Screenplay:** Curtis Kenyon and Ross; **Music:** Ralph Charmichael; **Cinematographer:** Ralph Woolsey; **Editor:** Eugene Pendleton; **Cast:** William Talman, James Craig, Kristine Miller, Darryl Hickman, Georgia Lee, Gregory Walcott.

A clergyman is forced to take up arms reluctantly in order to fight a band of mercenary outlaws.

PHANTOM COWBOY Republic, 1941, B&W, 56 min. **Producer:** George Sherman; **Director:** Sherman; **Screenplay:** Doris Schroeder; **Cinematographer:** Reggie Lanning; **Editor:** Tony Martinelli; **Cast:** Don "Red" Barry, Virginia Carroll, Milburn Stone, Neyle Marx, Rex Lease.

PHANTOM EMPIRE Mascot, 1935, B&W, 245 min, 12 chapters, VHS. **Producer:** Ned Levine; **Directors:** Otto Bower and B. Reeves Eason; **Screenplay:** John Rathmell and Armond Schaefer; **Music:** Lee Zahler; **Cinematographer:** Ernest Miller and William Nobles; **Editor:** Earl Turner; **Cast:** Gene Autry, Dorothy Christy, Smiley Burnette, Frankie Darro, Betsy King Ross, Wheeler Oakman.

A gang of crooks discovers a valuable mineral on a radio singer's ranch. The singer (Gene Autry) decides to fight the crooks, and in turn he finds a secret underground civilization. Autry's first starring venture is this fanciful 12-chapter Mascot serial combining the western and science fiction genres.

PHANTOM GOLD Columbia, 1938, B&W, 56 min. **Producer:** Larry Darmour; **Director:** Joseph Levering; **Screenplay:** Nate Gatzert; **Music:** Lee Zahler; **Cinematographer:** James S. Brown Jr.; **Editor:** Dwight Caldwell; **Cast:** Jack Luden, Beth Marion, Barry Downing, Slim Whitaker, Wally Wales.

When outlaws plan a gold rush by salting an old mine, they are thwarted by a cowboy, his two buddies, a young boy, and a dog the three men had rescued. Star Jack Luden, who would later die in San Quentin prison, appeared in a series of four films for Columbia in 1938 as a character named Breezy

Larkin. The other three films in the series include *Rolling Caravans*, *Stagecoach Days*, and *Pioneer Trail*.

PHANTOM OF THE DESERT Syndicate, 1930, B&W, 55 min. **Producers:** F. E. Douglas and Harry S. Webb; **Director:** Webb; **Screenplay:** Carl Krusada; **Cinematographer:** William Nobles; **Editor:** Frederick Bain; **Cast:** Jack Perrin, Eva Novak, Joseph Swickard, Lila Eccles, Ben Corbett, Edward Earle.

Horses are being stolen, presumably by a white stallion known as "The Phantom of the Desert." Cowboy Jack Saunders (Jack Perrin) sets out to find the horse, which he captures. He is then led to the missing horses and discovers who is really responsible for the spate of thefts. The tag line for this likable early Jack Perrin venture reads: "The First All-Talking Story of a Wild Horse."

PHANTOM OF THE PLAINS Republic, 1945, B&W, 56 min. **Producer:** R. G. Springsteen; **Director:** Leslie Selander; **Screenplay:** Charles Kenyon and Earle Snell; **Cinematographer:** William Bradford; **Editor:** Charles Craft; **Cast:** William "Wild Bill" Elliott, Robert Blake, Alice Fleming, Ian Keith, William Haade, Virginia Christine.

PHANTOM OF THE RANGE Victory, 1936, B&W, 57 min. **Producer:** Sam Katzman; **Director:** Robert F. Hill; **Screenplay:** Basil Dickey; **Cinematographer:** William Hyer; **Editor:** Charles Henkel Jr.; **Cast:** Tom Tyler, Beth Marion, Sammy Cohen, Soledad Jimenez, Forrest Taylor, Charles King.

PHANTOM PATROL Ambassador, 1936, B&W, 60 min. **Producer:** Maurice Conn; **Director:** Charles Hutchinson; **Screenplay:** Stephen Norris; **Cinematographer:** Arthur Reed; **Editor:** Richard G. Wray; **Cast:** Kermit Maynard, Joan Barclay, Harry Worth, Paul Fix, George Cleveland, Julian Rivero, Eddie Phillips.

PHANTOM PLAINSMEN, THE Republic, 1942, B&W, 56 min. **Producer:** Louis Gray; **Director:** John English; **Screenplay:** Barry Shipman and Robert Yost; **Music:** Cy Feuer; **Cinematographer:** Bud Thackery; **Editor:** William P. Thompson; **Cast:** Bob Steele, Tom Tyler, Rufe Davis, Rudolph Anders, Lois Collier.

PHANTOM RANGER Monogram, 1938, B&W, 53 min. **Producer:** Maurice Conn; **Director:** Sam Newfield; **Screenplay:** Joseph O'Donnell and Stanley Roberts; **Cinematographer:** Jack Greenhalgh; **Editor:** Richard G. Wray; **Cast:** Tim McCoy, Suzanne Kaaren, John St. Polis, Karl Hackett, Charles King, Tom London.

Lawman Tim McCoy is sent by the Treasury Department to rescue an engraver who is being held captive by a counterfeiting gang who wants him to make counterfeit plates for

Tim McCoy, one of the B westerns' most enduring and authentic cowboy stars (AUTHOR'S COLLECTION)

them. *Phantom Ranger* is yet another 1930s oater where the title has little or nothing to do with the plot or content of the film.

PHANTOM RIDER, THE Universal, 1936, B&W, 15 chapters. **Producer:** Henry MacRae; **Director:** Ray Taylor; **Screenplay:** Basil Dickey, Ella O'Neill, and George H. Plympton; **Music:** Karl Hajos, W. Frankie Harling, David Klatzkin, Sam Perry, Heintz Roemheld, and Oliver Wallace; **Cast:** Buck Jones, Maria Shelton, Diana Gibson, Joey Ray, Harry Woods.

In this 15-episode serial Buck Grant (Buck Jones), the Phantom Rider, helps a woman rancher fight off a band of outlaws out to seize her property. This well-made serial, while heavier in plot than action, should greatly please Jones's fans. Largely due to his charismatic screen presence, Buck Jones made four serials for Universal: *The Phantom Rider, Gordon of Ghost City* (1933); *The Red Rider* (1934); *The Roaring West* (1935).

PHANTOM STAGE, THE Universal, 1939, B&W, 58 min. **Producer:** Trem Carr; **Director:** George Waggner; **Screenplay:** Waggner (as Joseph West); **Cinematographer:** Harry Neumann; **Cast:** Bob Baker, Marjorie Reynolds, Forrest Taylor, Reed Howes, Glenn Strange.

PHANTOM STAGECOACH Columbia, 1957, B&W, 69 min. **Producer:** Wallace Macdonald; **Director:** Ray Nazarro; **Screenplay:** David Lang; **Cinematographer:** Henry Freulich; **Editor:** Edwin Bryant; **Cast:** William Bishop, Kathleen Crowley, Richard Webb, Hugh Sanders, John Doucette, Ray Teal, Frank Ferguson, Lane Bradford.

When two stage line owners have a dispute over travel routes, the result is gunplay.

PHANTOM STALLION Republic, 1954, B&W, 54 min. **Producer:** Rudy Ralston (associate); **Director:** Harry Keller; **Screenplay:** Gerald Geraghty; **Music:** R. Dale Butts; **Cinematographer:** Bud Thackery; **Editor:** Harold Minter; **Cast:** Rex Allen, Slim Pickens, Carla Balenda, Harry Shannon, Don Haggerty.

PHANTOM STOCKMAN (aka: THE RETURN OF THE PLAINSMAN) Astor Pictures, 1953, B&W, 67 min. **Producers:** George Heath and Chips Rafferty; **Director:** Lee Robinson; **Screenplay:** Robinson; **Music:** William Lovelock; **Cinematographer:** George Heath; **Editor:** Gus Lowry; **Cast:** Chips Rafferty, Victoria Shaw, Guy Doleman, Bob Darken, Bill Gregory, Hawkeye.

This Australian western has Chips Rafferty as the legendary bushman known as the Sundowner, who along with his aboriginal sidekick tracks down a gang of cattle rustlers. Released in the United States as *The Return of the Plainsman*, the picture is the first of two commercially successful collaborations between Rafferty and director Lee Robinson.

PHANTOM THUNDERBOLT World Wide, 1933, B&W, 63 min. **Producers:** Samuel Bischoff, Burt Kelly, and William Saal; **Director:** Alan James; **Screenplay:** James; **Cinematographer:** Jackson Rose; **Editor:** David Berg; **Cast:** Ken Maynard, Frances Lee, Frank Lee, William Gould, Bob Kortman.

Ken Maynard is The Thunderbolt Kid, a cowboy who comes to the aid of a town that is being threatened by a band of outlaws determined to prevent a railroad from going through it. This Maynard vehicle from World Wide Pictures is one of his better efforts between his two stints with Universal. After a prolific career at Universal (1920–30), the studio stopped its production of horse operas for a few years, leaving Maynard to work for some so-called poverty row producers like World Wide. In 1933 he returned to Universal, where he began making a series of fairly lavish pictures.

PHANTOM VALLEY Columbia, 1948, B&W, 53 min. **Producer:** Colbert Clark; **Director:** Ray Navarro; **Screenplay:** J. Benton Cheney; **Music:** Smiley Burnette; **Cinematographer:** George F. Kelley; **Editor:** Paul Borofsky; **Cast:** Charles Starrett, Virginia Hunter, Smiley Burnette, Michael Conrad, Sam Flint.

PILLARS OF THE SKY (aka: TOMAHAWK AND THE CROSS, UK) Universal, 1956, Color, 95 min. **Producer:** Robert Arthur; **Director:** George Marshall; **Screenplay:** Sam Rolfe; **Music:** William Lava, Heintz Roemheld, and Milton Rosen; **Cinematographer:** Harold Lipstein; **Editor:** Michael Carruth; **Cast:** Jeff Chandler, Dorothy Malone, Ward Bond, Keith Andes, Lee Marvin, Sydney Chaplin, Michael Ansara, Olive Carey, Martin Milner.

In the Oregon Country in 1868, several Indian tribes are placed on a reservation north of the Snake River. An American doctor (Ward Bond) builds a church, allowing many of the Indians to accept Christianity and to assume Christian names. Sergeant Emmett Bell (Jeff Chandler) is in charge of maintaining order, but eventually the inevitable clash occurs with the appearance of the U.S. cavalry, and hostile Indians attack in retaliation. Shot in CinemaScope, this standard 1950s adult oater benefits from a strong cast and Chandler's competent performance as the hard-drinking, hard-fighting sergeant.

PINTO BANDIT, THE PRC, 1944, B&W, 56 min. **Producer:** Alfred Stern; **Director:** Elmer Clifton; **Screenplay:** Clifton; **Music:** Lee Zahler; **Cinematographer:** Edward A. Kull; **Editor:** Charles Henkel Jr.; **Cast:** Dave O'Brien, James Newill, Guy Wilkerson, Mady Lawrence, James Martin.

PINTO CANYON Metropolitan, 1940, B&W, 55 min. **Producer:** Harry S. Webb; **Director:** Bernard B. Ray (as Raymond K. Johnson); **Screenplay:** Carl Krusada; **Cinematographer:** William Hyer and Edward Kull; **Editor:** Fred Bain; **Cast:** Bob Steele, Louise Stanley, Kenne Duncan, Ted Adams, Steve Clark.

See *FEUD OF THE RANGE.*

PINTO RUSTLERS Reliable, 1936, B&W, 56 min. **Producer:** Bernard B. Ray; **Director:** Harry S. Webb (as Henri Samuels); **Screenplay:** Robert Emmett Tansey; **Cinematographer:** William Hyer; **Editor:** Frederick Bain; **Cast:** Tom Tyler, George Walsh, Catherine Cotter, Earl Dwire, Al St. John.

PIONEER DAYS Monogram, 1940, B&W, 54 min. **Producer:** Harry S. Webb; **Director:** Webb; **Screenplay:** Bennett Cohen; **Cinematographer:** Edward A. Kull; **Editor:** Robert Golden; **Cast:** Addison Randall, June Wilkins, Frank Yaconelli, Nelson McDowell, Ted Adams.

PIONEER JUSTICE PRC, 1947, B&W, 56 min. **Producer:** Jerry Thomas; **Director:** Ray Taylor; **Screenplay:** Adrian Page; **Cinematographer:** Ernie Miller; **Editor:** Hugh Winn; **Cast:** Lash La Rue, Al St. John, Jennifer Holt, William Fawcett, Jack Ingram, Dee Cooper.

PIONEER MARSHAL Republic, 1949, B&W, 60 min. **Producer:** Melville Tucker; **Director:** Philip Ford; **Screen-play:** Bob Williams; **Music:** Stanley Wilson; **Cinematographer:** John MacBurnie; **Editor:** Robert M. Leeds; **Cast:** Monte Hale, Paul Hurst, Nan Leslie, Roy Barcroft, Myron Healey, Damian O'Flynn.

PIONEERS OF THE FRONTIER (aka: THE ANCHOR) Columbia, 1940, B&W, 58 min. **Producer:** Leon Barsha; **Director:** Sam Nelson; **Screenplay:** Fred Myton; **Cinematographer:** George Meehan; **Editor:** James Sweeney; **Cast:** William "Wild Bill" Elliott, Dorothy Comingore, Dick Curtis, Dub Taylor, Stanley Brown, Richard Fiske, Lafe McKee, Carl Stockdale, Al Bridge.

PIONEERS OF THE WEST Republic, 1940, B&W, 56 min. **Producer:** Harry Grey; **Director:** Lester Orlebeck; **Screenplay:** Karen DeWolf, Gerald Geraghty, and Jack Natteford; **Music:** Cy Feuer; **Cinematographer:** Jack A. Marta; **Editor:** Tony Martinelli; **Cast:** Robert Livingston, Raymond Hatton, Duncan Renaldo, Noah Beery, Beatrice Roberts.

PIONEER TRAIL Columbia, 1938, B&W, 59 min. **Producer:** Larry Darmour; **Director:** Joseph Levering; **Screenplay:** Nate Gatzert; **Music:** Mischa Bakaleinikoff, Ben Oakland, Louis Silvers, and William Grant Still; **Cinematographer:** James S. Brown Jr.; **Editor:** Dwight Caldwell; **Cast:** Jack Luden, Joan Barclay, Slim Whitaker, Leon Beaumon, Hal Taliaferro, Marin Sais, Eva McKenzie.

PIRATES OF MONTEREY Universal, 1947, Color, 77 min. **Producer:** Paul Malvern; **Director:** Alfred L. Werker; **Screenplay:** Sam Hellman, Bradford Ropes, and Margaret Buell Wilder; **Music:** Milton Rosen; **Cinematographer:** W. Howard Greene, Harry Hallenberger, and Hal Mohr; **Editor:** Russell F. Schoengarth; **Cast:** Maria Montez, Rod Cameron, Mikhail Rasumny, Philip Reed, Gilbert Roland, Gale Sondergaard.

A woman who journeys to California to marry a Spanish officer meets and falls in love with an American adventurer who is part of a movement to overthrow the Spanish in California. This Maria Montez venture was produced by Paul Malvern, who produced many early John Wayne B westerns in the 1930s. While the film lacks real excitement, it remains a testimony to the incredible beauty of Maria Montez, and it is also enhanced by solid performances from Rod Cameron and Gilbert Roland.

PIRATES OF THE PRAIRIE RKO, 1942, B&W, 57 min. **Director:** Howard Bretherton; **Screenplay:** Doris Schroeder and J. Benton Cheney; **Music:** Fred Rose and Ray Whitley (songs); **Cinematographer:** Nicholas Musuraca; **Editor:** John Lockert; **Cast:** Tim Holt, Cliff Edwards, Nell O'Day, John Elliott, Roy Barcroft, Karl Hackett, Ed Cassidy, Charles King.

One of Tim Holt's better RKO ventures has him as a U.S. marshal on the trail of a band of masked riders who are stealing land so they can get a top price when the railroad comes through. (See also *ALONG THE RIO GRANDE*.)

PIRATES ON HORSEBACK
Paramount, 1941, B&W, 69 min, VHS. **Producers:** Joseph W. Engel; **Director:** Lesley Selander; **Screenplay:** J. Benton Cheney and Ethel La Blanche; **Cinematographer:** Russell Harlan; **Editor:** Fred R. Feitshans Jr.; **Cast:** William Boyd, Russell Hayden, Andy Clyde, Eleanor Stewart, Morris Ankrum.

An entertaining mystery aura enhances this Hop-Along Cassidy entry in which Hoppy and the boys are after a gang of outlaws who are trying to locate a hidden gold mine. (See also *HOP-ALONG CASSIDY*.)

PISTOLERO OF RED RIVER
See *LAST CHALLENGE, THE*.

PISTOL HARVEST
RKO, 1951, B&W, 57 min. **Producer:** Herman Schlom; **Director:** Leslie Selander; **Screenplay:** Norman Houston; **Music:** Paul Sawtell; **Cinematographer:** J. Roy Hunt; **Editor:** Douglas Biggs; **Cast:** Tim Holt, Richard Martin, Joan Dixon, Robert Clarke, Mauritz Hugo, Robert J. Wilke.

PISTOL PACKIN' MAMA
Republic, 1943, B&W, 64 min. **Producer:** Edward J. White; **Director:** Frank Woodruff; **Screenplay:** Edward J. White; **Music:** Al Dexter; **Cinematographer:** Reggie Lanning; **Editor:** Tony Martinelli; **Cast:** Ruth Terry, Robert Livingston, Wally Vernon, Jack La Rue, Helen Talbot, Nat "King" Cole and His Trio, Kenne Duncan.

Western lady Sally Benson (Ruth Terry) is cheated out of her bankroll by Nick Winner (Robert Livingston), a gambler passing through town. When Nick opens up a combination night club/gambling establishment in New York, Sally (using the name Vicki Norris) gets a job singing there. When Nick tries to fire her, Sally/Vicki returns and coolly pulls out a gun to settle matters, but love prevails at the end.

This pleasant little musical oater is best known for Al Dexter's hit title song "Pistol Packin' Mama," which swept the country and is sung in the movie by Ruth Terry. Al Dexter had a big-selling recording of the song, as did Bing Crosby and the Andrews Sisters.

PLAINSMAN, THE
Paramount, 1936, B&W, 115 min, VHS. **Producers:** Cecil B. DeMille and William H. Pine; **Director:** DeMille; **Screenplay:** Harold Lamb, Jeanie MacPherson, Lynn Riggs, and Waldemar Young; **Music:** George Antheil; **Cinematographer:** Victor Miner and George Robinson; **Editor:** Anne Bauchens; **Cast:** Gary Cooper, Jean Arthur, James Ellison, Charles Bickford, Helen Burgess, Porter Hall, Paul Harvey, Victor Varconi, Harry Woods, Anthony Quinn, George "Gabby" Hayes, Fuzzy Knight, Francis Ford.

Following the Civil War, the unscrupulous John Lattimore (Charles Bickford) plans to sell repeating rifles to the Indians. In the meantime Wild Bill Hickok (Gary Cooper) learns from a wounded scout that Indians have attacked a nearby garrison. He reports his findings to General George Custer (John Miljan), who quickly sends Buffalo Bill Cody (James Ellison) with a wagon train of arms to the garrison. Hickok in turn is sent to talk to the chief of the Cheyenne, but on the way he sees Calamity Jane (Jean Arthur) being captured by Indians and tries to help her.

Wild Bill and Calamity are taken to the Indian camp, where Hickok is tortured because he won't give up information about the wagon train. But Calamity can't stand to see this abundance of torture, and she divulges the secret. Both are released, and each tries separately to correct the wrong created by Calamity's weakness. Hickok eventually faces Lattimore and kills him, but before the cavalry can arrive he is shot in the back during an infamous card game. Buffalo Bill and the cavalry arrive too late to save the dying Bill Hickok.

It was Cecil B. DeMille who brought the epic back to the western arena in 1936 with *The Plainsman*, a historically inaccurate but quite adept film adaptation loosely based on two books: *Wild Bill Hickok*, by Frank W. Wilstach; and *The Prince of Pistols*, by Courtney Riley Cooper and Grover Jones. The film was Gary Cooper's first for master showman Cecil B. DeMille.

Whatever historical license DeMille may have taken with the story, he more than compensates for it with an abounding enthusiasm for detail and a generally polished, though somewhat flawed finished project. Nor does he shy away from adding a name or two to help support his story line. For example, the film opens with the unlikely presence of Abraham Lincoln being dragged away from an all-important meeting, at which the destiny of the West is to be settled, by a nagging Mrs. Lincoln warning him that they will be late for the theater. Moreover, Ellison's Buffalo Billy Cody practically becomes a nonentity, given his depiction as a placid pal rather than a heroic hunter and celebrated Indian fighter.

Still, the result was an enormously popular film both in the United States and abroad. *Variety* called the *The Plainsman* "a big and good western . . . cowboys and Indians on a broad sweeping scale." An enthusiastic *London Times* is quoted in Homer Dickens's *The Films of Gary Cooper* as suggesting that ". . . If the West in its pioneer days is to be opened up again, Mr. Cooper and Miss Arthur, with the lavish assistance of Mr. Cecil DeMille, are certainly the people to do it." Little did it matter that the comely Jean Arthur in no way resembled the wizened and homely Calamity Jane. Audiences of the 1930s, as William Everson points out, did not carp at a top star like Miss Arthur taking on such a showcase role with beauty and glamour.

As for the enormously popular Cooper, his Cooperesque demeanor, combined with this surefire part, could only endear him further to the public at large. "By the simple expedient of being himself and not acting at all," *The New York American* observed, "[Gary Cooper] remains winning and effective." His death scene, with Calamity cradling his dead body while kissing him goodbye, brought tears to many in the audience.

Universal's 1966 remake of *The Plainsman*, helmed by David Nowell Rich and starring Don Murray, Abby Dalton, and Dean Stockwell, pales in comparison to the 1936 film.

PLAINSMAN AND THE LADY, THE   Republic, 1946, B&W, 87 min. **Producer:** Joseph Kane (associate); **Director:** Kane; **Screenplay:** Richard Wormser; **Music:** George Antheil; **Cinematographer:** Reggie Lanning; **Editor:** Fred Allen; **Cast:** William "Wild Bill" Elliott, Vera Hruba Ralston, Gail Patrick, Joseph Schildkraut, Andy Clyde, Don "Red" Barry, Paul Hurst, Jack Lambert.

Bill Elliott is a wealthy gambler named Sam Cotton. In search of new adventures, he joins with a local businessman and his daughter to start a Pony Express line between St. Joseph, Missouri, and Sacramento, California. However, he has to deal with a treacherous stagecoach operator (Joseph Shildkraut) and his cruel henchmen. This interesting, well-produced A-level Bill Elliott venture for Republic features good performances by Don "Red" Barry in the unusual role of a villain and Gail Patrick as heroine Vera Hruba Ralston's social-climbing sister.

PLAINSONG   Denali Films, 1982, Color, 76 min. **Producer:** Tiare Stack; **Director:** Ed Stable; **Screenplay:** Stable; **Cinematographer:** Richard Katz and Joe Ritter; **Editor:** Stable; **Cast:** Jessica Nelson, Teresanne Joseph, Lyn Steven Geiger, Carl Keilblock, Mary Smith.

The experiences of three young women settlers in pioneer Nebraska who find themselves in the midst of a range are starkly portrayed in this realistic low-budget drama, filmed, incredibly, in New Jersey.

PLUNDERERS, THE   Republic, 1948, Color, 87 min. **Producer:** Joseph Kane (associate); **Director:** Kane; **Screenplay:** Gerald Adams and Gerald Geraghty; **Music:** Dale Butts; **Cinematographer:** Jack Marta; **Editor:** Arthur Roberts; **Cast:** Rod Cameron, Ilona Massey, Lorna Gray (as Adrian Booth), Forrest Tucker, George Cleveland, Grant Withers, Taylor Holmes, Paul Fix, Francis Ford, Clayton Moore, Rex Lease.

Cavalry officer John Drum (Rod Cameron) tracks down outlaw Whit Lacy (Forrest Tucker) but finds that he must join forces with the outlaw to avoid an Indian raiding party and a Sioux massacre. Dependable character actor Paul Fix delivers well as a cynical villain, and the excellent supporting cast includes Grant Withers, Francis Ford, and George Cleveland. Lots of clichés and lots of action fill this top-budget western from Republic.

PLUNDERERS, THE   Allied Artists, 1960, B&W, 94 min. **Producer:** Lindsley Parsons; **Director:** Joseph Pevney; **Screenplay:** Bob Barbash; **Music:** Leonard Rosenman; **Cin-**ematographer:** Sol Polito; **Editor:** Tom McAdoo; **Cast:** Jeff Chandler, John Saxon, Dolores Hart, Marsha Hunt, Jay C. Flippen, Ray Stricklyn, James Westerfield.

Four rowdy cowhands ride into a small town to make trouble, and no one seems either willing or able to take them on—not even the toughest man in town. But things start changing once a murder is committed. Jeff Chandler coproduced this interesting oater while also starring as tough Civil War veteran Sam Christy.

PLUNDERERS OF PAINTED FLATS   Republic, 1959, B&W, 77 min. **Producer:** Albert C. Gannaway; **Director:** Gannaway; **Screenplay:** John Greene and Phil Shuken; **Cinematographer:** John M. Nickolaus Jr.; **Editor:** Asa Boyd Clark; **Cast:** Corinne Calvet, John Carroll, Skip Homeier, George Macready, Edmund Lowe, Madge Kennedy, Bea Benaderet.

When a town boss hires a notorious gunslinger to run settlers out of town, one of the settlers, a young man whose father had been murdered by the gunman, sets out to kill the gunslinger.

POCKET MONEY   First Artists, 1972, Color, 102 min, VHS. **Producer:** John Foreman; **Director:** Stuart Rosenberg; **Screenplay:** J. P. S. Brown and Terrence Malick; **Music:** Alex North; **Cinematographer:** Lazlo Kovacs; **Editor:** Bob Wyman; **Cast:** Paul Newman, Lee Marvin, Strother Martin, Christine Belford, Kelly Jean Peters, Wayne Rogers, Richard Farnsworth, Terrence Malick.

This modern-day western has Paul Newman as a Texas cowboy and Lee Marvin as his boozy pal and an inveterate con man. These two losers share a myriad of schemes that always manage to fail. The plot thickens when Newman, slow witted and gullible, is hired by a shifty and crooked businessman (Strother Martin) to go to Mexico and buy 200 head of cattle.

Terrence Malick, who cowrote the screenplay, also appears in the picture as an uncredited workman. The title song was written and performed in the film by Carol King. Directed by Stuart Rosenberg, *Pocket Money* was the first movie made by First Artists, the company formed by Paul Newman, Steve McQueen, Sidney Poitier, and Barbra Streisand.

PONY EXPRESS, THE   Paramount, 1925, B&W, 110 min. **Director:** James Cruze; **Screenplay:** Walter Woods; **Music:** Hugo Riesenfeld; **Cinematographer:** Karl Brown; **Cast:** Betty Compson, Ricardo Cortez, Ernest Torrence, Wallace Beery, George Bancroft.

Senator Glen of California attempts to create an empire built around the state of California and Sonora, Mexico. To do this he plots to have the new Pony Express system "fixed" at Julesburg, Mississippi, so that any political news from the East that might have a bearing on his plans can be delayed. However, the plan is exposed by a Pony Express rider. James

Cruze's 1925 western epic followed his landmark *THE COV-ERED WAGON* (1923), and while not of the same caliber as its predecessor, it was a precursor to such later "Company" epics as *WELLS FARGO* (1937), *UNION PACIFIC* (1939), and *WESTERN UNION* (1941).

PONY EXPRESS Paramount, 1953, Color, 101 min, VHS. **Producer:** Nat Holt; **Director:** Jerry Hopper; **Screenplay:** Charles Marquis Warren; **Music:** Paul Sawtell; **Cinematographer:** Ray Rennahan; **Editor:** Eda Warren; **Cast:** Charlton Heston, Rhonda Fleming, Jan Sterling, Forrest Tucker, Michael Moore, Porter Hall.

Charlton Heston and Forrest Tucker are Buffalo Bill Cody and Wild Bill Hickok. The two folk legends join together to establish the Pony Express across the West while also attempting to stop the secession of the state of California from the Union during the Civil War. This film boasts some great action scenes, beautiful Technicolor photography, and good screen interaction between Heston and Tucker as the two authentic American heroes.

However, while the picture is colorful and entertaining, it is also thoroughly inaccurate historically. For example, Hickok never got close to an Express pony, and Cody worked in Kansas as a boy messenger for Pony Express offices four miles apart. Nevertheless, a scene where Jan Sterling starts a mudfight with female lead Rhonda Fleming adds a great deal of fun and levity.

The film was the second western for the able Heston, who a year earlier had scored big points as the boss man in Cecil B. DeMille's *The Greatest Show on Earth*. He would go on to make a dozen genre films during his long and distinguished career. *The Pony Express* was one of two pictures he made in 1953 where he played an authentic historical figure, having also played Andrew Jackson in 20th Century Fox's 1953 film *The President's Lady*.

PONY EXPRESS RIDER Doty-Dayton, 1976, Color, 100 min, VHS. **Producers:** Lyman Dayton and Dan Green; **Director:** Robert Totten; **Screenplay:** Dan Greer, Hal Harrison Jr., and Totten; **Music:** Robert O. Ragland; **Cinematographer:** Bernie Abramson; **Editor:** Marsha Hendry; **Cast:** Stewart Peterson, Jack Elam, Henry Wilcoxon, Joan Caulfield, Slim Pickens, Dub Taylor, Buck Taylor, Maurine McCormick, Ace Reis.

Stewart Peterson plays a young man in search of his father's killer when he stumbles on a dead Pony Express Rider and decides to finish his mail run. Taut direction by Robert Totten, a genuinely authentic cast, and some good action help make for an interesting and underappreciated oater.

PONY POST Universal, 1940, B&W, 59 min. **Producer:** Will Cowan (associate); **Director:** Ray Taylor; **Screenplay:** Sherman L. Lowe; **Music:** Johnny Bond, Everette Carter and Milton Rosen; **Cinematographer:** William Sickner; **Editor:** Paul Landres; **Cast:** Johnny Mack

Brown, Fuzzy Knight, Nell O'Day, Dorothy Chatterton, Stanley Blystone, Ray Teal, Kermit Maynard, Charles King, Jimmy Wakely and his Rough Riders.

See *OLD CHISHOLM TRAIL, THE.*

PONY SOLDIER 20th Century Fox, 1952, Color, 82 min. **Producer:** Samuel G. Engel; **Director:** Joseph M. Newman; **Screenplay:** John C. Higgins; **Music:** Alex North; **Cinematographer:** Harry Jackson; **Editor:** John W. McCafferty; **Cast:** Tyrone Power, Cameron Mitchell, Thomas Gomez, Penny Edwards, Robert Horton, Richard Boone.

After Duncan MacDonald (Tyrone Power) joins the 300-member Mounted Police in 1876, he tries to keep the Cree Indians off the warpath as he escorts them back to the reservation. Some outstanding color photography highlights this better-than-average early 1950s western film.

The film was also a proving ground for two actors who would later gain enduring fame in television westerns. Robert Horton, who appears as Jess Calhoun in *Pony Soldiers*, went on to play Flint McCullough in the top-rated *Wagon Train* series of the late 1950s and early '60s, then starred in a second series, *A Man from Shenandoah*, in the mid-1960s. Similarly, Richard Boone, who appears in an uncredited role in *The Pony Soldiers*, would achieve TV immortality as Paladin in the popular western series *Have Gun, Will Travel* (1957–63).

POSSE Paramount, 1975, Color, 92 min, VHS. **Producer:** Kirk Douglas; **Director:** Douglas; **Screenplay:** Christopher Knopf and William Roberts; **Music:** Maurice Jarre; **Cinematographer:** Fred J. Koenekamp; **Editor:** John W. Wheeler; **Cast:** Kirk Douglas, Bruce Dern, Bo Hopkins, James Stacey, Luke Askew, David Canary.

Kirk Douglas's second film as a director has him starring as a Texas marshal named Howard Nightingale who wants to run for the U.S. Senate. Running on a law-and-order campaign, he travels around Texas with a six-man posse in a special train, dispatching villains and villainy along the way. To win all public relation battles, he even hires a photographer to travel with him.

Then, however, the film enters its "Watergate syndrome," and, overly obsessed with his political aspirations, Nightingale emerges as the film's villain. Conversely, the hero is an outlaw named Jake Strawhorn (Bruce Dern), a murderer who increasingly becomes the object of Nightingale's political campaign. Strawhorn's gang is no match for Nightingale's posse of professional gunmen in their well-pressed uniforms. Finally, though, the posse finds it very difficult to deal with Nightingale's corruption. Reviewers generally had a tough time identifying with Strawhorn as a hero in this all-too-political western in which all forms of authority are presented in a venal light.

POSSE Poly Gram/Working Title, 1993, Color, 109 min, VHS, DVD. **Producers:** Preston L. Holmes and Jim Steele;

Director: Mario Van Peebles; **Screenplay:** Sy Richardson and Dario Scardapane; **Music:** Michael Colombier; **Cinematographer:** Peter Menzies Jr.; **Editor:** Mark Conte; **Cast:** Mario Van Peebles, Stephen Baldwin, Charles Lane, Tom "Tiny" Lister Jr., Big Daddy Kane.

Mario Van Peebles directs and stars in this film about a black infantryman who leads his fellow troopers against a group of white supremacists headed by his extremely slimy former commanding officer. The film is another example of the pursuit-and-revenge plot line that had become increasingly in vogue within the genre. *Variety* reviewed it by stating, "Tag *The Magnificent Seven* on the end and paint it black, and you've got *Posse.*"

POSSE FROM HELL Universal, 1961, Color, 81 min. **Producer:** Gordon Kay; **Director:** Herbert Coleman; **Screenplay:** Clair Huffaker; **Music:** Irving Gertz, William Lava, Henry Mancini, Heintz Roemfeld, Henry Russell, Hans J. Slater, Frank Skinner, and Herman Stein; **Cinematographer:** Clifford Stein; **Editor:** Frederic Knudtson; **Cast:** Audie Murphy, John Saxon, Susan Cabot, Zohra Lampert, Vic Morrow, Rodolfo Acosta, Royal Dano, Frank Overton, Lee Van Cleef, Ray Teal, Allan Lane.

When four escaped convicts pillage and rape their way across the Old West, a reluctant Audie Murphy organizes an even more reluctant posse to hunt down the group of four who had recently killed his pal the sheriff.

POWDER RIVER RUSTLERS Republic, 1949, B&W, 60 min. **Producer:** Gordon Kay; **Director:** Philip Ford; **Screenplay:** Richard Wormser; **Music:** Stanley Wilson; **Cinematographer:** John MacBurnie; **Editor:** Robert M. Leeds; **Cast:** Allan Lane, Eddy Waller, Gerry Ganzer, Roy Barcroft, Francis McDonald, Cliff Clark.
See *BOLD FRONTIERSMAN, THE.*

POWDERSMOKE RANGE RKO, 1935, B&W, 72 min. **Producer:** Cliff Reid (associate); **Director:** Wallace Fox; **Screenplay:** Adele S. Buffington; **Cinematographer:** Harold Wenstrom; **Editor:** James Morley; **Cast:** Harry Carey, Hoot Gibson, Guinn "Big Boy" Williams, Bob Steele, Tom Tyler, Boots Mallory.

A crooked saloon owner and a crooked sheriff plan to steal land from three buddies. But when the Mesquiteers inadvertently come to the aid of an outlaw, they are framed for robbery. Stephen Foster's "Oh Susanna" plays as background music over the opening credits in RKO's screen adaptation of William Colt McDonald's *Three Mesquiteers.* This film features Harry Carey as Tucson Smith, Hoot Gibson as Stoney Brooke, and Guinn Williams as Lullaby Joslin. During this time RKO Radio maintained a fairly regular repertoire of medium-budget westerns that were usually stronger on plot than on action. Top-heavy with an all-star cast of current and former western stars, however, *Powdersmoke Range* leaves lit-

tle time for story or action. (See also *THREE MESQUITEERS, THE.*)

PRAIRIE BADMEN PRC, 1946, B&W, 55 min. **Producer:** Sigmund Neufeld; **Director:** Sam Newfield; **Screenplay:** Fred Myton; **Cinematographer:** Robert Cline; **Editor:** Holbrook N. Todd; **Cast:** Buster Crabbe, Al St. John, Patricia Knox, Charles King, Ed Cassidy, Kermit Maynard, John L. Cason.

PRAIRIE EXPRESS Monogram, 1947, B&W, 55 min. **Producer:** Barney A. Sarecky; **Director:** Lambert Hillyer; **Screenplay:** J. Benton Cheney and Anthony Coldway; **Cinematographer:** William Sickner; **Editor:** Fred Maguire; **Cast:** Johnny Mack Brown, Raymond Hatton, William Ruhl, Marshall Reed, Virginia Belmont, Hank Worden, Steve Darrell, Kenneth Adams.

PRAIRIE JUSTICE Universal, 1938, B&W, 58 min. **Producer:** Paul Malvern; **Director:** George Waggner; **Screenplay:** Waggner (as Joseph West); **Music:** Fleming Allen; **Cinematographer:** Gus Peterson; **Editor:** Carl Pierson; **Cast:** Bob Baker, Dorothy Fay, Wally Wales (as Hal Taliaferro), Jack Rockwell, Glenn Strange, Carlton Young.

PRAIRIE LAW RKO, 1940, B&W, 59 min. **Producer:** Bert Gilroy; **Director:** David Howard; **Screenplay:** Arthur V. Jones and Doris Schroeder; **Cinematographer:** J. Roy Hunt; **Editor:** Frederic Knudtson; **Cast:** George O'Brien, Virginia Vale, Dick Hogan, J. Farrell MacDonald, Slim Whitaker, Cy Kendall.

A band of crooks brings settlers onto range land with false promises of plenty of water, but they are thwarted when they encounter opposition from a group of cattlemen desirous of helping the homesteaders. This sturdy George O'Brien western is one of six he made with actress Virginia Vale as his leading lady. Vale left motion pictures in the early 1940s and rarely looked backed, only to be "rediscovered" in the 1990s, when she became a fan favorite at western film festivals across the country.

In a 1993 interview with the author, Vale explained what prompted her to leave the industry and explained her relatively short career as a B western leading lady: "You love the business, you love the attention, you love the slipping into somebody else's life when you play a part, even a small part. You miss it! Sure you miss it. But I'm a practical person, and having a regular paycheck coming in is pretty nice." (See also *RACKETEERS OF THE RANGE.*)

PRAIRIE MOON Republic, 1938, B&W, 58 min. **Producer:** Harry Grey; **Director:** Ralph Staub; **Screenplay:** Betty Burbridge and Stanley Roberts; **Music:** Alberto Columbo, William Lava, and Victor Young; **Cinematographer:** William Nobles; **Editor:** Lester Orlebeck; **Cast:** Gene

Autry, Smiley Burnette, Shirley Dean, Tommy Ryan, Walter Tetley, Tom London.

See *TUMBLING TUMBLEWEEDS.*

PRAIRIE PIONEERS Republic, 1941, B&W, 57 min. **Producer:** Louis Grey (associate); **Director:** Lester Orlebeck; **Screenplay:** Barry Shipman; **Music:** Cy Feuer; **Cinematographer:** Ernest Miller; **Editor:** Ray Snyder; **Cast:** Robert Livingston, Bob Steele, Rufe Davis, Esther Estrella, Robert Kellard.

See *THREE MESQUITEERS, THE.*

PRAIRIE RAIDERS Columbia, 1947, B&W, 58 min. **Producer:** Louis Gray (associate); **Director:** Lester Orlebeck; **Screenplay:** Barry Shipman; **Music:** Cy Feuer; **Cinematographer:** Ernest Miller; **Editor:** Ray Snyder; **Cast:** Charles Starrett, Smiley Burnette, Nancy Saunders, Robert E. Scott, Hugh Prosser, Lane Bradford.

See *DURANGO KID, THE.*

PRAIRIE ROUNDUP Columbia, 1951, B&W, 55 min. **Producer:** Colbert Clark; **Director:** Fred F. Sears; **Screenplay:** Joseph O'Donnell; **Cinematographer:** Fayte M. Browne; **Editor:** Paul Borofsky; **Cast:** Charles Starrett, Smiley Burnette, Mary Castle, Frank Fenton, Lane Chandler, Frank Sully.

See *DURANGO KID, THE.*

PRAIRIE RUSTLERS PRC, 1945, B&W, 56 min. **Producer:** Sigmund Neufeld; **Director:** Sam Newfield; **Screenplay:** Fred Myton; **Cinematographer:** Jack Greenhalgh; **Editor:** Holbrook N. Todd; **Cast:** Buster Crabbe, Al St. John, Evelyn Finley, I. Stanford Jolley, Karl Hackett, Kermit Maynard, Bud Osborne.

See *OUTLAW OF THE PLAINS.*

PRAIRIE SCHOONERS Columbia, 1940, B&W, 58 min. **Producer:** Leon Barsha; **Director:** Sam Nelson; **Screenplay:** Robert Lee Johnson and Fred Myton; **Music:** Sidney Cutner; **Cinematographer:** George Meehan; **Editor:** Al Clark; **Cast:** William 'Wild Bill' Elliott, Evelyn Young, Dub Taylor, Kenneth Harlan, Ray Teal, Bob Burns.

PRAIRIE STRANGER Columbia, 1941, B&W, 58 min. **Producer:** William A. Berke; **Director:** Lambert Hillyer; **Screenplay:** Winston Miller; **Music:** Lee Preston and Lopez Willingham; **Cinematographer:** Benjamin H. Kline; **Editor:** James Sweeney; **Cast:** Charles Starrett, Cliff Edwards, Patti McCarty, Forbes Murray, Frank La Rue, Archie Witchell.

The third and last of the Columbia series westerns based on the Medico stories of James L. Rubel, has Dr. Steven Monroe (Charles Starrett) and his friend "Bones" setting up an office in a new town. Before long they find themselves involved in a cattle-poisoning epidemic that has a rancher murdered and Dr. Monroe accused of the crime. (See also *GALLANT DEFENDER.*)

PRAIRIE SUNDOWN See *SUNDOWN ON THE PRAIRIE.*

PRAIRIE THUNDER Warner Bros., 1937, B&W, 54 min. **Producer:** Bryan Foy; **Director:** B. Reeves Eason; **Screenplay:** Ed Earl Rapp; **Music:** Howard Jackson; **Editor:** Harold McLernon; **Cast:** Dick Foran, Janet Shaw, Frank Orth, Wilfred Lucas, Albert J. Smith, Yakima Canutt, George Chesebro, Slim Whitaker.

A cavalry scout discovers that a freight operator has been inciting Indians to disrupt the construction of telephone lines. *Prairie Thunder* was Dick Foran's final series entry for Warner Bros. (See also *MOONLIGHT ON THE PRAIRIE.*)

PRESCOTT KID, THE Columbia, 1934, B&W, 60 min. **Director:** David Sellman; **Screenplay:** Ford Beebe and Claude Rister; **Cinematographer:** Benjamin H. Kline; **Editor:** Ray Snyder; **Cast:** Tim McCoy, Sheila Bromley, Joe Sawyer, Alden "Stephen" Chase, Hooper Atchley, Walter Brennan.

A man who rides into a small town is mistaken for the expected marshal. He quickly runs afoul a gang of crooks. This Tim McCoy venture for Columbia is one of his very best efforts. (See also *RIDING TORNADO, THE.*)

PRIDE OF THE WEST Paramount, 1938, B&W, 56 min. **Producer:** Harry Sherman; **Director:** Leslie Selander; **Screenplay:** Nate Watt; **Music:** Jack Stern and Harry Tobias; **Cinematographer:** Russell Harlan; **Editor:** Sherman Rose; **Cast:** William Boyd, George "Gabby" Hayes, Russell Hayden, Earle Hodgins, Charlotte Field, James Craig.

PRINCE OF THE PLAINS Republic, 1949, B&W, 60 min. **Producer:** Melville Tucker; **Director:** Philip Ford; **Screenplay:** Albert DeMond and Louise Rousseau; **Music:** Stanley Wilson; **Cinematographer:** Bud Thackery; **Editor:** Richard L. Van Enger; **Cast:** Monte Hale, Paul Hurst, Lane Bradford, George M. Carlton, Harry Lauter, Rory Mallinson.

PROFESSIONALS, THE Columbia, 1966, Color, 117 min, VHS, DVD. **Producer:** Richard Brooks; **Director:** Brooks; **Screenplay:** Brooks; **Music:** Maurice Jarre; **Cinematographer:** Conrad L. Hall; **Editor:** Peter Zinner; **Cast:** Burt Lancaster, Lee Marvin, Robert Ryan, Woody Strode, Jack Palance, Ralph Bellamy, Claudia Cardinale, Joe De Santis, Maria Gomez.

Railroad magnate J. W. Grant (Ralph Bellamy) hires four soldiers of fortune to rescue his wife, a sultry and disheveled Claudia Cardinale, from the clutches of a notorious Mexican bandit (Jack Palance). The quartet of "professionals" includes Burt Lancaster, Robert Ryan, Lee Marvin, and Woody Strode. This is a tale of the fading West, with an increasingly familiar theme, that of a dangerous mission being carried out in foreign territory by a group of tough, hand-picked specialists: the explosives expert, the horse handler, the marksman, and the guide.

Producer/director Richard Brooks chose his actors with uncanny precision. A near-perfect combination of physical presence and professional range befits the band of cynical mercenaries trying to survive in a world where the good guys and bad guys at times are hardly distinguishable. In her book *The Private Eye, the Cowboy, and the Very Naked Girl*, Judith Crist, describing the cast of *The Professionals*, noted that "They fulfill themselves because they are professionals in the fullest sense."

Although the plot is a bit of a stretch, even a little outrageous, *The Professionals* is generally considered one of the best westerns to come out of the 1960s, a film depicting symbols of bravery, glory, suffering, and the wisdom that comes from doing things the hard way. Moreover, Conrad Hall's photography is brilliant and deserving of the Academy Award nomination it received; while a constant stream of taut action, excitement, and suspense compensates for any glitch in the excessive plot.

In addition to Hall's Oscar nomination for Best Color Cinematography, Richard Brooks was nominated twice, as Best Director and for Best Screenplay Based on Material from Another Medium (Frank O'Rourke's novel *A Mule for the Marquesa*). In addition, *The Professionals* received a Golden Globe Nomination for Best Dramatic Motion Picture, and Maria Gomez (Chiquita in the film) was nominated as Most Promising Female Newcomer.

PROUD ONES, THE 20th Century Fox, 1956, 94 min. **Producer:** Robert Jacks; **Director:** Robert D. Webb; **Screenplay:** Edmund North and Joseph Petracca; **Music:** Lionel Newman; **Cinematographer:** Lucien Ballard; **Editor:** Hugh H. Fowler; **Cast:** Robert Ryan, Virginia Mayo, Jeffrey Hunter, Robert Middleton, Walter Brennan, Arthur O'Connell, Rodolfo Acosta, George Mathews, Whit Bissell.

Robert Ryan is Cass Silver, a man with a past who, after killing a man years earlier, was run out of town by a crooked saloon owner named Honest John Barrett (Robert Middleton). When Barrett arrives in Flat Rock, Kansas, where Cass Silver is now marshal, Cass sees an opportunity to right the previous injustice, and he prepares for a confrontation with Barrett.

Matters are complicated by the arrival of Thad (Jeffrey Hunter), an angry young gunslinger who drifts into town swearing vengeance on Cass for killing his father in the line of duty. But when Thad discovers that Cass was justified in killing his father in a fair fight, their relationship progresses from distrust to an uneasy admiration and finally to genuine affection as Thad becomes convinced of Cass's innocence.

As Cass prepares for a final showdown with Barrett and his gang, the town turns against him and the city council demands his resignation. Fort Rock had changed from a quiet Kansas frontier town to a boom town when the first trail herd arrived from Texas, and Cass's presence is no longer required. In a bitter diatribe, he denounces his erstwhile "friends" and the city council as blatant hypocrites.

This lesser-known western is unfortunately not available on VHS or DVD. Lucien Ballard's cinematography gives the film a better-than-average sense of realism, while veteran actor Robert Ryan again shows his enormous emotional range, this time in a more kindly and paternalistic role as a man beset by betrayal and indignation.

PROUD REBEL, THE Buena Vista, 1958, Color, 100 min, VHS, DVD, CD. **Producer:** Samuel Goldwyn Jr.; **Director:** Michael Curtiz, Lillie Hayward, and Joseph Petracca; **Music:** Jermome Moross; **Cinematographer:** Ted D. McCord; **Editor:** Aaron McCord; **Cast:** Alan Ladd, Olivia de Havilland, Dean Jagger, David Ladd, Cecil Kellaway, James Westerfield, John Carradine, Harry Dean Stanton, Tom Pittman, Eli Mintz, Henry Hull.

Alan Ladd is John Chandler, an ex-Confederate soldier seeking medical help for his young son (David Ladd), who was shocked into muteness when the Union forces sacked Atlanta and he saw his mother killed and his home destroyed by fire. The warmth of a father's love and faith and the devotion of a boy for his dog are prime ingredients in this suspenseful, exciting, and extremely touching film.

The action unfolds in a small southern Illinois community, where Ladd is drawn into a fight with the two ornery

Alan Ladd in The Proud Rebel (BUENA VISTA/ AUTHOR'S COLLECTION)

sons of Dean Jagger, a belligerent sheep raiser. Sentenced with a fine after his arrest, Ladd encounters unexpected support from Olivia de Havilland, a lonely farm woman whose property is coveted by Jagger and who offers to pay Ladd's fine. He agrees to pay her back by working her land and doing an assorted array of chores. Childless herself, she is captivated by the young boy's presence, and her attraction to his father grows.

Based on an original story by James Edward Grant (John Wayne's favorite writer) and backed up with some excellent color photography, *The Proud Rebel* is arguably a final showcase for Alan Ladd, who displays a depth of character and screen integrity not seen since *SHANE* (1953) five years earlier. Much of this centers on the scenes with his 11-year-old son David, who delivers a thoroughly appealing and difficult performance. The on-screen chemistry between father and son is marvelous, and the film has never received the recognition it rightly deserves.

"I'm sure my performance was enhanced because we were father and son," David Ladd recalled in a 1996 interview with the author for *Remember Magazine*. "He was on my side directing me in his own way. My father was very much a pure film actor, and as nice a man as you'd ever want to meet."

David Ladd was born in 1947, and his role in *The Proud Rebel* propelled him to stardom. Thereafter, he became a sought-after child star who made such films as *Misty* (1961) and *A Dog of Flanders* (1959). His much-publicized marriage to actress Cheryl Ladd ended in divorce. He continues to work in the film industry, having served as senior vice president of MGM's Worldwide Productions.

PROVED GUILTY   See *WYOMING HURRICANE*.

PUBLIC COWBOY NO. 1   Republic, 1937, B&W, 60 min, VHS. **Producer:** Sol C. Siegal; **Director:** Joseph Kane; **Screenplay:** Oliver Drake; **Music:** Drake, Fleming Allen, Felix Bernard, Alberto Colombo, Karl Hajos, Arthur Kay, William Lava, Hugo Risenfeld, Sam H. Stept, and Paul Francis Webster; **Cinematographer:** Jack A. Marta; **Editors:** Lester Orlebeck and George Reid; **Cast:** Gene Autry, Ann Rutherford, Smiley Burnette, William Farnum, Arthur Loft, House Peters Jr.

PURPLE HILLS, THE   20th Century Fox, 1961, Color, 60 min. **Producer:** Maury Dexter; **Director:** Dexter; **Screenplay:** Russ Bender and Edith Cash Pearl; **Cinematographer:** Floyd Crosby; **Editor:** Jodie Copelan; **Cast:** Gene Nelson, Kent Taylor, Danny Zapien, Medford Salway, Russ Bender, Joanna Barnes.

After a cowboy kills a wanted man in Indian Territory, he is hunted by Indians as he tries to take the dead man's body in for an award. Gene Nelson plays against type in this compact but undistinguished little oater.

PURPLE VIGILANTES, THE   Republic, 1938, B&W, 58 min. **Producer:** Sol C. Siegal; **Director:** George Sherman; **Screenplay:** Betty Burbridge and Oliver Drake; **Cinematographer:** Ernest Miller; **Editor:** Miller; **Cast:** Robert Livingston, Ray Corrigan, Max Terhune, Joan Barclay, Earl Dwire, Earle Hodgins.

PURSUED   Warner Bros., 1947, B&W, 101 min, VHS. **Producer:** Milton Sperling; **Director:** Raoul Walsh; **Screenplay:** Niven Busch; **Music:** Max Steiner; **Cinematographer:** James Wong Howe; **Editor:** Christian Nyby; **Cast:** Robert Mitchum, Teresa Wright, Judith Anderson, Dean Jagger, Alan Hale, Harry Carey Jr., Clifton Young, Ernest Severn, Charles Bates, Peggy Miller.

Robert Mitchum plays a Civil War veteran haunted and plagued by some unknown event from the past. While the setting is the Old West, the unusual structure of the picture is pure film noir. The plot motivation stems from a blood feud between two families, the Rands and the Callums. It begins when Dean Jagger, a Callum, wipes out Mitchum's family because a Callum woman (Judith Anderson) has dared to have an illicit affair with Mitchum's father, a Rand.

Mitchum is haunted by the inner demons of his childhood past and real killers in the present, and his passion for his stepsister (Teresa Wright) leads to a fatal gunfight with her brother. Embittered, she agrees to marry Mitchum so she can take revenge for his deed on their wedding night. Among the film's most memorable moments takes place that night as Mitchum's bride stalks and makes an abortive attempt to kill him, leading to a startling and unexpected climax.

Arguably one of the best, and clearly one of the most unusual, westerns to come out of the 1940s, the film has nary a flaw. The casting is superb, with Robert Mitchum so natural that he makes his complex character totally believable, while Teresa Wright delivers the type of honest portrayal that helped make her one of the top stars of the '40s. Deftly helmed by genre master Raoul Walsh, the film evolves into a crescendo of excitement and suspense, with a strong arsenal of psychological overtones. A prolific storyteller, Walsh could combine action drama with great moments of tenderness as few other directors, past or present.

Pursued was one of Mitchum's fine early post-World War II films, and it helped him gain rapid popularity as a rugged, nonchalant leading man. The film was also the western (and film) debut for 26-year-old Harry Carey Jr., who over the years evolved into one of the movie's finest all-purpose character actors, accumulating more than 50 western film credits alone, as well as scores of TV guest slots.

In an interview for *White Hats and Silver Spurs*, Harry Carey Jr. recalled his film debut. "[*Pursued*] was a wonderful western directed by Raoul Walsh. The whole cast was great. They tested about twenty-seven guys for the part of Prentice McComber, but it was made to order for me and I got it. My first three directors were Raoul Walsh, Howard Hawks [*Red River*], and John Ford [*The Three Godfathers*]. What a way for a guy to start out."

Director Martin Scorsese has included *Pursued* in his series "Martin Scorsese Presents," those films he considers to have shaped the life of American film. *Pursued* is "exceptional" and Robert Mitchum's performance "extraordinary." The film "inhabits a very unique position in film history, in that it is generally considered to be the first noir Western. . . .

Pursued resembles a Shakespearean drama with Freudian undertones."

PURSUIT See *APACHE BLOOD.*

QUANTEZ Universal, 1957, Color, 80 min. **Producer:** Gordon Kay; **Director:** Harry Keller; **Screenplay:** R. Wright Campbell; **Music:** Frederick Herbert, Arnold Hughes, and Herman Stein; **Cinematographer:** Carl E. Guthrie; **Editor:** Fred MacDowell; **Cast:** Fred MacMurray, Dorothy Malone, James Barton, Sydney Chaplin, John Gavin, John Larch, Michael Ansara.

Fred MacMurray is an easterner who is among those held captive in a western saloon by a band of sadistic bank robbers. Rather than romance pretty Dorothy Malone as one might expect, he helps her escape with her admirer, John Gavin. From 1955 through 1958, the versatile MacMurray made eight westerns for a variety of studios. Filmed in CinemaScope, this picture is a cut or two above the average 1950s western.

QUANTRILL'S RAIDERS Allied Artists, 1958, Color, 71 min. **Producer:** Ben Schwalb; **Director:** Edward Bernds; **Screenplay:** Polly James; **Music:** Martin Skiles; **Cinematographer:** William Whitley; **Editor:** William Austin; **Cast:** Steve Cochran, Diane Brewster, Leo Gordon, Gale Robbins, Will Wright, Myron Healey.

A Confederate captain is sent by General Robert E. Lee to make contact with William Quantrill about raiding a Kansas arsenal. This historically flawed but action-packed account of the life and times of William Quantrill features a good performance by Leo Gordon as the infamous guerrilla leader.

QUICK AND THE DEAD HBO, 1987, Color, 90 min, VHS. **Producer:** Phillip Cates; **Director:** Robert Day; **Teleplay:** James Lee Barrett; **Music:** Steve Doriff; **Cinematographer:** Dick Bush; **Editor:** Jay Freund; **Cast:** Sam Elliott, Kate Capshaw, Tom Conti, Kenny Morrison, Matt Clark.

Sam Elliott is the mysterious grizzled Con Vallian, who rides into a homesteading family's life when a ruthless gang attacks them. Great chemistry between Elliott and Capshaw and a solid story line makes this HBO production a top-flight endeavor. Sam Elliott has rarely been better than in this third entry in a trilogy of classy HBO shoot-'em-ups based on stories by Louis L'Amour, in a role that seems tailor-made for him.

QUICK AND THE DEAD, THE Columbia, 1995, B&W/Color, 105 min, VHS, DVD, CD. **Producer:** Joshua Donen, Patrick Markey, Allen Shapiro, and Sharon Stone; **Director:** Sam Raimi; **Screenplay:** Simon Moore; **Music:** Alan Silvestri; **Cinematographer:** Danti Spinotti; **Editor:** Pietro Scalia; **Cast:** Sharon Stone, Gene Hackman, Russell Crowe, Leonardo DiCaprio, Tobin Bell, Pat Hingle, Gary Sinise.

Coproducer Sharon Stone plays an avenger who returns to a western town owned by an evil gunslinger named Herod (Gene Hackman), who delights in hosting a round-robin elimination tournament accomplished through a series of gunfights.

Somehow the producers were able to obtain a quality cast to partake in this ode to cruelty and depredation. A pastiche of the "spaghetti westerns," this postmodern film with a selection of cardboard characters is little more than a study in spiritual and physical ugliness. Those who hated Gene Hackman's villainous role in *UNFORGIVEN* (1993) will detest him here.

As for Stone, the gunslinger out for revenge, she manages to fill out her designer jeans in grand fashion. Otherwise, for all true fans of the western genre, this inane film can best be described in one word: "Dreadful!"

QUICK GUN, THE Columbia, 1964, Color, 87 min. **Producer:** Grant Whytock; **Director:** Sidney Salkow; **Screenplay:** Robert E. Kent; **Music:** Richard LaSalle; **Cinematographer:** Lestor Shorr; **Editor:** Whytock; **Cast:** Audie Murphy, Merry Anders, James Best, Ted De Corsia, Walter Sande, Gregg Palmer, William Fawcet.

When a young cowboy returns home after a two-year absence, he encounters rejection from the townsfolk because he was forced to kill the son of a local land baron in self-defense. He nevertheless helps the ungrateful town fight off a raid by his former gang. Look for a young James Best in his pre-*Dukes of Hazzard* days.

QUICK ON THE TRIGGER Columbia, 1949, B&W, 54 min. **Producer:** Colbert Clark; **Director:** Ray Nazarro; **Screenplay:** Elmer Clifton; **Cinematographer:** Rex Wimpy; **Editor:** Paul Borofsky; **Cast:** Charles Starrett, Smiley Burnette, Ted Adams, Russell Arms, Al Bridge, Budd Buster, Helen Parish, Lyle Parish.

See *DURANGO KID, THE.*

QUIET GUN, THE (aka: FURY AT ROCK RIVER) 20th Century Fox, 1957, B&W, 77 min. **Producer:** Earle Lyon; **Director:** William F. Claxton; **Screen-** play: Lyon and Eric Norden; **Music:** Paul Dunlap; **Cinematographer:** John H. Mescall; **Editor:** Robert Fritch; **Cast:** Forrest Tucker, Mara Corday, Jim Davis, Kathleen Crowley, Lee Van Cleef, Tom Brown, Hank Warden.

A sheriff (Forrest Tucker) is called upon to investigate the charge that his rancher friend (Jim Davis) is having an affair with an Indian girl (Mara Corday) while his wife (Kathleen Crowley) is out of town. The impending scandal leads to Davis killing the town attorney (Lewis Martin), then being lynched by a band of angry townspeople. Later the sheriff discovers that a saloon owner (Tom Brown) and his cohort (Lee Van Cleef) started the rumors in order to gain the rancher's property. The sheriff faces both men down, shooting them dead in the street. This well-cast and unusual western was photographed in RegalScope.

QUIGLEY DOWN UNDER Pathé Entertainment/MGM, 1990, Color, 119 min, VHS, DVD, CD. **Producers:** Stanley O'Toole, Alexandra Rose, and Megan Rose; **Director:** Simon Wincer; **Screenplay:** John Hill; **Music:** Basil Poledouris; **Cinematographer:** David Eggby; **Editor:** Peter Burgess; **Cast:** Tom Selleck, Laura San Giacomo, Alan Rickman, Chris Haywood, Ron Haddrick, Tony Bonner.

Laura San Giacomo and Tom Selleck in Quigley Down Under (PATHÉ ENTERTAINMENT/AUTHOR'S COLLECTION)

A despotic Australian rancher hires American sharpshooter Matthew Quigley to shoot aborigines at a distance. Quigley wants no part of this practice and shows his disdain by throwing the rancher through a window. He soon finds himself in a near-lethal battle with the rancher. Beaten to a pulp and left to die in the desert, he is rescued and nursed to health by a group of aborigines, then becomes their self-appointed protector against the rancher and his band of thugs. His companion along the way is an addled young woman called "Crazy Cora" (Laura San Giacomo), who thinks Quigley is her estranged husband, a fellow named Roy who shipped her off to Australia in disgrace after their child's death.

Tom Selleck is splendid as Quigley, the cowboy from Wyoming with a rifle draped around his shoulder and a twinkle in his eye. Filmed at various locations in Australia and helmed by Emmy-winning director Simon Wincer (LONE-SOME DOVE, 1989), the film provides a goodly slice of old-fashioned action and adventure, where no scorecard is needed to delineate good from evil or hero from villain. The story line plays out well till the very end. Selleck is all cowboy and, like Sam Elliott, one of the very few contemporary actors capable of carrying the western into a new century.

QUINCANNON—FRONTIER SCOUT (aka: FRONTIER SCOUT, UK) United Artists, 1956, Color, 83 min. **Producers:** Howard W. Koch and Aubrey Schenck; **Director:** Leslie Selander; **Screenplay:** John C. Higgins and Don Martin; **Music:** Les Baxter, Hal Borne and Sammy Cahn; **Cinematographer:** Joseph F. Biroc; **Editor:** John F. Schreyer; **Cast:** Tony Martin, Peggie Castle, Morris Ankrum, John Bromfield, John Doucette, Edmund Hashim, Peter Mamokos.

Tony Martin (one of the best singing voices and top recording artists of the 1940s and '50s) stars as Linus Quincannon, a frontier scout hired by a young woman to help discover if her brother died in an Indian attack on a remote fort.

RACHEL AND THE STRANGER RKO, 1948, B&W, 93 min, VHS. **Producer:** Richard H. Berger; **Director:** Norman Foster; **Screenplay:** Waldo Salt; **Music:** Roy Webb; **Cinematographer:** Maury Gertsman; **Editor:** Les Millbrook; **Cast:** Loretta Young, William Holden, Robert Mitchum, Gary Gray, Tom Tully, Sara Hayden, Frank Ferguson.

Set in the frontier Northwest, a widower (William Holden) decides his son (Gary Gray) needs female care and looking after. He therefore buys and then marries an indentured servant (Loretta Young) who becomes his housekeeper/wife. But still mourning for his first wife, he fails to see the charms of the second.

When a wandering scout (Robert Mitchum) pays a visit, he immediately notices Young's feelings of neglect. He tries to woo her for himself, even strumming his guitar and singing a few songs to further his pursuit. Husband Holden now becomes jealous, and both men nearly lose her before they are forced to join together to fend off an impending Indian attack, providing this charming love story with an action-packed and exciting finale.

Based on the story "Rachel" by Howard Fast, this pleasant frontier tale features three attractive and increasingly popular stars. Overlooked by many film buffs today, *Rachel and the Stranger* was quite popular when first released to movie audiences in 1948. Nominated as the Best Written American Western by the Writers Guild of America, the film can also be seen in a computer-colored version.

RACKETEER ROUND-UP (aka: GUNNERS AND GUNS) Beaumont, 1935, B&W, 57 min. **Producer:** Nathan Hirsh and Murray Leichter; **Director:** Jerry Callahan and Robert Hoyt; **Screenplay:** J. S. Burrows, Martin Eldridge, and Ruth Runnell; **Cast:** Edmund Cobb, Edna Aselin, Edward Allen Bilby, Eddie Davis, Lois Glaze, Ned Horton, Black King (horse).

A rancher's daughter returns from college to marry the ranch foreman. However, she discovers that he has become involved with gangsters who are now after him because he hid their money and can't remember where he stashed it. This poorly produced film presents a rare opportunity to see Edmund Cobb in a starring sound role and the beautiful horse Black King. Fred Thompson Productions briefly released the film in 1934, with new footage added for general release the following year.

RACKETEERS OF THE RANGE RKO, 1939, B&W, 62 min. **Producer:** Bert Gilroy; **Director:** D. Ross Lederman; **Screenplay:** Oliver Drake; **Music:** Fred Rose and Ray Whitley; **Cinematographer:** Harry J. Wild; **Editor:** Frederic Knudtson; **Cast:** George O'Brien, Marjorie Reynolds, Robert Fiske, Chill Wills, Gay Seabrook, Ray Whitley, Robert Fiske.

A dishonest lawyer tries to cheat a girl out of her packing plant, so another meat packer takes over her operations to save local ranchers from being fleeced by crooks. This entertaining George O'Brien vehicle was made while he was RKO's resident cowboy star. O'Brien's costar Marjorie Reynolds gained notoriety as Bing Crosby's leading lady in the film *Holiday Inn*, the movie in which Bing Crosby introduced the ever-popular seasonal song "White Christmas."

O'Brien's tenure with RKO began with *Daniel Boone* in 1936 and continued through 1940, when the popular and sturdy star (nicknamed "The Chest") entered military service. Tim Holt then took his place as RKO's top B western star. O'Brien's films were unusually well made and far more expensive than the average B western. In addition, because they appealed to adults as well as children, they got far better bookings in big-circuit theaters than did most western programmers.

The best entries in this distinguished RKO series are *Racketeers of the Range* and *The Lawless Valley*. The others include HOLLYWOOD COWBOY (1937); PAINTED DESERT, RENEGADE RANGER, BORDER G-MEN, GUN LAW (1938); TIMBER STAMPEDE, TROUBLE IN SUNDOWN, THE LAWLESS VALLEY, THE MARSHAL OF MESA CITY, THE FIGHTING GRINGO, ARIZONA LEGION (1939); STAGE TO CHINO, LEGION OF THE LAWLESS, BULLET CODE, PRAIRIE LAW, TRIPLE JUSTICE (1940).

RAGE AT DAWN (aka: SEVEN BAD MEN) RKO, 1955, Color, 87 min, VHS, DVD. **Producer:** Nat Holt; **Director:** Tim Whelan; **Screenplay:** Horace McCoy; **Music:** Paul Sawtell; **Cinematographer:** Ray Rennahan; **Editor:** Harry Marker; **Cast:** Randolph Scott, Forrest Tucker, Mala Powers, J. Carrol Naish, Edgar Buchanan, Myron Healey, Howard Petrie, Ray Teal, William Forrest, Denver Pyle, Kenneth Tobey.

In post-Civil War Indiana, federal agent James Barlow (Randolph Scott) arrives undercover from Chicago to infiltrate a notorious outlaw gang headed by the cunning Reno brothers, who have the Midwest gripped with terror and the authorities helpless. The plot is complicated when agent Barlow falls for Laura Reno (Mala Powers), his adversaries' sister while also plotting the Renos' downfall.

What sets this film apart from other 1950s westerns of a similar theme is the inclusion of some familiar names and faces in supporting roles. For example, the infamous Reno brothers include Forrest Tucker (Frank), J. Carrol Naish (Slim), Myron Healey (John), and Denver Pyle (Clint). Top-flight character actors Edgar Buchanan and Ray Teal play the judge and the sheriff, respectively.

RAGTIME COWBOY JOE Universal, 1940, B&W, 68 min. **Producer:** Joseph G. Sanford (associate); **Director:** Ray Taylor; **Screenplay:** Sherman L. Lowe; **Music:** Hans J. Salter, Frank Skinner, Everette Carter, Robert Crawford, Ralph Freed, Milton Rosen, Hans J. Salter, Frank Skinner, and Franz Waxman; **Cinematographer:** Jerome Ash; **Editor:** Paul Landres; **Cast:** Johnny Mack Brown, Fuzzy Knight, Nell O'Day, Dick Curtis, Marilyn Merrick, Roy Barcroft.
See OLD CHISHOLM TRAIL, THE.

RAID, THE 20th Century Fox, 1954, Color, 82 min. **Producer:** Robert L. Jacks; **Director:** Hugo Fregonese; **Screenplay:** Sydney Boehm and Francis M. Cockrell; **Music:** Roy Webb; **Cinematographer:** Lucien Ballard; **Editor:** Robert Golden; **Cast:** Van Heflin, Anne Bancroft, Richard Boone, Lee Marvin, Tommy Rettig, Peter Graves, James Best, Claude Akins, Robert Eason.

Based on the book *Affair at St. Albans* by Herbert Ravenal Sass, this film deals with a group of Confederate soldiers who in 1864 enter Vermont from the Canadian border and pro-

ceed to the town of St. Albans. Posing as civilians, they plan to sack the town, then cross the border back into Canada, and sit out the remainder of the war. The diversionary tactic is designed to draw Union forces away from the front. Conflicts arise when their leader (Van Heflin) is torn between his sense of duty to the Confederacy and his affection for a Union war widow played by Anne Bancroft, who, along with her son Tommy Rettig, hopes to thwart his plans.

A fine reenactment of a factual event, this interesting and unusual film boasts an outstanding cast that delivers believable performances, a compelling story, and a well-written screenplay by Sidney Boehm.

RAIDERS, THE (aka: RIDERS OF VENGEANCE; THE RIDING KID) Universal, 1952, Color, 80 min. **Producer:** William Alland; **Director:** Leslie Selander; **Screenplay:** Lillie Hayward and Polly James; **Music:** Everett Carter, Henri Mancini, Milton Rosen, and Herman Stein; **Cinematographer:** Carl G. Guthrie; **Editor:** Paul Weatherwax; **Cast:** Richard Conte, Viveca Lindfors, Barbara Britton, Hugh O'Brien, Richard Martin, Gregg Palmer, William Reynolds, William Bishop, Morris Ankrum, Dennis Weaver.

In California during the gold rush days of 1849, two men wronged by the local authorities team up to destroy a crooked judge who is the leader of an outlaw gang.

RAIDERS, THE Universal, 1963, Color, 75 min. **Producer:** Howard Christie; **Director:** Hershall Daughtery; **Screenplay:** Gene L. Coon; **Music:** Morton Stevens; **Cinematographer:** Bud Thackery; **Editor:** Gene Palmer; **Cast:** Brian Keith, Robert Culp, Judi Meredith, Jim McMullan, Trevor Bardette, Harry Carey Jr., Paul Birch, Michael Burns, Richard Cutting, Richard Deacon, Addison Richards.

When a group of Texans is ambushed while trying to drive their cattle herds to the Kansas railheads, they receive some unexpected help from three western legends: Wild Bill Hickok (Robert Culp), Buffalo Bill Cody (Jim McMullan), and Calamity Jane (Judi Meredith). This taut fictionalized account of the western railroad expansion packs plenty of action.

RAIDERS OF OLD CALIFORNIA Republic, 1957, B&W, 72 min. **Producer:** Albert C. Gannaway; **Director:** Gannaway; **Screenplay:** Tom Hubbard and Samuel Rocca; **Cinematographer:** Charles Straumer; **Editor:** Carl Pingator; **Cast:** Jim Davis, Arleen Whelan, Faron Young, Marty Robbins, Lee Van Cleef.

Following the Mexican-American War, a group of cavalry officers conspire to set up their own empire in California.

RAIDERS OF RED GAP PRC, 1943, B&W, 60 min. **Producer:** Sigmund Neufeld; **Director:** Sam Newfield; **Screenplay:** Joseph O'Donnell; **Cinematographer:** Robert

E. Cline; **Editor:** Holbrook N. Todd; **Cast:** Robert Livingston, Al St. John, Myrna Dell, Ed Cassidy, Slim Whitaker, Kermit Maynard.

RAIDERS OF RED ROCK   See *FUGITIVE OF THE PLAINS.*

RAIDERS OF SAN JOAQUIN   Universal, 1943, B&W, 59 min. **Producer:** Oliver Drake; **Director:** Lewis B. Collins; **Screenplay:** Elmer Clifton and Morgan Cox; **Music:** Hans J. Salter and Drake (songs); **Cinematographer:** William A. Sickner; **Cast:** Johnny Mack Brown, Tex Ritter, Jennifer Holt, Fuzzy Knight, Henry Hall.

RAIDERS OF THE BORDER   Monogram, 1944, B&W, 53 min. **Producer:** Scott R. Dunlap; **Director:** Joseph McCarthy; **Screenplay:** Jess Bowers; **Cinematographer:** Harry Neumann; **Editor:** Carl Pierson; **Cast:** Johnny Mack Brown, Raymond Hatton, Ernie Adams, Richard Alexander, Ray Bennett, Lynton Brent, Edmund Cobb, Ellen Hall.

RAIDERS OF THE FRONTIER   See *GANGSTERS OF THE FRONTIER.*

RAIDERS OF THE RANGE   Republic, 1942, B&W, 54 min. **Producer:** Louis Grey; **Director:** John English; **Screenplay:** Barry Shipman; **Music:** Cy Feuer; **Cinematographer:** Ernest Miller; **Editor:** John Lockert; **Cast:** Bob Steele, Tom Tyler, Rufe Davis, Lois Collier, Frank Jaquet.

RAIDERS OF THE SOUTH   Monogram, 1946, B&W, 55 min. **Producer:** Scott R. Dunlap; **Director:** Lambert Hillyer; **Screenplay:** J. Benton Cheney; **Cinematographer:** Harry Neumann; **Editor:** Fred Maguire; **Cast:** Johnny Mack Brown, Raymond Hatton, Evelyn Brent, Reno Browne, Marshall Reed, John Hamilton, John Merton, Pierce Lyden.

RAIDERS OF THE WEST   PRC, 1942, B&W, 60 min. **Producer:** Sigmund Neufeld; **Director:** Sam Newfield (as Peter Stewart); **Screenplay:** Oliver Drake; **Music:** Bill "Cowboy Rambler" Boyd, Hal Burns, Aubrey Fisher, Johnny Lange, Earl Nunn, Lew Porter; **Cinematographer:** Jack Greenhalgh; **Editor:** Holbrook N. Todd; **Cast:** Lee Powell, "Cowboy Rambler" Boyd, Art Davis, Virginia Carroll, Charles King, Fred "Snowflake" Toones.

An outlaw gang hires two range detectives who pose as entertainers, but before they can get the goods and arrest the gang, they are found out and captured. Their partner must now find a way to rescue them before they are murdered.

Composer/actor Bill "Cowboy Rambler" Boyd should not be confused with Bill Boyd of Hop-Along Cassidy fame.

In 1942 Producers Releasing Corporation teamed Boyd and fellow musician Art Davis in its "Frontier Marshal" series. This entry includes five songs, three written by the team of Johnny Lange and Lew Porter, including "The Whispering Prairie." Other series films include *Along the Sundown Trail, Prairie Pals, Rolling Down the Great Divide, Raiders of the West, Texas Man Hunt,* and *Tumbleweed Trail* (1942).

RAIDERS OF TOMAHAWK CREEK   Columbia, 1950, B&W, 55 min. **Producer:** Colbert Clark; **Director:** Fred Sears; **Screenplay:** Barry Shipman; **Cinematographer:** Fayte M. Browne; **Editor:** Paul Borofsky; **Cast:** Charles Starrett, Smiley Burnette, Edgar Dearing, Kay Buckley, Billy Kimbley, Paul Marion.

RAILS INTO LARAMIE   Universal, 1954, B&W, 80 min. **Producer:** Ted Richmond; **Director:** Jessie Hibbs; **Screenplay:** D. D. Beauchamp and Joseph Hoffman; **Music:** Frederick Herbert, Arnold Hughes, and Henry Mancini; **Cinematographer:** Maury Gertsman; **Editor:** Ted J. Kent; **Cast:** John Payne, Dan Duryea, Mari Blanchard, Joyce Mackenzie, George Chandler, Myron Healey, Barton MacLane.

An army sergeant who attempts to get the railroad through to 1870s Laramie, Wyoming, has to contend with sabotage and a band of local crooks planning to thwart his mission. This colorful and entertaining western benefits from the presence of John Payne and Dan Duryea, both significant and sometimes underappreciated genre players. The versatile Payne, who began his career as a singer in the 1930s, made 12 of his 13 westerns in the 1950s. Duryea was featured in a total of 17 westerns starting in 1945, more often than not as a convincing villain.

RAINBOW OVER TEXAS   Republic, 1946, B&W, 65 min. **Producer:** Edward J. White; **Director:** Frank McDonald; **Screenplay:** Gerald Geraghty; **Music:** Jack Elliott, Gordon Forster, and Glenn Spencer; **Cinematographer:** Reggie Lanning; **Editor:** Charles Craft; **Cast:** Roy Rogers, George "Gabby" Hayes, Dale Evans, Sheldon Leonard, Robert Emmett, Kenne Duncan, Pierce Lyden, Bob Nolan.

When Roy visits his hometown on a personal appearance tour, he enters a pony express race. To keep him from winning, a band of crooks attempts to sabotage his entry. Based on a story by Max Brand, the film includes the songs "Smile for Me, Senorita" and "Rainbow over Texas." (See also *UNDER WESTERN STARS.*)

RAINBOW OVER THE ROCKIES   Monogram, 1947, B&W, 54 min. **Producer:** Oliver Drake; **Director:** Drake; **Screenplay:** Elmer Clifton; **Music:** Frank Sanucci (director); **Cinematographer:** Marcel Le Picard; **Editor:** Ralph Dixon; **Cast:** Jimmy Wakely, Jack Baxley, Budd Buster, Billy Dix, Bob Duncan.

See *ACROSS THE RIO GRANDE.*

RAINBOW'S END First Division, 1935, B&W, 55 min. **Director:** Norman Spencer; **Screenplay:** Rollo Ward; **Cinematographer:** Gilbert Warrenton; **Editor:** Ralph Dietrich; **Cast:** Hoot Gibson, June Gale, Oscar Apfel, Ada Ince, John Elliott.

A cowboy who has a falling out with his businessman father becomes the foreman of a ranch to which his father holds the mortgage. A crooked lawyer tries to get the old man to foreclose so he can gain possession of the land for himself. A modern story with some good comedy added makes this one a natural for the talents of Hoot Gibson. However, Gibson, a John Ford discovery, was never able to match the best of his earlier silent film work and had to compete with a newer crop of western stars, such as Johnny Mack Brown, George O'Brien, and two youngsters serving their apprenticeships to top stardom: Randolph Scott and John Wayne.

RAINBOW TRAIL, THE Fox, 1925, B&W, 58 min. **Presenter:** William Fox; **Director:** Lynn Reynolds; **Screenplay:** Reynolds; **Cinematographer:** Daniel B. Clark; **Cast:** Tom Mix, Anne Cornwell, George Bancroft, Lucien Littlefield, Mark Hamilton.

Tom Mix sets out to free his uncle, who has been trapped in a canyon in isolated Paradise Valley. One of Tom Mix's classic silent efforts, the film is a robust sequel to the very popular *Riders of the Purple Sage* (1925). Tom Mix was at the peak of his remarkable physical skills when this handsomely produced silent film was made. Zane Grey's *The Rainbow's Trail* was first filmed by Fox in 1918 with William Farnum in the lead role.

RAINBOW TRAIL, THE Fox, 1932, B&W, 60 min. **Director:** David Howard; **Screenplay:** Barry Conners and Philip Klein; **Cinematographer:** Daniel B. Clark; **Cast:** George O'Brien, Cecilia Parker, Minna Gombell, Roscoe Ates, J. M. Kerrigan, James Kirkwood, William L. Throne.

RAINBOW VALLEY Lone Star/Monogram, 1935, B&W, 52 min, VHS. **Producer:** Paul Malvern; **Director:** Robert N. Bradbury; **Screenplay:** Lindsley Parsons; **Cinematographer:** William Hyer and Archie Stout; **Cast:** John Wayne, Lucile Browne, LeRoy, George "Gabby" Hayes, Jay Wilsey, Bert Dillard.

Some shady individuals (actually the town leaders) are determined to prevent a road from being built from their small town to the county seat. In the process, innocent people are beaten, robbed, and forced to leave their property. As in many of his depression-era Monogram westerns, John Wayne becomes the hero of a West besieged by evil exploiters like ruthless merchants, greedy land barons, corrupt bankers, and even dangerous friends and relatives. Many of these "poverty row" oaters were produced by Paul Malvern and scripted by Lindsley Parsons, and they helped Wayne to learn his trade.

RAMONA 20th Century Fox, 1936, Color, 90 min. **Producer:** Sol M. Wurtzel; **Director:** Henry King; **Screenplay:** Lamar Trotti; **Music:** Alfred Newman; **Cinematographer:** William V. Skall; **Editor:** Alfred DeGaetano; **Cast:** Loretta Young, Don Ameche, Kent Taylor, Pauline Frederick, Jane Darwell, Katherine De Mille, John Carradine, J. Carrol Naish, Pedro de Cordoba.

A lovely half-Indian girl (Loretta Young) is brought up in the home of a wealthy aristocrat. However, when the son in the house falls in love with her, the parents are forced to reveal that she had been the offspring of a tragic affair between an Indian woman and a family member. After learning that she is really half-Indian, she feels free to love a handsome Indian man (Don Ameche) who is employed by the household. The ensuing love triangle dominates this romantic tale, which brings both happiness and tragedy to its protagonists.

This third remake of the Helen Hunt Jackson novel has been criticized as being little more than Hollywood fluff. Nevertheless, it continues to work as an appealing filmland costume piece, largely because of the richness of the original three-strip Technicolor. Set in early California, the film holds special significance for being 20th Century Fox's first full Technicolor feature.

Earlier versions of *Ramona* include Fox's 1928 feature directed by Edwin Carewe, with Dolores Del Rio and Warner Baxter featured as Ramona and Alessandro, the roles played by Loretta Young and Don Ameche. The popular song "Ramona" (Wolfe Gilbert and Mabel Wayne) was written to promote and accompany the 1928 silent film.

The Clune Producing Co. produced a 1916 version of *Ramona*. The director was future Oscar-winning actor Donald Crisp (*How Green was My Valley*, 1941), who later became one of the movies' premier character actors and supporting players. The four-year-old Ramona in the 1916 film was played by five-year-old Ann Revere, who went on to secure a number of fine roles as an adult in the 1930s, '40s, and '50s.

RAMROD United Artists, 1947, B&W, 95 min. **Producer:** Harry Sherman; **Director:** André De Toth; **Screenplay:** Jack Moffitt, G. Graham Baker, and Cecil Kramer; **Music:** Adolph Deutsch; **Cinematographer:** Russell Harlan; **Editor:** Sherman A. Rose; **Cast:** Joel McCrea, Veronica Lake, Don Defore, Donald Crisp, Preston Foster, Arleen Whelan, Charles Ruggles, Lloyd Bridges, Nestor Paiva, Ray Teal, Ward Wood.

Joel McCrea is Dave Nash, the ramrod (or foreman) of a ranch belonging to sultry and scheming Connie Dickson (Veronica Lake). While Nash contends with a tense range war, Lake's father wants her to marry the man who had recently intimidated her fiancé and forced him to leave town—a man who now plans to take her ranch away. To help her battle local cattle king and prime adversary Preston Foster, McCrea enlists the help of cohort and tough gunslinger Don Defore, who unexpectedly sacrifices his life for McCrea and Lake as the film zooms toward a suspenseful ending.

The first and perhaps the best of the André De Toth westerns (other works include *SPRINGFIELD RIFLE*, 1952; *MAN IN THE SADDLE*, 1951; and *CARSON CITY*, 1952) *Ramrod* is a picture that seems to improve with age and remains one of the most beautifully photographed westerns to come out of the 1940s. In his *A Pictorial History of the Western Film*, William Everson calls *Ramrod* "unusually appealing, dramatically strong, [and] intelligently written. . . ."

Bolstered by a superb supporting cast including Donald Crisp, Charles Ruggles, Ray Teal, and a young Lloyd Bridges, Joel McCrea delivers a fine performance with his usual unassuming excellence, and Veronica Lake is near perfect as the predatory rancher who, despite her scheming agenda, still manages to lose McCrea to nice girl Arleen Whelan, the town seamstress, at the final fadeout.

RANCHO DELUXE United Artists, 1975, Color, 93 min, VHS, DVD, CD. **Producer:** Elliott Kastner; **Director:** Frank Perry; **Screenplay:** Thomas McGuane; **Music:** Jimmy Buffett; **Cinematographer:** William A. Fraker; **Editor:** Sidney Katz; **Cast:** Jeff Bridges, Sam Waterson, Elizabeth Ashley, Clifton James, Slim Pickens, Charles Dallas, Harry Dean Stanton.

This light-hearted modern-day western stars Jeff Bridges and Sam Waterson as two drifters from diverse backgrounds (Waterson is half-Indian) who become Montana cattle rustlers. They manage to convince ranch hands Harry Dean Stanton and Richard Bright to join their plans for a big cattle heist, but the plan unravels when one of their gang gets involved with the daughter of range detective Slim Pickens, who is hired by ranch owner Clifton James to track them down. "Rancho Deluxe" is the name of the prison camp Bridges and Waterson wind up in. The two actors would be paired together for vastly different roles in Michael Cimino's controversial 1980 film *HEAVEN'S GATE*.

RANCHO GRANDE Republic, 1940, B&W, 68 min. **Producer:** William Berke; **Director:** Frank McDonald; **Screenplay:** Betty Burbridge, Bradford Ropes, and Peter Milne; **Music:** William Lava and Paul Sawtell; **Cinematographer:** William Nobles; **Editor:** Tony Martinelli; **Cast:** Gene Autry, Smiley Burnette, June Storey, Mary Lee, Ellen Lowe, The Pals of the Golden West, The Brewer Kids, St. Joseph Boys Choir.

RANCHO NOTORIOUS RKO, 1952, Color, 89 min, VHS, DVD. **Producer:** Howard Welsch; **Director:** Fritz Lang; **Screenplay:** Daniel Taradash; **Music:** Kim Darby; **Cinematographer:** Hal Mohr; **Editor:** Otto Ludwig; **Cast:** Marlene Dietrich, Arthur Kennedy, Mel Ferrer, Gloria Henry, William Fawley, Jack Elam, Lisa Feraday, Frank Furguson, George Reeves.

Marlene Dietrich plays Altar Keane, onetime fabulous saloon singer and mistress of a ranch used to hide notorious outlaws. Altar's house rule is "peace and quiet and no talk about the past." This is easier said than done, since almost everybody in the film gets killed.

An intensely emotional western helmed by Austrian-born director Fritz Lang, *Rancho Notorious* is based on the story "Gunsight Whitman" by Silvia Richards. Arthur Kennedy plays Vern Haskell, the essentially good fellow who is beset with revenge after tracking his fiancé's murderers to Dietrich's Chuck a-Luck Ranch, a haven named after a legendary game of chance.

Fritz Lang, who a decade earlier had directed THE *RETURN OF FRANK JAMES* (1940) and *WESTERN UNION* (1941), is helped by Kennedy's convincing portrayal of the prototypical Fritz Lang hero: of a man whose basic goodness gets twisted by his thirst for revenge and is consumed by a fate he cannot escape. Dietrich is at her sultry, throaty best, singing her song "Get Away Young Man" with an alluring style reminiscent of her work in *DESTRY RIDES AGAIN* (1939).

RANDY RIDES ALONE Monogram/Lone Star, 1934, B&W, 53 min, VHS, DVD. **Producer:** Paul Malvern; **Director:** Harry Fraser; **Screenplay:** Lindsley Parsons; **Cinematographer:** Archie Stout; **Editor:** Carl Pierson; **Cast:** John Wayne, Alberta Vaughn, George "Gabby" Hayes, Yakima Canutt, Earl Dwire.

Randy Bowers (John Wayne) rides into town after a long ride on the range and stops in the local saloon for the obligatory drink. But this is no ordinary saloon. The piano sound comes from a player piano running itself, and dead bodies are scattered everywhere. Accused of murder and robbery, he escapes from jail with the help of pretty Sally Rogers (Alberta Vaughn), sets out to hunt the real killers, and finds their secret hideout behind a waterfall.

This "poverty row" John Wayne western is a cut or two above the ordinary, partly because of its offbeat plot and eerie opening scene, partly because of the skilled scripting of screenwriter Lindsley Parsons, and finally because of the casting of "Gabby" Hayes as a villain. This film and nine other early John Wayne oaters are included in five separate paired releases under the banner "The John Wayne Collection" and are available on DVD. Volume 4 of this five-volume set includes *Randy Rides Alone* and *The Lawless Frontier* (1935).

RANGE BEYOND THE BLUE PRC, 1947, B&W, 53 min. **Producer:** Jerry Thomas; **Director:** Ray Taylor; **Screenplay:** Patricia Harper; **Cinematographer:** Robert E. Cline; **Editor:** Cline; **Cast:** Eddie Dean, Roscoe Ates, Helen Mowery, Bob Duncan, Ted Adams.

RANGE BUSTERS, THE Monogram, 1940, B&W, 55 min. **Producer:** George Weeks; **Director:** S. Roy Luby; **Screenplay:** John Rathmell; **Music:** Johnny Lang and Lew Porter; **Editor:** Luby (as Roy Claire); **Cast:** Ray Corrigan, John "Dusty" King, Max Terhune, LeRoy Mason, Luana Walters, Earle Hidgins, Frank La Rue.

The first of Monogram's Range Busters movies features the likable trio of Ray Corrigan, John King, and Max Terhune. The film opens when a cowboy midway through a song is shot through an open window by a mysterious villain called The Phantom. The Range Busters arrive on the scene and set out to hunt him down.

One of 24 Range Busters entries for Monogram (1940–43), this initial series venture provides good action, with added elements of mystery and suspense. Other Range Buster films include, *TRAILING DOWN TROUBLE*, *WEST OF PINTO BASIN* (1940); *FUGITIVE VALLEY*, *KID'S LAST RIDE*, *SADDLE MOUNTAIN ROUNDUP*, *TRAIL OF THE SILVER SPURS*, *TUMBLEDOWN RANCH IN ARIZONA*, *TONTO BASIN OUTLAWS*, *UNDERGROUND RUSTLERS*, *WRANGLER'S ROOST* (1941); *ARIZONA STAGECOACH*, *BOOT HILL BANDITS*, *ROCK RIVER RENEGADES*, *TEXAS TROUBLE SHOOTERS*, *THUNDER RIVER FEUD*, *TRAIL RIDERS* (1942); *COWBOY COMMANDOS*, *TWO-FISTED JUSTICE*, *HAUNTED RANCH*, *LAND OF HUNTED MEN*, *BULLETS AND SADDLES*, *BLACK MARKET RUSTLERS* (1943).

RANGE DEFENDERS Republic, 1937, B&W, 54 min. **Producer:** Sol C. Siegal; **Director:** Mack V. Wright; **Screenplay:** Joseph F. Poland; **Music:** Fleming Allen; **Cinematographer:** Jack A. Marta; **Editor:** Lester Orlebeck; **Cast:** Robert Livingston, Ray Corrigan, Max Terhune, Eleanor Stewart, Harry Woods.

RANGE FEUD Columbia, 1931, B&W, 64 min, VHS. **Producer:** Irving Briskin; **Director:** D. Ross Lederman; **Screenplay:** Milton Krims and George H. Plympton; **Cinematographer:** Ben Kline; **Editor:** Maurice Wright; **Cast:** Buck Jones, John Wayne, Susan Fleming, Edward Le Saint, Will Walling.

Sheriff Buck Gordon (Buck Jones) is forced to arrest his foster brother (John Wayne) for the murder of his girl's father. Harry Woods is again the villain who is responsible for all the killing and cattle rustling. The film has been promoted as a "westernized Romeo and Juliet," since the feud between two Arizona families and a land dispute threaten to destroy the romance between young Clint Turner (Wayne) and Judy Walton (Susan Fleming).

Range Feud is one of John Wayne's first westerns after the "failure" of *THE BIG TRAIL* (1930), marking the start of a long B western apprenticeship for Wayne that continued until his friend John Ford cast him in *STAGECOACH* (1939). The story goes that Wayne's western roles for Columbia lessened because of a conflict with studio boss Harry Cohn. Buck Jones, in the meantime, was in the process of evolving from a hero of the silent screen to one of the pillars of B western sound movies.

RANGE LAND Monogram, 1949, B&W, 56 min. **Director:** Lambert Hillyer; **Screenplay:** Adele Buffington; **Cinematographer:** Harry Neumann; **Editor:** John C. Fuller; **Cast:** Whip Wilson, Andy Clyde, Reno Browne, Leonard Penn, Reed Howes.

RANGELAND EMPIRE See *WEST OF THE BRAZOS*.

RANGER AND THE LADY, THE Republic, 1940, B&W, 59 min. **Producer:** Joseph Kane; **Director:** Kane; **Screenplay:** Stuart Anthony and Gerald Geraghty; **Music:** Peter Tinturin; **Cinematographer:** Reggie Lanning; **Editor:** Lester Orlebeck; **Cast:** Roy Rogers, George "Gabby" Hayes, Julie Bishop, Harry Woods (as Harry Wends), Henry Brandon, Yakima Canutt, Si Jerks, Noble Johnson.

RANGER COURAGE Columbia, 1937, B&W, 58 min. **Producer:** Larry Darmour; **Director:** Spencer Gordon Bennett; **Screenplay:** Nate Gatzert; **Cinematographer:** James S. Brown Jr. and Arthur Reed; **Editor:** Dwight Caldwell; **Cast:** Robert Allen, Martha Tibbetts, Walter Miller, Robert "Buzz" Henry, Bud Osborne.

RANGER OF CHEROKEE STRIP Republic, 1949, B&W, 60 min. **Producer:** Melville Tucker; **Director:** Philip Ford; **Screenplay:** Bob Williams; **Music:** Stanley Wilson; **Cinematographer:** Ellis W. Carter; **Editor:** Irving S. Schoenberg; **Cast:** Monte Hale, Paul Hurst, Roy Barcroft, George Meeker, Douglas Kennedy, Frank Fenton, Monte Blue.

RANGERS OF FORTUNE Paramount, 1940, B&W, 80 min. **Producer:** Dale Van Every; **Director:** Sam Wood; **Screenplay:** Frank Butler; **Music:** Frederick Hollander; **Cinematographer:** Theodor Sparkuhl; **Editor:** Eda Warren; **Cast:** Fred MacMurray, Patricia Morison, Betty Brewer, Albert Dekker, Gilbert Roland, Joseph Schildkraut, Dick Foran.

RANGERS RIDE, THE Monogram, 1948, B&W, 56 min. **Producer:** Louis Gray; **Director:** Derwin Abrahams; **Screenplay:** Basil Dickey; **Cinematographer:** Harry Neumann; **Editor:** John C. Fuller; **Cast:** Jimmy Wakely, Dub Taylor, Virginia Belmont, Riley Hill, Marshall Reed, Pierce Lyden, Steve Clark.

RANGER'S ROUND-UP, THE Spectrum, 1938, B&W, 57 min. **Producer:** Jed Buell; **Director:** Sam Newfield; **Screenplay:** George Plympton; **Music:** Lew Porter; **Cinematographer:** William Hyer; **Editor:** Robert Johns; **Cast:** Fred Scott, Al St. John, Christine McIntyre, Earle Hodgins.

Working undercover in search of a gang, ranger Tex Duncan (Fred Scott) successfully joins Dr. Aikman's traveling medicine show. A talented singer, Scott made a string of oaters for Spectrum Pictures (1937–39), an appendage of Stan Laurel Productions. (See also *MOONLIGHT ON THE RANGE*.)

RANGERS STEP IN, THE Columbia, 1937, B&W, 58 min. **Producer:** Larry Darmour; **Director:** Spencer Gordon

Bennet; **Screenplay:** Jesse Duffy, Nate Gatzert, and Joseph Levering; **Cinematographer:** James S. Brown Jr.; **Editor:** Dwight Caldwell; **Cast:** Robert Allen, Eleanor Stewart, John Merton, Wally Wales, Jack Ingram, Jack Rockwell.

RANGE WAR   Paramount, 1939, B&W, 64 min. **Producer:** Harry Sherman; **Director:** Leslie Selander; **Screenplay:** Sam Robins; **Music:** Victor Young; **Cinematographer:** Russell Harlan; **Editor:** Sherman A. Rose; **Cast:** William Boyd, Russell Hayden, Britt Wood, Pedro de Cordoba, Willard Robertson, Matt Moore.

RARE BREED, THE   Universal, 1966, Color, 97 min, VHS. **Producer:** William Alland; **Director:** Andrew V. McLaglen; **Screenplay:** Ric Hardman; **Music:** John Williams; **Cinematographer:** William H. Clothier; **Editor:** Russell F. Schoengarth; **Cast:** James Stewart, Maureen O'Hara, Brian Keith, Juliet Mills, Don Galloway, Jack Elam, David Brian, Ben Johnson, Harry Carey Jr., Perry Lopez, Gregg Palmer.

Upon the death of her husband, Martha Price (Maureen O'Hara) is determined to carry out his dream to introduce Hereford cattle into the American West. To aid her and her daughter in this arduous endeavor, she enlists the help of Sam "Bulldog" Burnett (James Stewart) to transport their lone bull, a Hereford named Vindicator, to a breeder in Texas. But the road is a tough one, and even the sturdy Burnett has doubts as to the survival potential of this rare breed of bull. Brian Keith dons a red beard and wig to portray Alexander Bowen, a Scottish rancher, while Jack Elam is his usual sinister self as the double-crossing gunman who engages Stewart in a fight to the finish.

Filmed in the Mojave Desert and containing an ample array of studio shots, *The Rare Breed* was one of three westerns teaming James Stewart and director Andrew V. McLaglen; the other two are *SHENANDOAH* (1965) and *BANDOLERO* (1968). Stewart had certainly appeared in better westerns, including McLaglen's *Shenandoah* the previous year earlier, but few scenes and sequences can top the one in this film where his character finds the calf that proves the validity of crossbreeding. In discussing this moment on film, Stewart biographer Donald Dewey, author of *James Stewart: A Biography*, has cited James Powers, whose review in *The Hollywood Reporter* opined: "The scene . . . with the camera entirely on Stewart's face is one of great poignancy and tenderness. . . . Stewart once again, as he has done hundreds of times, shows what it means to understand acting and to make it meaningful."

The Rare Breed was the first of four consecutive westerns Stewart made between 1966 and 1970. The story is based on the actual introduction of white-faced Hereford cattle from England to the U.S. western ranges. *Variety* found the picture to be "a generally successful fictionalized blend of violence, romance, comedy, inspiration and oater Americana."

RAWHIDE   20th Century Fox, 1938, B&W. **Producer:** Sol Lesser; **Director:** Ray Taylor; **Screenplay:** Jack Natte-

ford; **Cinematographer:** Allen Q. Thompson; **Editor:** Robert O. Crandall; **Cast:** Lou Gehrig, Smith Ballew, Evalyn Knapp, Arthur Loft, Dick Kendall.

All-time baseball great Lou Gehrig stars as a rancher who is being coerced to give up his properties to a band of outlaws. His sister (Evalyn Knapp) is in love with a young lawyer (Smith Ballew), and together they stand tall against an outlaw leader (Arthur Loft), the head of the Cattlemen's Protective Agency, who is running roughshod on the ranchers. This surprisingly interesting oater has Gehrig doing a yeoman's job as the sturdy rancher whose character's name in the film is also Lou Gehrig.

Lou Gehrig retired from baseball the following year, setting what was then a Major League record for playing in 2,130 consecutive games, a record broken only recently by the Baltimore Orioles' Cal Ripken Jr. Two years after his retirement, the disease that now carries his name claimed the life of this extraordinary athlete. When Gehrig's life story, *The Pride of the Yankees*, was released in 1942, it was Gary Cooper—no stranger to western films—who won an Oscar nomination for his moving portrayal of the great New York Yankee first baseman.

RAWHIDE   20th Century Fox, 1951, B&W, 89 min, VHS. **Producer:** Samuel G. Engel; **Director:** Henry Hathaway; **Screenplay:** Dudley Nichols; **Cinematographer:** Milton R. Krasner; **Editor:** Robert L. Simpson; **Cast:** Tyrone Power, Susan Hayward, Hugh Marlow, Dean Jagger, Edgar Buchanan, Jack Elam, George Tobias, Max Terhune.

Tyrone Power is the assistant to stagecoach way-station manager Edgar Buchanan. When news is received that a band of outlaws will soon reach the station, the manager advises a young woman (Susan Hayward) traveling with her infant niece to remain at the station and not continue her journey but to wait instead for the next stagecoach east. When the outlaws reach the way station, the manager is killed, while Hayward and Power are mistaken for a married couple and locked up. The outlaws then wait anxiously for the $100,000 gold shipment to arrive. They begin arguing with each other, while in the meantime the couple work at planning their escape so they might warn the oncoming stage. Tension builds as the stage pulls in, and Power and Hayward must pretend that nothing is wrong.

Helmed by Henry Hathaway, *Rawhide* was his one major foray into "serious" westerns. It is a film that William Everson calls "an interesting 'mood' and suspense western of the early fifties." Most of the action here is confined to a 24-hour period, employing the limited-time format that reached its cinematic apex in Fred Zinnemann's *HIGH NOON* (1952). Hugh Marlow performs particularly well as the leader of the outlaw gang, with Jack Elam in top form as the woman-hungry escaped ex-con who is a Marlow gang member.

RAWHIDE TERROR   Superior Talking Pictures, 1934, B&W, 52 min. **Producer:** Victor Adamson (as Denver Dixon); **Directors:** Bruce M. Mitchell and Jack Nelson;

Screenplay: Adamson (as Dixon) and Nelson; **Cinematographer:** A. J. Fitzpatrick and Bert Longenecker; **Cast:** Art Mix, Edmund Cobb, William Desmond, William Barrymore, Frances Morris.

A dozen renegades dressed like Indians kill the parents of two brothers. The brothers, who share similar birthmarks, then separate. Ten years later a man known only as "The Rawhide Terror" is murdering the renegades who are now town citizens. Everyone is after The Rawhide Terror, and the two brothers are destined to meet again.

Reputed to be a film only for cult lovers and "Z-move freaks," this Victor Adamson production began as a serial, but after a production halt it was converted into a B western. Nevertheless, ardent genre fans will appreciate the film as one of the few talkies with the great Art Mix in a starring role.

RAWHIDE TRAIL, THE   Allied Artists, 1958, B&W, 67 min. **Producer:** Earle Lyon; **Director:** Robert Gordon; **Screenplay:** Alexander J. Wells; **Music:** Andre Brummer; **Cinematographer:** Karl Strauss; **Editor:** Paul Borofsky; **Cast:** Rex Reason, Nancy Gates, Richard Erdman, Rusty Lane, Frank Chase.

Two men who are falsely accused of leading settlers into an Indian ambush prove their innocence as they await hanging and see the fort in which they are being held prisoner attacked by Indians.

RAWHIDE YEARS, THE   Universal, 1956, Color, 85 min. **Producer:** Stanley Rubin; **Director:** Rudolph Mate; **Screenplay:** Robert Presnell Jr., D. D. Beauchamp, and Earl Felton; **Music:** Hans J. Salter; **Cinematographer:** Irving Glassberg; **Editor:** Russell F. Schoengarth; **Cast:** Tony Curtis, Colleen Miller, Arthur Kennedy, William Demarest, William Gargan, Peter van Eyck.

Tony Curtis is Ben Mathews, a handsome riverboat gambler who gives up his flashy life to settle down in Galena with his girlfriend, a beautiful entertainer named Zoe (Colleen Miller). However, when Galena's leading citizen is murdered on the boat, Ben finds a lynch mob awaiting his arrival. He flees, wandering for three years until Zoe's letters suddenly stop coming. Ben returns to Galena hoping to find his wayward girlfriend and clear himself of murder charges.

One of Hollywood's handsomest young stars and reigning heartthrobs, Tony Curtis was on his way to proving that he had some real acting ability. Two years later, in 1958, he received an Oscar nomination for his role in Stanley Kramer's *The Defiant Ones*. Songstress/actress Peggy Lee wrote the lyrics for "The Gypsy with the Fire in His Shoe."

R.C.M.P. AND THE TREASURE OF GENGHIS KHAN   See *DANGERS OF THE CANADIAN MOUNTED*.

REBEL, THE   See *BUSHWHACKERS, THE*.

REBEL CITY   Allied Artists, 1953, B&W, 52 min. **Producer:** Vincent M. Fennelly; **Director:** Thomas Carr; **Screenplay:** Sidney Theil; **Music:** Raoul Kraushaar; **Cinematographer:** Ernest Miller; **Editor:** Sam Fields; **Cast:** William "Wild Bill" Elliott, Marjorie Lord, Robert Kent, Henry Rowland, Keith Richards, I. Stanford Jolley, Denver Pyle, Otto Waldis.

During the Civil War, when a man arrives in a Kansas town hoping to find the man who killed his father, he stumbles on a conspiracy of copperheads (Northerners) who desire to aid the Confederate cause in one of Bill Elliott's final B westerns. He made one more, *BITTER CREEK*, in 1954 as the B genre was rapidly dying out. Bill Elliott's career shifted to detective dramas. His last screen appearance was *Footsteps in the Night* in 1957. He died in 1965 at age 62.

REBEL IN TOWN   United Artists, 1956, B&W, 78 min. **Producer:** Howard W. Koch; **Director:** Alfred L. Werker; **Screenplay:** Danny Arnold; **Music:** Lex Baxter; **Cinematographer:** Gordon Avil; **Editor:** John F. Schever; **Cast:** John Payne, Ruth Roman, J. Carrol Naish, John Smith, James Griffith, Ben Johnson.

An ex-soldier, now a bank robber, accidentally kills a young boy, only to have his own life saved by the boy's father. The unusual plot line of this film sets it apart from many other period westerns.

REBELLION (aka: LADY FROM FRISCO)   Crescent, 1936, B&W, 62 min. **Producer:** E. B. Derr; **Director:** Lynn Shores; **Screenplay:** John T. Neville; **Music:** Abe Meyer; **Cinematographer:** Arthur Martinelli; **Editor:** Donald Barratt; **Cast:** Tom Keene, Rita Hayworth (as Rita Cansino), Duncan Renaldo, William Royle, Gino Corrado, Roger Gray.

RECKLESS RANGER   Columbia, 1937, B&W, 56 min. **Producer:** Larry Darmour; **Director:** Spencer Gordon Bennet; **Screenplay:** Nate Gatzert; **Cinematographer:** Bert Longenecker; **Cast:** Bob Allen, Louise Small, Mary MacLaren, Harry Woods, Jack Perrin, Slim Whitaker, Lane Chandler, Buddy Cox.

RED BLOOD OF COURAGE, THE   Ambassador, 1935, B&W, 55 min. **Producer:** Maurice Conn and Sam Neufeld; **Director:** Jack English; **Screenplay:** Barry Barringer; **Cinematographer:** Arthur Reed; **Editor:** Richard G. Wray; **Cast:** Kermit Maynard, Ann Sheridan, Reginald Barlow, Ben Hendricks, Charles King.

RED CANYON   Universal, 1949, Color, 82 min. **Producer:** Leonard Goldstein; **Director:** George Sherman; **Screenplay:** Maurice Geraghty; **Music:** Walter Scharf; **Cinematographer:** Irving Glassberg; **Editor:** Otto Ludwig; **Cast:** Ann Blyth, Howard Duff, George Brent, Edgar

Buchanan, John McIntyre, Chill Wills, Jane Darwell, Lloyd Bridges, James Seay, Denver Pyle, Hank Worden.

In this adaptation of Zane Grey's novel *Wildfire*, a reformed bad man and a farmer's tomboy daughter set out to tame Black Velvet, a "killer" stallion, so they can enter the horse in a race.

RED DESERT Lippert, 1949, B&W, 60 min. **Producer:** Ron Ormond; **Director:** Ford Beebe; **Screenplay:** Ormond and Daniel B. Ullman; **Cinematographer:** Ernest Miller; **Editor:** Hugh Winn; **Cast:** Don "Red" Barry (as Don Barry), Tom Neal, Jack Holt, Margia Dean, Tom London, Holly Bane.

Don Barry is the Pecos Kid, a government agent sent by President Ulysses S. Grant to track the outlaws who have stolen a treasure of gold bullion. His chase leads to a desolate desert region where he is forced to employ all his survival skills, battling two gambling house operators who use their business as a front for selling government gold.

RED GARTERS Paramount, 1954, Color, 91 min. **Producer:** Pat Duggan; **Director:** George Marshall; **Screenplay:** Michael Fessier; **Music:** Jay Livingston; **Cinematographer:** Arthur E. Arling; **Editor:** Arthur B. Schmidt; **Cast:** Rosemary Clooney, Jack Carson, Guy Mitchell, Pat Crowley, Gene Barry, Cass Daley, Frank Faylen, Reginald Owen, Buddy Ebsen, Joanne Gilbert.

A garish western musical, *Red Garters* tells the story of a man who rides into town hoping to find his brother's killer but discovers that the gun-happy citizens of the town are celebrating his brother's death instead. To complicate matters he finds himself involved in a romantic triangle with saloon singer Rosemary Clooney and town mayor Jack Carson. Eventually he discovers the murderer, and each man vows to shoot the other down—until, that is, their girlfriends team up to end the violence.

Though perhaps not for genre purists, this fast-paced western musical spoof still registers well, and it can be lots of fun. The film was made entirely on inside sets, and the lavish splashes of color garnered an Oscar nomination for Art Direction–Set Direction (color) for the team of Roland Anderson, Sam Comer, Ray Moyer, and Hal Pereira. The five musical numbers and excellent soundtrack were penned by the Oscar-winning team of Ray Evans and Jay Livingston ("Buttons and Bows") and are sung in grand manner, mainly by cast members Rosemary Clooney and Guy Mitchell, two of the top recording artists of the early and mid-1950s. Singing legend Clooney, who died in 2002, was the aunt of popular movie and TV star George Clooney.

REDHEAD AND THE COWBOY, THE Paramount, 1950, B&W, 82 min. **Producer:** Irving Asher; **Director:** Leslie Fenton; **Screenplay:** Jonathan Latimer and Liam O'Brien; **Music:** David Buttolph; **Cinematographer:** Daniel L. Fapp; **Editor:** Arthur P. Schmidt; **Cast:** Glenn Ford, Edmond O'Brien, Rhonda Fleming, Morris Ankrum, Ray Teal, Iron Eyes Cody.

A beautiful courier for the Confederacy during the closing days of the Civil War is pursued by two men—a cowboy who needs her testimony to clear him of a murder charge and a man who is actually a Union spy. The film features lots of action and star appeal, with Rhonda Fleming as Candace Bronson, the former dance-hall girl turned courier; and Glenn Ford as Gil Kyle, the apolitical cowboy who gets caught in a political quagmire.

REDHEAD FROM WYOMING, THE Universal, 1953, Color, 81 min, VHS. **Producer:** Leonard Goldstein; **Director:** Lee Sholem; **Screenplay:** Polly James and Herb Meadow; **Music:** Milton Rosen and Herman Stein; **Cinematographer:** Winton Hoch; **Editor:** Milton Carruth; **Cast:** Maureen O'Hara, Alex Nicol, William Bishop, Robert Strauss, Alexander Scourby, Gregg Palmer, Jack Kelly, Jeanne Cooper, Dennis Weaver.

Maureen O'Hara plays a feisty saloon proprietress caught between protecting a local cattle rustler (Bishop) and her love for sheriff Alec Nicol. When she frustrates Bishop's plan to start a range war, he frames her for murder, and Nicol helps her clear her name. This better than average 1950s western set in the Wyoming Territory benefits from Oscar-winner Winton Hoch's (*She Wore a Yellow Ribbon*, 1949; *The Quiet Man*, 1952) excellent camera work and an appealing cast.

RED MOUNTAIN Paramount, 1951, Color, 84 min. **Producer:** Hal B. Wallis; **Director:** William Dieterle; **Screenplay:** John Meredyth Lucas; **Music:** Franz Waxman; **Cinematographer:** Charles Lange; **Editor:** Warren Lowe; **Cast:** Alan Ladd, Lizabeth Scott, Arthur Kennedy, John Ireland, Jeff Corey, James Bell, Bert Freed, Walter Sandee, Neville Brand, Jay Silverheels, Iron Eyes Cody.

In 1865, Captain Brett Sherwood (Alan Ladd), a Confederate army officer, travels west to join William Quantrell in a last-ditch effort to prevent a Union victory. On the way Sherwood stops off in the town of Broken Bow in Colorado Territory to settle an old score with an assayer who had stolen his land claim before the war.

When the townspeople find the assayer dead from a Confederate-issue bullet, they are quick to blame Lane Waldron (Arthur Kennedy), an ex-Confederate soldier who had settled in Broken Bow as a private citizen. Sentenced to hang, he is rescued by Sherwood, and the two ride out to Waldron's mountainside cabin.

Discarding any gratitude, Waldron decides to bring his rescuer to justice in the supposed belief that it was Sherwood who really killed the assayer. He is supported in his decision by his fiancée Chris (Lizabeth Scott). However, when Waldron suffers a broken leg and lapses into a fever, the three protagonists are forced to take refuge in a cave. In their solitude, sparks start to fly between Sherwood and Chris.

Alan Ladd in Red Mountain (PARAMOUNT/AUTHOR'S COLLECTION)

However, before they are able to consummate their mutual attraction, they must first confront Quantrell, who now has designs on becoming the self-anointed overlord of the American West. After a well-staged climactic shoot-out, Waldron delivers a deathbed confession that in fact he was the assayer's killer. Brett and Chris are able to ride off and start a new life together.

John Ireland plays Quantrell with verve and conviction, joining the likes of Walter Pidgeon, Brian Donlevy (twice), and Leo Gordon as screen actors who have portrayed the infamous raider and plunderer. Because the film was so loosely based on historical fact, Paramount decided to change Quantrill's name by one letter. Thus the historical William Clark Quantrill becomes William Quantrell, so if challenged the studio could claim that the film was *not* really about Quantrill.

Ladd, as usual, is smooth in the role of Brett Sherwood, a man of action beset by serious doubt. The erotic sexual tension between Ladd and Lizabeth Scott was a harbinger of possible future screen efforts, but unfortunately they never worked together again. Scott, it might be recalled, had the same sultry demeanor and alluring presence as Veronica Lake, Ladd's prototype leading lady of the 1940s, when he and Lake were among the decade's classic screen couples.

In *The Films of Alan Ladd*, authors Marilyn Henry and Don DeSourdis quote Lizabeth Scott on the merits of Ladd's professional skills: "As an actor I found him quite involved with his craft. His intense concentration was impressive. Scenes were never done for his own self-aggrandizement. They were done with perspective."

RED RIDER, THE Universal, 1934, B&W, 15 chapters. **Producer:** Milton Gatzert and Henry MacRae; **Director:** Lew Landers; **Screenplay:** Basil Dickey, Vin Moore, Ella O'Neill, George H. Plympton, and W. C. Tuttle; **Cast:** Buck Jones, Marion Shilling, Grant Withers, Walter Miller, Richard Cramer, Edmond Cobb, Jim Thorpe.

A sheriff loses his job when he refuses to believe his pal committed a crime near the Mexican border. The villain leaves unwitting clues to his identity by discarding his marijuana cigarettes at the scene of the crime. Considered the best of the four 1930s Buck Jones serials for Universal, *The Red Rider* involves numerous plot twists and employs two notable elements extremely rare in the western serial: pleasant bantering comedy from both the good guys and the bad, and some good solid romance.

RED RIVER United Artists, 1948, B&W, 133 min. **Producer:** Howard Hawks; **Director:** Hawks; **Screenplay:** Borden Chase and Charles Schnee; **Music:** Dimitri Tiomkin; **Editor:** Christian Nyby; **Cast:** John Wayne, Montgomery Clift, Joanne Dru, Walter Brennan, Coleen Gray, Harry Carey, John Ireland, Noah Beery Jr., Harry Carey Jr., Chief Yowlachie, Paul Fix, Hank Warden, Wally Wales.

Howard Hawks's first major western, *Red River* tells the story of the first cattle drive over the Chisholm Trail from deep in Texas to Abilene, Kansas. It is also the story of the conflict between two determined men, Tom Dunson (Wayne) and his "adopted" son Matt Garth (Montgomery Clift), which erupts when Matt leads a revolt against Dunson, who is driving his men beyond the limit of human endurance.

Scripted by Chase and Charles Schnee, the film begins as Dunson leaves a wagon train and his girl behind, with the intent of heading south to Texas and the Red River to start his own cattle herd. He sets out with his pal Groot (Walter Brennan), but they are soon joined by a boy who was the sole survivor of the Indian massacre of the wagon train: a young Matt Garth (played by Mickey Kuhn).

Without missing a beat the film fast-forwards 14 years (it was 20 years in the original story). Dunson is now convinced he can lead a herd of 10,000 head of cattle to Missouri. Tough to the core, Dunson tells his men that if they are not willing to take the risk they can withdraw from the drive and still have a job waiting for them when he returns. But if they do sign on, it must be for the duration. There will be no quitting, and anyone who tries to quit will be dealt with harshly. This sets the stage for his eventual conflict with Matt.

A western masterpiece, *Red River* has been hailed as the picture that made John Wayne an actor rather than just a movie star. By playing a man who ages and hardens perceptibly during the film, Wayne paved the way for the marvelous character roles he would undertake later in his career, particularly the tough, hardened individualist who lived life on his own terms. In his most complex role to date, Wayne's Dunson emerges as the prototype rancher-hero, a man as tough as he is stubborn, a western trailblazer consumed by blinding ambition and a near-impossible task. The yelling that begins the cattle drive has become a classic scene echoed in numerous films.

Producer/director Howard Hawks had already distinguished himself as a first-rate director dating back to the silent era, with movies ranging from action and adventure to crime and comedy. Desirous of making a western, he purchased the film rights to Borden Chase's story "The Chisholm Trail," which first appeared in *The Saturday Evening Post*. Hawks originally leaned toward Gary Cooper for the part of Dunson and Cary Grant for the part of Cherry Valance, a more significant role than the one eventually taken

John Wayne, Montgomery Clift, and Walter Brennan in Red River, *Howard Hawks's first Western* (UNITED ARTISTS/AUTHOR'S COLLECTION)

by John Ireland in the movie. However, Cooper found the role to be too violent, and Grant simply did not want to take second billing to anyone. Hawks thereupon gave the part to John Wayne, who was offered $75,000 and a share of the profits.

For the role of young Matt Dunson, Hawks turned to the Broadway stage and selected 26-year-old Montgomery Clift, one of the founding members of the Actor's Studio. Total opposites in nearly every avenue including acting style, the on-screen interaction between Clift and Wayne is compelling. According to the late Pierce Lyden, the famous B western bad man who had an uncredited part in *Red River*, the Broadway-trained Clift had to be trained for everything, and he received lots of help from stuntman (later actor) Richard Farnsworth. In *Duke, We're Glad We Knew You*, Lyden asserts that Farnsworth "looked just enough like Montgomery Clift so they could do all the close-ups. He taught Montgomery Clift how to roll a cigarette and how to ride a horse."

The film also stars Joanne Dru and features Harry Carey (in his last film) and Harry Carey Jr. (in his second)—the only time these two fine character actors appeared in the same film (though they were in no scenes together). Also in the cast is Coleen Gray as the ill-fated Fen, the girl that Dunson left behind, and 26-year-old Shelley Winters in an uncredited role as a dance-hall girl. A few years later Clift and Winters would score brilliantly together in George Stevens's *A Place in the Sun* (1951).

If the film has any flaw, it is the somewhat tepid ending where Tess Millay (Dru), with whom Garth is in love, patches things up between the two protagonists in a rather simplistic way. Otherwise, *Red River* is a gem. The photography is superb, with Russell Harlan's camera vividly capturing the great outdoors in black and white. Dimitri Tiomkin's robust and melodic score is a treasure. Tiomkin and Hawks would work together four more times, with some of the movie's themes replicated by Tiomkin and Hawks in the 1959 western *RIO BRAVO*.

Old-line B western players Tom Tyler and Lane Chandler appear in the film in uncredited roles, Chandler in the role of the wagon master colonel. An alternate version, usually shown on television, substitutes Walter Brennan's spoken narration for the shots of a diary's turning pages in the uncut version, making the television entry eight minutes shorter than the original.

The movie was filmed in Elgin, Arizona, and nominated for two Academy Awards: Best Motion Picture Story (Borden Chase) and Best Editing (Christian Nyby). *Red River* remains a cinematic landmark, named to the National Film Registry in 1990 by the National Film Preservation Board, USA. It made Howard Hawks a main player in the western genre; Montgomery Clift emerged as one of the screen's most sympathetic leading men; and John Wayne, whose performance may rightly be described as brilliant, was clearly on his way to becoming one of the movies' top box-office stars. Eventually his legacy was unmatched in the American (and world) cinema.

RED RIVER RANGE   Republic, 1938, B&W, 56 min.
Producer: William A. Berke (associate); **Director:** George Sherman; **Screenplay:** Betty Burbridge, Stanley Roberts, and Luci Ward; **Music:** William Lava; **Cinematographer:** Jack D. Marta; **Editor:** Tony Martinelli; **Cast:** John Wayne, Ray Corrigan, Max Terhune, Polly Moran, Lorna Gray, Kirby Grant.
See *THREE MESQUITEERS, THE.*

RED RIVER RENEGADES   Republic, 1946, B&W, 53 min. **Producer:** Bennett Cohen (associate); **Director:** Thomas Carr; **Screenplay:** Norman S. Hall; **Cinematographer:** William Bradford; **Editor:** William P. Thompson; **Cast:** Sunset Carson, Peggy Stewart, Tom London, Ted Adams, LeRoy Mason, Kenne Duncan.

RED RIVER ROBIN HOOD   Republic, 1943, B&W, 57 min. **Producer:** Bert Gilroy; **Director:** Leslie Selander; **Screenplay:** Bennett Cohen; **Music:** Paul Sawtell; **Cinematographer:** J. Roy Hunt; **Editor:** Les Milbrook; **Cast:** Tim Holt, Cliff Edwards, Barbara Moffett, Ellen Drew, Otto Hoffman.

RED RIVER SHORE   Republic, 1953, B&W, 54 min. **Producer:** Rudy Ralston; **Director:** Harry Keller; **Screenplay:** Gerald Geraghty and Arthur Orloff; **Music:** R. Dale Butts; **Cinematographer:** Bud Thackery; **Editor:** Harold Minter; **Cast:** Rex Allen, Slim Pickens, Lyn Thomas, William Phipps, Douglas Fowley.

RED RIVER VALLEY (aka: MAN OF THE FRONTIER)   Republic, 1936, B&W, 60 min, VHS. **Producers:** B. Reeves Eason and Nat Levine; **Director:** Eason; **Screenplay:** Dorrell McGowan and Stuart E. McGowan; **Music:** Gene Autry, Smiley Burnette, Harry Gray, and Sam H. Stept; **Cinematographer:** William Nobles; **Editors:** Joseph H. Lewis and Carl Pierson; **Cast:** Gene Autry, Smiley Burnette, Frances Grant, Boothe Howard, Jack Kennedy, George Chesebro, Charles King.

Gene and Frog pretend to be ditchdiggers so they can find out who has been causing the accidents at a dam construction site. Using relatively high production standards, Republic deliberately gave nontraditional western settings to some of Gene Autry's better musical vehicles like *Red River Valley*.

RED RIVER VALLEY   Republic, 1941, B&W, 62 min. **Producer:** Joseph Kane (associate); **Director:** Kane; **Screenplay:** Malcolm Stuart Boylan; **Music:** Cy Feuer, Bob Nolan, and Tim Spencer; **Cinematographer:** Jack A. Marta; **Editor:** William P. Thompson; **Cast:** Roy Rogers, George "Gabby" Hayes, Sally Payne, Trevor Bardette, Gale Storm, Robert Homans, Wally Wales, Lynton Brent, Bob Nolan.

Roy helps a group of ranchers raise money to build a reservoir, but they soon lose it to a gambler through a crooked stock deal. With Gene Autry joining the armed forces, Republic got behind a big Roy Rogers campaign. Many of Roy's films like *Red River Valley* were basic remakes of earlier Autry successes but with bigger budgets than were allotted to Gene Autry.

The solid soundtrack includes the traditional "Red River Valley" sung by Roy and the Sons of the Pioneers; "Lily of the Valley," sung by Sally Payne; "When Payday Rolls Around," sung by the Sons of the Pioneers; "The Chant of the Wanderer," "Love Begins at the Sunset Trail," and "Springtime on the Range," all sung by Roy and the Sons of the Pioneers. (See also *UNDER WESTERN STARS.*)

RED ROPE, THE   Republic, 1937, B&W, 60 min, VHS. **Producer:** A. W. Hackel; **Director:** S. Roy Luby; **Screenplay:** George H. Plympton; **Cinematographer:** Bert Longenecker; **Editor:** S. Roy Luby; **Cast:** Bob Steele, Lois January, Forrest Taylor, Charles King, Karl Hackett.

A cowpoke comes to the aid of a young couple who want to be married but are being deterred by a man who wants the woman for himself and happens to hold the mortgage to her father's ranch. This A. W. Hackel entry for Republic is among Bob Steele's better entries, with fast-paced-action and a well-written script. (See also *LIGHTNIN' CRANDALL.*)

RED STALLION, THE   Eagle-Lion, 1947, Color, 81 min. **Producer:** Bryan Foy; **Director:** Lesley Selander; **Screenplay:** Robert E. Kent and Crane Wilbur; **Music:** Frederick Hollander; **Cinematographer:** Jack Greenhalgh and Virgil Miller; **Editor:** Fred Allen; **Cast:** Robert Paige, Noreen Nash, Ted Donaldson, Jane Darwell, Ray Collins, Guy Kibbee.

A young man raises an orphaned colt he finds in the woods. When he learns that his grandmother is going to have to sell her ranch to pay off her debts, the lad and a handler train "Red" to be a racehorse with the intention of selling the animal to help pay off his grandmother's debts.

RED STALLION IN THE ROCKIES
Eagle-Lion, 1949, B&W, 85 min. **Producer:** Aubrey Schenck; **Director:** Ralph Murphy; **Screenplay:** Tom Reed; **Music:** Lucien Caillet and Murphy; **Cinematographer:** John Alton; **Editor:** Norman Colbert; **Cast:** Arthur Franz, Ray Collins, Jim Davis, Wallace Ford, Jean Heather, Leatrice Joy, James Kirkwood.

Two circus performers go to work on a ranch and set out to round up a herd of wild horses. Problems arise when one of them falls in love with the owner's niece. This good outdoor drama benefits from a fine performance by Jim Davis as the ranch owner's son.

RED SUNDOWN
Universal, 1956, Color, 81 min. **Producer:** Albert Zugsmith; **Director:** Jack Arnold; **Screenplay:** Martin Berkeley; **Music:** Hans J. Salter; **Cinematographer:** William E. Snyder; **Editor:** Edward Curtiss; **Cast:** Rory Calhoun, Martha Hyer, Dean Jagger, Robert Middleton, Grant Williams, Lita Baron, Leo Gordon.

Rory Calhoun is Alec Longmire, the prototype bad man gone good, who becomes deputy sheriff in a small town and challenges a land baron and his hired killer. He succeeds in cleaning the town of its lawless elements, while managing to romance the cattle baron's pretty daughter in the process.

RED TOMAHAWK
Paramount, 1967, Color, 82 min. **Producer:** A. C. Lyles; **Director:** R. G. Springsteen; **Screenplay:** Andrew Craddock; **Music:** Jimmie Haskell; **Cinematographer:** W. Wallace Kelley; **Editor:** John F. Schreyer; **Cast:** Howard Keel, Joan Caulfield, Broderick Crawford, Scott Brady, Wendell Corey, Richard Arlen, Tom Drake, Tracy Olson, Ben Cooper, Don "Red" Barry, Henry Wills.

Following the Battle of Little Big Horn, an army captain attempts to warn the people of Deadwood that an Indian attack looms on the horizon. He must then convince the inhabitants of the town to turn over four Gatling guns in their possession.

Once again producer A. C. Lyles lines up cast of veteran players to star in this routine oater. While the production and script might be on the thin side, the presence of old-line stars still provides curious interest to genre fans. Reportedly Betty Hutton was signed for the lead role, but she could not endure the fast-paced shooting schedule and was replaced by Joan Caulfield.

REDWOOD FOREST TRAIL
Republic, 1950, B&W, 67 min. **Producer:** Franklin Adreon; **Director:** Philip Ford; **Screenplay:** Bradford Ropes; **Music:** Stanley Wilson; **Cinematographer:** John MacBurnie; **Editor:** Harold Minter; **Cast:** Rex Allen, Jane Darwell, Bob Burns, John L. Cason, Jeff Donnell, Jim Frasher, Dickie Jones.

RELENTLESS
Columbia, 1948, Color, 93 min. **Producer:** Eugene Rodney; **Director:** George Sherman; **Screenplay:** Winston Miller; **Music:** Martin Skiles; **Cinematographer:** Edward Cronjager; **Editor:** Gene Havlick; **Cast:** Robert Young, Marguerite Chapman, Willard Parker, Akim Tamiroff, Barton MacLane, Mike Mazurki, Clem Bevans, Frank Fenton.

A posse of men pursues a horse thief who has been framed for a murder he didn't commit. This fast-paced and well-done chase drama features Robert Young and Barton MacLane as the main protagonists and Marguerite Chapman as the girl who gives the suspected cowboy some unexpected help. This exciting little film reveals some good psychological give-and-take among the main players, with Young and MacLane fully believable in their roles.

REMEMBER ME
See *HORSEMEN OF THE SIERRAS*.

RENEGADE GIRL
Screen Guild, 1946, B&W, 65 min. **Producer:** William A. Berke; **Director:** Berke; **Screenplay:** Edwin K. Westrate; **Music:** Darrell Calker; **Cinematographer:** James S. Brown Jr.; **Cast:** Ann Savage, Alan Curtis, Russell Wade, Jack Holt, Edward Brophy, Chief Thundercloud, Claudia Drake, John "Dusty" King, Edmund Cobb.

Jean Shelby (Ann Savage) is a Confederate sympathizer in Missouri whose family has been supplying information to William Quantrill's raiders. In response, the Union army attempts to find the Shelby family, aided by an outcast Indian who has his own grudge against them. The plot of this semi-historical Civil War drama unfolds when Jean and Union captain Fred Raymond (Allan Curtis) fall in love with each other, and their respective loyalties come into question. Some good action here mixes with a fine cast of ex-genre players.

RENEGADE RANGER, THE
RKO, 1938, B&W, 60 min. **Producer:** Bert Gilroy; **Director:** David Howard; **Screenplay:** Oliver Drake; **Music:** Albert Hay Malotte and Willie Phelps (songs); **Cinematographer:** Harry J. Wild; **Editor:** Frederick Knudtson; **Cast:** George O'Brien, Rita Hayworth, Tim Holt, Ray Whitley, Lucio Villegas, William Royle.

Captain Jack Steele (George O'Brien) of the Texas Rangers is assigned to apprehend former ranch owner Judith Alvarez (Rita Hayworth), whose gang is waging a war against the crooked government officials who cheated the ranchers out of their land. Captain Steele manages to infiltrate the gang, and he gradually realizes Judith is innocent of the murder she was thought to have committed and was actually framed by the corrupt tax collector. Tim Holt plays ex-ranger Larry Corwin, who now works for Ms. Alvarez and realizes Steele's true identity. The film ends with the Mexican ranchers getting their land back from a band of greedy Texans.

This high-grade RKO vehicle stars the studio's two outstanding series cowboys, George O'Brien and Tim Holt (who took over from O'Brien when O'Brien's screen career went on hold during World War II). It is an entertaining remake of RKO Radio's 1932 film *Carry On Danger*, with Tom Tyler in the starring role. RKO remade *Carry On Danger* in 1942, this time with Tim Holt in the lead role. In this 1938 film, Rita Hayworth is absolutely lovely as bandit queen Alvarez in one of her early screen performances. (See also *RACKETEERS OF THE RANGE*.)

RENEGADES Color, 1946, Color, 87 min. **Producer:** Michael Kraike; **Director:** George Sherman; **Screenplay:** Francis Edward Faragoh and Melvin Levy; **Music:** Paul Sawtell; **Cinematographer:** William Snyder; **Editor:** Charles Nelson; **Cast:** Evelyn Keyes, Willard Parker, Larry Parks, Edgar Buchanan, Jim Bannon, Forrest Tucker, Ludwig Donath.

Hannah Brockway (Evelyn Keyes) is torn between two men: a respectable doctor (Willard Parker) and the youngest son of an outlaw family (Larry Parks), who wants to go straight but finds his family's reputation too difficult to overcome. A good cast that includes Parks and Keyes enhances this rather garish western. The two were also teamed more visibly in *The Jolson Story* (1946). Edgar Buchanan delivers an outstanding performance as Kirk Dembrow, the Bible-spouting bandit.

RENEGADES OF SONORA Republic, 1948, B&W, 60 min. **Producer:** Gordon Kay (associate); **Director:** R. G. Springstein; **Screenplay:** M. Coates Webster; **Music:** Stanley Wilson; **Cinematographer:** John MacBurnie; **Editor:** Tony Martinelli; **Cast:** Allan "Rocky" Lane, Eddy Waller, Roy Barcroft, Frank Fenton, Mauritz Hugo, Holly Bane, House Peters Jr.

RENEGADES OF THE RIO GRANDE Universal, 1945, Color, 88 min. **Producer:** Oliver Drake (associate); **Director:** Howard Bretherton; **Screenplay:** Ande Lamb; **Cinematographer:** Maury Gertsman; **Editor:** Edward Curtiss; **Cast:** Rod Cameron, Eddie Dew, Jennifer Holt, Fuzzy Knight, Ray Whitley, Glenn Strange, Edmund Cobb.

A ranger is assigned to stop an outlaw gang that is rustling cattle along the Mexican border. This solid B western from Universal is a good indication why Rod Cameron's film career began on an upswing. Tall and strong, Cameron made 39 westerns and was one of the sleeping giants of the genre—capable, genuine, and underappreciated.

RENEGADES OF THE SAGE Columbia, 1949, B&W, 56 min. **Producer:** Colbert Clark; **Director:** Ray Nazarro; **Screenplay:** Earle Snell; **Cinematographer:** Fayte M. Browne; **Editor:** Paul Borofsky; **Cast:** Charles Starrett, Smiley Burnette, Leslie Banning, Trevor Bardette, Douglas Fowley, Jock Mahoney.

RENEGADES OF THE WEST RKO, 1932, B&W, 55 min. **Producer:** David O. Selznick; **Director:** Casey Robinson; **Screenplay:** Albert S. Le Vino; **Cinematographer:** Allen Siegler; **Editor:** Holbrook N. Todd; **Cast:** Tom Keene, Roscoe Ates, Betty Furness, Jim Mason, Carl Miller, Max Wagner.

When cattle rustlers murder a rancher, his son returns from prison and sets out to find his father's killer. Based on the Frank Richardson Pierce story "The Miracle Baby," this early Tom Keene talkie is a cut above average. The interesting soundtrack includes "The Brahms Lullaby," played on a music box; "The Farmer in the Dell," sung a cappella by Roscoe Ates; and the traditional "Pop Goes the Weasel," played at the end of the picture.

RENEGADE TRAIL Paramount, 1939, B&W, 58 min, VHS. **Producer:** Harry Sherman; **Director:** Lesley Selander; **Screenplay:** Harrison Jacobs and John Rathmell; **Music:** Phil Ohman; **Cinematographer:** Russell Harlan; **Editor:** Sherman A. Rose; **Cast:** William Boyd, Russell Hayden, George "Gabby" Hayes, Charlotte Wynters, Roy Barcroft, Eddie Dean.

REPRISAL Columbia, 1956, Color, 71 min. **Producers:** Lewis J. Rachmil and Guy Madison; **Director:** George Sherman; **Screenplay:** David Dortort, David P. Harmon, and Raphael Hayes; **Music:** Mischa Bakaleinikoff; **Cinematographer:** Henry Freulich; **Editor:** Jerome Thoms; **Cast:** Guy Madison, Felicia Farr, Kathryn Grant, Michael Pate, Edward Platt, Otto Hulett.

When a powerful rancher is killed, Frank Madden (Guy Madison) is forced to clear himself of a murder charge and is saved from a lynch mob by two women who love him. A taut script and an appealing cast of good-looking stars highlight this mid-1950s B-quality western.

REQUIEM FOR A GUNFIGHTER Embassy Pictures, 1965, Color, 91 min. **Producer:** Alex Gordon; **Director:** Spencer Gordon Bennett; **Screenplay:** Ruth Alexander; **Music:** Ronald Stein; **Cinematographer:** Frederick E. West; **Editor:** Charles H. Powell; **Cast:** Rod Cameron, Stephen McNally; Mike Mazurki, Olive Sturgess, Tim McCoy, Johnny Mack Brown, Bob Steele, Lane Chandler, Raymond Hatton, Dickie Jones, Rand Brooks.

A judge is murdered before a trial is to take place, so an ex-gunman who is mistaken for the judge decides to see that justice will prevail. The grand cast of old-line genre favorites includes a still-virile Tim McCoy in his last screen appearance as Judge Irving Short. Independent producer Alex Gordon did a true service to tradition and nostalgia by uniting such veteran genre stars like McCoy, Bob Steele, Buster Crabbe, Rod Cameron, and even Broncho Billy Anderson in his various enterprises.

RESTLESS BREED, THE   20th Century Fox, 1957, Color, 86 min. **Producer:** Edward L. Alperson; **Director:** Allan Dwan; **Screenplay:** Steve Fisher; **Music:** Edward L. Alperson Jr.; **Cinematographer:** John W. Boyle; **Editor:** Merrill G. White; **Cast:** Scott Brady, Anne Bancroft, Jay C. Flippen, Jim Davis, Rhys Williams, Leo Gordon, Myron Healey.

Young, college-educated Mitch Baker (Scott Brady) rides into a tough Texas border town determined to avenge the death of his agent father by a band of gunrunners. The leader of these gunrunners (Jim Davis) resides on the Mexican side of the border. When his men fail to get rid of Mitch, he accepts the challenge himself. The result is a taut final showdown that ends his smuggling career. This tight little action-packed Allan Dwan western boasts an interesting early screen performance by Anne Bancroft as the half-breed Indian girl who wins Brady's heart.

RETURN OF A MAN CALLED HORSE, THE
United Artists, 1976, Color, 129 min, VHS. **Producers:** Richard Harris, Sandy Howard, and Terry Moore Jr.; **Director:** Irvin Kershner; **Screenplay:** Jack Dewitt; **Music:** Laurence Rosenthal; **Cinematographer:** Owen Roizman; **Editor:** Michael Kahn; **Cast:** Richard Harris, Gail Sondergaard, Geoffrey Lewis, William Lucking.

Richard Harris reprises his role as Lord John Morgan with a 17-minute foreword that recounts the events in the previous film (*A MAN CALLED HORSE*, 1970), which ends with his return to England. In this sequel, Lord Morgan returns to the West to find his adopted tribe in a bad way. Their land is being taken away by an unscrupulous trader, and their women and children are being sold into slavery. To cleanse himself and get rid of any evil spirits, he must again undergo the torturous Sun Vow Ceremony in a scene that lasts nearly 20 minutes. He teaches the Indians how to use guns and leads them in an assault on the trading post. Upon his return to their sacred land, he decides to stay this time. The film, like its predecessor, and later like *Triumphs of a Man Called Horse* (1983), has been condemned by those who believe the depiction of such Indian rites to be fraudulent.

The Return of a Man Called Horse marked a second return to the screen for actress Gale Sondergaard, who in 1936 was the first recipient of a Best Supporting Actress Award for her role in *Anthony Adverse*. Her career was cut short in 1951 after she refused to testify before the House Un-American Activities Committee.

RETURN OF DANIEL BOONE, THE   Columbia, 1941, B&W, 61 min. **Producer:** Leon Barsha; **Director:** Lambert Hillyer; **Screenplay:** Joseph Hoffman; **Music:** Sidney Cutner; **Cast:** William "Wild Bill" Elliott, Betty Miles, Ray Bennett, Melinda Rodik, Matilda Rodik, Walter Soderling.

Oddly this film has nothing to do with Daniel Boone. Instead "Wild Bill" Elliott plays Wild Bill Boone, a young man who goes to work for a tax collector only to discover that his boss is busy cheating settlers out of their properties.

RETURN OF DRAW EGAN, THE   Triangle, 1916, B&W, 55 min. **Producer:** Thomas Ince; **Director:** William S. Hart; **Screenplay:** C. Gardner Sullivan; **Cinematographer:** Joseph H. August; **Cast:** William S. Hart, Louise Glaum, Margerie Wilson, Robert McKim, J. P. Lockney, Dorothy Benhem, Hector Dion.

Outlaw Draw Egan turns up in the town of Yellow Dog and is mistaken for a fellow named William Blake, a tough, law-abiding man. They appoint him sheriff in order to rid Yellow Dog of the hoodlums who have taken over the town. He succeeds, and with the love of beautiful Margerie Wilson he becomes a genuinely respected citizen—until, that is, one of his former gang members arrives in town and threatens to blackmail him.

This entertaining William S. Hart silent effort once again has the stoic Hart as a bad fellow who is reformed by a heroine's gaze and the majesty of love. The plot would be reworked again and again in the sound era. (See also *HELL'S HINGES*.)

RETURN OF FRANK JAMES, THE   20th Century Fox, 1940, Color, 92 min, VHS. **Producer:** Darryl F. Zanuck; **Director:** Fritz Lang; **Screenplay:** Sam Hellman; **Music:** David Buttolph; **Cinematographer:** George Barnes; **Editor:** Walter Thompson; **Cast:** Henry Fonda, Gene Tierney, Jackie Cooper, Henry Hall, John Carradine, J. Edward Bromberg, Donald Meek.

In this sequel to Henry King's highly popular *JESSE JAMES* (1939), Henry Fonda continues his excellent characterization of Frank James, the quiet, tobacco-chewing farmer now determined to track down the killers of his brother after they are pardoned by the law. Directed by the skillful Fritz Lang, the film places more emphasis on mood and character than on blatant action, which sets it apart from most westerns and somehow manages to disturb certain critics.

A particularly well-crafted scene has Frank chasing Jesse's killer into a darkened barn. The killer is already dead when he finds him, but he doesn't know it and he doesn't have a gun at the ready; instead it lies calmly by his side. Unlike most directors who would have had the hero tensely holding his gun up, Lang's Frank James is perfectly relaxed and beautifully underplayed by Fonda.

A rare sequel that was up to—perhaps even better—than the original, the film marks the screen debut of Gene Tierney as the reporter who wants to tell the story of Frank James and comes to love him.

RETURN OF JACK SLADE, THE (aka: SON OF SLADE) Allied Artists, 1955, B&W, 79 min. **Producer:** Lindsley Parsons; **Director:** Harold Schuster; **Screenplay:** Warren Douglas; **Music:** Paul Dunlap; **Cinematographer:** William Sickner; **Editor:** Maurice Wright; **Cast:** John Ericson, Mari Blanchard, Neville Brand, Max Showalter, Angie Dickinson, Jon Sheppod.

In order to redeem his father's misdeeds, Jack Slade Jr. (John Ericson) joins the law in order to fight outlaws. With a good performance by Ericson and an unpretentious script by Warren Douglas, the film is another collaboration of writer Douglas, producer Lindsley Parsons, and director Harold Schuster, the latter two of whom mentored the talented Ericson as a young actor.

RETURN OF JESSE JAMES, THE
Lippert, 1950, B&W, 75 min. **Producer:** Carl K. Hittleman; **Director:** Arthur Hilton; **Screenplay:** Jack Natteford; **Music:** Ferde Grofe Sr.; **Cinematographer:** Karl Struss; **Editor:** Harry Coswick; **Cast:** John Ireland, Ann Dvorak, Henry Hull, Reed Hadley, Hugh O'Brien, Carlton Young, Tommy Noonan.

John Ireland is Johnny Callum, a Jesse James look-alike who tries to outdo the infamous outlaw, while Frank James (Reed Hadley) does everything he can to preserve his dead brother's reputation. Callum agrees to be used by a gang to rob a bank, seduced by excessive greed and the blind ambition of the saloon singer he loves. The film, which combines some good action with an interesting psychological bent, is a nice companion piece for Lippert's *I SHOT JESSE JAMES* (1949), with Ireland also in the lead role.

RETURN OF THE BAD MEN (aka: RETURN OF THE BADMEN)
RKO, 1948, B&W, 90 min. **Producer:** Nat Holt; **Director:** Ray Enright; **Screenplay:** Jack Natteford, Charles O'Neal, and Luci Ward; **Music:** Paul Sawtell; **Cinematographer:** J. Roy Hunt; **Editor:** Samuel E. Beetley; **Cast:** Randolph Scott, Robert Ryan, Anne Jeffreys, George "Gabby" Hayes, Steve Brodie, Tom Keene (as Richard Powers), Robert Bray, Lex Barker, Walter Reed, Michael Harvey, Dean White, Robert Armstrong.

A quasi-sequel to *BADMAN'S TERRITORY* (1946), a depraved Sundance Kid (Robert Ryan) assembles a gang of big-name outlaws to rampage through the Oklahoma Territory, including Cole Younger (Steve Brodie) and brothers Jim and John (Tom Keene and Ray Bray); Emmett, Bob, and Grat Dalton (Lex Barker, Walter Reed, Michael Harvey); and Billy the Kid (Dean White). Standing between the gang and brutal destruction is U.S. marshal Randolph Scott, sidekick "Gabby" Hayes, and female desperado Anne Jeffreys, whom Scott is able to reform when she falls in love with him.

This standard western is laden with the usual clichés, but the top-rate cast, Scott's taciturn presence, and especially Ryan's sadistic performance as the murderous Sundance—"a thoroughly hissable villain," according to *Time* magazine—make for good genre viewing. The film can also be seen in a computer-colored version.

RETURN OF THE CISCO KID, THE
20th Century Fox, 1939, B&W, 70 min. **Producer:** Kenneth Macgowan; **Director:** Herbert Leeds; **Screenplay:** Milton Sperling; **Music:** Cyril J. Mockridge; **Cinematographer:** Charles G. Clarke; **Editor:** James B. Clark; **Cast:** Warner Baxter, Lynn Bari, Cesar Romero, Henry Hull, Kane Richmond, Robert Barrat, Chris-Pin Martin.

The legendary Mexican bandit is vacationing in Arizona when he comes to the aid of a pretty young lady (Lynn Bari). She is trying to hold on to her ranch but is being manipulated by a crooked businessman. Cisco helps her because he thinks she has eyes for him, but when her boyfriend (Kane Richmond) gets preference, he plots to send his rival on a fatal mission. However, he changes his mind just in time, receives solace from an old flame, cleans up the town, and rides back to Mexico a hero.

Warner Baxter played the Cisco Kid for the first time in the extremely successful *IN OLD ARIZONA* (1929), the first "outdoor all talkie," for which he won an Oscar. He repeated the role in *THE ARIZONA KID* (1930), *THE CISCO KID* (1931), and *The Return of the Cisco Kid*, which also features future Cisco Kid Cesar Romero in a small part. (See also *CISCO KID, THE*.)

RETURN OF THE DURANGO KID
Columbia, 1945, B&W, 58 min. **Producer:** Colbert Clark; **Director:** Derwin Abrahams; **Screenplay:** J. Benton Cheney; **Music:** Ben Oakland and George Parrish; **Cinematographer:** Glen Gano; **Editor:** Aaron Stell; **Cast:** Charles Starrett, Tex Harding, Jean Stevens, John Calvert, Hal Price, Carl Sepulveda.

A passenger on a stagecoach being robbed takes on the masked guise of the Durango Kid and steals the money back from the gang leader. This is the film that started the Charles Starrett series, which would last for another decade. Despite the title, it is not a sequel to the 1940 film starring Starrett. (See also *DURANGO KID, THE*.)

RETURN OF THE FRONTIERSMAN
Warner Bros., 1950, Color, 74 min. **Producer:** Saul Elkins; **Director:** Richard L. Bare; **Music:** David Buttolph; **Cinematographer:** J. Peverell Marley; **Editor:** Frank Magee; **Cast:** Gordon MacRae, Jack Holt, Rory Calhoun, Julie London, Fred Clark, Edwin Rand.

A sheriff (Jack Holt) is forced to jail his son (Gordon MacRae), who is falsely accused of murder. But the son escapes with some aid from the real killer. Holt delivers a stellar performance as the sheriff father, with MacRae, Rory Calhoun, and Julie London, then ascending young stars, all performing well.

RETURN OF THE LASH
Eagle-Lion, 1947, B&W, 55 min. **Producer:** Jerry Thomas; **Director:** Ray Taylor; **Screenplay:** Joseph O'Donnell; **Music:** Walter Greene; **Cinematographer:** Ernest Miller; **Editor:** Hugh Winn; **Cast:** Lash La Rue, Al St. John, Mary Maynard, Buster Slaven, George Chesebro, Lane Bradford. See *LAW OF THE LASH*.

RETURN OF THE OUTLAW
See *PARSON AND THE OUTLAW, THE*.

RETURN OF THE PLAINSMEN
See *PHANTOM STOCKMAN*.

RETURN OF THE RANGERS PRC, 1943, B&W, 60 min. **Producer:** Arthur Alexander; **Director:** Elmer Clifton; **Screenplay:** Clifton; **Music:** Lee Zahler; **Cinematographer:** Robert E. Cline; **Editor:** Charles Henkel Jr.; **Cast:** Dave O'Brien, James Newill, Guy Wilkerson, Richard Alexander, Robert Barron, Nell O'Day, I. Stanford Jolley, Charles King.

RETURN OF THE SEVEN, THE (aka: RETURN OF THE MAGNIFICENT SEVEN; REGRESO DE LOS SIETE MAGNIFICOS, Spain) United Artists/Mirisch Co., 1966, Color, 96 min. **Producer:** Ted Richmond; **Director:** Burt Kennedy; **Screenplay:** Larry Cohen; **Music:** Elmer Bernstein; **Cinematographer:** Paul Vogel; **Editor:** Bert Bates; **Cast:** Yul Brynner, Robert Fuller, Julian Mateos, Warren Oates, Claud Akins, Rodolfo Acosta.

The first of three sequels to *THE MAGNIFICENT SEVEN* (1960) has Yul Brynner riding into town to gather a group of professional guns. "I never thought I'd come back," he muses. Their mission is to free the village's male population, who have been kidnapped by a group of bandits. Brynner (as Chris) is the only member of the original seven to return for the sequel; Robert Fuller assumes the role of Vin that belonged to Steve McQueen in the original production. Elmer Bernstein won an Oscar nomination for Best Scoring of Music—Adaptation or Treatment.

Directed by Burt Kennedy, *The Return of the Seven* was filmed in Alicante, Spain, a beautiful little seaport which was uncharted territory for location work. (The original *Magnificent Seven* was filmed in Mexico.) In his autobiography *Hollywood Trail Boss*, the late director recalled, "We were in the right country, but it took us four weeks driving all over hell to find where we wanted to build our various sets and shoot our picture." While certainly not of the calibre as the original, *Return of the Seven* still packs enough punch to be worth

Robert Fuller and Yul Brynner in Burt Kennedy's Return of the Seven *(UNITED ARTISTS/AUTHOR'S COLLECTION)*

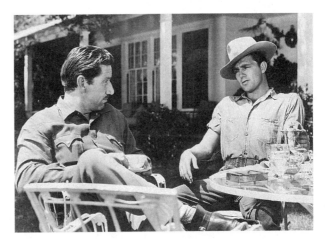

Richard Boone and Dale Robertson in Return of the Texan *(20TH CENTURY FOX/AUTHOR'S COLLECTION)*

the viewing. The film has also been known as *Return of the Magnificent Seven* and *Regreso de los siete magnificos* (in Spain).

RETURN OF THE TEXAN 20th Century Fox, 1952, B&W, 88 min. **Producer:** Frank Rosenberg; **Director:** Delmer Daves; **Screenplay:** Dudley Nichols; **Music:** Sol Kaplan; **Cinematographer:** Lucien Ballard; **Editor:** Louis R. Loeffler; **Cast:** Dale Robertson, Joanne Dru, Walter Brennan, Richard Boone, Tom Tully, Robert Horton, Helen Westcott, Lonnie Thomas.

Young widower Dale Robertson returns to his desolate Texas farm with his two sons and his father (Walter Brennan) hoping to start life anew. He takes a job with a crass neighbor (Richard Boone), whose sister-in-law (Joanne Dru) falls in love with him. Still haunted by memories of his wife, he manages to find love with a new woman and inner peace with his family.

Dale Robertson, in his virile prime, makes an appealing hero, and Joanne Dru a great-looking heroine. Not only would Robertson go on to television fame in two genre series—*Tales of the Wells Fargo* (1957–62) and *The Iron Horse* (1966–68)—but so would supporting players Richard Boone (*Have Gun Will Travel*, 1957–63) and Robert Horton (*Wagon Train*, 1957–65 and *A Man Called Shenandoah*, 1965–66). Add three-time Oscar winner Walter Brennan in *The Real McCoys* (1957–63), and the cast alone makes this hokey little oater lots of fun.

RETURN OF THE VIGILANTES See *VIGILANTES RETURN, THE*.

RETURN OF WILD BILL, THE Columbia, 1940, B&W, 60 min. **Producer:** Leon Barsha; **Director:** Joseph H. Lewis; **Screenplay:** Robert Lee Johnson and Fred Myton; **Cinematographer:** George Meehan; **Editor:** Richard Fantl;

Cast: William "Wild Bill" Elliott, Buel Bryant, Donald Haines, John Ince, Bruce Kellog, Frank La Rue.

Crooks try to get the owners of two ranches to gun each other down. One of the ranchers sends for his son, a famed gunfighter, but the rancher is shot before his son can arrive. This well-made Bill Elliott venture packs lots of excitement and provides good B western entertainment.

RETURN TO WARBOW Columbia, 1958, Color, 67 min. **Producer:** Wallace MacDonald; **Director:** Ray Nazarro; **Screenplay:** Lee Savage Jr.; **Music:** Mischa Bakaleinikoff; **Cinematographer:** Henry Freulich; **Editor:** Charles Nelson; **Cast:** Philip Carey, Frances De Sales, Andrew Duggan, Joseph Forte, James Griffith, Harry Lauter, William Leslie, Paul Picerni, Jay Silverheels, Robert J. Wilke.

When three outlaws return to the place where they buried the loot from a robbery, they find that the brother of one of them has already taken the money.

REVENGE RIDER, THE Columbia, 1935, B&W, 60 min. **Producer:** Harry L. Decker; **Director:** David Selman; **Screenplay:** Ford Beebe; **Cinematographer:** Benjamin H. Kline; **Editor:** Al Clark; **Cast:** Tim McCoy, Robert Allen, Billie Seward, Edward Earle, Jack Clifford.

When a man returns home, he finds that his brother, the sheriff, has been murdered. The culprits appear to be members of the local cattlemen's association. A good whodunnit plot and a bang-up shoot-out at the end make for an interesting Tim McCoy venture. (See also *RIDING TORNADO, THE*.)

REVENGERS, THE National General, 1972, Color, 107 min. **Producer:** Martin Rackin; **Director:** Daniel Mann; **Screenplay:** Wendell Mayes; **Music:** Pino Calvi; **Cinematographer:** Gabriel Torres; **Editors:** Walter Hannemann and Juan Jose Marino; **Cast:** William Holden, Ernest Borgnine, Susan Hayward, Woody Strode, Arthur Hunnicutt, John Kelly, Scott Holden.

A well-to-do rancher, William Holden, finds his family slaughtered and his horses stolen by a gang of renegade Indians led by two white men. The law is impotent, and the gang retreats across the Mexican border. Holden sets out alone on a mission of revenge. Realizing he needs help, he recruits six convicts from a Mexican prison, including Woody Strode and Ernest Borgnine. However, Holden is wounded by one of his recruits, and his mission put on hold. An Irish nurse (Susan Hayward) nurses him back to health and helps him put his violent and vengeful ways to rest.

This familiar western theme is boosted by a trio of big-name stars and good supporting players. Holden's son Scott plays a cavalry lieutenant in the picture. This was Susan Hayward's final film; she died in 1955 at age 56 after a two-year bout with brain cancer.

REVOLT AT FORT LARAMIE United Artists, 1957, Color, 73 min. **Producer:** Howard Koch; **Director:** Lesley Selander; **Screenplay:** Robert C. Dennis; **Music:** Les Baxter; **Cinematographer:** William Margulies; **Editor:** John F. Schreyer; **Cast:** John Dehner, Gregg Palmer, Frances Helm, Don Gordon, Robert Keyes, Harry Dean Stanton, Bill Barker, Kenne Duncan.

As the Civil War unfolds, Southern soldiers at a remote army fort want to leave and join the Confederacy, despite the threat of an impending Indian attack. Harry Dean Stanton makes his film debut (as Rinty) in this interesting and lesser-known oater.

RHYTHM OF THE RIO GRANDE Monogram, 1940, B&W, 53 min. **Producer:** Edward Finney; **Director:** Albert Herman; **Screenplay:** Robert Emmett Tansey (as Robert Tansey); **Music:** Frank Harford, Johnny Lange, Lew Porter, and Frank Sanucci; **Cast:** Tex Ritter, Suzan Dale, Martin Garralaga, Tristram Coffin, Forrest Taylor.

RHYTHM OF THE SADDLE Republic, 1938, B&W, 57 min. **Producer:** Harry Grey (associate); **Director:** George Sherman; **Screenplay:** Paul Franklin; **Cinematographer:** Jack A. Marta; **Editor:** Lester Orlebeck; **Cast:** Gene Autry, Smiley Burnette, Pert Kelton, Peggy Moran, LeRoy Mason, Arthur Loft, Ethan Ladlow.

RHYTHM ON THE RANCH See *ROOTIN' TOOTIN' RHYTHM*.

RHYTHM ON THE RANGE Paramount, 1936, B&W, 87 min, VHS. **Producer:** Bernard Glaser; **Director:** Norman Touring; **Screenplay:** Walter DeLeon, Francis Martin, Jack Moffitt, and Sidney Salkow; **Music:** J. Keirn Brennan, Walter Bullock, Bager Clark, Sam Coslow, Billy Hill, Frederick Hollander, Johnny Mercer, Ralph Rainger, Leo Robin, Gertrude Ross, and Richard Whiting; **Cast:** Bing Crosby, Frances Farmer, Martha Raye, Bob Burns, Samuel S. George E. Stone, Lucille Gleason.

Bing Crosby is a singing cowboy fresh from a rodeo in Madison Square Garden who, while returning to his ranch in the West, befriends society lady Frances Farmer, who is fleeing a bad marriage. When Farmer is kidnapped, Bing and buddy Bob Burns save the day. Among the musical numbers is the Johnny Mercer song "I'm an Old Cowhand (From the Rio Grande)," introduced in the film by Bing Crosby, who also had a hit recording of the song for Decca records. Roy Rogers also sang it in *King of the Cowboys* (1943) and also recorded it the same year. Crosby also sings "Empty Saddles (words J. Keirn Brennan, music Billy Hill), based on a poem written by Brennan and recorded on Decca by Crosby and then later by Roy Rogers and The Sons of the Pioneers.

This film was one of two westerns for the ever-popular Bing Crosby; the other was the 1966 remake of *Stagecoach*, although Crosby had cameo appearances in *Son of Paleface*,

1952, and *Alias Jesse James*, 1959. This lighthearted western musical also marks the film debut of Martha Raye and was one of the first screen appearances for the ill-fated Frances Farmer. Roy Rogers, under the name Dick Weston, appears with the Sons of the Pioneers in the film.

RIDE, RANGER, RIDE Republic, 1936, B&W, 63 min, VHS. **Producer:** Nat Levine; **Director:** Joseph Kane; **Screenplay:** Dorrell McGowan and Stuart E. McGowan; **Cinematographer:** William Nobles; **Cast:** Gene Autry, Smiley Burnette, Kay Hughes, Monte Blue, George J. Lewis, Max Terhune.

Gene is a Texas Ranger working undercover to protect an army wagon train full of ammunition and supplies. But when he warns of an impending Indian attack, the army doesn't believe him until the Comanche are almost upon them. This early Gene Autry entry for Republic provides a good blend of action, comedy, and music. (See also *TUMBLING TUMBLEWEEDS*.)

RIDE, RYDER, RIDE Eagle-Lion, 1949, Color. **Producer:** Jerry Thomas; **Director:** Lewis D. Collins; **Screenplay:** Paul Franklin; **Music:** Darrell Calker; **Cinematographer:** Gilbert Warrenton; **Editor:** Joseph Gluck; **Cast:** Jim Bannon, Don Kay Reynolds, Emmett Lynn, Peggy Stewart, Steve Pendleton.

RIDE, TENDERFOOT, RIDE Republic, 1940, B&W, 54 min. **Producer:** William A. Berke; **Director:** Frank McDonald; **Screenplay:** Winston Miller; **Cinematographer:** Jack Marta; **Editor:** Lester Orlebeck; **Cast:** Gene Autry, Smiley Burnette, June Story, Mary Lee, Warren Hall.

RIDE A CROOKED TRAIL Universal, 1958, Color, 87 min. **Producer:** Howard Pine; **Director:** Jesse Hibbs; **Screenplay:** Borden Chase; **Music:** Henry Mancini; **Cinematographer:** Harold Lipstein; **Editor:** Edward Curtiss; **Cast:** Audie Murphy, Gia Scala, Walter Matthau, Henry Silva, Joanna Cook Moore, Eddie Little, Leo Gordon, Morgan Woodward.

An outlaw assumes the identity of a dead lawman so he can pull off a bank robbery. This better-than-average Audie Murphy vehicle, with Murphy as the prototype good-hearted outlaw who is reformed by wearing a badge, boasts an excellent performance by Walter Matthau as the alcoholic judge. Filmed in CinemaScope, the picture was scripted by Borden Chase.

RIDE A DARK HORSE See *MAN AND BOY*.

RIDE A NORTHBOUND HORSE Walt Disney, 1969, Color, 79 min. **Producer:** Ron Miller; **Director:** Robert Totten; **Screenplay:** Herman Groves; **Cinematog-**

rapher: Robert Hoffman; **Cast:** Carroll O'Connor, Michael Shea, Ben Johnson, Andy Devine, Harry Carey Jr., Jack Elam, Edith Atwater, Dub Taylor.

A young man who wins and then loses a horse sets out to regain the animal in this film based on the novel by Richard Wormser. A lesser-known Walt Disney venture, the movie benefits from the authentic presence of western stalwarts Ben Johnson, Andy Devine, Harry Carey Jr., Jack Elam, and Dub Taylor, as well as from Bob Totten's able direction. Longtime pals Harry Carey Jr. and the late Ben Johnson made more than 10 films together, and seeing the two in the same picture is always a treat for genre fans.

RIDE A VIOLENT MILE 20th Century Fox, 1957, B&W, 80 min. **Producer:** Robert W. Sabler; **Director:** Charles Marquis Warren; **Screenplay:** Eric Norden; **Music:** Raoul Kraushnaar; **Cinematographer:** Brydon Baker; **Editor:** Leslie Vidor; **Cast:** John Agar, Penny Edwards, John Pickard, Bing Russell, Richard Shannon, Sheb Wooley.

This Civil War espionage story has Penny Edwards as a Union agent posing as a dance-hall girl. When she intercepts a Confederate plan to exchange a shipment of cattle for Mexican help, she and boyfriend John Agar manage to scatter the cattle and foil the Southerners' scheme.

RIDE BACK, THE United Artists, 1957, B&W, 79 min. **Producer:** William Conrad; **Director:** Allen H. Miner; **Screenplay:** Anthony Ellis; **Music:** Frank De Vol; **Cinematographer:** Joseph Biroc; **Editor:** Michael Luciano; **Cast:** Anthony Quinn, William Conrad, Lita Milan, Victor Millan, Jorge Treviño, Ellen Hope Monroe.

A lawman and his captured prisoner trek across hostile Indian territory and realize they must fight together against a common enemy and a hostile environment. Lots of suspense and fascinating character development mark this compelling western, which was produced with good results on a modest B budget.

RIDE BEYOND VENGEANCE Columbia, 1966, Color, 100 min. **Producer:** Andrew J. Fenady; **Director:** Bernard E. McEveety; **Screenplay:** Fenady; **Music:** Richard Markowitz; **Cinematographer:** Lester Short; **Editor:** Otto Lovering; **Cast:** Chuck Connors, Katherine Hays, Michael Rennie, Joan Blondell, Gloria Grahame, Gary Merrill, Bill Bixby, Claude Akins, Paul Fix, James MacArthur, Arthur O'Connell, Ruth Warrick, Buddy Baer, Frank Gorshin, Robert Q. Lewis.

Following an 11-year separation from his wife, a buffalo hunter returns home and is attacked and branded; his wife then rejects him. He sets out to find his attackers in this well-scripted, rugged picture, with lots of action, a good cast, and an outstanding performance by Chuck Connors as the returning hunter.

RIDE CLEAR OF DIABLO (aka: THE BRECK-ENRIDGE STORY) Universal, 1954, Color, 80 min, VHS. **Producer:** John Rogers; **Director:** Jesse Hibbs; **Screenplay:** George Zuckerman; **Music:** Henry Mancini, Milton Rosen, Hans J. Salter, Frank Skinner, Herman Stein, and Edward Ward; **Cinematographer:** Irving Glassberg; **Editor:** Edward Curtiss; **Cast:** Audie Murphy, Susan Cabot, Dan Duryea, Abbe Lane, Jack Elam, Denver Pyle, Russell Johnson, Paul Birch, William Pullen.

Audie Murphy is a railroad surveyor turned sheriff's deputy who goes after the rustlers who murdered his father and brother. The real scene-stealer in this one is Dan Duryea as the infamous black-clad outlaw Whitey Kincaid.

RIDE 'EM COWBOY Universal, 1942, B&W, 82 min, VHS. **Producer:** Alex Gottlieb (associate); **Director:** Arthur Lubin; **Screenplay:** True Boardman, John Grant (adaptation); **Music:** Frank Skinner; **Cinematographer:** John Boyle; **Editor:** Phillip Cahn; **Cast:** Bud Abbott, Lou Costello, Dick Foran, Anne Gwynne, Johnny Mack Brown, Ella Fitzgerald, Morris Ankrum, The Buckaroo Band, The Merry Macs, The High Hatters, The Ranger Chorus.

America's favorite 1940s comedy team has some fun with the American West. Bud and Lou, working as hot-dog vendors at a New York rodeo, accidentally let out a bull that gets in the way of the celebrated western hero "Broncho Bob" (Dick Foran). Shunted west with their former boss in hot pursuit, they become cowhands on a dude ranch.

Every available prop is employed to assist Abbott and Costello's zany slapstick, which is bolstered as always by the team's excellent timing and delivery as well as Lou's hilarious facial expressions. The film provides a good combination of comedy and music, and the outstanding sound track includes two would-be standards: "I'll Remember April," introduced in the film by Dick Foran; and "A-Tisket, A-Tasket," introduced by Ella Fitzgerald and the Merry Macs.

This film should not be confused with Universal's 1936 Buck Jones feature *Ride 'Em Cowboy*, about a wayward cowpoke who becomes a race car driver, which was produced by Jones and directed by Lesley Selander.

RIDE 'EM COWGIRL Grand National, 1939, B&W, 53 min. **Producer:** Arthur Dreifuss; **Director:** Samuel Diege; **Screenplay:** Arthur Hoerl; **Music:** Milton Drake, Walter Kent, and Alfred Sherman; **Cinematographer:** Mack Stengler; **Editor:** Guy V. Theyer Jr.; **Cast:** Dorothy Page, Milton Frome, Vince Barnett, Lynn Mayberry.

A girl is framed for having contraband silver on her property, but she escapes from jail to find the real culprit, who is after her father's ranch as a front for his operation. Dorothy Page's brief cowgirl series (the other two were *Water Rustlers* and *The Singing Cowgirl*) attempting to show that a woman could rope, ride, and yodel as well as any man failed to catch on with movie audiences.

RIDE HIM COWBOY (aka: THE HAWK) Warner Bros., 1932, B&W, 56 min. **Producer:** Leon Schleshinger; **Director:** Fred Allen; **Screenplay:** Scott Mason; **Editor:** William Clemens; **Cast:** John Wayne, Ruth Hall, Henry B. Walthall, Harry Gribbon, Otis Harlan, Frank Hagney.

Cowboy John Drury (John Wayne) saves a horse named "Duke the Devil Horse," who was being blamed for the death of a rancher, from being shot. Wayne tames the horse and with his help goes after the real murderer, a notorious bandit leader known as "The Hawk." However, he soon becomes the prime suspect himself.

The film was the first in a series of B westerns Wayne did for Warner Bros. Other films in his Warner Bros. series include *The Big Stampede* (1932); *Haunted Gold, The Telegraph Trail, Somewhere in Sonora,* and *Man from Monterey* (1933). The film is a remake of the Ken Maynard silent feature *The Unknown Cavalier* (1926), with "Duke the Devil Horse" looking very much like Maynard's horse "Tarzan." In fact, four films in the series are direct remakes of Maynard films, while two others use footage from them.

RIDE LONESOME Columbia, 1959, Color, 73 min. **Producer:** Harry Joe Brown; **Director:** Budd Boetticher; **Screenplay:** Burt Kennedy; **Music:** Heintz Roemheld; **Cinematographer:** Charles Lawton; **Editor:** Jerome Thoms; **Cast:** Randolph Scott, Karen Steele, Pernell Roberts, James Best, Lee Van Cleef, James Coburn.

Randolph Scott is sheriff-turned-bounty hunter Ben Brigade, whose interest in young murderer Billy John (James Best) appears to be the money he will receive upon delivering John to jail. Stopping at a trading post, he saves the manager's wife (Karen Steele) from an Indian attack and enlists two unwanted companions, outlaws Pernell Roberts and James Coburn, for help. It soon becomes obvious that Billy John's brother Frank (Lee Van Cleef), determined to rescue his brother, is on the trail with his gang. But the plot twists when we learn that Brigade might be more interested in settling a score with Frank who hanged his wife as revenge for Brigade having sent him to prison. Billy John is put on a horse with a noose around his neck, and they wait for Frank to arrive. The action is all packed into a compact 73 minutes.

A superb Budd Boetticher/Burt Kennedy collaboration, *Ride Lonesome* features beautifully raw, scenic landscape, a labyrinth of huge rounded rocks and the classic badlands terrain (a Boetticher trademark); several good plots and subplots; Kennedy's crisp, witty, immortal frontier dialogue, such as "There are some things a man just can't ride around;" and Boetticher's taut economical direction. There are also excellent performances from Best as Billy John, the whining killer; Roberts as the outlaw hoping for a new start; and Coburn in his screen debut as Robert's outlaw cohort.

Scott, of course, is perfect as the angular, tight-lipped hero whose laconic screen stature and William S. Hart persona was resurrected by Budd Boetticher in the mid-1950s,

Budd Boetticher and colleague Burt Kennedy directed and scripted Ride Lonesome, *a scene from which is shown here.* (COLUMBIA/COURTESY OF BUDD AND MARY BOETTICHER)

starting with his 1956 western masterpiece SEVEN MEN FROM NOW, which was produced by John Wayne.

RIDE ON VAQUERO 20th Century Fox, 1941, B&W, 64 min. **Producer:** Sol M. Wurtzel; **Director:** Herbert L. Leeds; **Screenplay:** Samuel G. Engel; **Cinematographer:** Lucien N. Andriot; **Editor:** Louis L. Loeffler; **Cast:** Cesar Romero, Mary Beth Hughes, Lynne Roberts, Chris-Pin Martin, Robert Lowery, Ben Carter, William Demarest.

Cesar Romero's final Cisco Kid adventure has the famed Mexican bandit thwarting a gang of kidnappers while managing to find enough time to romance dance-hall girl Mary Beth Hughes. (See also CISCO KID, THE.)

RIDE OUT FOR REVENGE United Artists, 1957, B&W, 78 min. **Producer:** Norman Retchin; **Director:** Bernard Girard; **Screenplay:** Retchin; **Music:** Leith Stevens; **Cinematographer:** Floyd Crosby; **Editor:** Leon Barsha; **Cast:** Rory Calhoun, Gloria Grahame, Lloyd Bridges, Joanne Gilbert, Frank DeKova, Vince Edwards.

A sheriff tries to help a group of Indians who are being forced off their land by a corrupt army officer who wants their gold deposits.

RIDER FROM TUCSON RKO, 1950, B&W, 60 min. **Producer:** Herbert Schlom; **Director:** Lesley Selander; **Screenplay:** Ed Earl Rapp; **Cinematographer:** Nicholas Musuraca; **Editor:** Robert Swink; **Cast:** Tim Holt, Richard "Chito" Martin, Elaine Riley, Douglas Fowley, Veda Ann Borg, Robert Shayne, William Phipps.

RIDER OF DEATH VALLEY, THE (aka: RIDERS OF THE DESERT) Universal, 1932, B&W, 78 min. **Producer:** Carl Laemmle Jr.; **Director:** Albert Rogell; **Screenplay:** Jack Cunningham; **Cinematographer:** Daniel B. Clark; **Editor:** Robert Carlisle; **Cast:** Tom Mix, Lois Wilson, Fred Kohler, Forrest Stanley.

When crooks murder a man for his Death Valley gold-mine claim, the rancher's friend tries to protect his daughter's claim to the mine and bring the murderers to justice. Based on a story by Max Brand, this beautifully photographed film contains some stunning scenery of Death Valley and is one of Tom Mix's better sound westerns.

RIDER OF THE LAW   Supreme, 1935, B&W, 56 min. **Producer:** A. W. Hackel; **Director:** Robert N. Bradbury; **Screenplay:** Jack Natteford; **Cinematographer:** Gus Peterson; **Editor:** S. Roy Luby; **Cast:** Bob Steele, Gertrude Messinger, Si Jenks, Lloyd Ingraham, John Elliott.

RIDERS FROM NOWHERE   Monogram, 1940, B&W, 47 min. **Producer:** Harry S. Webb; **Director:** Bernard B. Ray (as Raymond K. Johnson); **Screenplay:** Carl Krusada; **Music:** Johnny Lange and Lew Porter; **Cinematographer:** William Hyer and Edward A. Kull; **Editor:** Robert Golden; **Cast:** Addison Randall (as Jack Randall), Ernie Adams, George Chesebro, Jack Evans, Charles King, Tom London, Margaret Roach, Dorothy Vernon.

RIDERS IN THE SKY   Columbia, 1949, B&W, 69 min. **Producer:** Armand Schaefer; **Director:** John English; **Screenplay:** Gerald Geraghty; **Cinematographer:** William Bradford; **Editor:** Henry Batista; **Cast:** Gene Autry, Gloria Henry, Pat Buttram, Mary Beth Hughes, Robert Livingston, Steve Darrell, Alan Hale Jr., Tom London.

A rancher is framed on false evidence by a crooked gambler, so Gene sets out to clear the man's name and bring the real perpetrator to justice. The haunting song "Ghost Riders in the Sky," sung in the film by Gene Autry, was recorded by various artists, including Burl Ives, Peggy Lee, Bing Crosby, and Vaughn Monroe, who had the number one hit recording on the Decca label. Written by then-forest ranger Stan Jones while on duty one evening (he was as surprised as anyone by the song's enormous success), "Ghost Riders in the Sky" (sometimes titled "Riders in the Sky") remains one of the best-known cowboy ballads ever written.

RIDERS OF BLACK RIVER   Columbia, 1939, B&W, 59 min. **Producer:** Harry L. Decker; **Director:** Norman Deming; **Screenplay:** Bennett Cohen; **Music:** Bob Nolan and Tim Spencer; **Cinematographer:** George Meehan; **Editor:** William Lyon; **Cast:** Charles Starrett, Iris Meredith, Dick Curtis, Stanley Brown, Bob Nolan.
   See *GALLANT DEFENDER*.

RIDERS OF DESTINY   Lone Star/Monogram, 1933, B&W, 53 min, VHS, DVD. **Producer:** Paul Malvern; **Director:** Robert Bradbury; **Screenplay:** Bradbury; **Cinematographer:** Archie Stout; **Editor:** Carl Pierson; **Cast:** John Wayne, Cecilia Parker, Forrest Taylor, George Hayes, Al St. John, Heine Conklin, Yakama Canutt, Earl Dwire, Lafe McKee.

In his first western for Monogram, John Wayne plays a Secret Service agent on a mission to help ranchers whose water supply is being compromised by a gang of crooks. The film is Wayne's initial and only venture as "Singin' Sandy Saunders." Smith Ballew, who supposedly was way back in the brush, dubbed his voice, singing while Wayne was riding the open range. While Singin' Sandy Saunders never caught on with the public—nor with Wayne, who hated the charade—costar Cecilia Parker felt from the start that Wayne had real star potential. "You can tell when somebody has it and somebody doesn't. He had a certain aura about him. You knew he was going to go. He was a natural."

RIDERS OF PASCO BASIN   Universal, 1940, B&W, 56 min. **Producer:** Joseph Gershenson (as Joseph G. Sanford); **Director:** Ray Taylor; **Screenplay:** Forde Beebe; **Music:** Everette Carter and Milton Rosen; **Cinematographer:** William Sickner; **Editor:** Louis Sackin; **Cast:** Johnny Mack Brown, Bob Baker, Fuzzy Knight, Frances Robinson, Arthur Loft, Ted Adams, George Chesebro, Kermit Maynard.
   See *OLD CHISHOLM TRAIL, THE*.

RIDERS OF THE BADLANDS   Columbia, 1941, B&W, 57 min. **Producer:** William Berke; **Director:** Howard Bretherton; **Screenplay:** Betty Burbridge; **Cinematographer:** Benjamin H. Kline; **Editor:** Charles Nelson; **Cast:** Charles Starrett, Russell Hayden, Cliff Edwards, Betty Brewer, Kay Hughes, Roy Barcroft.

RIDERS OF THE BLACK HILLS   Republic, 1938, B&W, 55 min. **Producer:** William A. Berke; **Director:** George Sherman; **Screenplay:** Betty Burbridge; **Cinematographer:** William Nobles; **Editor:** Lester Orlebeck; **Cast:** Robert Livingston, Ray Corrigan, Max Terhune, Ann Evers, Roscoe Ates, Frank Melton, Maude Eburne.

RIDERS OF THE DAWN   Monogram, 1937, B&W, 55 min. **Producer:** Robert Bradbury; **Director:** Bradbury; **Screenplay:** Robert Emmett Tansey; **Music:** Bradbury; **Cinematographer:** Bert Longnecker; **Cast:** Addison (Jack) Randall, Warner P. Richmond, George Cooper, Peggy Keyes, Earl Dwire.

The notorious gunman Danti is terrorizing a lawless town, and two lawmen are assigned to clean things up in a good first series entry for Addison (Jack) Randall, with Warner Richmond excelling as the villain. The brother of B western star Robert Livingston, Addison Randall acted and sang on Broadway prior to entering films. He appeared in a number of movies, none of them westerns, before signing on with Monogram in 1937 as a singing cowboy under the name Jack Randall. Despite his considerable singing abilities, his musical westerns were poorly received and shelved by the studio. He continued playing leads in nonsinging B westerns. When his career began to falter, he found work in supporting roles, often as a villain. He died in 1945 at age 39 from a heart attack while shooting a riding scene in *The Royal Mounted Rides Again*.

In addition to *Riders of the Dawn*, Randall's Monogram series ventures include *Stars Over Arizona*, *Danger Valley* (1937); *Where the West Begins*, *Land of Fighting Men*, *Gunsmoke Trail*, *Man's Country*, *Mexicali Kid*, *Gun Packer*, *Wild Horse Canyon* (1938); *Drifting Westward*, *Trigger Smith*, *Across the Plains*, *Oklahoma Terror*, *Overland Mail*, *Nothing But Pleasure* (1939); *Pioneer Days*, *The Cheyenne Kid*, *Covered Wagon Trails*, *The Kid from Santa Fe*, *Wild Horse Range*, *Land of the Six Guns*, *Riders from Nowhere* (1940).

RIDERS OF THE DAWN Monogram, 1945, B&W, 58 min. **Producer:** Oliver Drake; **Director:** Drake; **Screenplay:** Louise Rousseau; **Music:** Johnny Bond, Spade Cooley, Jimmy Rodgers, and Jimmy Wakely; **Cinematographer:** William Sickner; **Editor:** William Austin; **Cast:** Jimmy Wakely, Lee "Lasses" White, John James, Sarah Padden, Horace Murphy, Phyllis Adair.

RIDERS OF THE DEADLINE United Artists, 1944, B&W, 70 min. **Producer:** Harry Sherman; **Director:** Leslie Selander; **Screenplay:** Bennett Cohen; **Music:** Irvin Talbot; **Cinematographer:** Russell Harlan; **Editors:** Fred W. Berger and Walter Hannemann; **Cast:** William Boyd, Andy Clyde, Jimmy Rogers, Richard Crane, Frances Woodward, Robert Mitchum, Montie Montana, Pierce Lyden.

RIDERS OF THE DESERT World Wide Pictures, 1932, B&W, 59 min. **Producer:** Trem Carr; **Director:** Robert N. Bradbury; **Screenplay:** Wellyn Totman; **Cinematographer:** Archie Stout; **Editor:** Carl Pierson; **Cast:** Bob Steele, Gertrude Messenger, Al St. John, George "Gabby" Hayes, John Elliott.

Bob Steele, as Arizona Ranger Bob Houston, is on the trail of an outlaw gang terrorizing the area. This action-packed early Bob Steele talkie boasts excellent photography, good locations, and a strong plot line. Directed by his prolific father Robert N. Bradbury, *Riders of the Desert* is one of 37 films Steele made with his father, dating back to 1920, when he played juvenile roles. Their final film together was *The Trusted Outlaw* for Republic in 1937.

Short, muscular and curly haired, Steele was a B western hero for 20 years before turning to character work. He remained popular throughout the 1930s, working for a number of independent studios such as World Wide, Tiffany, Supreme, Metropolitan, PRC, and Screen Guild. He also made a number of features for Monogram before signing on with Republic in the mid-1930s.

Steele's other early oaters for World Wide were also made in 1932 and include *Son of Oklahoma*, *South of Santa Fe*, and *The Man From Hell's Edges*. (See also KID COURAGEOUS; LIGHTNIN' CRANDALL; NEAR THE RAINBOW'S END; RIDERS OF THE SAGE.)

RIDERS OF THE DUSK Monogram, 1949, B&W, 60 min. **Producer:** Eddie Davis; **Director:** Lambert Hillyer; **Screenplay:** Adele Buffington (as Jess Bowers) and Robert Tansey; **Cinematographer:** Harry Neumann; **Editor:** John C. Fuller; **Cast:** Whip Wilson, Andy Clyde, Reno Browne, Tristram Coffin, Marshall Reed, Myron Healey.

RIDERS OF THE FRONTIER (aka: RIDIN' THE FRONTIER, UK) Monogram, 1939, B&W, 58 min. **Producer:** Edward Finney; **Director:** Spencer Gordon Bennet; **Screenplay:** Jesse Duffy and Joseph Levering; **Music:** Frank Harford and Frank Sanucci; **Cinematographer:** Marcel Le Picard; **Editor:** Frederick Bain; **Cast:** Tex Ritter, Jack Rutherford, Wally Wales, Glen Francis, Nolan Willis, Roy Barcroft, Mantan Moreland.

RIDERS OF THE LONE STAR Columbia, 1947, B&W, 55 min. **Producer:** Colbert Clark; **Director:** Derwin Abrahams; **Screenplay:** Barry Shipman; **Cinematographer:** George F. Kelley; **Editor:** Paul Borofsky; **Cast:** Charles Starrett, Smiley Burnette, Virginia Hunter, Steve Darrell, Edmund Cobb, Mark Dennis, Lane Bradford, Ted Mapes.

RIDERS OF THE NORTH Syndicate, 1931, B&W, 59 min. **Director:** J. P. McGowan; **Screenplay:** George Arthur Durlam; **Cinematographer:** Carl Himm; **Editor:** Charles J. Hunt; **Cast:** Bob Custer, Blanche Mehaffey, Frank Rice, Eddie Dunn, George Regas, Buddy Shaw, William Walling.

RIDERS OF THE PURPLE SAGE Fox, 1931, B&W, 58 min. **Director:** Hamilton MacFadden; **Screenplay:** Barry Conners, John Goodrich, and Philip Klein; **Cinematographer:** George Schneiderman; **Cast:** George O'Brien, Marguerite Churchill, Noah Beery, Yvonne Pelletier, Frank McGlynn Sr.

The first sound version of the popular Zane Grey novel stars George O'Brien and Marguerite Churchill (they would become husband and wife two years later). O'Brien plays a man who becomes a social outcast for killing his sister's murderer. He redeems himself later by saving a girl and her ranch from a band of outlaws.

Zane Grey's novels were extremely popular in the 1930s and made for frequent filming. *Riders of the Purple Sage* was filmed previously by Fox in 1918 with William Farnum and in 1925 with Tom Mix; 20th Century Fox would make yet another version in 1941. All versions (silent and sound) were well made and fine screen adaptations of the book. Interestingly, Zane Grey's sequel to his novel *The Rainbow Trail* was also filmed in 1918, 1925, and 1931 as sequels to the Farnum, Mix, and O'Brien films.

RIDERS OF THE PURPLE SAGE 20th Century Fox, 1941, B&W, 56 min. **Producer:** Sol Wertzel; **Director:** James Tingling; **Screenplay:** William Bruckner and Robert E. Metaler; **Cinematographer:** Lucien N. Androit; **Editor:**

Nick DeMaggio; **Cast:** George Montgomery, Mary Howard, Robert Barrat, Lynne Roberts, Kane Richmond, Patsy Patterson, Richard F. Metzler.

In perhaps the best version of Zane Grey's popular novel, George Montgomery is an avenging Jim Lassiter. As he looks for the man who wrecked his sister's life, he discovers that the judge (Robert Barrat) who cheated his niece out of her inheritance is also the leader of the band of vigilantes who are robbing and murdering in order to control the territory.

The ownership of several Zane Grey properties prompted Fox to begin a new series of program westerns in the 1940s. In little more than an hour, the film incorporates all of Grey's complicated plot and offers lots of action and good locations and photography. Star George Montgomery was promptly put into a follow-up film, THE LAST OF THE DUANES (1941), then later elevated to bigger pictures.

RIDERS OF THE PURPLE SAGE Amer/Rosemont/Zeke Productions, 1996, Color, 97 min. **Producers:** Ed Harris, Thomas John Kane, Amy Madigan, and David Rosemont; **Director:** Charles Haid; **Screenplay:** Gil Dennis; **Music:** Arthur Kempel; **Cinematographer:** William Wages; **Editor:** David Holden; **Cast:** Ed Harris, Amy Madigan, Henry Thomas, Robin Tunney, Norbert Weisser, G. D. Spradlin, Lynn Wanlass, Bob L. Harris, Jerry Wills.

This is the fifth adaptation of Zane Grey's 1912 novel of the same name, a made-for-TV movie starring coproducers Ed Harris and Amy Madigan (who are married in real life) as Lassiter and Jane Withersteen. The film follows the original story fairly closely, except here the Mormons are depicted only as a religious sect. For his lensing work William Wages won the Outstanding Achievement in Cinematography in a Made for TV Movie award from the ASC, and Harris was nominated by the Screen Actor's Guild for Best Performance by a Male Actor in a TV Movie or Miniseries.

RIDERS OF THE RANGE RKO, 1950, B&W, 60 min. **Producer:** Herman Schlom; **Director:** Lesley Selander; **Music:** Paul Sawtell; **Cinematographer:** J. Roy Hunt; **Editor:** Robert Swink; **Cast:** Tim Holt, Richard Martin, Jacqueline White, Reed Hadley, Robert Barrat.

RIDERS OF THE RIO GRANDE Republic, 1943, B&W, 55 min. **Producer:** Louis Gray (associate); **Director:** Howard Bretherton; **Screenplay:** Albert DeMond; **Music:** Mort Glickman; **Cinematographer:** Ernest Miller; **Editor:** Charles Craft; **Cast:** Bob Steele, Tom Tyler, Jimmie Dodd, Lorraine Miller, Edward Van Sloan.

See THREE MESQUITEERS, THE.

RIDERS OF THE ROCKIES Grand National, 1937, B&W, 56 min. **Producer:** Edward Finney; **Director:** Robert Bradbury; **Screenplay:** Norman Leslie; **Cinematographer:** Gus Peterson; **Editor:** Frederick Bain; **Cast:** Tex

Ritter, Louise Stanley, Horace Murphy, "Snub" Pollard, Earl Dwire.

See SONG OF THE GRINGO.

RIDERS OF THE SAGE Metropolitan, 1939, B&W, 57 min. **Producers:** Jack Broder and Harry S. Webb; **Director:** Harry S. Webb; **Cinematographer:** Edward A. Kull; **Editor:** Frederick Bain; **Cast:** Bob Steele, Claire Rochelle, Ralph Hooker, James Whitehead, Carleton Young.

Bob Burke (Bob Steele) is a cowboy who stops two outlaws from killing a man, and finds himself in the middle of a feud between sheepmen and cattlemen. Bob Steele made a short series of westerns for Metropolitan Pictures Corporation in 1939. In addition to *Riders of the Sage*, the films include *Feud of the Range, Mesquite Buckaroo,* and *Smoky Trails.* (See also RIDERS OF THE DESERT.)

RIDERS OF THE SUNSET TRAIL See CODE OF THE OUTLAW.

RIDERS OF THE TIMBERLINE Paramount, 1941, B&W, 59 min, VHS. **Producers:** Lewis J. Rachmil and Harry Sherman; **Director:** Lesley Selander; **Screenplay:** J. Benton Cheney; **Music:** Grace Hamilton, John Leipold, Jack Stern, and Irvin Talbot; **Cinematographer:** Russell Harlan; **Editor:** Fred R. Feitshans Jr.; **Cast:** William Boyd, Andy Clyde, Brad King, Victor Jory, Eleanor Stewart, J. Farrell MacDonald, Tom Tyler.

RIDERS OF THE WEST Monogram, 1942, B&W, 58 min. **Producer:** Scott R. Dunlap; **Director:** Howard Bretherton; **Screenplay:** Adele S. Buffington (as Jess Bowers); **Cinematographer:** Harry Neumann; **Editor:** Carl Pierson; **Cast:** Buck Jones, Tim McCoy, Raymond Hatton, Sarah Padden, Harry Woods, Charles King.

RIDERS OF THE WHISTLING PINES Columbia, 1949, B&W, 70 min, VHS. **Producer:** Armand Schaefer; **Director:** John English; **Screenplay:** Jack Townley; **Cinematographer:** William Bradford; **Editor:** Aaron Stell; **Cast:** Gene Autry, Patricia Barry, Jimmy Lloyd, Douglas Dumbrille, Damien O'Flynn, Clayton Moore, Loie Bridge.

A man (Gene Autry) believes falsely that he accidentally killed a forest ranger, but he soon learns that the ranger was actually murdered by a couple of nasties who are out to destroy the timberland. Gene is then framed on a cattle-rustling charge and is set up for murder. Gene fights and sings with the Forest Rangers in this entry, which is one of his better efforts for Columbia. (See also TUMBLING TUMBLEWEEDS.)

RIDERS OF THE WHISTLING SKULL Republic, 1937, B&W, 58 min, VHS. **Producer:** Nat Levine; **Director:** Mack V. Wright; **Screenplay:** Oliver Drake and

John Rathmell; **Music:** Jacques Aubran, Sidney Cutner, Karl Hajos, Arthur Kay, Hugo Riesenfeld, and Leon Rosebrook; **Cinematographer:** Jack A. Marta; **Editors:** Tony Martinelli and Murray Seldeen; **Cast:** Robert Livingston, Ray Corrigan, Max Terhune, Mary Russell, Roger Williams, Yakima Canutt, Iron Eyes Cody.

An archaeologist who is searching for a lost Indian city is reported missing. The Mesquiteers set out to find him in this excellent series entry with a supernatural bent. The story was reworked into a Charlie Chan film *The Feathered Serpent* (1948). (See also *THE THREE MESQUITEERS*.)

RIDERS OF VENGEANCE   See *RAIDERS, THE.*

RIDE THE HIGH COUNTRY (aka: GUNS IN THE AFTERNOON, UK)   MGM, 1962, Color, 94 min, VHS. **Producer:** Richard E. Lyons; **Director:** Sam Peckinpah; **Screenplay:** N. B. Stone Jr.; **Music:** George Bassman; **Cinematographer:** Lucien Ballard; **Editor:** Frank Santillo; **Cast:** Joel McCrea, Randolph Scott, Mariette Hartley, Ron Star, Edgar Buchanan, R. G. Armstrong, Jenie Jackson, L. Q. Jones, James Drury, John Anderson, John David Chandler, Warren Oates.

Genre veterans Joel McCrea and Randolph Scott came out of retirement to star as Steve Judd and Gil Westrum, two oldtimers striving to make ends meet in a changing West where they no longer belong. McCrea's focus is legitimate, Scott's is less scrupulous, yet at the end it is not so much the changing times that dominate the story but the personal integrity of each man and a code that must be preserved at all costs. Defending the old values against the new, their pride, dignity, and honor are at stake as they engage in one final moment of glory. One survives, the other does not. When death comes to Steve Judd, it is almost a blessed relief. "All I want is to enter my house justified," he says early in the film, paraphrasing Luke 18:14. The final scene remains one of the finest in the entire genre.

Scott and McCrea had known each other for years but had never worked in a picture together. The casting of these two western icons was perfect, though the story goes that McCrea was originally cast as Gil Westrum and Scott as Steve Judd. However, early in the production each actor, reportedly unbeknownst to the other, went to the producer on his own, expressing dissatisfaction and ready to quit if their roles were not reversed.

The film begins with Steve Judd riding into town. He hears the cheers from the street crowd and assumes they are for him. He acknowledges the townsfolk before realizing the hoopla and cheers are for a race that is in progress, and the crowd actually wants him to get off the street. Before he gets much further he is nearly run over by a car.

He has come to town to see about a job. The local bankers want him to pick up a shipment of gold from a new strike in the High Sierras at a place called Coarsegold. Fearing he is too old to do the job alone (he adjourns to a private room to delicately put on a pair of reading glasses), he looks up his old pal Gil Westrum, who like Steve is a former lawman down on his luck. Westrum is working in a carnival dressed as the Oregon Kid, a sad parody of his real past. He accepts Steve's offer because he's "hankering for a little old time excitement." He talks Steve into letting him bring the irascible Heck Longstreet (Ron Starr), a young friend who is handy with a gun.

Along the way they pick up a young girl, Elsa Knudson, played by Mariette Hartley in her first screen role. Eager to escape the oppressive life she faces with her religious father, she convinces the trio of men to take her to Coarsegold, where she can marry suitor Billy Hammond (James Drury).

Meanwhile, Westrum and Longstreet plan to steal the gold from under Steve's eyes. When they make their move, Steve catches them, puts them in cuffs, and plans to see that they are tried in a court of law. It's not just stealing that angers Steve; it is the betrayal of trust. "You were my friend," he tells Gill, his voice reverberating with his deep disappointment.

When the two eventually encounter Billy Hammond and his brothers in an old-time shoot-out, Steve and Gil recapture a final moment of glory. They win, but Steve is fatally wounded. "Don't worry about anything. I'll take care of it just like you would have," Gil assures his friend, promising that the gold will be returned to the bank. "Hell," says Steve, "I know that. I always did. You just forgot it for a while, that's all. . . . So long pardner. I'll see you later." Steve dies taking one last look at the hills on the horizon. He asks Gil to make sure nobody is around. "I don't want them to see this. I'll go it alone."

Ride the High Country might be the best western to come out of the 1960s, and it is arguably one of the best ever made, a picture that grows in stature with each successive viewing. The excessive violence so endemic to Sam Peckinpah's later film work is held in check until the final shoot-out, and it is merely an appendage to the evolving human drama.

Selected for the National Film Registry in 1992 by the National Film Preservation Board, *Ride the High Country* marked the final screen appearance for Randolph Scott, who had made his film debut as a bit player in 1928. One of Hollywood's richest men, due largely to wise investments in oil wells, real estate, and securities, he lived another 25 years before passing away in 1987 at age 89.

Joel McCrea retired from films once more after completing *Ride the High Country*. He eventually appeared in two more pictures, *CRY BLOOD APACHE* (1970) and *MUSTANG COUNTRY* (1976); and was the narrator for the documentary *The Great American Cowboy* (1974) and finally for another documentary, *George Stevens: A Filmmaker's Journey* (1985). A truly fine actor and an expert horseman, Joel McCrea died in 1990 at age 85.

RIDE THE MAN DOWN   Republic, 1953, Color, 90 min. **Producer:** Joseph Kane; **Director:** Kane; **Screenplay:** Mary C. McCall Jr.; **Music:** Ned Freeman; **Cinematographer:** Jack A. Marta; **Editor:** Fred Allen; **Cast:** Rod Cameron, Brian Donlevy, Ella Raines, Forrest Tucker, Barbara Britton, Chill Wills, J. Carrol Naish, Jim Davis, Paul Fix.

A rancher dies, and the feud between his daughter and local land grabbers results in a bloody range war, while the ranch foreman does his best to protect the dead man's property. A solid story with an exceptional cast makes this A-level project from Republic a good bet to enjoy.

RIDE VAQUERO! MGM, 1953, Color, 90 min. **Producer:** Steven Ames; **Director:** John Farrow; **Screenplay:** Farrow; **Music:** Bronislau Kaper; **Cinematographer:** Robert Surtees; **Editor:** Harold Kress; **Cast:** Robert Taylor, Ava Gardner, Howard Keel, Anthony Quinn, Kurt Kasner, Ted de Corsia, Jack Elam.

A gang of outlaws led by Anthony Quinn menaces western Texas around the town of Brownsville. Robert Taylor is Quinn's half-brother and lieutenant, a less flamboyant type but more deadly and introspective. Discovering that the times are changing as the West he once knew becomes rapidly settled, he begins to question his loyalty and allegiance to his outlaw brother and starts to doubt whether he wants to kill on Quinn's behalf any longer.

The plot thickens when Howard Keel tries to found a cattle empire and begins to bring in settlers. The outlaws in turn fight back, knowing that they will be finished if civilization comes to the land. Ava Gardner plays Keel's new bride, who arrives at their new homestead only to find it burned to the ground by Quinn's gang. Disenchanted, she makes more than one play for the handsome Taylor, who somehow manages to nix her advances.

The choice between a primitive way of life and the advent of civilization became a frequent thematic concern for the western film after World War II. *Ride Vaquero!* was one of MGM's few excursions into big-budget westerns. It also featured the first nonsinging role for Howard Keel, then one of the movies' most popular musical stars.

Although Quinn steals the acting honors, Taylor is also quite good in selling the quiet menace of his part. While reviews were generally mixed, *Newsweek* was more positive than many in praising the film's "interesting variation on the old formula, [providing] color and a cast that sets this Western well above the average."

RIDIN' DOWN THE CANYON Republic, 1942, B&W, 55 min. **Producer:** Harry Grey (associate); **Director:** Joseph Kane; **Screenplay:** Albert De Mond; **Music:** Bob Nolan (songs); **Cinematographer:** John Marta; **Editor:** Edward Mann; **Cast:** Roy Rogers, George "Gabby" Hayes, Bob Nolan (and the Sons of the Pioneers), Robert "Buzz" Henry, Linda Hayes, Addison Richards, Lorna Gray, Roy Barcroft.

RIDIN' DOWN THE TRAIL Monogram, 1947, B&W, 53 min. **Producer:** Bennett Cohen; **Director:** Howard Bretherton; **Screenplay:** Cohen; **Cinematographer:** James S. Brown; **Editor:** John C. Fuller; **Cast:** Jimmy Wakely, Dub Taylor, Douglas Fowley, John James, Charles King, Kermit Maynard.

RIDIN' FOR JUSTICE Columbia, 1932, B&W, 61 min. **Producer:** Irving Briskin; **Director:** R. Ross Lederman; **Screenplay:** Harold Shumate; **Music:** Irving Bibo and Milan Roder; **Cinematographer:** Benjamin H. Kline; **Editor:** Maurice Wright; **Cast:** Buck Jones, Mary Doran, Russell Simpson, Walter Miller.

RIDING KID, THE See *RAIDERS, THE.*

RIDING SHOTGUN Warner Bros., 1954, Color, 75 min. **Producer:** Ted Sherdeman; **Director:** André De Toth; **Screenplay:** Thomas Blackburn; **Music:** David Buttolph; **Cinematographer:** Bert Glennon; **Editor:** Rudi Fehr; **Cast:** Randolph Scott, Wayne Morris, Joan Weldon, Joe Sawyer, James Millican, Charles Bronson (as Charles Buchinsky), Dub Taylor, Budd Buster, Buddy Roosevelt.

In an attempt to find the outlaw responsible for his wife's death, Randolph Scott takes a job as a stagecoach driver, hoping to apprehend the man when he attempts to pull off another robbery.

RIDING THE CALIFORNIA TRAIL Monogram, 1947, B&W, 59 min, VHS. **Producer:** Scott R. Dunlap; **Director:** William Nigh; **Screenplay:** Clarence Upson Young; **Cinematographer:** Harry Neumann; **Editor:** Fred Maguire; **Cast:** Gilbert Roland, Martin Garralaga, Frank Yaconelli; Teala Loring, Inez Cooper, Ted Hecht, Marcelle Grandville.

RIDING THE WIND RKO, 1941, B&W, 60 min. **Producer:** Bert Gilroy; **Director:** Edward Killy; **Screenplay:** Morton Grant and Earle Snell; **Music:** Paul Sawtell, Fred Rose (songs), and Ray Whitley (songs); **Cinematographer:** Harry J. Wild; **Editor:** Frederic Knudtson; **Cast:** Tim Holt, Ray Whitley, Joan Barclay, Lee "Lasses" White, Eddie Dew.

Gilbert Roland as the Cisco Kid in Riding the California Trail *(MONOGRAM/AUTHOR'S COLLECTION)*

RIDING TORNADO, THE   Columbia, 1932, B&W, 64 min. **Producer:** Irving Briskin; **Director:** D. Ross Ledderman; **Screenplay:** Kurt Kempler; **Music:** Mischa Bakaleinikoff; **Cinematographer:** Benjamin H. Kline; **Editor:** Otto Meyer; **Cast:** Tim McCoy, Shirley Grey, Montagu Love, Wheeler Oakmont, Wallace MacDonald, Art Mix, Vernon Dent.

Tim McCoy is a championship rodeo rider who is having big trouble with a local boss who believes he is the mastermind behind a gang of cattle rustlers. There is plenty of action in this Tim McCoy entry for Columbia. At his peak McCoy, like his counterpart Buck Jones, helped Columbia produce some of the industry's highest quality B westerns. In the early 1930s Columbia, still a small studio, had both Tim McCoy and Buck Jones as its leading cowboy stars, with the two actors making simultaneous series.

After starring in Universal's first all-talking serial, *The Indians Are Coming* (1930), McCoy signed a contract with Columbia for a series of B westerns in 1931. He rose to the front rank of top western stars in the 1930s, and was reputed to be the fastest draw of any B screen hero in his day. During his four years with Columbia, he honed his screen persona, making more than 30 westerns. He remained with Columbia until 1935, when he left the studio to make westerns for studios such as Puritan, Victory, Monogram, and PRC.

Among McCoy's better entries for Columbia are *Texas Cyclone* (1931); *Trail of the End, Cornered* (1932); *Rusty Rides Alone* (1933); *The Prescott Kid* (1934); *Law Beyond the Range*, and *Revenge Rider* (1935).

His other series entries for Columbia are *One Way Trail, Shotgun Pass, The Fighting Marshal* (1931); *The Fighting Fool, Two-Fisted Law, Daring Danger, Western Code, Fighting for Justice* (1932); *Man of Action, Silent Men, Whirlwind* (1933); *Beyond the Law, The Westerner* (1934); *Square Shooter, Fighting Shadows, Justice of the Range, Outlaw Deputy, Riding Wild* (1935).

RIDING WEST   Columbia, 1944, B&W, 58 min. **Producer:** Jack Fier; **Director:** William Berke; **Screenplay:** Luci Ward; **Cinematographer:** Benjamin H. Kline; **Editor:** Jerry Thomas; **Cast:** Charles Starrett, Shirley Patterson, Arthur Hunnicutt, Ernest Tubb, Steve Clark, Wheeler Oakmont.

Some good excitement and pleasing music highlight this Charles Starrett oater about a gambler who tries to prevent a man from establishing a pony express business. (See also *GALLANT DEFENDER.*)

RIDING WILD   Columbia, 1935, B&W, 57 min. **Director:** David Selman; **Screenplay:** Ford Beebe; **Music:** Phil Boutelie and Louis Silvers; **Cinematographer:** Benjamin H. Kline; **Editor:** Al Clark; **Cast:** Tim McCoy, Billie, Niles Welch, Edward Le Saint, Richard Alexander.
See *RIDING TORNADO, THE.*

RIDIN' ON   Reliable, 1936, B&W, 60 min. **Producer:** Bernard B. Ray; **Directors:** Ray and Ira B. Webb; **Screenplay:** John T. Neville; **Cinematographer:** Pliny Goodfriend;

Editor: Frederick Bain; **Cast:** Tom Tyler, Joan Barclay, Rex Lease, John Elliott, Earl Dwire.

RIDIN' ON A RAINBOW   Republic, 1941, B&W, 79 min. **Producer:** Harry Grey; **Director:** Lew Landers; **Screenplay:** Doris Malloy; **Music:** Gene Autry and Fred Rose; **Cinematographer:** William Nobles; **Editor:** Tony Martinelli; **Cast:** Gene Autry, Smiley Burnette, Mary Lee, Carol Adams, Ferris Taylor, Georgia Caine, Tom London.

When a rancher completes a cattle drive, he puts his profits in the bank. The bank is robbed a short time later, so he joins an entertainment group aboard a showboat, suspecting that a veteran performer in the group is one of the robbers. This is a good Gene Autry action vehicle, and Autry and Fred Rose won an Oscar nomination for the song "Be Honest with Me."

RIDIN' THE CHEROKEE TRAIL   Monogram, 1941, B&W, 59 min. **Producer:** Edward Finney; **Director:** Spencer Gordon Bennet; **Screenplay:** Edmond Kelso; **Music:** Slim Andrews, Harry Blair, Jack Gilette, Johnny Lange, Lew Porter, Tex Ritter, and Frank Sanucci; **Cinematographer:** Marcel Le Picard; **Editor:** Robert Golden; **Cast:** Tex Ritter, Forrest Andrews, Fred Burns, Betty Miles, Bruce Nolan.
See *SONG OF THE GRINGO.*

RIDIN' THE FRONTIER   See *RIDERS OF THE FRONTIER.*

RIDIN' THE TRAIL   Spectrum, 1940, B&W, 57 min. **Producers:** C. C. Burr and Arthur Ziehm; **Director:** Bernard B. Ray (as Raymond Johnson); **Screenplay:** Phil Dunham; **Music:** June Hershey, Cactus Mack, and Don Swander; **Cinematographer:** Elmer Dyer and Harvey Gould; **Editor:** Charles Henkel Jr.; **Cast:** Fred Scott, Victor Adamson, Elias Gamboa, Harry Harvey, Gene Harvey.
See *MOONLIGHT ON THE RANGE.*

RIDIN' THRU   Reliable, 1934, B&W, 55 min. **Producer:** Bernard B. Ray; **Director:** Harry S. Webb; **Screenplay:** Rose Gordon; **Cinematographer:** J. Henry Kruse; **Editor:** Frederick Bain; **Cast:** Tom Tyler, Ruth Hiatt, Lafe McKee, Philo McCullough, Bud Corbett.

RIFLE, THE   See *TALL STRANGER, THE.*

RIMFIRE   Lippert, 1949, B&W, 63 min. **Producer:** Ron Ormond; **Director:** B. Reeves Eason; **Screenplay:** Ormond, Arthur St. Claire, and Frank Wisbar; **Music:** Walter Greene; **Cinematographer:** Ernest Miller; **Editor:** Hugh Winn; **Cast:** James Millican, Mary Beth Hughes, Reed Hadley, Henry Hull, Fuzzy Knight, Victor Kilian, Chris-Pin Martin, I. Stanford Jolley.

Charles Starrett and Arthur Hunnicutt star in Riding West (COLUMBIA/AUTHOR'S COLLECTION)

Set in post-Civil War Texas, this interesting and lesser-known western from Lippert tells the story of a cavalry officer who opposes a gang of crooked gamblers who are running a boom town.

RIM OF THE CANYON Columbia, 1949, B&W, 70 min. **Producer:** Armand Schaefer; **Director:** John English; **Screenplay:** John K. Butler; **Music:** Gene Autry, Hy Heath, and Johnny Lange; **Cinematographer:** William Bradford; **Editor:** Aaron Stell; **Cast:** Gene Autry, Nan Leslie, Thurston Hall, Clem Bevans, Walter Sande, Jock Mahoney, Alan Hale Jr., Denver Pyle.

See *TUMBLING TUMBLEWEEDS.*

RIO BRAVO Warner Bros., 1959, Color, 141 min, VHS, DVD. **Producer:** Howard Hawks; **Director:** Hawks; **Screenplay:** Leigh Brackett and Jules Furthman; **Music:**

Dimitri Tiomkin; **Cinematographer:** Russell Harlan; **Editor:** Folmar Blangsted; **Cast:** John Wayne, Dean Marin, Ricky Nelson, Angie Dickinson, Walter Brennan, Ward Bond, John Russell, Claude Akins.

In one of his best roles, John Wayne is Sheriff John T. Chance, who along with two deputies—one a toothless cripple (Walter Brennan) and the other a drunk (Dean Martin)—take on an army of gunmen set on springing a murderous sidekick from jail. They receive some unusual help from a young gunslinger named Colorado (Ricky Nelson) and an alluring dance-hall girl and gambler named Feathers (Angie Dickinson).

A near-perfect western example of good versus evil, *Rio Bravo* was John Wayne's first venture with director Howard Hawks since *RED RIVER* 10 years earlier. It highlights the dual themes of pride and professionalism, where men bond together under duress and adversity—in other words, vintage Howard Hawks. Wayne and company triumph in the end because, despite their human flaws, they are true professionals who use cool and cunning against a numerically superior array of arrogant amateurs. At no time do they try to enlist the help of townsfolk, whereas in period pieces like HIGH NOON (1952) and 3:10 TO YUMA (1957) the town members emerge as timid and cowardly.

In fact, both Hawks and Wayne had been critical of *High Noon*, despite its wide acclaim. Wayne objected to the portrayal of a town where citizens lacked courage and moral fiber, and he considered *High Noon* a specious depiction of the western character—a point he made clear in a 1971 interview with *Playboy* magazine. (It should be pointed out that most historians of the American West tend to agree with Wayne's thesis, and that when put to the test in times of trouble, most people stood by their lawmen).

What Hawks presents here is an entirely different type of beleaguered sheriff. Instead of Will Kane (Gary Cooper) in *High Noon* standing alone in the street, bitterly tossing his badge on the ground, Hawks's John T. Chance assembles a trustworthy group of men with disparate backgrounds who bond together to fight in a common cause. In Chance, Hawks finds his definitive western hero, the man who lives by his own imposed rules of honor and friendship.

Critics paid little attention to the film at the time of its release. The reviews, while good, were not outstanding. *Variety* noted that "Producer-director Howard Hawks makes handsome use of force in logically unraveling his hard hitting narrative," and called the film "a big, brawling western." Yet as Howard Hawks's star has risen in recent decades, so has the statue of *Rio Bravo*. Many critics now rank it as a genre classic, and a handful have even suggested that it is the best western ever.

The film certainly does belong among the front echelon of screen westerns. Award-winning director and film historian Peter Bogdanovich points to a defining moment in *Rio Bravo* that conveys Wayne's most enduring qualities. The scene has Wayne walking down the steps of the sheriff's office toward a group of men riding up to meet him, a scene that "finds him moving across the world of illusion he has more than conquered."

The excellent script by Leigh Brackett and Jules Furthman is based on a story by B. H. McCampbell. The film also did well at the box office, generating more than $10.5 million in ticket sales, making it the highest-grossing western of 1959. Wayne and Dean Martin (who delivers marvelously as Dude, the alcoholic deputy, in a role originally slated for Montgomery Clift) became fast friends, and a warm friendship developed between the two actors that would last until the end of Wayne's life.

Angie Dickinson takes her beauty a long way as the solid, endearing and enticing Feathers, who chagrins and then later charms a reluctant John T. Chance. Dickinson, then 26 years old, shared a few remembrances in a 1999 interview with the author:

> We were on location in Tucson, Arizona and hit a real heat wave with the temperature hitting 128° in the shade. We were sweating through our skin. Unlike many of his

[Wayne's] films where his scenes were short and tough, our scenes together in *Rio Bravo* were long and complex. They were very difficult but they ended up great.

Rio Bravo was full of suspense and is a delight to watch. What made it so special was the respect John Wayne and Howard Hawks had for each other. And that great cast: Duke, Dean Martin, Walter Brennan, and Ricky Nelson, who was a big teenage heart throb back then.

Not to be forgotten is Dimitri Tiomkin's excellent score. Dean Martin and Ricky Nelson add songs to the evolving drama, such as "My Rifle, My Pony, and Me," written by Tiomkin and Paul Francis Webster, a piece whose theme bears a blatant similarity to that from *Red River*. Ricky Nelson also strums his guitar and sings the melodic "Cindy," with vocal help from Martin and musical assistance from a harmonica-playing Walter Brennan. Screen veteran Brennan turns in a tremendous performance as Stumpy. In a delightful moment Chance tells Stumpy, "You're a treasure. I don't know what I'd do without you." Then he proceeds to plant a kiss on the old man's head.

Howard Hawks would rework the plot line of *Rio Bravo* twice more: with EL DORADO in 1967 and RIO LOBO in 1970, both times with Wayne in the lead role.

RIO CONCHOS 20th Century Fox, 1964, Color, 107 min, VHS. **Producer:** Joseph Weisbart; **Director:** Gordon Douglas; **Screenplay:** Claire Huffaker and Joseph Landon; **Music:** Jerry Goldsmith; **Cinematographer:** Joe MacDonald; **Editor:** Joseph Silver; **Cast:** Richard Boone, Stuart Whitman, Anthony Franciosa, Jim Brown, Edmond O'Brien, Rodolfo Acosta, House Peters Jr.

In Texas soon after the Civil War, the U.S. Army attempts to keep guns out of the hands of warlike Indians by releasing a sadistic Indian killer (Richard Boone) and a Mexican bandit (Anthony Franciosa) from a Mexican jail in the company of an army captain (Stuart Whitman). Determined to find out who is supplying the Indians with firearms, the trio follows a trail that takes them to the camp of a demented ex-Confederate general (Edmond O'Brien). It turns out the general is not only arming the Indians but is also building a mansion on the banks of the Rio Conchos, where he plans to retire in splendor.

Filmed in Arches National Park, Utah, this action-packed western marks the film debut of the surprisingly adept former college and pro football great Jim Brown. Anthony Franciosa was nominated for a Golden Globe Award in the category of Best Motion Picture Actor—Drama. Fast-paced and exciting, the film leads to an unexpected climax. Richard Boone is excellent as the vengeful ex-rebel soldier trying to avenge his family's killing.

RIO GRANDE Columbia, 1938, B&W, 58 min. **Producer:** Harry L. Decker; **Director:** Sam Nelson; **Screenplay:** Charles Francis Royal; **Music:** Bob Nolan; **Cinematographer:** Lucien Ballard; **Editor:** William A.

Lyon; **Cast:** Charles Starrett, Ann Doran, Bob Nolan and the Sons of the Pioneers, Dick Curtis, George Chesebro.

This standard B formula western has a cowboy and his pals coming to the aid of a girl being forced off her ranch by land grabbers. Bob Nolan and the Sons of the Pioneers offer lots of nice songs including "Tumbling Tumbleweeds," which was first introduced by Gene Autry in the film of the same name two years earlier. A short time later Nolan and the Sons would leave Starrett for the emerging Roy Rogers, who originally sang for the Sons of the Pioneers under the name Dick Western. (See also *GALLANT DEFENDER.*)

RIO GRANDE Lautem Productions, 1949, B&W, 56 min. **Producer:** Charles Lautem; **Director:** Norman Sheldon; **Screenplay:** Sheldon; **Music:** Gordon Clark and Marie Martino; **Cinematographer:** Jack Specht; **Editor:** Hugh Jamison; **Cast:** Sunset Carson, Evelyn Keyes, Lee Morgan, Bobby Clark, Bob Deats.

A cowboy comes to the aid of a rancher and his sister when two crooked brothers try to cheat them out of their water rights. Sunset Carson's last theatrically released film does not have much to recommend it. Filmed in Texas, the feature remains the only picture to be produced by the Lautem Productions company.

RIO GRANDE Republic, 1950, B&W, 105 min, VHS, DVD, CD. **Producers:** Merian C. Cooper, John Ford, and Herbert J. Yates; **Director:** Ford; **Screenplay:** James Kevin McGuinness; **Music:** Victor Young; **Cinematographer:** Bert Glennon; **Editor:** Jack Murray; **Cast:** John Wayne, Maureen O'Hara, Ben Johnson, Claude Jarman Jr., Harry Carey Jr., Chill Wills, Victor McLaglen, J. Carrol Naish,

John Wayne, Maureen O'Hara, and Claude Jarman Jr. in Rio Grande, *the third film in John Ford's cavalry trilogy and the first teaming of John Wayne and Maureen O'Hara* (REPUBLIC/AUTHOR'S COLLECTION)

Grant Withers, Fred Kennedy, Stan Jones, Chuck Roberson, Ken Curtis, Patrick Wayne (uncredited).

The third film in John Ford's celebrated cavalry trilogy has John Wayne as Lieutenant Colonel Kirby Yorke and Maureen O'Hara (in their first film together) as his estranged wife Kathleen. During the Civil War, Yorke, a Northerner, followed the orders of General Philip Sheridan (J. Carrol Naish) to burn down the plantation of his southern-born wife. As the film begins, Yorke has not seen his wife or son for 15 years. Meanwhile, Indians have been raiding settlements in the United States and then escaping across the river back to Mexico. Yorke finds himself frustrated over the continuing raids and the orders that prohibit him from crossing the Rio Grande into Mexico to pursue the Indians. To compound matters, Jeff Yorke (Claude Jarman Jr.) arrives at his father's post as a new recruit after flunking out of West Point. His mother has been attempting to use her influence to get the boy discharged. She comes to the post to bring him home, but he refuses to leave. When Jeff asks his mother what type of man his father is, she touchingly replies, "A lonely man." The happy ending has General Sheridan giving his tacit permission for Yorke to pursue the raiding Indians across the border. Kirby and Kathleen, after numerous altercations and moments of courting all over again, decide to reunite as husband and wife, and young Jeff proves his mettle at soldiering.

Why Ford gave Wayne's character the same name he had in *FORT APACHE* (the first of the cavalry trilogy films) has never been quite determined. Certainly, the two characters are different, and Ford teased a bit by adding an *e* to Yorke's name.

Rio Grande features many of the same players from Ford's famous stock company, including Harry Carey Jr., Chill Wills, Victor McLaglen, and Grant Withers. But the true laurels in the picture belong to former stuntman-wrangler Ben Johnson, who steals the show as Tyree, the trooper trying to stay one step behind the Indians and one step ahead of the hangman on a trumped-up manslaughter charge. (Johnson was Sergeant Tyree in *SHE WORE A YELLOW RIBBON* (1949), yet another interesting curiosity.) Reportedly Johnson and John Ford exchanged a few words while on location, a result of one of Ford's patented insults. Neither mentioned the incident again, and the problem seemed to have been mollified, but it would be another 13 years before the two men would work together again.

In a 1994 interview with the author, the genre legend discussed the film and the famous scene where he and fellow trooper Harry Carey Jr. engaged in a bit of Roman riding—riding two horses, standing, with one foot on each horse's back: "We had quite an experience with Roman riding. I always liked to ride a horse and did a lot of riding in that picture. We were supposed to come up with some riding we could use in the picture to beat the upper crust. Dobe [Harry Carey Jr.] came up with the Roman riding and took the prize."

Based on a *Saturday Evening Post* story by James Warner Bellah, the film is outdoor action at its best, delivered at a time when John Ford was at the absolute top of his cinematic game. What is also obvious in *Rio Grande* is John Wayne's

Reliable and durable, veteran character actor Harry Carey Jr. has appeared in nearly 100 movies and more than 50 Westerns (including Rio Grande*).* (HARRY CAREY JR. COLLECTION)

increasing level of maturity on the screen. In the 1948 *Motion Picture Herold* poll, Wayne ranked 33 among Hollywood's most popular stars. By 1950 he was number one—and *Rio Grande* was the only new John Wayne film to be released that year. Interestingly, Ford originally had never intended to make three John Wayne cavalry films. Rather it was a case of demand clearly dictating a product.

Wayne and costar Maureen O'Hara would be teamed together four more times and emerge as one of the most celebrated screen couples. They reached a high point two years later in *The Quiet Man* (1952), the film that won Ford an unprecedented fourth Best Director Oscar.

RIO GRANDE PATROL RKO, 1950, B&W, 60 min. **Producer:** Herman Schlom; **Director:** Leslie Selander; **Screenplay:** Norman Houston; **Music:** Paul Sawtell; **Cinematographer:** J. Roy Hunt; **Editor:** Desmond Marquette; **Cast:** Tim Holt, Richard Martin, Jane Nigh, John Holland, Tom Tyler.

RIO GRANDE RAIDERS Republic, 1946, B&W, 56 min. **Producer:** Bennett Cohen (associate); **Director:** Thomas Carr; **Screenplay:** Norton S. Parker; **Cinematog-**

rapher: Alfred Keller; **Editor:** William P. Thompson; **Cast:** Sunset Carson, Linda Stirling, Bob Steele, Tom London, Tristram Coffin, Edmund Cobb.
See *CALL OF THE ROCKIES.*

RIO GRANDE RANGER Columbia, 1936, B&W, 54 min. **Producer:** Larry Darmour; **Director:** Spencer Gordon Bennet; **Cinematographer:** James S. Brown Jr.; **Editor:** Dwight Caldwell; **Cast:** Robert Allen, Iris Meredith, Paul Sutton, Wally Wales, Robert "Buzz" Henry, John Elliott, Tom London.
See *LAW OF THE RANGER.*

RIO LOBO Batjac Productions/National General, 1970, Color, 114 min, VHS. **Producer:** Howard Hawks; **Director:** Hawks; **Screenplay:** Leigh Brackett; **Music:** Jerry Goldsmith; **Cinematographer:** William H. Clothier; **Editor:** John Woodcock; **Cast:** John Wayne, Jorge Rivero, Jennifer O'Neill, Jack Elam, Christopher Mitchum, Victor French, Susana Dosamantes, Sherry Lansing, Jim Davis, Edward Faulkner, Dean Smith, Robert Donner, Peter Jason, Don "Red" Barry.

When Confederate soldiers steal a gold shipment from a Union army train, Captain Cord McNally (John Wayne), the Union officer responsible for the gold shipment, goes after the thieves. He takes a fall from his horse and is captured by rebel soldiers. Although an amicable rapport is established between the Union captain and two important rebs, Lieutenant Pierre Cordona (Jorje Rivero) and Tuscarora (Chris Mitchum), neither will tell McNally the identity of the Union traitor who has been supplying secrets to the Confederacy.

After the war the three men meet again, and the former rebel leaders are now more conciliatory. Their quest brings them to the town of Rio Lobo, which is controlled by a gang of ruthless outlaws led by the very traitors for whom McNally is looking.

Taking a page out of the *RIO BRAVO* (1959) story book, this film is actually much better than genre purists tend to admit and critics care to cite. While many of the familiar ingredients of *Rio Bravo* and *EL DORADO* (1967) are present— the same screen writer, Leigh Brackett, the same star, and a similar climactic situation involving group trying to hold on to its prisoner in a besieged jailhouse—there are also significant differences. Hawks's female characters, for example, are forced to share the pain and suffering usually reserved for a disparate group of men acting alone, united by their sense of professionalism and loyalty. One of the corrupt sheriff's mistresses is brutally disfigured—a reversal from the Hawks style—in a scenario reminiscent of the evolving "spaghetti" influence beginning to permeate, then later to dominate, mainstream American westerns.

While John Wayne carries added poundage in *Rio Bravo*, his work is still convincing, and his bigger-than-life persona is forever tough. On a cold night, a younger Jennifer O'Neill prefers to snuggle up to him, now an aging avuncular figure, rather than the dashing and youthful Jorge Rivero, because

Edward Faulkner and John Wayne in Rio Lobo (NATIONAL GENERAL/COURTESY OF EDWARD FAULKNER)

Wayne is more "comfortable." However, true acting honors go to Jack Elam, who steals his scenes as Phillips, the shotgun-toting old jailer, a near copycat role to those played by Walter Brennan in *Rio Bravo* and Arthur Hunnicutt in *El Dorado*.

Rio Lobo was the final film for master director Howard Hawks, whose career dated back to 1926. While not one of his best efforts, *Rio Lobo* should not be dismissed as an inferior piece of work. Indeed, the French *auteur* critics have been especially kind to the Hawks trilogy (*Rio Bravo, El Dorado, Rio Lobo*), attributing their shared style to Hawks's distinct direction.

There is much to enjoy here: blunt action, crisp dialogue, escalating suspense, and Elam's vintage performance. *Rio Lobo* was John Wayne's fourth and final western collaboration with Howard Hawks, whom he admired greatly. The admiration was mutual. Hawks would later say in praise of the actor that "John Wayne represents more force, more power, than anyone else on the screen."

In a final postscript, *Rio Lobo* also marked the last acting appearance of future Paramount studio head Sherry Lansing.

RIO RATTLER Reliable, 1935, B&W. **Producer:** Bernard B. Ray; **Director:** Ray (as Franklin Shamray); **Screenplay:** Carl Krusada; **Cinematographer:** Pliny Goodfriend; **Editor:** William Austin; **Cast:** Tom Tyler, Eddie Gribbon, Marian Shilling, William Gould, Tom London, Lafe McKee.

See *MYSTERY RANCH.*

RIVER OF DESTINY See *FORLORN RIVER.*

RIVER OF NO RETURN 20th Century Fox, 1954, Color, 91 min, VHS. **Producer:** Stanley Rubin; **Director:** Otto Preminger; **Screenplay:** Frank Fenton; **Music:** Cyril Mockridge; **Cinematographer:** Joseph La Shelle; **Editor:** Louis Loefler; **Cast:** Robert Mitchum, Marilyn Monroe, Rory Calhoun, Tommy Rettig, Murvyn Vye, Douglas Spencer.

In Northwest Canada during the gold rush days, farmer Robert Mitchum is making his way to a homestead with his son (Tommy Rettig) when he rescues gambler Rory Calhoun and dance-hall girl Marilyn Monroe from a leaky raft.

Calhoun returns the favor by stealing Mitchum's horse and leaving him and his young son to deal with hostile Indians. Disapproving of Calhoun's brutality, Monroe decides to stay with the farmer and his son. He agrees to settle down with her once he catches up with the gambler and pays him back for leaving them in the lurch.

The main attractions of this film are the curvaceous Monroe, then at the height of her incomparable sensuality, and the gorgeous visual landscape of mountains and rapid rivers shot in CinemaScope. The title song, written by Lionel Newman (music) and Ken Darby (words), was introduced in the picture by Marilyn Monroe and Tennessee Ernie Ford, who would both record the song individually, Monroe for RCA and Ford on the Capital label.

ROAD AGENT Universal, 1941, B&W, 60 min. **Producer:** Ben Pivar (associate); **Director:** Charles Lamont; **Screenplay:** Morgan Cox, Arthur Strawn, and Maurice Tombragel; **Cinematographer:** Jerome Ash; **Editor:** Frank Gross; **Cast:** Dick Foran, Leo Carrillo, Andy Devine, Anne Gwynne, Samuel S. Hinds, Anne Nagel, Morris Ankrum.

Duke Masters and two pals hold up the men who had robbed a stage, deduct a finders' fee, and then return the money to the bank. But when two of the original holdup men are murdered, Masters and his pals are promptly tossed in jail on a fake murder charge. When they are released they set out to find the real culprits.

ROAD AGENT RKO, 1952, B&W, 60 min. **Producer:** Herman Schlom; **Director:** Lesley Selander; **Screenplay:** Norman Houston; **Music:** Paul Sawtell; **Cinematographer:** J. Roy Hunt; **Editor:** Paul Weatherwax; **Cast:** Tim Holt, Richard Martin, Dorothy Patrick, Mauritz Hugo, Noreen Nash.

ROAD TO DENVER, THE Republic, 1955, Color, 90 min. **Producer:** Herbert Yates; **Director:** Joseph Kane; **Screenplay:** Horace McCoy, Allen Rivkin, and R. Dale Butts; **Cinematographer:** Reggie Lanning; **Editor:** Richard L. Van Enger; **Cast:** John Payne, Mona Freeman, Lee J. Cobb, Skip Homeier, Ray Middleton, Andy Clyde, Lee Van Cleef.

John Payne and Skip Homeier are two brothers who find themselves on opposite sides of the law. Good characterizations and plenty of action elevate this Republic western and its obligatory final meeting, showdown, and shoot-out.

ROAMING COWBOY Spectrum, 1937, B&W, 56 min. **Producer:** Jed Buell; **Director:** Robert Hill; **Screenplay:** Fred Myton; **Music:** Stephen Foster and Rudy Sooter; **Cinematographer:** William Hyer; **Editor:** William Hess; **Cast:** Fred Scott, Al St. John, Lois January, Forrest Taylor, Roger Williams.

ROAMIN' WILD Reliable, 1936, B&W, 58 min. **Producer:** Bernard B. Ray; **Director:** Ray; **Screenplay:** Robert Tansey; **Cinematographer:** William Hyer; **Editor:** Freder-ick Bain; **Cast:** Tom Tyler, Carol Wyndham, Al Ferguson, George Chesebro, Lafe McKee.

ROARING FRONTIERS Columbia, 1941, B&W, 60 min. **Producer:** Leon Barsha (associate); **Director:** Lambert Hillyer; **Screenplay:** Robert Lee Johnson; **Cinematographer:** Benjamin H. Kline; **Editor:** Mel Thorsen; **Cast:** William "Wild Bill" Elliott, Tex Ritter, Ruth Ford, Frank Mitchell, Bradley Page, Tristram Coffin, Wally Wales, George Chesebro.

See *WILDCAT OF TUCSON.*

ROARING RANGERS (aka: FALSE HERO) Columbia, 1946, B&W, 55 min. **Producer:** Colbert Clark; **Director:** Ray Nazarro; **Screenplay:** Barry Shipman; **Cinematographer:** George Kelley; **Cast:** Charles Starrett, Smiley Burnette, Adele Roberts, Mickey Kuhn, Jack Rockwell, Edmund Cobb.

See *DURANGO KID, THE.*

ROARING WESTWARD (aka: BOOM TOWN BADMEN) Monogram, 1949, B&W, 58 min. **Producer:** Louis Gray; **Director:** Oliver Drake; **Screenplay:** Ronald Davidson; **Cinematographer:** Marcel Le Picard; **Editor:** Carl Pierson; **Cast:** Jimmy Wakely, Dub Taylor, Lois Hall, Dennis Moore, Claire Whitney, Jack Ingram.

See *ACROSS THE RIO GRANDE.*

ROAR OF THE IRON HORSE Columbia, 1950, B&W, 15 chapters. **Producer:** Sam Katzman; **Director:** Spencer Gordon Bennett and Thomas Carr; **Screenplay:** Royal K. Cole, Sherman L. Lowe, and George H. Plympton; **Music:** John Leipold; **Cast:** Jock Mahoney, Virginia Herrick, William Fawcett, Harold Landon, Jack Ingram, Myron Healey, Pierce Lydon, Dick Curtis.

In this action-filled serial, stuntman/actor Jock Mahoney stars as a special investigator from Washington who is assigned to find out what is causing a series of mishaps that are hindering the construction of a government-financed railroad.

ROBBERS OF THE RANGE RKO, 1941, B&W, 61 min. **Producer:** Bert Gilroy; **Director:** Edward Killy; **Screenplay:** Oliver Drake, Morton Grant, and Arthur V. Jones; **Music:** Fred Rose; **Cinematographer:** Harry J. Wild; **Editor:** Frederic Knudtson; **Cast:** Tim Holt, Virginia Vale, Ray Whitley, Emmett Lynn, Leroy Mason, Tom London.

ROBBERS' ROOST Fox, 1933, B&W, 64 min. **Producer:** Sol Lesser; **Director:** David Howard and Louis King; **Screenplay:** Dudley Nichols; **Cinematographer:** George Schneiderman; **Cast:** George O'Brien, Maureen O'Sullivan, Walter McGrail, Maude Eburne, Walter Pawley, Ted Oliver.

Tarzan's future Jane, Maureen O'Sullivan, stars with George O'Brien in this Zane Grey story about a ranch hand who suspects the foreman when his boss's cattle are rustled.

ROBBERS' ROOST   United Artists, 1955, Color, 83 min. **Producers:** Leonard and Robert Goldstein; **Director:** Sidney Salkow; **Screenplay:** Maurice Geraghty, John O'Dea, and Salkow; **Music:** Johnny Bradford, Barbara Hayden, and Tony Romano; **Cinematographer:** Jack Draper; **Editor:** George Gittens; **Cast:** George Montgomery, Richard Boone, Sylvia Findley, Bruce Bennett, Peter Graves, Tony Romano.

This is the second adaptation of the Zane Grey novel about two outlaw gangs battling each other for valuable range land.

In 1955 United Artists released the color film *Robber's Roost*, directed by Sidney Saklow and starring George Montgomery, Richard Boone, Bruce Bennett, Peter Graves, and Leo Gordon. Based on the Zane Grey story, the film tells the familiar story of two outlaw gangs battling each other for valuable range land.

ROBIN HOOD OF EL DORADO, THE   MGM, 1936, B&W, 85 min. **Producer:** John W. Considine Jr.; **Director:** William Wellman; **Screenplay:** Wellman, Joseph Calleia, and Melvin Levy; **Music:** Herbert Stothart and Esward Ward; **Cinematographer:** Chester Lyons; **Editor:** Robert Kern; **Cast:** Warner Baxter, Ann Loring, Bruce Cabot, Margo, J. Carrol Naish.

Set in California during the Gold Rush, William Wellman's *The Robin Hood of El Dorado* is one of the first westerns to portray a famous outlaw with sympathy. Based on the book by Walter Nobel Burns, the film tells the story of Joaquin Murietta, a victim of greedy financial interests and anti-Mexican prejudice, who ultimately became the champion of his downtrodden people.

Filmed on location, using some of Murietta's actual haunts, Wellman's romanticized movie nevertheless takes a tough look at one of the West's legendary figures. A Mexican farmer, Murietta becomes a bandit and rebel leader after his wife dies, the result of their being beaten and thrown off their land. After leading his brigands in a reign of terror against the settlers—there are 300 murders over a three-year period—he is hunted down and killed, dying at his wife's grave.

In dealing sympathetically with a famous outlaw, Wellman's *Robin Hood of El Dorado* had a direct influence on such later films as Nicholas Ray's *THE TRUE STORY OF JESSE JAMES* (1957) and Arthur Penn's *THE LEFT HANDED GUN* (1958). Film historian William Everson calls the film "the best of MGM's handful of Westerns [in the 1930s]."

ROBIN HOOD OF MONTEREY   Monogram, 1947, B&W, 71 min, VHS. **Producer:** Jeffrey Bernerd; **Director:** Christy Cabanne; **Screenplay:** Bennett Cohen; **Music:** Edward J. Kay; **Cinematographer:** William Sickner; **Editor:** Roy Livingston; **Cast:** Gilbert Roland, Chris-Pin Martin, Evelyn Brent, Nestor Paiva, Donna Martell (as Donna De Mario).

The Cisco Kid and Pancho (dubbed Chico and Pablo in TV prints) help a young man accused of killing his father, a Span-ish rancher. Star Gilbert Roland is given credit for some additional dialogue in this entertaining little film. (See also *CISCO KID, THE.*)

ROBIN HOOD OF TEXAS   Republic, 1947, B&W, 71 min. **Producer:** Sidney Picker; **Director:** Leslie Selander; **Screenplay:** John K. Butler and Earle Snell; **Cinematographer:** William Bradford; **Editor:** Harry Keller; **Cast:** Gene Autry, Lynne Roberts, Sterling Holloway, Adele Mara, James Cardwell, John Kellog, Ray Walker, Stanley Andrews.

ROBIN HOOD OF THE PECOS   Republic, 1941, B&W, 59 min, VHS. **Producer:** Joseph Kane; **Director:** Kane; **Screenplay:** Olive Cooper; **Music:** Cy Feuer; **Cinematographer:** Jack A. Marta; **Editor:** Charles Craft; **Cast:** Roy Rogers, George "Gabby" Hayes, Marjorie Reynolds, Cy Kendall, Sally Payne, Eddie Acuff.

ROCK ISLAND TRAIL (aka: TRANSCONTINENTAL EXPRESS, UK)   Republic, 1950, Color, 90 min. **Producer:** Paul Malvern; **Director:** Joseph Kane; **Screenplay:** James Edward Grant; **Music:** R. Dale Butts; **Cinematographer:** Jack A. Marta; **Editor:** Arthur Roberts; **Cast:** Forrest Tucker, Adele Mara, Lorna Gray (as Adrian Booth), Bruce Cabot, Chill Wills, Barbara Fuller, Grant Withers, Jeff Corey, Roy Barcroft.

Forrest Tucker is Reed Loomis, the president of the Rock Island Trail Company. When he tries to expand his rails into the Midwest, he finds malicious resistance from the stagecoach and steamship lines and especially from Kirby Morrow (Bruce Cabot), who does not shrink from engaging in acts of sabotage to stop Loomis. Only Constanza Strong (Adele Mara), the daughter of the local banker, has enough belief in him to allow him to see the project through.

ROCK RIVER RENEGADES   Monogram, 1942, B&W, 56 min, VHS. **Producer:** George W. Weeks; **Director:** S. Roy Luby; **Screenplay:** Earle Snell and John Vlahos; **Cinematographer:** Robert E. Cline; **Editor:** Luby (as Roy Claire); **Cast:** Ray Corrigan, John "Dusty" King, Max Terhune, Christine McIntyre, John Elliott, Kermit Maynard, Weldon Heyburn.

ROCKY MOUNTAIN   Warner Bros., 1950, B&W, 83 min. **Producer:** William Jacobs; **Director:** William Keighley; **Screenplay:** Alan Le May and Winston Miller; **Music:** Max Steiner; **Cinematographer:** Ted D. McCord; **Editor:** Rudi Fehr; **Cast:** Errol Flynn, Patrice Wymore, Scott Forbes, Guinn "Big Boy" Williams, Dickie Jones, Sheb Wooley, Peter Coe, Slim Pickens, Yakima Canutt, Grant Withers.

Confederate officer Lafe Barstow and his men are ordered to recruit outlaws to prepare for a Southern control of the area. Errol Flynn's final western, while not up to his earlier efforts, like *DODGE CITY* (1939) and *SANTA FE TRAIL* (1940) a decade earlier, still packs plenty of action, a strong cast, and stunning black and white photography of surrounding Gallup, New Mexico, where the picture was shot. The film was based on an actual incident.

Flynn met his third wife, Patrice Wymore, during the production. Wymore plays Johanna Carter, who is heading out West to join her Union soldier fiancé when Barstow and company rescue her from an Indian attack. All the Confederate soldiers die at the final fadeout, fighting Indians until the end.

ROCKY MOUNTAIN MYSTERY (aka: THE FIGHTING WESTERNER) Paramount, 1935, B&W, 63 min. **Producer:** Harold Hurley; **Director:** Charles Barton; **Screenplay:** Ethel Doherty and Edward Paramore Jr.; **Music:** Rudolph G. Kopp; **Cinematographer:** Archie Stout; **Cast:** Randolph Scott, Ann Sheridan, Charles "Chick" Sale, George F. Marion, Leslie Carter, Kathleen Burke.

Mining engineer Randolph Scott teams up with crusty sheriff "Chick" Sale to solve some killings at a mine. The element of a whodunnit mystery adds lots of zest to this mid-1930s oater, a good training ground for future genre great Randolph Scott.

Based very loosely on Zane Grey's novel *Golden Dream*, the film also marks an early screen appearance for future leading lady and box-office stalwart Ann Sheridan, who prior to 1935 was featured under her birth name, Clara Lou Sheridan. As the winner of Paramount's "Search for Beauty" contest in 1933, Sheridan was awarded with a bit part in the movie of the same name—the start of a big-name career.

RODEO Monogram, 1952, B&W, 70 min. **Producer:** Walter Mirisch; **Director:** William Beaudine; **Screenplay:** Charles R. Marion; **Music:** Marlin Skiles; **Cinematographer:** Harry Neumann; **Editor:** William Austin; **Cast:** John Archer, Jane Nigh, Wallace Ford, Gary Grey, Frances Rafferty, I. Stanford Jolley, Fuzzy Knight.

Crooked promoters run out on a rodeo still owing the owner some money, so a young woman takes over the show and makes it a big success.

RODEO KING AND THE SENIORITA Republic, 1951, B&W, 67 min. **Producer:** Melville Tucker (associate); **Director:** Philip Ford; **Screenplay:** John K. Butler; **Music:** Curley Fletcher, Fred Howard, Caroline Nirton, and Nat Vincent; **Cinematographer:** Walter Strenge; **Editor:** Robert M. Leeds; **Cast:** Rex Allen, Marry Ellen Kaye, Buddy Ebsen, Roy Barcroft, Tristram Coffin, Bonnie DeSimone, Don Beddoe.

RODEO RHYTHM PRC, 1941, B&W, 72 min. **Producer:** Leo J. McCarthy; **Director:** Fred C. Newmeyer; **Screenplay:** Eugene Allen and Gene Tuttle; **Music:** Eugene Moore, Morrill Moore, and Dave Oppenheim; **Cinematog-**

rapher: Edward A. Kull; **Editor:** George Halligan; **Cast:** Fred Scott, Pat Dunn, Lorie Bridge, Patricia Redpath, Jack Cooper, Gloria Morris.

ROGUE OF THE RANGE Supreme, 1936, B&W, 58 min, VHS. **Producer:** A. W. Hackel; **Director:** S. Roy Luby; **Screenplay:** Earl Snell; **Cinematographer:** Jack Greenhalgh; **Editor:** Luby (as Roy Claire); **Cast:** Johnny Mack Brown, Alden "Stephen" Chase, Jack Rockwell, Horace Murphy, George Ball.

ROLL ALONG, COWBOY 20th Century Fox, 1937, B&W, 57 min. **Producer:** Sol Lesser; **Director:** Gus Meins; **Screenplay:** Daniel Jarrett; **Music:** Lew Porter, Harry Tobias, and Lyle Womack; **Cinematographer:** Harry Neumann; **Editors:** Arthur Hilton and Albert Jordan; **Cast:** Smith Ballew, Cecilia Parker, Stanley Fields, Ruth Robinson, William "Wild Bill" Elliott (as Gordon Elliott), Wally Albright.

Singing cowboy Smith Ballew starts working on a ranch owned by a woman (Ruth Robinson), only to find her in trouble with a band of crooks. He sets things right and in the process falls in love with her daughter (Cecilia Parker).

ROLLING CARAVANS Columbia, 1938, B&W, 55 min. **Producer:** Larry Darmour; **Director:** Joseph Levering; **Screenplay:** Nate Gatzert; **Cinematographer:** James J. Brown Jr.; **Editor:** Dwight Caldwell; **Cast:** Jack Luden, Eleanor Stewart, Harry Woods, Lafe McKee, Buzz Barton, Slim Whitaker.

See *PHANTOM GOLD*.

ROLLING DOWN THE GREAT DIVIDE PRC, 1942, B&W, 62 min. **Producer:** Sigmund Neufeld; **Director:** Sam Newfield; **Screenplay:** Milton Raison (as George Milton) and George Wallace Sayre (as George Milton); **Music:** Bill "Cowboy Rambler" Boyd, Johnny Lange, Leon Payne, and Lew Porter; **Cinematographer:** Jack Greenhalgh; **Cast:** Bill "Cowboy Rambler" Boyd, Art Davis, Lee Powell, Wanda McKay, Glenn Stranger.

See *RAIDERS OF THE WEST*.

ROLLIN' PLAINS Grand National, 1938, B&W, 57 min. **Producer:** Edward Finney; **Director:** Albert Herman; **Screenplay:** Celia Jaccard, Jacques Jaccard, Edmond Kelso, and Lindsley Parsons; **Music:** Leonard Whitcup; **Cinematographer:** Gus Peterson; **Editor:** Frederick Bain; **Cast:** Tex Ritter, Hobart Bosworth, Harriet Bennet, "Snub" Pollard, Horace Murphy, Charles King.

See *SONG OF THE GRINGO*.

ROLL ON TEXAS MOON Republic, 1946, B&W, 54 min, VHS, DVD. **Producer:** Edward J. White (associate); **Director:** William Witney; **Screenplay:** Paul Ganglin;

Music: R. Dale Butts; **Cinematographer:** William Bradford; **Editor:** Lester Orlebeck; **Cast:** Roy Rogers, George "Gabby" Hayes, Dale Evans, Dennis Hoey, Elisabeth Risdon, Kenne Duncan, Tom London, Pierce Lyden, Bob Nolan and The Sons of the Pioneers.

See *UNDER WESTERN STARS.*

ROLL ON, UK   See *LAWLESS PLAINSMEN.*

ROLL, THUNDER, ROLL   Eagle-Lion, 1949, Color, 60 min. **Producer:** Jerry Thomas; **Director:** Lewis B. Collins; **Screenplay:** Paul Franklin; **Music:** David Chudnow and Raoul Kraushaar (as Ralph Stanley); **Cinematographer:** Gilbert Warrenton; **Editor:** Frank Baldridge; **Cast:** Jim Bannon, Don Kay Reynolds, Emmett Lynn, Marin Sais, I. Stanford Jolley, Nancy Gates, Glenn Strange, George Chesebro.

See *ADVENTURES OF RED RYDER, THE.*

ROLL, WAGONS, ROLL   Monogram, 1940, B&W, 52 min. **Producer:** Edward Finney; **Director:** Albert Herman; **Screenplay:** Victor Adamson, Edmond Kelso, and Roger Merton; **Music:** Frank Sanucci; **Cinematographer:** Marcel Le Picard; **Editor:** Frederick Bain; **Cast:** Tex Ritter, Frank Ellis, Nelson McDowell, Muriel Evans, Nolan Willis, Tom London, Reed Howes, Steve Clark.

See *SONG OF THE GRINGO.*

ROMANCE AND RHYTHM   See *COWBOY FROM BROOKLYN.*

ROMANCE OF THE RIO GRANDE   20th Century Fox, 1941, B&W, 72 min. **Producer:** Sol M. Wertzel; **Director:** Herbert L. Leeds; **Screenplay:** Harold Buchman and Samuel G. Engel; **Cinematographer:** Charles G. Clarke; **Editor:** Fred Allen; **Cast:** Cesar Romero, Patricia Morison, Lynn Roberts, Ricardo Cortez, Chris-Pin Martin, Tom London.

The Cisco Kid (Cesar Romero) meets his double when an aging cattle baron calls for his grandson to take over the operation of his empire. When the grandson is felled by an assassin, the Cisco Kid steps in to find out who is planning to inherit the ranch and its fortune. The culprit turns out to be another relative (Ricardo Cortez). (See also *THE CISCO KID.*)

ROMANCE OF THE ROCKIES   Monogram, 1937, B&W, 53 min. **Producer:** Robert N. Bradbury; **Director:** Bradbury; **Screenplay:** Robert Emmett Tansey; **Cinematographer:** Tansey; **Cast:** Tom Keene, Beryl Wallace, Don Orlando, Bill Cody, Franklin Farnum.

A young doctor living in cattle country gets mixed up in a battle over water rights in this well-made Monogram oater. (See also *WHERE TRAILS DIVIDE.*)

ROMANCE ON THE RANGE   Republic, 1942, B&W, 63 min. **Producer:** Joseph Kane; **Director:** Kane; **Music:** Sam Allen, Bob Nolan, Glenn Spencer, and Tim Spencer; **Cinematographer:** William Nobles; **Editor:** Lester Orlebeck; **Cast:** Roy Rogers, George "Gabby" Hayes, Sally Payne, Linda Hayes, Harry Woods, Hal Taliaferro, Glenn Strange, Roy Barcroft, Bob Nolan.

ROMANCE RIDES THE RANGE   Spectrum, 1936, B&W, 59 min. **Producer:** Jed Buell and George H. Callaghan; **Director:** Harry L. Fraser; **Screenplay:** Tom Gibson; **Editor:** Arthur A. Brooks; **Cast:** Fred Scott, Cliff Nazarro, Marion Shilling, Buzz Barton, Bob Kortman.

ROOSTER COGBURN (aka: ROOSTER AND THE LADY)   Universal, 1975, Color, 108 min, VHS, DVD. **Producers:** Hal B. Wallis and Paul Nathan; **Director:** Stuart Millar; **Screenplay:** Martin Julien; **Music:** Laurence Rosenthal; **Cinematographer:** Harry Stradling Jr.; **Editor:** Robert Swink; **Cast:** John Wayne, Katharine Hepburn, Anthony Zerbe, Richard Jordan, John McIntire, Paul Koslo, John Lormer, Richard Romancito, Lane Smith, Warren Vanders, Jerry Gatlin, Strother Martin, Richard Farnsworth, Tommy Lee.

Rooster Cogburn, eye patch and all, is back. This time he teams up with minister's daughter Eula Goodnight (Katharine Hepburn) to help her find her father's killers. The plot unfolds as District Court Judge Parker (John McIntire) removes the heavy-drinking Rooster's badge for being too quick on the draw. He had recently shot three outlaws, and it seems his penchant for the trigger might prevent newcomers from settling in the Northern District of Arkansas.

Rooster returns to his favorite haven, Chen Lee's grocery store, to down a few more beers with his beer-drinking cat General Price. However, when a group of outlaws ambush a cavalry escort and steal a wagon load of nitro and guns, Judge Parker offers Rooster a $2,000 reward plus reinstatement of his position if he brings the outlaws in alive. It is while trailing the outlaws to Fort Ruby that he meets Eula, a tough, Bible-toting spinster, and her escort Wolf (Richard Romancito), a young Indian boy. They join Rooster in pursuit of the outlaws, and the fun and adventure begin in earnest.

While it would have been nearly impossible for a sequel to replicate the magical quality of *TRUE GRIT* (1969) and Wayne's classic originality as the one-eyed marshal, it would be in error to pay too much attention to the tepid reviews harnessed on *Rooster Cogburn*. Called by some part *True Grit*, part *African Queen* (1951), the interplay between Wayne and Hepburn, two aging pillars of the silver screen, is masterful and charming, and Wayne is at his comedic best as this unlikely duo beat the bad guys.

When they are about to part company, Rooster's goodbye to Eula is endearing. The uncouth Rooster tells the no-longer-so-prim Eula the sadness he feels: "Well ma'am . . . I don't know too much about thoroughbreds, horses, or women.

Them that I did know I never liked. They're too nervous or spooky. They scare me! But you're one thoroughbred filly that don't. 'Course I don't know what you're talkin' about half the time, but that don't matter. Being around you pleases me."

In a September 17, 1977, *TV Guide* interview, Katharine Hepburn had this to say about her crusty costar: "As an actor he has an extraordinary gift. A unique naturalness. An unself-consciousness . . . he's a very good actor in the most high-brow sense of the word. You don't catch him at it."

ROOTIN' TOOTIN' RHYTHM (aka: RHYTHM ON THE RANCH) Republic, 1937, B&W, 60 min, VHS. **Producer:** Armand Schaefer; **Director:** Mark V. Wright; **Screenplay:** Jack Natteford; **Music:** Fleming Allen, Gene Autry, Al Clauser, Ted Hooper, and Natteford; **Editors:** William Nobles and Tony Martinelli; **Cast:** Gene Autry, Smiley Burnette, Armida, Monte Blue, Al Custer, Wally Wales, Charles King.

See *TUMBLING TUMBLEWEEDS.*

ROSE MARIE (aka: INDIAN LOVE CALL) MGM, 1936, B&W, 113 min, VHS. **Producer:** Hunt Stromberg; **Director:** W. S. Van Dyke; **Screenplay:** Frances Goodrich, Albert Hackett, and Alice D. G. Miller; **Music:** Rudolf Friml and Herbert Stothart; **Cinematographer:** William H. Daniels; **Editor:** Blanche Sewell; **Cast:** Jeanette MacDonald, Nelson Eddy, Reginald Owen, Allan Jones, James Stewart, Alan Mowbray, Gilda Gray, George Regas.

Opera star Jeanette MacDonald tours Canada and makes an appeal for her wayward brother's release from prison. However, the brother (a very young James Stewart in one of his earliest screen roles) escapes and kills a Mountie. The temperamental MacDonald leaves her stage work behind, and with the help of an Indian guide she pursues her brother deep into the forest, attracting the attention of Mountie Nelson Eddy. Romance blossoms, and so do a number of Rudolf Friml songs, including the keynote "Indian Love Call," "The Song of the Mounties," "Just for You," and the title song and lasting standard, "Rose Marie."

The most popular film made by the screen team of Jeanette MacDonald and Nelson Eddy, this 1936 version of the Rudolf Friml musical is arguably the best of the three turned out by MGM. The studio also filmed the story in 1928 with Joan Crawford and in 1954 with Ann Blyth and Howard Keel. In order not to have it confused with the 1954 CinemaScope color version, the MacDonald-Eddy version is retitled *Indian Love Call* when it is shown on television.

A major reason for this film's success is the vivid outdoor feeling established by director Woody Van Dyke. The location filming at Lake Tahoe on the California-Nevada border injects a genuine western feeling into the film. Interestingly, before James Stewart became a major western player in the 1950s, his only excursions into the genre were as the brother on the wrong side of the law in this Eddy-MacDonald musical, and the spoof remake of the early Tom Mix talkie, *DESTRY RIDES AGAIN.*

ROSE MARIE MGM, 1954, Color, 104 min. **Producer:** Mervyn Le Roy; **Director:** Le Roy; **Screenplay:** George Froeschel and Ronald Millar; **Music:** Rudolf Friml, Herbert Baker, George Stoll, and Herbert Stoddhart; **Cinematographer:** Paul Vogel; **Editor:** Harold Kress; **Cast:** Ann Blyth, Howard Keel, Fernando Lamas, Bert Lahr, Marjorie Main, Ray Collins, Chief Yowlachie, James Logan.

In this remake of the 1936 film, Ann Blyth is a native of the Canadian Rockies who is in love with a trapper (Fernando Lamas). However, Lamas is on the run from Mountie Howard Keel. The picture was filmed in lavish Cinema-Scope, with breathtaking views of the forests, lakes, and mountains. In his last film, there is one dance production choreographed by Busby Berkeley.

ROSE OF CIMARRON 20th Century Fox, 1952, Color, 72 min. **Producer:** Edward Alperson; **Director:** Harry Keller; **Screenplay:** Maurice Geraghty; **Music:** Alperson Jr.; **Cinematographer:** Karl Strauss; **Editor:** Arthur Roberts; **Cast:** Jack Buetel, Mala Powers, Bill Williams, Jim Davis, Art Smith, Bob Steele, Dick Curtis.

Mala Powers is Rose of Cimarron, a white brought up by Cherokee Indians after her parents were killed by the Comanche. When outlaws murder her Indian parents, she sets out for revenge. She teams up with a young marshal named Hollister (Jack Buetel), and together they bring the outlaws to justice. Lots of good action, vivid color, and the presence of old-line westerners like Bob Steele and Jim Davis add to the texture of this solid B vehicle told from a female angle.

ROSE OF THE RIO GRANDE (1931) See *GOD'S COUNTRY AND THE MAN.*

ROSE OF THE RIO GRANDE Monogram, 1938, B&W, 61 min. **Producer:** Scott Dunlap; **Director:** William Nigh; **Screenplay:** Ralph Bettinson; **Music:** Charles Rosoff; **Cinematographer:** Gilbert Warrenton; **Cast:** John Carroll, Movita, Antonio Moreno, Don Alavardo, Lina Basquette, George Cleveland, Duncan Renaldo.

A young man disguises himself as a bandit in order to find the men who killed his family. John Carroll takes a stab at being (a dubbed) singing cowboy in this B costume oater.

ROUGH NIGHT IN JERICHO Universal, 1967, Color, 104 min, DVD. **Producer:** Martin Rakin; **Director:** Arnold Laven; **Screenplay:** Sydney Boehm; **Music:** Don Costa and Phil Zeller; **Cinematographer:** Russell Metty; **Editor:** Ted J. Kent; **Cast:** Dean Martin, Jean Simmons, George Peppard, Carol Anderson, Dean Paul Martin.

Dean Martin is an ex-lawman named Alex Flood, who comes to clean up the town of Jericho. However, his ruthless disposition comes out, and he takes over the town, ruling it with an iron fist—more ruthlessly, in fact, than the previous regime he had kicked out. He destroys anyone who challenges his rule. The only one with the guts to stand up to him is female stage line owner Molly Lang (Jean Simmons). Martin plays against type with only limited success, since his natural charm works against him in this extremely violent film.

ROUGH RIDERS' ROUND-UP Republic, 1939, B&W, 55 min. **Producer:** Joseph Kane (associate); **Director:** Kane; **Screenplay:** Jack Natteford; **Music:** Cy Feuer, William Lava, Joseph Nussbaun, and Victor Young; **Cinematographer:** Jack A. Marta; **Editor:** Lester Orlebeck; **Cast:** Roy Rogers, Lynne Roberts, Raymond Hatton, Eddie Acuff, William Pawley, Dorothy Sebastion, George Meeker.

A group of Rough Rider soldiers who fought in the Spanish-American War regroup later to take on a gang involved with a gold shipment robbery. This adventurous Roy Rogers entry benefits from a good plot line. Strains of the traditional "When Johnny Comes Marching Home Again" highlight the patriotic theme. (See also *UNDER WESTERN STARS*.)

ROUGH RIDIN' JUSTICE Columbia, 1945, B&W, 58 min. **Producer:** Jack Fier; **Director:** Derwin Abrahams; **Screenplay:** Elizabeth Beecher; **Cinematographer:** George Meehan; **Editor:** Aaron Stell; **Cast:** Charles Starrett, Dub Taylor, Betty Jane Graham, Jimmy Wakely, Wheeler Oakman.

ROUGHSHOD RKO, 1949, B&W, 88 min. **Producer:** Richard A. Berger; **Director:** Mark Robson; **Screenplay:** Hugo Butler and Geoffrey Homes; **Music:** Roy Webb; **Cinematographer:** Joseph F. Biroc; **Editor:** Marston Fay; **Cast:** Robert Sterling, Gloria Grahame, Claude Jarman Jr., John Ireland, Jeff Donnell, Myrna Dell, Martha Hyer.

Robert Sterling and kid brother Claude Jarman Jr. head west to start a ranch. One the way they are derailed by four dancehall girls heading the same way but stranded in a stalled buggy. They take the girls to the nearest ranch, where it is discovered that one of the girls is the homesteader's wayward daughter. Before long they find themselves threatened by three outlaws on the run from the law. Matters are complicated when Sterling finds himself falling in love with one of the girls.

ROUGH TOUGH WEST, THE Columbia, 1952, B&W, 54 min. **Producer:** Colbert Clark; **Director:** Ray Nazarro; **Screenplay:** Barry Shipman; **Music:** Stan Jones; **Cinematographer:** Fayte M. Browne; **Editor:** Paul Borofsky; **Cast:** Charles Starrett, Jack Mahoney, Carolina Cotton, Pee Wee King, Smiley Burnette.

ROUNDERS, THE MGM, 1965, Color, 85 min, VHS. **Producer:** Richard E. Lyons; **Director:** Burt Kennedy; **Screenplay:** Kennedy; **Music:** Jeff Alexander; **Cinematographer:** Paul Vogel; **Editor:** John McSweeney Jr.; **Cast:** Henry Fonda, Glenn Ford, Sue Ane Langdon, Hope Holiday, Chill Wills, Edgar Buchanan, Kathleen Freeman, Denver Pyle, Barton MacLane, Doodles Weaver, Casey Tibbs, Warren Oates.

Henry Fonda and Glenn Ford are a couple of middle-age cowboys in the modern-day West who really don't like the cowboy life much. Rather, they long for a place "where there ain't no grass, ain't no horses." In fact, they dream of making enough money to open a bar in Tahiti. Down on their luck, they make various futile attempts to earn a dollar. They think they get their chance when they accept a mean, unbreakable horse from rancher Chill Wills. The two make a pile of money betting on the horse, but their dreams soon fade when their horse tears down the stable.

A cheerful and lighthearted western comedy directed and scripted by the late Burt Kennedy, *The Rounders* pairs Henry Fonda and Glenn Ford for the first time. The veteran leading men complement each other well as two cowpokes with opposite dispositions who are forever on the verge of settling down. A first-rate supporting cast including female interests Sue Ane Langdon and Hope Holiday add to the wild and wooly fun, making *The Rounders* one of the sleeper hits for 1965.

For costar Sue Ane Langdon, making *The Rounders* for Burt Kennedy was among her most favorite screen endeavors, albeit, in one scene, a somewhat embarrassing one:

> One scene had Hope Holiday and I supposedly swimming nude in a trout stream. On the bottom we were wearing our bikinis, but we had no covering for the top. So to assuage our modesty, Hope and I decided to get falsies for protection. We taped these almost transparent falsies on our bodies. However, after being in the water for a few minutes, the falsies came loose and floated up to the top of the stream. So they had to fish the falsies out of the trout stream and re-shoot the scene. This time there were two wardrobe people waiting with robes for us when we finished.

While making *The Rounders*, Henry Fonda, who was an accomplished artist in oil and watercolors, began a painting of the pickup truck used in the picture. He gave it to Burt Kennedy, and the director treasured it his entire life. In his autobiography *Hollywood Trail Boss*, Kennedy calls Fonda, "a multi-talented gentleman, a gentleman in every sense of the word. And one of the best actors that ever worked in Hollywood."

ROUNDUP, THE Paramount, 1941, B&W, 90 min. **Producers:** Joseph W. Engel and Harry Sherman; **Director:** Lesley Selander; **Screenplay:** Harold Shumate; **Music:** Foster Carling, Phil Ohman, and Victor Young; **Cinematographer:** Russell Harlan; **Editor:** Carroll Lewis and Sherman A. Rose; **Cast:** Richard Dix, Patricia Morison, Preston Foster, Don Wilson, Ruth Donnelly, Dick Curtis.

A rancher planning to wed the girl he loves must contend with her ex-lover, previously presumed dead, who returns on their wedding day in this remake of a romantic oater originally filmed in 1920 with Fatty Arbuckle.

ROUND-UP TIME IN TEXAS Republic, 1937, B&W, 63 min. **Producer:** Nat Levine; **Director:** Joseph Kane; **Screenplay:** Oliver Drake; **Music:** Arthur Kay, Raoul Kraushaar, Raffaello Penso, and Hugo Risenfeld; **Cinematographer:** William Nobles; **Editor:** Lester Orlebeck; **Cast:** Gene Autry, Smiley Burnette, Maxine Doyle, Le Roy Mason.

ROVING ROGUE See OUTLAWS OF THE ROCKIES.

ROVIN' TUMBLEWEEDS Republic, 1939, B&W, 62 min. **Producer:** William Berke (associate); **Director:** George Sherman; **Screenplay:** Betty Burbridge, Dorrell McGowan, and Stuart E. McGowan; **Music:** Gene Autry, Johnny Marvin, and Fred Rose; **Cinematographer:** William Nobles; **Editor:** Tony Martinelli; **Cast:** Gene Autry, Smiley Burnette, Mary Carlisle, Douglass Dumbrille, William Farnum, Lee "Lasses" White, Gordon Hart.

When corrupt politicians fail to pass a flood control bill and a massive flood follows, singer Gene Autry gets elected to Congress in order to get a flood bill passed. One of the top Autry entries for Republic, this one features Gene getting married at the finale. Gene also sings his signature theme song, "Back in the Saddle Again."

ROYAL MOUNTED PATROL (aka: GIANTS A'FIRE, UK) Columbia, 1941, B&W, 59 min. **Producer:** William A. Berke; **Director:** Lambert Hillyer; **Screenplay:** Winston Miller; **Cinematographer:** George Meehan; **Editor:** John Sweeney; **Cast:** Charles Starrett, Russell Hayden, Wanda McKay, Donald Curtis, Lloyd Bridges, Evan Thomas.

Two Mounties vie for the same girl, a teacher who works at a remote post and happens to be the sister of a corrupt lumber boss. The film was the first of a series for Columbia costarring the popular Charles Starrett and Russell Hayden. Other features in this series include *Bad Men of the Hills, Down Rio Grande Way, Overland to Deadwood, Riders of the Badlands, Riders of the Northland, West of Tombstone.*

RUGGLES OF RED GAP Paramount, 1935, B&W, 90 min. **Producer:** Arthur Hornblow Jr.; **Director:** Leo McCarey; **Screenplay:** Walter DeLeon and Harlan Thompson; **Music:** John Leipold and Heinz Roemheld; **Cinematographer:** Alfred Gilks; **Editor:** Edward Dmytryk; **Cast:** Charles Laughton, Mary Boland, Charles Ruggles, ZaSu Pitts, Roland Young, Leila Hyams.

While vacationing in Paris, Mr. and Mrs. Floud (Charles Ruggles and Mary Boland) win the Earl of Burnstead's butler Ruggles (Charles Laughton) in a card game. The uncouth Floud and his socially ambitious wife take the butler back to the town of Red Gap, where Laughton is mistaken for a British army officer and accorded celebrity status. Town spinster ZaSu Pitts takes a shine to the butler, and they fall in love. With his newfound freedom and confidence, Laughton marries Pitts, and together they open up a restaurant.

This filming of the Harry Leon Wilson novel is a sheer comedy delight and was nominated for an Academy Award as Best Picture. Charles Laughton won the New York Film Critics Award as Best Actor in 1935 for his work in both *Ruggles of Red Gap* and *Mutiny on the Bounty*. The story was filmed twice before: in 1918 by Essanay and in 1923 by Paramount. It was remade in 1950 as *Fancy Pants* with Bob Hope.

RUMPO KID, THE See CARRY ON COWBOY.

RUN FOR COVER Paramount, 1955, Color, 93 min. **Producers:** William H. Pine and William C. Thomas; **Director:** Nicholas Ray; **Screenplay:** Winston Miller; **Music:** Howard Jackson; **Cinematographer:** Daniel L. Flapp; **Editor:** Howard Smith; **Cast:** James Cagney, Viveca Lindfors, John Derek, Jean Hersholt, Grant Withers, Jack Lambert, Ray Teal, Denver Pyle.

James Cagney is Matt Dow, a tough westerner recently released from prison for a crime he did not commit. On the road he meets and befriends a younger man named Davey (John Derek). Soon, however, the two are mistaken for a couple of bank robbers, and in the ensuing strife Davey sustains a severe injury. The remorseful townspeople, eager to atone, respond for their misdeeds by making Matt sheriff and Davey his deputy.

The interplay between the two is interesting. Because he is anxious to turn Davey into the son he lost some 16 years ago, Matt overlooks the younger man's rebellious tendencies, and before long they are on opposite sides of the law. In the final showdown Matt is forced to kill Davey, whose antisocial behavior has reached beyond the extremes of decency. The grateful townspeople heap a monetary reward on Matt, who flings it back at their feet in disgust. "With Davey's compliments," he replies.

An interesting film with a familiar theme, *Run for Cover* succeeds in exploring the complex relationship between the two protagonists and the time-honored Code of the West, which the older man is called upon to enforce and then to endure. Author and film critic Richard Schickel calls Cagney's work in this film "his sunniest Fifties performance."

RUNNING WILD (aka: DELIVER US FROM EVIL) Golden Circle, 1973, Color, 104 min. **Producer:** Robert McCahon; **Director:** McCahon; **Screenplay:** Finley Hunt, McCahon, and Maurice Tombragel; **Music:** Luchi De Jesus; **Cinematographer:** Bill Butler; **Editor:** Arnold Freeman; **Cast:** Lloyd Bridges, Dina Merrill, Pat Hingle, Morgan Woodward, Gilbert Roland, Fred Betts, Slavio Martinez, R. G. Armstrong.

A woman journalist doing a photo story in Colorado becomes alarmed at the treatment accorded to wild horses. This entertaining, lesser-known film was reissued in 1976 by Dimension Pictures as *Deliver Us From Evil*.

RUN OF THE ARROW RKO, 1957, Color, 86 min. **Producer:** Samuel Fuller; **Director:** Fuller; **Screenplay:** Fuller; **Music:** Victor Young; **Cinematographer:** Joseph Biroc; **Editor:** Gene Fowler Jr.; **Cast:** Rod Steiger, Sarita Montiel, Brian Keith, Ralph Meeker, J. C. Flippen, Charles Bronson, Olive Carey, Tim McCoy, Frank DeKova.

A Confederate veteran (Rod Steiger with an Irish brogue) refuses to accept the surrender at Appomattox, deciding instead to live with the Sioux. He forsakes his country and takes a Sioux wife, but when the Sioux go to war with the U.S. Army, he is forced to make a choice regarding his real loyalty. The title comes from a scene in which he and an old scout are captured and then try to escape from a band of drunken Sioux by outrunning their arrows.

An interesting if uneven story bolstered by a good supporting cast, *Run of the Arrow* was originally advertised "as the first motion picture to portray American Indians with authentic realism," which it wasn't. Instead, it might have been the first film in which a white man not only wants to join the Indians but is willing to undergo a ferocious entrance exam. Reportedly Angie Dickinson dubbed the voice of Montiel, who plays Yellow Moccasin, Steiger's Indian wife.

RUSTLERS RKO, 1949, B&W, 61 min. **Producer:** Herman Schlom; **Director:** Lesley Selander; **Screenplay:** Jack Natteford and Luci Ward; **Music:** Paul Sawtell; **Cinematographer:** J. Roy Hunt; **Editor:** Frank Doyle; **Cast:** Tim Holt, Richard Martin, Martha Hyer, Steve Brodie, Lois Andrews, Harry Shannon, Addison Richards.

RUSTLER'S HIDEOUT PRC, 1945, B&W, 60 min. **Producer:** Sigmund Neufeld; **Director:** Sam Newfeld; **Screenplay:** Joseph O'Donnell; **Cinematographer:** Jack Greenhalgh; **Editor:** Holbrook N. Todd; **Cast:** Buster Crabbe, Al St. John, Ed Cassidy, Lane Chandler, Al Furguson, Charles King, Terry Frost.

RUSTLERS OF DEVIL'S CANYON Republic, 1947, B&W, 58 min. **Producer:** Sidney Picker; **Director:** R. G. Springsteen; **Screenplay:** Earle Snell; **Cinematographer:** William Bradford; **Editor:** Frank Arrigo; **Cast:** Allan Lane, Robert Blake, Martha Wentworth, Peggy Stewart, Arthur Space, Roy Barcroft, Tom London.

RUSTLERS OF THE BADLANDS Columbia, 1945, B&W, 55 min. **Producer:** Colbert Clark; **Director:** Derwin Abrahams; **Screenplay:** J. Benton Cheney; **Cinematographer:** George Meehan; **Editor:** Aaron Stell; **Cast:**

Charles Starrett, Carla Balenda (as Sally Bliss), Roy Barcroft, George Eldredge, Karl Hackett, Tex Harding.

RUSTLERS' PARADISE Ajax, 1935, B&W, 61 min, VHS. **Producer:** William Berke; **Director:** Harry L. Fraser; **Cinematographer:** Robert E. Cline; **Editor:** Arthur A. Brooks; **Cast:** Harry Carey, Gertrude Messinger, Edmund Cobb, Carmen Bailey.

Cheyenne Kincaid (Harry Carey) searches for his wife and daughter, who had been kidnapped by an outlaw years earlier. To find them he infiltrates the El Diablo gang, whose leader he suspects of being the kidnapper.

Western screen icon Harry Carey made four pictures for the independent Ajax Pictures in 1935. The others include *Last of the Clintons, Wagon Trail,* and *Wild Mustang.*

RUSTLERS' RANCH See *CHEYENNE CYCLONE.*

RUSTLERS' RHAPSODY Paramount, 1985, Color, 88 min, VHS. **Producers:** David Giler; **Director:** Hugh Wilson; **Screenplay:** Wilson; **Music:** Steve Dorff; **Cinematographer:** Jose Luis Alcaine; **Editors:** Zach Staenberg and Colin Wilson; **Cast:** Patrick Wayne, Tom Berenger, G. W. Bailey, Marilu Henner, Andy Griffith.

This satire on the old western musicals has a singing cowboy and his pal wandering through the West, when they come upon a small town where the sheepherders are being exploited by a corrupt cattle baron. Andy Griffith is especially funny as the effeminate cattle baron trying to take over the dusty old town.

What makes this film unique is the opening. The film begins with the audience watching a black-and-white horse opera. The narrator wonders what such a movie would be like today. Suddenly the screen turns to color, and singing cowboy Rex O'Herlenan (Tom Berenger) and pal Bob Barber (Patrick Wayne) enter the town run by Griffith. They also find an assortment of clichéd characters befitting the cowboy oaters of yesteryear, including Marilu Henner as the saloon dance-hall girl, G. W. Bailey as the town drunk, and a bevy of Italian cowboys in long raincoats.

RUSTLER'S ROUND-UP (aka: RUSTLER'S HIDEOUT) Universal, 1946, B&W, 57 min. **Producer:** Wallace Fox; **Director:** Fox; **Screenplay:** Jack Natteford; **Music:** Milton Rosen, Hans J. Salter, and Frank Skinner; **Cinematographer:** Maury Gertsman; **Editor:** Saul A. Goodkind; **Cast:** Kirby Grant, Jane Martin, Fuzzy Knight, Edmund Cobb, Ethan Ladlaw, Earle Hodgins, Kermit Maynard.

RUSTLERS' VALLEY Paramount, 1937, B&W, 61 min, VHS. **Producer:** Harry Sherman; **Director:** Nate Watt; **Screenplay:** Harry O'Hoyt; **Cinematographer:** Russell Harlan; **Editor:** Sherman Rose; **Cast:** William Boyd,

George "Gabby" Hayes, Russell Hayden, Morris Ankrum, Lee J. Cobb (as Lee Colt).

RUTHLESS FOUR, THE (aka: *OGNUNO PER SEE*; EVERY MAN FOR HIMSELF; EACH ONE FOR HIMSELF; SAM COOPER'S GOLD) MGM, 1968, Color, 97 min, VHS. **Producers:** Luciano Ercoli and Alberto Pugliese; **Director:** Giorgio Capitini; **Screenplay:** Augusto Caminito and Fernando Di Leo; **Music:** Carlo Rustichelli; **Cinematographer:** Sergio d'Offizi;

Editor: Renato Cinquini; **Cast:** Van Heflin, Gilbert Roland, George Hilton, Klaus Kinski, Sarah Ross.

This Italian/Spanish venture has an old prospector teaming with his grandson, a friend, and an old comrade to help search for the comrade's rich gold mine. However, the four fall out among themselves over the gold in a Nevada mine. Van Heflin is excellent as Sam Cooper in this interesting, foreign-made western that explores the ambiguous and complex relationship of four men hunting for gold.

SABRE AND THE ARROW, THE See *LAST OF THE COMANCHES.*

SACKETTS, THE NBC-TV/Media Productions, 1979, Color, 200 min. **Producers:** John Copeland and Douglas Netter; **Director:** Robert Totten; **Teleplay:** Jim Byrnes; **Music:** Jerrold Immel; **Cinematographer:** Jack Whitman; **Editor:** Howard A. Smith; **Cast:** Sam Elliott, Tom Selleck, Jeff Osterhage, Glenn Ford, Ben Johnson, Gilbert Roland, John Vernon, Ruth Roman, Jack Elam, Gene Evans, L. Q. Jones, Paul Koslo, Mercedes McCambridge, Slim Pickins, Pat Buttram, Buck Taylor.

Brothers Tell, Orrin, and Tyrell (Sam Elliott, Tom Selleck, and Jeff Osterhage) head out West from their home in Tennessee in this adaptation of two Louis L'Amour novels, *The Daybreakers* and *The Sacketts.* The eldest, Tell, is not heard from in years, as he is somewhere prospecting for gold. The two younger brothers, Orrin and Tyrell, are forced to leave home after Orrin's soon-to-be bride is killed on their wedding day, the result of a family blood feud, and Tyrell shoots the perpetrator dead. Eventually they start working as cattle herders under the supervision of ramrod Tom Sunday (Glenn Ford) and his top hand Cap Rountree (Ben Johnson). In time their paths merge with Tell's, and before the last fadeout the three Sackett brothers are forced to defend their honor and lives from a vengeful band of adversaries determined to do them in. The final shoot-out is a masterpiece.

Skillfully helmed by the late Emmy and Peabody award-winning director Robert Totten (TV productions of *The Red Pony*, 1973, and *The Adventures of Huckleberry Finn*, 1975), *The Sacketts* was voted one of the best TV western miniseries ever by the Western Writers Association. It was also named among the best westerns of the 1980s (TV or movies) by the National Cowboy Hall of Fame.

Totten's casting was near perfect, as he assembled a remarkable blend of young talent (Elliott, Selleck, and Osterhage) with solid screen veterans Glenn Ford and Ben Johnson and a supporting cast boasting the likes of Jack Elam, Gene Evans, Gilbert Roland, L. Q. Jones, John Vernon, and Pat Buttram. Moreover, Totten cast former Oscar-winning actress Mercedes McCambridge (as Ma Sackett) and ex-leading lady Ruth Roman (as Rosie).

In a 1995 interview with the author, Totten discussed his casting preferences: "What we did with *The Sacketts* because so much was going to be demanded of these guys, was to work in some not-too-nice-places. Nothing urban, it was to be super rural, and I wanted guys who looked like they belonged there. . . . A lot of guys auditioned. But the three guys who played in it—Tom Selleck, Sam Elliott, and Jeff Osterhage—didn't just show what great actors they were. They had to show how comfortable they were around horses."

A superb western with plenty of action, *The Sacketts* was a big impetus to the careers of Elliott and Selleck, both of whom went on to become major stars. For inexplicable reasons, Jeff Osterhage's career never took off to the extent that it should have. The three would appear again as the Sacketts in Andrew McLaglen's 1982 television western *THE SHADOW RIDERS.*

SADDLE BUSTER RKO, 1932, B&W, 60 min. **Director:** Fred Allen; **Screenplay:** Oliver Drake; **Cinematographer:** Ted D. McCord; **Editor:** William Clemens; **Cast:** Tom Keene, Helen Foster, Marie Quillan, Robert Frazer, Richard Carlyle.

SADDLE LEGION RKO, 1951, B&W, 60 min. **Producer:** Herman Schlom; **Director:** Lesley Sealnder;

Screenplay: Ed Earl Repp; **Music:** Paul Sawtell; **Cinematographer:** J. Roy Hunt; **Editor:** Desmond Marquette; **Cast:** Tim Holt, Dorothy Malone, Robert Livingston, Mauritz Hugo, James Bush, Movita, Cliff Clark.

SADDLEMATES Republic, 1941, B&W, 61 min. **Producer:** Louis Gray; **Director:** Lester Orlebeck; **Screenplay:** Herbert Dalmas and Albert DeMond; **Music:** Cy Feuer; **Cinematographer:** William Nobles; **Editor:** Tony Martinelli; **Cast:** Robert Livingston, Bob Steele, Rufe Davis, Gale Storm, Forbes Murray.

See *THREE MESQUITEERS, THE.*

SADDLE MOUNTAIN ROUNDUP Republic, 1941, B&W, 59 min. **Producer:** George W. Weeks; **Director:** S. Roy Luby; **Screenplay:** Earle Snell and John Vlahos; **Music:** Jean George and Joseph Winner; **Cinematographer:** Robert E. Cline; **Editor:** Luby (as Roy Claire); **Cast:** Ray Corrigan, John "Dusty" King, Max Terhune, Lita Conway, Willie Fung, George Chesebro.

SADDLE PALS Republic, 1947, B&W, 72 min. **Producer:** Sidney Picker (associate); **Director:** Lesley Selander; **Screenplay:** Jerry Sackheim and Bob Williams; **Music:** Ray Allen, Gene Autry, Perry Botkin Jr., Albert Gamse, Hy Heath, Joseph M. LcCalle, Harry Sosnik, and Britt Wood; **Cinematographer:** Budd Thackery; **Editor:** Harry Keller; **Cast:** Gene Autry, Lynne Roberts, Sterling Holloway, Irving Bacon, Daniel O'Flynn, Tom London.

SADDLES AND SAGEBRUSH Columbia, 1943, B&W, 54 min. **Producer:** Leon Barsha; **Director:** William A. Berke; **Screenplay:** Ed Earl Repp; **Music:** Cindy Walker and Bob Wills; **Cinematographer:** Benjamin Kline; **Editor:** William F. Claxton; **Cast:** Russell Hayden, Dub Taylor, Ann Savage, Bob Wills, William Wright.

Lucky Randall (Russell Hayden) and his pals come to the aid of a rancher and his daughter, who are being harassed by a gang of crooks. This good Hayden oater benefits from some nice music and songs by Bob Wills and His Texas Playboys.

Hayden, who gained fame playing Hop-Along Cassidy's womanizing sidekick Lucky in more than two dozen movies over a four-year period, also made starring features of his own, appearing in nearly 100 pictures with every Hollywood cowboy from Hoot Gibson to Roy Rogers.

He was somewhat of a rarity in the movie business. Had Hayden not become a movie cowboy, he had all the skills to have become a real one. Born on a ranch near Chino, California, he spent the first 17 years of life breaking horses and raising cattle. When his acting career ended, he produced the popular TV series *26 Men* (1957–59), the story of the original Arizona Rangers, starring Tris Coffin and Kelo Henderson.

SADDLE SERENADE Monogram, 1945, B&W, 57 min. **Producer:** Oliver Drake; **Director:** Drake; **Screenplay:** Frances Kavanaugh; **Music:** Drake, Bob Nolan, and Jimmy Wakely; **Cinematographer:** William Sickner; **Editor:** W. J. Austin; **Cast:** Jimmy Wakely, Lee "Lasses" White, Johnny James, Nancy Brinkman.

SADDLE THE WIND MGM, 1958, Color, 84 min. **Producer:** Armand Deutsch; **Director:** Robert Parish; **Screenplay:** Rod Serling; **Music:** Ray Evans and Jay Livingston; **Cinematographer:** George J. Folsey; **Editor:** John McSweeney Jr.; **Cast:** Robert Taylor, Julie London, John Cassavetes, Donald Crisp, Charles McGraw, Royal Dano, Douglas Spencer, Ray Teal.

Former gunman Robert Taylor settles down peacefully as a ranch owner until he has to deal with his quick-tempered, ill-mannered, and psychologically disturbed younger brother John Cassavetes. The story culminates in an ill-fated shoot-out between the two brothers.

Arguably Robert Taylor's best western—well acted, with a crisply written screenplay by Rod Serling (based on a screen story by Thomas Thompson) and a gripping, suspenseful plot—this Armand Deutsch production was filmed on location against a backdrop of the magnificent Colorado Rockies (in CinemaScope and Metro color). Julie London sings the lyrical title song written by the award-winning team of Ray Evans and Jay Livingston. In commenting on Cassavetes's performance as Taylor's unstable gun-toting younger brother, *Time* called him "a Stanislavsky-type buckaroo who looks sort of lost in all those wide open spaces."

As Robert Taylor wound down his long association with MGM, *Saddle the Wind* was one of two 1958 westerns (*The Law and Jake Wade* was the other) in which he played a reformed outlaw. "Robert Taylor didn't need much help, he was pretty good with guns," recalls actor Kelo Henderson, who was on the set to help the two stars with their gun work, and whose son Lars played Royal Dano's son in the film.

SADDLE TRAMP Universal, 1950, Color, 76 min. **Producer:** Leonard Goldstein; **Director:** Hugo Fregonese; **Screenplay:** Harold Shumate; **Cinematographer:** Charles Boyle; **Editor:** Frank Gross; **Cast:** Joel McCrea, Wanda Hendrix, John Russell, John McIntire, Jeanette Nolan, Russell Simpson, Ed Begley.

Joel McCrea takes the title role as a man who hires on as a ranch hand and becomes the guardian of four orphaned boys, to whom he reluctantly teaches the tools of survival. Hugo Fregonese's pleasant and taut little film concentrates on the less romantic everyday life of the American cowboy in the Old West. The realistic McCrea lends his patented authenticity to yet one more excellent role.

SAGA OF DEATH VALLEY Republic, 1939, B&W, 55 min. **Producer:** Joseph Kane; **Director:** Kane; **Screenplay:** Stuart Anthony and Karen De Wolf; **Cinematographer:** Jack A. Marta; **Editor:** Lester Orlebeck; **Cast:** Roy Rogers, George "Gabby" Hayes, Don "Red" Barry, Doris

Day, Jack Ingram, Hal Taliaferro, The Jimmy Wakely Trio, Frank M. Thomas, Lew Kelly, Lane Chandler.

In one of his best features, Roy Rogers returns to the ranch where his father was murdered to seek vengeance, but he finds the killer's chief henchman is his younger brother, played by Don "Red" Barry. The hidden identity or look-alike themes were common to Roy Rogers's films of the late 1930s. The Jimmy Wakely Trio consists of Wakely, Johnny Bond, and Dick Reinhart. (See also *UNDER WESTERN STARS.*)

SAGA OF HEMP BROWN, THE (aka: HEMP BROWN) Universal, 1958, Color, 80 min. **Producer:** Gordon Kay; **Director:** Richard Carlson; **Screenplay:** Robert Creighton Wiliams; **Cinematographer:** Philip H. Lathrop; **Editor:** Tony Martinelli; **Cast:** Rory Calhoun, John Larch, Russell Johnson, Fortunio Bonavona, Allan Lane.

Rory Calhoun is Lieutenant Hemp Brown, an officer in charge of the army payroll. When his convoy is robbed by outlaws who kill an innocent woman and his fellow soldiers in the process, Brown is branded a coward by a military court, stripped of all rank, and drummed out of the army. He then sets out to track down the man responsible and clear his disgraced name.

SAGA OF THE WEST See *WHEN A MAN'S A MAN.*

SAGEBRUSH LAW RKO, 1943, B&W, 56 min. **Producer:** Bert Gilroy; **Director:** Sam Nelson; **Screenplay:** Bennett Cohen; **Music:** Paul Sawtell; **Cinematographer:** Mack Stengler; **Editor:** John Lockert; **Cast:** Tim Holt, Cliff Edwards, Joan Barclay, John Elliott, Roy Barcroft, Ernie Adams, Ed Cassidy, John Merton, Edmund Cobb.

SAGEBRUSH TRAIL Monogram, 1933, B&W, 54 min, VHS, DVD. **Producer:** Paul Malvern; **Director:** Armand Schaefer; **Screenplay:** Lindsley Parsons; **Cinematographer:** Archie Stout; **Editor:** Carl Pierson; **Cast:** John Wayne, Nancy Shubert, Lane Chandler, Yakima Canutt, Henry Hull.

John Brant (John Wayne) is falsely convicted of a killing. Heading out west after making an escape, he finds and befriends the real killer, who eventually begins to suspect that Brant is not really an outlaw. Matters are complicated when both men fall for the same pretty shopkeeper. The film can also be seen in a computer-colorized version.

SAGEBRUSH TROUBADOR Republic, 1935, B&W, 68 min. **Producer:** Nat Levine; **Director:** Joseph Kane; **Screenplay:** Oliver Drake and Joseph F. Poland; **Music:** Gene Autry and Smiley Burnette; **Cinematographers:** Jack A. Marta and Ernest Miller; **Editor:** Lester Orlebeck; **Cast:** Gene Autry, Barbara Pepper, Smiley Burnette, Fred Kelsey, J. Frank Glendon.
See *TUMBLING TUMBLEWEEDS.*

SAGINAW TRAIL Columbia, 1953, B&W, 56 min. **Producer:** Armand Schaefer; **Director:** George Archainbaud; **Screenplay:** Dwight Cummins and Dorothy Yost; **Music:** Mischa Bakaleinikoff and Paul Mertz; **Cinematographer:** William Bradford; **Editor:** James Sweeney; **Cast:** Gene Autry, Smiley Burnette, Connie Marshall, Eugene Borden.

SALT LAKE RAIDERS Republic, 1950, B&W, 60 min. **Producer:** Gordon Kay; **Director:** Fred C. Brannon; **Screenplay:** M. Coates Webster; **Music:** Stanley Wilson; **Cinematographer:** John MacBurnie; **Editor:** Richard L. Van Enger; **Cast:** Allan Lane, Eddy Waller, Roy Barcroft, Martha Hyer, Byron Foulger, Myron Healey, Clifton Young.

SAM COOPER'S GOLD See *RUTHLESS FOUR, THE.*

SAM WHISKY United Artists, 1969, Color, 96 min. **Producers:** Arthur Gardner, Arnold Laven, and Jules Levy; **Director:** Laven; **Screenplay:** William W. Norton; **Music:** Herschel Burke Gilbert; **Cinematographer:** Robert C. Moreno; **Editor:** John Woodcock; **Cast:** Burt Reynolds, Clint Walker, Angie Dickinson, Ozzie Davis, William Shallert, Rick Davis.

A carefree gent falls under the spell of a beautiful widow who convinces him to take a million dollars in gold bars from a sunken riverboat and return it to the U.S. mint before the theft can be linked to her late husband. Reviews here have been mediocre at best, with a talented cast engaged in wasted energy. Character names are interesting: Burt Reynolds is Sam Whisky, while costar Clint Walker is O. W. Brandy.

SAN ANTONE Republic, 1953, B&W, 90 min. **Producer:** Joseph Kane; **Director:** Kane; **Screenplay:** Curt Carroll and Steve Fisher; **Music:** R. Dale Butts; **Cinematographer:** Bud Thackery; **Editor:** Tony Martinelli; **Cast:** Rod Cameron, Arleen Whelan, Forrest Tucker, Katy Jurado, Rodolfo Acosta, Roy Roberts, Bob Steele, Harry Carey Jr.

Texas cattleman Rod Cameron leads a cattle drive through enemy territory, not realizing that he is being used by his supposed allies. Forrest Tucker is the disreputable Confederate officer who double-crosses him, while Arleen Whelan is the disagreeable conniving southern belle who gives him plenty of grief as he journeys to Mexico to rescue a group of imprisoned cowboys. Good work by Cameron and the supporting cast as well as some nice songs add texture to this Republic oater.

SAN ANTONE AMBUSH Republic, 1949, B&W, 60 min. **Producer:** Melville Tucker (associate); **Director:** Philip Ford; **Screenplay:** Norman S. Hall; **Music:** Stanley Wilson; **Cinematographer:** Jack MacBurnie; **Editor:** Tony Martinelli; **Cast:** Monte Hale, Bette Daniels, Paul Hurst, Roy Barcroft, James Cardwell.

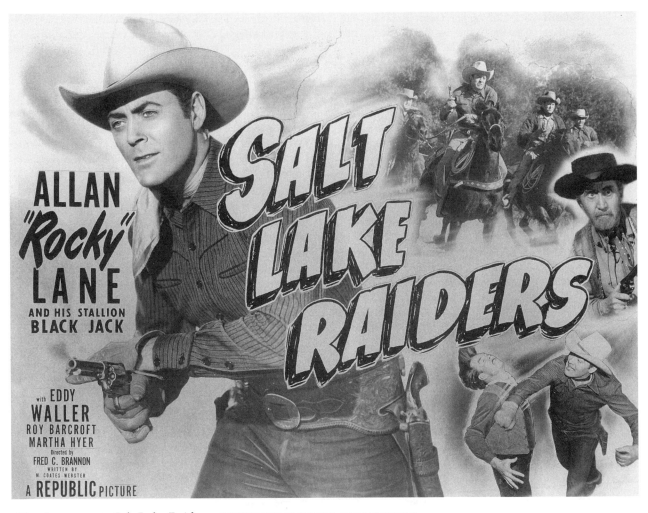

Allan Lane stars in Salt Lake Raiders (REPUBLIC/AUTHOR'S COLLECTION).

SAN ANTONIO Warner Bros., 1945, Color, 109 min, VHS. **Producer:** Robert Buckner; **Director:** David Butler; **Screenplay:** W. R. Burnette and Alan Le May; **Music:** Ray Heindorf, M. K. Jerome, and Max Steiner; **Cinematographer:** Bert Glennon; **Editor:** Irene Morra; **Cast:** Errol Flynn, Alexis Smith, S. Z. Sakall, Victor Francen, Florence Bates, John Litel, Paul Kelly, Robert Shayne, Monte Blue, Robert Barrat, Pedro de Cordoba, Tom Tyler.

Errol Flynn is cattleman Clay Hardin, who upon his return to San Antonio uncovers a rustling operation directed by saloon owner Roy Stewart (Paul Kelly). Alexis Smith is the tough dance-hall girl who sings in his saloon. Even though Flynn thinks she might be involved in the rustling scheme, he nevertheless finds time to romance her.

A true western of the old school without social significance or artistic trappings to encumber the plot, the film provides some good old-fashioned fun. The heroic Flynn is the ideal dashing hero, Kelly makes for a fine crafty villain, and an exciting barroom brawl enlivens the proceedings. *San Antonio* was scripted by W. R. Burnette and Alan LeMay

(who wrote the novel *The Searchers*), and it garnered two Academy Awards: for Best Song ("Some Sunday Morning," by Ray Heindorf, M. K. Jerome, and Ted Koehler); and Best (Color) Interior Art Direction (Jack McConaghy and Ted Smith).

SAN ANTONIO KID, THE Republic, 1944, B&W, 55 min. **Producer:** Steven Auer and William J. O'Sullivan (associates); **Director:** Howard Bretherton; **Screenplay:** Norman Hall; **Music:** Joseph Dubin; **Cinematographer:** William Bradford; **Editor:** Tony Martinelli; **Cast:** William "Wild Bill" Elliott, Robert Blake, Alice Fleming, Linda Stirling, Earle Hodgins, Glenn Strange, Duncan Renaldo, Tom London.

SAND (aka: WILL JAMES SAND) Republic, 1949, Color, 78 min. **Producer:** Robert Bassler; **Director:** Louis King; **Screenplay:** Martin Berkeley and Jerome Cady; **Music:** Daniele Amfitheatrof; **Cinematographer:** Charles

G. Clark; **Editor:** Nick DeMaggio; **Cast:** Mark Stevens, Coleen Gray, Rory Charles Grapewin, Bob Patten, Mike Conrad, Tom London, Paul Hogan, Jack Gallager.

Horseman Mark Stevens loses his prize stallion as a result of a railroad accident. He enlists the aid of another horse lover (Coleen Gray) in tracking the animal. The horse responds wildly to freedom and to anyone who might treat it badly. By the time Stevens locates the horse, he fears that the animal may have become a killer, but through care and kindness he is able to restore its confidence and continue its training. The film, which won an Oscar nomination for Charles G. Clark (Best Color Cinematography), is a must for all true horse lovers. It was filmed in the San Juan Mountains of Colorado and in Lake Arrowhead, California.

SAN FERNANDO VALLEY   Republic, 1944, B&W, 74 min. **Producer:** Armand Schaefer; **Directors:** Yakima Canutt and John English; **Screenplay:** Dorrell McGowan and Stuart E. McGowan; **Music:** Ken Carson, Charles Henderson, Gordon Jenkins, William Lava, Morton Scott, Tim Spencer, and Alyce Walker; **Cinematographer:** William Bradford; **Editor:** Ralph Dixon; **Cast:** Roy Rogers, Dale Evans, Jean Porter, Andrew Tombes, Charles Smith, Edward Gargan.

SAN FRANCISCO STORY, THE   Warner Bros., 1952, B&W, 80 min. **Producer:** Howard Welsch; **Director:** Robert Parrish; **Screenplay:** D. D. Beauchamp; **Music:** Paul Dunlap and Emil Newman; **Cinematographer:** John Seitz; **Editor:** Otto Ludwig; **Cast:** Joel McCrea, Yvonne De Carlo, Sidney Blackmer, Richard Erdman.

In the 1850s during the gold rush days, Yvonne De Carlo, the mistress of corrupt politician Sidney Blackmer, falls in love with mine owner Joel McCrea, who is out to get the goods on her crooked benefactor. Not surprisingly De Carlo switches her allegiance in this western melodrama where fortunes are made overnight and power is maintained by brutal frontier methods.

SANTA FE   Columbia, 1951, Color, 87 min, VHS. **Producer:** Harry Joe Brown; **Director:** Irving Pichel; **Screenplay:** Kenneth Gamet; **Music:** Paul Sawtell; **Cinematographer:** Charles Lawton Jr.; **Editor:** Gene Havlick; **Cast:** Randolph Scott, Janis Carter, Jerome Courtland, Peter M. Thompson, John Archer, Warner Anderson, Roy Roberts.

Following the Civil War, the four Canfield brothers take separate paths: Britt (Randolph Scott) goes to work building the Santa Fe Railroad; while younger brothers Terry, Tom, and Clint (Jerome Courtland, Peter M. Thompson, and John Archer) turn to a life of crime.

SANTA FE BOUND   Reliable, 1936, B&W, 58 min. **Producer:** Bernard B. Ray; **Director:** Harry Webb; **Screen-play:** Rose Gordon; **Cinematographer:** William Hyer; **Editor:** Carl Himm; **Cast:** Tom Tyler, Jeanne Martel, Richard Kramer, Slim Whitaker, Dorothy Woods, Charles King, Lafe McKee.

SANTA FE MARSHAL   Paramount, 1940, B&W, 68 min. **Producer:** Harry Sherman; **Director:** Leslie Selander; **Screenplay:** Harrison Jacobs; **Music:** John Leipold; **Cinematographer:** Russell Harlan; **Editor:** Sherman A. Rose; **Cast:** William Boyd, Russell Hayden, Marjorie Rambeau, Bernadine Hayes, Earl Hodgins, Eddie Dean.

SANTA FE PASSAGE   Republic, 1955, Color, 91 min. **Producer:** Herbert J. Yates; **Director:** William Witney; **Screenplay:** Lillie Hayward and Clay Fisher; **Music:** R. Dale Butts; **Cinematographer:** Bud Thackery; **Editor:** Tony Martinelli; **Cast:** John Payne, Faith Domergue, Rod Cameron, Slim Pickens, Irene Tedrow, George Keymas, Leo Gordon, Anthony Caruso.

A discredited scout (John Payne) and his sidekick (Slim Pickens) are hired to guide a wagon full of guns through hostile Indian territory. Despite Payne's hatred of Indians, he finds himself falling for a half-breed Indian girl who is a passenger on the wagon train. Lots of action and a fine cast highlight this exciting A-level Republic western.

SANTA FE SADDLEMATES   Republic, 1945, B&W, 56 min. **Producer:** Thomas Carr (associate); **Director:** Carr; **Screenplay:** Bennett Cohen; **Music:** Jack Elliott (songs); **Cinematographer:** William Bradford; **Editor:** Ralph Dixon; **Cast:** Sunset Carson, Linda Stirling, Olin Howard, Roy Barcroft, Bud Geary, Kenne Duncan, Henry Wills.

SANTA FE TRAIL   Warner Bros., 1940, B&W, 110 min, VHS, DVD. **Producer:** Hal B. Wallis; **Director:** Michael Curtiz; **Screenplay:** Robert Buckner; **Music:** Max Steiner; **Cinematographer:** Sol Polito; **Editor:** George Amy; **Cast:** Errol Flynn, Olivia de Havilland, Raymond Massey, Ronald Reagan, Alan Hale, William Lundigan, Van Heflin, Gene Reynolds, Henry O'Neill, Guinn "Big Boy" Williams, Alan Baxter, Ward Bond.

The third in a series of Warner Bros. westerns directed by Michael Curtiz begins with the West Point class of 1854. The leading protagonists are Jeb Stuart (Errol Flynn) and George Armstrong Custer (Ronald Reagan), two officer candidates from different sections of the country: Custer from the North and Stuart from the South.

The two classmates agree not to let politics interfere with their friendship, and they vie instead for the affections of pretty Kit Carson Holliday (Olivia de Havilland). The narrative follows the two officers as they leave West Point and are sent to serve at Fort Leavenworth, Kansas, where they encounter the fanatical John Brown (Raymond Massey) and his abolitionist activities. The evolving plot leads to Brown's seizure of the arsenal at Harpers Ferry, his capture, and his ultimate execution.

Recent critics too often attack the picture for its political ambiguity and for its treatment of Brown as little more than a religious fanatic (which, despite the nobility of his cause, he actually was). On the contrary, the film frequently implies that Brown's basic ideas and sentiments on the slavery question are sound. The picture has also been diminished as "worthless as history" and for an assortment of politically correct infractions endemic to our times.

The truth is that *Santa Fe Trail*, like many other Hollywood films, tried to straddle the fence and avoid pointing fingers as to who was responsible for the catastrophic Civil War. *Variety*, in its review of the film points out that the "picture shrewdly does not take sides on the slave issue" and called the film "a thrilling saga."

Officers Phil Sheridan, James Longstreet, Jeb Stuart, and George Custer were not all graduates of the West Point class of 1854. Nor are the ramifications of the Harpers Ferry episode given full and detailed exposition. Yet if *Santa Fe Trail* is not a particularly good history lesson, neither are its two predecessors. *DODGE CITY* (1939) and *VIRGINIA CITY* (1940) both relegated historical accuracy to the broader range of audience appeal and Hollywood flare. Michael Curtiz preferred to use historical characters and situations to enhance his story line. Interestingly, all three of these Curtiz-directed pictures featured the immensely popular Flynn in the lead roles. Robert Buckner wrote the screenplay and Max Steiner supplied the music for each film.

For sheer entertainment value, the film offers much, and there is enough action and suspense to keep it moving at an interesting pace. Flynn is dashing in his heroic assignments, and Reagan is pleasing as his good-natured sidekick. De Havilland, who also starred with Flynn in *Dodge City*, adds the right sparkle and chemistry in her tomboyish role.

Yet top acting honors go to 30-year-old Van Heflin as Rader, the erstwhile West Point cadet who casts his lot with John Brown; and to the charismatic Massey, who would repeat his role as John Brown in the 1955 film *SEVEN ANGRY MEN*. *Santa Fe Trail* can also be seen in a computer-colorized version.

SANTA FE UPRISING Republic, 1946, B&W, 54 min. **Producer:** Sidney Picker (associate); **Director:** R. G. Springstein; **Screenplay:** Earl Snell; **Cinematographer:** Bud Thackery; **Editor:** William P. Thompson; **Cast:** Allan Lane, Robert Blake, Martha Wentworth, Barton MacLane, Jack La Rue, Tom London, Dick Curtis.

SANTEE Vagabond Productions/Crown International Pictures, 1973, Color, 93 min, VHS. **Producers:** Caruth C. Byrd, Deno Paoli, and Edward Platt; **Director:** Gary Nelson; **Screenplay:** Brand Bell and Thomas W. Blackburn; **Music:** Don Randi; **Cinematographer:** Donald M. Morgan; **Editor:** George W. Brooks; **Cast:** Glenn Ford, Michael Burns, Dana Wynter, Jay Silverheels, Harry Townes, John Larch, Robert Donner.

Glenn Ford plays an aging bounty hunter seeking revenge for the murder of his son. However, when he kills the outlaw responsible for the deed, he adopts the man's son. This interesting western melodrama also contains a song by the popular 1960s rock group Paul Revere and the Raiders. It was filmed at various sections of New Mexico, including Albuquerque and Santa Fe.

SASKATCHEWAN Universal, 1954, Color, 87 min, VHS. **Producer:** Aaron Rosenberg; **Director:** Raoul Walsh; **Screenplay:** Gil Doud; **Music:** Henry Mancini and Hans J. Salter; **Cinematographer:** John F. Seitz; **Editor:** Frank Gross; **Cast:** Alan Ladd, Shelley Winters, Robert Douglas, J. Carrol Naish, Hugh O'Brien, Richard Long, Jay Silverheels.

While returning home from outpost duty, Canadian Mountain Police Inspector O'Rourke (Alan Ladd) rescues a tempestuous American girl (Shelley Winters) from an Indian attack. He returns with her to Fort Saskatchewan, only to discover that she is a fugitive from justice. U.S. Marshal Carl Smith (Hugh O'Brien) arrives to take her into custody, but a sudden Sioux uprising forces everyone to abandon Fort Saskatchewan and make the long trek to Fort Walsh. This is a dangerous mission to be sure, and one for which O'Rourke may well risk a court-martial for not surrendering the fugitive to Smith. The film's secondary theme concerns the relationship between O'Rourke and his Cree Indian half-brother Cajou (Jay Silverheels), whose friendship and trust is compromised as the film progresses.

Not among Ladd's better western endeavors, the film is made appealing by the brilliant Canadian Rockies setting and John Seitz's outstanding camera work, which highlights the magnificent splendor of the lovely landscape.

SATAN'S CRADLE United Artists, 1949, B&W, 60 min. **Producer:** Philip N. Krasne; **Director:** Ford Beebe; **Screenplay:** Jack Benton; **Music:** Albert Glasser; **Cinematographer:** Jack Greenhalgh; **Editor:** Martin G. Cohen; **Cast:** Duncan Renaldo, Leo Carillo, Ann Savage, Douglas Fowley, Byron Foulger.

SAVAGE, THE Paramount, 1953, Color, 95 min. **Producer:** Mel Epstein; **Director:** George Marshall; **Screenplay:** Sydney Boehm; **Screenplay:** John Taylor; **Music:** Paul Sawtell; **Editor:** Arthur Schmidt; **Cast:** Charlton Heston, Susan Morrow, Peter Hanson, Joan Taylor, Richard Rober, Donald Porter, Ted de Corsia.

Charlton Heston plays a white man whose family has been massacred by the Crow Indians and is brought up by the Sioux. He has learned every fighting trick in the Sioux warrior notebook, but when a war looms between the Indians and whites, he is faced with a crisis over where he really belongs. Based on a novel by L. L. Foreman, the film boasts excellent outdoor photography and a plethora of action-packed battle scenes.

SAVAGE PAMPAS Comet, 1967, Color, 99 min. **Producer:** Samuel Bronston; **Director:** Hugo Fregonese; **Screenplay:** Fregonese and John Melton; **Music:** Waldo de los Rios; **Cinematographer:** Manuel Berenguer; **Editor:** Juan Serra; **Cast:** Robert Taylor, Ty Hardin, Ron Randell, Rosenda Monteros, Marc Lawerence, Felicia Roc, Angel del Pozo.

Helmed and scripted (in part) by Argentine-born director Hugo Fregonese, and filmed in Spain, *Savage Pampas* features Robert Taylor as an army captain tracking an outlaw gang made up of deserters and Indians. He also persuades his military superiors to release prostitutes from prisons to serve as companions and morale boosters for his soldiers.

The film is a remake of the 1946 Argentine film *Pampa Barbera.* Care was given by the crew and production staff to find suitable locations in Spain to simulate corresponding terrain in Argentina.

SCALPHUNTERS, THE United Artists, 1968, Color, 102 min, VHS. **Producers:** Arthur Gardner, Arnold Laven, and Jules Levy; **Director:** Sydney Pollack; **Screenplay:** William Norton; **Music:** Elmer Bernstein; **Cinematographer:** Duke Callaghan and Richard Moore; **Editor:** John Woodcock; **Cast:** Burt Lancaster, Shelley Winters, Telly Savalas, Ossie Davis, Dabney Coleman, Paul Picerni, Dan Vadis.

When a trapper's furs are stolen by Indians, he joins forces with a runaway slave to get them back. Some good comedy and lots of plot twists highlight this overlooked late-1960s oater, in which Ossie Davis garnered a Golden Globe nomination as Best Supporting Actor. In the gaffe department, Burt Lancaster's character mentions the planet Pluto. The film was set in 1860, but the planet was discovered in 1930.

SCANDALOUS JOHN Buena Vista, 1971, Color, 113 min. **Producers:** Bill Walsh and Don DaGradi; **Director:** Robert Butler; **Screenplay:** Rod McKuen; **Cinematographer:** Frank V. Phillips; **Editor:** Cotton Warburton; **Cast:** Brian Keith, Alfonso Arau, Michelle Carey, Rick Lenz, Harry Morgan, Simon Oakland, Bill Williams, Edward Faulkner, Jimmy Lyden, John Ritter.

Brian Keith is John McCanless, a lovable, ornery, and eccentric elderly rancher, who refuses to sell to a land baron determined to flood his property. Instead, he prefers to fight the windmills of change as a modern-day Don Quixote in this spirited Walt Disney comedy western.

SCARLET RIVER RKO, 1933, B&W, 57 min. **Producers:** David Lewis and David O. Selznick; **Director:** Otto Brower; **Screenplay:** Harold Shumate; **Cinematographer:** Nicholas Musuraca; **Editor:** Frederic Knudtson; **Cast:** Tom Keene, Dorothy Wilson, Lon Chaney Jr. (as Creighton Chaney), Betty Furness, Roscoe Ates, Edgar Kennedy, Yakima Canutt, Myrna Loy, Joel McCrea, Bruce Cabot.

While on location filming a movie, a cowboy star tries to help a pretty rancher from being swindled by a crooked foreman. This entertaining Tom Keene series entry for RKO takes a glimpse at movie-making and features young stars Joel McCrea and Myrna Loy. (See also *BEYOND THE ROCKIES.*)

SEA OF GRASS, THE MGM, 1947, B&W, 131 min. **Producer:** Pandro S. Berman; **Director:** Elia Kazan; **Screenplay:** Vincent Lawrence and Marguerite Roberts; **Music:** Herbert Stothart; **Cinematographer:** Harry Stradling; **Editor:** Robert Kern; **Cast:** Spencer Tracy, Katharine Hepburn, Robert Walker, Melvyn Douglas, Phyllis Thaxter, Edgar Buchanan, Harry Carey, Ruth Nelson.

Based on the novel by Conrad Richter, the film deals with the turbulent years when farmers and cattlemen fought for control of New Mexico land. Spencer Tracy stars as the hard-nosed rancher determined to thwart the western push of farmers onto his grazing land—his "sea of grass." Katharine Hepburn plays Tracy's more cultured wife, a St. Louis belle who feels for the farm families her husband is forcing into starvation by illegally keeping them from the land. The plot thickens when Tracy learns that his son (Robert Walker) was actually fathered by longtime rival Brice Chamberlain (Melvyn Douglas), a lawyer and judge favorable to the farmers, with whom his wife, in despair, had once had an unguarded moment or two.

A pure western soap opera, the overlong film nevertheless benefits from its grand cast, some excellent acting, and from cinematographer Harry Stradling's marvelous outdoor sequences covering the epic panorama of the New Mexico prairie lands.

SEARCHERS, THE Warner Bros., 1956, B&W, 120 min, VHS, DVD. **Producer:** C. V. Whitney; **Director:** John Ford; **Screenplay:** Frank Nugent; **Music:** Max Steiner and Stan Jones (title song); **Cinematographer:** Winton C. Hoch; **Editor:** Jack Murray; **Cast:** John Wayne, Jeffrey Hunter, Vera Miles, Ward Bond, Natalie Wood, Harry Carey Jr., John Qualen, Henry Brandon, Ken Curtis, Pippa Scott, Patrick Wayne, Lana Wood.

This film was based originally on a 1954 *Saturday Evening Post* serial by Alan LeMay entitled *The Avenging Texan*, which was later published in book form as *The Searchers.* Frank Nugent's screenplay begins with Ethan Edwards (John Wayne), an ex-Confederate soldier, returning from the Civil War to his brother's home in Texas. The rider and horse had come a long way. It is 1868, the war has been over for three years, and Ethan's whereabouts over that period are never explained. He is vaguely mysterious, and there is something much darker lurking inside him, something not easy to fathom. "Don't believe in no surrender," is all he tells the family.

For the story's purposes Ethan's new journey begins when his brother, sister-in-law, and nephew are brutally murdered by marauding Indians, the result of a Comanche raid. Ethan and his adopted nephew Martin Pawley (Jeffrey Hunter), part Indian himself, set out in search for young Debbie, the one surviving niece who is presumed kidnapped by Scar, the Comanche chief. The journey lasts five years as the two travel the seasons, the elements, and the dangerous terrain. A tremendously complex man—independent, steadfast, dedicated to mission, obsessive, ever the outsider—Ethan Edwards evolves from an uncompromising Indian hater bent on revenge to a more sympathetic avuncular figure who at film's end lifts his frightened niece (Natalie Wood) high in the air and in one of the cinema's great moments says tenderly, "Let's go home, Debbie."

With a budget of $2.5 million, John Ford shot the picture in two installments. Even before Wayne had finished shooting *Blood Alley* (1955) for Warners and William Wellman, Ford sent a company to Gunnison, Colorado, and Alberta, Canada, in early 1955 to shoot the snow scenes so essential in delineating the grueling nature of the search. On May 31, 1955, construction began in secluded Monument Valley, the furthest spot from a railroad in the entire United States and John Ford's favorite shooting location. Ford also hired Navajo Indians to play the Comanche because the Navajo were excellent horsemen and complemented his stuntmen.

While reviews were mixed initially and the film has been analyzed and overanalyzed by a wide array of critics and pundits ever since, few movies—and precious fewer westerns—have come to enjoy such lavish acclaim over the years. Released on March 13, 1956, *The Searchers* has been credited with influencing the work of such contemporary directors as Steven Spielberg, Martin Scorsese, and George Lucas.

The film also reunited Wayne with John Ford for the first time since *The Quiet Man* four years earlier, and it was the first western they did together since *Rio Grande* in 1950. Both actor and director were at the height of their skills, and at no time during their long association were they closer personally and professionally. Actor Harry Carey Jr., who had already worked with Wayne and Ford in *RIO GRANDE* (1950), *SHE WORE A YELLOW RIBBON* (1949), and *THREE GODFATHERS* (1948), saw a different John Wayne in *The Searchers*. He recalled filming *The Searchers* in a 1995 interview with the author.

> The first scene I had with Duke, I discovered my family's prize bull had been slaughtered. When I looked up at Duke during rehearsal, it was into the meanest, coldest eyes I had ever seen. I don't know how he molded that character. Somehow Duke became Ethan Edwards, on the screen and off.
>
> I played a kid named Brad Jorgensen. Duke comes to tell me he found the girl I loved dead. He said, "What do you want me to do, draw you a picture, spell it out? Don't ever ask me. As long as you live, don't ever ask me more." It was a great line that Duke did particularly well. I run off and get killed. It was one of the most intense scenes I ever did with him.

Wayne's gesture at the end of the film was homage to the memory of his hero and mentor Harry Carey, as Carey Jr. related in the same interview.

> My mom Olive Carey played my screen mom. The movement Duke made when he closed the door at the end of the picture was a tribute to my father. That was John Ford's idea. But the idea of putting his left hand over his right elbow, that was his idea. He was to look and then just walk away. But just as he turned, he saw my mom, the widow of his all-time hero, standing behind the camera, He raised his left hand, reached across his chest and grabbed his right arm at the elbow. My dad did that a lot in movies when Duke was still a kid in Glendale.

While Frank Nugent's screenplay was written with John Wayne specifically in mind, two new characters were added to provide the film with some comic relief and to detract from the unabashed grimness of the original story: Mose Harper, a somewhat senile old man played by Hank Worden; and the Reverend Sam Clayton, played by Ward Bond. Wayne's catchphrase in the film, "That'll be the day," immediately entered the teenage jargon of the day, inspiring singer-songwriter Buddy Holly to write his 1957 hit song of the same name.

A masterpiece of cinematic art, *The Searchers* came up empty-handed at Oscar time, receiving nominations only for Best Editing (Jack Murray) and Best Original Musical Score (Max Steiner). However, it was later selected as a National Film Registry Outstanding Film, joining a handful of westerns including *HIGH NOON* (1952), *HOW THE WEST WAS WON* (1962), *MY DARLING CLEMENTINE* (1946), *THE OUTLAW JOSEY WALES* (1976), *RIDE THE HIGH COUNTRY* (1962), and *SHANE* (1953) to be accorded such an honor. In addition, the film has been named one of the American Film Institute Top 100 motion pictures.

SECRET OF TREASURE MOUNTAIN Columbia, 1956, B&W, 68 min, VHS. **Producer:** Wallace MacDonald; **Director:** Seymour Friedman; **Screenplay:** David Lang; **Music:** Mischa Bakaleinikoff; **Cinematographer:** Benjamin H. Kline; **Editor:** Edwin H. Bryant; **Cast:** Valerie French, Raymond Burr, William Prince, Lance Fuller, Susan Cummings, Pat Hogan.

This low-budget film from Columbia Pictures finds four men searching the desert for Indian treasure. Matters are complicated when they discover an old man and his daughter living next to the booty.

SECRET PATROL Columbia, 1936, B&W, 60 min. **Producer:** Kenneth J. Bishop (associate); **Director:** David Selman; **Screenplay:** J. P. McGowan and Robert Watson; **Cinematographers:** William Beckway and George Meehan; **Editor:** William Austin; **Cast:** Charles Starrett, Finis Bartton, J. P. McGowan, Henry Mollison.

SECRETS United Artists, 1933, B&W, 90 min. **Producer:** Mary Pickford; **Director:** Frank Borzage; **Screenplay:** Salisbury Field, Frances Marion, and Leonard Praskins; **Music:** Alfred Newman; **Cinematographer:** Ray June;

Editor: Hugh Bennett; **Cast:** Mary Pickford, Leslie Howard, C. Aubrey Smith, Blanche Frederici, Doris Lloyd.

A young couple, recently eloped, take a wagon train west and settle down as cattle ranchers. The husband becomes a rising star in politics until news of a love affair destroys his career. This well-made yet ponderous film is stronger on emotional qualities than on western action, with some of its biggest scenes being lifted directly from James Cruze's silent epic *THE COVERED WAGON* (1923). *Secrets* was the final screen outing for star Mary Pickford.

SECRETS OF THE WASTELAND Paramount, 1941, B&W, 66 min. **Producers:** Lewis J. Rachmil and Harry Sherman; **Director:** Derwin Abrahams; **Screenplay:** Gerald Geraghty; **Music:** Irvin Talbot; **Cinematographer:** Russell Harlan; **Editor:** Fred R. Feitshans Jr.; **Cast:** William Boyd, Andy Clyde, Soo Young, Barbara Britton, Douglas Fowley.

SEMINOLE Universal, 1953, Color, 86 min, VHS. **Producer:** Howard Christie; **Director:** Budd Boetticher; **Screenplay:** Charles K. Peck Jr.; **Music:** Joseph Gershenson; **Cinematographer:** Russell Metty and Virgil W. Vogel; **Editor:** Vogel; **Cast:** Rock Hudson, Barbara Hale, Anthony Quinn, Richard Carlson, Hugh O'Brien, Russell Johnson, Lee Marvin.

Rock Hudson is a West Point cavalry lieutenant who tries to help the Seminole Indians live their own lives free from the white man's law. Set at Fort King in the Florida Territory in 1835, *Seminole* starts with Hudson's court-martial for supposedly killing a sentry. The peaceful coexistence between settlers and Indians is compromised by the iron rule of the Indian-hating fort commander (Richard Carlson), who blames Hudson for killing the soldier while trying to restore the peace.

Barbara Hale is Hudson's childhood sweetheart, who allows him to meet Osceola (Anthony Quinn), now her fiancé and a mutual friend from their youth who had given up his own army career to become chief of the Seminole. Out of respect for his erstwhile friend Hudson, Osceola comes to the stockade under a flag of truce, but he is imprisoned by Carlson and dies in a detention pit.

Boetticher was among the pioneer Hollywood directors who gave the American Indian dignity on the screen in this thoughtful, well-crafted, and unusual film. Boetticher and Quinn would work together the following year in the director's 1954 film *The Magnificent Matador.* Both men both passed away in 2001, remaining friends until the end of their lives.

SEMINOLE UPRISING Columbia, 1955, Color, 71 min. **Producer:** Sam Katzman; **Director:** Earl Bellamy; **Screenplay:** Robert E. Kent; **Music:** Mischa Bakaleinikoff; **Cinematographer:** Henry Freulich; **Editor:** Jerome Thoms; **Cast:** George Montgomery, Karin Booth, William Fawcett, Steven Ritch, Ed Hinton.

There are no surprises in this familiar story of an army man who is raised by Indians and caught between bringing in the tribe's chief and securing the safety of his girlfriend, who has been kidnapped by errant braves.

SERENADE OF THE WEST See *GIT ALONG LITTLE DOGIES.*

SERGEANT RUTLEDGE Warner Bros., 1960, Color, 111 min, VHS. **Producers:** Patrick Ford and Willis Goldbrick; **Director:** John Ford; **Screenplay:** James Warner Belch and Goldbrick; **Music:** Howard Jackson; **Cinematographer:** Bert Glenn; **Editor:** Jack Murray; **Cast:** Jeffrey Hunter, Constance Towers, Billie Burke, Woody Strode, Carlton Young, Juano Hernandez, Willis Bouchey, Chuck Hayward, Walter Reed, Chuck Roberson.

Woody Strode plays Braxton Rutledge, a black cavalry sergeant and top soldier in the Ninth Cavalry Regiment, the great African-American unit that fought some of the hardest fights in the Indian wars of the 1800s. He is falsely accused of the rape and murder of a white woman. Much of the film takes place in the courtroom and is told through a series of flashbacks.

Ford, who was sympathetic to the struggle for black civil rights, was enthusiastic about the film early on. He was also aware of the potential commercial possibilities of the film, but he seemed to lose interest in the project once filming began, eventually calling it "just another job of work." Of the 50 working days Ford allotted for the film, a full 80 percent of the film was shot on the Warner Bros. lot and not on location in Monument Valley.

The picture was the first major Hollywood film with an African American as its hero, and it was Ford's tribute to the black cavalryman. Warner Bros., sensitive about possible criticism from the black community, screened the film for a number of civil rights leaders at various stages before its completion, always with positive results. Yet upon its release, the picture was generally not well received by critics, black and white alike, although *Variety* lauded it for dealing "frankly, if not too deeply, with racial prejudice in the post-Civil war era" and noted that "Ford expertly blends the action-pictorial and story elements to create lively physical excitement. . . ."

The film still holds up as a tense compelling western courtroom drama with a strong sense of mystery and escalating suspense. Another plus is Woody Strode's excellent performance in the title role. Ford gave Strode, a former football and track star at UCLA (where he was a teammate of Jackie Robinson's), his most challenging acting assignment, and Strode responded with a top-flight, endearing, and versatile portrayal of First Sergeant Rutledge. Ford would use Strode again in two more pictures: *TWO RODE TOGETHER* (1961), as an Indian scout; and *The Man Who Shot Liberty Valance* (1962), as Pompeii, Tom Donophon's (John Wayne) loyal hired hand and sidekick.

SERGEANTS 3   United Artists, 1962, Color, 112 min. **Producer:** Howard Koch; **Director:** John Sturges; **Screenplay:** W. R. Burnett; **Music:** Billy May; **Cinematographer:** Winton Hoch; **Editor:** Ferris Webster; **Cast:** Frank Sinatra, Dean Martin, Sammy Davis Jr., Joey Bishop, Peter Lawford, Ruta Lee, Buddy Lester, Phillip Crosby, Dennis Crosby, Lindsay Crosby, Dick Simmons, Michael Pate.

John Sturges's comedy western based on Kipling's poem *Gunga Din* stars Frank Sinatra, Dean Martin, and Peter Lawford as three madcap cavalry sergeants in the West. A warmed-over version of the 1939 film featuring Cary Grant, Douglas Fairbanks Jr., and Victor McLaglen as the three soldiers of fortune, this later entry has Sammy Davis Jr. as Jonah Williams, the Gunga Din part played by Sam Jaffe in George Stevens's masterpiece. Here, however, he appears as a freed slave who rides a mule instead of an elephant. He attaches himself to the three sergeants, helping them become heroes by thwarting an Indian attack on a group of settlers.

Interestingly, no mention is made of the obvious source (Kipling's poem) in the screen credits, although W. R. Burnett's screenplay not only owes its foundation to the story but faithfully adheres to it, but for the glaring exception that Davis, unlike Jaffe, does not die for his heroism. As *Variety* rightly points out in its review, ". . . the emphasis in *Gunga* was serious, with tongue-in-cheek overtones, whereas the emphasis in *Sergeants* is tongue-in-cheek, with serious overtones."

SEVEN ALONE   Doty-Dayton, Color, 97 min, VHS. **Producer:** Lyman Dayton; **Director:** Earl Bellamy; **Screenplay:** Eleanor Lamb and Douglas G. Stewart; **Music:** Robert O. Ragland; **Cinematographer:** Robert Stum; **Editor:** Dan Greer; **Cast:** Dewey Martin, Aldo Ray, Ann Collings, Dean Smith, Stewart Peterson, James Griffith.

A frontier family crosses the United States by wagon train, hoping to find a better life in the Oregon Territory. However, when their parents die en route, the seven children, led by the 13-year-old eldest boy, continue to make the perilous 2,000-mile trek from Missouri to their final destination in the West.

SEVEN ANGRY MEN   Allied Artists, 1958, B&W, 90 min. **Producer:** Vincent Fennelly; **Director:** Charles Marquis Warren; **Screenplay:** Daniel Ulman; **Music:** Carl Brandt; **Cinematographer:** Ellsworth Fredericks; **Editor:** Lester A. Sansom; **Cast:** Raymond Massey, Debra Paget, Jeffrey Hunter, Larry Pennell, Leo Gordon, John Smith, James Best, Dennis Weaver, Guy Williams, Tom Irish.

Abolitionist John Brown (Raymond Massey) and his sons fight zealously to free slaves during the pre-Civil War period. But when this leads to a massacre of slave owners, Brown and his family become hunted fugitives. Massey delivers an outstanding performance in this taut historical drama, a role he first played 18 years earlier in Warner Bros.' *SANTA FE TRAIL* (1940).

SEVEN BAD MEN   See *RAGE AT DAWN*.

SEVEN BRIDES FOR SEVEN BROTHERS
MGM, 1954, Color, 103 min, VHS, DVD, CD. **Producer:** Jack Cummings; **Director:** Stanley Donen; **Screenplay:** Albert Hackett, Frances Goodrich, and Dorothy Kingsley; **Music:** Gene de Paul; **Cinematographer:** George J. Fosley; **Editor:** Ralph E. Winters; **Cast:** Jane Powell, Howard Keel, Jeff Richards, Julie Newmar, Jacques d'Amboise, Nancy Kilgas, Russ Tamblyn, Tommy Rall, Marc Platt, Matt Mattox, Betty Carr, Virginia Gibson, Ruta Lee, Norma Doggett, Ian Wolfe.

Howard Keel is the eldest of seven brothers who run a ranch in Oregon in the mid-1800s. It is a lonely life for the Pontipee brothers, who crave female companionship. When oldest brother Adam (Keel) ventures into town, he convinces unsuspecting lass Jane Powell to marry him and accompany him to the ranch. However, he fails to tell her that he shares his house with his six unwashed, unwed brothers.

Powell cleans up the house and the brothers, and soon the grateful six start yearning for their own feminine company. They therefore decide to run off with six girls from town and take them back to the ranch for some old-fashioned fun and frolic. Conveniently, an avalanche strands the entire group at the ranch for the winter. The result is lots of songs, some absolutely brilliant dancing, and a mass marriage at winter's end that seals the charming story.

One of MGM's very best in its long catalogue of great musicals, *Seven Brides for Seven Brothers* garnered five Academy Award nominations, including Best Picture, Best Screenplay, Best (Color) Cinematography, and Best Editing; it won an Oscar for Best Music, Scoring of a Musical Picture (Saul Chaplin and Adolph Deutsch). It was also nominated for a British Academy Award by the BAFTA in the category of Best Film from Any Source, and was named the Best Written American Musical (1955) by the Writers Guild of America. Four of the songs for this sprightly musical were written by Gene de Paul with lyrics by the incomparable Oscar-winning wordsmith Johnny Mercer.

SEVEN CITIES OF GOLD   20th Century Fox, 1955, Color, 103 min. **Producers:** Richard D. Webb and Barbara McLean; **Director:** McLean; **Screenplay:** Robert C. Breen and John C. Higgins; **Music:** Hugo Friedlander; **Cinematographer:** Lucien Ballard; **Cast:** Richard Egan, Anthony Quinn, Michael Rennie, Jeffrey Hunter, Rita Moreno, Eduardo Norega, Leslie Bradley, John Doucette.

While looking for seven great deposits of gold made by the California Indians, the military commander of the Spanish conquistadors (Anthony Quinn) comes into conflict with Father Junipero Serra (Michael Rennie), the revered cleric who founded California's string of missions and who protected the Indians. One of Quinn's officers (Richard Egan) trifles with an Indian girl (Rita Moreno) and is forced to subject himself to unbearable tortures in order to keep the Indians from rising against his comrades.

Interesting, adventurous, and beautifully photographed by Lucien Ballard in De Lux Color and CinemaScope, this film offers some good historical insight into early California history.

SEVEN GUNS TO MESA Allied Artists, 1957, B&W, 68 min. **Producer:** William Broidy; **Director:** Edward Dein; **Screenplay:** Edward Dein, Mildred Dein, and Myles Wilder; **Cast:** Charles Quinlivan, Lola Albright, James Griffith, Jay Adler, John Cliff.

Stagecoach passengers are taken prisoners by a gang of outlaws intent on robbing a gold shipment. The limited material on this obscure oater suggests that it is a dull and poorly conceived picture.

SEVEN MEN FROM NOW Warner Bros./Batjac Productions, 1956, Color, 78 min. **Producers:** Andrew V. McLaglen, Robert E. Morrison, and John Wayne; **Director:** Budd Boetticher; **Screenplay:** Burt Kennedy; **Music:** Henry Vars; **Cinematographer:** William H. Clothier; **Editor:** Everett Sutherland; **Cast:** Randolph Scott, Gail Russell, Lee Marvin, Walter Reed, John Larch, Don "Red" Barry, Fred Graham, John Beradino, John Phillips, Chuck Roberson, Stuart Whitman.

Randolph Scott is Ben Stride, a grim ex-lawman whose wife has been killed in a holdup at a courier station and whose mission now is to track the seven men who were responsible for the murder. Making his way through the desert, he comes across a married couple (Gail Russell and Walter Reed) and two of the outlaws, (Lee Marvin and Donald Barry) who are after the stolen gold the couple is carrying.

The first of a series of extraordinary westerns Budd Boetticher made with Randolph Scott in the mid-to-late 1950s, *Seven Men from Now* is arguably the best of the superb lot. It was this film that helped elevate Boetticher to the front rank of western film directors (although he helmed a number of quality nonwesterns as well). It also began a successful and fruitful collaboration between Boetticher and writer (later director) Burt Kennedy.

Randolph Scott (left) stars in Seven Men from Now. (COLUMBIA/COURTESY OF BUD AND MARY BOETTICHER)

Yet it was John Wayne who set the wheels in motion for the film by asking Boetticher to take a look at Kennedy's story. The treatment impressed the director immensely and in an interview with the author he recalled a meeting with Kennedy and Wayne.

Duke actually produced two of the very best of my fifty-two films: *The Bullfighter and the Lady* and *Seven Men From Now*. That's the film that started Lee Marvin's career, and the first of the seven films I did with Randolph Scott. Five of those were written by Burt Kennedy.

When Duke's Production Company, Batjac, wanted to make *Seven Men From Now*, Duke called Burt Kennedy and me. I think Duke was always sorry he didn't play the hero in *Seven Men from Now*. I recall that Duke came in to have coffee with Burt and me one morning. He said "'Bood' and Burt, who do you think should play this fellow in the picture?" Out of respect to him we said, "Duke, we want you to do it." But for some reason he suggested Randolph Scott.

For Randolph Scott, *Seven Men from Now* began a cluster of movies that exemplified his best work, giving the actor a new image as the lone figure on a mission of vengeance or a similar private quest and solidifying his stature as a genre superstar. Lee Marvin's performance as the villain whom Scott fells with a single bullet is as interesting as it is compelling.

In his last public appearance at Hollywood's Egyptian Theater in September 2001, three months before his death, Boetticher lauded Lee Marvin's work in *Seven Men from Now* as one of true Oscar calibre. Ironically, Boetticher's favorite collaborator and good friend Burt Kennedy—who wrote both story and screenplay for *Seven Men from Now*—had passed away earlier in the year, with an ailing Boetticher driving to Los Angeles from his home in Ramona, California, three weeks before Kennedy's death, for one final visit with his dear friend and erstwhile colleague.

An exceptionally stylish film, brilliantly photographed by Lucien Ballard, *Seven Men from Now* was Boetticher's personal favorite among his western ventures. Until recently, the film had been unavailable for 40 years, remaining instead within the protected archives of Batjac Productions. Recent public screenings, however, have informed newer audiences what serious pundits, critics, and film historians have long known: that *Seven Men from Now* is truly one of the finest westerns ever made.

SEVENTH CAVALRY Columbia, 1956, Color, 75 min. **Producer:** Harry Joe Brown; **Director:** Joseph H. Lewis; **Screenplay:** Peter Packer; **Cinematographer:** Ray Rennahan; **Editor:** Gene Havlick; **Cast:** Randolph Scott, Barbara Hale, Jay C. Flippen, Jeanette Nolan, Frank Faylen, Leo Gordon, Denver Pyle, Harry Carey Jr., Michael Pate, Donald Curtis.

Randolph Scott plays an officer who returns from furlough to find that his regiment, Custer's Seventh Cavalry, has been wiped out by Indians. Accused of cowardice, he sets out to find out the true cause of the massacre at Little Big Horn and to bring back General Custer's body. Matters are complicated when the father of Scott's fiancée (Barbara Hale), Colonel Kellogg, becomes the new commander of the regiment and the man charged with investigating the recent military debacle.

SEVEN WAYS FROM SUNDOWN Universal, 1960, Color, 96 min. **Producer:** Gordon Kay; **Director:** Harry Keller; **Screenplay:** Clair Huffaker; **Music:** Irving Gertz and William Lava; **Cinematographer:** Ellis W. Carter; **Editors:** Carter and Tony Martinelli; **Cast:** Audie Murphy, Barry Sullivan, Venetia Stevenson, John McIntire, Kenneth Tobey, Mary Field, Ted Rooney, Suzanne Lloyd, Jack Kruschen.

Audie Murphy is a lawman charged with bringing bad guy Barry Sullivan to town to hang. Along the way, however, the two men become friends. The elegant outlaw teaches the naive lawman a lesson or two about life, while lawman Murphy teaches the dapper bad man a few things about morality. This well-written film remains among Murphy's best outings for Universal, with the two leads delivering good performances and an ending that borders on the unusual.

SHADOW OF BOOT HILL See *SHOWDOWN AT BOOT HILL*.

SHADOW RANCH Columbia, 1930, B&W, 64 min. **Producers:** Harry Cohen and Sol Lesser; **Director:** Louis King; **Screenplay:** Frank Howard Clark, George M. Johnson, and Clark Silvernail (dialogue); **Cinematographer:** Ted McCord; **Editor:** James Sweeney; **Cast:** Buck Jones, Marguerite De La Motte, Kate Price, Albert J. Smith, Robert McKenzie.

"All Talking Whirlwind Western" is the tag line for this very early Buck Jones talkie that has Buck taking on a crooked saloon owner who murders the foreman of a ranch run by a young girl. Filmed on location, it features songs such as "When it's Roundup Time in Texas" and "Ragtime Cowboy Jones." (See also *WHITE EAGLE*.)

SHADOW RIDERS, THE (aka: LOUIS L'AMOUR'S THE SHADOW RIDERS) CBS-TV, 1982, Color, 100 min. **Producers:** Hugh Benson, Dennis Durney, and Verne Nobles; **Director:** Andrew V. McLaglen; **Teleplay:** Jim Byrnes and Verne Nobles; **Music:** Jerrold Immel; **Cinematographer:** Jack Whitman; **Editor:** Bud Friedgen; **Cast:** Tom Selleck, Sam Elliott, Ben Johnson, Jeff Osterhage, Gene Evans, Katharine Ross, R. G. Armstrong, Jane Greer, Harry Carey Jr., Ben Fuhrman, Marshall R. Teague.

Based on a story by Louis L'Amour, this film tells the tale of two brothers searching for family members kidnapped by rebel guerrillas during the Civil War. This time Tom Selleck, Sam Elliott, and Jeff Osterhage (the Sackett Brothers in the

1979 film), as brothers Mac, Del, and Jesse Traven, take on a white slave trader (Gene Evans) and his cronies. Ben Johnson delivers a real showcase performance as the boys' irascible Uncle BlackJack Craven in this excellent made-for-TV western. It is also nice to see old-line players Jane Greer and Harry Carey Jr., as Ma and Pa Craven, the boys' parents. The movie is sometimes called *Louis L'Amour's The Shadow Riders*. (See also SACKETTS, THE.)

SHADOWS OF DEATH PRI, 1945, B&W, 1945. **Producer:** Sigmund Neufeld; **Director:** Sam Newfield; **Screenplay:** Fred Myton; **Cinematographer:** Jack Greenhalgh; **Editor:** Holbrook N. Todd; **Cast:** Buster Crabbe, Al St. John, Charles King, Eddie Hall, Dona Dax.

See OUTLAW OF THE PLAINS.

SHADOWS OF THE WEST Monogram, 1949, B&W, 60 min. **Producer:** Barney A. Sarecky; **Director:** Ray Taylor; **Cinematographer:** Harry Neumann; **Editor:** John C. Fuller; **Cast:** Whip Wilson, Andy Clyde, Riley Hill, Reno Browne, Bill Kennedy, Pierce Lyden, Keith Richards.

See ABILENE TRAIL.

SHADOWS OF TOMBSTONE Republic, 1953, B&W, 54 min. **Producer:** Rudy Ralston; **Director:** William Witney; **Screenplay:** Gerald Geraghty; **Music:** R. Dale Butts; **Cinematographer:** Bud Thackery; **Editor:** Richard L. Van Enger; **Cast:** Rex Allen, Slim Pickens, Jeanne Cooper, Roy Barcroft, Emory Parnell.

SHADOWS ON THE SAGE Republic, 1942, B&W, 57 min. **Producer:** Louis Gray (associate); **Directors:** John English and Les Orlebeck; **Screenplay:** J. Benton Cheney; **Music:** Mort Glickman; **Cinematographer:** Edgar Lyons; **Editor:** William P. Thompson; **Cast:** Bob Steele, Tom Tyler, Jimm Dodd, Cheryl Walker, Tom London, Yakima Canutt.

See THREE MESQUITEERS, THE.

SHADOW VALLEY PRI, 1947, B&W, 59 min. **Producer:** Jerry Thomas; **Director:** Rod Taylor; **Screenplay:** Arthur Sherman; **Music:** Pete Gates; **Cinematographer:** Ernest Miller; **Editor:** Joseph Gluck; **Cast:** Eddie Dean, Roscoe Ates, Jennifer Holt, George Chesebro, Eddie Parker.

See SONG OF OLD WYOMING.

SHADOW VALLEY (1954) See FOUR GUNS TO THE BORDER.

SHAKIEST GUN IN THE WEST Universal, 1968, Color, 101 min, VHS. **Producer:** Edward J. Montague; **Director:** Alan Rafkin; **Screenplay:** James Fritzell, Everett Greenbaum, Edmund L. Hartmann, and Frank Tashlin; **Cinematographers:** Vic Mizzy and Andrew Jackson; **Editor:** Tony Martinelli; **Cast:** Don Knotts, Barbara Rhoades,

Jackie Coogan, Don "Red" Barry (as Donald Barry), Dub Taylor, Ed Faulkner, Pat Morita, Ruth McDevitt, Myron Healey.

Don Knotts is Jesse W. Haywood, a dental-school graduate from Philadelphia who heads out west and finds himself involved with dangerous gunslingers and a beautiful girl. Don Knotts is at his funniest in this remake of Bob Hope's 1948 comedy classic PALEFACE. While not as entertaining as Hope's venture, this film supplies lots of laughs and offers some good family fun.

SHALAKO Cinerama, 1968, Color, 113 min, VHS, DVD. **Producers:** Artur Brauner and Euan Lloyd; **Director:** Edward Dmytryk; **Screenplay:** J. J. Griffith, Scott Finch, and Hal Hopper; **Music:** Robert Farnon; **Cinematographer:** Ted Moore; **Editor:** Bil Blunden; **Cast:** Sean Connery, Brigitte Bardot, Stephen Boyd, Jack Hawkins, Peter van Eyck, Honor Blackman, Woody Strode, Eric Sukes, Alexander Knox, Valerie French, Julian Mateos, Don "Red" Barry.

Filmed in Spain, helmed by Edward Dmytryk, and based on a story by Louis L'Amour, *Shalako* follows a group of Europeans on a sheep-hunting expedition who are attacked by Indians after being double-crossed by their guide (Stephen Boyd). Shalako (Sean Connery) is the lone gunfighter, knowledgeable in the ways of the Indian, who comes to their rescue. The romantic element pairs Connery with French siren Brigitte Bardot, who plays the Countess Irena Lazaar. Not only does he rescue the alluring Bardot, but he must also pit his wits against both the harassing Indians on the one hand and members of the expedition on the other, before finally saving the party from total destruction.

It took nearly four years for the film's producers to obtain the $5 million necessary for financing. But neither the all-star international cast nor the leading presence of Connery and Bardot resulted in the monetary and critical success their backers had anticipated.

SHANE Paramount, 1953, Color, 118 min, VHS. **Producer:** George Stevens; **Director:** Stevens; **Screenplay:** A. B. Guthrie; **Music:** Victor Young; **Cinematographer:** Loyal Griggs; **Editor:** William Horbeck; **Cast:** Alan Ladd, Van Heflin, Jean Arthur, Brandon De Wilde, Jack Palance, Ben Johnson, Emile Meyer, Elisha Cook Jr., John Dierkes.

The snowcapped peaks of the Grand Tetons provide the backdrop for this film set in a desolate Wyoming valley at the end of the 19th century. A small boy, his face perched flush between the antlers of a stately deer, watches as a man on horseback rides slowly toward the Starrett family farm. The stranger approaches, and the boy's blue eyes widen with awe. Outfitted in buckskin, a pearl-handled revolver packed solidly into his studded holster, the stranger resembles a knight-errant from another world.

Considered by many to be the greatest western ever made, George Stevens's *Shane* bypasses story and goes directly to the legend. Alan Ladd, in a definitive role, arrives out of nowhere to fight the final battle between ranchers led by Rufe Ryker (Emile Meyer) and homesteaders led by Joe Starrett. A beautifully crafted motion picture, *Shane* reflects a decency of spirit with a rare ending that truly tugs at the heart.

Though the subject matter in *Shane* is out of the familiar traditions of popular westerns—the conflict between cattlemen and homesteaders—there is nothing familiar with the way the material has been handled. Everywhere one sees indications of the barren and drab life of the homesteaders: the starkly realistic frontier town, the mud in the streets, the artifacts in the general store, the authentic items outfitted in the Starretts' kitchen. Images of sunlight, the shadow of rainstorms, and the eerie lights of night pervade Victor Young's beautifully melodic yet dramatically stirring musical score. (William Everson, calling it "incurably romantic," is a bit shortsighted and negates its overall excellence and impact.)

Producer/director George Stevens called Alan Ladd's performance in the title role one of the best ever by an American actor in a western. Ladd, he argued, had the capacity to convey to audiences a large measure of reserve, dignity, and decency. In fact, Stevens was so impressed with his work that he offered Ladd the opportunity to become associated with another classic, but Ladd refused to accept any role that would not give him star billing. The role of Jett Rink in *Giant* was therefore taken instead by a far-too-young James Dean.

"He loved the film and working with George Stevens whom he admired greatly," says Ladd's daughter Alana. "It was his favorite role by far." Unfortunately, Ladd did not have press agents working for his Oscar campaign. Paramount did little in promoting Ladd, who had broken from the studio to become a freelance actor, and the studio threw its full support behind ultimate Oscar winner William Holden for his work in *Stalag 17*.

Ben Johnson (a John Ford protégé) was handpicked by Stevens to play Chris Calloway, the tough ornery cowpoke who evolves from barroom bully to unlikely hero with great aplomb. William Everson, not overly fond of the film itself, considers Johnson's performance to have been the best among the film's strong cast, which includes top performances by stars Van Heflin, Jean Arthur, Brandon De Wilde, and Jack Palance; and supporting players Edgar Buchanan, Elisha Cook Jr., Emile Meyer, John Dierkes, and Paul McVey.

The fight scene between Chris and Shane (Johnson and Ladd) in Grafton's saloon remains one of the very best ever put on film. Johnson recalled staging the fight in a 1993 interview with the author.

> Stevens was a very patient director. He took a lot of time with that fight scene. It took about seven days to do it and he shot it from every angle and direction possible.
>
> Alan [Ladd] did a wonderful job. I'm the first tall guy that Alan ever let work in a scene with him. It was George Stevens that made him let me in there. What they did was

Alan Ladd (in a definitive performance) and Academy Award nominee Brandon De Wilde in George Stevens's Shane. *The film was nominated for six Academy Awards, including Best Picture.* (PARAMOUNT/AUTHOR'S COLLECTION)

> build a platform about yea high for Alan to work around on. And I'm down in this hole. I really liked Alan. He was a good actor—a very underrated actor.

Few films have integrated script, narrative, photography, music, and drama so successfully, including a closing scene that remains among the most haunting and memorable in American cinema. As the injured gunfighter rides alone into the wilderness, a heartbroken young boy with tears streaking down his face calls out to him, and the hills echo the boy's pleading but futile cry, "Shane, come back! Shane . . . Shane . . ."

The *New York Times* opined that *Shane* had "the quality of a fine album of paintings of the frontier." The *New York Post* argued that "it's only a Western in the sense that *Romeo and Juliet* is only a love story." *Variety* was equally enthusiastic: "Director George Stevens handles the story and players with tremendous integrity. Alan Ladd's performance takes on dimensions not hitherto noticeable in his screen work."

Ben Johnson, who that same year won the World's Rodeo Championship, had nary a doubt that he was involved in the making of a true classic:

> I felt we were involved with something great because everything about the picture was so real. [*Shane*] was made with a lot of integrity. To give you an idea, when it hits the air now,

it still plays as well as it did forty years ago. It was so real, it's just incredible. It stays with you. I was in it and I still like to watch it.

Based on Jack Schaefer's first novel, *Shane* garnered an Academy Award for Loyal Griggs for Best Color Cinematography. It also received five other Oscar nominations: Best Picture; Best Director (Stevens); Best Screenplay (A. B. Guthrie); and two nominations for Best Supporting Actor: 10-year-old Brandon De Wilde as Joey Starrett, the young boy in awe of the mysterious gunman; and Jack Palance as Wilson, clad ominously in black, speaking just 16 lines of dialogue, yet so menacing that even the dog slinks across the barroom floor, head bowed, as Wilson enters Grafton's saloon.

When Shane dispatches Wilson as well as the Rykers at the finale, Wilson collapses across the table. "Was that him, Shane?" Joey asks. "Was that Jack Wilson?"

"Yes, that was Wilson, all right," Shane replies. "He was fast, fast on the draw."

Selected to the National Film Registry, *Shane* was recently voted the Best Western of the Century by the Western Writers of America. It made the American Film Institute's controversial list of 100 greatest movies (#69)—a selection woefully short of western entries with only *HIGH NOON* (1952, #33), *BUTCH CASSIDY AND THE SUNDANCE KID* (1969, #50), *STAGECOACH* (1939, #63), *DANCES WITH WOLVES* (1990, #79), *THE WILD BUNCH* (1969, #80), *THE SEARCHERS* (1956, #96), and *UNFORGIVEN* (1992, #98) listed among the celebrated Top 100.

Released in theaters as late as 1967, *Shane* was the third highest-grossing film for 1953, behind *The Robe* and *From Here to Eternity*. The main musical theme (also known as "The Call of the Far-Away Hills," words added by Mack David) became a hit recording for Paul Weston and his Orchestra. *Shane* also marked the final film appearance for actress Jean Arthur, whose career dated back to 1923 and who came out of a seven-year retirement to play the role of Marian Starrett.

SHANGHAI NOON Touchstone Pictures, 2000, Color, 110 min, VHS, DVD, CD. **Producers:** Jules Daly and Ned Dowd; **Director:** Tom Dey; **Screenplay:** Miles Millar and Alfred Gough; **Music:** Randy Edelman; **Cinematographer:** Daniel Mindel; **Editor:** Richard Chew; **Cast:** Jackie Chan, Owen Wilson, Luci Liu, Brandon Merrill, Roger Yuan, Xander Berkeley.

It is 1881 in the Forbidden City of China, and Jackie Chan is a member of the Chinese Imperial Guard who heads to Carson City, Nevada, in the western United States to rescue a beautiful kidnapped princess. When he meets up with a laid-back outlaw (Owen Wilson), the fun and excitement begins as these two mismatched new buddies, with spectacular stunts and blatant irreverence, find themselves involved in a series of brawls and bordellos, an assortment of villains and Indians, and a never-ending array of adventures, misadventures, and martial arts.

This is an unusual western spoof, billed for promotion purposes as an "Eastern Western." There is fun to be had in the collision of two cultures when Jackie Chan's East meets Owen Wilson's American West. While it is certainly not for genre purists, Chan fans and less serious western aficionados should enjoy this film.

SHEEPMAN, THE (aka: STRANGER WITH A GUN) MGM, 1958, Color, 85 min. **Producer:** Edmund Grainger; **Director:** George Marshall; **Screenplay:** William Bowers and James Edward Grant; **Music:** Jeff Alexander; **Cinematographer:** Robert Bonner; **Editor:** Ralph E. Winters; **Cast:** Glenn Ford, Shirley MacLaine, Leslie Nielsen, Mickey Shaughnessy, Edgar Buchanan, Willis Bouchey, Slim Pickens, "Buzz" Henry.

It's the age old battle of sheepmen versus cattlemen in this underrated western blend of parody and traditional action. Glenn Ford (in the same year he was the country's number one box-office draw) is an aggressive sheep farmer who anticipates—with perfect timing—the opposition he will incur in a thriving cattle town run by the corrupt Leslie Nielsen. Mickey Shaughnessy is hilarious as Jumbo McCall, town boob and resident tough guy, who to his chagrin finds himself constantly outmaneuvered by sheepman Ford. This fine family film has some of the funniest sequences to be seen in any western, with Glenn Ford delivering one of his best performances. Unfortunately, this extremely enjoyable film scripted by veteran screenwriters William Bowers and James Edward Grant never received very wide distribution.

SHENANDOAH Universal, 1965, Color, 105 min, VHS. **Producer:** Robert Arthur; **Director:** Andrew V. McLaglen; **Screenplay:** James Lee Barrett; **Music:** Frank Skinner; **Cinematographer:** William H. Clothier; **Editor:** Otho Lovering; **Cast:** James Stewart, Doug McClure, Glenn Corbett, Patrick Wayne, Rosemary Forsyth, Philip Alford, Katharine Ross, Charles Robinson, Paul Fix, Denver Pyle, Harry Carey Jr., George Kennedy, Edward Faulkner, Dabbs Greer.

James Stewart is Charles Anderson, a Virginia widower who works his farm with his six sons and a daughter and is indifferent to the Civil War, which is raging all around him. The family tranquility is shattered when Anderson's youngest son (Philip Alford) is mistaken for a Confederate by a Union patrol and carted away as a prisoner. Leaving his son James (Patrick Wayne) and his second wife Ann (Katharine Ross, in her film debut) to attend the farm, Anderson, his daughter Jennie (Rosemary Forsyth, also in her film debut) and his other sons set out to find their missing family member. After freeing Sam (Doug McClure), a Southern officer whose wedding ceremony with Jennie was interrupted by a call to arms, they continue their search but to no avail.

Another son, Jacob, is killed in a Rebel ambush as the party heads home. But the worst is yet to come when Anderson discovers that James and Ann have been murdered by two deserters. His only consolation is that their baby had been spared. Then, in church the following Sunday, young Boy, having escaped from a Union prison, stumbles into church on crutches, uniting the remainder of the family.

Stewart is magnificent in a role that required enormous range and dimension to make it work well. In the best of the four films Stewart did for Andrew McLaglen, the director was miffed that Stewart was denied an Oscar nomination. "To the day they put me in my grave, I will never understand why Jimmy didn't get at least an Oscar nomination for what he did in *Shenandoah*. The range of the man was never clearer, his conviction never more moving," McLaglen was quoted as saying.

Filmed in Oregon, *Shenandoah* received an Oscar nomination for Best Sound (Waldon O. Watson), while Rosemary Forsyth received a Golden Globe nomination in the category of Most Promising Newcomer—Female. The film later formed the basis for the Tony award-winning Broadway musical of the same name.

SHEPHERD OF THE HILLS, THE
Paramount, 1941, Color, 97 min. **Producer:** Jack Moss; **Director:** Henry Hathaway; **Screenplay:** Grover Jones and Stuart Anthony; **Music:** Girard Carbonara; **Cinematographer:** Charles Lang; **Editor:** Ellsworth Hogland; **Cast:** John Wayne, Betty Field, Harry Carey, Beulah Bondi, James Barton, Samuel S. Hinds, Marjorie Main, Ward Bond, Marc Lawrence, John Qualen, Fuzzy Knight, Tom Fadden.

John Wayne is Matt Mathews, a hot-tempered mountaineer who vows to kill the man he holds responsible for destroying his mother's life—his own father. However, he soon learn that the man he is looking for is a stranger (Harry Carey) called "the shepherd of the hills" by the mountain people because of his many kindnesses to them. The two men finally come to an understanding, as Carey helps clear the way for Wayne to live happily with his mountain sweetheart Sammy (Betty Field).

Helmed by Henry Hathaway, who nearly three decades later directed Wayne's Oscar-winning role in *TRUE GRIT* (1969), *Shepherd of the Hills* was John Wayne's first color production. The actor received a piece of advice that would serve him well his entire professional life. According to Harry Carey Jr., his mother Olive was sitting on the set when the senior Carey (Wayne's hero) was sitting off by himself.

> Duke came up to my mom and they started talking. He began [belaboring] the fact that he was falling into a niche. He felt he was the same in every picture and that was bothering him.
>
> My mom said, "Now wait a minute. You are a big good-looking outdoor guy. You are more or less in the mold of Harry." She pointed at my father who was sitting a little over by the way and said, "Would you like to see him change on the screen?" And Duke went, "Well, hell no! Not in any way!" She said, "Well that's the way you are."

SHERIFF, THE
See *SILVER STAR, THE*.

SHERIFF OF CIMARRON
Republic, 1945, B&W, 54 min. **Producer:** Thomas Carr (associate); **Director:** Yakima Canutt; **Screenplay:** Bennett Cohen; **Cinematographer:** Bud Thackery; **Editor:** Tony Martinelli; **Cast:** Sunset Carson, Linda Stirling, Olin Howard, Riley Hill, Jack Ingram, Tom London, Jack Kirk.

SHERIFF OF FRACTURED JAW, THE
20th Century Fox, 1959, Color, 103 min. **Producer:** Daniel M. Angel; **Director:** Raoul Walsh; **Screenplay:** Arthur Dales; **Music:** Robert Farnon and Harry Harris; **Cinematographer:** Otto Heller; **Editor:** John Shirley; **Cast:** Kenneth More, Jayne Mansfield, Henry Hull, Bruce Cabot, Ronald Squire, William Campbell, Robert Morley, Sidney James, Reed de Rouen, David Horne, Enyon Evans.

Kenneth More is a gentlemanly English firearms salesman on the Texas frontier, and Jayne Mansfield is a saloon singer. Mistaken for a gunman, he is appointed sheriff of a rowdy town after winning a poker game with the mayor. He goes on to enforce the law with a derringer up his sleeve. More is delightful as the staunch Brit who imposes his manners and concepts on a group of wild westerners and eventually stops a range war. The exteriors for this 20th Century Fox western spoof were shot in Spain. Jayne Mansfield's songs were dubbed by Connie Francis.

SHERIFF OF GUNSMOKE
See *MARSHAL OF GUNSMOKE*.

SHERIFF OF LAS VEGAS
Republic, 1944, B&W, 55 min. **Producer:** Stephen Auer (associate); **Director:** Leslie Selander; **Screenplay:** Norman Hall; **Cinematographer:** Bud Thackery (as Ellis Thackery); **Editor:** Charles Craft; **Cast:** William "Wild Bill" Elliott, Robert Blake, Alice Fleming, Peggy Stewart, Kenne Duncan, Bob Wilke, William Haade, Selmer Jackson, John Hamilton.

SHERIFF OF MEDICINE BOW
Monogram, 1948, B&W, 55 min. **Producer:** Barney A. Sarecky; **Director:** Lambert Hillyer; **Screenplay:** J. Benton Cheney; **Cinematographer:** Harry Neumann; **Editor:** Carl Pierson; **Cast:** Johnny Mack Brown, Raymond Hatton, Max Terhune, Evelyn Finley, Bill Kennedy.

SHERIFF OF REDWOOD VALLEY
Republic, 1946, B&W, 54 min. **Producer:** Sidney Picker (associate); **Director:** R. G. Springsteen; **Screenplay:** Earle Snell; **Cinematographer:** Reggie Lanning; **Editor:** Ralph Dixon; **Cast:** William "Wild Bill" Elliott, Robert Blake, Bob Steele, Alice Fleming, Peggy Stewart, Tom London.

SHERIFF OF SAGE VALLEY
PRC, 1942, B&W, 57 min. **Producer:** Sigmund Neufeld; **Director:** Sam Newfield (as Sherman Scott); **Screenplay:** Milton Raison and George

Wallace Sayre; **Music:** Johnny Lange and Lew Porter; **Cinematographer:** Jack Greenhalgh; **Editor:** Holbrook N. Todd; **Cast:** Buster Crabbe, Al St. John, Dave O'Brien, Maxine Leslie, Charles King, Kermit Maynard, John Merton.

SHERIFF OF SUNDOWN Republic, 1944, B&W, 55 min. **Producer:** Steven Auer (associate); **Director:** Leslie Selander; **Screenplay:** Norman S. Hall; **Music:** Joseph Dubin; **Cinematographer:** Bud Thackery (as Ellis Thackery); **Editor:** Harry Keller; **Cast:** Allan Lane, Linda Stirling, Max Terhune, Twinkle Watts, Roy Barcroft, Duncan Renaldo, Tom London.

A group of cowboys lead a herd into a small town and find themselves opposing a corrupt and murderous town boss. Before he achieved stardom as Red Ryder, Allan "Rocky" Lane starred in this early series entry. Other early Allan Lane ventures for Republic include *Silver City Kid*, *Stagecoach to Monterey* (1944); *Trail of Kit Carson, Corpus Christi Bandits, Bells of Rosarita* (1945); and *The Topeka Terror* (1946).

SHERIFF OF TOMBSTONE Republic, 1941, B&W, 54 min. **Producer:** Joseph Kane; **Director:** Kane; **Screenplay:** Olive Cooper; **Music:** Cy Feuer; **Cinematographer:** William Nobles; **Editor:** Tony Martinelli; **Cast:** Roy Rogers, George "Gabby" Hayes, Elyse Knox, Addison Richards, Wally Wales, Sally Payne, Harry Woods.

SHERIFF OF WICHITA Republic, 1949, B&W, 60 min. **Producer:** Gordon Kay (associate); **Director:** R. G. Springsteen; **Screenplay:** Bob Williams; **Music:** Stanley Wilson; **Cinematographer:** John MacBurnie; **Editor:** Tony Martinelli; **Cast:** Allan "Rocky" Lane, Eddy Walker, Roy Barcroft, Lyn Wilde, Clayton Moore, House Peters Jr., Eugene Roth, Trevor Bardette.

SHE WORE A YELLOW RIBBON RKO, 1949, Color, 103 min, VHS, DVD. **Producers:** John Ford and Merian C. Cooper; **Director:** Ford; **Screenplay:** Frank Nugent and Laurence Stallings; **Cinematographer:** Winton Hoch; **Editor:** Jack Murray; **Cast:** John Wayne, Joanne Dru, John Agar, Ben Johnson, Harry Carey Jr., Victor McLaglen, Mildred Natwick, George O'Brien, Arthur Shields, Tom Tyler, Michael Dugan, Chief John Big Tree.

In this film set in an unnamed cavalry post deep in Indian Territory, John Wayne plays Captain Nathan Brittles, a veteran officer set to retire in a short time. However, with Indian trouble looming ahead he is reluctant to leave his command and the men whom he has trained. His one last mission before returning to civilian life is to stop an impending Indian war. In time he ends the Indian uprising by stampeding the tribe's horses. At film's end he rides away, only to be stopped and informed that he has been appointed chief of scouts. The romantic element in the film concerns two young lieutenants (John Agar and Harry Carey Jr.), both in love with pretty Olivia Dandridge (Joanne Dru). Each wants her to wear his yellow ribbon as a token of love.

Many of the cast members were at various times part of John Ford's famed stock company, including young protégés Agar, Carey Jr., and Ben Johnson (whose horsemanship and riding skills have rarely been duplicated on screen); and veteran regulars Arthur Shields, Francis Ford, Mildred Natwick, and Victor McLaglen, who provides a good supply of robust Irish humor as Sergeant Quincannon. Ford also gave George O'Brien, former leading man and star of his silent epic *The Iron Horse* (1924) the strong supporting part of Major Allshard.

John Wayne has never been better than in this beautifully crafted film with its masterful Ford imprint and a landscape worthy of a fine Remington painting. In fact, Ford deliberately tried to duplicate the look of Frederic Remington's style as a standard for the film's composition. "I tried to get his [Remington's] color and movement and I think I succeeded partly," Ford later confided to Peter Bogdanovich.

The second entry in John Ford's celebrated Cavalry Trilogy (it followed FORT APACHE, 1948, and preceded RIO GRANDE, 1950), *She Wore a Yellow Ribbon* remains the most sentimental of all John Ford westerns, a film that warrants repeated viewing on a multitude of levels. Filmed in Monument Valley and released in July 1949, it garnered Winton Hoch an Oscar for Color Cinematography.

The movie also presents an opportunity to see the composite John Wayne: his maturity, strength, sentiment, and dignity. Nowhere is this better exemplified than when the troopers under his command give Captain Brittles a watch on the day he is to retire. Visibly moved, Brittles fumbles nervously for his glasses. Fighting back tears, he reads the simple inscription, "Lest We Forget!" Wayne's Nathan Brittles epitomizes strength, valor, honor, decency, and courage, the foundations of Ford's ideal screen hero. An excellent scene has him visiting his wife's grave, placing flowers beside her stone, and speaking to her with direct unassuming candor about the losses at Little Big Horn and his own plans for the future.

"Mr. Wayne, his hair streaked with silver and wearing a dashing mustache, is the ideal of the legendary cavalryman," wrote an appreciative Bosley Crowther in the *New York Times*. "[In] this big Technicolored Western Mr. Ford has superbly achieved a vast composite illustration of all the legends of the frontier cavalryman."

Actor John Agar, who played Lieutenant Flint Cohill, worked with Wayne in six films, including *Sands of Iwo Jima* (1949). Yet he insists that *She Wore a Yellow Ribbon* was the best thing John Wayne ever did. "I strongly feel he should have received an Academy Award nomination for the role of Captain Nathan Brittles. He was just brilliant. Remember I had a lot of scenes with him. He played a guy 20 years older than he was at the time. At the time Duke was 41 and was playing a guy in his later 50s or 60s."

Purists, especially lovers of John Ford films, are most impressed by the storm scene, particularly a sequence in which a cavalry doctor (Arthur Shields) is operating on a soldier (Tom Tyler) inside a moving wagon train. What makes the scene special is that much of sequence was filmed in the dark, with only flashes of lightning to illuminate the camera—a gamble, to be sure.

"It was a Technicolor breakthrough," Harry Carey Jr. (Lieutenant Pennell) reminds us in his excellent autobiographical book *Company of Heroes*. "Back in those days, the film was not nearly as sensitive to light as it is today. Now, over forty-years later, the cameraman would have no problem."

SHINE ON HARVEST MOON Republic, 1938, B&W, 55 min. **Producer:** Charles E. Ford; **Director:** Joseph Kane; **Screenplay:** Jack Natteford; **Cinematographer:** William Nobles; **Editor:** Lester Orlebeck; **Cast:** Roy Rogers, Lynne Roberts, Lulubelle, Stanley Andrews, William Farnum, George Montgomery.

SHOOTING, THE AIP, 1967, Color, 82 min, VHS, DVD. **Producers:** Monte Hellman and Jack Nicholson; **Director:** Hellman; **Screenplay:** Carole Eastman (as Adrien Joyce); **Music:** Richard Markowitz; **Cinematographer:** Gregory Sandor; **Editor:** Hellman; **Cast:** Jack Nicholson, Will Hutchins, Warren Oates, Millie Perkins, Charles Eastman.

A young woman (Millie Perkins) engages a bounty hunter (Warren Oates) and a man named Colby (Will Hutchins) to help her cross the desert and avenge the death of her husband and child. They find themselves followed by a mystery gunman (Jack Nicholson), who eventually joins them. The ending has a very strange (inexplicable, some might argue) twist.

The fragmented narrative adds levels of confusion to this Monte Hellman entry, which has often been described as an existential western. It was shot simultaneously with Hellman's *Ride the Whirlwind* (1965), which also starred Nicholson and Perkins. Writer Adrien Joyce (Carole Eastman) later scripted *Five Easy Pieces* (1970).

Will Hutchins, who played Colby, recalled *The Shooting* in a 1995 interview with the author: "*The Shooting* was a lot of fun to work on, very strenuous. [Monte Hellman] made us do everything over and over again. It was very hard dialogue to memorize. It was written in a strange poetic vernacular, and I've never seen that kind of role again."

The film was given a television airing before being released to the theaters.

SHOOTING HIGH 20th Century Fox, 1940, B&W, 65 min. **Producer:** John Stone; **Director:** Alfred Green; **Screenplay:** Lou Breslow and Owen Francis; **Music:** Samuel Kaylin; **Cinematographer:** Ernest Palmer; **Editor:** Nick DeMaggio; **Cast:** Jane Withers, Gene Autry, Marjorie Weaver, Robert Lowery, Kay Aldridge, Hobart Cavanaugh, Jack Carson, Charles Middleton, Tom London, Hamilton MacFadden, Eddie Acuff, George Chandler.

A movie company arrives in a small town to make a film about a legendary sheriff, and they hire his grandson (Gene Autry) for the actor who is playing the role of the sheriff. But the grandson's friend (Jane Withers) scares the leading man (Robert Lowery) out of town so that Autry can get the star-

ring part and the love of her sister (Marjorie Weaver). Gene then proves himself a worthy hero by thwarting a bank robbery in this Hollywood spoof of itself.

The picture is one of the rash of films in the mid-1930s and early '40s that dealt with making westerns. Others include *The Cowboy Star* (1936) with Charles Starrett, *The Big Show* (1936) with Gene Autry, *Hollywood Roundup* (1937) with Buck Jones, *It Happened in Hollywood* (1937) with Richard Dix, and *Hollywood Cowboy* (1937) with George O'Brien.

SHOOTIST, THE Universal, 1976, Color, 100 min. **Producers:** M. J. Frankovich and William Self; **Director:** Don Siegel; **Screenplay:** Miles Hood Swarthout and Scott Hale; **Music:** Elmer Bernstein; **Cinematographer:** Bruce Surtees; **Editor:** Douglas Stewart; **Cast:** John Wayne, Lauren Bacall, Ron Howard, James Stewart, Richard Boone, Hugh O'Brien, Bill McKinney, Harry Morgan, John Carradine, Sheree North, Rick Lenz, Scatman Crothers, Greg Palmer.

"I won't be wronged. I won't be insulted and I won't be laid a hand on. I don't do these things to other people and I require the same of them."

Such was the code of John Bernard Books, the man they called The Shootist. It is 1901, and the prairie-hardened gunfighter enters a new century, knowing the times have passed him by. Encumbered by recurring pain, he pays a visit to the town doctor (James Stewart), who confirms the worst: Books has cancer and in all probability will die an excruciating death.

Forced to confront his own legacy and give his death meaning, he hopes only to live out his remaining days in dignity. He takes a room in the home of the widow Bond Rogers (Lauren Bacall), where after some initial conflicts he manages to cement a kindly relationship with her and her son Gillom (Ron Howard). Their interaction and resulting friendship dominates much of the story.

The Shootist, *John Wayne's final film* (UNIVERSAL/ AUTHOR'S COLLECTION)

The Shootist is a marvelous film—an elegy both for the western and for its star. John Wayne would die of cancer three years later, but contrary to popular lore he did not have cancer at the time this movie was made. His health problems then were related to pneumonia and a damaged valve in his heart.

No actor ever had a more poignant a screen epitaph than John Wayne nor as enduring a role as John Bernard Books. The opening credits of *The Shootist* relives Books's journey as a gunman with nostalgic clips from four of Wayne's films—*RED RIVER* (1948), *HONDO* (1953), *RIO BRAVO* (1959), and *EL DORADO* (1967). The climactic showdown has Books setting up a fight in the saloon with three nasty characters played by Richard Boone, Hugh O'Brien, and Bill McKinney. The three gunmen represent Book's past. The present and future are represented by Bond and Gillom Rogers (Bocall and Howard). Through their eyes that we see the full tapestry that is John Bernard Books, culminating in Books's "merciful" death at the hands of the bartender. Focusing on character development rather than providing a spate of action scenes, the film becomes a testament to the life and times of John Bernard Books. When the film was completed it marked the end of John Wayne's 50th year in motion pictures.

According to Wayne's costumer and good friend Luster Bayless, there was some mild friction between actor and director over the last scene, in which Gillom shoots the bartender who kills Books. In the original script Ron Howard was to take the gun at Wayne's request and, knowing that he was badly wounded, would kill the shootist himself. "Duke insisted that Ron look at him when he was dying, look back at the gun he had lived by with blood on the tip, then take the gun and throw it out of his life. Duke would not compromise on that scene. 'I will not compromise!' I remember those exact words. And that was how the scene was finally shot."

Variety called *The Shootist* "one of John Wayne's towering achievements. Don Siegel's terrific film is simply beautiful

Ron Howard and John Wayne in The Shootist
(UNIVERSAL/AUTHOR'S COLLECTION)

and beautifully simple, in its quiet, elegant and sensitive telling of the last days of a dying gunfighter. . . . Wayne and Lauren Bacall are both outstanding. . . . Atop this comes an emerging tenderness . . . which is articulated in careful politeness and the artful exchange of expressions that evoke memories of great silent films."

The best western to come out of the 1970s, *The Shootist* presented Wayne with one of his strongest roles. Had the political climate in Hollywood not been so hostile, he might have garnered a second Oscar. As it was, he didn't even receive what would have been a well-deserved nomination. The film came up empty at Oscar time, receiving an Academy Award nomination only for Best Art Direction. However, Lauren Bacall was nominated for a British Academy Award (Best Actress), while Ron Howard received a Golden Globe nomination for Best Motion Picture Actor in a Supporting Role.

A film that can be enjoyed again and again, *The Shootist* is a testament to John Wayne's incredible growth as an actor and a presence. It reflects his long journey through the world of film, and like his character John Bernard Books, no one has ever gone out with more stature and dignity. As Books tells Mrs. Rogers when she asks him about his remarkable life: "In general," he replies, "I've had a hell of a good time."

SHOOT OUT Universal, 1971, Color, 95 min, VHS, DVD. **Producer:** Hal B. Wallis; **Director:** Henry Hathaway; **Screenplay:** Marguerite Roberts; **Music:** Dave Grusin; **Cinematographer:** Earl Rath; **Editor:** Archie Marshek; **Cast:** Gregory Peck, Robert F. Lyons, Susan Tyrrell, Jeff Corey, James Gregory, Rita Gam, Paul Fix, Arthur Hunnicutt.

Clay Lomax (Gregory Peck) is released from prison after a six-year sentence in this film based on Will James's novel *Lone Cowboy*. Bent on revenge against the former partner who

John Wayne as John Bernard Books, the man they call The Shootist (UNIVERSAL/AUTHOR'S COLLECTION)

betrayed him, his anger begins to dissipate when he is "adopted" by a little girl. Produced, directed, and scripted by the same trio (Hal B. Wallis, Henry Hathaway, and Marguerite Roberts) responsible for *TRUE GRIT* (1969), this familiar entry about a cowboy and a girl has too much talking and too little action. The picture is a remake of Paramount's 1934 film *Lone Cowboy*, starring Jackie Cooper.

SHOOT-OUT AT MEDICINE BEND Warner Bros., 1957, B&W, 87 min. **Producer:** Richard Whorf; **Director:** Richard L. Bare; **Screenplay:** John Tucker Battle and D. D. Beauchamp; **Music:** Ray Heindorf, Paul Sawtell, Wayne Shanklin, and Roy Webb; **Cinematographer:** Carl E. Guthrie; **Editor:** Clarence Kolster; **Cast:** Randolph Scott, James Craig, Angie Dickinson, Dani Crayne, James Garner, Gordon Jones, Trevor Bardette, Myron Healey.

A cavalry troop, not able to defend itself because of faulty ammunition, is wiped out in a Sioux massacre. The brother of the troop commander leaves the service along with two pals and sets out to find the men responsible. This lesser-known mid-50's Randolph Scott venture features James Garner and Angie Dickinson before they became big-name stars. Ray Heindorf and Wayne Shanklin wrote the song "Kiss Me Quick."

SHORT GRASS Allied Artists, 1950, B&W, 82 min. **Producer:** Scott Dunlap; **Director:** Leslie Selander; **Screenplay:** Tom W. Blackburn; **Music:** Edward J. Kay; **Cinematographer:** Harry Neumann; **Editor:** Otto Lovering; **Cast:** Rod Cameron, Cathy Downs, Johnny Mack Brown, Raymond Walburn, Alan Hale Jr., Morris Ankrum, Jonathon Hale, Harry Woods, Myron Healey, Tristram Coffin, Jack Ingram.

A sheriff (Johnny Mack Brown) joins forces with a rancher to stop a crooked land scheme and a deadly grazing dispute west of Santa Fe. Rod Cameron is the drifter who comes to New Mexico just as it is to be opened to federal law and to commerce with the oncoming railroad and who suddenly finds himself the intended scapegoat in a saloon robbery. A good taut script and an interesting cast help make this little film a well-kept secret.

SHOTGUN Allied Artists, 1955, Color, 80 min, VHS. **Producer:** John Champion; **Director:** Leslie Selander; **Screenplay:** Rory Calhoun and Clark Reynolds; **Music:** Carl Brandt; **Cinematographer:** Ellsworth Fredericks; **Editor:** John C. Fuller; **Cast:** Sterling Hayden, Yvonne De Carlo, Zachary Scott, Robert J. Wilke, Guy Prescott, Ralph Sanford.

A sheriff and a bounty hunter battle for the love of a half-breed girl (Yvonne De Carlo) while trying to track down a killer. Rory Calhoun, who cowrote the script, was originally slated to star in this film, best remembered for De Carlo's provocative bathing scene.

SHOTGUN PASS Columbia, 1931, B&W, 58 min. **Director:** J. P. McGowan; **Screenplay:** Robert Quigley; **Cinematographer:** Benjamin H. Kline; **Editor:** S. Roy Luby; **Cast:** Tim McCoy, Virginia Lee Corbin, Monte Vandergrift, Frank Rice, Joe Smith Marba, Ben Corbett.

SHOWDOWN Paramount, 1940, B&W, 65 min. **Producer:** Harry Sherman; **Director:** Howard Bretherton; **Screenplay:** Donald Kusel and Harold Daniel Kusel; **Cinematographer:** Russell Harlan; **Editor:** Carroll Lewis; **Cast:** William Boyd, Russell Hayden, Britt Wood, Morris Ankrum, Jan Clayton, Wright Kramer, Donald Kirke, Roy Barcroft, Eddie Dean, Kermit Maynard.

SHOWDOWN Universal, 1963, B&W, 79 min. **Producer:** Gordon Kay; **Director:** R. G. Springsteen; **Screenplay:** Bronson Howitzer; **Music:** Hans J. Salter; **Cinematographer:** Ellis W. Carter; **Editor:** Jerome Thoms; **Cast:** Audie Murphy, Kathleen Crowley, Charles Drake, Harold Stone, Skip Homeier, L. Q. Jones, Charles Horvath, Henry Will, Dabs Greer, Henry Wills.

When two convicts escape from prison, they head for the Mexican border and get involved in a robbery.

SHOWDOWN Universal, 1973, Color, 90 min, VHS. **Producer:** George Seaton; **Director:** Seaton; **Screenplay:** Theodore Taylor; **Music:** David Shire; **Cinematographer:** Ernest Laszlo; **Editor:** John W. Holmes; **Cast:** Rock Hudson, Dean Martin, Susan Clark, Donald Moffat, John McLiam, Charles Baca.

In George Seaton's final film, Rock Hudson and Dean Martin play two childhood friends who are in love with the same girl and who go separate ways. Chuck Jarvis (Hudson) becomes a sheriff who is forced to hunt down former friend Billy Massey (Martin), now a robber. However, the two eventually join forces against the other robbers who have come for the loot that Billy had taken. The ensuing gun battle results in Martin's death.

Filmed on location in New Mexico and set at the turn of the century, the film received neither good promotion nor first-class distribution. Hudson received a few broken bones and a concussion as a result of an automobile accident during the location shooting. Even though production was shut down for a few weeks, he managed to deliver one of his better screen performances.

SHOWDOWN, THE Republic, 1950, B&W, 86 min, VHS. **Producer:** William J. O'Sullivan; **Directors:** Dorrell McGowan and Stuart E. McGowan; **Screenplay:** McGowan and McGowan; **Music:** Stanley Wilson; **Cinematographer:** Reggie Lanning; **Editor:** Harry Keller; **Cast:** William "Wild Bill" Elliott, Walter Brennan, Marie Windsor, Harry Morgan, Jim Davis, Leif Ericson, Rhys Wiliams.

Bill Elliott is Shadrock Jones, a mysterious loner (actually an ex-Texas Ranger) out to find the man who murdered his brother and stole his money. To accomplish this he joins a cattle drive to Montana headed by Cap McKellar (Walter Brennan), and in his capacity as trail-herd boss he hopes to uncover the murderer, whom he believes to be one of McKellar's cowhands.

Elliott is outstanding in this A-level Republic western with an underlying darkness and film-noir setting. Marie Windsor and Walter Brennan deliver top-flight supporting performances, Windsor as Adelaide, the saloon gal who points Shadrock in the right (or wrong) direction, and Brennan as the enigmatic cattle drive leader who tries to convince Shadrock that he should forget about revenge and instead let the law take care of the killer.

SHOWDOWN AT ABILENE (aka: GUN SHY)

Universal, 1956, color, 80 min. **Producer:** Howard Christie; **Director:** Charles S. Haas; **Screenplay:** Berne Giler; **Music:** Henry Mancini and Herman Stein; **Cinematographer:** Irving Glassberg; **Editor:** Ray Snyder; **Cast:** Jock Mahoney, Martha Hyer, Lyle Bettger, David Janssen, Grant Williams, Ted de Corsia.

When former sheriff Jim Trask (Jock Mahoney) returns to Abilene after fighting for the Confederacy, he is surprised to learn that the townsfolk believed him to be dead. To compound matters he learns that his old pal, one-armed Dave Mosely (Lyle Bettger) is engaged to his former sweetheart and has become a cattle tycoon. With the increasing tension between cattlemen and the original farmers about to boil over, Trask is persuaded to again sign on as sheriff. Plenty of problems and some sordid discoveries loom ahead for Trask.

Former stuntman Mohoney gives a thumbs-up performance. The strong supporting cast includes Martha Hyer as Peggy and David Janssen as Deputy Vern Ward.

SHOWDOWN AT BOOT HILL (aka: SHADOW OF BOOT HILL)

20th Century Fox, 1958, B&W, 71 min, VHS. **Producer:** Harold E. Knox; **Director:** Gene Fowler Jr.; **Screenplay:** Louis Vittes; **Music:** Albert Harris; **Cinematographer:** John M. Nickolaus; **Editor:** Frank Sullivan; **Cast:** Charles Bronson, Robert Hutton, John Carradine, Carole Mathews, Paul Maxey, Thomas Browne Henry, George Pembroke, William Stevens.

U.S. Marshal Luke Welsh (Charles Bronson) tracks a murderer to a western town, where he kills him. However, he discovers that the man had no local criminal record and contrary to his belief was quite popular there. Because there is a bounty to be collected, the townspeople refuse to identify the dead man. Consequently, the marshal now has reason to sit back and reflect on his lifestyle and the reasons he has chosen to be a bounty hunter. Charles Bronson gives a first-rate performance as the gunman who must now search his soul in this underappreciated 1950s western.

SIEGE AT RED RIVER, THE (aka: GATLING GUN)

20th Century Fox, 1954, Color, 86 min. **Producer:** Leonard Goldstein; **Director:** Rudolph Mate; **Screenplay:** Sidney Boehrn; **Music:** Lionel Newman; **Cinematographer:** Edward Cronjager; **Editor:** Betty Steinberg; **Cast:** Van Johnson, Joanne Dru, Richard Boone, Milburn Stone, Jeff Morrow, Craig Hill, Lyle Talbot, Roland Winters, Rico Alaniz, Robert Burton, Pilar Del Rey, Ferris Taylor, John Clift.

Van Johnson and Milburn Stone are Confederate spies who commandeer some Gatling guns from Union forces and take them back to the lines in a medicine-show wagon. But a renegade outlaw (Richard Boone) steals the guns and sells them to the Shawnee Indians, who use them to attack a Union fort. When the Union army catches the Confederate officers, they help defeat the Shawnee and retrieve the guns.

The Siege at Red River offers a good share of action bolstered by its capable cast.

SIERRA

Universal, 1950, Color, 83 min, VHS. **Producers:** Michael Kraike and Walter Kraike; **Director:** Alfred E. Green; **Screenplay:** Edna Anhalt and Milton Gunzburg; **Music:** Arnold Hughes, Walter Scharf, and Frank Skinner; **Cinematographer:** Russell Metty; **Editor:** Ted J. Kent; **Cast:** Wanda Hendrix, Audie Murphy, Burl Ives, Dean Jagger, Richard Rober, Tony Curtis (as Anthony Curtis), Housley Stevenson, Elliott Reid.

Lawyer Riley Martin (Wanda Hendrix) stumbles on the hideout of a man and his son (Dean Jagger and Audie Murphy) who are on the run from the law after being falsely accused of murder. Burl Ives appears as "Lonesome" and sings six songs. Costars Audie Murphy and Wanda Hendrix were a young married couple at the time. The picture is based on the novel *Mountains Are My Kingdom*, by Stuart Hardy.

SIERRA BARON

20th Century Fox, 1958, Color, 80 min. **Producer:** Plato A. Skouras; **Director:** James B. Clark; **Screenplay:** Houston Branch; **Music:** Paul Sawtell and Bert Shefter; **Cinematographer:** Alex Phillips; **Editor:** Frank Baldridge; **Cast:** Brian Keith, Rick Jason, Rita Gam, Mala Powers, Allan Lewis, Pedro Steve Brodie, Pedro Galvan.

It is mid-19th century California, and unscrupulous easterners are moving into the territory, trying to fleece the residents of their land. Land promoter Steve Brodie brings in gunman Brian Keith to hassle Rick Jason, the proprietor of a large Spanish land tract. When Jason allows the exhausted members of a wagon train to rest on his land long enough to grow crops, the grateful settlers come to his aid in fending off the scheming Brodie. The Texas gunman changes sides when he falls for Rita Gam, Jason's sister. Although filmed in Mexico, the picture covers a large slice of California history.

SIERRA PASSAGE

Monogram, 1950, B&W, 81 min. **Producer:** Lindsley Parsons; **Director:** Frank McDonald; **Screenplay:** Thomas W. Blackburn, Warren Douglas, Samuel Roeca, and Warren D. Wandbert; **Music:** Edward J.

Kay; **Cinematographer:** William Sickner; **Editor:** Ace Herman (as Leonard Herman); **Cast:** Wayne Morris, Lola Albright, Lloyd Corrigan, Alan Hale Jr., Roland Winters, Jim Bannon, Billy Gray.

Wayne Morris grows to adulthood determined to wreak vengeance on the man who killed his father years earlier. To do this he postpones his impending marriage and sets off with a traveling variety show to find the culprit.

SIERRA SUE   Republic, 1941, B&W, 64 min. **Producer:** Harry Grey; **Director:** William Morgan; **Screenplay:** Earl Felton and Julian Zimet; **Music:** Fleming Allen, Gene Autry, J. B. Carey, Fred Rose, and Nelson Shawn; **Cinematographer:** Jack A. Marta; **Editor:** Lester Orlebeck; **Cast:** Gene Autry, Smiley Burnette, Fay McKenzie, Frank M. Thomas, Robert Homans, Earle Hodgins, Dorothy Christy, Kermit Maynard, Eddie Dean, Bud Buster, Rex Lease.

Gene Autry is a government inspector investigating why cattle are being killed, but he meets opposition from the head of the local cattleman's association. A standard Autry mix of action, romance, comedy, and song, *Sierra Sue* marks one of five successive films in which actress Fay McKenzie was Autry's leading lady. The other four are *Down Mexico Way* (1941); *Cowboy Serenade, Heart of the Rio Grande,* and *Home in Wyomin'* (1942). (See also *TUMBLING TUMBLEWEEDS.*)

SILENT CONFLICT   United Artists, 1948, B&W, 61 min. **Producers:** Lewis Rachmil and Harry Sherman; **Director:** George Archainbaud; **Screenplay:** Charles Belden; **Music:** Darrell Calker and Ralph Stenley; **Cinematographer:** Mack Stengler; **Editor:** Fred W. Berger; **Cast:** William Boyd, Andy Clyde, Rand Brooks, Virginia Belmont, Earle Hodgins, James Harrington.
   See *HOP-ALONG CASSIDY.*

SILVERADO   Columbia, 1985, Color, 132 min, VHS, DVD. **Producer:** Lawrence Kasdan; **Director:** Kasdan; **Screenplay:** Kasdan and Mark Kasdan; **Music:** Bruce Broughton; **Cinematographer:** John Bailey; **Editor:** Carol Littleton; **Cast:** Kevin Kline, Scott Glenn, Kevin Costner, Danny Glover, John Cleese, Rosanna Arquette, Brian Dennehy, Linda Hunt, Jeff Goldblum.

After meeting in the desert, two drifters (Kevin Kline and Scott Glenn) join forces and set out for Silverado to take on the McKendrick boys. Along the way they spring Glenn's gun-happy brother (Kevin Costner) out of jail, outwitting Sheriff Langston (John Cleese). The unlikely trio is then joined by an itinerant black man (Danny Glover), who is out to rejoin what is left of his family. An archvillain emerges in the person of Cobb, the sheriff of Silverado and puppet of MacKendrick, played superbly by the burly Brian Dennehy.
   Considering the paucity of quality westerns during the previous 20 years, Lawrence Kasdan's *Silverado* (he produced, directed, and cowrote the film) plays extremely well, with a disparate cast of characters and shades of almost every conven-

tional theme in the genre arena ensconcing the film. He adapts Howard Hawks's theme of men bonding together in a common cause, combining conventional drama with irreverent humor. As Ted Sennett notes in his *Great Hollywood Westerns* (1991), "Kasdan's film took the familiar situations of classic Westerns and gave them a flippant, contemporary spin."
   The film, which has outstanding visual effects, won two Oscar nominations: Best Original Score (Bruce Broughton) and Best Sound (Donald O. Mitchell, Rick Kline, Kevin O'Connell, David Rome).

SILVER BULLET   Reliable, 1935, B&W, 58 min. **Producer:** Bernard Ray; **Director:** Ray; **Screenplay:** Rose Gordon and Carl Krusada; **Cinematography;** J. Henry Kruse; **Editor:** Frederick Bain; **Cast:** Tom Tyler, Jayne Regan, Lafe McKee, Charles King, George Chesebro, Wally Wales, Slim Whitaker, Lew Meehan, Franklyn Farnum.
   See *MYSTERY RANCH* (1934).

SILVER BULLET, THE   Universal, 1942, B&W, 58 min. **Producer:** Will Cowan (associate); **Director:** Joseph H. Lewis; **Screenplay:** Elizabeth Beecher; **Music:** Hans J. Salter; **Cinematographer:** Charles Van Enger; **Editor:** Maurice Wright; **Cast:** Johnny Mack Brown, Fuzzy Knight, William Farnum, Jennifer Holt, LeRoy Mason, Rex Lease, Grace Lenard, Claire Whitney, Slim Whitaker.

A cowboy heads for the town where his father was murdered to uncover the identity of those responsible. The soundtrack songs were supplied by Oliver Drake, Milton Rosen, and Jimmy Wakely. (See also *OLD CHISHOLM TRAIL.*)

SILVER CANYON   Columbia, 1951, B&W, 70 min. **Producer:** Armand Schaefer; **Director:** John English; **Screenplay:** Gerald Geraghty; **Music:** Mischa Bakaleinikoff, Sidney Cutner, George Duning, Irving Gertz, Werner R. Heymann, John Leipold, Arthur Morton, and Heintz Roemheld; **Cinematographer:** William Bradford; **Editor:** James Sweeney; **Cast:** Gene Autry, Pat Buttram, Gail Davis, Bob Steele, Edgar Dearing, Richard Dearing, Richard Alexander, Terry Frost, Peter Mamakos.
   See *TUMBLING TUMBLEWEEDS.*

SILVER CITY (aka: HIGH VERMILION, UK)   Paramount, 1951, Color, 90 min. **Producer:** Nat Holt; **Director:** Byron Haskin; **Screenplay:** Frank Gruber; **Music:** Paul Sawtell; **Cinematographer:** Ray Rennahan; **Editor:** Elmo Billings; **Cast:** Edmond O'Brien, Yvonne De Carlo, Richard Arlen, Barry Fitzgerald, Gladys George, Laura Elliott, John Dierkes, Myron Healey.

When a miner attempts to help a beautiful girl and her father develop their gold claim, they are opposed by a wealthy rancher who wants both the girl and the gold for himself.

SILVER CITY BONANZA   Republic, 1951, B&W, 67 min, VHS. **Producer:** Melville Tucker (associate); **Director:**

George Blair; **Screenplay:** Bob Williams; **Music:** Stanley Wilson; **Cinematographer:** John MacBurnie; **Editor:** Robert M. Leeds; **Cast:** Rex Allen, Buddy Ebsen, Mary Ellen Kay, Billy Kimbley, Alix Ebsen, Bill Kennedy, Gregg Barton, Clem Bevans, Frank Jenks, Harry Lauter.

A blind man is murdered at a "haunted ranch," and cowboy Rex Allen sets out to find the killer. One of the best-written Rex Allen series ventures, the film provides some genuine suspense. (See also *ARIZONA COWBOY.*)

SILVER CITY KID Republic, 1944, B&W, 55 min, VHS. **Producer:** Stephen Auer; **Director:** John English; **Screenplay:** Taylor Caven; **Music:** Joseph Dubin; **Cinematographer:** Reggie Lanning; **Editor:** Charles Craft; **Cast:** Allan Lane, Peggy Stewart, Wally Vernon, Twinkle Watts, Harry Woods, Frank Jaquet, Lane Chandler, Glenn Strange.

SILVER CITY RAIDERS (aka: LEGAL LAR-CENY) Columbia, 1943, B&W, 55 min. **Producer:** Leon Barsha; **Director:** William Berke; **Screenplay:** Ed Earl Repp; **Cinematographer:** Benjamin Kline; **Editor:** Jerome Thoms; **Cast:** Russell Hayden, Bob Wills, Dub Taylor, Alma Carroll, Paul Sutton, Luther Wills, Jack Ingram, Edmond Cobb.

SILVER DOLLAR See *OVERLAND PACIFIC.*

SILVER LODE RKO, 1954, Color, 81 min. **Producer:** Benedict Bogeaus; **Director:** Allan Dwan; **Screenplay:** Karen Wolfe; **Music:** Louis Forbes; **Cinematographer:** John Alton; **Editor:** James Leicester; **Cast:** John Payne, Lizabeth Scott, Dan Duryea, Dolores Moran, Emile Meyer, Harry Carey Jr., Alan Hale Jr., John Hudson, Robert Warwick.

Dan Ballard (John Payne), a respected citizen of Silver Lode, is about to be married to lovely Rose Evans (Lizabeth Scott). It is Independence Day, and Marshal Ned McCarthy rides into town claiming that he has been sent to arrest Ballard for the murder of his brother and the theft of $20,000. At first the townspeople stand behind Ballard, but soon their loyalty begins to waver, and his erstwhile friends start to desert him—with only Rose and a former flame saloon girl (Dolores Moran) left to support him.

Helmed by longtime director Allan Dwan, who began his film career in 1909 writing scenarios for Essanay Company, the film is an overt play on the *HIGH NOON* (1952) theme. It has been called "an astonishing anti-McCarthy Western" by the *Village Voice* and an "obvious allegory of HUAC (The House Un-American Activities Committee)" by Leonard Maltin in his *Video Guide.* Whether this was Dwan's deliberate intention or merely an evolutionary by-product of the film is uncertain, but with villain Dan Duryea bearing the name McCarthy, the supposition at least deserves some merit.

SILVER ON THE SAGE Paramount, 1939, B&W, 68 min, VHS. **Producer:** Harry Sherman; **Director:** Lesley Selander; **Screenplay:** Maurice Geraghty; **Music:** John Leipold and Stephan Pasternacki; **Cinematographer:** Russell Harlan; **Editor:** Robert Warwick; **Cast:** William Boyd, Russell Hayden, George "Gabby" Hayes, Ruth Rogers, Stanley Ridges, Roy Barcroft, Buzz Barton.

SILVER QUEEN United Artists, 1942, B&W, 80 min. **Producer:** Harry Sherman; **Director:** Lloyd Bacon; **Screenplay:** Cecile Kramer and Bernard Schubert; **Music:** Victor Young; **Cinematographer:** Russell Harlan; **Editor:** Sherman B. Rose; **Cast:** George Brent, Priscilla Lane, Bruce Cabot, Lynn Overton, Eugene Pallette, Guinn "Big Boy" Williams, Roy Barcroft, Eleanor Stewart, Arthur Hunnicutt.

The Civil War is over, and a girl gambles to raise money to pay off her father's debts, but her fiancé invests her winnings in a worthless silver mine instead. A decent piece of film entertainment, this picture captured Oscar nominations for Best Interior Direction—Black and White (Ralph Berger, Emile Kuri), and Best Scoring of a Dramatic or Comedy Picture (Victor Young).

SILVER RANGE Monogram, 1946, B&W, 53 min. **Producer:** Scott Dunlap; **Director:** Lambert Hillyer; **Screenplay:** J. Benton Cheney; **Cinematographer:** Harry Neumann; **Editor:** Fred Maguire; **Cast:** Johnny Mack Brown, Raymond Hatton, I. Stanford Jolley, Terry Frost, Eddie Parker, Ted Adams.

SILVER RIVER Warner Bros., 1948, B&W, 110 min, VHS. **Producer:** Owen Crump; **Director:** Raoul Walsh; **Screenplay:** Steven Longstreet and Harriet Frank Jr.; **Music:** Max Steiner; **Cinematographer:** Sid Hickox; **Editor:** Alan Crosland Jr.; **Cast:** Errol Flynn, Ann Sheridan, Thomas Mitchell, Bruce Bennett, Tom D'Andrea, Barton MacLane, Monte Blue, Jonathon Hale, Al Bridge, Arthur Space.

When he is unjustly discharged from the cavalry, Mike McComb (Errol Flynn) sets out for Nevada, where he ruthlessly works his way up to become one of the most powerful silver magnates in the West. He goes so far as having one of his men (Bruce Bennett) sent to his death so McComb can marry his wife. However, when McComb's empire begins to fall apart, the other mining combines rise up against his arrogant and greedy ways, and he loses even the support of his wife and his friends. It is his wife's departure that leads him onto the path of restoration.

A good cast of movie veterans helps to move this film along, but it is far from one of Errol Flynn's better Warner Bros. westerns. In fact, Flynn fans were aghast at seeing their hero playing such a heel. Filmed on location in Bronson Canyon (near Hollywood), the Sierra, and at the Calabasas Ranch, *Silver River* marked the last time Errol Flynn and director Raoul Walsh would work together. It was also a comedown for Flynn and Ann Sheridan, who sparkled so well together a decade earlier in *DODGE CITY* (1939).

While intriguing in its Civil War sequences, which utilized scenes from *Birth of a Nation* (1915), the film never seems to put on steam. Thomas Pryor wrote in his *New York Times* review (cited in *The Great Westerns*): "[Walsh] handicapped himself unmercifully in filming *Silver City* by cramming all the excitement into the first ten minutes or so. As a consequence the new picture . . . runs downhill for most of its remaining length."

SILVER SPURS (aka: SILVERSPURS) Universal, 1936, B&W, 60 min. **Producer:** Buck Jones; **Director:** Ray Taylor; **Screenplay:** Joseph F. Poland; **Cinematographer:** Herbert Kirkpatrick and Allen Thompson; **Editor:** Bernard Loftus; **Cast:** Buck Jones, George "Gabby" Hayes (as George Hayes), J. P. McGowan, Bruce Lane, Beth Marion, W. E. Lawrence, Earl Askam.

SILVER SPURS Republic, 1943, B&W, 68 min. **Producer:** Harry Grey; **Director:** Joseph Kane; **Screenplay:** John K. Butler and J. Benton Cheney; **Music:** Smiley Burnette, Hugh Farr, Bob Nolan, and Tim Spencer; **Cinematographer:** Reggie Lanning; **Editor:** Tony Martinelli; **Cast:** Roy Rogers, Smiley Burnette, John Carradine, Phyllis Brooks, Jerome Cowan, Joyce Compton, Bob Nolan and the Sons of the Pioneers.

SILVER STAR, THE (aka: THE SHERIFF) Lippert Pictures, 1955, B&W, 73 min. **Producers:** Richard Bartlett and Earle Lyons; **Director:** Bartlett; **Screenplay:** Bartlett and Ian MacDonald; **Music:** Leo Klatzkin; **Cinematographer:** Guy Roe; **Editors:** George Reed and Merrill G. White; **Cast:** Edgar Buchanan, Marie Windsor, Lon Chaney Jr., Richard Bartlett, Barton MacLane, Morris Ankrum, Edith Evanson.

When three gunmen threaten his town, a frontier marshal doubts his own courage. Advised to leave town, he is forced to search his own moral fortitude. Only when he is shamed by his girlfriend and her father does he come to terms with his responsibilities. This low-budget film from Lippert may perhaps be described as an anti-*High Noon* western. Interestingly, it was scripted by the same Ian Macdonald who played Gary Cooper's nemesis Frank Miller in HIGH NOON (1952) three years earlier. The title song was written and sung by Jimmy Wakely.

SILVER TRAILS Monogram, 1948, B&W, 53 min. **Producer:** Louis Gray; **Director:** Christy Cabbanne; **Screenplay:** J. Benton Cheney; **Music:** Jimmy Rogers, Jimmy Wakely, and Don Weston; **Cinematographer:** Harry Neumann; **Editor:** John C. Fuller; **Cast:** Jimmy Wakely, Dub Taylor, Christine Larson, Whip Wilson, Pierce Lyden, George J. Lewis, William Bailey.
See *ACROSS THE RIO GRANDE*.

SILVER WHIP, THE 20th Century Fox, 1953, B&W, 73 min. **Producers:** Michael Abel and Robert Bassler;

Director: Harmon Jones; **Screenplay:** Jesse Lasky Jr., and Jack Schaefer; **Music:** Lionel Newman; **Cinematographer:** Lloyd Ahern; **Editor:** George A. Gittens; **Cast:** Dale Robertson, Rory Calhoun, Robert Wagner, Kathleen Crowley, James Millican, Lola Albright, J. M. Kerrigan, John Kellogg, Harry Carter, Ian MacDonald.

A young stagecoach driver (Robert Wagner) is fired from his first big job when a bandit (John Kellogg) holds him up. Injured by the bandit, the stage's guard (Dale Robertson) vows revenge. As the plot develops, Wagner becomes a deputy to sheriff Rory Calhoun. When bandit Kellogg is captured and jailed, a mob led by Robertson descends on the jail with lynching on its agenda. The deputy must now choose between his longtime friendship with Robertson or upholding the law and the wheels of justice.

Based on a story by Jack Schaefer, author of the novel *Shane* (1953). This interesting, offbeat western features three handsome rising stars in their professional primes; an assortment of familiar faces; and a taut, well-developed script.

SING, COWBOY, SING Grand National, 1937, B&W, 59 min, VHS. **Producer:** Edward Finney; **Director:** Robert N. Bradbury; **Screenplay:** Robert Emmett Tansey (as Robert Emmett); **Music:** Bradbury, Ted Choate, Tex Frank Sanucci, and Rudy Sooter; **Cinematographer:** Gus Peterson; **Editor:** Frederick Bain; **Cast:** Tex Ritter, Louise Stanley, Al St. John, Charles King, Karl Hackett, Robert McKenzie.
See *SONG OF THE GRINGO*.

SINGING BUCKAROO, THE Spectrum, 1937, B&W, 50 min. **Producers:** Jed Buell and George Callaghan; **Director:** Tom Gibson; **Screenplay:** Gibson; **Cinematographer:** Robert Doran; **Editor:** Dan Milner; **Cast:** Fred Scott, Victoria Vinton, William Faversham, Cliff Nazarro, Howard Hill, Dick Curtis.

SINGING COWBOY Republic, 1936, B&W, 56 min. **Producer:** Nat Levine; **Director:** Mack V. Wright; **Screenplay:** Dorrell McGowan and Stuart E. McGowan; **Music:** Smiley Burnette, Oliver Drake, Harry Grey, and Arthur Kay; **Cinematographer:** Edgar Lyons; **Editor:** Lester Orlebeck; **Cast:** Gene Autry, Smiley Burnette, Lois Wilde, Lon Chaney Jr., Ann Gillis, Earle Hodgins, Harvey Clark, John Van Pelt.

SINGING COWGIRL, THE Grand National, 1939, B&W, 59 min. **Producer:** Don Lieberman; **Director:** Samuel Diege; **Screenplay:** Arthur Hoerl; **Music:** Ross DiMaggio, Milton Drake, Walter Kent, and Alfred Sherman; **Cinematographer:** Mack Stengler; **Editor:** Guy V. Thayer Jr.; **Cast:** Dorothy Page, Dave O'Brien, Vince Barnett, Dorothy Short, Dix Davis, Warner P. Richmond.

A young woman takes in a boy whose parents have been killed by rustlers. She then sets out to round up the gang that is responsible. This feature was the last of a trio of a series of cowgirl oaters starring Dorothy Page; the first two were *Water Rustlers* and *Ride 'Em Cowgirl* (1939).

SINGING GUNS Republic, 1950, Color, 91 min. **Producer:** Abe Lyman; **Director:** R. G. Springsteen; **Screenplay;** Dorrell McGowan and Stuart McGowan; **Music:** Nathan Scott; **Cinematographer:** Reggie Lanning; **Editor:** Richard L. Van Enger; **Cast:** Vaughn Monroe, Ella Raines, Walter Brennan, Ward Bond, Jeff Corey, Barry Kelley, Harry Shannon.

An outlaw who saves the life of the man he is tracking decides to change his ways and his name. With his new identity he settles down to become the sheriff of a small town. Singer/bandleader Vaughn Monroe does extremely well as a cowboy. Through the course of the picture he sings three songs, including the Oscar-nominated hit song "Mule Train," written by Johnny Lange, Fred Glickman, and Hy Heath. Although the song was recorded by Monroe, one of the best crooners in the business, it was Frankie Laine who had the number one hit recording. The song also appeared in the movie of the same name starring Gene Autry.

SINGING HILL, THE Republic, 1941, B&W, 75 min. **Producer:** Harry Grey (associate); **Director:** Lew Landers; **Screenplay:** Olive Cooper; **Cinematographer:** William Nobles; **Editor:** Lester Orlebeck; **Cast:** Gene Autry, Smiley Burnette, Virginia Dale, Mary Lee, Spencer Charters, Gerald Oliver Smith.

SINGING OUTLAW Universal, 1937, B&W, 60 min. **Producers:** Trem Carr, Glenn Cook, and Paul Malvern; **Director:** Joseph H. Lewis; **Screenplay:** Harry O. Hoyt; **Music:** Charles Previn; **Cinematographer:** Virgil Miller; **Editor:** Charles Craft; **Cast:** Bob Baker, Joan Barclay, Fuzzy Knight, Harry Woods, Carl Stockdale, LeRoy Mason, Bob Card, Edward Peil Sr., Glenn Strange, Budd Buster.

SINGING SHERIFF, THE Universal, 1944, B&W, 63 min. **Producer:** Bernard W. Burton (associate); **Director:** Leslie Goodwins; **Screenplay:** Henry Blankfort and Eugene Conrad; **Music:** Dave Franklin, William Lava, Sidney Miller, Don Rave, and Gene de Paul; **Cinematographer:** Charles Van Enger; **Editor:** Edward Curtiss; **Cast:** Bob Crosby, Fay McKenzie, Fuzzy Knight, Iris Adrian, Samuel S. Hinds, Edward Norris, Andrew Tombes, Joe Sawyer, Walter Sande, Doodles Weaver.

Bob Crosby is a singer and son of a prominent citizen who arrives in a western town incognito but unwittingly has a run-in with a gang of desperadoes. Somehow he manages to bring them to justice. The plot of this innocuous little film is only a ploy to give Crosby an opportunity to sing some songs (which he always did quite well). The younger brother of Bing, Bob Crosby was a top talent in his own right as was his

band, the Bobcats, although it was Spade Cooley & His Orchestra who appeared in this picture.

SINGING VAGABOND, THE Republic, 1935, B&W, 55 min. **Producer:** Nat Levine; **Director:** Carl Pierson; **Screenplay;** Betty Burbridge and Oliver Drake; **Music:** Arthur Kay; **Cinematographer:** William Nobles; **Cast:** Gene Autry, Ann Rutherford, Smiley Burnette, Barbara Pepper, Niles Welch, Grace Goodall.

SINISTER JOURNEY United Artists, 1948, B&W, 59 min, VHS. **Producers:** William Boyd and Lewis J. Rachmil; **Director:** George Archainbaud; **Screenplay:** Doris Schroeder; **Music:** Darrell Calker; **Cinematographer:** Mack Stengler; **Editor:** Fred W. Berger; **Cast:** William Boyd, Andy Clyde, Rand Brooks, Elaine Riley, John Kellogg, Don Haggerty, Stanley Andrews.

SIN TOWN Universal, 1942, B&W, 73 min. **Producer:** George Waggner; **Director:** Ray Enright; **Screenplay:** Scott Darling, Gerald Geraghty, and Richard Brooks; **Music:** Hans J. Salter; **Cinematographer:** George Robinson; **Editor:** Edward Curtiss; **Cast:** Constance Bennett, Broderick Crawford, Anne Gwynne, Patric Knowles, Andy Devine, Leo Carillo, Ward Bond.

Broderick Crawford and Constance Bennett are two grifters who arrive in a boomtown, hoping to clean up big via the confidence route. After they save Rock Delaney (Ward Bond) from the hangman's noose, they gain ownership of the local saloon. However, when the local newspaper editor (Anne Gwynne) is murdered after beginning an investigation into their dealings, the town goes into an uproar. This quick-paced shoot-'em-up western set in 1910 benefits from an excellent cast and taut early writing by Richard Brooks, who supplied some of the additional dialogue.

SIOUX CITY SUE Republic, 1946, B&W, 69 min, VHS. **Producer:** Armand Schaefer (associate); **Director:** Frank McDonald; **Screenplay:** Olive Cooper; **Music:** R. Dale Butts; **Cinematography;** Reggie Lanning; **Editor:** Fred Allen; **Cast:** Gene Autry, Lynne Roberts, Sterling Holloway, Richard Lane, Ralph Sanford, Ken Lundy, Helen Wallace, Pierre Watkin, Kenne Duncan.

Hollywood scout Sue Warner (Lynne Roberts) is looking for a singing cowboy and discovers cattle rancher Gene Autry. She offers him a contract if he will agree to go to Hollywood, and Gene agrees, but with one proviso. There will have to be a part for his horse too.

Sue City Sue marked Gene's return to films following his wartime stint in the army air corps. The movie was based on the script *She Married a Cop* (1939) and a 1946 Hit Parade song. Written by Dick Thomas and Ray Freedman, the song was sung in the film by Gene with the Cass County Boys as his backup. The big hit recording of "Sioux City Sue" was by

Bing Crosby with The Jesters and Bob Haggart's Orchestra on the Decca label.

Other vocals in the film have Gene singing the popular hit standards "Yours" and "Someday (You'll Want Me to Want You)," with the traditional "The Old Chisholm Trail" performed by the Cass County Boys. (See also *TUMBLING TUMBLEWEEDS*.)

SITTING BULL   United Artists, 1954, Color, 105 min, DVD. **Producer:** W. R. Frank; **Director:** Sidney Salkow; **Screenplay:** Jack DeWitt and Salkow; **Music:** Raoul Kraushaar; **Cinematographer:** Charles Van Enger; **Cast:** Dale Robertson, Mary Murphy, J. Carrol Naish, Iron Eyes Cody, Joel Fluellen, John Litel, William Hooper, Douglas Kennedy.

Major Bob Parish (Dale Robertson) clashes with his superiors over their treatment of the Sioux prior to the events leading up to the Battle of Little Big Horn. After Sitting Bull, chief of the Sioux, is forced to take up arms against an Indian-hating General Custer, slaughtering troops at Little Big Horn, Major Parish is court-martialed for "collaborating with the enemy." However, Sitting Bull (in a slice of pure historical hokum) manages to intercede with President Ulysses S. Grant on Parish's behalf and meets with the chief executive to set up a state of peaceful coexistence between the two races.

Despite the film's rampant historical inaccuracies, J. Carrol Naish delivers a splendid performance in the title role, a part that he also played with a more comical touch in the western musical *ANNIE GET YOUR GUN* (1950). Unfortunately, the movie tells little that is factual about Sitting Bull's life either before or after the Battle at Little Big Horn. Decidedly pro-Sioux in its take, the film is compatible with the prevailing fad of the early 1950s to provide screen biographies of tribal leaders.

SIX BLACK HORSES   Universal, 1962, Color, 80 min. **Producer:** Gordon Kay; **Director:** Harry Keller; **Screenplay:** Burt Kennedy; **Music:** Joseph Gershenson; **Cinematographer:** Maury Gertsman; **Editor:** Aaron Stell; **Cast:** Audie Murphy, Dan Duryea, Joan O'Brien, Roy Barcroft, Phil Chambers, Bob Steele, Henry Wills, Charlita, Richard Pasco.

A cowboy befriends a fellow drifter who rescues him from a lynch mob, and a mysterious woman hires the two to take her across Indian territory. However, it turns out that the woman has an ulterior motive. She plans to kill one of them.

SIX GUN DECISION   Allied Artists, 1953, B&W. **Producer:** Wesley Barry; **Director:** Frank McDonald; **Screenplay:** William Raynor; **Cinematographer:** William Sickner; **Cast:** Guy Madison, Andy Devine, Gloria Saunders, Lyle Talbot, David Sharpe, Zon Murray.

It's Guy Madison as Marshal James Butler "Wild Bill" Hickok and Andy Devine as Deputy Aloysius "Jingles" P.

Jones. Madison appeared in more than 85 films and starred in the TV series *Adventures of Wild Bill Hickok* (1951–58). He played the famed lawman in a number of films, including *Yellow Haired Kid, Trail of the Arrow, Ghost of Crossbones Canyon, Behind Southern Lines* (1952); *Two-Gun Marshal, Secret of Outlaw Flats, Border City Rustlers* (1953); *The Two Gun Teacher, Trouble on the Trail, Outlaw's Son, Marshals in Disguise* (1954); *The Titled Tenderfoot, Timber County Trouble, Phantom Trails. The Matchmaking Marshal* (1955).

SIX-GUN GOLD   RKO, 1941, B&W, 57 min. **Producer:** Bert Gilroy; **Director:** David Howard; **Screenplay:** Norton S. Parker; **Music:** Fred Rose and Ray Whitley; **Cinematographer:** Harry J. Wild; **Editor:** Frederic Knudtson; **Cast:** Tim Holt, Ray Whitley, Jan Clayton, Lee "Lasses" White, LeRoy Mason, Eddy Waller, Fern Emmett.

SIX-GUN LAW   Columbia, 1948, B&W, 54 min. **Producer:** Colbert Clark; **Director:** Ray Nazarro; **Screenplay:** Barry Shipman; **Cinematographer:** George F. Kelley; **Editor:** Henry DeMond; **Cast:** Charles Starrett, Smiley Burnette, Nancy Saunders, Paul Campbell, Hugh Prosser, George Chesebro.

SIX-GUN RHYTHM   Grand National, 1939, B&W, 57 min. **Producer:** Sam Newfield; **Director:** Newfield; **Screenplay:** Fred Myton (as Fred Richmond); **Music:** Johnny Lange and Lew Porter; **Cinematographer:** Arthur Reed; **Editor:** Robert O. Crandall; **Cast:** Tex Fletcher, Ralph Peters, Joan Barclay, Reed Howes, Malcom "Bud" Taggart, Ted Adams.

Football player Tex Fletcher arrives home and finds that his father is missing. In reality his father has been killed, and the killer is about to stake out Tex. When Tex kills one of the outlaw's henchmen, the stooge sheriff puts him in jail. Along the way he manages to sing a few tunes, including Lonesome Cowboy" and "Git Along Little Dogies."

A singing cowboy on the radio at the height of the singing cowboy craze, Tex Fletcher was given a screen test and signed to do a series of horse operas for Grand National Productions. Upon the release of *Six Gun Rhythm*, the studio went under, leaving the only existing prints of the film unreleased. Fletcher therefore went on a one-man promotional tour for the film in the Northeast, personally booked the film, and traveled to each movie house, where he opened the show with a couple of songs and signed autographs when the feature ended. He turned down all future Hollywood offers to do a series and instead enlisted during World War II, after which returned home to marry and raise a family. Nicknamed the "Lonely Cowboy," Fletcher returned to radio and nightclubs and also did some television. He released his last record album in 1964, but he never again appeared on the big screen.

SIX-GUN SERENADE   Monogram, 1947, B&W, 55 min. **Producer:** Barney Sarecky; **Director:** Ford Beebe;

Screenplay: Ben Cohen; **Music:** Wanda Daniels, Arthur "Fiddlin" Smith, and Lee "Lasses" White; **Cinematographer:** Marcel Le Picard; **Editor:** Edward A. Biery Jr.; **Cast:** Jimmy Wakely, Lee "Lasses" White, Kay Morley, Jimmy Martin, Steve Clark, Pierce Lyden, Bud Osborne, Rivers Lewis, Arthur "Fiddlin" Smith.

See *ACROSS THE RIO GRANDE.*

SKIN GAME Warner Bros., 1971, Color, 102 min, VHS. **Producer:** Harry Keller; **Director:** Paul Bogart; **Screenplay:** Pierre Marton; **Music:** David Shire; **Cinematographer:** Fred J. Koenekamp; **Editor:** Walter Thompson; **Cast:** James Garner, Louis Gossett Jr., Susan Clark, Edward Asner, Andrew Duggan, Henry Jones, Royal Dano, Neva Patterson, Parley Baer, George Tyne.

James Garner and Louis Gossett Jr. operate an unusual con game, posing as master and slave during the pre-Civil War years. Operating around Kansas and Missouri, Garner is a crafty con man pretending to be a ruined plantation owner who is forced by destitution to sell his loyal slave (Gossett) to the highest-bidding slave owner. Garner then helps him escape, and the two move on to the next town, where they repeat their ruse. They eventually hook with a woman con artist (Susan Clark) with a few tricks of her own. The fleecing continues until they encounter villainous Ed Asner, who catches on to their ruse with a chilling effect.

This deftly made western sociocomedy packs a serious punch and should not be confused with the 1931 Alfred Hitchcock thriller *The Skin Game.*

SKIPALONG ROSENBLOOM Eagle Lion, 1951, B&W, 72 min. **Producer:** Wally Kline; **Director:** Sam Newfield; **Screenplay:** Eddie Forman and Dean Riesner; **Music:** Jack Kenney; **Cinematographer:** Ernest Miller; **Editor:** Victor Lewis; **Cast:** Maxie "Slapsie" Rosenbloom, Max Baer, Jackie Coogan, Fuzzy Knight, Hillary Brooke, Raymond Hatton, Jacqueline Fountain.

The tag line for this western spoof reads, "With a Gun, a Gal, or a Rope . . . He's a Dope!" The citizens of the town of Buttonhole Bend are in the clutches of the ruthless Butcher Baer (Max Baer) gang, which has knocked off every sheriff and robbed every bank in the territory. The brains behind the whole operation is Square Deal Sal (Hillary Brooke), the owner of the Square Deal Saloon. Enter eastern gunman Skipalong Rosenbloom (Maxie Rosenbloom), who comes to town and is tricked into becoming sheriff.

This high-camp little spoof is filled with lots of slapstick and fun. What makes it an oddity is that both Max Baer and Maxie Rosenbloom were boxing champions. Rosenbloom was the light heavyweight champion of the world (1932–34), while Max Baer was the heavyweight champion of the world for 364 days, winning the championship by knocking out Primo Carnera on June 14, 1934, and then losing it to Jim Braddock on June 3, 1935. Max Baer makes for a pretty tough villain. After all, he KO'd 50 opponents during his professional career. Maxie Rosenbloom went on to a long career as an entertainer.

SLAUGHTER TRAIL RKO, 1951, Color, 78 min. **Producer:** Irving Allen; **Director:** Allen; **Screenplay:** Sid Kuller; **Music:** Terry Gilkyson and Lyn Murray; **Cinematographer:** Jack Greenhalgh; **Editor:** Fred Allen; **Cast:** Brian Donlevy, Gig Young, Andy Devine, Virginia Grey, Robert Hutton, Terry Gilkyson, Lois Hall, Myron Healey.

Brian Donlevy is a cavalry officer determined to track down the outlaw gang that murdered three Indians and the Fort commander after committing a robbery. The unique feature of this western film is its balladlike sound track.

SMOKE SIGNAL Universal, 1955, Color, 88 min. **Producer:** Howard Christie; **Director:** Jerry Hopper; **Screenplay:** George W. George and George F. Slavin; **Music:** Irving Gertz, William Lava, and Henry Mancini; **Cinematographer:** Clifford Stine; **Editor:** Milton Carruth; **Cast:** Dana Andrews, Piper Laurie, Rex Reason, William Talman, Milburn Stone, Douglas Spencer, Gordon Jones.

The surviving members (including one woman) of an Indian massacre trek downstream on the Colorado River aboard flatboats in an escape attempt. The plot twist here is that among the survivors is a reputed army traitor (Dana Andrews) and the cavalry captain (William Talman) who had been assigned to bring him in. Piper Laurie adds the female equation to this zesty adventure, and like Andrew and Talman she turns in a first-rate performance.

SMOKE TREE RANGE Universal, 1937, B&W, 55 min. **Producer:** Buck Jones; **Director:** Lesley Selander; **Screenplay:** Francis Guihan; **Cinematographer:** Allen O. Thompson; **Editor:** Bernard Loftus; **Cast:** Buck Jones, Muriel Evans, John Elliott, Dickie Jones, Ted Adams, Ben Hall.

Buck Jones and director Lesley Selander are at their best in this story of a cowboy who aids an orphaned girl whose cattle are being rustled by an outlaw gang. (See also *STONE OF SILVER CREEK.*)

SMOKEY SMITH Supreme, 1935, B&W, 57 min. **Producer:** A. W. Hackel; **Director:** Robert Bradbury; **Screenplay:** Bradbury; **Cinematographer:** William Nobles; **Editor:** S. Roy Luby; **Cast:** Bob Steele, Mary Kornman, George "Gabby" Hayes, Warner Richmond, Earle Dwire, Horace B. Carpenter.

SMOKING GUNS Universal, 1934, B&W, 65 min. **Producer:** Ken Maynard; **Director:** Alan James; **Screenplay:** Maynard and Nate Gatzert; **Cinematographer:** Ted McCord; **Editor:** Charles Harris; **Cast:** Ken Maynard, Gloria Shea, Jack Rockwell, Walter Miller, William Gould, Harold Goodwin, Robert Kortman.

Ken Maynard is a cowboy, falsely accused of a crime, who heads for the jungles of South America. He is followed by a

Texas Ranger, and the two become friends. But when the ranger is killed by a crocodile, Ken assumes his identity and returns home to clear his name. This was Ken Maynard's final film for Universal. (See also *LUCKY LARKIN*.)

SMOKY 20th Century Fox, 1946, Color, 87 min. **Producer:** Robert Bassler; **Director:** Louis King; **Screenplay:** Lily Hayward, Dwight Cummins, and Dorothy Yost; **Music:** David Raskin; **Cinematographer:** Charles Clarke; **Editor:** Emil Newman; **Cast:** Fred MacMurray, Anne Baxter, Burl Ives, Bruce Cabot, Esther Dale, Roy Roberts, J. Farrell MacDonald.

Fred MacMurray is a roving cowboy who spots a beautiful black stallion as it defies a roundup. After capturing the horse, he trains it to respond to him alone, but then it is stolen during a cattle raid. The cowboy is never deterred in his quest to find the horse, which has been mistreated and ends up pulling a junk wagon. One day during a parade the horse responds to the sound of music, and quite coincidentally the cowboy is there to see him.

Filmed in Utah, this beautiful and delightful modern western is the second based on Will James's classic horse story. A perfect family film, the picture grossed more than $4 million at the box office (not an inconsiderable sum by 1946 standards).

The first film treatment of *Smoky* was made by Fox in 1933, with Eugene Ford directing and Victor Jory in the lead role. 20th Century Fox did a remake of *Smoky* in 1966, directed by George Sherman and featuring Fess Parker, Diana Hyland, and Katy Jurado. The 1946 version is clearly the best.

SMOKY CANYON Columbia, 1952, B&W, 55 min. **Producer:** Colbert Clark; **Director:** Fred F. Sears; **Screenplay:** Barry Shipman; **Music:** Mischa Bakaleinikoff; **Cinematographer:** Fayte M. Browne; **Editor:** Paul Borofsky; **Cast:** Charles Starrett, Smiley Burnette, Jock Mahoney, Dani Sue Nolan, Chris Alcaide, Tristram Coffin, Sandy Sanders.
See *DURANGO KID, THE*.

SMOKY MOUNTAIN MELODY Columbia, 1948, B&W, 61 min. **Producer:** Colbert Clark; **Director:** Ray Nazarro; **Screenplay:** Barry Shipman; **Cinematographer:** Rex Wimpy; **Editor:** Paul Borofsky; **Cast:** Roy Acuff, Guinn Williams, Russell Arms, Sybil Merritt, Jason Robards, Harry V. Cheshire, Fred Sears, Trevor Bardette, Carolina Cotton, Tommy Ivo, Jock Mahoney, John Elliott, Sam Flint.

When a singer gets a three-month trial period to run a ranch, the late owner's son does all he can to sabotage his chances. This fun-packed country-music western features a lively array of talent, including Roy Acuff and his Smoky Mountain Boys and young Carolina Cotton, who when it came to yodeling was among the very best in the business.

SNAKE RIVER DESPERADOES Columbia, 1951, B&W, 54 min. **Producer:** Colbert Clark; **Director:** Fred F. Sears; **Screenplay:** Barry Shipman; **Cinematographer:** Fayte M. Browne; **Editor:** Paul Borofsky; **Cast:** Charles Starrett, Smiley Burnette, Monte Blue, Don K. Reynolds, Tommy Ivo, Boyd "Red" Morgan, George Chesebro, Frank Wayne.
See *DURANGO KID, THE*.

SNOW FIRE Allied Artists, 1955, Color, 73 min. **Producers:** Darrell McGowan and Stuart E. McGowan; **Directors:** McGowan and McGowan; **Screenplay:** McGowan and McGowan; **Music:** Albert Glasser; **Cinematographer:** Brydon Baker; **Editor:** Arthur H. Nadel and Jerry Young; **Cast:** Don McGowan, Molly McGowan, Claire Kelly, John Cason, Michael Vallon, Melody McGowan.

A father captures a wild white stallion, but his young daughter decides to set it free and earns its friendship. This fine low-budget family film touches at the heartstrings and is a joy to see. Unfortunately, according to most reports it is almost impossible to find a print of the film today.

SOLDIER BLUE Avco-Embassy, 1970, Color, 112 min, VHS. **Producers:** Harold Loeb and Gabriel Katzka; **Director:** Ralph Nelson; **Screenplay:** John Gay; **Music:** Roy Budd; **Cinematographer:** Robert Hauser; **Editor:** Alex Beaton; **Cast:** Candice Bergen, Peter Strauss, Donald Pleasence, John Anderson, Jorge Rivero, Dana Elcar.

Based on the novel *Arrow in the Sun* by Theodore V. Olson, the film deals with a massacre of the Cheyenne at the hand of the U.S. cavalry. "Soldier Blue" of the title is private Honus Gent (Peter Strauss), who joins forces with a white woman (Candice Bergen) after the paymaster party with which they have been traveling has been ambushed and slaughtered by the Cheyenne. Together they make the long trek to reach an army post, where Bergen reminds one and all that the white man is far more beastly than the Indians. Previously she had lived among the Cheyenne for two years, so when she discovers an army plot to wipe out the Indians, she rides out to warn them.

Decidedly pro-Indian in scope and gratuitously violent, the climax of the film makes the army the complete villain and the Cheyenne the complete innocents. The excessively bloody action meant to recreate the Sand Creek Massacre of the Cheyenne in 1864 shows the U.S. cavalry at its brutal worst. The gory climax defies any semblance of balance and objectivity, such as cavalrymen slicing off the breast of a squaw and tossing it back and forth on the ends of their sabers in scenes so graphic that people actually reported becoming ill in the theaters.

Soldier Blue was filmed during the height of the Vietnam War, when anti-American sentiment was rampant among vocal segments at home and abroad. The strong suggestion here is that the behavior of the cavalry against the American Indians was closely related to that of some American soldiers in Vietnam. *Variety* was quick to notice the film's heavy-handed manner and incongruities, stating that "It would appear obvious that director Ralph Nelson is trying to correlate this allegedly historical incident with more contemporaneous events."

SOMBRERO KID, THE
Republic, 1942, B&W, 56 min. **Producer:** George Sherman (associate); **Director:** Sherman; **Screenplay:** Norman Hall; **Cinematographer:** William Bradford; **Editor:** William P. Thompson; **Cast:** Don "Red" Barry, Lynn Merrick, Robert Homans, John James, Joel Friedkin, Rand Brooks.

See *WYOMING OUTLAW*.

SOMETHING BIG
National General, 1971, Color, 108 min. **Producers:** James Lee Barrett and Andrew V. McLaglen; **Director:** McLaglen; **Screenplay:** Barrett; **Music:** Marvin Hamlisch; **Cinematographer:** Harry Stradling; **Editor:** Robert L. Simpson; **Cast:** Dean Martin, Brian Keith, Honor Blackman, Carol White, Ben Johnson, Albert Salmi, Don Knight, Harry Carey Jr., Joyce Van Patten, Denver Pyle, Edward Faulkner, Merlin Olson, Paul Fix.

Dean Martin plays an outlaw named Joe Baker, who comes out West determined to do "something big." Traveling with a dog strapped to his saddle, he decides his something big will be to steal a bundle of gold from the villa of a Mexican bandit. He needs a Gatling gun for his mission to succeed. But to trade for the gun he has to find a woman for the Gatling's owner (Albert Salmi). So Baker holds up four different stagecoaches (he doesn't harm anyone or take anything) in search of the right woman. He finally finds a woman to his liking on the fifth stage, but she happens to be the wife of the retiring fort commander, Colonel Morgan (Brian Keith), and a woman known for her frigidity. After much hassle Morgan gets his wife back; Cobb (Salmi) gets two lascivious sisters; and Baker, making good use of his Gatling, gets the loot and rides off into the sunset a rich man.

Directed by Andrew V. McLaglen, who had directed Martin a decade earlier in *BANDOLERO*, the film may well have been made because of the enormous success of *BUTCH CASSIDY AND THE SUNDANCE KID*, which had succeeded in part because of its lighthearted look at comic outlaws. However, unlike Butch and Sundance, who play for their outlaw ways with their lives, Joe Baker is able to get away with robbery and murder.

According to *The Hollywood Reporter*, "Dear old Dino is a way-out robber, kind of cute in his own way," and it that the film was "clever but suggestive, violent without blood . . . precisely the same sort of mindless goo that corrodes TV airwaves." Marvin Hamlisch composed the musical score; the title song was written by Burt Bacharach. In most sources the movie is listed entirely in lower case, that is, something big.

SOMEWHERE IN SONORA
Warner Bros., 1933, B&W, 59 min. **Producer:** Leon Schlesinger; **Director:** Mack V. Wright; **Screenplay:** Will Levington Comfort; **Cinematographer:** Ted McCord; **Editor:** William Clemens; **Cast:** John Wayne, Shirley Palmer, Henry B. Walthall, Paul Fix, Ann Faye, Billy Franey, Ralph Lewis, Frank Rice, J. P. McGowan.

Falsely accused of cheating during a rodeo race, John Wayne goes to Mexico and redeems himself by joining an outlaw gang to help uncover a plot to rob the mine owned by the father of the girl he loves. A remake of the 1927 Ken Maynard/First National Film of the same title, the picture was the first of many Wayne would make with versatile character actor Paul Fix.

SONG OF ARIZONA
Republic, 1946, B&W, 68 min. **Producer:** Edward J. White (associate); **Director:** Frank McDonald; **Screenplay:** M. Coates Webster; **Music:** Jack Elliott, Gordon Foster, Bob Nolan (songs), Ira Schuster, and Larry Stock; **Cinematographer:** Reggie Lanning; **Editor:** Arthur Roberts; **Cast:** Roy Rogers, George "Gabby" Hayes, Dale Evans, Lyle Talbot, Tommy Cook, Johnny Calkins, Bob Nolan and The Sons of the Pioneers.

SONG OF NEVADA
Republic, 1944, B&W, 75 min. **Producer:** Armand Schaefer; **Director:** Joseph Kane; **Screenplay:** Olive Cooper and Gordon Kahn; **Music:** Morton Scott; **Cinematographer:** Jack Marta; **Editor:** Tony Martinelli; **Cast:** Roy Rogers, Dale Evans, Mary Lee, Lloyd Corrigan, Thurston Hall, John Eldredge.

SONG OF OLD WYOMING
PRC, 1945, Color, 65 min. **Producer:** Robert Emmett Tansey (as Robert Emmett); **Director:** Tansey (as Emmett); **Screenplay:** Frances Kavanaugh; **Music:** Eddie Dean, Carl Hoefle, Milt Mabie, Ralph Rainger, and Leo Robin; **Cinematographer:** Marcel Le Picard; **Editor:** Hugh Winn; **Cast:** Eddie Dean, Sarah Padded, Ian Keith, Lash La Rue (as Al La Rue), Jennifer Holt, Emmett Lynn.

A singing cowboy (Eddie Dean) comes to the aid of a woman, the owner of a cattle ranch and publisher of a newspaper, when rustlers steal her cattle and attempt to bankrupt her. This Dean series western benefits from Cinecolor and a scene-stealing performance by Al (not yet Lash) La Rue as the rancher's long-lost outlaw son.

Eddie Dean made a number of series oaters for Producers Releasing Corporation, including *Tumbleweed Trail, Down Missouri, Stars Over Texas, Wild West, Romances of the West, COLORADO SERENADE, THE CARAVAN TRAIL* (1946); *Wild Country, Range Beyond the Blue, West to Glory, My Pal Ringeye, Shadow Valley, HARMONY TRAIL* (1947); *CHECK YOUR GUNS Tornado Range, Black Hills, The Westward Trail, The Tioga Kid, The Hawk of Powder River* (1948).

SONG OF TEXAS
Republic, 1943, B&W, 69 min, VHS. **Producer:** Harry Grey (associate); **Director:** Joseph Kane; **Screenplay:** Winston Miller; **Music:** Fleming Allen, Ben Black, C. Fernandez, Edward H. Lemare, Neil Moret, Helen Stone, and Jack Tinney; **Cinematographer:** Reggie Lanning; **Editor:** Tony Martinelli; **Cast:** Roy Rogers, Sheila Ryan, Barton MacLane, Harry Shannon, Pat Brady, Bob Nolan and The Sons of the Pioneers, Yakima Canutt.

SONG OF THE BUCKAROO Monogram, 1938, B&W, 58 min, VHS. **Producer:** Edward Finney; **Director:** Albert Herman; **Screenplay:** John Rathmell; **Music:** Frank Sanucci; **Cinematographer:** Francis Corby; **Editor:** Frederick Bain; **Cast:** Tex Ritter, Jinx Falkenburg, Mary Ruth, Frank La Rue, Tom London, Snub Pollard.

SONG OF THE CABALLERO Universal/Ken Maynard Productions, 1930, B&W, 73 min. **Producer:** Ken Maynard; **Director:** Harry Joe Brown; **Screenplay:** Bennett Cohen; **Music:** Sam Perry; **Cinematographer:** Ted D. McCord; **Editor:** Fred Allen; **Cast:** Ken Maynard, Doris Hill, Francis Ford, Gino Corrado, Evelyn Sherman.

SONG OF THE DRIFTER Monogram, 1948, B&W, 53 min. **Producer:** Louis Gray; **Director:** Lambert Hillyer; **Screenplay:** Frank Young; **Cinematographer:** Harry Neumann; **Editor:** Fred Maguire; **Cast:** Jimmy Wakely, Dub Taylor, Mildred Coles, Patsy Moran, William Ruhl, Marshall Reed, Frank La Rue, Carl Mathews.

SONG OF THE GRINGO (aka: THE OLD CORRAL UK) Grand National, 1936, B&W, 62 min. **Producer:** Edward Finney; **Director:** John McCarthy; **Screenplay:** Al J. Jennings, John P. McCarthy, and Robert Emmett; **Music:** Jose Pacheco; **Cinematographer:** Gus Peterson; **Editor:** Frederick Bain; **Cast:** Tex Ritter, Joan Woodbury, Fuzzy Knight, Monte Blue, Warner P. Richmond, Al J. Jennings.

Tex Ritter's film debut has him as an investigator who is sent to look into the killings of a number of miners. He poses as a cowboy to infiltrate the gang and ends up being accused of murdering a ranch owner.

Following the success of singing cowboy Gene Autry, Tex Ritter was signed to star in a series of westerns, beginning with *Song of the Gringo* for Grand National and then for Monogram. Steeped in Texas history, he began singing on the radio and the stage and developed a penchant for singing authentic sagebrush songs. Quite popular for a while, his series of low-budget westerns include HEADIN' FOR THE RIO GRANDE (1936); ARIZONA DAYS, TROUBLE IN TEXAS, HITTIN' THE TRAIL, SING COWBOY SING, RIDERS OF THE ROCKIES, MYSTERY OF THE HOODED HORSEMEN, TEX RIDES WITH THE BOY SCOUTS (1937); FRONTIER TOWN, ROLLIN' PLAINS, UTAH TRAIL, *Where the Buffalo Roam, Starlight Over Texas, Song of the Buckaroo,* (1938); *Rollin' Westward, Sundown on the Prairie, Man from Texas, Down Wyoming Trail, Westbound Stage,* RIDERS OF THE FRONTIER (1939); PALS OF THE SILVER SAGE, COWBOY FROM SUNDOWN, THE GOLDEN TRAIL, *Rainbow Over the Range,* ROLL WAGONS ROLL, ARIZONA FRONTIER, *Take Me Back to Oklahoma, Rolling Home to Texas,* RHYTHM OF THE RIO GRANDE (1940); RIDIN' THE CHEROKEE TRAIL, *The Pioneers* (1941).

Ritter then went on to support Bill Elliott (Columbia, 1941–42) and Johnny Mack Brown (Universal, 1942–44) in a series of films. His final appearances were in a series of eight low-level Texas Ranger films (PRC, 1944–45).

SONG OF THE RANGE Monogram, 1944, B&W, 55 min. **Producer:** Philip N. Krasne; **Director:** Wallace Fox; **Screenplay;** Betty Burbridge; **Cinematographer:** Marcel Le Picard; **Editor:** Martin Cohn; **Cast:** Jimmy Wakely, Dennis Moore, Lee "Lasses" White, Sam Flint, Kay Forrester, Hugh Prosser, Steve Clark.

SONG OF THE SIERRA See *SPRINGTIME IN THE SIERRAS.*

SONG OF THE SIERRAS Monogram, 1946, B&W, 58 min. **Producer:** Oliver Drake; **Director:** Drake; **Screenplay:** Elmer Clifton; **Music:** Arthur "Fiddlin" Smith and Jimmy Wakely; **Cinematographer:** Marcel Le Picard; **Editor:** Ralph Dixon; **Cast:** Jimmy Wakely, Lee "Lasses" White, Jack Baxley, Jean Carlin, Iris Clive, Zon Murray, Budd Buster.

SONG OF THE TRAIL Ambassador, 1936, B&W, 59 min. **Producer:** Maurice Cohn; **Director:** Russell Horton; **Screenplay:** Barry Barringer and George Wallace Sayre; **Cinematographer:** Arthur Reed; **Editor:** Kermit Maynard; **Cast:** Kermit Maynard, Evelyn Brent, Fuzzy Knight, George "Gabby" Hayes, Wheeler Oakman, Andrea Leeds.

SONG OF THE WASTELAND Monogram, 1947, B&W, 58 min. **Producer:** Barney A. Sarecky; **Director:** Thomas Carr; **Screenplay:** J. Benton Cheney; **Cinematographer:** Harry Neumann; **Editor:** Fred Maguire; **Cast:** Jimmy Wakely, Lee "Lasses" White, John James, Dottye Brown, Holly Bane, Henry Hall, Marshall Reed.

SONGS AND BULLETS Spectrum, 1938, B&W, 57 min. **Producer:** Jed Buell; **Director:** Sam Newfield; **Screenplay:** Joseph O'Donnell; **Music:** Lew Porter; **Cinematographer:** Mack Stengler; **Editor:** Robert Johns; **Cast:** Fred Scott, Al St. John, Alice Ardell, Charles King, Karl Hackett, Frank La Rue, Budd Buster.

SON OF A BAD MAN Screen Guild, 1949, B&W, 64 min. **Producer:** Ron Ormond; **Director:** Ray Taylor; **Screenplay:** Ron Ormond and Ira Webb; **Music:** Walter Greene; **Cinematographers:** Ron Ormond and Ira Webb; **Editor:** Ernest Miller; **Cast:** Lash La Rue, Al St. John, Noel Neill, Michael Whalen, Zon Murphy.

Marshalls Lash and Fuzzy come to the aid of a town whose citizens are being plagued by a gang led by the mysterious El Sombre. This fast-paced little Lash La Rue oater marked his final Screen Guild series film.

SON-OF-A-GUN, THE G. M. Anderson, 1919, B&W, 68 min. **Producer:** Gilbert M. "Broncho Billy" Anderson; **Director:** Anderson; **Screenplay:** Anderson and Jess Robbins; **Cast:** "Broncho Billy" Anderson, Joy

Lewis, Fred Church, Frank Whitson, A. E. Witting, Maggie Eitting.

Swindlers are about to fleece a man of his savings in a crooked card game when a cowboy intercedes on the man's behalf. The picture is most noteworthy because it is the final film of the screen's first cowboy star, "Broncho Billy" Anderson.

SON OF BELLE STAR Allied Artists, 1953, Color, 70 min. **Producer:** Peter Scully; **Director:** Frank McDonald; **Screenplay:** D. D. Beauchamp; **Cinematographer:** Harry Nuemann; **Editor:** Bruce Schoengarth; **Cast:** Keith Larsen, Dona Drake, Peggie Castle, Regis Toomey, Myron Healey, James Seay, Frank Puglia.

Belle Starr's son grows to adulthood having to prove that he is not an outlaw like his infamous mom.

SON OF BILLY THE KID Screen Guild, 1949, B&W, 64 min. **Producer:** Ron Ormond; **Director:** Ray Taylor; **Screenplay:** Ron Ormond and Ira Webb; **Music:** Walter Greene; **Cinematographer:** Ernest Miller; **Editor:** Hugh Winn; **Cast:** Lash La Rue, Al St. John, Marion Colby, June Carr, George Baxter, Terry Frost, House Peters Jr., Clark Stevens, John James.

SON OF DAVY CROCKETT Columbia, 1941, B&W, 59 min. **Producer:** Leon Barsha; **Director:** Lambert Hillyer; **Screenplay:** Hillyer; **Cinematographer:** Benjamin H. Kline; **Editor:** Mel Thorsen; **Cast:** Bill Elliott, Iris Meredith, Dub Taylor, Richard Fiske, Kenneth MacDonald, Eddy Waller, Lloyd Bridges.

SON OF GOD'S COUNTRY Republic, 1948, B&W, 60 min. **Producer:** Melville Tucker; **Director:** R. G. Springsteen; **Screenplay:** Paul Gangelin; **Music:** R. Dale Butts; **Cinematographer:** John MacBurnie; **Cast:** Monte Hale, Pamela Blake, Paul Hurst, Jason Robards, Jay Kirby, Jim Nolan, Steve Darrell, Fred Graham.

SON OF OKLAHOMA World Wide, 1932, B&W, 57 min. **Producer:** Trem Carr; **Director:** Robert N. Bradbury; **Screenplay:** George Hull and Burl Tuttle; **Cast:** Bob Steele, Josie Sedgwick, Julian Rivero, Carmen LaRouix, Earl Dwire, Robert Homans, Henry Rocquemore.

SON OF PALEFACE Paramount, 1952, Color, 95 min. **Producer:** Robert L. Welch; **Director:** Frank Tashlin; **Screenplay:** Joseph Quillan, Tashlin, and Welch; **Music:** Jack Brooks, Ray Evans, Jay Livingston, and Lyn Murray; **Cinematographer:** Harry J. Wild; **Editor:** Eda Warren; **Cast:** Bob Hope, Jane Russell, Roy Rogers, Bill Williams, Lloyd Corrigan, Paul E. Burns, Douglas Dumbrille, Harry von Zell, Iron Eyes Cody.

In a sequel to the 1948 hit film, Bob Hope plays the son of his character in PALEFACE. This time he is a bumbling Ivy leaguer named Junior Potter who heads West to claim the inheritance left by "Painless" Potter, his frontier dentist dad. He and Roy Rogers hunt down a crook who has been holding up gold shipments, while curvaceous Jane Russell is again the object of his affections so that Junior prances and romances in another zany romp. The musical score includes a reprisal of Ray Evans and Jay Livingston's Oscar-winning song, "Buttons and Bows."

While not up to Hope's original comedic masterpiece, there is still lots of frolic and laughter in this winning sequel, which *Variety* calls "a freewheeling, often hilarious, rambunctious followup to *The Paleface*." The film was the first directorial assignment for former cartoonist Frank Tashlin, who also cowrote the original picture.

SON OF ROARING DAN Republic, 1940, B&W, 63 min. **Producer:** Joseph G. Sanford; **Director:** Ford Beebe; **Screenplay:** Clarence Upson Young; **Music:** Hans Salter and Frank Skinner; **Cinematographer:** William A. Sickner; **Editor:** Paul Landres; **Cast:** Johnny Mack Brown, Fuzzy Knight, Nell O'Day, Jean Brooks, Robert Homans, Tom Chatterton, Lafe McKee.

See *OLD CHISHOLM TRAIL*.

SON OF SLADE See *RETURN OF JACK SLADE, THE*.

SON OF THE BORDER RKO, 1933, B&W, 55 min. **Producer:** David Lewis (associate); **Director:** Lloyd Nosler; **Screenplay:** Harold Shumate and Wellyn Totman; **Music:** Max Steiner; **Cinematographer:** Nicholas Musuraca; **Editor:** Fred Knudtson; **Cast:** Tom Keene, Julie Haydon, Edgar Kennedy, Lon Chaney Jr. (as Creighton Chaney), David Duran, Al Bridge, Charles King.

SONS OF KATIE ELDER Paramount, 1965, Color, 122 min, VHS, DVD. **Producer:** Hal B. Wallis; **Director:** Henry Hathaway; **Screenplay:** William H. Wright, Allan Weiss, and Harry Essex, **Music:** Elmer Bernstein; **Cinematographer:** Lucien Ballard; **Editor:** Warren Low; **Cast:** John Wayne, Dean Martin, Martha Hyer, Michael Anderson Jr., Earl Holliman, James Gregory, Jeremy Slate, George Kennedy, Dennis Hopper, Sheldon Allman, John Litel, John Doucette, James Westerfield, Strother Martin, Rodolfo Acosta, John Qualen.

The four adult sons of Katie Elder return home for their mother's funeral and burial. Dismayed because their mother died in poverty, they also learn that their homestead had been lost in a card game by their late father, who was killed the same night. The Elder brothers are an assorted lot: John (John Wayne) is a gunfighter; Tom (Dean Martin) is a gambler; Matt (Earl Holliman) is quiet, yet tough; and Bud (Michael Anderson Jr.), the youngest, is a college student. It is now time to settle the score and bring the culprits to justice but not before a bitter land war claims the lives of two of the brothers as well as the bad men.

The Sons of Katie Elder remains one of John Wayne's most popular films, partly because it is a straightforward western full of action and adventure, one where no scorecard is needed to separate the good guys from the bad. However, its popularity stems mostly from the fact that it was John Wayne's first film after licking his initial bout with cancer in the mid-1960s.

Based on a story by Talbot Jennings and filmed in Durango, Mexico, this movie was John Wayne's 135th and director Henry Hathaway's 84th picture. (Four years later, Hathaway would direct Wayne to an Oscar-winning role in *TRUE GRIT*. The crusty director was a blessing in disguise for Wayne. Having survived colon cancer and being a tough taskmaster himself, Hathaway was not about to soft-pedal his star. In fact, Wayne would later credit the director for pushing him through, sparing him little comfort but making sure the actor could finish filming at the remote locations.

"Duke had the greatest respect for Henry both as a director and a man," recalls Luster Bayless, who outfitted Wayne for many of his pictures. "In fact, Duke told me that Henry helped save his life because he hadn't shown him any damn sympathy following his surgery. Henry made him work like nothing had happened."

The press coverage of *The Sons of Katie Elder* exceeded that for *The Alamo* five years earlier. But if critics expected to see a depleted and faltering John Wayne, they were sadly mistaken. Instead they saw a leaner Wayne who appeared in better shape than he had been in some previous films.

SONS OF NEW MEXICO   Columbia, 1949, B&W, 71 min. **Producer:** Armand Schaefer; **Director:** John English; **Screenplay:** Paul Gangelin; **Cinematographer:** William Bradford; **Editor:** Henry Batista; **Cast:** Gene Autry, Gail Davis, Robert Armstrong, Dickie Jones, Frankie Darro, Russell Arms, Irving Bacon.

SONS OF THE PIONEERS   Republic, 1942, B&W, 55 min. **Producer:** Joseph Kane; **Director:** Kane; **Screenplay:** M. Coates Webster; **Music:** Cy Feuer, Bob Nolan (songs), and Tim Spencer; **Cinematographer:** Bud Thackery; **Editor:** Edward Schroeder; **Cast:** Roy Rogers, George "Gabby" Hayes, Maris Wrixon, Forrest Taylor, Bob Nolan, Pat Brady, Hugh Farr.

SOUL OF NIGGER CHARLEY   Paramount, 1973, Color, 109 min. **Producer:** Larry Spangler; **Director:** Spangler; **Screenplay:** Harold Stone; **Music:** Don Costa; **Cinematographer:** Richard C. Glouner; **Editor:** Howard Kuperman; **Cast:** Fred Williamson, D'Urville Martin, Denise Nichols, Pedro Armendáriz Jr., Kirk Calloway, George Allen, Kevin Hagen, Richard Farnsworth.

This followup to Paramount's *The Legend of Nigger Charley* (1972) has stars Fred Williamson and D'Urville Martin battling ex-Confederate soldiers out west.

SOUTH OF ARIZONA   Columbia, 1938, B&W, 56 min. **Producer:** Harry L. Decker; **Director:** Sam Nelson; **Screenplay:** Bennett Cohen; **Music:** Bob Nolan; **Cinematographer:** Benjamin H. Kline; **Editor:** William A. Lyon; **Cast:** Charles Starrett, Iris Meredith, Bob Nolan, Dick Curtis, Edmund Cobb, Art Mix, Dick Botiller.

SOUTH OF CALIENTE   Republic, 1951, B&W, 67 min. **Producer:** Edward J. White (associate); **Director:** William Witney; **Screenplay:** Eric Taylor; **Music:** R. Dale Butts; **Cinematographer:** Jack Marta; **Editor:** Harold Minter; **Cast:** Roy Rogers, Dale Evans, Pinky Lee, Douglas Fowley, Ric Roman, Leonard Penn.

SOUTH OF DEATH VALLEY   Columbia, 1949, B&W, 54 min. **Producer:** Colbert Clark; **Director:** Ray Nazarro; **Screenplay:** Earle Snell; **Music:** Smiley Burnette, Milton Drake, and Marie Duncan; **Cinematographer:** Fayte Browne; **Editor:** Paul Borofsky; **Cast:** Charles Starrett, Gail Davis, Fred F. Sears, Lee Roberts, Richard Emory, Clayton Moore, Tommy Duncan, Smiley Burnette, Western All Stars.

SOUTH OF SANTA FE   Republic, 1942, B&W, 60 min. **Producer:** Joseph Kane; **Director:** Kane; **Screenplay:** James R. Webb; **Cinematographer:** Harry Neumann; **Editor:** William Thompson; **Cast:** Roy Rogers, George "Gabby" Hayes, Linda Hayes, Paul Fix, Authur Loft, Charles F. Miller, Sam Flint, Jack Kirk, Sons of the Pioneers.

SOUTH OF ST. LOUIS   Warner Bros., 1949, Color, 84 min. **Producer:** Milton Sperling; **Director:** Ray Enright; **Screenplay:** Zachary Gold and James R. Webb; **Music:** Max Steiner; **Cinematographer:** Karl Freund; **Editor:** Clarence Kolster; **Cast:** Joel McCrea, Alexis Smith, Zachary Scott, Douglas Kennedy, Alan Hale, Victor Jory, Bob Steele, Art Smith, Monte Blue.

Joel McCrea, Zachary Scott, and Douglas Kennedy are three ranching partners who run blockades for the South during the Civil War. But they have a big falling-out when one of them gets greedy and kills several soldiers for a gun shipment. Dorothy Malone and Alexis Smith provide the love interests in this well-cast and exciting western melodrama.

SOUTH OF THE BORDER   Republic, 1939, B&W, 71 min, VHS. **Producer:** William Berke (associate); **Director:** George Sherman; **Screenplay:** Betty Burbridge and Gerald Geraghty; **Cinematographer:** William Nobles; **Editor:** Lester Orlebeck; **Cast:** Gene Autry, Smiley Burnette, June Storey, Lupita Tovar, Mary Lee, Duncan Renaldo, Alan Edwards, William Farnum.

Gene Autry is a federal agent sent to Mexico (with his sidekick Frog) to prevent foreign powers from gaining control of

Mexican oil refineries and fomenting a revolution among the Mexican people. This is one of Autry's best-known outings, containing strong overtones of patriotism. The most remembered item in the film is its popular title song "South of the Border (Down Mexico Way)" (words and music by Jimmy Kennedy and Michael Carr). Autry first introduced it as a recording before he sang the film's title song, and it became both the number one sheet-music seller and top record seller of the year. Because of the song and the picture's added production value, Autry's films were temporarily upgraded into bigger, longer, larger, and more musical productions without sacrificing an iota of his popularity.

SPATS TO SPURS   See *HENRY GOES TO ARIZONA.*

SPEED BRENT WINS   See *BREED OF THE BORDER.*

SPOILERS, THE   Selig-Poliscope, 1914, B&W, nine reels. **Producer:** William Selig; **Director:** Colin Campbell; **Screenplay:** Campbell; **Cast:** William Farnum, Kathlyn Williams, Bessie Eyton, Frank Clark, Jack McDonald, Tom Santschi, Wheeler Oakman, Norvel MacGregory, William H. Ryno.

Despite the fact that five versions of the Rex Beach novel *The Spoilers* have been filmed, this 1914 silent production is the one usually noted by film scholars. The film deals with the adventures of participants in the Alaskan gold rush and the events that occur in a brawling mining town. William Farnum is Roy Glennister, a tough gent who tries to stop lawlessness and claim jumping in the vicinity. Considered a silent screen classic, it is best remembered for its raw and realistic atmosphere as well as a landmark climactic brawl between Franum and Tom Sanyschi. The production was adapted from Beach's 1906 novel and the Beach-James MacArthur stage play.

SPOILERS, THE   Goldwyn, 1923, B&W, 8020 feet. **Director:** Lambert Hillyer; **Screenplay:** Fred Kennedy Myton, Elliott Clawson, and Hope Loring; **Cinematographer:** John Stumer and Dwight Warren, **Cast:** Milton Sills, Anna Q. Nilsson, Barbara Bedford, Robert Edeson, Ford Sterling, Wallace MacDonald, Noah Beery, Mitchell Lewis.

Issued by Samuel Goldwyn, this second silent version of Rex Beach's novel stars Milton Sills as Roy Glennister and Anna Q. Nilsson as Cherry. It was directed by Lambert Hillyer, who helmed many of William S. Hart's films. *Photoplay* called this remake "as thrilling as ever."

SPOILERS, THE   Paramount, 1930, B&W, 86 min. **Producer:** Edward Carewe; **Director:** Carewe; **Screenplay;** Bartlett Cormack and Agnes Brand Leahy; **Music:** Karl Hajos and John Leipold; **Cinematographer:** Harry Fischbeck; **Editor:** William Shea; **Cast:** Gary Cooper, Kay Johnson, Betty Compson, William "Stage" Boyd, Harry Green, Slim Summerville, James Kirkwood.

The third of five screen versions (and the first sound production) of Rex Beach's novel has Gary Cooper and James Kirkwood as partners in an Alaskan gold mine. On the way to Nome, they meet a girl (Kay Johnson), the niece of a crooked judge (Harry Green) who is in cahoots with an arch swindler (William "Stage" Boyd.)

The obligatory brawl, by which all versions of the film are measured, is between Cooper and Boyd. With technical assistance from William Farnum and Tom Santschi, the actors who duked it out in the 1914 original silent version, the fight succeeds quite well and is without a doubt the film's highlight.

Although Gary Cooper was filmland's ascending All-American hero at the time, he was in fact a last-minute replacement for George Bancroft in the role of Roy Glennister, and he may have been too clean-cut looking for the part. Twelve years later the role of Glennister went to a rugged and battle-tested John Wayne. Nevertheless, *Motion Picture News* opined that "Cooper does perhaps the finest work of his career under the experienced direction of Edwin Carewe. James Kirkpatrick is most convincing as is Betty Compson in a small supporting role. Kay Johnson's acting is above reproach. She is excellent as the love interest."

SPOILERS, THE   Universal, 1942, B&W, 87 min, VHS. **Producer:** Frank Lloyd; **Director:** Ray Enright; **Screenplay:** Lawrence Hazard and Tom Reed; **Music:** Hans J. Salter; **Cinematographer:** Milton R. Krasner; **Editor:** Clarence Kolster; **Cast:** Marlene Dietrich, Randolph Scott, John Wayne, Margaret Lindsay, Harry Carey, Richard Barthelmess, George Cleveland, Samuel S. Hinds, Russell Simpson, William Farnum, Marietta Canty.

The fourth version of Rex Beach's popular western about Alaskan gold prospectors has John Wayne and Harry Carey as two mine owners whose claim is questioned by shady gold commissioner Randolph Scott. Consequently, the two prospectors plot to steal back their own assets from the bank. Marlene Dietrich is Cherry Malotte, the saloon girl who helps Wayne in a key moment, winning him away from the scheming Margaret Lindsay. The bare-knuckle fight between Wayne and Scott is a humdinger and provides one of the biggest slambang fight climaxes ever put on film, prompting the *New York Times* to note, "The he-men are back." *Variety* commented that "Scott and Wayne are typical of the great outdoors men for which the parts call."

William Farnum, who played Glennister in 1914 and was a technical advisor on the 1930 film, has a supporting role as the lawyer who works for Glennister (Wayne) and Dextry (Carey). Rumors abounded about Wayne and Dietrich, who were constant companions off the set, making numerous appearances together at trendy restaurants, sporting events, and weekend hunting and fishing trips.

The Spoilers received an Oscar nomination in the category of Best Art-Interior Decoration, Black & White.

Randolph Scott, Marlene Dietrich, and John Wayne star in The Spoilers. (UNIVERSAL/AUTHOR'S COLLECTION)

SPOILERS, THE Universal, 1955, Color, 84 min. **Producer:** Ross Hunter; **Director:** Jesse Hibbs; **Screenplay:** Oscar Brodney and Charles Hoffman; **Cinematographer:** Maury Gertsman; **Editor:** Paul Weatherwax; **Cast:** Anne Baxter, Jeff Chandler, Rory Calhoun, Ray Danton, Barbara Britton, John McIntire, Wallace Ford, Carl Benton Reid.

Jeff Chandler is Glennister and Anne Baxter is Cherry in the first color version and last filmed adaptation of *The Spoilers*. While not the same caliber of its predecessors, the elaborate fight scene, this time between Chandler and Rory Calhoun, is quite effective.

SPOILERS OF THE PLAINS Republic, 1951, B&W, 68 min. **Producer:** Edward J. White (associate); **Director:** William Witney; **Screenplay:** Sloan Nibley; **Music:** R. Dale Butts; **Cinematographer:** Jack Marta; **Editor:** Tony Martinelli; **Cast:** Roy Rogers, Penny Edwards, Gordon Jones, Grant Withers, William Forrest, Don Haggaety, Fred Kohler, House Peters Jr.
See *UNDER WESTERN STARS.*

SPOILERS OF THE RANGE Columbia, 1939, B&W, 57 min. **Producer:** Harry L. Decker; **Director:** Charles C. Coleman; **Music:** Bob Nolan and Tim Spencer; **Cinematographer:** Allen G. Siegler; **Editor:** William B. Lyon; **Cast:** Charles Starrett, Iris Meredith, Dick Curtis, Kenneth MacDonald, Hank Bell, Nolan, Edward Le Saint.
See *GALLANT DEFENDER.*

SPOOK TOWN PRC, 1944, B&W, 59 min. **Producer:** Arthur Alexander; **Director:** Elmer Clifton; **Screenplay:** Clifton; **Music:** Lee Zahler; **Cinematographer:** Robert E. Cline; **Editor:** Charles Henkel Jr.; **Cast:** Dave O'Brien, James Newill, Guy Wilkerson, Mady Lawrence, Dick Curtis.

SPRINGFIELD RIFLE Warner Bros., 1952, Color, 93 min, VHS. **Producer:** Louis F. Edleman; **Director:** André De Toth; **Screenplay:** Frank Davis and Charles Marquis Warren; **Music:** Max Steiner; **Cinematographer:** Edwin DuPar; **Editor:** Robert L. Swanson; **Cast:** Gary Cooper, Phyllis Thaxter, David Brian, Paul Kelly, Lon Chaney Jr., Philip Carey, James Millican, Guinn "Big Boy" Williams, Alan Hale Jr., Martin Milner.

This film concerns the development of the Army Intelligence Department during the Civil War. Gary Cooper is Major Lex Kearney, a Union officer who infiltrates a band of raiders that is stealing horses needed for a spring offensive. His main objectives are to uncover the efficient spy network responsible for the raids and learn the identity of the "mole" within the Union ranks who has betrayed the cause.

The film, released the same year as *HIGH NOON*, helped cement a series of four successful westerns (*DISTANT DRUMS*, 1951, *SPRINGFIELD RIFLE*, *High Noon*, *VERA CRUZ*, 1954) during the early 1950s that put Cooper's career in high gear again after a run of less distinguished films. Unfortunately, it did not receive the press attention it might have had it not followed *High Noon*, the raves for which were still reverberating. Nevertheless, *Springfield Rifle* packs some solid entertainment, an excellent score by Max Steiner, capable performances from a fine cast, and steady director by the Hungarian-born André De Toth. The title *Springfield Rifle* refers to the special weapon used to round up the Confederate horse thieves and is ancillary to the main plot line.

SPRINGTIME IN TEXAS Monogram, 1945, B&W, 55 min. **Producer:** Oliver Drake; **Director:** Drake; **Screenplay:** Frances Kavanaugh; **Cinematographer:** William A. Sickner; **Editor:** William Austin; **Cast:** Jimmy Wakely, Dennis Moore, Lee "Lasses" White, Marie Harmon, Rex Lease, Hal Taliaferro, I. Stanford Jolley, Pearl Early, Horace Murphy.
See *ACROSS THE RIO GRANDE.*

SPRINGTIME IN THE ROCKIES Republic, 1937, B&W, 56 min. **Producer:** Sol C. Siegal; **Director:** Joseph Kane; **Screenplay:** Betty Burbridge and Gilbert Wright; **Music:** Alberto Columbo, Karl Hajos, Frank Harford (songs), Ted Koehler, William Lava, Johnny Marvin (songs), and Sam H. Stept; **Cinematographer:** Ernest Miller; **Editor:** Lester Orlebeck; **Cast:** Gene Autry, Smiley Burnette, Polly Rowles, Ula Love, Ruth Bacon, Jane Hunt, George Chesebro, Al Bridge.
See *TUMBLING TUMBLEWEEDS.*

SPRINGTIME IN THE SIERRAS (aka: SONG OF THE SIERRA) Republic, 1947, B&W, 75 min. **Producer:** Edward J. White (associate); **Director:** William Witney; **Screenplay:** Sloan Nibley; **Music:** Bob Nolan (songs); **Cinematographer:** Jack Marta; **Editor:** Tony Martinelli; **Cast:** Roy Rogers, Jane Frazee, Andy Devine, Stephanie Bachelor, Harold Landon, Roy Barcroft, Bob Nolan, Harry Cheshire, Chester Conklin.
See *UNDER WESTERN STARS.*

SPURS Universal, 1930, B&W, 60 min. **Producer:** Hoot Gibson; **Director:** B. Reeves Eason; **Screenplay:** Eason; **Cinematographer:** Eason; **Editor:** Gilmore Walker; **Cast:** Hoot Gibson, Helen Wright, Robert Homans, Philo McCullough, C. E. Anderson, Buddy Hunter, Gilbert Holmes.

A cowpoke and a young lad attempt to track down a band of outlaws, while the cowboy also tries his hand at winning a rodeo and wooing a pretty young girl. This exciting early sound Hoot Gibson venture is one of nine films produced by the actor. The other include *THE THRILL CHASER* (1923); *KING OF THE RODEO, THE LONG, LONG, TRAIL* (1929); *TRAILING TROUBLE, ROARING RANCH, TRIGGER TRICKS, THE CONCENTRATION KID* (1930).

SQUARE DANCE JUBILEE Lippert, 1949, B&W, 79 min. **Producers:** June Carr and Ron Ormond; **Director:** Paul Landres; **Screenplay:** Ormond and Daniel B. Ullman; **Music:** Walter Greene; **Cinematographer:** Ernest Miller; **Editor:** Hugh Winn; **Cast:** Don "Red" Barry (as Donald Barry), Mary Beth Hughes, Wally Vernon, Spade Cooley, Max Terhune, John Eldredge, Thurston Hall, Clyde Clute, Tom Tyler, Carolina Cotton, Johnny Downs, Tom Kennedy, Marshall Stevens.

A New York-based country music TV show called "Square Dance Jubilee" sends two talent scouts out west to find authentic western singing acts. However, they manage to get involved in some cattle rustling and a case of murder as well. Don "Red" Barry served as executive producer for this curio of old-time country music acts, and he even sings a song himself.

SQUARE SHOOTER Columbia, 1935, B&W, 57 min. **Producer:** Irving Briskin; **Director:** David Selman; **Screenplay:** Harold Shumate; **Cinematographer:** George Meehan; **Editor:** Al Clark; **Cast:** Tim McCoy, Julie Bishop, Erville Alderson, Charles Middleton, J. Farrell MacDonald, Warner Oakman.

See *RIDING TORNADO, THE.*

SQUAW MAN, THE Paramount, 1914, B&W, six reels. **Producers:** Cecil B. DeMille and Jesse L. Lasky; **Directors:** Oscar Apfel and DeMille; **Screenplay:** Apfel and DeMille; **Cinematographer:** Alfred Gandolfi; **Editor:** Mamie Wagner; **Cast:** Dustin Farnum, Monroe Salsbury, Winifred Kingston, Red Wing, William Elmer, Hal Roach.

Thirty-three-year old Cecil B. DeMille must have been enamored of Edwin Milton Royal's 1906 play because he filmed it three times. He chose *The Squaw Man* to be his first full-length feature film, then he remade it in 1918, and finally he filmed it in 1930 as a talking picture.

The story concerns a high-born Englishman named James Wynnegate (Dustin Farnum), who leaves England for America when he is accused of embezzling charity funds (a crime actually committed by his cousin). Once in America he heads for Wyoming, where he clashes with a cattle rustler and rescues an Indian girl from the outlaw's clutches. After she saves him in a battle and kills the evil rustler, Wynnegate weds the girl, who by now is bearing his child.

When Wynnegate's cousin dies in England, making a death-bed confession that clears Wynnegate of any complicity in the crime, his English sweetheart journeys to Wyoming to inform Wynnegate that he has inherited the title Earl of Kerhill. His Indian wife commits suicide, believing that she stands in the way of Wynnegate's happiness and their son's birthright. Wynnegate then returns to England with his half-breed son to start life anew.

An enormous hit, *The Squaw Man* was filmed in Southern California and helped establish Hollywood as the matrix of the emerging film industry. In 1917 Lasky-Paramount produced a sequel directed by Edward J. Le Saint, *The Squaw Man's Son*, with Wallace Reid as the son of an Indian who leaves his English wife, returns to his tribe, and marries an Indian maiden after his white wife dies from a morphine injection.

SQUAW MAN, THE Paramount, 1918, B&W, six reels. **Producer:** Cecil B. DeMille; **Director:** DeMille; **Screenplay:** Beulah Marie Dix; **Cast:** Elliott Dexter, Thurston Hall, Katharine McDonald, Helen Dunbar, Winter Hall, Julia Faye, Herbert Standing.

This second version of DeMille's film stars Elliott Dexter and Katherine MacDonald in lead roles. Following closely the plot of the earlier film, *Photoplay* opined that the picture "marks Cecil B. DeMille at his best."

SQUAW MAN, THE MGM, 1931, B&W, 105 min. **Producer:** Cecil B. DeMille; **Director:** DeMille; **Screenplay:** Lucien Hubbard and Lenore Coffee; **Cinematography;** Harold Rosen; **Editor:** Anne Bauchens; **Cast:** Warner Baxter, Lupe Velez, Eleanor Boardman, Paul Cavanaugh, Lawrence Grant, Roland Young, Charles Bickford, Desmond Roberts.

Produced as part of his short-term pact with MGM, Cecil B. DeMille expanded his film of Edwin Milton Royle's Milton Play from six reels to 12 reels. The plot again follows a young English nobleman (Warner Baxter) who abandons his title and escapes to the American frontier after pleading guilty to a crime to protect the woman he loves (Eleanor Boardman). Once in America he marries a beautiful Indian woman (Lupe Velez), but when his former love arrives in America, he finds himself torn between two worlds.

So infatuated was DeMille with *The Squaw Man* story that upon the release of the first version in 1914 he planned to remake the story every 10 years. But with just lukewarm reviews to his 1931 edition, his enthusiasm for the production cooled and was finally shelved.

STAGECOACH United Artists, 1939, B&W, 96 min, VHS, DVD. **Producer:** Walter Wanger; **Director:** John Ford; **Screenplay:** Dudley Nichols; **Music:** Leo Shuken, John Leipold, Richard Hageman, W. Frank Harling, and

Louis Gruenberg; **Cinematographer:** Bert Glennon; **Editors:** Dorothy Spencer and Walter Reynolds; **Cast:** Claire Trevor, John Wayne, Thomas Mitchell, Andy Devine, George Bancroft, John Carradine, Louise Platt, Donald Meek, Berton Churchill, Tim Holt.

It is a cinematic certainty that *Stagecoach* made a star out of John Wayne, who was cast by John Ford after many years of working his trade. Wayne's Ringo Kid is the key character and the romantic lead in this western classic that revitalized and revamped the genre for years to come.

By using the *Grand Hotel* formula of placing a group of unrelated characters together in common settings and creating dangerous situations; by engaging some of the industry's finest character actors; and by employing the magnificent setting of Monument Valley and Yakima Canutt's marvelous stuntwork, John Ford lifted the western to new heights.

The plot, based on Ernest Haycox's story "Stage to Lordsburg," concerns the adventures of a disparate group of passengers aboard a stagecoach caught between two frontier settlements during an Apache uprising. On board are Dallas, a dance-hall girl forced by the "good ladies" to leave town (Claire Trevor); Buck, the robust stagecoach driver (Andy Devine); Curly, the determined yet kindly marshal (George Bancroft); Hatfield, the obsessed cardsharp and gambler (John Carradine); Doc Boone, the inebriated frontier medic (Thomas Mitchell); Peacock, the diminutive whisky salesman (Donald Meek); Gatewood, the corrupt banker absconding with the bank's money (Berton Churchill); Lucy Mallory, the pregnant wife of an army officer en route to his post (Louise Platt); and the Ringo Kid (Wayne), an escaped prisoner with avenging appointment in Lordsburg.

Wayne's entrance is stunning, a cinematic landmark. As the stage approaches, the camera focuses perfectly on his

A cast shot of Stagecoach. *John Ford's landmark 1939 western made a star of John Wayne and earned Thomas Mitchell a Best Supporting Actor Oscar. It was nominated for five Academy Awards, including Best Picture.* (UNITED ARTISTS/ AUTHOR'S COLLECTION)

Claire Trevor and John Wayne were a romantic team in Stagecoach, Allegheny Uprising, *and* Dark Command. (AUTHOR'S COLLECTION)

sweat-filmed face. Set against the classic western backdrop—sky, desert, and the abundant buttes of Monument Valley—Ringo's world is black and white. His parameters are firmly established. "There are some things a man can't run away from."

By all accounts, Ford was far from easy on his protégé. In fact, he was downright cruel and often humiliating. But as biographer Dan Ford relates in *Pappy: The Life of John Ford*, there was a proverbial method to his granfather's madness. "As a newcomer and an actor with no formal training, Wayne already felt insecure playing with such seasoned professionals as Thomas Mitchell, Claire Trevor, and George Bancroft. [Ford] made it even worse by bullying him in front of the entire company calling him a 'dumb bastard,' a 'big oaf,' and the like. He even criticized the way Wayne moved; 'Can't you walk for Chrissake, instead of skipping like a goddamn fairy?'"

In the end Ford engendered a masterful performance from Wayne, a portrayal where true actor's best qualities—charisma, physical grace, and vulnerability—come shining through. A master storyteller and poet, Ford maintains an intensely dramatic pace throughout the film with presentations of personal struggle; an Indian chase in which the sound of thundering horse hooves, with no whoops or war cries, adds measurably to the feeling of speed; a hacienda

sequence steeped in pathos and tenderness; and a climactic shoot-out at Lordsburg between Ringo and Luke Plummer (Tom Tyler), when "John Wayne [kills] three men with a carbine as he was falling to the dusty street in *Stagecoach*," Walker Percy as remembered in his novel *The Moviegoer.*

The Oscar-winning score by Richard Hageman, Frank Harding, John Leipold, and Leo Shuken, consisting of traditional American folk songs with full orchestration, defines perfectly the sense of time and place. In a year that gave the world such enduring classics as *Wuthering Heights; Goodbye, Mr. Chips; Mr. Smith Goes to Washington; The Wizard of Oz; Of Mice and Men;* and *Gone with the Wind*, which many consider the best film of all time, *Stagecoach* was nominated for seven Academy Awards, including Best Picture.

Thomas Mitchell won a Best Supporting Actor Oscar as Dr. Josiah Boone, a physician too fond of his liquor. Additional nominations included Best Cinematography (Bert Glennon), Best Editing (Otto Lovering, Dorothy Spencer, and Walter Reynolds), and Best Director (Ford). Ford's direction was honored by the New York Film Critics, (the Oscar went instead to Victor Fleming, who had directed *Gone with the Wind*). But Ford would win back-to-back Oscars the two following years for *The Grapes of Wrath* (1940) and *How Green Was My Valley* (1941), and he won again for his direction of *The Quiet Man* (1952).

Variety has called this film "a display of photographic grandeur." *Newsweek* labeled it "a rare screen masterpiece." Lindsay Anderson, the late director and film critic, maintained that "as narrative [*Stagecoach*] is one of the finest films ever made." Andre Bazin has called it an "ideal example of the maturity of style brought to classic perfection."

In his reevaluation, film historian J. A. Place argues in *The Western Films of John Ford* (1973) "that when placed within the context of Ford's body of work, and judged by that high standard, the film does not measure up." Nevertheless, the film remains after 60 years the standard for all subsequent westerns, a point made by Pauline Kael when she wrote that "just about every good western made since 1939 has imitated *Stagecoach* or has learned something from it" and called the film "a mixture of reverie and reverence about the American past that made the picture seem almost folk art. . . ."

Stagecoach marked John Ford's first use of Monument Valley, which played such a strong part in future location work. It also cemented the cinematic partnership between the director and star that was synonymous with the genre itself, and it almost single-handedly renewed the western's popularity beyond the B series fold. "In one superbly expansive gesture, John Ford has swept aside 10 years of artifice and talkie compromise and has made a motion picture that sings a song of camera," wrote Frank Nugent in the *New York Times.* Because he was impressed with Ford's use of chiaroscuro lighting and low ceilings, Orson Welles watched *Stagecoach* over and over again when preparing for *Citizen Kane* (1941).

In the 1940s and 1950s Ford made a series of unsurpassed westerns, most with his protégé John Wayne. Following *Stagecoach* they made 13 more pictures together, and in time both men became living legends. *Stagecoach* was selected to the National Film Registry in 1995 by the National Film Preservation Board. More recently, it was named among the American Film Institute's Top 100 Movies, though many might argue that at number 63 the AFI shortchanged Ford's innovative masterpiece.

By capturing the imagination of the public and critics alike, *Stagecoach* ushered in the biggest single cycle of large-scale westerns that the industry had ever seen. The by-product was that top-name stars who hitherto had avoided appearing in westerns now found a new and vital market-place for their work.

STAGECOACH 20th Century Fox, 1966, Color, 114 min, VHS. **Producer:** Martin Rackin; **Director:** Gordon Douglas; **Screenplay:** Joseph Landon; **Music:** Jerry Goldsmith; **Cinematographer:** William H. Clothier; **Editor:** Hugh S. Fowler; **Cast:** Ann-Margret, Red Buttons, Michael Connors, Alex Cord, Bing Crosby, Bob Cummings, Van Heflin, Stephanie Powers, Slim Pickens, Keenan Wynn.

Alex Cord is Ringo and Ann-Margret is Dallas (the roles made famous by John Wayne and Claire Trevor) in this remake of John Ford's 1939 film masterpiece. The disparate group of passengers on board the stagecoach to Lordsburg include Robert Cummings as Hatfield, the devious bank manager; Bing Crosby as Doc Boone, the alcoholic frontier doctor; Red Buttons as Mr. Peacock; Michael Connors as Hatfield the gambler; Stephanie Powers as Mrs. Mallory; Van Heflin as Curly, the marshal; and Slim Pickens as Buck, the stagecoach driver.

The biggest drawback to the film was the very fact that it was a unremarkable remake of a remarkable classic. Taken in its entirety, however, this version of *Stagecoach* is not as bad as many critics have suggested. The performances are generally good, especially that of Ann-Margret as Dallas, and Robert Cummings is pleasantly effective as a heavy. Then there is the surprising presence of an unshaven Bing Crosby in the role of Doc Boone.

There is some robust action as well, especially a gory two-minute kick-off sequence to establish the full extent of the Indian menace. But all told, the film pales in comparison with the original and would have best been left unmade.

A TV western was made in 1986 starring Willie Nelson, Kris Kristofferson, Johnny Cash, and Waylon Jennings. Supposedly a remake of *Stagecoach*, this made-for-TV production bears little resemblance to John Ford's 1939 original.

STAGECOACH BUCKAROO Universal, 1942, B&W, 58 min. **Producer:** Will Cowan (associate); **Director:** Ray Taylor; **Screenplay:** Al Martin; **Music:** Hans J. Salter; **Cinematographer:** Jerome Ash; **Cast:** Johnny Mack Brown, Fuzzy Knight, Nell O'Day, Anne Nagel, Herbert Rawlinson, Glenn Strange.

STAGECOACH EXPRESS Republic, 1942, B&W, 57 min. **Producer:** George Sherman; **Director:** Sherman; **Screenplay:** Arthur V. Jones; **Music:** Cy Feuer; **Cinematographer:** John MacBurnie; **Editor:** William P. Thompson; **Cast:** Don "Red" Barry, Lynn Merrick, Al St. John, Robert Kent, Emmett Lynn, Guy Kingsford, Ethan Laidlaw, Wheaton Chambers.

STAGECOACH KID RKO, 1949, B&W, 60 min. **Producer:** Herman Schlom; **Director:** Lew Landers; **Screenplay:** Norman Houston; **Music:** Paul Sawtell; **Cinematographer:** Nicholas Musuraca; **Editor:** Less Milbrook; **Cast:** Tim Holt, Richard Martin, Jeff Donnell, Joe Sawyer, Thurston Hall, Carol Hughes.

STAGECOACH OUTLAWS PRC, 1945, B&W, 58 min. **Producer:** Sigmund Neufeld; **Director:** Sam Newfield; **Screenplay:** Fred Myton; **Cinematographer:** Jack Greenhalgh; **Editor:** Holbrook N. Todd; **Cast:** Buster Crabbe, Al St. John, Frances Gladwin, Ed Cassidy, I. Stanford Jolley, Kermit Maynard.

See *OUTLAWS OF THE PLAINS*.

STAGECOACH TO DANCERS' ROCK Universal, 1962, B&W, 72 min. **Producer:** Earl Bellamy; **Director:** Bellamy; **Screenplay:** Kenneth Darling; **Music:** Franz Steininger; **Cinematographer:** Eddie Fitzgerald; **Cast:** Warren Stevens, Martin Landau, Judy Dan, Bob Anderson, Holly Bane, Tim Bolton, Rand Brooks.

Six passengers on a stagecoach are abandoned in the desert when the driver takes off after learning that one of them is infected with smallpox.

STAGECOACH TO DENVER Republic, 1946, B&W, 56 min. **Producer:** Sidney Picker (associate); **Director:** R. G. Springsteen; **Screenplay:** Earle Snell; **Cinematographer:** Edgar Lyons; **Editor:** Les Orlebeck; **Cast:** Allan Lane, Robert Blake, Martha Wentworth, Roy Barcroft, Peggy Stewart, Emmett Lynn.

STAGECOACH TO FURY 20th Century Fox, 1956, B&W, 75 min. **Producer:** Earle Lyon; **Director:** William F. Claxton; **Screenplay:** Eric Norden; **Music:** Paul Dunlap; **Cinematographer:** Walter Strenge; **Editor:** Carl Pierson; **Cast:** Forrest Tucker, Mari Blanchard, Wallace Ford, Margia Dean, Rodolfo Hoyos Jr., Paul Fix.

A cavalry officer organizes his fellow passengers when a band of Mexican outlaws hold them hostage at a stagecoach stop. The bandits are awaiting a gold shipment due to arrive on the next stage. Through a series of flashbacks more is learned about the passengers and their abilities to meet the crisis. This 1956 western was given an Academy Award nomination for Best Black and White Cinematography. It marked the last year that black and white cinematography was categorized separately for Oscar consideration.

STAGECOACH WAR Paramount, 1940, B&W, 63 min. **Producer:** Harry Sherman; **Director:** Lesley Selander;

Screenplay: Norman Houston; **Music:** Foster Carling, John Leipold, and Phil Ohman; **Cinematographer:** Russell Harlan; **Editor:** Sherman A. Rose; **Cast:** William Boyd, Russell Hayden, Julie Carter, Harvey Stevens, J. Farrell MacDonald, Britt Wood.

See *HOP-ALONG CASSIDY.*

STAGE TO BLUE RIVER Monogram, 1951, B&W, 56 min. **Producer:** Vincent Fennelly; **Director:** Lewis Collins; **Screenplay:** Joseph Poland; **Cinematographer:** Ernest Miller; **Editor:** Sam Fields; **Cast:** Whip Wilson, Fuzzy Knight, Phyllis Coates, Lee Roberts, Pierce Lyden, Lane Bradford, John Hart, Lyle Talbot, Terry Frost, I. Stanford Jolley.

See *ABILENE TRAIL.*

STAGE TO CHINO RKO, 1940, B&W, 59 min. **Producer:** Bert Gilroy; **Director:** Edward Killy; **Screenplay:** Morton Grant and Arthur V. Jones; **Music:** Fleming Allen (song), Robert Russell Bennett, Dave Dreyer, and Roy Webb; **Cinematographer:** J. Roy Hunt; **Editor:** Frederic Knudtson; **Cast:** George O'Brien, Virginia Vale, Hobart Cavanaugh, Roy Barcroft, William Haade, Carl Stockdale, Glenn Strange, Tom London, Harry Cording, Martin Garralaga.

STAGE TO MESA CITY PRC, 1947, B&W, 56 min. **Producer:** Jerry Thomas; **Director:** Ray Taylor; **Screenplay:** Joseph F. Poland; **Music:** Walter Greene; **Cinematographer:** James S. Browne Jr.; **Editor:** Hugh Winn; **Cast:** Lash La Rue, Al St. John, Jennifer Holt, George Chesebro, Buster Slaven, Marshall Reed.

See *LAW OF THE LASH.*

STAGE TO THUNDER ROCK Paramount, 1964, Color, 82 min. **Producer:** A. C. Lyles; **Director:** William F. Claxton; **Screenplay:** Charles A. Wallace; **Music:** Paul Dunlap; **Cinematographer:** W. Wallace Kelley; **Editor:** Jodie Copelan; **Cast:** Barry Sullivan, Marilyn Maxwell, Scott Brady, Keenan Wynn, Lon Chaney Jr., Anne Seymour, John Agar, Wanda Hendrix, Ralph Taeger, Allan Jones, Laurel Goodwin, Robert Strauss, Robert Lowery.

A retiring sheriff (Barry Sullivan) is forced by events to hunt down two brothers who have robbed a bank. He kills one and takes the other prisoner. When the prisoner's father (Keenan Wynn) vows revenge, the sheriff takes him to an isolated way station to wait for the next stage back to town. When the stage arrives, special deputy Sam Swope (Scott Brady) tries to get the reward money for his wife and small daughter.

Others on the stage include a prostitute (Marilyn Maxwell), the older daughter of way station owner Lon Chaney Jr.; and the driver Dan Carrouthers (John Agar) who is with Chaney's youngest daughter, Julie (Laurel Goodwin). After a night of unrest, the vengeful Wynn arrives on the scene to save his no-good son, and the sheriff is forced to kill him. All ends well, however, when the reward money is used to save the way station. Station owner Chaney promises to remain sober, and Agar and Goodwin announce their love for one another.

Stage to Thunder Rock is one of the best of the A. C. Lyle's low-budget westerns of the 1960s, and as usual the screen is filled with familiar faces and onetime big-name stars whose careers had seen their better days.

STALKING MOON, THE National General, 1968, Color, 109 min, VHS. **Producer:** Alan J. Pakula; **Director:** Robert Mulligan; **Screenplay:** Alvin Sargent; **Music:** Fred Karlin; **Cinematographer:** Charles Lange; **Editor:** Aaron Stell; **Cast:** Gregory Peck, Eva Marie Saint, Robert Forster, Noland Clay, Russell Thorson, Frank Silvera, Lonny Chapman, Lou Frizell, Henry Beckman, Charles Tyner, Nathaniel Narcisco, Richard Bull, Sandy Wyeth, Richard Farnsworth.

A veteran frontier scout (Gregory Peck) who is about to retire becomes involved in one last Apache roundup. In the process he finds a white woman (Eva Marie Saint) and her nine-year-old half-breed son (Noland Clay). He decides to help the two to a railroad station, but when it becomes clear that they cannot fend for themselves he takes them to his New Mexico ranch and a plot of land he had bought by mail order.

Soon they find themselves stalked across hundreds of miles by the boy's father, a relentless Apache warrior who leaves a trail of blood, murder, and carnage each step along the way, although the audience never sees him in full view. They wait nervously for the crazed Apache father to find them. When he does there is the inevitable fight to the finish between an extremely fit 52-year-old Gregory Peck and his brutal and determined Indian antagonist (Nathaniel Narcisco).

Helmed by Robert Mulligan (*To Kill a Mockingbird*, 1963) and based on the novel by Theodore Olson, the film failed to generate much suspense and earned weak reviews. Yet the picture is beautifully photographed, and Peck and Saint deliver excellent performances as Varner the scout and Sarah the captive woman. It is a film worth viewing.

STALLION CANYON Astor, 1949, Color, 72 min. **Producers:** H. R. Brandon and Robert L. Fenton; **Director:** Harry Fraser; **Screenplay:** Hy Heath; **Music:** Heath (song); **Cinematographer:** Jack McCluskey; **Editor:** Ray Snyder; **Cast:** Ken Curtis, Carolina Cotton, Shug Fisher, Forrest Taylor, Ted Adams.

A cowboy who tries to help an Indian is framed on a murder charge, just as he is attempting to win a big cash prize at the annual race.

STAMPEDE Columbia, 1936, B&W, 57 min. **Director:** Ford Beebe; **Screenplay:** Robert Barton; **Music:** R. H. Bassett and Jack Virgil; **Cinematographers:** William Beckway and George Meehan; **Editor:** William Austin; **Cast:** Charles Starrett, Finis Barton, J. P. McGowan, Le Strange Millman, Reginald Hincks.

See *GALLANT DEFENDER.*

STAMPEDE Allied Artists, 1949, B&W, 78 min. **Producers:** John C. Champion and Blake Edwards; **Director:**

Lesley Selander; **Screenplay:** Champion and Edwards; **Music:** Edward Kay; **Cinematographer:** Harry Neumann; **Editor:** Richard Heermance; **Cast:** Rod Cameron, Gale Storm, Don Castle, Johnny Mack Brown, Donald Curtis, Jonathan Hale, John Eldredge, Kermit Maynard, Kenne Duncan, Adrian Wood, Wes Christensen, Steve Clark.

Rod Cameron and Don Castle are feuding brothers Mike and Tim McCall, who become involved with settlers being cheated out of their water rights by a gang of crooks. Skillfully helmed by Leslie Selander and based on a book by E. B. Mann, this robust film features B western star Johnny Mack Brown in a supporting role as the sheriff and Gale Storm (who later achieved TV fame as the title character in *My Little Margie*, 1952) as the heroine Connie Dawson.

STAMPEDE   See *BIG LAND, THE.*

STAND AT APACHE RIVER, THE   Universal, 1953, Color, 77 min. **Producer:** William Alland; **Director:** Lee Schlom; **Screenplay:** Arthur Ross; **Music:** Frank Skinner; **Cinematographer:** Charles P. Boyle; **Editor:** Leonard Weiner; **Cast:** Stephen McNally, Julie Adams, Hugh Marlow, Jaclynne Greene, Hugh O'Brien, Russell Johnson, Jack Kelly, Forrest Lewis.

Eight people stranded at a stagecoach way station await an attack by rampaging Apaches. Two future pillars of the TV western, Hugh O'Brien (*The Life and Legend of Wyatt Earp*, 1955–61) and Jack Kelly (*Maverick*, 1957–62), are among the cast members in this standard little action-packed oater.

STAND UP AND FIGHT   MGM, 1939, B&W, 105 min. **Producer:** Mervyn LeRoy; **Director:** W. S. Van Dyke; **Screenplay:** James M. Cain, Jane Murfin, and Harvey Furguson; **Music:** Dr. William Axt; **Cinematographer:** Leonard Smith; **Editor:** Frank Sullivan; **Cast:** Wallace Beery, Robert Taylor, Florence Rice, Helen Broderick, Charles Bickford, Barton MacLane, Charley Grapewin, John Qualen.

In this railroad-versus-stagecoach western directed by Woody Van Dyke, Robert Taylor is Blake Cantrell, a fallen aristocrat who goes into bankruptcy and temporarily turns to drink. He feuds bitterly with Wallace Beery, the railroad owner, after losing his plantation. When he discovers that Beery is unknowingly giving aid and comfort to people dealing in stolen slaves, he mends his drunken ways and puts in with those who are trying to get the railroad to sell away its rights. After a series of realistic knock-'em-down brawls with Beery, the two finally become friends, and Taylor is ready to seriously romance pretty Florence Rice. Taylor and Beery are excellent as the two protagonists who skillfully pull their robust punches assuring that Taylor's handsome face would not be damaged.

STAR IN THE DUST (aka: LAW MAN)   Universal, 1956, Color, 80 min). **Producer:** Albert Zugsmith;

Director: Charles F. Haas; **Screenplay:** Oscar Brodney; **Music:** Frank Skinner; **Cinematographer:** John L. Russell; **Editor:** Ray Snyder; **Cast:** John Agar, Mamie Van Doren, Richard Boone, Coleen Gray, Leif Ericson, James Gleason, Randy Stuart, Terry Gilkyson, Paul Fix, Harry Morgan.

When the local sheriff (John Agar) plans to hang a gunman for killing three farmers, the citizens of the town refuse to support him.

STARLIGHT CANYON   See *DESERT PASSAGE.*

STARLIGHT OVER TEXAS (aka: MOON-LIGHT OVER TEXAS, UK)   Monogram, 1938, B&W, 58 min. **Producer:** Edward Finney; **Director:** Albert Herman; **Screenplay:** Harry MacPherson and Harry Rathmell; **Music:** Frank Sanucci; **Cinematographer:** Francis Corby; **Editor:** Frederick Bain; **Cast:** Tex Ritter, Salvatore Damino, Carmen Laroux, Rosa Turich, Horace Murphy, "Snub" Pollard, Charles King, George Chesebro.
   See *SONG OF THE GRINGO.*

STAR OF TEXAS   Allied Artists, 1953, B&W, 68 min. **Producer:** Vincent Fennelly; **Director:** Thomas Carr; **Screenplay:** Daniel B. Ullman; **Music:** Raoul Kraushaar; **Cinematographer:** Ernest Miller; **Cast:** Wayne Morris, Paul Fix, Frank Ferguson, Rick Vallin, Jack Larson, James Flavin, William Fawcett.

An outlaw gang begins recruiting members from prison, so a Texas Ranger pretends to be an escaped convict in order to track down the crooks. Filmed in a semidocumentary style, *Star of Texas* is the first entry in Wayne Morris's series for Allied Artists, which was the final official B western series.

STAR PACKER, THE (aka: HE WORE A STAR, UK)   Monogram/Lone Star, 1934, B&W, 60 min, VHS, DVD. **Producer:** Paul Malvern; **Director:** Robert N. Bradbury; **Screenplay:** Bradbury; **Cinematographer:** Archie Stout; **Editor:** Carl Pierson; **Cast:** John Wayne, Verna Hille, George Hayes, Yakima Canutt, Billy Franey, Eddie Parker, Earl Dwire.

John Travers (John Wayne) rides into town and organizes the ranchers who are being terrorized by The Shadow and his gang. Look for lots of action and "Gabby" Hayes cast out of type as the mysterious hooded gang leader known as The Shadow. Yakima Canutt, emerging as one of the movies' premier stuntmen, appears as Yak, Travers's Indian sidekick.

STAR SAID NO, THE   See *CALLAWAY WENT THAT-AWAY.*

STARS OVER TEXAS   PRC, 1946, B&W, 59 min. **Producer:** Robert Emmett Tansey; **Director:** Tansey; **Screenplay:** Frances Kavanaugh; **Music:** Hal Blair (songs), Eddie Dean (songs), and Glenn Strange (songs); **Cine-**

matographer: Ernest Miller; **Editor:** Hugh Winn; **Cast:** Eddie Dean, Roscoe Ates, Shirley Patterson, Lee Bennett, Kermit Maynard, Jack O'Shea, Hal Smith.

See *SONG OF OLD WYOMING.*

STATE POLICE See *WHIRLWIND RAIDERS.*

STATION WEST RKO, 1948, B&W, 80 min. **Producer:** Robert Sparks; **Director:** Sidney Lanfield; **Screenplay:** Frank Fenton and Winston Miller; **Music:** Heinz Roemheld; **Cinematographer:** Harry J. Wild; **Editor:** Frederic Knudtson; **Cast:** Dick Powell, Jane Greer, Agnes Moorehead, Tom Powers, Gordon Oliver, Steve Brodie, Guinn "Big Boy" Williams, Raymond Burr, Regis Toomey, Olin Howlin, John Berkes, Burl Ives, Grant Withers.

Dick Powell is an army officer who works undercover in a small town to find out who is behind a series of hijackings and a murder. He infiltrates the criminal operation and falls in love with its notorious leader, a gal named Charlie, played to the hilt by beautiful Jane Greer.

A must-see movie with grand performances and a suspenseful plot, *Station West* was nominated for a Writers Guild of America award as the Best Written American Western. Look for Burl Ives in an uncredited part as the hotel clerk who moonlights as the film's balladeer, and there is some unusual screen chemistry between tough guy Powell and the seductive Greer.

STICK TO YOUR GUNS Paramount, 1941, B&W, 63 min. **Producers:** Lewis J. Rachmil and Harry Sherman; **Director:** Lesley Selander; **Screenplay:** J. Benton Cheney; **Music:** John Leipold; **Cinematographer:** Russell Harlan; **Editor:** Earl Moser; **Cast:** William Boyd, Andy Clyde, Brad King, Jennifer Holt, Dick Curtis, Weldon Heyburn, Kermit Maynard, Henry Hall, Ian MacDonald, Tom London.

See *HOP-ALONG CASSIDY.*

STONE OF SILVER CREEK Universal, 1935, B&W, 63 min, VHS. **Producer:** Buck Jones; **Director:** Nick Grinde; **Screenplay:** Earle Snell; **Music:** Howard Jackson, Charles Rosoff, Oliver Wallace, and Lee Zahler; **Cinematographers:** Joseph Novak and Ted D. McCord; **Editor:** B. T. Loftus; **Cast:** Buck Jones, Noel Francis, Niles Welch, Marion Shilling, Peggy Campbell.

When a saloon owner gets religion, he suddenly finds himself at odds with a preacher over his affections for a pretty girl. There are some touches of William S. Hart in this offbeat and somber Buck Jones venture.

Jones joined Universal in 1934 and made 22 features and four serials, producing many himself, before escalating costs and studio infighting drove him back to Columbia in 1937. His Universal productions include: *ROCKY RHODES* (1934); *THE IVORY-HANDLED GUN, THE CRIMSON TRAIL, BORDER BRIGAND, OUTLAWED GUNS, THE THROWBACK, SUNSET OF POWER* (1935); *SILVER SPURS, FOR THE SERVICE, THE COWBOY AND THE KID, BOSS RIDER OF GUN CREEK, EMPTY SADDLES* (1936); *SANDFLOW, LEFT-HANDED LAW, THE LAW FOR TOMBSTONE, SMOKE TREE RANGE, BLACK ACES, BOSS OF LONELY VALLEY, SUDDEN BILL DORN* (1937).

STORM OVER WYOMING RKO, 1950, B&W, 61 min. **Producer:** Herman Schlom; **Director:** Lesley Selander; **Screenplay:** Ed Earl Repp; **Music:** Paul Sawtell; **Cinematographer:** J. Roy Hunt; **Editor:** Robert Swink; **Cast:** Tim Holt, Richard Martin, Noreen Nash, Tom Keene, Betty Underwood, Kenneth MacDonald, Holly Bane.

STORM RIDER, THE 20th Century Fox, 1957, B&W, 72 min. **Producer:** Bernard Glasser; **Director:** Edward Bernds; **Screenplay:** Bernds; **Music:** Les Baxter; **Cinematographer:** Brydon Baker; **Editor:** John F. Link; **Cast:** Scott Brady, Mala Powers, Bill Williams, John Goddard, William Fawcett, Roy Engel, George Keymas, Olin Howlin, Bud Osborne, James Dobson, Rocky Lundy, Hank Patterson, Wayne Mallory.

Scott Brady, a former gunman, is hired by a group of small ranchers to fend off a big ranching mogul who wants their land. The caveat is that they are unaware he is the man who killed their leader. Matters are further complicated when he falls in love with the man's widow (Mala Powers). He succeeds in bringing peace to the community when he guns down a killer employed by the big rancher. Yet despite his love for the widow, he rides away knowing that the killing of her husband could never stand the test of time and would always be a wedge between them.

A real sleeper, this taut little western blends drama, action, and romance. Les Baxter's musical score is based on orchestral variation of the old English folk ballad "Greensleeves" and fits the mood of the feature beautifully.

STORMY Universal, 1935, B&W, 69 min. **Producer:** Carl Laemmle; **Director:** Lew Landers (as Louis Friedlander); **Screenplay:** Bennett Cohen, Ben Grauman Kohn, and George H. Plympton; **Music:** Heinz Roemheld; **Cinematographer:** Richard Fryer; **Editor:** Murray Seldeen; **Cast:** Noah Beery, Jean Rogers, J. Farrell MacDonald, Raymond Hatton, Walter Miller, Fred Kohler.

A young man searches for a beautiful stallion that broke free after a train wreck. As a result of his pursuit he manages to save a herd of wild horses.

STORMY TRAILS Colony/Grand National, 1936, B&W, 58 min. **Producers:** Arthur Alexander and Matt Alexander; **Director:** Sam Newfield; **Screenplay:** Phil Durham; **Cinematographer:** Robert E. Cline; **Editor:** Charles Henkel Jr.; **Cast:** Rex Bell, Lois Wilde, Karl Hackett, Murdock MacQuarrie, Earle Ross, Bob Hodges, Lloyd Ingraham, Earl Dwire, Lane Chandler.

A band of crooks is after a ranch owned by two brothers because the land contains some valuable gold deposits. This basic low-budget Rex Bell oater is one of 23 he made during the 1930s. Married for many years to actress Clara Bow, Bell also served a stint as lieutenant governor of New Mexico. In 1936 he made six features under the Colony/Grand National and First Division/Grand National banner. They include *Men of the Plains, Law and Lead, The Idaho Kid, Too Much Beef, West of Nevada*. (See IDAHO KID, THE.)

STRAIGHT SHOOTER Victory, 1939, B&W, 54 min. **Producer:** Sam Katzman; **Director:** Sam Newfield; **Screenplay:** Basil Dickey and Joseph O'Donnell; **Music:** Oliver Wallace; **Cinematographer:** Arthur Reed; **Editor:** Holbrook N. Tood; **Cast:** Tim McCoy, Julie Sheldon, Ben Corbett, Ted Adams, Reed Howes, Forrest Taylor.

STRAIGHT SHOOTING Universal, 1917, B&W, 57 min. **Producer:** Carl Laemmle; **Director:** John Ford (as Jack Ford); **Screenplay:** George Hively; **Cinematographer:** George Scott; **Cast:** Harry Carey, Duke Lee, George Berrell, Molly Malone, Ted Brooks, Hoot Gibson.

Made for Universal in 1917, *Straight Shooting* is John Ford's very first full-length feature; he was 22 years old at the time. The basic plot concerns a range war between cattlemen and homesteaders and the intervention of a professional gunman on behalf of the homesteaders. The film made a star out of actor Harry Carey, whose "good bad man" characterization somewhat overlaps that of William S. Hart. Carey and Ford made 26 westerns, many with Carey playing a wily, good-natured character named Cheyenne Harry. This film is one of the very few John Ford silent pictures extant.

STRANGE INCIDENT See OX BOW INCIDENT, THE.

STRANGE LADY IN TOWN Warner Bros., 1955, Color, 112 min. **Producer:** Mervyn LeRoy; **Director:** LeRoy; **Screenplay:** Frank Butler; **Music:** Dimitri Tiomkin; **Cinematographer:** Harold Rosson; **Editor:** Folmar Blangsted; **Cast:** Greer Garson, Dana Andrews, Cameron Mitchell, Lois Smith, Walter Hampden, Adele Jergens, Earl Holliman, Joan Camden, Pedro Gonzales-Gonzales, Gregory Walcott, Douglas Kennedy, Nick Adams, Robert J. Wilke, Frank DeKova.

Greer Garson is Dr. Julia Winslow Garth, a physician who arrives in Santa Fe in the 1880s and begins the fight against social prejudice and male recalcitrance. Her medical prowess allows her to treat Billy the Kid (Nick Adams) and Lew Wallace, the governor of New Mexico and future author of *Ben Hur* (Ralph Moody), while accomplishing medical wonders in just a short time. In the process she discovers that her brother is an outlaw, and she is courted by fellow doctor Dana Andrews. The title song, written by the *High Noon* (1952) team of Dimitri Tiomkin and Ned Washington, is

sung by Frankie Laine, who also recorded it on the Columbia label.

STRANGE LAW See CHEROKEE STRIP, THE.

STRANGER AT MY DOOR Republic, 1956, B&W, 85 min. **Producer:** Sidney Picker (associate); **Director:** William Witney; **Screenplay:** Barry Shipman; **Music:** R. Dale Butts; **Cinematographer:** Bud Thackery; **Editor:** Howard B. Smith; **Cast:** Macdonald Carey, Patricia Medina, Skip Homeier, Stephen Wooton, Louis Jean Heydt, Howard Wright, Slim Pickens, Malcolm Atterbury.

An outlaw (Skip Homeier) and his gang rob a bank and flee in separate directions. However, when his horse goes lame he is forced to pull up at the farm of the local preacher (Macdonald Carey), his new wife, and a son from a previous marriage. The preacher hopes to change the outlaw's criminal tendency, but the outlaw has other things on his mind. Macdonald Carey delivers a fine performance as the idealistic preacher with an overdose of faith and patience.

STRANGER FROM ARIZONA, THE Columbia, 1938, B&W, 54 min. **Producer:** Monroe Shaff; **Director:** Elmer Clifton; **Screenplay:** Shaff; **Cinematographer:** Edward Linden; **Editor:** Holbrook N. Todd; **Cast:** Buck Jones, Dorothy Fay, Hank Mann, Hank Worden, Roy Barcroft, Bob Terry, Horace Murphy.

STRANGER FROM PONCA CITY, THE Columbia, 1947, B&W, 56 min. **Producer:** Colbert Clark; **Director:** Derwin Abrahams; **Screenplay:** Ed Earl Repp; **Cinematographer:** George F. Kelley; **Editor:** Burton Kramer; **Cast:** Charles Starrett, Smiley Burnette, Virginia Hunter, Paul Campbell, Forrest Taylor, Jock Mahoney.

STRANGER FROM TEXAS, THE Columbia, 1940, B&W, 54 min. **Producer:** Harry L. Decker; **Director:** Sam Nelson; **Screenplay:** Paul Franklin; **Music:** Bob Nolan and Tim Spencer; **Cinematographer:** George Meehan; **Editor:** Mel Thorson; **Cast:** Charles Starrett, Lorna Gray, Bob Nolan, Richard Fiske, Dick Curtis, Edmund Cobb, Al Bridge, Jack Rockwell, Wally Wales.

Working incognito, a lawman sets out to discover who is behind a series of fence cuttings and cattle rustling for which his rancher father is being blamed. This Charles Starrett entry for Columbia is a remake of his 1936 film *Mysterious Avenger*, but it does not pack the same punch. (See also GALLANT DEFENDER.)

STRANGER ON HORSEBACK United Artists, 1955, Color, 66 min. **Producer:** Robert Goldstein; **Director:** Jacques Tourneur; **Screenplay:** Don Martin and Herb Meadow; **Music:** Paul Dunlap; **Cinematographer:** Ray Rennahan; **Editor:** William C. Murphy; **Cast:** Joel McCrea,

Miroslava, Kevin McCarthy, John McIntire, Nancy Gates, John Carradine, Emile Meyer.

Joel McCrea is a circuit court judge who is sent to a small town to restore law and order. But when he tries to bring a suspected killer to justice, he runs afoul of the killer's rich cattle baron father.

STRANGER WITH A GUN See *SHEEPMAN, THE.*

STRANGER WORE A GUN, THE Columbia, 1953, Color, 83 min. **Producer:** Harry Joe Brown; **Director:** André De Toth; **Screenplay:** Kenneth Gamet; **Music:** Mischa Bakaleinikoff; **Cinematographer:** Lester White; **Editors:** Gene Havlick and James Sweeney; **Cast:** Randolph Scott, Claire Trevor, Joan Weldon, George Macready, Alfonso Bedoya, Lee Marvin, Ernest Borgnine, Pierre Watkin, Joseph Vitale, Clem Bevans, Roscoe Ates, Rayford Barnes.

Jeff Travis (Randolph Scott) works as a spy for Confederate guerrilla leader William Quantrill until he discovers Quantrill's venal nature. He quits but then is attacked by three men who know his past. When his life is saved by an unknown stranger, he proceeds to Prescott, Arizona, where he encounters his previously unseen savior (George Macready). The problem is that the rescuer wants Travis to resume his spying activities this time by going to work for the stage line and making sure that the stages are vulnerable to ambush attacks.

STRAWBERRY ROAN Universal, 1933, B&W, 60 min. **Producers:** Ken Maynard and Leon Schlesinger; **Director:** Alan James; **Screenplay:** Nate Gatzert and Harry O. Hoyt; **Music:** Curley Fletcher; **Cinematographer:** Ted D. McCord; **Editor:** Charles Harris; **Cast:** Ken Maynard, Ruth Hall, Harold Goodwin, Frank Yaconelli, James A. Marcus, William Desmond, Charles King.

See *LUCKY LARKIN.*

STRAWBERRY ROAN, THE Columbia, 1948, Color, 79 min. **Producers:** Louis H. Jackson and Dorothy Yost; **Director:** John English **Screenplay:** Dwight Cummins and Yost; **Cinematographer:** Fred Jackman Jr.; **Editor:** Henry Batista; **Cast:** Gene Autry, Gloria Henry, Dickie Jones, Pat Buttram, Rufe Davis, John McGuire, Eddy Waller, Reed Harper.

Gene Autry is a horse breaker who tires to stop a rancher from killing a beautiful wild roan, unaware that the horse had paralyzed the rancher's son. Among Autry fans, *The Strawberry Roan* remains one of his best and most popular Columbia entries.

STREETS OF GHOST TOWN Columbia, 1950, B&W, 54 min. **Producer:** Colbert Clark; **Director:** Ray Nazarro; **Screenplay:** Barry Shipman; **Music:** Mischa Bakaleinikoff; **Cinematographer:** Fayte M. Browne; **Editor:**

Paul Borofsky; **Cast:** Charles Starrett, Smiley Burnette, George Chesebro, Mary Ellen Kay, Stanley Andrews, Frank Fenton.

See *DURANGO KID, THE.*

STREETS OF LAREDO Paramount, 1949, Color, 93 min. **Producer:** Robert Fellows; **Director:** Leslie Fenton; **Screenplay:** Elizabeth Hill, Louis Stevens, King Vidor, and Charles Marquis Warren; **Music:** Victor Young; **Cinematographer:** Ray Rennahan; **Editor:** Archie Marshek; **Cast:** William Holden, Macdonald Carey, Mona Freeman, William Bendix, Stanley Ridges, Alfonso Bedoya, Ray Teal, Clem Bevans, James Bell.

Three outlaw pals from Texas (William Holden, Macdonald Carey, William Bendix) rescue an orphan girl (Mona Freeman) from a band of rustlers. When the three finally separate, Carey pursues his outlaw ways, while Holden and Bendix reluctantly join the Texas Rangers. Because of their erstwhile friendship they avoid any conflict with each other. But a showdown becomes inevitable when the spunky orphan girl grows into a beautiful young woman who must now choose between the affections of Ranger Holden and outlaw Carey.

A remake of King Vidor's sturdy 1936 film *THE TEXAS RANGERS*, this film was nominated by the Writers Guild of America in the category of Best Written American Western (1950). But it was thoroughly panned by film historian William Everson, who called it a "dull Technicolor forties remake . . . [with] overdoses of sex and brutality . . . added." The title song (based on the traditional tune) was written by the Academy Award-winning team of Jay Livingston and Ray Evans and is sung in the film by Dick Foote and a chorus.

This 1949 film is not the source of nor related to the excellent 1995 TV miniseries *Streets of Laredo,* Larry McMurtry's official sequel to his highly acclaimed *Lonesome Dove* (1989).

SUDDEN BILL DORN Universal, 1937, B&W, 60 min. **Producer:** Buck Jones; **Directors:** Ray Taylor and Frances Guihan; **Music:** David Klazkin and Oliver Wallace; **Cinematographer:** Allen Thompson; **Cast:** Buck Jones, Evelyn Brent, Noel Francis, Frank McGlynn Sr., Harold Hodge, Ted Adams.

SUDDEN DEATH See *FAST ON THE DRAW.*

SUGARFOOT (aka: SWIRL OF GLORY) Warner Bros., 1951, Color, 80 min. **Producer:** Saul Elkins; **Director:** Edwin Marin; **Screenplay:** Russell S. Hughes; **Music:** Max Steiner; **Cinematographer:** Wilfred M. Cline; **Editor:** Clarence Kolster; **Cast:** Randolph Scott, Adele Jergons, Raymond Massey, S. Z. Sakall, Robert Warwick, Arthur Hunnicutt, Hugh Sanders, Hank Worden, Gene Evans.

When an ex-Confederate officer wants to settle down peacefully as a rancher in Arizona, he finds that he is the sworn enemy of a local crook who was once his rival. Saddled with a rather familiar Randolph Scott plot, the film nevertheless packs a goodly share of excitement.

SUNDOWNERS, THE Eagle Lion, 1950, Color, 83 min, VHS. **Producer:** Alan Le May; **Director:** George Templeton; **Screenplay:** Le May; **Music:** Alberto Colombo, Leonid Raab, and Rudy Schrager; **Cinematographer:** Winton B. Hoch; **Editor:** Jack Ogilvie; **Cast:** Robert Preston, Robert Sterling, Chill Wills, Cathy Downs, John Drew Barrymore, Jack Elam, John Litel.

Brothers Robert Sterling and John Drew Barrymore try to survive on their land while big cattlemen attempt to squeeze them out. Complications arise when "Kid Wichita," the gunman sent to harass them, turns out to be their rogue older brother (Robert Preston).

This western was based on Alan Le May's story "Thunder in the Dust" and filmed at various Texas locations. Robert Preston performs well as a corrupt yet likable heavy. Good performances by all (especially Barrymore) and a compelling script provide an effective western melodrama with brother pitted against brother.

SUNDOWN IN SANTA FE Republic, 1948, B&W, 60 min. **Producer:** Melville Tucker (associate); **Director:** R. G. Springsteen; **Screenplay:** Norman S. Hall; **Music:** Stanley Wilson; **Cinematographer:** John MacBurnie; **Editor:** Irving Schoenberg; **Cast:** Allan "Rocky" Lane, Eddy Waller, Roy Barcroft, Trevor Bardette, Russell Simpson, Rand Brooks, Lane Bradford.

SUNDOWN KID, THE Republic, 1942, B&W, 59 min. **Producer:** Edward J. White (associate); **Director:** Elmer Clifton; **Screenplay:** Norman S. Hall; **Music:** Mort Glickman; **Cinematographer:** Ernest Miller; **Editor:** William P. Thompson; **Cast:** Don "Red" Barry, Ian Keith, Helen MacKellar, Linda Johnson, Emmett Lynn, Wade Crosby, Ted Adams.

SUNDOWN ON THE PRAIRIE (aka: PRAIRIE SUNDOWN, UK) Monogram, 1939, B&W, 58 min. **Producer:** Edward Finney; **Director:** Albert Herman; **Screenplay:** Edmond Kelso and William L. Nolte; **Music:** Frank Sanucci; **Cinematographer:** Bert Longenecker; **Editor:** Holbrook N. Todd; **Cast:** Tex Ritter, Dorothy Fay, Horace Murphy, Hank Warden, Charles King, Dave O'Brien, Karl Hackett.

SUNDOWN RIDER, THE Columbia, 1932, B&W, 65 min. **Director:** Lambert Hillyer; **Screenplay:** Hillyer and John T. Neville; **Cinematographer:** John W. Boyle; **Cast:** Buck Jones, Barbara Weeks, Pat O'Malley, Niles Welch, Ward Bond, Wheeler Oakman, Bradley Page, Edward Brady, Harry Todd, Frank La Rue, George Chesebro, Jack Lumen.
See *WHITE EAGLE.*

SUNDOWN SAUNDERS Supreme, 1935, B&W, 59 min. **Producer:** A. W. Hackel; **Director:** Robert N. Bradbury; **Screenplay:** Bradbury; **Cinematographer:** Bert Longenecker; **Editor:** S. Roy Luby; **Cast:** Bob Steele, Catherine Cotter, Earl Dwire, Ed Cassidy, Jack Rockwell, Milburn Morante, Frank Ball, Hal Price, Budd Buster, Edmund Cobb.
See *KID COURAGEOUS.*

SUNDOWN TRAIL RKO, 1931, B&W, 56 min. **Producer:** Fred Allen; **Director:** Robert F. Hill; **Screenplay:** Hill; **Cinematographer:** Ted M. McLord; **Cast:** Tom Keene, Marion Shilling, Nick Stuart, Hooper Atchley, Stanley Blystone, Alma Chester, William Welsh.

SUNDOWN VALLEY Columbia, 1944, B&W, 55 min. **Producer:** Jack Fier; **Director:** Benjamin Kline; **Screenplay:** Luci Ward; **Cinematographer:** George Meehan; **Editor:** Aaron Stell; **Cast:** Charles Starrett, Dub Taylor, Jeanne Bates, Tennessee Ramblers, Jimmy Wakely, Budd Buster, Jesse Arnold.

This Charles Starrett vehicle was directed toward World War II audiences. Steve Denton (Starrett) is a war hero who wants to close down a gambling den because its owners are causing high absenteeism at the local gun-manufacturing plant. Not wanting any interference from Denton, the owners of the casino send a gunman to do him in.

SUNSET IN EL DORADO Republic, 1945, B&W, 65 min, VHS. **Producer:** Louis Grey (associate); **Director:** Frank McDonald; **Screenplay:** John K. Butler; **Music:** Ken Carson; **Cinematographer:** William Bradford; **Editor:** Tony Martinelli; **Cast:** Roy Rogers, George "Gabby" Hayes, Dale Evans, Hardie Albright, Margaret Dumont, Roy Barcroft, Tom London, Bob Nolan and the Sons of the Pioneers.
See *UNDER WESTERN STARS.*

SUNSET IN THE WEST Republic, 1950, Color, 67 min. **Producer:** Edward J. White (associate); **Director:** William Witney; **Screenplay:** Gerald Geraghty; **Music:** R. Dale Butts; **Cinematographer:** Jack Marta; **Editor:** Tony Martinelli; **Cast:** Roy Rogers, Estelita Rodriguez, Penny Edwards, Gordon Jones, Will Wright, Pierre Watkin.
See *UNDER WESTERN STARS.*

SUNSET IN WYOMING Republic, 1941, B&W, 65 min. **Producer:** Harry Grey (associate); **Director:** William Morgan; **Screenplay:** Anne Morrison Chapin and Ivan Goff; **Music:** Raoul Kraushaar; **Cinematographer:** Reggie Lanning; **Editor:** Tony Martinelli; **Cast:** Gene Autry, Smiley Burnette, Maris Wrixon, George Cleveland, Robert Kent, Sarah Edwards, Monte Blue, Dick Elliott, John Dilson, Stanley Blystone, Eddie Dew.
See *TUMBLING TUMBLEWEEDS.*

SUNSET ON THE DESERT Republic, 1942, B&W, 83 min. **Producer:** Joseph Kane; **Director:** Gerald Geraghty; **Screenplay:** Geraghty; **Music:** Cy Feuer, Bob Nolan (songs), and Tim Spencer (songs); **Cinematographer:** Lester Orlebeck; **Cast:** Roy Rogers, George "Gabby" Hayes, Lynne Carver, Frank M. Thomas, Beryl Wallace, Glenn Strange, Douglas Fowley, Fred Burns, Roy Barcroft, Henry Hill, Bob Nolan and the Sons of the Pioneers.

See *UNDER WESTERN STARS*.

SUNSET PASS Paramount, 1933, B&W, 61 min. **Producer:** Adolph Zucker; **Director:** Henry Hathaway; **Screenplay:** Jack Cunningham and Gerald Geraghty; **Music:** John Leipold; **Cinematographer:** Archie Stout; **Cast:** Randolph Scott, Tom Keene, Kathleen Burke, Harry Carey, Fuzzy Knight, Noah Beery, Vince Barnett, Kent Taylor, Tom London, Patricia Farley, Charles Middleton.

While working undercover as a cowpoke, a government agent falls in love with a girl whose brother is suspected of heading a rustling operation. This remake of Zane Grey's novel was first filmed in 1929, starring Jack Holt, and remade in 1946 by RKO Radio. This entry was among the first for Henry Hathaway, who made his directorial debut in 1932 helming a series of Zane Grey westerns, many of which starred Randolph Scott. Hathaway directed Scott in seven features between 1932 and 1943.

SUNSET PASS RKO, 1946, B&W, 64 min. **Producer:** Herbert Schlom; **Director:** William Berke; **Screenplay:** Norman Houston; **Music:** Paul Sawtell and Roy Webb; **Cinematographer:** Frank Redman; **Editor:** Samuel Beetley; **Cast:** James Warren, Nan Leslie, John Laurenz, Jane Greer, Robert Barrat, Harry Woods, Robert Clarke, Steve Brodie.

This third screen version of the Zane Grey novel has James Warren and John Laurenz as two government agents on the trail of a stolen good shipment they were hired to protect.

SUNSET SERENADE Republic, 1942, B&W, 58 min. **Producer:** Joseph Kane (associate); **Director:** Kane; **Screenplay:** Robert Felton; **Music:** Bob Nolan and Tim Spencer; **Cinematographer:** Bud Thackery; **Editor:** Arthur Roberts; **Cast:** Roy Rogers, George "Gabby" Hayes, Bob Nolan and the Sons of the Pioneers, Joan Woodbury, Helen Parrish, Onslow Stevens, Roy Barcroft, Frank M. Thomas, Jack Kirk, Dick Wessel, Rex Lease.

See *UNDER WESTERN STARS*.

SUNSET TRAIL Paramount, 1938, B&W, 69 min. **Producer:** Harry Sherman; **Director:** Leslie Selander; **Screenplay:** Norman Houston; **Music:** Stanley Cowan and Bobby Worth (songs); **Cinematographer:** Russell Harlan; **Editor:** Robert Warwick; **Cast:** William Boyd, George "Gabby" Hayes, Russell Hayden, Charlotte Winters, Jan Clayton (as Jane Clayton), Robert Fiske, Kenneth Harlan.

See *HOP-ALONG CASSIDY*.

SUN VALLEY CYCLONE Republic, 1946, B&W, 56 min. **Producer:** Sidney Picker (associate); **Director:** R. G. Springsteen; **Screenplay:** Earle Snell; **Cinematographer:** Bud Thackery; **Editors:** Charles Craft and Harry Keller; **Cast:** William "Wild Bill" Elliott, Robert Blake, Alice Fleming, Roy Barcroft, Monte Hale, Kenne Duncan, Eddy Waller, Edmund Cobb, Tom London, Ed Cassidy, George Chesebro, Rex Lease.

See *ADVENTURES OF RED RYDER, THE*.

SUPPORT YOUR LOCAL GUNFIGHTER United Artists, 1971, Color, 91 min, VHS, DVD. **Producer:** Bill Finnegan; **Director:** Burt Kennedy; **Screenplay:** James Edward Grant; **Music:** Jack Elliott and Allyn Ferguson; **Cinematographer:** Harry Stradling Jr.; **Editor:** William B. Gulick; **Cast:** James Garner, Suzanne Pleshette, Harry Morgan, Joan Blondell, John Dehner, Henry Jones, Dub Jones, Marie Windsor, Jack Elam, Chuck Connors, Kathleen Freeman.

James Garner is Latigo Smith, a con man and gigolo escaping a matrimonial entanglement. He drifts into the town of Purgatory, which is controlled by two competing companies. Because he is mistaken as a dreaded gunfighter, both companies want his services to drive the other out of town. While he play-acts at being a cold-blooded gunslinger, he hopes to bide his time until he has enough money to skip town.

The film has its moments, but it is not on par with Kennedy's 1969 ribald western spoof *Support Your Local Sheriff*, starring James Garner in the lead role and Jack Elam and Harry Morgan in supporting parts. Director Burt Kennedy originally wanted to title the film *Hell Bent on Purgatory*, but he was overruled by others associated with the project.

SUPPORT YOUR LOCAL SHERIFF United Artists, 1969, Color, 92 min, VHS, DVD. **Producer:** William Bowers; **Director:** Burt Kennedy; **Screenplay:** Bowers; **Music:** Jeff Alexander; **Cinematographer:** Harry Stradling Jr.; **Editor:** George W. Brooks; **Cast:** James Garner, Joan Hackett, Walter Brennan, Harry Morgan, Jack Elam, Henry Jones, Bruce Dern, Willis Bouchey, Gene Evans, William Burke, Chubby Johnson.

James Garner is Jason McCullough, a cool cowboy on his way to Australia who strolls into a robust gold-rush town and assumes the job of sheriff. Immediately he arrests a hot-headed but confused young killer (Bruce Dern), arousing the ire of the killer's pappy, Pa Danby (Walter Brennan), and his equally ineptly brutish brothers. Meanwhile Garner takes on a series of aspiring gunslingers with aplomb and increasing exasperation, finally pelting one wannabe gunman with rocks while chasing him out of town. "Sure is a childish way for a grown man to make a living," he chides.

This is among the best western spoofs ever to be put on film. Jack Elam provides one of his first comic roles as Garner's perfect foil, a character named Deputy Jake. It was a landmark role for the ever-capable Elam. "[Jack] was so

SWING IN THE SADDLE

identified with being a heavy that United Artists thought I was crazy when I wanted him for the comic deputy in *Support Your Local Sheriff*," director Burt Kennedy recalled in his autobiography *Hollywood Trail Boss*. "I knew that Jack was a riot personally and that he'd be great. He was, and it started a new career for him. Jack was so funny in that, I had a hard time casting him in a straight role from then on."

Unlike the many spoofs to follow, where nonstop vignettes are thrown at audiences a mile a minute and reduced in time to banal avenues of slapstick and silliness, Kennedy's film reflects the work of a man richly schooled in the genre. He began his career as an actor and then worked as a writer for John Wayne's Batjac Productions Co. before earning his full spurs by teaming with director Budd Boetticher in such masterful westerns as SEVEN MEN FROM NOW (1956), THE TALL T (1957), BUCHANAN RIDES ALONE (1958), RIDE LONESOME (1959), and COMANCHE STATION (1960). Consequently, he is able to convey a wealth of hilarity by exaggerating the type of improbable situations that the classic western tends to portray without sinking to a base level of bawdiness.

James Garner again shows why he is one of the industry's top acting craftsmen, equally adept at rich subtle comedy and strong, effective drama. "James Garner is delightful as the 'stranger' riding into town on his way to Australia, so modest, yet so perfect in his various abilities," says *Variety Movie Guide* (2001).

Support Your Local Sheriff proved popular with both critics and audiences and earned over $5 million in distribution for U.S. and Canadian rentals, making it one of the top 20 moneymakers for 1969.

SUSANNA PASS
Republic, 1949, Color, 67 min, VHS. **Producer:** Edward J. White (associate); **Director:** William Witney; **Screenplay:** John K. Butler and Sloan Nibley; **Music:** R. Dale Butts and Stanley Wilson; **Cinematographer:** Reggie Lanning; **Editor:** Tony Martinelli; **Cast:** Roy Rogers, Dale Evans, Estelita Rodriguez, Martin Garralaga, Robert Emmett Keane, Lucien Littlefield, Douglas Fowley, David Sharpe, Robert Bice, Foy Willing and the Riders of the Purple Sage.

An escaped convict joins with an unscrupulous newspaper owner to take over another man's property so they can mine the oil that lies beneath a lake. They go so far as to murder an old man, with the villain shooting a bullet into a boat, causing the old fellow to drown. This extremely well-done Roy Rogers vehicle, expertly helmed by William Witney, packs plenty of action and lots of good songs.

The hit song "Brush Those Tears from Your Eyes" (Oakley Haldeman, Clem Watts, and Jimmy Lee) is sung in the film by Roy Rogers with Foy Willing and The Riders of the Purple Sage. It became a best-selling record for a number of artists, including Buddy Clark and the Modernaires, Billy Vaughn and his Orchestra, Barry Green, Evelyn Knight and the Starlighters, and Al Trace and his Orchestra.

SUTTER'S GOLD
Universal, 1936, B&W, 94 min. **Producer:** Edmund Granger; **Director:** James Cruze; **Screenplay:** Blaise Cendras, Bruno Frank, Jack Kirkland, George O'Neil, and Walter Woods; **Music:** Heinz Roemheld, Clifford Vaughn, and Franz Waxman; **Cinematographer:** John P. Fulton and George Robinson; **Editor:** Philip Cahn; **Cast:** Edward Arnold, Lee Tracy, Binnie Barnes, Katharine Alexander, Montagu Love, Addison Richards, Harry Carey.

Universal's one big-budget spectacular of the 1930s, *Sutter's Gold* tells the story of Johann August Sutter, a Swiss immigrant who builds an empire in the American West with Mexican and California land grants, only to have it destroyed when gold is discovered on his land in 1949. Designed as a vehicle for actor Edward Arnold (in the title role), it was hoped that the film might revamp the career of director James Cruze and be the talkie equivalent of his silent epic THE COVERED WAGON (1923)—though it should be noted that the project was originally designed with Russian director Sergei M. Eisenstein in mind.

Unfortunately the film did not play well or pay off for the studio. Its lack of big-name stars and a larger than anticipated budget resulted in financial failure. The receipts from the film were so disappointing, in fact, that Universal might have gone under had it not been for the release that same year of the musical *Show Boat*, which proved a true blockbuster for the studio.

Frank Nugent in his *New York Times* review called the film " . . . one of the major disappointments of the season. . . ." Similarly, film historian William Evernson notes that despite its crowded canvas and good intentions "it was a jerky episodic tale, frequently held together by old fashioned subtitles, and with its action sequences staged on a big scale but disappointingly underplayed."

SWIFTY
Diversion/Grand National, 1935, B&W, 62 min. **Producer:** Walter Futter; **Director:** Alan James; **Screenplay:** Roger Allman and Bennett Cohen; **Cinematographer:** Carl Himm; **Cast:** Hoot Gibson, June Gale, George "Gabby" Hayes, Bob Kortman, William Gould, Wally Wales, Lafe McKee, Art Mix.

Swifty Wade (Hoot Gibson) is framed for murder by a crooked lawyer and the victim's stepson. When the culprits incite an angry lynch mob, Swifty gets some unexpected help from sheriff Gabby Hayes (listed in the credits as George F. Hayes).

SWING IN THE SADDLE (aka: SWING AND SWAY)
Columbia, 1944, B&W, 69 min. **Producer:** Jack Fier; **Director:** Lew Landers; **Screenplay:** Elizabeth Beecher, Morton Grant, and Bradford Ropes; **Music:** Oliver Drake, Edgar Leslie, Raymond McKee, Phil Moore, Gabriel Ruiz, Sunny Skyler, Fred Stryker, and Harry Warren; **Cinematographer:** Glen Gano; **Editor:** Aaron Stell; **Cast:** Jane Frazee, Guinn Williams, Slim Summerville, Carla Balenda (as Sally

Bliss), Mary Treen, Red River Dave (McEnery), Nat "King" Cole Trio, Jimmy Wakely and His Oklahoma Cowboys.

A pretty girl comes to a ranch through a misunderstanding, ends up engaged to the ranch foreman, and wins a local singing contest. With more music than action, this fun-filled oater is the only feature film starring long-ignored western singer/songwriter Red River Dave McEnery.

SWIRL OF GLORY   See *SUGARFOOT.*

TAGGART Universal, 1965, Color, 65 min. **Producer:** Gordon Kay; **Director:** R. G. Springsteen; **Screenplay:** Robert Creighton Williams; **Music:** Herman Stein; **Cinematographer:** Will Margulies; **Editor:** Tony Martinelli; **Cast:** Tony Young, Dan Duryea, Dick Foran, Elsa Cardenas, Jean Hale, Emile Meyer, David Carradine, Peter Duryea, Harry Carey Jr., Ray Teal, Claudia Barrett.

In this film based on a novel by Louis L'Amour Kent Taggart (Tony Young) plays a young man looking for the outlaws who murdered his parents. He is tracked through Indian country by a gunman. Dan Duryea does his usually excellent job as the top villain, but the big plus is the fine casting of Dick Foran, who appeared in more than 100 films. He would appear in one more picture three years later, ending a four-decade film career that included a series of films as an established singing cowboy.

Directed by R. G. Springsteen, this well-made little western has rarely been given its proper due. Unfortunately it is very difficult to find, although there are many genre enthusiasts awaiting any type of showing.

TAKE A HARD RIDE 20th Century Fox, 1975, Color, 103 min, VHS. **Producers:** Harry Bernsen and Leon Chooluck; **Director:** Antonio Margheriti (as Anthony Dawson); **Screenplay:** Eric Bercovi and Jerrold L. Ludwig; **Music:** Jerry Goldsmith; **Cinematographer:** Ricardo Pallottini; **Editor:** Stanford C. Allen; **Cast:** Lee Van Cleef, Jim Brown, Fred Williamson, Catherine Spaak, Jim Kelly, Dana Andrews, Barry Sullivan, Harry Carey Jr., Robert Donner, Charles Mcgregor.

Black cowboy Jim Brown promises his dying boss Dana Andrews that he will deliver the profits of Andrews's last cattle drive to his wife in Mexico. After Brown sets out he is joined by smooth gambler Fred Williamson, who has other ideas about the money. Together they fend off numerous attacks set to trap and kill them by evil bounty hunter Lee Van Cleef, with a posse led by sheriff Barry Sullivan also in hot pursuit. The film concludes with the usual blood-and-gore finish characteristic of the spaghetti genre.

Filmed in the Canary Islands and directed by Antonio Margheriti, this Italian entry came near the end of the spaghetti western cycle, which had somewhat dominated the genre for nearly a decade. A cut above the average, the movie's major asset is an effective cast, mostly Americans, many of whom had come to depend on the Italian film market for their income.

TAKE ANOTHER HARD RIDE See *KID VENGEANCE.*

TAKE ME BACK TO OKLAHOMA Monogram, 1940, B&W, 57 min, VHS. **Producer:** Edward Finney; **Director:** Albert Herman; **Screenplay:** Robert Emmett; **Music:** Frank Sanucci; **Cinematographer:** Marcel Le Picard; **Editor:** Frederick Bain; **Cast:** Tex Ritter, Bob Wills, Slim Andrews, Terry Walker, Robert McKenzie, Karl Hackett, Donald Curtiss, Gene Alsace, Olin Francis.

See *SONG OF THE GRINGO.*

TAKE THE STAGE See *CURTAIN CALL AT CACTUS CREEK.*

TAKING SIDES See *LIGHTNING GUNS.*

TALL IN THE SADDLE RKO, 1944, B&W, 87 min, VHS, DVD. **Producer:** Robert Fellows; **Director:** Edwin L. Marin; **Screenplay:** Paul P. Fix and Michael Hogan; **Music:**

Roy Webb; **Cinematographer:** Robert De Grasse; **Editor:** Philip Martin Jr.; **Cast:** John Wayne, Ella Raines, Ward Bond, George "Gabby" Hayes, Audrey Long, Elizabeth Risdon, Donald Douglas, Paul Fix, Emory Parnell, Raymond Hatton.

When Rocklin (John Wayne) arrives in Santa Inez to take over as foreman of the KC Ranch, he discovers that the man who hired him has been murdered. Because the ranch will now be owned by Clara Cardell (Audrey Long), a well-bred woman from the East, and her acerbic aunt (Elizabeth Risdon), he refuses to work for them (women as a gender seem to bother him). Yet he soon finds himself embroiled in a confrontation between greedy landowners and honest but helpless settlers. Compounding Rocklin's problems is fiery frontier gal Ella Raines, who makes the taciturn, free-spirited Rocklin the object of her desire.

The element of mystery, escalating suspense, and a romantic triangle with a surprising result makes for one of RKO's finest westerns. *Time* magazine called it ". . . a Western made up of the traditional ingredients and served with a trifle more than the traditional style . . .," while Philip T. Hartung in *Commonweal* called it ". . . the fastest and toughest Western of the season." William Everson in *Rediscovering The American Cinema* opines that *Tall in the Saddle* is among the more imposing westerns John Wayne ever made, ". . . literate, sober, and well acted—and has a couple of Wayne's roughest fistic scraps. . . ."

Coscripted by character actor and long-time Wayne friend Paul Fix, the film also helped to cement an eventual and successful business partnership between Wayne and producer Robert Fellows.

TALLION See *EYE FOR AN EYE, AN.*

TALL MEN, THE 20th Century Fox, 1955, Color, 122 min, VHS. **Producers:** William A. Bacher and William B. Hawks; **Director:** Raoul Walsh; **Screenplay:** Sydney Boehm and Frank Nugent; **Music:** Victor Young; **Cinematographer:** Leo Tover; **Editor:** Louis R. Loeffler; **Cast:** Clark Gable, Jane Russell, Robert Ryan, Cameron Mitchell, Juan Garcia, Harry Shannon, Emile Meyer, Steve Darell.

Ex-Confederate brothers Clark Gable and Cameron Mitchell, drifting toward Montana, hope to make a fortune in the gold fields. Instead they end up working for an unscrupulous businessman (Robert Ryan) whom they had originally intended to fleece, joining him in an uneasy alliance and then together driving a herd of cattle to its final destination in Montana. On the way they fight off bandits and rescue a buxom beauty (Jane Russell) from an Indian attack. Her affection alternates between Ryan and Gable as Ryan attempts to double-cross his hearty trail boss.

The film's biggest assets are its saleable cast and its CinemaScope and Technicolor photography. The story line and script falter quickly, and despite some good action sequences the film's most memorable scenes might well be the voluptuous Russell attempting with enormous difficulty to take off her tight boots with Gable and Ryan being called upon to assist her at strategic moments. *New York Times* critic Bosley Crowther called the film "a depressingly hackneyed horse opera," with Gable and Ryan going at it "as though they were acting in a deathless tragedy."

Not all reviews were so negative. *Photoplay* called the film a "big, amiable Western" in its review of December 1955. At the time of its release, *The Tall Men* was touted as "the biggest production in Fox's history," by its makers, and critic Andrew Sarris noted in *Film Culture* that "there is a pathos and vulnerability in [director] Walsh's characters. . . ."

TALL MEN RIDING Warner Bros., 1955, Color, 83 min. **Producer:** David Weibart; **Director:** Leslie Selander; **Screenplay:** Joseph Hoffman; **Music:** Paul Sawtell; **Cinematographer:** Wilfred M. Cline; **Editor:** Irene Morra; **Cast:** Randolph Scott, Dorothy Malone, Peggie Castle, William Ching, Robert Barrat, John Baragrey, Lane Chandler.

Randolph Scott returns home after 14 years to take revenge on the land baron who had stolen his lands and destroyed his intended marriage. This familiar theme benefits from a well-written script and Scott's inimitable screen presence.

TALL STRANGER, THE (aka: THE RIFLE; WALK TALL) Allied Artists, 1957, Color, 81 min. **Producers:** Richard Heermance and Walter Mirisch; **Director:** Thomas Carr; **Screenplay:** Christopher Knopf; **Music:** Hans J. Salter; **Cinematographer:** Wilfred M. Cline; **Editor:** William Austin; **Cast:** Joel McCrea, Virginia Mayo, Barry Kelly, Michael Ansara, Whit Bissell, James Dobson, George Neise, Leo Gordon, Ray Teal.

When passengers of a wagon train save a man's life, he agrees to help them with the settlement of their new lands, but he is opposed by a band of crooks. The film does not deliver much excitement, but it is good enough to please Joel McCrea's legion of fans.

TALL T, THE Columbia, 1957, Color, 78 min. **Producer:** Harry Joe Brown; **Director:** Budd Boetticher; **Screenplay:** Burt Kennedy; **Cinematographer:** Charles Lawton Jr.; **Editor:** Al Clark; **Cast:** Randolph Scott, Richard Boone, Maureen O'Sullivan, Arthur Hunnicutt, Skip Homeier, Henry Silva, John Hubburd, Robert Burton.

Based on a novel by Elmore Leonard, this Budd Boetticher/Burt Kennedy collaboration has Pat Brennan (Randolph Scott), a former ace ramrod, returning to his ranch on board a special stage belonging to honeymoon couple Willard and Doretta Mims (John Hubbard and Maureen O'Sullivan). When Brennan stops off at an isolated way station to deliver some candy to a young boy, the stage is commandeered by ruthless outlaw Frank Usher (Richard Boone) holds the passengers hostage with the assistance of his brutal henchmen Chink (Henry Silva) and Billy Jack (Skip Homeier).

Willard Mims, however, proves his cowardly stripes by making a deal with Usher in which the outlaw writes a ransom

Randolph Scott and Maureen O'Sullivan star in Budd Boetticher's The Tall T. (COLUMBIA/COURTESY OF BUDD AND MARY BOETTICHER)

note demanding $50,000 to Mrs. Mims's father, the richest man in the territory, with an additional promise to let Mims escape. But even Usher finds Mims so contemptuous that he has Chink shoot him after Mims makes the agreement. After this happens, Pat and Doretta conspire against the outlaws and pit one against the other. The nexus of the film is a deft character study of the two main protagonists (Scott and Boone), leading to an action-packed finale with an ironic twist.

Randolph Scott in a scene from The Tall T, *a Budd Boetticher–Burt Kennedy collaboration based on a novel by Elmore Leonard* (COLUMBIA/COURTESY OF BUDD AND MARY BOETTICHER)

Selected to the National Film Registry by the National Film Preservation Board (2000), *The Tall T* is the second in a series of superb pictures helmed by Boetticher, scripted by Kennedy, and starring Scott as the recalcitrant loner. *Variety* applauded the film as "an unconventional western [that] passes up most oater cliches." Richly praised for years in Europe, the film is receiving increasing critical acclaim in the United States. Both the film and Boetticher's remarkable and uncompromising artistry are studied in Martin Scorsese's highly touted retrospective *A Personal Journey Through American Movies* (1995).

TALL TEXAN, THE Lippert, 1953, B&W, 83 min. **Producers:** Robert L. Lippert Jr. and Samuel Roeca; **Director:** Elmo Williams; **Music:** Bert Shefter; **Cinematographer:** Joseph F. Biroc; **Editor:** Elmo Williams; **Cast:** Lloyd Bridges, Lee J. Cobb, Marie Windsor, Luther Adler, Syd Saylor, Samuel Herrick, George Steele, Dean Train.

A group of travelers bands together to search for gold on a sacred Indian burial ground. When greed and anger become a prime motivator, Ben Trask (Lloyd Bridges)—a newly-captured convict on his way back to prison—emerges as the man to maintain order within the group. The eclectic group of passengers aboard the wagon train include the obligatory lady of ill repute and a flawed lawman commissioned to bring in the prisoner (Trask). Directed by Elmo Williams, who a year earlier had edited *HIGH NOON* (in which Lloyd Bridges also had a strong supporting role as Harv, the deputy), *The Tall Texan* is considered by many genre enthusiasts to be a well-crafted B western and one of Lippert Studio's very best feature films.

TALL TIMBER See *PARK AVENUE LOGGER*.

TALL TROUBLE, THE See *HELL CANYON OUTLAWS*.

TAMING OF THE WEST Columbia, 1939, B&W, 55 min. **Producer:** Leon Barsha; **Director:** Norman Deming; **Screenplay:** Robert Lee Johnson and Charles F. Royal; **Cinematographer:** George Meehan; **Editor:** Otto Meyer; **Cast:** Bill Elliott, Iris Meredith, Dick Curtis, Dub Taylor, James Craig, Stanley Brown, Ethan Allen.
See *WILDCAT OF TUCSON*.

TAZA, SON OF COCHISE Universal, 1954, Color, 79 min. **Producer:** Ross Hunter; **Director:** Douglas Sirk; **Screenplay:** Gerald Drayson Adams and George Zuckerman; **Music:** Frank Skinner; **Cinematographer:** Russell Metty; **Editor:** Milton Carruth; **Cast:** Rock Hudson, Barbara Rush, Gregg Palmer, Rex Reason, Morris Ankrum, Ian MacDonald, Jeff Chandler, Robert Hoy.

The son of the great Apache chief promises at his father's deathbed that he will try to keep the peace that Cochise painstakingly made with the white men. However, his younger brother is equally determined to see that the tribe takes to the warpath again. Jeff Chandler, who played

Budd Boetticher's The Tall T, *recently selected to the National Film Registry, is the second in a series of superb westerns helmed by Boetticher, scripted by Burt Kennedy, and starring Randolph Scott.* (COLUMBIA/COURTESY OF BUDD AND MARY BOETTICHER)

Cochise in Universal's BATTLE AT APACHE PASS (1952), repeats the character in a single uncredited deathbed scene.

Taza, Son of Cochise, filmed amidst the spectacular scenery of Mohab, Utah, marked Rock Hudson's second and final role as an American Indian, and he was not very happy about it. When asked how he felt playing Indians onscreen, he replied, "Lousy." Moreover, Universal's makeup department didn't make matters any better in their efforts to make him look more authentic. He was said to have replied, "I looked like Joe College with a long wig and dark makeup. It was ridiculous."

TELEGRAPH TRAIL, THE Warner Bros., 1933 B&W, 54 min. **Producer:** Leon Schlesinger; **Director:** Tenny Wright; **Screenplay:** Kurt Kempler; **Music:** Leo F. Forbstein; **Cinematographer:** Ted McCord; **Editor:** Wm. Clemens; **Cast:** John Wayne, Frank McHugh, Marceline Day, Otis Harlan, Albert J. Smith, Yakima Canutt, Lafe McKee.

John Trent (John Wayne) is a government scout who attempts to get a supply train through to the camp of the men who are constructing the first telegraph line. Some good comedy work by Frank McHugh and Otis Harlan save this early Wayne "poverty row" oater. Much of the action footage was culled from *The Red Raiders* (1927), a Ken Maynard silent film.

TELL THEM WILLIE BOY IS HERE (aka: WILLIE BOY) Universal, 1969, Color, 98 min, VHS. **Producers:** Jennings Lang and Philip A. Waxman; **Director:** Abraham Polonsky; **Screenplay:** Polonsky; **Music:** Dave Grusin; **Cinematographer:** Conrad Hall; **Editor:** Melvin Shapiro; **Cast:** Robert Redford, Katharine Ross, Robert Blake, Susan Clark, Barry Sullivan, John Vernon, Charles Aidman, Charles McGraw, Shelly Novack.

Willie Boy, a young Paiute Indian (Robert Blake), kills his girlfriend's father and sets off with her in this film based on Harry Lawton's book, *Willie Boy . . . A Desert Manhunt.* The

Indians consider it "marriage by capture," but American law deems it murder. Led by Sheriff Cooper (Robert Redford), a posse is organized to track Willie down. The hunt escalates when it is announced that President Taft (1909–13) is to pay a visit to the area.

Willie Boy's way of life is crumbling all around him. His girlfriend Lola (Katharine Ross), fearing that her continued presence will slow Willie Boy down, dies off camera, a purported suicide. Sheriff Cooper gives him one last opportunity to surrender but is forced to kill the fleeing Willie, much to the chagrin of Dr. Elizabeth Arnold (Susan Clark), a liberal physician with whom Redford has a brief romance. In an action almost obligatory to the times, the dismayed sheriff flings his gun to the ground and helps carry Willie's body down the mountain.

This movie was the first for director Abraham Polonsky since his 1951 film *Force of Evil*. He had been blacklisted for failing to confirm or deny his membership in the Communist Party. Reviews of *Willie Boy* were generally lukewarm. Some have argued that the film offered Polonsky a vehicle to compare his own plight with that of Willie Boy's in the early 20th century. This may be so, but Polonsky becomes far too preachy, with each character's point of view conveyed in pat little speeches.

As the British *Monthly Film Bulletin* perceived: "For a film dealing with human fallibility, *Willie Boy* is just a fraction *too* infallible. Everybody says the right things, and in the right way, and it's the very rightness that turns out wrong." Nevertheless, the BAFTA (British Academy Awards) voted Robert Redford Best Actor and Katharine Ross Best Actress for their respective roles.

TENNESSEE'S PARTNER

RKO, 1955, Color, 87 min, VHS, DVD. **Producer:** Benedict Bogeaus; **Director:** Allan Dwan; **Screenplay:** C. Graham Baker, D. D. Beauchamp, Dwan, Milton Krims, and Teddi Sherman; **Music:** Louis Forbes and Dave Franklin; **Editor:** James Leicester; **Cast:** John Payne, Ronald Reagan, Rhonda Fleming, Coleen Gray, Anthony Caruso, Morris Ankrum, Chubby Johnson, Joe Devlin, Myron Healey, John Mansfield.

A stranger named Cowpoke (Ronald Reagan) rides into a western town in time rescue a gambler named Tennessee (John Payne) from being gunned down from behind. The two quickly become friends. When Tennessee learns that Cowpoke plans to marry a conniving woman who has pulled the wool over his partner's smitten eyes, he decides to lure the shady lady (Coleen Gray) to San Francisco to rescue Cowpoke from her nefarious scheme. With that task accomplished, Tennessee hopes to return to his own ladylove, a fiery saloon owner named The Duchess (Rhonda Fleming). But by then both Tennessee and Cowpoke find they have been framed on a murder charge involving a gold-mine claim.

Tennessee's Partner was the third screen and first talking version of the Bret Hart story (the others being two silent features, *Tennessee's Partner* [1916] and *The Flaming Forties* [1924]). Allan Dwan's film is a quiet and comfortable little western with enough action to keep the story flowing. Payne

(with a moustache) and Reagan are convincing buddies, each ready to sacrifice his life for the other if the occasion requires.

TENSION AT TABLE ROCK

RKO, 1956, Color, 91 min, VHS. **Producer:** Sam Wiesenthal; **Director:** Charles Marquis Warren; **Screenplay:** Winston Miller; **Music:** Dimitri Tiomkin; **Cinematographer:** Joseph F. Biroc; **Editor:** Dean Harrison and Harry Marker; **Cast:** Richard Egan, Dorothy Malone, Cameron Mitchell, Billy Chapin, Royal, Dano John Dehner, DeForest Kelly, Royal Dano, Angie Dickinson, Joe De Santis.

Wes Tancred (Richard Egan), who killed his best friend, a wanted man, in self-defense, is accused by his friend's wife of murdering him. With Tancred's reputation now destroyed, he is forced to leave town and start life anew. He takes a new identity and settles in the town of Table Rock, where he befriends a young orphaned boy (Billy Chapin) whose father had been killed at a way-station robbery. But Tancred's new identity is blown away when he stands up to a local gang that is terrorizing the town, helping the sheriff whose courage has been compromised.

Though not of the same caliber as *SHANE* (1953), this film explores many of the themes we see in that classic: a young boy's hero worship for an ex-gunslinger, the gunslinger's attraction to the wife of the man he chooses to protect, and the showdown with the hired gun. There is also an anti-*HIGH NOON* (1952) finish in which the town stands behind its sheriff and the gunslinger's decision to ride out of town, leaving the sheriff a redeemed man and a town reclaimed for its citizens.

Based on Frank Gruber's novel *Bitter Sage*, this forgotten little western packs plenty of suspense and features an understated performance by Cameron Mitchell as the self-doubting sheriff Fred Miller, as well as an excellent musical score by Dimitri Tiomkin. The title song "Ballad of Wes Tancred" is sung in the film by country music legend Eddie Arnold.

TENTING TONIGHT ON THE OLD CAMP GROUND

Universal, 1943, B&W, 62 min. **Producer:** Oliver Drake (associate); **Director:** Lewis D. Collins; **Screenplay:** Elizabeth Beecher; **Music:** Harold Adamson, Everett, June Hershey, Walter Kittredge, Jimmy McHugh, Milt Rosen, and Hans J. Salter; **Cinematographer:** William Sickner; **Editor:** Charles Maynard; **Cast:** Johnny Mack Brown, Tex Ritter, Fuzzy Knight, Jennifer Holt, Jimmy Wakely and the Jimmy Wakely Trio, Earl Hodgins, Rex Lease, Lane Chandler.

See *OLD CHISHOLM TRAIL, THE.*

TERROR IN A TEXAS TOWN

MGM, 1958, B&W, 80 min. **Producer:** Frank N. Seltzer; **Director:** Joseph H. Lewis; **Screenplay:** Ben L. Perry; **Music:** Gerald Fried; **Cinematographer:** Tay Rennahan; **Editor:** Stefan Arnsten and Frank Sullivan; **Cast:** Sterling Hayden, Sebastian Cabot, Carol Kelly, Gene Martin, Nedrick Young, Victor Millan.

Sterling Hayden stars as a whaler who returns to his prairie homeland to find it overrun by duplicitous oilmen and his father murdered by a ruthless land baron. A complex story with a surprising climactic twist featuring a showdown between a man with a six-gun and another with a harpoon, this inventive little Western marked the last film of the great low-budget stylist-director Joseph H. Lewis.

TERROR OF THE PLAINS   Reliable, 1935, B&W, 55 min. **Producer:** Bernard B. Ray; **Director:** Harry S. Webb; **Screenplay:** Carl Keusada and Jane Regan; **Cinematographer:** J. Henry Kruse; **Editor:** Frederick Bain; **Cast:** Tom Tyler, Roberta Gale, William Gould, Slim Whitaker, Fern Emmett, Nelson McDowell.

   See *MYSTERY RANCH* (1934).

TERRORS ON HORSEBACK   PRC, 1946, B&W, 55 min. **Producer:** Sigmund Neufeld; **Director:** Sam Newfield; **Screenplay:** George Milton; **Cinematographer:** Jack Greenhalgh; **Editor:** Holbrook N. Todd; **Cast:** Buster Crabbe, Al St. John, Patti McCarty, I. Stanford Jolley, Kermit Maynard, Henry Hall, Karl Hackett.

   See *OUTLAW OF THE PLAINS*.

TERROR TRAIL, THE   Columbia, 1946, B&W, 57 min. **Producer:** Colbert Clark; **Director:** Ray Nazarro; **Screenplay:** Ed Earl Repp; **Music:** Smiley Burnette; **Cinematographer:** George B. Meehan; **Editor:** Aaron Stell; **Cast:** Charles Starrett, Smiley Burnette, Barbara Pepper, Lane Chandler, Zon Murray, Elvin Eric Field, Tommy Coats, George Chesebro, Robert Barron, Budd Buster.

   See *DURANGO KID, THE*.

TEXAN, THE   Paramount, 1930, B&W, 79 min. **Producer:** Hector Turnbull (associate); **Director:** John Cromwell; **Screenplay:** Daniel Nathan Rubin; **Music:** Abel Baer and L. Wolfe Gilbert; **Cinematographer:** Victor Milner; **Editor:** Verna Willis; **Cast:** Gary Cooper, Emma Dunn, Oscar Apfel, James A. Marcus, Fay Wray, Donald Reed, Soledad Jimenez, Russ Columbo.

Gary Cooper plays the Llano Kid, an arrogant bandit with a price on his head in 1855 Texas. While playing poker he catches a young cardsharp cheating and kills him in self-defense. Then, on the train to Galveston, the Kid meets a man named Thacker (Oscar Apfel) who makes him an offer he can't refuse. Thacker tells the Kid of a wealthy aristocrat whose only son ran away when he was 10. She had offered Thacker a handsome reward if he could find her boy, so Thacker convinces and then trains the Llano Kid to pose as her son.

   The Kid accepts the ruse and pulls it off easily. But matters change when he discovers that the lady's real son was the same man he killed in the saloon brawl. He calls off the deal with Thacker, who promptly hires some desperadoes to attack the ranch. When the Kid is wounded and Thacker is killed, the sheriff realizes that the Kid has gone straight and

agrees to let the dead Thacker assume the identity of the Llano Kid. The former Kid is now free to court his lovely "cousin" Consuelo (Fay Wray).

   Based on O. Henry's story "The Doubled Eyed Deceiver," the film was the third teaming for Gary Cooper and Fay Wray. Of Cooper's performance, *Screenplay* noted, "This big boy is becoming a real actor." Paramount remade *The Texan* in 1939 as *THE LLANO KID*, with Tito Guizar in the starring role. Popular crooner and recording star Russ Columbo appears in an uncredited role as a singing cowboy at the campfire.

TEXAN, THE   Principal, 1932, B&W, 55 min. **Producer:** William M. Pizor; **Director:** Clifford Smith; **Cinematographer:** Ross Fisher; **Editor:** Murray Seldeen; **Cast:** Jay Wilsey (as Buffalo Bill Jr.), Lucile Browne, Bobby Nelson, Lafe McKee, Jack Mower, Art Mix, Duke Lee.

A cowboy running from the law gets mixed up in a crooked horse race scheme. He is eventually redeemed by love. Jay Wisley appeared as Buffalo Bill Jr., in more than 50 films (1924–37). This entry is the only film Principal Attractions ever produced.

TEXAN MEETS CALAMITY JANE, THE   Columbia, 1950, Color, 71 min. **Producer:** Ande Lamb; **Director:** Lamb; **Screenplay:** Lamb; **Music:** Rudy De Saxe; **Cinematographer:** Karl Struss; **Editor:** George McGuire; **Cast:** Evelyn Ankers, James Ellison, Lee "Lasses" White, Grace Lee Whitney, Jack Ingram.

Evelyn Ankers is yet another actress to play the female sharpshooter. In this inept outing. Calamity Jane learns that her ownership of the Prairie Queen saloon is being challenged by the niece of the man who bequeathed the saloon to Calamity. But when the niece and her lawyer discover that a rival saloon owner is out to take over the property, they change sides and lend Calamity their support.

TEXANS, THE   Paramount, 1938, B&W, 92 min, VHS. **Producer:** Lucien Hubbard; **Director:** James Hogan; **Screenplay:** William Wister Haines, Bertram Millhauser, and Paul Sloane; **Music:** Gerard Carbonara; **Cinematographer:** Theodor Sparkuhl; **Editor:** Le Roy Stone; **Cast:** Randolph Scott, Joan Bennett, May Robson, Walter Brennan, Robert Cummings, Robert Barrat, Harvey Stephens, Francis Ford.

In this film set in the post-Civil War era, carpetbaggers try to cheat Texas ranchers out of their land claims. The ranchers in turn are forced to lead a cattle drive from Texas to Abilene, Kansas, thus opening the Chisholm Trail. The leader of the drive is Kirk Jordan (Randolph Scott), a former rebel soldier attempting to carve a new life as a trail boss. In addition to battling rustlers, carpetbaggers, and hostile Indians, Scott must also contend with female gunrunner Joan Bennett, who wants to reignite a war between the states.

   Filmed in Cotulla, Texas, the picture includes a blizzard, a number of dust storms, and Indian and cavalry raids. It is a remake of Emerson Hough's 1924 novel *North of '36*, which Paramount filmed first in 1924 with Jack Holt in the lead role.

TEXANS NEVER CRY Columbia, 1951, B&W, 66 min. **Producer:** Armand Schaefer; **Director:** Frank McDonald; **Screenplay:** Norman S. Hall; **Cinematographer:** William Bradford; **Editor:** James Sweeney; **Cast:** Gene Autry, Pat Buttram, Mary Castle, Russell Hayden, Gail Davis, Tom Keene, Don C. Harvey.

See *TUMBLING TUMBLEWEEDS*.

TEXAS Columbia, 1941, B&W, 94 min. **Producer:** Samuel Bischoff; **Director:** George Marshall; **Screenplay:** Michael Blankfort, Horace McCoy, and Lewis Meltzer; **Music:** Sidney Cutner, Ross DiMaggio, and Carmen Dragon; **Cinematographer:** George Meechan; **Editor:** William A. Lyon; **Cast:** William Holden, Glenn Ford, Claire Trevor, George Bancroft, Edgar Buchanan, Andrew Tombes, Addison Richards, Edmund MacDonald.

Two young Virginians (Glenn Ford and William Holden) witness a stagecoach robbery. They decide to rob the robbers and make off with the loot themselves. To escape the posse and avoid a lynching, they split up and go their separate ways, not seeing each other for many years. When they finally meet up again they find themselves on the opposite sides of the law: Todd (Ford) has joined the law-abiding ranchers and is now a ranch foreman, while Dan (Holden) has become involved with an outlaw gang of rustlers headed by Doc Thorpe (Edgar Buchanan). To compound matters they both vie for the affections of the same woman (Claire Trevor), the daughter of a ranch owner.

Columbia made this film as a follow-up to its more costly *ARIZONA* (1940), also starring Holden. An entertaining and underrated western that makes good use of stock footage, it was originally issued in a blue-tinted sepia print. William Everson in *A Pictorial History of the Western Film* calls *Texas* ". . . lively, fast, and full of rather refreshingly grisly black humor." The 25-year-old Ford and the 23-year-old Holden (both rising young stars) make an appealing pair of youthful buddies. After service in World War II, the two appeared

Glenn Ford and William Holden (seated on stage) face Claire Trevor at the piano in Texas. (COLUMBIA/AUTHOR'S COLLECTION)

together seven years later in Columbia's THE MAN FROM COLORADO (1948).

TEXAS ACROSS THE RIVER Universal, 1966, Color, 1966, 101 min, VHS. **Producer:** Harry Keller; **Director:** Michael Gordon; **Screenplay:** Wells Root, Harold Greene, and Ben Starr; **Music:** Frank De Vol; **Cinematographer:** Russell Metty; **Editor:** Gene Milford; **Cast:** Dean Martin, Alain Delon, Rosemary Forsythe, Joey Bishop, Tina Augment, Peter Graves, Michael Ansara, Andrew Prine, Linden Chiles, Richard Farnsworth.

A Spanish nobleman (Alain Delon), accused of murdering the fiancé of the girl he loves, heads across the border to Texas. Along the way he meets a gunrunner (Dean Martin), who is transporting guns across Comanche territory, and an Indian ally named Kronk (Joey Bishop), who pops up from time to time in the film. Both Don Andrea (Delon) and Sam Hollis (Martin) have a keen eye for the ladies, and what follows is pure fun and frolic heightened by some hilariously romantic and convoluted twists and turns.

A well-crafted spoof helmed by former stage actor Michael Gordon, *Texas Across the Border* garnered good reviews. *Variety* calls it ". . . a rootin', tootin' comedy western with no holds barred . . . a gag man's dream, with a choice assemblage of laughs, many of the belly genre."

TEXAS BAD MAN Universal, 1932, B&W, 63 min. **Producer:** Carl Laemmle Jr.; **Director:** Edward Laemmle; **Screenplay:** Jack Cunningham; **Cinematographer:** Daniel B. Clark; **Editor:** Philip Cahn; **Cast:** Tom Mix, Lucille Powers, Willard Robertson, Fred Kohler, Joseph W. Griard.

Tom Mix is an undercover lawman who poses as a bad man in order to infiltrate an outlaw gang and identify their mysterious leader. A sidebar has him dressing up in a garish Mexican outfit to romance the heroine (Lucille Powers). One of Tom Mix's better sound movies, the film features some first-rate riding stunts by Mix and his horse Tony.

TEXAS BAD MAN Allied Artists, 1953, B&W, 62 min. **Producer:** Vincent M. Kennelly; **Director:** Lewis D. Collins; **Screenplay:** Joseph Poland; **Music:** Raoul Kraushaar; **Cinematographer:** Gilbert Warrenton; **Editor:** Sam Fields; **Cast:** Wayne Morris, Frank Ferguson, Elaine Riley, Myron Healey, Denver Pyle, Sheb Wooley, Nelson Leigh, Mort Mills.

When an outlaw leader and his gang attempt to rob the proceeds from a gold mine, the gang leader's son tries to stop them.

TEXAS CITY Monogram, 1952, B&W, 54 min. **Producer:** Vincent M. Fennelly; **Director:** Lewis B. Collins; **Screenplay:** Joseph D. Collins; **Cinematographer:** Ernest Miller; **Editor:** Sam Fields; **Cast:** Johnny Mack Brown, James Ellison, Lois Hall, Lyle Talbot, Terry Frost, Pierce Lyden, John Hart.

See *UNDER ARIZONA SKIES*.

TEXAS KID, THE Monogram, 1943, B&W, 57 min, VHS. **Producer:** Scott R. Dunlap; **Director:** Lambert Hillyer; **Screenplay:** Jess Bowers (Adele Buffington); **Cinematographer:** Harry Neumann; **Editor:** Carl Pierson; **Cast:** Johnny Mack Brown, Raymond Hatton, Marshall Reed, Shirley Patterson, Robert Fiske, Edmund Cobb.

See *UNDER ARIZONA SKIES*.

TEXAS KID OUTLAW See *KID FROM TEXAS, THE* (1950).

TEXAS LADY RKO, 1955, Color, 86 min, VHS. **Producers:** Nat Holt and Lewis P. Rosen; **Director:** Tim Whelan; **Screenplay:** Horace McCoy; **Music:** Paul Sawtell; **Cinematographer:** Ray Rennahan; **Editor:** Richard W. Farrell; **Cast:** Claudette Colbert, Barry Sullivan, Ray Collins, James Bell, Horace McMahon, Gregory Walcott, John Litel, Douglas Fowley, Don Haggerty.

Prudence Webb (Claudette Colbert), a gambling queen from New Orleans, inherits a local newspaper in an isolated western town. Not surprisingly, the local menfolk are not exactly happy when she arrives and starts exposing the many existing

Gregory Walcott and Claudette Colbert in Texas Lady (RKO/COURTESY OF GREGORY WALCOTT)

avenues of corruption while also challenging the iron rule of the two men who had wrested the territory from the Indians 25 years earlier. Forced to contend with the corrupt town bigwigs and the amorous advances of ornery Deputy Jess Foley (Gregory Walcott), she gets some unexpected help from Chris Mooney (Barry Sullivan), the same suave gambler she bested in a big-stakes poker game in New Orleans before making her way west.

Actor Gregory Walcott, who had a distinguished 40-year career as a character actor, was some 20 years younger than leading lady Claudette Colbert when they teamed together in a romantic scene. In an interview he recalled being paired with one of the silver screen's all-time leading ladies: "At first I was scared of her. She was a very big star and I heard she could chew up actors at the drop of a hat. However, I discovered that she was a bit intimidated by me. There was that age difference and I think that made her feel a little insecure. I don't think she knew exactly what to make of me."

TEXAS LAWMEN Monogram, 1951, B&W, 57 min. **Producer:** Vincent Fennelly; **Director:** Lewis Collins; **Screenplay:** Collins, and Joseph Poland; **Cinematographer:** Ernest Miller; **Editor:** Sammy Fields; **Cast:** Johnny Mack Brown, Jimmy Ellison, I. Stanford Jolley, Lee Roberts, Terry Frost, Marshall Reed, Lane Bradford, Lyle Talbot, John Hart, Stanley Price, Pierce Lyden.

See UNDER ARIZONA SKIES.

TEXAS LEGIONNAIRES See MAN FROM MUSIC MOUNTAIN.

TEXAS MARSHAL, THE PRC, 1941, B&W, 59 min. **Producer:** Sigmund Neufeld; **Director:** Sam Newfield; **Screenplay:** William Lively; **Music:** Johnny Lange and Lew Porter; **Cinematographer:** Jack Greenhalgh; **Editor:** Holbrook N. Todd; **Cast:** Tim McCoy, Karl Hackett, Charles King, Dave O'Brien, Kay Leslie, Edward Peil Sr., Budd Buster.

When local ranchers are being knocked off one by one, Marshal "Trigger Tim" Rand (Tim McCoy) is called in to investigate the terrorism. But his efforts are compromised by his singing partner, who is being misled by the crooked perpetrators. McCoy's final solo series film includes four original western-swing numbers by Art Davis and His Rhythm Riders.

TEXAS MASQUERADE United Artists, 1944, B&W, 58 min. **Producer:** Harry Sherman; **Director:** George Archainbaud; **Screenplay:** Norman Houston and Jack Lait Jr.; **Cinematographer:** Russell Harlan; **Editors:** Walter Hannemann and Carrol Lewis; **Cast:** William Boyd, Andy Clyde, Jimmy Rogers, Mady Correll, Don Costello, J. Farrell MacDonald, Pierce Lyden, Robert McKenzie, June Pickerell, Bill Hunter.

See HOP-ALONG CASSIDY.

TEXAS RANGER, THE Columbia, 1931, B&W, 61 min. **Producer:** Sol Lessor; **Director:** D. Ross Lederman;

Screenplay: Forrest Sheldon; **Cinematographer:** Teddy Tetzlaff; **Editor:** Gene Milford; **Cast:** Buck Jones, Carmelita Geraghty, Harry Woods, Edward Brady, Nelson McDowell, Harry Todd.

Buck Jones is a Texas Ranger trying to stop a feud between two factions in the Texas cattle country. This fast-paced and exciting early Jones talkie venture is a couple of cuts above the usual early sound-era B oater. (See also WHITE GAGLE.)

TEXAS RANGERS Price Entertainment/Dimension Films, 2001, Color, 93 min, VHS, DVD. **Producers:** Alan Greisman and Frank Price; **Director:** Steve Miner; **Screenplay:** Scott Busby and Martin Copeland; **Music:** Trevor Rabin; **Cinematographer:** Daryn Okada; **Editor:** Gregg Feathermaan; **Cast:** James Van Der Beek, Rachael Leigh Cook, Dylan McDermott, Usher Raymond, Ashton Kutcher, Leonor Varela, Tom Skerritt, Alfred Molina, Randy Travis, Matt Keesler, Jon Abrahams, Vincent Spano, Marco Leonardi, Kate Newby.

A bunch of ragtag young men who join together after the Civil War to form the Texas Rangers are charged with the task of cleaning up the West—sometimes in ruthless fashion. The film opens in 1875 with real-life Ranger Leander McNelly (Dylan McDermott), whose wife and three children had been kidnapped by bandidos years earlier, recruiting men to make the lawless territory safe. They succeed in their task only through much carnage and lots of bloodshed—and with predictable results. In his review of December 3, 2001, *Los Angeles Times* critic Kevin Thomas notes, "Any one of the half-hour episodes in the old radio serial 'Tales of the Texas Rangers' starring Joel McCrea or 'The Lone Ranger' hold more interest than this 93-minute bore." The film, he concludes, "seems like a nail in the coffin of a genre so integral to the history of the American cinema."

TEXAS RANGERS, THE Paramount, 1936, B&W, 98 min, VHS. **Producer:** King Vidor; **Director:** Vidor; **Screenplay:** Louis Stevens; **Music:** Phil Boutelje, Sam Coslow, and Jack Scholl ; **Cinematographer:** Edward Cronjager; **Cast:** Fred MacMurray, Jack Oakie, Jean Parker, Lloyd Nolan, Edward Ellis, Benny Bartlett, George "Gabby" Hayes, Elena Martinez, Frank Shannon.

Fred MacMurray, Jack Oakie, and Lloyd Nolan are three train robbers who are separated after committing the robbery in this movie produced and directed by King Vidor and filmed to commemorate the state of Texas's centennial year. While Jim Hawkins (MacMurray) and Wahoo Jones (Oakie) redeem themselves and become Texas Rangers, the third, Sam McGee (Nolan) becomes an infamous bandit. Jean Parker, the pretty daughter of Ranger commander Bailey (Edward Ellis), is the object of MacMurray's affections and the woman he returns to once he carries out his mission to bring McGee to justice.

While the plot is familiar, Vidor's skillful helming and rugged sense of landscape as well as some solid action provide for an interesting film. Based on Walter Prescott's book *The Texas Rangers*, the film's story was concocted by Vidor, himself a Texan and a man who understood the West, and his wife Elizabeth Hill. It was Vidor's first western since *BILLY THE KID* (1930), and it is generally considered the best of Paramount's four westerns made in the 1930s.

Called an ". . . exhilarating Western with a refreshing schoolboy vigor" by William Everson, *The Texas Rangers* boasts one of the most callous yet memorable scenes in a 1930s feature film: Lloyd Nolan's murder of his friend Jack Oakie, shooting him in the stomach from under a table while talking in terms of friendship and devotion. Filmed in Santa Fe County, New Mexico, this picture garnered an Oscar for Best Sound Recording (Franklin Hansen). A sequel, *THE TEXAS RANGERS RIDE AGAIN*, was issued in 1941, while the 1936 original was remade by Paramount in 1949 as *STREETS OF LAREDO*.

TEXAS RANGERS, THE Paramount, 1951, Color, 74 min. **Producer:** Bernard B. Small; **Director:** Phil Karlson; **Screenplay:** Richard Shayer; **Music:** George Duning and Paul Sawtell; **Cinematographer:** Ellis Carter; **Editor:** Al Clark; **Cast:** George Montgomery, Gale Storm, Jerome Courtland, Noah Beery Jr., William Bishop, John Litel, Ian MacDonald, Douglas Kennedy, John Dehner, John Doucette, Jock Mahoney, Myron Healey, Joe Fallon, Trevor Bardette.

Three outlaws—George Montgomery, Noah Beery Jr., and Ian MacDonald (as the Sundance Kid)—start out robbing a bank in Waco, but Sundance double-crosses his two cohorts, who soon find themselves languishing in a Texas jail. Major Jones of the Texas Rangers makes the two men an offer they can't refuse. He will free them and make them Rangers if they agree to track down the outlaws who are terrifying the townspeople.

TEXAS RANGERS RIDE AGAIN, THE Paramount, 1941, B&W, 68 min, VHS. **Producer:** William LeBaron; **Director:** James Hogan; **Screenplay:** Walter R. Lipman and Horace McCoy; **Music:** Gerard Carbonara and John Leipold; **Cinematographer:** Archie Stout; **Editor:** Arthur Schmidt; **Cast:** Ellen Drew, John Howard, Akim Tamiroff, May Robson, Broderick Crawford, Charlie Grapewin, John Miljan, Anthony Quinn, Eddie Foy Jr., Monte Blue.

With cattle by the thousands being rustled from the White Sage Ranch, the Texas Rangers are called in to investigate the matter. One of the Rangers manages to infiltrate the gang by making them think he is the infamous Pecos Kid. The good cast provides the film's best offering.

TEXAS SERENADE See *OLD CORRAL, THE.*

TEXAS STAGECOACH Columbia, 1940, B&W, 60 min. **Producer:** Leon Barsha; **Director:** Joseph H. Lewis; **Screenplay:** Fred Myton; **Music:** Bob Nolan and Tim Spencer; **Cinematographer:** George Meehan; **Editor:** Charles Nelson; **Cast:** Charles Starrett, Irish Meredith, Bob Nolan, Kenneth MacDonald, Pat Brady, Edward Le Saint, George Becinita, Don Beddoe.

See *GALLANT DEFENDER.*

TEXAS STAMPEDE Columbia, 1939, B&W, 57 min. **Producer:** Harry L. Decker; **Director:** Sam Nelson; **Screenplay:** Charles F. Royal; **Music:** Bob Nolan and Ben Oakland; **Cinematographer:** Lucien Ballard; **Editor:** William Lyon; **Cast:** Sam Nelson, Iris Meredith, Fred Kohler, Nolan, Lee Prather, Ray Bennett, Blackjack Ward.

See *GALLANT DEFENDER.*

TEXAS TERROR Monogram/Lone Star, 1935, B&W, 58 min, VHS, DVD. **Producer:** Paul Malvern; **Director:** R. N. Bradbury; **Screenplay:** Bradbury; **Cinematographer:** William Hyer and Archie Stout; **Editor:** Carl Pierson; **Cast:** John Wayne, Lucile Browne, LeRoy Mason, Fern Emmett, George "Gabby" Hayes, Jay Wilsey (as Buffalo Bill Jr.), John Ince, Frank Ball, Yakima Canutt.

Sheriff John Higgins (John Wayne) is a Texas lawman who retires from law enforcement when he thinks he killed his best friend in an accident. Desolate, he seeks solace in the lonely life of a prospector. But fate intervenes when he saves the life of the sister of the man he presumes he had killed as bandits are attacking her. He goes with her to town and finds a clue that leads him to those who actually killed his friend. Exonerated now, he returns to the desert with the woman to start life anew.

TEXAS TERRORS Republic, 1940, B&W, 57 min. **Producer:** George Sherman (associate); **Director:** Sherman; **Screenplay:** Anthony Coldeway and Doris Schroeder; **Music:** Cy Feuer; **Cinematographer:** John MacBurnie; **Editor:** Tony Martinelli; **Cast:** Don "Red" Barry, Julie Duncan, Arthur Loft, Al St. John, Eddy Waller, William Ruhl, Ann Pennington, Sammy McKim, Jimmy Wakely and his Roughriders (Johnny Bond & Dick Rinehart).

See *WYOMING OUTLAW.*

TEXAS TO BATAAN Monogram, 1942, B&W, 56 min. **Producer:** George W. Weeks; **Director:** Robert Tansey; **Screenplay:** Arthur Hoerl; **Music:** John "Dusty" King (songs); **Cinematographer:** Robert E. Cline; **Editor:** Roy Claire; **Cast:** John "Dusty" King, David Sharpe, Max Terhune, Margorie Manners, Budd Buster, Kenne Duncan.

The Range Busters find themselves opposed by enemy agents when they attempt to take a shipment of horses to the Philippines for the U.S. Army. The trio of John "Dusty" King, David Sharpe, and Max Terhune appeared together as "The Range Busters" in three other films: *Trail Riders* (1942), *Haunted Ranch* (1943), and *Two Fisted Justice* (1943).

TEXAS TRAIL   Paramount, 1937, B&W, 54 min, VHS. **Producer:** Harry Sherman; **Director:** David Selman; **Screenplay:** Harrison Jacobs, Jack Merserveau, and Jack O'Donnell; **Music:** Gerard Carbonara; **Cinematographer:** Russell Harlan; **Editor:** Sherman Rose and Robert Warwick; **Cast:** William Boyd, George "Gabby" Hayes, Russell Hayden, Judith Allen, Alexander Cross, Bob Kortman.

See *HOP-ALONG CASSIDY.*

TEXAS WILDCATS   Victory, 1939, B&W, 57 min. **Producer:** Sam Katzman; **Director:** Sam Newfield; **Screenplay:** George Plympton; **Cinematographer:** Marcel Le Picard; **Editor:** Holbrook N. Todd; **Cast:** Tim McCoy, Joan Barclay, Ben Corbett, Forrest Taylor, Ted Adams, Avando Reynaldo.

TEXICAN, THE (aka: TEXAS KID, Spain)   Columbia, 1966, Color, 90 min, VHS. **Producers:** John C. Champion and Bruce Balaban; **Director:** Lesley Selander; **Screenplay:** Champion, Jose Antonio de la Loma, and Nico Fidenco; **Cinematographer:** Francisco Marin; **Editor:** Teresa Alcocer; **Cast:** Audie Murphy, Broderick Crawford, Diana Lorys, Luis Induni, Victor Israel, Antonio Casas.

Jess Carlin (Audie Murphy) is living peacefully as an exile in Mexico when he is forced to cross the border to learn the truth about his brother's murder. He arrives in Rim Rock, a town beset by fear and under the control of brutal town boss Luke Starr (Broderick Crawford). Jess discovers it was Starr who murdered his brother, a crusading newspaperman bent on exposing the boss's brutality and corruption. Matters are complicated when Jess finds himself attracted to beautiful dance-hall girl Kit O'Neal (Diane Lorys), the same gal the villainous Starr pines for. The pairing of the heroic Murphy and an overweight Crawford (both in the declining years of their respective careers) is interesting and rather effective. The movie was filmed in Spain.

TEX RIDES WITH THE BOY SCOUTS   Grand National, 1937, B&W, 66 min. **Producers:** Edward L. Alperson and Edward Finney; **Director:** Ray Taylor; **Screenplay:** Edmond Kelso and Lindsley Parsons; **Music:** Ted Choate, Curley Fletcher, Tex Ritter, and Frank Sanucci; **Cast:** Tex Ritter, Marjorie Reynolds, "Snub" Pollard, Tommy Bupp, Charles King, Forrest Taylor, Karl Hackett.

See *SONG OF THE GRINGO.*

THERE WAS A CROOKED MAN   Warner Bros., 1970, Color, 126 min, VHS. **Producer:** Joseph L. Mankiewicz; **Director:** Mankiewicz; **Screenplay:** Robert Benton and David Newman; **Music:** Charles Strouse; **Cinematographer:** Harry Stradling Jr.; **Editor:** Gene Milford; **Cast:** Kirk Douglas, Henry Fonda, Hume Cronyn, Warren Oates, Burgess Meredith, Arthur O'Connell, Martin Gabel, Alan Hale Jr., Lee Grant, Gene Evans, Jeanne Cooper.

Kirk Douglas is Paris Pittman Jr., a charming, capable, seductive crook with a fortune of gold stashed in some unknown place. Unfortunately he is serving time in the territorial penitentiary, which is controlled by straitlaced, nononsense, reform-minded Warden Woodward Lopeman (Henry Fonda). Determined to best the warden in a clever battle of wits and deceit, the duplicitous Paris engineers an escape from the slammer, in the process betraying his fellow convicts, including the naïve and sad sycophant Floyd Moon (Warren Oates) who believes that in Paris Pitmann he at long last found a true friend. It all leads to a cynical finale with some interesting character studies and a good amount of and twists and turns.

Douglas and Fonda pair off well in adversarial roles, playing two determined men caught in a game of one-upmanship. Produced and helmed by award-winning director/writer Joseph Mankiewicz (*A Letter to Three Wives,* 1949; *All About Eve,* 1950; *Julius Caesar,* 1953), with a script by Robert Benton and David Newman (their first since *Bonnie and Clyde,* 1967), and shot in the desert location of La Joya, New Mexico, the film did not do well at the box office and generally received poor reviews. In fact, the picture was reportedly shelved for more than a year before being released almost as a Christmas season afterthought in 1970. Today it is finding an increased stature and popularity through TV and video showings. Trini Lopez sings title song by Charles Strouse and Lee Adams.

THESE THOUSAND HILLS   20th Century Fox, 1959, Color, 96 min. **Producer:** David Weisbart; **Director:** Richard Fleischer; **Screenplay:** Alfred Hayes; **Music:** Leigh Harline; **Cinematographer:** Charles G. Clark; **Editor:** Hugh S. Fowler; **Cast:** Don Murray, Richard Egan, Lee Remick, Patricia Owens, Stuart Whitman, Albert Dekker, Harold Stone, Royal Dano, Fuzzy Knight.

Don Murray plays an ambitious cowboy who saves his money and, with a loan from a dance-hall girl (Lee Remick), buys a ranch and marries the niece of a banker and his wife (Albert Dekker and Patricia Owens). Now a leading citizen and political candidate, he is forced to join a posse led by a brutish rancher (Richard Egan in an uncharacteristically villainous part). The posse tracks down then hangs the cowboy's former buddy (Stuart Whitman). Unable to save his friend, the cowboy begins rethinking what he has done with his life. It results in a final showdown between the cowboy and the rancher who had persuaded him to join the posse. This introspective little western deserves some high marks for its insightful content and interesting character studies. The title song, written by Ned Washington and Harry Warren, is performed by Randy Sparks.

THEY CAME TO CORDURA   Columbia, 1959, Color, 123 min, VHS. **Producer:** William Goetz; **Director:** Robert Rossen; **Screenplay:** Ivan Moffat and Rossen; **Music:** Elie Siegmeister; **Cinematographer:** Burnett Guffey; **Editor:** William A. Lyon; **Cast:** Gary Cooper, Rita Hayworth, Van Heflin, Tab Hunter, Richard Conte, Michael Callan, Dick York, Robert Keith.

In his final western, Gary Cooper stars as Major Thomas Thorn, an army officer accused of cowardice and demoted to presenting awards to braver men for their courageous valor against Pancho Villa in the Mexican Expedition of 1916. He selects a battery of heroes for the Congressional Medal of Honor, but when he is forced to escort them safely back to Cordura through dangerous back-road Mexican country, the candidates' true colors begin to emerge.

Rita Hayworth, in an outstanding performance (some consider it her finest dramatic role), is detested by the entire group for providing a haven to Villa and his men. Accused of treason, she is forced to accompany the men on their difficult journey back to Cordura.

Despite its first-rate cast, *They Came to Cordura* never quite hits its mark, tending instead to be overlong, laborious, and even monotonous at times. Unfortunately, Cooper at age 59 was too old for his role (a fact clearly noted by the critics). Unbeknownst to the public, his health was in a precarious state, making it difficult for him to perform the many grueling tasks the film required, such as dragging a wagon along the railroad tracks through the desert.

Nonetheless, the pairing of Gary Cooper and Rita Hayworth, two of the cinema's most charismatic personalities, is enough to recommend the 28th and final western of Cooper's illustrious film career. *They Came to Cordura* still provides some solid glimpses of Cooper's remarkable affinity for the movie camera. The songs were provided by the team of Sammy Cahn and Jimmy Van Heusen.

THEY DIED WITH THEIR BOOTS ON
Warner Bros., 1941, B&W, 140 min, VHS. **Producers:** Hal B. Wallis and Robert Fellows; **Director:** Raoul Walsh; **Screenplay:** Wally Kline and Eneas MacKenzie; **Music:** Max Steiner; **Cinematographer:** Bert Glennon; **Editor:** William Holmes; **Cast:** Errol Flynn, Olivia de Havilland, Arthur Kennedy, Sidney Greenstreet, Charley Grapewin, Gene Lockhart, Anthony Quinn, John Litel, Walter Hampden, Regis Toomey.

This fictionalized biography of George Armstrong Custer traces Custer's life from his tenure as an unruly cadet at West Point through the Civil War, culminating with his death at the Battle of Little Big Horn. Everything in the exciting film is geared toward the rousing final battle, with Bert Glennon's camera providing a focused panoramic sweep as Custer leads his troops into the climactic Battle of Little Big Horn.

Errol Flynn is superb in a role that requires all the dash and daring a major film studio like Warner Bros. had to offer. Olivia de Havilland supplies romance as Libby Bacon Custer, the only time where the romantic screen couple of de Havilland and Flynn are actually man and wife. The prototype military wife, she allows herself to faint only after becoming aware that her husband has gone on his last mission, one that would provide him no return.

Raoul Walsh, who had supplanted Michael Curtiz as Flynn's main actor director, helmed this rousing, action-packed western adventure. The flamboyant Flynn is a far nobler and valiant figure than the one presented in later films, particularly in the past 30 years when the famed Boy General has been depicted in various degrees of complexity, with derision or as a downright butcher. It should be noted that Flynn portrayed Confederate officer Jeb Stuart in Warner's *SANTA FE TRAIL*, with Ronald Reagan playing a lighthearted and more benign George Custer. Sidney Greenstreet lends verve to his portrayal of General Winfield Scott, George Custer's main benefactor in the film, and a young Anthony Quinn makes for an interesting Chief Crazy Horse.

The biggest and most expensive of Warner Bros.' epic westerns, *They Died with Their Boots On* was the studio's last western spectacular for years to come. Future genre films would become neatly packed programmers rather than grand-scale, historical epics. While the film is flawed history, it still provides for superb and grandiose entertainment. A stirring musical score incorporates strains of some of our most patriotic and best-loved melodies. The enormous cast of supporting players and extras also meant a movie paycheck for lots of previously unemployed industry people.

THEY RODE TOGETHER
Columbia, 1954, Color, 84 min. **Producer:** Louis Batista; **Director:** Phil Karlson; **Screenplay:** Frank S. Nugent and De Vallon Scott; **Music:** Paul Sawtell; **Cinematographer:** Charles Lawton Jr.; **Editor:** Henry Batista; **Cast:** Robert Francis, Donna Reed, Mae Wynn, Philip Carey, Onslow Stevens, Peggy Converse, Roy Roberts, Jack Kelly.

When a post doctor wants to treat a local Indian tribe during an outbreak of malaria, he finds himself at odds with the army camp commander.

THIRTEEN FIGHTING MEN
20th Century Fox, 1960, B&W, 69 min. **Producer:** Jack Leewood; **Director:** Harry W. Gerstead; **Screenplay:** Robert Hammer and Jack W. Thomas; **Music:** Irving Gertz; **Cinematographer:** Walter Strenge; **Editor:** John A. Bushelman; **Cast:** Grant Williams, Brad Dexter, Carole Mathews, Robert Dix, Richard Garland, Richard Crane.

As the Civil War ends, returning Confederates seize a Union gold shipment with the idea that it will remove the hardships they anticipate when they return home. However, their leader (Brad Dexter) must now keep them from drifting into full-time banditry. Matters are compounded when the Union commander (Grant Withers) discovers that the lure of gold has a demoralizing effect on his troops as well.

THOSE REDHEADS FROM SEATTLE
Paramount, 1953, Color, 90 min. **Producers:** William H. Pine and William C. Thomas; **Director:** Lewis R. Foster; **Screenplay:** Lionel Lindon; **Music:** Hoagy Charmichael, Sidney Cutner, Ray Evans, Jay Livingston, Jerry Livingston, Louis W. Pritzkow, and Leo Shuken; **Editor:** Archie Marshek; **Cast:** Rhonda Fleming, Gene Barry, Agnes

Moorehead, Guy Mitchell, Teresa Brewer, Cynthia Strother, Kay Strother, Walter Reed, Roscoe Ates.

A woman takes her four daughters from Seattle to Alaska during the Gold Rush to join her newspaper editor husband, but when they get there they learn that he has been murdered. Hoping now to make their fortunes, they manage to find love and romance. Originally filmed in 3-D, this sprightly musical film offers an opportunity to see two of the top pop recording stars of the 1950s, Teresa Brewer and Guy Mitchell, onscreen at the peaks of their respective careers.

THREE AMIGOS HBO/Orion, 1986, Color, 110 min. **Producers:** George Folsey Jr. and Lorne Michaels; **Director:** John Landis; **Screenplay:** Steve Martin, Michaels, and Randy Newman; **Music:** Elmer Bernstein and Newman; **Cinematographer:** Ronald W. Browne; **Editor:** Malcom Campbell; **Cast:** Chevy Chase, Steve Martin, Martin Short, Joe Mantegna, Patrice Martinez, Philip Gordon, Jon Lovitz, Phil Hartman.

Three unemployed silent-screen cowboys accept an invitation to a Mexican village to replay their roles as bandit fighters. However, they are unaware that the villagers are inviting them for the real thing, as they are expected to save the village from the clutches of some bloodthirsty bandidos.

THREE BAD MEN (aka: 3 BAD MEN) Fox, 1926, B&W, 92 min. **Producer:** John Ford; **Director:** Ford; **Screenplay (titles):** Malcom Stuart Boylan and Ralph Spence; **Cinematographer:** George Schneiderman; **Cast:** George O'Brien, Olive Borden, Lou Tellegen, Tom Santschi, J. Farrell MacDonald.

Adapted from the Herman Whitaker novel *Over the Border* and set during the Dakota land rush of 1876, this notable Ford effort follows three "bad men" who join a family of settlers and, at the sacrifice of their own lives, help them to oppose a band of outlaws and a crooked sheriff. A story of redemption and sacrifice, John Ford's final and best silent western was originally intended to be a costarring vehicle for popular action stars Tom Mix, Buck Jones, and George O'Brien. Only O'Brien emerged as the nominal hero and romantic lead, with character actors Tom Santschi, Frank Campeau, and J. Farrell MacDonald lending critical support as the bad men heroes.

Filming began in Jackson Hole, Wyoming, in March 1926. Despite its rave critical reviews, stunning photography, and impressive land rush sequences, upon the film's release in October that year, it did not meet with the anticipated public popularity. It remained Ford's only western for 13 years, until *STAGECOACH* revitalized the A western in 1939.

THREE GODFATHERS, THE Universal, 1916, B&W, six reels. **Director:** Edward J. Le Saint; **Screenplay:** Le Saint and Harvey Gates; **Cast:** Harry Carey, Stella Razeto, George Berrell, Frank Lanning, Jack Hoxie, Joe Ricksen.

Three outlaws who are being chased by a posse risk their lives to save an infant child. Written by Peter B. Kyne and originally published in 1910 as a short story in *The Saturday Evening Post*, it was first brought to the screen by "Broncho" Billy Anderson. Shot in one day, it was called *Broncho Billy and the Baby*. It was so successful that in 1913 Kyne rewrote his story as a novel, the basis of this film by Edward J. Le Saint with Harry Carey in the lead role. Carey and Winifred Westover later starred in a 1919 silent version called *MARKED MEN*. The first talking version of the story was William Wyler's *HELL'S HEROES* in 1930.

THREE GODFATHERS, THE (aka: MIRACLE IN THE SAND) MGM, 1936, B&W, 82 min. **Producer:** Joseph L. Mankiewicz; **Director:** Richard Boleslawski; **Screenplay:** Edward E. Paramore, Jr.; **Music:** William Axt; **Cinematographer:** Joseph Ruttenberg; **Editor:** Frank Sullivan; **Cast:** Chester Morris, Lewis Stone, Walter Brennan, Irene Hervey, Dorothy Tree, Robert Livingston, Joseph Marievsky, Jean Kirchner, Willard Robertson, Sidney Toler.

Three outlaws led by Chester Morris rob a bank, absconding with a man's Christmas savings. Riding into the desert anticipating their freedom, they come upon a dying woman and her infant baby and promise to return to the town of New Jerusalem with the child. In time the life of the young child becomes more important to them than either the money they have stolen or their lives. John Ford repeated the western parable of the Three Wise Men in 1948 with John Wayne, Pedro Armendáriz, and Harry Carey Jr. (See also *HELL'S HEROES.*)

THREE GODFATHERS MGM, 1948, Color, 106 min., VHS. **Producers:** John Ford and Merian C. Cooper; **Director:** Ford; **Screenplay:** Lawrence Stallings and Frank S. Nugent; **Music:** Richard Hageman; **Cinematographers:** Winton B. Hoch and Charles P. Boyle; **Editor:** Jack Murray; **Cast:** John Wayne, Pedro Armendáriz, Harry Carey Jr., Ward Bond, Mildred Natwick, Charles Halton, Jane Darwell, Ben Johnson, Hank Warden, Jack Pennick.

This time it is John Wayne, Pedro Armendáriz, and Harry Carey Jr. as the three bandits who discover a dying woman (Mildred Natwick) in the desert with an unborn child ready to be delivered. At her request the outlaws promise to care for the child as its three godfathers. What follows is a picture that is touching, brave, sentimental, and rich in pathos as the outlaws contend with a myriad of obstacles in the scorching desert heat, pushing on to New Jerusalem while taking their instructions from the Bible. Two perish along the way (Armendáriz and Carey), but the third (Wayne) reaches "the promised land" with the child intact, stumbling through the doors of the Last Chance Saloon on Christmas Eve.

John Ford's first color feature was dedicated to the memory of his dear friend Harry Carey, "Bright Star of the Early Western Sky." For the role of the Abilene Kid, he chose Harry Carey Jr., the son of his friend and early film collabo-

Harry Carey Jr., Pedro Armandáriz, and John Wayne in John Ford's Three Godfathers. *The film was dedicated to the memory of Ford's good friend Harry Carey.* (MGM/AUTHOR'S COLLECTION)

rator. Carey Jr. responded with what is arguably his finest performance in a long and distinguished career, which has now entered its second half-century. His performance was widely praised by Bosley Crowther in his *New York Times* review of March 4, 1949. Crowther specifically cited Carey Jr.'s "touching job as a tow headed boy from Texas who gets mixed up in banditry" and commended the film as being "visually beautiful."

However, Ford was a harsh taskmaster and made the young actor's life miserable. "He rode me something awful, and I wanted to quit a few times," Carey Jr. recalled in an interview with the author. "Duke [John Wayne] was a great help. He told me that I'd just have to take it, that Ford did the same thing to him in *Stagecoach*. He said to listen very carefully to him, because sometimes you couldn't understand what Ford was saying."

Three Godfathers marked the film debut of future Oscar-winning actor and western screen icon Ben Johnson. Johnson too recalled the ordeal of making *Three Godfathers*, calling it one of the toughest pictures he had ever worked on, and like Harry Carey Jr. he credits John Wayne for helping him along. "We were working in the sand dunes all the time. Sometimes I thought Ford was trying to destroy us. It was my first movie and Duke was real good to me. 'Ford is a mean son of a buck,' Duke would say. But he's my son of a buck.' If you listened to him, he [Ford] was a good education."

An allegory of the Nativity, the film uses the Christmas story to convey a tale of self-sacrifice and redemption on the western frontier. John Ford's *Three Godfathers* is the best screen adaptation of Peter Tyne's story. Others include Edward Le Saint's version of 1916; John Ford's version of 1919, entitled MARKED MEN; William Wyler's version of 1929, entitled HELL'S HEROES; and Richard Boleslawski's version of 1936. Kyne's story was utilized for a sixth time as an ABC-TV feature called *The Godchild* (1974), with Jack Palance, Jose Perez, and Ed Lauter as the three bandits.

THREE GUNS FOR TEXAS Universal, 1968, Color, 99 min. **Producer:** Richard Irving; **Directors:** Earl Bellamy, David Lowell Rich, and Paul Stanley; **Screenplay:** John D. F. Black; **Music:** Russell Garcia; **Cinematographer:** Andrew Jackson; **Editor:** Richard G. Wray; **Cast:** Neville Brand, Peter Brown, William Smith, Martin Milner, Philip Carey, Albert Salmi, Dub Taylor.

The Texas Rangers are on the trail of an outlaw gang led by an Indian woman. This theater entry was put together from three segments of *Laredo*, an NBC-TV series (1956–57).

THREE HOURS TO KILL Columbia, 1954, Color, 77 min. **Producer:** Harry Joe Brown; **Director:** Alfred L. Werker; **Screenplay:** Roy Huggins and Richard Alan Smmons; **Music:** Paul Sawtell; **Cinematographer:** Charles Lawton Jr.; **Editor:** Gene Havlick; **Cast:** Dana Andrews, Donna Reed, Stephen Elliott, Richard Coogan, Laurence Hugo, James Westerfield, Richard Webb, Carolyn Jones, Charlotte Fletcher, Whit Bissell, Filipe Turich.

Many years after he is falsely accused of killing his fiancée's brother, a man returns home to clear himself of the murder. Dana Andrews gives his usual steady and convincing performance as the accused stagecoach driver who is almost lynched by an angry mob. Attempting to prove his innocence, he becomes a gunman and dedicates himself to finding the real killer.

Alfred Werker's career started with silent features, beginning and ending with smaller westerns. His later westerns include *The Last Posse, Devil's Canyon* (1953); *Canyon Crossroads, At Gunpoint* (1954); and *Rebel in Town* (1956).

THREE IN THE SADDLE PRC, 1945, B&W, 61 min. **Producer:** Arthur Alexander; **Director:** Harry Frazer; **Screenplay:** Elmer Clifton; **Music:** Frank Hartford, Tex Ritter, and Ernest Tubbs (songs); **Cinematographer:** Robert Cline; **Editor:** Holbrook Todd; **Cast:** Tex Ritter, Dave O'Brien, Guy Wilkerson, Lorraine Miller, Charles King, Edward M. Howard.

The Texas Rangers come to the aid of a girl who is threatened by a ruthless land grabber after her ranch. Tex Ritter joined Dave O'Brien and Guy Wilkerson in 1944 as one of the three Texas Rangers in this PRC series. Other Ritter, O'Brien, and Wilkerson series outings include *Dead or Alive, Gangsters of the Frontier, The Whispering Skull* (1944); *Enemy of the Law, Flaming Bullets, Frontier Fugitives*, and *Marked for Murder* (1945). (See also *FIGHTING VALLEY*.)

THREE MEN FROM TEXAS Paramount, 1940, B&W, 76 min, VHS. **Producer:** Harry Sherman; **Director:** Lesley Selander; **Screenplay:** Norton Parker; **Music:** Victor Young; **Cinematographer:** Russell Harlan; **Editor:** Carroll Lewis and Sherman A. Rose; **Cast:** William Boyd, Russell Hayden, Andy Clyde, Morris Ankrum, Morgan Wallace, Thornton Edwards.

Hoppy and company bust up Morris Ankrum's plan to gain control over the Mexican border territory. Benefiting from a strong script and some unusual plot twists, this excellent feature is generally considered among the very best Hop-Along Cassidy series entries. (See also *HOP-ALONG CASSIDY*.)

THREE MESQUITEERS, THE Republic, 1936, B&W, 61 min, VHS. **Producer:** Nat Levine; **Director:** Ray Taylor; **Screenplay:** Jack Natteford; **Music:** Harry Grey; **Cinematographer:** William P. Nobles; **Editors:** Murray Seldeen and William B. Thompson; **Cast:** Robert Livingston, Ray Corrigan, Syd Saylor, Kay Hughes, J. P. McGowan, Al Bridge.

Three cowboys find themselves in the midst of a feud between rival cattlemen. Based on characters created by William Colt MacDonald, Republic's *Three Mesquiteers* series helped put the studio on the map. Obviously inspired by Alexander Dumas's *Three Musketeers* ("harmless plagiarisms," as William Everson calls them), with stories initially based on MacDonald's novels, the series was enormously popular with audiences. It is generally agreed that the heroic trio of Ray Corrigan, Bob Livingston, and Max Terhune provided the best entries in the series. Other participants included John Wayne (who replaced Livingston), Tom Tyler, Bob Steele, Duncan Renaldo, Rufe Davis, and Raymond Hatton.

Yet no matter who made up the trio, they all seemed to possess a similar romantic and adventurous camaraderie, despite the inconsistencies of the series. Some features were set in the old West, some were set during the Civil War, and there were even post-World War I and World War II settings. Until their inevitable decline in the mid-1940s, *The Three Mesquiteers* movies had excellent stuntwork (usually organized and performed by Yakima Canutt) and consistent, uncomplicated action, and they spawned many imitations.

Among the better entries in the long-running series are *HEART OF THE ROCKIES, RANGE DEFENDERS*, and *OUTLAWS OF SONORA* (Livingston, Corrigan, Terhune); *WYOMING OUTLAW* (Wayne, Corrigan, Hatton); and *UNDER TEXAS SKIES* (Livingston, Steele, Davis).

The Three Mesquiteers series includes: *Powdersmoke Range, Law of the .45s* (1935); *The Three Mesquiteers, GHOST-TOWN GOLD, Roarin' Lead* (1936); *RANGE DEFENDERS, HEART OF THE ROCKIES, Wild Horse, WILD HORSE RODEO, THE TRIGGER TRIO, RIDERS OF THE WHISTLING SKULL, HIT THE SADDLE, GUNSMOKE RANCH, COME ON COWBOYS* (1937); *RED RIVER RANGE, THE PURPLE VIGILANTES, CALL THE MESQUITEERS, OVERLAND STAGE RAIDERS, OUTLAWS OF SONORA, RIDERS OF THE BLACK HILLS, PALS OF THE SADDLE* (1938); *NEW FRONTIER, THE COWBOYS FROM TEXAS, The Kansas Terrors, WYOMING OUTLAW, THREE TEXAS STEERS, THE NIGHT RIDERS* (1939); *THE TRAIL BLAZERS, HEROES OF THE SADDLE, PIONEERS OF THE WEST, COVERED WAGON DAYS, Rocky Mountain Rangers, OKLAHOMA RENEGADES, UNDER TEXAS SKIES, Lone Star Raiders* (1940); *Pals of the Pecos, PRAIRIE PIONEERS, SADDLEMATES, Gauchos of El Dorado, OUTLAWS OF THE CHEROKEE TRAIL, WEST OF CIMARRON, Gangs of Sonora* (1941); *CODE OF THE OUTLAW, VALLEY OF HUNTED MEN, SHADOWS ON THE SAGE, THE PHAN-*

TOM PLAINSMEN, WESTWARD HO, RAIDERS OF THE RANGE (1942), *The Blocked Trail, RIDERS OF THE RIO GRANDE, Santa Fe Scouts, THUNDERING TRAILS* (1943).

THREE ON THE TRAIL   Paramount, 1936, B&W, 67 min, DVD. **Producer:** Harry Sherman; **Director:** Howard Bretherton; **Screenplay:** Doris Schroeder and Vernon Smith; **Cinematographer:** Archie Stout; **Editor:** Edward Schroeder; **Cast:** William Boyd, James Ellison, Onslow Stevens, Muriel Evans, George "Gabby" Hayes, Claude King, William Duncan.

See *HOP-ALONG CASSIDY.*

THREE OUTLAWS, THE   Associated Film Releasing, 1956, B&W, 75 min. **Producer:** Sigmund Neufeld; **Director:** Sam Newfield; **Screenplay:** Orville H. Hampton; **Music:** Paul Dunlap; **Cinematographer:** William A. Bradford; **Editor:** Dwight Caldwell; **Cast:** Neville Brand, Alan Hale Jr., Bruce Bennett, Jose Gonzales-Gonzales, Jeanne Carmen, Rodolfo Hoyos Jr., Robert Tafur, Lillian Molieri.

A federal lawman pursues Butch Cassidy and his gang into Mexico, where they are posing as honest citizens. This time it is Neville Brand as the infamous Butch and Alan Hale Jr.

Neville Brand and Jeanne Carmen in The Three Outlaws (ASSOCIATED FILM RELEASING/COURTESY OF JEANNE CARMEN)

as the Sundance Kid. The most appealing thing about this low-budget oater is sensuous Jeanne Carmen (in dark hair) as Serelda.

3:10 TO YUMA (aka: THREE TEN TO YUMA) Columbia, 1957, B&W, 92 min. **Producer:** David Heilweil; **Director:** Delmer Daves; **Screenplay:** Halsted Welles; **Music:** George Duning and Ned Washington; **Cinematographer:** Charles Lawton Jr.; **Editor:** Al Clark; **Cast:** Glenn Ford, Van Heflin, Felicia Farr, Leora Dana, Henry Jones, Richard Jaeckel, Robert Emhardt, Sheridan Comerate.

When rancher Dan Evans (Van Heflin) desperately needs money to pay the debt on his failing ranch, he agrees to take captured outlaw Ben Wade (Glenn Ford) on the 3:10 train from Contention City to Yuma, where Wade is to stand trial. Wade's gang has pledged to release him, and the rest of the townsfolk will not assist Evans, so the inevitable tension builds toward a deadly confrontation between Evans and Wade's gang.

Skillfully helmed by Delmer Daves, *3:10 to Yuma* is yet another *HIGH NOON* (1952) clone. The familiar formula has minutes and seconds ticking away until the 3:10 train to Yuma arrives in town. Like Gary Cooper in *High Noon*, Heflin finds himself standing alone and outnumbered. If the climax is as disappointing as many critics contend, the blame rests with Halsted Welles, whose screenplay had been rather faithfully adapted from Elmore Leonard's original story.

Van Heflin and Glenn Ford (soon to be the country's top box-office star for 1958) offer solid performances; the genre had become a benchmark for their acting talents. Frankie Laine sings the title song by Ned Washington and George Dunning.

THREE TEXAS STEERS   Republic, 1939, B&W, 59 min, VHS. **Director:** George Sherman; **Screenplay:** Betty Burbridge and Stanley Roberts; **Cinematographer:** Ernest Miller; **Editor:** Tony Martinelli; **Cast:** John Wayne, Carole Landis, Ray Corrigan, Max Terhune, Colette Lyons, Roscoe Ates, Lew Kelly, David Sharpe.

The Mesquiteers come to the aid of a young girl and a ranch in the Mesquite country. The film's main interest is future leading lady Carole Landis starring as the beleaguered young woman. John Wayne's *THREE MESQUITEERS* entries also include *Pals of the Saddle, Overland Stage Raiders, Santa Fe Stampede, Red River Range* (1938); *The Night Riders, Wyoming Outlaw,* and *New Frontier* (1939).

THREE VIOLENT PEOPLE   Paramount, 1956, Color, 100 min, VHS. **Producer:** Hugh Brown; **Director:** Rudolph Mate; **Screenplay:** James Edward Grant; **Music:** John Leipold and Walter Scharf; **Cinematographer:** Roy Webb; **Editor:** Alma Macrorie; **Cast:** Charlton Heston, Anne Baxter, Gilbert Roland, Tom Tryon, Forrest Tucker, Bruce Bennett, Elaine Stritch, Barton MacLane, Peter Hansen, Robert Blake.

Charlton Heston is a Confederate soldier returning to post-Civil War Texas, where he marries a woman who is, unbeknownst to him, a former prostitute (Anne Baxter). However, a member of the occupation army camp followers recognizes her and relays tales of her shady past to all. The familiar theme of the post-Civil War divided family plays out in a series of squabbles between Heston and his one-armed brother, played by Tom Tryon. Gilbert Roland as the lovable Mexican lends an aura of warmth, and Elaine Stritch makes an early colorful appearance as the saloon keeper. There is also a salty and sensuous chemistry between costars Heston and Baxter as they battle each other while taking on greedy land barons.

THREE YOUNG TEXANS 20th Century Fox, 1954, Color, 77 min. **Producer:** Leonard Goldstein; **Director:** Henry Levin; **Screenplay:** Gerald Drayson Adams; **Cinematographer:** Harold Lipstein; **Editor:** William B. Murphy; **Cast:** Mitzi Gaynor, Keefe Brasselle, Jeffrey Hunter, Michael Ansara, John Harmon, Vivian Marshall, Alex Montova, Dan Riss, Aaron Spelling, Harvey Stephens, Helen Wallace, Frank Wilcox.

A young Texan (Jeffrey Hunter) robs a train with his girlfriend's (Mitzi Gaynor) help in an effort to prevent his father from complying with a blackmailer's demand. Yet once they have the money, a cowboy friend (Keefe Brasselle) takes it for himself. After a few obligatory killings, Hunter shoots it out with villain Michael Ansara and clears himself of all culpability.

THRILL HUNTER, THE Columbia, 1933, B&W, 60 min. **Producer:** Irving Briskin; **Director:** George Seitz; **Screenplay:** Harry O. Hoyt; **Cinematographer:** Ted Tetzlaff; **Editor:** Gene Milford; **Cast:** Buck Jones, Dorothy Revier, Edward Le Saint, Eddie Kane, Arthur Rankin, Frank La Rue.

See WHITE EAGLE.

THROWBACK, THE Universal, 1935, B&W, 61 min. **Producer:** Buck Jones; **Director:** Ray Taylor; **Screenplay:** Frances Guihan; **Cinematographers:** Herbert Kirkpatrick, William Sickner, and Allen Thompson; **Editor:** Bernard Loftus; **Cast:** Buck Jones, Muriel Evans, George "Gabby" Hayes, Bryant Washburn, Eddie Phillips, Paul Fix.

Buck Jones is a man whose father had been unjustly accused of theft 15 years earlier. When he returns to town he now finds that he is being framed on a similar charge. (See also STONE OF SILVER CREEK.)

THUNDERBOLT Regal Pictures, 1935, B&W, 55 min. **Producer:** Sherman S. Krellberg; **Director:** Stuart Paton; **Screenplay:** Jack T. O. Gevne; **Cinematographer:** Roland Price; **Editor:** Charles Craft; **Cast:** Kane Richmond, Bobby Nelson, Fay McKenzie, Barney Furey, Robert McKenzie, Frank Hagney, Hank Bell, Lafe McKee.

A cowboy is blamed when a pair of crooked deputies steal a gold shipment and kill a young boy's father. The murdered man's son and his dog set out to prove the cowboy's innocence and prevent the real killer from trying to force a comely young girl into marrying him.

THUNDERCLOUD See COLT .45.

THUNDERING FRONTIER Columbia, 1940, B&W, 57 min. **Producer:** Leon Barsha (associate); **Director:** R. Ross Lederman; **Screenplay:** Paul Franklin; **Music:** Bob Nolan and Tim Spencer; **Cinematographer:** George Meehan; **Editor:** Arthur Seid; **Cast:** Charles Starrett, Iris Meredith, Ray Bennett, Alex Callam, Pat Brady, Bob Nolan and The Sons of the Pioneers, Fred Burns, John Dilson.

See GALLANT DEFENDER.

THUNDER GAP OUTLAWS See BAD MEN OF THUNDER GAP.

THUNDERING GUNSLINGERS PRC, 1944, B&W, 59 min. **Producer:** Sigmund Neufeld; **Director:** Sam Newfield; **Screenplay:** Fred Myton; **Cinematographer:** Robert Cline; **Editor:** Holbrook Todd; **Cast:** Buster Crabbe, Al St. John, Frances Gladwin, Charles King, Jack Ingram, Karl Hackett, Kermit Maynard, Budd Buster.

See OUTLAW OF THE PLAINS.

THUNDERING HERD (aka: BUFFALO STAMPEDE, THE) Paramount, 1933, B&W, 62 min. **Producer:** Harold Hurley; **Director:** Henry Hathaway; **Screenplay:** Jack Cunningham and Mary Flannery; **Music:** Karl Hajos and John Leipold; **Cinematographer:** Ben Reynolds; **Cast:** Randolph Scott, Judith Allen, Larry "Buster" Crabbe, Noah Beery, Raymond Hatton, Blanche Frederici, Harry Carey, Monte Blue, Barton MacLane, Al Bridge.

In this remake of Paramount's 1925 silent version helmed by Henry Hathaway, Randolph Scott stars as buffalo hunter Tom Doan, who joins a wagon train heading west. On the journey he tries to prevent an impending attack by Indians who have been incited to war due to the needless slaughter of their buffalo. Noah Beery repeats his original role as the lecherous villain Randall Jett, and much of the stock footage from the original 1925 version is employed here as well.

Hathaway, who had a penchant for outdoor action films (25 years later he would direct John Wayne to an Oscar in *True Grit*), has a solid cast, including genre stalwarts Harry Carey, Monte Blue, and a young Buster Crabbe. Filmed in the Alabama Hills at Lone Pine, California, the movie's reissue title is *Buffalo Stampede*.

While Paramount usually filmed Zane Grey's properties more than once, *The Thundering Herd* was filmed only twice. The 1925 silent version of *The Thundering Herd* was directed by William K. Howard and starred Jack Holt as Tom Doan, a Kansas farmer who in 1876 joins a band of buffalo hunters. Noah Beery is the evil Randall Jett, whose minions have been robbing the buffalo hunters, eventually incurring the wrath of warring Indians. Presented by Adolph Zucker and Jesse Lasky, this silent oater which *Photoplay* magazine reported as being "equally as good as *The Covered Wagon*," includes among its cast future genre greats Tim McCoy (in the supporting role of Burne Hudnall) and 25-year-old Gary Cooper (as a cowboy extra).

THUNDER IN GOD'S COUNTRY Republic, 1951, B&W, 67 min. **Producer:** Melville Tucker (associate); **Director:** George Blair; **Screenplay:** Arthur E. Orloff; **Music:** Stanley Wilson; **Cinematographer:** John MacBurnie; **Editor:** Harold Minter; **Cast:** Rex Allen, Mary Ellen Kay, Buddy Ebsen, Ian MacDonald, Paul Harvey, Harry Lauter, John Doucette.

THUNDERING TRAILS Republic, 1943, B&W, 60 min. **Producer:** Louis Grey (assistant); **Director:** John English; **Screenplay:** Norman Hall and Robert Yost; **Music:** Mort Glickman and Paul Sawtell; **Cinematographer:** Reggie Lanning; **Editor:** William P. Thompson; **Cast:** Bob Steele, Tom Tyler, Jimmie Dodd, Nell O'Day, Sam Flint, Karl Hackett, Charles F. Miller.
See *THREE MESQUITEERS, THE.*

THUNDERING WEST, THE Columbia, 1939, B&W, 57 min. **Producer:** Harry I. Decker; **Director:** Sam Nelson; **Screenplay:** Bennett Cohen; **Music:** Bob Nolan; **Cinematographer:** Lucien Ballard; **Editors:** William Ballard and William A. Lyon; **Cast:** Charles Starrett, Iris Meredith, Dick Curtis, Hank Bell, Bob Nolan and The Sons of the Pioneers, Edward Le Saint, Wally Wales.
See *GALLANT DEFENDER.*

THUNDER IN THE PINES Lippert, 1948, B&W, 61 min. **Producer:** William Stephens; **Director:** Robert Edwards; **Screenplay:** Maurice Tombragel; **Music:** Lucien Cailliet; **Cinematographer:** Carl Berger; **Editor:** Norman Cerf; **Cast:** George Reeves, Ralph Byrd, Lyle Talbot, Denise Darcel, Marion Martin, Roscoe Ates, Greg McClure, Michael Whalen, Tom Kennedy.

Two loggers (including future TV Superman George Reeves) compete for a mail-order bride by way of a timber-cutting contest, but they abandon their mutual hostilities when outsiders endanger their interests. The picture marks an early screen appearance for actress Denise Darcel.

THUNDER IN THE SUN Paramount, 1959, Color, 81 min. **Producer:** Clarence Greene; **Director:** Russell Rouse; **Screenplay:** Rouse and Stewart Stern; **Music:** Cyril J. Mockridge; **Cinematographer:** Stanley Cortez; **Editor:** Chester W. Schaeffer; **Cast:** Susan Hayward, Jeff Chandler,

Jacques Bergerec, Blanche Yurka, Carl Esmond, Fortunio Bonanova, Felix Locher.

In 1850 a wagon train of Basques head for California, where they hope to plant vineyards and make wine. On board is a pretty girl being romanced by two men, including the wagon master. When the wagon train is attacked by Indians, the Basques, wearing berets, defeat their would-be captors through a series of fancy guerrilla tactics. Jeff Chandler and Susan Hayward add an attractive star appeal to this benign yet entertaining feature.

THUNDER MOUNTAIN 20th Century Fox, 1935, B&W, 68 min. **Producer:** Sol Lesser; **Director:** David Howard; **Screenplay:** Daniel Jarrett and Don Swift; **Cinematographer:** Frank B. Good; **Editor:** Robert O. Crandall; **Cast:** George O'Brien, Frances Grant, Barbara Fritchie, Morgan Wallace, William Bailey, Edward Le Saint, George "Gabby" Hayes, Sid Jordan, Dean Benton.

George O'Brien plays a gold prospector who stakes a claim to a gold mine with his partner. However, aided by a scheming saloon keeper, the partner double-crosses him. The fighting O'Brien is now determined to set matters straight in this interesting mining story set in timber country.

THUNDER MOUNTAIN RKO, 1947, B&W, VHS, DVD. **Producer:** Herman Schlom; **Director:** Lew Landers; **Screenplay:** Norman Houston; **Music:** Paul Sawtell; **Cinematographer:** Jack MacKenzie; **Editor:** Philip Martin; **Cast:** Tim Holt, Martha Hyer, Richard Martin, Steve Brodie, Virginia Owen, Jason Robards Sr., Harry Woods, Tom Keene.

College boy Tim Holt returns home to find himself in the midst of a feud being manipulated by a dishonest saloon keeper and his cohort. This exciting and fast-moving Holt vehicle has little to do with the Zane Grey novel from which it is supposedly taken. (See also *ALONG THE RIO GRANDE.*)

THUNDER OF DRUMS, A MGM, 1961, Color, 97 min. **Producer:** Robert Enders; **Director:** Joseph M. Newman; **Screenplay:** James Warner Bellah; **Music:** Harry Sukman; **Cinematographer:** William W. Spencer; **Editor:** Ferris Webster; **Cast:** Richard Boone, George Hamilton, Luana Patten, Arthur O'Connell, Charles Bronson, Richard Chamberlain, Duane Eddy, Slim Pickens, Casey Tibbs.

Richard Boone delivers a sympathetic and inspiring performances as an aging cavalry officer who because of an earlier mistake has been denied promotion beyond the rank of captain. He must shape up a young lieutenant now assigned to his remote cavalry post, a brash young officer only too eager to challenge the mettle of his seasoned, wiser, and battle-tested commanding officer.

THUNDER OVER TEXAS Beacon, 1934, B&W, 61 min, VHS. **Producers:** Matt Alexander and Max Alexander;

Director: John Warner (Edgar G. Uhmer); **Screenplay:** Eddie Granemann; **Cinematographer:** Harry Forbes; **Editor:** George M. Merrick; **Cast:** Guinn "Big Boy" Williams, Marion Shilling, Helen Westcott, Philo McCullough, Victor Potel, Ben Corbett.

A cowboy rescues a kidnapped girl whose father has been murdered in a dispute over valuable maps. Guinn "Big Boy" Williams, a longtime character actor and sidekick in both B and A movies, is the film's hero. Director Edgar G. Ulmer's wife Alice wrote the original story.

THUNDER OVER THE PLAINS Warner Bros., 1953, Color, 82 min. **Producer:** David Weisbart; **Director:** André De Toth; **Screenplay:** Russell S. Hughes; **Music:** David Buttolph; **Cinematographer:** Bert Glennon; **Editor:** James C. Moore; **Cast:** Randolph Scott, Phyllis Kirk, Charles McGraw, Henry Hull, Elisha Cook Jr., Hugh Sanders, Lane Chandler, James Brown, Fess Parker, Trevor Bardette, Mark Dana.

Randolph Scott is an army officer in post-Civil War Texas assigned to bring in a bandit who has been terrorizing carpetbaggers. His dilemma is that while he sympathizes with the fellow he is bringing to justice, he still must carry out his job.

This good André De Toth/Randolph Scott feature has lots of action. The Hungarian-born director carved a small niche in westerns, working mostly with Scott, whom he used in a series of films.

THUNDER OVER THE PRAIRIE Columbia, 1941, B&W, 60 min. **Producer:** William A. Berke; **Director:** Lambert Hillyer; **Screenplay:** Betty Burbridge; **Music:** Billy Hughes and Cal Shrum; **Cinematographer:** Benjamin H. Kline; **Editor:** Burton Kramer; **Cast:** Charles Starrett, Cliff Edwards, Eileen O'Hearn, Stanley Brown, Cal Shrum and His Rhythm Rangers, Donald Curtis, Joe McGuinn.
See *GALLANT DEFENDER.*

THUNDER PASS Lippert, 1954, B&W, 76 min, VHS. **Producer:** A. Robert Nunes; **Director:** Frank MacDonald; **Screenplay:** Fred Eggers and Tom Hubbard; **Cast:** Dane Clark, Dorothy Patrick, Andy Devine, Raymond Burr, John Carradine, Mary Ellen Kay, Raymond Hatton, Nestor Paiva.

Dane Clark is a cavalry commander who attempts to bring a group of travelers through hostile Indian territory safely. Time is working against him: He has just two days to accomplish his task before being overrun by hostile Indians. A pretty standard oater, this Lippert entry sports a substantial cast of genre players.

THUNDER TRAIL Paramount, 1937, B&W, 58 min. **Director:** Charles Barton; **Screenplay:** Stuart Anthony and Robert Yost; **Music:** George Antheil and Boris Morros; **Cinematographer:** Karl Struss; **Editor:** John F. Link Sr.; **Cast:** Gilbert Roland, Charles Bickford, James Craig, Marsha Hunt, Monte Blue, J. Carrol Naish, Barlowe Borland.

Bandits kill everyone aboard a wagon train except two young brothers, played as adults by Gilbert Roland and James Craig. The brothers join forces to bring the bandit leader to justice, 15 years later. Based on Zane Grey's short story *Arizona Ames,* this solid B level production is packed with action and adventure.

TICKET TO TOMAHAWK, A 20th Century Fox, 1950, Color, 90 min. **Producer:** Richard Bassler; **Director:** Richard Sale; **Screenplay:** Mary Loos and Sale; **Music:** Cyril Mockridge; **Cinematographer:** Harry Jackson; **Editor:** Harmon Jones; **Cast:** Dan Dailey, Anne Baxter, Rory Calhoun, Walter Brennan, Charles Kemper, Connie Gilchrist, Arthur Hunnicutt, Will Wright, Chief Yowlachie, Victor Sen Young, Robert Adler, Jack Elam, Marilyn Monroe, Guy Wilkerson.

This western spoof revolves around a rivalry between a stagecoach line and a new railroad trying to establish a line in the Colorado Territory. The stage line promoter (Rory Calhoun) uses bandits and a touring troupe of actors to keep the railroad from meeting its deadline. However, proponents of the train are led by a sharpshooting young woman (Anne Baxter), the granddaughter of the injured train owner. Aided by an enterprising traveling salesman (Dan Dailey) she conspires to get the train in on time.

Highlighted by the magnificent Colorado scenery, a fine cast, and a pleasant, sprightly script, the film features an early uncredited screen appearance by Marilyn Monroe as a chorus girl in the traveling theatrical company. *A Ticket to Tomahawk* was nominated by the Writers Guild of America (WGA) in the category of Best Written American Western (1951).

TIMBERJACK Republic, 1955, Color, 94 min. **Producer:** Herbert J. Yates; **Director:** Joseph Kane; **Screenplay:** Allen Rivkin; **Music:** Hoagy Carmichael, Johnny Mercer, Ned Washington, Paul Francis Webster, and Victor Young; **Cinematographer:** Jack Marta; **Editor:** Richard L. Van Enger; **Cast:** Sterling Hayden, Vera Hruba Ralston, David Brian, Adolph Menjou, Hoagy Carmichael, Chill Wills, Jim Davis, Howard Petrie, Ian MacDonald, Elisha Cook Jr.

A logger is being cheated out of his inherited timberland by a ruthless land baron. This rather standard Republic oater benefits from a bevy of award-winning and Oscar-nominated composers and lyricists (Hoagy Carmichael, Johnny Mercer, Ned Washington, Paul Francis Webster, and Victor Young) who contributed a series of original songs for the film.

TIMBER STAMPEDE RKO, 1939, B&W, 59 min. **Producer:** Bert Gilroy; **Director:** David Howard; **Screenplay:** Morton Grant; **Cinematographer:** Harry J. Wild; **Editor:** Frederic Knudtson; **Cast:** George O'Brien, Chill Wills, Marjorie Reynolds, Morgan Wallace, Robert Fiske, Guy Usher.

TIMBER TRAIL, THE Republic, 1948, Color, 67 min. **Producer:** Melville Tucker (associate); **Director:** Philip Ford; **Screenplay:** Bob Williams; **Music:** Phil Ohman, Tim Spencer, and Ned Washington; **Cinematographer:** Reggie Lanning; **Editor:** Tony Martinelli; **Cast:** Monte Hale, Lynne Roberts, James Burke, Roy Barcroft, Francis Ford, Robert Emmett Keane, Steve Darrell.

TIMBER WAR Ambassador, 1936, B&W, 60 min. **Producers:** Maurice Conn and Sigmund Neufeld; **Director:** Sam Newfield; **Screenplay:** Barry Barringer and Joseph O'Donnell; **Cinematographer:** Jack Greenhalgh; **Editor:** Richard G. Wray; **Cast:** Kermit Maynard, Lucille Lund, Lawrence Gray, Robert Warwick, Lloyd Ingraham, Wheeler Oakman.

TIME FOR DYING, A Corinth Films, 1971, Color, 73 min. **Producer:** Audie Murphy; **Director:** Budd Boetticher; **Screenplay:** Boetticher; **Music:** Harry Betts; **Cinematographer:** Lucien Ballard; **Editor:** Harry V. Knapp; **Cast:** Audie Murphy, Victor Jory, Beatrice Kay, Richard Lapp, Ron Masak, Burt Mustin, Anne Randall, Robert Random.

A young man who is trained by his father to be a fast gun travels through the West and saves a girl from a life of prostitution. A problem arises when Judge Roy Bean (Victor Jory) forces him to marry her. Audie Murphy produced the film, and he does a very credible job as Jesse James, the same character he played in KANSAS RAIDERS (1950). It would be his final screen role. The collaboration between Budd Boetticher and Murphy (who had suffered career and business misfortunes in the late '60s) ended with the star's untimely death in 1971, when he and five others perished in a small plane crash.

It had been hoped that the film, directed and scripted by Boetticher, would rejuvenate the careers of both actor and director. Boetticher had returned to Hollywood in 1967, after spending seven years in Mexico creating his masterful documentary *Arruza* (1972), based on the life and career of his dear friend, the great matador Carlos Arruza. *A Time for Dying* was released in 1971, shortly after Murphy's death.

TIME FOR KILLING, A Columbia, 1967, Color, 1967. **Producer:** Harry Joe Brown; **Director:** Phil Karlson; **Screenplay:** Halsted Wells; **Music:** Van Alexander and Mundell Lowe; **Cinematographer:** Kenneth Peach; **Editor:** Roy V. Livingston; **Cast:** Inger Stevens, Glenn Ford, George Hamilton, Paul Peterson, Timothy Carey, Kenneth Tobey, Richard X. Slattery, Harrison Ford, Emile Meyer, Harry Dean Stanton, Max Baer Jr.

As the Civil War is ending, several Confederate prisoners escape from their Union captors and take the fiancée of the Union captain as their hostage. The film was a showcase of sorts for actor George Hamilton (Confederate captain Dorrit Bentley), who had achieved headlines in 1966 when he became the steady companion of Lynda Bird Johnson, President Lyndon Johnson's daughter.

Based on the novel *The Southern Blade* by Nelson and Shirley Wolford, the film's theme song "The Long Ride Home" by Ned Washington and Van Alexander is sung in the film by legendary country & western great Eddie Arnold.

TIN STAR, THE Paramount, 1957, B&W, 93 min, VHS. **Producers:** William Perlberg and George Seaton; **Director:** Anthony Mann; **Screenplay:** Dudley Nichols; **Music:** Elmer Bernstein; **Cinematographer:** Loyal Griggs; **Editor:** Alma Macrorie; **Cast:** Henry Fonda, Anthony Perkins, Betsy Palmer, Michel Ray, Neville Brand, John McIntyre, Mary Webster, Lee Van Cleef, Peter Baldwin.

Henry Fonda is a bitter ex-sheriff turned bounty hunter who comes to town to collect his reward for shooting a wanted outlaw. Forced to stay in town to wait for the reward to arrive, he takes it upon himself to educate an insecure and bumbling young sheriff (Anthony Perkins). He teaches him that a gun is only a tool and that the real work is in reading your enemy. He becomes a mentor and surrogate father to the unsteady young man, carefully teaching him the "code of the west." When it comes to a final showdown between Ben Owens (Perkins) and hardened thug Bart Bogardus (Neville Brand), Morg Hickman (Fonda) stays on the sidelines knowing that his young protégé must stand alone and finally show his mettle.

Fonda and Perkins are exceptionally good in their respective roles as the former lawman and the diffident young sheriff determined to keep his badge despite the pleadings of his sweetheart to abandon the job and all its hazards. Anthony Mann directed this intelligent, low-key examination of law-enforcement psychology and social dynamics in a small frontier town. More concerned with character development and story line than nonstop action and gunplay, *The Tin Star* garnered two Academy Award nominations, for Best Original Story and Best Screenplay.

TIOGA KID, THE PRC/Eagle Lyon, 1948, B&W, 54 min. **Producer:** Jerry Thomas; **Director:** Ray Taylor; **Screenplay:** Ed Earl Repp; **Music:** Eddie Dean and Walter Greene; **Cinematographer:** Ernest Miller; **Editor:** Hugh Winn; **Cast:** Eddie Dean, Roscoe Ates, Jennifer Holt, Dennis Moore, Lee Bennett, William Fawcett, Eddie Parker, Bob Woodward.

See *SONG OF OLD WYOMING*.

TOLL GATE, THE Paramount/Art Craft, 1920, B&W, 55 min, VHS, DVD. **Producer:** William S. Hart; **Director:** Lambert Hillyer; **Screenplay:** Hart and Hillyer; **Cinematographer:** Joe August; **Editor:** LeRoy Stone; **Cast:** William S. Hart, Anna Q. Nilsson, Joseph Singleton, Jack Richardson, Richard Headrick.

William S. Hart is Black Deering, a betrayed outlaw who falls in love with the wife of his betrayer after saving her child. Embittered, angry, and true to his "good bad man" screen persona, he is eventually reformed by love. At film's end, when the woman learns of his innocence, she tells him, "They may call you Black Deering, but by God, you're white!"

Lambert Hillyer, one of the American cinema's most prolific and least pretentious directors, wrote and directed many of the silent westerns of William S. Hart and later Tom Mix and Buck Jones and other cowboy stars. The film was produced by Hart, who cowrote the story with Hillyer. (See also *HELL'S HINGES*.)

TOMAHAWK (aka: BATTLE OF POWDER RIVER, UK) Universal, 1951, Color, 82 min, VHS. **Producer:** Leonard Goldstein; **Director:** George Sherman; **Screenplay:** Silvia Richards and Maurice Geraghty; **Music:** Hans J. Salter; **Cinematographer:** Charles P. Boyle; **Editor:** Danny B. Landres; **Cast:** Van Heflin, Yvonne De Carlo, Alex Nichol, Preston Foster, Jack Oakie, Tom Tully, Rock Hudson, Susan Cabot, John Wareagle, Ann Doran.

Much to the chagrin of frontier scout Jim Bridger (Van Heflin), in 1886 the U.S. Army decides to build a road and a fort in territory ceded by a previous treaty to the Sioux after a new gold discovery in the region. A conflict escalates to the point of violence despite the efforts of the peace-loving fron-

tier scout. Future superstar Rock Hudson has eighth billing as a soldier who loves an Indian girl named Monahseetah (Susan Cabot). The film parallels many 1950s westerns that began showing the American Indian in a more sympathetic light.

TOMAHAWK AND THE CROSS See *PILLARS OF THE SKY*.

TOMBSTONE Hollywood/Cinergi, 1994, Color, 127 min, VHS, DVD. **Producers:** James Jacks, Sean Daniel, and Bob Misiorowski; **Director:** George Cosmotos; **Screenplay:** Kevin Jarre; **Music:** Bruce Broughton; **Cinematographer:** William A. Fraker; **Editors:** Frank J. Uriste, Roberto Silvi, and Harvey Rosenstock; **Cast:** Kurt Russell, Val Kilmer, Sam Elliott, Bill Paxton, Michael Biehn, Charlton Heston, Harry Carey Jr., Jason Priestley, Lisa Collins, Joanna Pacula, Billy Bob Thornton.

Wyatt Earp (Kurt Russell), recently retired as marshal of Dodge City, looks for a more peaceful and lucrative career with brothers Morgan (Bill Paxton) and Virgil (Sam Elliott). He seems to find the opportunity in the saloon world of Tombstone. But a peaceful life becomes an illusion when

Val Kilmer (Doc Holliday), Sam Elliott, Kurt Russell (Wyatt Earp), and Bill Paxton in Tombstone, *the first 1990s retelling of the oft-told Wyatt Earp/Doc Holliday saga* (HOLLYWOOD/CINERGI PICTURES/AUTHOR'S COLLECTION)

they are forced to combat a band of thugs led by the Clantons called The Cowboys, garbed in long coats and red sashes, who delight in slaughtering a Mexican wedding party (priest included).

Tombstone beautifully chronicles the events leading to the famous gunfight at the O.K. Corral and the reign of terror inflicted by the Earps on the Cowboys. They are joined in their quest by the consumptive Doc Holliday, played by Val Kilmer, whose memorably eccentric portrayal of the dying gunman, though controversial, is well worth the price of admission.

Filmed on location around Tucson, Arizona, where the story's major incidents occurred, the movie's visuals are excellent. *Tombstone* was the first 1990s version of the oft-told adventures of the legendary Wyatt Earp and Doc Holliday. In a salute to historical accuracy, the film, which played to mixed reviews, was also first to make Virgil Earp (played to perfection by Sam Elliott) the leader of the Earp clan. Kurt Russell's Wyatt Earp is a more complex figure than in other films, a loyal family man who nonetheless abandons his demure wife for an actress, who became the love of his life.

TOMBSTONE, THE TOWN TOO TOUGH TO DIE Paramount, 1942, B&W, 79 min. **Producer:** Harry Sherman; **Director:** William C. McGann; **Screenplay:** Albert S. Le Vino and Edward E. Paramoe, Jr.; **Cinematographer:** Russell Harlan; **Editors:** Carroll Lewis and Sherman A. Rose; **Cast:** Richard Dix, Edgar Buchanan, Frances Gifford, Don Castle, Rex Bell, Kent Taylor, Victor Jory, Chris-Pin Martin, Dick Curtis.

A gun accident results in a child's death, so Wyatt Earp (Richard Dix) agrees to take over as sheriff of Tombstone. Together with his brothers he succeeds in cleaning up the town. Kent Taylor is Doc Holliday and Victor Jory is Ike Clanton in yet another historically flawed but otherwise entertaining saga about the Earps and the Clantons.

TOM HORN Warner Bros./First Artists, 1979, Color, 97 min, VHS. **Producer:** Fred Weintraub; **Director:** William Wiard; **Screenplay:** Thomas McGuane and Bud Shrake; **Music:** Ernest Gold; **Cinematographer:** John A. Alonzo; **Editor:** George Grenville; **Cast:** Steve McQueen, Linda Evans, Richards Farnsworth, Billy Green Bush, Slim Pickens, Peter Canon, Elisha Cook Jr., Roy Jenson.

Steve McQueen is Tom Horn, a Wyoming legend and western hero who at various times of his life had been a cowboy, deputy sheriff, Rough Rider in Cuba, Pinkerton detective, frontier scout, and range detective. The film covers the last three years of Horn's life (1901–03), when an association of Wyoming cattlemen hires him to get rid of some rustlers. But Horn's school is of the Old West, and his murderous methods start to embarrass the cattlemen (the so-called representatives of law and order), and they frame him for the murder of a young shepherd. He died on the gallows in Cheyenne, Wyoming, on November 20, 1903.

The film is based on Horn's autobiography, *Tom Horn, Government Scout and Interpreter, Written by Himself*, written during his final days in jail. All the ingredients were in place for a top-quality film: a major star, a fine cast of supporting players, a real-life legend to build upon, and the cold visual excellence of the landscape. Interestingly, Slim Pickens, who plays the sheriff, claimed that during his rodeo days he had met the sheriff who had hanged the real Tom Horn.

Most of *Tom Horn* was filmed outdoors in Mescal, Arizona, a few miles from the Mexican border, to provide the rustic look of the Old West. The costumes were meticulously researched by Luster Bayless, one of the best in the business. With McQueen as the film's executive producer, the final product should certainly have been better. But a sustaining plot was lacking from the start, and there was little real sense of continuity. *Variety* found *Tom Horn* lacking, calling it "a sorry ending to the once high hopes of the star-studded First Artists Prods. . . ." Similarly, Joseph Roquemore in *History Goes to the Movies* calls the film "oddly indecisive . . . a strange lifeless film worth a look only because of fine period detail, beautiful photography, and authentic turn-of-the century atmosphere."

With westerns no longer the vogue, *Tom Horn* suffered public apathy and tanked at the box office, earning a mere $12 million. On a more positive note, the film seems to have gained stature as new filmgoers, who were not alive or old enough to see it when the film came out, have come to respect its grit and toughness. A veritable megastar with enormous screen charisma, Steve McQueen would make just one more picture (*The Hunter*, 1980) before his death from cancer in 1980 at age 50.

TONTO BASIN OUTLAWS Monogram, 1941, B&W, 60 min. **Producer:** George W. Weeks; **Director:** S. Roy Luby; **Screenplay:** John Vlahos; **Music:** Frank Sanucci; **Cinematographer:** Robert F. Cline; **Editor:** S. Roy Claire; **Cast:** Ray Corrigan, John "Dusty" King, Max Terhune, Jan Wiley, Tristram Coffin, Edmund Cobb.

TONTO KID, THE Resolute, 1934, B&W, 61 min. **Producer:** Alfred T. Mannon; **Director:** Harry Fraser; **Screenplay:** Harry C. Crist; **Cinematographer:** Holbrook N. Todd; **Cast:** Rex Bell, Ruth Mix, Buzz Barton, Theodore Lorch, Joseph Girard, Barbara Roberts.

A scheming lawyer shoots the owner of a ranch he wants, puts the blame on a younger man, then gets a circus performer to pose as the victim's daughter. This is one of four pictures starring Rex Bell, Ruth Mix, and Buzz Barton.

TOPEKA Allied Artists, 1953, B&W, 69 min. **Producer:** Vincent Fennelly; **Director:** Thomas Carr; **Screenplay:** Milton Raison; **Music:** Raoul Kraushaar; **Cinematographer:** Ernest Miller; **Editor:** Sam Fields; **Cast:** William "Wild Bill" Elliott, Phyllis Coates, Fuzzy Knight, Rick Vallin, John James, Denver Pyle, Harry Lauter, Dale Van Sickel, Ted Mapes, I. Stanford Jolley.

"Wild Bill" Elliott is perfect as an outlaw who becomes sheriff of a town and gets the support of his former gang members when it comes to cleaning up the place.

TOPEKA TERROR, THE Republic, 1945, B&W, 55 min. **Producer:** Stephen Auer (associate); **Director:** Howard Bretherton; **Screenplay:** Norman Hall and Patricia Harper; **Cinematographer:** Bud Thackery; **Editor:** Charles Craft; **Cast:** Allan Lane, Linda Stirling, Earle Hodgins, Twinkle Watts, Roy Barcroft, Tom London, Frank Jaquet, Robert J. Wilke.

A special investigator takes on the guise of vagabond cowboy while he is on the trail of a band of outlaws. There is lots of action in this Republic oater, with an early screen appearance by future B western star Monte Hale in an uncredited part. (See also *SHERIFF OF SUNDOWN*.)

TOP GUN United Artists, 1955, B&W, 73 min. **Producer:** Edward Small; **Director:** Ray Nazarro; **Screenplay:** Richard Shayer; **Music:** Irving Gertz; **Cinematographer:** Lester White; **Editors:** Henry Adams and Dwight Caldwell; **Cast:** Sterling Hayden, William Bishop, Karin Booth, James Millican, Regis Toomey, Hugh Sanders, John Dehner, Rod Taylor.

After a man is cleared of murder charges, he is elected to the post of town sheriff. But with the new job he undergoes a change of character.

TORNADO RANGE PRC, 1948, B&W, 56 min. **Producer:** Jerry Thomas; **Director:** Ray Taylor; **Screenplay:** William Lively; **Music:** Eddie Dean and Walter Greene; **Cinematographer:** James S. Brown Jr.; **Editor:** Joseph Gluck; **Cast:** Eddie Dean, Roscoe Ates, Jennifer Holt, George Chesebro, Buster Slaven, Marshall Reed, Terry Frost, Lane Bradford, Russell Arms.

See *SONG OF OLD WYOMING*.

TO THE LAST MAN Paramount, 1933, B&W, 70 min, VHS. **Producer:** Harold Hurley; **Director:** Henry Hathaway; **Screenplay:** Jack Cunningham; **Cinematographer:** Ben F. Reynolds; **Cast:** Randolph Scott, Esther Ralston, Noah Beery, Jack La Rue, Buster Crabbe, Fuzzy Knight, Barton MacLane, Muriel Kirkland, Shirley Temple, John Carradine, Harlan Knight.

A family feud extends from Kentucky to Nevada in this thoughtful story set in the post-Civil War era. As part of Paramount's highly popular Zane Grey series in the 1930s, this early Henry Hathaway outing is one of the best, especially with its unusual climactic fight between villain Jack La Rue and heroine Esther Ralston. And what an opportunity it is to see Randolph Scott, Buster Crabbe, John Carradine, and Shirley Temple (whose doll's head is shot off) on the same screen. A contract director with Paramount, Hathaway started directing a series of westerns in 1932, often starring Randolph Scott and based on stories by Zane Grey.

TOUGHEST GUN IN TOMBSTONE United Artists, 1958, B&W, 72 min. **Producer:** Robert E. Kent; **Director:** Earl Bellamy; **Screenplay:** Orville H. Hampton; **Music:** Paul Dunlap; **Cinematographer:** Kenneth Peach; **Editor:** Grant Whytock; **Cast:** George Montgomery, Jim Davis, Beverly Tyler, Gerald Milton, Don Beddoe, Hank Worden, Harry Lauter, Lane Bradford, Rodolfo Hoyos Jr., Gregg Barton.

A captain in the Texas Rangers pretends to be an outlaw so he can infiltrate the Johnny Ringo gang.

TOUGHEST MAN IN ARIZONA Republic, 1952, B&W, 85 min. **Producer:** Sidney Picker; **Director:** R. G. Springsteen; **Screenplay:** John K. Butler; **Music:** R. Dale Butts; **Cinematographer:** Reggie Lanning; **Editor:** Richard L. Van Enger; **Cast:** Vaughn Monroe, Joan Leslie, Edgar Buchanan, Victor Jory, Jean Parker, Harry Morgan, Ian Macdonald, Lee MacGregor.

Vaughn Monroe is a widower sheriff who falls in love with a beautiful girl while he also tries to track down a notorious outlaw. Monroe, one of the era's top crooners who recorded such hit songs as "Ghost Riders in the Sky" and "Dance Ballerina Dance," adds a taste of charm to this pleasant little film, his second A-level production for Republic.

TOWN TAMER Paramount, 1965, Color, 89 min. **Producer:** A. C. Lyles; **Director:** Lesley Selander; **Screenplay:** Frank Gruber; **Music:** Jimmy Haskell; **Cinematographer:** W. Wallace Kelley; **Editor:** George A. Gittens; **Cast:** Dana Andrews, Terry Moore, Pat O'Brien, Lon Chaney Jr., Bruce Cabot, Lyle Bettger, Richard Arlen, Barton MacLane, Richard Jaeckel, Phillip Carey, Sonny Tufts, Coleen Gray, De Forrest Kelley, Jeanne Cagney, Don "Red" Barry, James Brown, Richard Webb.

After a gunman murders his wife, a man travels from town to town bringing peace and searching for the killer. When he finds him he discovers that the man he was searching for is the marshal of a small community. Producer A. C. Lyles once again gathered a top-notch cast of fine players whose days of stardom were behind them. The film was adapted from the novel by Frank Grober.

TRACK OF THE CAT Warner Bros., 1954, Color, 102 min. **Producers:** Robert Fellows and John Wayne; **Director:** William A. Wellman; **Screenplay:** A. I. Bezzerides; **Music:** Roy Webb; **Cinematographer:** William H. Clothier; **Editor:** Fred MacDowell; **Cast:** Robert Mitchum, Teresa Wright, Diana Lynn, Tab Hunter, Beulah Bondi, Philip Tonge, William Hopper, Carl Switzer.

When the eldest son of a feuding mountain farm family is killed by a murderous panther, his two brothers set out to destroy the animal. This film reunites Robert Mitchum and Teresa Wright, who teamed so well in Raoul Walsh's *Pursued* (1947). Yet as good as they are in this unusual psychological melodrama, top acting honors here belong to Beulah Bondi as the mean-spirited mother of the troubled brood. Also in the cast are William Hopper, Hedda Hopper's son; and Carl "Alfalfa" Switzer, playing a mystical 100-year-old Indian.

Based on a novel by Walter Van Tilburg Clark, who also penned *The Ox Bow Incident* (filmed in 1943), and produced by John Wayne and his partner Robert Fellows, *Track of the Cat* features an unusual visual experiment: making a black-and-white movie in color—that is, shooting the picture in color film but designing a palette of nothing but black and white.

The location filming at Mount Rainier was difficult to the extreme. According to Mitchum biographer Lee Server in *Robert Mitchum: "Baby I Don't Care,"* it presented Mitchum with the worst and most difficult conditions he ever experienced in making a film: roaring snow and whipping winds that were "bitterly cold, physically exhausting, all day sinking or falling over into the bottomless drifts."

Despite the innovative camera work by William Clothier, which includes some of most amazing and starkly beautiful images ever put on film; an excellent cast and realistic performances; and a director the caliber of William Wellman, *Track of the Cat* failed to go over well with audiences, in part because the director and screenwriter A. I. Bezzerides found it difficult to agree on certain rewrites and because Wellman insisted that all scenes stay intact as he saw fit.

TRACY RIDES Reliable, 1935, B&W, 60 min. **Producer:** Bernard B. Ray; **Director:** Harry S. Webb; **Screenplay:** Betty Burbridge and Rose Gordon; **Cinematographer:** J. Henry Kruse; **Editor:** Frederick Bain; **Cast:** Tom Tyler, Virginia Brown Faire, Edmund Cobb, Charles K. French, Carol Shandrew, Lafe McKee, Jimmy Aubrey.

See *MYSTERY RANCH.*

TRAIL BEYOND Monogram/Lone Star, 1934, B&W, 55 min, VHS, DVD. **Producer:** Paul Malvern; **Director:** Robert Bradbury; **Screenplay:** Lindsley Parsons; **Music:** Sam Perry; **Cinematographer:** Archie Stout; **Editor:** Charles Hunt; **Cast:** John Wayne, Verna Hillie, Noah Beery, Noah Beery Jr., Robert Frazer, Iris Lancaster.

One of John Wayne's "poverty row" oaters finds Wayne fighting outlaws who have kidnapped a young girl and are attempting to steal a gold mine. Produced by Paul Malvern, who used Wayne in numerous low-budget westerns, the film presents a rare opportunity to see father and son actors Noah Beery and Noah Beery Jr. working together.

TRAIL BLAZERS, THE Republic, 1940, B&W, 58 min. **Producer:** Harry Grey (associate); **Director:** George Sherman; **Screenplay:** Barry Shipman and Earle Snell; **Music:** Cy Feuer; **Cinematographer:** William Nobles; **Editor:** Tony Martinelli; **Cast:** Robert Livingston, Bob Steele, Rufe Davis, Pauline Moore, Weldon Heyburn, Carroll Nye, Tom Chatterton, Si Jenks, John Merton, Rex Lease.

See *THREE MESQUITEERS, THE.*

TRAIL DRIVE, THE Universal, 1933, B&W, 60 min. **Producer:** Ken Maynard; **Director:** Alan James; **Screenplay:** Nate Gatzert and James; **Cinematographer:** Ted D. McCord; **Cast:** Ken Maynard, Cecilia Parker, William Gould, Frank Rice, Bob Kortman, Fern Emmett, Lafe McKee, Jack Rockwell.

See *LUCKY LARKIN.*

TRAIL DUST Paramount, 1936, B&W, 77 min. **Producer:** Harry Sherman; **Director:** Nate Watt; **Screenplay:** Al Martin; **Music:** Claudia Humphrey, Jack Stern, and Harry Tobias; **Cinematographer:** Archie Stout; **Editor:** Robert Warwick; **Cast:** William Boyd, Jimmy Ellison, George "Gabby" Hayes, Morris Ankrum, Gwynne Shipman, Britt Wood, Al St. John.

See *HOP-ALONG CASSIDY.*

TRAIL GUIDE RKO, 1952, B&W, 60 min. **Producer:** Herman Schlom; **Director:** Lesley Selander; **Screenplay:** William Lively and Arthur E. Orloff; **Music:** Paul Sawtell; **Cinematographer:** Nicholas Musuraca; **Editor:** Samuel E. Beetley; **Cast:** Tim Holt, Richard Martin, Linda Douglas, Frank Wilcox, Robert Sherwood, John Pickard, Kenneth MacDonald, Wendy Waldren, Tom London, Patricia Wright.

TRAILING DANGER Monogram, 1947, B&W, 58 min. **Producer:** Barney Sarecky; **Director:** Lambert Hillyer; **Screenplay:** J. Benton Cheney; **Cinematographer:** Harry Neumann **Editor:** Roy V. Livingston; **Cast:** Johnny Mack Brown, Raymond Hatton, Peggy Wynne, Patrick Desmond, Steve Darrell, Marshal Reed.

See *UNDER ARIZONA SKIES.*

TRAILING DOWN TROUBLE Monogram, 1940, B&W, 56 min, VHS. **Producer:** George W. Weeks; **Director:** S. Roy Luby; **Screenplay:** Oliver Drake and George H. Plympton; **Music:** Johnny Lange and Lew Porter; **Cinematographer:** Edward Linden; **Editor:** Luby (as Roy Claire); **Cast:** John "Dusty" King, Max Terhune, Lita Conway, Nancy Louise King, Roy Barcroft, Jack Rutherford, Tom London.

TRAILIN' WEST Warner Bros., 1936, B&W, 59 min. **Producer:** Bryan Foy; **Director:** Noel M. Smith; **Screenplay:** Anthony Coldway; **Music:** M. K. Jerome and Jack Scholl; **Cinematographer:** Sidney Hickox and Ted D. McCord; **Editor:** Frank McGee; **Cast:** Dick Foran, Paula Stone, William "Wild Bill" Elliott (as Gordon Elliott), Addison Richards, Robert Barrat, Joseph Crehan, Jim Thorpe, Milton Kibbee.

A Secret Service agent is assigned to track down an outlaw gang in the West during the Civil War. Dick Foran fans will enjoy this action-packed little oater with a musical flavor. (See also *MOONLIGHT ON THE PRAIRIE.*)

TRAIL OF ROBIN HOOD Republic, 1950, Color, 67 min, VHS. **Producer:** Edward J. White (associate);

Director: William Witney; **Screenplay:** Gerald Geraghty; **Music:** Nathan Scott; **Cinematographer:** John MacBurnie; **Editor:** Tony Martinelli; **Cast:** Roy Rogers, Penny Edwards, Jack Holt, Rex Allen, Allan Lane, Monte Hale, William Farnum, Tom Tyler, Ray Corrigan, Kermit Maynard, George Chesebro, Tom Keene.

Roy Rogers and an assortment of contemporary western heroes come to the aid of Jack Holt (playing himself) to provide Christmas trees for needy families in time for the holidays. Cameo appearances by Rex Allen, Allan Lane, Monte Hale, and Ray Corrigan add to this thoroughly enjoyable seasonal oater that never stops playing well. (See also *UNDER WESTERN STARS.*)

TRAIL OF TERROR   Supreme, 1935, B&W, 54 min. **Producer:** A. W. Hackel; **Director:** Robert Bradbury; **Screenplay:** Bradbury; **Cinematographer:** E. M. MacManigal; **Editor:** S. Roy Luby; **Cast:** Bob Steele, Beth Marion, Forrest Taylor, Charles King, Frank Lyman, Charles K. French, Lloyd Ingraham.
   See *KID COURAGEOUS.*

TRAIL OF TERROR   PRC, 1943, B&W, 60 min. **Producers:** Arthur Alexander and Alfred Stern; **Director:** Oliver Drake; **Screenplay:** Drake; **Music:** James Newill and Dave O'Brien; **Cinematographer:** Ira H. Morgan; **Editor:** Charles Henkel Jr.; **Cast:** Dave O'Brien, James Newill, Guy Wilkerson, Patricia Knox, I. Stanford Jolley, Budd Buster, Robert Hill, Kenne Duncan, Frank Ellis.

TRAIL OF THE LAW   See *GOD'S COUNTRY AND THE MAN.*

TRAIL OF THE RUSTLERS   Columbia, 1950, B&W, 55 min. **Producer:** Colbert Clark; **Director:** Ray Navarro; **Screenplay:** Victor Arthur; **Cinematographer:** Fayte M. Browne; **Editor:** Paul Borofsky; **Cast:** Charles Starrett, Smiley Burnette, Gail Davis Tommy Ivo, Mira McKinney, Don C. Harvey, Myron Healey, Chuck Roberson, Gene Roth, Eddie Cletro.
   See *DURANGO KID, THE.*

TRAIL OF THE SILVER SPURS   Monogram, 1941, B&W, 57 min. **Producer:** George W. Weeks; **Director:** S. Roy Luby; **Screenplay:** Earle Snell; **Music:** Johnny Lange and Lew Porter; **Cinematographer:** Robert E. Cline; **Editor:** Roy Claire (S. Roy Luby); **Cast:** Ray Corrigan, John "Dusty" King, Max Terhune, Dorothy Short, Milburn Morante, I. Stanford Jolley, George Chesebro, Eddie Dean.

TRAIL OF THE VIGILANTES   Universal, 1940, B&W, 75 min. **Producer:** Allan Dwan; **Director:** Dwan; **Screenplay:** Harold Shumate; **Music:** Ralph Freed, Charles Previn, and Frank Skinner; **Cinematographer:** Milton Krasner and Joseph Valentine; **Editor:** Edward Curtiss; **Cast:** Franchot Tone, Warren William, Broderick Crawford, Andy Devine, Mischa Auer, Porter Hall, Peggy Morgan, Paul Fix.

Tenderfoot Franchot Tone joins up with Broderick Crawford, Andy Devine, and Mischa Auer to bust smooth racketeer Warren William. Allan Dwan's sprightly film combines some good action with a strong dose of humor. Interestingly, Dwan tries to recapture the spirit of *DESTRY RIDES AGAIN* (1932, 1939) using a similar theme and many of the same character actors. Film historian William Everson suggests that while the film is an enjoyable romp, it never becomes true satire because it is divided into two distinct halves, with most of the comedy in the first half and all of the action in the second, but "whether intended or not, [it emerges] as good, straight Western fare."

TRAIL RIDERS   Monogram, 1942, B&W, 55 min. **Producer:** George W. Weeks; **Director:** Robert Emmett Tansey; **Screenplay:** Frances Kavanaugh and Tansey; **Cinematographer:** Robert E. Cline; **Editor:** S. Roy Luby (as Roy Claire); **Cast:** John "Dusty" King, David Sharpe, Mac Terhune, Evelyn Finley, Forrest Taylor, Charles King, Kermit Maynard.

TRAIL STREET   RKO, 1947, B&W, 84 min. **Producer:** Nat Holt; **Director:** Ray Enright; **Screenplay:** Norman Houston and Gene Lewis; **Music:** Stanley Carter, Ben Oakland, and Paul Sawtell; **Cinematographer:** J. Roy Hunt; **Editor:** Lyle Boyer; **Cast:** Randolph Scott, Robert Ryan, Anne Jeffreys, George "Gabby" Hayes, Madge Meredith, Steve Brodie, Billy House, Virginia Sale.

Robert Ryan's first film after returning from service with the U.S. Marines in World War II has him as land agent Allen Harper, a good-natured easterner who comes to lawless Kansas to farm, not to fight, in the 1870s. However, a band of ruthless land grabbers led by the devious Logan Maury (Steve Brodie) and the black-clad villain Lance Larkin (Harry Woods) thwarts him. Matters are finally resolved by Bat Masterson (Randolph Scott), who arrives in town, subdues the villains almost single-handedly, and makes things right for Ryan and ladylove Madge Meredith.
   Trail Street was the second of 19 westerns in which Robert Ryan appeared. By the end of his career they composed nearly a third of his film repertory. More action than substance, the film was one of RKO's few profitable releases of 1947.

TRAIL TO LAREDO   Columbia, 1948, B&W, 54 min. **Producer:** Colbert Clark; **Director:** Ray Nazzaro; **Screenplay:** Barry Shipman; **Cinematographer:** Henry Freulich; **Editor:** Paul Borofsky; **Cast:** Charles Starrett, Smiley Burnette, Jim Bannon, Virginia Maxey, Tommy Ivo, Hugh Prosser.
   See *DURANGO KID, THE.*

TRAIL TO MEXICO   Monogram, 1946, B&W, 56 min. **Producer:** Oliver Drake; **Director:** Drake; **Screen-**

play: Drake; **Cinematographer:** James Brown; **Editor:** Ralph Dixon; **Cast:** Jimmy Wakely, Lee "Lasses" White, Julian Rivero, Dolores Castelli, Dora Del Rio.

See *ACROSS THE RIO GRANDE.*

TRAIL TO SAN ANTONE Republic, 1947, B&W, 67 min, VHS. **Producer:** Armand Schaefer; **Director:** John English; **Screenplay:** Luci Ford and Jack Natteford; **Music:** Gene Autry, Spade Cooley, Joseph Dubin, Sid Robbin, Deuce Spriggins, and Cindy Walker; **Cinematographer:** William Bradford; **Editor:** Charles Craft; **Cast:** Gene Autry, Peggy Stewart; Sterling Holloway, William Henry, Johnny Duncan, Tristram Coffin, Dorothy Vaughn.

See *TUMBLING TUMBLEWEEDS.*

TRAIL TO VENGEANCE Universal, 1945, B&W, 54 min. **Producer:** Wallace Fox; **Director:** Fox; **Screenplay:** Bob Williams; **Music:** Everett Carter; **Cinematographer:** Maury Gertsman; **Editor:** Russell F. Schoengarth; **Cast:** Kirby Grant, Fuzzy Knight, Jane Adams, Tom Fadden, Frank Jaquet, Pierce Lyden, Beatrice Gray, Roy Brent.

See *BAD MEN OF THE BORDER.*

TRAIN ROBBERS, THE Warner Bros., 1973, Color, 92 min, VHS, DVD. **Producer:** Michael Wayne; **Director:** Burt Kennedy; **Screenplay:** Kennedy; **Music:** Dominic Frontiere; **Cinematographer:** William Clothier; **Editor:** Frank Santillo; **Cast:** John Wayne, Ann-Margret, Ben Johnson, Rod Taylor, Christopher George, Bobby Vinton, Jerry Gatlin, Ricardo Montalban.

A trio of Civil War veterans (John Wayne, Ben Johnson, and Rod Taylor) become involved in an elaborate ruse concerning a hidden cache of gold stolen from a train and an alluring young widow (Ann-Margret). En route to Mexico to retrieve the loot, they discover they are being followed by a group of riders led by an increasingly visible mystery figure (Ricardo Montalban). With the widow's help, they fight off the mysterious riders, and in appreciation Wayne decides to leave his share of the loot to the widow's little boy—only to discover that she isn't really a widow and that he and his pals have been duped.

Written and directed by Burt Kennedy, this later John Wayne venture combines suspense, comedy, and altruism, qualities well suited to Kennedy, an enormously gifted writer and able director. His characters have a rich dimension, and the interplay between Wayne and Johnson—a screen association going back to the great John Ford westerns of the late 1940s—is sheer pleasure. The casting of Rod Taylor has something of a twist. Kennedy very much wanted Jack Elam for the part, but Wayne fought him on the issue, insisting on Taylor instead. Elam, it seems, had stolen the show from Wayne in *RIO LOBO* (1970), and the Duke was not about to let that happen again, a fact revealed by Kennedy in a 1995 interview with the author.

Nevertheless, Wayne was able to deliver what was perhaps his best one-liner ever in *The Train Robbers.* Bewildered by Ann-Margret's charm and seductive ploy, he says, "I have a saddle older than you are, Mrs. Lowe."

In a 1995 interview Ben Johnson also related an interesting sidebar during the filming of *The Train Robbers:* "They called me from Hollywood and said I better get back there because I might win an Academy Award. Well, I was a cowboy and no cowboy had ever won an Academy Award, so I knew I couldn't. Well anyhow, Duke lent Ann-Margret (nominated for *Carnal Knowledge*) and me his new airplane to go to the awards. We come up there and I win that old Oscar for *The Last Picture Show.* That's the big thing in my life."

TRAIN TO TOMBSTONE Lippert, 1950, B&W, 56 min. **Producer:** William Berke; **Director:** Berke; **Screenplay:** Orville Hampton and Victor West; **Music:** Albert Glasser; **Cinematographer:** Ernest Miller; **Editor:** Carl Pierson; **Cast:** Don "Red" Barry, Robert Lowery, Wally Vernon, Tom Neal, Judith Allen, Minna Phillips, Jack Perrin.

Don Barry is protecting a large shipment of gold on a train traveling from Albuquerque to Tombstone by posing as an outlaw. But one of the passengers on the train has masterminded a robbery, having his men dressed as Indians when they attack. When Don "Red" Barry's popularity started to decline, he made a series of similar low-budget entries for Lippert.

TRAITOR, THE Puritan, 1936, B&W, 56 min. **Producer:** Sigmund Neufeld and Leslie Simmonds; **Director:** Sam Newfield; **Screenplay:** John T. Neville and Joseph O'Donnell; **Cinematographer:** Jack Greenhalgh; **Editor:** John English; **Cast:** Tim McCoy, Frances Grant, Frank Melton, Pedro Regas, Soledad Jimenez, Karl Hackett, Dick Curtis, Roger Williams, J. Frank Glendon.

TRANSCONTINENTAL EXPRESS See *ROCK ISLAND TRAIL.*

TRAVELING SALESWOMAN (aka: TRAVELING SALESLADY) Columbia, 1950, B&W, 75 min. **Producer:** Tony Owen; **Director:** Charles F. Reisner; **Screenplay:** Howard Dimsdale; **Music:** Lester Lee and Allan Roberts; **Cinematographer:** George E. Diskant; **Editor:** Viola Lawrence; **Cast:** Joan Davis, Andy Devine, Adele Jergens, Joe Sawyer, Dean Riesner, John L. Cason, Chief Thundercloud, Minerva Urecal.

A girl and her boyfriend set out to sell her father's soap so that his business might survive. The two go out West, where they get involved with crooks and find themselves in the midst of an Indian attack. Joan Davis and Andy Devine provide some fun, but the film is ordinary and outdated at best.

TREACHERY RIDES THE RANGE Warner Bros., 1936, B&W, 56 min. **Producer:** Bryan Foy; **Director:** Frank McDonald; **Screenplay:** William Jacobs; **Music:**

M. K. Jerome and Jack Scholl; **Cinematographer:** L. William O'Connell; **Editor:** Frank Magee; **Cast:** Dick Foran, Paula Stone, Craig Reynolds, Monte Blue, Carlyle Moore Jr., Henry Otho, Jim Thorpe, Monte Montague, Don Barclay, Frank Bruno.

The Plains Indians threaten to go on the warpath when they are about to be defrauded by a band of crooks, so a cowboy sets out to make peace. Dick Foran, Warner Bros.' resident cowboy in the mid-1930s, delivers well in this top-notch vehicle with a nice blend of music and action. (See also *MOONLIGHT ON THE PRAIRIE.*)

TREASON Columbia, 1933, B&W, 63 min. **Producer:** Irving Briskin; **Director:** George Seitz; **Screenplay:** Gordon Battle; **Cinematographer:** John W. Boyle; **Editor:** Otto Meyer; **Cast:** Buck Jones, Shirley Grey, Robert Ellis, Ivor McFadden, Edward Le Saint, Frank Lackteen, T. C. Jack.

Buck Jones is an army scout who tries to infiltrate a band of Confederate sympathizers led by a woman who wants to get back the land she had lost unjustly in Kansas. This high-quality early Buck Jones offering is among the best of his many sound films.

TREASURE OF PANCHO VILLA RKO, 1955, Color, 92 min. **Producer:** Edward Grainger; **Director:** George Sherman; **Screenplay:** Gladys Atwater, J. Robert Bren, and Niven Busch; **Music:** Leith Stevens; **Cinematographer:** William E. Snyder; **Editor:** Harry Marker; **Cast:** Rory Calhoun, Shelley Winters, Gilbert Roland, Joseph Calleia, Fanny Shiller, Tony Carbajal, Carlos Muzquiz, Pasquel Pena.

Rory Calhoun is an American mercenary who sells himself and his machine gun to Pancho Villa's band of revolutionaries in 1913. Together with Mexican patriot Gilbert Roland they rob a shipment of gold from a government train with the intention of giving the loot to the revolutionaries. But Calhoun starts thinking that the money would look better in his pockets, and the action begins. Calhoun and Roland both deliver well in this action-packed, offbeat little film.

TREASURE OF RUBY HILLS Allied Artists, 1955, B&W, 71 min. **Producer:** William F. Broide; **Director:** Frank McDonald; **Screenplay:** Fred Eggers and Tom Hubbard; **Music:** Edward J. Kay; **Cinematographer:** John J. Martin; **Editor:** Ace Herman; **Cast:** Zachary Scott, Carole Mathews, Barton MacLane, Dick Foran, Lola Albright, Gordon Jones, Lee Van Cleef, Steve Darrell.

As crooked cattlemen battle for control of range land, a rancher tries to stop their criminal activity. Zachary Scott is convincing in the unusual role of a hero. One of the screen's underappreciated talents, Scott's nonvillainous roles were rather rare since his outstanding performance in *The Southerner* (1945) a decade earlier.

TREASURE OF THE AZTECS, THE (aka: SCHATZ DER AZTEKEN [WEST GERMANY]) CCC Filmkunst/Franco-London/Serena/Avala Film, 1965, Color, 102 min. **Producer:** Artur Brauner; **Director:** Robert Siodmak; **Screenplay:** Ladislas Fodor, Georg Marischka, Robert A. Stemmle, and Paul Jerrico; **Music:** Erwin Halletz; **Cinematographer:** Siegfried Hold; **Editor:** Walter Wischniewsky; **Cast:** Lex Barker, Gerard Barray, Michele Girardon, Rik Battaglia, Kelo Henderson, Jeff Corey, Theresa Lorca, Allessandra Panaro, Fausto Tozzi, Ralf Wolter.

Based on a story by German western novelist Karl May (known as the German Zane Grey), this film is set in Mexico during the Civil War. Dr. Sternau (Lex Barker) tries to get financial support for deposed President Benito Juarez to topple the government of Emperor Maximilian, who had been put on the Mexican throne by the French. Various parties are trying to get a cache of gold, the source of Aztec wealth, but it all culminates in a free-for-all inside a pyramid as their search for the gold is complicated by an active volcano.

Robert Siodmak (*The Spiral Staircase, The Killers, The Dark Mirror,* 1946) made his way to Hollywood just before the German occupation of Paris because of his Jewish heritage. He directed a number of fine films before returning to France in 1953 and to Germany the following year.

Actor Kelo Henderson, who had scored big with the popular TV series *26 Men* (1957–59), and a true westerner with all the requisite cowboy skills, played Frank Wilson, an American cowboy, in the film. In an interview excerpted from *White Hats and Silver Spurs,* he discussed the picture, which had been filmed in Dubrovnik, Belgrade, and Titograd. This location filming was more interesting because neither producer Arthur Brauner, president of Central Cinema Company in West Berlin, nor author Karl May had ever been to the Southwest.

Director Robert Siodmak (left) and actors Ralf Wolter (top) and Kelo Henderson (right) on location in Yugoslavia (1964), shooting two films back to back: The Treasure of the Aztecs *and* Pyramid of the Sun-God (AVALA FILM/COURTESY OF KELO HENDERSON)

Lex [Barker] and I were called in for lots of consultation. Actually the films were typical Westerns with a decidedly European flavor. Actors and actresses from Spain, Italy, and France added to the international ambience.

An interesting story has to do with the casting of the Indians. The Indians were played by the Belgrade Ballet Company. They had peacock feathers in the Indian head-dresses. We had to correct that immediately.

The most remarkable thing about Karl May's stories, many of which were made into movies, is not just the fact that the author had never been to the American West but that he wrote a whole series of western books while serving a prison term for forgery.

Designed by Siodmak to be a grandiose tale featuring Dr. Sternau's search for the legendary Aztec treasure, this picture (Part One) and *Pyramid of the Sun God* (Part Two) were shot back-to-back, or perhaps simultaneously. The cast and the crew remained the same except for Fausto Tozzi. American actor Jeff Corey plays President Abraham Lincoln. These two films are Robert Siodmak's only contribution to the western genre.

TRIBUTE TO A BAD MAN MGM, 1956, Color, 95 min, VHS. **Producer:** Sam Zimbalist; **Director:** Robert Wise; **Screenplay:** Michael Blankfort; **Music:** Miklos Roza; **Cinematographer:** Robert Surtees; **Editor:** Ralph E. Winters; **Cast:** James Cagney, Don Dubbins, Stephen McNally, Irene Papas, Vic Morrow, James Griffith, Jeanette Nolan, Chubby Johnson, Royal Dano, Lee Van Cleef.

In a role originally intended for Spencer Tracy, James Cagney is outstanding as Jeremy Rodock, a tough and gruff horse rancher who built a livestock empire out of nothing and as a middle-aged man lords over his domain as if it were his personal kingdom. Rustlers caught in the act are hanged summarily. Others are rounded up and dealt the same fate. Imprisoned by his omnipotence, he eventually loses the respect of his Greek-born companion Jocasta (Irene Papas in her screen debut). His story unfolds through the eyes of a young easterner named Steve Millar (Dan Dubbins), who initially saves Rodock from a band of bushwhackers. Millar comes to work on the ranch, and he and the alienated Jocasta develop a deep mutual attraction and fondness. They are about to leave together when Rodock has a change of heart. In a memorable scene of contrition, he acknowledges his fallen ways, begs Jocasta to return, and promises a better day. Millar rides off alone, never to see either again but a more rounded man with an episodic tale he will carry all his life.

Based on a short story by Jack Schaefer, the film is set against the scenically striking Colorado Rockies. Cagney's Jeremy Rodock is not "Cody Jarett in chaps," as Richard Shickel suggests, referring to the psychopathic character Cagney portrayed to perfection in *White Heat* (1949), but rather a complex, hard-bitten pioneer who had to learn to enforce his own law on a limitless land range, a man caught within himself yet not beyond learning the errors of his way and finding redemption. The film was the third and final

western for director Robert Wise, who cracked the genre for the first time with *BLOOD ON THE MOON* (1948).

TRIGGER FINGERS Victory, 1939, B&W, 54 min. **Producer:** Sam Katzman; **Director:** Sam Newfield; **Screenplay:** Basil Dickey; **Cinematographer:** William Hyer; **Editor:** Holbrook N. Todd; **Cast:** Tim McCoy, Ben Corbett, Harlene Wood, Joyce Bryant, Carleton Young, Ted Adams, John Elliott, Malcolm "Bud" McTaggart.

TRIGGER FINGERS Monogram, 1946, B&W, 56 min. **Producer:** Scott R. Dunlap; **Director:** Lambert Hillyer; **Screenplay:** Frank H. Young; **Cinematographer:** Harry Neumann; **Editor:** Fred Maguire; **Cast:** Johnny Mack Brown, Raymond Hatton, Jennifer Holt, Riley Hill, Steve Clark, Eddie Parker, Pierce Lyden, Ted Adams, Cactus Mack, Ed Cassidy.
See *UNDER ARIZONA SKIES.*

TRIGGER, JR. Republic, 1950, Color, 68 min, VHS. **Producer:** Edward White (associate); **Director:** William Witney; **Screenplay:** Gerald Geraghty; **Music:** R. Dale Butts, Darol Rice, Peter Tinturin, and Foy Willing; **Cast:** Roy Rogers, Dale Evans, Pat Brady, Gordon Jones, Grant Withers, Peter Miles, George Cleveland, T. Stanford Jolley.
See *UNDER WESTERN STARS.*

TRIGGERMAN Monogram, 1948, B&W, 58 min. **Producer:** Barney A. Sarecky; **Director:** Howard Bretherton; **Screenplay:** Ronald Davidson; **Cinematographer:** Harry Neumann; **Editor:** Johnny Fuller; **Cast:** Johnny Mack Brown, Raymond Hatton, Virginia Carroll, Bill Kennedy, Marshall Reed.
See *UNDER ARIZONA SKIES.*

TRIGGER PALS See *BILLY THE KID'S FIGHTING PALS.*

TRIGGER SMITH Monogram, 1939, B&W, 59 min. **Producer:** Robert Emmett Tansey; **Director:** Alan James; **Screenplay:** Tansey; **Cinematographer:** Bert Longenecker; **Editor:** Howard Dillinger; **Cast:** Addison Randall, Joyce Bryant, Frank Yaconelli, Ed Cassidy, Bobby Clark, Dave O'Brien.
See *RIDERS OF THE DAWN* (1937).

TRIGGER TOM Reliable, 1935, B&W, 57 min. **Producer:** Bernard B. Ray; **Director:** Harry S. Webb (as Henri Webb); **Screenplay:** Tom Gibson; **Cinematographer:** Pliny Goodfriend; **Editor:** William Austin; **Cast:** Tom Tyler, Al St. John, William Gould, John Elliott, Bernadene Hayes, Bud Osborne.
See *MYSTERY RANCH* (1934).

TRIGGER TRICKS Universal, 1930, B&W, 61 min. **Producer:** Hoot Gibson; **Director:** B. Reeves Eason; **Screenplay:** Eason; **Cinematographer:** Harry Neumann;

Editor: Gilmore Walker; **Cast:** Hoot Gibson, Sally Eilers, Robert Homans, Jack Richardson, Monte Montague, Neal Hart, Max Asher, Walter Perry.

Tim Brennan (Hoot Gibson) sets out to avenge the death of his brother at the hands of a ruthless band of cattlemen. This lighthearted picture was popular at the time of its release because of the much-publicized romance between Hoot Gibson and leading lady Sally Eilers, whom he married and later divorced. (See also *SPURS*.)

TRIGGER TRIO, THE Republic, 1937, B&W, 60 min. **Producer:** Sol C. Siegal; **Director:** William Witney; **Screenplay:** Oliver Drake and Joseph F. Poland; **Music:** Alberto Colombo, Karl Hajos, William Lava, and Hugo Riesenfeld; **Cinematographer:** Ernest Miller; **Editor:** Tony Martinelli; **Cast:** Ray Corrigan, Max Terhune, Ralph Byrd, Sandra Corday, Robert Warwick, Cornelius Keefe, Sammy McKim, Wally Wales, Willie Fung.

A rancher who is trying to prevent authorities from discovering that his cattle have hoof and mouth disease kills a range inspector. Ralph Byrd replaced Robert Livingston in this exciting Three Mesquiteers series entry. This entry also marked the directorial debut of William Witney, one of the most capable B western directors of his era. (See also *THREE MESQUITEERS, THE*.)

TRIPLE JUSTICE RKO, 1940, B&W, 66 min. **Director:** David Howard; **Screenplay:** Morton Grant and Arthur V. Jones; **Music:** Fred Rose, Paul Sawtell, and Ray Whitley; **Cinematographer:** J. Roy Hunt; **Editor:** Frederic Knudtson; **Cast:** George O'Brien, Virginia Vale, Peggy Shannon, Paul Fix, LeRoy Mason, Glenn Strange, Malcolm "Bud" McTaggart.

A rancher on his way to a friend's wedding meets a trio of men who rob the local bank and throw the blame on him. This fast-paced RKO venture marks George O'Brien's final starring B western series role. (See also *RACKETEERS OF THE RANGE*.)

TRIUMPHS OF A MAN CALLED HORSE Jensen Farley Pictures, 1982, Color, 90 min. **Producer:** Derek Gibson; **Director:** John Hough; **Screenplay:** Carlos Aured, Ken Blackwell, and Jack Dewitt; **Music:** Georges Garvarentz; **Cinematographer:** John Alcott and John Cabrera; **Cast:** Richard Harris, Michael Beck, Ana De Sade, Vaughn Armstrong, Anne Seymour, Buck Taylor.

TROOPER HOOK United Artists, 1957, B&W, 81 min. **Producer:** Sol Baer Fielding; **Director:** Charles Marquis Warren; **Screenplay:** Martin Berkeley, Herbert Little Jr., and David Victor; **Music:** Gerald Fried; **Cinematographer:** Ellsworth Fredericks; **Editor:** Fred W. Berger; **Cast:** Joel McCrea, Barbara Stanwyck, Earl Holliman, Edward Andrews, John Dehner, Susan Kohner, Royal Dano, Stanley Adams, Rodolfo Acosta, Sheb Wooley.

Trooper Clovis Hook (Joel McCrea) captures a notorious Apache leader, whose wife (Barbara Stanwyck) is a white woman with an Indian child. His job is to bring the woman and child back to he real husband (John Dehner), but her own people scorn her for having a child fathered by an Apache. The tough but good-natured Trooper Hook then finds himself in the predicament of falling in love with the woman.

This film is yet another example of a better-than-average western starring Joel McCrea, whose genre credits remain among the strongest of any major screen star. Tex Ritter sings the title song, which was written by Gerald Fried and Mitzi Cummings.

TROUBLE BUSTERS Majestic Pictures, 1933, B&W, 55 min. **Producers:** Larry Darmour and Henry L. Goldstein; **Director:** Lewis D. Collins; **Screenplay:** Collins and Oliver Drake; **Cinematographer:** William Nobles; **Editor:** S. Roy Luby; **Cast:** Jack Hoxie, Lane Chandler, Kaye Edwards, Harry Todd, Ben Corbett, Slim Whitaker, William Burt, Roger Williams.

See *GOLD*.

TROUBLE IN SUNDOWN RKO, 1939, B&W, 60 min. **Producer:** Bert Gilroy; **Director:** David Howard **Screenplay:** Oliver Drake, Dorrell McGowan, and Stuart E. McGowan; **Music:** Ray Whitely; **Cinematographer:** Harry J. Wild; **Editor:** Frederic Knudtson; **Cast:** George O'Brien, Rosalind Keith, Ray Whitley, Ward Bond, Cy Kendall.

TROUBLE IN TEXAS Grand National, 1937, B&W, 63 min, VHS. **Producer:** Edward Finney; **Director:** Robert N. Bradbury; **Screenplay:** Robert Emmett Tansey (as Robert Tansey); **Music:** Frank Sanucci; **Cinematographer:** Gus Peterson; **Editor:** Frederick Bain; **Cast:** Tex Ritter, Rita Hayworth, Yakima Canutt, Charles King, Dick Palmer, Horace Murphy, Earl Dwire, Tom Cooper.

See *SONG OF THE GRINGO*.

TROUBLE SHOOTER, THE See *MAN WITH THE GUN*.

TRUE GRIT Paramount, 1969, Color, 128, VHS, DVD, CD. **Producer:** Hal Walis; **Director:** Henry Hathaway; **Screenplay:** Marguerite Roberts; **Music:** Elmer Bernstein; **Cinematographer:** Lucien Ballard; **Editor:** Warren Low; **Cast:** John Wayne, Glen Campbell, Kim Darby, Jeremy Slate, Robert Duvall, Dennis Hooper, Alfred Ryder, Strother Martin, Jeff Corey, Ron Soble, John Fielder.

The fat old man with one good eye shouts, "Fill your hands you son of a bitch!" Then with a pistol in one hand, a rifle in another, and his horse's reins between his teeth, he rides into the Ned Pepper gang and kills them one by one. For his performance as Rooster Cogburn in Henry Hathaway's *True Grit*, John Wayne was accorded that elusive Oscar that many felt had been denied him far too long.

With a screenplay by Marguerite Roberts based on the novel by Charles Portis, the story centers on young Mattie Ross (Kim Darby), who starts out from Arkansas to avenge the murder of her father. She enlists the help of Marshal Rooster Cogburn, whose record at apprehending criminals is somewhat suspect but whose efficiency is well established—a man of true grit. Though he is overweight and has an overly healthy liking for the bottle, she seeks out the one-eyed Marshal because she believes he has the grit to track her father's murderer into hostile Indian territory. They are joined by LaBoeuff, a handsome Texas Ranger played by Glen Campbell in his film debut.

The unlikely trio pools their even more unlikely resources against Ned Pepper (Robert Duvall) and his gang as well as the evil Tom Cheney (Jeff Corey), the murderer of Mattie Ross's father. The result is an excellent film—sad, exciting, sweet, and bittersweet, with an ending more poignant than any Wayne film, except, perhaps, *THE SEARCHERS* (1956). John Wayne towers over the entire production, beyond even Lucien Ballard's majestic Colorado and California location filming and Elmer Bernstein's movingly melodic musical score. *True Grit* has only one brief studio "exterior."

John Wayne's Oscar was well earned, not just because he was being honored for the complete body of his long time film work, as some claim, but equally for his well-crafted and memorable performance, which only seems to get better with each new viewing. "Wow!" exclaimed the grateful Wayne at Oscar time, "If I had put that [eye] patch on thirty-five years earlier..."

The now-famous eye patch was the work of costumer Luster Bayless, who recalled it in an interview with the author.

> We were out in the desert and Duke needed an eye patch he could see through and [I was] all out of leather. So I worked all night and came up with an idea. I cut the eye patch out, put a screen inside then took the gauze and sprayed it. So now you could see through it and with no light behind you, you never saw the hole. Duke used several of those through the course of the day. Each morning he would check the thing to see if there was any makeup inside it.

After collecting his Oscar, when Wayne returned to Tucson to resume filming *RIO LOBO* (1970) for Howard Hawks, everyone was wearing an eye patch—the crew, the actors, and even his horse. When he arrived, they all turned around, and Wayne found himself staring at a sea of eye patches. Reportedly, he was quite amused.

TRUE STORY OF JESSE JAMES, THE (aka: THE JAMES BROTHERS, UK) 20th Century Fox, 1957, Color, 92 min. **Producer:** Herbert B. Swope Jr.; **Director:** Nicholas Ray; **Screenplay:** Nunnally Johnson and Walter Newman; **Music:** Leigh Harline; **Cinematographer:** Joe MacDonald; **Editor:** Robert Simpson; **Cast:** Robert Wagner, Jeffrey Hunter, Hope Lange, Agnes Moorehead, Alan Hale Jr., Allan Baxter, John Carradine.

This film chronicles the last 18 years of Jesse James's life, from his home life in Missouri through his experiences with Quantrill's Raider's to his career of banditry and his attempt to settle down after the failed robbery of the bank at Northfield, Minnesota, on September 7, 1876. It culminates with James's death at the hands of an assassin eager to pick up the $25,000 reward offered by the Remington Detective Agency.

The idea here is that Jesse (Robert Wagner) and Frank James (Jeffrey Hunter) were led into a life of crime because of the family's Confederate sympathies while living among Union neighbors in post-Civil War Missouri. Finding work difficult to obtain, they become involved in a robbery with the idea of leaving Missouri but soon become addicted to robbing trains and banks. The story is told through the eyes of the people who knew them. Director Nicholas Ray effectively uses some action clips from Henry Hathaway's *Jesse James* (1939).

TRUSTED OUTLAW, THE Republic, 1937, B&W, 57 min. **Producer:** A. W. Hackel; **Director:** Robert Bradbury; **Screenplay:** Fred Myton and George Plympton; **Cinematographer:** Bert Longenecker; **Editor:** S. Roy Luby; **Cast:** Bob Steele, Lois January, Joan Barclay, Earl Dwire, Charles King, Richard Cramer, Hal Price.

TUCSON RAIDERS Republic, 1944, B&W, 55 min. **Producer:** Eddie White (associate); **Director:** Spencer Bennet; **Screenplay:** Anthony Coldeway; **Music:** Joseph Dubin; **Cinematographer:** Reggie Lanning; **Editor:** Harry Keller; **Cast:** William "Wild Bill" Elliott, George "Gabby" Hayes, Robert Blake, Alice Fleming, Ruth Lee, Peggy Stewart, LeRoy Mason.
See *ADVENTURES OF RED RYDER, THE.*

TULSA Eagle Lion, 1949, 90 min, VHS. **Producer:** Walter Wanger; **Director:** Stuart Heisler; **Screenplay:** Frank S. Nugent and Curtis Canyon; **Music:** Frank Skinner; **Cinematographer:** Winton C. Hoch; **Editor:** Terry Morse; **Cast:** Susan Hayward, Robert Preston, Chill Wills, Ed Begley, Lloyd Gough, Pedro Armendáriz, Harry Shannon, Jimmy Conlon, Paul E. Burns.

Susan Hayward is a rancher's daughter who fights with the oil prospector she blames for killing her father. She then becomes a wildcatter herself as a result of ending up with a large share of land leases. With the help of a geologist (Robert Preston) and an Indian rancher (Pedro Armendáriz), she builds her own oil empire, but by working with her onetime nemesis she compromises her existing relationships. The film won an Academy Award nomination for Best Special Effects.

TULSA KID, THE Republic, 1940, B&W, 57 min. **Producer:** George Sherman (associate); **Director:** Sherman; **Screenplay:** Anthony Coldway and Oliver Drake; **Cinematographer:** Jack MacBurnie; **Editor:** William P. Thompson; **Cast:** Don "Red" Barry, Noah Beery, Luana Walters, Dave Durand, George Douglas, Ethan Laidlaw, Stanley Blystone.
See *WYOMING OUTLAW.*

TUMBLEDOWN RANCH IN ARIZONA Monogram, 1941, B&W, 60 min. **Producer:** George W. Weeks; **Director:** S. Roy Luby; **Screenplay:** Milton Raison; **Cinematographer:** Robert E. Cline; **Editor:** Luby (Roy Claire); **Cast:** Ray Corrigan, John "Dusty" King, Max Terhune, Sheila Darcy, Marian Kirby, Quen Ramsey, James Craven.

TUMBLEWEED Universal, 1953, Color, 79 min. **Producer:** Ross Hunter; **Director:** Nathan Juran; **Screenplay:** John Meredyth Lucas; **Music:** Milton Rosen, Herman Stein, and Henry Mancini; **Cinematographer:** Russell Metty; **Editor:** Virgil V. Vogel; **Cast:** Audie Murphy, Lori Nelson, Chill Wills, Roy Roberts, Russell Johnson, K. T. Stevens, Madge Meredith.

Jim Harvey (Audie Murphy) is a guard on a small wagon train as it makes its way west. When Indians attack the wagon train, Harvey tries to negotiate with their chief, Aguila, whose son's life he had once saved. He is captured and the rest of the wagon train is wiped out, except for two sisters. Escaping his captors, he eventually shows up in town, where he is declared a deserter and nearly hanged. Escaping again, Harvey is eventually caught by the sheriff and his posse, but then they are attacked by the raiding Indians once more. This time, the Indians are defeated, and as he dies Aguila exonerates Harvey by identifying the white man who staged the initial attack on the wagon train.

TUMBLEWEEDS United Artists, 1925, B&W, 82 min. **Producer:** William S. Hart; **Director:** King Baggot; **Screenplay:** Gardner Sullivan; **Cinematographer:** Joseph H. August; **Cast:** William S. Hart, Barbara Bedford, Lucien Littlefield, J. Gordon Russell, Richard Neill, Jack Murphy.

In his farewell to the silver screen, William S. Hart is a ranch boss who falls in love with a pretty girl. Together they decide to stake a claim in the Oklahoma Territory when it is opened up to settlers. The well-crafted land-rush sequences have yet to be duplicated, with Hart giving one of his finest exhibitions of horse riding at full speed. At the beginning of the film, he remarks prophetically to his companions as they leave the Cherokee Strip, "Boys, it's the last of the West." There is a scrupulous attention to detail, exemplified in a scene where Hart exposes a fellow who illegally anticipated the land rush and staked his claim too soon by testing the sweat on the man's horse. The sweat turned out to be soap suds.

Hart never tried to top this remarkable example of filmmaking. *Tumbleweeds* was reissued in 1939 to cash in on the great new cycle of westerns established that year by *STAGECOACH*. For this reissue Hart again faced the camera to present a memorable 10-minute introduction, outlining the historical facts behind the opening up of the Cherokee Trail. Then, as a moviemaker proud of his record, he recalled the past with a deep blend of emotional and honest sentiment

before finally bidding farewell to his audience for the last time. (See also *HELL'S HINGES*.)

TUMBLEWEED TRAIL PRC, 1946, B&W, 59 min. **Producer:** Robert Emmett Tansey; **Director:** Tansey; **Screenplay:** Frances Kavanaugh; **Music:** Johnny Bond, Eddie Dean, Bob Sheldon, Glenn Strange, Ernest Tubb, and Lou Wayne; **Cinematographer:** Ernest Miller; **Editor:** Hugh Winn; **Cast:** Eddie Dean, Roscoe Ates, Shirley Patterson, Johnny McGovern, Ted Adams, Jack O'Shea, Kermit Maynard, William Fawcett.

See *SONG OF OLD WYOMING*.

TUMBLING TUMBLEWEEDS Republic, 1935, B&W, 61 min. **Producer:** Nat Levine; **Director:** Joseph Kane; **Screenplay:** Ford Beebe; **Cinematographer:** Ernest Miller; **Editor:** Lester Orlebeck; **Cast:** Gene Autry, Smiley Burnette, Lucile Browne, George "Gabby" Hayes, Norma Taylor, Edward Hearn, Eugene Jackson, George Chesebro, Jack Rockwell, Frankie Marvin, Slim Whitaker.

Billed as "The Screen's New Cowboy Singing Star," Gene Autry returns home to find his father murdered and his boyhood pal being blamed for the crime. Autry's first starring feature film is a fast-paced, pleasant affair in which he introduced the popular title song "Tumbling Tumbleweeds," which has become a genre standard and the theme song for Bob Nolan and The Sons of the Pioneers; it was written by Nolan in 1934. The film also set the pattern of giving action and songs an equal amount of screen time, making Gene Autry a household name and paving the way for the likes of Tex Ritter, Roy Rogers, and a slew of other singing cowboys.

Born in Tioga, Texas, on September 29, 1907, Autry began singing on a local radio station in 1928. Three years later he had his own show and was making his first recordings. His screen debut was as an entertainer at a dude ranch in Ken Maynard's 1934 film *IN OLD SANTA FE*, followed the same year by *MYSTERY MOUNTAIN*, another Maynard film. He followed these appearances with his own 13-part serial, *PHANTOM EMPIRE* (1935), which led to his being signed to a contract by Republic when that company was formed as a result of a merger of four minor studios.

Autry's personal success helped Republic flourish, and the studio purchased many hit songs for him to sing and yodel in such films as *Round Up Time in Texas* (1937); *South of the Border, In Old Monterey, Mexicali Rose* (1939); and *Back in the Saddle* (1941), in which he introduced his famous theme song. His popularity remained unabated until 1942, when he joined the armed services and Roy Rogers began to take over his mantle.

Following his service in World War II, Autry returned briefly to Republic and then in 1947 he signed on with Columbia, where he made dozens of musical westerns before turning to television in the early 1950s. With sidekicks Smiley Burnette and Pat Buttram as well as his horse Champion, he delighted filmgoers for more than two decades; keeping the B westerns of the 1930s and 1940s alive despite the presence of automobiles, radios, and airplanes. These films often grossed more than 10 times their $50,000 production costs.

All told Gene Autry made more than 100 films. His post-*Tumbling Tumbleweeds* filmography includes: *Melody Trail, Sagebrush Troubadour, The Singing Vagabond* (1935); RED RIVER VALLEY, COMIN' ROUND THE MOUNTAIN, *Singing Cowboy,* GUNS AND GUITARS, *Oh Susanna*; RIDE, RANGER, RIDE; THE BIG SHOW, THE OLD CORRAL (1936); *Git Along, Little Dogies, Round-Up Time in Texas, Yodelin' Kid From Pine Ridge,* BOOTS AND SADDLES, *Manhattan Merry-Go-Round, Springtime in the Rockies, Rootin' Tootin' Rhythm, Public Cowboy No. 1* (1937); GOLD MINE IN THE SKY, *Man from Music Mountain, Prairie Moon, Rhythm of the Saddle, Western Jamboree, The Old Barn Dance* (1938); *Home on the Prairie, Mountain Rhythm,* COLORADO SUNSET, SOUTH OF THE BORDER, ROVIN' TUMBLEWEEDS, MEXICALI ROSE, IN OLD MONTEREY, BLUE MONTANA SKIES (1939); *Men with Steel Faces,* GAUCHO SERENADE; *Ride, Tenderfoot, Ride;* MELODY RANCH, *Rodeo Dough, Unusual Occupations,* SHOOTING HIGH, *Rancho Grande,* (1940); BACK IN THE SADDLE, *The Singing Hill, Meet Roy Rogers, Under Fiesta Stars, Sunset in Wyoming,* SIERRA SUE, RIDIN' ON A RAINBOW, DOWN MEXICO WAY (1941); *Carolina Moon, Home in Wyomin', Cowboy Serenade,* HEART OF THE RIO GRANDE, *Stardust on the Sage,* CALL OF THE CANYON, BELLS OF CAPISTRANO, (1942); SIOUX CITY SUE, (1946); *Trail to San Antone, Saddle Pals, Robin Hood of Texas, Twilight on the Rio Grande, The Last Round-Up* (1947); THE STRAWBERRY ROAN, LOADED PISTOLS (1948); THE COWBOY AND THE INDIANS, *Sons of New Mexico, Rim of the Canyon,* RIDERS OF THE WHISTLING PINES, *Riders in the Sky.* THE BIG SOMBRERO (1949); MULE TRAIN, *Indian Territory,* COW TOWN, *The Blazing Sun,* BEYOND THE PURPLE HILLS (1950); *Gene Autry and the Mounties, Texans Never Cry, Silver Canyon, Valley of Fire, Whirlwind, The Hills of Utah* (1951); NIGHT STAGE TO GALVESTON, APACHE COUNTRY, *Wagon Team,* BLUE CANADIAN ROCKIES, THE OLD WEST, *Barbed Wire* (1952); ON TOP OF OLD SMOKEY, *Winning of the West, Saginaw Trail, Pack Train,* LAST OF THE PONY RIDERS, GOLDTOWN *Ghost Riders* (1953).

Gene Autry also appeared as himself in the 1956 feature *Hollywood Bronc Buster* and had a cameo role as himself in ALIAS JESSE JAMES (1951) starring Bob Hope.

TWILIGHT IN THE SIERRAS Republic, 1949, Color, 67 min, VHS. **Producer:** Edward J. White (associate); **Director:** William Nibley; **Screenplay:** Sloan Nibley; **Music:** Sid Robbins, Foy Willing, and Stanley Wilson; **Cinematographer:** John MacBurnie; **Editor:** Anthony Martinelli; **Cast:** Roy Rogers, Dale Evans, Estelita Rodriguez, Pat Brady, Russ Vincent, George Meeker, Pierce Lyden, Fred Kohler Jr., House Peters Jr.

See UNDER WESTERN STARS.

TWILIGHT ON THE PRAIRIE Universal, 1944, B&W, 62 min. **Producer:** Warren Wilson (associate); **Director:** Jean Yarbrough; **Screenplay:** Clyde Bruckman; **Music:** Hans J. Salter; **Cinematographer:** Jerome Ash; **Edi-**tor: Fred R. Feitshans Jr.; **Cast:** Johnny Downs, Vivian Austin, Leon Errol, Connie Haines, Eddie Quillan, Milburn Stone, Jimmie Dodd, Olin Howard, Perc Launders, Dennis Moore, Ralph Peters, Jack Teagarden and His Orchestra, Foy Willing and the Riders of the Purple Sage, The Eight Buckaroos.

A cowboy band on its way to Hollywood to break into the movies gets stranded on a ranch and agrees to work there through harvest time. Lots of songs and good times fill this glossy little Universal feature. Original songs are provided by Frankie Brown, Redd Evans, Lew Porter, Jack Teagarden, and Foy Willing.

TWILIGHT ON THE RIO GRANDE Republic, 1947, B&W, 71 min. **Producer:** Armand Schaefer (associate); **Director:** Frank McDonald; **Screenplay:** Dorrell McGowan and Stuart E. McGowan; **Music:** Smiley Burnette, Dick Charles, Jack Elliott, Larry Marks, Nat Simon, and Charles Tobias; **Cinematographer:** William Bradford; **Editor:** Harry Keller; **Cast:** Gene Autry, Sterling Holloway, Adele Mara, Bob Steele, Charles Evans, Martin Garralaga.

See TUMBLING TUMBLEWEEDS.

TWILIGHT ON THE TRAIL Paramount, 1941, B&W, 58 min. **Producer:** Harry Sherman; **Director:** Howard Bretherton; **Screenplay:** J. Benton Cheney, Ellen Corby, and Cecile Kramer; **Music:** John Leipold; **Cinematographer:** Russell Harlan; **Editor:** Fred R. Fetishes Jr.; **Cast:** William Boyd, Andy Clyde, Brad King, Wanda McKay, Jack Rockwell, Tom London, Jimmy Wakely, Johnny Bond, Dick Rinehart (Jimmy Wakely Trio).

See HOP-ALONG CASSIDY.

TWINKLE IN GOD'S EYES, THE Republic, 1955, B&W, 73 min. **Producer:** Mickey Rooney; **Director:** George Blair; **Screenplay:** P. J. Wolfson; **Music:** Van Alexander; **Cinematographer:** Bud Thackery; **Editor:** Tony Martinelli; **Cast:** Mickey Rooney, Coleen Gray, Hugh O'Brian, Joey Forman, Don "Red" Barry, Mike Connors, Ruta Lee, Raymond Hatton.

A minister (Mickey Rooney) returns to the town of Lodestone, where his father had been killed 25 years ago, determined to spread the word of God through humor.

TWO-FISTED JUSTICE Monogram, 1931, B&W, 63 min. **Producer:** Trem Carr; **Director:** George Arthur Durlam; **Screenplay:** Durlam; **Cinematographer:** Archie Stout; **Editor:** J. Logan Pearson; **Cast:** Tom Tyler, Barbara Weeks, Bobby Nelson, Will Walling, John Elliott, Gordon De Main, Yakima Canutt.

Kentucky Carson (Tom Tyler), a scout sent by President Lincoln to protect settlers, uncovers an outlaw gang led by Nick Slovenia (Will Walling). He gets some help from Poncho Rider (Yakima Canutt).

TWO-FISTED JUSTICE Monogram, 1943, B&W, 54 min. **Producer:** George Weeks; **Director:** Robert Tansey; **Screenplay:** William L. Nolte; **Music:** John "Dusty" King; **Cinematographer:** Robert Cline; **Editor:** Roy Claire (S. Roy Luby); **Cast:** "Dusty" King, David Sharpe, Max Terhune, Owen Gaze, Charles King, George Chesebro, John Elliott.

TWO-FISTED LAW Columbia, 1932, B&W, 64 min, VHS, DVD. **Producer:** Irving Briskin; **Director:** D. Ross Lederman; **Screenplay:** Kurt Kempler; **Music:** Mischa Bakaleinikoff and Sam Perry; **Cinematographer:** Benjamin H. Kline; **Editor:** Otto Meyer; **Cast:** Tim McCoy, Alice Day, Wheeler Oakman, Tully Marshall, Wallace MacDonald, John Wayne, Walter Brennan.

Tim McCoy is a rancher who is cheated out of his ranch by a crooked cattleman. He is finally able to pin the crime on his nemesis and sundry other culprits who are upsetting the community. This early Tim McCoy (sound) oater presents a rare opportunity to see McCoy, John Wayne, and three-time Oscar winner Walter Brennan on the same western screen.

TWO-FISTED RANGERS Columbia, 1940, B&W, 62 min. **Producer:** Leon Barsha; **Director:** Joseph H. Lewis; **Music:** Bob Nolan and Tim Spencer; **Cinematographer:** George Meehan; **Editor:** Charles Nelson; **Cast:** Charles Starrett, Iris Meredith, Bob Nolan and the Sons of Pioneers, Kenneth MacDonald, Dick Curtis, Wally Wales, Bill Cody Jr., Pat Brady.
  See *GALLANT DEFENDER.*

TWO-FISTED SHERIFF Columbia, 1937, B&W, 60 min. **Producer:** Harry L. Decker; **Director:** Leon Barsha; **Screenplay:** Paul Perez; **Music:** R. H. Bassett, Milan Roder, and Louis Silvers; **Cinematographer:** Allen G. Siegler; **Editor:** William A. Lyon; **Cast:** Charles Starrett, Barbara Weeks, Bruce Lane, Edward Peil Sr., Allan Sears, Walter Downing, Ernie Adams.
  See *GALLANT DEFENDER.*

TWO FLAGS WEST 20th Century Fox, 1950, B&W, 92 min. **Producer:** Casey Robinson; **Director:** Robert Wise; **Screenplay:** Robinson; **Music:** Hugo Friedhofer; **Cinematographer:** Leon Shamroy; **Editor:** Louis Loeffler; **Cast:** Joseph Cotten, Linda Darnell, Jeff Chandler, Cornel Wilde, Dale Robertson, Jay C. Flippen, Noah Beery, Harry von Zell, John Sands, Arthur Hunnicutt, Jack Lee.

A contingent of Confederate prisoners led by their colonel (Joseph Cotten) agree to serve in the Union Army with the proviso that they are used in the Indian campaigns against the Kiowa, who are taking advantage of the Civil War to try to take back their land. The Confederates are sent to a New Mexico post where the commandant (Jeff Chandler) is an embittered, uncompromising rebel hater, his brother having been killed by rebel troops. Matters are complicated by his torturous love for his sister-in-law (Linda Darnell). He refuses at first to employ the Confederates in the post's

defense but changes his mind when Indians viciously attack the fort. However, the attack was very much a personal matter, since the commandant had brutally killed the chief's son. Realizing this, he sacrifices himself to the Indians and saves the fort from further danger.

The factual basis for the film's plot comes from a story by Frank S. Nugent and Curtis Kenyon relating how in 1864 the Union Army recruited Confederate prisoners to man western army outposts under Union command. It is an interesting story that benefits from a top-quality cast and the steady directorial hand of Robert Wise. This is one of three westerns helmed by Wise, sandwiched between *BLOOD ON THE MOON* (1949) and *TRIBUTE TO A BAD MAN* (1957).

TWO GUN CUPID See *BAD MAN, THE.*

TWO GUN JUSTICE Monogram, 1938, B&W, 57 min. **Producer:** Maurice Conn; **Director:** Alan James; **Screenplay:** Fred Myton; **Cinematographer:** Jack Greenhalgh; **Editor:** Richard Wray; **Cast:** Tim McCoy, Betty Compson, John Merton, Joan Barclay, Lane Chandler, Al Bridge, Tony Patton, Al Craven, Harry Strang, Earl Dwire.

Lawman Tim Carson (Tim McCoy) takes on the guise of a Mexican bandit called The Vulture in an attempt to break up a notorious gang.

TWO-GUN LADY Associated Release Corporation, 1956, B&W, 71 min. **Producer:** Richard Bartlett **Director:** Richard Bartlett; **Screenplay:** Norman Jolley; **Music:** Leo Klatzkin; **Cinematographer:** Guy Roe; **Editor:** Carl Pierson; **Cast:** Peggie Castle, William Talman, Robert Lowery, Marie Windsor, Ian MacDonald, Earle Lyon.

A young woman learns to become a sharpshooter so she can hunt down the three men who murdered her parents. Fortunately she finds a sheriff who is willing to help her.

TWO-GUN LAW Columbia, 1937, B&W, 56 min. **Producer:** Harry L. Deeker; **Director:** Leon Barsha; **Screenplay:** John Rathmell; **Cinematographer:** George Meehan; **Editor:** William A. Lyon; **Cast:** Charles Starrett, Peggy Stratford, Hank Bell, Edward Le Saint, Charles Middleton, Al Bridge, Lee Prather, Dick Curtis, Victor Potel, George Chesebro, Art Mix, Tex Cooper, George Morrell.
  See *GALLANT DEFENDER.*

TWO GUN MAN FROM HARLEM Merit, 1938, B&W, 65 min. **Producers:** Richard C. Kahn and Alfred N. Sack; **Director:** Kahn; **Screenplay:** Kahn; **Music:** Herbert Jeffrey; **Cinematographer:** Harvey Gould and Marcel Le Picard; **Editor:** William Faris; **Cast:** Herb Jeffries, Marguerite Whitten, Clarence Brooks, Mantan Moreland, Tom Southern, Spencer Williams.

TWO GUNS AND A BADGE Allied Artists, 1954, B&W, 69 min. **Producer:** Vincent M. Fennelly; **Director:** Lewis D. Collins; **Screenplay:** Daniel B. Ullman; **Music:**

Raoul Kraushaar; **Cinematographer:** Joe Novak; **Editor:** Sam Fields; **Cast:** Wayne Morris, Morris Ankrum, Beverly Garland, Roy Barcroft, William Phipps, Damian O'Flynn, I. Stanford Jolley, Robert J. Wilke.

An ex-convict who is mistaken for a deputy sheriff when he rides into a small town soon finds himself pitted against a corrupt rancher while falling in love with the man's daughter. Considered to be the last B western series vehicle, this film proves to be a worthy genre finale.

TWO GUN SHERIFF Republic, 1940, B&W, 56 min. **Producer:** George Sherman (associate); **Director:** Sherman; **Screenplay:** Bennett Cohen; **Music:** Cy Feuer; **Cinematographer:** William Nobles; **Editor:** Tony Martinelli; **Cast:** Don "Red" Barry, Lynn Merrick, Jay Novello, Milton Kibbee, Fred Kohler Jr., Fred "Snowflake" Toones, Dick Thane, Archie Hall Sr.

See *WYOMING OUTLAW.*

TWO GUYS FROM TEXAS Warner Bros., 1948, Color, 86 min. **Producer:** Alex Gottlieb; **Director:** David Butler; **Screenplay:** Allen Boretz, and I. A. L. Diamond; **Music:** Sammy Cahn and Julie Styne; **Cinematographer:** Arthur Edeson and William V. Skall; **Editor:** Irene Morra; **Cast:** Dennis Morgan, Jack Carson, Dorothy Malone, Penny Edwards, Forrest Tucker, Fred Clark, Gerald Mohr, John Alvin, Monte Blue.

Two vaudeville entertainers (Dennis Morgan and Jack Carson) are stranded on a Texas ranch where they fight crooks and become involved with two pretty girls. As usual, Morgan and Carson provide an appealing team, this time in a light-hearted musical romp with western trappings. The film is a reworking of *COWBOY FROM BROOKLYN* (Warner Bros., 1938).

TWO MULES FOR SISTER SARA Universal, 1970, Color, 105 min, VHS. **Producer:** Martin Rankin; **Director:** Don Siegal, **Screenplay:** Albert Maltz; **Music:** Ennio Morricone; **Cinematographer:** Gabriel Figueroa; **Editor:** Robert Shugrue; **Cast:** Clint Eastwood, Shirley MacLaine, Manolo Fabregas, Alberto Morin, Armando Silvestre, John Kelly, Enrique Lucero.

American mercenary Clint Eastwood happens on a group of bandits about to rape a woman (Shirley MacLaine). After dispatching them quickly, he is surprised to discover she is a nun. He is then duped into delivering her to the Mexican revolutionaries whom she is helping in their battle against the French. As he falls under her influence, the two form a plan to sabotage a French supply train by climbing high up a bridge to plant dynamite. Along the way they take refuge at a brothel, where it is revealed that the cigar-smoking Sister Sara is really a prostitute disguised as a nun.

Based on a story by Budd Boetticher (who was hardly pleased with the mutilation of his original work), the film reunited Clint Eastwood with director Don Siegel, an association dating back to 1968 when Siegel directed Eastwood

in the entertaining and successful cowboy-turned-city-cop story *Coogan's Bluff.* It was Eastwood's second western after ending his association with Sergio Leone (*HANG 'EM HIGH* (1957) was the first).

Filming took place in Mexico over a four-month period, and the location shooting proved difficult for the cast, the vast majority of whom suffered various bouts of "Montezuma's Revenge." The final product met with mixed reviews, though Eastwood felt that the scene in which MacLaine had to liquor him up to the point of inebriation in order to remove an arrow presented him with his best acting to date.

Reviews were mixed, but Eastwood's presence and some exciting though overly violent action scenes resulted in a profitable venture.

TWO RODE TOGETHER Columbia, 1961, Color, 109 min, VHS. **Producers:** John Ford and Stanley Shpetner; **Director:** Ford; **Screenplay:** Frank Nugent; **Music:** George Duning; **Cinematographer:** Charles Lawton Jr.; **Editor:** Jack Murray; **Cast:** James Stewart, Richard Widmark, Shirley Jones, Linda Cristal, Andy Devine, Woody Strode, John McIntire, Paul Birch, Willis Bouchey, Henry Brandon, Harry Carey Jr., Olive Carey, Ken Curtis, Anna Lee, David Kent.

Marshal James Stewart (in his first John Ford film) and cavalry lieutenant Richard Widmark team together to help bring back people whom the Comanche had taken prisoner as children years before. Stewart—whose concern is less with the captives and more with monetary reward—explains to relatives gathered at the fort that they should not expect too much. Not surprisingly, therefore, when he and Widmark reach the Comanche camp a short time later, the captives (including silent screen star Mae Marsh) do not want to return.

They do manage to bring two captives back to white civilization: a young boy (David Kent) who is so inculcated in his Comanche identity that he kills the woman who claims him, a deed for which he is hanged; and a Spanish woman (Linda Cristal), the mistreated squaw of the Comanche chief (Woody Strode), who finds herself shunned and faced with bigotry once she is thrust into white civilization.

According to Dan Ford in *Pappy, The Life of John Ford*, his grandfather rapidly lost interest in the project, which he liked less and less as filming went on, eventually calling it "the worst piece of crap I've done in twenty years." Any lingering enthusiasm faded with the news that Ward Bond (a Ford protégé) had died from a heart attack in Dallas while watching a football game. The grief-stricken director shut down production of *Two Rode Together* to fly back to Los Angeles and make funeral arrangements.

The film was a commercial failure. With the exception of the performances by James Stewart and Linda Cristal, it was poorly received by most critics, although William Everson at least commends Ford for keeping his film "visually on the move, playing out the long dialogue scenes on horseback or against picturesque locations." *Variety* notes that while the story, based on a novel by Will Cook, provides a fairly fresh slice of sagebrush fiction that examines a relatively untapped corner of American history, "the production misfires in the process."

ULZANA'S RAID Universal, 1972, Color, 103 min, VHS, DVD. **Producers:** Harold Hecht and Burt Lancaster; **Director:** Robert Aldrich; **Screenplay:** Alan Shapre; **Music:** Frank De Vol; **Cinematographer:** Joseph Biroc; **Editor:** Michael Luciano; **Cast:** Burt Lancaster, Bruce Davison, Jorge Luke, Richard Jaeckel, Joaquin Martinez, Lloyd Bochner, Dean Smith, Larry Randles.

Ulzana, a brilliant and brutal Indian warrior, perpetrates a reign of terror against Arizona settlers as the U.S. cavalry is continually frustrated in its attempts to stop him. Therefore they employ an introspective veteran army scout named McIntosh (Burt Lancaster), who has more respect than hate for his enemy. McIntosh must mentor a green and naïve West Point lieutenant (Bruce Davison) who becomes increasingly shocked by Ulzana's bestial tactics: torturing male homesteaders to death, raping the women, and leaving a trail of mutilated corpses, causing the lieutenant's Christian values to spiral downward into blind hatred.

The film reunited Burt Lancaster with director Robert Aldrich, with whom he had worked in the 1954 film *APACHE*. In that film Lancaster had portrayed a sympathetic Apache warrior. This time all sentimentality was removed from the story. Violence and hate are pervasive in the film, as the ultimate battle of cultures is reduced to the base level of sheer survival.

Unlike *THE WILD BUNCH* (1969), in which Sam Peckinpah graphically displays horrific acts of brutality in slow motion, Aldrich leaves the violence offscreen, allowing the audience to see only the aftermath of the horror, which to some degree is even more disturbing. A particularly galling scene has some Indians cutting out a man's heart and playing catch with it. Many find the film to be compelling and powerful, a grimly realistic and fast-paced story and a testimony to man's brutal inhumanity against his fellow man. *Variety*, on the other hand, considers it "simply another exploitive western which crassly exploits the potential in physical abuse, and in which plot suspense is not what is going to happen, but how bestial it can be." Many pundits at the time likened Ulzana's tactics to the guerrilla attacks by the Viet Cong against American troops during the Vietnam War.

UNCONQUERED BANDIT, THE Reliable, 1935, B&W, 59 min. **Producer:** Bernard B. Ray; **Director:** Harry S. Webb; **Screenplay:** Lon Borden and Rose Gordon; **Cinematographer:** J. Henry Kruse; **Editor:** Frederick Bain; **Cast:** Tom Tyler, Lillian Gilmore, Slim Whitaker, William Gould, John Elliott, Earl Dwire, Joe De La Cruz, George Chesebro.

See *MYSTERY RANCH*.

UNDEFEATED, THE 20th Century Fox, 1969, Color, 119 min. **Producer:** Robert L. Jacks; **Director:** Andrew V. McLaglen; **Screenplay:** James Lee Barrett; **Music:** Hugo Montenegro; **Cinematographer:** William Clothier; **Cast:** John Wayne, Rock Hudson, Antonio Aguilar, Roman Gabriel, Marion McCargo, Lee Meriwether, Merlin Olsen, Ben Johnson, Melissa Newman, Dub Taylor, Bruce Cabot, Edward Faulkner, Harry Carey Jr., Jan-Michael Vincent, Paul Fix, Robert Donner, John Agar, Gregg Palmer, Chuck Roberson.

A Confederate colonel (Rock Hudson) sets fire to his plantation house at the end of the Civil War rather than let it fall into the hands of carpetbaggers. He sets off to Mexico with his family and a group of proud southerners who hope to start new lives and find new homes. They are saved from the attacks of Mexican bandits by a former Union colonel (John Wayne) and his adopted Cherokee son (Roman Gabriel), who have decided to take a herd of 3,000 horses into Mexico rather than allow crooked army agents to take advantage of them. The two former enemies, Hudson and Wayne, then join forces in fighting off the soldiers of Maximilian and the rebel leader Juarez. When the Mexican rebels take the Confederates prisoner, Wayne and his Union men come to their aid, sacrificing their horses to free the southerners.

Although not of the same caliber as other Andrew V. McLaglen ventures such as *MCLINTOCK!* (1963); *CHISUM* (1970), and his superb *SHENANDOAH* (1965), this big (some have called it "lumbering") production does benefit from a reliable group of character actors (many of them Wayne film regulars) and an excellent performance by Dub Taylor as the cook. Of added interest are the appearances of former Los Angeles Rams quarterback Roman Gabriel and All-Pro football star Merlin Olsen, both of whom acquit themselves quite well.

UNDER ARIZONA SKIES Monogram, 1946, B&W, 59 min. **Producer:** Scott R. Dunlap; **Director:** Lambert Hillyer; **Screenplay:** J. Benton Cheney and John McCarthy; **Cinematographer:** Harry Neumann; **Editor:** Fred Maguire; **Cast:** Johnny Mack Brown, Reno Blair, Raymond Hatton, Riley Hill, Tristram Coffin, Reed Howes, Ted Adams, Ray Bennett.

A rancher who heads an outlaw rustling gang is out to get another rancher's cattle.

After stints with Universal and Republic, in 1943 cowboy star Johnny Mack Brown signed with Monogram, where he made some 65 westerns, beginning with *The Ghost Rider* and continuing for nine years. His character name started out as "Nevada Jack McKenzie" in the Rough Riders series, but it was soon changed to "Johnny." Other Monogram ventures include *Outlaws of Stampede Pass, The Texas Kid, The Stranger from Pecos, Six-Gun Gospel* (1943); *Partners of the Trial, Law Men, Land of the Outlaws, Law of the Valley, Ghost Guns, West of the Rio Grande, Range Law, Raiders of the Border* (1944); *The*

Johnny Mack Brown lands a punch in Under Arizona Skies, *one of more than 50 features the cowboy star made for Monogram Pictures. The movie also stars Reno Blair, Raymond Hatton, Smith Ballew and the Sons of the Sage.* (MONOGRAM/AUTHOR'S COLLECTION)

Navajo Trail, Forever Yours, Gun Smoke, Flame of the West, The Lost Trail, Frontier Feud, Stranger from Santa Fe (1945); *Border Bandits, Drifting Along, The Haunted Mine, Gentleman from Texas, Silver Range, Trigger Fingers, Shadows on the Range, Raiders of the South* (1946); *Valley of Fear, Land of the Lawless, The Law Comes to Gunsight, Code of the Saddle, Flashing Guns, Prairie Express, Gun Talk, Trailing Danger* (1947); *Crossed Trails, Overland Trails, Frontier Agent, Triggerman, Back Trail, The Fighting Ranger, Sheriff of Medicine Bow, Gunning for Justice, Hidden Danger* (1948); *Law of the West, Stampede, Western Renegades, West of El Dorado, Trail's End, Range Justice* (1949); *Over the Border, Six Gun Mesa, Law of the Panhandle, Outlaw Gold, West of Wyoming, Short Grass* (1950); *Colorado Ambush, Man from Sonora, Blazing Bullets, Montana Desperado, Outlaw Justice, Whistling Hills, Texas Lawmen* (1951); *Texas City, Man From the Black Hills, Dead Man's Trail, Canyon Ambush, Man from Black Hills* (1952).

UNDER A TEXAS MOON Warner Bros., 1930, B&W, 82 min. **Director:** Michael Curtiz; **Screenplay:** Gordon Rigby; **Music:** Ray Perkins; **Cinematographer:** William Rees; **Editor:** Ralph Dawson; **Cast:** Frank Fay, Raquel Torres, Myrna Loy, Armida, Noah Beery, George E. Stone, Fred Kohler, Betty Boyd.

A Mexican adventurer and his pals romance two pretty girls at a ranch where they also plan to earn a reward by capturing the outlaws who are rustling the owner's cattle. This very early Michael Curtiz sound film features a 25-year-old Myrna Loy as south-of-the-border siren Lolita Romero.

UNDER CALIFORNIA STARS (aka: UNDER CALIFORNIA SKIES) Republic, 1948, Color, 70 min, VHS. **Producer:** Edward J. White (associate); **Director:** William Witney; **Screenplay:** Sloan Nibley; **Cinematographer:** Jack Marta; **Editor:** Anthony Martinelli; **Cast:** Roy Rogers, Jane Freeze, Andy Devine, George Lloyd, Wade Crosby, Michael Chapin, House Peters Jr., Steve Clark, Joseph A. Garro, Bob Nolan and the Sons of the Pioneers.

See *UNDER WESTERN STARS*.

UNDERCOVER MAN Republic, 1936, B&W, 57 min. **Producer:** A. W. Hackel; **Director:** Albert Ray; **Screenplay:** Andrew Benison; **Cast:** Johnny Mack Brown, Suzanne Kaaren, Ted Adams, Horace Murphy, Ed Cassidy, Frank Ball, Margaret Mann, Frank Darien, Dick Morehead, George Morrell.

UNDERCOVER MAN United Artists, 1942, B&W, 68 min. **Producer:** Harry Sherman; **Director:** Lesley Selander; **Screenplay:** J. Benton Cheney; **Music:** Irvin Talbot; **Cinematographer:** Russell Harlan; **Editor:** Carroll Lewis; **Cast:** William Boyd, Andy Clyde, Jay Kirby, Antonio Moreno, Nora Lane, Chris-Pin Martin, Pierce Lyden, Esther Estrella, John Vosper.

See *HOP-ALONG CASSIDY*.

UNDERCOVER MEN Booth Productions, 1935, B&W, 60 min. **Producers:** J. B. Booth, Arthur Gottlieb; **Director:** Sam Neufeld; **Screenplay:** Murison Dunn; **Cinematographer:** Sam Leavitt; **Editor:** Alex Meyers; **Cast:** Charles Starrett, Adrienne Dore, Kenne Duncan, Wheeler Oakman, Eric Clavering, Philip Brandon, Austin Moran, Grace Webster, Gilmore Young.

A Mountie working as an undercover agent is on the trail of an outlaw in the wilds of Canada. This Canadian-made western predates Charles Starrett's Columbia series.

UNDER FIESTA STARS Republic, 1941, B&W, 64 min. **Producer:** Harry Grey (associate); **Director:** Frank McDonald; **Screenplay:** Karl Brown and Eliot Gibbons; **Music:** Darrell Calker; Leo Erody, Albert Glasser, Mort Glickman, and Marlin Skiles; **Cinematographer:** Harry Neumann; **Editor:** Tony Martinelli; **Cast:** Gene Autry, Smiley Burnette, Carol Hughes, Frank Darien, Joe Strauch Jr., Paulene Drake, Ivan Miller, Sam Flint, Hal Taliaferro, Elias Gamboa, John Merton.

See *TUMBLING TUMBLEWEEDS*.

UNDERGROUND RUSTLERS Monogram, 1941, B&W, 57 min. **Producer:** George W. Weeks; **Director:** S. Roy Luby; **Screenplay:** Elizabeth Beecher, Bud Tuttle, and John Vlahos; **Music:** Mickey Ford; **Cinematographer:** Robert E. Cline; **Editor:** Roy Claire; **Cast:** Ray Corrigan, John "Dusty" King, Max Terhune, Gwen Gaze, Robert Blaire, Forrest Taylor, Tom London, Steve Clark.

UNDER MEXICALI STARS Republic, 1950, B&W, 67 min. **Producer:** Meville Tucker (associate); **Director:** George Blair; **Screenplay:** Bob Williams; **Music:** Stanley Wilson; **Cinematographer:** John MacBurnie; **Editor:** Harold Minter; **Cast:** Rex Allen, Dorothy Patrick, Roy Barcroft, Buddy Ebsen, Percy Helton, Walter Coy, Steve Darrell.

UNDER NEVADA SKIES Republic, 1946, B&W, 69 min. **Producer:** Edward J. White (associate); **Director:** Frank McDonald; **Screenplay:** J. Benton Cheney and Paul Gangelin; **Music:** Dale Butts; **Cinematographer:** William Bradford; **Editor:** Edward Mann; **Cast:** Roy Rogers, George "Gabby" Hayes, Dale Evans, Douglas Dumbrille, Leyland Hodgson, Tristram Coffin, Rudolph Anders, LeRoy Mason, George Lynn, Bob Nolan and the Sons of the Pioneers.

See *UNDER WESTERN STARS*.

UNDER STRANGE FLAGS Crescent, 1937, B&W, 64 min. **Producer:** F. B. Derr; **Director:** Irwin Wilt; **Screenplay:** Mary Ireland; **Cinematographer:** Arthur Martinelli; **Editor:** Donald Barratt; **Cast:** Tom Keene, Luana Walters, Budd Buster, Maurice Black, Roy D'Arcy, Paul Sutton, Paul Barrett, Donald Reed, Jane Wolfe, Anthony Quinn, Manuel Ziroga.

See *GLORY TRAIL, THE*.

UNDER TEXAS SKIES Republic, 1940, B&W, 57 min. **Producer:** Harry Grey (associate); **Director:** George Sherman; **Screenplay:** Betty Burbridge and Anthony Coldway; **Music:** Cy Feuer; **Cinematographer:** William Nobles; **Editor:** Tony Martinelli; **Cast:** Robert Livingston, Bob Steele, Rufe Davis, Lois Ranson, Henry Brandon, Wade Boteler, Rex Lease, Jack Ingram, Walter Tetley, Yakima Canutt, Earle Hodgins, Curley Dresden.

See *THREE MESQUITEERS, THE.*

UNDER THE PAMPAS MOON Fox, 1935, B&W, 78 min, VHS. **Producer:** Buddy DeSylva; **Director:** James Tinning; **Screenplay:** Bradley King and Ernest Pascal; **Music:** Arthur Lange; **Cinematographer:** Chester A. Lyons; **Editor:** Alfred DeGaetano; **Cast:** Warner Baxter, Keith Galleon, J. Carrol Naish, John Miljan, Armida, Ann Codee, Jack La Rue, George Irving, Rita Hayworth (as Rita Cansino), Tito Guizar.

A gaucho's horse is stolen by crooks who want to run him in the big race held in Buenos Aires. However, the South American cowboy heads to Buenos Aires in an attempt to get him back. The most noteworthy thing about this film is that it marked Rita Hayworth's first screen appearance.

UNDER THE TONTO RIM Paramount, 1933, B&W, 63 min. **Director:** Henry Hathaway; **Screenplay:** Jack Cunnington; **Cinematographer:** Archie Stout; **Cast:** Stuart Erwin, Raymond Hatton, Fuzzy Knight, Kent Taylor, Fred Kohler.

A slow-moving cowpoke manages to capture a murderer and win the hand of the boss's daughter. The Zane Grey story was originally filmed in 1924 as a silent movie directed by Herman Raymaker and starring Richard Arlen and Mary Brian. RKO made its version of Zane Grey's *Under Tonto's Rim* in 1947 with resident cowboy Tim Holt in the starring role and Lew Landers directing.

UNDER WESTERN SKIES Universal, 1945, B&W, 57 min. **Producer:** Warren Wilson; **Director:** Jean Yarbrough; **Screenplay:** Clyde Bruckman and Stanley Roberts; **Music:** Lloyd Ackridge, Milton Rosen, and Paul Sawtell; **Cinematographer:** Charles Van Enger; **Editor:** Arthur Hilton; **Cast:** Martha O'Driscoll, Noah Beery Jr., Leo Carrillo, Leon Errol, Irving Bacon, Ian Keith, Jennifer Holt, Edna May Wonacott.

The citizens of a small western town oppose the staging of a traveling show when it becomes known that the show's comely little lady has become involved with the town's school teacher and a masked outlaw. Some lively music and a plot more intricate than most B westerns make this little Universal oater worthy to watch. Cowriter Clyde Bruckman earlier had a part in creating some of Buster Keaton's finest films.

UNDER WESTERN STARS Republic, 1938, B&W, 65 min, VHS. **Producer:** Sol C. Siegal; **Director:** Joseph Kane; **Screenplay:** Betty Burbridge, Doral McGowan and Stuart E. McGowan; **Music:** Eddie Cherkose, Jack Lawrence, Johnny Marvin, Charles Rosoff, and Peter Tinturin; **Cinematographer:** Jack A. Marta; **Editor:** Lester Orlebeck; **Cast:** Roy Rogers, Smiley Burnette, Carol Hughes, Guy Usher, Tom Chatterton, Kenneth Harlan, Alden "Stephen" Chase.

In his first starring role, Roy Rogers plays a newly elected young congressman trying to obtain water power for the Dust Bowl. A colleague in Congress whose support he needs proves to be the pawn of a large water company that is overcharging ranchers during a drought. Roy sings "That Pioneer Mother of Mine," and Johnny Marvin's song "Dust" was nominated for an Academy Award.

A member of the original Sons of the Pioneers, Rogers made almost 100 films. When Gene Autry went on strike for more money in 1938, Republic held auditions for a replacement, and Leonard Slye rechristened Roy Rogers, got the job. *Under Western Stars* was an instant hit, and Republic retained its new star even after Autry came to terms with the studio. Rogers made eight westerns per season, playing historical figures in *BILLY THE KID* (1938); *Young Buffalo Bill, Young Bill Hickok* (1940); and *JESSE JAMES AT BAY* (1941).

Roy Rogers and Trigger, billed as "the smartest horse in the movies." The future King of the Cowboys became a big-time western star in Under Western Stars. *(REPUBLIC/ AUTHOR'S COLLECTION)*

In 1938 Rogers began riding a beautiful palomino named Golden Cloud, which had carried Olivia de Havilland in *The Adventures of Robin Hood*. He renamed the palomino Trigger for his films. He also obtained the services of grizzled long-standing sidekick George "Gabby" Hayes. When Gene Autry entered the service in 1942, Republic bought more hit songs and upped the size of its production budgets, beginning with HEART OF THE GOLDEN WEST, with Rogers backed up now by his old singing partners The Sons of the Pioneers. In 1944 he was cast opposite a feisty blond named Dale Evans in the film THE COWBOY AND THE SENORITA. Roy Rogers was now the acknowledged "King of the Cowboys," and his best-remembered series westerns for Republic included DON'T FENCE ME IN, ALONG THE NAVAJO TRAIL (1945); MY PAL TRIGGER, and ROLL ON, TEXAS MOON (1946).

By the late 1940s Rogers's films were enhanced by beautiful "True Color," although the plots and action became increasingly violent. The Sons of the Pioneers left and were replaced by Foy Willing and the Riders of the Purple Sage. When Gabby Hayes departed in 1947, a succession of sidekicks followed, including Andy Devine, Gordon Jones, and Pinky Lee. Rogers's final series western, *Pals of the Golden West*, was released in 1951. His long-running television show ran from 1951 to 1957, and he made numerous personal appearances.

The first Roy Rogers films was helmed by Joseph Kane, and director and actor teamed together for more than 40 pictures (1938–44). William Witney later directed Rogers in more than 25 features (1946–51).

Following *Under Western Stars*, Roy Rogers's films for Republic include *Shine on Harvest Moon*, BILLY THE KID RETURNS, COME ON, RANGERS (1938); *Southward Ho, Wall Street Cowboy*, ROUGH RIDERS ROUND-UP, *Jeepers Creepers, In Old Caliente*, FRONTIER PONY EXPRESS, *Day of Jesse James, Saga of Death Valley*, THE ARIZONA KID (1939); *Rodeo Dough*, THE BORDER LEGION, *Young Bill Hickok, Young Buffalo Bill, The Ranger and the Lady* (1940); *In Old Cheyenne, Meet Roy Rogers*, RED RIVER VALLEY, *Sheriff of Tombstone, Robin Hood of the Pecos, Nevada City, Jesse James at Bay*, BAD MAN OF DEAD-WOOD, ARKANSAS JUDGE (1941); *Man from Cheyenne, South of Santa Fe, Sunset on the Desert, Sunset Serenade, Sons of the Pioneers, Romance on the Range, Ridin' Down the Canyon*, HEART OF THE GOLDEN WEST (1942); *Idaho*, KING OF THE COWBOYS, *Song of Texas, Silver Spurs, Man from Music Mountain*, HANDS ACROSS THE BORDER (1943); THE YELLOW ROSE OF TEXAS, *Song of Nevada, San Fernando Valley*, LIGHTS OF OLD SANTA FE, *Lake Placid Serenade*, THE COWBOY AND THE SENORITA (1944); THE MAN FROM OKLAHOMA, ALONG THE NAVAJO TRAIL, *Utah, Sunset in El Dorado*, DON'T FENCE ME IN, BELLS OF ROSARITA (1945); *Under Nevada Skies, Song of Arizona, Roll On Texas Moon*, RAINBOW OVER TEXAS, *Out California Way*, MY PAL TRIGGER, *Home in Oklahoma, Heldorado* (1946); *Springtime in the Sierras, On the Old Spanish Trail*, BELLS OF SAN ANGELO, APACHE ROSE (1947); *The Gay Ranchero, Under California Stars, Pecos Bill, Melody Time, Night Time in Nevada*, GRAND CANYON TRAIL, EYES OF TEXAS (1948); SUSANNA PASS, DOWN DAKOTA WAY, *Twilight in the Sierras, The Golden Stallion*, THE FAR FRONTIER (1949); *Trigger Jr.,*

Formerly Leonard Slye of the Sons of the Pioneers, Roy Rogers became the movies' premier singing cowboy when Gene Autry entered military service in 1942. He made scores of lively westerns for Republic through the early 1950s. (REPUBLIC/AUTHOR'S COLLECTION)

Trail of Robin Hood, Sunset in the West, North of the Great Divide, BELLS OF CORONADO (1950); *Spoilers of the Plains, South of Caliente*, PALS OF THE GOLDEN *West, In Old Amarillo, Heart of the Rockies* (1951).

UNFORGIVEN Warner Bros., 1992, Color, 131 min, VHS, DVD, CD. **Producer:** Clint Eastwood; **Director:** Eastwood, **Screenplay:** David Webb Peoples; **Music:** Lennie Niehaus; **Cinematographer:** Jack N. Green; **Editor:** Joel Cox; **Cast:** Clint Eastwood, Gene Hackman, Morgan Freeman, Richard Harris, Jaimz Woolvett, Saul Rubbing, Frances Fisher, Anna Levine, Anna Thomson.

In the town of Big Whiskey, Wyoming, a prostitute (Anna Thomson) is mutilated, and Sheriff Little Billy Daggett (Gene Hackman) releases the perpetrators with practically no punishment. The other prostitutes post a reward for the murder of the criminals, and the bounty attracts a number of gunmen and would-be gunmen, much to Little Billy Daggett's consternation.

Reluctantly drawn into the bounty hunt is William Munny (Clint Eastwood), once a murderous outlaw, now

Clint Eastwood (left) and Morgan Freeman in Unforgiven. *Winner of four Academy Awards—Best Picture, Best Director (Eastwood), Best Supporting Actor (Gene Hackman), and Editing—the film garnered six additional Oscar nominations.* (WARNER BROS./AUTHOR'S COLLECTION)

haunted by his past. Attempting to pursue a legitimate life as a pig farmer, he runs into hard times after the death of his beloved wife. Although he has turned away from all forms of violence, he holsters up one final time in pursuit of the bounty money needed to support his two motherless children and to find the men who brutalized the prostitute. He enlists the aid of his onetime partner in crime Ned Logan (Morgan Freeman), a semiretired outlaw turned farmer himself. They are joined by a young braggart calling himself The Schofield Kid (Jaimz Woolvette), who seeks to emulate the ways of Will Munny's past.

The result is tragedy for all concerned. Munny's return to gunplay opens old psychological wounds previously held dormant. The Schofield Kid pales at the advent of real violence and falls apart physically and emotionally. Logan is killed by a vengeful Daggett, who in turn is coldly shot to death by Munny, who places the barrel of his rifle into Daggett's mouth, tells him he'll see him in hell, and blows him away. Munny returns to his family a wiser man but not necessarily a better one. A postscript notes that he moves his family to a distant location with hopes of again starting a new life far removed from the violent one he had reentered. It is

also notes that a certain former prostitute left town at about the same time, leaving a rather clear implication.

The film received many rave reviews. "A gripping and haunting work of art that should finally establish Eastwood as one of America's finest directors," Kathleen Carroll noted in the *New York Daily News. Variety's* Todd McCarthy called it ". . . a classic western for the ages. . . ." By the end of 1992, *Unforgiven* had been named one of the year's best films by more than 200 critics, and it proved one of the top-grossing films of Eastwood's career.

Unforgiven scored big at Oscar time, winning four Academy Awards: Best Picture, Best Supporting Actor (Gene Hackman), Best Director (Clint Eastwood), and Best Film Editing (Joel Cox). Nominations also went to Eastwood for Best Actor, Jack N. Green for Best Cinematography, and David Webb Peoples for Best Screenplay Written Directly for the Screen, with two more in the categories of Best Art Direction–Set Design and Best Sound.

The film is perhaps the ultimate revisionist western, and no genre work since has come close to approaching its overall excellence. The story's dark nature might not meet everyone's tastes, but few westerns have ever been crafted any better. It was Eastwood's 10th foray into a genre that had made him famous more than 25 years earlier.

UNFORGIVEN, THE United States, 1960, Color, 125 min, VHS. **Producer:** James Hill; **Director:** John Huston; **Screenplay:** Ben Maddow; **Music:** Dimitri Tiomkin; **Cinematographer:** Franz Planer; **Editor:** Russell Lloyd; **Cast:** Burt Lancaster, Audrey Hepburn, Audie Murphy; John Saxon, Charles Bickford, Lillian Gish, Albert Salmi, Joseph Weisman, June Walker, Kipp Hamilton, Arnold Merritt, Doug McClure, Carlos Rivas.

In the Texas Panhandle after Civil War, the Zacharys, a Texas family headed by Lillian Gish, struggles to raise cattle while coping with the incessant threat of hostile Indians. When suspicions start to surface that her adopted daughter Rachel (Audrey Hepburn) may be of Indian birth, she kills the messenger but cannot stop the Kiowa from trying to reclaim the girl once it becomes known that she is a full-blooded Indian. The family splits from within as son Cash (Audie Murphy is a surprisingly strong performance) refuses to defend his adopted sister and abandons the family, while eldest brother Ben (Burt Lancaster), always her protector, falls in love with his Kiowa sister.

Plots that addressed the problem of a half-breed cut off from society became a central genre theme in the 1960s. Based on Alan Le May's novel *The Siege at Dancing Bird* and filmed in Mexico, John Huston's *The Unforgiven* combines an intriguing study of human relationships with a strong share of action and adventure. Despite its enormous potential, the film met with mixed reviews and fell short at the box office. It had been beset by problems from the start. During the course of the shooting Audrey Hepburn injured her back and had a miscarriage, Audie Murphy nearly drowned, and three members of the crew died in a plane crash.

UNION PACIFIC Paramount, 1939, B&W, 136 min, VHS. **Producer:** Cecil B. DeMille; **Director:** DeMille; **Screenplay:** Jack Cunningham, Walter DeLeon, C. Gardner Sullivan, and Jesse Lasky Jr., **Music:** George Antheil, Sigmund

Barbara Stanwyck and Joel McCrea in Cecil B. DeMille's Union Pacific (PARAMOUNT/AUTHOR'S COLLECTION)

Krumgold, and John Leipold; **Cinematographer:** Victor Milner; **Editor:** Anne Bauchens; **Cast:** Barbara Stanwyck, Joel McCrea, Akim Tamiroff, Robert Preston, Lynne Overman, Brian Donlevy, Robert Barrat, Anthony Quinn, Stanley Ridges, Evelyn Keyes, Fuzzy Knight, Harry Woods, Lon Chaney Jr.

Cecil B. DeMille recreates the story of the first transcontinental railroad in epic style. Joel McCrea portrays Captain Jeff Butler, a construction foreman who tries to thwart rival Robert Preston's attempts to slow construction of the Union Pacific through theft and vice. Former friends, McCrea and Preston both vie for the affections of Mollie Monahan (Barbara Stanwyck), the Union Pacific's postmistress, who proves she can sling lead with the best of men when the going gets tough during an Indian attack.

Though not as widely acclaimed as John Ford's STAGE-COACH (1939), DeMille's *Union Pacific* was the western blockbuster of 1939. Virtually a remake of THE IRON HORSE (1924), more attention was paid to its empire-building theme, and histrionics aside, the film remains one of DeMille's crowning screen glories. Replete with action, it includes a raucous saloon brawl, merciless Indian attacks, a train smash-up in a snowbound canyon, and a final holdup and shoot-out in which Preston dies after saving McCrea's life.

Laced with DeMille's patriotic fervor and his obligatory flag-waving, *Union Pacific* was a timely film. America was slipping out of the Great Depression, fascism was dominating much of Europe and Asia, and the American public was ready to take part in a surge of national pride and progress embodied by such slices of Americana as the building of the great Union Pacific Railroad. The film was nominated for an Academy Award for Best Special Effects. William Everson has called *Union Pacific* "a good film by any standard . . . its box office potential boosted by a wave of national feeling with which it coincided in so timely a fashion." The impressive musical score also features slices of old Americana folk favorites such as "I've Been Working on the Railroad" and "My Darling Clementine."

UNKNOWN RANGER, THE Columbia, 1936, B&W, 57 min. **Producer:** Larry Darmour; **Director:** Spencer Gordon Bennet; **Screenplay:** Nate Gatzert; **Music:** Dave Ormont and Lee Zahler; **Cinematographer:** James S. Brown Jr.; **Cast:** Robert Allen, Martha Tibbets, Harry Woods, Wally Wales, "Buzz" Henry, Bob Card, Horace B. Carpenter, Allan Cavan, Oscar Gahan.

When rustlers plan to use a wild stallion to steal a rancher's horse herd, a Ranger (posing as a cowboy) working on the ranch gets wind of the plan. Wally Wales sings a novelty tune in "Ranger Bob" Allen's first series film for Columbia. (See also *LAW OF THE RANGER*.)

UNKNOWN VALLEY Columbia, 1933, B&W, 69 min. **Director:** Lambert Hillyer; **Screenplay:** Hillyer; **Cinematographer:** Allen G. Siegler; **Editor:** Clarence Kolster;

Cast: Buck Jones, Cecilia Parker, Frank McGlynn Sr., Ward Bond, Arthur Wanzer.

Buck Jones plays an ex-army scout lost in the desert while searching for his father. He is rescued by a girl belonging to a strange sect. A well-written script and that inimitable Buck Jones presence makes for an extremely impressive early 1930s oater.

UNTAMED FRONTIER Universal, 1952, Color, 78 min. **Producer:** Leonard Goldstein; **Director:** Hugo Fregonese; **Screenplay:** Gerald Drayson Adams, Gwen Bagni, John Bagni, and Polly James; **Music:** Hans J. Salter; **Cinematographer:** Charles P. Boyle; **Editor:** Virgil Vogel; **Cast:** Joseph Cotten, Shelley Winters, Scott Brady, Suzan Ball, Minor Watson.

A wealthy cattle baron employs all means necessary to prevent settlers from taking free government land he wants for his herds.

UNTAMED WEST See *FAR HORIZONS*.

UTAH Republic, 1945, B&W, 78 min, VHS. **Producer:** Donald H. Brown (associate); **Director:** John English; **Screenplay:** John K. Butler and Jack Townley; **Music:** Ken Carson, Dave Franklin, Charles Henderson, Bob Nolan, Glenn Spencer, and Tim Spencer; **Cast:** Roy Rogers, George "Gabby" Hayes, Dale Evans, Peggy Stewart, Beverly Lord, Wally Wales, Bob Nolan & The Sons of the Pioneers, Grant Withers.
See *UNDER WESTERN STARS*.

UTAH BLAINE Columbia, 1957, B&W, 75 min. **Producer:** Sam Katzman; **Director:** Fred F. Sears; **Screenplay:** James B. Gordon and Robert Kent; **Music:** Ross DiMaggio and George Duning; **Cinematographer:** Benjamin H. Kline; **Editor:** Charles Nelson; **Cast:** Rory Calhoun, Susan Cummings, Max Baer, Angela Stevens, Paul Langton, George Keymas, Ray Teal, Gene Roth, Dean Fredericks.

A rancher who is being harassed by marauders out to control the territory receives aid from a sympathetic gunman. Based on a novel by Louis L'Amour, this above-average little oater should please Rory Calhoun fans.

UTAH KID, THE Monogram, 1930, B&W, 53 min. **Producer:** William Strohbach; **Director:** Vernon Keays; **Screenplay:** Victor Hammond; **Cinematographer:** Harry Neumann; **Editors:** Ray Curtiss and John Fuller; **Cast:** Hoot Gibson, Bob Steele, Beatrice Grey, Ralph Lewis, Evelyn Eaton, Mauritz Hugo.

A U.S. marshal and his new deputy investigate a gang that has a habit of winning big events on the rodeo circuit. This little Monogram oater featuring Hoot Gibson and Bob Steele employs lots of stock footage.

UTAH TRAIL Grand National, 1938, B&W, 56 min. **Producer:** Edward Finney; **Director:** Albert Herman; **Screenplay:** Edmond Kelso and Lindsley Parsons; **Music:** Frank Sanucci; **Cinematographer:** Francis Corby; **Editor:** Frederick Bain; **Cast:** Tex Ritter, Horace Murphy, "Snub" Pollard, Pamela Blake, Karl Hackett, Charles King, Ed Cassidy, Dave O'Brien, Bud Osborne. See *SONG OF THE GRINGO*.

UTAH WAGON TRAIN Republic, 1951, B&W, 67 min. **Producer:** Melville Tucker (associate); **Director:** Philip Ford; **Screenplay:** John K. Butler; **Music:** Stanley Wilson and Rex Allen; **Cinematographer:** John MacBurnie; **Editor:** Edward H. Schroeder; **Cast:** Rex Allen, Penny Edwards, Buddy Ebsen, Roy Barcroft, Sarah Padden, Grant Withers, Arthur Space.

V

VALDEZ IS COMING United Artists, 1971, Color, 90 min, VHS, DVD. **Producer:** Ira Steiner; **Director:** Edward Sherin; **Screenplay:** Roland Kibbee and David Rayfiel; **Music:** Charles Gross; **Cinematographer:** Gabor Pogany; **Editors:** James T. Heckert and George Rohrs; **Cast:** Burt Lancaster, Susan Clark, Frank Silvera, Jon Cypher, Richard Jordan, Barton Heyman, Hector Elizondo.

Burt Lancaster is Bob Valdez, a Mexican-American ex-constable who now makes his living riding shotgun on a stagecoach. He kills a black man as the result of a calculated plan designed by a cruel cattleman who wanted the man dead. When Valdez tries to collect money for the man's Indian widow, he is tortured by the cattleman's henchmen. Escaping, he becomes a self-appointed lawman with the gunmen in hot pursuit. One by one he takes them out, exacting revenge on murder and racial injustice.

Based on the Elmore Leonard novel about an ethnic southwestern constable who accidentally kills a suspected murderer, this film made in Spain marked Edward Sherin's first film directorial effort after years as a stage director. *Variety* found the debut to be "unimpressive," calling the film "a sluggish [melodrama which] collapses from [the] premise of a man attempting to right a wrong, to reels of boring mayhem." Ted Sennett notes in his *Great Hollywood Westerns* that in attempting to touch all minority bases (black, Mexican, Indian), "the movie diffused rather than expanded its impact."

VALERIE United Artists, 1957, B&W, 84 min. **Producer:** Hal L. Makelim; **Director:** Gerd Oswald; **Screenplay:** Leonard Heideman and Emmett Murphy; **Music:** Albert Glasser; **Cinematographer:** Ernest Laszlo; **Editor:** David Bretherton; **Cast:** Sterling Hayden, Anita Ekberg, Peter Walker, John Wengraf, Iphigenie Castiglioni, Jerry Barclay, Robert Barclay.

When a man's wife is wounded and her parents are murdered, the ensuing trial becomes a confusing affair. However, the wife finally unravels the puzzle by testifying to a nightmarish marriage, constant brutality, and her unreasonable suspicion against a minister who had befriended her in her misery.

VALIANT HOMBRE United Artists, 1948, B&W, 60 min. **Producer:** Philip N. Krasne; **Director:** Wallace Fox; **Screenplay:** Adele Buffington; **Music:** Albert Glasser; **Cinematographer:** Ernest Miller; **Editor:** Martin Cohn; **Cast:** Duncan Renaldo, Leo Carrillo, John Litel, Barbara Billingsley, Stanley Andrews.

VALLEY OF FEAR Monogram, 1947, B&W, 54 min. **Producer:** Charles J. Bigelow; **Director:** Lambert Hillyer; **Screenplay:** J. Benton Cheney; **Cinematographer:** Harry Neumann; **Editor:** Roy Livingston; **Cast:** Johnny Mack Brown, Christine McIntyre, Ed Cassidy, Tristram Coffin, Ted Adams, Steve Darrell, Pierce Lyden, Eddie Parker, Cactus Mack, Robert O'Byrne.

See *UNDER ARIZONA SKIES*.

VALLEY OF FIRE Columbia, 1951, B&W, 70 min. **Producer:** Armand Schaefer; **Director:** John English; **Screenplay:** Gerald Geraghty; **Cinematographer:** William Bradford; **Editor:** James Sweeney; **Cast:** Gene Autry, Pat Buttram, Gail Davis, Russell Hayden, Christine Larsen, Harry Lauter, Terry Frost.

See *TUMBLING TUMBLEWEEDS*.

VALLEY OF FURY See *CHIEF CRAZY HORSE*.

VALLEY OF HUNTED MEN Republic, 1942, B&W, 60 min. **Producer:** Louis Grey (associate); **Director:**

John English; **Screenplay:** Albert DeMond and Morton Grant; **Music:** Mort Glickman; **Cinematographer:** Bud Thackery; **Editor:** William P. Thompson; **Cast:** Bob Steele, Tom Tyler, Jimmie Dodd, Edward Von Sloan, Roland Varno, Anna Marie Stewart, Rand Brooks, Budd Buster, Kermit Maynard.

See *THREE MESQUITEERS, THE.*

VALLEY OF TERROR Ambassador, 1937, B&W, 59 min. **Producer:** Maurice Conn; **Director:** Al Herman; **Screenplay:** James Oliver Curwood; **Cast:** Kermit Maynard, Harley Wood, John Merton, Jack Ingram, Hank Bell, Dick Curtis, Frank McCarroll.

VALLEY OF THE LAWLESS Supreme, 1936, B&W, 56 min. **Producer:** A. W. Hackel; **Director:** Robert N. Bradbury; **Screenplay:** Bradbury and Charles F. Royal; **Cinematographer:** Bert Longenecker; **Editor:** S. Roy Luby; **Cast:** Johnny Mack Brown, Joyce Compton, George "Gabby" Hayes, Frank Hagney, Dennis Moore.

VALLEY OF THE SUN RKO, 1942, B&W, 78 min. **Producer:** C. Graham Baker; **Director:** George Marshall; **Screenplay:** Horace McCoy; **Music:** Paul Sawtell; **Cinematographer:** Harry J. Wild; **Editor:** Desmond Marquette; **Cast:** Lucille Ball, James Craig, Cedric Hardwick, Dean Jagger, Peter Witney, Bill Gilbert, Tom Tyler, Antonio Moreno, Iron Eyes Cody, Stanley Andrews, Tom London.

In the Arizona Territory a government agent poses as a renegade Indian scout to learn the malevolent intentions of a crooked Indian agent. An interesting bit of casting has Tom Tyler in the role of Geronimo.

VALLEY OF VENGEANCE PRC, 1944, B&W, 57 min. **Producer:** Sigmund Neufeld; **Director:** Sam Newfield; **Screenplay:** Jack Greenhalgh; **Editor:** Holbrook N. Todd; **Cast:** Buster Crabbe, Al St. John, Evelyn Finley, Jack Ingram, Glenn Strange, Lynton Brent, Donald Mayo, David Polonsky, Bud Osborne.

See *OUTLAW OF THE PLAINS.*

VALLEY OF WANTED MEN Conn Pictures, 1942, B&W, 62 min. **Producer:** Maurice Conn; **Director:** Alan James; **Screenplay:** Forrest Barnes and Barry Barringer; **Cinematographer:** Arthur Reed; **Editor:** Richard G. Wray; **Cast:** Frankie Darro, Grant Withers, Drue Leyton, LeRoy Mason, Russell Hopton, Paul Fix, Walter Miller.

Frankie Darro plays a young man who tries to bring peace to his hometown, a community populated by outlaws with prices on their head, in this film based on the story *All for Love* by Peter B. Kyne.

VANISHING AMERICAN, THE Republic, 1955, B&W, 90 min. **Producer:** Herbert J. Yates; **Director:** Joseph Kane; **Screenplay:** Alan Le May; **Music:** R. Dale Butts; **Cin-**ematographer: John L. Russell; **Editor:** Richard L. Van Enger; **Cast:** Scott Brady, Audrey Totter, Forrest Tucker, Gene Lockhart, Jim Davis, John Dierkes, Gloria Castillo.

This remake of George B. Seitz's venerable silent picture, relating the history of the West from prehistoric times to the present, strays from the original plot of the Zane Grey novel on which it is based. Instead it tells the story of a land war in New Mexico, where whites and Navajo Indians band together to thwart the unholy ambitions of white land grabbers and their renegade Apache allies. Richard Dix starred in the 1925 original, which is looked upon as one of the last of the silent genre epics.

VANISHING FRONTIER Paramount, 1932, B&W, 65 min. **Producer:** Sam Jaffe; **Director:** Phil Mason; **Screenplay:** Stuart Anthony; **Cinematographer:** James S. Browne; **Cast:** Johnny Mack Brown, Evalyn Knapp, ZaSu Pitts, Ben Alexander, Wallace MacDonald, George Irving, Raymond Hatton, J. Farrell MacDonald.

An American residing in Old California tries to aid officials to stop military abuse in Johnny Mack Brown's last preseries western film feature. Unable to land the plum leading man roles he had hoped for, the former All-American football star found steady work and enduring genre fame as a B western movie hero. Ben Alexander, who in the 1950s became Jack Webb's partner in both the movie and TV series productions of *Dragnet*, is cast as Lucien Winfield.

VANISHING OUTPOST, THE Western Adventures Productions, 1951, B&W, 56 min. **Producer:** Ron Ormond; **Director:** Ormond; **Screenplay:** Alexander White; **Music:** Walter Greene; **Cinematographer:** Ernest Miller; **Editor:** Hugh Winn; **Cast:** Lash La Rue, Al St. John, Riley Hill, Sue Hussey, Bud Osborne, Sharon Hall, Clark Stevens, Lee Morgan, Ted Adams.

See *LAW OF THE LASH.*

VANISHING RIDERS Spectrum, 1935, B&W, 58 min. **Producer:** Ray Kirkwood; **Director:** Bob Hill; **Screenplay:** Oliver Drake; **Cinematographer:** Bill Hyers; **Editor:** Holbrook Todd; **Cast:** Bill Cody, Ethel Jackson, Bill Cody Jr., Wally Wales, Donald Reed, Budd Buster, Roger Williams, Ace Cain, Colin Chase.

A cowboy and his young pal set out to round up a rustling gang, which has been terrorizing ranchers. The main point of interest here is the teaming of Bill Cody and son Bill Cody Jr.

VANISHING WESTERNER, THE Republic, 1950, B&W, 60 min. **Producer:** Melville Tucker (associate); **Director:** Philip Ford; **Screenplay:** Bob Williams; **Music:** Stanley Wilson; **Cinematographer:** Ellis W. Carter; **Editor:** Richard L. Van Enger; **Cast:** Monte Hale, Paul Hurst, Aline Towne, Roy Barcroft, Arthur Space, Richard Anderson, William Phipps, Dan Haggerty, Dick Curtis, Rand Brooks, Edmund Cobb, Harold Goodwin.

VENGEANCE OF RANNAH Reliable, 1936, B&W, 56 min. **Producer:** Bernard B. Ray; **Director:** Ray (as Raymond Samuels); **Screenplay:** Joseph O'Donnell; **Cinematographer:** Paul Ivano; **Editor:** Holbrook N. Todd; **Cast:** Bob Custer, Victoria Vinton, Ed Cassidy, Eddie Phillips, Oscar Gahan, Roger Williams.

When an insurance detective investigates a stagecoach robbery, he finds the driver murdered and the man's dog holding the clue to the killing.

VENGEANCE OF THE WEST Columbia, 1942, B&W, 61 min. **Producer:** Leon Barsha; **Director:** Lambert Hillyer; **Screenplay:** Luci Ward; **Cinematographer:** George Meehan; **Editor:** Burton Kramer; **Cast:** Bill "Wild Bill" Elliott, Tex Ritter, Frank Mitchell, Adele Mara, Dick Curtis, Robert Fiske, Ted Mapes, Guy Wilkerson.

When his family is murdered, Joaquin Murietta (Bill Elliott) begins raiding gold shipments, eventually teaming up with a ranger (Tex Ritter) who has been sent to capture him. Together they try to stop the gang that was responsible for the killing. The most memorable scene has Elliott receiving a vigorous lashing from the bad guys; the grimaces on his face are very convincing.

This feature was the last in Columbia's series costarring Bill Elliott and Tex Ritter. The other seven series entries include *Roaring Frontiers, King of Dodge City* (1941); *Bullets for Bandits, Devil's Trail, Lone Star Vigilantes, North of the Rockies,* and *Prairie Gunsmoke* (1942).

VENGEANCE VALLEY MGM, 1951, Color, 83 min, VHS, DVD. **Producer:** Nicholas Nayfack; **Director:** Richard Thorpe; **Screenplay:** Irving Ravetch; **Music:** Rudolph G. Kopp; **Cinematographer:** George J. Fosley; **Editor:** Conrad A. Nervig; **Cast:** Burt Lancaster, Robert Walker, Joanne Dru, Sally Forrest, John Ireland, Carlton Carpenter, Ray Collins, Ted de Corsia, Hugh O'Brian.

Robert Walker is the no-good son of a rich cattle baron, and Burt Lancaster is the good foster son who tries to protect him until the venal Walker turns on him. Some great cattle sequences appear in this wide-screen take of cattle ranchers coping with jealousy and family pathology while trying to work their herd. Based on a novel by Luke Short, the film is set in the range country of the Rockies.

VERA CRUZ United Artists, 1954, Color, 94 min. **Producers:** James Hill Harold Hecht, and Burt Lancaster; **Director:** Robert Aldrich; **Screenplay:** Roland Kibbee and James R. Webb; **Cinematographer:** Ernest Laszlo; **Editor:** Alan Crosland, Jr.; **Cast:** Gary Cooper, Burt Lancaster, Denise Darcel, Cesar Romero, Sarita Montiel, George Macready, Jack Elam, Ernest Borgnine, James McCallion, Morris Ankrum.

Gary Cooper and Burt Lancaster are two American adventurers who join forces during the Mexican revolution of 1866, fighting for whichever side pays them more. Nina (Sarita Montiel), an idealistic peasant girl, falls for Trane (Cooper) and implores the two to fight for the rebels. The Marquis de Labordere (Cesar Romero), an aide to the Emperor Maximilian, asks them to fight on his side.

While attending a ball in the Chapultepec Palace, the two adventurers meet the beautiful countess Marie Duvarre (Denise Darcel), and they agree to escort her on the arduous journey to Vera Cruz. In time she confesses that she is actually transporting a gold shipment to the emperor's forces. A little later, however, she agrees to steal the gold and split it with the Americans. Overhearing the plan, the marquis flees with the gold, but Trane and his unprincipled pal Erin (Lancaster) storm the fort, with Erin getting the gold. The saucy Nina succeeds in convincing Trane that the gold rightfully belongs to the people, forcing a final showdown with Erin. Trane is forced to kill his erstwhile pal, who has become consumed with greed.

Lancaster was willing to take second billing to the venerable Cooper in order to get box-office punch from Cooper's name and to have a strong actor play opposite him. Enhanced by Ernest Laszlo's stunning photography and Hugo Friedhofer's stirring musical score (Sammy Cahn penned the lyrics for the title song), the film received high marks from audiences but less than enthusiastic reviews from critics. Some critics and film scholars consider *Vera Cruz* a veritable blueprint for the Italian spaghetti westerns of the 1960s.

VIGILANTE HIDEOUT Republic, 1950, B&W, 60 min. **Producer:** Gordon Kay (associate); **Director:** Fred C. Bannon; **Screenplay:** Richard Wormser; **Music:** Stanley Wilson; **Cinematographer:** John MacBurnie; **Editor:** Robert M. Leeds; **Cast:** Allan Lane, Eddy Waller, Roy Barcroft, Virginia Heroic, Cliff Clark, Don Haggerty, Paul Campbell, Guy Teague, Art Dillard.

See *BOLD FRONTIERSMAN, THE.*

VIGILANTES OF BOOMTOWN Republic, 1947, B&W, 56 min. **Producer:** Sidney Picker (associate); **Director:** R. G. Springsteen; **Screenplay:** Earle Snell; **Cinematographer:** Alfred Keeler; **Editor:** William P. Thompson; **Cast:** Allan Lane, Robert Blake, Martha Wentworth, Roscoe Karns, Roy Barcroft, Peggy Stewart, George Turner, Eddie Lou Simms, George Chesebro, John Dehner.

See *ADVENTURES OF RED RYDER, THE.*

VIGILANTES OF DODGE CITY Republic, 1944, B&W, 54 min. **Producer:** Stephen Auer (associate); **Director:** Wallace Grissell; **Screenplay:** Anthony Coldeway and Norman S. Hall; **Music:** Joseph Dubin; **Cinematographer:** William Bradford; **Editor:** Charles Craft; **Cast:** William "Wild Bill" Elliott, Robert Blake, Alice Fleming, Linda Fleming, LeRoy Mason, Wally Wales, Tom London, Steve Barclay, Kenne Duncan, Robert J. Wilke, Bud Geary.

See *ADVENTURES OF RED RYDERS, THE.*

VIGILANTES RETURN, THE (aka: RETURN OF THE VIGILANTES, UK) Columbia, 1943, B&W, 56 min. **Producer:** Howard Welsch; **Director:** Ray Taylor; **Screenplay:** Roy Chanslor; **Music:** Jack Brooks and Milton Schwarzwald (songs); **Cinematographer:** Virgil Miller; **Editor:** Paul Landres; **Cast:** Jon Hall, Margaret Lindsay, Andy Devine, Paula Drew, Robert Wilcox, Jack Lambert, Jonathan Hale, Arthur Hohl, Jon Hart.

A marshal who is sent to a frontier town to investigate a rash of murders is caught up in a murder himself.

VIGILANTES RIDE, THE Columbia, 1944, B&W, 55 min. **Producer:** Leon Barsha; **Director:** William Berke; **Screenplay:** Ed Earl Repp; **Cinematographer:** Benjamin Kline; **Cast:** Russell Hayden, Dub Taylor, Bob Wills, Shirley Patterson, Tristram Coffin, Jack Rockwell, Bob Kortman.

Russell Hayden leaves the Arizona Rangers when his younger brother is killed by outlaws. He pretends to become a bandit in order to infiltrate and bring in the gang that he holds responsible. This better-than-average Hayden venture benefits from the music of Bob Wills and the Texas Playboys as well as a fine array of genre bad guys.

VIGILANTE TERROR Allied Artists, 1953, B&W, 70 min. **Producer:** Vincent Fennelly; **Director:** Lewis B. Collins; **Screenplay:** Sidney Theil; **Music:** Raoul Kraushaar; **Cinematographer:** Ernest Miller; **Editor:** Sam Fields; **Cast:** William "Wild Bill" Elliott, Mary Ellen Kay, Myron Healey, Fuzzy Knight, I. Stanford Jolley, Henry Rowland, George Wallace, Denver Pyle.

When masked vigilantes pull of a successful gold hijacking and blame it on an innocent storekeeper, a cowboy comes to his defense. Nothing new in the plot, but Bill Elliott's manly presence and adept acting makes for a worthwhile B effort.

VILLA! 20th Century Fox, 1958, Color, 72 min. **Producer:** Plato A. Skouras; **Director:** James B. Clark; **Screenplay:** Louis Vittes; **Music:** Ken Darby, Margia Dean, Walter Kent, Lionel Newman, Paul Sawtell, Bert Shefter, and Tom Walton; **Cinematographer:** Alex Phillips; **Editor:** Benjamin Laird; **Cast:** Brian Keith, Cesar Romero, Margia Dean, Rodolfo Hoyos Jr., Carlos Muzquiz, Ben Wright, Elisa Loti, Enrique Lucero, Rosenda Monteros, Mario Navarro, Jose Espinoza.

Pancho Villa (Rodolfo Hoyos Jr.) is simply a young playboy desperado until he witnesses the government's excesses backing oppressive landowners against the peons. As he is egged on by his sadistic lieutenant (Cesar Romero), he becomes more determined in his quest to stifle brutal oppression. He is joined by an American gunrunner (Brian Keith), who persuades him to join the forces of Francisco Madero, the leader of the revolution. Hoyos delivers a good performance in the title role in yet another example of an appealing adventure film that at best is faulty history.

VILLAIN, THE Columbia, 1979, Color, 93 min, VHS, DVD. **Producer:** Mort Engleberg; **Director:** Hal Needham; **Screenplay:** Robert G. Kane; **Music:** Bill Justice; **Cinematographer:** Bobby Byrne; **Editor:** Walter Hannemann; **Cast:** Kirk Douglas, Ann-Margret, Arnold Schwarzenegger, Paul Lynde, Foster Brooks, Ruth Buzzi, Jack Elam, Strother Martin, Ray Bickel, Robert Tessier, Mel Tillis, Laura Lizer Sommers.

A live-action spoof on the cartoon series *The Roadrunner*, this film has a cast of characters with names like Cactus Jack (Kirk Douglas), Charming Jones (Ann-Margret), and Handsome Stranger (Arnold Schwarzenegger) playacting their way through a loose plot, less-than-glib dialogue, a number of one-liners, and a few zany gags. The plot has Handsome Stranger escorting Miss Charming Jones to get a large sum of money from her father Parody Jones (Strother Martin). The wealthy Jones hires old cowboy Cactus Jack to rob them, but the evil Jack proves himself to be an inept robber.

In his 1978 autobiography *The Ragman's Son*, Douglas recalls how he used the same name for his horse in this 1979 satire as that of his beautiful palomino Whiskey in his favorite film *LONELY ARE THE BRAVE* (1962). "We got a joke out of it. I walk into a saloon, pound on the bar, demand 'Whiskey!'—and my horse ambles through the swinging door." Nevertheless, according to *Variety*, "Rarely has so much talent been used to so little purpose."

VILLA RIDES Paramount, 1968, Color, 125 min. **Producer:** Ted Richmond; **Director:** Buzz Kulik; **Screenplay:** Sam Peckinpah and Robert Towne; **Music:** Maurice Jarre; **Cinematographer:** Jack Hildyard; **Editor:** David Bretherton; **Cast:** Yul Brynner, Robert Mitchum, Charles Bronson, Maria Grazia Buccello, Bob Carricart.

Yul Brynner stars as Mexican revolutionary leader Pancho Villa. He is aided in his fight by a murderous lieutenant named Ferro (Charles Bronson), who kills as many as 300 prisoners at a time. Robert Mitchum is a freelance aviator who uses his rickety plane to sell guns to counterrevolutionary forces, but when captured by Villa he becomes a one-man air force under Villa's command.

This film was released shortly after the assassination of Bobby Kennedy. Critics who felt that excessive violence would not play well to audiences were quite wrong. The screenplay by Sam Peckinpah and Robert Towne is in part an orgy of bloodletting, where the good guys are every bit as murderous as the villains. Yet the film, shot in Spain, is an uneven attempt to capitalize on the Villa legend while shortchanging the historical wealth of the real story.

VIOLENT MEN, THE Columbia, 1955, Color, 95 min. **Producer:** Lewis J. Rachmil; **Director:** Rudolph Mate; **Screenplay:** Harry Kleenex; **Music:** Max Steiner;

Cinematographer: W. Howard Greene and Burnett Guffey; **Editor:** Jerome Thomas; **Cast:** Glenn Ford, Barbara Stanwyck, Edward G. Robinson, Dianne Foster, Brian Keith, May Wynn, Warner Anderson, Basil Ruysdael, Lita Milan, Richard Jaeckel, James Westerfield, Jack Kelly, Willis Bouchey.

Edward G. Robinson is Lew Wilison, owner of the Anchor Ranch, who carved an empire out of pure wilderness and battled Indians with his bare hands before becoming a cripple and being confined to a wheelchair. His duplicitous wife, played by Barbara Stanwyck, is having a long-term affair with his brother (Brian Keith).

Trouble begins with the arrival of John Parish (Glenn Ford), an ex-Civil War cavalry man turned pacifist bent on selling his property to Wilison and heading east. But the more he learns the more he becomes increasingly aware that Wilison's men are employing terror against the smaller ranchers, stampeding their property and murdering their ranch hands. In response, Parish employs the guerrilla tactics he learned during the war to lead the small ranchers to ultimate victory over Wilison's hired thugs. A twist at the end places Parish and Wilison on the same side against Wilison's two-timing wife and devious brother.

Nearly perfectly cast, with an excellent performance by Richard Jaeckel as venal hired gun Wade Matlock, this compelling CinemaScope production combines an interesting story line with some exciting action scenes and a hefty degree of sexual tension. Max Steiner's musical score is of almost symphonic proportion.

VIOLENT ONES, THE

VIOLENT ONES, THE   Feature Film Corporation of America, 1967, Color, 84 min. **Producer:** Robert Stabler; **Director:** Fernando Lamas; **Screenplay:** Charles Davis and Doug Wilson; **Music:** Marlin Skiles; **Cinematographer:** Fleet Southcott; **Editor:** Fred W. Berger; **Cast:** Fernando Lamas, Aldo Ray, Tommy Sands, David Carradine, Lisa Gaye, Melinda Marx Gaye, Melinda Marx.

The sheriff of a small New Mexico town runs into trouble with its Mexican population when three men are arrested as suspects in the rape and murder of a young woman. A joint USA-Argentina production, this independent film with some recognizable names (Fernando Lamas, Aldo Ray, Tommy Sands) and a modern-day western setting touches on such late-1960s themes as rape, lynching, and prejudice.

VIRGINIA CITY

VIRGINIA CITY   Warner Bros., 1940, B&W, 118 min, VHS. **Producer:** Hal Wallis; **Director:** Michael Curtiz; **Screenplay:** Robert Buckner; **Music:** Max Steiner; **Cinematographer:** Sol Polito; **Editor:** George Amy; **Cast:** Errol Flynn, Miriam Hopkins, Randolph Scott, Humphrey Bogart, Frank McHugh, Alan Hale, Guinn "Big Boy" Williams, John Litel, Douglas Dumbrille, Moroni Olsen, Dickie Jones, Charles Middleton, Ward Bond, Lane Chandler, Paul Fix.

Michael Curtiz's Civil War follow-up to *DODGE CITY* (1939) has Errol Flynn as a Union officer who escapes from a Confederate prison camp. Making his way to Virginia City, Nevada, he finds that the former commander of the prison camp (Randolph Scott) is planning to send $5 million in gold to stir up a rebel uprising in a last-ditch attempt to save the Confederacy. Flynn's mission now is to see that the gold never reaches Confederate hands. Along the way he fights off Mexican outlaw Humphrey Bogart (in a paper-thin moustache and a weak Spanish accent) and beautiful rebel spy Miriam Hopkins, who is out to set a trap for him, thus forcing him to put patriotism before love. Alan Hale and Guinn "Big Boy" Williams are terrific as Flynn's raucous and affable sidekicks; and Flynn, Hopkins, and Scott are effective as participants in the predictable romantic triangle.

Like Curtiz's two other Errol Flynn Westerns (*Dodge City* and *SANTA FE TRAIL*, 1940), *Virginia City* is an action-packed adventure bustling with excitement—a bit short on historical accuracy, perhaps, but a real pleasure to watch. Inserted into Max Steiner's melodic score are such musical slices of Americana as "Battle Hymn of the Republic," sung by townsmen in Virginia City; "The Battle Cry of Freedom," sung by Miriam Hopkins and the chorus girls in the saloon; "Oh Susanna"; and "We Will Hang Jeff Davis from a Sour Apple Tree," sung to the tune of "Battle Hymn of the Republic" by Union troops and Northern sympathizers in Virginia City. Charles Middleton, best known as Ming the Merciless in the *Flash Gordon* series, is featured as Jefferson Davis.

VIRGINIAN, THE

VIRGINIAN, THE   Paramount, 1929, B&W, 91 min, VHS. **Producer:** Louis D. Lighton; **Director:** Victor Fleming; **Screenplay:** Howard Easterbrook; **Music:** Karl Hajos, John Leipold, and Leo Robin; **Cinematographer:** J. Roy Hunt and Edward Cronjager; **Editor:** William Shea; **Cast:** Gary Cooper, Walter Huston, Richard Arlen, Mary Brian, Chester Conklin, Eugene Pallette, E. H. Calvert, Helen Ware, Tor Potel, Tex Young, Charles Stevens, Jack Pennick, George Chandler, Randolph Scott.

In this film based on the play by Owen Wister and Kirk La Shelle, Gary Cooper is the Virginian, foreman of the Box H Ranch, who gives his old buddy Steve (Richard Arlen) a job. Soon thereafter the two pals meet Molly Wood (Mary Brian), the new schoolteacher from Vermont, and both take a fancy to her. Later the Virginian meets the nefarious Trampas (Walter Huston) at a local saloon, and the two clash over a dancing girl.

The years of bantering and friendship between Steve and the Virginian start unraveling when the Virginian catches Steve putting Trampas's brand on Box H stock. Believing that his friend has repented his act, the Virginian admonishes him only with a warning. But when a posse of ranchers seize Steve and two other rustlers in the act, the Virginian is forced to oversee the hanging of the three men. Knowing that Trampas is behind their deeds, the Virginian swears vengeance.

When Mary learns that the Virginian participated in Steve's hanging, she initially spurns him. However, when he is wounded by Trampas she nurses him back to health, and they affirm their love for each other. On their wedding day,

Dustin Farnum in The Virginian, *an early silent version of the Owen Wister classic. This 1914 film was a pioneering western for Cecil B. DeMille, and it remains one of the most advanced features of its time.* (PARAMOUNT/AUTHOR'S COLLECTION)

Randolph Scott, a Virginia native and an uncredited extra in the film, worked with Cooper to get the proper accent required of a Virginian. The movie was helmed with gusto by Victor Fleming, and two future front-line directors also had a hand in it: Henry Hathaway, who later worked with Cooper in many films served as Fleming's assistant; and Joseph Mankiewicz, who wrote all the transition titles, which were still employed even though sound had already arrived. While Owen Wister's story is set at the Box H Ranch near Medicine Bow, Wyoming, actual filming was done on location near Sonora and the High Sierras.

The Virginian solidified Cooper's reign as one of the screen's most popular and enduring leading men. Paramount reissued *The Virginian* in 1935 by popular demand. The original play by Wister and La Shelle opened in New York on January 5, 1904, and ran for 138 performances.

VIRGINIAN, THE Paramount, 1946, Color, 90 min, VHS. **Producer:** Paul Jones; **Director:** Stuart Gilmore; **Screenplay:** Frances Goodrich and Albert Hackett; **Music:** Daniele Amfitheatrof; **Cinematographer:** Harry Hallenberger; **Editor:** Everette Douglas; **Cast:** Joel McCrea, Sonny Tufts, Brian Donlevy, Barbara Britton, Fay Bainter, Tom Tully, Henry O'Neill.

For the 1946 remake of *The Virginian*, Paramount cast Joel McCrea in the title role, with Sonny Tufts (in possibly his best role) as his errant pal Steve, whom he is forced to hang. The story remains basically intact: a romance with enough shooting and suspense to keep things from moving too slowly, as the schoolmarm from Vermont and the cowboy from Virginia meet and wed, but not until the hero has disposed of the evil Trampas (Brian Donlevy) and his gang of rustlers.

Trampas comes to town and orders the Virginian to leave by sundown. The two shoot it out on a dusty western street. Trampas dies, felled by the Virginian's fast-drawn gun. Molly rushes to the Virginian's arms, and the two are free to love one another forever.

Most memorable is a card-playing scene during which the Virginian is insulted by the words "When I want to know anything from you, I'll tell you, you long-legged son of a——." The Virginian responds by laying his gun on the table and saying, "If you want to call me that, smile." (The line has often been misquoted as, "When you call me that, smile.") Included in the soundtrack are the traditional children's songs "Pop Goes the Weasel," played at the dance; "Three Blind Mice," sung by the children in school; and the traditional western ballad "Bury Me Not on the Lone Prairie."

The Virginian was Gary Cooper's first all-talking picture and the third film version of the Owen Wister classic. Dustin Farnum was the first Virginian in 1914, followed shortly by Kenneth Harlan in 1923. It was remade in 1946 with Joel McCrea (see below). In 1962 it was adapted into a weekly 90-minute television series with James Drury, which ran until 1970. Finally in 1999 it became a TNT original movie directed by and starring Bill Pullman.

Joel McCrea and Sonny Tufts star in the 1946 remake of The Virginian. (PARAMOUNT/AUTHOR'S COLLECTION)

McCrea delivers well in the title role, following in the able footsteps of Dustin Farnum and Gary Cooper. The adaptation benefits from the use of color, resplendent costumes of the eastern 1870s, early-style railroads, and the rolling Montana hills, each element adding to the film's nostalgic flavor. Critics generally favor the Cooper version, but genre fans should not be deterred from enjoying this entry as well.

VIVA CISCO KID   20th Century Fox, 1940, B&W, 65 min. **Producer:** Sol M. Wurtzel; **Director:** Norman Foster; **Screenplay:** Samuel G. Engel and Hal Long; **Cinematographer:** Charles G. Clarke; **Editor:** Norman Colbert; **Cast:** Cesar Romero, Jean Rogers, Chris-Pin Martin, Minor Watson, Stanley Fields, Francis Ford, Charles Jules.

The Cisco Kid (Cesar Romero) and sidekick Gordito (Chris-Pin Martin) rescue a stagecoach from a robbery attempt. When Cisco falls for one of the passengers (Jean Rogers), it turns out that the girl's father is involved in a crime with a vicious partner who plans to kill him. Cisco prevents the crime from occurring and sees to it that the villain's career comes to an abrupt end. (See also *CISCO KID, THE.*)

VIVA VILLA   MGM, 1934, B&W, 115 min, VHS. **Producer:** David O. Selznick; **Director:** Jack Conway; **Screenplay:** Ben Hecht; **Music:** Herbert Stothart; **Cinematographer:** Charles G. Clark and James Wong Howe; **Editor:** Robert Kern; **Cast:** Wallace Beery, Leo Carillo, Fay Wray, Donald Cook, Stuart Erwin, Henry B. Walthall, Joseph Schildkraut, Katharine De Mille, George E. Stone.

Young Pancho Villa takes to the hills after he kills the overseer responsible for the death of his father. In 1910, with American reporter Johnny Sykes as the intermediary, he meets with Father Francisco Madero and is transformed from an avenging bandit to a revolutionary general.

From the time the young Villa watched his father being whipped by soldiers, he has seethed with anger toward the rich landowners who control Mexico. He earns the praise and support of the downtrodden peasants by robbing from the landowners and distributing some of the booty to the poor. But while Villa's rebels sweep to victory, internal rivalries lead to dissension and murder.

Filmed on location in Mexico, *Viva Villa* was among the first Hollywood films to undertake prolonged, full-scale, first-unit location filming in foreign lands. It was also an early indication of the Hollywood view of Mexican politics. The film was initially directed by Howard Hawks, but then his friend Jack Conway took the helm, reportedly as a result of a rift between Hawks and MGM chief Louis Mayer. According to Hawks biographer Todd McCarthy, the director later said, "It could have really been one hell of a picture. I tried to make a strange man, humorous but vicious, out of Villa, as he was in real life, but Conway's version had Wallace Beery playing Santa Claus."

Wallace Beery's performance in the title role presents a complex man, at once childish, romantic, patriotic, and excessively brutal, which according to *Variety* makes Villa "a somewhat sympathetic and quasi-patriotic bandit." The film garnered an Academy Award for John Waters as Best Assistant Director and three additional Oscar nominations, including Best Picture. The Venice Film Festival also nominated director Jack Conway for its Mussolini Cup. (Benito Mussolini was the Fascist dictator of Italy at the time and Hitler's ally during World War II.) Included in the soundtrack of this fictionalized biography is the song "La Cucaracha," sung by the chorus at intervals throughout the film, and the tune of which is heard as Villa's victorious armies sweep into Mexico City.

WACO Monogram, 1952, B&W, 68 min. **Producer:** Vincent M. Fennelly; **Director:** Lewis Collins; **Screenplay:** Dan Ullman; **Music:** Raoul Kraushaar; **Cinematographer:** Ernest Miller; **Editor:** Sam Fields; **Cast:** William "Wild Bill" Elliott, I. Stanford Jolley, Pamela Blake, Paul Fierro, Rand Brooks, Richard Avonde, Pierce Lyden, Ian Bradford, Terry Frost, Stanley Price.

After he kills a dishonest man in a fair fight, a man is denied a fair trial, but he manages to escape and is forced to go on the run. A literate script and Bill Elliott's sturdy presence make for an engrossing B western. Monogram was then in the process of changing itself into Allied Artists, and it had begun concentrating on a better movie product. One such endeavor was an intelligent and interesting series starring Bill Elliott that provided an excellent blend of good action and well-written scripts. Other Bill Elliott films in the series include *The Longhorn* (1951), *Kansas Territory* (1952), and *Fargo* (1952).

WACO Paramount, 1966, Color, 85 min. **Producer:** A. C. Lyles; **Director:** R. G. Springsteen; **Screenplay:** Steve Fisher; **Music:** Jimmy Haskell; **Cinematographer:** Robert Pittack; **Editor:** Bernard Matis; **Cast:** Howard Keel, Jane Russell, Brian Donlevy, Wendell Corey, Terry Moore, John Smith, John Agar, Gene Evans, Richard Arlen, Ben Cooper, De Forrest Kelley, Anne Seymour, Fuzzy Knight, Robert Lowery, Willard Parker, Jeff Richards.

Howard Keel plays a psychologically tormented man torn between his violent past, his love for a woman, and a new-found faith in God. Tension abounds when he is hired to bring peace to a Wyoming community and finds his ex-girl-friend (Jane Russell) married to the local preacher (Wendell Corey).

Once again producer A. C. Lyles assembled an all-star cast of mainly fading veteran stars to make this rudimentary little western a cut above the average oater. The film was helmed by veteran director R. G. Springsteen, who after years as an assistant director began directing Wild Bill Elliott and Allan "Rocky" Lane westerns for Republic in 1945.

WAGON MASTER RKO, 1950, B&W, 86 min, VHS. **Producers:** Merian C. Cooper and John Ford; **Director:** Ford; **Screenplay:** Patrick Ford and Frank S. Nugent; **Music:** Richard Hageman and Stan Jones (songs); **Cinematographer:** Bert Glennon; **Editor:** Jack Murray; **Cast:** Ben Johnson, Joanne Dru, Harry Carey Jr., Ward Bond, Charles Kemper, Alan Mowbray, Jane Darwell, Ruth Clifford, Russell Simpson, Kathleen O'Malley, James Arness, Francis Ford, Jim Thorpe, Hank Worden, Cliff Lyons.

A group of Mormons led by Elder Jonathon Wiggs (Ward Bond) hires two young horse traders named Travis and Sandy (Ben Johnson and Harry Carey Jr.) to lead a disparate group of people beyond the San Juan River and into Utah. Along the way they are joined by a wagon troupe of traveling actors and a family of hardened outlaws called the Cleggs, who are running away from a posse.

Reportedly this small-scale classic, filmed on a low budget of $500,000, was John Ford's favorite film. It has a basic simplicity and a poetic symmetry at its core that escapes most other feature films. Ford incorporates Bert Glennon's black-and-white photography along with a bevy of traditional western folk songs and hymns—including four musical entries provided by ex-forest ranger Stan Jones, who a few years earlier had written the popular hit song "Ghost Riders in the Sky." Ford conveys the essence of the pioneer experience in a series of lyrical images with repeated views of wagons etched into the majestic background of a western sky.

Ben Johnson and Joanne Dru in John Ford's Wagon Master *(RKO/ARGOSY/AUTHOR'S COLLECTION)*

first picture company ever in Mohab, Utah. Some people associate Monument Valley with *Wagon Master*, but it wasn't. . . . There was just one motel . . . a lot of the guys stayed at rented houses. There was a big catering company called Anderson. They came up here and built these marvelous tin cities with wooden floors. It was called an Anderson Camp. That was where the crew stayed and where the Navajo stayed."

A gem of a motion picture, *Wagon Master* has received much praise over the years. William Everson in his *A Pictorial History of the Western Film* considers it one of the finest A westerns ever produced and, along with Henry King's THE GUNFIGHTER (1950) and Delmer Daves' BROKEN ARROW (1950), one of the three best westerns to come out of the 1950s. Everson calls *Wagon Master* "a lovely, leisurely movie full of romanticized reincarnation of the pioneer

Reputed to be the best horseman in Hollywood, Ben Johnson, a World Rodeo champion and John Ford protégé, won a Best Supporting Actor Oscar for his excellent work in The Last Picture Show *(1971). He took great pride in being the "only cowboy to ever win an Academy Award."* (AUTHOR'S COLLECTION)

The feeling of community, so endemic in Ford's films, is seen most everywhere in this one, particularly in a sequence where Mormon pilgrims dance to a tune called "Chukaswanna Swing." Later they join in a dance with the Indians, the disparate groups circling around a fire. Despite some bursts of violence (the Cleggs are a brutal lot), the Mormons manage to defy outlaws, hostile Indians, and errant nature along the way. When they finally reach the "the promised land," having won over adversity, their faces glow in happiness and relief.

As wagon master Travis Blue, future Oscar winner Ben Johnson carries off one of his few lead roles with a quiet aplomb, and according to *Variety* he "sits in his saddle mighty easily and gives the same kind of performance, natural and likeable." He receives capable assistance from cohort Harry Carey Jr. as Sandy, his hotheaded sidekick (the emerging friendship between the two young actors would last until Johnson's death nearly 50 years later). Both agree, however, that it was Ward Bond as the Mormon elder who walked away with acting laurels. Bond would later play the role of the wagon master in the hit TV series *Wagon Train* (1957–65).

Actor Harry Carey Jr. believes that John Ford enjoyed making *Wagon Master* more than any picture before or since. As he relates in *White Hats and Silver Spurs*, "*Wagon Master* was just a fabulous film and a great experience. We were the spirit, all beautiful images and stirring ballads . . . a fond nostalgic look backwards." Similarly, the *New York Times* reviewed the film as "a trip well worth taking." *Wagon Master* remains a must-see film for both fans and students of the western genre.

WAGON MASTER, THE
Universal, 1929, B&W, 70 min. **Producer:** Ken Maynard; **Director:** Harry Joe Brown; **Cinematographer:** Ted G. McCord; **Editor:** Fred Allen; **Cast:** Ken Maynard, Edith Roberts, Tom Santschi, Jack Hanlon, Al Ferguson, Bobby Dunn, Frank Rice, Frederick Dana, Chief Whitehorse.

In what is basically a silent movie with some talking sequences, Ken Maynard plays a character called the Rambler, who joins a wagon train and then takes over command when its leader is killed. The tag line reads, "See Ken Maynard's First Talking Picture," and it proved that the great cowboy star could adapt to sound.

WAGONS EAST
Carolco/Outlaw, 1994, Color, 106 min, VHS. **Producers:** Gary Goodman, Barry Rosen, and Robert Newmeyer; **Director:** Peter Markle; **Screenplay:** Mathew Carlson; **Music:** Michael Small; **Cinematographer:** Frank Tidy; **Editor:** Scott Conrad; **Cast:** John Candy, Richard Lewis, John C. McGinley, Robert Picardo, Ellen Greene, William Sanderson.

John Candy plays a disgruntled wagon-train master who finds a chance to regain his sobriety and self-respect by leading a band of alienated frontier settlers back east. The vastly overweight Candy died on the set of this film, whose only merit is in showing how low the western spoof had sunk since the days of *SUPPORT YOUR LOCAL SHERIFF* (1969), *BLAZING SADDLES* (1974), and the more serious *SILVERADO* (1985) in the 1960s, 1970s, and 1980s.

Wagons East is an appalling slice of ultra-politically correct hogwash. *Variety* calls it a "woeful outing," noting that "the dialogue and characters' neuroses are insistently contemporary, with colloquialisms and '90s urban lingo cascading out of everyone's mouth." The silly plot has happy-go-lucky Indians escorting a group of disillusioned palefaces out of their territory, only to be vehemently opposed by the big-money rail interests who fear bad publicity if word of the malcontents gets around. This is not just a poor film; it is not a very funny one either.

WAGONS WEST
Monogram, 1952, Color, 70 min. **Producer:** Vincent Fennelly; **Director:** Ford Beebe; **Screenplay:** Dan Ullman; **Music:** Marlin Skyles; **Editor:** Walter Hannnemann; **Cast:** Rod Cameron, Noah Beery Jr., Peggie Castle, Michael Chapin, Henry Brandon, Sara Haden, Frank Ferguson, Anne Kimbell, Wheaton Chambers, Riley Hill, Effie Laird, I. Stanford Jolley, Glenn Strange.

A wagon master leading a group of passengers westward from Missouri discovers that some of them are selling guns to the Indians. Part of a Rod Cameron series for Monogram, this average oater contains lots of stock footage from *Fort Osage*, another 1952 Cameron/Monogram entry.

WAGONS WESTWARD
Republic, 1940, B&W, 69 min. **Producer:** Armand Schaefer (associate); **Director:** Lew Landers; **Screenplay:** Harrison Jacobs and Joseph Moncure March; **Cinematographer:** Ernest Miller; **Editor:** Ernest J. Nims; **Cast:** Chester Morris, Anita Louise, Ona Munson, Buck Jones, George "Gabby" Hayes, Guinn "Big Boy" Williams, Douglas Fowley, John Gallaudet.

Twin brothers grow up on opposite sides of the law. The dishonest one is being protected by a crooked sheriff, but when he is eventually arrested, the honest brother takes his place in order to round up the remainder of his gang. Chester Morris does a nice job in a dual role, while audiences will have a rare opportunity to see Buck Jones on the wrong side of the law.

WAGON TEAM
Columbia, 1952, B&W, 61 min. **Producer:** Armand Schaefer; **Director:** George Archainbaud; **Screenplay:** Gerald Geraghty; **Cinematographer:** William Bradford; **Editor:** James Sweeney; **Cast:** Gene Autry, Pat Buttram, Gail Davis, Dickie Jones, Gordon Jones, Harry Harvey, Henry Rowland, George J. Lewis, Pierce Lyden, John L. Cason.

WAGON TRACKS WEST
Republic, 1943, B&W, 55 min. **Producer:** Louis Grey (assistant); **Director:** Howard Bretherton; **Screenplay:** William Lively; **Music:** Mort Glickman; **Cinematographer:** Reggie Lanning; **Editor:** Charles Craft; **Cast:** William "Wild Bill" Elliott, George "Gabby" Hayes, Tom Tyler, Anne Jeffreys, Rick Vallin, Robert Frazer, Roy Barcroft, Charles F. Miller, Tom London, Cliff Lyons, Hank Bell, Fred Burns.

When a crooked Indian agent tries to cheat the Pawnee out of their land, a cowboy comes to the tribe's aid. However, he runs into opposition from a medicine man as well as the agent, who has been providing the "bad water" that is being used as an excuse to take over the land for grazing. The teaming of Bill Elliott and Gabby Hayes (who was soon to become Roy Rogers's sidekick) provides top-notch B western entertainment.

WAGON TRAIL
Ajax, 1935, B&W, 55 min. **Producer:** William Berke; **Director:** Harry Fraser; **Screenplay:** Monro Talbot; **Cinematographer:** Robert E. Cline; **Editor:** Arthur A. Brooks; **Cast:** Harry Carey, Gertrude Messenger, Edward Norris, Roger Williams, Earl Dwire, Chuck Morrison, John Elliott, Chief Thundercloud.

Harry Carey plays a lawman coming to the aid of his gambler son when the young man is falsely accused of murder.

WAGON TRAIN
RKO, 1940, B&W, 62 min. **Producer:** Bert Gilroy; **Director:** Edward Killy; **Screenplay:**

Morton Grant; **Music:** Paul Sawtell; **Cinematographer:** Harry J. Wild; **Editors:** Frederic Knudtson and Harry Marker; **Cast:** Tim Holt, Ray Whitley, Emmett Lynn, Martha O'Driscoll, Malcom "Bud" McTaggart, Cliff Clark, Ellen Lowe.

In his first series film for RKO, Tim Holt is the young owner of a wagon train who becomes the target of the operator of a trading post who killed his father and wants to buy his business. The film is not just the first of Holt's RKO series but also among his best—although it might have been originally written with George O'Brien in mind. With World War II brewing, the patriotic O'Brien had left the RKO lot to serve in the U.S. Navy. (See also *ALONG THE RIO GRANDE*.)

WAGON WHEELS   Paramount, 1934, B&W, 56 min. **Producer:** Harold Hurley; **Director:** Charles Barton; **Screenplay:** Carl A. Bass, Jack Cunningham, and Charles Logan; **Music:** Billy Hill and John Leipold; **Cinematographer:** William C. Mellor; **Cast:** Randolph Scott, Gail Patrick, Billy Lee, Monte Blue, Raymond Hatton, Jan Duggan, Leila Bennett, Olin Howard.

In this film based on Zane Grey's *Fighting Caravans*, three scouts lead a band of settlers westward to Oregon while a half-breed tries to stop them in order to preserve his fur-trade business. A good entry in Paramount's early Zane Grey series, the film is a remake of Gary Cooper's 1931 film *FIGHTING CARAVANS*. Much of the stock footage of the original feature is used in this production.

WAGON WHEELS (1943)   See *KANSAN, THE*.

WAGON WHEELS WESTWARD   Republic, 1945, B&W, 56 min. **Producer:** Sidney Picker (associate); **Director:** R. G. Springsteen; **Screenplay:** William Bradford; **Editor:** Fred Allen; **Cast:** William "Wild Bill" Elliott, Robert Blake, Alice Fleming, Linda Stirling, Roy Barcroft, Emmett Lynn, Dick Curtis, Jay Kirby.

See *ADVENTURES OF RED RYDER, THE*.

WALKING HILLS, THE   Columbia, 1949, B&W, 78 min. **Producers:** Harry Joe Brown and Randolph Scott; **Director:** John Sturges; **Screenplay:** Alan Le May; **Music:** Arthur Morton; **Cinematographer:** Charles Lawton; **Editor:** William Lyon; **Cast:** Randolph Scott, Ella Raines, William Bishop, Edgar Buchanan, Arthur Kennedy, John Ireland, Jerome Courtland, Josh White, Russell Collins.

As this film opens in a Mexican border town, several men accidentally stumble on some information pointing to the desert location of a 100-year-old wagon train loaded with gold bullion. Joined by a beautiful woman (Ella Raines), they set out for Death Valley in search of the gold. As the film progresses the psychological backgrounds of each character are revealed, and hatred develops among the men. Among the crosscurrents of greed and gold, there is the obligatory

romantic triangle, which helps establish the sharp human conflicts slowly evolving within the intriguing plot.

Randolph Scott, William Bishop, Edgar Buchanan, and Arthur Kennedy deliver outstanding performances in this overlooked and underrated western assisted by the steady, skillful helming of John Sturges. As he does so well Sturges explores the theme of characters trapped in a hostile environment, from which violent confrontation offers the only escape.

WALK LIKE A DRAGON   Paramount, 1960, B&W, 95. **Producer:** James Clavell; **Director:** Clavell; **Screenplay:** Clavell and Daniel Mainwaring; **Music:** Paul Dunlap; **Cinematographer:** Loyal Griggs; **Editor:** Howard A. Smith; **Cast:** Jack Lord, Nobu McCarthy, James Shigeta, Mel Tormé, Josephine Hutchinson, Rodolfo Acosta, Benson Fong.

A man who saves a young Chinese girl from prostitution takes her to his home town, where she is predictably snubbed by the townsfolk. The plot centers on an interracial romantic triangle consisting of a tall, strapping American (Jack Lord); a proud, rebellious Chinese (James Shigeta); and a frail slave girl (Nobu McCarthy). Produced, directed, and coscripted by best-selling author James Clavell (*Shogun, Tai-Pan, Brother Rat*), the film is unusual for its day in boasting a Chinese gunfighter and for the offbeat casting of singer/songwriter Mel Tormé as the gun-totin', scripture-spoutin' deacon.

WALK TALL (1957)   See *TALL STRANGER, THE*.

WALK TALL   20th Century Fox, 1960, Color, 50 min. **Producer:** Maury Dexter; **Director:** Dexter; **Screenplay:** Joseph Fritz; **Music:** Dick Aurandt; **Cinematographer:** Floyd Crosby; **Editor:** Eddie Dutko; **Cast:** Willard Parker, Joyce Meadows, Kent Taylor, Russ Bender, Dave DePaul, Felix Locher.

An army captain (Willard Parker) brings in a cocky gunman and Indian killer (Kent Taylor) whose irresponsible behavior seems likely to instigate an Indian uprising.

WALK THE PROUD LAND (aka: APACHE AGENT)   Universal, 1956, Color, 89 min, VHS. **Producer:** Aaron Rosenberg; **Director:** Jesse Hibbs; **Cinematographer:** Harold Lipstein; **Editor:** Sherman Todd; **Cast:** Audie Murphy, Anne Bancroft, Pat Crowley, Charles Drake, Tommy Rall, Robert Warwick, Jay Silverheels, Eugene Mazzola, Anthony Caruso.

Audie Murphy plays John P. Clum, an honest Indian agent who is trapped between Geronimo's Apache, the U.S. Army, and land-grabbing pioneers. To bring peace he sets out to capture Geronimo and engineer his surrender. Matters are compounded when Apache squaw Anne Bancroft takes a fancy to him. Jay Silverheels, better known as Tonto of *Lone*

Ranger fame, plays Geronimo in this engrossing Audie Murphy venture.

WANDA NEVADA United Artists, 1979, Color, 109 min, VHS. **Producers:** Neal Dobrofsky and Dennis Hackin; **Director:** Peter Fonda; **Screenplay:** Hackin; **Music:** Ken Lauber; **Cinematographer:** Michael Butler; **Editor:** Scott Conrad; **Cast:** Peter Fonda, Brooke Shields, Fiona Lewis, Luke Askew, Ted Markland, Henry Fonda, Severn Darden.

A cowboy (Peter Fonda) wins an orphaned girl (Brooke Shields) in a poker game, and together they set out to the Grand Canyon looking for gold. However, they are pursued by a gang looking for the same loot. The film marks Peter Fonda's directorial debut and is the only time he and father Henry Fonda worked together in a movie. The elder Fonda appears as a grizzled gold prospector.

WANDERER OF THE WASTELAND Paramount, 1924, B&W, 5775 feet. **Producer:** Lucien Hubbard; **Director:** Irvin Willat; **Screenplay:** George C. Hull and Victor Irvine; **Cinematographer:** Arthur Ball; **Cast:** Jack Holt, Noah Beery, Kathlyn Williams, George Irving, Billie Dove, James Mason, Richard R. Neill, James Gordon, William Carroll, Willard Cooley.

Mining engineer Adam Larey (Jack Holt) wanders into the desert alone, distraught because he thinks he has killed his brother, but an old prospector (Noah Beery) helps him survive. He finds his sweetheart's parents in the desert, where her father has virtually imprisoned her mother because of his obsessive jealousy. After some misunderstandings, Adam reunites with his sweetheart Ruth Virey (Billie Dove), and with his brother, who is alive after all.

Wanderer of the Wasteland, an adaptation of the 1923 Zane Grey novel, is most notable for being the first screen western (and first feature film) shot entirely in color. Paramount used this film to test an early Technicolor process, feeling that the extra cost was justified because there was always a movie audience for Grey's work and because the story is set partially in Arizona's Painted Desert and California's Death Valley. Unfortunately, this is one of many silent westerns now considered lost. (See also *WANDERER OF THE WASTELAND* [1937].)

WANDERER OF THE WASTELAND Paramount, 1935, B&W, 62 min. **Producer:** Harold Hurley; **Director:** Otho Lovering; **Screenplay:** Stuart Anthony; **Cinematographer:** Ben Reynolds; **Editor:** Everette Douglas; **Cast:** Dean Jagger, Gail Patrick, Edward Ellis, Monte Blue, Bennie Baker, Buster Crabbe, Trixie Friganza, Raymond Hatton, Fuzzy Knight, Charles Waldon Sr., Jim Thorpe, Anna Q. Nillson, Stanley Andrews.

A man who mistakenly thinks he killed his brother in an argument heads to the desert, where he falls in love with a pretty girl. The first of two sound versions of the original Grey novel stars Dean Jagger as Adam Larey.

WANDERER OF THE WASTELAND RKO, 1945, B&W, 67 min. **Producer:** Herman Schlom; **Directors:** Edward Killy and Wallace Grissell; **Screenplay:** Norman Houston; **Music:** Paul Sawtell; **Cinematographer:** Harry J. Wild; **Editor:** J. B. Whittredge; **Cast:** James Warren, Audrey Long, Richard Martin, Robert Barrett, Robert Clarke, Harry Woods, Minerva Urecal, Henry D. Brown, Tommy Cook, Harry McKim, Jason Robards Sr.

When his father is killed, a young man grows up vowing revenge on the murderer and spends years searching for the culprit. RKO made this second talking version of *Wanderer of the Wasteland* as part of its Zane Grey series. It is almost a complete rewrite of the original Grey story.

WANDERERS OF THE WEST Monogram, 1941, B&W, 58 min. **Producer:** Robert Emmett Tansey (as Robert Emmett); **Director:** Robert Hill; **Screenplay:** Tansey (as Robert Tansey); **Cinematographer:** Jack Young; **Editor:** Fred Bain; **Cast:** Tom Keene, Betty Miles, Sugar Dawn, Slim Andrews, Tom Seidel, Stanley Price, Gene Alsace, Tom London.

Tom Keene poses as a wanted man as he searches for the cattle rustler who killed his father. His only clue is the name "Westy Mack." Along the way he befriends a man who turns out to be the person he is trailing. (See also *WHERE TRAILS DIVIDE.*)

WANTED: DEAD OR ALIVE Monogram, 1951, B&W, 58 min. **Producer:** Vincent M. Fennelly; **Director:** Thomas Carr; **Screenplay:** Clint Johnson; **Cinematographer:** Ernest Miller; **Editor:** Sam Fields; **Cast:** Whip Wilson, Fuzzy Knight, Jim Bannon, Christine McIntyre, Leonard Penn, Lane Bradford.

See *ABILENE TRAIL.*

WAR ARROW Universal, 1953, Color, 78 min, VHS. **Producer:** John W. Rogers; **Director:** George Sherman; **Screenplay:** John Michael Hayes; **Cinematographer:** William H. Daniels; **Editor:** Frank Gross; **Cast:** Maureen O'Hara, Jeff Chandler, Suzan Ball, Noah Beery Jr., Charles Drake, Henry Brandon, Dennis Weaver, Jay Silverheels.

As the Kiowa threaten to overrun their Seminole neighbors, the U.S. cavalry sends a soldier to train the Seminole to fight their traditional enemy. The unusual aspects of this otherwise average oater are its Indian-versus-Indian plot and its pro-Native American theme, which was a bit ahead of its time. Jeff Chandler, who had scored so well two years earlier in his Oscar-nominated performance as Cochise in Delmer Daves's *BROKEN ARROW* (1950), plays Major Howard Brady, the cavalry officer who advises the Seminole.

WAR DRUMS United Artists, 1957, Color, B&W, 75 min. **Producer:** Howard W. Koch; **Director:** Reginald Le Borg; **Screenplay:** Gerald Grayson Adams; **Cinematographer:** William Marguiles; **Editor:** John A. Bushelman; **Cast:**

Whip Wilson (left) in Wanted: Dead or Alive (MONOGRAM/AUTHOR'S COLLECTION)

Lex Barker, Joan Taylor, Ben Johnson, Larry Chance, Richard H. Cutting, John Pickard, James Parnell, Jeanne Carmen, Tom Monroe, Mauritz Hugo.

At the start of the Civil War the Apache go on the warpath when gold seekers invade their lands and a cavalry officer is assigned to stop the trouble.

WARLOCK 20th Century Fox, 1959, Color, 122 min, VHS, DVD. **Producer:** Edward Dmytryk; **Director:** Dmytryk; **Screenplay:** Robert Allen Arthur; **Music:** Leigh Harline; **Cinematographer:** Joe MacDonald; **Editor:** Jack W. Holmes; **Cast:** Henry Fonda, Richard Widmark, Anthony Quinn, Dorothy Malone, Dolores Michaels, Wallace Ford, Tom Drake, Richard Arlen, DeForest Kelley, Regis Toomey, Vaughn Taylor, Don Beddoe, Whit Bissell, Bartlett Robinson.

When top frontier marshal Clay Blaisdel (Henry Fonda) comes to the town of Warlock to protect it, he also expects a share of the town's graft and privileges. Deputy Johnny Gannon (Richard Widmark), himself a former outlaw, is now dedicated to a peaceful life and has the support of the townspeople when it comes to cleaning up Warlock of its lawless elements. This includes getting rid of the new marshal and his neurotic, clubfooted, gambling sidekick Tom Morgan (Anthony Quinn). To compound matters Deputy Gannon is seeing a lot of Lillie Dollar (Dorothy Malone), an ex-mistress of Morgan's who hates both Morgan and Blaisdel for having shot the man she had intended to marry.

In yet another minor variation on the *High Noon* theme, when the chips are down the men of Warlock back their deputy when he is forced to confront the villains. Although the plot and subplots are a bit convoluted, this psychological western benefits from top performances by its three frontline stars. Henry Fonda delivers yet another marvelously understated performance as Blaisdel, the melancholy gunslinger with a killer reputation, a man forced to confront his personal demons and his entire value structure. With the passing years Fonda's screen work only seemed to grow richer. His place in the genre was now fully secured, and the actor was equally at home in all aspects of the western. *Warlock* marked Fonda's return to 20th Century Fox after a

12-year hiatus from the studio. Interestingly, he had second billing after Richard Widmark.

WAR OF THE WILDCATS   See *IN OLD OKLAHOMA.*

WAR PAINT   United Artists, 1953, Color, 89 min. **Producer:** Howard W. Koch; **Director:** Lesley Selander; **Screenplay:** Martin Berkeley and Richard Allen Simmons; **Music:** Arthur Lange and Emil Newman; **Cinematographer:** Gordon Avil; **Editor:** John F. Schreyer; **Cast:** Robert Stack, Joan Taylor, Charles McGraw, Keith Larson, Peter Graves, Robert W. Wilke, Walter Reed, John Douchette, Douglas Kennedy, Charles Nolte, James Parnell.

Lieutenant Billings (Robert Stack) is the hardened commanding officer of an army company entrusted to deliver a peace treaty to the Indian commissioner. If the treaty is not received in nine days, Chief Gray Cloud will go to war. The Chief's son Taslik (Keith Larson) offers to guide them, but as the water supply dwindles and internal conflicts escalate, the commissioner is murdered and Taslick begins to don his warpaint. The song "Elaine," written by Emil Newman with lyrics by Johnny Lehmann, is sung by the cast and chorus.

WAR PARTY   20th Century Fox, 1965, B&W, 73 min. **Producer:** Hal Klein; **Director:** Lesley Selander; **Screenplay:** William Marks and George Williams; **Music:** Richard LaSalle; **Cinematographer:** Gordon Avil; **Editor:** John F. Schreyer; **Cast:** Michael T. Milker, Davey Davison, Donald Barry, Laurie Monk, Dennis Robertson, Charles Horvath, Guy Wilkerson, Michael Carr, Fred Krone.

A cavalry patrol headed by a tough sergeant (Don "Red" Barry) and a veteran scout (Michael T. Milker) rides through Indian country to deliver a message that will prevent a massacre. Along the way they pick up the daughter (Davey Davison) of a missionary. By the time they deliver the message, only the girl and the scout have survived the ride.

WARPATH   Paramount, 1951, Color, 95 min. **Producer:** Nat Holt; **Director:** Byron Haskin; **Screenplay:** Frank Gruber; **Music:** Paul Sawtell; **Cinematographer:** Ray Rennahan; **Editor:** Philip Martin; **Cast:** Edmond O'Brien, Dean Jagger, Forrest Tucker, Harry Carey Jr., Polly Bergen, James Millican, Wallace Ford, Paul Fix, Monte Blue.

Edmond O'Brien is John Vickers, a man on a quest for revenge. After he hunts down one of the three men who had killed his sweetheart, the dying miscreant tells him that his accomplices have joined the cavalry. Therefore Vickers, a former officer, also joins up. Filmed on location in Montana, this unheralded western set against the backdrop of Custer's Last Stand has enough plot twists and action to commend. Future Oscar winner Edmond O'Brien gives an excellent early performance.

WAR WAGON, THE   Universal/Batjac Production, 1967, Color, 101 min, VHS, DVD. **Producer:** Marvin Schwartz; **Director:** Burt Kennedy; **Screenplay:** Clair Huffaker; **Music:** Dimitri Tiomkin; **Cinematographer:** William H. Clothier; **Editor:** Harry Gerstad; **Cast:** John Wayne, Kirk Douglas, Howard Keel, Robert Walker Jr., Keenan Wynn, Bruce Cabot, Joanna Barnes, Valora Noland, Bruce Dern, Gene Evans, Sheb Wooley, Terry Wilson, Don Collier.

Antagonists Taw Jackson (John Wayne) and Lomax (Kirk Douglas) join together to liberate a shipment of gold bullion from the claws of villain Frank Pierce (Bruce Cabot), the man who stole Wayne's ranch and gold mine and then framed him into a jail sentence. The double-dealing Lomax, who had shot Jackson five years ago, has been offered $12,000 by Pierce to kill Taw Jackson, but he realizes that he can make more profit from robbing the war wagon carrying the gold. The menacing wagon is actually an early version of an armored car, complete with a revolving turret and a Gatling gun.

Director Burt Kennedy allowed Wayne and Douglas to play off each other with maximum efficiency in this solid western of the old school. Although the two men were miles apart on social and political issues, there was genuine mutual respect for each other as acting professionals, and according to Kennedy the two got along well. Screen heavyweights Wayne and Douglas also costarred in Otto Preminger's 1965 war drama *In Harm's Way* and in Melville Shavelson's 1966 film *Cast a Giant Shadow.*

Nevertheless, Kennedy had his hands full with the project and especially with Wayne, who by this time in his career did not like to take direction from any director other than John Ford and to a lesser degree from "old eagles" like Howard Hawks and Henry Hathaway. As Kennedy told the author in a 1995 interview, "I had such a rough time with Duke in *War Wagon.* He was going to begin *The Green Berets.* Some people were asking if I'd like to direct him in *The Green Berets.* I told them other things being equal, I'd rather *join* the Green Berets."

John Wayne and Kirk Douglas (with Joanna Barnes) are unlikely colleagues in Burt Kennedy's The War Wagon. (UNIVERSAL/AUTHOR'S COLLECTION)

Based on Clair Huffaker's novel *Badmen* and adapted by the author into a good screenplay, *War Wagon* was filmed in fall 1966 and released in May 1967. It did well at the box office and was the 16th top-grossing film for 1967. Over all, the reviews tended to be favorable. Arthur Knight in *Saturday Review* found it "a bit like the Western of old, with action all the way. . . ." In a similar vein *Variety* praised the film's scripting and performances, calling *War Wagon* "an entertaining, exciting western drama of revenge, laced with action and humor. . . ." The title song is written by the award-winning team of Dimitri Tiomkin and Ned Washington.

WATERHOLE #3 (aka: WATERHOLE THREE, UK) Paramount, 1967, Color, 95 min, VHS. **Producer:** Joseph Steck; **Director:** William Graham; **Screenplay:** Steck and R. R. Young; **Music:** Dave Grusin; **Cinematographer:** Robert Burks; **Editor:** Warren Low; **Cast:** James Coburn, Carroll O'Connor, Margaret Blye, Claude Akins, Timothy Carey, Bruce Dern, Joan Blondell, James Whitmore, Harry Davis.

Three Confederate soldiers rob the Union army of a fortune in gold and bury it at a deserted waterhole. After a gambler obtains a map showing the location of the buried loot, what follows is a series of well-crafted adventures and misadventures that tickle the funnybone. Then-popular singer/songwriter Roger Miller is the uncredited narrator, and onetime front-line star Joan Blondell is cast as Lavinia, the cathouse madam. *Variety* has called *Waterhole #3* "a slow moving deliberate oater comedy blending satire, slapstick and double entendre dialogue for laughs." The title song, "The Ballad of Waterhole #3," was written by the team of Dave Grusin (music) and Robert Wells (lyrics).

WATER RUSTLERS Grand National, 1939, B&W, 54 min. **Producer:** Don Lieberman; **Director:** Samuel Diege; **Screenplay:** Arthur Hoerl; **Music:** Milton Drake, Walter Kent, and Alfred Sherman; **Cinematographer:** Mack Stengler; **Editor:** Guy V. Theyer Jr.; **Cast:** Dorothy Page, Dave O'Brien, Stanley Price, Leonard Trainor, Vince Barnett, Edward Gordon, Warner P. Richmond, Ethan Allen, Edward Peil Sr., Lloyd Ingraham, Merill McCormick.

When a woman rancher discovers that a crooked land owner is diverting water from the valley and her cattle are dying, she and her foreman try to set matters straight. This is the initial entry for a short-lived series starring Dorothy Page; the last two were *Ride 'Em Cowgirl* and *The Singing Cowgirl* (1939).

WAY OF A GAUCHO 20th Century Fox, 1952, Color, 88 min. **Producer:** Phillip Dunne; **Director:** Jacques Tourneur; **Screenplay:** Dunne; **Music:** Sol Kaplan; **Cinematographer:** Harry Jackson; **Editor:** Robert Fritch; **Cast:** Rory Calhoun, Gene Tierney, Richard Boone, Hugh Marlowe, Everette Sloane, Enrique Chaico.

Set and filmed in Argentina and filmed there as well, *Way of a Gaucho* tells the story of a likable gaucho (Rory Calhoun) in

the 1870s who resents the intrusion of civilization and its restrictions on his pristine homeland. Forced to choose service in the army rather than serve a jail sentence, he deserts and organizes a band of outlaws whose aim is to hold back the railroad. The head of the police (Richard Boone)—also his commanding officer in the army—makes it a personal mission to bring him in. With most of his friends gone and his men scattered, he realizes that he must now yield to progress and turns himself in. The police officer is contrite and leaves him to marry the beautiful society girl (Gene Tierney) with whom he has fallen in love.

The pleasant plot line is short on substance, and romance rules the day. The scenery and photography are absolutely breathtaking and evocative, with stunning vistas of the pampas and the snow-capped Andes shot in magnificent color.

WAY OF THE WEST, THE First Division/Superior, 1934, B&W, 52 min. **Producer:** Robert Emmett (Tansey); **Director:** Emmett; **Screenplay:** Barry Barringer; **Cinematographer:** Brydon Baker; **Editor:** Arthur Cohen; **Cast:** Wally Wales, Bobby Nelson, Myrla Bratton, Fred Parker, William Desmond, Art Mix, James Sheridan.

Wally Wales is an undercover government agent sent to investigate a war between cattlemen and sheepmen. In the course of his duties he tries to stop the cattlemen from using an outlaw to harass sheepherders leasing government lands.

WAY OUT WEST MGM, 1930, B&W, 71 min. **Director:** Fred Niblo; **Screenplay:** Joe Farnham and Ralph Spence; **Music:** Joseph Meyer; **Cinematographer:** Henry Sharp; **Editors:** William S. Gray and Jerome Thoms; **Cast:** William Haines, Leila Hyams, Polly Moran, Cliff Edwards, Francis X. Bushman Jr., Vera Marshe, Charles Middleton, Jack Pennick, Buddy Roosevelt, Jay Wilsey, Ann Dvorak.

This almost forgotten and very dated early talkie stars then-Hollywood box-office king William Haines as a carnival sharpie who cheats some cowboys out of their money with a crooked roulette wheel. In retaliation they kidnap him and take him back to their ranch, where they force him to work off the debt.

WAY OUT WEST MGM, 1937, B&W, 65 min, VHS, DVD. **Producers:** Stan Laurel and Hal Roach; **Director:** James W. Horne; **Screenplay:** Felix Adler, James Parrot, and Charles Rogers; **Music:** Marvin Hatley, J. L. Hill, Leroy Shield, and Egbert Van Alstyne; **Cinematographer:** Art Lloyd and Walter Lundin; **Editor:** Bert Jordan; **Cast:** Stan Laurel, Oliver Hardy, Sharon Lynn, James Finlayson, Rosina Lawrence, Stanley Fields, Vivien Oakland, Harry Bernard.

Laurel and Hardy go west as the boys are commissioned to deliver a deed to a gold mine. After handling it over they discover that the valuable paper has been given to the wrong girl, thus beginning a mad race to rectify matters. This film marks the great comedy team's only foray into the western genre, and it proved more successful than other movie lampoons from the likes of Buster Keaton, the Marx Brothers, Abbott and Costello, Martin and Lewis, and others.

Marvin Hatley received an Academy Award nomination for his musical score. Film historian William K. Everson opined that "with the possible exception of *Sons of the Desert*, *Way Out West* must rank as the best of all the Laurel & Hardy features. . . ." *Variety*, on the other hand was not so enthusiastic, commenting that the "manner in which this comedy falters and stumbles along is probably due both to formula direction and scripting . . . there's too much driving home of gags." In the long run what makes good comedy is so often in the eye of the beholder that viewers are recommended here to make up their own minds.

WAY WEST, THE United Artists, 1967, Color, 122 min, VHS, CD. **Producer:** Harold Hecht; **Director:** Andrew V. McLaglen; **Screenplay:** Mitch Lindemann and Ben Maddow; **Music:** Bronislau Kaper; **Cinematographer:** William H. Clothier; **Editor:** Otho Lovering; **Cast:** Kirk Douglas, Robert Mitchum, Richard Widmark, Lola Albright, Sally Field, Katherine Justice, Jack Elam, Stubby Kaye, Harry Carey Jr., Connie Sawyer, Michael Witney, William Lundigan, Elizabeth Fraser, John Mitchum, Patric Knowles, Roy Barcroft, Peggy Stewart.

In Missouri in 1843, ex-senator William J. Tadlock (Kirk Douglas) and scout Dick Summers (Robert Mitchum) lead a band of settlers on a 2,500-mile trek to Oregon. Through snow, ice, and hostile Indian terrain, Tadlock drives his people mercilessly. When his blind ambition results in loss of life, his ability to lead is questioned, and settler Lije Evans (Richard Widmark) takes over command.

By the time he made this film, director Andrew V. McLaglen had become a genre standard bearer, and he assembled a first-rate cast for this ambitious project. Among them were three of the industry's biggest stars in Kirk Douglas, Robert Mitchum, and Richard Widmark; a gala array of supporting players, including B western heroine Peggy Stewart (as Mrs. Turley); and 20-year-old Sally Field (in her film debut) as Mercy.

According to most accounts the production was complicated by arduous physical terrain. Everything was filmed on location, with one month in Eugene, Oregon, and two months in Bend. There were no interiors or studio shots. Rivers had to be forded, and wagons had to be raised from tops of cliffs. "Physically, it was as tough as it could possibly be," according to longtime supporting actor Jack Elam. Nevertheless, director McLaglen was a master at handling such matters and kept the production on schedule.

But there were problems among the actors. According to Mitchum biographer Lee Server, there was tension between Mitchum and Douglas. The two had first worked together two decades earlier in *Out of the Past* (1947), and subsequently both had appeared in *The List of Adrian Messenger* (1963) in the mid-1960s. Douglas had rapidly made himself unpopular with many of the cast and crew, and he was particularly galling to Widmark and actor Harry Carey Jr. Mitchum, Lee Server reports, basically laughed things off.

"It was very dumb of him to try to provoke a confrontation with me . . . all I have to do is whack him one between the horns and it would be all over. And he knows it," Mitchum reportedly told an associate.

Yet despite the film's good intentions, its remarkable star trio, and some splendid action scenes, *The Way West* fell far short of expectations and played to mixed reviews at best. Certainly the film hardly measures up to A. B. Guthrie Jr.'s fine novel, and it was a financial bust.

WELCOME TO HARD TIMES (aka: KILLER ON A HORSE) MGM, 1967, Color, 103 min. **Producers:** David Karr and Max E. Youngstein; **Director:** Burt Kennedy; **Screenplay:** Kennedy; **Music:** Harry Sukman, Jr.; **Cinematographer:** Harry Stradling Jr.; **Editor:** Aaron Stell; **Cast:** Henry Fonda, Janice Rule, Keenan Wynn, Janis Paige, John Anderson, Warren Oates, Fay Spain, Edgar Buchanan, Aldo Ray, Denver Pyle, Michael Shea, Arlene Golonka, Lon Chaney Jr., Royal Dano, Paul Fix, Elisha Cook Jr.

Henry Fonda plays Mayor Will Blue, a man unwilling to stand up to the evil Man From Bodie (Aldo Ray), who pillages the apathetic town of Hard Times, terrorizing and killing its citizens, then burning the town to the ground as he rides away. After he leaves, the good people of Hard Times rebuild the town, but just as they begin to take pride in what they accomplished, the Man From Bodie rides into town again for a second round of death and destruction. The benign Mayor Blue must show his mettle or be disgraced a second time.

This bleak revisionist western based on a novel by E. L. Doctorow has little to recommend it. It is an excessively grim film which people either enjoy or detest. Aldo Ray is excellent as the personification of evil, a far call from the role of the heroic, good-natured tough guy that made him so popular in the 1950s.

WELLS FARGO Paramount, 1937, B&W, 97 min. **Producer:** Frank Lloyd; **Director:** Lloyd; **Screenplay:** Gerald Geraghty and Paul Schofield; **Music:** Victor Young; **Cinematographer:** Theodor Sparkuhl; **Editor:** Hugh Bennett; **Cast:** Joel McCrea, Bob Burns, Frances Dee, Lloyd Nolan, Henry O'Neill, Mary Nash, Ralph Morgan, Johnny Mack Brown, Porter Hall, Robert Cummings, Granville Bates, Peggy Stewart, Harry Davenport.

Frank Lloyd's epic 1937 film deals with the founding of the nation's first express company, formed by two enterprising businessmen named Henry Wells and Will Fargo. Most of the narrative concerns the adventures of the company's main advance man and messenger, Ramsey MacKay (Joel McCrea), as he makes his first Wells Fargo trip from Tipton, Missouri, to San Francisco, and his relationship over the year with his wife, Justine (Frances Dee, McCrea's real-life wife). While not all it might have been, the film provides for a fairly good history lesson about the expansion of the country. McCrea does his usual capable job—strong, tough, and taciturn; like Randolph Scott, he is a throwback to the William S. Hart type of hero.

Nominated for an Academy Award in the category of Best Sound, the film's original release was 20 minutes longer than the 97 minutes listed in most credits. Within the genre, Paramount was the most epic-minded producer of the period with such films as *Wells Fargo* and THE PLAINSMAN (1936), THE TEXAS RANGERS (1936), and THE TEXANS (1938).

WELLS FARGO GUNMASTER Republic, 1951, B&W, 60 min. **Producer:** Gordon Kay; **Director:** Philip Ford; **Screenplay:** M. Coates Webster; **Music:** Stanley Wilson; **Cinematographer:** John MacBurnie; **Editor:** Robert M. Leeds; **Cast:** Allan Lane, Chubby Johnson, Mary Ellen Kaye, Michael Chapin, Roy Barcroft, Walter Reed, Stuart Randall, William Bakewell, George Meeker.

See BOLD FRONTIERSMAN, THE.

WESTBOUND Warner Bros., 1958, Color, 72 min. **Producer:** Henry Blanke; **Director:** Budd Boetticher; **Screenplay:** Berne Giler; **Music:** David Buttolph; **Cinematographer:** J. Peverell Marley; **Editor:** Philip W. Anderson; **Cast:** Randolph Scott, Virginia Mayo, Karen Steele, Michael Dante, Andrew Duggan, Michael Pate, Wally Brown, John Daheim, Walter Barnes.

In this film set during the Civil War, Randolph Scott is Captain John Hayes, who sets up a stage line to protect gold shipments to the North. But a rich rancher, whose beautiful wife was once Scott's girlfriend, opposes him. This very well-made Budd Boetticher–Randolph Scott western is an enjoyable film with strong characterizations. Director Boetticher, however, was disappointed with the finished project and considered *Westbound* to be the weakest of his string of seven westerns with Randolph Scott. It was also the only one of the seven that Columbia did not produce and one of two that was not scripted by Burt Kennedy; DECISION AT SUNDOWN (1957) was the other.

WESTBOUND MAIL Columbia, 1937, B&W, 54 min. **Director:** Folmar Blangsted; **Screenplay:** Frances Guihan; **Cinematographer:** Benjamin H. Kline; **Editor:** Richard Fantl; **Cast:** Charles Starrett, Rosalind Keith, Edward Keene, Arthur Stone, Ben Weldon, Al Bridge, Art Mix, George Chesebro.

See GALLANT DEFENDER.

WESTBOUND STAGE Monogram, 1939, B&W, 57 min. **Producer:** Edward Finney; **Director:** Spencer Gordon Bennet; **Screenplay:** Robert Emmett (Tansey); **Music:** Frank Sanucci, Johnny Lange (song), and Lew Porter (song); **Cinematographer:** Marcel Le Picard; **Editor:** Frederick Bain; **Cast:** Tex Ritter, Nelson McDowell, Muriel Evans, Nolan Willis, Steve Clark, Tom London, Reed Howes, Frank Ellis, Kenne Duncan, Frank La Rue.

See SONG OF THE GRINGO.

WESTERN CARAVANS Columbia, 1939, B&W, 58 min. **Director:** Sam Nelson; **Screenplay:** Bennett Cohen;

Music: Bob Nolan and Tim Spencer; **Cinematographer:** George A. Cooper; **Editor:** William A. Lyon; **Cast:** Charles Starrett, Iris Meredith, Dick Curtis, Russell Simpson, Wally Wales, Hank Bell, Bob Nolan, Sammy McKim, Edmund Cobb, Ethan Laidlaw, Sons of the Pioneers.

See GALLANT DEFENDER.

WESTERN CODE, THE Columbia, 1932, B&W, 60 min. **Director:** John P. McCarthy; **Screenplay:** Milton Krims and William Colt McDonald; **Cinematographer:** Benjamin H. Kline; **Editor:** Otto Meyer; **Cast:** Tim McCoy, Mischa Auer, Nora Lane, Dwight Frye, Wheeler Oakman, Matthew Betz, Gordon De Main, Emilio Fernandez.

See RIDING TORNADO, THE.

WESTERN COURAGE Columbia, 1935, B&W, 61 min. **Producer:** Larry Darmour; **Director:** Spencer Gordon Bennett; **Screenplay:** Nate Gatzert; **Cinematographer:** Herbert Kirkpatrick; **Editor:** Dwight Caldwell; **Cast:** Ken Maynard, Geneva Mitchell, Charles K. French, Betty Blyth, Cornelius Keefe, Ward Bond, E. H. Calvert, Renee Whitney.

The foreman of a dude ranch falls for a guest, but she turns out to be a spoiled brat. Then she is kidnapped by a nasty fellow who has been wooing her.

WESTERN CYCLONE (aka: FRONTIER FIGHTERS) PRC, 1943, B&W, 62 min. **Producer:** Sigmund Newfield; **Director:** Sam Newfield; **Screenplay:** Patricia Harper; **Cinematographer:** Robert E. Cline; **Editor:** Holbrook N. Todd; **Cast:** Buster Crabbe, Al St. John, Glenn Strange, Charles King, Karl Hackett, Marjorie Manners, Hal Price, Martin Kibbee, Jack Ingram, Steve Clark, Frank Ellis, Kermit Maynard.

See BILLY THE KID TRAPPED.

WESTERNER, THE Columbia, 1934, B&W, 58 min. **Director:** David Selman; **Screenplay:** Walt Coburn and Harold Shumate; **Music:** Louis Silvers; **Cinematographer:** George Meehan; **Editor:** Ray Snyder; **Cast:** Tim McCoy, Marion Shilling, Joe Sawyer, Hooper Atchley, John Dilson, Edward Le Saint.

See RIDING TORNADO, THE.

WESTERNER, THE United Artists, 1940, B&W, 100 min, VHS, DVD. **Producer:** Samuel Goldwyn; **Director:** William Wyler; **Screenplay:** Niven Busch and Jo Swerling; **Music:** Dimitri Tiomkin; **Cinematographer:** Gregg Toland; **Editor:** Daniel Mandell; **Cast:** Gary Cooper, Walter Brennan, Doris Davenport, Fred Stone, Forrest Tucker, Paul Hurst, Chill Wills, Lillian Bond, Dana Andrews, Charles Halton, Trevor Bardette, Tom Tyler, Lucien Littlefield.

Cole Hardin (Gary Cooper) is a drifter falsely accused of stealing a horse. He is brought into the saloon courthouse of Judge Roy Bean (Walter Brennan) where the judge represents the only law "west of the Pecos." While the jury is deliberating, Cole discovers that the judge idolizes Lillie Langtry, the beautiful "Jersey Lily." As Bean's kangaroo court is about to pass a guilty verdict, Cole lets on that he knows Lilie well. The judge is so stunned that he arranges to have Cole reprieved on the condition that he get him a lock of Lilie's hair.

Cole spends the night watched by the judge and only escapes because he steals the old fellow's gun. On his way to California, he stops at the farm of Caliphet Matthews (Fred Stone), whose daughter Jane-Ellen (Doris Davenport) convinces Cole that he should help the homesteaders, whom she insists are in the right in their fight against cattlemen. Cole returns to town declaring his support for the farmers. As Judge Bean is about to arrest him, he recalls his promise of a lock of Langtry's hair, and just before they set out to round up the cattle, he gives the judge some of Jane-Ellen's tresses under the guise that it belongs to Lillie. A few nights later, however, Bean's men start burning the farmers' crops and homes and they kill Jane-Ellen's father.

Cole goes after Bean but learns that the judge has gone to nearby Fort Davis to see Langtry on stage; he has, in fact, bought out the entire house so that he might be the sole person in the audience. After the overture the curtain rises, exposing Cole with both guns drawn. He and Bean shoot it out, with Bean falling to the floor mortally wounded. Cole picks him up and escorts him to Lillie's dressing room where he kisses the hand of the Jersey Lily before he dies.

Director William Wyler opted for characterization over action, with Cooper and Brennan in total command, and although Brennan steals the show, Cooper's easy, laconic style pleased reviewers and audiences alike. For his work in playing one of the silver screen's most salty and memorable villains, Walter Brennan became the first actor in screen history to win a third Academy Award for Best Supporting Actor. Oscar nominations also went to James Basevi (Best Art Direction–Black and White) and Stuart Lake (Best Writing, Original Story). Wyler also brought in cinematographer

Gary Cooper relaxing on the set of The Westerner
(AUTHOR'S COLLECTION)

Gregg Toland, who had assisted him in his superlative production of *Wuthering Heights* a year earlier. Toland's deft black and white photography provided the film with a visual sheen.

The Westerner marked the debut of Forrest Tucker, then age 25, and Dana Andrews, age 29, as hotheaded farm youths. Although composer Dimitri Tiomkin was given screen credit for the score, producer Sam Goldwyn did not like it and had his friend Alfred Newman completely rewrite the music; Newman received no screen credit because of prior contractual agreements.

There might be better pure westerns than this 1940 classic, but few have ever been more entertaining. Cooper was then at the height of his popularity, and the U.S. Treasury Department reported that in 1939 he was the nation's top wage earner, at $482,819. He was deemed too expensive for *STAGECOACH* (1939). William Wyler and Gary Cooper worked together again 16-years later in Wyler's Oscar-nominated film, *FRIENDLY PERSUASION* (1956).

Walter Brennan (left, in his Oscar-winning role as Judge Roy Bean) and Gary Cooper in William Wyler's The Westerner (UNITED ARTISTS/AUTHOR'S COLLECTION)

WESTERN FRONTIER Columbia, 1935, B&W, 59 min. **Producer:** Larry Darmour; **Director:** Albert Herman; **Screenplay:** Nate Gatzert; **Music:** Lee Zahler; **Cinematographer:** James S. Brown Jr. and Herbert Kirkpatrick; **Editor:** Dwight Caldwell; **Cast:** Ken Maynard, Lucile Browne, Nora

Lane, Robert "Buzz" Henry, Frank Yaconelli, Otis Harlan, Harold Goodwin.

Ken Masters (Ken Maynard) and his sister are separated as youngsters when Indians attack their wagon train. Years later Ken is sent to pursue an outlaw known only as the Golden Hair Girl, not knowing that she is the sister he had lost years earlier.

WESTERN GOLD (aka: MYSTERIOUS STRANGER) 20th Century Fox, 1937, B&W, 57 min. **Producer:** Sol Lesser; **Director:** Howard Bretherton; **Screenplay:** Forrest Barnes and Earl Snell; **Music:** Arthur Lange; **Cinematographer:** Harry Neumann; **Cast:** Smith Ballew, Heather Angel, LeRoy Mason, Howard C. Hickman, Ben Alexander, Frank McGlynn Sr., Ottis Harlan, Victor Potel, Lew Kelly, Al Bridge, Tom London, Fred Burns, Steve Clark, Paul Fix, Wesley Giraud, Art Lasky, Horace Murphy, Bud Osborne, Harry Semels.

During the Civil War, a westerner serving in the Union army is assigned to discover how gold shipments from the West are being waylaid by Southerners. He finds that their leader is his onetime friend and school chum, who is murdered before they can meet. Smith Ballew's fine singing voice is revealed in this initial series entry based on a book by Harold Bell Wright.

WESTERN HERITAGE RKO, 1948, B&W, 61 min. **Producer:** Herman Schlom; **Director:** Wallace Grissell; **Screenplay:** Norman Houston; **Music:** Paul Sawtell; **Cinematographer:** Alfred Keller; **Editor:** Desmond Marquette; **Cast:** Tim Holt, Nan Leslie, Richard Martin, Lois Andrews, Tony Barrett, Walter Reed, Harry Woods, Tom Keene.

WESTERN JAMBOREE Republic, 1938, B&W, 60 min. **Producer:** Harry Grey; **Director:** Ralph Staub; **Screenplay:** Gerald Geraghty; **Cinematographer:** William Nobles; **Editor:** Lester Orlebeck; **Cast:** Gene Autry, Smiley Burnette, Jean Rouverol, Esther Muir, Frank Darien, Margaret Armstrong, Harry Holman, Kermit Maynard, Ray Teal.
See *TUMBLING TUMBLEWEEDS.*

WESTERN JUSTICE Supreme, 1935, B&W, 56 min. **Producer:** A. W. Hackel; **Director:** Robert N. Bradbury; **Screenplay:** Bradbury; **Cinematographer:** William Hyer; **Editor:** S. Roy Luby; **Cast:** Bob Steele, Rene Borden, Julian Rivero, Arthur Loft, Lafe McKee, Jack Cowell, Perry Murdock, Vane Calvert, Earl Dwire.
See *KID COURAGEOUS.*

WESTERN PACIFIC AGENT Lippert, 1950, B&W, 64 min. **Producer:** Sigmund Neufeld; **Director:** Sam Newfeld; **Screenplay:** Fred Myton; **Cinematographer:** Ernest W. Miller; **Editor:** Carl Pierson; **Cast:** Kent Taylor, Sheila Ryan, Robert Lowery, Mickey Knox, Morris Carnovsky, Sid Melton, Frank Richards.

A modern day western where a railroad detective is murdered during a robbery, and a fellow agent hunts down the killer.

WESTERN RENEGADES Monogram, 1949, B&W, 58 min. **Producer:** Eddie Davis; **Director:** Wallace Fox; **Screenplay:** Adele S. Buffington; **Cinematographer:** Harry Neumann; **Editor:** John C. Fuller; **Cast:** Johnny Mack Brown, Max Terhune, Jane Adams, Hugh Prosser, Riley Hill, Marshall Reed, Constance Worth, Steve Clark, Terry Frost, William Ruhl, John Merton.
See *UNDER WESTERN SKIES.*

WESTERN UNION 20th Century Fox, 1941, Color, 92 min. **Producer:** Harry Joe Brown (associate); **Director:** Fritz Lang; **Screenplay:** Robert Carson; **Cinematographer:** Edward Cronjager and Allen M. Davey; **Editor:** Robert Bischoff; **Cast:** Robert Young, Randolph Scott, Dean Jagger, Virginia Gilmore, John Carradine, Slim Summerville, Chill Wills, Barton MacLane, Russell Hill, Victor Kilian, Minor Watson, George Chandler.

Another western epic of early American history, *Western Union* is a fictionalized account of connecting the telegraph wires between Omaha, Nebraska, and Salt Lake City, Utah, in the 1860s. Vance Shaw (Randolph Scott) gives up his outlaw ways to help Western Union chief engineer Edward Creighton (Dean Jagger) set up this pioneering endeavor. Shaw's ex-partner in crime Jack Slade (Barton MacLane) heads the gang that tries to foil its completion. Hired to protect Western Union from Indians and marauders, Shaw falls in love with Creighton's sister (Virginia Gilmore), but he must compete for her affections with dandified Harvard educated easterner Richard Blake (Robert Young). The film ends in a dramatic shoot-out with some surprising twists.

This is a superior western that should not be missed. Director Fritz Lang develops his characters skillfully, and Randolph Scott delivers what is arguably his best performance until his superb string of Budd Boetticher westerns in the 1950s. Shot on location in Utah and photographed in stunning color, the film's characters and plot evolve in a deliberate cadence, with Indian raids, outlaw interference, and a big forest fire to keep the action moving with nary a lull. It was purportedly based on the novel by Zane Grey, and it has been suggested that Grey may have finished the book a few days before he died or possibly that it may have been put together by some ghostwriter to cash in on the film's popularity—a popularity validated by *Variety,* which called *Western Union* "a lusty and actionful outing."

WEST OF ABILENE (aka: THE SHOWDOWN) Columbia, 1940, B&W, 58 min. **Producer:** Leon Barsha; **Director:** Ralph Ceder; **Screenplay:** Paul Franklin; **Music:** Bob Nolan; **Cinematographer:** George Meehan; **Editor:** Charles Nelson; **Cast:** Charles Starrett, Marjorie Cooley, Bruce Bennett, William Pawley, Don Beddoe, George Cleveland.
See *GALLANT DEFENDER.*

WEST OF CARSON CITY Universal, 1940, B&W, 56 min. **Producer** Joseph G. Sanford (associate); **Director:** Ray Taylor; **Screenplay:** Jack Bernhard, Sherman L. Lowe, and Milton Raison; **Music:** Everette Carter (song); **Cinematographer:** Jerome Ash; **Cast:** Johnny Mack Brown, Bob Baker, Fuzzy Knight, Peggy Moran, Harry Woods, Robert Homans, Al K. Hall, Roy Barcroft, Charles King.

See *OLD CHISHOLM TRAIL, THE*.

WEST OF CHEYENNE Columbia, 1938, B&W, 59 min. **Director:** Sam Nelson; **Screenplay:** Ed Earl Repp; **Music:** Bob Nolan; **Cinematographer:** Benjamin H. Kline; **Editor:** William A. Lyon; **Cast:** Charles Starrett, Iris Meredith, Bob Nolan, Pat Brady, Dick Curtis, Edward Le Saint, Edmund Cobb, Art Mix, Ernie Adams, Jack Rockwell, Sons of the Pioneers.

See *GALLANT DEFENDER*.

WEST OF CIMARRON Republic, 1941, B&W, 56 min. **Producer:** Louis Gray (associate); **Director:** Les Orlebeck; **Screenplay:** Albert De Mond and Don Ryan; **Music:** Cy Feuer; **Cinematographer:** Ernest Miller; **Editor:** Howard O'Neill; **Cast:** Bob Steele, Tom Tyler, Rufe Davis, Lois Collier, James Bush, Guy Usher, Hugh Prosser, Roy Barcroft.

See *THREE MESQUITEERS, THE*.

WEST OF DODGE CITY Columbia, 1947, B&W, 57 min. **Producer:** Colbert Clark; **Director:** Ray Nazarro; **Screenplay:** Bert Horswell; **Music:** Mischa Bakaleinikoff; **Cinematographer:** George F. Kelley; **Editor:** Paul Borofsky; **Cast:** Charles Starrett, Smiley Burnette, Nancy Saunders, Fred F. Sears, I. Stanford Jolley, George Chesebro, Robert J. Wilke.

See *DURANGO KID, THE*.

WEST OF EL DORADO Monogram, 1949, B&W, 58 min. **Producer:** Barney A. Sarecky; **Director:** Ray Taylor; **Screenplay:** Adele Buffington; **Editor:** John C. Fuller; **Cast:** Johnny Mack Browne, Max Terhune, Reno Brown, Milburn Morante, Teddy Infuhr, Terry Frost, Marshall Reed.

See *UNDER ARIZONA SKIES*.

WEST OF MONTANA See *MAIL ORDER BRIDE*.

WEST OF PINTO BASIN Monogram, 1940, B&W, 60 min. **Producer:** George W. Weeks; **Director:** S. Roy Luby; **Screenplay:** Elmer Clifton and Earle Snell; **Music:** Johnny Lange and Lew Porter; **Cinematographer:** Edward Linden; **Editor:** Luby (as Roy Claire); **Cast:** Ray Corrigan, John "Dusty" King, Max Terhune, Gwen Gaze, Tristram Coffin, Dirk Thane, George Chesebro, Jack Perrin.

WEST OF RAINBOW'S END Monogram, 1938, B&W, 57 min. **Producer:** Maurice Conn; **Director:** Alan James; **Screenplay:** Genera Rea, Stanley Roberts, and Robert Emmett Tansey; **Music:** Connie Lee; **Cinematographer:** Jack Greenhalgh; **Cast:** Tim McCoy, Kathleen Eliot, Walter McGrail, Frank La Rue, George Chang, Mary Carr, Ed Coxen.

Tim McCoy is an ex-ranger who comes out of retirement to investigate the murder of his foster father, who had been investigating a series of train robberies.

WEST OF SONORA Columbia, 1948, B&W, 57 min. **Producer:** Colbert Clark; **Director:** Ray Nazarro; **Screenplay:** Barry Shipman; **Cinematographer:** Ira H. Morgan; **Editor:** Jerome Thoms; **Cast:** Charles Starrett, Smiley Burnette, Anita Castle, George Chesebro, Steve Darrell, Lloyd Ingraham, Emmett Lynn, Wally Wales, Robert J. Wilke.

See *DURANGO KID, THE*.

WEST OF TEXAS PRC, 1943, B&W, 61 min. **Producers:** Arthur Alexander and Alfred Stern; **Director:** Oliver Drake; **Screenplay:** Drake; **Cinematographer:** Ira Morgan; **Editor:** Charles Henkel Jr.; **Cast:** Dave O'Brien, James Newill, Guy Wilkerson, Frances Gladwin, Marilyn Hare.

WEST OF THE ALAMO Monogram, 1946, B&W, 57 min. **Producer:** Oliver Drake; **Director:** Drake; **Screenplay:** Louise Rousseau; **Cinematographer:** Harry Neumann; **Editor:** William Austin; **Cast:** Jimmy Wakely, Lee "Lasses" White, Iris Clive, Jack Ingram, Rod Holton, Budd Buster, Ray Whitley.

See *ACROSS THE RIO GRANDE*.

WEST OF THE BRAZOS (aka: RANGELAND EMPIRE) Lippert, 1950, B&W, 58 min. **Producer:** Ron Ormond; **Director:** Thomas Carr; **Screenplay:** Ormond and Maurice Tombragel; **Music:** Walter Greene; **Cinematographer:** Ernest Miller; **Editor:** Hugh Winn; **Cast:** Jimmy Ellison, Russell Hayden, Raymond Hatton, Fuzzy Knight, Julie Adams, Tom Tyler, George J. Lewis, John L. Cason.

Two cowboys attempt to stop a crook who is out to fleece a man of his oil-rich lands.

WEST OF THE DIVIDE Monogram/Lone Star, 1934, B&W, 54 min, VHS, DVD. **Producer:** Paul Malvern; **Director:** Robert N. Bradbury; **Screenplay:** Bradbury; **Cinematographer:** Archie Stout; **Editor:** Carl Pierson; **Cast:** John Wayne, Virginia Faire Brown, George "Gabby" Hayes, Lloyd Whitlock, Yakima Canutt, Lafe McKee, Billy O'Brien, Dick Dickinson, Earl Dwire.

Tex Hayden (John Wayne) returns to the scene of his youth pretending to be wanted criminal Gat Ganns so he can find the man who had murdered his father and kidnapped his younger brother. One of 24 early Wayne B westerns produced by Paul Malvern and one of 13 Wayne ventures directed by Robert N. Bradbury (only John Ford helmed Wayne in more features), *West of the Divide* features some good fight scenes, with Yakima Canutt working as Wayne's stunt double.

In 1985 Fox/Lorber Associates copyrighted a version of the film with an original score composed and orchestrated by William Barber, running 48 minutes. The picture is also available in a computer-colorized version.

WEST OF THE LAW Monogram, 1942, B&W, 60 min. **Producer:** Scott R. Dunlap; **Director:** Howard Bretherton; **Screenplay:** Jess Bowers; **Cinematographer:** Harry Neumann; **Editor:** Carl Pierson; **Cast:** Buck Jones, Tim McCoy, Raymond Hatton, Evelyn Cook, Milburn Morante, Malcolm "Budd" McTaggart, Jack Daley, Harry Woods, Roy Barcroft, George De Normand.

Three marshals go undercover in a small town where outlaws have made attacks on the local newspaper. In the process they uncover a gold smuggling operation. Lots of fast action fills this eighth and final entry in the popular "Rough Riders" series. (See also ARIZONA BOUND.)

WEST OF THE PECOS RKO, 1935, B&W, 68 min. **Producer:** Cliff Reid; **Director:** Phil Rosen; **Screenplay:** Milton Krims and John Twist; **Music:** Max Steiner and Roy Webb; **Cinematographer:** Walter Metty and James Van Trees; **Editor:** Archie Marshek; **Cast:** Richard Dix, Martha Sleeper, Samuel S. Hinds, Fred Kohler, Willie Best, Louise Beavers, Maria Alba, Pedro Regas.

In RKO's first version of the Zane Grey story, Richard Dix is Pecos Smith, a cowboy who fights lawlessness in Texas. The studio remade the film in 1945, with budding star Robert Mitchum featured as the Texas cowboy. The film is just one of a number of 1930s westerns where the title had little to do with the storyline.

WEST OF THE PECOS RKO, 1945, B&W, 66 min. **Producer:** Herbert Schlom; **Director:** Ed Killy; **Screenplay:** Norman Houston; **Music:** Paul Sawtell; **Cinematographer:** Harry J. Wild; **Editor:** Roland Gross; **Cast:** Robert Mitchum, Barbara Hale, Richard Martin, Thurston Hall, Rita Corday, Russell Hopton, Bill Williams, Bruce Edwards, Harry Woods.

Outlaws hold up a stagecoach carrying a rich Chicagoan who is heading west with his daughter on his doctor's advice. When the thieves kill the driver, the Chicagoan's cowboy friend Pecos Smith (Robert Mitchum) and his pal set out to get the villains. Following much of the same story line as Tim Holt's later RKO venture *The Stagecoach Kid* (1949), the plot involves costar Barbara Hale (the beautiful young woman who had been on the stage with her father when it was held up) disguised as a young cowboy and the fallout as she travels across the frontier with the gunslinging Pecos.

West of the Pecos proved to be a watershed film for 29-year-old Robert Mitchum. Pleased with what they had seen in NEVADA (1944), producers Herman Schlom and Sid Rogell decided to schedule another Zane Grey remake for Mitchum and assembled much of the *Nevada* crew, including director Ed Killy, screenwriter Norman Houston, and cinematogra-

pher Harry Wild. Actor Richard Martin reprised his role of Chito Rafferty, the Irish-Mexican sidekick.

In *Nevada* Mitchum was indistinguishable from other deadpan B cowboy stars. In *West of the Pecos* he revealed many of the qualities that would one day propel him to the front rank of major movie stars: the charm, the humor, the laid-back demeanor, and not least the rugged good looks. He would soon go far beyond the long line of Zane Grey horse operas that the studio had in mind for him.

WEST OF THE RIO GRANDE Monogram, 1944, B&W, 57 min. **Producers:** Charles Bigelow and Scott R. Dunlap; **Director:** Lambert Hillyer; **Screenplay:** Betty Burbridge; **Cinematographer:** Arthur Martinelli; **Editor:** John C. Fuller; **Cast:** Johnny Mack Brown, Raymond Hatton, Dennis Moore, Christine McIntyre, Lloyd Ingraham, Kenneth MacDonald, Hugh Prosser, Edmund Cobb, Frank La Rue.
See UNDER ARIZONA SKIES.

WEST OF TOMBSTONE Columbia, 1942, B&W, 59 min. **Producer:** William Berke; **Director:** Howard Bretherton; **Screenplay:** Maurice Geraghty; **Cinematographer:** George Meehan; **Editor:** Mel Thorsen; **Cast:** Charles Starrett, Russell Hayden, Cliff Edwards, Marcella Martin, Gordon De Main, Clancy Cooper, Jack Kirk, Budd Buster, Tom London, Lloyd Bridges, Horace B. Carpenter.
See GALLANT DEFENDER.

WEST OF WYOMING Monogram, 1950, B&W, 57 min. **Director:** Wallace W. Fox; **Screenplay:** Adele Buffington; **Cinematographer:** Harry Neumann; **Editor:** John C. Fuller; **Cast:** Johnny Mack Brown, Gail Davis, Milburn Morante, Myron Healey, Dennis Moore, Stanley Andrews, Carl Mathews, Paul Cramer, John Merton, Holly Bain.
See UNDER ARIZONA SKIES.

WEST SIDE KID Republic, 1943, B&W, 57 min. **Producer:** George Sherman; **Director:** Sherman; **Screenplay:** Albert Beich and Anthony Coldeway; **Cinematographer:** Jack Marta; **Editor:** Ernest Nims; **Cast:** Don "Red" Barry, Henry Hull, Dale Evans, Chick Chandler, Matt McHugh, Nana Bryant, Walter Catlett, Edward Gargan, Chester Clue, Peter Lawford.
See WYOMING OUTLAW.

WEST TO GLORY PRC, 1947, B&W, 56 min. **Producer:** Jerry Thomas; **Director:** Rod Taylor; **Screenplay:** Robert B. Churchill and Elmer Clifton; **Music:** Karl Hajos, Hal Blair (songs), Eddie Dean (songs), and Pete Gates (songs); **Cinematographer:** Milford Anderson; **Editor:** Hugh Winn; **Cast:** Eddie Dean, Roscoe Ates, Dolores Castle, Gregg Barton, Jimmy Martin, Zon Murray.
See SONG OF OLD WYOMING.

WESTWARD BOUND Monogram, 1944, B&W, 54 min. **Producer:** Robert Tansey; **Director:** Tansey; **Screen-**

play: Elizabeth Beecher and Frances Kavanaugh; **Cinematographer:** Marcel Le Picard; **Editor:** John C. Fuller; **Cast:** Ken Maynard, Hoot Gibson, Bob Steele, Barry Miles, Harry Woods, Weldon Heyburn.

A trio of marshals (Ken Maynard, Hoot Gibson, and Bob Steele as themselves) come to the aid of ranchers who are being forced off their land. The outlaws are led by a government official who wants the area for its resale value once Montana becomes a state. This film is part of Monogram's popular "Trail Blazers" series. (See also *DEATH VALLEY RANGERS*.)

WESTWARD HO Republic, 1935, B&W, 61 min, VHS. **Producer:** Paul Malvern; **Director:** Robert N. Bradbury; **Screenplay:** Harry Friedman, Lindsley Parsons, and Robert Emmett Tansey; **Music:** Heinz Roemheld and Clifford Vaughan; **Cinematographer:** Archie Stout; **Editor:** Carl Pierson; **Cast:** John Wayne, Sheila Bromley, Frank McGlynn Jr., Jim Farley, Jack Curtis, Bradley Metcalfe.

John Wayne is a young man who had been separated from his younger brother years before when outlaws attacked their wagon and killed their parents. He now goes west with settlers and becomes friends with another man working as a spy for the outlaws, not knowing that the man is really his brother. Wayne's first Republic western is an entertaining and action-packed Paul Malvern production.

WESTWARD HO Republic, 1942, B&W, 56 min. **Producer:** Louis Gray; **Director:** John English; **Screenplay:** Morton Grant and Doris Schroeder; **Music:** Cy Feuer; **Cinematographer:** Reggie Lanning; **Editor:** William P. Thompson; **Cast:** Bob Steele, Tom Tyler, Rufe Davis, Evelyn Brent, Donald Curtis, John James, Lois Comer, Emmett Lynn, Tom Seidel, Jack Kirk.

See *THREE MESQUITEERS, THE*.

WESTWARD HO THE WAGONS Walt Disney/Buena Vista, 1956, Color, 90 min. **Producer:** Bill Walsh; **Director:** William Beaudine; **Screenplay:** Tom Blackburn; **Music:** Blackburn, George Bruns, Gil George, Stan Jones, Fess Parker, and Paul J. Smith; **Cinematographer:** Charles P. Boyle; **Editor:** Cotton Warburton; **Cast:** Fess Parker, Kathleen Crowley, Jeff York, David Stollery, Sebastian Cabot, George Reeves, Doreen Tracey, Morgan Woodward.

Fess Parker is "Doc" Grayson, a clear-thinking pioneer leading a wagon train through territory occupied by the Pawnee and the Sioux in this adaptation of a novel by Mary Jane Carr. The settlers' hopes of reaching Oregon diminish as they face such hardships as horse thieves, kidnappers, and unpredictable Indian attacks. The soundtrack contains a number of songs that include "Green Grow the Lilacs" by Tex Ritter and "Wringle Wrangle" by Stan Jones.

WESTWARD THE WOMEN MGM, 1951, B&W, 118 min, VHS. **Producer:** Dore Schary; **Director:** William Wellman; **Screenplay:** Charles Steno; **Music:** Jeff Alexander and Henry Russell; **Cinematographer:** William Mellor; **Editor:** James E. Newcom; **Cast:** Robert Taylor, Denise Darcel, Hope Emerson, John McIntire, Julie Bishop, Lenore Lonergan, Henry Nakamura, Marilyn Erskine, Beverly Dennis, Renata Vanni.

Robert Taylor is Buck Wyatt, a rugged trail boss who in 1851 is hired by a visionary California landowner (John McIntire) to deliver several dozen mail-order brides on a 2,000-mile trek from Chicago to California. What follows is a survival-at-any-cost journey where the women under Taylor's harsh command display courage and fortitude, enduring Indian raids, nature's wrath (dust and rain storms), and unwanted advances from the dozen or so men who agree to accompany them. Among the women are two former show girls (Denise Darcel and Julie Bishop) and a hearty widow (Beverly Dennis).

William Wellman helmed this film with a deliberate and unpretentious hand, enhancing it with stark black-and-white photography. The female characters are shot using mostly flat, natural lighting sources—a daring choice considering the intensified glamour aura of the 1950s. Despite a few false notes and generally mixed reviews, Wellman delivered a compelling film, ahead of its time in exploring the vital role of women as a part of the nation's frontier. While some of the gritty women perish along the way from a variety of causes, the picture nevertheless ends on an upbeat note when the depleted party finally make it to California to meet and wed their men. If the finale is a bit fabricated, it touches the romantic heart deeply, with strains of the traditional "Believe Me if All Your Endearing Young Charms" and "Drink to Me Only With Thine Eyes" follow each couple as they pair off to exchange vows.

There are two interesting sidebars. The film lacks any musical score except for a title melody and the aforementioned incidental music near the end, and the scenario is based on a story by veteran director Frank Capra.

WHEELS OF DESTINY Universal, 1934, B&W, 64 min. **Producer:** Ken Maynard; **Director:** Alan James; **Screenplay:** Nate Gatzert; **Music:** Maynard (song); **Cinematographer:** Ted D. McCord; **Editor:** Charles Harris; **Cast:** Ken Maynard, Dorothy Dix, Philo McCullough, Frank Rice, Jay Wilsey (as Buffalo Bill Jr.), Edward Coxen, Fred Sale Jr.

See *LUCKY LARKIN*.

WHEN A MAN'S A MAN (aka: SAGA OF THE WEST) Fox, 1935, B&W, 60 min. **Producers:** Sol Lesser and John Zanft; **Director:** Edward F. Cline; **Screenplay:** Frank Mitchell Dazey, Daniel Jarrett, and Agnes Christine Johnston; **Cinematographer:** Frank B. Good; **Editor:** W. Donn Hayes; **Cast:** George O'Brien, Dorothy Wilson, Paul Kelly, Harry Woods, Jimmy Butler, Richard Carlyle, Clarence Wilson, Edgar Norton.

In a small western town a cowboy comes to the aid of a female ranch owner whose water supply has been taken over by outlaws. (See also *DUDE RANGER, THE*.)

WHEN A MAN SEES RED Universal, 1934, B&W, 60 min. **Producer:** Buck Jones; **Directors:** Alan James and Alfred Raboch; **Screenplay:** James; **Music:** Mischa Bakaleinikoff; **Cinematographer:** Ted D. McCord and Joe Novak; **Editor:** Bernard Loftus; **Cast:** Buck Jones, Peggy Campbell, Dorothy Revier, LeRoy Mason, Syd Saylor, Libby Taylor.

See *WHITE EAGLE.*

WHEN LEGENDS DIE 20th Century Fox, 1972, Color, 107 min. **Producers:** Gene Lasko and Stuart Millar; **Director:** Millar; **Screenplay:** Robert Dozier; **Music:** Glenn Paxton; **Cinematographer:** Richard H. Kline; **Editor:** Louis San Andrews; **Cast:** Richard Widmark, Frederic Forrest, Luana Anders, Vito Scotti, Herbert Nelson, John War Eagle, John Gruber, Garry Walberg.

Aging rodeo rider Red Dillon (Richard Widmark) discovers the remarkable rodeo talents of a rebellious Ute Indian named Tom Black Bull (Frederic Forrest) and turns the young rider into a bronc-busting contender. However, Red's tendencies to gamble and drink lead to a rift in the relationship. Once he makes it to national competition, Tom Black Bull begins questioning the values of the white men's ways, finds them wanting, rejects Dillon's friendship, and returns to his own people.

Contemporary westerns about the aging rodeo cowboy became quite popular in the early 1970s with such films as Cliff Robertson's *J. W. COOP* (1972), Steve Inhat's *THE HONKERS* (1972), and Sam Peckinpah's *JUNIOR BONNER* (1972). Unlike the others, this one has a stinging and reflective social message, with Richard Widmark delivering perhaps the best performance of his later period roles. The location work in Colorado and New Mexico is beautifully filmed. Frederic Forrest received a Golden Globe nomination (1973) as the screen's Most Promising Male Newcomer.

WHEN THE DALTONS RODE Universal, 1940, B&W, 81 min. **Director:** George Marshall; **Screenplay:** Harold Shumate; **Music:** Frank Skinner; **Cinematographer:** Hal Mohr; **Editor:** Ed Curtiss; **Cast:** Randolph Scott, Kay Francis, Brian Donlevy, George Bancroft, Broderick Crawford, Stuart Erwin, Andy Devine, Frank Albertson, Mary Gordon.

When young lawyer Tod Jackson (Randolph Scott) arrives in pioneer Kansas, he pays a visit to his friends the Dalton brothers, who are prosperous ranchers but are also in danger of losing their land to a crooked development company. A fake murder charge is leveled against them, which pushes the brothers toward a life of crime. Matters are complicated when Jackson, who is set to defend the Daltons before their trial for murder, falls in love with the fiancée of one of them.

Five years later, the studio reworked much of the same material in *THE DALTONS RIDE AGAIN* (1945).

WHEN THE REDSKINS RODE Columbia, 1951, Color, 78 min. **Producer:** Sam Katzman; **Director:** Lew Landers; **Screenplay:** Robert E. Kent; **Cinematographer:** Lester White; **Editor:** Richard Fantl; **Cast:** Jon Hall, Mary Castle, James Seay, John Ridgely, Sherry Moreland, Pedro de Cordoba, John Dehner, Lewis L. Russell, William Bakewell.

Prior to the Revolutionary War, Virginia Governor Dinwiddle and George Washington try to get local Indian tribes to ally with the British against the French. But a pretty spy tries to convince the Indian chief's son to do the opposite.

WHEN THE WEST WAS YOUNG See *HERITAGE OF THE DESERT* (1932).

WHERE THE BUFFALO ROAM Monogram, 1938, B&W, 61 min. **Producer:** Edward Finney; **Director:** Albert Herman; **Screenplay:** Robert Emmett (Tansey); **Music:** Frank Sanucci; **Cinematographer:** Francis Corby; **Editor:** Frederick Bain; **Cast:** Tex Ritter, Dorothy Short, Horace Murphy, "Snub" Pollard, John Merton, Richard Alexander, Karl Hackett, Louise Massey, Dave O'Brien, Bob Terry.

See *SONG OF THE GRINGO.*

WHERE THE RIVER BENDS See *BEND OF THE RIVER.*

WHERE THE WEST BEGINS Monogram, 1938, B&W, 54 min. **Producer:** Maurice Conn; **Director:** J. P. McGowan; **Screenplay:** Gennaro Rea; **Music:** Johnny Lange, Connie Lee, and Fred Stryker; **Cinematographer:** Jack Greenhalgh; **Editor:** Richard G. Wray; **Cast:** Addison Randall, Fuzzy Knight, Luana Walters, Arthur Housman, Richard Alexander, Ralph Peters.

See *RIDERS OF THE DAWN.*

WHERE TRAILS DIVIDE Monogram, 1937, B&W, 60 min. **Producer:** Robert N. Bradbury; **Director:** Bradbury; **Screenplay:** Robert Emmett (Tansey); **Music:** Mischa Bakaleinikoff; **Cinematographer:** Bert Longnecker; **Cast:** Tom Keene, Warner P. Richmond, Eleanor Stewart, Lorraine Randall, David Sharpe, Hal Price, James Sheridan, Richard Cramer, Jim Mason.

An express company lawyer is made sheriff of a small town in order to stop an outlaw gang. This is one of Tom Keene's early entries in his Monogram series, which also included *God's Country and the Man, Romance of the Rockies* (1937), *The Painted Trail* (1938), *Wanderers of the West, Dynamite Canyon, The Driftin' Kid, Riding the Sunset Trail, Lone Star Law Men* (1941); *Western Mail, Arizona Round-Up, Where Trails End* (1942).

WHERE TRAILS END Monogram, 1942, B&W, 55 min. **Producer:** Robert Emmett Tansey; **Director:** Tansey; **Screenplay:** Robert Cline; **Editor:** Fred Bain; **Cast:** Tom Keene, Joan Curtis, Frank Yaconelli, Don Stewart, Charles King, Wilhelm von Brincken, Steve Clark, Horace B. Carpenter, Nick Moro, Gene Alsace.

When a mysterious outlaw gang drives settlers from their homes, a U.S. marshal is sent to investigate. He finds that enemy agents are after recently discovered tungsten. This film is Tom Keene's final series entry for Monogram. (See also *WHERE TRAILS DIVIDE*.)

WHIRLWIND Columbia, 1951, B&W, 70 min. **Producer:** Armand Schaefer; **Director:** Norman S. Hall; **Screenplay:** Norman Hall; **Music:** John Leipold, Arthur Morton, Heinz Roemheld, Paul Sawtell, and Marlin Skiles; **Cinematographer:** William Bradford and Paul Borofsky; **Cast:** Gene Autry, Smiley Burnette, Gail Davis, Harry Lauter, Dick Curtis, Harry Harvey, Gregg Barton, Tommy Ivo, Kenne Duncan, Al Wyatt Sr.

See *TUMBLING TUMBLEWEEDS*.

WHIRLWIND RAIDERS (aka: STATE POLICE, UK) Columbia, 1948, B&W, 54 min. **Producer:** Colbert Clark; **Director:** Vernon Keays; **Screenplay:** Norman Hall; **Cinematographer:** M. "Andy" Anderson; **Editor:** Paul Borofsky; **Cast:** Charles Starrett, Fred F. Sears, Smiley Burnette, Jack Ingram, Don Reynolds, Philip Morris, Nancy Saunders.

See *DURANGO KID, THE*.

WHISPERING SMITH Paramount, 1948, Color, 88 min. **Producer:** Mel Epstein (associate); **Director:** Leslie Fenton; **Screenplay:** Frank Butler and Karl Lamb; **Music:** Adolph Deutsch; **Cinematographer:** Ray Rennahan; **Editor:** Archie Marshek; **Cast:** Alan Ladd, Robert Preston, Brenda Marshall, Donald Crisp, William Demarest, Fay Holden, Murvyn Vye, Frank Faylen, John Eldredge, Robert Wood, J. Farrell MacDonald, Will Wright, Don Barclay, Eddy Waller, Ray Teal.

Alan Ladd is the iron-willed, soft-spoken railroad detective Whispering Smith. His good friend Murray Sinclair (Robert Preston), who has been fired from the railroad, starts helping a band of crooks led by Barney Rebstock (Donald Crisp) to wreck the railroad trains, which forces Smith to go after his friend. There also seems to be more than a passing attraction between Smith and Murray's wife Marian (Brenda Marshall).

Whispering Smith was Alan Ladd's first color film and first starring western. Taken from a novel by Frank H. Spearman, the film is based on a real-life railroad detective who earned the nickname of "Whispering Smith" because he was fast on the draw and spoke in a low, hard voice. While the character of "Whispering Smith" was purified by the scriptwriters, it was well suited for Ladd, then Paramount's hottest male star. He looks wonderful in color and manages to convey strength, warmth, steadiness, and tenderness, while still remaining every bit a man alone and apart.

While there has been a tendency to downplay Ladd's film work in recent times, there was no doubt about his charisma and talent, and as an actor he was more than solid. *Newsweek* opined that the film was "a deserving if desperately orthodox Western. . . . Facially and vocally, the new role fits Ladd to perfection and, for all his deceptive deadpan and almost fastidious gunplay, there is never any doubt that he is as lethal as any Western star since William S. Hart."

Movie fans were enthusiastic about Ladd's foray into the western. It would soon become one of his genre staples, with Ladd subsequently starring in 10 more westerns, including his superb performance in *SHANE* (1953), which many consider his definitive role. The Screen Writers Guild nominated *Whispering Smith* as the Best Written American Western of the Year.

During the silent era, two adaptations of *Whispering Smith* were released, Mutual's 1916 version starring J. P. McGowan as the title character, and PDC's 1926 entry, produced by Cecil B. DeMille, with H. B. Warner playing the railroad detective. Some works using the title departed from the original novel; George O'Brien's *Whispering Smith Speaks* (1935), for example, had little to do with Spearman's story, and the NBC series debuting in 1962 with Audie Murphy playing Tom "Whispering" Smith, a Denver criminologist, had no connection to any of the film versions nor the novel by Spearman.

WHISPERING SMITH SPEAKS Fox Film Corporation, 1935, B&W, 65 min. **Producer:** Sol Lesser; **Director:** David Howard; **Screenplay:** Dan Jarrett and Don Swift; **Cinematographer:** Frank B. Good; **Editor:** Robert O. Crandall; **Cast:** George O'Brien, Irene Ware, Kenneth Thomson, Maude Allen, Spencer Charters, Victor Potel.

George O'Brien is the son of a railroad president who chooses to work as a trackwalker in order to learn the business. He encounters a girl (Irene Ware) who is about to sell some land, unaware that it contains valuable deposits.

WHISTLING BULLETS Ambassador, 1937, B&W, 57 min. **Producer:** Maurice Conn; **Director:** John English; **Screenplay:** Joseph O'Donnell; **Music:** Connie Lee (songs); **Cinematographer:** Jack Greenhalgh; **Editors:** Kermit Maynard, Harley Wood, Karl Hackett, Maston Williams, Jack Ingram, Bruce Mitchell, James Sheridan, Cliff Parkinson.

WHISTLING HILLS Monogram, 1951, B&W, 59 min. **Producer:** Vincent M. Fennelly; **Director:** Derwin Abrahams; **Screenplay:** Fred Myton; **Cinematographer:** Ernest Miller; **Editor:** Sammy Fields; **Cast:** Johnny Mack Brown, James Ellison, Pamela Duncan, Noel Neill, I. Stanford Jolley, Pierce Lyden, Lane Bradford, Lee Roberts, Marshall Reed.

See *UNDER ARIZONA SKIES*.

WHITE BUFFALO (aka: HUNT TO KILL) De Laurentis, 1977, Color, 97 min, VHS. **Producer:** Pancho Kohner; **Director:** J. Lee Thompson; **Screenplay:** Richard Sale; **Music:** John Barry; **Cinematographer:** Paul Lohman; **Editor:** Michael F. Anderson; **Cast:** Charles Bronson, Will Sampson, Jack Warden, Kim Novak, Clint Walker, Stuart Whitman, Slim Pickens, John Carradine, Cara Williams.

Wild Bill Hickok (Charles Bronson) leaves Buffalo Bill Cody's Wild West Show, returns to the West, and forms an uneasy alliance with Crazy Horse (Will Sampson) in order to hunt down an albino buffalo that has been haunting his dreams. Hickok and Crazy Horse (whose daughter has been killed in an attack and who must purge himself of dishonor) assume aliases to pursue their prey. Much of the action takes place in the snow and includes the obligatory avalanche and a blinding snow blizzard. According to *Variety*, "The title beast looks on, a hung-over-carnival prize, despite attempts to camouflage via hokey sound track noise, busy John Barry scoring, murky photography and fast editing."

WHITE EAGLE Columbia, 1932, B&W, 64 min. **Director:** Lambert Hillyer; **Screenplay:** Fred Myton; **Editor:** Gene Milford; **Cast:** Buck Jones, Barbara Meeks, Ward Bond, Robert Ellis, Jason Robards Sr., Jim Thorpe, Frank Campeau, Bob Kortman, Robert Elliott, Clarence Geldart, Jimmy House.

An Indian who is really white tries to protect his tribe from a band of horse thieves. This sturdy Buck Jones vehicle was remade by Columbia as a serial in 1941, with Jones in the title role once again.

Buck Jones's enormous popularity as a big star began to wane when his attempt to produce his own talkie film, *The Big Hop* (1928), flopped badly. He revitalized his career in 1930 with a string of above-average, low-budget films for Columbia before moving on to Universal in 1934. In 1937 he returned to Columbia, where over the next two years his film series was of a lesser quality.

Jones's Columbia filmography includes: *The Lone Rider, Shadow Ranch, Men Without Law, The Dawn Trail* (1930); *Desert Vengeance, The Avenger, The Texas Ranger, The Fighting Sheriff, Branded, Border Law, The Deadline, Range Feud* (1931); *Ridin' for Justice, One Man's Law, South of the Rio Grande, High Speed, Hello Trouble, McKenna of the Mounted, Forbidden Trail, The Sundown Rider* (1932); *Treason, The California Trail, The Thrill Hunter, Unknown Valley, Gordon of Ghost City, The Fighting Code, Child of Manhattan* (1933); *The Fighting Ranger, The Man Trailor, When a Man Sees Red* (1934).

WHITE FEATHER 20th Century Fox, 1955, Color, 102 min. **Producers:** Leonard Goldstein and Robert L. Jacks; **Director:** Robert D. Webb; **Screenplay:** Delmer Daves and Leo Townsend; **Music:** Hugo Friedhofer; **Cinematographer:** Lucien Ballard; **Editor:** George A. Gittens; **Cast:** Robert Wagner, John Lund, Debra Paget, Jeffrey Hunter, Eduard Franz, Noah Beery Jr., Virginia Leith, Emile Meyer, Hugh O'Brien, Milburn Stone, Iron Eyes Cody.

White Feather tells the tale of an 1877 campaign in Wyoming to contain the Indians by persuading them to sign treaties, leave the plains, and move to reservations. The colonel in charge (John Lund) is aided by a surveyor (Robert Wagner) who has made two strong Indian friends: Jeffrey Hunter, the chief's son; and his warrior pal, Hugh O'Brien. Matters are complicated when a beautiful Indian girl (Debra Paget), who is engaged to one of the young bucks, falls in love with Wagner. When the time comes to sign the treaty,

the two men jeopardize the meeting when they challenge the army to fight. Matters are settled only when Wagner offers a personal challenge to the two, whom he kills, thus saving the day.

Based on a John Preeble story about the Cheyenne Indians, this fair and sympathetic treatment of the American Indian, coscripted by *Broken Arrow*'s (1950) Delmer Daves, boasts an outstanding performance by Eduard Franz as the venerable Chief Golden Hand as well as some breathtaking on-location photography in colorful CinemaScope.

WHITE SQUAW, THE Columbia, 1956, B&W, 75 min. **Producer:** Wallace MacDonald; **Director:** Ray Nazarro; **Screenplay:** Les Savage Jr.; **Music:** Mischa Bakaleinikoff; **Cinematographer:** Henry Freulich; **Editor:** Edwin H. Bryant; **Cast:** David Brian, May Wynn, William Bishop, Nancy Hale, William Leslie, Myron Healey, Robert C. Ross, Frank DeKova, George Keymas, Grant Withers.

A rancher seeks revenge when the government tells him that he did not properly file his land claim and that they are going to use the area for an Indian reservation.

WHITE STALLION See *HARMONY TRAIL*.

WICHITA Allied Artists, 1955, Color, 81 min. **Producer:** Walter Mirisch; **Director:** Jacques Tourneur; **Screenplay:** Daniel B. Ullman; **Music:** Hans J. Salter; **Cinematographer:** Harold Lipstein; **Editor:** William Austin; **Cast:** Joel McCrea, Vera Miles, Lloyd Bridges, Wallace Ford, Edgar Buchanan, Peter Graves, Keith Larson, Carl Benton Reid, John Smith, Jack Elam, Robert J. Wilke, Walter Sande.

Wyatt Earp (Joel McCrea) arrives in the lawless town of Wichita, where his skill as a gunfighter makes him a perfect candidate for marshal. However, he refuses the offer until events beyond his control makes it a necessity. This is an interesting look at the early career of Wyatt Earp during his pre-Dodge City days. Stuart N. Lake, whose biography of Earp was the basis for many films, served as technical advisor. Helmed by Jacques Tourneur, this fine film won a Golden Globe Award for Best Outdoor Drama (1956).

WIDE OPEN TOWN Paramount, 1941, B&W, 79 min. **Producer:** Harry Sherman; **Director:** Leslie Selander; **Screenplay:** J. Benton Chaney and Harrison Jacobs; **Music:** John Leipold and Irvin Talbot; **Cinematographers:** Harrison Jacobs and J. Benton Cheney; **Editor:** Carroll Lewis; **Cast:** William Boyd, Russell Hayden, Andy Clyde, Evelyn Brent, Victor Jory, Morris Ankrum, Bernice Kay, Kenneth Harlan, Roy Barcroft, Glenn Strange, Ed Cassidy.
See *HOP-ALONG CASSIDY*.

WILD AND THE INNOCENT, THE Universal, 1959, Color, 84 min. **Producer:** Sy Gomberg; **Director:** Jack Sher; **Screenplay:** Gomberg and Sher; **Music:** Hans J.

Salter; **Cinematographer:** Harold Lipstein; **Editor:** George A. Gittens; **Cast:** Audie Murphy, Joanne Dru, Gilbert Roland, Jim Backus, Sandra Dee, George Mitchell.

Audie Murphy is a mountaineer getting his first taste of big-city life. He reluctantly hooks up with perky Sandra Dee, who is fleeing the oppressive constraints of her family. Thoroughly mismatched, they manage to get into all types of trouble in town, with Audie having to shoot the sheriff in order to rescue Sandra from her job as a dance-hall girl. Entertaining and surprisingly charming, this film should please more than just the usual Audie Murphy fans.

WILD AND WOOLLY 20th Century Fox, 1937, B&W, 65 min. **Producer:** John Stone; **Director:** Albert Werker; **Screenplay:** Lynn Root and Howard Fenton; **Music:** Samuel Kaylin, Sidney Clare (songs), and Harry Akst (songs); **Cinematographer:** Harry Jackson; **Cast:** Jane Withers, Walter Brennan, Pauline Moore, Carl "Alfalfa" Switzer, Jackie Searl, Benton Churchill, Douglas Fowley, Robert Wilcox, Douglas Scott, Lon Chaney Jr., Frank Melton, Syd Saylor.

This western comedy has Jane Withers as a lovely lass delighting in the celebrations of her hometown's 50th anniversary. Walter Brennan, her grandfather and once a bad man, has an ongoing feud with a local politician (Berton Churchill), whom he challenges to a duel. For unknown reasons, though, Brennan doesn't show up. He gets a chance to save face when Jane and her friend (Carl "Alfalfa" Switzer) overhear a pair of crooks planning to stage a bank robbery during the festivities, and with this knowledge grandfather saves the day. While short on action, this comedy western is generally considered one of Jane Withers's better features.

WILD BILL United Artists/MGM, 1995, B&W, 98 min, VHS, DVD. **Producers:** Lili Fini Zanuck and Richard Z. Zanuck; **Director:** Walter Hill; **Screenplay:** Hill; **Music:** Van Dyke Parks; **Cinematographer:** Lloyd Ahern; **Editor:** Freeman A. Davies; **Cast:** Jeff Bridges, Ellen Barkin, John Hurt, Diane Lane, Keith Carradine, David Arquette, Christina Applegate, Bruce Dern, James Gannon.

In Deadwood, South Dakota, James Butler "Wild Bill" Hickok (Jeff Bridges) must face a mysterious stranger (David Arquette) who arrives in town announcing that he will not leave until Hickok is dead. Bridges's Hickok is a hard-drinking, quick-shooting gunslinger living on the edge, "one ornery sore-headed s.o.b," according to *Variety*. In the film's initial 20 minutes, he cuts down a succession of men "in an elongated montage that spans nine years up to 1876 and locations from Abilene to Cheyenne to New York City."

Bridges delivers very well in his role, in which Wild Bill's psyche is dissected and trisected as he heads toward his final hand of poker in Deadwood. There is a series of flashbacks (in black and white) to his younger days and the events that led to his reputation as a feared gunman—even as he copes with encroaching blindness caused by syphilis.

Director Walter Hill gives a cinematic debunking of Wild Bill Hickok. Certainly Hill's presentation is a long way from William S. Hart's sympathetic and more accurate portrayal of James Butler Hickok in his 1923 silent feature *WILD BILL HICKOK*. Basing his film on both Pete Dexter's novel *Deadwood* and Thomas Babe's play *Fathers and Son*, director/screenwriter Hill included some twisted romantic scenarios. Hickok, for instance, carries on an old quasi-romance with Calamity Jane (Ellen Barkin) while he is still obsessed with his lost love (Diane Lane), the mother of his mysterious adversary (Arquette)—who, it appears, may also be Wild Bill's son.

The film will not sit well with genre purists who might well see it as a companion piece to Robert Altman's inept *BUFFALO BILL AND THE INDIANS*. But whatever artistic merit *Wild Bill* may or may not have (including a dream sequence in an opium den), one can only wonder what prompted its making. A structurally awkward and gratuitously violent film, *Variety* calls it "an art Western that manages to shoot itself in both feet."

WILD BILL HICKOK Paramount, 1923, B&W, 6890 feet. **Producer:** William S. Hart; **Director:** Clifford S. Smith; **Screenplay:** J. G. Hawk; **Cinematographers:** Dwight Warren and Arthur Reeves; **Cast:** William S. Hart, Ethel Grey Terry, Kathleen O'Connor, James Farley, Jack Gardner, Carl Gerard, William Dyer, Bert Sprotte, Leo Willis, Naida Carle, Herschel Mayall.

In his preface to this movie, William S. Hart apologizes to his audience for not looking more like the real Bill Hickok. The film has gunfighter Hickok heading to Dodge City, where he becomes a gambler but also agrees to fight lawlessness in the community. When outlaw leader Jack Queen escapes from jail, Hickok must hunt him down. In the climactic showdown Hickok kills the escaped outlaw, but when he finds himself falling in love with a married woman he leaves town to avoid causing a scandal.

The film has two well-staged gunfights and a reasonable respect for historical data, including the little-known fact that Bill Hickok was going blind. The real Hickok had been a stagecoach driver, Union scout, and U.S. marshal of no particular repute until an article in the February issue of *Harper's News Monthly* magazine, written by Colonel George Ward Nichols, bestowed the hero mantle upon him. Neither hero nor villain, "Wild Bill" Hickok became an American legend based on Nichols's fanciful stories of Hickok's battles and skirmishes. Hart's film was shot in Victorville, California, today the home of the Roy Rogers Museum.

WILD BILL HICKOK (1938) See *GREAT ADVENTURES OF WILD BILL HICKOK, THE*.

WILD BILL HICKOK RIDES Warner Bros., 1941, B&W, 81 min. **Producer:** Edmund Grainger; **Director:** Ray Enright; **Screenplay:** Charles Grayson, Raymond Schrock, and Paul Girard Smith; **Music:** Howard Jackson;

Ethel Grey Terry and William S. Hart in Wild Bill Hickok. *Hart produced and wrote the original story for this 1923 silent film.* (PARAMOUNT/THE MUSEUM OF MODERN ART; THE FILMS OF PORTER, INCE, AND HART COLLECTION)

Cinematographer: Ted McCord; **Editor:** Clarence Kolster; **Cast:** Constance Bennett, Bruce Cabot, Warren Williams, Betty Brewer, Walter Catlett, Ward Bond, Howard da Silva, Frank Wilcox, Faye Emerson, Lucia Carroll, Julie Bishop, Russell Simpson, J. Farrell MacDonald, Ray Teal.

Character actor Bruce Cabot takes his turn as Wild Bill Hickok as the famed lawman tries to stop a ruthless entrepreneur from establishing an empire. A standard early 1940s western adventure, the picture is bolstered by good production values and a strong cast of reliable supporting players.

WILD BUNCH, THE Warner Bros., Seven Arts, 1969, Color, 140 min. **Producer:** Phil Feldman; **Director:** Sam Peckinpah; **Screenplay:** Peckinpah, Walon Green, and Roy N. Sickner; **Music:** Jerry Fielding; **Cinematographer:** Lucien Ballard; **Editor:** Louis Lombardo; **Cast:** William Holden, Ernest Borgnine, Robert Ryan, Edmond O'Brien, Warren Oates, Jaime Sanchez, Ben Johnson, Emilio Fernández, Strother Martin, L. Q. Jones, Albert Dekker, Bo Hopkins, Dub Taylor, Paul Harper.

In 1913, when old style outlaw gangs are becoming a thing of the past, an aging Pike Bishop (William Holden) and his band of desperadoes ride into the Texas border town of San Rafael to rob the railway office. Dressed like U.S. cavalrymen, a band of mercenaries led by Zeke Thornton (Robert Ryan) is poised waiting for them. As the two sides face off against each other, a group of temperance workers is caught in the crossfire. Bishop and his gang escape into Mexico, while Thornton's bounty hunters stop their pursuit in order

to pilfer loot from the corpses. Only when Bishop stops to meet an old confederate named Sykes (Edmond O'Brien) does he realize that the money bag they have taken from the railway office does not contain gold but rather a bunch of iron washers.

While in Mexico, Pike's men encounter General Mapache (Emilio Fernández), a vicious opponent of Pancho Villa, and they are forced to rob an army gun-supply train and sell its contents to the bandits for a mere $10,000. Worried about a double-cross, Pike has each of his men arrive in town with only a part of the rifle supply, and in turn each receives only part of the money due them. Angel (Jaime Sanchez), the last of Pike's men to make his delivery, is held captive by Mapache; he had once tried to take the general's life but killed instead the girl who had betrayed him.

Realizing they have little to live for but their pride and loyalty, Pike's men decide to fight for Angel's release. But when Mapache slits Angel's throat, Pike kills him. In the melee that follows, 200 Mexicans are killed and Pike and his men are wiped out. Thornton and his men arrive to collect the corpses and receive their bounty, but the people of Angel's village ambush them. At the end, Sykes and Thornton, who now have the gold, decide to join forces.

Rarely has a film stirred such controversy and dissension among critics. What is certain is that *The Wild Bunch* has become a landmark within the genre, and it has risen in stature through the ensuing years. When the film is at its best, Peckinpah deftly reconstructs the period, with precise attention to realistic detail and a compelling commentary on the men, good and bad, who had a share in building the West but also lived long enough to wither with its passing.

When costar Ernest Borgnine (Dutch) was asked his opinion at the prestigious Golden Boot Awards a few years ago, he proclaimed *The Wild Bunch* to be one of the best westerns ever and his own personal favorite. William Holden defended the excessive bloodletting and gore by proclaiming that such violence was cathartic. And indeed *The Wild Bunch* found its share of champions among contemporary critics. *Time* listed it as "one of the year's best." The *New York Times* agreed that it was "a fascinating movie," while the *Los Angeles Times* declared it "an extraordinary accomplishment . . . a highly personal vision of what a man is and how he relates to the world."

The negatives were also high. Arthur Knight in *Saturday Review* found the violence revolting, while Joseph Gelmis was even more direct, writing in *Newsday* that *The Wild Bunch* "is the bloodiest movie I've ever seen, maybe the bloodiest ever made." Judith Crist concurred, proclaiming, "The film winds up with a with a shootdown that is the bloodiest and most sickening display of slaughter that I can ever recall in a theatrical film. . . ." Andrew Sarris in the *Village Voice* skirts the violence issue, criticizing the production itself as being ". . . too long, the plot too lumpy, [and] the acting wildly uneven. . . ."

Film historian William Everson dismisses those (like Peckinpah, Holden, and others) who insisted that the director *had* to depict violence graphically in order to condemn it.

Nor does he place much stock in the contention that the film's artistry necessitated presenting detailed bloodletting in slow motion, arguing instead that it cannot "counteract, or justify the effect of revulsion and nausea it created."

Ben Johnson and Warren Oates were the raucous Gorch brothers in the film. Twenty-five years later, in a 1994 interview with the author, Johnson recalled making *The Wild Bunch* and the director with whom he worked more than a few times: "Peckinpah was a good director, but he was different, he was a fatalist. Only thing was that he was so violent. I think the violence was in his nature. He was a fatalist all the way. He tried to kill himself for forty years before he got it done. Drinking that old whiskey and taking all those pills and stuff like that."

Still an enormously popular western, and to some a defining film in the genre, *The Wild Bunch* was nominated for two Academy Awards: Best Original Story and Screenplay (Walon Green, Roy N. Sickner, Sam Peckinpah); and Best Original Music Score (Jerry Fielding).

WILDCAT See *GREAT SCOUT AND CATHOUSE THURSDAY.*

WILDCAT OF TUCSON, THE Columbia, 1940, B&W, 59 min. **Producer:** Leon Barsha; **Director:** Lambert Hillyer; **Screenplay:** Fred Myton; **Cinematographer:** George Meehan; **Editor:** Charles Nelson; **Cast:** Bill Elliott, Evelyn Young, Stanley Brown, Dub Taylor, Kenneth MacDonald, Ben Taggart, Edmond Cobb, George Lloyd, Sammy Stein, Bert Young.

When his brother is jailed on a phony charge of attempted murder, Wild Bill Hickok returns to help him. After launching to genre stardom in *THE GREAT ADVENTURES OF WILD BILL HICKOK* (1938), "Wild Bill" Elliott played his namesake Hickok in 13 films for Columbia, beginning with the 1938 serial *The Great Adventures of Wild Bill Hickok.* Other films include *Beyond the Sacramento, Prairie Schooners, Wildcat of Tucson* (1940); *Across the Sierras, Hands Across the Rockies, King of Dodge City, North from the Lone Star, Roaring Frontiers,* (1941); *Bullets for Bandits, Devil's Trail, Lone Star Vigilantes, Prairie Gunsmoke* (1942).

Elliott assumed the name "Wild Bill" Saunders in four other Columbia ventures: *Taming of the West* (1939); *Pioneers of the Frontier, The Man from Tumbleweeds,* and *The Return of Wild Bill* (1940).

WILD COUNTRY PRC, 1947, B&W, 59 min. **Producer:** Jerry Thomas; **Director:** Ray Taylor; **Screenplay:** Arthur E. Orloff; **Music:** Karl Hajos; **Cinematographer:** Robert Cline; **Editor:** Hugh Winn; **Cast:** Eddie Dean, Roscoe Ates, Peggy Wynne, Douglas Fowley, I. Stanford Jolley, Lee Roberts.
See *SONG OF OLD WYOMING.*

WILD COUNTRY (aka: THE NEWCOMERS) Walt Disney/Buena Vista, 1971, Color, 100 min. **Producer:** Ron Miller; **Director:** Robert Totten; **Screenplay:** Calvin Clements Jr. and Paul Savage; **Music:** Robert F. Brunner; **Cinematographer:** Frank Phillips; **Editor:** Robert Stafford; **Cast:** Steve Forrest, Jack Elam, Ron Howard, Frank DeKova, Morgan Woodward, Vera Miles, Clint Howard, Dub Taylor, Woody Chambliss, Karl Swenson.

In the 1880s a Pittsburgh, Pennsylvania, family makes the long trek westward to Wyoming in this pleasant family film directed by Robert Totten (*THE SACKETTS*, 1979). Totten sponsored Ron Howard years later for membership in the Directors Guild.

WILD DAKOTAS, THE Associated Film, 1956, B&W, 73 min. **Producers:** Sigmund Neufeld and Sam Newfield; **Directors:** Neufeld and Newfield; **Screenplay:** Thomas W. Blackburn; **Music:** Paul Dunlap; **Cinematographer:** Kenneth Peach; **Editor:** Holbrook N. Todd; **Cast:** Bill Williams, Coleen Gray, Jim Davis, Dickie Jones, John Miljan, Lisa Montell, I. Stanford Jolley.

A trail guide and a corrupt wagon train boss are at odds with one another when the boss wants to settle down in a valley belonging to Indians who will fight to protect their land.

WILDFIRE Screen Guild, 1945, Color, 57 min, VHS. **Producer:** William B. David; **Director:** Robert Tansey; **Screenplay:** Frances Kavanaugh; **Cinematographer:** Marcel Le Picard; **Editor:** Charles Henkel Jr.; **Cast:** Bob Steele, Sterling Holloway, John Miljan, Eddie Dean, Virginia Maples, Sarah Padden, Gene Alsace, Francis Ford, William Farnum, William "Wee Willie" Davis.

This colorful outdoor outing has a band of outlaws rustling a group of horses while blaming their disappearance on a wild horse named Wildfire. Bob Steele takes it upon himself to save the beautiful Wildfire and protect the right of the wild horses as he sets out to apprehend the culprits.

WILD FRONTIER, THE Republic, 1947, B&W, 59 min. **Producer:** Gordon Kay (associate); **Director:** Philip Ford; **Screenplay:** Albert DeMond; **Cinematographer:** Alfred Keller; **Editor:** Less Orlebeck; **Cast:** Allan "Rocky" Lane, Jack Holt, Eddy Waller, Pierre Watkin, Roy Barcroft, Tom London, Sam Flint.
See *BOLD FRONTIERSMAN, THE.*

WILD HORSE Allied Pictures, 1931, B&W, 77 min. **Producer:** M. H. Hoffman Jr.; **Director:** Sidney Algiers and Richard Thorpe; **Screenplay:** Jack Natteford; **Cinematographer:** Ernest Miller; **Editor:** Mildred Johnston; **Cast:** Hoot Gibson, Alberta Vaughn, Stepin Fetchit, Neal Hart, Edmund Cobb, George Bunny, Edward Peil Sr., Skeeter Bill Robins, Joe Reckon, Fred Gilman.

A dishonest rodeo bronc buster murders a cowboy who, along with his partner, had captured a wild horse. The murdered man's partner now finds himself blamed for the crime.

WILD HORSE AMBUSH Republic, 1952, B&W, 54 min. **Producer:** Rudy Ralston; **Director:** Fred C. Bannon; **Screenplay:** William Lively; **Music:** Stanley Wilson; **Cinematographer:** John MacBurnie; **Editor:** Harold Minter; **Cast:** Michael Chapin, Eilene Janssen, James Bell, Richard Avonde, Roy Barcroft, Julian Rivero, Movita.

Two youngsters help the law track down a counterfeiting ring in this average entry to Republic's "Rough Ridin' Kids" series.

WILD HORSE CANYON Monogram, 1938, B&W, 57 min. **Producer:** Robert Emmett Tansey; **Director:** Robert Hill; **Screenplay:** Robert Emmett (Tansey); **Cinematographer:** Bert Longenecker; **Editor:** Howard Dillinger; **Cast:** Addison Randall, Dorothy Short, Frank Yaconelli, Warner P. Richmond, Walter Long.
    See *RIDERS OF THE DAWN*.

WILD HORSE MESA Paramount, 1932, B&W, 65 min. **Producer:** Harold Hurley; **Director:** Henry Hathaway; **Screenplay:** Frank Howard Clark and Harold Shumate; **Music:** John Leipold; **Cinematographer:** Arthur L. Todd; **Cast:** Randolph Scott, Sally Blane, Fred Kohler, Lucille La Verne, Charley Grapewin, James Bush, Jim Thorpe, George "Gabby" Hayes, Buddy Roosevelt, E. H. Calvert.

A horse trainer objects to the round-up methods of using barbed wire, which might injure a wild horse herd. Zane Grey's story was originally filmed as a silent feature by Paramount in 1925 with Jack Holt in the lead role.

WILD HORSE MESA RKO, 1947, B&W, 61 min. **Producer:** Herbert Schlom; **Director:** Wallace A. Grissell; **Screenplay:** Norman Houston; **Music:** Paul Sawtell; **Cinematographer:** Frank Redman; **Editor:** Desmond Marquette; **Cast:** Tim Holt, Nan Leslie, Richard Martin, Tom Keene, Jason Robards Sr., Tony Barrett, Harry Woods, William Gould, Robert Bray, Dick Foote, Frank Yaconelli.

WILD HORSE PHANTOM PRC, 1944, B&W, 56 min. **Producer:** Sigmund Neufeld; **Director:** Sam Newfield; **Screenplay:** George Milton; **Cinematographer:** Robert E. Cline; **Editor:** Holbrook; **Cast:** Buster Crabbe, Al St. John, Elaine Morey, Kermit Maynard, Budd Buster, Hal Price, Robert Meredith, Frank Ellis.
    See *OUTLAW OF THE PLAINS*.

WILD HORSE RANGE Monogram, 1940, B&W, 58 min. **Producer:** Harry S. Webb; **Director:** Raymond K. Johnson; **Screenplay:** Carl Krusada; **Music:** Johnny Lange (songs) and Lew Porter (songs); **Cinematographer:** William Hyer and Edward A. Kull; **Editor:** Robert Golden; **Cast:** Addison Randall, Frank Yaconelli, Phyllis Ruth, Marin Sais, Ralph Hoopes, Forrest Taylor, Charles King, Tom London.
    See *RIDERS OF THE DAWN* (1937).

WILD HORSE RODEO Republic, 1937, B&W, 55 min. **Producer:** Sol C. Siegal; **Director:** George Sherman; **Screenplay:** Betty Burbridge and Oliver Drake; **Music:** Alberto Columbo, Karl Hajos, and William Lava; **Cinematographer:** William Nobles; **Editor:** Lester Orlebeck; **Cast:** Robert Livingston, Ray Corrigan, Max Terhune, June Martel, Walter Miller, Edmund Cobb, William Gould, Jake Ingram, Roy Rogers (as Dick Weston).
    See *THREE MESQUITEERS, THE*.

WILD HORSE ROUND-UP Ambassador, 1937, B&W, 58 min. **Producer:** Maurice Conn; **Director:** Alan James; **Screenplay:** Joseph O'Donnell; **Music:** Connie Lee (songs); **Cinematographer:** Arthur Reed; **Editor:** Richard G. Wray; **Cast:** Kermit Maynard, Beth Marion, Dickie Jones, John Merton, Frank Hagney, Roger Williams, Dick Curtiss, Budd Buster.

WILD HORSE RUSTLERS PRC, 1943, B&W, 58 min. **Producer:** Sigmund Neufeld; **Director:** Sam Newfield; **Screenplay:** Joe O'Donnell and Steve Braxton; **Cinematographer:** Robert Cline; **Editor:** Holbrook N. Todd; **Cast:** Robert Livingston, Al St. John, Lane Chandler, Linda Johnson, Frank Ellis, Stanley Price, Karl Hackett, Jimmy Aubrey.

WILD HORSE STAMPEDE Monogram, 1943, B&W, 59 min. **Producer:** Robert Tansey; **Director:** Alan James; **Screenplay:** Elizabeth Beecher; **Cinematographer:** Marcel Le Picard; **Editor:** Fred Bain; **Cast:** Ken Maynard, Hoot Gibson, Betty Miles, Bob Baker, Ian Keith, Si Jenks, Robert McKenzie, John Bridges, Kenneth Harlan, I. Stanford Jolley.
    See *DEATH VALLEY RANGERS*.

WILD MUSTANG Ajax, 1935, B&W, 62 min. **Producer:** William Berke; **Director:** Harry L. Fraser; **Screenplay:** Fraser (as Weston Edwards); **Cinematographer:** Robert Cline; **Editor:** Arthur A. Brooks; **Cast:** Harry Carey, Barbara Fritchie, Del Gordon, Katheryn Johns, Bob Kortman, George Chesebro, Chuck Morrison.

An outlaw gang leader brands his son so the young man will be forced to work with him. However, an old-time lawman takes up his badge again and sets out to round up the crooks.

WILD NORTH, THE (aka: THE BIG NORTH) MGM, 1952, Color, 97 min. **Producer:** Stephen Aims; **Director:** Andrew Marton; **Screenplay:** Frank Fenton; **Music:** Bronislau Kaper; **Cinematographer:** Robert Surtees; **Editor:** John D. Dunning; **Cast:** Stewart Granger, Wendell Corey, Cyd Charisse, Morgan Farley, J. M. Kerrigan, Howard Petrie, Houseley Stevenson, Lewis Martin, John War Eagle, Ray Teal, Clancy Cooper.

Falsely accused of murder, a trapper is followed by a Mountie into the north country. Along the way he falls in love with a beautiful Indian girl. The film, shot on location in Idaho, is bolstered by Robert Surtees's excellent cinematography.

WILD ROVERS MGM, 1971, Color, 136 min, VHS, CD. **Producers:** Blake Edwards and Ken Wales; **Director:** Edwards; **Screenplay:** Edwards; **Music:** Jerry Goldsmith; **Cinematographer:** Philip Lathrop; **Editor:** John F. Burnett; **Cast:** William Holden, Ryan O'Neal, Karl Malden, Lynn Carlin, Tom Skeritt, Joe Don Baker, James Olson, Leora Dana.

In this film directed and scripted by comedy master Blake Edwards, two disenchanted cowboys, old-timer William Holden and youngster Ryan O'Neal, grow tired and bored working on Karl Malden's ranch, so to brighten their drab existence they decide to rob a bank. After the robbery nets them a mere $36, they head to Mexico intent on having a wild spree, but they soon find themselves followed by the sons of a ranch boss and a relentless posse.

Ryan O'Neal was at the height of his star appeal following the remarkable success of *Love Story* (1970). Yet the pairing of O'Neal with Holden, one of the screen's solid veterans, was lacking, and although there are some compelling and sentimental sequences, the film is uneven, and it played to mixed reviews at best.

WILD STALLION Monogram, 1952, Color, 70 min. **Producer:** Walter Mirisch; **Director:** Lewis D. Collins; **Screenplay:** Daniel B. Ullman; **Music:** Martin Skiles; **Cinematographer:** Harry Neumann; **Editor:** William Austin; **Cast:** Ben Johnson, Edgar Buchanan, Martha Hyer, Hayden Rorke, Hugh Beaumont, Orley Lindgren, Don Haggerty, Susan Odin, John Hart, John Halloran, I. Stanford Jolley, Barbara Woodell.

A young cavalry officer (Ben Johnson) recalls his life in military school and how another man helped him settle into the service. Johnson was a rodeo champion as well as a future Oscar winner, and his skill with horses makes this mundane story somewhat appealing. Andrew V. McLaglen, later a major director of TV and screen westerns, served as second-unit director for the film.

WILD WEST Monogram, 1946, B&W/Color (1948 reissue), 73 min. **Producer:** Robert Emmett Tansey; **Director:** Tansey; **Screenplay:** Frances Kavanaugh; **Music:** Dorcas Cochran (songs), Eddie Dean (songs), Lou Herscher (songs), Ruth Herscher (songs), and Charles Rosoff (songs); **Cinematographer:** Fred Jackman Jr.; **Editor:** Hugh Winn; **Cast:** Eddie Dean, Roscoe Ates, Sarah Padden, Lash La Rue, Robert "Buzz" Henry, Louise Currie, Jean Carlin, Lee Bennett, Terry Frost.

See *SONG OF OLD WYOMING*.

WILD WEST DAYS Universal, 1937, B&W, 13 episodes. **Producers:** Ben Koenig and Henry MacRae (associate producers); **Directors:** Ford Beebe and Clifford Smith; **Screenplay:** Wyndham Gittens, Norman S. Hall, and Ray Trampe; **Music:** Kay Kellogg (songs); **Cinematographer:**

Richard Fryer; **Editors:** Saul A. Goodkind, Louis Sackin, and Alvin Todd; **Cast:** Johnny Mack Brown, Lynn Gilbert, Russell Simpson, George Shelley, Frank Yaconelli, Bob Kortman, Al Bridge, Charles Stevens, Frank McGlynn, Walter Miller, Bruce Miller, William Royle, Jack Clifford.

Three frontiersmen come to the aid of a girl and her brother, whose ranch is being raided by outlaws trying to find gold. To achieve their objective, they frame the girl's brother on a murder charge. Based on W. R. Burnette's novel *Saint Johnson*, the story had been previously filmed in 1932 under the title *LAW AND ORDER*, and later Universal produced another *Law and Order* in 1940, also with Johnny Mack Brown. While this later version claimed to be based on the Burnette novel, it is a formula B western which bears little resemblance to the original, with comedy and musical sequences.

WILD WESTERNERS, THE Columbia, 1962, Color, 70 min. **Producer:** Sam Katzman; **Director:** Oscar Rudolph; **Screenplay:** Gerald Drayson Adams; **Music:** Duane Eddy; **Cinematographer:** Gordon Avil; **Editor:** Jerome Thoms; **Cast:** James Philbrook, Nancy Kovack, Duane Eddy, Guy Mitchell, Hugh Sanders, Elizabeth MacRae, Marshal Reed, Nestor Paiva, Harry Lauter, Bob Steele, Lisa Burkett, Terry Frost, Hans Wedemeyer.

A marshall and his new wife try to carry gold across the desert for the Union cause, but they are opposed by Indians as well as a renegade lawman and his cohorts. An interesting sidebar is the casting of pop singers Guy Mitchell and Duane Eddy (who also composed the original score) as deputy marshals.

WILLIE BOY See *TELL THEM WILLIE BOY IS HERE*.

WILL JAMES SAND See *SAND*.

WILL PENNY Paramount, 1968, Color, 108 min, VHS, DVD. **Producers:** Fred Engel and Walter Seltzer; **Director:** Tom Gries; **Screenplay:** Gries; **Music:** David Raskin; **Cinematographer:** Lucien Ballard; **Editor:** Warren Low; **Cast:** Charlton Heston, Joan Hackett, Donald Pleasence, Lee Majors, Bruce Dern, Anthony Zerbe, Ben Johnson, Slim Pickens, Clifton James.

In arguably his best western role, Charlton Heston is Will Penny, an aging cowboy who knows no other way but life on the open range. After an arduous cattle drive, he joins with two other cowpokes (Lee Majors and Anthony Zerbe) in seeking employment for the winter. While out hunting they are attacked by a crazed preacher (Donald Pleasance) and his three equally nasty sons. When Will kills one of them in self-defense he ignites a blood feud.

Things seem to be more to his satisfaction as he proceeds to the mountain cabin he is to use as his winter headquarters. There he meets lovely Joan Hackett, who is living in the cabin with her young son. For the first time in his life Will feels the pangs of romance and develops a growing fondness for the young boy, who increasingly looks upon Will as a surrogate for his real father, who is long gone.

Pleasance and his sons return to reap vengeance and leave Will close to death (in an unnecessarily brutal scene). Hackett helps nurse him back to health. She agrees to abrogate her vows for her wayward husband and marry the penniless cowboy, but Will must ultimately leave and return to the only life he knows and understands, fully aware that this is as close as he will ever come to loving a woman and having a family. "I'm damn near 50 years old," he tells her. "What do I know about love? It's too late for me. . . . I don't have them years no more. . . . As for farmin', I'm a cowboy. I've been one all my life."

This film is a compelling elegy to the cowboy way of life—the cold, the solitude, and the dreariness—and Heston's performance borders on brilliant. Moreover, in many recent interviews he lauds the work of the late Joan Hackett, calling her one of the best and most underrated actresses he has ever worked with. *History Goes to the Movies* calls *Will Penny* "an accurate, absorbing rendition of cowboy life and the line rider's isolated, enervating work. . . ." While the film remains Tom Gries's finest screen effort, it only grossed $1.3 million domestically, which was barely enough money to pay back production costs.

WINCHESTER '73 Universal, 1950, B&W, 92 min, VHS. **Producer:** Aaron Rosenberg; **Director:** Anthony

James Stewart in Winchester '73, *the first of a series of outstanding westerns the actor made for director Anthony Mann in the 1950s.* (UNIVERSAL/AUTHOR'S COLLECTION)

Mann; **Screenplay:** Borden Chase and Robert L. Richards; **Cinematographer:** Williams Daniels; **Editor:** Edward Curtiss; **Cast:** James Stewart, Shelley Winters, Dan Duryea, Stephen McNally, Millard Mitchell, Charles Drake, John McIntire, Will Geer, J. C. Flippen, Rock Hudson, Steve Brodie, Tony Curtis (as Anthony Curtis), James Best.

The first in a series of westerns Anthony Mann made with Jimmy Stewart begins in Dodge City on July 4, 1876. Central to the celebration is a shooting contest, the prize being a special presentation model Winchester '73—a repeating rifle with great power and accuracy, known as "the gun that won the West." The overseer of the proceedings is Wyatt Earp (Will Geer).

Lin McAdam (Stewart) rides into town looking for the man who killed his father. The man happens to be his brother Dutch Henry (Stephen McNally), although not until near the end does the viewer realize that the two are brothers. They shoot to a technical draw, but as a result of some trick shooting McAdam is awarded the rifle. A short time later Dutch and his men rob him of it. The rifle passes from hand to hand as the story progresses: to an arms trader (John McIntyre); a warring Indian (Rock Hudson); a coward and his fiancée (Charles Drake and Shelley Winters); and a vicious bandit (Dan Duryea). Millard Mitchell as High-Spade Frankie Wilson is McAdam's dependable and steady sidekick; his performance matches the fine character work he did in THE GUNFIGHTER that same year.

The climactic mountain shoot-out and the long rifle duel at the finish is one of the best ever put on screen. Dan Duryea is superbly despicable as swaggering villain Waco Johnny Dean. The twisted look of rage on Stewart's face as he confronts Duryea in a saloon, banging the bandit's head down on the bar, brought grasps from the audience quite unaccustomed to seeing such hate emanating from Stewart. According to screenwriter Borden Chase, that scene more than any other single moment marked the beginning of a toughened-up Jimmy Stewart. (Stewart had been an authentic air ace during World War II, and he later rose to the rank of general in the California Air National Guard.)

Based on a story by Stuart N. Lake, with a screenplay by Borden Chase and Robert L. Richards, *Winchester '73* signaled Stewart's ascendancy into the western genre and introduced a whole new aspect to the great actor's film résumé. In addition it assuaged some early skeptics who thought Stewart did not have the rough edges necessary for a western star. The New York *Herald Tribune* was quick to note that Jimmy Stewart took to the chaps and saddles of a cowboy "as if he had been doing nothing else through-out his illustrious career."

Director Anthony Mann took over the project only after the Austrian-born Fritz Lang pulled out. Much like the Budd Boetticher–Randolph Scott partnership later in the decade, *Winchester '73* began a string of classic westerns from director Anthony Mann and star Jimmy Stewart that included BEND OF THE RIVER (1952), THE NAKED SPUR (1953), THE FAR COUNTRY (1954), and THE MAN FROM LARAMIE (1955). The film was also the first in which an actor forsook a huge up-front salary in favor of a share of the profits, a strategy that made Stewart a rich man and forever changed the way Hollywood did business.

WINDS OF THE WASTELAND

Republic, 1936, B&W, 54 min, VHS, DVD. **Producer:** Nat Levine; **Director:** Mack V. Wright; **Screenplay:** Joseph Poland; **Music:** Arthur Kay, Heintz Roemheld, and Paul Van Loan; **Cinematographer:** William Nobles; **Editor:** Robert Jahns; **Cast:** John Wayne, Phyllis Fraser, Lew Kelly, Douglas Cosgrove, Lane Chandler, Sam Flint, Ed Cassidy, Jon Hall.

John Wayne and his buddy Lane Chandler purchase a broken-down stagecoach and repair it so they can enter it in a race with a rival stage line, with a winning prize of $25,000. Despite the nefarious efforts of villains to stop them, Wayne and Chandler win the race to Sacramento and set their business on solid footing. One of John Wayne's better early westerns, the film captures the flavor and ambience of the Old West and provides an exciting stagecoach race to boot.

WINGS OF THE HAWK

Universal, 1953, Color, 81 min. **Producer:** Aaron Rosenberg; **Director:** Budd Boetticher; **Screenplay:** Kay Leonard and James E. Moser; **Music:** Frank Skinner; **Cinematographer:** Clifford Stine; **Editor:** Russell F. Schoengarth; **Cast:** Van Heflin, Julie Adams, Abbe Lane, George Dolenz, Noah Beery Jr., Rodolfo Acosta.

Van Heflin is "Irish" Gallagher, an American engineer whose gold mine is confiscated by the Mexican provisional governor. Heflin joins the revolutionary forces and ends up destroying his own mine. Glenn Ford, who had recently starred in director Budd Boetticher's *MAN FROM THE ALAMO* (1953), was slated to star in *Wings of the Hawk*. However, he was hurt in a fall and the part went to Heflin, who had just finished his role in *SHANE* (1953). Set in Mexico in 1911 during the Pancho Villa insurrection, the film's title is a reference to the falcon on the flag of Mexico. *Wings of the Hawk* marks the film debut of actress Abbe Lane. The film was originally issued in 3-D.

WINGS OVER WYOMING

See *HOLLYWOOD COWBOY* (1937).

WINNING OF BARBARA WORTH, THE

United Artists, 1926, B&W, 8 reels. **Producer:** Samuel Goldwyn; **Director:** Henry King; **Screenplay:** Frances Marion; **Music:** Ted Henkel; **Cinematographer:** George Barnes and Gregg Toland; **Editor:** Viola Lawrence; **Cast:** Ronald Coleman, Vilma Banky, Charles Lane, Paul McAllister, E. J. Ratcliffe, Gary Cooper, Clyde Cook, Erwin Connelly, Sam Blum, Edwin Brady.

Jefferson Worth finds an orphaned child in the desert and raises her as his daughter Barbara (Vilma Banky). As a woman now grown, she is loved by her father's ranch foreman Abe Lee (Gary Cooper). However, when a rich land developer arrives with plans to irrigate the desert, Worth joins forces with him. The irrigation project is put under the charge of Willard Holmes (Ronald Coleman), an engineer from the East. He too falls in love with Barbara, and a rivalry begins between Willard and Abe for Barbara's affections. But when Abe Lee discovers that financier James Greenfield (E. J. Ratcliffe) plans to double-cross his partners and that the dam is about to burst, he runs exhaustedly to tell Holmes. Holmes in turn manages to save the day in the nick of time. Abe Lee dies in Barbara's arms, the victim of his own courage.

Loosely based on Harold Bell Wright's popular 1911 novel, *The Winning of Barbara Worth* is probably best remembered for Gary Cooper's first memorable screen role. While the film was one of the big box-office hits of 1926, it is of relatively minor importance today. However, both the public and critics liked Cooper, whose star was then on the rise.

WINTERHAWK

Howco-International, 1976, Color, 98 min, VHS. **Producer:** Charles B. Pierce; **Director:** Pierce; **Screenplay:** Pierce; **Music:** Lee Holdridge; **Cinematographer:** James Robertson; **Editor:** Tom Boutross; **Cast:** Leif Ericson, Michael Dante, Woody Strode, Denver Pyle, L. Q. Jones, Arthur Hunnicutt, Elisha Cook Jr., Dennis Fimple, Dawn Wells, Chuck Pierce Jr.

Chief Winterhawk (Michael Dante), in need of smallpox serum to help his people, comes to a white settlement in search of help. However, when his companion is killed, Winterhawk abducts a woman and her small brother. Filmed in Montana on a limited budget, *Winterhawk* marked the final screen appearance for Arthur Hunnicutt, one of the industry's truly fine character actors.

WISTFUL WIDOW OF WAGON GAP, THE

Universal, 1947, B&W, 78 min, VHS. **Producer:** Robert Arthur; **Director:** Charles T. Barton; **Screenplay:** John Grant, Robert Lees, and Frederic I. Rinaldo; **Music:** Walter Schumann; **Cinematographer:** Charles Van Enger; **Editor:** Frank Gross; **Cast:** Bud Abbot, Lou Costello, Marjorie Main, Audrey Wilder, George Cleveland, Gordon Jones, Peter Thompson, Olin Howlin, Bill Clauson.

Bud Abbott and Lou Costello, film's most popular comedy team in the 1940s, take a trip west, as salesman Chester Wooley (Costello) accidentally kills a man and finds that legally he must support the widow and six children. Problems abound when he finds that the widow and his bride-to-be is no-nonsense Marjorie Main. A solid cast makes for some good, old-fashioned Abbott and Costello fun, with the boys battling the raucous Main and an array of Montana tough guys.

WOLF DOG

20th Century Fox, B&W, 1958. **Producer:** Sam Newfield; **Director:** Newfield; **Music:** Jonathon Bath; **Cinematographer:** Frederick Ford; **Editor:** Douglas

Robertson; **Cast:** Jim Davis, Allison Hayes, Tony Brown, Don Garrard, John Hart, Juan Root.

An ex-convict moves his family to a ranch in a remote area of Canada but finds that he has to deal with an obstinate neighbor who wants all the land for himself.

WOLVES OF THE RANGE PRC, 1943, B&W, 60 min. **Producer:** Sigmund Neufeld; **Director:** Sam Newfield; **Cinematographer:** Robert Cline; **Editor:** Holbrook N. Todd; **Cast:** Robert Livingston, Al St. John, Frances Gladwin, I. Stanford Jolley, Karl Hackett, Howard Cassidy, Jack Ingram, Kenne Duncan, Budd Buster, Bob Hill.

WOMAN FOR CHARLIE, A See *COCKEYED COWBOYS OF CALICO COUNTY.*

WOMAN OF THE TOWN, THE United Artists, 1943, B&W, 90 min, VHS. **Producer:** Harry Sherman; **Director:** George Archainbaud; **Screenplay:** Eneas MacKenzie; **Music:** Miklos Rozsa; **Cinematographer:** Russell Harlan; **Editor:** Carroll Lewis; **Cast:** Claire Trevor, Albert Dekker, Barry Sullivan, Henry Hull, Marion Martin, Porter Hall, Percy Kilbride.

Claire Trevor is the saloon girl who tries to get Bat Masterson (Albert Dekker) to give up his guns and take up journalism instead. Barry Sullivan is Masterson's befuddled friend who also vies for Trevor's affections. Miklos Rozsa won an Oscar nomination for scoring the film.

WOMAN THEY ALMOST LYNCHED, THE Republic, 1953, B&W, 90 min. **Producer:** Allan Dwan; **Director:** Dwan; **Screenplay:** Michael Fessier and Steve Fisher; **Music:** Peggy Lee, Sidney D. Mitchell, Sam H. Stept, Stanley Wilson, and Victor Young; **Cinematographer:** Reggie Lanning; **Editor:** Fred Allen; **Cast:** John Lund, Brian Donlevy, Audrey Totter, Joan Leslie, Ben Cooper, Nina Varela, Ellen Corby, Fern Hall, Minerva Urecal, Jim Davis, Reed Hadley, Ann Savage, Dick Simmons.

After she inherits a saloon in a town controlled by bandits, a city girl becomes a bandit herself and is almost hanged. Brian Donlevy (as Quantrill) and Audrey Totter (as Kate Quantrill) deliver strong performances in this better-than-average little film.

WONDERFUL COUNTRY, THE United Artists, 1959, Color, 96 min. **Producer:** Chester Erskine; **Director:** Robert Parrish; **Screenplay:** Robert Ardrey; **Music:** Alex North; **Cinematographer:** Floyd Crosby and Alex Phillips; **Editor:** Michael Luciano; **Cast:** Robert Mitchum, Julie London, Gary Merrill, Albert Dekker, Jack Oakie, Charles McGraw, Leroy "Satchel" Paige, Anthony Caruso, Pedro Armendáriz.

Robert Mitchum (who was also executive producer) stars as a man who at age 13 killed a man to avenge his father's death.

He subsequently becomes a pistolero in the employ of a local dictator. Sent across the river to buy weapons, he breaks his leg in a fall and becomes involved with curvaceous Julie London, the wife of a cavalry officer. After refusing to carry out the assassination he was hired to do, he returns to Mexico. He now finds himself with a price on his head in the United States, while his Mexican associates are after him as well.

Based on a novel by Tom Lea, the film features the author in a small part as the town barber who gives Mitchum a bath and a shave. Robert Mitchum was actually a third choice for the lead role. Both Lea and director Robert Parrish felt that Henry Fonda would be ideal as Martin Brady, the alienated pistolero, but Fonda wasn't interested. They then sought Gregory Peck, but he had just married and had no interest either. Mitchum, however, *was* interested, and in time he took control of much of the project, serving as the film's executive producer.

Baseball fans and all true students of Americana will delight in seeing the great Leroy "Satchel" Paige as Sergeant Todd Sutton. Since the screenplay called for an all-black cavalry regiment, it was Mitchum who suggested the use of the Hall of Fame baseball legend.

WRANGLER'S ROOST Monogram, 1941, B&W, 57 min. **Producer:** George W. Weeks; **Director:** S. Roy Luby; **Screenplay:** Robert Hinkle and John Vlahos; **Cinematographer:** Robert E. Cline; **Editor:** Luby (as Roy Claire); **Cast:** Ray Corrigan, John "Dusty" King, Max Terhune, Forrest Taylor, Gwen Gaze, George Chesebro, Frank Ellis, Jack Holmes, Walter Chummy.

WRATH OF GOD MGM, 1972, Color, 111 min. **Producer:** Peter Katz; **Director:** Ralph Nelson; **Screenplay:** Nelson; **Music:** Ariel Ramirez and Lalo Schifrin; **Cinematographer:** Alex Phillips Jr.; **Editors:** Richard Braken, J. Terry Williams, and Albert P. Wilson; **Cast:** Robert Mitchum, Frank Langella, Rita Hayworth, John Colicos, Victor Buono, Ken Hutcheson, Paula Pritchett.

A band of seedy adventurers led by a renegade machine-gun-toting priest (Robert Mitchum) are hired to assassinate a Latin American despot. This offbeat film was the veteran actor's sixth time filming in Mexican locations. Hearing that his former leading lady Rita Hayworth was having financial and professional problems, Mitchum persuaded director-screenwriter Ralph Nelson to give her the part of villain Victor Buono's mother. However, the 54-year-old Hayworth was impossible to work with. Reportedly she was unable to remember more than one word at a time. It would be her final motion picture; she would later succumb to Alzheimer's disease in 1987. To compound matters, actor Ken Hucheson cut his arm on some broken glass and nearly bled to death before being saved by Dorothy Mitchum (Robert's wife). Hucheson had to be rushed to the hospital, temporarily shutting down the picture. While Mitchum's work is strong, the film lost its balance and symmetry as a result of these problems. Nevertheless, much of its tongue-in-cheek quality remains intact.

WYATT EARP Warner Bros., 1994, Color, 189 min, VHS. **Producers:** Kevin Costner, Lawrence Kasdan, and Jim Wilson; **Director:** Kasdan; **Screenplay:** Dan Gordon and Kasdan; **Music:** James Newton Howard; **Cinematographer:** Owen Roizman; **Editor:** Carol Littleton; **Cast:** Kevin Costner, Dennis Quaid, Gene Hackman, Jeff Fahey, Mark Harmon, Michael Madsen, Dave Andrews, Linden Ashby, Catherine O'Hara, Bill Pullman, Isabella Rossellini, Jo Beth Williams, Mare Winningham.

This Lawrence Kasdan–Kevin Costner epic tries to cover the whole life of the famed lawman in just over three hours. The film follows Wyatt Earp from his birth and childhood in the Iowa cornfields to his relationship with his father (Gene Hackman) to the family law practice he joined in Missouri to his move west and his employment as a Wells Fargo man and finally to his stints as a lawman in Dodge City and Tombstone.

Reviews were generally lukewarm. Many insisted that, in addition to being too long, the film was overplotted and understaged. Its attempt to leave no stone untouched reduces it to an exercise in boredom, and in spite of all the screen time, the characters remain vague and poorly developed. Reviewer Rita Kempley in the *Washington Post* argued that as "a bio-pic that lasts more than three hours and moves with the urgency of a grazing buffalo [*Wyatt Earp*] lacks everything from a coherent dramatic structure to a clearly articulated point of view." Roger Ebert writing in the *Chicago Sun Times* called the film "rambling and unfocused."

Kevin Costner joined the ranks of such stars as Richard Dix, Randolph Scott, Burt Lancaster, James Gardner, Henry Fonda, Joel McCrea, and Kurt Russell who over the years have played Wyatt Earp on the silver screen. His portrayal did not fare well with critics, who generally awarded kudos only to Dennis Quaid for his performance as Doc Holliday. Quaid dropped nearly 40 pounds and grew a mustache for the part, making him almost unrecognizable to some. The film garnered an Oscar nomination for Best Cinematography.

WYOMING (aka: BAD MAN OF WYOMING) MGM, 1940, B&W, 89 min. **Producer:** Milton Bren; **Director:** Richard Thorpe; **Screenplay:** Jack Jeyne and Hugo Butler; **Music:** David Snell; **Cinematography:** Clyde De Vinna; **Editor:** Robert J. Kern; **Cast:** Wallace Beery, Leo Carillo, Ann Rutherford, Lee Bowman, Joseph Calleia, Bobs Watson, Marjorie Main, Paul Kelly, Henry Travers.

The army is after him and his partner has deserted him, so "Reb" Harkness (Wallace Beery) opts for a change of scenery and heads to Wyoming. Once there he gets involved with a female blacksmith and ends up on the right side of the law. The teaming of Beery, Leo Carillo, and Marjorie Main, each a scene stealer in his or her own right, packs lots of interest and enjoyment.

WYOMING Republic, 1947, B&W, 84 min. **Producer:** Joseph Kane (associate); **Director:** Kane (as Joe Kane); **Screenplay:** Gerald Geraghty and Lawrence Hazard; **Music:** Ernest Gold and Nathan Scott; **Cinematographer:** John Alton; **Editor:** Arthur Roberts; **Cast:** Bill Elliott, Vera Hruba Ralston, John Carroll, George "Gabby" Hayes, Albert Dekker, Virginia Grey, Maria Ouspenskaya, Grant Withers, Harry Woods, Dick Curtis, Roy Barcroft, Trevor Bardette, Minna Gombell.

A Wyoming land baron finds squatters on his property. His foreman quits in their defense, and his college-educated daughter deserts him as well. Small farmers battle against the rich land baron once more, but this time the story is told from the land baron's point of view. This solid Republic production has a great cast, lots of action, and Yakima Canutt, the second-unit director, supervising the stunt work.

WYOMING BANDIT, THE Republic, 1949, B&W, 60 min. **Producer:** Gordon Kay; **Director:** Philip Ford; **Screenplay:** M. Coates Webster; **Music:** Stanley Wilson; **Cinematographer:** John MacBurnie; **Editor:** Harold Minter; **Cast:** Allan Lane, Eddy Waller, Trevor Bardette, Victor Kilian, Rand Brooks, William Haade, Lane Bradford, Robert J. Wilke, Harold Goodwin.

See *BOLD FRONTIERSMAN, THE.*

WYOMING HURRICANE (aka: PROVED GUILTY, UK) Columbia, 1944, B&W, 58 min. **Producer:** Leon Barsha; **Director:** William Berke; **Screenplay:** Fred Myton; **Cinematographer:** Benjamin Kline; **Editor:** Charles Nelson; **Cast:** Russell Hayden, Dub Taylor, Bob Wills (and the Texas Playboys), Alma Carroll, Tristram Coffin, Joel Friedkin, Paul Sutton.

When a dishonest café operator murders a local lawman, the blame is placed on the boyfriend of the dead man's daughter. True to the B western tradition of bloodless brutality, Russell Hayden and Paul Sutton become engaged in a furious fistfight with neither protagonist incurring a mark on his body, and Hayden sends three slugs into Sutton's left arm but produces no trace of blood. Another fight follows, during which Sutton manages to conceal the fact that his left arm is riddled with bullets.

WYOMING MAIL Universal, 1950, Color, 87 min. **Producer:** Aubrey Schenck; **Director:** Reginald Le Borg; **Screenplay:** Harry Essay and Leonard Lee; **Music:** Lester Lee (songs), Dan Shapiro (songs), and Harry Lubin; **Cinematographer:** Russell Metty; **Editor:** Edward Curtiss; **Cast:** Stephen McNally, Alexis Smith, Howard Da Silva, Ed Begley, Dan Riss, Roy Roberts, James Arness, Whit Bissell, Richard Jaeckel, Gene Evans, Frankie Darro, Armando Silvestre.

The United States opens a railroad mail service to the West Coast that proves highly tempting to a gang of train robbers working with one of the mail service's guardians in their pay. Prize fighter Steve Davis (Stephen McNally), formerly an army intelligence man, is hired to track down the culprits and save the Territorial Mail Service. He goes undercover in the territorial prison, where he learns Morse Code from a fellow prisoner. When he infiltrates the gang, however, he falls in love with its female member.

WYOMING OUTLAW

WYOMING OUTLAW Republic, 1939, B&W, 56 min. **Producer:** William Berke (associate); **Director:** George Sherman; **Screenplay:** Betty Burbridge and Jack Natteford; **Music:** William Lava; **Cinematographer:** Reggie Lanning; **Editor:** Tony Martinelli; **Cast:** John Wayne, Ray Corrigan, Raymond Hatton, Don "Red" Barry (as Donald Barry), Pamela Blake, LeRoy Mason, Charles Middleton.

The Three Mesquiteers take on a band of crooked politicians who are cheating ranchers. A subplot has Will Parker (Donald Barry) as a young man drawn into crime for self-protection.

This extremely well-done Mesquiteers series entry has a finale that predates *High Sierra* (1941). The film brought Don "Red" Barry to the screen forefront and was his first movie for Republic. Elmo Lincoln, the screen's first *Tarzan*, appears as a U.S. marshal. Stunts were handled by two of the industry's very best, Yakima Canutt and David Sharpe.

Don Barry went on to star in numerous Republic westerns during the 1940s, gaining stature as Red Ryder in Republic's popular serial THE ADVENTURES OF RED RYDER. (The nickname "Red" followed him throughout his career, even though he did not have red hair.) He also featured as the Cyclone Kid and the Tulsa Kid, and for many years he was one of the top ten money making western stars. In 1939 he appeared in the Roy Rogers film *The Days of Jesse James* (1939), stealing the show as the famed outlaw. He also appeared in another 1939 Roy Rogers venture, *Saga of Death Valley*.

Barry's Republic filmography includes *Frontier Vengeance* (1937); *Ghost Valley Raiders, One Man's Law, Two Gun Sheriff, The Tulsa Kid, Texas Terrors* (1940); *The Apache Kid, Death Valley Outlaws, Desert Bandit, Phantom Cowboy, Missouri Outlaws, Kansas Cyclone, Wyoming Wildcat* (1941); *Jesse James Jr., Stagecoach Express, Outlaws of Pine Ridge, The Sundown Kid, The Sombrero Kid, The Cyclone Kid, Jesse James Jr., Arizona Terrors* (1942); *West Side Kid, Dead Man's Gulch, Carson City Cyclone, Black Hills Express, California Joe, The Man from the Rio Grande, Days of Old Cheyenne, Fugitive from Sonora* (1943): *Outlaws of Santa Fe* (1944); *Bells of Rosarita* (with Roy Rogers, 1945); *The Plainsman and the Lady* (with Bill Elliott), and *Out California Way* (with Monte Hale, 1946).

In 1949 Barry began a series of westerns for Lippert: *Red Desert, The Dalton Gang* (1949); *I Shot Billy the Kid, Train to Tombstone, Border Rangers*, and *Gunfire* (1950).

WYOMING ROUNDUP

WYOMING ROUNDUP Monogram, 1952, B&W, 53 min. **Producer:** Vincent M. Fennelly; **Director:** Thomas Carr; **Screenplay:** Daniel Ullman; **Music:** Raoul Kraushaar; **Cinematographers:** Ernest Miller and Charles Van Enger; **Editor:** Sam Fields; **Cast:** Whip Wilson, Tommy Farrell, Phyllis Coates, Richard Emory, Robert J. Wilke, House Peters Jr., I. Stanford Jolley.

See *ABILENE TRAIL*.

WYOMING WILDCAT

WYOMING WILDCAT Republic, 1941, B&W, 56 min. **Producer:** George Sherman (associate); **Director:** Sherman; **Screenplay:** Bennett Cohen; **Cinematographer:** William Nobles; **Editor:** Lester Orlebeck; **Cast:** Don "Red" Barry, Julie Duncan, Frank M. Thomas, Sid Saylor, Dick Botiller, Edmund Cobb, Edward Brady, Ed Cassidy.

See *WYOMING OUTLAW*.

YAQUI DRUMS Allied Artists, 1956, B&W, 71 min. **Producer:** William F. Broidy; **Director:** Jean Yarbrough; **Screenplay:** D. D. Beauchamp and Jo Pagano; **Cinematographer:** John J. Martin; **Editor:** Carl Pierson; **Cast:** Rod Cameron, Mary Castle, J. Carrol Naish, Roy Roberts, Robert Hutton, Denver Pyle, Keith Richards, Ray Walker, Donald Kerr.

A rancher who is fighting a corrupt saloon owner gets some unexpected help from a Mexican outlaw gang who were thwarted in a stagecoach robbery. Rod Cameron and J. Carrol Naish offer solid genre performances.

YELLOW DUST RKO, 1936, B&W, 68 min. **Producer:** Cliff Reid; **Director:** Wallace Fox; **Screenplay:** Cyril Hume and John Twist; **Music:** Alberto Colombo; **Cinematographer:** Edward Cronjaeger; **Editor:** James B. Morley; **Cast:** Richard Dix, Leila Hyams, Moroni Olsen, Jessie Ralph, Andy Clyde, Onslow Stevens.

A miner falls in love with a saloon girl and tries to woo her away from the saloon owner, even after he is falsely accused of robbing a stagecoach.

YELLOW MOUNTAIN, THE Universal, 1954, Color, 77 min. **Producer:** Ross Hunter, **Director:** Jesse Hibbs; **Screenplay:** Robert Blees, Russell S. Hughes, and George Zuckerman; **Music:** Henry Mancini; **Cinematographer:** George Robinson; **Editor:** Edward Curtiss; **Cast:** Lex Barker, Mala Powers, Howard Duff, William Demarest, John McIntire, Leo Gordon, Dayton Lummis, Hal K. Dawson, William Fawcett, James Parnell.

Two men vie for the same girl and for a share in a valuable gold claim.

YELLOW ROSE OF TEXAS, THE Republic, 1944, B&W, 69 min, VHS. **Producers:** Harry Grey and Armand Schaefer (associates); **Director:** Joseph Kane; **Screenplay:** Jack Townley; **Cinematographer:** Jack A. Marta; **Editor:** Tony Martinelli; **Cast:** Roy Rogers, Dale Evans, Grant Withers, Harry Shannon, George Cleveland, William Haade, Weldon Heyburn, Wally Wales, Tom London, Bob Nolan.

A man who is falsely accused of robbing a stagecoach goes on the run. He is sought by his daughter, an entertainer on a showboat, and by an insurance investigator masquerading as an entertainer to see if she knows her father's whereabouts. One of the better Roy Rogers ventures, the film delivers a good story complemented by some fine music. (See also *UNDER WESTERN STARS.*)

YELLOW ROSE OF TEXAS, THE (1956) See *GUNSLINGER.*

YELLOW SKY 20th Century Fox, 1948, B&W, 98 min. **Producer:** Lamar Trotti; **Director:** William A. Wellman; **Screenplay:** Trotti; **Music:** Alfred Newman; **Cinematographer:** Joe MacDonald; **Editor:** Harmon Jones; **Cast:** Gregory Peck, Anne Baxter, Richard Widmark, Robert Arthur, John Russell, Harry Morgan, James Barton, Charles Kemper, Hank Warden, Jay Silverheels.

After robbing an Arizona bank, a group of outlaws arrives at a ghost town in a state of exhaustion only to find it occupied by an old man and his daughter. When they discover there is gold on the premises they make a deal with the old man to share it. However, a few of the men, lead by double-dealing Richard Widmark, choose instead to cheat him. The leader of outlaws (Gregory Peck) has a fondness for the girl (Anne Baxter) and becomes increasingly appalled by Widmark's perfidious dealings. It all culminates in a battle to the finish between the two stars.

Based on the novel by W. R. Burnette and filmed entirely in the California desert and Death Valley, this outstanding western is skillfully helmed by William Wellman. A taut script by Lamar Trotti provides lots of passion and excitement, and stunning black-and-white photography by Joe MacDonald beautifully frames the outdoor locations. Peck and Baxter turn in wonderful performances, with Widmark patently cold-blooded as Peck's double-crossing partner in crime. Lamar Trotti was given the WGA Screen Award for the year's Best Written Western Film.

YELLOWSTONE KELLY Warner Bros., 1959, Color, 91 min. **Producer:** (uncredited); **Director:** Gordon Kelly; **Screenplay:** Burt Kennedy; **Music:** Howard Jackson; **Cinematographer:** Carl Guthrie; **Editor:** William Ziegler; **Cast:** Clint Walker, Edd Byrnes, John Russell, Ray Danton, Andrea Martin, Claude Akins, Gary Vinson, Warren Oates.

Based on a book by Clay Fisher, *Yellowstone Kelly* tells the story of a fabled fur trader (Clint Walker) who is on good terms with the Sioux. He refuses to help the U.S. cavalry in its punitive 1876 expedition, but ultimately he is forced into the fray when some white men are slaughtered at the hands of Indians.

Much of the film's appeal at the time of its release came from the casting of two 1950s television favorites, Clint Walker (*Cheyenne*) as the stolid Kelly and Edd Byrnes (*77 Sunset Strip*) as the confused tenderfoot. Yet director Gordon Douglas keeps the story going at a sprightly pace, helming a very good western and getting strong performances from his cast—including a surprisingly sympathetic turn by Byrnes. TV's John Russell (*The Lawman*, 1958–62) appears as an Indian chief.

YELLOW TOMAHAWK, THE United Artists, 1954, Color, 82 min. **Producers:** Howard W. Koch and Aubrey Schenck; **Screenplay:** Richard Alan Simmons; **Music:** Les Baxter; **Cinematographer:** Gordon Avil; **Editor:** John F. Schreyer; **Cast:** Rory Calhoun, Peggie Castle, Noah Beery Jr., Warner Anderson, Peter Graves, Lee Van Cleef, Rita Moreno, Walter Reed, Dan Riss, Adams Williams, Ned Glass.

A guide warns the builders and settlers of a new army outpost that they will be wiped out by unfriendly Indians. He is ridiculed and snubbed by the army authority until he is proved right. Some good action scenes and exciting hand-to-hand combat distinguish this mid-1950s oater.

YODELIN' KID FROM PINE RIDGE (aka: HERO OF PINE RIDGE) Republic, 1937, B&W, 62 min, VHS. **Producer:** Armand Schaefer; **Director:** Joseph Kane; **Screenplay:** Dorrell McGowan, Stuart E. McGowan, and Jack Natteford; **Music:** Gene Autry, Smiley Burnette, Frank Harford, and William Lava (all uncredited); **Cinematographer:** William Nobles; **Editor:** William Lava; **Cast:** Gene Autry, Smiley Burnette, Betty Bronson, LeRoy Mason,

Charles Middleton, Russell Simpson, Jack Dougherty, Guy Wilkerson.

See *TUMBLING TUMBLEWEEDS*.

YOUNG BILL HICKOK Republic, 1940, B&W, 59 min. **Producer:** Joseph Kane (associate); **Director:** Kane; **Screenplay:** Olive Cooper and Norton S. Parker; **Cinematographer:** William Nobles; **Editor:** Lester Orlebeck; **Cast:** Roy Rogers, George "Gabby" Hayes, Julie Bishop, John Milian, Sally Payne, Archie Twichell, Monte Blue, Wally Wales.

See *UNDER WESTERN STARS*.

YOUNG BILLY YOUNG United Artists, 1969, Color, 89 min, VHS. **Producer:** Max E. Youngstein; **Director:** Burt Kennedy; **Screenplay:** Kennedy; **Music:** Shelly Manne; **Cinematographer:** Harry Stradling Jr.; **Editor:** Otho Lovering; **Cast:** Robert Mitchum, Angie Dickinson, Robert Walker Jr., David Carradine, Jack Kelly, John Anderson, Paul Fix, Willis Bouchey.

Ben Kane (Robert Mitchum), a peace-loving man, takes a job as deputy marshal because he has an old score to settle with the man who killed his son during a jailbreak. He jails his adversary's son, but the boy's father makes plans to break him out. In the process Kane takes a trigger-happy young gunslinger, the Billy Young of the title (Robert Walker Jr.), under his wing because Billy reminds him of his murdered son. Director Burt Kennedy showcases solid performances and plenty of gunplay in this film based on the novel *Who Rides with Wyatt* by Will Henry. Robert Mitchum sings the title song written by Shelly Manne and Ernie Sheldon.

YOUNG BUFFALO BILL Republic, 1940, B&W, 59 min. **Producer:** Joseph Kane; **Director:** Kane; **Screenplay:** Gerald Geraghty, Harrison Jacobs, and Robert Yost; **Music:** Cy Feuer; **Cinematographer:** William Nobles; **Editor:** Tony Martinelli; **Cast:** Roy Rogers, George "Gabby" Hayes, Pauline Moore, Hugh Sothern, Chief Thundercloud, Julian Rivero, Trevor Bardette.

See *UNDER WESTERN STARS*.

YOUNG DANIEL BOONE Monogram, 1950, Color, 71 min. **Producer:** James S. Burkett; **Director:** Reginald LeBorg; **Screenplay:** Clint Johnston and LeBorg; **Cinematographer:** G. Warrenton; **Editors:** Charles Craft and Otho Lovering; **Cast:** David Bruce, Kristine Miller, Damian O'Flynn, Don Beddoe, Mary Treen, John Mylong.

Frontier scout Daniel Boone (David Bruce) is sent out to locate the only two of General Braddock's men who are believed to have survived an Indian attack. He discovers that a French spy has been responsible for the Indians' uprising.

YOUNGER BROTHERS, THE Warner Bros., 1949, Color, 78 min. **Producer:** Saul Elkins; **Director:** Edwin L. Marin; **Screenplay:** Edna Anhalt; **Music:** William Lava; **Cinematographer:** William Snyder; **Edi-**

tor: Frederick Richards; **Cast:** Wayne Morris, Janice Paige, Bruce Bennett, Geraldine Brooks, Robert Hutton, Alan Hale, Fred Clark, James Brown, Monte Blue, Tom Tyler, William Forrest, Ian Wolfe.

The Younger Brothers (Cole, Jim, Johnny, and Bob) are waiting for a pardon from the governor when the youngest is forced to kill a man in self-defense. Consequently the rest of the clan resume their lawless ways. Wayne Morris plays Cole Younger, but in an interesting tidbit, Bruce Bennett, who plays Jim Younger, would play the part of Cole two years later in THE GREAT MISSOURI RAID (1951).

YOUNG FURY Paramount, 1965, Color, 80 min. **Producer:** A. C. Lyles; **Director:** Christian Nyby; **Screenplay:** Steve Fisher; **Music:** Paul Dunlap; **Cinematographer:** Haskell B. Boggs; **Editor:** Marvin Coil; **Cast:** Rory Calhoun, Virginia Mayo, William Bendix, Lon Chaney Jr., John Agar, Richard Arlen, Linda Foster, Merry Anders, Joan Huntington, Jody McCrea, Rex Bell Jr., William Wellman Jr.

When a group of thugs rides into the town of Dawson and take it over, a cowardly sheriff is unable to restore control. The father of the gang's leader therefore takes it upon himself to enforce the law. An ex-gunslinger, he straps on his holster once again and faces the possibility of having to square off against his own son. This A. C. Lyles film marked the screen swan song for actor William Bendix. Among the industry's most prolific character actors during the 1940s and '50s, Bendix died in 1964, a short time before the film was released.

YOUNG GUNS, THE Warner Bros., 1956, B&W, 84 min. **Producers:** Albert Brand and Richard V. Heermance; **Director:** Albert Band; **Screenplay:** Louis Garfinkle; **Music:** Marlin Skiles; **Cinematographer:** Ellsworth Fredericks; **Editor:** George White; **Cast:** Russ Tamblyn, Gloria Talbot, Perry Lopez, Scott Marlow, Wright King, Walter Coy, Chubby Johnson, Myron Healey.

Russ Tamblyn is the son of a famous gunman who is torn between leading a peaceful life and living up to his father's lofty status. Scott Marlow plays the sheriff who tries to get the young lad on the straight and narrow and away from a gang of young thugs. Perhaps an attempt to link the perceived juvenile delinquency problems of the 1950s with the Old West, the film never quite comes together and is generally slow moving. Nevertheless, it still holds interest, possibly due to the splendid noir-style camera work by Ellsworth Fredericks, who that same year lensed *The Invasion of the Body Snatchers*.

YOUNG GUNS Morgan Creek, 1988, Color, 107 min, VHS. **Producer:** Joe Roth and Christopher Cain; **Director:** Cain; **Screenplay:** John Fusco; **Music:** Anthony Marinelli and Brian Banks; **Cinematographer:** Dean Semler; **Editor:** Jack Hofstra; **Cast:** Emilio Estevez, Kiefer Sutherland, Lou Diamond Phillips, Charlie Sheen, Jack Palance, Terence Stamp.

Emilio Estevez takes a shot at being Billy the Kid, costarring with Charlie Sheen (his real-life brother) in what has been called an MTV western and an attempt to create a "brat pack" *Wild Bunch*. A British do-gooder (Terence Stamp) tries to make gentlemen out of Billy and other renegade boys by teaching them to read and having them call each other "gentlemen." However, when Stamp is murdered by town big shots, Billy and his trigger-happy friends seek vengeance and retaliation. The film's hard-rock musical score is a first for a western. As *Variety* notes, "Music's every appearance on the scene throws one right out of the scene and serves to remind that this is a high tech artifact of the 1980s." Clearly aimed at younger audiences, the movie includes a drug-oriented episode with Billy and the gang getting high on peyote, as well as an interracial romance between Kiefer Sutherland and a Chinese girl. All in all, *Young Guns* shows little respect for the genre and departs too far from its best traditions.

YOUNG GUNS II Morgan Creek, 1990, Color, 103 min, VHS. **Producers:** Paul Schiff and Irby Smith; **Director:** Geoff Murphy; **Screenplay:** John Fusco; **Music:** Alan Silvestri; **Cinematographer:** Dean Semler; **Editor:** Bruce Green; **Cast:** Emilio Estevez, Kiefer Sutherland, Lou Diamond Phillips, Christian Slater, William Peterson, James Coburn.

The 1990 sequel to the original *Young Guns* is a little more ambitious but achieves the same results: a glossy MTV-style western with Estevez, Sutherland, and Phillips returning from the first film. The story picks up on Billy Bonney's Lincoln County gang a few years after the conclusion of the 1988 film. Conveyed in a series of flashbacks, the plot involves the gang's rush toward the perceived safety of Mexico as a band of government men led by Pat Garrett (Billy's former ally, now turned adversary) pursue them. The picture received an Oscar nomination for Best Song, "Blaze of Glory." Like the original film, the sequel is loaded with violence and profanity.

YOUNG GUNS OF TEXAS 20th Century Fox, 1962, color, 78 min. **Producer:** Maury Dexter; **Director:** Dexter; **Screenplay:** Harry Spalding; **Music:** Paul Sawtell and Bert Shefter; **Cinematographer:** John M. Nickolaus Jr.; **Editor:** Richard Einfeld; **Cast:** James Mitchum, Alana Ladd, Jody McCrea, Chill Wills, Gary Conway, Barbara Mansell, Robert Lowery, Troy Melton.

James Mitchum is an outlaw brought up by the Comanche who falls in love with the daughter (Alana Ladd) of a mean rancher. Included in his band is a young man (Jody McCrea) who has stolen army funds and whose brother (Gary Conway) is out to find him. Most of the characters die at the hands of the Apache at film's end. The main interest in this film is the casting of the three leads, all offspring of famous stars: Robert Mitchum, Alan Ladd, and Joel McCrea.

YOUNG JESSE JAMES 20th Century Fox, 1960, B&W, 73 min. **Producer:** Jack Leewood; **Director:** William

Claxton; **Screenplay:** Orville Hampton and Jerry Sackheim; **Music:** Irving Gertz; **Cinematographer:** Carl Berger; **Cast:** Ray Stricklyn, Willard Parker, Merry Anders, Robert Dix, Emile Meyer, Jacklyn O'Donnell, Rayford Barnes, Rex Holman, Bob Palmer, Sheila Bromley.

Brothers Frank and Jesse James (Ray Stricklyn and Robert Dix) find it hard to adjust to post-Civil War life. When the Yankees hang their father, they join Quantrill's Raiders and meet up with Cole Younger (Willard Parker) and Belle Starr (Merry Anders). While somewhat less sanitized than the 1939 version with Tyrone Power and Henry Fonda as Frank and Jesse, the overall merit of the film falls far from the original. Emile Meyer delivers yet another top performance as the outlaw leader William Quantrill.

YOUNG LAND, THE Columbia, 1959, Color, 89 min, VHS. **Producers:** Patrick Ford and C. V. Whitney; **Director:** Ted Tetzlaff; **Screenplay:** Norman S. Hall; **Music:** Dimitri Tiomkin; **Cinematographers:** Winton C. Hoch and Henry Sharp; **Editor:** Tom McAdoo; **Cast:** Patrick Wayne, Yvonne Craig, Dennis Hopper, Dan O'Herlihy, Cliff Ketchum, Ken Curtis, Pedro Gonzales-Gonzales, Ed Sweeney, Miguel Comancho.

Lots of trouble is brewing in the Republic of Texas when a citizen is about to be tried for the murder of a Mexican. The song "Strange are the Ways of Love," written by Dimitri Tiomkin and Ned Washington (the same team that wrote the Oscar-winning song "High Noon"), is sung by Randy Sparks.

ZACHARIAH Cinerama Releasing Corporation, 1970, Color, 93 min, VHS, DVD. **Producers:** George Englund and Lawrence Kubik; **Director:** Englund; **Screenplay:** Phillip Austin, Peter Bergman, Joe Massot, David Ossman, and Philip Proctor; **Music:** Jimmie Haskell; **Cinematographer:** Jorge Stahl; **Editor:** Gary Griffen; **Cast:** John Rubenstein, Patricia Quinn, Barry Melton, Don Johnson, Country Joe McDonald.

An uncredited adaptation of Herman Hesse's *Siddhartha*, *Zachariah* follows the trail of two gunfighters on their psychedelic journeys through the old west. One gives up his guns for peace, and eventually the two are forced into a showdown. Somewhat of a cult film today, *Zachariah* features music by such groups as Country Joe and the Fish, The New Rock Ensemble, and White Lightnin'. This "rock-musical" western, advertised as the "the first electric Western," will probably not have much appeal to fans of the genre. John Rubenstein, who plays Zachariah, is the son of classical piano legend Artur Rubenstein.

ZANDY'S BRIDE Warner Bros., 1974, Color, 116 min, VHS. **Producer:** Harry Matofsky; **Director:** Jan Troell; **Screenplay:** Marc Norman; **Music:** Michael Franks and Fred Karlin; **Cinematographers:** Jordan Croenweith and Frank Holgate; **Editor:** Gordon Scott; **Cast:** Gene Hackman, Liv Ullmann, Eileen Heckart, Susan Tyrrell, Harry Dean Stanton, Joe Santos, Frank Cady, Sam Bottoms, Vivian Gordon.

This film is set in mid-19th-century California in the Big Sur area, where people eke out livings as small-scale cattlemen and dirt farmers, making only limited contact with the outside world. Lonely Zandy Allan decides to solve his problems by ordering a mail-order bride. But Zandy sees the woman as only another one of his possessions until she proves herself, earning his respect and his love. A compelling human interest story, this engaging film relies almost entirely on its characters for its interest. There are no shoot-outs, Indian attacks, or stampedes. Based on Lillian Bos Ross's novel *The Stranger*, the film is a joint American-Scandinavian production.

ZORRO RIDES AGAIN Republic, 1959, B&W, 69 min. **Producer:** Robert M. Beecher; **Directors:** John English and William Witney; **Screenplay:** Franklyn Adreon, Morgan Cox, Ronald Davidson, John Rathmell, and Barry Shipman; **Cinematographer:** William Nobles; **Editor:** DeWitt McCann; **Cast:** John Carroll, Helen Christian, Richard Alexander, Duncan Renaldo, Reed Howes, Nigel De Burlier, Bob Kortman, Jack Ingram, Roger Williams, Mona Rico, George Mori, Tom London.

This is an edited-down feature film derived from the 12-chapter 1937 Republic serial. (See also *MARK OF ZORRO, THE*.)

Appendixes

Appendix I

SPAGHETTI WESTERNS A–Z

Over the years the American western has inspired filmmakers from countries all over the world. Yet today when one speaks of non-Hollywood westerns it is inevitable to refer to a phenomena that began in Germany in the 1960s. It was swiftly taken over and turned into a boom industry in Italy, where these films have been labeled with a degree of affectionate scorn as "spaghetti westerns."

In the early 1960s Germany began to successfully produce full-blooded imitations of the American western. The first efforts were adaptations of works by native author Karl May, who had written several enormously popular western novels around the turn of the century. Ironically, May, who died in 1912, had never been anywhere near the real West, but he was a passionate disciple of Zane Grey whom he had read voraciously while serving time in prison. The characters from May's fiction, Old Shatterhand, the Indian Brave Winnetou, and Old Surehand, were portrayed on the German screen by British, French, and American actors such as Stewart Granger, Lex Barker, Anthony Steele, and Pierre Brice, and additional Yugoslav assistance. The themes of May's films basically involved legendary figures of the American West such as Buffalo Bill (Gordon Scott) in *Buffalo Bill, Hero of the Far West* (1964); Wyatt Earp (Guy Madison) in *Duel at Rio Bravo* (1965); and Calamity Jane and Wild Bill Hickok (Gloria Milland and Adrian Hoven) in *Seven Hours of Gunfire* (1965).

On the other hand, the Italian westerns drifted away from the traditional mold and established a quasi-western style of their own. The trailblazer film was Sergio Leone's *A Fistful of Dollars* (1964) starring American actor Clint Eastwood, who at the time was enjoying TV fame as Rowdy Yates in the popular television series *Rawhide* (1959–66).

Due to some early apprehension as to how the films would be received, many in the cast and crew assumed English or American pseudonyms. For example, Sergeo Leone became "Bob Robertson," and celebrated composer Ennio Morricone was dubbed "Dan Savio."

Generally, the Italian western had a Texas-Mexico border setting and sadistic-looking Mexican bandits as the villains. The environment was usually the desert, and the time frame was the Civil War or post-Civil War. Violence, torture, rape, and mur-

der usually dominated the action. The main protagonist was an antihero who subscribed to few of the gentlemanly codes.

Much of the spaghetti westerns' success was clearly due to the willingness of top commercial directors to make them, including Sergio Corbucci, Joaquin L. Romero, Carlo Lizzani (alias Lee W. Beaver), Sergio Sollima, Duccio Tessari, Diamiano Damiani, Giulio Questri, and Tonio Cervi. Moreover, the spaghettis provided ample work for actors, and just about every western star and heavy available cashed in from time to time. For some the spaghetti was an avenue that kept their fading careers alive. Other used it as a springboard for a hopeful comeback.

Lee Van Cleef, Lex Barker, and Guy Madison joined Clint Eastwood as major players in the spaghetti circuit. Other American stars who made an impact include Alex Nicol (*Ride and Kill*, 1963); Cameron Mitchell (*Killer's Canyon*, 1964 and *Minnesota Clay*, 1965); Henry Silva and Dan Duryea (*The Hills Run Red*, 1966); Joseph Cotten (*The Tramplers*, 1966; *The Hellbenders*, 1966; *White Comanche*, 1968); Eli Wallach (*The Good, the Bad and the Ugly*, 1966; *Revenge in El Paso*, 1968); John Ireland (*Hate for Hate*, 1967); Alex Cord, Robert Ryan, and Arthur Kennedy (*Deal or Alive*, 1968); John Philip Law (*Death Rides a Horse*, 1968); Jeffrey Hunter (*Find a Place to Die*, 1968); Chuck Connors (*Kill Them All and Come Back Alone*, 1968); Jack Palance (*A Professional Gun*, 1968); and Ernest Borgnine (*A Bullet for Sandoval*, 1969). The irony is that the American westerns to follow bore a marked spaghetti influence in films like *Hang 'Em High, Lawman,* and *The Hunting Party.*

By the late 1970s the spaghetti western had burned itself out, but not before many U.S.-made films began using the format. Within the course of this work, many of the major spaghetti westerns have been included as full entries—*Ace High; Django; A Fistful of Dollars; For a Few Dollars More; The Good, the Bad, and the Ugly; Once Upon a Time in the West;* and so on. For purposes of brevity, and because a full study of the spaghetti western would warrant a volume(s) of its own, we have included the rest in this appendix.

Listed below are nearly 500 spaghetti westerns (mainly, though not entirely, Italian-made features) in alphabetical order.

Ace High (1967), Italy, Director: Giuseppe Colizzi
Adios Cjamango (1969), Italy/Spain, Director: Harry Freeman
Adios Gringo (1965), Director: George Finley
Adios Hombre (1966), Italy, Director: Mario Caiano
Adios Sabata (1970), Italy, Director: Frank Kramer
Alive or Preferably Dead (1969), Italy, Director: Duccio Tessari
All Out (1968), Italy, Director: Umberto Lenzi
Among Vultures (1964), Italy, Director: Alfred Vohrer
And God Said to Cain (1969), Italy, Director: Anthony Dawson
And the Crows Will Dig Your Grave (1971), Italy, Director: John Wood
And They Smelled the Strange, Exciting, Dangerous Scent of Dollars (1973), Italy, Director: Italo Alfaro
Animal Called Man, An (1973), Italy, Director: Roberto Mauri
Another Man, Another Woman (1977), France, Director: Claude Lelouch
Anything for a Friend (1973), Italy, Director: Miles Deem
Apache's Last Battle (1964), Italy, Director: Hugo Fregonese
Apache Woman (1976), Italy, Director: George McRoots
Apocalypse Joe (1970), Italy, Director: Leopoldo Savona
Arizona (1970), Italy, Director: Sergio Martino
Arizona Colt (1966), Italy, Director: Michele Lupo
Arizona Kid, The (1971), Italy, Director: Luciano Carlos
Armed and Dangerous (1977), Russia, Director: Vladimir Vainstok
Awkward Hands (1968), Italy, Director: Rafael Romero Marchent
Bad Kids of the West (1967), Italy, Director: Tony Good
Bad Man's River (1971), Italy, Director: Eugenio Martin
Ballad of a Gunman (1967), Italy, Director: Alfio Caltabiano
Bandera Bandits (1973), Italy, Director: Sergio Corbucci
Bandidos (1968), Italy, Director: Massimo Dallamano
Bandits, The (1967), Mexico, Directors: Robert Conrad and Alfred Zacharias
Bang Bang Kid, The (1968), Italy, Director: Luciano Lelli
Bastard, Go and Kill (1971), Spain, Director: Gino Mangini
Beast, The (1970), Italy, Director: Mario Costa
Behind the Mask of Zorro (1965), Italy, Director: Ricardo Blasco
Belle Starr Story, The (1968), Italy, Director: Nathan Wich
Ben and Charlie (1970), Italy, Director: Michele Lupo
Between God, the Devil and a Winchester (1968), Italy, Director: Dario Silvestri
Beyond the Law (1968), Italy, Director: Giorgio Stegani
Big Gundown, The (1966), Italy, Director: Sergio Sollima
Big Ripoff (1967), Spain/Italy, Director: Franco Rossetti
Big Showdown, The (1972), Italy, Director: Giancarlo Santi
Billy the Kid (1962), Italy, Director: Leon Klimovsky
Black Eagle of Santa Fe, The (1964), Germany/Italy/France, Director: Ernst Hofbauer
Black Jack (1968), Italy, Director: Gianfranco Baldanello
Black Killer (1971), Italy, Director: Lucky Moore
Black Tigress (1967), Italy, Director: Siro Marcellini
Blindman (1971), Italy, Director: Ferdinando Baldi
Blood and Guns (1968), Spain, Director: Giulio Petroni

Blood at Sundown (1967), Italy, Director: José Antonio De La Loma
Blood Calls to Blood (1968), Italy, Director: Lewis King
Blood for a Silver Dollar (1965), Italy, Director: Calvin J. Padget
Blood River (1974), Italy, Director: Gianfranco Baldenello
Boldest Job in the West, The (1969), Spain/Italy/France, Director: José Antonio De La Loma
Boot Hill (1969), Italy, Director: Giuseppe Colizzi
Born to Kill (1967), Italy, Director: Tony Mulligan
Bounty Hunter in Trinity, A (1972), Italy, Director: Oskar Faradine
Brother Outlaw (1971), Italy, Director: Edward G. Muller
Brothers Blue (1973), Italy, Director: Marc Meyer
Buddy Goes West (1981), Italy, Director: Michele Lupo
Buffalo Bill, Hero of the Far West (1964), Italy, Director: John W. Fordson
Bullet for Sandoval, A (1969), Italy/Spain, Director: Julio Buchs
Bullet for the General, A (1966), Italy, Director: Damiano Damiani
Bullets and the Flesh (1965), Italy, Director: Fred Wilson
Bullets Don't Argue (1964), Italy/West Germany/Spain, Director: Mike Perkins
Bury Them Deep (1968), Italy, Director: John Byrd
Calibre .38 (1971), Italy, Director: Toni Secchi
California (1976), Italy, Director: Michele Lupo
Canadian Wilderness (1969), Spain/Italy, Director: Armando De Ossorio
Captain Apache (1971), England, Director: Alexander Singer
Carambola (1974), Italy, Director: Ferdinando Baldi
Carambola's Philosophy: in the Right Pocket (1974/75), Italy, Director: Ferdinando Baldi
Cavalry Charge (1964), Spain, Director: Ramon Torrado
Cemetery Without Crosses (1968), Italy, Director: Robert Hossein
Challenge of the Mackennas (1969), Italy, Director: León Klimovsky
Charge of the Seventh Cavalry (1965), Italy/Spain/France, Director: Herbert Martin
Charley One-Eye (1972), England/Spain, Director: Don Chaffey
Chetan, Indian Boy (1972), Germany, Director: Mark Bohm
China 9, Liberty 37 (1978), Italy/Spain/US, Director: Monte Kellman
Chino (1973), Italy/Spain/France, Director: John Sturges
Christmas Kid, The (1967), Spain/Italy, Director: Sidney Pink
Chrysanthemums for a Bunch of Swine (1968), Italy, Director: Sergio Pastore
Chuck Moll (1970), Italy, Director: E. B. Clucher
Ciccio Forgives, I Don't (1968), Italy, Director: Frank Reed
Cipolla Colt (1975), Italy, Director: Enzo G. Castellari
Cisco (1966), Italy, Director: Sergio Bergonzelli
Cjamango (1967), Italy, Director: Edward G. Muller
Clint the Stranger (1968), Italy/Spain/West Germany, Director: Alfonso Balcazar
Coffin for the Sheriff, A (1965), Italy, Director: William Hawkins

Colorado Charlie (1965), Italy, Director: Robert Johnson

Colt 45, Five Dollars, and a Bandit (1967), Italy, Director: Richard Chardon

Colt in the Hand of the Devil (1967), Italy, Director: Sergio Bergonzelli

Colt in the Hand of the Devil (1972), Italy, Director: Frank G. Carrol

Colt is the Law (1965), Italy/Spain, Director: Al Bradly

Comin' at Ya (1981), Italy, Director: Ferdinando Baldi

Compañeros (1970), Italy/Spain/West Germany, Director: Sergio Corbucci

Cost of Dying (1968), Italy, Director: Sergio Merolle

Cowards Don't Pray (1968), Italy/Spain, Director: Marlon Sirko

Coyote (1964), Spain/Italy, Director: Joaquin L. Romero

Cry for Revenge (1968), Italy/Spain, Director: Rafael Romero Marchent

Cut-Throats Nine (1973), Spain, Director: Joaquin Romero Marchent

Dallas (1972), Italy, Director: Juan Bosch

Damned Pistols of Dallas (1964), Italy, Director: Joseph Trader

Day of Anger (1967), Italy, Director: Tonino Valerii

Days of Violence (1967), Italy, Director: Al Bradly

Dead Are Countless (1969), Italy, Director: Rafael Romero Marchent

Dead for a Dollar (1968), Italy, Director: Osvaldo Civirani

Deadlock (1970), Italy, Director: Roland Klick

Deadly Trackers (1972), Italy, Director: Americo Anton

Dead Men Ride (1970), Italy, Director: Aldo Florio

Deaf Smith and Johnny Ears (1972), Italy, Director: Paolo Cavara

Death at Owell Rock (1967), Italy, Director: George Lincoln

Death is Sweet for the Soldier of God (1972), Italy, Director: Robert Johnson

Death Knows No Time (1968), Italy, Director: Leon Klimovsky

Death on High Mountain (1969), Italy, Director: Fernando Cerchio

Death Played the Flute (1972), Italy, Director: Elo Panaccio

Death Rides a Horse (1967), Italy, Director: Giulio Petroni

Death Rides Alone (1968), Italy, Director: Joseph Warren

Death Sentence (1967), Italy, Director: Mario Lanfranchi

Death Walks in Laredo (1966), Italy/Spain, Director: Enzo Peri

Deguello (1966), Italy, Director: Joseph Warren

Deserter (1970), Italy, Director: Niska Fulgozzi/Burt Kennedy

Desperado (1972), Spain/Italy, Director: Al Bagrain

Dick Luft in Sacramento (1975), Italy, Director: Anthony Ascott

Dig Your Grave Friend . . . Sabata's Coming (1970), Italy/Spain/France, Director: John Wood

Django (1966), Italy, Director: Sergio Corbucci

Django, a Bullet for You (1966), Italy, Director: Leon Klimovsky

Django and Sartana Are Coming . . . It's the End (1970), Italy, Director: Dick Spitfire

Django Challenges Sartana (1970), Italy, Director: William Redford

Django Does Not Forgive (1967), Italy, Director: Julio Buchs

Django, Kill . . . If You Live, Shoot! (1967), Italy, Director: Giulio Questi

Django Kills Softly (1968), Italy, Director: Max Hunter

Django, Last Killer (1967), Italy, Director: Joseph Warren

Django Shoots First (1966), Italy, Director: Alberto De Martino

Django Strikes Again (1987), Italy, Director: Ted Archer

Django the Bastard (1969), Italy, Director: Sergio Carrone

Djurado (1966), Italy, Director: Gianni Narzisi

Do Not Touch the White Woman (1974), Italy, Director: Marco Ferreri

Dollar for a Fast Gun (1968), Spain/Italy, Director: Joaquin Romero Marchent

Dollar of Five (1967), Italy, Director: Nick Nostro

Don't Turn the Other Cheek (1971), Italy/Spain/West Germany, Director: Duccio Tessari

Don't Wait, Django . . . Shoot! (1969), Italy, Director: Edward G. Muller

Drummer of Vengeance (1971), Italy, Director: Robert Paget

Duck You Sucker (1971), Italy, Director: Sergio Leone

Duel at Sundown (1965), France/Germany, Director: Leopoldo Lahola

Duel in the Eclipse (1967), Italy, Director: Eugenio Martin/José Luis Merino

Durango is Coming, Pay or Die (1972), Italy, Director: Roberto Bianchi Montero

Dust in the Sun (1971), Italy, Director: Richard Balducci

Dynamite Jack (1963), Italy, Director: Jean Batista

Dynamite Jim (1966), Italy, Director: Alfonso Balcazar

Dynamite Joe (1966), Italy, Director: Anthony Dawson

Eagle's Wing (1980), England/Spain, Director: Anthony Harvey

Even Django Has His Price (1971), Italy, Director: Paolo Solvay

Execution (1968), France, Director: Domenico Paolella

Eye for an Eye (1972), Italy, Director: Albert Marshall

Face to Face (1967), Italy, Director: Sergio Sollima

Fasthand (1972), Italy/Spain, Director: Frank Bronston

Few Dollars for Django (1966), Italy, Director: Leon Klimovsky

Fifteen Scaffolds for the Killer (1968), Italy, Director: Nunzio Malasomma

Fighters from Ave Maria (1970), Italy, Director: Al Albert

Fighting Fists of Shanghai Joe (1973), Italy, Director: Mario Caiano

Find a Place to Die (1968), Italy, Director: Anthony Ascott

Finders Killers (1968), Italy, Director: Gianni Crea

Finger on the Trigger (1965), Spain/Italy/U.S., Director: Sidney Pink

Fistful of Death (1971), Italy, Director: Miles Deem

Fistful of Dollars, A (1964), Italy, Director: Sergio Leone

Five Dollars for Ringo (1968), Italy, Director: Ignacio Iquiono

Five Giants From Texas (1966), Italy, Director: Aldo Florio

Five Man Army (1969), Italy, Director: Don Taylor

Five Thousand Dollars on One Ace (1965), Italy, Director: Alfonso Balcazar

Flaming Frontier (1965), Germany, Director: Alfred Vohrer

For a Book of Dollars (1973), Italy/Spain, Director: Renzo Spaziani

For a Few Dollars Less (1966), Italy, Director: Mario Mattòli

For a Few Dollars More (1965), Italy, Director: Sergio Leone

For a Fist in the Eye (1965), Italy, Director: Michele Lupo

Forewarned, Half Killed . . . The Word of the Holy Ghost (1971), Italy, Director: Anthony Scott

Forgotten Pistolero (1970), Spain, Director: Ferdinando Baldi

For One Thousand Dollars Per Killing (1967), Italy, Director: Sidney Lean

For One Thousand Dollars Per Day (1966), Italy, Director: Silvio Amadio

Fort Yuma Gold (1966), Italy, Director: Calvin J. Padget

Four Came to Kill Sartana (1969), Italy, Director: Miles Deem

Four Dollars for Vengeance (1965), Italy, Director: Alfonso Balcazar

Four Gunmen of the Apocalypse (1975), Italy, Director: Lucio Fulci

Four Gunmen of the Holy Trinity (1971), Italy, Director: Giorgio Cristallini

Four Rode Out (1969), Italy, Director: John Peyser

Frenchie King (1971), France, Director: Christian-Jaque

Fury of Johnny Kid (1967), Italy, Director: Gianni Puccini

Fury of the Apache (1964), Spain, Director: José María Elorrieta

Fury of the Apaches (1966), Italy, Director: Joe Lacy

Garter Colt (1967), Italy, Director: Gian Andrea Rocco

Genius (1975), Italy, Director: Damiano Damiani

Gentleman Killer (1969), Italy, Director: George Finley

Get Mean (1975), Italy, Director: Ferdinando Baldi

Get the Coffin Ready (1968), Italy, Director: Ferdinando Baldi

Girl Is a Gun, A (1970), France, Director: Luc Moullet

Go Away! Trinity Has Arrived in Eldorado (1972), Italy, Director: Dick Spitfire

God Does Not Pay on Saturday (1968), Italy, Director: Amerigo Anton

God Forgives, I Don't (1966), Italy, Director: Giuseppe Colizzi

God in Heaven . . . Arizona on Earth (1972), Italy, Director: John Wood

God is My Colt .45 (1972), Italy, Director: Dean Jones

God Made Them . . . I Kill Them (1968), Italy, Director: Paolo Bianchi

✓*God's Gun* (1976), Italy, Director: Frank Kramer

God Will Forgive My Pistol (1969), Italy, Director: Mario Giazzo/Leopoldo Savona

Gold of the Heroes (1971), Italy, Director: Don Reynolds

Go Kill and Come Back (1968), Italy, Director: Enzo E. Castellari

Good, the Bad, and the Ugly, The (1966), Italy, Director: Sergio Leone

Go with God, Amigo (1966), Italy, Director: Edward G. Muller

Grandsons of Zorro (1968), Italy, Director: Mariano Laurenti

Greatest Robbery in the West (1968), Italy, Director: Maurizio Lucidi

Great Silence (1968), Italy, Director: Sergio Corbucci

Great Treasure Hunt (1967), Italy, Director: Tonino Ricci

Gunfight at High Noon (1963), Italy, Director: Joaquin Romero Marchent

Gunfight at O Q Corral (1974) (X rated), France, Director: Jean-Marie Pallardy

Gunfight at Red Sands (1963), Italy, Director: Ricardo Blasco

Gunfighters of Casa Grande (1965), Spain, Director: Roy Rowland

Gunman of One Hundred Crosses (1971), Italy/West Germany, Director: Lucky Moore

Gunmen and the Holy Ghost (1973), Italy, Director: Roberto Mauri

Gunmen of Rio Grande (1964), Italy, Director: Tullio Demichelli

Guns for San Sebastian (1967), France, Director: Henri Verneuil

Half Breed (1966), Germany, Director: Harald Phillipp

Halleluja and Sartana Strike Again (1972), Italy, Director: Mario Siciliano

Halleluja to Vera Cruz (1973), Italy, Director: Newman Rostel

Hands of a Gunman (1965), Italy, Director: Rafael Romero Marchent

Handsome, the Ugly, and the Stupid, The (1967), Italy, Director: Giovanni Grimaldi

Hannie Caulder (1971), England/Spain/France, Director: Burt Kennedy

Hate for Hate (1967), Italy, Director: Domenico Paolella

Hate Thy Neighbor (1969), Italy, Director: Ferdinando Baldi

Hatred of God (1967), Italy/West Germany, Director: Claudio Gora

Have a Good Funeral, My Friend . . . Sartana Will Pay (1971), Italy, Director: Anthony Ascott

Heads or Tails (1969), Italy, Director: Peter E. Stanley

Heads You Die . . . Tails I Kill You (1971), Italy, Director: Anthony Ascott

Hellbenders (1966), Italy, Director: Sergio Corbucci

Here We Go Again, Eh Providence? (1973), Italy, Director: Alberto De Martino

Heroes of the West (1964), Italy, Director: Steno

Hero Was Called Allegria (1971), Italy, Director: Dennis Ford/Slim Alone

He Was Called the Holy Ghost (1972), Italy, Director: Robert Johnson

Hey Amigo! A Toast to Your Death! (1971), Italy, Director: Paul Maxwell

Hills Run Red (1966), Italy, Director: Lee W. Beaver

His Name Was Holy Ghost (1970), Italy/Spain, Director: Anthony Ascott

His Name Was King (1971), Italy, Director: Don Reynolds

His Name Was Sam Wabash, But They Call Him Amen (1971), Italy, Director: Miles Deem

Hole in the Forehead (1968), Italy, Director: Joseph Warren

Holy Water Joe (1971), Italy, Director: Mario Gariazzo

Hour of Death (1968), Spain, Director: Paul Marchenti

Hunting Party (1971), Italy, Director: Don Medford

I Am Sartana, Trade Your Guns for a Coffin (1972), Italy, Director: Anthony Ascott

I Am Sartana, Your Angel of Death (1969), Italy, Director: Anthony Ascott

I Came, I Saw, I Shot (1968), Italy, Director: Enzo G. Castellari

I Do Not Forgive . . . I Kill! (1968), Italy, Director: Joaquin R. Marchent/Giovanni Simonelli/Victor Aux

If One Is Born a Swine . . . Kill Him (1968), Italy, Director: Al Bradly

If You Shoot . . . You Live! (1974), Spain, Director: Joe Lacy

If You Want to Live . . . Shoot! (1967), Italy, Director: Willy S. Regan

I'll Sell My Skin Dearly (1968), Italy, Director: Ettore Fizarotti

In a Colt's Shadow (1965), Italy, Director: Giovanni Grimaldi

In the Name of the Father (1968), Italy, Director: Ruggero Deodato

In the Name of the Father, the Son and the Colt (1972), France, Director: Frank Bronston

It Can Be Done . . . Amigo (1971), Italy, Director: Maurizio Lucidi

I Want Him Dead (1968), Italy, Director: Paolo Bianchi

Jaguar (1964), Spain, Director: Jess Franco

Jesse and Lester, Two Brothers in a Place Called Trinity (1972), Italy, Director: James London

Jesse James' Kid (1966), Spain/Italy, Director: Antonio Del Amo

Joe Dexter (1965), Italy, Director: Ignacio Iquino

Johnny Colt (1966), Italy, Director: Giovanni Grimaldi

Johnny Hamlet (1968), Italy, Director: Enzo G. Castellari

Johnny Yuma (1966), Italy, Director: Romolo Guerrieri

John the Bastard (1967), Italy, Director: Armando Crispino

Judge Roy Bean (1970), France, Director: Richard Owens

✓*Keoma* (1975), Italy, Director: Enzo E. Castellari

Kid Rodelo (1966), Italy, Director: Richard Carlson

Kid Vengeance (1976), Italy, Director: Joe Manduke

Kill Django . . . Kill First (1971), Italy, Director: Willy S. Regan

Killer Caliber .32 (1967), Italy, Director: Al Bradly

Killer Goodbye (1969), Italy/Spain, Director: Primo Zeglio

Killer Kid (1967), Italy, Director: Leopoldo Savona

Kill Johnny Ringo (1966), Italy, Director: Frank G. Carrol

Kill or Die (1966), Italy, Director: Amerigo Anton

Kill the Poker Player (1972), Italy, Director: Frank Bronston

Kill Them All and Come Back Alone (1967), Italy, Director: Enzo G. Castellari

Kitosch, the Man Who Came from the North (1967), Italy/Spain, Director: Joseph Marvin

Kung Fu Brothers in the Wild West (1973), Italy/Hong Kong, Director: Yeu Ban Yee

Land Raiders (1969), U.S./Spain, Director: Nathan Juran

Last Gun (1964), Italy, Director: Sergio Bergonzelli

Last of the Mohicans (1965), Italy/Spain/West Germany, Director: Matteo Cano

Last Rebel (1971), Italy, Director: Denys McCoy

Last Ride to Santa Cruz (1969), Germany, Director: Rolf Olsen

Last Tomahawk (1965), West Germany/Italy/Spain, Director: Harald Reinl

Law of Violence (1969), Italy, Director: Gianni Crea

Left Handed Johnny West (1965), Italy, Director: Frank Kramer

Legacy of the Incas (1965), West Germany/Italy, Director: Georg Marischka

Lemonade Joe (1966), Czechoslovakia, Director: Oldrich Lipsky

Let's Go and Kill Sartana (1972), Spain, Director: Mario Pinzauti

Let Them Rest (1967), Italy, Director: Carlo Lizzani

Light the Fuse . . . Sartana Is Coming (1971), Italy, Director: Anthony Ascott

Long Day of the Massacre (1968), Italy, Director: Albert Cardiff

Long Days of Vengeance (1967), Italy, Director: Stan Vance

Long Ride From Hell (1968), Italy, Director: Alex Burkes

Lost Treasure of the Incas (1965), Italy, Director: Piero Pierotti

Lucky Johnny: Born in America (1973), Italy, Director: José Antonio Balanos

Machine Gun Killers (1968), Italy/Spain, Director: Paolo Bianchini

Macho Killers (1977), Italy, Director: Mark Andrew

Mad Dog Morgan (1975), Australia, Director: Philippe Mora

Magnificent Brutes of the West (1964), Italy, Director: Fred Wilson

Magnificent Texan (1967), Italy, Director: Lewis King

Magnificent Three (1963), Italy, Director: Joaquin R. Marchent

Magnificent West (1972), Italy, Director: Gianni Crea

Mallory Must Not Die (1971), Italy, Director: Mario Moroni

Man and a Colt, A (1967), Italy, Director: Tullio Demichelli

Man Called Amen, A (1972), Italy, Director: Alfio Caltabiano

✓*Man Called Blade, A* (1977), Italy, Director: Sergio Martino

Man Called Django, A (1971), Italy, Director: Edward G. Muller

Man Called Gringo, A (1964), West Germany/Spain, Director: Roy Rowland

Man Called Invincible, The (1973), Italy, Director: Anthony Ascott

Man Called Noon, The (1974), Italy, Director: Peter Collinson

Man Called Sledge, A (1970), Italy, Director: Vic Morrow

Man From Canyon City, The (1965), Italy, Director: Alfonso Balcazar

Man From Oklahoma, The (1965), Italy, Director: Robert M. White

Man: His Pride and His Vengeance (1967), Italy, Director: Luigi Bazzoni

Manhunt (1984), Italy, Director: Larry Ludman

Man of the Cursed Valley, The (1964), Italy, Director: Omar Hopkins

Man of the East (1973), Italy, Director: E. B. Clucher

Man Who Cried for Revenge, The (1969), Italy, Director: William Hawkins

Man Who Killed Billy the Kid, The (1969), Italy, Director: Julio Buchs

Man with the Golden Pistol (1966), Spain/Italy, Director: Alfonzo Balcazar

Massacre at Fort Grant (1963), Spain, Director: J. Douglas

Massacre at Fort Holman (1972), Italy, Director: Tonino Valerii/Ernesto Gastaldi

Massacre at Grand Canyon (1963), Italy, Director: Stanley Corbett

Massacre at Marble City (1964), Italy, Director: Franz J. Gottlieb

Massacre Time (1966), Italy, Director: Lucio Fulci

Matalo! (1971), Spain, Director: Cesare Canavari

May God Forgive You . . . But I Won't (1968), Italy, Director: Glenn Vincent Davis

Mercenary (1968), Italy, Director: Sergio Corbucci

Minnesota Clay (1964), Italy, Director: Sergio Corbucci

Minute to Pray, a Second to Die (1967), Italy, Director: Franco Giraldi

Miss Dynamite (1972), Italy, Director: Sergio Grieco

Moment to Kill, The (1968), Italy, Director: Anthony Ascott

Montana Trap (1976), Germany, Director: Peter Schamoni

More Dollars for the MacGregors (1970), Italy, Director: J. L. Merino

Murieta (1963), Italy, Director: George Sherman

Mutiny at Fort Sharp (1966), Italy, Director: Fernando Cerchio

My Colt, Not Yours (1972), Italy, Director: Steve McCohy

My Horse, My Gun, Your Widow (1972), Italy, Director: John Wood

My Name is Nobody (1973), Italy, Director: Tonino Valerii

My Name Is Pecos (1966), Italy, Director: Maurice A. Bright

Navajo Joe (1966), Italy, Director: Sergio Corbucci

Ned Kelly (1970), England, Director: Tony Richardson

Nephews of Zorro (1969), Italy, Director: Frank Reed

Night of the Serpent (1969), Italy, Director: Giulio Petroni

No Graves on Boot Hill (1968), Italy, Director: Willy S. Regan

None of Three Were Called Trinity (1974), Spain, Director: Pedro L. Ramirez

No Room to Die (1969), Italy, Director: Willy S. Regan

Nude Django (1968), Germany, Director: Ron Elliot

Once Upon a Time in the West (1968), Italy, Director: Sergio Leone

Once Upon a Time in the Wild, Wild West (1969), Italy, Director: Enzo Matassi

One After Another (1968), Italy, Director: Nick Howard

One Against One . . . No Mercy (1968), Italy, Director: Rafael Romero Marchent

One Damned Day at Dawn . . . Django Meets Sartana (1971), Italy, Director: Miles Deem

One Hundred Thousand Dollars for Ringo (1966), Italy, Director: Alberto De Martino

On the Third Day Arrived the Crow (1972), Italy, Director: Gianni Crea

Outlaw of Red River (1966), Spain, Director: Maury Dexter

Paid in Blood (1972), Italy, Director: Paolo Solvay

Pancho Villa (1972), Spain/England, Director: Eugenio Martin

Paths of War (1969), Italy, Director: Gianni Grimaldi

Patience Has a Limit (1974), Italy, Director: Armando Morandi

Payment in Blood (1968), Italy, Director: E. G. Rowland

Pecos Cleans Up (1967), Italy, Director: Maurizio Lucidi

Piluk, the Timid One (1968), Italy, Director: Guido Celano

Pirates of the Mississippi (1963), West Germany/Italy/France, Director: Jürgen Roland

Pistol for a Hundred Coffins (1968), Italy, Director: Umberto Lenzi

Pistol for Ringo (1965), Italy, Director: Duccio Tessari

Pistol Packin' Preacher (1972), Italy, Director: Leopoldo Savona

Place Called Glory (1965), West Germany/Spain, Director: Ralph Gideon

Poker with Pistols (1967), Italy, Director: Joseph Warren

Porno-Erotic Western (1978), Italy, Director: Gerard B. Lennox

Prairie in the City (1971), Germany, Director: Claus Timney

Prey of Vultures (1973), Spain/Italy, Director: Rafael Romero Marchent

Price of Death (1972), Italy, Director: Vincent Thomas

Price of Power (1969), Italy/Spain, Director: Tonino Valerii

Pyramid of the Sun God (1965), Germany, Director: Robert Siodmak

Quinta: Fighting Proud (1969), Italy, Director: Leon Klimovsky

Quintana: Dead or Alive (1969), Italy, Director: Glenn Vincent Davis

Raise Your Hands, Dead Man . . . You're Under Arrest (1971), Italy, Director: Leon Klimovsky

Ramon the Mexican (1966), Italy/Spain, Director: Maurizio Pradeaux

Rampage at Apache Wells (1965), West Germany/Yugoslavia, Director: Harald Phillipp

Rattler Kid (1968), Italy, Director: Leon Klimovsky

Reach You Bastard! (1971), Italy, Director: Lucky Dickerson

Rebels of Arizona (1969), Spain, Director: José Maria Zabalza

Red Blood, Yellow Gold (1968), Italy/Spain, Director: Nando Cicero

Red Coat (1975), Italy, Director: Joe D'Amato

Red Hot Zorro (1972), France/Belgium, Director: William Russell

Red Sun (1971), Italy/France/Spain, Director: Terence Young

Relentless Four (1966), Italy, Director: Primo Zeglio

Requiem for a Bounty Hunter (1970), Italy, Director: Mark Welles

Return of Clint the Stranger (1971), Italy, Director: George Martin

Return of Halleluja (1972), Italy, Director: Anthony Ascott

Return of Ringo (1966), Italy, Director: Duccio Tessari

Return of Sabata (1972), Italy, Director: Frank Kramer

Return of Shanghai Joe (1974), West Germany/Italy, Director: Bitto Albertini

Revenge for Revenge (1968), Italy, Director: Ray Calloway

Reverend Colt (1970), Italy, Director: Leon Klimovsky

Reward's Yours, the Man's Mine, The (1970), Italy, Director: Edward G. Muller

Rick and John, Conquerors of the West (1967), Italy, Director: Osvaldo Civirani

Ride and Kill (1964), Italy, Director: J. L. Boraw/Mario Caiano

Ringo and Gringo Against All (1966), Italy, Director: Bruno Corbucci

Ringo and His Golden Pistol (1966), Italy, Director: Sergio Corbucci

Ringo: Face of Revenge (1966), Italy, Director: Mario Caiano

Ringo, It's Massacre Time (1970), Italy, Director: Mario Pinzauti

Ringo, the Lone Rider (1967), Italy, Director: Rafael R. Marchent

Ringo's Big Night (1966), Italy, Director: Mario Maffei

Rita of the West (1967), Italy, Director: Ferdinando Baldi

Road to Fort Alamo (1966), Italy/France, Director: Mario Bava

Rojo (1966), Spain, Director: Leo Coleman

Roy Colt and Winchester Jack (1970), Italy, Director: Mario Bava

✓ *Run Man, Run* (1967), Italy/France, Director: Sergio Sollima

Ruthless Colt of the Gringo (1967), Italy, Director: José Luis Madrid

Ruthless Four, The (1968), Italy, Director: Giorgio Capitani

✓ *Sabata* (1969), Italy, Director: Frank Kramer

Sabata the Killer (1970), Italy/Spain, Director: Tullio Demichelli

Saguaro (1968), Italy, Director: Amerigo Anton

Sartana (1968), Italy/West Germany, Director: Frank Kramer

Sartana Does Not Forgive (1968), Italy, Director: Alfonso Balcazar

Sartana in the Valley of Death (1970), Italy, Director: Roberto Mauri

Sartana Kills Them All (1970), Italy, Director: Rafael Romero Marchent

Savage Gringo (1966), Italy, Directors: Mario Bava and Antonio Romano

Savage Guns (1961), Spain, Director: Michael Carreras

Savage Pampas (1966), Spain, Director: Hugo Fregonese

Scalps (1987), Germany, Director: Werner Knox

Secret of Captain O'Hara (1965), Italy, Director: Arturo Castillo

Seven Dollars on the Red (1968), Italy, Director: Alberto Cardone

Seven for Pancho Villa (1966), Spain, Director: José M. Ellorieta

Seven Guns for the MacGregors (1965), Italy, Director: Frank Garfield

Seven Guns for Timothy (1966), Spain/Italy, Director: Rod Gilbert

Seven Guns from Texas (1964), Spain/Italy, Director: Joaquin Romero Marchent

Seven Hours of Gunfire (1964), Italy, Director: José Hernandez

Seven Nuns in Kansas City (1973), Italy, Director: Marcello Zeanile

Seven Pistols for a Gringo (1967), Italy/Spain, Director: Juan Xiol Marchel

Shadow of Sartana . . . Shadow of Your Death (1968), Italy, Director: Sean O'Neal

Shadow of Zorro (1963), Spain/Italy, Director: Joaquin Romero Marchent

Shalako (1968), England, Director: Edward Dmytryk

Shango (1969), Italy, Director: Edward G. Muller

Sheriff of Rock Spring (1971), Italy, Director: Anthony Green

Sheriff Was a Lady (1965), Germany, Director: Söbey Martin

Sheriff With the Gold (1966), Italy, Director: Richard Kean

Sheriff Won't Shoot (1967), Italy/France/England, Director: J. Luis Monter

Shoot, Gringo . . . Shoot! (1968), Italy, Director: Frank B. Gorlish

Shoot Joe, and Shoot Again (1972), Italy, Director: Hal Brady

Shoot the Living . . . Pray for the Dead (1971), Italy, Director: Joseph Warren

Shoot to Kill (1963), Spain, Director: Ramon Torrado

Shotgun (1969), Italy, Director: Roberto Mauri

Shots Ring Out! (1965), Italy, Director: Augustin Navarro

Showdown for a Badman (1972), Italy, Director: Miles Deem

Sign of Coyote (1964), Italy, Director: Mario Caiano

Sign of Zorro (1964), Italy, Director: Mario Caiano

Silver Saddle (1978), Italy, Director: Lucio Fulci

Sky Full of Stars for a Roof, A (1968), Italy, Director: Giulio Petroni

Sometimes Life is Hard, Right Providence? (1972), Italy, Director: Giulio Petroni

Son of a Gunfighter (1966), Spain, Director: Paul Landres

Son of Django (1967), Italy, Director: Osvaldo Cicivani

Son of Zorro (1973), Italy, Director: Gianfranco Baldanello

Specialists (1969), Italy, Director: Sergio Corbucci

Sting of the West (1972), Italy, Director: Enzo G. Castellari

Stranger and the Gunfighter (1973), Italy, Director: Anthony Dawson

Stranger in Japan (1969), Italy/U.S./Japan, Director: Vance Lewis

Stranger in Paso Bravo (1968), Italy, Director: Salvatore Rosso

Stranger in Sacramento (1964), Italy, Director: Serge Bergon

Stranger in Town (1966), Italy, Director: Vance Lewis

Stranger Returns (1967), Italy/Spain/U.S., Director: Vance Lewis

Stranger That Kneels Beside the Shadow of a Corpse (1971), Italy, Director: Miles Deem

Sugar Colt (1966), Italy, Director: Franco Giraldi

Sunscorched (1966), Spain/Germany, Director: Alfonzo Balcazar

Take a Hard Ride (1974), Italy, Director: Anthony Dawson

Talent for Loving (1969), Spain, Director: Richard Quine

Tall Women (1966), Italy, Director: Sidney Pink

Taste for Killing (1966), Italy, Director: Torino Valerii

Taste of Violence (1961), France, Director: Robert Hossein

Ten Thousand Dollars Blood Money (1966), Italy, Director: Romolo Guerrieri

Tequila (1974), Italy/Spain, Director: Tullio Demichelli

Terrible Sheriff (1963), Italy, Director: Antonio Momplet

Terror of Oklahoma (1961), Italy, Director: Mario Amendola

Terror of the Black Mask (1963), Italy, Director: Umberto Lenzi

Tex and the Lord of the Deep (1985), Italy, Director: Duccio Tessari

Texas, Adios (1966), Italy, Director: Ferdinando Baldi

Texican (1966), U.S./Spain, Director: José L. Espinosa

They Called Him Trinity (1972), Italy/Spain, Director: Fred Lyon Morris

They Call Him Cemetery (1971), Italy, Director: Anthony Ascott

They Call Him Veritas (1972), Italy, Director: Luigi Perelli

They Call Me Trinity (1970), Italy, Director: E. B. Clucher

They Still Call Me Amen (1972), Italy, Director: Alfio Caltabiano

Thirteen is a Judas (1971), Italy, Director: Joseph Warren

Thirty Winchesters for El Diablo (1967), Italy, Director: Frank G. Carrol

This Man Can't Die (1968), Italy, Director: Gianfranco Baldanello

Thomson 1880 (1966), Italy/West Germany, Director: Albert Moore

Those Dirty Dogs! (1973), Italy/Spain, Director: Giuseppe Rosati

Three Bullets for a Long Gun (1970), Germany, Director: Peter Henkel

Three from Colorado (1967), Spain, Director: Armando de Ossorio

Three Graves for a Winchester (1966), Italy, Director: Erminio Salvi

Three Musketeers of the West (1972), Italy, Director: Bruno Corbucci

Three Silver Dollars (1968), Italy, Director: Irving Jacobs

Three Supermen of the West (1974), Italy, Director: Italo Martinenghi

Three Swords of Zorro (1963), Italy, Director: Ricardo Blasco

Thunder Over El Paso (1972), Italy, Director: Roberto Montero

Time and Place for Killing (1968), Italy, Director: Vincent Eagle

Time of Vultures (1967), Italy, Director: Nando Cicero

Today It's Me . . . Tomorrow You (1968), Italy, Director: Tonino Cervi

To Hell and Back (1968), Italy/Spain, Director: Giovanni Fago

Too Much Gold for One Gringo (1974), Italy/Spain, Director: Juan Bosch

Torrejon City (1961), Italy, Director: Leon Klimovsky

Town Called Hell (1971), England/Spain, Director: Robert Parrish

Trail of the Falcon (1968), East Germany/U.S.S.R., Director: Gottfried Kölditz

Train for Durango (1967), Italy/Spain, Director: William Hawkins

Tramplers (1965), Italy, Director: Albert Band

Treasure of Silver Lake (1962–63), Germany, Director: Harald Reinl

Treasure of the Aztecs (1965), Germany, Director: Robert Siodmak

Trinity and Sartana Are Coming (1972), Director: Mario Siciliano

Trinity Is Still My Name (1974), Italy, Director: E. B. Clucher

Trinity Plus the Clown and a Guitar (1975), Italy/Austria/France, Director: François Legrand

Trinity Sees Red (1971), Italy, Director: Mario Camus

Twenty Paces to Death (1970), Italy/Spain, Director: Ted Mulligan

Twenty Thousand Dollars for Seven (1968), Italy, Director: Alberto Cardone

Twice A Judas (1968), Italy, Director: Nando Cicero

Twins from Texas (1964), Italy, Director: Steno [Stefano Vanzina]

Two Crosses at Danger Pass (1968), Italy/Spain, Director: Rafael R. Marchent

Two Gangsters in the Wild West (1965), Italy, Director: Giorgio Simonelli

Two Gunmen (1964), Italy, Director: Anthony Greepy

Two Pistols and a Coward (1967), Italy, Director: Calvin J. Padget

Two R-R-Ringos from Texas (1967), Italy, Director: Frank Martin

Two Sergeants of General Custer (1965), Italy, Director: Giorgio Simonelli

Two Sides of the Dollar (1967), Italy, Director: Roberto Montero

Two Sons of Ringo (1966), Italy, Director: Giorgio Simonelli

Two Sons of Trinity (1972), Italy, Director: Glenn Eastman

Two Thousand Dollars for Coyote (1965), Spain, Director: Leon Klimovsky

Ugly Ones (1966), Spain/Italy, Director: Eugenio Martin

Up the MacGregors! (1967), Italy, Director: Frank Garfield

Valley of the Dancing Widows (1974), Germany, Director: Volker Vogeler

Vendetta at Dawn (1971), Italy, Director: Willy S. Regan

Vengeance (1968), Italy/West Germany, Director: Anthony Dawson

Vengeance Is a Dish Served Cold (1971), Italy, Director: William Redford

Viva Cangaceiro (1971), Spain/Italy, Director: Giovanni Fago

Viva Maria (1965), France/Italy, Director: Louis Malle

Wanted (1968), France, Director: Calvin J. Padget

Wanted Johnny Texas (1971), Italy, Director: Erminio Salvi

Wanted Sabata (1970), Italy, Director: Robert Johnon

Watch Out Gringo! Sabata Will Return (1972), Italy, Director: Alfonso Balcazar

What Am I Doing in the Middle of the Revolution? (1973), Italy, Director: Sergio Corbucci

White Apache (1984), Italy, Director: Vincent Dawn

White Comanche (1967), Italy/Spain/U.S., Director: Gilbert Lee Kay

White, the Yellow, and the Black (1974), Italy, Director: Sergio Corbucci

Who Killed Johnny R.? (1966), Italy/Spain, Director: José Luis Madrid

Who's Afraid of Zorro (1975), Italy, Director: Franco Lo Cascio

Winchester Does Not Forgive (1968), Director: Adelchi Bianchi

Winnetou and Shatterhand in the Valley of Death (1968), Germany, Director: Harald Reinl

Winnetou: Last of the Renegades (1964), France/Italy/West Germany, Director: Harald Reinl

Winnetou: The Desperado Trail (1965), Germany, Director: Harald Reinl

Winnetou the Warrior (1963), Germany, Director: Harald Reinl

Winnetou: Thunder at the Border (1967), Germany, Director: Alfred Vohrer

With Friends, Nothing is Easy (1971), Spain/Italy, Director: Steve MacCohy

Woman for Ringo (1966), Italy/Spain, Director: Rafael R. Marchent

Wrath of God (1968), Italy/Spain, Director: Alberto Cardone

Yankee (1967), Italy, Director: Tinto Brass

Yankee Dudler (1973), Germany, Director: Volker Vogeler

You're Jinxed, Friend, You Just Met Sacramento (1970), Italy, Director: Giorgio Cristallini

Zorro (1974), Italy, Director: Duccio Tessari

Zorro, Rider of Vengeance (1971), Italy, Director: José Luis Merino

Zorro, the Navarra Marquis (1969), Italy/Spain, Director: Jean Monty

Appendix II

WESTERNS AND THE OSCARS

When it comes to the western genre it is apparent that Oscar has taken an unwarranted holiday. It is a sad but true fact that the American western has been all but ignored at Oscar time. Only a cursory look at some basic facts should suffice. Until *Dances With Wolves* and *Unforgiven* were awarded gold statuettes in the 1990s, it had been 62 years since a western film (*Cimarron* in 1930) had been named the year's Best Movie.

Moreover, John Ford, a four-time Oscar-winning director and acknowledged master of the western genre, never won an Academy Award for helming a western film—not for *Stagecoach*, not for *My Darling Clementine*, not for *The Searchers*. Excluding *Stagecoach*, which was nominated in 1939, no Ford western received an Oscar nomination as Best Picture of the Year.

Actors as well have experienced a paucity of recognition. Since the inception of the Academy Awards in 1927–28, only four actors have claimed Best Actor statuettes for a performance in a Western film: Warner Baxter (*In Old Arizona* (1927–28); Gary Cooper (*High Noon*, 1952); Lee Marvin (*Cat Ballou*, 1965); and John Wayne (*True Grit*, 1969). On the other side of the gender equation, Patricia Neal won a Best Actress Oscar for her work in *Hud* (1963).

The reasons for this failure to give adequate recognition to the western have been wide and varied and are beyond the purview of this work to explore in greater depth. Suffice it to say that with the passing years, film scholars and movie fans have generally come to an increased appreciation of the overall artistic merit of the western film and of the talented actors, directors, cinematographers, and editors who have contributed so much to the genre.

Thus, it was not until the politically correct and revisionist era of the 1990s did a director receive an Oscar for helming a western. Today only Kevin Costner (*Dances with Wolves*, 1990) and Clint Eastwood (*Unforgiven*, 1992) can claim that honor. In the nearly 65 years of the Academy Awards, the combined total of Oscars meted out in the four major categories (Best Picture, Best Actor, Best Actress, Best Director) number a scant 10—remarkable but true.

Add Best Supporting Actor, a category that appeared for the first time in 1936, and the total swings upward to 16, with the inclusion of Thomas Mitchell (*Stagecoach*, 1939); Walter Brennan (*The Westerner*, 1940); Burl Ives (*The Big Country*, 1958); Melvyn Douglas (*Hud*, 1963); Jack Palance (*City Slickers*, 1991); and Gene Hackman (*Unforgiven*, 1992).

WESTERN OSCARS AND NOMINATIONS (1929–2001)

1929
In Old Arizona (Fox)
Oscar: Best Actor (Warner Baxter)
Nominations: Best Picture (Winfield Sheehan); Best Director (Irving Cummings); Writing (Tom Barry); Cinematography (Arthur Edison)

1931
Cimarron (RKO)
Oscars: Best Picture (William Lebaron); Writing/Adaptation (Howard Estabrook); Interior Decoration, (Max Ree)
Nominations: Best Director (Wesley Ruggles); Best Actor (Richard Dix); Best Actress (Irene Dunne); Cinematography (Edward Cronjager)

1934
Viva Villa (MGM)
Nominations: Best Picture (David O. Selznick); Writing/adaptation (Ben Hecht)

1935
Barbary Coast (UA)
Nomination: Cinematography (Ray June)
Ruggles of Red Gap (Paramount)
Nomination: Best Picture (Arthur Hornblower Jr.)

1936
The Texas Rangers (Paramount)
Nomination: Sound Recording (Franklin Hansen)
Trail of the Lonesome Pine (Paramount)
Nomination: Song, "A Melody from the Sky" (words, Sidney Mitchell; music, Louis Alter)

1938
The Cowboy and the Lady (Paramount)
Oscar: Sound Recording (Thomas Moulton)
Nominations: Original Score (Lionel Newman); Song, "The Cowboy and the Lady" (words, Arthur Quenzer; music, Lionel Newman)
Under Western Stars (Republic)
Nomination: Song, "Dust" (words and music, Johnny Marvin)

1939
Stagecoach (UA)
Oscar: Best Supporting Actor (Thomas Mitchell); Best Score (Richard Hagman, Frank Harling, John Leipold, and Leo Shuken)
Nominations: Best Picture (Walter Wanger); Director (John Ford); Cinematography, Black and White (Bert Glennon); Interior Decoration (Arthur Toluboff); Editing (Otho Lovering and Dorothy Spencer)
Drums Along the Mohawk (20th Century Fox)
Nomination: Cinematography, Color (Ray Rennahan and Bert Glennon); Best Actress in a Supporting Role (Edna May Oliver)
Man of Conquest (Republic)
Nomination: Sound Recording (C. L. Lootens)
Union Pacific (Paramount)
Nomination: Special Effects, Photographic (Farciot Edouart and Gordon Jennings); Sound (Loren Ryder)

1940
The Westerner (UA)
Oscar: Best Supporting Actor (Walter Brennan)
Nominations: Writing/Original Story (Stuart N. Lake); Interior Decoration (James Basevi)
North West Mounted Police (Paramount)
Oscar: Editing (Anne Bauchens)
Nominations: Cinematography, Color (Victor Milner and W. Howard Greene); Interior Decoration, Color (Hans Dreier, Roland Anderson); Sound Recording (Loren Ryder); Original Score (Victor Young)
Arizona (Columbia)
Nominations: Interior Decoration, Black and White (Lionel Banks and Robert Peterson); Original Score (Victor Young)
Dark Command (Republic)
Nominations: Interior Decoration, Black and White (John Victor Mackey); Original Score (Victor Young)
The Mark of Zorro (20th Century Fox)
Nomination: Original Score (Alfred Newman)
Northwest Passage (MGM)
Nomination: Cinematography, Color (Sidney Wagner and William Skall)

1941
Billy The Kid (MGM)
Nomination: Cinematography, Color (William V. Skall and Leonard Smith)
Ridin' On a Rainbow (Republic)
Nomination: Best Song, "Be Honest with Me" (words and music, Gene Autry)

1942
The Gold Rush (UA)
Nomination: Sound Recording (James Field); Scoring, Drama or Comedy (Max Terr)
The Spoilers (Universal)
Nomination: Interior Direction, Black and White (John B. Goodman, Jack Otterson, Russell A. Gausman, and Edward R. Robinson)

1943
In Old Oklahoma (Republic)
Nominations: Scoring of a Dramatic of Comedy Picture (Walter Sharf); Sound Recording (Daniel J. Blomberg)
The Kansan (UA)
Nomination: Scoring of a Dramatic or Comedy Picture (Gerard Carbonara)
The Ox Bow Incident (20th Century Fox)
Nomination: Best Picture (Lamar Trotti)

1945
Flame of the Barbary Coast (Republic)
Nominations: Sound Recording (Daniel B. Bloomberg); Scoring of a Dramatic or Comedy Picture (Dale Butts and Morton Scott)
San Antonio (WB)
Nominations: Interior Decoration, Color (Ted Smith and Jack McConaghty); Best Song: "Some Sunday Morning" (music, Ray Heindorf, M. K. Jerome; words, Ted Kohler)
The Harvey Girls (MGM)
Oscar: Best Song "On the Atchison Topeka and Santa Fe" (music, Harry Warren; words, Johnny Mercer)
Nomination: Scoring of a Musical Picture (Lennie Hayton)
Canyon Passion (Universal)
Nomination: Best Song "Ole Buttermilk Sky" (music, Hoagy Charmichael; words, Jack Brooks)
Duel in the Sun (Selznick International)
Nominations: Best Actress (Jennifer Jones); Best Supporting Actress (Lillian Gish)

1948
The Paleface (Paramount)
Oscar: Best Song "Buttons and Bows" (words and music, Jay Livingston and Ray Evans)
Red River (UA)
Nominations: Writing, Motion Picture Story (Borden Chase); Editing (Christian Nyby)

1949
She Wore a Yellow Ribbon (Argosy, RKO)
Oscar: Cinematography, Color (Winton Hoch)

1950
Annie Get Your Gun (MGM)
Oscar: Scoring of a Musical Picture (Adolph Deutsch and Roger Edens)
Nominations: Cinematography, Color (Charles Rosher); Art/Set Direction (Cedric Gibbons, Paul Groesse, Edwin B. Willis, Richard A. Pefferle)
Broken Arrow (20th Century Fox)

Nominations: Best Supporting Actor (Jeff Chandler); Screenplay (Michael Blankfort)
The Furies (Paramount)
Nomination: Cinematography, Black and White (Victor Milner)
The Gunfighter (20th Century Fox)
Nomination: Writing, Motion Picture Story (William Bowers and André de Toth)
Singin' Guns (Republic)
Nomination: Best Song "Mule Train" (words and music, Fred Glickman, Hy Heath, Johnny Lange)

1952
High Noon (UA)
Oscars: Best Actor (Gary Cooper); Best Song "High Noon/Do Not Forsake Me, Oh My Darlin'" (music, Dimitri Tiomkin; words, Ned Washington); Best Scoring of a Dramatic or Comedy Picture (Dimitri Tiomkin); Editing (Elmo Williams and Harry Gerstad)
Nominations: Best Picture (Stanley Kramer); Best Director (Fred Zinnemann); Screenplay (Carl Foreman)
The Big Sky (RKO)
Nominations: Best Supporting Actor (Arthur Hunnicutt); Cinematography, Black and White (Russell Harlan)
Navajo (Lippert)
Nomination: Cinematography, Black and White (Virgil E. Miller)

1953
Shane (Paramount)
Oscar: Cinematography, Color (Loyal Griggs)
Nominations: Best Picture (George Stevens); Best Director (George Stevens); Best Supporting Actor (Jack Palance); Best Supporting Actor (Brandon De Wilde); Screenplay (A. B. Guthrie)
Calamity Jane (WB)
Oscar: Best Song "Secret Love" (music, Sammy Fain; words, Ray Heindorf)
Nomination: Scoring of a Musical Picture (Ray Heindorf)
Hondo (WB)
Nominations: Best Supporting Actress (Geraldine Page); Writing, Motion Picture Story (Louis L'Amour ineligible for nomination under Academy bylaws)
The Naked Spur (MGM)
Nomination: Story and Screenplay (Sam Rolfe and Harold Jack Bloom)

1954
Broken Lance (20th Century Fox)
Oscar: Writing, Motion Picture Story (Philip Yordan)
Nomination: Best Supporting Actress (Katy Jurado)
Red Garters (Paramount)
Nomination: Art Direction/Set Direction (Hal Pereira, Roland Anderson, Sam Comer, Ray Moyer)
Seven Brides for Seven Brothers (MGM)
Nominations: Best Picture (Jack Cummings); Screenplay (Albert Hackett, Frances Goodrich, Dorothy Kingsley); Cinematography, Color (George Folsey); Scoring of a Musical

Picture (Adolph Deutsch and Saul Chaplin); Editing (Ralph P. Winters)

1955
Oklahoma! (Magna)
Oscar: Scoring of a Musical Picture (Robert Russell Bennett, Jay Blackstone and Adolph Deutsch); Sound Recording (Todd-AO Sound Department; Fred Hynes, sound director)
Nominations: Cinematography, Color (Robert Surtees); Editing (Gene Roggiero and George Boemler)
Bad Day at Black Rock (MGM)
Nominations: Best Actor (Spencer Tracy); Best Director (John Sturges); Screenplay (Millard Kaufman)

1956
Friendly Persuasion (Allied Artists)
Nominations: Best Picture (William Wyler); Director (William Wyler); Best Supporting Actor (Anthony Perkins); Screenplay-Adapted (Writer Michael Wilson ineligible for nomination under Academy bylaws); Best Song, "Friendly Persuasion" (music, Dimitri Tiomkin; words, Paul Francis Webster); Sound Recording (Gordon R. Glennan, Gordon Sawyer)
Stagecoach to Fury (20th Century Fox)
Nomination: Cinematography, Black and White (Walter Strenge)

1957
Gunfight at the OK Corral (Paramount)
Nomination: Editing (Warren Low)
The Tin Star (Paramount)
Nomination: Story and Screenplay Written Directly for the Screen (Barney Slater, Joel Kane, and Dudley Nichols)

1958
The Big Country (UA)
Oscar: Best Supporting Actor (Burl Ives)
Nomination: Scoring of a Dramatic or Comedy Picture (Jerome Moross)
Cowboy (Columbia)
Nomination: Editing (William A. Lyons and Al Clark)
The Sheepman (MGM)
Nomination: Story and Screenplay Written Directly for the Screen (James Edward Grant and William Bowers)

1959
The Hanging Tree (WB)
Nomination: Best Song, "The Hanging Tree" (music, Jerry Livingston; words, Mack David)

1960
The Alamo (Batjac, UA)
Oscar: Sound (Gordon E. Sawyer and Fred Hynes)
Nominations: Best Picture (John Wayne); Best Supporting Actor (Chill Wills); Cinematography, Color (William Clothier); Best Song, "The Green Leaves of Summer" (music, Dimitri Tiomkin; words, Paul Francis Webster); Scoring of a Dramatic or Comedy Picture (Dimitri Tiomkin); Editing (Stuart Gilmore)

Cimarron (MGM)
Nomination: Art Direction/Set Decoration, Color (George W. Davis, Addison Hehr, Henry Grace, Hugh Hunt, and Otto Siegel)

1961

One Eyed Jacks (Paramount)
Nomination: Cinematography, Color (Charles Lang Jr.)

1963

How the West Was Won (MGM/Cinerama)
Oscars: Story and Screenplay Written Directly for the Screen (James R. Webb); Sound (Franklin E. Milton); Editing (Harold F. Kress)
Nominations: Best Picture (Bernard Smith); Cinematography, Color (William H. Daniels, Milton Krasner, Charles Lange Jr., and Joseph LaShelle); Art Decoration/Set Decoration, Color (George W. Davis, William Ferrari, Addison Hehr, Henry Grace, Don Greenwood Jr., and Jack Mills); Music Score (Alfred E. Newman and Ken Darby); Costume Design (Walter Plunkett)
Hud (Paramount)
Oscars: Best Actress (Patricia Neal); Best Supporting Actor (Melvyn Douglas); Cinematography, Black and White (James Wong Howe)
Nominations: Best Actor (Paul Newman); Screenplay Based on Material From Another Medium (Irving Ravetch and Harriet Frank Jr.); Art Decoration Set Decoration, Black and White (Hal Pereira and Tambi Larsen, Sam Comer, and Robert Benton)

1965

Cat Ballou (Columbia)
Oscar: Best Actor (Lee Marvin)
Nominations: Screenplay Based on Material from Another Medium (Walter Newman and Frank R. Pierson); Best Song, "The Ballad of Cat Ballou" (music, Jerry Livingston; words, Mack David); Scoring of Music, Adaptation or Treatment (Frank De Vol); Editing (Charles Nelson)

1966

The Professionals (Pax Enterprise/Columbia)
Nominations: Best Director (Richard Brooks); Screenplay Based on Material From Another Medium (Richard Brooks); Cinematography, Color (Conrad Hall)

1969

Butch Cassidy and the Sundance Kid (20th Century Fox)
Oscars: Best Song, "Raindrops Keep Falling on my Head" (music, Burt Bacharach; words, Hal David); Original Score (Burt Bacharach); Cinematography (Conrad Hall); Story and Screenplay Based on Material Not Previously Published or Produced (William Goldman)
Nominations: Best Picture (John Foreman); Best Director (George Roy Hill); Sound (William Edmundson and David Dockendorf)
True Grit (Paramount)

Oscar: Best Actor (John Wayne)
Nomination: Best Song, "True Grit" (music, Elmer Bernstein; words, Don Black)
Paint Your Wagon (Paramount)
Nomination: Score, Original or Adaptation (Nelson Riddle)
The Wild Bunch (WB)
Nominations: Story and Screenplay Based on Material Not Previously Published or Produced (Walon Green, Roy N. Sickner, and Sam Peckinpah); Original Score For a Motion Picture Not a Musical (Jerry Fielding)

1970

Little Big Man (National General)
Nomination: Best Supporting Actor (Chief Dan George)

1971

McCabe and Mrs. Miller (WB)
Nomination: Best Supporting Actress (Julie Christie)

1972

The Life and Times of Judge Roy Bean (National General)
Nomination: Best Song, "Marmalade, Molasses, & Honey" (music, Maurice Jarre; words, Marilyn and Alan Bergman)

1974

Blazing Saddles (WB)
Nominations: Best Supporting Actress (Madeline Kahn); Best Song, "Blazing Saddles" (music, John Morris; words, Mel Brooks); Editing (John C. Howard and Danford Greene)

1976

The Shootist (Paramount)
Nomination: Art Direction/Set Direction (Robert F. Boyle and Arthur Jeph Parker)

1978

Comes a Horseman (UA)
Nomination: Best Supporting Actor (Richard Farnsworth)

1979

Butch and Sundance: The Early Days (20th Century Fox)
Nomination: Costume Design (William Theis)
The Electric Horseman (Columbia)
Nomination: Sound (Arthur Piantadosi, Les Fresholtz, Michael Minkler, and Al Overton)

1985

Silverado (Columbia)
Nominations: Sound (Donald O. Mitchell, Rick Kline, Kevin O'Connell, and David Ronne); Original Score (Bruce Broughton)

1990

Last of the Mohicans (20th Century Fox)
Oscar: Best Sound (Chris Jenkins, Doug Hemphill, Mark Smith, and Simon Kaye)
Dances With Wolves (Tig/Orion)

Oscars: Best Picture (Jim Wilson and Kevin Costner); Best Director (Kevin Costner); Sound (Russell Williams II, Jeffrey Perkins, Bill W. Benton, and Greg Watkins); Screenplay Based on Material From Another Medium (Michael Blake); Original Score (John Barry); Editing (Neil Travis)
Nominations: Best Actor (Kevin Costner); Best Supporting Actor (Graham Greene); Best Supporting Actress (Mary McDonnell); Art/Set Direction (Jeffrey Beecroft and Lisa Dean); Costume Design (Elsa Zamparelli)
Young Guns II (20th Century Fox)
Nomination: Best Song, "Blaze of Glory" (words and music, Jon Bon Jovi)

1991

City Slickers (Castle Rock Entertainment)
Oscar: Best Supporting Actor (Jack Palance)

1992

Unforgiven (WB)
Oscars: Best Picture (Clint Eastwood); Best Supporting Actor (Gene Hackman); Best Director (Clint Eastwood); Editing (Joel Cox)
Nominations: Best Actor (Clint Eastwood); Screenplay Written Directly for the Screen (David Webb Peoples); Art/Set Direction (Henry Bumstead and Janice Blackie-Goodine); Sound (Les Fresholtz, Vern Poore, Dick Alexander, and Rob Young)

1994

Wyatt Earp (WB)
Nomination: Sound (Owen Roizman)

Appendix III

WESTERN MOVIES AND LITERATURE

As with most film genres, a number of western movies have been based on independent literary sources. The following films (in Roman type) are listed alphabetically, followed by the literary sources that inspired them and their authors.

A

Abilene Town: *Trail Town*, Ernest Haycox

Across the Wide Missouri: *Across the Wide Missouri*, Bernard DeVoto

Advance to the Rear: *The Company of Cowards*, William Chamberlain, Jack Schaefer

Along Came Jones: *Along Came Jones*, Alan Le May

Along the Navajo Trail: *Sleepy Horse Range*, William Colt MacDonald

Allegheny Uprising: *The First Rebel*, Neil Swanson

Annie Get Your Gun: *Annie Get Your Gun*, Irving Berlin

Apache Territory: *The Last Stand at Papago Wells*, Louis L'Amour

Arizona Kid, The: *The Arizona Kid*, O. Henry

Arizona Mahony: *Stairs of Sand*, Zane Grey

Arizona Raiders, The: *Raiders of the Spanish Peaks*, Zane Grey

Arrowhead: *Adobe Wells*, W. R. Burnette

B

Badlanders, The: *The Asphalt Jungle*, W. R. Burnett

Bend of the River: *Bend of the Snake*, William Gulick

Big Sky, The: *Big Sky*, A. B. Guthrie Jr.

Billy the Kid (1930): *Saga of Billy the Kid*, Walter Noble Burnes

Blackjack Ketchum, Desperado: *Kilkenny*, Louis L'Amour

Blood on the Moon: *Gunman's Chance*, Luke Short

Border Legion, The: *The Border Legion*, Zane Grey

Born to the West: *Born to the West*, Zane Grey

Branded: *Montana Rides*, Max Brand (as Evan Evans)

Broken Arrow: *Blood Brother*, Elliott Arnold

Burning Hills, The: *The Burning Hills*, Louis L'Amour

C

Canyon Passage: *Canyon Passage*, Ernest Haycox

Catlow: *Catlow*, Louis L'Amour

Cheyenne Autumn: *Cheyenne Autumn*, Mari Sandoz

Cheyenne Kid, The: *Sir Piegan Passes*, W. C. Tuttle

Chip of the Flying U: *Chip of the Flying U*, B. M. Bower

Cimarron: *Cimarron*: Edna Ferber

Cisco Kid: *The Cisco Kid*, O. Henry

Code of the West: *Code of the West*, Zane Grey

Colorado Territory: *High Sierra*, W. R. Burnett

Comancheros, The: *The Comancheros*, Paul Wellman

Cowboy from Brooklyn, The: *Howdy Stranger*, Robert Sloane and Louis Pelletier Jr.

Cowboys, The: *The Cowboys*, William Dale Jennings

D

Dark Command: *The Dark Command*, W. R. Burnett

Deerslayer, The: *The Deerslayer*, James Fenimore Cooper

Desert Gold: *Desert Gold*, Zane Grey

Desperadoes, The: *The Desperadoes*, Max Brand

Destry: *Destry Rides Again*, Max Brand

Destry Rides Again: *Destry Rides Again*, Max Brand

Distant Drums: *Distant Drums*, Niven Busch

Drift Fence: *Drift Fence*, Zane Grey

Drums Along the Mohawk: *Drums Along the Mohawk*, Walter D. Edmonds

Dude Ranger, The: *The Dude Ranger*, Zane Grey

Duel in the Sun: *Duel in the Sun*, Niven Busch

E

El Dorado: *The Stars in Their Courses*, Harry Brown

End of the Trail: *Outlaws of Palouse*, Zane Grey

F

Fargo Kid, The: *Sir Piegan Passes*, W. C. Tuttle

Far Horizons, The: *Sacajawea of the Shoshones*, Della Gould Emmons

Fighting Caravans: *Fighting Caravans*, Zane Grey

Flaming Guns: *Flaming Guns*, Peter B. Kyne

Flaming Star: Flaming Star, Clair Huffaker

Forlorn River: *Forlorn River*, Zane Grey

Four Guns to the Border: *Four Guns to the Border*, Louis L'Amour

Friendly Persuasion: *The Friendly Persuasion*, Jessamyn West

From Hell to Texas: *The Hell Bent Kid*, Charles O. Locke

Frontier Marshal: *Frontier Marshal*, Stuart N. Lake
Furies, The: *The Furies*, Niven Busch

G

Ghost-Town Gold: *Ghost-Town Gold*, William Colt MacDonald
Gordon of Ghost City: *Oh Promise Me*, Peter Kyne
Gunfight at the O.K. Corral: *The Killer*, George Scullin
Gunfighter, The: *The Gunfighter*, William Bowers and André de Toth
Gunfighters, The: *Twin Sombreros*, Zane Grey
Guns of Timberland: *Guns of Timberland*, Louis L'Amour

H

Hallelujah Trial, The: *The Hallelujah Trail*, William Gulick
Hanging Tree, The: *The Hanging Tree*, Dorothy Johnson
Heller With Pink Tights: *Heller With a Gun*, Louis L'Amour
Hell's Heros: *The Three Godfathers*, Peter Kyne
Heritage of the Desert: *Heritage of the Desert*, Zane Grey
High Noon: "The Tin Star," John W. Cunningham
Hit the Saddle: *Hit the Saddle*, William Colt MacDonald
Home on the Range: *Code of the West*, Zane Grey
Hondo: *The Gift of Cochise*, Louis L'Amour
Hop-Along Cassidy: *Hopalong Cassidy*, Clarence Mulford
Horse Soldiers: *The Horse Soldiers*, Harold Sinclair
Hour of the Gun: *Tombstone's Epitaph*, Douglas D. Martin
How the West Was Won: "How the West Was Won," *Life* Magazine
Hundred Rifles (*aka* 100 Rifles): *100 Rifles*, Robert MacLeod

I

In Old Arizona: "The Caballero's Way," O. Henry
Iron Mistress: *The Iron Mistress*, Paul Wellman

J

Just Tony: *Just Tony*, Max Brand

K

Knights of the Range: *Knights of the Range*, Zane Grey

L

Last Hard Men: *Gun Down*, Brian Garfield
Last Hunt: *The Last Hunt*, Milton Lott
Last of the Duanes: "Last of the Duanes," Zane Grey
Last of the Mohicans, The: *The Last of the Mohicans*, James Fenimore Cooper
Last Round-Up, The: *Border Legion*, Zane Grey
Last Sunset: *Sundown at Cochise*, Howard Rigsby
Last Trail, The: *The Trail*, Zane Grey
Law and Jake Wade: *The Law and Jake Wade*, Marvin H. Albert
Law and Order: *Saint Johnson*, W. R. Burnett (as William R. Burnett)
Light of the Western Stars: *Light of the Western Stars*, Zane Grey
Llano Kid, The: "Double Dyed Deceiver," O. Henry
Lonesome Dove: *Lonesome Dove*, Larry McMurtry

Lone Star Ranger: *Lone Star Ranger*, Zane Grey
Lone Texan, The: *Lone Texan*, James Landis

M

Man Called Horse, A: *A Man Called Horse*, Dorothy Johnson
Man in the Saddle: *Man in the Saddle*, Ernest Haycox
Man of the West: *Man of the West*, Will C. Brown
Man Who Shot Liberty Valance, The: *The Man Who Shot Liberty Valance*, Dorothy Johnson
Mark of Zorro, The: *The Curse of Capistrano*, Johnston McCulley
Massacre River: *When a Man's a Man*, Harold Bell Wright
Maverick Queen, The: *The Maverick Queen*, Zane Grey
Michigan Kid, The: *The Michigan Kid*, Rex Beach
Monte Walsh: *Monte Walsh*, Jack Schaefer
My Darling Clementine: *Wyatt Earp, Frontier Marshal*, Stuart N. Lake and Sam Hellman
My Outlaw Brother: *South of the Rio Grande*, Max Brand
Mysterious Rider: *Mysterious Rider*, Zane Grey

N

Nevada: *Nevada*, Zane Grey
Nevada Smith: *Nevada Smith*, John Michael Hayes
North of the Rio Grande: *Cottonwood Gulch*, Clarence Mulford
North to Alaska: *Birthday Gift*, Laszlo Fodor
North West Mounted Police: *Royal Canadian Mounted Police*, R. C. Featherstonhaugh

O

Oklahoma!: *Oklahoma!*, Richard Rodgers, Oscar Hammerstein II (adapted from the folk play *Green Grow the Lilacs*, Lynn Riggs)
One Eyed Jacks: *The Authentic Death of Hendry Jones*, Charles Neider
Outlaw Josey Wales, The: *Gone to Texas*, Forrest Carter

P

Paint Your Wagon: *Paint Your Wagon*, Frederick Loewe, Alan Jay Lerner
Panamint's Bad Man: "Panamint's Bad Man," Edmund Kelso and Lindsley Parsons
Parson of Panamint: *Parson of Panamint*, Peter B. Kyne
Plainsman, The: "Wild Bill Hickok," Frank J. Wilstach and "The Prince of Pistoleers," Courtney Riley Cooper
Powdersmoke Range: *Powdersmoke*, William Colt MacDonald
Professionals, The: *A Mule for the Marquesa*, Frank O'Rourke
Proud Ones, The: *The Proud Ones*, Verne Athanas

R

Rainbow Over Texas: *Rainbow Over Texas*, Max Brand
Red Canyon: *Wildfire*, Zane Grey
Red River: *The Chisholm Trail*, Borden Chase
Return of a Man Called Horse, The: *A Man Called Horse*, Dorothy Johnson
Return of the Texan: *The Home Place*, Fred Gipson
Riders of Death Valley, The: *The Riders of Death Valley*, Max Brand

Riders of the Purple Sage: *Riders of the Purple Sage*, Zane Grey
Rio Conchos: *Rio Conchos*, Clair Huffaker
Rio Grande: "Mission with No Record," James Warner Bellah
Rocky Mountain Mystery: *Golden Dreams*, Zane Grey
Roll Along Cowboy: *The Dude Ranger*, Zane Grey
Romance of the Rio Grande: *Conquistador*, Katherine Fullerton
Rooster Cogburn: *True Grit*, Charles Portis
Rounders, The: *The Rounders*, Max Evans

S

Sacketts, The: *Sacketts* and *The Daybreakers*, Louis L'Amour
Savage Pampas: *Pampas Barbara*, Homero Manzi and Ulises Petit De Murat
Sea of Grass, The: *The Sea of Grass*, Conrad Richter
Searchers, The: *The Searchers*, Alan Le May
Seven Ways from Sundown: *Seven Ways from Sundown*, Clair Huffaker
Shalako: *Shalako*, Louis L'Amour
Shane: *Shane*, Jack Schaefer
Shepherd of the Hills, The: *The Shepherd of the Hills*, Harold Bell Wright
She Wore a Yellow Ribbon: "War Party" and "The Big Hunt" James Warner Bellah
Shootist, The: *The Shootist*, Glendon Swarthout
Silver Horde: *The Silver Horde*, Rex Beach
Singing Guns: *Singing Guns*, Max Brand
Spoilers, The: *The Spoilers*, Rex Beach
Springfield Rifle: "Springfield Rifle," Sloan Nibley
Stagecoach: *Stage to Lordsburg*, Ernest Haycox
Stranger on Horseback: *Stranger on Horseback*, Louis L'Amour
Sunset Pass, *Sunset Pass:* Zane Grey

T

Taggart: *Taggart*, Louis L'Amour
Tall Men, The: *The Tall Men*, Clay Fisher
Tall Stranger, The: *Showdown Trail*, Louis L'Amour
Tennessee's Partner: *Tennessee's Partner*, Bret Hart
Texan, The: "Double Eyed Deceiver," O. Henry
Texas Rangers, The (1936): *The Texas Rangers*, Walter Prescott Webb
They Came to Cordura: *They Came from Cordova*, Glendon Swarthout
Three Godfathers (1948): *The Three Godfathers*, Peter Kyne

Three Godfathers, The (1916 and 1936): *The Three Godfathers*, Peter Kyne
Thundering Herd, The: *The Thundering Herd*, Zane Grey
Thunder Mountain: *Thunder Mountain*, Zane Grey
Thunder Trail: *Arizona Ames*, Zane Grey
Trail Dust: *Trail Dust*, Clarence Mulford
Trail of the Lonesome Pine: *Trail of the Lonesome Pine*, John Fox Jr.
Treasure of Ruby Hills: *Treasure of Ruby Hills*, Louis L'Amour
True Grit: *True Grit*, Charles Portis
Two Mules for Sister Sara: "Two Mules for Sister Sara," Budd Boetticher
Two Rode Together: *Comanche Captives*, Will Cook

U

Undefeated, The: *The Undefeated*, Lewis B. Patten
Under Tonto Rim: *The Bee Hunter*, Zane Grey
Unforgiven, The: *The Unforgiven*, Alan Le May
Union Pacific: *Trouble Shooters*, Ernest Haycox
Utah Blaine: *Utah Blaine*, Louis L'Amour

V

Vera Cruz: "Vera Cruz," Borden Chase

W

Wagon Wheels: *Fighting Caravans*, Zane Grey
Wanderer of the Wasteland: *Wanderer of the Wasteland*, Zane Grey
Warlock: *Warlock*, Oakley Hall
War Wagon, The: *Badman*, Clair Huffaker
Way West, The: *The Way West*, A. B. Guthrie Jr.
Welcome to Hard Times: *Welcome to Hard Times*, E. L. Doctorow
Western Gold: *Helen of the Old House*, Harold Bell Wright
Western Union: *Western Union*, Zane Grey
West of the Pecos: *West of the Pecos*, Zane Grey
Whispering Smith: *Whispering Smith*, Frank Spearman
Whistling Bullets: *The Fifth Man*, James Oliver Curwood
Wild Horse Mesa: *Wild Horse Mesa*, Zane Grey
Winchester '73: "Winchester '73," Stuart N. Lake
Wonderful Country: *The Wonderful Country*, Tom Lea

Y

Yellow Sky: *Yellow Sky*, W. R. Burnette
Young Billy Young: *Who Rides With Wyatt*, Will Henry

Appendix IV

SOUND ERA SUPPLEMENTARY LISTINGS

Following is a supplementary, year-by-year list of westerns from the sound era not covered among the A–Z entries. Information about some of these films proved too scarce for a full entry, and others simply did not merit full coverage. They are listed with their studio and director. The overwhelming majority of the westerns produced from 1965 through 1972 were spaghetti westerns, and consequently many titles from those years appear in Appendix A.

1930

Apache Kid's Escape
    Horner Productions, Robert J. Horner
Bar L Ranch
    Big 4 Picture, S. Harry Webb
Beau Bandit
    RKO, Lambert Hillyer
Breezy Bill
    Syndicate, J. P. McGowan
Call of the Desert
    Syndicate, J. P. McGowan
Call of the West
    Columbia, Albert Ray
Canyon of Missing Men, The
    Syndicate, J. P. McGowan
Cheyenne Kid, The
    West Coast Productions, Jacques Jaccard
Code of Honor
    Syndicate, J. P. McGowan
Dude Wrangler
    Sono-Art World Wide, Richard Thorpe
Firebrand Jordan
    Big 4, Alvin J. Neitz
Hunted Men
    Syndicate, J. P. McGowan
Indians are Coming, The
    Universal, Henry McRae
Lightning Express
    Universal, Henry MacRae
Lone Rider, The
    Columbia, Louis King

Lone Star Ranger, The
    Fox, A. F. Ericson
Men Without Law
    Columbia, Louis King
Mountain Justice
    Universal, Harry Joe Brown
Mounted Stranger, The
    Universal, Arthur Rosson
Oklahoma Cyclone
    Tiffany, J. P. McGowan
The Oklahoma Sheriff
    Syndicate, J. P. McGowan
O'Malley Rides Alone
    Syndicate, J. P. McGowan
Pardon My Gun
    Pathé, Robert De Lacy
Parting of the Trails
    Syndicate, J. P. McGowan
Riders of Rio
    Round-Up Pictures, Robert Emmett Tansey
Ridin' Law
    Big 4-Biltmore, Harry S. Webb
Rivers End
    Warner Bros., Michael Curtiz
Roaring Ranch
    Universal, B. Reeves Eason
Rogue of the Rio Grande
    Sono-Art World Wide, Spencer Gordon Bennett
Romance of the West
    Arthur Hammond Production, John Tansey and Robert Emmett Tansey

Rough Romance
    Fox, A. F. Ericson
Sagebrush Politics
    Hollywood Pictures, Victor Adamson
Sante Fe Trail, The
    Paramount, Edwin Knoph and Otto Brower
Song of the West
    Warner Bros., Ray Enright
Storm, The
    Universal, William Wyler
Trailing Trouble
    Universal, Arthur Rosson
Trails of Peril
    Big 4, Alan James
Under a Texas Moon
    Warner Bros., Michael Curtiz
Under Montana Skies
    Tiffany, Richard Thorpe
Westward Bound
    Syndicate, Robert Emmett Tansey

1931

Alias, The Bad Man
    Tiffany, Phil Rosen
Arizona Terror
    Tiffany, Phil Rosen
At the Ridge
    Tiffany, J. P. McCarthy
Avenger, The
    Columbia, Roy William Neill
Branded Men
    Tiffany, Phil Rosen

Cheyenne Cyclone
    Kent, Armand Schaefer
Dugan of the Badlands
    Monogram, Robert N. Bradbury
Flying Lariats
    Big 4, Alan James and David
    Kirkland
Galloping Thru
    Monogram, Lloyd Nosler
Headin' For Trouble
    Big 4, J. P. McGowan
Hell's Valley
    Big 4, Alan James
Heroes of the Flames
    Universal, Robert F. Hill
Hurricane Horseman
    Kent, Armand Schaefer
In Old Cheyenne
    World Wide Pictures, Stuart
    Patton
Kid from Arizona, The
    Cosmos, Robert Horner
Land of Wanted Men
    Monogram, Harry S. Fraser
Lariats and Six Shooters
    Cosmos, Alan James
Lightning Warrior, The
    Mascot, Benjamin Kline and
    Armand Schaefer
Lightnin' Smith Returns
    Syndicate, Jack Irwin
Montana Kid, The
    Sono-Art World, Stuart Paton
Mounted Fury
    Syndicate, Stuart Patton
Mystery Trooper, The
    Syndicate, Stuart Patton and Harry
    Webb
Near the Trail's End
    Tiffany, Wallace Fox
Nevada Buckaroo, The
    Tiffany, John P. McCarthy
Oklahoma Jim
    Monogram, Harry L. Fraser
One Way Trail, The
    Columbia, Ray Taylor
Partners of the Trail
    Monogram, Wallace Fox
Phantom of the West
    Mascot, D. Ross Lederman
Pocatello Kid, The
    Tiffany, Phil Rosen
Pueblo Terror
    Cosmos, Alan James
Quick Trigger Lee
    Big 4, J. P. McGowan

Range Law
    Tiffany, Phil Rosen
Red Fork Range
    Big 4, Alan James
Riders of the Cactus
    Big 4, David Kirkland
Riders of the Plains
    Arrow, Jacques Jaccard
Riders of the Rio Grande
    Round-Up, Robert Emmett
    Tansey
Ridin' Fool, The
    Tiffany, John P. McCarthy
Secret Menace
    Imperial, Richard C. Kahn
Sheriff's Secret, The
    Cosmos, James P. Hogan
Son of the Plains
    Syndicate/Trem Carr, Robert N.
    Bradbury
So This is Arizona
    Big 4, J. P. McGowan
Sunrise Trail
    Tiffany, John P. McCarthy
Three Rogues
    Fox, Benjamin Stoloff
Trail of the Golden West
    Cosmos, Leander De Cordova
Two-Gun Caballero
    Imperial, Jack Nelson
Two-Gun Man
    Tiffany, Phil Rosen
Vanishing Legion
    Mascot, Ford Beebe and Yakima
    Canutt

1932

Arm of the Law
    Monogram, Louis King
Battling Buckaroo
    Kent, Armond Shaefer
Beyond the Rockies
    RKO, Oliver Drake
Black Ghost
    RKO, Spencer Gordon Bennett
Diamond Trail, The
    Monogram, Harry Fraser
Dynamite Ranch
    World Wide, Forrest Sheldon
Forbidden Trail
    Sunset, Robert N. Bradbury
Forty-Five Calibre Echo
    Horner Production, Bruce
    Mitchell
Galloping Kid
    Imperial, Robert Emmet Tansey

Hell Fire Austin
    Tiffany, Forrest Sheldon
Honor of the Mounted
    Monogram, Harry Fraser
Law of the North
    Monogram, Harry Fraser
Lone Trail, The
    Syndicate, Harry S. Webb and
    Forrest Sheldon
Lucky Larrigan
    Monogram, J. P. McCarthy
Man from Arizona
    Monogram, Harry Fraser
Man from Hell's Edges
    World Wide, Robert N. Bradbury
Man from New Mexico
    Metropolitan, J. P. McCarthy
Man's Land, A
    Allied, Phil Rosen
Mason of the Mounted
    Monogram, Harry Fraser
McKenna of the Mounted
    Columbia, Ross Lederman
Men of America
    RKO, Ralph Ince
Night Rider
    Supreme, Fred Newmeyer and
    William Nigh
One Man Law
    Columbia, Lambert Hillyer
Outlaw Justice
    Majestic, Armand Schaefer
Reckless Rider, The
    Kent, Armand Schaefer
Riders of the Golden Gulch
    West Coast Studios, Clifford
    Smith
Single Handed Sanders
    Monogram, Lloyd Nosler
South of Santa Fe
    World Wide, Bert Glennon
South of the Rio Grande
    Columbia, Lambert Hillyer
Spirit of the West
    Allied, Otto Brower
Sunset Trail
    Tiffany, B. Reeves Eason
Texas Buddies
    World Wide, Robert N. Bradbury
Texas Cyclone
    Columbia, D. Ross Lederman
Texas Gunfighter
    Tiffany, Phil Rosen
Texas Tornado
    Kent, Oliver Drake
Tombstone Canyon
    World Wide, Alan James

Two Fisted Law
Columbia, D. Ross Lederman
Whistlin' Dan
Tiffany, Phil Rosen
Without Honor
Art Class, William High
Wyoming Whirlwind
Kent, Armand Schaefer
Young Blood
Monogram, Phil Rosen

1933
Drum Taps
World Wide, J. P. McGowan
Fargo Express
World Wide, Alan James
Fiddlin' Buckaroo
Universal, Ken Maynard
Fighting Cowboy, The
Superior, Denver Dixon
Fugitive, The
Monogram, Harry Fraser
King of the Arena
Universal, Alan James
King of the Wild Horses
Columbia, Earl Haley
Mysterious Rider
Paramount, Fred Allen
Rainbow Ranch
Monogram, Harry Fraser
Ranger's Code
Monogram, Robert N. Bradbury
Rustlers Roundup
Universal, Henry MacRae
Rusty Rides Alone
Columbia, D. Ross Lederman
Silent Men
Columbia, D. Ross Lederman
Smoke Lightning
Fox, David Howard
Terror Trail
Universal, Armand Schaefer
Trailing North
Monogram, J. P. McCarthy
Trails of Adventure
American, Jay Wilsey
Via Pony Express
Majestic, Lewis Collins
War of the Range
Monarch, J. P. McGowan
When a Man Rides Alone
Monarch, Oliver Drake
Whirlwind
Columbia, D. Ross Lederman

1934
Arizona Cyclone
Imperial, Robert Emmett Tansey

Arizona Nights
Reliable, Bennett Cohen
Beyond the Law
Columbia, D. Ross Lederman
Border Menace
Aywon, Jack Nelson
Brand of Hate
Supreme, Lewis D. Collins
Cactus Kid
Reliable, Harry S. Webb
Ferocious Pal
Principal, Spencer Gordon
Fighting Hero
Reliable, Harry S. Webb
Fighting to Live
Principal, Edward F. Cline
Last Round-Up
Paramount, Henry Hathaway
Law of the Wild
Mascot, B. Reeves Eason
Lightning Bill
Superior, Victor Adamson
Lightning Range
Superior, Victor Adamson
Lone Bandit
Empire/Kinematrade, J. P. McGowan
Lone Rider, The
Imperial, Robert Emmett Tansey
Outlaw's Highway
Trop Productions, Robert Hill
Outlaw Tamer, The
Empire/Kinematrade, J. P. McGowan
Rainbow Riders
Reliable, Bennett Cohen
Rawhide Mail
Reliable, Bernard Ray
Rawhide Romance
Superior, Victor Adamson
Riding Speed
Superior, Jay Wisley
Rocky Rhodes
Universal, Al Raboch
Sundown Trail
Imperial, Robert Emmett Tansey
Western Racketeers
Aywon, Robert J. Horner
When the Kellys Rode
Harry Southwell

1935
Alias John Law
Supreme, Robert N. Bradbury
Arizona Trails
Superior, Alan James

Cheyenne Tornado
Kent, William A. O'Connor
Courage of the North
Stage and Screen, Robert Emmett Tansey
Desert Mesa
Security, Alan James
Devil's Canyon
Sunset Productions, Clifford Smith
Fighting Pioneers
Resolute, Harry Fraser
Five Bad Men
Sunset, Clifford Smith
His Fighting Blood
Ambassador, John English
Judgment Book
Beaumont, Charles Hutchinson
Laramie Kid, The
Reliable, Harry S. Webb
Lawless Borders
Spectrum, John P. McCarthy
Lawless Riders
Columbia, Spencer Gordon Bennet
Loser's End
Reliable, Bernard B. Ray
No Man's Range
Supreme, Robert N. Bradbury
North of Arizona
Reliable, Harry S. Webb
Old Homestead
Liberty, William Nigh
Outlaw Rule
Kent, S. Roy Luby
Pals of the Range
Superior, Elmer Clifton
Pals of the West
Imperial, Robert Emmett Tansey
Pecos Kid, The
Commadore, William Berke
Phantom Cowboy
Aywon, Robert J. Horner
Range Warfare
Kent, S. Roy Luby
Reckless Buckaroo, The
Spectrum, Harry Fraser
Roaring West, The
Universal, Ray Taylor
Rough Riding Ranger
Superior, Robert Clifton
Rustlers of Red Dog
Universal, Louis Friedlander
Saddle Aces
Resolute, Harry C. (Fraser) Crist
Silent Code
Stage and Screen, Stuart Paton

Silent Valley
    Reliable, Bernard B. Ray
Six Gun Justice
    Spectrum, Robert F. Hill
Skull and Crown
    Reliable, Elmer Clifton
Smokey Smith
    Supreme, Robert N. Bradbury
Sunset of Power
    Universal, Ray Taylor
Sunset Range
    First Division, Ray McCarey
Test, The
    Reliable, Bernard B. Ray
Texas Rambler, The
    Spectrum, Robert Hill
Timber Terrors
    Empire/Stage and Screen, Robert
    Emmett Tansey
Toll of the Desert
    Commodore, Lester Williams (aka
    William Berke)
Tombstone Terror
    Supreme, Robert N. Bradbury
Trail's End
    Beaumont, Albert Herman
Trails of the Wild
    Ambassador, Sam Newfield
Twisted Rails
    Imperial, Albert Herman
Under the Pampas Moon
    Fox, James Tinging
Valley of Wanted Men
    Conn Pictures, Alan James
Wanderer of the Wasteland
    Paramount, Otho Levering
Wilderness Mail
    Ambassador, Forrest Sheldon
Wolf Riders
    Reliable, Harry S. Webb

1936

Avenging Waters
    Columbia, Spencer Gordon
    Bennet
Caryl of the Mountains
    Reliable, Bernard B. Ray
Cavalcade of the West
    Diversion, Harry L. Fraser
Dodge City Trail
    Columbia, Charles C. Coleman
Feud of the West
    Diversion, Harry Fraser
Fugitive Sheriff, The
    Columbia, Spencer Gordon
    Bennet

Gun Grit
    Atlantic, Lester Williams (William
    Berke)
Heart of the West
    Paramount, Howard Bretherton
Heroes of the Range
    Columbia, Ray Taylor
Hi Gaucho
    RKO, Thomas Atkins
Irish Gringo, The
    Keith, William C. Thompson
Law and Lead
    Colony, Robert Hill
Law Rides, The
    Supreme, Robert N. Bradbury
Men of the Plains
    Grand National, Robert Emmett
    (Tansey)
Mine with the Iron Door
    Columbia, David Howard
Outlaws of the Range
    Spectrum, Al Herman
Riddle Ranch
    Beaumont, Charles Hutchison
Ride 'Em Cowboy
    Universal, Lesley Selander
Riding Avenger, The
    Diversion, Harry Fraser
Rio Grande Romance
    Victory, Robert Hill
Rip Roarin' Buckaroo
    Victory, Robert Hill
Roaring Guns
    Puritan, Sam Newfield
Roarin' Lead
    Republic, Mack V. Wright
Rose of the Rancho
    Paramount, Marion Gering
Song of the Saddle
    Warner Bros., Louis King
Tenderfoot Goes West, A
    Hofberg, Maurice O'Neill
Too Much Beef
    First Division/Grand National,
    Robert Hill
West of Nevada
    Colony, Robert F. Hill
Wildcat, Trooper
    Ambassador, Elmer Clifton

1937

Bar-Z Bad Men
    Republic, Sam Newfield
Battle of Greed
    Crescent, Howard Higgin
Black Aces
    Universal, Buck Jones

Doomed at Sundown
    Republic, Sam Newfield
Drums of Destiny
    Crescent, Ray Taylor
Feud of the Trail
    Victory, Robert Hill
Fighting Deputy, The
    Spectrum, Sam Newfield
Galloping Dynamite
    Ambassador, Harry Fraser
It Happened Out West
    20th Century Fox, Howard
    Bretherton
Lost Ranch
    Victory, Sam Katzman
Luck of the Roaring Camp
    Monogram, Irvin W. Willat
Mystery Range
    Victory, Robert Hill
Orphan of the Pecos
    Victory, Sam Katzman
Painted Stallion, The
    Republic, William Witney, Alan
    James, James Taylor
Phantom of Santa Fe
    Burroughs-Tarzan Enterprises,
    Jacques Jaccard
Roaring Six Guns
    Ambassador, J. P. McGowan
Rootin' Tootin' Rhythm
    Republic, Mack V. Wright
Rough Riding Rhythm
    Ambassador, J. P. McGowan
Sandflow
    Universal, Lesley Selander
Santa Fe Rides
    Reliable, Raymond Samuels
    (Bernard B. Ray)
Secret Valley
    20th Century Fox, Howard
    Bretherton
Silver Trail, The
    Reliable, Raymond Samuels
    (Bernard B. Ray)
Stars Over Arizona
    Monogram, Robert N. Bradbury
Trailin' Trouble
    Grand National, Robert Rosson
Trail of Vengeance
    Republic, Sam Newfield
Trapped
    Columbia, Leon Barsha

1938

California Frontier
    Columbia, Elmer Clifton

Painted Trail, The
Monogram, Robert Emmett
Tansey

1939
Across the Plains
Monogram, Spencer Gordon
Bennet
Down the Wyoming Trail
Monogram, Al Herman
Drifting Westward
Monogram, Robert Hill
El Diablo Rides
Metropolitan, Ira Webb
Feud of the Range
Metropolitan, Harry S. Webb
Fighting Gringo, The
RKO, David Howard
Fighting Renegade
Victory, Sam Newfield
Honor the West
Universal, George Waggner
Kansas Terrors
Republic, George Sherman
Outlaws Paradise
Victory, Sam Newfield
Outpost of the Mounties
Columbia, C. C. Coleman Jr.
Pal From Texas, The
Metropolitan, Harry S. Webb
Rollin' Westward
Monogram, Al Herm
Smoky Trails
Metropolitan, Bernard B. Ray
Trigger Pals
Grand National, Sam Newfield
Two Gun Troubadour
Spectrum, Raymond Sherman
Wall Street Cowboy
Republic, Joseph Kane
Western Caravans
Columbia, Sam Nelson
Zorro's Fighting Legion
Republic, William Witney and
John English

1940
Billy the Kid Outlawed
PRC, Sam Newfield
Billy the Kid's Gun Justice
PRC, Peter Stewart (Sam
Newfield)
Blazing Six Shooters
Columbia, Joseph H. Lewis
Carolina Moon
Republic, Frank McDonald

Hi-Yo Silver
Republic, John English and
William Witney
Pinto Canyon
Metropolitan, Raymond Johnson
Queen of the Yukon
Monogram, Phil Rosen
Rainbow Over Texas
Monogram, Al Sherman
Rocky Mountain Rangers
Columbia, George Sherman
Sagebrush Family Trails West
Distribution Corporation, Peter
Stewart (Sam Newfield)

1941
Billy the Kid Wanted
PRC, Herman Scott
Doomed Caravan
Paramount, Lesley Selander
Down Mexico Way
Republic, Joseph Stanley
Driftin' Kid
Monogram, Robert Emmett
Tansey
Gunman from Bodie
Monogram, Spencer Gordon
Bennett
Lone Rider Fights Back, The
PRC, Sam Newfield
Lone Rider Rides On, The
PRC, Sam Newfield
Lone Star Law Men
Monogram, Robert Emmett
Tansey
Men of Timberland
Universal, John Rawlins
Missouri Outlaw, A
Republic, George Sherman
Mormon Conquest
Victor Adamson
Outlaws of the Rio Grande
PRC, Peter Stewart
Pinto Kid, The
Columbia, Lambert Hillyer
Pirates on Horseback
Paramount, Lesley Selander
Riders of Death Valley
Universal, Ford Beebe and Ray
Taylor
Riding the Sunset Trail
Monogram, Robert Emmett
Tansey
Silver Stallion
Monogram, Robert Emmett
Tansey
Thundering Hoofs
RKO, Lesley Selander

West of Cimarron
Republic, Lester Orleback
White Eagle
Columbia, James W. Horne

1942
Along the Sundown Trail
PRC, Sam Newfield
Arizona Roundup
Monogram, Robert Emmett
Tansey
Arizona Stagecoach
Monogram, S. Roy Luby
Arizona Terrors
Republic, George Sherman
Bad Men of the Hills
Columbia, William Berke
Billy the Kid's Smoking Gun
PRC, Sam Newfield
Bullets and Bandits
Columbia, Wallace Fox
Down Rio Grande Way
Columbia, William Berke
Down Texas Way
Monogram, Howard Bretherton
King of the Stallions
Monogram, Edward Finney
Law and Order
PRC, Sherman Scott
Lone Rider and the Bandit
PRC, Sam Newfield
Lone Rider in Cheyenne
PRC, Sam Newfield
Lone Star Ranger
20th Century Fox, A. F. Ericson
Mysterious Rider
PRC, Sam Newfield
North of the Rockies
Columbia, Lambert Hillyer
Prairie Gunsmoke
Columbia, Lambert Hillyer
Rangers Take Over
PRC, Albert Herman
Riding through Nevada
Columbia, William Berke
Shadows on the Sage
Republic, Lester Orlebeck
Shut My Big Mouth
Columbia, Charles Barton
Stardust on the Sage
Republic, William Morgan
Texas Manhunt
PRC, Peter Stewart (Sam
Newfield)
Texas Trouble Shooters
Monogram, S. Roy Luby
Thunder River Feud
Monogram, S. Roy Luby

Tornado in the Saddle
Columbia, William Berke
Tumbleweed Trail
PRC, Sam Newfield
Valley of Vanishing Men, The
Columbia, Spencer Gordon
Bennet
Western Mail
Monogram, Robert Emmett
Tansey
West of Tombstone
Columbia, Howard Bretherton

1943

Arizona Trail
Universal, Vernon Keays
Avenging Rider, The
RKO, Sam Nelson
Black Hills Express
Republic, John English
Border Buckeroos
PRC, Oliver Drake
King of the Cowboys
Republic, Joseph Kane
Law of the Northwest
Columbia, William Berke
Man from the Rio Grande
Republic, Howard Bretherton
Man from Thunder River
Republic, John English
Outlaws of Stampede Pass
Monogram, Wallace Fox
Raiders of Sunset Pass
Republic, John English
Rangers Take Over
PRC, Albert Herman
Red River Robin Hood
RKO, Lesley Salender
Renegade, The
PRC, Sam Newfield
Robin Hood of the Range
Columbia, William Berke
Stranger from Pecos, The
Monogram, Lambert Hillyer
Wolves of the Range
PRC, Sam Newfield

1944

Arizona Whirlwind
Monogram, Robert Emmett
Tansey
Beneath Western Skies
Republic, Spencer Gordon Bennet
Black Arrow
Columbia, B. Reeves Easin
Drifter, The
PRC, Sam Newfield

Guns of the Law
PRC, Elmer Clifton
Lumberjack
United Artists, Lesley Selander
Phantom Outlaws
Derwin Abrahams
Pride of the Plains
Republic, Philip Ford
Raiders of Ghost City
Universal, Ray Taylor and Lewis
Collins
Range Law
Monogram, Lambert Hillyer
Riders of Santa Fe
Universal, Wallace Cox
Saddle Leather Law
Columbia, Benjamin Kline
Sonora Stagecoach
Monogram, Robert Emmett
Tansey
Stagecoach to Monterey
Republic, Lesley Selander
Sundown Valley
Columbia, Benjamin Kline
Swing in the Saddle
Columbia, Lew Landers
Utah Kid, The
Monogram, Vernon Keyes

1945

Bandits and Badlands
Republic, Thomas Carr
Blazing the Western Trail
Columbia, Vernon Keays
Fighting Bill Carson
PRC, Sam Newfield
Frontier Feud
Monogram, Lambert Hillyer
Frontier Fugitives
PRC, Harry Fraser
Jeep Herders
Planet, Richard Talmadge and
Harvey Perry
Law of the Badlands
RKO, Leslie Selander
Navajo Kid
PRC, Harry Fraser
Navajo Trail, The
Monogram, Howard Bretherton
Northwest Trail
Screen Guild, Derwin Abrahams
Rockin' in the Rockies
Columbia, Vernon Keays
Royal Mounted Rides Again, The
Universal, Ray Taylor and Lewis
Collins
South of the Rio Grande
Monogram, Lambert Hillyer

Texas Panhandle
Columbia, Ray Nazarro
Topeka Terror
Republic, Howard Bretherton

1946

Ambush Trail
PRC, Harry L. Fraser
Border Bandits
Monogram, Lambert Hillyer
Don Ricardo Returns
PRC, Terry Morse
Drifting Along
Monogram, Derwin Abrahams
Driftin' River
PRC, Robert Emmett Tansey
El Paso Kid
Republic, Thomas Carr
Gay Cavalier, The
Monogram, William Nigh
Gentlemen with Guns
PRC, Sam Newfield
Landrush
Columbia, Vernon Keays
North of the Border
Screen B, Reeves Eason
Phantom Rider
Republic, Spencer Gordon Bennett
Romance of the West
PRC, Robert Emmett (Tansey)
Scarlet Horseman
Universal, Ray Taylor and Lewis
Collins
Shadows of the Range
Monogram, Lambert Hillyer
Sheriff of Redwood Valley
Republic, R. G. Springsteen
Six Gun Man
PRC, Harry Fraser
South of Monterey
Monogram, William Nigh
Thunder Town
PRC, Harry Fraser
Wild Beauty
Universal, Wallace Fox

1947

Bandits of Dark Canyon
Republic, Philip Ford
Buffalo Bill Rides Again
Screen Guild, B. Ray
Cheyenne
Warner Bros., Raoul Walsh
Code of the West
RKO, William Berke
Flashing Guns
Monogram, Lambert Hillyer

Gas House Kids Go West
　　PRC, William Beaudine
Ghost Town Renegades
　　PRC, Ray Taylor
Gunsmoke
　　Standard/Astor, Fred King
Gun Talk
　　Monogram, Lambert Hillyer
Heaven Only Knows
　　United Artists, Albert Rogell
Hollywood Barn Dance
　　Screen Guild, Bernard B. Ray
Jesse James Rides Again
　　Republic, Fred C. Brannon and
　　Thomas Carr
Law Comes to Gunsight
　　Monogram, Lambert Hillyer
Northwest Outpost
　　Republic, Allan Dwan
Over the Santa Fe Trail
　　Columbia, Ray Nazarro
Prairie, The
　　Screen Guild, Frank Wisbar
Smoky River Serenade
　　Columbia, Derwin Abrahams
Song of The Wasteland
　　Monogram, Thoms Carr
Son of Zorro
　　Republic, Spencer Gordon Bennett
Stranger from Ponca City
　　Columbia, Derwin Abrahams
Under Colorado Skies
　　Republic, R. G. Springsteen
Under the Tonto Rim
　　RKO, Lew Landers
Unexpected Guest
　　United Artists, George
　　Archainbaud
Vigilantes Return, The
　　Universal, Ray Taylor
West of Dodge City
　　Columbia, Ray Nazarro
Where the North Begins
　　Screen Guild, Howard Bretherton

1948

Angel in Exile
　　Republic, Allan Dwan
Frontier Agent
　　Monogram, Lambert Hillyer
Hawk of the Powder River
　　Eagle Lion, Ray Taylor
Last of the Wild Horses
　　Lippert, Robert L. Lippert
Range Renegades
　　Monogram, Lambert Hillyer
Return of Wildfire, The
　　Lippert, Ray Taylor

Strange Gamble
　　United Artists, George
　　Archainbaud
Sundown Riders
　　Film Enterprises, Lambert Hillyer
Sunset Carson Rides Again
　　Astor, Oliver Drake
Tex Granger
　　Columbia, Derwin Abrahams
Untamed Breed
　　Columbia, Charles Lamont
Valiant Hombre
　　United Artists, Wallace Fox
West of Sonora
　　Columbia, Ray Nazarro
Westward Trail
　　Eagle Lion, Ray Taylor

1949

Bandits of El Dorado
　　Columbia, Ray Nazarro
James Brothers in Missouri, The
　　Republic, Fred C. Brannon
Kid from Gower Gulch, The
　　Friedgen, Oliver Drake
Law of the Barbary Coast
　　Columbia, Lew Landers
Outlaw County
　　Screen Guild, Ray Taylor
Range Justice
　　Monogram, Ray Taylor
Red Rock Outlaw
　　Friedgen, Elmer Pond
Riders of the Pony Express
　　Kayson/Screencraft, Michael Salle
Silver Bandit, The
　　Friedgen, Elmer Clifton
South of Rio
　　Republic, Philip Ford

1950

Battling Marshal
　　Republic, Oliver Drake
Border Rangers
　　Lippert, William Burke
Fighting Stallion
　　Eagle Lion, Robert Tansey
Hostile Country
　　Lippert, Thomas Carr
Kangaroo Kid, The
　　Allied Artists, Lesley Selander
Lightning Guns
　　Columbia, Fred F. Sears
Marshal of Heldorado
　　Lippert Thomas Carr
Outlaws of Texas
　　Monogram, Thomas Carr

Palomino
　　Columbia, Ray Nazarro
Rogue River
　　Eagle Lion, John Rawlins
Rustlers on Horseback
　　Republic, Fred C. Brannon
Singing Guns
　　Republic, R. G. Springsteen
Stage to Tucson
　　Columbia, Ralph Moody
Stars in My Crown
　　MGM, Jacques Tourneur
Surrender
　　Republic, Allan Dwan
Texas Dynamo
　　Columbia, Ray Nazarro
Timber Fury
　　Eagle Lion, Bernard B. Ray
Trigger Jr.
　　Republic, William Witney

1951

Badman's Gold
　　Eagle Lion, Robert Emmett
　　Tansey
Border Fence
　　Astor Pictures/Gulf Coast Pro,
　　Howard Kier and Norman
　　Sheldon
Fort Savage Raiders
　　Columbia, Ray Nazarro
Gene Autry and the Mounties
　　Columbia, John English
Gunplay
　　RKO, Leslie Selander
Heart of the Rockies
　　Republic, William Witney
Hot Lead
　　RKO Stuart Gilmore
Inside Straight
　　MGM, Gerald Mayer
Kid from Amarillo
　　Columbia, Ray Nazarro
King of the Bullwhip
　　Western Adventure, Ron Ormond
Last Outpost, The
　　Paramount, Lewis R. Foster
Pecos River
　　Columbia, Fred F. Sears
Ridin' the Outlaw Trail
　　Columbia, Fred F. Sears
Rough Riders of Durango
　　Republic, Fred C. Brannon
Secret of Convict Lake
　　20th Century Fox, Michael
　　Gordon
Stagecoach Driver
　　Monogram, Louis D. Collins

Thundering Trail, The
   Western Adventure, Ron Ormond
Treasure of Lost Canyon, The
   Universal, Ted Tetzlaff
Vanishing Outpost
   Western Adventure, Ron Ormond

1952

Barbed Wire
   Columbia, George Archainbaud
Black Hills Ambush
   Republic, Harry Keller
Desperadoes' Outpost
   Republic, Philip Ford
Face to Face
   Warner Bros., William A. Graham
Gold Fever
   Monogram, Leslie Goodwins
Gunman, The
   Monogram, Lewis B. Collins
Hired Gun
   Monogram, Thomas Carr
Leadville Gunslinger
   Republic, Harry Keller
Man from Black Hills
   Monogram, Thomas Carr
Old Oklahoma Plains
   Republic, William Witney
Savage, The
   Paramount, George Marshall
Scorching Fury
   Fraser Productions, Rick Freers
Smoky Canyon
   Columbia, Fred Sears
Son of Geronimo
   Columbia, Spencer Gordon
   Bennett
Target
   RKO, Stuart Gilmore
Thundering Caravans
   Republic, Harry Keller
Trail of the Arrow
   Monogram, Thomas Carr

1953

Bandits of the West
   Republic, Harry Keller
Down Laredo Way
   Republic, William Witney
Fighting Lawman, The
   Allied Artists, Thomas Carr
Iron Mountain Trail
   Republic, William Witney
Last Posse, The
   Columbia, Alfred L. Werker
Marksman, The
   Allied Artists, Louis D. Collins
Marshal's Daughter, The
   United Artists, William Berke

Northern Patrol
   Monogram, Rex Bailey
Powder River
   20th Century Fox, Louis King
Savage Frontier
   Republic, Harry Keller
Secret of Outlaw Pass
   Allied Artists, Wesley Barry and
   Frank McDonald
Son of the Renegade
   United Artists, Reg Brown
Take Me to Town
   Universal, Douglas Sirk
Two-Gun Marshal
   Allied Artists, Frank McDonald
Vanquished, The
   Paramount, Edward Ludwig
Winning of the West
   Columbia, George Archainbaud

1954

Jesse James vs. The Daltons
   Columbia, William Castle
Lawless Rider, The
   United Artists, Yakima Canutt
Man with the Steel Whip
   Republic, Franklyn Adreon
Marshals in Disguise
   Allied Artists, Frank McDonald
Massacre Canyon
   Columbia, Fred F. Sears
Riding with Buffalo Bill
   Columbia, Spencer Gordon
   Bennett
They Rode West
   Columbia, Phil Karlson
Trouble on the Trail
   Allied Artists, Frank McDonald
The Two-Gun Teacher
   Allied Artists, Frank McDonald
Wyoming Renegades
   Columbia, Fred F. Sears

1955

Canyon Crossroads
   United Artists, Alfred Werker
Fort Yuma
   United Artists, Lesley Selander
Frontier Woman
   Top Pictures, Ron Ormond
Fury in Paradise
   Filmmakers/Alfonso, Sanchez-
   Tello and George Bruce
Lawless Street, The
   Columbia, Joseph H. Lewis
Lonesome Trail, The
   Lippert, Richard Bartlett

Outlaw Treasure
   American Releasing Corporation,
   Oliver Drake
Phantom Trails
   Allied Artists, Welsey Barry and
   Frank McDonald
Second Greatest Sex, The
   Universal, George Marshal
Tall Men Riding
   Warner Bros., Lesley Selander
Ten Wanted Men
   Columbia, Bruce Humberstone
Timber Country Trouble
   Allied Artists, Frank McDonald

1956

Frontier Gambler
   Associated Releasing Corporation,
   Sam Newfield
Perils of the Wilderness
   Columbia, Spencer Gordon
   Bennet
Running Target
   United Artists, Marvin R.
   Weinstein
Thunder Over Arizona
   Republic, Joseph Kane
White Squaw
   Columbia, Ray Nazarro

1957

Buckskin Lady, The
   United Artists, Carl K.
   Himmleman
Hell's Crossroads
   Republic, Franklyn Adreon
Iron Sheriff, The
   United Artists, Sidney Salkow
Outlaw Queen
   Globe/Ashcroft and Associate,
   Herbert S. Greene
Robbery Under Arms
   Lopert, Jack Lee
Sierra Stranger
   Columbia, Richard Sholem
Tall Stranger, The
   Allied Artists, Thomas Carr
Tomahawk Trail
   Bel Air/United Artists, Lesley
   Selander

1958

Ten Days to Tulara
   United Artists, George Sherman

1959

The Bandit of Zhobe
   Columbia, John Gilling

1965
Bounty Killer
Embassy, Spencer Gordon Bennet
Kid Rodelo
Paramount, Richard Carlson
Peace for a Gunfighter
Crown International, Raymond
Boley
Ride in the Whirlwind
Jack H. Harris Enterprises, Monte
Hellman
Town Tamer
Paramount, Lesley Selander

1967
Far Out West
Universal, Joe Connely

1968
Day of the Evil Gun
MGM, Jerry Thorpe
Journey to Shiloh
Universal, William Hale

1969
Land Raiders
Columbia, Nathan Juran
Moon Zero Two
Warner Bros., Michael Carreas
More Dead than Alive
United Artists, Robert Spar
Talent for Loving, A
Richard Quine

1970
King of the Grizzley
Buena Vista, Ron Yelly

1972
Red Sun
Oceana, Terrence Young

Appendix V

Following is a year-by-year list of silent films not covered in the A–Z section of this book. Many of them have short running times. Sadly, most of these titles are now lost.

1898
Cripple Creek Barroom

1904
A Brush between Cowboys and Indians
The Hold-up of the Leadville Stage

1905
Pendaison á Jefferson City (aka *Hanging at Jefferson City*)

1906
Holdup of the Rocky Mountain Express
The Life of a Cowboy
A Race for Millions

1907
The Bad Man
The Bandit King
The Bandit Makes Good
Girl from Montana
Pony Express
The Tenderfoot
Western Justice

1908
A Bank Robbery
The Cattle Rustlers
A Cowboy Escapade
The Girl and the Outlaw
The Life of an American Cowboy
Misadventures of a Sheriff
The Red Man and the Child
The Stage Rustler

1909
Bill Sharkey's Last Game

Boots and Saddles
Comata the Sioux
The Corporal's Daughter
The Cowboy Millionaire
Custer's Last Stand
The Friend in Need
The Heart of a Cowboy
The Indian Runner's Romance
In the Badlands
The Mended Lute
A Mexican's Gratitude
On the Border
Pet of the Big Horn Ranch
Pine Ridge Feud
The Ranchman's Rival
The Red Man's View
Red Wing's Gratitude
The Road Agents
The Squaw's Revenge
Stampede
A Tale of the West
The Tenderfoot
The True Heart of an Indian
A Western Hero

1910
The Angel of Dawson's Claim
The Bandit's Wife
The Boys of Topsy-Turvy Ranch
Broncho Billy's Redemption
A Cheyenne Brave
The Cowboy and the Squaw
The Cowboy's Sweetheart
A Cowboy's Vindication
The Girl from Arizona
Hidden under Campfire
In Old California

The Indian Scout's Revenge
The Outlaw's Redemption
Over Silent Paths
Pride of the Range
Ranch Life in the Great Southwest
The Ranch Rider
The Red Girl and the Child
Romantic Redskins
The Sheriff's Law
That Chink at Golden Gulch
The Two Brothers
Western Chivalry

1911
Back to the Primitive
The Best Man Wins
Billy The Kid
A Branded Indian
Branding a Bad Man
The Cowboy and the Lady
The Cowboy Coward
The Crimson Scars
The Curse of the Redman
Dad's Girls
The Fall of the Alamo
Fate
Fighting Blood
Flaming Arrows
For the Squaw
His Mother's Scarf
In the Days of the '49
Kit Carson's Wooing
The Last Drop of Water
The Law of the Range
The Lonedale Operator
Mary's Strategem
Maude Muller

On the Warpath
The Outlaw and the Child
The Outlaw's Deputy
The Ranchman's Nerve
A Range Romance
A Romance of the Rio Grande
Saved by the Pony Express
The Sheriff and the Man
The Sheriff's Brother
The Sheriff's Chum
The Sheriff's Daughter
The Squaw's Love
The Totem Mark
A True Westerner
Under the Stars and Bars
Was He a Coward?
A Western Girl's Sacrifice
When the Tables Turned
The White Medicine Man
Why the Sheriff is a Bachelor
A Young Squaw's Bravery

1912

The Altar of Death
The Apache Renegade
At Cripple Creek
The Ball Player and the Bandit
The Band Cashier
The Battle of the Red Men
The Boy Rangers
The Brand
The Brand Blotter
The Bravery of Dora
Broncho Billy and the Bandits
Broncho Billy's Mexican Wife
Chicago in 1812
The Chief's Blanket
Custer's Last Fight
Custer's Last Raid
The Deserter
Double Trail
The Driver of the Deadwood Coach
The Fear
For the Honor of the Seventh
Friends
The Goddess of Sagebrush Gulch
The Half Breed Scout
The Heart of an Indian
Her Indian Hero
His Only Son
His Squaw
An Indian Ishmael
An Indian Legend
Indian Raiders
The Indian Uprising in Santa Fe
An Indian Vendetta
In the Service of the Stage
The Invaders

Juan and Juanita
The Lieutenant's Last Fight
The Life of Buffalo Bill
Maiden and Men
The Minister and the Outlaw
My Hero
Red Wing and the Paleface
The Renegade
The Renegades
The Sheriff's Inheritance
The Sheriff's Mistake
Star Eyes' Stratagem
The Tattoo
A Temporary Truce
Their Hero Son
Through Death's Valley
War on the Plains
Western Girls
When Uncle Sam was Young
The White Vaquero

1913

The Accusation of Broncho Billy
An Apache Father's Vengeance
An Apache's Gratitude
Arizona
The Battle at Fort Laramie
The Battle of Bull Run
The Branded Six Shooter
The Call of the Blood
The Capture of Bad Brown
Children of the Forest
The Claim Jumper
Diamond Cut Diamond
Down on the Rio Grande
During the Round-Up
Exposure of the Land Swindlers
Fifty Miles from Tombstone
From Dawn Till Dark
A Frontier Mystery
A Frontier Providence
Hearts and Horses
An Indian's Loyalty
The Jealousy of Miguel and Isabella
Love and the Law
The Making of Broncho Billy
The Man from the Golden West
Man's Duty
The Marshal's Capture
Massacre
Modern Snare
Mona of the Modocs
The Opal Stealers
Pride of Lonesome
The Ranchero's Revenge
The Range Law
The Rattlesnake
The Red Girl's Sacrifice

A Romance of the Ozarks
The Rustler's Reformation
Sallie's Sure Shot
Saved from the Vigilantes
The Schoolmarm's Shooting Match
A Shadow of the Past
The Sheriff and the Rustler
The Sheriff's Baby
The Sheriff's Child
The Snake
The Stolen Moccasins
Taming a Tenderfoot
The Tattooed Arm
Texas Kelly at Bay
Three Friends
Tobias Wants Out
The Tonopah Stampede for Gold
The Trail of the Cards
Two Men of the Desert
When Jim Returned
When Luck Changes
Wynona's Vengeance
The Yaqui Cur
Youth and Jealousy

1914

The Adventures of Buffalo Bill
The Bad Buck of Santa Ynez
The Battle of Elderbush Gulch
The Rifle Smugglers
The Two-Gun Man in the Bargain
Beating Back
The Brand
Broncho Billy and the Greaser
Broncho Billy's Bible
Buck Parvin in the Movies
By the Sun's Rays
Cactus Jack Heartbreaker
Captured by Mexicans
Chip of the Flying U
Daughter of the Redskins
Doc
Dodge City Trail
The Flower of Faith
For the Freedom of Cuba
The Good-For-Nothing
Her Grave Mistake
His Hour of Manhood
Jimmy Hayes and Muriel
The Little Angel of Canyon Creek
The Man from the East
The Man Within
The Mexican
A Miner's Romance
The Mountain Rat
The Moving Picture Cowboy
The Mysterious Hand
The Mysterious Shot

The Foreman's Deceit
The Outlaw Reforms
The Passing of Black Pete
The Passing of Two-Gun Hicks
A Ranch Romance
The Ranger's Romance
The Real Thing in Cowboys
The Redemption of Broncho Billy
Red Riding Hood of the Hills
The Rival Stage Lines
Rose of the Rancho
Salomy Jane
Sands of Fate
Saved by a Watch
The Scapegoat
The Sheriff's Reward
Shorty's Escape from Matrimony
Sierra Jim's Reformation
Snakeville's New Doctor
Strongheart
The Telltale Knife
The Thundering Herd
The Tragedy of Whispering Creek
The Virginian
The Way of the Redman
When Cook Fell Ill
Where the Trail Divides

1915
And They Called Him Hero
Athletic Ambitions
The Auction Sale of Run Down Ranch
Bad Man Bobbs
The Bandit and the Preacher
Bandits of Death Valley
The Boundary Line
Broncho Billy and the Card Sharp
Broncho Billy and the False Note
Broncho Billy and the Land Grabber
Broncho Billy and the Lumber King
Broncho Billy and the Posse
Broncho Billy and the Vigilante
Broncho Billy Begins Life Anew
Broncho Billy Evens Matters
Broncho Billy Misled
Broncho Billy's Brother
Broncho Billy's Cowardly Brother
Broncho Billy's Greaser Deputy
Broncho Billy Sheepman
Broncho Billy's Love Affair
Broncho Billy's Marriage
Broncho Billy's Parents
Broncho Billy's Protégé
Broncho Billy's Sentence
Broncho Billy Steps In
Broncho Billy's Surrender
Broncho Billy's Teachings
Broncho Billy's Vengeance

Broncho Billy's Word of Honor
Broncho Billy Well Repaid
Buckshot John
Buck's Lady Friend
Cactus Jim's Shopgirl
Captain Courtesy
Child of the Prairie
Chimmie Fadden Out West
Colorado
The Conversion of Smiling Tom
The Convert
The Cowboy and the Lady
The Cowboy's Conquest
A Cowboy's Sweetheart
The Cowpuncher
The Curse of the Desert
The Desert Breed
The Disciple
Double Crossed
The Eagle's Nest
Environment
The Exile of Bar-K Ranch
Fatherhood
The Folly of a Life of Crime
The Foreman's Choice
The Gambler of the West
The Girl and the Mail Bag
The Girl I Left Behind Me
The Girl of the Golden West
The Gold Dust and the Squaw
The Greaser
The Great Divide
Her Slight Mistake
The Impersonation of Tom
The Indians' Narrow Escape
The Iron Street
The Lamb
The Last Card
Lillian's Atonement
The Lily of Poverty Flat
The Long Chance
The Love Route
The Lure of Woman
Man Afraid of his Wardrobe
A Man and his Mate
The Man from Texas
Martyrs of the Alamo
M'Liss
Never Again
On the Eagle Trail
The Outlaw's Bridge
Passing of the Oklahoma Outlaws
The Plunderer
Quits
The Race for a Gold Mine
The Range Girl and the Cowboy
Ranson's Folly
Roping a Bride

Satan McAllister's Heir
Saved by her Horse
Sealed Valley
The Sheriff's Streak of Yellow
Square Deal
Sweeter than Revenge
The Taking of Luke McVane
The Tenderfoot's Triumph
This is the Life
Three Bad Men and a Girl
The Valley of Lost Hope
A Western Governor's Humanity

1916
Across the Rio Grande
All Man
Along the Border
An Angelic Attitude
The Aryan
At Medicine Bend
The Bandit's Wager
A Bear of a Story
Ben Blairr
Blue Blood and Red
The Bugle Call
Canbyhill Outlaws
The Carquinez Woods
A Close Call
A Corner in Water
The Cowpuncher's Peril
Crooked Trails
Davy Crockett
The Dawn Maker
The Desert Calls Its Own
The Deserter
The Devil's Double
An Eventful Evening
A Five-Thousand Dollar Elopement
The Girl of Gold Gulch
God's Crucible
Going West to Make Good
The Golden Thought
Hair Trigger Casey
His Bitter Pill
His Hereafter
His Majesty Dick Turpin
Honor Thy Country
Humanizing Mr. Winsby
Jim Grimsby's Boy
A Knight of the Range
The Lass of the Lumberlands
A Law Unto Himself
Legal Advice
Liberty, Daughter of the U.S.A.
Local Color on the A-1 Ranch
Love Mask
Love's Lariat
A Lucky Gold Piece

Making Good
The Man from Bitter Roots
The Man Within
The Mediator
A Mistake in Rustlers
Mister 44
Mixed Blood
A Mix-Up in Movies
The Night Riders
The Parson of Panamint
The Passing of Hell's Crown
The Passing of Pete
Passing Through
The Patriot
The Pony Express Rider
The Primal Lure
The Quitter
The Raiders
Reclamation
The Return of Draw Egan
The Sheriff's Blunder
A Sheriff's Duty
Shooting Up the Movies
Silent Shelby
A Sister of Six
Some Duel
The Stain in the Blood
Starring in Western Stuff
Taking a Chance
The Taming of Grouchy Bill
The Target
Tennessee's Pardner
The Three Godfathers
Tom's Sacrifice
Tom's Strategy
Too Many Chefs
Trilby's Love Disaster
Truthful Tulliver
Twisted Trails
Two Men of Sandy Bar
A Western Masquerade
When Cupid Slipped
Whispering Smith
The Winning Pair
The Yaqui

1917
'49-'17
Anything Once
Ashes of Hope
The Blue Streak
The Bond of Fear
The Boss of the Lazy Y
The Bronze Bridge
Bucking Broadway
By Right of Possession
Captain of the Gray Horse Troop
The Cold Deck

The Conqueror
Dead Shot Baker
Delayed in Transit
The Desert Man
The Desire of the Moth
The Devil Dodger
The Divorcee
Durand of the Bad Lands
The Empty Gun
Fancy Jim Sherwood
Fighting Back
The Fighting Gringo
Fighting Mad
The Fighting Trail
The Firefly of Tough Luck
Follow the Girl
The Girl Angle
The Golden Fetter
The Golden Rule Kate
Guardian of El Dorado
The Gun Fighter
Hands Up!
Hearts and Saddles
Her God
The Hero of the Hour
The Highway of Hope
Humanity
Indian's Last Testament
Jack and Jill
The Jaguar's Claws
John Ermine of Yellowstone
The Kill-Joy
The Learnin' of Jim Benton
The Luck of Roaring Camp
The Luck That Jealousy Brought
The Mad Stampede
Madame Bo-Peep
Marked Man
Me of the Desert
Nan of Music Mountain
The Narrow Trail
One Shot Ross
One Touch of Sin
On the Level
Open Places
The Outlaw and the Lady
Pioneer Days
The Plow Woman
The Price of Pride
The Primitive Call
The Range Boss
The Round U
Salt of the Earth
The Secret of Black Mountain
The Silent Man
Single Shot Parker
The Siren
Six Cylinder Love

Six Shooter Justice
The Sky Pilot
Slam Bang Jim
A Soft Tenderfoot
The Square Deal Man
Straight Shooting
Sunlight's Last Raid
The Tenderfoot
Their Compact
Tom and Jerry Mix
The Tornado
The Trail of the Shadow
Trooper of Troop K. A
Under Handicap
Up or Down?
The Vulture of Skull Mountain
Who Knows?
Wild and Woolly
Wolf Lowry
The World Apart

1918
Beyond the Law
Blue Blazes Rawden
Bobby Bumps Out West
The Border Legion
Border Raiders
The Border Wireless
The Branded Man
Branding Broadway
By Proxy
Cactus Crandall
Cupid's Roundup
A Daughter of the West
The Dawn of Understanding
Denny from Ireland
Desert Law
Deuce Duncan
The Eagle
Faith Endurin'
Fame and Fortune
The Fast Mail
The Fighting Grin
Flare-Up Sal
The Fly God
A Good Loser
Go West, Young Man
The Grand Passion
The Gun Woman
Hands Down
Heart of the Sunset
Hell Bent
The Hell Cat
The Hell's Crater
The Home Trail
Hungry Eyes
Keith of the Border
The Lady of the Dugout

Lawless Love
The Law's Outlaw
The Light of the Western Stars
The Man Above the Law
The Man From Funeral Range
Mr. Logan, U.S.A.
Naked Hands
Oh Johnny!
The Only Road
Out West
Paying his Debit
Perfectly Fiendish Flanagan
Petticoats and Politics
The Phantom Riders
The Pretender
The Rainbow Trail
The Ranger
The Red Haired Cupid
The Red, Red Heart
Revenge
Riddle Gawne
Rimrock Jones
Rose of Wolfville
Rough and Ready
Ruggles of Red Gap
The Scarlet Drop
Selfish Yates
Shootin Mad
The Silent Rider
Six Shooter Andy
Smashing Through
The Squaw Man
Staking his Life
The Sunset Princess
Thieves' Gold
Three Mounted Men
The Tiger Man
Tongues of Flame
The Trail to Yesterday
True Blue
Two-Gun Betty
Unclaimed Goods
Untamed
Western Blood
Whatever the Cost
When a Man Rides Alone
Wild Honey
Wild Life
Wild Women
The Winding Trail
Winner Takes All
The Winning of the Mocking Bird
With Hoops of Steel
Wolves of the Border
Wolves of the Rail
A Woman's Fool
The Younger Brothers

1919

Ace of the Saddle
The Arizona Cat Claw
As the Sun Went Down
At the Point of a Gun
Bare-Fisted Gallagher
Bare Fists
The Best Bad Man
Brass Buttons
Breed of Men
Breezy Jim
Brother Bill
Caliber 38
The Challenge of Chance
Chasing Rainbows
The Coming of the Law
The Cowboy and the Rajah
A Debtor to the Law
Desert Gold
The End of the Game
A Fight for Love
Fighting for Gold
The Fighting Line
The Forfeit
God's Outlaw
The Gray Towers Mystery
A Gun Fightin' Gentleman
Heart of Juanita
The Heart of Wetona
Hell-Roarin' Reform
High Pockets
In Mizzoura
It's a Bear
Jack, Sam and Pete
Jubilo
Just Squaw
The Kid and the Cowboy
The Knickerbocker Buckaroo
The Lady of Red Butte
Lasca
The Last of the Duanes
The Last Outlaw
Leave It to Susan
Lightning Bryce
The Lone Star Ranger
Love Call
A Man's Country
Marked Men
The Midnight Stage
Miss Arizona
The Money Corral
Nugget Nell
The Outcasts of Poker Flat
Partners Three
The Peace of Roaring River
The Poppy Girl's Husband
The Prodigal Liar
Put Up Your Hands

Red Blood and Yellow
Rider of the Law
Rider of Vengeance
The Root of Evil
Roped
Rough Riding Romance
Rowdy Ann
Rustlers
The Rustlers
Rustling a Bridge
A Sagebrush Hamlet
Sandy Burke of the U-Bar-U
Scarlet Days
The Sheriff's Son
The She Wolf
Six Feet Four
The Sleeping Lion
Some Liar
The Son of a Gun
The Speed Maniac
Speedy Meade
Square Deal Sanderson
The Sundown Trail
Terror of the Range
This Hero Stuff
Told in the Hills
The Trail's End
Treat 'Em Rough
Two Men of Tinted Butte
The Unbroken Promise
Wagon Tracks
The Westerners
When a Girl Loves
When Big Dan Rides
When the Desert Smiles
Where the West Begins

1920

Blazing the Way
Blue Streak McCoy
A Broadway Cowboy
The Broncho Kid
Bullet Proof
Crossed Trails
Cupid the Cowpuncher
Dangerous Love
Dangerous Trails
Daredevil
The Daughter of Dawn
Death Valley Kid
The Deerslayer and Chingachgook
Desert Love
Desert Scorpion
Drag Harlan
Fight It Out
Fighting Cressy
The Fighting Shepherdess
The Flame of Hellgate

Forbidden Trails
Frontier Days
The Galloping Devil
A Gamblin' Fool
Get Your Man
The Girl Who Dared
The Gun Game
The Heart of Big Dan
Hell's Oasis
Honest Hutch
Honeymoon Ranch
Human Stuff
"If Only" Jim
The Invisible Hand
The Iron Rider
The Joyous Troublemakers
Just Pals
Lahoma
The Last Straw
The Lone Hand
Lone Hand Wilson
The Man from Nowhere
The Moon Riders
The Orphan
Out of the Dust
Overland Red
Pinto Prairie Trails
Riders of the Dawn
Ruth of the Rockies
The Sagebrusher
Sand!
Sheriff Nell's Comeback
Shod with Fire
Square Shooter
The Stranger
Sundown Slim
The Terror
The Testing Block
The Texan
The Third Woman
Three Gold Coins
Toll Gate
Trailed by Three
The Twins of Suffering Creek
The Two-fisted Lover
Two Kinds of Love
Under Sentence
The Unknown Ranger
The Untamed
The U.P. Trail
Vanishing Trails
The Veiled Mystery
Vengeance and the Girl
West is West
The White Rider
Wolf Tracks
A Woman's Man
Across the Divide

Action
After Your Own Heart
Another Man's Boots
Bar Nothin'
The Beautiful Gambler
Black Sheep
The Border Raider
Brand of Courage
The Bull-Dogger
Colorado
The Cowboy Ace
The Crimson Skull
Crossed Clues
Crossing Trails
Cyclone Bliss
Desperate Trails
Double Crossed
The Double O
Duke of Chimney Butte
The Fighting Breed
The Fighting Stranger
Fightin' Mad
The Fire Eater
The Fox
The Freeze-Out
Ghost City
God's Gold
Hands Off
Hearts o' the Range
Hearts Up
Hills of Hate
The Hunger of the Blood
The Jack Rider
Jesse James as the Outlaw
Jesse James under the Black Flag
Judge Her Not
The Killer
A Knight of the West
The Last Chance
The Last Trail
The Man from Texas
Man of the Forest
Montana Bill
The Mysterious Rider
The Night Horsemen
No Man's Woman
O'Malley of the Mounted
The One-Man Trail
On the High Card
The Outlaw
Outlawed
Out of the Depths
Penny of Top Hill Trail
The Primal Law
The Range Pirate
The Ranger and the Law
Red Courage
A Riding Romeo

Riding with Death
Riding with Romeo
The Ropin' Fool
The Rough Diamond
The Ruse of the Rattler
Rustlers of the Night
The Sage Hen
The Sheriff of Hope Eternal
Singing River
The Stampede
Steelheart
Strait from the Shoulder
Struggle
Sure Fire
That Girl Montana
Three Word Brand
To a Finish
Trail to Red Dog
The Trigger Trail
Under Western Skies
The Vengeance Trail
The Wallop
A Western Adventurer
Western Firebrands
Western Hearts
West of the Rio Grande
Where Men are Men
The White Horseman
The White Masks
White Oak
The Winding Trail
Winners of the West
The Wolverine
Wolves of the Range

1922

The Ableminded Lady
Across the Border
Backfire
Back to Yellow Jacket
Barb Wire
Barriers of Folly
Battling King
The Bearcat
Behind the Mask
Bells of San Juan
The Better Man Wins
Big Stakes
Billy Jim
Blaze Away
Blazing Arrows
Blue Blazes
Boomerang Justice
Branded Man
Butterfly Range
The Cowboy and the Lady
The Cowboy King
The Crimson Challenge

Crimson Clue
Cross Roads
The Crow's Nest
The Crusader
Daring Danger
The Desert Bridegroom
Desert's Crucible
Do and Dare
False Brands
The Fighting Streak
The Firebrand
Flaming Hearts
Fools of Fortune
For the Big Stakes
Four Hearts
The Galloping Kid
The Girl Who Ran Wild
Gold Grabbers
Golden Silence
Good Men and True
Gun Shy
The Gypsy Trail
The Half Breed
Headin' West
The Heart of a Texan
Hellhounds of the West
In the Days of Buffalo Bill
Iron to Gold
The Kickback
The Kingfisher's Roost
Lights of the Desert
Little Brother of God
The Loaded Door
The Lone Hand
The Lone Rider
The Long Chance
The Love Gambler
Lure of Gold
The Man from Hell's River
Man of Courage
Man to Man
The Man Who Waited
The Masked Avenger
The Milky Way
Moonshine Valley
Nine Points of the Law
North of the Rio Grande
One Eight Apache
Pals of the West
Pardon My Nerve!
Partners of the Sunset
Peaceful Peters
The Prairie Mystery
The Purple Riders
Rangeland
Ridin' Wild
Roughshod
Rounding Up the Law

The Sagebrush Trail
Sheriff of Sun Dog
Silver Spurs
Sky High
Step on it!
The Stranger of the Hills
Table Top Ranch
The Test
Texas
Texas Angel Citizens
Thorobred
The Three Buckaroos
Tracked to Earth
Tracks
Trail of Hate
Trail's End
Trapped in the Air
Travelin' On
Trimmed
Two-Fisted Jefferson
Two Kinds of Women
A Western Demon
The Western Musketeer
Western Speed
A Western Thoroughbred
West of Chicago
West of the Pecos
West vs East
When Danger Smiles
When East Comes West
While Justice Waits
While Stan Sleeps
Without Compromise
The Yosemite Trail

1923

At Devil's Gorge
The Bad Man
Battling Bates
Below the Rio Grande
Big Dan
Blinky
Blood Test
Brass Commandments
The Buster
The Call of the Canyon
Crashin' Thru
Crimson Gold
Cyclone Jones
Dead Game
Desert Driven
Desert Rider
The Devil's Bowl
Don Quickshot of the Rio Grande
The Eagle's Feather
End of the Rope
Eyes of the Forest
Fighting Jim Grant

The Fighting Strain
The Footlight Ranger
The Forbidden Range
The Forbidden Trail
The Garage
The Girl from the Golden West
Girl from the West
The Grail
The Gunfighter
Hell's Hole
In the West
It Happened Out West
Kindled Courage
King's Creek Law
The Law Rustlers
Lone Fighter
The Lone Horseman
The Lone Star Ranger
The Lone Wagon
The Love Brand
The Man from New York
The Man Getter
The Man Who Won
Men in the Raw
Mile-a-Minute Romeo
The Miracle Baby
The Mysterious Witness
The Old Fool
$1,000 Reward
The Oregon Trail
Pioneer Trails
Playing It Wild
Pure Grit
The Ramblin' Kid
The Ranchers
The Range Patrol
The Red Warning
Riders at Night
Riders of the Range
Romance Land
Ruggles of Red Gap
The Rum Runners
Salomy Jane
Salty Saunders
The Santa Fe Trail
Scars of Hate
The Secret of the Pueblo
The Seventh Sheriff
Shadows of the North
Shootin' for Love
Slow as Lightning
Stepping Fast
Sting of the Scorpion
The Sunshine Trail
Three Jumps Ahead
Three Who Paid
To the Last Man
The Vengeance of Pierre

The Virginian
The Web of the Law
Western Blood
Western Justice
Where Is This West?
Wild Bill Hickok
With Naked Fists
Wolf's Tracks
Wolves of the Border

1924

Ace of Cactus Range (aka *Ace of Cactus*)
Ace of the Law
Against All Odds
The Avenger
The Back Trail
Baffled
Battlin' Buckaroo
Battlin' Buddy
Behind Two Guns
The Beloved Brute
Biff Bang Buddy
Black Gold
The Border Legion
Border Women
Branded a Bandit
The Breed of the Border
Bringin' Home the Bacon
Buckin' the West
Calibre 45
California in '49
Code of the Wilderness
Come on Cowboys! (aka *His Glorious Romance*)
Courage
The Covered Trail
The Cowboy and the Flapper
Coyote Fangs
Crashin' Through
Crossed Trails
Cupid's Rustler
Cyclone Buddy
The Dangerous Coward
Daring Chances
Days of '49
The Deadwood Coach
The Desert Hawk
The Desert Outlaw
The Desert Secret
A Desperate Adventure
The Diamond Bandit
Down by the Rio Grande
The Eagle's Claw
False Trails
Fast and Fearless
$50,000 Reward (aka *Fifty Thousand Dollar Reward*)
Fighter's Paradise

Fighting for Justice
Fighting Fury
The Fighting Sap
The Flaming Crisis
The Flaming Forties
Flashing Spurs
The Galloping Ace
Galloping Gallagher (aka *The Sheriff of Tombstone*)
Galloping Hoofs
Hard Hittin' Hamilton
Headin' Through
The Hellion
The Heritage of the Desert
His Own Law
Hook and Ladder
Horse Sense
Huntin' Trouble
The King of the Wild Horses
The Lash of Pin Duanes
The Left Hand Brand
The Lightning Rider
The Lone Hand Texan
Looped for Life
The Loser's End
The Love Bandit
Man from God's Country
The Man from Wyoming
The Man Who Played Square
The Mask of Lopez
Midnight Shadows
The Millionaire Cowboy
The Mine with the Iron Door
The Night Hawk
The No-Gun Man
North of Nevada
Not Built for Runnin'
Oh, You Tony!
The Passing of Wolf MacLean
Payable on Demand
Perfect Alibi
The Phantom Horseman
Pioneer's Gold
The Plunderer
Pot Luck Pards
Rainbow Rangers
Range Blood
Rarin' to Go
Reckless Riding Bill
The Riddle Rider
Ride for Your Life
Ridgeway of Montana
Ridin' Fool
Riding Double (aka *Ridin' Double*)
The Ridin' Kid From Powder River (aka *The Lone Outlaw*)
Ridin' Mad
Ridin' West

Rip Roarin' Robber
A Rodeo Mixup
Romance of the Wasteland
Rough Ridin'
Sagebrush Gospel
Sawdust Trail
Sell 'Em Cowboy (aka *Alias Texas Pete Owens*)
Shootin' Square
The Silent Stranger
Singer Jim McKee
The Smoking Trail
Sundown
The Sunset Trail
Teeth
The Terror of Pueblo
That Wild West
Thundering Hoofs
Thundering Romance
Tiger Thompson
Trail Dust
Travelin' Fast
Treasure Canyon
Trigger Finger
The Troubleshooter
Trucker's Top Hand
Two Fisted Justice (aka *Two-fisted Justice*)
Two Fisted Tenderfoot
The Vagabond Trail
Valley of Vanishing Men
Walloping Wallace
Wanderer of the Wasteland
Wanted by the Law
The Way of a Man
Westbound
Western Fate
Western Feuds
Western Grit
Western Luck
Western Vengeance
The Western Wallop
Western Yesterdays
West of Hot Dog
When a Man's a Man
The Whirlwind Ranger
The Wildcat
Yankee Speed

1925

Across the Deadline
Action Galore (aka *Men Without Fear*)
Adventures of Texas Jack
All Around Frying Pan
Always Ridin to Win
The Bad Lands
The Bandit's Baby
The Bandit Tamer
Bashful Whirlwind

Battling Travers
Beauty and the Bad Man
Beauty and the Bandit
The Best Bad Man
Beyond the Border
Black Cyclone
Blood and Steel
Blood Bond
Border Intrigue
Border Justice
Border Vengeance
The Boundary Line
Brand of Cowardice
Braveheart
Bulldog Courage
The Burning Trail
Bustin' Thru
The Cactus Cure
Cactus Trails
The Calgary Stampede
The Call of Courage
The Cherokee Strip
A Chocolate Cowboy
The Circus Cyclone
Code of the West
Cold Fury
Cold Nerve
Cowboy Courage
Cowboy Grit
The Cowboy Musketeer
Dangerous Fists
Dangerous Odds
Daniel Boone Through the Wilderness
Daring Days
A Daughter of the Sioux
The Demon Rider
The Desert Demon
The Desert Flower
Desert Madness
The Desert's Price
Desperate Odds
Don X
Double-Fisted
Durand of the Badlands
The Empty Saddle
The Everlasting Whisper
Fangs of Fate
Fast Fightin'
Fear-Bound
Fighting Courage
The Fighting Romeo
The Fighting Sheriff
The Fighting Smile
Fightin' Odds
Flaming Love (aka Frivolous Sal)
Flashing Steeds
Flash o'Lightning
Flying Hoofs

Fugitive
Galloping Jinx (aka The Fearless Jinx)
Galloping On
Galloping Vengeance
Gambling Fool
The Ghost Rider
The Girl of the West
Gold and Grit
Gold and the Girl
The Golden Princess
The Golden Strain
The Gold Hunters
The Great Divide
Hearts and Spurs
Hearts of the West
Hidden Loot
The Human Tornado
The Hurricane Horseman
The Hurricane Kid
Kit Carson Over the Great Divide (aka With Kit Carson Over the Great Divide)
Knockout Kid
Let'er Buck
Let's Go Gallagher
The Light of Western Stars
Love on the Rio Grande
Luck and Sand
The Lucky Horseshoe
Lure of the West
The Man from Lone Mountain
The Man from Red Gulch
A Man of Nerve
The Meddler
Moccasins
My Pal
The Mystery of the Lost Ranch
One Law for the Woman
One Shot Ranger
On the Go
The Outlaw's Daughter
The Pony Express
The Prairie Pirate
The Prairie Wife
Queen of Spades
Quicker'n Lightnin'
The Rainbow Trail
Ranchers and Rascals
Range Buzzards
Range Justice
The Range Terror
Ranger Bill
Ranger of the Big Pines
Range Vultures
The Rattler
Reckless Courage (aka Flying Courage)
Red Blood and Blue
Red Love

The Red Rider (aka The Open Trail)
Renegade Holmes, M.D.
Riders of Mystery
Riders of the Purple Sage
Riders of the Sand Storm
Ridin' Easy
The Riding Comet (aka Ridin' Comet; The Riding Contest)
Ridin' Pretty
Ridin' the Wind
Ridin' Thunder
Ridin' Wild
The Rip Snorter
A Roaring Adventure
Romance and Rustlers
Roped by Radio
A Ropin' Ridin' Fool
Rose of the Desert
Rough Going
Saddle Cyclone
The Saddle Hawk
Sagebrush Lady
Sand Blind
Santa Fe Pete
Scar Hanan (aka The Man with the Scar)
The Scarlet West
The Secret of Black Canyon
The Shield of Silence
The Sign of the Cactus
Silent Pal
Silent Sanderson
Silent Sheldon
A Son of His Father
Stampede Thunder
Starlight Untamed
Straight Through (aka Ridin' Through)
The Strange Rider
A Streak of Luck
The Taming of the West
Tearin' Loose
The Texas Bearcat
The Texas Trail
That Devil Quemado
That Man Jack!
Three in Exile
The Thundering Herd
Thundering Through
Timber Wolf
Tonio, Son of the Sierras
The Trail Rider
Tricks
Triple Action
The Trouble Buster
Tumbleweeds
A Two Fisted Sheriff
Vanishing American (aka The Vanishing Race)
The Verdict of the Desert

Vic Dyson Pays
Warrior Gap
A Western Engagement
West of Arizona
West of Mojave
Where Romance Rides
Whistling Jim
White Fang
The White Outlaw
White Thunder
Who Is the Guilty?
The Wild Bull's Lair
Wild Horse Canyon
Wild Horse Mesa
Wild West
Win, Lose or Draw
Winning a Woman
Wolfheart's Revenge
Wolves of the Road
The Wyoming Wildcat
Zander the Great

1926

Ace of Action
The Ace of Clubs
Across the Pacific
Ahead of the Law
Alice in the Wooly West
Ambushed
The Arizona Streak
Arizona Sweepstakes
Bad Man's Bluff
Baited Trap
The Bandit Buster
The Bar-C Mystery
Battling Kid
Beyond the Rockies
Beyond the Trail
Blind Trail
Blue Blazes
Blue Streak O'Neil
The Bonanza Buckaroo
The Border Sheriff
Border Whirlwind
Born to Battle
Born to the West
The Buckaroo Kid
Bucking the Truth
Buffalo Bill on the U.P. Trail
Buried Gold
Chasing Trouble
Chip of the Flying U
Coming an' Going
The Cowboy and the Countess
Cyclone Bob
The Dangerous Dub
Davy Crockett at the Fall of the Alamo
The Dead Line

The Demon
Desert Gold
Desert Greed
The Desert's Toll
Desert Valley
Desperate Chance
The Desperate Game
Deuce High
The Devil Horse
The Devil's Gulch
Double Daring
Driftin' Through
The Dude Cowboy
Easy Going
The Enchanted Hill
Escape
The Fighting Boob
The Fighting Cheat
The Fighting Failure
The Fighting Gob
Fighting Jack
Fighting Luck
The Fighting Peacemaker
The Fighting Ranger
The Fighting Stallion
Fighting with Buffalo Bill
The Fire Barrier
The Flaming Frontier
The Flying Horseman
Forlorn River
Fort Frayne
The Frontier Trail
The Galloping Cowboy
General Custer at Little Big Horn
The Gentle Cyclone
The Great K & A Train Robbery
The Grey Devil
The Grey Vulture
Hair Trigger Baxter
Hands Across the Border
Hard Boiled
Haunted Range
Hell Hounds of the Plains
The High Hand
Hi-Jacking Rustlers
Hoodoo Ranch
The Iron Rider
Jim Hood's Ghost
King of the Rodeo
King of the Saddle
The Lady from Hell
Lash of the Whip
The Last Chance
The Last Frontier
Lawless Trails
Lazy Lightning
Lightning Bill
The Little Warrior

Lone Hand Saunders
Looking for Trouble
Lost, Strayed or Stolen
A Man Four-Square
The Man from Oklahoma
The Man from the Rio-Grande
The Man from the West
The Man in the Saddle
Man of the Forest
Man Rustlin'
The Masquerade Bandit
Moran of the Mounted
My Own Pal
No Man's Gold
One Man Trail
The Outlaw Breaker
The Outlaw Express
Out of the West
Paths of Flame
The Phantom Bullet
Pony Express Rider
Prince of the Saddle
Prowlers of the Night
The Ramblin Galoot
Rawhide
Red Blood
Red Hot Hoofs
Red Hot Leather
A Regular Scout
A Ridin' Gent
Riding for Life
Riding Romance
The Ridin' Rascal
Road Agent
Roaring Bill Atwood
The Roaring Rider
Rustlers' Ranch
Rustling for Cupid
Salt Lake Trail
Satan Town
The Scrappin' Kid
Senor Daredevil
The Set-Up
The Seventh Bandit
Sheep Trail
The Shoot 'Em Up Kid
Signal Fires
The Silent Guardian
A Six Shootin' Romance
Sky High Corral
Stacked Cards
Starlight's Revenge
The Stolen Ranch
Tangled Herds
Temporary Sheriff
The Terror
Tex
The Texas Streak

The Texas Terror
That Girl from Oklahoma
3 Bad Men
The Thunderbolt Strikes
Thundering Speed
Tony Runs Wild
The Tough Guy
Trumpin Trouble
Twin Six O'Brien
The Twin Triggers
Twisted Triggers
Two Fisted Buckaroo
The Two-Gun Man
Under Fire
Under Western Skies
The Unknown Cavalier
Unseen Enemies
The Valley of Bravery
Vanishing Hoofs
Walloping Kid
War Paint
West of Broadway
West of the Law
West of the Rainbow's End
Western Pluck
Western Trails
Whispering Smith
The Wildcat
The Wild Horse Stampede
Wild to Go
The Winking Idol
The Winning of Barbara Worth
Without Orders
Wolves of the Desert
The Yankee Senor
The Yellow Back

1927
Action Craver
Arizona Bound
Arizona Nights
The Arizona Whirlwind
The Arizona Wildcat
Between Dangers
Black Jack
Blazing Days
Blood Will Tell
Border Blackbirds
The Border Cavalier
The Boy Rider
The Broncho Twister
The Brute
Bulldog Pluck
California
Code of the Cow Country
Code of the Range
Cross Country Run
The Cyclone Cowboy

Cyclone of the Range
Daze of the West
Death Valley
The Denver Dude
Desert Dust
The Desert of the Lost
The Desert Pirate
The Devil's Saddle
The Devil's Twin
Don Desperado
Fangs of Destiny
The Fightin' Come Back
The Fighting Hombre
The Fighting Three
The Flying U Ranch
The Frontiersman
Galloping Fury
The Galloping Gogs
Galloping Thunder
The Golden Stallion
Gold from Weepah
Good as Gold
Grinning Guns
Gun Gospel
Gun-Hand Garrison
Gun Justice
Hands Off
Hard Fists
The Haunted Homestead
Hawk of the Hills
Heroes of the Wild
A Hero on Horseback
Hey! Hey! Cowboy
Hills of Peril
The Home Trail
Hoof Marks
The Interferin' Gent
Jesse James
Jim Conqueror
Just Travelin'
King of the Herd
The Laffin' Fool
The Land Beyond the Law
Land of the Lawless
The Last Outlaw
The Last Trail
Lightning
Lightning Lariats
Loco Luck
The Long Loop on the Pecos
The Man from Hard Pan
The Meddlin' Stranger
Men of Daring
The Mojave Kid
The Mysterious Rider
Nevada, No Man's Law
The Obligin' Buckaroo
One Glorious Scrap

A One Man Game
Open Range
The Ore Raiders
Outlaws of Red River
The Overland Stage
Painted Ponies
Pals in Peril
Pals of the West
The Phantom Outlaw
Pioneers of the West
The Prairie King
Prince of the Plains
Range Courage
The Range Raiders
Ride 'Em Cowboy
Ride 'Em High
Rider of the Law
Riders of the West
Ridin' Luck
The Ridin' Rowdy
Roarin' Broncs
Rough and Ready
The Rough Riders
Saddle Jumpers
Set Free
Shootin' Irons
Shootin' Straight
The Silent Partner
The Silent Rider
Silver Comes Through
Silver Valley
Sitting Bull at the Spirit Lake Massacre
Skedaddle Gold
Soda Water Cowboy
Speeding Hoofs
Splitting the Breeze
Spoilers of the West
Spurs and Saddles
The Square Shooter
Tearin' into Trouble
Tenderfoot Courage
The Terror of Bar X
Thunderbolt's Tracks
Tom's Gang
Tumbling River
Two-Gun of the Tumbleweed
The Valley of Hell
Wanderer of the West
Western Courage
The Western Rover
The Western Whirlwind
Whispering Sage
White Gold
White Pebbles
Wild Beauty
Wild Born
A Yellow Streak

1928

Across the Plains
The Apache Raider
Arizona Cyclone
Arizona Days
Arizona Speed
Avalanche
The Avenging Rider
The Ballyhoo Buster
The Battling Bookworm
Beauty and Bullets
Beyond the Sierras
The Big Hop
The Black Ace
The Border Patrol
The Boss of the Rustler's Roost
The Branded Sombrero
The Brand of Courage
Breed of the Sunsets
The Bronc Stomper
The Bullet Mark
Burning Bridges
Call of the Heart
The Clean-Up Man
Clearing the Trail
The Cowboy Cavalier
The Cowboy Kid
Crashing Through
The Crimson Canyon
The Danger Rider
Daredevil's Reward
Desperate Courage
Devil's Tower
Double Action Daniels
Driftin' Sands
The Fearless Rider
The Fightin' Redhead
Flyin' Buckaroo
The Flyin' Cowboy
Forbidden Grass
The Four-Footed Ranger
A Gentlemen Preferred
Girl-Shy Cowboy
The Glorious Trail
Greased Lightning
Guardians of the Wild
Headin' for Danger
Hello Cheyenne
His Destiny
A Horseman of the Plains
King Cowboy
Kit Carson
Laddie Be Good
Land of the Silver Fox
The Law of the Range
The Little Buckaroo
Made-To-Order Hero
Manhattan Cowboy

Man in the Rough
Mystery Valley
The Old Oregon Trail
On the Divide
Orphan of the Sage
Painted Post
Painted Trail
The Phantom City
The Phantom Flyer
Phantom of the Range
The Pinto Kid
Pioneer Scout
The Price of Fear
Put 'Em Up
Quick Triggers
Ranger's Oath
The Rawhide Kid
Riders of the Dark
Riders of Vengeance
Riding for Flame
The Ridin' Renegade
Rough Ridin' Red
The Rustler's End
Saddle Mates
Secrets of the Range
Silent Trail
The Sunset Legion
Taking a Chance
Terror
Texas Flash
Texas Tommy
The Texas Tornado
The Thrill Chaser
Thunder Riders
Tracked
Tracy the Outlaw
Trailin' Back
The Trail of '98
Trail of Courage
Trail Riders
Trails of Treachery
A Trick of Hearts
Two Gun O'Brien
The Two Outlaws
Under the Tonto Rim
The Upland Rider
The Vanishing Pioneer
Vanishing Rider
The Vanishing West
The Wagon Show
The Water Hole
West of Paradise
West of Santa Fe
When the Law Rides
The Wilderness Patrol
Wild West Romance
The Wild West Show
Wizard of the Saddle

Wyoming
Young Whirlwind

1929

The Amazing Vagabond
The Arizona Kid
Bad Men's Money
Border Romance
The Border Wildcat
Born to the Saddle
The Boy and the Bad Man
Bride of the Desert
Bullets and Justice
Captain Cowboy
Code of the West
Courtin' Wildcats
The Cowboy and the Outlaw
The Desert Rider
The Drifter
False Fathers
Fighters of the Saddle
The Fighting Terror
The Forty-five Caliber War
The Freckled Rascal
The Great Divide
Grit Wins
Gun Law
The Harvest of Hate
Hawk of the Hills
Headin' Westward
Hoofbeats of Vengeance
Idaho Red
In Old California
The Invaders
King of the Rodeo
The Lariat Kid
The Last Roundup
Law of the Plains
The Lawless Legion
The Lone Horseman
The Long, Long Trail
The Man from Nevada
Morgan's Last Raid
An Oklahoma Cowboy
The Oklahoma Kid
Outlawed
Overland Bound
The Overland Telegraph
Pals of the Prairie
The Phantom Rider
Pioneers of the West
Plunging Hoofs
Points West
The Pride of the Pawnee
The Rainbow
Rainbow Range
Redskin
Riders of the Rio-Grande

Riders of the Storm
The Ridin' Demon
The Ridin' Streak
Romance of the Rio Grande
The Royal Rider
The Saddle King
Senor Americano
Sin Town
Sioux Blood
The Smiling Terror

Smilin' Guns
Stairs of Sand
Sunset Pass
A Texan's Honor
A Texas Cowboy
The Three Outcasts
Thundering Thompson
Tide of Empire
Trail Horse Thieves
The Unknown Rider

The Virginian
The Wagon Master
Western Methods
West of the Rockies
The White Outlaw
Wild Blood
The Winged Horseman
Wolf Song
Wyoming Tornado

Selected Bibliography

Anderson, Lindsay. *About John Ford*. New York: McGraw Hill, 1981.

Andrew, Geoff. *The Director's Vision*. Chicago: A Cappella Books, 1999.

Bogdanovich, Peter. *John Ford*. Berkeley, Calif.: University of California Press, 1968.

Carey, Harry Jr. *Company of Heroes*. Metuchen, N.J.: Scarecrow Press, 1994.

Case, Christopher. *The Ultimate Movie Thesaurus*. New York: Henry Holt and Company, 1996.

Dewey, Donald. *James Stewart, a Biography*. Atlanta, Ga.: Turner Publishing Company, 1996.

Dickens, Homer. *The Films of Gary Cooper*. New York: The Citadel Press, 1970.

Douglas, Kirk. *The Ragman's Son: An Autobiography*. New York: Simon & Schuster, 1988.

Elley, Derek, ed. *Variety Movie Guide, 2000*. New York: Penguin/Putnam, 2000.

Everson, William. *A Pictorial History of the Western Film*. New York: Citadel Press, 1970.

———. *The Films of Laurel & Hardy*. New York: Citadel Press, 1967.

Fagen, Herb. *Duke, We're Glad We Knew You*. Secaucus, N.J.: Birch Lane Press, 1996.

———. *White Hats and Silver Spurs*. Jefferson, N.C.: McFarland, 1996.

Ford, Dan. *Pappy: The Life of John Ford*. Englewood Cliffs, N.J.: Prentice Hall, 1979.

Hardy, Phil. *The Western*. New York: William Morrow, 1983.

Henry, Marilyn, and Ron De Sourdis. *The Films of Alan Ladd*. Secaucus, N.J.: Citadel Press, 1981.

Higham, Charles. *Brando: The Unauthorized Biography*. New York: New American Library, 1987.

Hyams, Jay. *The Life and Times of the Western Movie*. New York: Gallery Books, 1983.

Jarlett, Franklin. *Robert Ryan: A Biography and Critical Filmography*. Jefferson, N.C.: McFarland, 1990.

Katz, Ephraim. *The Film Encyclopedia*, 3rd ed., revised by Fred Klein and Ronald Dean Nolen. New York: Harper Perennial, 1998.

Kennedy, Burt. *Hollywood Trail Boss*. New York: Boulevard Books, 1997.

Kitses, Jim, and Gregg Rickman, eds. *The Western Reader*. New York: Limelight, 1998.

Lemza, Douglas, ed. *Rediscovering American Cinema*. New York: Films Incorporated, 1977.

Maltin, Leonard. *Leonard Maltin's Movie and Video Guide*. New York: Signet, 1992.

Martin, Nick, and Marsha Porter. *Video Movie, 2002 Guide*. New York: Ballantine Books, 2002.

McCarthy, Todd. *Howard Hawks*. New York: Grove Press, 1997.

Mitchum, John. *Them Ornery Mitchum Boys*. Pacifica, Calif. Creatures of a Larger Press, 1989.

Moses, Robert, ed. *American Movie Classic's Classic Movie Companion*. New York: Hyperion, 1999.

Nowlan, Robert A., and Gwendolyn W. Nowlan. *Film Quotations*. Jefferson, N.C.: McFarland, 1994.

Parish, James, and Don E. Stanke. *The All Americans*. New Rochelle, N.Y.: Arlington House Publishers, 1977.

——— and Michael Pitts. *The Great Western Pictures*. Metuchen, N.J.: Scarecrow Press, 1976.

Parkinson, Michael, and Clyde Jeavons. *A Pictorial History of the Western*. London: Hamlin Publishing Group, 1972.

Pitts, Michael. *Western Movies: A TV and Video Guide to 4200 Genre Films*. Jefferson, N.C.: McFarland, 1997.

Place, J. A. *The Western Films of John Ford*. New York: Citadel Press, 1974.

Quirk, Lawrence J. *The Films of Robert Taylor*. Secaucus, N.J.: The Citadel Press, 1975.

Ricci, Mark, et al. *The Complete Films of John Wayne*. New York: Citadel Press, 1995.

Roberts, Randy, and James Olson. *John Wayne, American*. New York: Free Press, 1995.

Roquemore, Joseph. *History Goes to the Movies*. New York: Doubleday, 1999.

Schickel, Richard. *James Cagney*. Boston: Little Brown Company, 1985.

Schoell, William. *Martini Man: The Life and Times of Dean Martin*. Dallas: Taylor Publishing, 1999.

Sennett, Ted. *Great Hollywood Westerns*. New York: AFI Press, 1990.

———. *Great Movie Directors*. New York: AFI Press, 1986.

Server, Lee. *Robert Mitchum: "Baby, I Don't Cry."* New York: St. Martin's, 2001.

Smith, Harold. *Saturdays Forever: A Personal Journey through the Era of B-Western Films*. Knoxville, Tenn.: National Paperback Books Inc., 1985.

Terrill, Marshal. *Steve McQueen: Portrait of an American Rebel*. New York: Donald I. Fine, 1993.

Thomas, Tony, and Aubrey Soloman. *The Films of Twentieth Century Fox*. Secaucus, N.J.: Citadel Press, 1979.

Walsh, Raoul. *Each Man in His Own Time*. New York: Farrar, Straus and Giroux, 1974.

Wellman, William. *A Short Time for Insanity: An Autobiography*. New York: Hawthorn Books, 1974.

Wiley, Mason, and Daniel Bona. *Inside Oscar*, 10th ed. New York: Ballantine, 1996.

Weisser, Thomas. *Spaghetti Westerns—The Good, The Bad and the Violent*. Jefferson, N.C.: McFarland, 1992.

Zmijewsky, Boris, and Lee Pfeiffer. *The Films of Clint Eastwood*. Secaucus, N.J.: Carol Publishing Edition, 1994.

Index

Boldface page numbers indicate major treatment of a subject. Page numbers followed by an *f* indicate a photograph.

Brauner, Arthur, *The Treasure of the Aztecs* produced by 445
Bravados, The **59**
Brave Warrior **59**
Bray, Ray, in *The Return of the Bad Men* 346
Breakheart Pass **59**
Breckenridge Story, The. See Ride Clear of Diablo
Breed of the Border (Speed Brent Wins) **60**
Breed of the West **60**
Brendel, Ed, in *The Big Trail* 40
Brennan, Walter
  in *Along the Great Divide* 9
  in *The Big Country* 37
  in *Brimstone* 60
  in *Cornered* 103
  in *The Far Country* 149
  in *My Darling Clementine* 286–287
  in *Red River* 341–342
  in *Return of the Texan* 347
  in *Rio Bravo* 358–359
  in *The Showdown* 392
  in *Support Your Local Sheriff* 416
  in *Two-Fisted Law* 451
  in *The Westerner* 255, 478–479, 479f
  in *Wild and Wooly* 487
Brent, Evelyn, in *Hop-Along Cassidy Returns* 217
Brent, George
  in *Gold Is Where You Find It* 184
  in *Montana Belle* 284
Brewer, Teresa, in *Those Redheads from Seattle* 431
Brian, David
  in *Ambush at Tomahawk Gap* 10
  in *Fury at Gunsight Pass* 175
Brian, Mary
  in *The Light of Western Stars* 257

in *Under the Tonto Rim* 456
in *The Virginian* 466
Bride Wasn't Willing, The. See Frontier Gal
Bridge, Alan, *God's Country and the Man* by 183
Bridges, Jeff
  in *Bad Company* 23
  in *Hearts of the West* 205
  in *Rancho Deluxe* 335
  in *Wild Bill* 487
Bridges, Lloyd
  in *Abilene Town* 1
  in *Apache Women* 16
  in *Hail to the Rangers* 200
  in *Ramrod* 335
  in *The Tall Texan* 421
Brigham Young (Brigham Young—Frontiersman [UK]) **60**
Bright, Richard, in *Rancho Deluxe* 335
Brimley, Wilfred, in western genre x
Brimstone **60**
Bring Me the Head of Alfredo Garcia **60**
Brix, Herman, in *The Lone Ranger* 260
Broadway to Cheyenne (From Broadway to Cheyenne) **60–61**
Brodie, Steve
  in *Badman's Territory* 25–26
  in *Brothers in the Saddle* 62
  in *The Return of the Bad Men* 346
  in *Sierra Baron* 392
  in *Trail Street* 443
Broken Arrow 3–4, **61**
Broken Lance **61**
Broken Land, The **61**
Broken Star **61**
Brolin, James, in *Bad Jim* 24
Broncho Billy, in *The Bandit Makes Good* 28

Broncho Billy and the Baby **61**
Bronco Apache (Wellman) 14
Bronco Billy **61–62**
Bronco Buster **62**
Bronson, Charles
  in *Apache* 14
  in *Breakheart Pass* 59
  in *Chato's Land* 83
  in *Chino* 86
  in *Drum Beat* 137
  in *Four for Texas* 169
  in *Jubal* 230
  in *The Magnificent Seven* 267
  in *Once Upon a Time in the West* 300
  in *Showdown at Boot Hill* 392
  in *Villa Rides* 465
  in *White Buffalo* 485
Bronze Buckaroo, The **62**
Brooke, Hillary, in *Skipalong Rosenbloom* 398
Brooks, Louise, in *Empty Saddles* 145
Brooks, Mel, in *Blazing Saddles* 46–47
Brooks, Richard
  The Professionals directed by 325
  Sin Town written by 396
Brothers O'Toole, The **63**
Brothers in the Saddle **62**
Brothers of the West **62**
Brown, Barry, in *Bad Company* 23
Brown, Forrest, *Boss of Lonely Valley* by 56
Brown, Harry, *Stand at Spanish Boot* by 14
Brown, Harry Joe
  Buchanan Rides Alone produced by 63
  The Doolins of Oklahoma produced by 135
  Hangman's Knot produced by 202
  Lawless Street produced by 250
Brown, Jim
  in *El Condor* 142

in *100 Rifles* 301
in *Rio Conchos* 359
in *Take a Hard Ride* 419
Brown, Johnny Mack
  in *Apache Uprising* 15
  in *Arizona Cyclone* 18
  in *Bad Man from Red Butte* 25
  in *Bell of the Nineties* 32
  in *Between Men* 35
  in *Billy the Kid* 41–42, 41f
  in *Blazing Bullets* 46
  in *Boothill Brigade* 50
  in *Born to the West* 55–56
  in *Boss of Bullion City* 56
  in *Branded a Coward* 58
  in *Bury Me Not on the Lone Prairie* 67
  in *Canyon Ambush* 75
  in *Chip of the Flying U* 86, 87f
  in *Code of the Saddle* 95
  in *Colorado Ambush* 96
  in *Dead Man's Trail* 123
  in *Deep in the Heart of Texas* 125
  in *Desperate Trails* 130
  in *Fighting Bill Fargo* 152
  in *The Fighting Ranger* 156
  in *Fighting with Kit Carson* 157
  in *Flame of the West* 160
  in *Flaming Frontiers* 161
  in *The Gambling Terror* 178
  in *The Ghost Rider* 180
  in *The Great Meadow* 188
  as Kit Carson 237
  in *Lasca of the Rio Grande* 240
  in *Law and Order* 247, 491

Clothier, William
  Chisum filmed by 89
  The Horse Soldiers
    filmed by 219
  Track of the Cat filmed
    by 442
  Wayne, John, and 49
*Clue, The. See Outcasts of
  Black Mesa*
Clyde, Andy
  in *Abilene Trail* 1
  in *Bar 20* 29
Coates, Phyllis
  in *Blood Arrow* 48
  in *The Longhorn* 263f
Cobb, Edmund
  in *The Cherokee Strip*
    83
  in *Racketeer Round-Up*
    331
Cobb, Lee J.
  in *Buckskin Frontier* 64
  in *The Man of the West*
    274
  in *The Man Who Loved
    Cat Dancing* 274
Coburn, Charles, in *Green
  Grass of Wyoming* 190
Coburn, James
  in *Bite the Bullet* 43–44
  in *The Cherokee Kid* 83
  in *Fistful of Dynamite*
    159
  in *The Honkers* 216
  in *The Last Hard Men*
    241
  in *The Magnificent
    Seven* 267
  in *Maverick* 279
  in *Pat Garrett and Billy
    the Kid* 315
  in *Ride Lonesome* 350
Cochran, Steve, in *The
  Deadly Companions* 122
*Cockeyed Cowboys of Calico
  County (A Woman for
  Charlie* [UK]*)* 94
Code of the Cactus 94
Code of the Fearless 94
Code of the Lawless 94
Code of the Mounted 95
Code of the West (Grey)
  214

*Code of the Outlaw (Riders
  of the Sunset Trail)* 95
Code of the Prairie 95
Code of the Range 95
Code of the Rangers 95
Code of the Saddle 95
Code of the Silver Age
  95–96
Code of the West 96
Cody, Bill
  in *Border Guns* 52
  in *Frontier Days* 172
  in *Ghost City* 180
  in *Vanishing Riders* 463
Cody, Bill, Jr., in *Vanishing
  Riders* 463
Cody, Iron Eyes, in *El
  Condor* 142
Cody of the Pony Express
  95
Cohn, Harry, Dale
  Robertson and xiii
Colbert, Claudette
  in *Drums Along the
    Mohawk* 137
  in *Texas Lady* 426, 426f
Cole, Nat King, in *Cat
  Ballou* 79
Coleman, Ronald, in
  Winds of the Wasteland
  493
Cole Younger, Gunfighter
  96
Colizzi, Giuseppi, *Ace
  High* directed by 1–2
Collins, Denver John, in
  Doc 134
Colorado 96
Colorado Ambush 96
Colorado Kid, The 96
Colorado Pioneers 96
*Colorado Ranger (Guns of
  Justice)* 96
Colorado Serenade 96–97,
  97f
Colorado Sundown 97
Colorado Sunset 97
Colorado Territory 98
Colorado Trail 98
Colt Comrades 98
Colt .45 (Thundercloud) 98
Columbia Pictures
  Elliott, Bill, with 3,
    489

Jones, Buck, with 486
  McCoy, Tim, at 357
  Starrett, Charles, at 63
Columbo, Russ, in *The
  Texan* 424
Column South 98
Comanche 98
Comancheros, The 98–99
Comanche Station 99–100,
  99f, 100f
Comanche Territory 100
Come on Cowboys 100
Come on Danger (1932)
  100
Come on Danger (1942)
  101
Come on Rangers 101
Comes a Horseman 101
Come on, Tarzan 101
*Comin' Round the
  Mountain* 101
Command, The 101
*Company of Cowards. See
  Advance to the Rear*
Compson, Betty, in *The
  Spoilers* 404
Conagher 101–102
Concentration Kid, The
  102
Connery, Sean, in *Shalako*
  384
Connors, Chuck
  in *Geronimo* 179
  in *Pancho Villa* 313
  in *Ride Beyond
    Vengeance* 349
Connors, Michael, in
  Stagecoach 409
Conquering Horde, The
  102
Conquerors, The 102
Conquest of Cheyenne 102
Conquest of Cochise 102
Conrad, William, *Chisum*
  narrated by 89
Conried, Hans, in *New
  Mexico* 293
Conte, Richard, in *Big
  Jack* 37
Conway, Gary, in *Young
  Guns of Texas* 499
Conway, Jack, *Viva Villa*
  and 468

Conway, Tim
  in *The Apple Dumpling
    Gang* 16
  in *The Apple Dumpling
    Gang Rides Again* 16
Coogan, Jackie, in *Home
  on the Range* (1935) 214
Cook, Elisha, Jr., in *Shane*
  x, 385
Cook, Fielder, *Big Hand
  for the Little Lady*
  directed by 37
Cooley, Spade, in *Border
  Outlaws* 53
Cooper, Ben
  in *Arizona Raiders* 19
  in *Lightning Jack* 256
  in *Outlaw's Son* 307
Cooper, Courtney Ryley
  The Last Frontier by
    241
  The Prince of Pistols by
    320
Cooper, Floyd, *High Noon*
  filmed by 211
Cooper, Gary
  in *Along Came Jones* 8
  in *Arizona Bound* 17
  The Big Trail and 40
  in *The Cowboy and the
    Lady* 106, 106f
  in *Dallas* 116
  in *Distant Drums* 133
  in *Fighting Caravans*
    153
  in *Friendly Persuasion*
    170
  in *Garden of Evil* 178
  in *The Hanging Tree*
    201
  in *High Noon* 210, 210f
  in *The Man of the West*
    34, 273
  in *Northwest Mounted
    Police* 295
  in *The Plainsman* 320
  in *Pride of the Yankees*
    337
  in *The Spoilers* 404
  in *Springfield Rifle* 405
  in *The Texan* 424
  in *They Came to
    Cordura* 430
  in *Vera Cruz* 464

Crawford, Broderick
  in *The Fastest Gun Alive*
    150
  in *Last of the Comanches*
    242
  in *Lone Star* 262
  in *Men of Texas* 281
  in *Sin Town* 396
  in *The Texican* 429
  in *Trail of the Vigilantes*
    443
Crawford, Joan
  Brown, Johnny Mack,
    and 42
  in *Johnny Guitar* 229
  in *Montana Moon* 284
Crawford, Oliver, *The*
  Man from the Alamo
  story by 272
Crenna, Richard, in
  Catlow 80
Crime's Highway. See
  Desert Justice
Crimson Trail, The **111**
Cripple Creek **111**
Cripple Creek Barroom
  111
Crisp, Donald
  in *The Man from*
    Laramie 270
  Ramona directed by
    334
  in *Ramrod* 335
  in *Whispering Smith*
    485
Cristal, Linda, in *Two Rode*
  Together 452
Cronjager, Edward, *The*
  Conquerors filmed by
  102
Crooked River (The Last
  Bullet) **111**
Crooked Trail, The **111**
Crosby, Bing, in *Stagecoach*
  409
Crosby, Bob
  in *Rhythm on the Range*
    348
  in *The Singing Sheriff*
    396
Crossed Trails **111**
Crossfire **111–112**
Crossfire (Shumate)
  111–112

Crossfire Trail **112**
  land in x
  ratings for x
Crow Killer (Thorp and
  Bunker) 228
Crowley, Kathleen
  in *Curse of the Undead*
    112
  in *The Quiet Gun* 329
Cruze, James
  The Covered Wagon
    directed by 41, 105
  The Pony Express
    directed by 321–322
  Sutter's Gold directed
    by 417
Cry Blood, Apache **112**
Cry for Me, Billy. See Face
  to the Wind
Crystal, Billy, in *City*
  Slickers 93
Cugat, Xavier, *The*
  Americano score by 11
Cukor, George, *Heller in*
  Pink Tights directed by
  207
Culp, Robert
  in *The Castaway Cowboy*
    79
  in *Great Scout and*
    Cathouse Thursday
    189
  in *Hannie Caulder* 202
  in *The Raiders* 332
Culpepper Cattle Company,
  The **112**
Cummings, Irving
  The Cisco Kid directed
    by 92
  In Old Arizona directed
    by 224
Cummings, Robert
  in *Arizona Mahoney* 19
  in *Desert Gold* 127
  in *Heaven Only Knows*
    205
  in *Stagecoach* 409
Cummins, Peggy, in *Green*
  Grass of Wyoming 190
Cunningham, John W.,
  "Tin Star" by 211
Curse of Capistrano, The
  (McCulley) 277

Curse of the Undead (Mark
  of the West) **112**
Curtain Call at Cactus
  Creek (Take the Stage
  [UK]) **112–113**
Curtis, Alan
  in *The Daltons Ride*
    Again 117
  in *Renegade Girl* 343
Curtis, Dick, in *Across the*
  Sierras 3
Curtis, Ken
  in *The Alamo* 7
  in *Cheyenne Autumn* 84
Curtis, Tony
  in *Kansas Raiders* 233
  in *The Rawhide Years*
    338
Curtiz, Michael
  Dodge City directed by
    135
  The Hangman directed
    by 202
  Santa Fe Trail directed
    by 376–377
  Under a Texas Moon
    directed by 455
  Virginia City directed
    by 466
Curwood, James Oliver
  Fangs of the Arctic by
    148
  God's Country by 183
  Wheels of Fate by 95
Custer, Bob
  in *Ambush Valley* 10
  in *Covered Wagon Trails*
    105
  in *Law of the Rio*
    Grande 252
Custer Massacre, The. See
  Great Sioux Massacre, The
Custer's Last Fight **113**
Custer's Last Stand **113**
Custer of the West (Good
  Day for Fighting) **113**
Cyclone Fury **113**
Cyclone on Horseback **114**
Cyclone Kid **113**
Cyclone Kid, Barry,
  Donald, as 5
Cyclone Kid, The **113**
Cyclone Prairie Rangers
  114

Cyclone Ranger **114**
Cyclone of the Saddle
  113–114

D

Dahl, Arlene, in *Ambush*
  10
Dailey, Dan, in *Ticket to*
  Tomahawk 437
Dakota **115**
Dakota Incident **115**, 116f
Dakota Kid, The **116**
Dakota Lil **116**
Dallas **116–117**
Dalton Gang, The (The
  Outlaw Gang) **117**
Dalton Girls, The **117**
Daltons Ride Again, The
  117
Daltons' Women, The **117**
Damita, Lily, in *Fighting*
  Caravans 153
Damon, Matt, in
  Geronimo: An American
  Legend 180
Dan Candy's Law (Alien
  Thunder) **117**
Dances With Wolves x,
  117–118
Dan George, Chief
  in *Little Big Man* 258
  in *The Outlaw Josey*
    Wales 305
Danger Ahead **118**
Dangerous Venture **118**
Danger Patrol **118**
Dangers of the Canadian
  Mounted (R.C.M.P. and
  the Treasure of Genghis
  Khan) **118**
Danger Trails **118**
Danger Valley **118–119**
Daniel Boone **119**
Daniel Boone, Trail Blazer
  119
Daniels, Bebe, in *Heritage*
  of the Desert 209
Danner, Blythe, in *Hearts*
  of the West 205
Dano, Royal, in *Saddle the*
  Wind 373
Dante, Michael, in
  Winterhawk 493

Kennedy, Burt *(continued)*
  Mail Order Bride
    directed by 268
  Return of the Seven
    directed by 347
  Ride Lonesome written
    by 350
  The Rounders written by
    368
  Seven Men from Now
    written by 382–383
  *Support Your Local
    Gunfighter* directed by
    416
  *Support Your Local
    Sheriff* directed by
    417
  The Tall T written by
    420–421
  The Train Robbers
    directed by 7, 444
  The War Wagon
    directed by 7, 475
  Young Billy Young
    directed by 498
Kennedy, Douglas, in
  South of St. Louis 403
Kennedy, Fred, in *The
  Horse Soldiers* 219
Kennedy, George
  in *Bandolero* 28–29
  in *Cahill: United States
    Marshal* 70
  in *Dirty Dingus Magee*
    133
  in *Good Guys and Bad
    Guys* 185
  in *Guns of the
    Magnificent Seven* 198
*Kenny Rogers as the
  Gambler (The Gambler)*
  234
Kent, David, in *Two Rode
  Together* 452
Kent, Willis, *Lightning
  Triggers* produced by
  257
Kentuckian, The **234**
Kentucky Rifle **234**
Kenyon, Curtis, *Two Flags
  West* by 451
Kern, Jerome, *Annie Get
  Your Gun* and 13

Kerrigan, J. Warren, in
  Girl of the Golden West
  181
Keyes, Evelyn
  in *Beyond the
    Sacramento* 36
  in *Renegades* 344
Keymas, George, as
  Apache Kid 15
Keystone Cops, Wesley
  Ruggles in 17
Kid Blue **234**
Kid from Broken Gun, The
  234
Kid Courageous **234**
Kid Ranger, The **235**
*Kid Rides Again, The (Billy
  the Kid Rides Again)* **235**
Kid from Santa Fe, The
  234
Kid's Last Ride **235**
Kid from Texas, The (1939)
  234
*Kid from Texas, The (Texas
  Kid Outlaw* [UK]*)* (1950)
  234–235
*Kid Vengeance (Take
  Another Hard Ride)* **235**
Kilbride, Percy, in *Black
  Bart* 44
Kilkenny (L'Amour) 45
"Killer, The" (Scullin)
  193
*Killer on a Horse. See
  Welcome to Hard Times*
*Killer and 21 Men, The. See
  Parson and the Outlaw,
  The*
Killy, Ed, *West of the Pecos*
  directed by 482
Kilmer, Val, in *Tombstone*
  439f, 440
King, Charles
  in *Along the Sundown
    Trail* 10
  in *Death Rides the Range*
    125
  in *The Last of the
    Warrens* 244
  in Lone Rider series
    261
King, Henry
  The Gunfighter directed
    by 193

Jesse James directed by
  228
King, John
  in *The Range Busters*
    335–336
  in *Texas to Bataan* 428
King, Paul, *Black Noon*
  and 45
King, Pee Wee, in *Flame
  of the West* 160
*King of the Arena (King of
  the Range)* **235**
King of the Bandits **235**
King of the Bullwhip
  235–236
King of the Cowboys **236**
King of Dodge City **235**
King and Four Queens, The
  235
*King Gun. See Gatling
  Gun, The*
King of the Mounties **236**
King of the Pecos **236**
*King of the Range. See
  Marauders, The*
King of the Wild Horses
  236
King of the Wild Stallions
  236
Kipling, Rudyard, *Gunga
  Din* by 381
Kirby, Bruno, in *City
  Slickers* 93
Kirkwood, James, in *The
  Spoilers* 404
Kissing Bandit, The **236**
Kit Carson **236–237**
Kline, Kevin, in *Silverado*
  393
Klondike Kate **237**
Knapp, Evelyn, in *Rawhide*
  337
Knight, Fuzzy
  in *Chip of the Flying U*
    87f
  in *The Old Chisholm
    Trail* 298
Knights of the Range **237**
Knotts, Don
  in *The Apple Dumpling
    Gang* 16
  in *The Apple Dumpling
    Gang Rides Again* 16

  in *The Shakiest Gun in
    the West* 384
Knowles, Patric, in
  Chisum 88
Kohler, Fred
  in *Arizona Mahoney* 19
  in *The Lawless Valley*
    250
Kohler, Fred, Jr., in *The
  Lawless Valley* 250
Konga, the Wild Stallion
  237
Kopit, Arthur, *Indians* by
  65
Korman, Harvey, in
  Blazing Saddles 46–47
Kortman, Robert
  in *Fugitive Valley* 175
  in *The Miracle Rider*
    282
Kovacs, Ernie, in *North to
  Alaska* 293
Kristofferson, Kris
  in *Another Pair of Aces*
    13–14
  in *Heaven's Gate* 206
  in *Pat Garrett and Billy
    the Kid* 315
  in *Stagecoach* 409
Kuhn, Mickey, in *Red
  River* 341
Kyne, Peter B.
  All for Love by 463
  Flaming Guns by 161
  The Three Godfathers by
    207, 431

L

Ladd, Alan
  in *The Badlanders* 24
  in *The Big Land* 38–39
  in *Branded* 58, 58f
  in *The Carpetbaggers*
    292
  in *Drum Beat* 137
  in *Guns of the
    Timberland* 198
  in *The Iron Mistress*
    226
  in *The Light of Western
    Stars* 257
  in *One Foot in Hell* 301
  in *The Proud Rebel* 325,
    325f

Moore, Roger, in *Gold of the Seven Saints* 184

Moran, Dolores, in *Silver Lode* 394

More, Kenneth, in *The Sheriff of Fractured Jaw* 387

Moreau, Jeanne, in *Monte Walsh* 285

Moreno, Antonio, in *Border Legion* 52

Moreno, Rita
in *Garden of Evil* 178
in *Seven Cities of Gold* 381

Morgan, Dennis
in *Bad Men of Missouri* 26
in *Cattle Town* 81
in *Two Guys from Texas* 452

Morgan, Frank, *Annie Get Your Gun* and 13

Morgan, Harry
in *How the West Was Won* 220
in *Support Your Local Gunfighter* 416

Moriarty, Michael, in *Pale Rider* 312

Moross, Jerome, *The Big Country* scored by 37

Morricone, Ennio, *Navajo Joe* score by 291

Morris, Chester
in *The Three Godfathers* 431
in *Wagons Westward* 471

Morris, Wayne
in *Bad Men of Missouri* 26
in *Buffalo Gun* 65
in *The Bushwhackers* 67
in *Sierra Passage* 393
in *Star of Texas* 411
in *The Younger Brothers* 499

Morrison, Robert, *Escort West* produced by 146

Morrow, Jeff, in *Copper Sky* 103

Moss, William, in *Badman's Territory* 25–26

Mountain Man (Fisher) 228

Mountain Men **286**

Mountain Rhythm **286**

Mountains Are My Kingdom (Hardy) 392

Mule for the Marquesa, A (O'Rourke) 325

Mule Train **286**

Mulford, Clarence E., Hop-Along Cassidy books by 73, 216
Borderland by 52

Mulhall, Jack, in *The Bad Man* 24

Mulligan, Richard, in *Little Big Man* 258

Mulligan, Robert, *The Stalking Moon* directed by 410

Murder on the Yukon **286**

Murdock, Perry, in *Headin' North* 204

Murlock, Al, in *Once Upon a Time in the West* 300

Murphy, Audie
in *Apache Rifles* 15
in *Arizona Raiders* 19
in *Bullet for a Badman* 66
in *Cast a Long Shadow* 79
in *The Cimarron Kid* 91
in *Destry* 130
in *Drums Across the River* 137
in *40 Guns to Apache Pass* 168
in *Gunfight at Comanche Creek* 192
in *Gunsmoke* 197
in *Guns of Fort Petticoat* 198
in *Hell Bent for Leather* 206
in *Kansas Raiders* 233
in *The Kid from Texas* 235
in *Night Passage* 293
in *No Name on the Bullet* 293
in *Posse from Hell* 323

in *Ride Clear of Diablo* 350

in *Ride a Crooked Trail* 349

in *Seven Ways from Sundown* 383

in *Sierra* 392

in *The Texican* 429

in *A Time for Dying* 438

in *Tumbleweed* 449

in *The Unforgiven* 459

in *Walk the Proud Land* 472

in *The Wild and the Innocent* 487

Murphy, Mary, in *The Man Alone* 268

Murray, Don
in *From Hell to Texas* 171
in *One Foot in Hell* 301
in *These Thousand Hills* 429

Murray, Ken, in *The Man Who Shot Liberty Valance* 275

Mustang Country **286**

My Darling Clementine **286–287**
Back to the Future, Part III and 22
Holt, Tim, in 9
influence of ix–x

My Friend Flicka **287**

My Heroes Have Always Been Cowboys **287**

My Little Chickadee **287–288**

My Pal, the King **288**

My Pal Trigger **288**

My Reminiscences as a Cowboy (Harris) 105

Mysterious Avenger **288**

Mysterious Desperado, The **288**

Mysterious Mr. Sheffield, The. See Law of the .45s

Mysterious Stranger. See Western Gold

Mystery of the Hooded Horseman **289**

Mystery Mountain **288–289**

Mystery Ranch (1932) **289**

Mystery Ranch (1934) **289**

N

Nagel, Conrad, in *The Michigan Kid* 282

Naish, J. Carrol
in *Bad Bascomb* 23
in *Canadian Pacific* 75
in *Rage at Dawn* 332
in *Rio Grande* 360
in *Sitting Bull* 397
in *Yaqui Drums* 497

Naked Dawn, The **290**

Naked Gun (The Hanging Judge) **290**

Naked Hill, The **290**

Naked Spur, The **290–291**

Naked in the Sun **290**

Namath, Joe, in *Last Rebel* 244

Narcisco, Nathaniel, in *The Stalking Moon* 410

Natwick, Mildred
in *She Wore a Yellow Ribbon* 388
in *Three Godfathers* 431

Navajo Joe (A Dollar a Head) **291**

Navarro, Ramon, in *Heller in Pink Tights* 207

Nazarro, Ray, *Apache Territory* directed by 15

Neal, Patricia, in *Hud* 220

Neal, Tom, in *The Great Jesse James Raid* 188

Near the Rainbow's End **291**

'Neath Arizona Skies **291**

Nebraskan, The **291**

Ned Kelly (Ned Kelly, Outlaw) **291**

Neilson, James, *Night Passage* directed by 293

Nelson, Gene, in *The Purple Hills* 326

Nelson, Lori, in *Pardners* 314

Nelson, Ralph
Soldier Blue directed by 399–400
Wrath of God directed by 494

Scott, Randolph
(continued)
in *The Bounty Hunter*
57
in *Buchanan Rides Alone*
63
in *Canadian Pacific*
74–75
in *The Cariboo Trail*
xiii, 78
in *Carson City* 78
in *Colt .45* 98
in *Comanche Station* 99,
100, 100f
in *Corner Creek* 103
in *Decision at Sundown*
125
in *The Desperadoes* 129
in *The Doolins of
Oklahoma* 135
in *Fighting Man of the
Plains* xiii, 155
in *Fort Worth* 168
in *Frontier Marshal*
173
in *The Gunfighters* 193
in *Hangman's Knot* 202
in *High, Wide, and
Handsome* 211
in *Home on the Range*
(1935) 214
in *The Last of the
Mohicans* 243
in *The Last Roundup* 53
in *The Last Round-Up*
245
in *Lawless Street* 250
in *The Man Behind the
Gun* 269
in *Man in the Saddle*
272
in *Man of the Forest*
273
in *The Nevadan* 292
in *Rage at Dawn* 332
in *The Return of the Bad
Men* 346
in *Ride Lonesome* 350
in *Ride the High
Country* 355
in *Riding Shotgun* 356
in *Rocky Mountain
Mystery* 365
in *Santa Fe* 376

in *Seven Men from Now*
382–383, 382f
in *Seventh Cavalry* 383
in *Shoot-Out at
Medicine Bend* 391
in *The Spoilers* 404,
405f
in *The Stranger Wore a
Gun* 414
in *Sugarfoot* 414
in *Tall Men Riding* 420
in *The Tall T* 420,
421f, 422f
in *The Texans* 424
in *Thundering Herd*
435
in *Thunder Over the
Plains* 437
in *To the Last Man* 441
in *Trail Street* 443
in *Virginia City* 466
in *The Virginian* 467
in *The Walking Hills*
472
in *Westbound* 478
in *Western Union* 480
in *When the Daltons
Rode* 484
Scott, Zachary
in *Bandido* 27
in *Colt .45* 98
in *South of St. Louis*
403
in *Treasure of Ruby Hills*
445
Scullin, George, "The
Killer" by 193
Sea of Grass, The **378**
Searchers, The **378–379**
Sears, Fred, *Fury at
Gunsight Pass* directed by
175
Seaton, George, *Showdown*
directed by 391
Seberg, Jean, in *Paint Your
Wagon* 311–312
Secret Patrol **379**
Secrets **379–380**
Secrets of the Wasteland
380
Secret of Treasure Mountain
379

Sedgwick, Edward, *The
Flaming Frontier* and
161
Segal, George, in
Invitation to a Gunfight
225
Seitz, George
Desert Gold directed by
127
The Fighting Ranger
directed by 156
The Last Frontier
directed by 241
Selander, Leslie
Arrow in the Dust
directed by 20
Belle Starr's Daughter
directed by 32
*The Light of Western
Stars* directed by 257
*The Lone Ranger and the
Lost City of Gold*
directed by 261
Ride 'Em Cowboy
directed by 350
Smoke Tree Range
directed by 398
Stampede directed by
411
Selleck, Tom
in *Crossfire Trail* 112
in *Last Stand at Saber
River* 245
in *Quigley Down Under*
329f, 330
in *The Sacketts* 372
in *The Shadow Riders*
383–384
in westerns xiii–xiv
on westerns ix–xi
Selmier, Dean, in *Hunting
Party* 220
Selznick, David O.
Beyond the Rockies
produced by 36
Duel in the Sun
produced by 140
Seminole **380**
Seminole Uprising **380**
Sennett, Mack xviif
Ruggles, Wesley, and
17
western spoofs of 130

Sennett, Ted
on *Gunfight at the O.K.
Corral* 193
on *The Life and Times of
Judge Roy Bean* 255
on *The Man of the West*
274
on *Silverado* 393
on *Valdez Is Coming* 462
*Serenade of the West. See
Git Along Little Dogies*
Sergeant Rutledge **380**
Sergeants 3 **381**
Serling, Rod, *Saddle the
Wind* written by 373
Seven Alone **381**
Seven Angry Men **381**
*Seven Bad Men. See Rage at
Dawn*
*Seven Brides for Seven
Brothers* **381**
Seven Cities of Gold
381–382
Seven Guns to Mesa **382**
Seven Men from Now
382–383, 382f
*Seven Samurai, The, The
Magnificent Seven* and
267
Seventh Cavalry **383**
Seven Ways from Sundown
383
Severance, Joan, in
Another Pair of Aces
13–14
*Shadow of Boot Hill. See
Showdown at Boot Hill*
Shadow Ranch **383**
*Shadow Riders, The (Louis
L'Amour's The Shadow
Riders)* ix, **383–384**
Shadows of Death **384**
Shadows on the Sage **384**
Shadows of Tombstone **384**
Shadows Valley (1947) **384**
Shadows Valley (1954) **384**
Shadows of the West **384**
Shahan, James "Happy,"
The Alamo and 6–7
Shakiest Gun in the West
384
Shalako **384**
Shallert, William, in
Lonely Are the Brave 259